ISBN 978-1-331-13904-1
PIBN 10149461

1 MONTH OF
FREE
READING

at

www.ForgottenBooks.com

By purchasing this book you are eligible for one month membership to ForgottenBooks.com, giving you unlimited access to our entire collection of over 1,000,000 titles via our web site and mobile apps.

To claim your free month visit:

www.forgottenbooks.com/free149461

English
Français
Deutsche
Italiano
Español
Português

www.forgottenbooks.com

Mythology Photography **Fiction**
Fishing Christianity **Art** Cooking
Essays Buddhism Freemasonry
Medicine **Biology** Music **Ancient**
Egypt Evolution Carpentry Physics
Dance Geology **Mathematics** Fitness
Shakespeare **Folklore** Yoga Marketing
Confidence Immortality Biographies
Poetry **Psychology** Witchcraft
Electronics Chemistry History **Law**
Accounting **Philosophy** Anthropology
Alchemy Drama Quantum Mechanics
Atheism Sexual Health **Ancient History**
Entrepreneurship Languages Sport
Paleontology Needlework Islam
Metaphysics Investment Archaeology
Parenting Statistics Criminology
Motivational

REPORTS

OF

CASES DETERMINED

IN

THE SUPREME COURT

OF THE

STATE OF ILLINOIS,

DURING THE YEARS 1861 AND 1862.

BY E. PECK,
COUNSELOR AT LAW.

VOLUME XXVII.

CHICAGO:
PUBLISHED BY CALLAGHAN & COMPANY.

1877.

STEREOTYPED AND PRINTED
BY THE
CHICAGO LEGAL NEWS CO.

JUDGES OF THE SUPREME COURT.

CHIEF JUSTICE.

JOHN D. CATON.

ASSOCIATE JUSTICES.

PINKNEY H. WALKER.
SIDNEY BREESE.

292670

RESOLUTIONS OF RESPECT TO THE MEMORY OF W. H. L. WALLACE.

The following proceedings are published by request of the bar attending the Supreme Court at Ottawa:

A meeting of the Members of the Bar was held at the Supreme Court Room, on the 23rd of April, 1862.

Hon. N. H. PURPLE was called to the Chair. Hon. WM. C. GOUDY was appointed Secretary.

On motion, a committee of seven was appointed by the Chair to report resolutions to an adjourned meeting.

The Chair appointed THOMAS HOYNE, B. C. COOK, GEO. CAMP-BELL, EBENEZER PECK, JAMES ROBERTS, H. M. WEAD, and W. W. ORME.

At the adjourned meeting, Mr. HOYNE reported the following resolutions:

Resolved, That in the recent death of our esteemed friend and brother, the late W. H. L. WALLACE, from wounds received while gallantly leading a division at the battle of Pittsburgh Landing, the Bar of Illinois, in common with the people of the whole State, deplore the loss of a soldier, who, as well in his life, as by the manner of his death on the field, has sealed by his blood this new testimony of the ineradicable devotion which the people of Illinois are manifesting in heroic deeds and patriotic sacrifices to that form of free government on this continent, which domestic traitors are so wickedly attempting to overthrow.

Resolved, That while as citizens, the State may regret the loss of the experienced chief who could successfully inspire by his personal daring and valor, the troops committed to his charge, and by his example and bravery command success in the desperate charge or assault of battle,—and while to the grateful history of his country is now committed that fame, which to remote ages will rank his name with the other heroic defenders and founders of the Republic;—yet the Bar of Illinois have a sadder tribute to render now to his memory, by an expression of the profound grief which they feel at this final parting, and loss of a friend and brother.

Resolved, That they knew in the late W. H. L. WALLACE, one who, while possessing all the virtues that adorn a private life of exemplary excellence, in his professional character he was also a man without spot or blemish. Of a persevering industry, a very high order of legal attainment, and the very highest order of intellectual capacity, he seemed above all to shine in the very spirit of intellectual, moral and professional rectitude. This was "the daily beauty of his life," which never ceased to distinguish him in that career of professional triumphs which had placed him already in the very front rank of eminent professional men, in all his intercourse with his brethren of this Bar and the State. As brethren, therefore, of the profession which he honored in his life as well as by his glorious death, we may well pause as we now do, in the midst of our professional and other avocations, to drop a tear upon his tomb, and inscribe this·brief tablet by recalling a few of the many virtues of his life.

Resolved, That we tender our deepest sympathies to the widow and family of our departed brother. In their bereavement we are impressed with the conviction, that all mere words are inadequate to express that deep sense of affliction which the loss of such a *husband* must have caused to the bereaved and stricken one. We humbly commend her to the guardianship and care of Him from whom alone, at such a time, can come the only solace for hearts so afflicted. He only can "temper the wind to the shorn lamb."

Resolved, That Hon. NORMAN H. PURPLE, the chairman of this meeting, be appointed to present a copy of these Resolutions to the Supreme Court of this State, at its present session, and request that they be entered of record among the proceedings of said Court.

Resolved, That the Secretary of this meeting furnish a copy of the proceedings of the meeting, and that they be presented to the family of deceased.

FRIDAY, April 25, 1862.

The above resolutions were presented to the Court by Hon. N. H. PURPLE, who made the following remarks:

May it please the Court:

At a meeting of the Members of the Bar of the State of Illinois, held in the Court House of the Supreme Court, at Ottawa, on the 23rd day of April, A. D. 1862, for the purpose of testifying their respect for the memory and regret at the untimely decease of their late friend and brother, GENERAL WM. H. L. WALLACE, the following resolutions were unanimously adopted:

(Here Judge PURPLE read the resolutions to the Court.)

As Chairman of this meeting, I have been desired to present these resolutions to this Court, with the request that they may be entered upon the records thereof.

In doing this, I cannot forbear to add my feeble personal testimony to the intellectual ability, unflinching integrity, exalted patriotism, and sterling moral worth of our deceased friend. It has been my good fortune to know him long and well. We have often met, both here and in other courts of the State. As lawyers we have often had contests, but collisions—never. His very countenance was to me a sure guaranty of honesty and truthfulness—an index to a heart that knew no guile. I trusted him ever, and, neither professionally nor otherwise, did he ever deceive me.

I never inquired where he was born, or whence he came, nor knew aught of his parentage or ancestry; but I loved the man because I knew that he had head, and soul, and intellect, and honor—because he was, in all respects, a MAN. And when I was first assured of his untimely fate—selfish as it may appear—I do believe that I felt more deeply and keenly the misfortune that I had lost a friend, than that the country had lost a gallant soldier, and a brave, meritorious and most accomplished chieftain.

I felt that one of the bright lights of the profession to which I had devoted my life, was at once extinguished; that a link in the chain that had bound me to its arduous duties, and enlivened its dull routine, had been severed and forever broken.

I believe that these feelings and sentiments of the worth, character and virtue of the deceased, are common to all, and find an echo in the hearts of all who have enjoyed the pleasure and honor of his acquaintance and friendship; and that the grief which, in the resolutions just read, we declare that we feel, is as real and profound as the language of the resolutions import.

But why speak of our sorrows or regret, while there is one, at least, who knew him far better than any one of us, to whom his loss is irreparable—one whose deep anguish and unmitigated grief approaches nearly the boundaries of despair?

Yet even she should draw consolation from the reflection that he died bravely fighting in defense of his country, and his country's constitution; that during his whole life his honor has remained untarnished; that victory, though dearly bought, finally crowned his dying struggle; and that posterity will bless, revere and honor his name forever.

Valor and bravery in him was not a virtue—it was a necessity—an essential part of his moral and physical constitution.

When his country's call to arms was sounded, he was compelled to go; and where the fight raged thickest and fiercest, the very impulses of his nature forced him to be foremost in the conflict.

But he sleeps now, the sleep that knows no waking, until the trump of God shall call him. In the maturity of his strong intellect, in the full vigor of his manhood, he has sacrificed his life upon the altar of his country, and now reposes quietly and silently in his last resting-place, without a blot upon his fair fame, or a stain upon his memory.

> " So sleep the brave who sink to rest,
> With all their country's honors blest."

Whereupon Chief Justice CATON responded:

The Court receives the announcement of the death of General WALLACE with emotions, for the expression of which we find no

adequate words. In his death the Bar has lost one of its brightest
ornaments, the court one of its safest advisers, and our country one
of its ablest defenders. His whole professional life has been passed
among us, and we have known him well. All your words of encom-
ium are but simple justice, and we know they proceed from the deepest convictions of their truth. All his instincts were those of a
gentleman. All his impulses were of a noble and lofty character,
his sensibilities refined and generous. He was certainly a man of a
very high order of talent, and he was a very excellent lawyer. By
his industry he studied the law closely, and by his clear judgment
he applied it properly. He did honor to his profession ; it is meet
that his professional brethren should honor his memory. Scarcely
a year ago he was with us, engaged in a lucrative practice—the
ornament and the delight of a large circle of friends, and enjoying
the quiet endearments of domestic life, loving and beloved by a
family worthy of him, now made desolate. At the very first call of
his country for defenders, he abandoned his practice, he withdrew
from his associates and friends at home, and tore himself from the
domestic circle, and pledged his energies and his life to the vindica-
tion of his country's flag, which had been torn down and dishonored
by rebel hands at Sumter,—to the defense of that constitution and
those laws, the maintenance of which is indispensable to national
greatness and happiness. For these he fought ; for these he died.

  For myself, I may say, he was my near neighbor and my dear
friend. He honored me with his confidence, and disclosed to me
fully the patriotic impulses which led him to abandon all, to defend
his native land. If he was an able lawyer, so was he an able com-
-mander. If we mourn him as a departed friend and brother, so
does the country mourn him as one of her ablest generals gone.

  With the glad news of victory came the sad lament of his death.
Our gladness was turned to mourning. So it ever is, and so
must it ever be, in this sublunary world. With all our joys are
mingled strains of sorrow. Happiness unalloyed is reserved for
that brighter and better world, promised to those who act well their
part on earth, into the full fruition of which those who knew him
best doubt not he is accepted.

  The resolutions which have been adopted by the Bar, will be
entered upon the records of the Court, as a perpetual memorial of
our appreciation of the worth of the late GENERAL WALLACE, and
the clerk will furnish a copy of them, and a copy of this order, to
the widow and family of the deceased. And out of respect to his
memory, this Court will now adjourn.

TABLE OF CASES.

DECISIONS

OF

THE SUPREME COURT

OF THE

STATE OF ILLINOIS,

OF CASES ARGUED AT

NOVEMBER TERM, 1861, AT MOUNT VERNON.

THE OHIO AND MISSISSIPPI RAILROAD COMPANY, Appellant, *v.* JAMES McCUTCHIN, Appellee.

ERROR FROM CLAY.

The case of *Swingley* v. *Haynes*, 22nd Illinois, 216, examined and approved. An appeal from the decision of a justice of the peace, gives the appellate court jurisdiction of the party, although he was not served with process in the case appealed from; and the appellate court can proceed to a trial on the merits.

THIS was an appeal from a judgment of a justice of the peace in Clay county, rendered against the railroad company on the 16th of April, 1859. Summons was issued, and the return of the constable thereon showed that the process was served on "Charles Weir, Station Agent of the Ohio and Mississippi Railroad Company at Xenia," etc.

At the October term of the Circuit Court of Clay county, the defendant below filed a plea in abatement, and moved to dismiss the cause. The motion was overruled, and cause continued.

NOTE.—Mr. Justice Breese did not take any part in the decisions of this term. His absence was by reason of a severe domestic affliction.

At the March special term, the defendant below renewed the motion to dismiss the cause, on plea in abatement denying [*10] the jurisdiction of the justice. The order overruling the motion at October term was set aside.

At the regular May term, 1860, it was agreed between the parties that the facts averred in the plea of abatement were true; that Charles Weir was not the agent, and never has been the agent of the railroad company at Xenia; and that no service had been had upon the company. Upon this agree. ment the cause was tried by the court without any other evidence, and judgment rendered in favor of the plaintiff below. Defendant excepted, and appealed.

The errors assigned are, that the court erred in overruling the motion of the defendant below to dismiss the cause for want of jurisdiction in the justice; and the court erred in rendering judgment in favor of the plaintiff below.

W. Homes, and Edwin Beecher, for Appellant.

J. G. Bowman, for Appellee.

Walker, J. We are asked in this case to review the grounds of our decision in the case of *Swingley* v. *Haynes*, 22 Ill. 216. Lest we may in that case, have overlooked some rule that might have induced a different conclusion from that announced, we cheerfully undertake the careful reconsideration of the question, and have given to it such thought and reflection as time and opportunity have permitted. The question is, whether under our statute, the Circuit Court acquired jurisdiction of a party, not served with process before a justice of the peace, but who appeals from a judgment rendered by the justice. Or must there be service or appearance before the justice, to authorize the trial of a cause taken by appeal to that court? That a judgment rendered against a defendant without either actual or constructive notice or appearance is void, there can be no question. But does he, by presenting an appeal from such a judgment, confer upon the Circuit Court jurisdiction of his person, and thereby authorize the Circuit Court to proceed to a trial on the merits? It not, what is his standing in that court? He is there for some purpose, and so is his case. He cannot say he is not in that court, after he has brought his appeal. Then is such an appeal only a writ of error, or is it an appeal for all purposes?

From the sixty-sixth and sixty-seventh sections of the statute regulating justices of the peace and constables, it is manifest that the design of the General Assembly was to give a trial *de novo* on the merits in all appeal cases. It was to dispense with all technicalities, and to afford a speedy trial on the merits. It would also seem that it was designed that the [*11] Circuit Court should not be a court for the correction of errors, appearing on the records of judgments of justices of the peace. From all the legislation in reference to appeals it is the manifest design to give a new trial on the merits.

But it is supposed that the case of *Bines v. Proctor,* 4 Scam. 174, the first case that arose under the provision of these sections, announces a different rule. In that case, the question was, whether a defect in a justice's summons, which omitted to name a time when the defendant should appear, was subject to exception in the Circuit Court on appeal, and it was held that it was not. This seems to have been the only question properly presented to the court in that case, and yet the court say, that by this enactment, " the appellant is prevented from excepting in the Circuit Court to any proceeding before the justice, except such as are not only wholly without authority of law, but also, had without notice to, or the knowledge and consent of the defendant." "And that he may object when no summons or other process has been issued against him, where there has been no service of the summons, or other process issued by the justice, upon the defendant, and no notice to him, actual or constructive, of the pendency before the justice, of the suit against him, in which the judgment has been rendered." It now seems to us, that what is there said was unnecessary to the decision of any question in that case. It in effect holds, that no exception can be taken for the want of a summons.

But if it were conceded, that in the case of *Bines v. Proctor,* it was designed to give the construction, indicated by the language employed, has the court subsequently acted upon it, as the proper construction? In the case of *Rogers* v. *Blanchard*, 2 Gil. 335, it was held that when the justice's jurisdiction is doubtful, as to amount, that it is the duty of the Circuit Court, on appeal to hear the evidence, in order to determine the question. To the same effect are the cases of *Ballard* v. *McCarty*, 11 Ill. 501, and *Vaughn* v. *Thompson*, 15 Ill. 39. These decisions are strictly in accordance with the requirements of the sixty-seventh section. It provides that if it appears that the justice had no jurisdiction of the subject matter of the suit, it shall be dismissed at the costs of the plaintiff.

The statute provides that upon the trial of all appeals, no exception shall be taken to the form or service of the justice's summons; but the court shall hear and determine the same in a summary way according to the justice of the case. But if [*12] it shall appear that the justice had no jurisdiction of the subject matter, then the court shall dismiss the suit. This case was an appeal, and is undeniably embraced within the statute, as it includes all appeals. Being an appeal, it is required that the court should hear and determine it in a summary way according to the justice of the case. Not to dismiss it if there was a want of service, but only when the justice did not have jurisdiction of the subject matter of the suit. The statute has prohibited exceptions to the form of the summons, or to the service. Now to permit the defendant on appeal to question the sufficiency of the service, would be to violate the terms of the statute. The language of the act does not refer to the form of the service, but to the service itself. If it had prohibited an exception to the form of the service, then a different question would have been presented. But the legislature, to guard against all doubt, has prohibited all exception to any proceeding before the justice. Now this service, or want of it, was a part of the proceedings before the justice, and is manifestly embraced within the prohibition. How language more comprehensive or unequivocal could have been employed it is difficult to perceive, unless this very case had been specified.

It is however urged that the justice of the peace could only

Ohio and Mississippi R. R. Co. *v.* McCutchin.

acquire jurisdiction of the subject matter by service of the summons. It is not the parties, the justice of the peace, the summons, or the service, which confers that jurisdiction, but it is the statute. It has provided that justices of the peace shall have jurisdiction to hear and determine certain causes of action, which are specified. This jurisdiction is inherent in his office, yet he is unable to exercise it until called upon to adjudicate such a cause of action between the proper parties, who are properly before him. Until jurisdiction over the person has been acquired, he cannot exercise his jurisdiction over the subject matter.

It is not perceived that this construction can work any possible injury, for if the summons was served upon an improper person, and the knowledge of that fact did not come to the knowledge of the defendant, in time to perfect an appeal, there is no construction that could be given which would afford any relief. When there is such a service and an appeal is prosecuted, no reason is perceived why a trial on the merits should not be had. When all the parties are in the Circuit Court, and when a full and fair trial may be had, and complete justice done between the parties, why send them back to the justice of the peace, unless it be simply to afford delay? If the judgment appealed from is unjust, a trial on the [*13] appeal will correct it. It is manifest that the legislature designed to give a speedy trial, and this effectuates the object.

After giving the question all the consideration which we have been able to bestow upon it, we can perceive no sufficient reason why we should not adhere to the rule announced in the case of *Swingley* v. *Haines*, as the true exposition of the intention of the legislature. The judgment of the court below must therefore be affirmed.

Judgment affirmed.

NATHAN HORNER, and BENJAMIN HYPES, Plaintiffs in Error, *v.* MARY C. STARKEY, Administratrix of the Estate of William C. Starkey, deceased, Defendant in Error.

ERROR TO MONROE.

If the maker of a note says to the payee, that if he will wait awhile he will pay the note; and that he will pay when he "makes a raise," not being at the time in a condition to pay; the note will be taken out of the statute of limitations.

THE plaintiffs in error filed the two notes sued on in this case, in the County Court of Monroe county, for allowance in the case of the decedent. The County Court refused to allow the claim. The plaintiffs in error took an appeal to the Circuit Court, where the cause was tried by the court without a jury, OMELVENY, Judge, presiding, at May term, 1861, the court affirming the judgment of the County Court, and sustaining the plea of the statute of limitations interposed by the defendant.

On the trial, the plaintiffs introduced a promissory note under seal, dated November 14, 1838, made by Wm. A. Strong and Wm. C. Starkey, for the payment of fifty-one dollars and seventeen cents one day after date, with interest at twelve per cent. from date, and payable to Horner & Hypes. Also, another promissory note under seal, dated November 14, 1838, made by Wm. C. Starkey and Wm. A. Strong, for the payment of twelve dollars and sixty-eight cents, with twelve per cent. interest from date, and payable one day after date to Horner & Hypes.

Henry Horner, for plaintiffs, testified that he was collecting agent for them, and as such handed to, or sent said notes to Thomas Quick, an attorney of Monroe county, for collection, in the year 1848 or 1849; that Starkey left Lebanon and re-[*14] moved to Waterloo in 1839, and Horner & Hypes dissolved partnership in 1840, and that in these notes were all their accounts against Starkey.

Thomas Quick testified, that Horner placed in his hands evidences of indebtedness against Starkey for collection in 1848 or 1849. Believed they were sent in a letter, and are the ones now sued on. It was an old claim of about the amount of these notes, sixty dollars and interest. In 1848 witness went, saw Starkey, and told him the notes were placed in his hands for collection. Starkey said, if Hypes would wait awhile he would pay it to witness. He said, I am not in a condition now to pay it, but say to Mr. Hypes, that when I make a raise I'll pay it. Witness thinks he was not at that time able to pay it. Witness told Starkey at the time of conversation, the amount and nature of the indebtedness. Witness afterwards sent the papers back to Hypes, with a statement of what Starkey said.

Plaintiffs assign for error: That the court erred in finding for defendant, and in refusing to grant a new trial.

Wm. H. Underwood, for Plaintiffs in Error.

Omelveny & Kennedy, for Defendant in Error.

Caton, C. J. Here is not a simple admission or recognition of the existence of the debt, leaving us to infer a promise to pay, in order to take it out of the statute of limitations, but we have a direct promise to pay it, not then, it is true, but in the future. The maker of the notes said, if the payee would wait a while he would pay them. He said he was not in a condition then to pay them, but that *when he made a raise* he would do so. This the defendant insists was a conditional promise, to be performed upon the happening of an event, which is not shown to have transpired. Much as we are disinclined to fritter away this statute of repose, we cannot adopt this, as the meaning of the party. If his language is properly reported, he meant to convey the idea that he would certainly pay the debt, but wanted further time to do so. The idea he designed to convey was, that he would make exertions, and as soon as possible, would pay the debt; and he did not intend to convey the meaning, that he would pay only upon the condition that his circumstances should subsequently so improve, as to place in his hands the means of doing so. If we disapprove of the rule originally adopted for taking cases out of the statute of limitations, that rule is well settled now, and we must not attempt to evade it, but [*15] give it as fair an application as if it met with our cordial approbation.

The judgment is reversed, and the cause remanded.

Judgment reversed.

HENRY B. LUCAS, Plaintiff in Error, *v.* DANIEL R. SPENCER *et al.*, Defendants in Error.

ERROR TO WASHINGTON.

By the act of 31st January, 1857, relating to interest, a forfeiture of all interest, legal or illegal, is incurred for usury; no other penalty can be recovered for a breach of the law.

If a party has had an opportunity, which he has neglected, to prevent the recovery of a judgment, which includes usurious interest, he cannot relieve himself by a resort to chancery.

The sixth section of the interest law of 1845, only applies to cases where the money has been paid; and not as a defense to usury due and unpaid.

After usurious money has been paid, the parties are not competent witnesses in a suit to recover it back.

A party who voluntarily submits to a default, impliedly admits that the demand against him is just.

THE plaintiff in error, who was complainant in the court below, filed his bill in the Circuit Court of Washington county against defendants in error, in the Court below, alleging that at the September term, 1860, of the Washington Circuit Court, defendant, Daniel R. Spencer, recovered three judgments, by default, against plaintiff and others, to wit: one judgment for $276.77 and costs, against plaintiff and defendant, William M. Logan; one other judgment against plaintiff and defendants, Edmund C. Dew and Alexander P. Shipley, for $1,222.75 and costs of suit; and one judgment against plaintiff alone, for $115.33. Said judgments were all rendered on promissory notes, as follows: the first, for $235.25, dated February 25th, 1858, payable one day after date; the second, for $1,000, payable twelve months after date; and the third, for $102.52, payable one day after date. Since the making of the $1,000 note, plaintiff has paid defendant Spencer, $675; and that the said note was executed in consideration of only $925, instead of $1,000. That plaintiff is justly entitled to a credit of $675, and the other two notes referred to were executed for interest on the $1,000 note, at a greater rate then ten per cent. per annum. That ·there is now only due defendant Spencer, $175, or thereabouts, [*16] balance on the $1,000 note, he having forfeited all claim to interest. Plaintiff charges, that defendant has by the law of the land not only forfeited all claim to interest on· the $1,000 note, for money loaned, but three times the interest so illegally taken and received; charges further, defendant Spencer has not only forfeited all claim to recover on the other two notes, but three times their amount, together with all interest claimed on them. Charges that the judgments aforesaid are illegal, unjust and inequitable, there not being one cent due said defendant Spencer, after deducting the credits for the cash paid and the forfeitures aforesaid claimed by plaintiff, but that plaintiff has a right to recover of defendant Spencer a judgment for $1,000 at least. Plaintiff further charges, that his co-defendants in said judgment are in no way interested in this suit, being only securities of plaintiff on said notes, and are made defendants nominally, because defendant Spencer has caused executions to be issued on said judgments. That injunction was prayed against defendants.

Defendant Spencer then filed a motion in writing to dismiss the plaintiff's bill for want of equity on the face, which was allowed by the court and the bill was dismissed; and the plaintiff brings this cause into this court by writ of error, alleging that the court below erred in dismissing said bill.

R. S. NELSON, for Plaintiff in Error.

J. H. GUNN, and H. K. S. OMELVÉNY, for Defendants in Error.

WALKER, J. We are of the opinion that this decree should be affirmed. The bill was exhibited in the court below for the purpose of enjoining the collection of three several judgments, recovered on promissory notes given by plaintiff in error and his securities to Spencer. The bill alleges that a portion of the consideration of each note was for usurious interest. It appears from the copies of the judgments filed with the bill as exhibits, that the defendants in each case, permitted judgment to go by default. Spencer appeared to this suit in the court below, and filed a motion to dissolve the injunction and dismiss the bill for want of equity. On a hearing the motion was allowed, and a decree accordingly entered. From that decree complainant prosecutes this writ of error.

The act of the 31st January, 1857, (Sess. Laws, p. 45,) regulating the rate of interest in this State, has adopted [*17] six per cent. per annum, unless a larger rate is fixed by agreement. But the second section of that act allows the parties to agree upon any rate not exceeding ten per cent. per annum. The third section provides that if a greater rate than ten per cent. is taken or reserved, the creditor shall forfeit the whole interest, and only recover the principal sum due. And the fourth section repeals all other laws imposing penalties for receiving or contracting for a greater rate of interest than is allowed by law. Under this enactment, there can be no pretense that a penalty can be recovered for a violation of the statute. It only creates a forfeiture of all the interest, legal as well as illegal, which has accumulated on the debt. And it repeals the penalty imposed by the act of 1845, for taking or reserving a greater rate of interest than is allowed by law. This then disposes of the question of the right to enforce the penalty claimed by the bill.

It is however urged that equity will interpose to prevent the collection of the usurious interest reserved in these notes. The reason of the creation of courts of equity, at their foundation, was to supply the deficiencies, and to relieve the severities of the law. We are informed by Grotius, that equity was for " the correction of that wherein the law, (by reason of its universality) is deficient." This being the object and scope of

Lucas *v.* Spencer *et al.*

equity jurisdiction, courts of equity have at all times, adhered to this as the general rule. Whilst in some instances courts of law have acted upon equity principles, and courts of chancery have assumed concurrent jurisdiction with courts of law, for the purpose of affording more ample relief, to prevent a multiplicity of suits, and to afford relief against fraud, accident or mistake in the recovery of judgments at law, yet, unless it be for some such purpose, they never assume jurisdiction to revise judgments at law, but leave the party to his legal remedy. Where the party has had the opportunity of interposing his defense at law, and his remedy in that forum is complete, and he from carelessness or inattention has failed to make it, courts of equity never afford relief. The law only favors the vigilant. In this case the plaintiff in error had ample opportunity and means to make his defense if he had any, in the court of law; yet he failed to appear and make it, nor does he give any reason or excuse for his negligence. It is not the policy of the law to permit a party to slumber upon his rights, when he has the opportunity, and is required to assert them in a court of justice, and then seek them in another forum.

But it is supposed, that, whilst such is the general rule, the sixth section of the interest law of 1845, has conferred the jurisdiction, and afforded the means of obtaining the relief at [*18] any time by bill. That section gives the debtor, who has paid or delivered a greater sum or value than is allowed to be reserved for interest, the right to maintain an action of debt or a bill in chancery, to recover it from the creditor. This provision by is terms, seems to apply alone to cases where the money has been paid, and not as a defense to usury due and unpaid. The whole policy of our statutes prior to the passage of the act of January 31st, 1857, has been that the defense of usury should be made alone by plea, as authorized by the fifth section of that act. *Hadden v. Innes*, 24 Ill. 381. And under such a plea the plaintiff in error could have had the benefit of a discovery, by calling the plaintiff in the action at law as a witness, as fully as by a bill. After the money had been paid however, in a suit to recover it back the parties are not made competent witnesses, and it was to give the benefit of a discovery that a recovery was authorized by bill in chancery.

In any point of view the defense is as complete at law as in equity. And hence the General Assembly could not have designed to authorize it to be made in equity. But only to prevent a resort to that forum, when the money has already been paid, for a recovery of it from the creditor. Again, a party who voluntarily permits a default to be taken, thereby impliedly admits that the demand is just, and that he has no defense. And unless he can show some sufficient reason for the interposition of the chancellor, he cannot be heard to impugn the judgment at law. Inasmuch as there is no pretense that the principal and legal interest was paid, or any portion of the usury, and as the plaintiff in error had an opportunity to make his defense at law, we can perceive no reason for reversing the decree of the court below, and it must be affirmed.

Decree affirmed.

Ninian S. Moore, Plaintiff in Error, *v.* George Goelitz, Defendant in Error.

ERROR TO MONROE.

A continuance will not be granted because a witness has said that he would be present at the trial and had been subpoenaed by the opposite party. The party desiring the testimony of the witness, should secure his presence at the trial.

This was an action of trespass by Goelitz against Moore for assault and battery, tried at the Monroe Circuit Court. Pleas [*19] of the general issue and *son assault demesne* were filed, and issue joined. At the October term, 1859, judgment was rendered in favor of Goelitz for $600 and costs. The case is brought here by writ of error.

Before the trial, Moore applied for a continuance, and filed an affidavit, setting forth, "That Jacob Lavo was a material witness for him on the trial of his suit; that said witness resided in Georgetown, St. Clair county, in this State, and promised the affiant to be present at the term of court to testify in said case, and said he was subpœnaed for plaintiff, and was absent against his (defendant's) will and consent. That defendant expected to prove by said absent witness, who had testified before a justice of the peace in said case, that said witness was present at the time the supposed trespass sued for was committed, and that defendant at that time used no more force than was necessary for the defense of his person, on that occasion." Affiant further swore that the witnesses who saw the said supposed trespass, differ materially as to the circumstances attending the same, and affiant could not safely proceed to trial in the absence of said witness, and this affidavit was made to enable affiant to have a fair trial on the merits, and that he expected to procure the attendance of said absent witness at the next term of said court.

The court overruled the said motion for a continuance, to which Moore, the defendant below, at the time excepted, and assigns said decision for error.

W. H. UNDERWOOD, for Plaintiff in Error.

R. S. NELSON and OMELVENY & KENNEDY, for Defendant in Error.

CATON, C. J. The plaintiff in error complains, that his motion for a continuance was overruled. The feature that distinguishes this case from that of *Day v. Gelston*, 22 Ill. 102, is, that here the witness told the party, that he was subpœnaed by the opposite party, as a witness in the same cause; while in that case, the witness merely promised to attend without a subpœna. We there held that if a party would rely upon the promise of the witness to attend, he must run the hazard of having the promise violated. Nor is this case any better for the party complaining. He had no right to appropriate the diligence used by the opposite party, to his own use. He knew that his adversary had a right to tell the witness that he need not attend in obedience to the subpœna, and

[*20] thus relieve him from his obligation to obey it. Indeed, he might well expect if the party who subpœnaed the witness found his opponent wanted him upon the trial, that he would relieve him from the trouble of attending.

The judgment is affirmed.

Judgment affirmed.

ANDREW J. BROMLEY, indicted with Dempsey Abels, and Smith Sullivan, Plaintiff in Error, *v.* THE PEOPLE, Defendants in Error.

ERROR TO MARION.

This court will not disturb a verdict, which the evidence justifies.

At the July special term of Marion Circuit Court, 1861, the plaintiff, Andrew J. Bromley, was indicted with Dempsey Abels and Smith Sullivan for larceny, in stealing one shoulder of bacon, of the value of two dollars, one ham of bacon, of the value of two dollars and fifty cents, and eight sides of bacon, of the value of three dollars each, the property of John Wood. The indictment was in proper form, and the plaintiff was tried separately before BRYAN, Judge and a jury.

The jury found the defendant guilty, and sentenced him to imprisonment in the penitentiary for one year; whereupon the defendant moved for an arrest of judgment and for a new trial, for several reasons; but the ground relied upon for a new trial was, that the verdict was contrary to the law and evidence. The court overruled the motions in arrest of a new trial, and rendered judgment upon the verdict of the jury.

R. S. NELSON, for Plaintiff in Error.

T. S. CASEY, State's Attorney for the People.

CATON, C. J.   The only point relied on for the reversal of this judgment is, that the evidence did not sustain the verdict. In this we cannot agree with the counsel for the prisoner.

That a larceny was committed as charged in the indictment, is not questioned. And the tracks of the prisoner's horses from his stable to the place where the meat was stolen, and back to the stable, which was distinctly proved, would seem to leave no doubt, that the meat was carried away, and [*21] to the premises of the prisoner, on his horses. In addition to this, a portion of the stolen meat was found on the prisoner's premises, secreted under a stack. The only explanation of this, is the prisoner's own declaration, that the other prisoners indicted with him, had taken his horses and brought away the meat without his knowledge, and the testimony of one or two witnesses, that they had never heard anything against his character; while another witness had heard him suspected of counterfeiting. Upon this evidence the jury convicted the prisoner, and we think they were justified in doing so.

The judgment is affirmed.

Judgment affirmed.

WILLIAM WINKELMAN, and NICHOLAS KISER, Plaintiffs in Error, *v.* MATHIAS KISER, for the use of Noah B. Harlow, Defendant in Error.

ERROR TO MONROE.

A person who holds the beneficial interest in a mortgage should be made the complainant, yet when the use is declared the suit need not be dismissed if the bill should be amended by striking out the name of the nominal complainant; and such an amendment would not produce injury.

A decree should not be pronounced against a party not before the court.

A decree should not be entered against the purchaser of mortgaged premises, whether he be or not a purchaser with notice; the decree should direct a sale of the premises and a distribution of the proceeds. If he held the equity of redemption, the sale might bar it, if he failed to redeem.

THIS was a suit in chancery, brought in the Monroe Circuit Court, at the May term thereof, 1861, by Mathias Kiser, who sued for the use of Noah B. Harlow, against Nicholas Kiser and William Winkelman, to foreclose a mortgage, made by Nicholas Kiser to Mathias Kiser, dated September 7th, 1858, to secure to said Mathias Kiser the payment of a certain promissory note of that date. Said mortgage conveyed certain town lots in the town of Harrisonville in said county. Winkelman claims said lands by a title subsequent to said mortgage. Said bill prays for a foreclosure and sale of the premises in the usual form.

Summons was issued in the usual way, and notice given by publication to said Nicholas Kiser, he being a non-resident of this State. Summons was served upon Winkelman and the following return thereon indorsed, to wit: "This writ executed [*22] by leaving copy with Winkelman, and by reading the same to the above named Winkelman. Kiser not found. March 15, 1861. WM. BOURKE, Dep. Sheriff."

And afterwards, on the second Monday of said term of court, the defendants having failed to appear and answer, the bill was taken as confessed against them, and decree rendered by said court for $173.10 in favor of plaintiffs below, and the land ordered to be sold.

William Winkelman brings this case to this court, and assigns for error: That the court below erred in rendering a decree against defendants without their appearance or their being duly served with process. That the proceedings are irregular and erroneous in this, that the suit should have been brought in the name of the party for whose use it was instituted.

W. H. UNDERWOOD, for Plaintiffs in Error.

OMELVENY & KENNEDY, for Defendant in Error.

WALKER, J. It is urged that this bill was improperly exhibited in the name of Mathias Kiser for the use of Harlow. Whilst it is true that the person holding the beneficial interest should be made the complainant, we are not prepared to hold, that when the use is declared, that the suit should be dismissed, if the bill should be amended by striking out the name of the nominal complainant, and let it proceed in the name of the

Moore *et al. v.* Bracken.

person having the beneficial interest. To permit an amendment to that extent, at any stage of the proceeding, would produce no injury to any party to the record.

The bill alleges that Nicholas Kiser executed the note and mortgage to Mathias Kiser, and alleges that Harlow claimed to have some interest in the mortgaged premises. Service was only had upon Harlow, but on the bill being taken as confessed, a decree for the payment of the money was rendered against both defendants. There can be no pretense that the decree against the defendant not served or in any way entering his appearance, was authorized. Until he was in court in some appropriate mode it was error to render a decree against him. It was also error to render a decree against Harlow for the payment of the money. If his interest was subsequently acquired with actual or constructive notice, it would be proper to order the premises to be sold, and if his claim was a mortgage or deed of trust, to decree his payment out of any surplus remaining after satisfying complainant's demand. Qr if he had become the owner of the equity of redemption, to order the sale of the property, and if he [*23] failed to redeem, the sale would bar his equity of redemption.

The decree of the court below must be reversed, and the cause remanded.

Decree reversed.

ROBERT MOORE, and PRESLEY P. HAMILTON, Plaintiffs in Error, *v.* JOHN BRACKEN, Defendant in Error.

ERROR TO MARION.

It is erroneous to decree a sale of premises in thirty days, where there is not any redemption from the sale.

In chancery all matters, whether of discretion or of positive law, are subject to review in a superior court. A bill of review may also be filed in the same court to correct an error in the original decree.

Moore *et al. v.* Bracken.

Where the attorney of a party becomes the purchaser at a forced sale, he stands in the shoes of his client; and though the attorney designed to purchase for his own benefit, the client may claim the purchase for himself.

THE bill in this cause, filed in Marion Circuit Court, for review and general relief, states that the complainant Bracken is a non-resident.

That on the 27th of February, 1861, defendant Moore filed his petition for a mechanics' lien in said court, which states that on the 12th of October, 1860, said Bracken contracted with him (Moore) to pay him $377, if he would by the first of November, 1860, erect a house, of certain dimensions stated, one story high, or, if two stories high, to be paid for additional in proportion. Said $377 to be paid when the work was completed according to contract. The building to be erected on a piece of ground known as lots 91, 92, 69, and 70, in block 6, in Urial Mills' Addition to Salem, more fully described as follows, etc.; which real estate said Bracken purchased, and held a title bond for, from one Urial Mills.

That Moore, pursuant to said contract, did erect said house, and finish and deliver it to Bracken before the 1st of November, 1860.

That Moore did, in addition to said contract, at Bracken's request, make and deliver certain parts of work in and about said house over and above the original contract, which are set out in petition, which additional work amounted to $92, which amount Bracken, on the 5th of January, 1861, promised to pay.

That Bracken paid on said contract and extra work, at various [*24] times before said 5th of January, 1861, about $300, leaving, on said day, due on said contract and extra work, $169, and being so indebted, Bracken on said day promised to pay same, which he has failed to pay.

Prays that Bracken be made defendant; that summons issue; that he make answer; that on final hearing, plaintiff Moore be decreed to have a valid and subsisting mechanics' lien on said house and lot; that same be ordered to be sold for cash, the proceeds to be applied in payment of amount due plaintiff; and for further relief.

The bill then sets out the decree thereon, of March 27th, 1861,

Moore *et al. v.* Bracken.

which states, that defendant Bracken made default to answer as ruled. That the suit being on an account, a jury was called to assess damages. That the jury assessed the same at $171.11. Decree—That defendant pay said $171.11 and costs in thirty days. In default of which, that James S. Martin, master in chancery, sell the premises in petition described, (the description is given at length as in petition,) at public auction to the highest and best bidder for cash, first advertising according to law. Sale to be at south door of court house in Salem. That master execute conveyance to the purchaser. Said sale to be for judgment of the damages and costs in the first place, the overplus to be paid to Bracken. That master report; and cause continued for report.

The bill then states, that on the 23rd of May, 1861, the master published a notice of sale, which notice is set out, and states, that pursuant to said decree, he (the master) would sell, on the 14th of June then next, lots, 91, 92, 69 and 70, in block 6, in U. Mills' Addition to Salem, with the buildings thereon. Sale for cash. Purchaser to get deeds.

The bill states, that said master did, on said 14th June, 1861, sell said premises *en masse*, without offering to sell them separately. That defendant, P. P. Hamilton, one of the attorneys in said cause for said Moore, bought said four lots with the improvements, for $193.

That said house is on but one of said lots, and the said house is worth in cash, $800. That Bracken paid said Moore $300 for same, and about $200 to others for work and labor done and materials purchased.

That he (Bracken) did not appear and defend said suit, at March term, 1861, because that shortly before said term, it was understood and agreed between him, Moore and said Hamilton, that Moore should have a lien for balance on said contract, of $97. That Moore would give time to pay same, and not force sale for a reasonable time, on pretense of friendship, and assurances that no advantage would be taken. That Bracken would save expense of attorney to defend him—[*25] otherwise he would have defended said suit.

That immediately after said sale, said Hamilton took forcible

31

possession of said premises, evicted the tenant, and deprived Bracken of the use and rents thereof, worth from $4 to $10 per month.

The bill states errors in the record and decree in said original suit, as follows:

It does not appear what estate Bracken had in the premises ordered to be sold.

The judgment is for $171, while the pleading shows only $77 due on the contract.

The decree limits the time of payment to thirty days.

The decree ordered sale of four lots without limitation, and accordingly the sale was *en masse.*

The premises were sold to the plaintiff's attorney in the cause, who knew all the errors in decree.

The bill prays, that Moore & Hamilton be parties; that summons issue; that they answer; that on final hearing the decree in said mechanics' lien suit be set aside; that the complainant Bracken be allowed to defend same; that Hamilton be decreed to pay rent for the time he held said premises, and be decreed to surrender possession to complainant; and for further relief.

Decree of August term, 1861, is set out, which shows that on the 19th of August, 1861, defendant Moore appeared, by defendant Hamilton, his attorney. That on the 30th of August, 1861, demurrer was argued and overruled in all particulars except that the bill herein be verified by oath or affidavit. Defendants except, and stand by their demurrer, which is still on file.

That on the 31st of August, in said August term, came complainant, by his solicitor, and amended his bill by attaching affidavit. Defendants ruled to answer, etc., to amended bill by 8 o'clock in the evening. That at 8 o'clock P. M. cause called. Defendants failed to answer, and bill taken for confessed by them. Court hears the cause on bill as confessed, and finds apparent error on the face of the decree on mechanics' lien in two particulars: In not giving longer time to pay the debt; and in ordering sale of all the premises when a part would have paid the debt and discharged the lien.

Decree that said decree on mechanics' lien be set aside;

that the sale be set aside; that defendant Hamilton surrender the premises sold, which are described as in said bill for mechanics' lien. The parties consent that the said demurrer be considered as refiled to said amended bill—be overruled—defendants stand thereby—and that the decree be con- [*26] sidered as amended in these respects and join in error. The said appellants, Moore and Hamilton, assign for error in said decree as follows:

The court erred in overruling the demurrer to bill of review.

The court erred on bill of review in allowing the bill to be sworn to, after its filing and argument on demurrer.

The court erred in admitting bill of review to be sworn to on affidavit of attorney in the form filed. The bill should have been dismissed.

The court erred in assigning two insufficient reasons for error as the basis of its decree on bill of review.

The court erred in setting aside the original decree and sale.

The court erred in overlooking the fundamental principles regulating bills of review, to-wit, error in original decree or newly discovered facts, not known on original hearing. After decree *pro confesso* in original suit, Bracken should not be allowed to defend on insufficient cause shown.

The court erred in overlooking and setting aside the sound discretion of the chancellor in original decree.

The court erred in making no provision for repayment of purchase money to Hamilton. It does not do equity, and has not decreed a resale.

The court erred in divesting Moore of his equity without making Bracken in equity respond to him by payment.

The court erred in not declaring to whom Hamilton should surrender his possession.

The decree makes no provision for costs.

P. P. HAMILTON, for self and Moore, Plaintiffs in Error.

E. BEECHER, for Defendant in Error.

CATON, C. J. We now decide directly, what we have on a

former occasion intimated, that it was error to order a sale of the premises within thirty days after the decree, where, as in this case, there is no redemption from the sale. In most cases, upon judgments at law or decrees in chancery, the debtor is allowed twelve months within which to redeem after the sale, and his judgment creditor three months longer. In this particular case, and it may be the only case in this State, the law has made no provision for redemption, but the sale is absolute. It is discretionary in the court, no doubt, to fix the time for the sale, and were it in a proceeding at law, we might not have power to review the exercise of that discretion, [*27] but in chancery, all matters, whether of discretion or positive law, are subject to review in a superior court. Or the party may file his bill of review to correct the error in the original decree, as was done in this case.

As the solicitor of the complainant in the original bill was the purchaser, there is no question about the intervening rights of third persons or innocent purchasers. When the attorney or solicitor of a party becomes the purchaser, he occupies the position of the party himself, and although he may design the purchase for himself, the client may claim it to his own use.

The Circuit Court properly overruled the demurrer to the bill of review, and the party standing by the demurrer, the decree was properly entered and must be affirmed.

Decree affirmed.

THE PEOPLE OF THE STATE OF ILLINOIS, who sue for the use of Titus Buffington, Treasurer of Schools of Township Two South, Range Seven East, etc., Plaintiffs in Error, *v.* HENRY A. ORGAN *et al.*, Defendants in Error.

ERROR TO CLAY.

Where it appears that the treasurer of schools, the obligor of a bond, presented it signed and sealed in blank for approval, the penalty not being expressed, but was afterwards inserted in his presence and with his approval, but in the absence of his sureties; *Held*, that while he was estopped by his consent, his sureties were not holden.

An executed deed may be avoided by erasure, interlineation or other material alteration; or by an intentional destruction of the seal.

A deed signed and sealed in blank, with verbal authority to fill the blank, will be void, unless it has been subsequently acknowledged or adopted by the party executing it.

In debt, recovery must be had against all or none of the defendants.

THIS was an action of debt brought by plaintiffs against defendants in the Wayne Circuit Court, on the official bond of defendant Organ, as collector of Wayne county for the year 1859. The venue was subsequently changed to Clay county.

The declaration is in the usual form against Organ as principal, and the other defendants as his securities, and alleges the non-payment of certain moneys belonging to the school fund.

The plea of all but two of the defendants denies the execution of the bond, and is verified by the affidavits of the de- [*28] fendants.

A certified copy of the bond sued on was read on trial, and contains the usual conditions. This bond purports to be in the sum of forty thousand dollars.

It was agreed by the parties, that the plea denying the execution of the bond sued on, should be considered on file for all the defendants.

S. J. R. Wilson, being sworn, said, that at the date of the bond sued on, he was judge of the County Court of Wayne county, Illinois. That said defendant Organ, as collector of said county for the year 1859, presented to said County Court, at its November term, 1859, the bond sued on in the case, for approval. That when said bond was presented to said court, there was no amount stated as the penalty therein, but it was, as to the amount for which the bond was given, *a blank*. That he, as one of the court, insisted that the bond was invalid, unless the securities would appear and acknowledge their signatures after the blank was filled up; but as they had no trouble the former year with said Organ as collector, they finally agreed to receive it. That the sum of forty thousand dollars was then inserted in said bond as the penalty. That none of the securities to said bond were present when the same was filled up, nor was any authority produced authorizing any one to fill it up, nor does he know of any such authority having been given to any one. That at that time the tax books had not been made out, and they could not ascertain the amount for which it ought to be taken, but insisted that it ought to be for more than the amount for which it was finally filled up.

Thomas M. Scott, being sworn, said, he was also a member of said court. He confirms the foregoing statement of Judge Wilson. He further says that he also objected to receiving said bond, but finally consented to accept it for the reason stated.

It was admitted by the parties defendants, that the signatures to the bond were genuine, but insisted that when such signatures were written, the bond was blank.

The plaintiffs also introduced a certificate of the clerk of the county Court of said county of Wayne, showing that there was due from said collector to said township, (for whose use this suit is brought,) the sum of $25 belonging to district No. 3, and $60 to district No. 2.

It was also agreed by the parties that all objections which could have been legally taken to the introduction of any of [*29] the foregoing evidence, should be considered as having been made at the time, and that the parties should be entitled to the same benefit therefrom as if the same had been formally objected to, and objections overruled by the court and exceptions taken thereto.

This was all the evidence in the cause; and the court, ALLEN, Judge, presiding, (a jury having been waived by the parties,) thereupon gave judgment for the defendants for costs. To which opinion of the court the plaintiffs at the time, by their counsel, excepted.

HANNA, WHITING & COOPER, for Plaintiffs in Error.

E. BEECHER, for Defendants in Error.

WALKER, J. It appears that Organ, the principal obligor in

36

this bond, presented it, signed and sealed, in blank for approval. The penalty was not then inserted, and some question arose as to the legality of filling in the amount in the absence of the securities, and without competent authority for the purpose. It was, however, finally agreed that the amount should be inserted in the bond, which was done. Organ seems to have been present, and it was done at his request, with his approbation and consent. He cannot therefore be heard to object to the validity of the bond. Whether it was, after the blank was filled, binding upon his sureties, can make no difference, as what he did at the time amounts to a re-delivery by him, after the blank was filled.

But the question is still presented, whether the filling the blank with the amount of the penalty, after the sureties had executed it, without their knowledge or consent, rendered it void as to them. Cases may no doubt be found which hold that the filling a blank promissory note under seal, with the amount agreed upon, does not release the indorser. And that such is the case with commercial paper generally, is certainly true. But such cases are exceptions to, and not the rule. After a deed has been executed, it may be avoided by erasure, interlineation or other alteration in a material part; or by an intentional breaking or defacing of the seal by the obligee. A deed to be binding must be in writing, signed, sealed and delivered by the parties. It has been held that a paper signed and sealed in blank, with verbal authority to fill the blank, which is afterwards done, is void as to the parties so signing and sealing unless they afterwards deliver, or acknowledge or adopt it. *Gilbert v. Anthony*, 1 Yerg. 69; *Wayne v. Govenor*, ib. 149; *Myers v. McClanahan*, 6 Gill & John. 250; *Parminter v. Mc-* [*30] *Daniel*, 1 Hill, 267; *Boyd v. Boyd*, 2 N. & M. 125; *United States v. Nelson*, 2 Brock, 64; *Ayres v. Harness*, 1 Ham. 368; *McKee v. Hicks*, 2 Dev. 379.

It is believed that these decisions fully accord with the rule announced by the British courts. And it is for the plain reason that after the blank has been filled up, the deed ceases to be that which the parties executed. It is then of a different tenor, and is another instrument, as much so as if it was executed in a penalty for one sum, and was changed to a different and larger sum. And without consent, re-delivery, or a subsequent ratification, no one would suppose that such an alteration could be made without releasing the parties. In this case, there is no evidence that the sureties consented to the change, re-delivered the bond, or in any manner ratified the act done. And these cases held, that even if they had agreed that the blank might be filled after they had executed the bond, still they would not be bound, unless they had been present and consented, or had adopted the act by a subsequent delivery, or by a ratification of the change. As the plaintiff must however recover against all of the defendants sued upon a contract, or against none, the court below decided correctly in rendering judgment for costs in favor of the defendants, which is affirmed.

Judgment affirmed.

The Ohio and Mississippi Railroad Company, Appellant, *v.* Milly Meisenheimer, Appellee.

APPEAL FROM CLAY.

A party who sues a railroad company, under the statute, for injuries to cattle, resulting from omission to fence a road, should show that the road had been opened more than six months prior to the injury complained of.

This was an action brought before a justice of the peace in Clay county, and taken by appeal to the Circuit Court, where a judgment was obtained by Meisenheimer against the railroad company for eighty dollars, the value of a horse killed at a road crossing. There was entire absence of proof, in reference to the time when the railroad was opened for use.

William Homes, for Appellant.

W. B. Cooper, for Appellee.

[*31] Caton, C. J. The plaintiff relies upon the statute requiring railroad companies to fence certain portions of their

road within six months after the road is open, and it is not pretended that unless he made out a case under this statute, the action could be sustained. This he undoubtedly failed to do. He did not show that the road had been opened for six months before the casualty of which the plaintiff complained. This was indispensable. The proof, too, that the damage was done on the defendant's road, was very slight if not totally deficient.

The judgment is reversed, and the cause remanded.

Judgment reversed.

JAMES M. MORGAN *et al.*, Plaintiffs in Error, *v.* CHARLES B. FALLENSTEIN *et al.*, Defendants in Error.

ERROR TO JACKSON.

Parol evidence is admissible, to show that the consideration of a note has wholly or partially failed.

THE record in this case shows that an action of assumpsit was brought in the Jackson Circuit Court, at May term, 1860, by the appellees against the appellants. The declaration counts first upon a promissory note for $886.55, with the usual money counts added.

The defendants pleaded first the general issue, and secondly, a plea of partial failure of consideration to the first count; the second plea alleging that the "sum of fifty-nine dollars was included in said note, and in consideration of the agreement and promise of the said plaintiff at the time of making said note, and contemporaneously therewith, that they, the said plaintiffs, would not institute a suit upon said note, or attempt by legal process to collect it of said defendants, or demand payment thereof of them, until after the first day of June, 1860, and which said time has not yet elapsed, and plaintiffs have instituted this suit and demanded payment of the said sum of $59 before the said first day of June, 1860, by means whereof, the consideration of the said note has failed, and this they are ready to verify; wherefore they pray judgment," etc.

To this second plea a general demurrer was filed, and the court sustained the demurrer. A trial was then had upon the general issue, and the jury returned a verdict against the appellants, for $897.62. Motion for new trial was overruled by [*32] the court, and judgment was rendered upon the verdict of the jury. From this judgment, Morgan and Hundley appealed to this court.

The errors assigned are: That the court erred in sustaining demurrer to second plea. That the court erred in overruling motion for new trial, and entering judgment upon the verdict.

WILLIAM J. ALLEN, for Appellants.

C. S. WARD, for Appellees.

CATON, C. J. The second plea to which the court sustained a demurrer, presents precisely the same question that was decided in *Hill* v. *Enders*, 19 Ill. 163. It may be that, strictly speaking, the agreement to pay the money mentioned in the note at the time there stated, and the agreement not to enforce the payment of that amount till after the first of June, 1861, all being made at the same time, constituted but one agreement, only that part of it which is embodied in the note being reduced to writing, the rest being allowed to rest in parol, and that by the general rule of law, this latter part which was not embraced in the writing, could not be shown by parol. If that rule is to be applied in this case, then it must in all similar cases, and it would be impossible in any case to show a total or partial failure of consideration of a note by parol, for the consideration of a note must necessarily form a part of the agreement in pursuance of which the note is given, and when the note is given, that part of the agreement which constitutes the consideration, is never reduced to writing, and it must be shown by parol if it is ever shown. If I agree with you to deliver you my horse to-morrow, and you give me your note for one hundred dollars in consideration thereof, here only one part of the agreement is reduced to writing by the execution and delivery of the note, and that portion which required me to deliver the horse to-morrow, is left in parol. Shall it be said that when I refuse to deliver the

40

horse, I may turn round and say, you shall never prove it because that portion of the agreement was not put into the writing? The truth is, that even the common law made an exception to that rule of evidence, in cases where notes or other instruments for the absolute payment of money are given. It has always been admissible to show by parol, the consideration upon which such instruments were executed. But whatever may have been the rule of the common law, our statute has expressly provided for this defense, and necessarily, to give effect to the statute, parol evidence must be admitted to show what that consideration was, as well as to show [*33] that that consideration has failed. The statute has made no exception, and we can make none. A note or bond to pay money, is necessarily but a part of the agreement between the parties, leaving out as it does all that portion of the agreement which induced the undertaking to pay the money, and if this part could not be shown by parol, there must ever be a liability to a failure of justice. Nor is the exception to the general rule upon which the counsel here rely, confined to showing by parol a failure of consideration. Usury, and, in fine, any other defense arising out of the original agreement upon which the note was given, or of which the note constitutes a part, may be shown by parol in order to establish a defense to the note.

The demurrer to the plea should have been overruled, and the judgment must be reversed, and the cause remanded.

Judgment reversed.

RACHEL ANN HOLLIDAY *et al.*, Plaintiffs in Error, *v.* ROBERT DIXON, Jr., Defendant in Error.

ERROR TO PERRY.

Held, that the following words of devise in a will gave the devisee an estate of inheritance: "I will and bequeath to my oldest daughter, Margaret Jane Elizabeth Holliday, eighty acres of land where my house and well stands, never to to her and and heirs forever, never to be mortgaged nor sold forever."

In construing wills, the court will gather the meaning of the testator from the language used, if it be possible to do so.

41

Holliday *et al. v.* Dixon.

Robert Dixon, Junior, the plaintiff in the court below, and defendant in error, at the April term of the Perry Circuit Court, 1860, filed his petition in the Circuit Court of Perry county, setting forth that he was the husband of Margaret Jane Elizabeth Holliday, eldest daughter of Matthew Holliday deceased, and that on the 2nd December, 1848, said Holliday, being seized in fee of the following described real estate, viz., east half north-west quarter section 21, town 4 south, range 4 west, 3rd principal meridian, in said county of Perry, made his will, in substance as follows: "I will and bequeath to my oldest daughter, Margaret Jane Elizabeth Holliday, the eighty acres of land where my house and well stands, *never to her and her heirs forever never to be mortgaged and sold forever;*" that on the 1st April, 1859, petitioner intermarried with the said Margaret Jane Elizabeth Holliday, deceased, and lived [*34] with her as her lawful husband until she died, which was on the 11th July, 1860; that there was no issue of the marriage born alive; and the defendants in the court below were brothers and sisters of his said wife, and her only surviving heirs-at-law, and as such interested in said estate, and that the defendants in the court below are minor children of the said Matthew Holliday, deceased, by a second wife, excepting the defendant Samuel, who is their lawful guardian.

The petitioner claims by his petition that he is entitled by law to one undivided half of the above described eighty acre tract of land, (it being the same eighty acre tract in the will referred to,) as heir by statute of his said wife, the fee simple therein being by the terms of said Matthew's will devised to said Margaret Jane Elizabeth, the wife of petitioner, as above stated, and prayed a partition thereof accordingly.

At the September term, 1860, of the Perry Circuit Court, a final decree for the partition of the premises was entered according to the prayer of the petitioner, and partition made by commissioners, who, at the April term, 1861, of said court, made their final report, which was filed and approved by the court, but excepted to at the same term by plaintiff in error.

The defendants in the court below bring the cause by writ of error into this court.

E. Beecher, and R. S. Nelson, for Plaintiffs in Error.

Marshall & Wall, for Defendant in Error.

Caton, C. J. The clause of the will upon the construction of which this clause depends, is this: " I will bequeath to my eldest daughter, Margaret Jane Elizabeth Holliday, eighty acres of land, where my house and well stands, never to to her and and heirs forever, never to be mortgaged nor sold forever." It is insisted by the appellant that·it was the intention of the testator to create a life estate only in his daughter, and to forbid her heirs from inheriting the estate, upon her decease. It may be remarked that as the will was executed by the testator by affixing his mark, it musť have been written by another, and that he must have been illiterate, or very careless, or both. Evidently here are words inserted, not designed to be used, and others which were intended are omitted. Still we must gather the meaning of the testator from the language used, if that be ·possible. There is one thing which may be safely assumed in the beginning, and that is, the testator intended to make some provision for his daughter Margaret, out of the premises described, and the only question is, what was the extent of that provision? What estate in the land did [*35] he design to create in her? It is admitted on all hands that he intended to create in her either a life estate or an estate of inheritance. The appellant insists that it was the former. By the will the testator first gives the land to her, and then specifies the estate, thus—" never to to her and and heirs forever, never to be mortgaged nor sold forever." Now here are two qualifying words of opposite meaning, one of limitation and the other of extension, both of which cannot stand, and we must determine which to reject, in order to arrive at the meaning of the testator. These words are "never" and "forever." If we give effect to the former and reject the latter, we not only defeat the estate in the heirs but in the devisee also. The negation or prohibition expressed by the word *never* applies as much to the estate created in her as in her heirs. It is *never* to her as well as never to her heirs. This was manifestly not the intention of the testator, unless we conclude that he meant nothing by this second clause of the will — that he intended to give nothing whatever to his eldest daughter. But this is not contended. All admit that he meant to give her some estate in this land. So that we are obliged, in order to give effect to the acknowledged intent of the testator, to strike out the word *never* where it first occurs, as having been inserted by mistake. And when once stricken out so as to allow her to take the devise, we have no warrant by any intimation of the intention or desire of the testator, to insert the word in another place for the purpose of excluding her heirs. On the contrary the word *forever* following the word heirs, shows an intention, that not only she but her heirs should take an estate of unlimited duration, restricted only by the words which follow, that they should never mortgage or sell it.

We have no doubt that this was the intention of the testator, and the decree must be affirmed.

Judgment affirmed.

WILLIAM STEPHENS *et al.*, Plaintiffs in Error, *v.* THOMAS CROSS, and RICHARD BROWN, Defendants in Error.

ERROR TO PERRY.

Upon an appeal from a justice of the peace, the Circuit Court should try the cause *de novo*. and it is error to dismiss the suit because the justice rendered judgment against two defendants when he had only obtained jurisdiction over the person of one of them.

[*36] If a justice of the peace renders judgment against two defendants when only one has been brought into court, and the defendant who was served appeals the case and fails to prosecute his appeal, the Circuit Court may affirm the judgment as to him, and reverse it as to the other who has not been served.

THE plaintiffs in error commenced a suit before a justice of the peace in Perry county, on an account under $100 against the defendant in error and Richard Brown, which account was for goods sold by the plaintiffs to the said Cross and Brown as partners.

The defendant in error was regularly served with process in the suit so commenced before the justice, but although both defendants were named in the summons, and the summons was regular in form, Brown was not served with process, nor did he appear or in anywise waive the service of the process or confess judgment, but the justice on the day of trial rendered judgment against the defendant in error and Brown.

The defendant appealed to the Circuit Court of Perry county, Brown not joining in the appeal, and on motion of defendant in error, the suit before the justice was dismissed as to both the defendant in error, and Brown, his co-defendant before the justice.

The plaintiffs in error bring the case by writ of error into this court, and seek to reverse the judgment of the Circuit Court of Perry county, because they say that the said court erred in dismissing the suit before the justice on the motion of the defendant in error.

This cause was submitted *ex parte.*

R. S. NELSON, for Plaintiffs in Error.

WALKER, J. Plaintiffs in error instituted a suit before a justice of the peace of Perry county, on an account against defendant in error, and Richard Brown, as partners. The summons was regularly served on defendant in error, but Brown was not served, nor did he enter his appearance before the justice of the peace. The plaintiffs in error proceeded to trial, and recovered a judgment against both defendants. An appeal was prosecuted to the Circuit Court, and on motion of defendants in error the suit was dismissed. The plaintiffs prosecute this writ of error to reverse that judgment.

The 20th section of the act regulating the duties of justices of the peace and constables, authorized the rendition of judgment against such defendants as have been served with process. It provides, that, " Where there are several joint debtors, and all cannot be served with process, the justice may render judgment against such as are served with process." From this

45.

[*37] provision it is perfectly manifest, that the justice of the peace had power to proceed to trial and render judgment against defendant Cross, but had no power, unless Brown had entered his appearance, to render judgment against him. As to him there was no jurisdiction. But the 66th section of the same act provides, that on the trial of appeals in the Circuit Court, no exception shall be taken to the form or service of the summons, nor to any proceeding before that officer; but the court shall hear and determine the same, in a summary manner, according to the justice of the case.

This latter section has expressly prohibited the allowance of any exception to the proceedings before the justice. It has required a trial *de novo*. And in this case, notwithstanding the justice of the peace erred in rendering judgment against Brown, he had jurisdiction of Cross, and by his appeal the Circuit court acquired the same jurisdiction which the justice had, and as required by the 66th section of the statute aforesaid, should have heard the cause and rendered judgment on the merits. The court below erred in allowing exception to the judgment of the justice, and in dismissing the suit. The trial should have been had against Cross. Or if the defendant had failed to prosecute his appeal, and the court had not acquired jurisdiction of the person of Brown, the judgment might have been affirmed as to Cross, and reversed as to the other defendant.

The judgment of the Circuit Court must be reversed, and the cause remanded.

Judgment reversed.

W. W. WILLARD, Appellant, *v.* JAMES BASSETT, Administrator *de bonis non* of the Estate of N. C. Merrill, deceased, Appellee.

APPEAL FROM MARION.

An attorney, who is an administrator, is not entitled to an allowance against the estate for professional services he may have rendered it. If he perform such services, they will be regarded as a gratuity.

THE appellant, who was an attorney at law, and Minerva Merrill, the widow of the decedent, took out letters of administration on the estate of N. C. Merrill, deceased. They subsequently resigned, and the appellee was appointed administrator *de bonis non*.

The appellant presented an account for $218, against the estate, nearly all of which was for legal services rendered [*38] by him, while administrator, in cases in which the estate was interested as plaintiff or defendant. The County Court refused to allow this account, but finally allowed Willard and Minerva Merrill, the administratrix, the sum of one hundred and fifty dollars for their services, which was about sixty-three dollars above the regular per cent. to which they would be entitled; this sum, however, was not apportioned between them.

Willard appealed from this order to the Circuit Court of Marion county, and the cause was submitted, by consent, to OMELVENY, Judge, upon an agreed statement of facts.

The Circuit Court affirmed the judgment of the County Court, but ordered the cause to be remanded in order that the amount allowed might be apportioned between Willard and the administratrix, according to their respective services.

Willard, the appellant, brings the cause to this court, and assigns for error, that the Circuit Court erred in affirming the decision of the County Court, and in remanding the cause back to the County Court to amend its order and judgment by apportioning the judgment between the administrators— and in refusing to allow the appellant his fees for services rendered as attorney for the estate.

W. STOKER, for Appellant.

JAMES BASSETT, *pro se*.

CATON, C. J. The only question in this case is, whether an attorney of this court, who is an administrator, is entitled to an allowance against the estate, for professional services, in cases which he prosecutes or defends as such administrator. The authorities are uniform that this should not be allowed, and every principle of sound policy forbids it. The law cannot permit the idea that a person can take the office of executor or administrator as a business, or as a means of making money. It must ever associate with that place, to a certain extent, the idea of benevolence or philanthropy. We must ever assume that whoever takes such a position is actuated by an impulse of generosity and a desire to do good to others, rather than to make it a source of profit to himself. He must not be expected to suffer loss in the discharge of his duties, hence he must be allowed his necessary disbursements, and a reasonable compensation for the time and trouble bestowed upon the business of the estate. But beyond this the court should never go. If he chooses to exercise his professional [*39] skill as a lawyer in the business of the estate, that must be considered a gratuity. To allow him to become his own client and charge for professional services in his own cause, although in a representative or trust capacity, would be holding out inducements for professional men to seek such representative places to increase their professional business, which would lead to most pernicious results. This is forbidden by every sound principle of professional morality as well as by the policy of the law.

We think the decision of the court below was proper, and it must be affirmed.

Judgment affirmed.

CHARLES HENCKLER, impleaded, etc., Appellant, *v.* THE COUNTY COURT OF MONROE COUNTY, for the use of John E. Schuetze, and Charles F. Eggers, Appellee.

APPEAL FROM MONROE.

The statute has not made it the duty of a constable to collect money except by virtue of process; and an action will not lie upon his bond for money collected by him without process for that purpose.

The Circuit Court should not, in cases of appeal from a justice of the peace, authorize an amendment of the summons, by changing the names of parties.

Henckler, impl., etc., *v.* County Court of Monroe County.

THIS was an appeal from a justice of the peace, tried in the Monroe Circuit Court, at the May term thereof, 1861. The suit was upon a constable's bond against Scheuermann and the others as his securities. The case was tried by the court by consent, and judgment was rendered for plaintiffs below for the sum of one thousand dollars debt, and forty-three dollars and fifty-five cents damages, to be satisfied upon the payment of said damages and costs.

Before the trial of the case, plaintiffs asked and obtained leave of the Circuit Court to change the name of the plaintiffs so as to read: County Court of Monroe county for the use of said plaintiffs below, to which the defendants below excepted.

Plaintiffs below proved that the account sued on was presented by witness to George Scheuermann, who acknowledged that the same was correct, except that the interest was too much. (Interest was computed at ten per cent.) This was before suit was brought before the justice of the peace. Witness further stated, that said sum was collected by Scheuermann in 1856, on an account of Schuetze, and Eggers against Dr. Hoffmann, and witness thought it was collected without [*40] suit, and that said Scheuermann was constable when he received and collected said accounts. This was all the evidence in the case, on which evidence the court found for the plaintiffs below. Motion for new trial was then made because the verdict was contrary to law and evidence, which motion was overruled by the court.

Charles Henckler, one of the defendants below, appealed to this court, and assigns for error: That the court below erred in allowing the name of the plaintiffs' parties to be changed. That the court below erred in finding for plaintiffs below, and in refusing a new trial.

W. H. UNDERWOOD, for Appellant.

OMELVENY & KENNEDY, for Appellee.

WALKER, J. This was an action before a justice of the peace on a constable's bond. It was removed by appeal to the Circuit Court, where a trial was had, resulting in a judgment against the constable and his sureties, for the amount of the penalty as debt and forty-three dollars and fifty-five cents damages, and the costs of suit. The evidence discloses the fact, that Scheuermann as constable received a claim due Schuetze and Eggers against Dr. Hoffman, which was collected without suit. This presents the question whether the sureties on a constable's bond are liable for money received on claims placed in his hand for collection, when suit has not been instituted. Does the statute impose that as a duty upon that officer except upon process? If it does, then it is an official act, for which his sureties are unquestionably responsible.

No reference has been made to any such statute, nor have we been able to find any such duty imposed. When a summons is placed in his hands, the statute has authorized the defendant to pay the amount indorsed thereon with the costs, in discharge of the claim. The constable is also by the command of an execution required to levy the amount of the judgment and costs. Money thus received, is in his official character, and a failure to pay it to the plaintiff or justice of the peace would be a breach of duty, against which his sureties have undertaken. On the contrary, the statute has made the justice of the peace a collecting officer, independent of legal process, and with him and his sureties it is otherwise. But the statute having failed to impose such a duty upon a constable, and as he derives all of his authority from it, the liability of his sureties can be no more extensive than his duties. [*41] They cannot be held liable for this or any other unofficial act. If a claim be placed in his hands for collection, and he receives the money without process, and fails to account for it, the creditor must look alone to the constable for its payment, as to any other agent.

Again, the court erred in permitting an amendment of the summons, by authorizing a change in the parties to the suit. *Lake* v. *Moss*, 11 Ill. 589. Unless there was something in the record by which to amend, the names of the plaintiffs could not be changed. To this effect is the uniform current of adjudged cases.

The Circuit Court therefore erred in rendering judgment in

favor of the appellees, and it must be reversed and the cause remanded.

Judgment reversed.

The Ohio and Mississippi Railroad Company, Appellant, *v.* Levi H. Jones, Appellee.

APPEAL FROM CLAY.

Before a party can recover for injury to property, he must show that he is either the absolute or qualified owner of it.

In an action against a railroad corporation resulting from injuries to property, because of an omission to fence its road, it should appear that the road has been open for use for six months prior to the injury.

This was an action on the case against the Ohio and Mississippi Railroad Company, to recover the value of certain horses killed on the road of the company. The declaration contained four counts inartificially drawn. There was a plea of the general issue, and a recovery by the plaintiff below.

The cause was tried before Kitchell, Judge, and a jury, at October term, 1860, of the Clay Circuit Court.

W. Homes, for Appellant.

W. B. Cooper, for Appellee.

Walker, J. To authorize a party to recover for an injury to property, he must show that he is the absolute or qualified owner. Unless he shows himself to be owner of the property, no injury appears to have been inflicted, and he cannot recover. In this case we have examined the record with care, and have been unable to find any evidence which tends in the slightest degree to prove that appellee was the owner or had the [*42] possession of the property, for the injury to which a recovery is sought in this case. If he was the owner, it was an affirmative fact easy of proof by possession at least, and in its absence a jury had no right to assume the fact. It was an essential

51

Farnsworth *v.* Agnew.

fact, the proof of which is absolutely indispensable to a recovery. For the want of this evidence the verdict of the jury was not warranted, and should have been in favor of appellant.

Again, by the second instruction the court fails to inform the jury that the company were not bound to fence their road until it has been open for use six months. Although the company may have failed to fence their track as specified by the act, still if it had not been open for use for that period, it would not be liable for injury to animals for merely not fencing. This was a fact essential to a recovery under the statute, and one upon which the jury should pass, and the question whether the road had been in use for that period, should have been submitted by instruction, and in this the court erred.

It is a matter of regret that we feel ourselves compelled to reverse a judgment on purely technical grounds; but we are equally powerless, either to supply evidence which has no doubt been omitted in preparing the bill of exceptions, as to amend an instruction so as to conform to the requirements of the law arising upon the evidence. We can only decide upon the record presented, and leave parties to seek their rights by a further trial, in the court below. For the errors above indicated the judgment of the court below is reversed and the cause remanded.

Judgment reversed.

NATHAN H. FARNSWORTH, Plaintiff in Error, *v.* MILTON M. AGNEW, Defendant in Error.

ERROR TO MONROE.

An action of ejectment is within the purview of the statute requiring security for costs; and if the plaintiff is a non-resident he must give security for costs before instituting suit; which is commenced by serving the declaration and notice.

If it appears from the bill of exceptions that a plaintiff in ejectment was a non-resident at the time of the service of the declaration and notice, although the affidavit of the defendant to that fact is not saved in the bill of exceptions, the judgment dismissing the action for want of security will be upheld.

52

Farnsworth *v.* Agnew.

THIS was an action of ejectment, in the Monroe Circuit Court, to recover certain land lying in that county. The plaintiff in error filed his declaration, with the usual no- [*43] tice, on the 12th day of April, 1858, and also a bond for costs in the usual form. On the same day plaintiff moved for a rule on defendant to plead in twenty days, and defendant entered a cross-motion to dismiss said suit for want of a bond for costs. On these motions an affidavit, by Morrison, defendant's attorney, was presented to the court, and then amended by striking out certain words, being in effect that the bond for costs was indorsed on the original declaration filed, and not on the copy served on defendant. That affiant told plaintiff's attorney on the first day of the term, that he did not believe that said bond for costs was put on the declaration when it was served, and was informed by said attorney that it was not written on it at the time of service, but was put on as soon as he ascertained plaintiff was a non-resident. George Abbott presented an affidavit that the bond for costs was filed with the declaration. This was all the evidence; and judgment was rendered against said plaintiff for costs, and said suit dismissed; to which decision of the court, plaintiff below at the time excepted, and appealed to this court, assigning for error that the court below erred in dismissing said suit.

W. H. UNDERWOOD, for Plaintiff in Error.

OMELVENY & KENNEDY, for Defendant in Error.

WALKER, J. The bond for costs in this case was not filed, until after the service of the declaration and notice on defendant in error. A motion was entered to dismiss the suit for want of such a bond filed before suit was instituted, which motion was allowed and the suit dismissed, which is assigned for error. The first section of the cost act, requires, that in all cases of law or equity where the plaintiff or person for whose use an action is commenced, shall not be a resident of this State, the plaintiff or person for whose use the action is to be commenced, shall, before he institutes such suit, file or cause to be filed with the clerk of the Circuit or Supreme Court in which the action is to be commenced, an instrument in writing of some responsible person, a resident of the State, to be approved by the clerk, whereby such person shall acknowledge himself bound to pay or cause to be paid all costs which may accrue to the opposite party or to any of the officers of the court. That this is an action contemplated by the statute is undeniably true. And if the plaintiff was a non-resident of the State when it was commenced, he was bound to conform to [*44] this requirement, by filing such an instrument before suit was commenced.

But as there is no process issued by the clerk, to be served upon the defendant, as in other cases, the question arises, when is an action of ejectment commenced? By the fifth section of the chapter regulating that proceeding, it is provided that " the action shall be commenced by the service of a declaration, in which the name of the real claimants shall be inserted as plaintiffs." The tenth section, provides that a written notice shall be annexed to the declaration, directed to the defendant. The eleventh section requires the service to be made upon the defendant by delivering a copy of the declaration and notice, etc. Now there seems to be no question that when a copy of the declaration and notice shall be served as required, that the suit is commenced. And if so, the first section of the cost act is imperative that the bond for costs must be filed before that time, or the suit may be dismissed on motion of the defendant. If the plaintiff in this case was a non-resident, then this suit was properly dismissed, as the bond was not filed in time.

It is, however, urged, that the affidavit that plaintiff was a non-resident when suit was commenced not being embodied in the bill of exceptions, is no part of the record. This is certainly true as has been uniformly held by this court. And unless there is something otherwise appearing in the record from which it may be inferred, the court erred in dismissing the suit. It appears that the defendant entered a motion to dismiss because the plaintiff was a non-resident and had not filed a bond for costs before the suit was commenced. To this motion plaintiff's attorney filed his affidavit which is embodied in the bill of exceptions, alleging that the bond for costs was filed with the original declaration, as an answer to the motion to dismiss. It also appears from the bill of exceptions that plaintiff's attorney informed defendant's attorney, that the bond was written upon the declaration before it was filed and as soon as he ascertained. that plaintiff was a non-resident. From this it appears that plaintiff was admitted to be a non-resident, and there is nothing which rebuts that admission. This is sufficient to warrant the conclusion that he was not a resident of the State. The court below therefore did right in dismissing the suit, and the judgment is affirmed.

Judgment affirmed.

ISHAM E. WALLACE, Plaintiff in Error, *v.* THE [*45] PEOPLE, Defendants in Error.

ERROR TO MONROE.

An indictment upon a lost paper, which it is averred was a forgery, should set out the substance and effect of the instrument; that the court may see that it was such an instrument, that the forgery of it would constitute a crime.

WALLACE was indicted for forgery in the Monroe Circuit Court, at May term, 1861.

The indictment avers, that Wallace, on the thirtieth day of September, in the year of our Lord one thousand eight hundred and sixty, at and in the county of Monroe aforesaid, unlawfully, willfully, knowingly, falsely and feloniously, did then and there forge a certain certificate, purporting to be a certificate of qualification, purporting to be issued by John H. Breemer, school commissioner of Monroe county aforesaid, to him the said Isham E. Wallace; which said false, forged and fraudulent certificate purported to authorize said Isham E. Wallace to keep a school in any of the school districts and draw the public school funds, in any school district in said county of Monroe, in which he, the said Isham E. Wallace, should be

employed by the school directors of any school district, for the
space of two years from the date of said forged certificate; the
date of which said forged certificate is some day in the month
of September aforesaid; the said date and substance of which
said forged certificate is unknown to the jurors aforesaid, the
said forged certificate being lost; with intent thereby then and
there unlawfully, willfully, knowingly and feloniously, to cheat
and defraud William Rush, etc., school directors of school district number six, in township number four, etc., in said county,
etc., contrary to the form of the statute, etc.

Wallace was tried, convicted and sentenced to the penitentiary for one year. Motions for a new trial, and in arrest of
judgment were overruled. Thereupon Wallace sued out this
writ of error.

H. K. S. OMELVENY, and W. H. UNDERWOOD, for Plaintiff in
Error.

T. S. CASEY, District Attorney, for The People.

CATON, C. J. This indictment was undoubtedly insufficient
[*46] and should have been quashed. It was designed to be
upon a forged certificate of qualification to teach a common
school, by the school commissioner of Monroe county, to the
prisoner; which was lost. The indictment does not set forth the
tenor or substance of such a certificate as would authorize the
prisoner to be employed as a teacher and draw the public money.
The law requires such a certificate to state that the person is of
good moral character, and is qualified to teach orthography,
reading in English, penmanship, arithmetic, English gram-
mar, modern geography, and the history of the United States.
The indictment does not find that the forged paper contained
any such statements, or the substance of them. All it states is,
that the certificate purported to authorize the prisoner to keep a
school in any of the districts and draw the public school funds,
in any school district in Monroe county. If this was the substance of the paper, it was not such a certificate as the law required, to authorize the directors to employ the prisoner as a
teacher. It does not appear that it contained any statement of

his qualifications to teach a school, as is specified in the law. But more than this, the indictment expressly avers that the *substance* of the certificate was unknown to the grand jurors. Where an indictment is upon a lost instrument, which is a forgery, it should set out the substance and effect of the instrument that the court may see that it was such an instrument as to forge which constitutes a crime. In this respect, the indictment upon which the prisoner was convicted is entirely defective.

But the proof was as insufficient as the indictment. Had the indictment set out such a certificate as the law requires, the proof would not have sustained it. For this reason we shall not remand the case. The judgment is reversed, and the prisoner ordered to be discharged.

Judgment reversed.

HARRISON RAYBURN *et al.*, Appellants, *v.* GEORGE W. DAY *et al.*, Appellees. .

APPEAL FROM PERRY.

The giving of a note and mortgage by one of two copartners in settlement of a joint debt, does not discharge an account against the firm, unless they were received in satisfaction of it.

If a note is given not under seal, by one of several parties, it will not satisfy the account, unless the parties so intended; and a recovery may be had upon the account, if the note is surrendered. A recovery cannot be had on the account if the note is still held by the creditor.

A custom on the part of a creditor to charge interest on an account [*47] past due, will not authorize its recovery, unless the debtor was informed of the custom.

THE facts of this case are stated in the opinion of the Court, delivered by Mr. Justice WALKER.

E. L. HOWETT, for Appellants.

W. B. COOPER, for Appellees.

WALKER, J. This was an action of assumpsit instituted by appellees against appellant and Jesse Barbre, the latter of whom was not served with process. The declaration contained a count on a promissory note against appellant and Jesse Barbre, and the common counts. On the trial, it appeared that Barbre signed the firm name to the note, after the partnership had ceased to exist, and to secure the same gave a mortgage on two hundred and forty acres of land, which mortgage had been foreclosed, and a decree for the sale of the land rendered. The note when offered in evidence, was rejected, and the appellees then proceeded, against the objection of appellant, to prove the account for which the note and mortgage was given. The court rendered judgment for the sum of $1,279.73 and costs of suit. A motion for a new trial was entered and overruled.

It is now insisted that the giving of the note and mortgage by Barbre in settlement of the account and the foreclosure of the mortgage, released appellant from all liability for its payment. It is a well-settled rule that the merely giving a note not under seal, unless received as a satisfaction, does not discharge an account. This is equally true of a note given by one of several partners on the settlement of a partnership account. Yet when the parties design that the execution of the note shall be a satisfaction of the account, there can be no question that such is the effect. When the note given is under seal it satisfies the account, and the creditor must rely upon the note alone for a recovery. The intention of the parties may be ascertained by their acts, as well as their declarations. After the note is given, to be able to recover on the account the note must be surrendered. The creditor cannot be permitted to recover on the account and still hold the note against the debtor.

Story, in his treatise on Partnership, lays down the rule, that the mere fact of a creditor taking additional security from a new firm without releasing the old debt, or receiving interest from the new firm, will not absolve a retiring partner from his [*48] original responsibility. The taking of the note and mortgage could not be regarded as anything more than taking additional security. The attorney for appellee testifies that he did not intend it as a discharge of appellant. And as it was not so agreed or intended, it did not have that effect.

It is likewise urged, that the court below erred in allowing interest on the account. The witness who proved the sale and delivery of the goods, testified that it was the custom of appellees to charge interest after accounts became due. But there is no evidence in the record from which it appears that appellee was informed of that custom. In the case of *Simms* v. *Clark*, 13 Ill. 544, it was held that a delay of payment from 1845 to 1848 did not show a vexatious delay. To the same effect is the case of *Hitt* v. *Allen*, ib. 592, and *Aldrich* v. *Dunham*, 16 Ill. 403. These cases are decisive of this question, and the decision of the court below, being in violation of the rule then established, the judgment was erroneous to the extent of the interest allowed, and must be reversed, and the cause remanded.

Judgment reversed.

THE ILLINOIS CENTRAL RAILROAD COMPANY, Appellant, *v.* ABNER WILLIAMS, Appellee.

APPEAL FROM PERRY.

If an action is brought against a railroad company under the statute, and the negligence charged results from an omission to erect a fence, the declaration should show that the accident did not happen at a place where the company is not bound to maintain a fence.

A town or village, within the meaning of the statute requiring railroad corporations to construct fences, may exist, although there is no plat of the same, dedicating streets, etc., in the manner pointed out by the statute in that regard.

WILLIAMS filed his declaration in case, against the Illinois Central Railroad Company, in the Perry Circuit Court, to recover damages for the loss of a cow, killed on the road of the company in July, A. D. 1856.

There were several counts in the declaration, substantially as follows: averring "that it was in consequence of the negligence of the defendant in not keeping the fence which inclosed the track of said railroad in good repair, and permitting gates and cattle-guards to remain open, that said animal en [*49] tered upon said railroad track, and was killed, whereby,' etc. No averment, in the declaration, that the place where the accident occurred, was not in a village, etc., or at a crossing.

A demurrer to the declaration was overruled. The defendant then pleaded not guilty, and some special pleas. There was trial by jury, and a finding for the plaintiff below. The defendant below prayed this appeal.

An erroneous instruction, given on the trial, is set out in the opinion of the court. The cause was tried before PARRISH, Judge.

HAYNIE & GREEN, for Appellant.

R. S. NELSON, for Appellee.

CATON, C. J. As this action was brought under the statute, and the negligence charged, is not fencing the road, the declaration is defective in not stating that the place where the accident happened is not within a city, town or village, or at a road crossing, for at those places the company was not bound to maintain a fence, and it was necessary to show affirmatively, that it was the duty of the company to maintain the fence at the particular place, by negativing all those provisions of the statute exempting it from fencing in particular places.

The court also erred in its instruction, as to what constitutes a town or village, under the statute. The instruction is this: "To constitute a town, city or village, there should be something more than simply a place or point at which people live. There must be a dedication of the streets, alleys, etc., to the public." This was substantially telling the jury that no matter how many people lived at the place, or what business was done there, it could not be a town or village unless it was laid out and platted under our statute. Such is not the law. Any small assemblage of houses, for dwellings, or business, or both, in the country, constitutes a village, whether they are situated upon regularly laid out streets and alleys, or not. And the proof abundantly shows that this was a village. It was called

St. Johns. There was at this point, a railroad station, a mill, a blacksmith shop, a store, and a grocery. The number of dwellings is not given, but the reasonable presumption is, that they were sufficient at least to accommodate the persons doing business in the village. But there was no proof that there were streets and alleys laid off and dedicated to the public, hence the jury were bound to find that St. Johns was not a village, according to the instructions of the court. The judgment is reversed and the cause remanded, with leave to [*50] the plaintiff to amend his declaration.

Judgment reversed.

The Ohio and Mississippi Railroad Company, Appellant, *v.* Lawrence County, Appellee.

APPEAL FORM LAWRENCE.

A railroad company cannot appeal to the Circuit Court from an assessment of its property for taxation by a board of supervisors. If any remedy exists, it may be by *certiorari.*

The provision of the constitution granting the right of appeal, needs legislative action to make it available.

The Ohio and Mississippi Railroad Company filed with the clerk of Lawrence county, Illinois, its schedule of property, with valuation, for the year 1859.

At the December term, 1859, of the board of supervisors for that county, the board, regarding the valuation of the company as too low, increased, by more than double, the valuation, and so notified the company.

The company applied for a hearing and a reduction, at a meeting of the board granted for the purpose. The board refused the reduction asked, and affirmed the order increasing the valuation; whereupon the company prayed an appeal to the Circuit Court of Lawrence county, and filed bond, which was approved.

At the September term, 1860, of the Circuit Court of Lawrence county, the cause was tried by the court without a jury. After hearing evidence as to value of property, and argument, the court took the case under advisement, reserving its decision until the April term, 1861, of the court.

At the April term, 1861, motion was made by counsel for the board of supervisors to dismiss the cause for want of jurisdiction, and thereupon the court allowed the motion and dismissed the cause. It should be stated that counsel for the board at the first term of the docketing of the cause, moved to dismiss for want of jurisdiction; which motion, after argument, and time taken for deliberation by the court, was overruled, and the cause set down for trial.

The error assigned is, the dismissal of the cause for want of jurisdiction.

W. HOMES, for Appellant.

TANNER & CASEY, for Appellee.

[*51] WALKER, J. This record presents but a single question. That is, whether a railroad company may appeal from an assessment of its property for taxation by the board of supervisors, to the Circuit Court. The ninth section of the revenue law of the 27th February, 1847, (Scates' Comp. 1010), gives the right of appeal from an application to the Commissioners' Court, for a reduction of the valuation on an assessment. That section also requires the Circuit Court trying the appeal to hear the evidence, and if too high, make the proper reduction, which shall be certified to the collector by the clerk of that court. The thirty-fourth section of the revenue law of 12th Feb., 1853, (Scates' Comp. 1040), provides that in an application for this purpose, to the County Court, if the court shall hold that the property is not liable to taxation, it shall not be final unless approved by the auditor. If he shall, however, be dissatisfied with the decision of the County Court, he may give notice to the county clerk, and apply to this court for an order to set aside and vacate the order of the County Court. The thirty-third section of the revenue law, (Scates' Comp. 1057,) applica-

ble to counties under township organization, contains substantially the same provisions.

It will be perceived that the act of February, 1853, gives the
right to apply to the County Court for a reduction of the valuation, and for an abatement on property not liable for assessment.
If the court holds the property exempt, then application may
be made to the Supreme Court to vacate the order of the County
Court. But it will be observed that there is no provision for an
application to this or any other court, in reference to an over valuation on an assessment. This then leaves the right to appeal to
the Circuit Court, as given by the act of February, 1847, unre-
pealed.

It however remains to determine whether an appeal is allowed
in such a case from an over valuation in a county acting under
township organization. The thirty-second section of the revenue act, (Scates' Comp. 1056), in force in such counties, provides that on the last Saturday in June the assessor, town clerk
and supervisor, shall attend at the office of the town clerk for
the purpose of reviewing the assessment list, and when any person objecting thereto shall make an affidavit that his property
is of the value of a specified sum, the assessor shall reduce the
same to the sum specified. This section contains no provision
for an appeal from the decision of the board, either to the board
of supervisors, or Circuit Court. But if the board were to refuse to make the reduction, we are inclined to think that the
decision could be reviewed on a *certiorari*.

When the legislature conferred the duty of making the [*52]
assessment of railroad property, on the board of supervisors,
(Scates' Comp. 1105), they substituted that body for the assessor. And when it required the board to give the road notice
of any change they might make in the lists furnished, it was no
doubt to enable them to apply to the supervisors for a reduction, as they might have done to the board of auditors, before
the adoption of this enactment. When the law was changed,
exempting the roads from returning a list to the assessor, and
requiring it to be furnished to the county clerk, as the basis of
an assessment by the board of Supervisors, it could not have
been designed to deprive the roads of any right they previously

enjoyed.   And by substituting the board of supervisors first as
the assessor, and then as the board of auditors, the assessment
of their property could be more conveniently and uniformly
made in the county, and still have the same means of redress as
if the change had not been made.

It is however urged, that our constitution has, by the 8th section, article 5, conferred jurisdiction upon the Circuit Courts in
all cases of appeals from inferior courts, and that the right exists in this case by force of that provision.   As a general proposition, subject, however, to some exceptions, it may be safely
asserted, that the constitution cannot execute its own provisions,
independent of legislative enactment.   In this case it no doubt
not only authorizes but requires the General Assembly to make
all necessary provisions to carry this requirement into effect.
If, independent of legislation, an appeal were attempted, it
would be found that innumerable difficulties would be presented
to its accomplishment.   If this constitutional provision stood
alone, unaided by legislation, and an appeal were attempted,
how could it be perfected? Would it be accomplished by simply filing a transcript of the record in the superior court; or
would bond, with security have to be given? If so, in what sum,
with what conditions?   Which court should impose them?
Within what time would it have to be prayed and perfected?
And when in the appellate court how would the trial be had, on
the transcript or *de novo* on the merits? It will be readily perceived that these form not a few of the obstacles, that present
themselves at the very threshold of this question.

From these considerations it appears to be perfectly apparent that this provision of the constitution cannot be carried
into effect unaided by legislative enactment.   Then an appeal
in this case cannot exist for want of legislative action.   Until
the legislature by a late enactment gave the right, it did not
[*53] exist, or if it did, it was in so imperfect a condition that
courts were unable to recognize and enforce it.

It was again urged, that this court had recognized the right.
Upon examination it will be found that where a new jurisdiction has been conferred upon a court, from which under general laws a party might appeal to a superior court, that the leg-

islature intended also to confer the right of appeal.   Or in cases
where the law not having given an appeal, the question was not
raised in this court.   We have been referred to no decision, nor
are we aware of any, which holds that under this constitutional
provision an appeal may be prosecuted although unprovided for
by statute.   Nor is the right of appeal recognized by the common law.   It is the creature of statutory enactment.   We are
therefore of the opinion that the appellant could only, if at all,
be relieved by writ of *certiorari,* and that the appeal was improperly taken, and the court below did right in dismissing it.
The judgment of the court below is affirmed,

Judgment affirmed.

LEHIGH D. GOSNEY, Appellant, *v.* ZARDA FROST, Appellee.

APPEAL FROM PERRY.

The purchaser of personal property is not to presume, by a vague statement
made, that the vendor is a trifling fellow, and had not money, in the opinion of the person making the remark, to buy the property; that the title of
the vendor is defective.   A purchaser is not bound to take mere suspicions
unsupported by facts, in his business affairs, as a warning; though the
statement of facts touching the manner of the acquisition of property by
his vendor, might be sufficient to put him on his guard.

ZARDA FROST, the appellee, who was the plaintiff in the court
below, brought his action of trover against the appellant, who
was defendant in the court below, for the recovery of the value
of a horse, to which action the defendant in the court below
filed his plea of not guilty.   The cause was tried at the April
term, 1860, of Perry Circuit Court, by a jury, JENKINS, Judge,
presiding.   A verdict was rendered in favor of the appellee for
seventy dollars damages; a motion was entered by the appellant for a new trial; the motion was overruled, and judgment
was rendered upon the verdict.

Gosney bought the horse at auction.   Some conversation

occurred at the time of the sale and afterwards, as to the ownership of the horse; which was sold as the property of one
David Martin.

[*54] *James Martin* testified, that appellant told him that he
had purchased the horse at auction, but had not then paid for him,
that David Martin was the nephew of James, and that the horse
had been purchased of appellee; and asked the advice of James
Martin as to what he (appellant) should do; James Martin told
him he had better keep his money in his pocket, that David
Martin was a trifling fellow, and had not money enough to buy
such a horse, and feared that he (David Martin) had got the
horse dishonestly—that before appellant paid for the horse, he
had better see Frost; that at this conversation David Martin
came up, and offered to go with appellant and see Frost the
next day, but could not go that day, as he (David) had to make
a payment on the day in question, upon the purchase of a mill,
for which purpose he had sold the horse; but that if appellant
on the next day should not desire to keep the horse, he (David
Martin) would take him back; that his only object in selling
the horse was to raise money with which to pay for the mill.

There was much testimony as to the value of the horse. It
did not appear by the evidence, that there was any suspicion, at
the time of the sale, in regard to David Martin's title to the
horse.

R. S. Nelson, for Appellant.

G. W. Wall, for Appellee.

Caton, C. J. Assuming, without determining, that the
purchaser of personal property may be charged with constructive notice of a fraud, by which his vendor obtained the
property, whenever there is sufficient to put him on inquiry
the same as a purchaser of real estate, we are satisfied that ·
the evidence in this case, does not show enough to charge the
purchaser with such constructive notice. All the evidence
there is, showing anything calculated to excite the suspicion of
the purchaser, is in the testimony of James Martin. From this
it appears that an uncle of the vendor, some hours after the

horse was purchased and before the purchase money was paid, told the defendant, that the vendor had bought the horse of Frost, that he was a trifling fellow, and had not money enough to buy such a horse, and that he feared he came by him dishonestly, and advised him to keep his money till he 'had seen Frost. The auctioneer who sold the horse for the vendor, says he was present at the same conversation, and that subsequently, on the same day, the purchaser met the vendor and asked him to go and see Frost with him, to ascertain if all was right. The vendor said he would go with him next day, but he had [*55] got to make a payment on a mill he had purchased in another county; that he must raise the money that day and make the payment or forfeit the mill, and showed the contract of purchase to that effect. This explanation, the witness Lord says, convinced him that David Martin had a good title. And it seems to have allayed any suspicions which the statements of James Martin had excited in the mind of the purchaser, and he paid for the horse. Indeed, without this explanation, we do not think that the vague statements of James Martin, that David Martin was a trifling fellow and he did not believe he had money enough to buy such a horse, imposed the duty on Gosney to go and hunt up Frost, before paying for the horse. A purchaser should not be bound to take the mere suspicions, unsupported by facts stated, warranting such suspicion, and interrupt his regular business and run about the country to see if they are well or ill founded. If James Martin had told the purchaser that David Martin had acquired the horse fraudulently, or stated any facts inconsistent with the assumption that he had obtained him honestly, the case might have been different. But as it was, we think a reasonably cautious man might have completed the purchase by paying for the horse as the defendant did,

The judgment is reversed, and the cause remanded.

Judgment reversed.

THE ILLINOIS CENTRAL RAILROAD COMPANY, Appellant,
v. JOHN F. DICKERSON, Appellee.

APPEAL FROM JACKSON.

A railroad company is not required to keep a patrol at night along the road, to see that the fence is not broken down. If the fence is sufficient, and all reasonable diligence is used to keep it up, the company will not be guilty of negligence in that particular.

THIS was an action commenced by appellee against appellant to recover the value of three animals, alleged to have been killed, upon the road of appellant. The action was commenced before a justice of the peace, and taken by appeal to the Circuit Court of Jackson county, where it was heard before JENKINS, Judge, without the intervention of a jury, the court finding against the corporation, and rendering a judgment against it for forty-eight dollars and costs. From this judgment the corporation appealed.

[*56] A witness stated that there was a gap in the fence near where the cattle were killed; that the company had fenced the road, and kept the fence up, and put up gaps, whenever the fence was found down. That he passed by the place where the fence was down on the evening before the animals were killed, after six o'clock, and the fence was all right. He also stated that the fence might have been down, and he not notice it, that it was the business of the witness to keep the fence, but that he did not think it was down the evening before the cattle were killed.

Another witness stated, that right close to where the cattle were killed, he had noticed before that, that the fence was not good—that a while before the accident he had observed that the fence was down, both north and south of the place where the cattle were killed, at places where ties had been hauled out—that he did not recollect whether he had seen the fence down at the place where the cattle were killed before or after they were killed, but had seen the fence down there.

HAYNIE & GREEN, for Appellant.

C. S. WARD, for Appellee.

CATON, C. J. The appellant's counsel is mistaken in the supposition that the proof does not show that the place where the cattle were killed was not in a town or village or at a road crossing. The proof does clearly show that at the place where the accident happened, the company was bound to maintain a good and sufficient fence.

If the fact were clearly established, that the fence was up, the night before, at the point where the cattle actually got in, we think that would be a sufficient compliance with the duty imposed by the law, which is, to maintain a good and sufficient fence. When up, the proof does not show that the fence at this point was not good and sufficient. It cannot be the duty of the railroad company to keep a patrol all night the whole length of their road to see that the fence is not broken down by breachy cattle, by evil men, or by a whirlwind. If the company use all reasonable diligence to keep up the fence, that is all the law requires, and it is not guilty of negligence in that particular. Although the proof in this case tends to show, that the fence was up the night before, it is by no means of so conclusive a character as to require us to set aside the finding of the court below, for that reason. The foreman in charge of the repairs of the road at that point, whose duty it was also to keep up the fence, first states that he passed down the road about six o'clock the night be- [*57] fore, and that the fence at the point where the cattle got in was then up, and that at six o'clock the next morning he found it down, and put it up. He afterwards states that it might have been down the night before, but that he did not see it down, and he thinks it was not. This shows that he depended on his general observation, and that his attention was not directed to this particular point; nor does he state that his mind was on the subject, and that he expressly examined the fence on his way down, to see that it was up. The witness Penrod says, that he had seen the fence down at that point, but whether before or after the night in question he could not say. But as the witness Burnes says he put up the fence as soon as he found it down on the morning when the cattle were killed, this tends to fix the time when Penrod saw it down, as having been before that morning. At any rate the evidence tending to show that the fence was up the night before, is not sufficiently conclusive, to justify a reversal of the judgment for this cause.

The judgment must be affirmed.

Judgment affirmed.

BENJAMIN F. ANDERSON, Plaintiff in Error, *v.* WILLIAM WHITE, Defendant in Error.

ERROR TO MARION.

An agreement to submit a cause upon briefs, to be decided in vacation, order and decree to be entered as of that or the next term, will be construed as a submission of the whole controversy, and not of the submission of a motion to dissolve an injunction.

When parties make a new agreement, revoking an old one, and a horse is paid as a part of the consideration on the new agreement, one of the parties cannot refuse to execute it because the other has not executed a reconveyance of land, no time being fixed for that purpose. A reasonable time will be allowed for performance, and a tender of the reconveyance was not an indispensable preliminary to the enforcement of the new agreement. The parties must be restored to their original rights before either can insist upon a rescinding of the new contract.

THIS bill, which was for general relief and for an injunction, states that White was the owner of lot No. 3, of block 2, Cunningham's Addition to Salem, Marion county, Illinois; that he sold said lot to Anderson, on the 11th of November, 1858, and conveyed it by warranty deed. States that the consideration for said lot was to be seven hundred dollars, to be paid as [*58] follows: one hundred dollars down, which was paid in cash, and the balance to be paid in equal payments in one and two years, by two promissory notes, which were executed on the day of said sale: one payable in one year, for the sum of

70

three hundred dollars with ten per cent. interest; the other in two years for the same sum with like interest, to said White.

That said notes were secured by a mortgage on the lot, executed on the day aforesaid and duly recorded. That one of said notes for the sum of three hundred dollars, became due on the 11th of November, 1859, and was not paid. That White brought a suit at law on said note, together with a book account against Anderson, and got judgment at the March term of the Marion Circuit Court, A. D. 1860, for the sum of three hundred and eighty-three dollars and sixty-six cents. That execution was issued on said judgment, and that on or about the 20th of April, 1860, defendant White entered into a new contract with Anderson, by which White agreed to discharge said judgment and return said execution satisfied, and to deliver up to Anderson said note, and cancel said mortgage for three hundred dollars given by Anderson and dated 11th November, 1860. It was agreed by both parties, that the one hundred dollars paid by Anderson to White at the time of sale, should be applied by said White as rent for the use of said lot, at the rate of eight dollars per month.

That White then charged to Anderson's account in said White's book, one hundred dollars, rent for said lot, and gave Anderson credit for that amount received as rent for the lot. That White exercised ownership over said lot, and has since tried to rent it to other persons. That it was further agreed by the parties that Anderson should give White a horse worth one hundred dollars, and pay the costs of the suit, and reconvey the lot to White, in consideration of which, White agreed to satisfy the execution, and deliver up the note and cancel said mortgage note then not due.

That White accepted said horse, and ordered the Sheriff in writing, to return the execution satisfied.

That Anderson has paid the costs of the suit at law, and has made a deed to White for the lot and tendered the same to White, and demanded the note, and well and truly performed all his part of the agreement.

That White refused the deed offered him by Anderson, and refused to deliver said note, and without Anderson's consent

Anderson *v.* White.

has repudiated the contract and ordered the sheriff to levy on the goods and chattels of complainant, which the sheriff has done; that the property levied upon is to be sold at public sale on the 11th day of August, 1860.

[*59] Prays that White be made a party to petition, and, waiving oath, that he answer allegations in petition; that White, his attorneys, and agents, and the sheriff Shultz, be enjoined from selling said property; that the property be released; that White be ordered by the court to deliver up the note and mortgage not due, and to accept the deed, and that the execution be returned satisfied; that White be summoned to appear at the August term, 1860, to answer said petition, and that White, and Shultz, and attorney, be enjoined from all further proceedings in said execution; and prays general relief.

Affidavits for and against the injunction were filed.

Admits that he was the owner of the lot and house described in the bill, and that he made a deed to complainant for same on the 11th November, 1858, which was recorded. Admits the consideration and mode of payment as is set forth in the bill, and that the notes and mortgage were made as set forth in bill. Admits that judgment was had on first $300 note, and another note of complainant for medical services. That bill states truly when execution issued on said judgment; that on the 12th of April, 1860, defendant and complainant made a new contract by parol. Denies that by said new contract defendant was to discharge said judgment and return said execution satisfied, and deliver to complainant said note and cancel said mortgage for $300 on said 11th November, 1860; and denies that it was agreed that the $100 paid by complainant down, should be applied on rent at the rate of eight dollars per month for said property; and denies that he charged complainant's account on his books $100, rent for said lot, and gave credit for same as received for said rent; and denies that it was agreed at all by defendant that complainant should give defendant one horse worth $100 or $125, and pay the rent of said lot to defendant, in consideration of which defendant agreed to have said execution satisfied, and deliver up said note, and cancel said mortgage, and avers that said contract is untruly stated in said bill.

72

Alleges that said contract was thus: That if said new contract was complied with by complainant forthwith and without delay, defendant would rescind said original contract; that in consideration that complainant was in possession and had the use of said property from 11th of November, 1858, to 12th April, 1860, the $100 paid down as part of purchase money of said property, should be applied, as far as it went, to rent of said house at $8 per month from date of sale; that said complainant should be considered as tenant from date of new contract, and should continue such tenant. That complainant should pay the costs of said judgment suit, and all taxes on said house, and should execute a deed of warranty to said [*60] property to defendant; that complainant should give defendant a horse worth $100, not $125; that it was distinctly agreed that each and all the terms of said contract should be complied with fully, forthwith and without delay, and that the first contract should remain intact, and said judgment stand as a security till said new contract should be performed fully; that the new contract should be done forthwith, then, and not before then, said defendant was to satisfy said judgment, return said execution satisfied, surrender said note, and cancel said mortgage.

Defendant denies that he made the entry on his book account. That said credit depended on the fulfillment of said contract by complainant. Denies that he has exercised ownership over said property since 11th November, 1858, or that he has offered said lots since said time, for rent. Admits that other parties applied to him to rent, which he refused to act on.

Denies that he made a written order in the terms or to the effect in bill alleged, directed to the sheriff having said execution in his hands. But admits that he gave a written order to sheriff, that when said terms stated by this answer were complied with, to satisfy said execution, etc.

That he was ready forthwith on his part to perform his part of said contract, and frequently urged said complainant to perform his part of said contract. But avers that it was the essence of the contract that it should be done forthwith, and that he never altered or waived or extended the time or terms of fulfillment. Alleges that said contract was not performed forthwith, or within a reasonable time, and is now unfulfilled on complainant's part.

Denies that said deed was ever tendered to defendant by complainant or any person for him—and denies that said deed was ever made at the time agreed, or said costs paid. Admits that he received a horse worth $100, not $125. Denies that said costs were paid, or that said taxes were paid, or said deed made within a reasonable time, or forthwith.

That more than ninety days elapsed after said contract was made, and that said contract was not performed by complainant; that he ordered a new execution and the old one returned, on the 7th July, 1860. That not until after new execution issued, and ninety days had elapsed, did complainant pay the costs, and have deed made, if it was made, and not until said execution was levied, did the complainant pay said costs; that said deed has never been tendered to defendant, nor did complainant pay said taxes as agreed.

[*61] Submits that he had a right to disregard said contract and rely on his said judgment, and says that he had a right to treat said horse as a credit on said execution, and that he is willing to treat said horse as such credit. Denies that payment of said costs was in compliance with the contract; and that said deed had not been made pursuant to contract. Admits the levy of said execution and advertisements for sale, but denies the alleged value of said property levied on.

Alleges that Joseph Shultz, sheriff, is not made a party to said bill, though injunction is prayed as to him.

That the injunction is prayed to continue until the hearing of the case, only; that complainant has made no offer to do equity, and is not entitled to relief. Denies all fraud and combination; denies each and all and every allegation not confessed, and asks to be dismissed with costs.

Whereupon the court made the following order, August 23, 1860. The defendant, by Parrish & Bassett, his solicitors, enters a motion to dissolve the injunction herein, which is set for Thursday next; also on the date aforesaid, 23rd August, 1860, defendant, by his attornies, filed certain affidavits, signed by J. O. Chance, O. W. Baker and H. W. Eagan.

Complainant filed his replication to the answer of White.

On the 30th August, 1860, the following order was made, to wit : This cause is submitted to the judge upon briefs to be decided at chambers in vacation; order in decree may be entered of this or next term as to the court may seem just and equitable; and on the 1st September, 1860, White, by his attorney, submitted a brief on motion to dissolve injunction.

On the 10th November, 1860, the court below made the following order :

With a view that full justice be done to the parties, the court doth decree, that in the first place the complainant, within twenty days, to wit, by the 10th day of November, 1860, tender to defendant a warranty deed, made by himself and wife, of the lot in said bill described—Lot 3, Block 2, in Cunningham's Addition to Salem, to defendant, his heirs and assigns. That complainant, within twenty days, pay to defendant the sum of $36, the residue of his rent of said premises, up to the 15th of April, 1860. That complainant, within said twenty days, deliver to said defendant the possession of said premises, and pay the costs of these proceedings within said time; and on the payment of said $36, and said costs, and said tender of said deed, as aforesaid, and on said surrender of said premises, it is ordered and decreed, that said defendant do surrender the note and mortgage in bill described, and that the judgment therein be satisfied.

But in case of failure of said complainant to perform [*62] his part of this decree, specifically, within twenty days from this date, to wit, the 10th November, 1860, it is in that case further decreed that the injunction be dissolved and forever held for nought, and that White have leave to take execution on his judgment, and pursue his remedies in his note and mortgage as if no other contract had been made, provided that the price of the horse ($100) be credited on said *fi. fa.* in case the same sued out in default of said complainant executing said decree.

That said injunction be dissolved without costs to Joseph Shultz, and that complainant pay the costs of this suit, etc. And leave is granted to either party to appeal or prosecute writ of error on entering into bonds of $500, to be approved, etc.

Whereupon White sued out this writ of error, and says the Circuit Court erred in pronouncing a final decree,

1. Because all that was submitted to the court for decision, was a motion for dissolution of the injunction.

2. Because, though answer and replication were filed, no testimony was taken, nor was the cause set for hearing at the then next term.

3. Because it was not set down for final hearing at all, neither by consent, nor by operation of law, so as to have final decree.

4. Because all the court could do in the cause at that stage of submission, was to allow or deny the motion for dissolution of the injunction, and could not decide the merits by plenary decree.

5. Because the equity of the bill was fully denied, and that denial in the answer substantially sustained by the affidavits.

BASSETT, HAYNIE & SMITH, for Plaintiff in Error.

WILLARD & STOKER, for Defendant in Error.

WALKER, J. The first question presented is, whether this cause was submitted on the motion to dissolve the injunction, or upon its merits. The order of submission is this: "This cause is submitted to the judge upon brief, to be decided at chambers in vacation; order and decree may be entered of this or next term as to the court may seem just and equitable." What was submitted? The cause and not the motion alone. What was to be decided? The cause as well as the motion. The cause was the suit in all its parts, including the motion [*63] as well as all other questions. The bill had been filed, the answer interposed, and affidavits supporting each, produced, and it was upon this state of facts that the cause was submitted. And whatever may have been the design of the parties, the order of submission will not bear the construction that the motion to dissolve the injunction was alone submitted. There was therefore no error in trying the case on the merits.

But it remains to determine whether the court below erred in the decree which was rendered. When the agreement was

Anderson *v.* White.

made to rescind the contract, reconvey the property and to pay rent by the complainant, satisfy the judgment and cancel the note, by defendant below, a horse was paid as a part of the consideration. It was appropriated on the rent under the new agreement, and not upon the price of the property. As far as it applied it was a part performance of the new agreement, and as no time seems to have been fixed for a reconveyance, each party had a reasonable time within which to perform his part of the contract. And to put the other in default he should have offered to perform on his part. And then to have rescinded he should have refunded what had been received on the agreement.

In this case appellant retained the horse, without an offer to perform or restore it to the appellee. He cannot be permitted to retain all of the benefits resulting from the contract, and yet repudiate and avoid its performance. Unless he had rescinded the contract, appellee had a right to enforce its specific performance, and appellant having failed to rescind, he must be held to its performance, unless appellee has been guilty of laches that render it inequitable to insist upon its enforcement.

It is however urged that as appellee failed to make a tender of the deed, and is in default, he cannot have the relief sought. In the case of *Webster* v. *French*, 11 Ill. 254, it was held that a court of chancery is not bound by any fixed rule in relation to the tender of money, in bills, for a specific performance. That the court may order the money to be paid into court when the interest of the parties may require it. As this bill was for the specific performance of an agreement, no reason is perceived why a tender of the deed was essential to the relief sought, especially as the appellant had failed to offer to perform on his part, or to restore the horse and declare the contract rescinded. The evidence seems to rebut the supposition, that the appellant regarded the contract rescinded for the want of the immediate tender of the deed, as he afterwards offered both to sell and to rent the property. He also repeatedly declared that it was [*64] his, and that the first contract had been rescinded.

On this entire record no error is perceived, and the decree must be affirmed.

Decree affirmed.

State of Illinois *v.* Illinois Central R. R. Co.

THE STATE OF ILLINOIS *v.* THE ILLINOIS CENTRAL RAILROAD COMPANY.

ORIGINAL SUIT.

For purposes of taxation property should be assessed at its present value, and not at its prospective value.

In assessing the value of a railroad, for purposes of taxation, the inquiry should be, what is the property worth, to be used for the purposes for which it was designed, and not for any other purposes to which it might be applied?

In such a case, if the property is devoted to the use for which it was designed, and is in a condition to produce its maximum income, one very important element for ascertaining its present value, is the amount of its net profits.

This, however, should not be the absolute standard of value. There should be taken in connection with it, the inquiry, what would a prudent man give for the property as a permanent investment, with a view to present and future income?

ALL the facts of this case are fully set out in the opinion of the Court by Mr. Justice BREESE.

The case was originally commenced in the Second Grand Division, but by consent, was finally heard and determined at Mount Vernon in the First Grand Division.

J. B. WHITE, State's Attorney, S. T. LOGAN and M. HAY, for The People.

J. M. DOUGLAS, and A. LINCOLN, for the Railroad Company.

BREESE, J.* This is an action of debt originally brought in this court, against the defendants, for taxes alleged to be due to the State, for the year 1857, by the defendants, and unpaid.

To the declaration, the defendants have pleaded the general issue, payment, and set-off for over-payments, on which issues are made up. It is these issues, and these only, we are called upon to try.

After the instititution of this suit, on the 31st of January,

---

* NOTE.—This case was heard at a term anterior to that named in the caption.

State of Illinois *v.* Illinois Central R. R. Co.

1859, it was agreed between the parties, that in order to comply with the 22d section of the charter of the Illinois [*65] Central Railroad Company, (Session Laws 1851, page 72), requiring them, after the expiration of six years from the grant of the charter, to list their stock, property and assets for the purpose of State taxation, the defendants, on the 13th day of August, 1857, filed with the Auditor of State, a paper, of which Exhibit A filed in the cause, is a true copy. But upon this, the auditor assessed a tax for that year, amounting to the aggregate sum of one hundred and thirty-two thousand and sixty-seven and forty-four one-hundredths dollars, being so assessed at sixty-seven cents on the one hundred dollars on the aggregate sum of nineteen million seven hundred and eleven thousand five hundred and fifty-nine, and fifty-nine one hundredths dollars, and that for the non-payment of this assessment, this suit is brought. It was further agreed, that for the year 1857, the defendants paid into the State treasury, the sum of one hundred and forty-five thousand six hundred and forty-five and thirty-two one-hundredths dollars, a portion of which, namely, one hundred and eight thousand. and eighteen and sixty-one one-hundredths dollars, was to apply to the five per cent. of gross proceeds provided for in section eighteen of the charter, and the remainder, namely, thirty-seven thousand six hundred and twenty-seven and twenty-one one-hundredths dollars, was to apply to the object of the assessment above mentioned. It was then agreed, that on the trial, this court might receive evidence from both the parties, or either of them, as to the true value of the stock, property and assets contained in the list, at the time of filing it, and might, if this court should be of opinion the true value at the time of listing, is the true legal basis for the assessment, modify the assessment so as to conform to such basis, provided that in this case, the aggregate value of the stock, property and assets shall not be reduced below thirteen million of dollars, and provided further, that this case shall not, as fixing a basis of assessment, be claimed as a binding precedent in any future case, in or out of court. It was further agreed, that the only questions to be submitted to the court and to be decided, are,

First. Whether by the charter of said company, that company is liable to pay any taxes exceeding in amount two per cent. on their gross receipts, and whether if the taxes assessed on their property, exceed the amount of the two per cent. on the gross receipts of the road, the company is bound to pay the balance of the taxes.

Second. The court is to decide on evidence, whether the property of the railroad has been estimated too high, and if [*66] too high, how much it should be reduced to make it conform to its real taxable value, provided it is expressly agreed that the valuation shall not be reduced below thirteen million of dollars; and,

Third. If the court decides that the company is bound to pay taxes if they exceed two per cent. of the gross proceeds of the road, then the court shall give judgment in favor of the plaintiff for such amount as the taxes, at the rate of sixty-seven cents on the one hundred dollars, on the assessed value as fixed by the court, exceed the two per cent. aforesaid of the gross receipts of the road paid into the treasury for that fiscal year.

At the date of this agreement, a bill was pending before the legislature then in session, for an act in relation to assessments of the Illinois Central Railroad Company, when it was stipulated by these parties on the 18th February, that in the event of the passage of that bill, there should be no revaluation of the property of the company, nor any appeal from the assessment for the year 1857, but the counsel for the State agreed to remove the limit of thirteen million of dollars, and leave the valuation as entirely open to the court. The bill referred to became a law on the 21st of February, 1859.

Exhibit A is nothing more than the list of the property owned by the company, and its valuation, as made by them and returned to the auditor.

The argument on the first proposition was not presented fully to the court, but alluded to only by the counsel for the State. It was considered, as the case then stood, it would be unnecessary to make up any decision upon it. The case turned upon the second proposition, as to the valuation of the property, and on that point it was agreed that the evidence heard by this court, at the last November term, held for the first grand division, should be considered as before the court now here. That testimony was taken on an appeal from the assessment of the auditor, as prescribed by the Act of 1859, (Session Laws of 1859, pages 206–7), and full evidence was produced and examined, both on the part of the People, and on the part of the defendants. The most experienced and intelligent railroad men in the West, were fully examined on all the elements of value, as subsisting in a railroad concern, and in this road particularly, ample notes of which we have preserved.

There being no conflicting testimony before the court on the question of value, the court could not hesitate in its judgment on that point, but, like a jury, were compelled to find on the evidence. Accordingly, the court directed the following order to be entered in the cause:

"THE ILLINOIS CENTRAL RAILROAD CO. } An Appeal from the As- [*67]
vs.
THE PEOPLE OF THE STATE OF ILLINOIS. } sessment of the Auditor.

" And now at this day come the said parties, by their attorneys, and a certified copy of the list and valuation of the stock, property and assets owned by said company, as made by the auditor of public accounts of the State of Illinois, having been filed, and from which this appeal is taken and prosecuted by said company; and the court proceeding to hear the evidence presented by the State, and by said company, as to said valuation, do find, that the aggregate value of the stock, property and assets owned by said company, to be listed for taxation, is four million nine hundred and fifty-two thousand dollars and no more, and the clerk of this court will certify the said aggregate value so found by the court, to the auditor of public accounts, in pursuance of the statute in such case made and provided."

Some of the witnesses confined their valuation of the railroad to its present value, whilst others embraced, in their testimony, its prospective value also, but in their aggregates they do not essentially differ. We understood the witness called on the part of the State, to include its prospective value in his estimate, and with that in view he would not desire to be one of a company to take the road and operate it, at five millions.

It was urged, on the argument, by the counsel for the State, that the prospective value of the road should be taken into the estimate, and not its income. Such value is purely speculative, it must be admitted, and we very much question, if it is a proper element in the present, or any like case. The assessment is for the time being only, and the value of the property for such purpose should be limited to that time, the more especially, as in the efflux of time, other valuations are required to be made. At any subsequent assessment, the proofs adduced may show a much higher valuation. The law does not design this to be permanent by any means. The ninth section of the act, under which the appeal was taken by the company, (Session Laws 1859, p. 207,) provides, " that all the provisions of this act shall apply to the listing, valuations and assessments of said years (1857 and 1858), as well as to all future listings, valuations and assessments." If then, the property is more valuable in 1859 or in 1860, than as now found, or in subsequent years, the taxes will be assessed accordingly, so that the injunction of the constitution, " that every person and corporation shall pay a tax in proportion to the value of his or her property," will be regarded. This clause has been understood to mean, the value at the time of taxa-[*68] tion or assessment. Values are fluctuating and changeable, as all experience shows. Nor is it easy, at any one period of time, to lay down a general and satisfactory rate of certain application, in all cases, for the purpose of ascertaining the value of many kinds of property, subject to taxation. Where property has a known and determinate value ascertained by commerce in it, as in most kinds of personal property, or fixed by law as money, there can be no difficulty. But there are many kinds of property, as to which the assessor has no such satisfactory guide. Such is peculiarly the case with railroad property, and other similar property, constructed not only for the profit of the owners, but for the accommodation of the public, under the sanction and by the exercise of the sovereign power of the State. In such cases, the inquiry should be, what is the property worth to be used for the purposes for which it is constructed, and not for any other purpose to which

State of Illinois *v.* Illinois Central R. R. Co.

it might be applied or converted, or for which it might be used. In such cases, if the property is devoted to the use for which it was designed, and is in a condition to produce its maximum income, one very important element for ascertaining its present value is discovered, and that is its net profits. When property is thus improved, it is manifest that it is more or less valuable, as it yields a greater or less profit, in its product and economical use. No prudent purchaser of such property would neglect, in the first instance, to look at the income the property yields, so that he might thereby judge what profits he might, in the future, reasonably expect from his investment. To ascertain what he might safely give for the property, no doubt he would, and ought, prudently, to anticipate the future, as well as regard the past, and yet, should he give more than the value as indicated by the present income, such enhanced value would be rather speculative than real, depending on a great variety of circumstances and casualties. The anticipation that in a given time in future, the property would yield a larger income, would be the inducement to give more than its present actual value. We are not prepared to say, that an assessor, making yearly valuations of property for taxation, can, or ought to take into consideration, anything more than the value of the property at the time he is called upon to value it, since, if it does increase in value in process of time, advantage can be taken of it in future valuations, as they may be periodically made. But if he can, and does, look to the future, for the purpose of ascertaining the present value of property, he should do it with extreme caution. In this country at least, hope is so seductive, and the future so bright, and so full of promise, there is the [*69] greatest danger that the most prudent may be mistaken, and the most considerate be misled, and it is much safer to rely upon practical demonstration, to determine the present value of such property, rather than, speculatively, enter into the unknown future, whose dark veil it is not given to us to lift, and look beyond. It is safer surely, to say, that, when the future shall be revealed, and practically exhibit an increased value of the property, then would be the proper time to assess it at such increased value.

To illustrate the argument, by the counsel for the State, that the income of the road afforded no criterion for determining its value, it was said that an uncultivated tract of land was always worth something, and often very valuable, when producing no income. This is very true, but why? It is because the land has a capacity to produce an income whenever the owner shall desire to cultivate it, and put it up to the top of that capacity. It was in proof that the railroad was already put to the extent of its capacity to yield income, and producing the utmost it can now be made to produce. If the road was lying idle, there would then be a proper comparison between it and an uncultivated tract of land or farm. If the farm is cultivated to the extent of its power of production, as the road is, the income of the farm would be a criterion of its value. It is often the case, that a farm has a fanciful value, beyond and apart from its productive capacity. It may have beautiful scenery, it may have grottoes and fountains and groves, and well fitted to be the abode of luxury and pride, or adjoin a growing city or town; but railroads and farms are not generally luxuries, or the offspring or seats of pride, and are only valuable from their power to produce income. They are matters of mere utility, and nothing else. When property is in a condition to develop its full productiveness, it is then only that such productiveness can be relied upon, as exhibiting its real value. If a railroad has only one-half the rolling stock required for its business, its productiveness would be delusive, as a criterion of value. In such a case the assessor would very properly inquire, what would be the value of the property, if fully equipped to do a maximum business, and consider the result of such inquiry in determining its present value. This road is doing its best, and it is proved, it has no net income—no profit on its cost, and is not a good investment at a value greater than that fixed by its owners, and proved on this trial. In process of time it may produce a greater income, when its value for taxation will be fixed proportionably higher. [*70] Under the law it must be valued and assessed every

State of Illinois *v.* Illinois Central R. R. Co.

year, and whenever it shall produce twice as great an income as it does at present, it will be valued, of course, twice as high. Then, too, may arise the necessity, if it ever can arise, of determining the other question, whether, in any event, the company are liable to the State for anything beyond seven per cent. of the gross earnings of their road. We decide now only the case before us, as made in the declaration filed by the State, and the pleadings of the parties. We do not wish to be understood as asserting that the productiveness of property when fully improved, is an absolute standard of valuation, but that it forms a very important element in ascertaining its actual value. In connection with this, and possibly of even greater importance in forming a just opinion of real value, would be the inquiry, what would prudent men give for the property, as a permanent investment, with a view to present and future income? Both these elements were taken into the consideration of the witnesses in this case, and weighed with the court in making up its judgment. It is admitted by the auditor that the company has overpaid all that was due from it to the State, on the valuation of their property as established by the testimony. The company makes no claim for the overplus. The judgment of the court is, therefore, in favor of the defendants, that they are not indebted to the State for any portion of the taxes of 1857, but have fully paid and discharged the same.

Judgment for the Defendant.

DECISIONS

OF

THE SUPREME COURT

OF THE

STATE OF ILLINOIS,

OF CASES ARGUED AT

JANUARY TERM, 1862, AT SPRINGFIELD.

THE ÆTNA INSURANCE COMPANY, Plaintiff in Error, *v.* WILLIAM PHELPS, Defendant in Error.

ERROR TO MASON.

In an action upon an insurance policy; which contains a condition that in the event of a loss, the company may at its option restore the building; it is unnecessary to negative the performance of this condition, in the declaration. It is a condition subsequent, and if performed, the company should allege it in defense of the action.

Upon a default, a writ of inquiry issues to have the damages assessed, which may be executed in court or be directed to the sheriff to execute in vacation. It would be regular for the sheriff to summon a jury from the bystanders, and have the damages assessed in the presence of the court.

THIS was a suit brought by Phelps, in the Circuit Court of Mason county, against the Ætna Insurance Company, upon a fire policy issued by said company.

The declaration contains four special counts. The first upon the policy according to its alleged legal effect. The other counts are upon the policy in "*hæc verba.*"

In each count the allegation of the interest of Phelps in the

87

premises destroyed by fire, is as in the first count, "said plaintiff was interested," etc., without otherwise setting forth the nature of the interest.

[*72] The breach of each count is the same as alleged in first count, to wit: " Said defendant has never paid said plaintiff the sum of twenty-five hundred, or any part thereof."

To each of the counts the defendant below filed a demurrer. The demurrer to the first count, craving oyer of and setting out the policy with its conditions—the causes of demurrer, that the counts do not sufficiently disclose the interest of the plaintiff below; that the contract or policy of insurance declared on, discloses a contract in the disjunctive, viz., the 12th condition, and the first count fails to set out said condition, and this and each of the other counts fail to allege any breach of this condition.

The 12th condition of the policy is as follows: "Payment of losses shall be made in sixty days after the loss shall have been ascertained and proved, and in case differences shall arise touching any loss, it may be submitted to the judgment of arbiters indifferently chosen, whose award, in writing, shall be binding on the parties. In case of any loss on, or damage to, the property insured, it shall be optional with the company to replace the articles lost or damaged with others of the same kind and equal goodness; and to rebuild or repair the building or buildings within a reasonable time, giving notice of their intention so to do within thirty days after the preliminary proof shall have been received at the office of the company."

The last clause of the policy is, " And that this policy is made and accepted in reference to the conditions hereto annexed, which are to be used and resorted to, in order to explain the rights and obligations of the parties hereto, in all cases not herein otherwise specially provided for."

The court overruled the demurrer, and judgment thereupon was entered for the amount of damages assessed by a jury and costs. The regular jury had all been discharged, and upon the order of the court, the sheriff summoned twelve jurors, who made this assessment.

The errors assigned, question the correctness of the decision of the court below in overruling the demurrer, and the right of the court to summon a jury after all the regular panel had been discharged.

STUART, EDWARDS & BROWN, for Plaintiff in Error.

JAMES ROBERTS, for Defendant in Error.

WALKER, J. It is urged, that the declaration in this case was insufficient, and that the court below erred in overruling the defendant's demurrer. The policy upon which suit [*73] was brought, contains this amongst other provisions: "In case of any loss on, or damage to, the property insured, it shall be optional with the company to replace the articles lost or damaged, with others of the same kind and equal goodness; and to rebuild or repair the building or buildings within a reasonable time, giving notice of their intention so to do within thirty days after preliminary proof shall have been received at the office of the company." It is insisted, that the declaration is substantially defective, for the want of an averment, negativing this clause. By the common law rules of pleading, in declaring upon a bond with a condition annexed, breaches were alone required to be assigned upon the bond. If there had been a performance of the defeasance or condition, it was held to be matter of defense. And this is certainly true of all conditions subsequent. 1 T. R. 640. It is however otherwise, with conditions precedent. Gould, in his treatise on Pleading, 177, states the rule thus: "It is never necessary, by the common law, for the plaintiff, in his declaration to state or in any manner to take notice of any condition subsequent annexed to the right he asserts. For the office of such condition is not to *create* the right on which the plaintiff founds his demand; but to *qualify* or *defeat* it. The condition therefore, if performed or complied with, is matter of defense, which it is for the defendant to plead."

In this case the defendant in error became, according to the covenants contained in the policy, entitled to recover at the time the loss occurred. But by this condition the company had

Town of Paris v. People.

the right to defeat the recovery, by rebuilding the property destroyed. If they performed this subsequent condition, they should have pleaded the performance. This condition was inserted solely for the benefit of the company, its performance was to be subsequent to any loss which might occur, and after notice of that fact, and was purely a matter of defense. *Howard Fire and Marine Ins. Co.* v. *Cornick*, 24 Ill. 455.

It is also urged that the court erred in impaneling a jury to assess the damages, after the regular panel had been discharged for the term. At common law, the court had the unquestioned right to issue a *venire facias*, at any time during its session, returnable to the term, whenever the business of the court might require it. And we must suppose if it was designed to constitute this a regular panel, that such a writ was issued. But if that were not so, still upon a default, a writ of inquiry may issue to have the damages assessed, which may be executed in court, or be directed to the sheriff to execute in vacation. If the [*74] sheriff executed the writ, by summoning the jury, and having the damages assessed in the presence of the court, it would certainly be as regular as if done in vacation. So that whether it were executed before the court, or the sheriff, with a portion of the regular panel or bystanders, can make no difference. We are unable to perceive any error in this record requiring the judgment of the court below to be reversed, and it is therefore affirmed.

Judgment affirmed.

THE TOWN OF PARIS, Plaintiff in Error, *v.* THE PEOPLE OF THE STATE OF ILLINOIS, Defendants in Error.

ERROR TO EDGAR.

Where an indictment concludes against the form of the statute, etc., it clearly indicates a prosecution under a statute, and not at common law.

The offense of keeping and maintaining a "*calaboose*," by an incorporated town, is not an offense against the statute, for which an indictment will lie.

Town of Paris *v.* People.

THIS was a prosecution by the People against the town of Paris for keeping and maintaining a nuisance.

An indictment was found at the August special term, 1862, of the Edgar Circuit Court, containing but one count, charging the town of Paris, described therein as a corporation, with having 'kept and maintained "a disorderly house, known as a calaboose," and with having kept and confined "in said house, divers disorderly and noisome persons, to the great damage and common nuisance of the said citizens of the town of Paris and the People of the State of Illinois, in returning, passing, repassing, riding, laboring and residing near the said house, contrary," etc.

Upon this indictment being found, a capias issued, commanding the sheriff, etc., "to take *the body of the town of Paris* and it safely keep, so that" he should "have *its body* before the judge," etc.

The sheriff returned this capias, "executed by arresting and taking bail from Walter Booth, the President of the Town Council," etc.

Aferwards, the defendant below appeared and moved to quash the indictment, which motion was overruled by the court.

A plea of not guilty was then entered, and a trial had before a jury, resulting in a verdict of guilty.

The evidence heard on the trial preserved in the bill of [*75] exceptions showed that the town of Paris had erected in the fall of 1860, on the back part, fifteen or twenty feet from the west end of lot number thirty-five owned by the town, on the west side of the public square, a calaboose, which was still there; that an alley sixteen feet wide separated the lot on which the calaboose stood from that on which Mr. Metcalf lived; that the calaboose was about forty feet from Mr. Metcalf's residence, which was there when the calaboose was built, one hundred feet from the street, eighty feet distant from J. K. Douglas' residence. The witnesses referred to a map, a copy of which is contained in the record, to show the situation of surrounding residences, buildings, streets and alleys. They described the calaboose as having walls of thick oak plank, ceiled inside, having two small grated windows, one on the west and the other on the east end, and stated that there was a tight plank fence eight feet high on the south side of the lot, next to the alley, and one so high that a man standing on the ground could not look over it on the north side. Drunken, disorderly persons had been confined there, but not over twelve hours. Some who were drunk when arrested had been confined there awaiting trial, to allow them to get sober. Witnesses for the prosecution testified, that some who were confined there made noises by hallooing and blackguarding, and used vulgar and obscene language in the day time and at night, which could be heard in their houses and on the streets; not so bad lately as in the latter part of 1860 and fore part of 1861. The town constable testified, that he had kept one person there eight hours. The police magistrate, Otis Brown, testified, that a good many offenders had been confined there, but thought that only three had been noisy. Hoge was one of these. He was intoxicated, enraged and abusive of Logan, a policeman. A majority had been quiet. The calaboose had been carefully managed and kept clean. His office was on the same lot, and he had been police magistrate ever since it was built.

The ordinances of the town of Paris were read in evidence, one of which provides for the confinement of persons in the calaboose in certain cases to await trial.

THOMAS C. W. SALE, and SHERIDAN P. REED, for Plaintiff in Error.

J. B. WHITE, State's Attorney, for the People.

WALKER, J. This indictment concludes, "contrary to the [*76] form of the statute in such case made and provided." This clearly designates it as a prosecution under the statute and not at the common law. When an indictment contains this conclusion, a recovery can only be had on a statutory offense. And if no statute exists creating the offense, then the indictment is vicious, and should be quashed on motion, or a demurrer sustained if interposed. Such a motion was interposed and overruled. Without stopping to inquire whether the 10th section

Town of Paris *v.* People.

of article 13 of the constitution, prohibits the city from adopting ordinances for the imprisonment of persons, or justices of the peace or police magistrates from committing them under such ordinances or a law of the State, we shall proceed to the consideration of the question whether the court below erred in refusing to quash the indictment.

In determining this question, it will become necessary to determine, whether the indictment describes any offense, created by the statute. It is urged that it may be sustained under the 127th section of the act regulating criminal jurisprudence. That section prohibits and defines the punishment of "open lewdness, or other notorious act of public indecency, tending to debauch the public morals," or the keeping open a tippling house on the Sabbath day or night, or maintaining or keeping a lewd house or place for the practice of fornication, or keeping a common ill-governed and disorderly house, to the encouragement of idleness, gaming, drinking, fornication or other misbehavior. The indictment was not designed to embrace any of these offenses, as it nowhere describes either of them. Nor can we perceive, notwithstanding there was undoubtedly disorderly conduct in this *calaboose*, that it was a tippling house, lewd house for the practice of fornication, or a common ill-governed and disorderly house, to the encouragement of idleness, gaming, drunkenness, fornication, or other misbehavior. Now the design in erecting and maintaining this building, however obnoxious and objectionable to the residents in the vicinity, was the very opposite of these misdemeanors. It was intended to reform by punishment, those confined in the building.

Then can it be sustained under the 134th section of the same act? That section prohibits the obstruction or injury of public roads, bridges, navigable streams, so as to render them inconvenient or dangerous to pass; the erection or establishment of any offensive trade, manufacture or business, or to continue the same after it has been erected, or to pollute or obstruct any water-course, lake, pond, marsh or common sewer, so as to render the same offensive to the county, town, village or neighborhood. Whilst all these acts are designated nuisances, and although this *calaboose* may have been so [*77] managed or situated as to be a nuisance, still it is in nowise embraced or enumerated in this section. If an offense at all, it was so by the common law, and not by statute. And as the indictment concludes against the form of the statute, and there being no such statutory offense, the motion to quash should have been sustained. The judgment of the court below is therefore reversed.

Judgment reversed.

WILLIAM S. MAUS, Plaintiff in error, *v.* THE LOGANS-PORT, PEORIA AND BURLINGTON RAILROAD, CHARLES L. FROST, EDWARD WESTON, and HENRY G. MAR-QUAND, Defendants in Error.

ERROR TO TAZEWELL.

In construing an amendatory statute, it is a fixed rule that the old law must be considered, the mischief arising under that law, and the remedy for it, which the new law may be supposed to provide.

The act of February 14th, 1855, amendatory of the revenue law, which directs that the track or superstructure of a railroad shall be denominated "fixed and stationary personal property," was intended to create a species of personal property not before known to the law. For non-payment of taxes upon this property, the collector may levy upon the rails and remove them from the track, for the purpose of selling them.

This act has reference only to the collection of the revenue, and does not change the character of such property for other purposes.

Section 14, of the amendatory act of 1853, which provides that real property shall be liable for taxes on personal property and *vice versa*, has no application to this "fixed and stationary personal property;" such property must bear its own burden of taxation.

It is within the province of the legislature to provide that property, which is attached to the freehold, so as to become a part of it by the common law, may be regarded as personal property, for all purposes, or for any special purpose. Of this character is the act of Feb. 14th, 1855, which directs that the track and superstructure of a railroad, together with the improvements at stations, shall be denominated personal property, for the purposes of collecting the revenue.

THE opinion of the court contains a full statement of the case.

JAMES ROBERTS, for the Plaintiff in Error.

BREESE, J. This was a bill in chancery filed by the defendants in error, August 17th, 1861, in the Circuit Court of Tazewell county, alleging that the complainants had been duly incorporated by the legislature of Illinois, and were the [*78] owners of the franchise and reversionary interest, in a line of railway extending from the eastern boundary line of the State, through the county of Tazewell and the city of Peoria, to the Mississippi river opposite the city of Burlington, in the State of Iowa; that said railroad connects at the eastern terminus with a railroad extending eastward to Logansport, in the State of Indiana; that said railroad is now, and has been for several years past, in active operation, and is used for the purpose of transporting freight, passengers, the United States mail, etc.; that there is no other railroad parallel on the north, nearer than the Chicago and Rock Island Railroad, and none nearer south than the Great Western Railroad, and that it is the only route over and by which the United States mails for that portion of the State of Illinois can be carried. That Charles L. Frost, Edward Weston, and Henry G. Marquand, own an interest in the property of said railroad, and have the actual possession and control of the same, with all its revenues, in trust for the payment of certain liabilities created in the construction of, and operating said road; that William S. Maus, claiming to be the treasurer of Tazewell county—a large amount of taxes assessed upon said railroad or its track, superstructure and improvements, by Tazewell county and the State of Illinois, being due and unpaid—threatens to take and remove from said road-bed, lying and being in said county of Tazewell, the iron rails laid and fixed thereupon, and constituting the track of said railway, and to sell the same by virtue of his authority as *ex officio* collector of said county, for the purpose of enforcing payment of said taxes, and pretends that he has been authorized and required to adopt said proceeding, by the board of supervisors of Tazewell county, and threatens to use the whole power of the county to carry his threats into execution unless the taxes so claimed by him shall be immediately paid; charges that the proceedings of said Maus are illegal, in violation of, and without any authority of law whatever; that such proceedings would tend to the breach of the peace, and be of irreparable injury to the railway; that it would be a flagrant violation of the criminal laws of the State under color of authority; that damages to be recovered at law would not compensate for the threatened injury; and concludes with a prayer for an injunction to restrain the said Maus from carrying his threats into execution.

At the September term, 1861, when the cause came on to be heard, it was submitted upon the following statement of facts:

It is agreed, that the complainant is a regularly incorpo-[*79] rated company, for the purposes and objects stated in the bill. And that it has connections, and runs for the carriage of passengers and freight and United States mails, as stated in the bill; and that said company was formerly known as the Eastern Extension of the Peoria and Oquawka Railroad Company. It is further admitted, that the length of the main track and side tracks of said road in Tazewell county, liable to taxation, is sixteen and 35-100 miles; that the value of the fixed and stationary personal property in said county, as returned by said company, was $70,000, for the year 1857, upon which there was legally assessed for state, county and special taxes for that year, $863.76. For the year 1858 the value of the fixed and stationary personal property was $38,450, upon which there was assessed for that year, for state, county and special taxes, the sum of $439.64. For the year 1859, the value of the fixed and stationary personal property was $40,875, upon which there was legally assessed for that year upon the same, the sum of $457.-79; and that the value of the fixed and stationary personal property for the year 1860 was $40,875, upon which there was legally assessed for taxes for that year the sum of $396.48. That no part of said taxes was ever paid by said company, but that there is now due for taxes on said fixed and stationary personal property, besides interest, the sum of $2,157.67; that the complainants were requested to pay said taxes, and that the defendant, on the 17th of August, 1861, after notifying the agents of said company, and upon their refusal to pay, was proceeding by warrant in due form of law to collect said taxes; and that the complainant had no personal property whatever, out of which said taxes could be collected; and that Tazewell county has adopted township organization; and that said defendant was, at the time stated, and still is, treasurer of said Tazewell county, and said defendant was proceeding to take up and remove the rails of said road, that composed and formed the track of said road, and which were affixed with spikes and chairs to the ties imbedded in the bed of said railroad, to take them to a convenient place for the purpose of sale, when he was stopped by injunction from so doing. It is further agreed, that this statement shall stand in lieu of an answer and bill of exceptions, and that this cause shall be submitted to the Circuit Court of Tazewell county, upon this statement of facts, and that the judge of said court may render his decision therein in term time, or vacation, as of the present term; and that either party may except to the decree rendered by said judge, without making any further bill of exceptions; and that a writ of error may be sued out of the Supreme Court for the Second Grand Division; and that whichever of said parties shall be defendant in error, will enter their appearance without service of pro- [*80] cess; and that the bill, summons, and all orders and decrees made in this cause by said Circuit Court of Tazewell county, and this agreement, shall be certified as a complete record in said cause; and if said Supreme Court shall be of opinion that the defendant had no right, under the laws of the State as collector of taxes, where said railroad company had no personal property, out of which the taxes could be made, to take and remove the rails of said road, fixed to the ties and bed of the road, and used as the track thereof, for the taxes upon the fixed and stationary personal property, said injunction shall be made perpetual; otherwise to be dissolved, and said defendant be at liberty to proceed as aforesaid.

It is further agreed, that the rolling stock, and other moveable property, on the railroad, belong to said Frost, Weston and Marquand, who are operating the railroad in the name of the corporators, : nd that the rolling stock, and moveable property, have never belonged to said corporators.

Whereupon the court rendered a decree making the injunction perpetual. The plaintiff in error brings the cause to this court, and assigns for error, this decision of the Circuit Court.

The facts agreed, involve an inquiry into the revenue law as applicable to railroads in this State, constructed in counties which have adopted township organization, as the county of Tazewell had, at the time of filing and hearing this bill of complaint.

Previous to the act of Feb. 14th, 1853, the terms "real property" and "land" were held to mean and include, not only the land itself, whether laid out in town lots or otherwise, with all things contained within the land, but also, all buildings, structures and improvements, and other fixtures of every kind thereon, and all rights and privileges belonging, or in an any wise appertaining thereto. The term "personal property" was held to mean and include every tangible thing which was the subject of ownership, whether animate or inanimate, other than money, and forming part or parcel of real property, as above defined. (Scates' Comp. 1046, 1047, Sec. 2, Act of Feb. 12, 1853.) This act applied to counties under township organization. By section 22, it was provided, "that the president, secretary or principal accounting officer of every railroad company, etc., shall list for taxation, at its actual value, its real and personal property, moneys and credits within this State, in the manner following: In all cases returns shall be made to the assessor of each of the respective counties where such property may be situated, together with a statement of the amount of said property, which is situated in each county, town, city [*81] or ward therein. The value of all moveable property shall be added to the stationary and fixed property, and real estate, and apportioned to such wards, cities and counties, *pro rata*, in proportion to the value of the real estate and fixed property in said ward, town, city or county. The remainder of the section authorizes the county assessor to whom returns are made, if he is of opinion that false or incorrect valuations have been made, or that the property has not been listed at its full value, or has not been listed in its proper location, or in cases where no returns have been made to him, to provide to have the same valued and assessed in the same manner as is prescribed in the several sections of the same act, regulating the duties of county assessors, in cases where there has been neglect or refusal to list property. (Ib. 1055.) By section 14 of an amendatory act of the same session, it is provided that personal property shall be liable for taxes levied on real property, and real property shall be liable for taxes levied on personal property, but the tax on personal property shall not be charged against real property, except in cases of removals, or when the tax cannot be made out of the personal property. (Ib. 1070.) Sections from fifteen to forty-three inclusive, have reference, chiefly, to providing for the sale of delinquent and forfeited lands, and their redemption. The thirty-eighth section provides that every tract of land, or town lot offered at public sale, for the taxes due thereon, and not sold for want of bidders, shall be declared to be forfeited to the State. The fortieth section provides for the redemption of such forfeited lands.

On the 14th February, 1855, this act was amended, and by the second section the return of the schedule or list of taxable property of a railroad company must be made to the county clerk instead of to the assessor, and the clerk is required to lay the list before the board of supervisors, at their meeting to equalize assessments, and if a majority of the board is satisfied that the return is correct, the property is to be assessed accordingly—but if not, the board can assess it, etc.

The fourth section is as follows:

"The schedule or list of the taxable property of railroad companies shall set forth a description of all the real property, owned or occupied by the company, in each county, town, and city, through which such railroad may run; and the actual value of each lot or parcel of land, including the improvements thereon, (except the track or superstructure of said road), shall be annexed to the description of such lot or parcel of land. Said list shall set forth the number of acres taken for right of way, stations, or other purposes, from each tract of land through which said road may run, describing said

99

[*82] land, as near as practicable, in accordance with the surveys of the United States, giving the width of the strip, or parcel of land, and its length through each tract; also, the whole number of acres, and the aggregate value thereof, in said county, town, and city.   All of the property mentioned in this section shall be denominated 'real property.' The list aforesaid shall set forth the length of the main track, and the length of all side tracks, and turn-outs, in each county, city, and town, through which the road may run, with the actual value of the same, and the value of the improvements at each of the several stations, when said stations are not a part of city or town lots.   The said stations and track shall be denominated 'fixed and stationary personal property.' The list shall contain an inventory of the rolling stock belonging to said company, with the value thereof; said rolling stock shall be denominated 'personal property;' also, a statement of the value of all the personal property, owned by said company, in each county, city, and town.   The length of the whole of the main track within this State, and the total value of the rolling stock, shall be set forth in said list.   The rolling stock shall be listed and taxed in the several counties, towns, and cities, *pro rata*, in proportion as the length of the main track in such county, town, or city, bears to the whole length of the road.   All other property shall be listed and taxed in the county, town, or city, where the same is located or used."   The remainder of the section is directory to the assessor as to the manner in which he shall enter the description of the right of way, or land for station purposes, on his books, and "when advertised by any sheriff or collector to be sold for taxes, or when so sold, no other description shall be necessary." (Ib. 1106-7.)

We have quoted this section at length, for the reason that this controversy arises upon the construction to be placed upon it.   It classifies railroad property somewhat differently from the act of 1853.   In that act, railroad property was known only as real property and personal property, and subjected to taxes as such, and to compulsory payment of them, in the same manner as property of natural persons, each description of property being liable for the taxes assessed upon any one description.   In construing any amendatory act, it is a fixed rule that the old law must be considered—the mischiefs arising under that law, and the remedy for them which the new law may be supposed to provide.   We have seen in what manner the old law classified such property.   We apprehend the evils resulting from it were found to be, that the government was liable to the loss of its sustenance by the obstacles thrown in the way of the speedy collection of the taxes, by the very law itself there being no other mode [*83] provided than by the sale of their real property, in default of personal property, with a redemption of two years allowed after the sale, or, in case of no sale, a forfeiture to the State, then by carring it, from year to year, on the assessor's books, as forfeited land, to be again sold as such for the taxes assessed. It is a part of the public history of this State, that purchasers could not be found to buy for taxes such property, who were willing to take the risk of the legality of the sales, and other risks, the consequence of which was, a forfeiture to the State; and the counties, through which the roads ran, were deprived of their annual taxes due them from such property.   The object of the amendatory law was, as we conceive, to provide some remedy for this, which they have done by giving a description other than "real property," and other attributes, to a portion of such property, thereby rendering it susceptible of immediate transfer and delivery, on a sale of it for the taxes assessed upon it.

The complainants contend, that the only object of the legislature in so classifying railroad property, was for the purpose of valuation, with a view to increase the aggregate of the revenue.   We do not precisely understand, how the aggregate of revenue can be increased by classifying this kind of property.   It is very evident the statute, in the valuation, requires the road bed to be separated from the track and superstructure placed upon it, and to be valued separately.   Now is it possible they could produce more revenue, by being valued separately, than if valued together?   Suppose the value of the road bed be, ten thousand dollars per mile, and the value of the superstructure, six thousand dollars per mile, do these

two sums produce more revenue than would be produced by
a valuation of the road bed and superstructure, jointly, at sixteen thousand dollars per mile? As in the case of improved
property owned by individuals, by separating the house from
the lot, the State would derive no more revenue from them
separately, than it would from them together. The valuation in
each respect, controlling the amount of the revenue to be derived from the property. If such was the only design of this
amendatory act, it need not have been passed, as it is no improvement whatever on the old law. It is quite manifest, we
think, that the legislature had something more in view, in thus
classifying railroad property, and in denominating a portion
of its fixtures, placed by artificial means upon the land owned
by it, " personal property," than mere facility in its valuation.
The road bed and right of way is denominated " real property." For delinquency in paying the taxes assessed upon
[*84] them, they can be sold, and redeemed in two years after
the sale. The main track, the side tracks, the turn-outs, and
the buildings of the several stations, are to be scheduled separately, and denominated " fixed and stationary personal property." The rolling stock shall be denominated " personal
property."

Here is, evidently, a design on the part of the legislature
to create a species of personal property, not before known to
the law, and with the purpose, as we think, of subjecting it,
in certain contingencies, to a separation from the soil on which
it may be fixed. If not, why call it personal property, at all?
If, though " fixed and stationary," it was never to be, under
any circumstances, subject to removal, and to all intents, and
for every purpose, of the same nature and character as land
itself, why not call it real estate? What is gained by designating it as personal property, when it shall never, under any
circumstances, or for any purpose, public or otherwise, possess
any of the attributes of such property? We are at a loss to
discover any good reason for the distinction, unless it be, in
view of the loss of revenue to the State and counties, by the
neglect of such companies to pay the taxes assessed on such
property, that the legislature has endowed it with the attri-

Maus *v.* Logansport, Peoria and Burlington R. R. *et al.*

butes of personal property, so that it might be removed and sold for the taxes, an attempt to do which, would bring delinquent or reluctant companies to a performance of their obligations to the State.   To make the road bed, on which the superstructure is placed, personal property, would have been, for this purpose, of no practical benefit, as it could not be removed, and though sold for the taxes, the company would continue in its enjoyment.   Not so with the main and side tracks, turn-outs, and improvements at the several stations. They are placed there by artificial means, and easily removed. It is true, they are stationary and fixed, but surely it will not be contended, that although fixtures of a certain kind, which, by the common law, are deemed a part of the freehold and cannot be removed, that the legislature may not destroy this character, and make them personal property liable to be sold for taxes, or upon execution to pay a private debt.   It is a question of expediency, and of policy only, whether the dwelling-house shall not, for purposes of taxation, be deemed personal property, to be severed from the land if the taxes assessed upon the house are not duly paid, and the house exposed to sale on that account.

It cannot be denied, that this " fixed and stationary personal property," is liable for the taxes assessed upon it—the defendants do not deny that—it follows then, like all other property, it is liable to be sold for the assessments.   The defendants, however, insist, that for the taxes assessed on this property [*85] and unpaid, the land is liable, and that this property is liable for the tax assessed upon the land—that there is a mutual liability under section fourteen already quoted.   That section does not so provide, as we understand it.   The provision is, that personal property of the kind and nature denominated in that act, shall be liable for the taxes on real estate, and *vice versa*, but it nowhere provides that land or personal property shall be subject to the taxes assessed upon " fixed and stationary personal property," that new description of personal property, so by the act created.   This kind of property stands by itself, isolated from real and from personal property, and is made, by the law, to bear its own burdens, and if it cannot be sold and removed, as the defendants contend it cannot be, then the new law is of less avail than the old law, for under the old law the real property could be sold to pay the taxes assessed on the personal property in certain cases. Under the new law this kind of personal property is not so liable, and no taxes assessed upon it can be collected, unless authority is conceded to the collector to take it and sell it. This property is a new species of property, created by the legislature, made distinct from all other property, and assessed and valued as such, and as the lands and personal property are not made liable for the taxes assessed upon this kind of property, as they clearly are not, it must follow, that this new description of property must be liable for the assessments upon it, to be collected, on default, by a sale of the property. Surely, the legislature did intend, that this new description of property should be liable to taxation, and to be sold, if the taxes were not duly paid, else how could it be subjected to this burden?

It seems to follow, as a necessary consequence from these premises, that the sheriff or collector, to put the property in a position to be sold, may sever the superstructure from the freehold, and take it into his possession precisely the same as he could any other fixtures which the legislature may have declared to be personal property, and subject to removal. In taking personal property for taxes, the collector, in all cases, has the right to remove the property. His right to do so, cannot be questioned, and it is no argument against it, that he may exercise it in a riotous manner, or at an improper hour. Nor as to the quantity of such personal property to be removed to satisfy the taxes, can the collector be restricted, unless his act, in this regard, should be oppressive, and wanton, and done with a design unnecessarily to vex and harrass the delinquent.

That the State should have this power, vast and destruc-
[*86] tive as it may be to some great interests of the country when exercised, there seems great propriety. In considering such questions as have arisen in this case, we must bear in mind the maxim, that the government must not be deprived of the aliment indispensable to its life—that it must be sustained at all hazards, regardless of the individual suffering which may

be produced, the derangement of the business affairs of the community, or the crippling of corporate powers, for whatever purposes they may have been granted. All must yield to the inexorable demands of the government. Taxation, in some form, must exist in every civilized community, and must be enforced upon property, if not paid in money. It is a public burden, which all persons and corporations should be willing to bear, since all receive a just compensation in the benefits conferred by the government. Nay, it is a duty which all should be prompt to perform. Taxation is the breath of its life—if that be stopped, anarchy, ruin and death, would be the inevitable catastrophe. As was said by the Supreme Court of the United States in the case of *Priestman* v. *The United States*, 4 Dallas, 28, " Public policy, national purposes, and the regular operations of government, require that the revenue system should be faithfully observed and strictly executed."

We know of no principle that will exonerate an individual from the prompt payment of his taxes, if he has property out of which they can be made, nor of any applicable to railroad corporations, however conducive they are admitted to be, to the development of the resources of a State, or however necessary to the transaction of its widely extended business. Nor is it an argument in favor of relieving the company from the taxes imposed upon their property, that they have become embarrassed for its construction and equipment, incurring therefor, heavy debts. It is no fault of the State, that it has become embarrassed, and contracted debts beyond its ability to pay, but it is the just claim of the State, that the dues of the company to it, shall be first paid, in preference to all other claims upon it.

The conduct of this road furnishes a strong argument, in favor of the view of the case we have presented. Keeping in view the principle, that taxes must be paid before all other obligations, this record shows, this road has not paid one dollar of taxes assessed upon its fixed and stationary personal property for the last four years, having been delinquent for the years 1857, 1858, 1859 and 1860, until the amount due the county of Tazewell, has reached the very considerable

[*87] sum of two thousand one hundred and fifty-seven and sixty-seven one-hundredths dollars, exclusive of interest. This preferred and paramount claim of the public has been postponed, year after year, by the company, and they now contend, when the attempt to collect it is made in good earnest, that the mode adopted is illegal—that great public interests will be destroyed —and a wanton sacrifice of property inevitable.

The legality of the mode proposed to be adopted by the collector, we do not question. He can take these rails from their bed and sell them, in the same manner as he could take a horse from the stable of an individual owner, for the payment of taxes, and if the property be sacrificed, if great public interests be injured, we have only to say, all these considerations must yield to the paramount claim of the State to be sustained in its existence—a claim so great and overriding, as to dwarf all others, which may be set off against it. It is a good law, and should be strictly enforced, doing as little injury as possible in the execution of its provisions.

We think it may be said, with truth, that the railroad companies of this State have discharged their taxes with commendable promptitude, and performed their obligations in a manner, generally, satisfactory. This road is the only one, so far as we are informed, which has manifested a disposition to postpone the just claims of the State, to those of other creditors, and to evade its responsibility to the power which protects it in the enjoyment of its franchise. We are slow to believe that other railroad companies, operating in this State, desire such a construction should be placed on the revenue law as the appellees contend for, by which they may avoid the payment of their taxes, and, to that extent, assume an attitude of hostility to the government.

The views here expressed are not intended to apply to a levy and sale, by execution, of this species of property, or to retract, or qualify, in the slightest degree, former decisions of this court, on that question. This species of property is made personalty, to a limited extent and for revenue purposes only, and the attributes of personal property only attach to it for such purposes. The General Assembly, in regulating the liability of property to taxation, sought to prescribe the mode in which it was to be subjected to that burden, and were not seeking to change, wholly, its incidents. Was such a provision found in the act regulating sales on execution, or in the law regulating chattel mortgages, or had the legislature declared, in those statutes, this description of fixtures to be "fixed and stationary personal property," then it would assume the attributes of personalty, for these several pur- [*88] poses. No such design has been indicated, except in this revenue law, and for purposes of revenue, and since no other property, real or personal, is made liable to the burden imposed upon this species, we are forced to conclude, the legislature designed that, on delinquency, it should be subject to sale and removal.

The decree of the Circuit Court is reversed, and a decree here, that the injunction be dissolved and the bill dismissed.

Decree reversed.

CATON, C. J. I do not understand that it was the intention of the legislature that, in any event, the rails should be severed from the track, and the public deprived of its use, which was the great object in view in granting the franchise. This the law would not allow either creditor or owner to do. While it is made personal property for the convenience of assessment, it is fixed and stationary for the purpose of securing its permanent location, that it may subserve the public good. It seems to me that the entire track should be sold to pay the tax, rather than destroy it by tearing up the rails.

SAMUEL C. GIBSON, Plaintiff in Error, *v.* JOHN E. ROLL, Defendant in Error.

ERROR TO SANGAMON.

Infants are bound by proceedings by an administrator to sell real estate, although they are not nominally made parties to the proceeding. The case *Ex parte Sturms*, 25th Illinois R. 390, overruled in part.

If the proceedings of a guardian to sell the estates of infants have not been regular and in conformity to law, they must have an opportunity to correct the errors. But such proceedings are not adverse to the interests of the infant, and if they have been regular. the infant will be bound by them. The case of *Mason* v. *Wait,* 4 Scam. 127, examined.

A proceeding by an administrator to sell the real estate of his decedent, is adverse to the infants, and he must follow the statute in his petition, and give proper notice; if he does this, the sale will be good. The court is to pass upon the sufficiency of the statements in the notice, which calls upon parties to object to the proceedings.

PLAINTIFF filed his declaration in ejectment, against Henry R. Richardson, for the recovery of the undivided half of the east twenty feet of lot No. 7, in block No. 10, in the city of Springfield.

The defendant plead the general issue, and Roll was substi- [*89] tuted in his stead, and possession of premises was by him admitted. It is also admitted that Benjamin F. Jewett died intestate, on or about the 20th day of December, 1848, seized in fee simple of the premises, and that defendant has chain of title, perfect and complete, from the heirs of said Jewett, to the premises.

Plaintiff offered in evidence a transcript of the record of the County Court of Tazewell county, of the proceedings of said court, in the matter of William S. Maus, administrator of Benjamin F. Jewett, dating from the 9th day of September, 1856, and setting forth the petition of said administrator for sale of real estate of said Jewett, including the premises, the order of sale, and report of sale of premises, and approval of sale by the court.

Plaintiff also offered in evidence a deed from said administrator to John D. Bail, conveying premises; also a deed from said Bail to Ninian E. Primm, and plaintiff, for said premises. Defendant objecting to said evidence, his objections were sustained, and plaintiff excepted.

The defendant offered in evidence a transcript of the record of the proceedings of the County Court of Tazewell county, in the matter of William S. Maus, administrator of Benjamin F. Jewett, showing a notice in words and figures following:

"ADMINISTRATOR'S NOTICE.

"Notice is hereby given, that I will make application to the County Court of Tazewell county, on the 3rd day of September next, for a decree to sell all or so much of the real estate of Benjamin F. Jewett, deceased, late of Tazewell county, as will be sufficient to pay the debts of said estate. All persons interested are requested to appear and show cause, if any they have, why such decree should not be granted. WM. S. MAUS,

"PEKIN, July 24, 1856. Adm'r of BENJAMIN F. JEWETT, dec'd."

Accompanied by the following certificate:

"We, Young & Underwood, printers and publishers of the '*Weekly Plaindealer*,' do hereby certify that the annexed advertisement was published in the '*Weekly Plaindealer*' for six weeks successively—the first publication being on the 24th day of July, 1856, and the last publication on the 4th day of September, A. D. 1856. YOUNG & UNDERWOOD, Publishers and Printers."

It is admitted that said notice was the only one given and published previous to said sale, under the order of sale, in the record, offered as evidence by plaintiff. The plaintiff objected to said notice as evidence. The court overruled said objection, and plaintiff excepted.

Verdict and judgment for defendant.

E. B. HERNDON, for Plaintiff in Error. [*90]

W. H. HERNDON, and E. L. GROSS, for Defendant in Error.

CATON, C. J.* The plain question is now presented, whether in proceedings by an administrator to sell the real estate of his intestate, it is necessary to make the heirs formal parties defendants in the petition, and to name them as such defendants in the notice. In *Ex parte Sturms*, 25 Ill. 390, which was a proceeding by a guardian to sell the lands of his wards, we dismissed the writ of error brought by the infants to reverse the order of sale, because the infants had not been made parties, from which it would seem to follow that they were not bound by the proceeding. If this consequence follows that decision, then we are satisfied that it was unadvisedly made and ought not to be adhered to. This whole subject of the sale of the

---

* NOTE. — See the case of *Smith* v. *Race*, in this volume.

Gibson *v.* Roll.

property of wards, by their guardians, in pursuance of laws authorizing proceedings for such sales is examined in *Mason* v. *Wait*, 4 Scam. 127, and we think it is there satisfactorily shown, that infants are bound, although not nominally made parties to the proceeding. Why then, when they attain their majority, may they not bring their writ of error to reverse the order for the sale, for errors and irregularities in the proceeding? The reasoning in this last case might answer this inquiry, for it is there said, that it is not a proceeding adverse to the heir, but is a proceeding by his guardian for his benefit, and should be treated as if the proceeding were by the heir himself. Now if this is so to its full extent, he should never afterwards be allowed to complain, that in his own proceeding there is error. But the reasoning in that case upon this point, should only be applied, where, as in that case, the proceeding is regular and in conformity to law, and only to that extent should the act of the guardian be considered the act of the ward, and whatever the guardian does in such a proceeding, which is not in conformity to law, is adverse to the infant, and he must have an opportunity of correcting that error in proper time.

These, it may be repeated, were cases of sales by guardians ostensibly, at least, for the benefit of their wards. The case before us is a sale of an administrator of the estate, descended to the heirs, and not for their benefit, but to enable him to pay the debts of the ancestor. As to the heirs it is essentially hostile in every respect, hence it is the duty of the courts to see that the law which authorizes this proceeding is complied [*91] with. This it is our duty to do, but more than this, we have no right to require. Has the law required the heirs to be made parties by notice, either in the petition or in the notice? This proceeding is authorized by the one hundred and third section of the statute of wills. That requires that the administrator "shall make out a petition to the Circuit Court of the county in which administration shall have been granted, stating therein what real estate the testator or intestate died seized of, or so much thereof as will be necessary to pay his or her debts as aforesaid. and request the aid of the court in the premises." This is all that the statute requires shall be stated in the petition, and by what authority shall we require more to be stated? There is not a word said about the heirs. They are not requested to be mentioned or alluded to in the petition. This petition, however, does set out the names of the widow and heirs, but it does not formally ask that they may be made parties defendants. Nor was this necessary. The portion of the statute quoted, has all the elements of an *ex parte* proceeding. When a petition is filed, the court acquires jurisdiction of the subject matter. The balance of the section shows, that it was not designed that it should be necessarily *ex parte*. The section proceeds: "and it shall be the duty of such administrator or executor, to give at least thirty days' notice, of the time and place of presenting such petition, by serving a written or printed notice of the same, together with a copy of said account and petition, on each of the heirs, or their guardians, or the devisees of said testator or intestate, or by publishing a notice in the nearest newspaper for three weeks successively, commencing at least six weeks before the presenting of said petition, of the intention of presenting the same to the Circuit Court, for the sale of the whole or so much of the real estate of the said testator or intestate, as will be sufficient to pay his or her debts, and requesting all persons interested in said real estate, to show cause why it should not be sold for the purposes aforesaid." Now here is prescribed the modes by which the court may acquire jurisdiction of the persons, so to speak, of those whose interests may be affected by the proceeding. The administrator is given the alternative of one of two ways, by which he may bring into court all adverse parties. One is, by serving a written or printed notice, together with a copy of the account and petition, on all of the heirs or devisees, in whom the title of the land proposed to be sold may be vested; and the other is, by publishing a notice to all parties interested, to come in and show cause why the land should not be sold, according to the prayer of the petition. Either mode is equally efficacious to give the court complete jurisdiction, and equally satisfies the re- [*92] quirements of the law, although the notices are substantially different. The first requires a copy of the petition and account to be served with the notice on the heirs or devisees only.

Gibson *v.* Roll.

While the statute does not require these to be set out in the published notice, but that is required to be addressed to all persons interested in the subject matter. Not only heirs and devisees, but their guardians and creditors, and, in fine, everybody, whose interest might be affected by a sale of the land under the petition. But it must be observed, that in neither of these notices is it required that the names of the heirs or others, interested parties, shall be inserted. It leaves the door wide open for all who may conceive themselves interested, and whenever they choose, to come in, when they become in fact parties to the proceeding in name, as well as in substance. It was for the legislature to say in what mode parties interested should be brought into court, and they had an undoubted right to declare that a notice by publication should be as effectual to bind the parties, as a personal service. In this case the notice was by publication, and was as follows:

"ADMINISTRATOR'S NOTICE.

" Notice is hereby given, that I will make application to the County Court of Tazewell county, on the 3rd day of September next, for a decree to sell all or so much of the real estate of Benjamin F. Jewett, deceased, late of Tazewell county, as will be sufficient to pay the debts of said estate. All persons interested are requested to appear and show cause, if any they have, why such decree should not be granted. WM. S. MAUS,
"*Pekin, July* 24, 1856. Adm'r of BENJAMIN F. JEWETT, dec'd."

The statute has not declared what this notice shall contain, and it is for the court to determine whether its statements are sufficient. This notice gives the information that at a specified time and place, the administrator would apply to the Circuit Court, for authority to sell the whole, or so much as was necessary for the purpose stated, of the real estate of the intestate. This, we think, was sufficient for all practical purposes. This was quite as sure to put persons interested on their guard, as if the property had been described by its numbers or boundaries. On the whole, we are unable to find anything even irregular in this proceeding, for which we should reverse it on a direct application for that purpose, much less to hold it void, in a collateral action as this is.

We strongly intimated, in *Turney* v. *Turney*, 24 Ill. 625,
112

that the heirs should be made formal parties in the petition, but the decision of that question was not necessary to the determination of that case. The case had already been [*93] decided upon the ground that there had been no sufficient notice, and what was afterwards said about the form of the petition was unnecessary, and we now think unadvised. The evidence should have been admitted. The judgment is reversed, and the cause remanded.

Judgment reversed.

RICHARD BLUNT, Plaintiff in Error, *v.* THOMPSON TOMLIN, DAVID HILLYARD, and SAMUEL BLUNT, Defendants in Error.

ERROR TO MASON.

Where a purchaser, under a verbal contract for the sale of land, takes possession by consent of the vendor, and makes valuable improvements, and within the time agreed upon for payment, tenders the purchase money, the case is taken out of the statute of frauds and the purchaser is entitled to a specific performance of the oral agreement.

It is no defense for third parties who subsequently purchased of the vendor with full notice, and before the time for payment had expired, that the vendor had disaffirmed the verbal contract, and sold to them before the purchase money was actually paid or tendered. The purchaser is entitled to protection, if he paid or tendered the money within the time agreed upon.

Where a purchaser of land under an oral agreement, has five years in which to make his payments, so that the contract conflicts with two sections of the statute of frauds, he may nevertheless be entitled to a specific performance. The same facts which would take the case out of one section of the statute, will take it out of the other. In such a case, the court should be more cautious in examining the evidence of the oral contract.

A party who makes a tender for a deed under a contract, need not part with the money, until he receives his deed. If the vendor offers to take the money but refuses to make the deed, this is a refusal of the tender, and it is a useless ceremony to count out the money after that.

A tender made in pursuance of a contract for a deed, fixes the rights of the parties, as conclusively as if the money had been actually paid.

.PLAINTIFF filed a bill in Mason Circuit Court, May, 1856, to enjoin Tomlin and Hillyard from ejecting plaintiff from land described in bill, and for specific performance of an oral contract. The bill alleges, that in the fall of 1851, plaintiff purchased of Samuel Blunt land described therein; paid part of the purchase money; took possession under and by virtue of the contract, by actual occupancy with his family, erected dwelling-house, fenced and broke eighty acres, and made other valuable improvements. That the land and improvements are worth over $2,000. That complainant was to pay $3 per acre for the prairie (about 150 acres), and $100 for ten acres of [*94] timber. That he was to have from three to five years to complete payment, as it suited his convenience. That within the five years he tendered the full amount of purchase money to Samuel Blunt, and demanded deed. Kept tender good by deposit with clerk. That long before the expiration of the five years, Samuel Blunt sold the land to Tomlin and Hillyard, they having full knowledge of all the facts. Charges the defendants with fraud, and prays for specific performance of contract, and that the injunction remain perpetual.

Defendants answer, (not on oath.) Admit contract, part payment, making improvements, and actual occupancy, under and by virtue of contract. But allege that contract was made by Samuel with Richard and Alexander Blunt, his son. That they were to pay $3.50 per acre for prairie, (no controversy as to timber.) That they were to pay in installments annually, and to complete payment in three years from December 25, 1851. That they did not comply with contract, and rely on statute of frauds as if plead. Deny notice as to Tomlin and Hillyard. Deny tender and an attempt to defraud complainant.

Replications filed December, 1856. Referred to master to take proof.

George Wandall testifies, that in Spring of 1852, Samuel Blunt told him that he had sold the land to Richard in the Fall of 1851, at $3 per acre for the prairie, and $10 per acre for timber. That Richard had paid $32 on contract, and was to pay the residue in three years, if he (Richard) could, but if he could not, he was to have five years to complete payment.

That Richard took possession under the contract, and had resided on the land with his family ever since the Fall of 1853.
That Richard had fenced and broke eighty acres of the land,
and erected two dwelling-houses, and made other improvements
to the value of $600.   That defendants all resided in the same
neighborhood, and that all the settlement knew where Richard
lived.   That the witness had frequently seen Hillyard at Richard Blunt's house, and that he heard Tomlin, the other defendant, say that at the time they purchased the land of Samuel,
they knew of the sale by Samuel to Richard, but that the contract was not valid, because it was not in writing.   On cross-
examination, says the use of the land was worth $250.

Erastus How testifies, that Richard bought the land in 1851,
and commenced improving in 1852.   That he (Richard) was to
pay $3 for prairie.   Plaintiff has resided on land since 1853.
That Samuel had told witness that Richard had paid
$32.50 on contract.   On cross-examination, says he does not
know whether Alexander had any interest or not.   [*95]
Never heard that he had any interest.   That witness is satisfied
that if Alexander had an interest, he would have known it
Satisfied that Alexander had no interest in the land.

Alexander Blunt testifies, that Richard bought the land in
1851, of Samuel, at $3 per acre for prairie (no controversy as
to price of timber.)   That witness paid, for his father, $20, on
contract.   That in 1852, Richard took possession and commenced improving the land.   That in 1853, Richard moved his
family on the land, and has continued to reside thereon ever
since.   That witness and E. How commenced making rails for
Richard on the timber in 1851, to fence the prairie.   That witness had no interest in the land purchased, and has none now;
(describes the section of land.)   That witness helped Sweney
survey the land, and the land described and surveyed was the
land sold by Samuel to Richard.   That Tomlin and Hillyard
both knew of the sale to Richard by Samuel, at the time they
bought the land in controversy, of Richard.   That Tomlin and
Hillyard had seen, prior to their purchase, Richard in possession
of the land.   That witness was present at the time when the
sale was made by Samuel to Richard, and heard the contract.

Says that Richard was to pay for the land in three years if he could, and if he could not, Richard was to have five years to pay. On cross-examination, says there was no written contract.

John M. Sweney, surveyor, testifies as to the survey and plat, and that Samuel told witness that he (Samuel) had sold the land to Richard, but expected that he would have to take it back, as Richard would not be able to pay for it. No controversy as to the description of the land. And that witness obtained his information, as to the land surveyed being the land in controversy, from Alexander Blunt and Samuel.

J. H. Wandall testifies, that Samuel told him that he had sold the land that Richard lived on, to Richard, and had given him from one to five years to pay for it, and had received some money on the sale. That he was afraid that Richard would not be able to pay, and he would have to take it back. This conversation took place in January, 1856.

Wm. Swiger testifies, that Samuel told him that he (Samuel) had sold the land that Richard lived on, to Richard. That he had given Richard a better chance than he would have given a stranger. That he had given Richard from one to five years to pay for the land in. That Richard was a poor man, and that he was to have from one to five years to pay for all the land. The first conversation was in Fall of 1851, the last some time [*96] in 1855. On cross-examination, says that the first talk was in Fall of 1851, and the last conversation in 1855. That they were standing on the prairie land that Richard now lives on.

Jacob Propst testifies, that Samuel told him in 1853 that he (Samuel) had sold the land on which Richard now resides, to Richard. That Richard was a poor man, and that Samuel had given him from three to five years to pay for the land. That Richard had paid $20. On cross-examination, says Richard was not on the land, but was making improvements.

Geo. Wandall testifies, that T. P. Cowan asked Samuel if he did not sell the land to Richard. Samuel said that he did, but Richard would not be able to pay for it. Mr. Cowan replied, "just make out a deed, and your money is ready for you in three minutes." Samuel replied, "I will take the money, but I will be damned if I will make the deed." This was in January,

1856. Witness heard S. M. Green, attorney for Richard, say, "Samuel, just make out the deed to Richard for that land, and you shall have your money as quick as I can count it; here, I have the gold." Witness says he saw $100 in gold in Green's hand. This was in May, 1856. Witness says he also heard Mr. Cowan tell Samuel that his money was ready for him, and had been for two years if he would have taken it. Mr. Blunt said he would not take the money. This last conversation took place in January, 1856.

Theodore Howell testifies, that he heard L. M. Green, attorney for Richard, tell S. C. Conwell, attorney for Tomlin and Hillyard, that if they would make out a deed for this land, their money would be ready for them in twenty-five minutes. This was in the Spring of 1856.

Thomas P. Cowan testifies, that in the Winter of 1855–56, he, as the attorney of Richard Blunt, demanded a deed for plaintiff, to the land described in the bill, and offered to pay Samuel the amount, or balance on the land, on the rendition of the deed. Samuel said he would receive the money, but he never would make the deed. And also, in February, witness heard L. M. Green tell Samuel that he had the money ready, and would pay it over to him if Samuel would make out the deed to the land in controversy to Richard. Samuel said he would be damned if he would ever make the deed. Cross-examined—Says that at the conversation referred to, he, as attorney for Richard, demanded a deed for the lands on which Richard now resides, stating to Samuel that the witness had the money ready and would pay all that was [*97] due on the land, on the rendition of deed. Also, says he is security for costs.

On behalf of the defendant, *William Pelham* testifies, that he heard Richard say that he had bought the land of Samuel, and that he had to make up money to pay on the land; that the money was due. This was in the Fall of 1854. On cross-examination, says he does not know the amount said to be due at the time.

Thomas Blunt testifies, that four or five years ago, he heard Richard say he had bought 140 acres of prairie, and ten acres of

Blunt *v.* Tomlin *et al.*

timber. That Richard was to pay $100 for ten acres of timber, and $3.50 per acre for prairie; to pay $100 25th December next after contract, and was to have three years to pay the balance, in installments. That he had bought the land for himself and Alexander his son. That Alexander was to have half the land. At another time Richard said he had let Alexander have $50 to pay his half of the $100 payment. Witness says he talked the whole matter all over with Richard, and Richard said the reason he got the land so low, was that Samuel was in debt, and wanted to get out of debt. That Richard told him that they had not entered into writing, but were to do so when the $100 payment was made at Christmas. Witness says, about one year after the first payment was to have been made, heard Richard say that he was going to be so hard run that he feared he would not be able to pay Samuel the payments on the land. Heard Alexander say that he was to have half the land. Heard Alexander say, sometime after the installments were due, that he (Alexander) saw that his father could not pay for the land, and that he would have nothing more to do with it, and let his father sweat it out himself. That they had paid scarcely anything on the land. A short time before the commencement of this suit, he heard Alexander say that his father had gone to get the money, and that he (Richard) intended to have the land yet. Witness said to Alexander that there were no writings, and that they had not paid scarcely anything on the land, and how could they expect to hold the land. Witness heard Tom Cowan say that Samuel was trying to swindle Richard out of his land, and that he (Cowan) intended to wear him (Samuel) out at law, and that he (Cowan) was to have two hundred dollars. On cross-examination, says that Richard had told him that he bought the land for him and Alexander, and that they were to pay for the land. Says that Alexander was under age at the time of contract. Witness says he has not visited Richard's house since he moved on the land. If there [*98] is any hard feeling between him and Richard, he does not know it.

Daniel Moslander testifies, that in 1852 he heard Samuel tell Richard he had better get his wheat threshed, and pay him

118

for his land.   Richard replied, " Samuel, I know your money is
due.   I will pay you all off this Fall, and you may go to hell with
it."   On cross-examination, says this conversation took place
five years ago last Fall.   Says that Samuel told him that Richard was to have three years to pay for the land. and that if he
(Richard) would not pay for it in that time, he (Samuel) was to
give him (Richard) two years longer, provided Richard would
pay all he could without distressing himself, and enough to lift
a mortgage on the land within three years.   Says that
Richard commenced improving the next Summer after he
bought the land, and moved his family on in the Spring of 1854.
That Samuel made no objection, and both lived on same farm.

John Tomlin testifies, that on 1st March, 1860, Samuel gave
witness forty dollars.   Told witness to offer it to Richard as a
tender of the money paid by Richard to Samuel as a payment
made some four years ago on the land.   Witness made the
tender, and Richard refused to receive it.

John Barton testifies, that in Fall of 1853, he heard Richard
say that he (Richard) was coming to town to get Geo. Walker
to close a mortgage on this land, or that he (Richard) would,
witness don't know which, and that he would get George
Walker to make him a deed, and he would pay Walker.   In
1854-55, he heard Richard say that he had not paid for the
land, and could not get it, but that he would have the scamp off
of it.   On cross-examination, says that he is son-in-law to Samuel.   Says Richard moved on the land in 1854.

Matthew Tomlin says, that in January, 1856, L. M. Green
told Tomlin that he would lose his suit for the land, and that
he (Green) and Cowan were engaged to attend to the suit, and
if Richard gained the suit, he (Green) would sell the land to
Tomlin for the same.   Tomlin was to pay Samuel.   Witness
has heard both Samuel and Richard say that Richard and
Alexander were partners in buying the land.

Powell Ingle, on the 18th April, 1857, testifies, that in April,
1855, he heard Samuel say that he had sold Richard same land
that Richard lived on.   That he had received about $70 in part
payment, and that he was not going to let Richard have the
land, but would sell it all together.

119

Geo. Wandall says, that he has known Richard and Samuel about five years, and Alexander as long. Has had frequent conversations with them about this land. Has never heard [*99] either of them say that Alexander had any interest in the land. That Alexander never acted like he had any interest in the land, and that witness did not believe Alexander had any interest. Also, told Samuel that witness would loan Richard $100 to pay on the land, if he wanted it. Samuel said he would not receive it. This was in Fall of 1854, and in 1855 Samuel told witness that he would not receive any more money on the land from Richard, but that he intended to take the land from Richard. Says that Alexander has been doing business for himself some four years. On cross-examination, says that Samuel told him that he would not receive the $100 that witness offered to loan Richard, because Samuel had sold cattle and sheep, and had enough money to pay Walker. This was at first conversation, and at second, Samuel did not assign any reason why he would not receive any more money on the land.

Alanson Robinson testifies, that he heard Samuel say that he had sold the land to Richard, and that Richard was to have from three to five years to pay for it. And that after Samuel had sold the land to Tomlin and Hillyard, Samuel said that all that Richard could get back was the money that he had paid, with interest.

Alexander Blunt testifies, that he did not, at any time that he knows of, tell Thomas Blunt that he (Alexander) was interested in the purchase of the land. Never told Thomas Blunt that he (witness) was to pay any part of the purchase money. That he never had, directly or indirectly, any interest in the land. And also, that Thomas and Richard are mad at each other, and have been for six or seven years.

Thomas P. Cowan says, that he never told Thomas Blunt that he was to receive $200 as fee in this suit. Never told Thomas Blunt that he (witness) would wear Samuel out at law. But he (witness) was to receive $100 if he gained the suit.

N. Powell, master in chancery, testifies, that at a trial before him, as justice of the peace, the question as to the sale of this land came up, when Thomas P. Cowan, attorney for plaintiff in this suit, addressed himself either to Samuel, or his attorney, "You make out a deed to Richard Blunt for this land, and your money is ready in five minutes." He made use of one or the other of these expressions. This took place February 18, 1856.

The court dissolved the injunction, dismissed the bill, and rendered judgment for the defendants; and plaintiff brings the cause to this court.

THOMAS P. COWAN, for Plaintiff in Error.　　　　[*100]

LYMAN LACEY, for Defendants in Error.

CATON, C. J. We have rarely considered a case addressing itself stronger to the equitable consideration of the court, than this. The case made by the bill, is either admitted by the answers, or is proved by an overwhelming preponderance of the testimony. Indeed the whole case is admitted, except as to the time of payment, and the price of the prairie land. Upon the former point, the bill is sustained by the testimony of one witness, who heard the bargain made, and three or four other witnesses, who testify to the admissions of the defendant, and one witness only, testifies to the admissions of the complainant, tending to support the answer; and upon the second point, the bill is sustained by the testimony of the witness who heard the bargain, and by two other witnesses, who heard the defendant admit, that the price of the prairie land was three dollars per acre, as stated in the bill, and one states that the complainant said he was to give three dollars and fifty cents per acre. That Tomlin and Hillyard had notice, both actual and constructive, no question can be made.

The case then is this: In 1851, the complainant by a parol agreement, purchased the land in question of the defendant, and was to pay him for the timber lot one hundred dollars, and for the prairie three dollars per acre. That he was to have at his option five years, within which to pay the purchase money, and that upon the payment of the purchase money, the defendant should convey the land to the complainant. That at the time the bargain was made, the complainant paid the defendant twenty dollars, and afterwards a steer worth twelve dollars, or twelve dollars and fifty cents, upon the purchase. Soon after the purchase was made, the complainant took possession of the land under the purchase, with the consent of the defendant, built a house thereon, and enclosed and broke eighty acres of the land, and made other improvements, of the value, in all, of six hundred dollars. That in 1853, the complainant moved his family on to the premises, and has continued to reside thereon ever since. Before the expiration of the five years, the complainant offered to pay and tendered to the defendant the balance of the purchase money upon receiving a conveyance. The defendant said he would receive the money, but refused, with imprecation, to make the deed.

Does this take the case out of the statute of frauds, which is relied upon by the defendant in his answer? We think it [*101] unquestionably does. The only condition that any case or *dictum* has ever required, and which is not entirely fulfilled here, is that the whole of the purchase money was not actually paid, before Samuel Blunt sold the same land to the other defendant, and thus repudiated the contract with the complainant. But we have met with no case where the purchaser has been required to make payment or tender of the purchase money, before it was due by the terms of the agreement, in order to secure the right of his purchase, where he has taken possession with the consent of the vendor, and made valuable and lasting improvements. Here the complainant, in the confidence of the integrity and good faith of the defendant, took possession of the land, made improvements upon it of greater value than the price of the land itself, and made of it, as he supposed, a permanent home for himself and family. All this the defendant encouraged, at least by his acquiescence, until these valuable improvements were completed—until a piece of wild land was converted into an improved farm, with a comfortable home, and then, as the time for the final payment of the purchase money was approaching, he turned round and sold the land, with all these improvements, to other parties, who have commenced an action of ejectment against the complainant to expel him from his home. The simple statement of the case is revolting to one's sense of moral justice, and shows that here is an attempt to use the statute passed to prevent frauds, for the purpose of perpetrating a gross fraud. It was one of these extreme cases, so revolting to our sense of justice, which first induced the court to set aside the statute, for the very reason just stated, and while we may in general regret that courts have ever been influenced by any consideration, so far as to break in upon the statute, yet, when we meet cases like this, we feel quite resigned to follow the precedents which were well understood when our law was passed, and have thus become a part of it.

Here, if there was not an actual payment of the purchase money, there was a tender of it, within the time in which he had a right by the agreement to make the payment, and a refusal by the defendant. We have said, in *Doyle* v. *Teas*, 4 Scam. 202, that he who tenders for a deed, need not part with his money till he can touch the deed; so he need run no risk for the safety of his money. A refusal to make the deed was, virtually, a refusal to accept the tender, and rendered it even unnecessary for the complainant to go through the formality of counting out the money, for the doing so, after the peremptory refusal by the defendant, would have been an idle form, unnecessary and contemptible in the eye of a court of equity. The offer to pay, was equivalent to actual pay- [*102] ment, so far as fixing the right of the parties in this court is concerned.

One other objection we may notice, and that is, that as this contract was not to be performed in one year, it was obnoxious to another section of the statute of frauds, and that no contract should be enforced which has been declared void by two statutes, and for two reasons. We might answer to this last objection, that it is not relied upon for a defense in the answer, but if it were, it would be as repugnant to the promptings of an enlightened conscience to allow the defendant to succeed in his fraud by the use of one statute, as the other. This feature of the contract may, and no doubt should, make the court more cautious in examining the evidence to prove the contract, but when that is once established to the entire satisfaction of the court, as here, it necessarily passes from the consideration of the case. The complainant was entitled to a decree. The decree of the Circuit Court is reversed, and the suit remanded, with instructions to that court to proceed with the suit consistently with the principles here stated.

Judgment reversed.

Separate Opinion by Breese, J. Whilst I admit the opinion of the majority of the Court is in accordance with repeated decisions of the courts of our sister States, and of England, still I cannot concur in it, for the reason, that I feel myself controlled above and beyond all judicial decisions, by the express law of this State, solemnly enacted by the people, through their representatives, and which I deem of imperative and paramount obligation.

The statute is in these words:

" No action shall be brought, whereby to charge any executor or administrator upon any special promise to answer any debt or damages out of his own estate; or whereby to charge the defendant upon any special promise to answer for the debt, default or miscarriage of another person; or to charge any person upon any agreement made upon consideration of marriage, or upon any contract for the sale of lands, tenements or hereditaments, or any interest in, or concerning them, for a longer term than one year; or upon any agreement that is not to be performed within the space of one year from the making thereof, unless the promise or agreement upon which such action shall be brought, or some memorandum or note thereof, shall be in writing, and signed by the party to be charged therewith, or some other person thereunto by him lawfully authorized." (Scates' Comp. 541, Sec. 1.)

[*103] This is the will of the people of the State, emphatically declared, by the use of words of no doubtful meaning, and inhibitory in their character. No words of inhibition, more imperious than these, could be used in a statute, and it is, in my opinion, the duty of all courts to give full effect to them. The question presented to me is, shall a solemn act of the legislature, containing no ambiguous or doubtful terms, prevail—be carried into full effect—or shall it be evaded, in deference to

the authority of respectable courts? Of all the evils incident to our system, that of judicial legislation, going so far as to nullify an act of the legislature, is one of the most pernicious. The apology for this decision, and all similar ones in such cases, is, that this act of the legislature was passed with full knowledge of the decisions of the courts upon it, and that the legislature must be presumed. when making the enactment, to have adopted the judicial construction placed upon it. This is a dangerous principle, where no words are used of doubtful meaning, and where it goes to repeal a statute. My view is, that the legislature, in disregard of those decisions, declared what the law should be, and conferred no power upon the courts to repeal it, or evade it. If they entertained the opinion that it was good policy and wise, that part performance, by payment of part of the purchase money, making improvements, etc., should be proof, equivalent to a note or memorandum in writing, of the contract, it was quite easy for them to say so, and thus save the courts from legislating, and relieve them from the necessity of seeking pretexts, by which to evade or nullify the law.

The courts, not only in Great Britain, but in this country, have often expressed regret, that parol testimony had ever been allowed to take cases out of the operation of this statute. The books abound in such cases. And it is worthy of consideration, how the courts could, in the first instance, be brought to nullify it, and render it, in practice, of but little force or effect. It requires more than an ordinary share of boldness, to declare, judicially, in the teeth of a statute, that an action may be brought and maintained on a contract, not in writing, for the sale of land, when the statute declares. "no such action shall be brought"! I have fully considered and debated this question, in the separate opinion filed, in the case of *Keener* v. *Crull and Wife*, 19 Ill. 192, in reference to the statute of limitations, which has also been frittered away, and "evaded" by the courts. These judicial evasions have not my sanction, and so long as those acts remain on the statute book, I shall feel it my bounden duty to defer to them, yielding to them implicit obedience.

[*104] It may be said, as it has often been said, to justify these evasions of this statute, that frauds might be committed by allowing the vendor to retain the payments made on account, and also the benefit of the improvements, and thus fraud would be promoted, rather than prevented. This result need not happen, for the vendee claiming under a parol contract, has his remedy at law or in equity, for the moneys he has advanced, and for the value of his improvements, and such decree, or judgment, as he may obtain, might be made a lien on the land, until he is fully reimbursed all his expenses and outlays. Complete justice, in most cases, might be thus rendered between the parties, and the act preserved inviolate. If not, the fault is not with the law. Let the contracting parties obey the law, and no bad consequences can follow. Judicial legislation is the work of danger; to steer clear of it, is the part of wisdom.

Lewis W. Ross, Plaintiff in Error, *v.* James H. Hole, Defendant in Error.

ERROR TO MASON.

The certificate of a county clerk, showing that A. B. was not a justice of the peace, at the date of an acknowldgement, purporting to have been taken by him, is some though not conclusive evidence of such fact.

A deed may be valid though not recorded; and may be offered as proof in ejectment; and then the fact of knowledge of its existence, may be brought home to subsequent purchasers, as touching their good faith, and the duty of making inquiries as connected with them.

This was an action of ejectment, commenced by Ross at the May term of the Mason Circuit Court. A. D. 1856, for the recovery of town lot No. 4, in block No. 19, in the town of Havana, in said county.

At the October term, 1861, the cause was tried before Harriot, Judge, and a jury, and on the trial of the cause the plaintiff offered and read in evidence,

 1. A patent from the United States to Ossian M. Ross, for

 126

the tract of land on which the said town of Havana is situated, dated December 8, 1827.

2. A plat of the town of Havana, laid off, executed and acknowledged by Ossian M. Ross, on said land, dated June 2, 1835.

3. A will from Ossian M. Ross to Lewis W. Ross, Harriett M. Ross, Harvey L. Ross, Lucinda C. Ross, Leonard F. Ross, and Pike C. Ross, dated January 19, 1837, and admitted [*105] to probate, February 3, 1837, bequeathing all his real and personal estate to the above named heirs.

4. A deed from the heirs of Ossian M. Ross to the plaintiff, dated April 16, 1845.

Which said deed and evidences of title were permitted by the court to be read to the jury.

The defendant offered in evidence a deed from Ossian M. Ross and wife, to Joshua Aiken and Robert E. Little, for sundry town lots in Havana, including the lot in controversy, purporting to have been acknowledged before Eli Fisk, a justice of the peace of Tazewell county, in 1836. The plaintiff objected to the reading of said deed in evidence, and offered a certificate from the clerk of the County Court of Tazewell county, dated November 2, 1859, under the seal of the said court, certifying that " there was no such justice of the peace in Tazewell county, in 1836, as Eli Fisk, as appears from the files and records in my office, after a full and careful examination." But the court overruled said objection, and permitted the deed to be read to the jury.

The plaintiff then stated, that inasmuch as the last deed vested the title by decision of the court, in Joshua Aiken and Robert E. Little, the plaintiffs in one count in the declaration, he would also rest the case on his part.

The plaintiff then offered in evidence a deed from Clarissa P. Little and George W. Little, to Lewis W. Ross, dated December 2, 1847, commissioner appointed by the Circuit Court of Peoria county, to sell and convey the title in and to said lot of Joshua Aiken and Robert E. Little; also, a certified copy of the record from Peoria county, a certificate of magistracy, and an agreement of Walker and Conwell, attorneys for Hole, the defendant, were offered in connection with said deed; which said deed and other evidence offered therewith, were admitted by the court, and vested the title to said lot in said Ross.

The plaintiff then offered in evidence a deed from Clarissa P. Little and Henry A. Little, to Lewis W. Ross, for the lot in controversy, dated June, 1852, together with the certificate thereto attached, the affidavit of Theodore Tarlton, and the agreement of defendant's attorneys thereto attached; to the reading of which deed, affidavit, and agreement, the defendant objected, and the court sustained such objection.

The defendant then read in evidence a deed from Lewis W. Ross and wife to R. S. Patterson, for said lot, dated December 15, 1851. The defendant then offered in evidence a deed from R. S. Patterson and wife, to William Walker and S. C. Con-[*106] well, the defendant's attorneys in this case, dated May 1, 1861; to the reading of which deed in evidence the plaintiff objected, but the court overruled said objection, and permitted the same to be read to the jury.

The plaintiff then offered in evidence a deed and certificate of acknowledgment from R. S. Patterson and wife to Lewis W. Ross, for the lot in controversy, dated March 15, 1852, and also, in connection with said deed, the plaintiff had C. J. Dilworth sworn as witness, who testified that he was well acquainted with R. S. Patterson and his handwriting, that he had frequently seen him write, and that the signature to the said deed is in the proper handwriting of the said R. S. Patterson.

And it was then and there agreed, between the parties in the case, (to save the trouble of taking testimony on that point that Wm. Walker and S. C. Conwell (to whom said deed from R. S. Patterson and wife purported to be made) were the attorneys for defendant in this ejectment suit, and filed the plea in this case, and that they knew on the first day of May, 1861, at the time the deed was read in evidence, from R. S. Patterson and wife to said Walker and Conwell, that L. W. Ross, the plaintiff in this suit, claimed the said lot in controversy, and was prosecuting an ejectment suit in this court for the recovery of the same. And the said defendant objected to the reading of said deed to the jury, for the reason that it had not been recorded, and the court sustained such objection, and would not permit the said plaintiff to read the said deed to the jury.

The court then, at the request of the defendant, gave the jury the following instruction, to wit: "The court instructs the jury that if the defendant has proved title to lot 4, in block 19, in Walker and Conwell, the jury will find the defendant not guilty."

The jury retired, and returned a verdict in favor of the defendant.

The plaintiff now prosecutes his writ of error to this court.

Lewis W. Ross, *pro se.*

W. Walker, for Defendant in Error.

Caton, C. J.   There are several errors in this record, for which the judgment must be reversed.   In the first place, we think it was competent to show by the certificate of the county clerk, the state of the county records, for the purpose of proving that Fisk, before whom the acknowledgment of the deed was taken, was not, at the time the acknowledg- [*107] ment purported to have been taken, a justice of the peace.   It seems to us as competent to make it appear by the certificate of the county clerk that his records show that there was no such justice in the county at the time, as that a particular person was at a particular time a justice of the peace.   Such certificate would not establish, conclusively, that Fisk was not a justice, but it was competent evidence, as tending to show that fact. He may have been a justice *de facto*, although there was not any record of his commission.   This certificate should have been admitted.

We shall pass over some other errors in the record, which will not be likely to arise on another trial; and consider the exception taken to the decision of the court in refusing to permit the plaintiff to introduce in evidence, the deed from Patterson and wife to L. W. Ross, dated the 15th of March, 1852. The execution of this deed had been proved, but it had never been recorded.   The defendant's attorneys, Walker and Conwell,

had, for the purpose of proving title in themselves and consequently out of the plaintiff, introduced a deed from Patterson
and wife, executed in 1861. The defendant objected to the
reading of the deed in evidence which was offered by the plaintiff, on the ground that it had not been recorded, and the court
sustained the objection. In this the court undoubtedly erred.
The recording could have no possible effect upon its validity.
The recording laws might postpone it in favor of subsequent
bona fide purchasers, but the deed was nevertheless valid. It
should have been admitted in evidence, and then the question
would have been fairly open to controversy, whether the subsequent purchasers had, before they purchased, such notice of the
plaintiff's claim of title to the lot, as made it incumbent on
them, in good faith, to have inquired of him what title he had.

The judgment must be reversed, and the cause remanded.

Judgment reversed.

MICHAEL MULLETT, Appellant, *v.* DOROTHEA SHRUMPH,
and WILLIAM SHRUMPH, Administratrix and Administrator of the estate of John E. Mullett, deceased,
Appellees.

APPEAL FROM BOND.

A promise by the defendant that he will settle with the plaintiff as soon as he
receives his pay for certain work, is a conditional promise; and does not
waive the statute of limitations, unless it is proved that he has received his
pay.

[*108] THIS was a suit instituted by appellees against appellant, at the February term, A. D. 1861, of the Bond County
Court, in assumpsit, for work and labor, care and diligence and
attention, performed by John E. Mullett, deceased, in his lifetime. Declaration, one common count.

Appellant pleaded the general issue, and statute of limitations.

Verdict for appellees for $245.

130

Mullett *v.* Shrumph *et al.*

Upon the trial, *Samuel Mullett,* being sworn for the plaintiff, stated, that John E. Mullett, deceased, worked himself, with his team, on the Mississippi and Atlantic Railroad, for defend. ant, 108 days. Said work was worth $2.75 per day. Said work was commenced sometime in the month of June, 1854, and ended in the month of November or December of the same year. On cross-examination, witness states, that he did not keep account of time, but was present when John E. Mullett and defendant agreed upon the amount of work, about the time they quit work; and defendant offered to give John E. Mullett $200 for his work. Witness states, it was for the work; he did not know of any partnership; witness worked with them on the road.

Benedict Mullett, for the plaintiff, testified, that John E. Mullett, deceased, between the months of June and December, 1854, worked with his team 108 days for defendant; that said work was worth $2.75 per day; that it was done on the Mississippi and Atlantic Railroad; that he knew of no partnership between John E. Mullett and defendant in relation to the work; that the work was done on two sections of said road, in Madison county, which defendant had taken to grade; that he and preceding witness both worked on said road, at said time, with John E. Mullett, deceased.

Gaspar Britt, for the plaintiff, testified, that shortly after the death of John E. Mullett, which occurrred in the fall of 1858, (the said John E. Mullett having been his son-in-law, and the administratrix being his daughter), he conversed with the defendant about this account; that he then had John E. Mullett's memorandum book, containing the account of their work on railroad, amounting to ninety-eight days, which he showed defendant; that defendant said that John worked more days than that; that he could not pay it then, for he had no money; that he was going to have some parts of the work measured, and expected to get some money soon, and then he would settle the account. On cross-examination, witness states,' that defendant, in the conversation, claimed that there was a partnership arrangement between him and John E. Mullett; that defendant spoke of measuring the work, and

Mullett v. Shrumph et al.

[*109] also about a suit for the railroad work, but did not know whether the suit was commenced at that time; that defendant said, when he got the money for the work he would settle.

On behalf of the defendant, *John Wickenhousen* stated, that during the summer and fall of 1854, he did the smithing work for the firm of Mullett & Co., who were at work on a contract of grading on the Mississippi and Atlantic Railroad. That the said smith work was done sometimes at the request of one, and sometimes at the request of others of the Mulletts. That he understood that defendant, John E. Mullett, deceased, Samuel Mullett, and Benedict Mullett, were partners, and comprised the firm of Mullett & Co. That he had often, during that time, heard each of them speak of the partnership, and that it was generally known in the neighborhood that they were partners in said work.

One *Mohman* testified, that in the summer of 1854, he worked as a day laborer in grading on the Atlantic and Mississippi Railroad for the Mulletts; worked two or three days; that said firm was composed of Michael Mullett, (defendant), John E. Mullett, deceased, Samuel Mullett, and Benedict Mullett; (the two last mentioned being the two witnesses first examined for plaintiff); that he was hired by defendant, and discharged by John E. Mullett, deceased; and that it was at the time generally understood in the neighborhood, that the above persons were partners in said work on the railroad.

John Schlup testified, that he, in the year 1854, carried on a wagon shop in Highland, Madison county, in partnership with Michael Mullett, defendant, and did wagon work for the Mulletts while at work on the railroad. Knows that they were partners, from frequent conversations with defendant and John E. Mullett; had heard John E. Mullett often speaking of himself as partner in said work, and say how much he expected to make out of it; he thought it would be very profitable. The work was charged to Mullett & Co.

As rebutting testimony for the plaintiff, *Samuel Mullett* testified, that in the spring, before work on railroad was commenced, Michael Mullett proposed to witness, John E. Mullett, and Benedict Mullett, to take an interest in building part of the road, of which Michael Mullett was sub-contractor, and the four should build it in partnership; that afterwards, just before they were ready to commence work, he proposed to Michael Mullett, defendant, that they should make the agreement of partnership before talked of; defendant replied that he would make an agreement with him (witness); but he would not make any agreement with the boys, meaning John E. Mullett, [*110] deceased, and Benedict Mullett, for he (defendant) would retain authority to dismiss them (John E. and Benedict Mullett) at any time. There was no attempt to close the partnership afterwards, and no agreement made.

Benedict Mullett testified. that there was no partnership agreement ever made between defendant, Samuel Mullett, John E. Mullett, and witness; that it was talked of in the spring, but no partnership ever formed as he knew of, and he worked all the time with them.

This was all the testimony submitted in the cause.

By agreement of parties, this cause to be tried by the Supreme Court, at Springfield.

George W. Shutt, and L. Stevenson, for Appellant.

S. C. Moore, for Appellee.

Caton, C. J. Whatever promise there was in this case, was an express promise. So no implied promise to pay the debt can be raised from an admission that it was due. The express promise was sworn to by Mr. Britt. He says, the defendant said he was going to have the work measured, and expected to get some money soon, then he would settle the account. Again, " that defendant said when he got the money for the work he would settle." This was a conditional promise, and could neither serve for the foundation of an action itself, nor waive the statute of limitations, without at least proving that the defendant had received the money for the work.

The judgment must be reversed, and the cause remanded.

Judgment reversed.

JOHN A. METCALF, Appellant, v. ANDREW B. FOUTS, Appellee.

APPEAL FROM EDGAR.

On a settlement of partnership affairs, if it is agreed that one of the partners shall collect a note and accounts, for the benefit of both, it will be presumed, that the money, as fast as received, should be divided between the parties.

In cases tried by the court, errors may be assigned as to the law and fact upon the judgment.

THIS was an action of assumpsit, brought by Andrew B. [*111] Fouts against John A. Metcalf. The declaration contains only the common counts. The one relied on in the trial below, was the count for money had and received. To the declaration the defendant pleaded the general issue. A jury was waived, and the cause tried by the court, who rendered judgment in favor of the plaintiff for the sum of $321.35, from which the defendant below prayed an appeal to this court, which was granted.

On the trial of the cause, the plaintiff below introduced as a witness *John J. Fouts*, who testified that he was clerk for defendant, Metcalf; that said Metcalf and plaintiff, Fouts, had been partners, trading in horses and mules. Fouts, the plaintiff, had sold a lot of them in Iowa, and taken notes for a part of the proceeds, in his own name. Metcalf became afraid about the safety of his interest in the notes. He had furnished the capital and they were to divide the profits. Witness passed several times between the parties in proposing terms. Metcalf wanted security, and demanded interest on the capital advanced by him. At last the plaintiff, Fouts, agreed that, if Metcalf would settle up the partnership matters finally, he would arrange matters. There was some difference about interest, and at last Fouts agreed that if Metcalf would pay a note which he (Fouts) owed to one Redmon for $770, and would make settlement of the partnership, as stated, that he would allow Metcalf the interest in controversy; and they

134

made a computation of their accounts as to everything except an account due the firm in Cincinnati, for feeding mules, and found there would be due the plaintiff on the final adjustment of the matters as stated, three hundred dollars of the six hundred dollar note in Iowa. The amount of the Cincinnati account was not known at the time. It was agreed that when the account was collected, it should be divided between the parties equally. Metcalf was to collect the account. Metcalf afterwards collected between seventy and eighty dollars of the account. There was one note in Iowa for six hundred dollars, as I understood from the parties, and it was agreed that it should be placed in the hands of the witness for collection, and when collected, to be paid by witness, to each the amount due them—three hundred and fifteen dollars to be paid to the plaintiff, Fouts, as balance due him as aforesaid. The plaintiff then gave witness an order for the note or proceeds thereof. And afterwards, Henry S. Metcalf was about to go to Iowa to collect some notes which had been transferred to his father; the defendant remarked, that witness had better get Henry S. Metcalf to collect it also, as it would save costs; and witness transferred his order to Henry S. Metcalf, at the suggestion of the defendant. Witness identified the order, [*112] which was read in evidence, viz.:

Messrs. Isett & Bruster:

" Pay to John J. Fouts, or order, the proceeds of a certain note against the St. Johns, which Phelps left with you for collection, in favor of me; or if protested, deliver said note to him or his order.
" *September* 9, 1857.   .   A. B. FOUTS."

On the back of the order was the following indorsement:

"Deliver to H. S. Metcalf the proceeds of the within named notes for me.
" *October* 23, 1857.   JOHN J. FOUTS."

On cross-examination, witness admitted that he was, by agreement of the parties, to collect the six hundred dollar note, and pay to each three hundred and fifteen dollars, that being the amount due to each by the settlement. The plaintiff was to pay it.

Henry S. Metcalf testified: There had been four hundred dollars collected on the note; three hundred at one time, and one hundred at another. Witness don't know whether the money was sent to him or his father, but his father had got the money through witness. Witness received the order from John J. Fouts, who said, when he transferred it to witness, he knew he (witness) would do what was right in the matter. On that order witness got the note from the bankers whose hands it was in, and left it with a friend for collection, who agreed to do so and charge nothing for it. The money above stated was collected and remitted, and received by defendant.

Some three hundred and fifty dollars remain uncollected, a good deal of interest having accrued on the note. The note is held subject to the order of witness, and never was under the control of the defendant, Metcalf. Witness acted in obtaining note under the authority conferred by the assignment of the order to him by John J. Fouts; was present part of the time on the 9th of September, when the adjustment was made, and the agreement entered into, that John J. Fouts should collect the six hundred and thirty dollars and pay to each one-half of it; did not understand it to be a full settlement of the partnership transactions. The books were not squared, nor any entry of a settlement made. The account on the books was introduced in evidence.

There was an account due the firm for feeding mules in Cincinnati, which was not known at the time. Witness made a trip to Iowa to collect notes which had been transferred to [*113] defendant, and the six hundred dollar note. (Defendant here offered to prove what witness' time was worth in collecting said note, or trying to collect it, which the court refused to admit, and to which ruling of the court, in rejecting said evidence, the defendant at the time excepted.) Witness proved that he made two trips to Iowa in collecting or trying to collect notes which had been transferred to defendant, and the six hundred dollar note. One trip cost $28.50 and the other $33.

The errors assigned are, that,

The court erred in rejecting evidence of the value of the

time of Henry S. Metcalf in collecting, or trying to collect, the six hundred dollar note.

The judgment of the court is contrary to the law and evidence in the case.

The finding of the court is contrary to the evidence in the case.

The court erred in overruling the defendant's motion for a new trial.

A. GREEN, for Appellant.

JOHN SCHÒLFIELD, for Appellee.

WALKER, J. This cause was tried, in the court below, without the intervention of a jury, by consent of the parties. It is assigned for error, that the court below, excluded evidence of the expenses of collecting the money sued for, and that the finding is against the evidence.

It appears from the evidence contained in the record, that the parties had been jointly engaged in the purchase and sale of horses and mules. That on a settlement of their firm business, there remained to be collected a note, on parties in Iowa, for the sum of $630; also an account against some person in Cincinnati, for feeding mules, the amount of which, at the time of the settlement, was not known. It also appears, that on the settlement, there was due appellant three hundred and fifteen dollars of the Iowa note. It was then agreed that the account should be equally divided, when collected. It appears, that the witness Fouts was to collect the note for the parties, and pay to each of the parties one-half. It also appears, that an order was given to John J. Fouts, on persons in Iowa who had the note for collection, for the note or its proceeds, which he afterwards transferred to Henry S. Metcalf, who collected at one time three hundred, and at another one hundred dollars, which he paid to appellant. It likewise appears, that [*114] appellant collected on the account, seventy-five dollars.

From a reasonable and fair construction of the arrangement we have no hesitation in saying, that the parties designed the money to be equally divided, as the same should be collected.

It cannot be, that it was their intention, that the different payments which might be received should remain in the hands of
the agent or of either party, until the entire sum was received,
before a division should be had.   Nor had the appellant the
right to receive his full share out of the first moneys collected,
but only an equal portion as it should be received.   The evidence shows that there had been collected and was in the hands
of appellant, from four hundred and seventy-five to seventy-
eight dollars, one-half of which, according. to the settlement,
belonged to appellee, and which he had a right to recover.   It
would therefore appear, that this judgment was too large, and
the court erred in its finding.

It is, however urged, that the appellant cannot assign error
on this judgment, because no reasons for a new trial were filed
in the court below.   Under the 22nd section of the practice
act, the parties are authorized to assign error on the final judgment, upon both the law and the evidence, in cases of trial by
the court without a jury.   Even if error cannot be assigned for
the overruling the motion for a new trial, in such a case, yet
as error may be assigned on the final judgment, there can be no
force in the objection.   The court under that section is authorized to consider both the law and evidence, and determine
whether error has intervened in rendering the judgment.

It is also urged, that the court below should have received
evidence of the value of Henry S. Metcalf's time in collecting,
and trying to collect the Iowa note.   The proof shows that he
was going to Iowa on other business, and was to attend to this
matter without charge.   It, therefore, would have been improper to make any allowance for his time, unless it had been
proved that a different arrangement had been made.   No such
proof was offered, and there was no error in excluding this evidence.

The judgment of the court below is reversed, and the cause
remanded.

Judgment reversed.

W. B. WARREN, Appellant, *v.* A. C. DICKSON, [*115] and JOHN H. DICKSON, Appellees.

APPEAL FROM MORGAN.

It is error to instruct the jury, that if the defendant purchased lumber from the plaintiffs without disclosing the fact that he was purchasing as the agent of another, he became personally liable for the price of the lumber —because the plaintiffs may have known all the time that the defendant was merely an agent; in which event, he would not be personally liable.

It does not follow that a judgment will be reversed, because an improper instruction has been given for the plaintiff and appellee, if the other instructions on his behalf, put the whole case fairly before the jury.

The statute of frauds must be pleaded, if it is to be relied upon by the defendant. He cannot set it up, for the first time, in an instruction.

THIS was an action of assumpsit on an account for lumber. The first item in the account is in the following words: "1856, Jan. 25th. To amount per P. Warren, $68.59." Then an account for lumber, amounting to $361.24, running from April 19, 1856, to September 2, 1858.

The defendant pleaded the general issue.

Upon the trial of the case, the plaintiffs introduced as a witness *Samuel Markoe*, who testified that he had no personal knowledge of any of the items of plaintiffs' account sued for in this case, excepting those commencing November 10, 1857, and ending December 4, 1857; that these items were selected by the defendant and were delivered by witness, who was at the time a clerk for plaintiffs at their lumber yard, to a man by the name of Hobson, who then lived upon the farm where they were used. Witness heard nothing said by defendant at the time about the lumber being charged to any other person. Witness also stated, that in a conversation he had with the defendant during the present term of the court, defendant admitted the correctness of the account, excepting one item, to wit, the siding charged at $30, which he said he did not obtain. Witness, upon his cross-examination, stated, that the first item in plaintiffs' account, was for an account of that amount against Phil. Warren, which was transferred and charged on plaintiffs' books against defendant. , Witness also stated, that the defendant, in the conversation above spoken of, also said that the item of lumber delivered to Hobson for the farm ought to have been charged to his son, William M. Warren, and not to him (defendant); that defendant did not, in the conversation alluded to, speak of the account as "the account sued for in this case," or . "the account in suit," or "in court," or attached to any decla- [*116] ration; he said it was not necessary to call me as a witness, because he would admit the charges I had made. He had no doubt they were correct. I understood him to speak of the account in suit.

Plaintiffs then introduced *James H. Dickson*, who testified, that he is a son of Plaintiff, Archimedes C. Dickson; that witness saw the defendant in St. Louis last winter, on the 13th of February, at the office of A. C. Dickson & Co.; that defendant left the office to visit some of his friends, and saying that he would return again; that after defendant left, father requested witness to secrete himself in the office for the purpose of hearing what might be said by defendant on his return; that father notified witness when defendant was returning, and witness secreted himself in the stairway leading up stairs out of the office, locking the door after him; that when defendant came in, witness heard him say that John had sued him up here, that he knew that he owed the account, and if he had the money he would pay it then, but he hadn't it, and he wanted the case continued until he could get the money; father gave him a paper; defendant wanted the words "and son" added to it, and father went back to the desk and witness supposed he added those words. The plaintiffs here rested their case.

The defendant, with the consent of the plaintiffs, then read in evidence to the jury the following letter, to wit:

I. L. MORRISON:

*Dear Sir—*You will continue the suits as to *A. C. Dickson & Son v. W. B. Warren and W. M. Warren,* until I come up and have the matter arranged.   A. C. DICKSON & SON.

St. Louis, February 13, 1861.

The defendant then introduced *Wm. M. Warren* as a witness, who testified, that he is a son of the defendant; that the items contained in the account sued for in this case, commencing Nov. 10, 1857, and ending Dec. 4, 1857, were engaged and contracted for by witness, with the plaintiff, A. C. Dickson, and were by agreement to be furnished witness in part payment of the indebtedness of the plaintiff to him, witness, for the purpose of being used upon a farm owned by witness and his father, and then occupied by one Hobson; and witness notified plaintiff at that time that his father or said Hobson would come and get them; that soon after the above items had been obtained, the plaintiff, John H. Dickson, on meeting witness said to him, "You must be building a large house; your father has got a large quantity of lumber on your account, which we have charged to you." To which witness replied, "No, it was only for a small house for a tenant." Witness further testified, on cross-examination, that the [*117] indebtedness of plaintiffs to him, above spoken of, was for witness' interest in lumber left at the time of the dissolution of the firm of A. C. Dickson and witness, Wm. M. Warren, at their lumber yard in Jacksonville, to which firm the plaintiffs were successors in the same business and at the same lumber yard.

The defendant here rested his case.

Whereupon plaintiff introduced *Isaac L. Morrison,* who testified, that the firm of A. C. Dickson and Son was dissolved some time previous to February 13, 1861, and that he had for some time previous held the books and accounts of said firm; and that by arrangement between said plaintiffs, said John H. Dickson had the control of the business of the former firm.

The instructions asked for by the plaintiff and given on his behalf, are set out in the opinion of the Court.

The defendant asked the court to instruct the jury as follows, to wit:

2.   The court further instructs that for so much of plaintiffs' account as the jury shall believe, from the evidence, is for lumber furnished on the account, or on the credit of Wm. M. Warren, the plaintiffs have no right to recover in the case.

3. The court further instructs that the defendant is not liable for the account against Phil. Warren, charged in plaintiffs' account, unless the jury find from the evidence that the defendant has promised in writing to pay the same.

The court refused to give defendant's instruction No. 3, and also refused to give defendant's instruction No. 2, until the same was modified by adding the words "unless they shall believe that defendant admitted its correctness or promised to pay it;" and when so modified, gave the same. To which refusal to give said instruction, and to the action of the court in modifying the said instruction No. 2, and giving the same as modified by the court, the defendant, by his counsel, then and there excepted.

The jury found a verdict for plaintiff. Motion by defendant for new trial overruled, and appeal granted.

The errors assigned are: The verdict was against all the evidence; the court erred in giving instructions asked by plaintiff; also in giving instructions asked by defendant; the court erred in modifying defendant's instructions; and in overruling motion for new trial, and rendering judgment against defendant.

SCHOLFIELD & EDMUNDS, for Appellant.

I. L. MORRISON, for Appellee.

[*118] BREESE, J. The principal errors assigned on this record, question the correctness of the instructions given by the court. The first instruction given for the plaintiff is as follows:

"The court instructs the jury for the plaintiffs, that if they find from the evidence in the case that the defendant called at the yard of plaintiffs for any of the lumber in the bill of items filed in this case, and that he agreed upon the prices of the lumber, and had the same selected; and that said items of lumber were charged at the time of its sale and delivery by plaintiffs to defendant, and that defendant did not then disclose the fact to plaintiffs, that he, defendant, was purchasing said lumber for and on account of W. M. Warren, then defendant became personally liable for the value of said lumber, notwithstanding they may find from the evidence in the case that defendant, at

142

the time of the sale and delivery aforesaid, was in fact acting as the agent of W. M. Warren, in the purchase of the same."

This instruction was clearly wrong, for the plaintiffs may have known perfectly well, that the defendant was getting the lumber for another, and not on his own account. In such a case, it surely was not necessary for the defendant to disclose his agency. If the plaintiffs knew that fact, why disclose it, on receiving the lumber? The instruction shuts out of view this consideration.

We see no objection to the modification of defendant's second instruction, nor in the refusal to give the third instruction. The statute of frauds was not pleaded, or in any shape set up, as a defense. Consequently, according to the rulings of this, and other courts, it can not be set up in the form of instructions.

But though the first instruction of plaintiffs was wrong, does it follow the judgment should be reversed? The second instruction asked by plaintiff, puts the whole case fairly and squarely before the jury, and to which we see no objection, and we have been pointed to none. It is this: "That if they find, from the evidence in the case, that the defendant admitted the account sued on in this case to be correct and unpaid, and promised to pay the same, that such admissions are sufficient evidence to entitle the plaintiffs to recover the amount of said account, unless they further find from the evidence that defendant when he made the admission, was as a fact mistaken in the facts in regard to said account."

The statute of frauds not having been pleaded and relied on, it was competent, by the defendant's unqualified promise to pay the debt, to charge him with it. The jury have found the defendant made the admissions and promise, with a full knowledge of all the facts in regard to the account, and it [*119] ought to bind him. The testimony of James H. Dickson, relied on by the jury, fully establishes the liability growing out of an express promise to pay the account. The judgment must be affirmed.

Judgment affirmed.

QUINTUS TIBBS, and AMELIA J. TIBBS, his Wife, impleaded with Amelia Allen, Georgiana Allen, Onick S. Allen, Laura Allen, Frank V. Allen, and Tandy Allen, Plaintiffs in Error, *v.* CHARLES H. ALLEN, Defendant in Error.

ERROR TO SANGAMON.

Where an answer is filed for infant defendants, by one purporting to be their guardian *ad litem*, and the decree recites that he was so appointed, but the record shows no separate order of appointment, it will be presumed that the appointment was regularly made.

Where the record shows a notice by publication in a chancery cause, which recites the fact that an affidavit of the non-residence of the defendants was duly filed, but the affidavit does not appear in the record, this court will regard that recital as an official declaration by the clerk, and will presume that the affidavit was duly filed.

Where there are infant and adult defendants, and the adults alone prosecute a writ of error, they cannot assign for error those proceedings which only affect the interests of the infants.

Upon a bill for a partition brought by one of the heirs at law, in which it is suggested that the widow is entitled to dower in the lands sought to be divided, but the prayer does not ask that her dower be assigned, the court cannot decree an assignment of dower and appoint commissioners to set it off. Nor can the court give the widow an estate in fee in one-third of the land, in lieu of her life estate, for dower.

Where the affidavit and report of commissioners appointed to make partition bear date one day prior to the order of their appointment, and no specific objection is raised to this, it will be regarded as a mistake of the clerk in making up the record.

Commissioners appointed to make partition, should take the oath as provided by the statute, "to make partition in accordance with the judgment of the court as to the rights and interests of the parties." It is irregular for them to be sworn, merely to divide the land impartially.

Commissioners appointed to make partition, reported, "that from all the circumstances surrounding the pecuniary condition of the family, and the locality of the lands, they cannot be divided without prejudice to the owners." *Held*, that this report was not in conformity with the statute, and did not justify the court in ordering a sale of the lands.

A bill in chancery for a partition should set out the title of the petitioner, or show the interest he claims in the premises sought to be divided.

The decree in a chancery proceeding for partition, should set out the respective interests and titles of the parties, and it is erorr for the decree to provide for an equal division among the defendants without finding [*120] that they have equal interests in the land.

Infants are not bound by a decree unless all of the evidence necessary to establish it, is preserved in the record.

THIS was a bill in chancery for a partition of lands, filed by the defendant in error in the Circuit Court of Sangamon county.

The opinion of the Court contains a full statement of all the points arising in the case.

J. GRIMSHAW, for the Plaintiffs in Error.

M. HAY, for the Defendant in Error

BREESE, J. This was a petition filed in the Sangamon Circuit Court on the 11th of September, 1848, by Charles H. Allen, setting forth that the petitioner, together with Amelia Jane Tibbs, one of the plaintiffs in error here, and other persons named, were the children and heirs at law of one Tandy Allen, deceased, and Amelia Allen, his widow. That Tandy Allen was, at his death, seized of certain lands which are particularly described, situate in Sangamon county, all of which had descended to his said children, subject to the dower of his widow, Amelia Allen. The petition further states, that no partition has ever been made of the lands, and on account of the minority of most of the heirs, they are incapable of making partition. And that it is not certain from the nature and situation of the lands, that a partition can be made amongst the heirs, without prejudice to their interests, and diminishing the value of the land. The petitioner therefore prays that partition of the lands may be made by an order and decree of the court, between him and the other heirs and the widow, if it can be done without prejudice to their interest, and if partition cannot be made, that the lands may be sold and the proceeds divided amongst the petitioner and the other heirs and widow. The widow, Amelia Allen, and Amelia Jane Tibbs, with her husband, Quintus Tibbs, together with the other heirs, are made defendants, and a summons prayed to be issued against them, and "that they be compelled to answer the petition."

The petition was sworn to by Elijah Iles, on the day it was filed.

Summons was issued against the widow and heirs at law, dated on the same day, 11th September, 1848, and returned by the sheriff on the 14th, that the defendants were not found in his bailiwick.

[*121] The record then recites, that on the 11th September, 1848, there was made, and the same is now among the papers in the case, a notice and certificate of publication, which, after the statement of the venue and of the court, and the title of the cause and names of parties, is as follows: "Affidavit having been filed in the office of the clerk of the Circuit Court for the county and State aforesaid, that all of the defendants in the above entitled cause are non-residents of the State of Illinois, notice is hereby given to the said defendants, that a suit is pending in the Circuit Court in and for the county and State aforesaid, on the chancery side thereof, wherein Charles H. Allen is complainant and you are defendants; that a subpoena in chancery has been issued in said cause, returnable on the first day of the next term of said court, to be holden at the court house in the city of Springfield, on the third Monday in the month of November, A. D. 1848, at which time and place you are required to appear," etc. September 11, 1848.

"We certify that the attached notice was published in the Illinois Journal, a weekly newspaper printed in Springfield, Illinois, four weeks successively, the first publication being made on the 13th day of September, 1848, and the last on the 11th day of October, same year."

The record then recites, that on a subsequent day of the term there was filed in open court an answer of guardian *ad litem* as follows: "The answer of Georgiana Allen, Onick S. Allen, Laura Allen, Frank V. Allen, and Tandy Allen, by B. S. Edwards, their guardian *ad litem.* These defendants, being minors, know nothing of the facts stated in the petition, and require proof so far as proof is necessary to be made."

146

These are all the proceedings in the court, preliminary to the decree. That was passed on the twenty-third of November, and is substantially as follows: The court finds the petition duly sworn to, and that notice of the petition has been duly given by publishing the same four weeks successively in the Sangamon Journal, a public newspaper printed and published in Springfield, commencing more than sixty days before the first day of the present term of the court, and Benjamin S. Edwards, who was appointed guardian *ad litem* for the defendants (naming them) who are minors, having filed the answer of said minors, and the court being satisfied that the lands in the petition mentioned (describing them) are owned jointly by the petitioners and the defendant, Amelia Jane Tibbs, (and the other defendants, naming the children,) and that the defendant, Amelia Allen, is entitled to dower in said lands. It is therefore ordered by the court, that William Butler, Erastus Wright, and Washington Iles, be ap- [*122] pointed commissioners to make partition of said lands; that they lay off and assign to the said Amelia Allen her dower, being one-third of the land aforesaid, by metes and bounds, according to quantity and quality. And it is further ordered, that said commissioners divide said lands equally, among the other defendants, assigning to said Charles H. Allen, Amelia Jane Tibbs (and the other children, naming them) each, one equal part of said land, and that they make their report to this court.

On the next day, (Nov. 24, 1848,) the commissioners reported, prefixing to their report an affidavit, as follows: We, William Butler, Erastus Wright, and Washington Iles, commissioners appointed by the foregoing decree, do solemnly swear that we will fairly and impartially make partition of the lands in said decree mentioned, according to the rights and interests of the parties, if the same can be done consistently with the interests of the parties. Sworn to and subscribed this 22nd day of November, 1848.

The report then recites: We, the commissioners undersigned, having made ourselves fully acquainted with the following list of lands, belonging to the estate of the late

Tandy Allen, deceased—(describing them)—being the same
as described in the order attached hereto and forming part of
this report. From all the circumstances surrounding the
pecuniary condition of the family, and locality of the land, we
are of opinion that said lands cannot be divided without prejudice to the interest of the owner. Given under our hands
and seals, this 22nd day of November, 1848.

On the same day, 22nd November, 1848, upon the coming in
of the report, this order was made:

The commissioners appointed in this case, to make partition
of the lands in the petition mentioned, to wit:—(describing
them)—having made their report that said lands cannot be
divided without manifest prejudice to the proprietors of the
same; it is therefore ordered by the court, that said lands be
sold, and that Erastus Wright be appointed commissioner to
sell said lands; that he sell the same at public auction, to the
highest bidder, for cash in hand; that he sell the same at the
door of the court house, in the city of Springfield, and that
he give notice of the sale by advertising the same in some
public newspaper, in Springfield, for twenty days, and that he
make deed or deeds to the purchaser or purchasers, and report
the same to this court.

No other order appears until at the March term, 1850, when
an order of continuance was entered—and no other order in
[*123] the cause, until March term, 1852, when the following
order was entered: "Ordered, by the court, that this cause be
stricken from the docket."

The foregoing is a full abstract of the whole record in this
cause, on which the plaintiffs in error have assigned these
errors:

First. In permitting the answer of guardian *ad litem* to be
filed for minors without order appointing guardian.

Second. In rendering a decree for partition and sale, without service of process or affidavit of non-residence, and due
publication of notice on such affidavit.

Third. In rendering decrees against defendants for partition and sale, without notice, either actual or constructive, to
defendants, of pendency of suit.

Fourth. In rendering decrees against minor defendants, without proof of truth of allegations contained in bill.

Fifth. In ordering commissioners to assign dower to Amelia Allen, widow, when bill contained no prayer, either general or special, for such assignment of dower.

Sixth. In ordering partition of land amongst heirs of Tandy Allen, and assignment to Amelia . Allen, widow, her dower being one-third of lands, thereby giving to widow one-third in fee instead of use of one-third for life.

Seventh. In decreeing a sale upon an insufficient report of commissioners.

Eighth. In decreeing a sale upon a report which showed that commissioners did not go upon premises, and in which they do not report that premises are so situated that partition cannot be made, but only that "from circumstances surrounding the pecuniary condition of the family, and the locality of the land, such lands cannot be divided."

Ninth. In ordering partition and sale without fully adjudicating upon rights of all parties to suit.

Tenth. Ordering partition and sale, and establishing interest of Amelia Allen, widow, to be one-third, when by law her share was a mere dower interest.

Eleventh. Ordering a sale as well for benefit of Amelia Allen, the doweress, as of the other parties, instead of ascertaining the yearly value of such dower, and ordering a sale, subject to such yearly value.

Twelfth. Ordering a sale without disposing of the interest of Amelia Allen, the doweress.

Thirteenth. Error assigned by leave: In rendering decrees in the cause, either against minors or adults, without preserving in record the evidence upon which such decrees are based.

We will dispose of the errors in the order in which [*124] they are assigned.

The record does not show by any separate order entered therein, that a guardian *ad litem* was appointed by the court, as the statute in such cases imperatively requires. (Scates' Comp. 160, Sec. 6; ib. 155, Sec. 22.) An answer, however,

by a person styling himself guardian *ad litem* and assuming
that character, appears in the record, and he is recognized by
the court, as such, in the decree. It may happen that the clerk
will omit entering upon his minutes, this preliminary proceeding, and we see no reason why it may not be supplied by the
recital in the order of the court. The court certainly knew
Mr. Edwards was acting as guardian *ad litem*, and with that
knowledge recognized his authority. The record states the
fact that he was appointed, and that must be held equivalent to
a formal appointment, for it is but a form, the infants being in
no way affected by the answer of the guardian. In the case of
Cost v. *Rose*, 17 Ill. 277, it appears that the answer of a person assuming to act as guardian *ad litem* was put in, after a
default had been taken against all the defendants, and without
any formal appointment by the court. This was clearly irregular, as the bill then stood as confessed. That case did not go
off upon that ground, nor do we think had the answer of the
guardian *ad litem* been put in before the default, and recognized by the court as the answer, that it would have been
deemed such an irregularity as to reverse a decree. That case
was reversed for want of a sufficient return of service of summons, and because the commissioners made partition of a tract
of land not in the petition, and the court approved it. The appointment is one, more of form than substance, and so long as
the court sees the interests of minors have been attended to, by
a competent person assuming to act as guardian *ad litem*, and
as his acts do not bind the infants, and he is recognized by the
court, we should not deem it such an irregularity as should reverse a decree, regular in all other respects.

The second and third errors assigned, bring before us the
notice of the pendency of the suit. This is a jurisdictional
fact, and lies at the foundation of the case, the rule being that
no party can be bound by a judgment or decree, who never
had notice of the proceeding, either actual or constructive.
The record shows affirmatively, that a subpœna was issued,
and returned *non est*, and a notice published in the Illinois
Journal, a public newspaper, printed at the place of holding
the court, the number of weeks required by law, and in the

time required. This notice takes the place of process, and is furnished to the newspaper by the clerk, and is his act. [*125] In the notice, it is recited that, " Affidavit having been filed in the office of the clerk of the Circuit Court, for the county and State aforesaid, that all of the defendants in the above entitled cause, are non-residents of the State of Illinois: Notice is hereby given," etc.

The affidavit does not appear in the record. It is a loose paper in the cause, quite liable to be lost or mislaid, and we should be very unwilling to reverse a decree or judgment if it did not appear in the record, when the clerk has affirmed, in his official character, that the affidavit was filed in his office, and the fact is so recited in the record. We must place reliance on the official acts of the clerk, and on his official declarations, and we must presume something to sustain his acts. It is his duty to require the affidavit—he states in the notice it was filed in his office, and we must take the fact to be so, unless the contrary shall be made to appear. The presumption must obtain, from all that appears on the record, that the required affidavit was made, and that the defendants were properly before the court by the published notice. The certificate of the publisher of the paper may well be likened to the return of an officer. Great loss might result to parties, if the affidavit of non-residence, in a case like this, could not be produced after the lapse of years. The case of *Randall* v. *Songer*, 16 Ill. 28, does not disturb this view of the question. In that case, the record recited only that, "it appears to the satisfaction of the court, that due notice has been given by publication of the pendency of this suit." Neither a summons or advertisement was shown in that case; here, both are found in the record.

The writ of error being prosecuted by two of the adult defendants only, we do not well see how they can assign as error, such proceedings of the court as affect the infant defendants. When they complain, we will consider the errors affecting them, should there be any. " Sufficient unto the day, is the evil thereof." The plaintiffs in error cannot be injured by any proceedings against the infants, however, irregular they may have been, and therefore we consider the fourth error not well assigned.

The fifth error assigned, questions the correctness of that part of the decree which directs the commissioners to assign to the widow her dower in the lands, the bill containing no prayer to that end.

Other errors are assigned upon this order of the court, being the sixth, tenth, eleventh and twelfth, which we will dispose of together.

[*126] The bill is for partition only, with a suggestion of the petitioners, that Amelia Allen, the widow, is entitléd to dower in the land sought to be divided, but there is no averment that she claims dower, and no prayer that her dower be set off and assigned to her.

The court finds, upon what proof we do not know, as none is preserved in the record, that the widow was entitled to dower in all the lands described in the petition, and the commissioners appointed to divide the lands among the heirs at law, were ordered, in addition, " to lay off and assign " to her, " her dower, being one-third of the lands aforesaid, by metes and bounds, according to quantity and quality." On a bill for mere partition among the heirs at law of a decedent, without any prayer that dower be assigned the widow, we know of no law or practice authorizing the court to decree an assignment of dower, and appoint commissioners to set it off to her. Nor do we recognize the propriety of a decree which shall, on such a petition, assign to the widow as her own absolutely, one-third of the lands, dividing the residuum among the heirs at law. A proceeding in partition in chancery may undoubtedly contain a prayer for the assignment of dower to the widow, and if the court adjudges that she shall have her dower, it must be so entered of record, together with a description of the land out of which she is to be endowed, and the commissioners appointed to make partition, and assign dower, and so sworn, can set off to the widow her dower, by metes and bounds, according to the judgment of the court, which she can hold and enjoy during her natural life, and at the same time, allot and set off to each owner his proper share, according to quantity and quality, every one of which shares may be incumbered by the dower interest in it, set off to the widow. If, however, the commissioners report, the land cannot be divided without great injury thereto, nor the dower set off by metes and bounds, the court then directs the yearly value of the widow's dower to be ascertained by a jury empaneled and sworn for that purpose, and their finding is a yearly charge upon the lands during her natural life, and that the lands be sold, subject to this charge. (Scates' Comp. 156, Sec. 28.) It was error in the court to decree, on this petition, to the widow one-third of the land absolutely, but no injury resulted from this, because the commissioners were not sworn to set off and assign the widow's dower, nor did they do so. The estate of the plaintiffs has not been lessened in any decree, nor in any manner affected by this portion of the decree determining the widow's dower, or in ordering a sale without regard to it; they therefore cannot complain if there be error therein.

The seventh and eighth errors, assigned, question the [*127] report of the commissioners, as not in conformity to the statute under which they were appointed to act.

The ninth section of the act regulating partition, provides, when the court shall order a partition, it shall appoint three disinterested commissioners, each of whom shall take an oath fairly and impartially to make partition in accordance with the judgment of the court, as to the rights and interests of the parties, if the same can be done consistently with the interests of the estate, and the said commissioners shall go upon the premises and make partition of said lands, tenements and hereditaments, assigning to each party his or her share by metes and bounds; and may make report, etc.

It is provided by section eleven, when any lands, etc., are so circumstanced that a division cannot be made without manifest prejudice to the proprietors, and the commissioners shall so report to the court, the court shall thereupon give an order to the same commissioners, or other person or persons, to sell such lands, etc., and make report. (Scates' Comp., ch. 79, page 161).

It may be objected, that the commissioners did not take the oath prescribed by the statute. They were not sworn to make partition, "in accordance with the judgment of the court as to the rights and interests of the parties," but only sworn to divide the land according to their own opinions of those rights and interests, without regard to the judgment of the court. It may be remarked here too, that the affidavit of the commissioners, and their report, bear date one day prior to their appointment—their appointment by the decree having been made on the twenty-third of November, whilst the affidavit, and report, bear date the twenty-second of that month. But no point is made on this, and we will assume there is a mistake by the clerk in making up the record.

But now, as to the report itself. It seems to us so objectionable, as to preclude the right to ask for, and obtain an order of sale upon it. It fails to come up to the reasonable requirements of the statute, in the most important particulars.

It does not state, they went upon the premises they were required to divide—it does not state they had such a personal knowledge of the lands, and of such tract, as to render it unnecessary to comply, strictly, with the statute—it does not state that the lands, and each tract thereof, are so circumstanced that a division could not be made without manifest prejudice to the proprietors of the land, nor does it contain a syllable or word respecting the circumstances which might prevent a division.

[*128] They report merely, that from all the circumstances surrounding the pecuniary condition of the family and locality of the lands, they cannot be divided without prejudice to the interests of the owners. We infer from this, that the lands were unimproved, yielding no income to the family, and that money was needed for their support, and being in a good " locality," near the city of Springfield, they would bring money if offered for sale. The court was not justified in ordering a sale on such a report as this. It is not only, not in accordance with the statute, but in the face of the statute. The pecuniary condition of the family and the locality of the land are not elements to be regarded by sworn commissioners appointed to divide the land. The case shows there were, including the petitioner, seven heirs at law of Tandy Allen, each one supposed to have an equal interest in those lands, the whole subject to the dower of the widow. It appears there were eight tracts of land to be divided, containing, in the aggregate, seven hundred

Tibbs *et al. v.* Allen.

and twenty acres, all in a rich and populous neighborhood, and near the city of Springfield. It would require much proof to induce the belief that so much land could not be divided fairly and equally, according to quantity and quality, among seven claimants. We are justified in believing, that it was not the real design of the proceeding in partition that the lands should be divided, the report of the commissioners informing us, that the pecuniary condition of the family was such,—or in other words, some one or more members of the family were so much in want of money,—that it was necessary, in order to supply the want, to bring these rich and valuable lands to the hammer. There is no law for it, nor justice in it, and a sale should not have been ordered on this report.

When it is considered, that titles to valuable lands can be divested by this statutory proceeding, it is essential the statute should be observed, the courts not tolerating any essential departure from it. In this case it seems to have been wholly disregarded.

It is also objected, that the court did not ascertain and declare the rights, titles and interests of the parties by the decree, nor is the evidence shown, on which the decree was based. It might be said also, that the petitioner did not set out his title in the petition, or make exhibits of any rights and titles the defendants may have claimed to possess to the lands. The decree finds nothing proved— not even heirship of the parties, nor the interests of the several parties, by any evidence in the record. The court orders that the lands be divided equally among the defendants, after taking out one-third as dower of the widow, [*129] there being nothing in the record to show, they were entitled equally. The whole proceeding is defective. The infant heirs were not bound by the decree, for no proof was made of the truth of the bill as to them, which has been always held to be necessary, as against them. *McClay* v. *Norris,* 4 Gilman, 385; *Carr* v. *Fielden,* 18 Ill. 18, and cases there cited. The circumstances requiring a sale of the lands, were not such as the statute regards. By the decree, the widow is given one-third of the land absolutely, when by law, she is entitled only to a life estate in one-third. The decree does not find the interests of the several parties. *Greenup* v. *Sewall*, 18 Ill. 53; *Herdman* v. *Short*, ib. 59. For these errors, the decree must be reversed, and the cause remanded.

Judgment reversed.

JOSEPH VEILE, Administrator of the Estate of Leonard Koch, deceased, *v.* MICHAEL KOCH, Guardian of the minor heirs of Leonard Koch, deceased.

AGREED CASE FROM ST. CLAIR.

A, being in feeble health and a resident of Missouri, was brought by B to Illinois, and lived in the house of B, as a guest, furnishing his own room and a part of his food, but occupying the room at the sufferance of B. A had two daughters, within the age prescribed by the fourth section of the act, entitled, "An Act to amend an act relative to wills and testaments, executors and administrators, and the settlement of estates," page 597, Revised Statutes of 1845, one of whom remained with him, the other living apart from him with a relative—A, during his lifetime, declaring his intention to return to Missouri, to pursue his former occupation: *Held*, that A was not a housekeeper within the meaning of the said fourth section, and that his children could not receive the same amount of property that would have been by law allowed to the widow of A.

"ORDERED by the court, that all the property mentioned in the appraisement bill and inventory of said administrator, be forthwith delivered up by said administrator to Michael Koch, guardian, for the use of his wards, children and heirs at law of Leonard, deceased."

It is hereby agreed by the attorneys on both sides of this case, that the foregoing is a correct transcript and order of the St. Clair County Court, and that the said St. Clair Circuit Court affirmed the same on appeal at its Spring term, 1861; and that the following was all the material evidence introduced in said trial, in said Circuit Court, to wit:

[*130] Leonard Koch died intestate in said county, September 30, 1860. Joseph Veile, his brother-in-law, took out letters of administration in said county, on his estate, December

10, 1860. About the same time, Michael Koch, brother of deceased, took out letters of guardianship, in said county, for the two minor children of deceased, who are his only heirs at law, and who at the commencement of this suit had the custody of said children. Said Leonard Koch, deceased, left, at the time of his death, Anne Maria Koch and Rosa Koch, the one four years of age, the other ten years of age, his only children and heirs at law, and no widow, and no more property than the quantity and amount mentioned in Act 37, page 597, Revised Statutes of the year 1845, and the amendments thereto, consisting of household furniture and musical instruments. That said deceased, about a year before his death, had a wife, with whom he was keeping a hotel in St. Louis, Mo.; that soon afterwards his wife died, and he moved with said children to another part of the city of St. Louis, Mo., where he rented a couple of rooms, and he and his children kept house for about nine months, he teaching music for a livelihood. About two months before his death, and while so situated, his brother and brother-in-law, who are the plaintiff and defendant in this suit, being informed that said Leonard Koch was confined to his room, and part of the time to the bed, with consumption, and having obtained his consent, went over from St. Clair county aforesaid, where they resided, to St. Louis, Mo., about fourteen miles, with a two-horse wagon, and moved the said Leonard, his children, and all his property, over to St. Clair county, and placed the same at the residence of said Joseph Veile, whose wife is the sister of said deceased, said Michael Koch remarking at the time that it would be inconvenient for deceased to go to his house, as his wife was sick. Deceased was so far advanced with sickness at that time that he was placed on a bed in the wagon while being brought over. Deceased was placed in a room in the house of Veile, which was furnished from that time till his death, partly with the furniture of Veile, and partly with deceased's furniture; the bed, table, one bureau, and chairs, belonged to Veile; one bureau, a stand, the lounge on which deceased generally laid, as well as some other things, belonged to deceased. Deceased, while there, till his death, was sometimes walking about, but generally confined to his room or bed. After being there about two weeks, he told Mr. Von Bernum he might take his youngest child and keep it till he got well, but he would not part with her permanently; the older one would not be so much trouble to Mrs. Veile, and [*131] could help him some, and that she might stay with him. Thereupon the youngest one went and lived with Mr. Von Bernum, about half a mile distant, until deceased died, and the older one remained at Veile's—was frequently seen to make soup for and to bring it to her father, and waited upon him generally; she slept in another room (up stairs) with Veile's daughter, and ate at Veile's table, with his children, several times. Michael Koch, who is a butcher, sent meat to his brother Leonard, with which to make soup, which soup was used by deceased, and the meat by Veile's family. The cooking was all done on Veile's stove, with Veile's fire-wood. Michael lived in Centreville, and Veile lived about a half a mile from there. Leonard, while at Veile's, remarked that if he should get well, he thought he would move back to St. Louis, where he would follow music teaching again. Said daughter also assisted Mrs. Veile in cooking, and washed generally for her father with the material and implements of Veile. There was no agreement made about charging for board or rent. The daughter testified, that Mrs. Veile did not generally wait upon deceased on account of his offensive smell.

Now it is further agreed, that this suit stand as appealed by said Veile to the Supreme Court, to be tried at Springfield, the said Veile having filed an appeal bond, which is hereby accepted. And it is further agreed, that if the said Supreme Court is of opinion that the said Leonard Koch was a housekeeper, the head of a family, at the time of his death, under the evidence, within the meaning of section four of Act No. 37, page 597, of the Revised Statutes of 1845, and that the said children were then residing with him, within the meaning of said section, so that they became thereby entitled to the property mentioned in said act, then said court shall affirm the judgment below. If the court, however, is of a contrary opinion, then said judgment below is to be reversed.

J. B. UNDERWOOD, for Veile.

W. B. UNDERWOOD, and J. B. HAY, for Koch, Guardian.

WALKER, J. This record presents upon the agreed facts in the case, the question, whether the property left by deceased passes to the administrator or to the guardian. It is urged, that by the operation of the fourth section of the Act of 21st February, 1849, (Scates' Comp. 1202), the property in controversy belong to the minor heirs of deceased. That section provides that any person dying intestate, being "a house-keeper and the head of a family, and shall leave no widow, [*132] there shall be allowed to the children of the intestate, residing with him, (including all males under eighteen years of age, and all females), at the time of his death, the same amount of property as is allowed to the widow by this act, and the act to which this is an amendment." It is conceded, that the property consists of such articles as are enumerated in the law, and that the children are such as are provided for in the act; if the deceased was a housekeeper and his children resided with him, within the meaning of the statute.

It is shown by the evidence, that the deceased being at the time in feeble and declining health, the present parties to this record brought him from St. Louis, in Missouri, to this State. He then remained with and accepted a room in the house of appellant until his death. He was, when he came to the State, feeble, and was confined a greater portion of his time to his room or bed. His elder daughter remained with him, and waited upon and attended to him, until his death. The younger was placed with a friend, with the understanding that, on her father's recovery, she should return to him. The daughter who remained with him, sometimes ate at the table of appellant, and slept with his daughter in a different apartment from that occupied by deceased. Appellees furnished deceased with meat, from which soup was made, and which deceased ate, but the meat was used by appellant's family. The cooking was done on his stove, and with his wood. Deceased, before his death, expressed the intention of again returning to St. Louis, when he should regain his health, and there to resume his profession of teaching music.

From this evidence it is apparent, that the arrangement for deceased to remain with appellant, was temporary and not permanent. The evidence fails to show any design to reside in Illinois as his home, but on the contrary, he expressed the design of returning to Missouri, to pursue his profession. And it must have been his purpose to make that State his permanent home. So far as we can gather his intention from all the facts in the record, he never intended to make this State his residence. He obviously came to this State, with the design of remaining for a limited period only, and then to return. We find no fact in the record which indicates any intention to abandon his residence in Missouri. And to entitle his children to the beneficent provisions of this statute, he should manifestly have been a resident of this State. This law was not designed to operate, nor can it operate, upon residents of other States. Residents of other jurisdictions, although they may be in the condition specified by the act, [*133] are not embraced within its provisions, and hence have no right to claim its benefits.

Nor does the evidence show that he was a householder. He, it is true, occupied one room of appellant's dwelling, and so far as appears from the evidence, he and his daughter were its only occupants. He was not a lessee of the room. He paid no rent, nor does it appear that any arrangement existed, giving him any legal right to continue its occupancy, against the consent of appellant. Notwithstanding he furnished it in part, it does not appear that he was there in any other relation than that of a visitor. Appellant had the undoubted right to control its use. He had the power at any time to require it to have been vacated. He could have had deceased removed to another room in the house, as convenience or necessity might have required. If appellant had the right to perform these acts, they were certainly inconsistent with the authority of a housekeeper, who may certainly control his household affairs as he may choose, independent of the will of another. This was by no means the condition of deceased, with reference to the room which he occupied.

To bring the parties claiming its benefits within the provisions of the act, deceased must also have been the head of a family, and that family should have resided with him. In this case, we think the evidence shows that appellant was the head of the family, and not the deceased, during his life. Deceased and his daughter were, it might be only temporarily, a part of his family, and his younger daughter was for the time being a part of another family, residing in a separate and distinct tenement. Deceased, being himself a guest, we think he was in no sense a resident, and his children were not residing with him. If they were, it was in Missouri, and not in this State, as that was his residence.

Whilst an act so beneficent in its character, and directed to objects of the tenderest care of the law, should receive a reasonably liberal construction, yet it cannot be perverted to purposes or objects not contemplated by its framers. To give the act such a construction as to embrace this property, would be calculated to work injustice to creditors in other cases, if not in this. However much we might be inclined to permit the guardian to hold this property for the benefit of his wards, they are not within the provisions of the statute, and the judgment of the court below must be reversed, and the cause remanded.

Judgment reversed.

JOHN GAUCHE, Plaintiff in Error, *v.* FREDERICK [*134] MAYER, impleaded with Walter Wright, Defendant in Error.

ERROR TO ST. CLAIR.

A party may maintain trespass, if he has at the time of the act, such a title as draws after it a constructive possession.

A had placed goods with an auctioneer for sale, reserving to himself the right to resume possession at his pleasure, the auctioneer not having any claim to or charge upon such goods: *Held*, that A had a right of action in trespass against a sheriff for making a levy upon those goods as the property of another, the sheriff having been notified of the facts before the levy.

PLAINTIFF in error filed his declaration against Mayer and Wright in trespass for carrying away certain articles of chinaware and crockery, and other merchandise, fully described therein. Wright filed his plea of general issue. Mayer justified as sheriff under an execution issued from Cook county, in favor of Wright and against the property of Nolin, Belt and Galbreath, which said execution he had levied upon the goods, etc., etc., claimed by plaintiff in error in his declaration, as the goods of Nolin, one of the defendants in the said execution.

Plaintiff filed two replications to said special plea; one denying the execution, and the other averring, that the said property was the property of plaintiff, and not of Nolin.

Upon trial, jury found defendants guilty, and assessed damages at $276.64. The plaintiff's counsel discharged the said defendant Wright.

Defendant moved for and obtained a new trial.

Before second trial, plaintiff dismissed the case as to Wright.

Upon the trial, plaintiff proved that in the spring of 1859, the merchandise in question was given to Nolin & Belt, auctioneers in the city of Belleville, to sell on commission. Some months before the goods were levied upon, Nolin & Belt sold out to one Bates, who was also carrying on the auctioneering business. Nolin & Belt, at the time of selling out, informed plaintiff that his goods had been left in the store, and plaintiff made arrangements with Mr. Bates to sell them on commission. Nolin, at the time of the levy, was in the store, having still some things of his own in the store, and he told the sheriff, that the goods levied upon were the goods of Gauche. Bates stated, that about 20th July, 1859, about two weeks before the levy, an agent of Gauche came over

and asked him whether he would take the commission of
goods on the same terms that Nolin & Belt had had [*135]
them; that he agreed to it, and he was to sell the goods at auction or otherwise, to the best advantage, for ten per cent. commission. The goods levied upon as invoiced by him at half
the original prices, amounted to $319. He told the sheriff that
the goods were not Nolin's, but belonged to plaintiff at St.
Louis; they were apart under the counter, and he repeatedly
informed the sheriff that they were commission goods, and the
sheriff said he did not know, nor did he care, or words to that
effect. He could, as he understood it, return the goods at any
time, and Gauche could have called for them at any time. The
old sign of the firm of Nolin & Belt was still painted over the
door, but Bates had ordered the painter to paint the names of
the new firm, but the painter had disappointed him. The
goods were sold by the sheriff.

Defendant proved that Mayer was acting sheriff, produced
execution, and also the return thereon; to the reading of which
return, the plaintiff objected, but objection was overruled.

Case was by consent tried by court, who took the case under
advisement, for the purpose of examining witness Bates again,
which the court did, while plaintiff's counsel was not in court,
at a subsequent day, and gave verdict for defendant, overruled
motion for a new trial, and gave judgment for costs.

The plaintiff assigns the following errors: That the court
admitted improper evidence; admitted evidence improperly;
refused motion for new trial; and gave judgment for defendant
and not for plaintiff.

Gustavus Kœrner, for Plaintiff in Error.

J. B. Underwood, for Defendant in Error.

Breese, J. To entitle a person to maintain an action of
trespass, he must, at the time when the act, constituting the
trespass, was done, either have the actual possession in him of
the thing which is the object of the trespass, or else he must
have a constructive possession, by reason of the right or title
to the thing being actually vested in him, such title or right,

163

drawing after it, a constructive possession. If the general owner parts with his possession, and the bailee, at the time when the injury was committed, has a right exclusively to use the thing, the inference of a constructive possession is rebutted, and the general owner cannot maintain trespass, his possession [*136] being in reversion only. The action is founded on possession, or on such a title as draws after it a constructive possession. What are the facts in this case? The goods in question had been deposited by the plaintiff, a resident of St. Louis, with the firm of Nolin & Belt, of Belleville, to sell on a certain stipulated commission, but within no specified time. The firm made sale of some of the goods, and having sold out their concern to Bates, he agreed to sell the remainder on the same terms that Nolin & Belt had stipulated. Soon after this sale, Bates being in possession of the goods, an execution against Nolin & Belt was levied, by the defendant, as sheriff of St. Clair county, on them, he being informed at the time, both by Nolin and by Bates, that they were the goods of the plaintiff, and not the property of Nolin & Belt, or either of them. The goods were taken by the sheriff and sold, and this action of trespass brought by the owners.

On the trial, it was proved by Bates, that he had agreed with the plaintiff, some weeks before the levy, to sell these goods at auction for a commission of ten per cent. He states he understood the contract with the plaintiff to be, that he could return the goods at any time, and that plaintiff could have called for them at any time. At a separate examination of this witness by the court, on the following day, the court stating, that his decision would turn on the nature of the contract the witness had made with the plaintiff, the witness stated, there was nothing said specially about the keeping the goods, or the right of plaintiff to call for them at any time — he took the goods on general commission to sell for the plaintiff. This the court deemed sufficient evidence, to rebut the claim of a right of possession in the plaintiff, and accordingly decided that he could not maintain his action of trespass.

It is undoubtedly true, that Bates, the bailee of these goods, might have maintained trespass against the defendant for taking

the goods out of his actual possession — trespass being founded
on possession. But does it follow, that the real owner might
not also maintain the action? The defendant was a wrong-
doer, both as it regards the bailee, and the real owner of the
goods, though the force was actually against the bailee's possession. The question then is, had the plaintiff, by reason
of his being the real owner of the goods, such a constructive possession as to enable him to maintain trespass? To
answer this, we must inquire, was there any bar to his taking actual possession? Was there any subsisting right or
claim to the goods in any other person, sufficient to override
or postpone the right of plaintiff to the possession of the goods
at the time of the levy? We cannot find from the testimony,
that any such bar existed, or that there was anything [*137]
in the way to prevent the plaintiff from taking immediate
possession, at the time of the levy. The bailee sets up no
claim for storage, commissions, or any lien whatever upon the
goods, and according to his view of the contract, though nothing special was said about it, the plaintiff had a right to re-
possess himself of the goods whenever he pleased, and so had
the bailee the right to return them, whenever he thought proper.
The defendant is a stranger to the goods and a wrong-doer, and
it does not rest with him to say, that the bailee had a lien on
the goods, when the bailee disclaims any such lien, and proofs
show that the bailee had no claim of any kind upon the goods.

We think then, the plaintiff being the real owner of the
goods, and having the right, at the time of the levy and depor-
tation of the goods, to have the immediate possession of them,
can maintain trespass against a stranger and wrong-doer for
taking them and carrying them away. The case of *Cannon*
v. *Kinney*, 3 Scam. 10, and cases there cited, sustain the view
we have taken of this case. It is urged, however, by the defendant, that the bill of exceptions does not purport to contain
all the evidence in the cause. This court has repeatedly decided,
that if the bill of exceptions does not contain all the evidence,
the ruling of the court on a motion for a new trial will not be
considered. This is, undoubtedly, the general rule and a salutary one; but when a record discloses the fact that the cause

was tried by the court without a jury, and the judge certifies that he based his decision on one part of the testimony only, and that part is decisive of the case, this court, it would seem, could inquire into the propriety of the decision on that testimony, it being fully stated in the bill of exceptions and made the turning point of the judgment. There is no serious question made about any other point in the cause.

The judgment of the court below is reversed, and the cause remanded, with directions to award a new trial.

Judgment reversed.

[*138] ABNER LEITCH, Appellant, *v.* EDMON CAMPBELL, Appellee.

APPEAL FROM EDGAR.

An award of arbitrators arising out of a suit before a justice of the peace, will not be set aside, because the arbitrators did not see the account filed with the justice; or because they allowed proof of a delivery of articles beyond what was stated therein, such proofs having been made to countervail an unexpected claim for a payment for articles previously delivered.

THIS was a suit originally brought by Campbell against Leitch, on an account, before a justice of the peace, who rendered a judgment in behalf of the defendant below for costs, from which judgment Campbell appealed to the Circuit Court.

On trial being had in the Circuit Court, resulting in favor of plaintiff, and a new trial awarded, the case was afterwards, by an agreement made an order of court, referred to three arbitrators, viz.: Michael O'Hair, C. B. McAnnally, and S. H. Elliott, who awarded that Leitch should pay to Campbell the sum of $31.24 and all costs.

Upon the filing of said award, the defendant excepted to the same for the following reasons: the arbitrators made a mistake in making their award, as to the amount found to be due from the defendant to the plaintiff; and the arbitrators, in making their award, allowed the plaintiff for a greater number of bushels of corn than was claimed by the plaintiff in his account filed in the case.

The defendant introduced *Silas H. Elliott* as a witness, who testified that he was one of the arbitrators to whom this case was submitted, and who joined in making the award; that he heard the evidence in the case when tried before the arbitrators; that in making their award, they found that the plaintiff had delivered the defendant about two hundred and sixteen bushels of corn, or nine loads, of twenty-four bushels to each load, at thirty-three and one-third cents per bushel, and they allowed the defendant a credit of forty dollars, which was proved or admitted before the arbitrators to have been paid by the defendant to the plaintiff; that the evidence as to the amount of corn which was delivered by the plaintiff to the defendant varied, some witnesses stating that there were eight wagon-loads delivered, and some nine, and the quantity of bushels to the load being variously estimated at eighteen, twenty and twenty-four bushels. The witness did not recollect that he saw any account on the trial before the arbitrators, and did not think any of the papers in [*139] the case were shown to the arbitrators.

Sheridan P. Read, another witness then introduced by defendant, testified that he had been counsel for defendant, Leitch, in this case from its commencement; that the account which is now filed with the papers was the only account which had ever been filed in the case, so far as he knew, which account, then shown to the court, is in the following words and figures:

"ABNER LEITCH,
Bo't of EDMON CAMPBELL,
March, 1857, 160 Bu. Corn, 33⅓c..$53.33."

Witness further testified that the account is in the handwriting of Charles Summers, who was the plaintiff's counsel when the suit was first brought before the magistrate, and thinks that it is the original account filed in the case. At the time of the trial before the arbitrators, the papers in the case were there, and witness thinks he had them open, and, as he left the room before the trial was concluded, he laid them on the table near

Leitch *v.* Campbell.

which the arbitrators were sitting, but does not know whether their attention was called to them or not.

· The court overruled the defendant's exceptions to the award, and rendered judgment on the same, for the sum of $31.24 and all the costs; the defendant then and there excepting to the decision of the court in overruling said exceptions to the award and rendering said judgment.

· The defendant assigns for error, the overruling by the court below of the exceptions to the award, and the judgment of the court below upon said award.

, SHERIDAN P. READ, for Appellant.

JOHN SCHOLFIELD, for Appellee.

CATON, C. J.   This action was brought before a justice of the peace, whence it was appealed to the Circuit Court, where it was referred to arbitrators, who reported to the court that there was due to the plaintiff thirty-one dollars and twenty-four cents. The defendant moved to set aside the report, upon the ground that the arbitrators had allowed the plaintiff for more corn than he had claimed in the account filed with the justice, when he commenced his action. The account filed, was for one hundred and sixty bushels of corn, at thirty-three and one-third cents per bushel, amounting to fifty-three dollars and thirty-three [*140] cents.   One of the arbitrators states, that they allowed the plaintiff for two hundred and sixteen bushels of corn, at thirty-three and one-third cents per bushel, and charged him with forty dollars, paid by the defendant, leaving the balance due as stated in the report.   That their attention was never called to, nor did they see the account filed before the justice. Under such circumstances, we are by no means prepared to say, that the award of the arbitrators should have been set aside, if it clearly appeared that they had allowed the plaintiff more than the amount of his account filed before the justice.   If the defendant desired the arbitrators to be influenced in their decision by the account, he should have brought it to their attention. But in this case they did not exceed the claim filed. The award was more than twenty dollars less than the amount of the plaintiff's account. True, he proved the delivery of more corn than was charged in the account, but this he was obliged to do, in order to meet the forty dollar payment proved by the defendant. The corn paid for by the forty dollars, had no ear marks by which he could show that it was not the corn charged in the account, and there was no possible way of doing that, but by showing that he had delivered more corn than he had charged in that account. When the whole evidence was considered, instead of showing that the plaintiff had not charged for enough corn to sustain the award, it showed that he had charged for more than was actually due him, and hence the arbitrators cut down the account by more than twenty dollars. The judgment must be affirmed.

Judgment affirmed.

THE COMMISSIONERS OF HIGHWAYS OF THE TOWN OF SONORA, Plaintiffs in Error, *v.* THE SUPERVISORS OF CARTHAGE, PRAIRIE AND MONTEBELLO, and GEORGE BLACK, J. J. GARDNER and J. DARBY, Defendants in Error.

ERROR TO HANCOCK.

The only office which the common law writ of certiorari performs, is to certify the record of a proceeding from an inferior to a superior tribunal. It is the duty of the inferior body to whom it is directed, to transmit a complete transcript of the record properly certified, to the court awarding the writ; without any statement of facts *dehors* the record.

The superior tribunal, upon an inspection of the record alone, determines whether the inferior tribunal had jurisdiction of the parties and of the subject matter, and whether it has exceeded its jurisdiction, or has [*141] otherwise proceeded in violation of law.

This proceeding is wholly different from a trial under our statutory writ of *certiorari*, inasmuch as that is a trial *de novo*.

Upon an appeal to the board of supervisors from the decision of the commissioners of highways, as to the laying out of a road, it is not necessary that the supervisors should examine the entire road. It will be sufficient if they examine that portion of the road against which the objections are urged.

Commissioners, etc., of Sonora *v.* Supervisors of Carthage, etc., *et al.*

Where the commissioners of highways make themselves parties to a proceeding to reverse a decision of the supervisors, by a writ of certiorari, and are
unsuccessful, a judgment against them for costs is proper.

If they were acting in behalf of the town, they should have appeared in its
name and not in their own.

THIS was a common law certiorari, brought by the commissioners of highways of the town of Sonora, Hancock county, in
the Hancock Circuit Court, to review and reverse a decision of
the supervisors of the towns of Carthage, Prairie and Montebello, on appeal said Black, Gardner and Darby, reversing a
decision of the plaintiff, in laying out a highway in said town
of Sonora.

The writ was allowed upon the affidavit of Fulton, one of the
petitioners for the road, which shows that on the 18th of April,
1855, fourteen legal voters of the town of Sonora, Hancock
county, Illinois, residing within three miles of the proposed
road, petitioned the commissioners of highways of said town to
lay out a road on or near the line between sections 16 and 21, 15
and 22, 14 and 23, and 13 and 24, in said town. That on the
7th May, 1858, petition, and proof of posting, was presented to
said commissioners.

Notice of hearing petition on 17th May, 1858, at the house
of W. H. Fulton, between 8 o'clock a. m. and 4 p. m., and affidavit of posting.

That on 17th May, 1858, commissioners met and laid out
road, and on the 18th filed petition, affidavit of posting notices,
affidavit of posting order laying out road, and survey thereof.

Appeal by Black, Gardner and Darby, to supervisors of
Carthage, Prairie and Montebello, on 14th June, 1858.
Appeal papers delivered to Ruggles, supervisor of Montebello,
and notice of hearing fixed for the 30th of July, 1858.

July 30th, 1858, supervisors met. The petitioners for the
road and commissioners of highways, as well as the appellants,
also met at the house of George Black, one of the appellants.
The commissioners of highways presented the petition, affidavit
of posting notice, affidavit of posting order laying out road, survey, and order as to damages.

170

Commissioners requested the supervisors to examine [*142] the route of said road as laid out by them, and insisted that it was the duty of the supervisors to do so. That said supervisors started, went one-half mile and returned, and wholly neglected and refused to examine the other three and a half miles; the half mile examined was within Black's inclosure, and a good route for a road; that other parts of the route were inclosed, no part of which were examined by said supervisors, and said supervisors refused to examine the same. The appellants insisted that the commissioners of highways and petitioners for the road held the affirmative—that unless they made out by the oaths of witnesses that the road was necessary, that the supervisors must reverse the decision of the commissioners in laying out said road *in toto*—and refuse to offer any proof on their part, and submitted said cause.

The commissioners of highways insisted that the supervisors were to act upon the petition and other papers brought before them by the appeal, and examine the route, the same as commissioners of highways are required to do; and that no further act or proof was necessary on their part, or on the part of the petitioners for the road, to sustain the same, unless made so to rebut proof offered by the appellants; that the appeal was brought to reverse an act of the commissioners of highways done within their jurisdiction, and the supervisors must affirm the same unless they should be satisfied by proof, or an examination of the route, that the road was improper and inexpedient.

The supervisors, without examining route, and disregarding the petition and order of the commissioners of highways, on the same day filed with the clerk of said town an order reversing *in toto* the order of said commissioners laying out said road, and taxed the costs to the town of Sonora at $23.

In their order said supervisors say, " Whereas, neither of the parties offered any proofs, but submitted the same without proofs, and we being fully advised in the premises, do order and determine that the order and determination of the commissioners be and the same is hereby in all things reversed."

The following is the return to the writ of certiorari:

171

Commissioners, etc., of Sonora *v.* Supervisors of Carthage, etc., *et al.*

"The undersigned, for return to the within writ, say that the facts stated in affidavit on which this writ was allowed, are literally and substantially true in every respect, and pray that the same may be considered our return hereto, with this addition, that we examine the road as far as we deemed it necessary.

DENNIS SMITH,)
T. RUGGLES, - Supervisors."
C. WINSTON,)

"I understood from some one present, but from whom I [*143] cannot state, that we had examined the route as far as there was any dispute."—D. Smith, Sup. of Prairie.

The court found for the defendants, and rendered judgment for costs against the commissioners of highways. To reverse which, this writ of error is prosecuted.

The following are the errors assigned:

The court erred in finding the issues for the defendants.

The court erred in rendering judgment against the plaintiffs for costs.

The court erred in not deciding it to be the duty of the supervisors, on appeal, to perform the same duties required of commissioners of highways on petition to them for a road, and in not reversing the decision of said supervisors because they refused to perform that duty.

The court erred in not reversing the decision of the supervisors, on the ground that said supervisors admit by their return that they did not do any act, except to meet, required by law of them on appeal.

The court erred in not either reversing the decision of said supervisors and affirming the decision of the commissioners of highways, or reversing said order and remanding said proceedings to said supervisors, commanding them to act upon the same, and decide " whether it is proper and expedient to locate said road," and to make and file with the town clerk of said town their order thereon.

GEO. EDMUNDS, JR., for Plaintiffs in Error.

GRIMSHAW & WILLIAMS, for Defendants in Error.

WALKER, J. The only office which the common law writ of *certiorari* performs, is to certify the record of a proceeding from an inferior to a superior tribunal. When issued and served, it becomes the duty of the inferior court or body, to whom it is directed, to transmit a full and complete transcript of the record of the proceeding, of which complaint is made, properly certified, to the court awarding the writ. It is not the duty of the jurisdiction to which it is directed, to certify or return facts *dehors* the record, but simply the record itself. Upon the return when made, the superior court tries the case upon the record alone, and it is not admissible to try it upon the allegations contained in the petition for the writ, or on facts, not contained in the record so returned. In this proceeding no trial can be had upon any issue of fact. It must be by an inspection of the record, returned in obedience to the writ.

When the return is sufficient, it is the duty of the [*144] court to try and determine, whether the inferior tribunal had jurisdiction of the parties and the subject matter, and whether it has exceeded its jurisdiction, or has otherwise proceeded in violation of law. If from the record it shall appear that the proceeding is irregular in any of these particulars, the court should quash and vacate the entire proceeding, otherwise dismiss the writ. A trial on a return of this character, is in many respects like a trial on a writ of error, it being a trial upon an issue of law and not of fact. This proceeding is wholly different from a trial on our statutory writ of *certiorari*, inasmuch as that is a trial *de novo*.

In this case no question is raised, as to the jurisdiction of the supervisors over the subject matter. Nor is it denied that they had legal authority to reverse the action of the commissioners of highways in locating the road. But it is insisted that it appears from the return, that they did not conform their action to the requirements of the law, by failing to pass over and view the entire road, before they reversed the order by which it had been located. The return does show, that the supervisors examined the road so far as they deemed it necessary, and one of them returns specially, that it was examined as far as there was any dispute. The legal presumption would be, that they had acted in conformity with the duty imposed by the statute, if it appeared from the record that they had acquired jurisdiction, although the return had been silent as to the view.

The 3rd⁻ Sec., Art. 24, of the chapter entitled Counties, (Scates' Comp. 353,) requires the commissioners to "personally examine the proposed alteration, discontinuance, or route for the new road proposed to be laid out, and shall hear any reasons that may be offered for or against altering, discontinuing or laying out the same." The twelfth section of the same article provides, that the supervisors on an appeal, shall convene at the time and place mentioned in the notice, and hear the proofs and allegations of the parties. The act confers power to issue process to compel the attendance of witnesses, and it provides that their decision shall embrace the whole matter in controversy. They are first to consider the propriety and expediency of locating, altering or discontinuing the road; and secondly, the subject of damages, if embraced in the appeal. Even if the provisions of the third section apply to the action of the supervisors trying the appeal, it would only require them to make a personal examination of the road, so far as might be necessary to arrive at a just and fair conclusion. [*145] It is not imperative that they shall pass over every part of the proposed road. It might be, that the whole objection urged against the road, referred to a specified point in the route. As if the crossing a stream might involve too large an outlay of money and labor, to justify its location. In such a case, they by passing over a small portion of the line of the road, could determine the question in dispute, as accurately as if they passed over every part of it. Or the evidence adduced might be so clear and satisfactory, as to render a personal examination of the entire route useless. They might, by passing over a part, be able to inspect the remainder as satisfactorily as by traveling over it. As this return shows that the road was examined as far as they deemed it necessary, we must presume they examined the portion about which the controversy existed, or so far as was necessary to convince them that the road was inexpedient, and not required by public necessity. Upon this return we do not perceive anything which indicates that they exceeded the¹ jurisdiction, or decided against the law.

The commissioners were the parties plaintiffs in this proceeding, or at any rate, they made themselves such. They instituted and continued the proceeding in their own name, and are estopped now, to complain that they have been mulcted in costs. If they were only appearing on behalf of the town, they should have acted in· its name and not their own, but there is nothing to show that such was their design. The judgment against them for costs was properly rendered in the court below.

The judgment of the court below is therefore affirmed.

Judgment affirmed.

MARY REDDICK, MARY ANN REDDICK, ELIZA ANN REDDICK, and JOSEPH HOWARD, Guardian of the said Mary Ann and Eliza Ann Reddick, minors, Plaintiffs in Error, *v.* THE PRESIDENT, DIRECTORS AND COMPANY OF THE STATE BANK OF ILLINOIS, Defendants in Error.

ERROR TO MACON.

Where a default has been taken and a decree entered, *pro confesso*, which recites that the defendants have been regularly notified of the pendency of the suit, by summons or advertisement, a *bona fide* purchaser under the decree will be protected, although the record may not furnish any evidence of a summons or advertisement. The cases of *Randall* v. *Songer*, 16 Ill. 27, and *Vairin* v. *Edmonson*, 5 Gilm. 272, modified.

Upon writ of error in a chancery cause, the Supreme Court will not [*146] pres..me that any evidence was given in the court below, except what appears in the record.

Strict proof is required against infant defendants, and the record must furnish the evidence to sustain a decree against them, whether their guardian answers or not.. No confession by their guardian can bind them.

THIS was a bill in chancery to foreclose a mortgage filed by the defendants in error against the plaintiffs in error, in the Circuit Court of Macon county. The opinion of the Court contains a full statement of the case.

Reddick *et al. v.* President, etc., State Bank of Illinois.

B. F. SMITH, for Plaintiffs in Error.

TUPPER & NELSON, for Defendants in Error.

BREESE, J. This record may be truly said to be a very barren one, as it contains neither bill, subpœna, note, mortgage, nor any of the evidence, if any was produced. The first recital in the record before us, is the following:

In the Macon Circuit Court, October term, October 18, A. D. 1841.

STATE BANK OF ILLINOIS,
vs. } In Chancery.
MARY REDDICK AND OTHERS.

And now this day comes the complainant by his solicitor, and on his motion, it appearing to the satisfaction of the court that process has 'been duly served on defendants herein, it is ordered that Mary Reddick, and the said defendants, Mary Ann Reddick, and Eliza Ann Reddick, by their guardian, Joseph Howard, be ruled to answer, plead or demur to complainants' said bill of complaint, on or before the meeting of court to-morrow morning and that in default thereof, said bill be taken for confessed.

And at the said term of said court, further proceedings were had, as appears of record in said court, as follows, to wit:

The President, Directors and Company of the State Bank of Illinois, Complainants, *vs.* Mary Reddick, and Mary Ann Reddick, and Eliza Ann Reddick, children and heirs at law of William G. Reddick, deceased, and Joseph Howard, Guardian of the said Mary Ann and Eliza Ann Reddick, minors under the age of twenty-one years, Defendants. } In Chancery.

And now at this day come the said complainants by their solicitor, and the said defendant, Mary Reddick, widow of William G. Reddick, deceased, and the said Mary Ann and Eliza Ann Reddick, by Joseph Howard, their guardian, having wholly failed to answer, demur or plead to the complainants' said bill of complaint, in conformity to the rule heretofore taken on them: It is therefore considered and [*147] adjudged by the court, that the complainants' said bill of complaint be taken *pro confesso* against said defendants. And thereupon this cause coming on to be heard, on bill and exhibits, and it appearing to the satisfaction of the court that default has been made in the payment of the sum of money secured by the indenture of mortgage and promissory note, in said bill of complaint mentioned, and that, in fact, the sum of two hundred dollars, the principal debt in said indenture of mortgage and promissory note mentioned, and the further sum of thirty-eight and fifty one-hundredths dollars, interest thereon, amounting in all to the sum of two hundred and thirty-eight and fifty one-hundredths dollars, remain due and unpaid on the said indenture of mortgage and promissory note, to the said complainants; it is therefore considered, adjudged and decreed, that the said complainants recover of the said defendants the sum last aforesaid, together with their costs, etc. Time, until the first day of December ensuing, is given, within which to pay the money, " and in default thereof, the right and equity of redemption of the defendants in the land in the indenture of mortgage mentioned and described, is forever barred and foreclosed, and a sale ordered, by a commissioner appointed for that purpose."

At the May term, 1842, the commissioner made his report of sale, which was approved. The complainants were the purchasers.

This is the substance of the record, on which the heirs of Reddick assign these errors:

1. That there was no summons against the defendants, and the record does not show how they were served, and the summons ought to be a part of the record.

2. There was no mortgage or note, or other evidence, to show the liability of the defendants to complainants, and no evidence thereof appears of record.

3. The records do not show any facts to justify the court in entering a decree against the defendants.

4. That the defendants were infants, and no confession or answer of guardian *ad litem* could bind them, but strict proof of every fact alleged against them should have been made.

The record is very barren, and we must take it as it appears.

Upon the first error assigned, this court has decided that a complainant is not entitled to a decree *pro confesso*, until the

Reddick *et al. v.* President, etc., State Bank of Illinois.

defendant has been served with process, or has been regularly notified of the pendency of the suit, and that it is not enough for a decree to recite that the defendant has been duly served with process, or that he has been regularly notified of the pen-[*148] dency of the suit, but the summons or advertisement should appear in the record, so that this court may determine whether the statute has been complied with. This is the ruling in the case of *Randall* v. *Songer,* 16 Ill. 27, and in the previous case of *Vairin* v. *Edmonson,* 5 Gilm. 272, and which we think, on mature consideration, requires some modification, in view of the vast interests to be affected by it. It does not seem reasonable to require a party who has purchased land under the judgment of a court of competent jurisdiction, *bona fide,* and with no notice of any such defects as the absence of a summons or notice, to be put in jeopardy of his title, or be required to take the risk of the loss or abstraction of a loose paper from the files, when the decree, or judgment of the court recites the fact, that process was duly served, or the required notice duly given. These are facts lying at the very threshold of the case, and on which the court is required to be informed and to pronounce, just as much as upon any other facts which may be developed, and no reason can be perceived why the rights of parties, depending upon those facts, should not be as secure, as upon any other adjudicated facts in the cause, especially after the lapse of many years.

It is to be presumed no court would state of record, the existence of facts which had no existence, or pass a decree, or render a judgment, unless proof of service or notice was actually produced. The record therefore, stating such facts, and nothing to the contrary appearing, it should be received as evidence of their existence. We think the rule which has obtained, should be thus modified, and this disposes of the first error assigned.

As to the second error assigned, this court has repeatedly decided, that in chancery causes, we are not allowed to presume that any evidence was given in the cause in the court below except what appears in the record. *White* v. *Morrison,* 11 Ill. 361; *Ward* v. *Owens et al.,* 12 Ill. 283; *Osborne et al.* v. *Ho-*

rine, 17 Ill. 92; *Cost* v. *Rose*, id. 276. And so far as infants are defendants, it has been settled by the court that strict proof is required, and the record must furnish evidence to sustain a decree against them, whether the guardian answers or not. *Masterson et al.* v. *Wiswould and Wife*, 18 Ill. 48; *Reavis and Reavis, Minors,* v. *Fielden,* id. 77.

The remaining errors assigned, are disposed of by the decision upon the first two. No facts are shown to justify a decree against these plaintiffs, and, no confession by their legal guardian could bind them, and strict proof of all facts necessary to make them liable, should have been made. *Cochran* v. *McDowell,* 15 Ill. 10; *Hitt* v. *Ormsbee,* 12 Ill. 169; *Hamilton* v. *Gilman,* id. 260; *Tuttle* v. *Garrett,* 16 Ill. 354; *Green-* [*149] *ouyh* v. *Taylor,* 17 Ill. 602.

The record does not show the whole case upon which the court below decided. Taking it as it is, on its face, there is not sufficient to sustain the decree, on the principles established by the cases cited. The decree must be reversed, and the cause remanded.

Judgment reversed.

· BENJAMIN M. TRUMBULL, Plaintiff in Error, *v.* AARON · B. NICHOLSON, Defendant in Error.

ERROR TO SANGAMON.

An attorney has no power to receive depreciated money, in satisfaction of a judgment.

If an attorney should accept from the sheriff depreciated money, in satisfaction of an execution, the owner of the judgment is not bound by such acceptance; and may compel the sheriff to return the amount in legal currency. If the sheriff has been injured by the conduct of the attorney, he must look to him for redress.

An assignment of a judgment, is a revocation of the authority of the plaintiff's attorney to receive the money on the execution, or to control the judgment.

THE plaintiff in error moved the Sangamon Circuit Court for a rule upon the defendant in error, who was the sheriff of Logan county, to return an execution in his hands, in favor of the plaintiff in error and against one Thomas G. Taylor—which rule being granted, and the execution returned, indorsed, "satisfied in full," a motion was entered at the same term, for a rule upon the sheriff to bring into court the money made on the execution.

The facts upon which this motion was based, are fully stated in the opinion of the Court.

The court ordered the sheriff to bring or return into court the money collected on the execution, or pay it to the plaintiff, except the amount of the two checks (which was $231) sent by the sheriff to Zane. To which decision the plaintiff in error excepted, and brings the case to this court.

W. H. HERNDON, for Plaintiff in Error.

J. C. CONKLING, for Defendant in Error.

CATON, C. J. Even if we should come to the conclusion, that the attorney was authorized to receive depreciated bank [*150] bills, in satisfaction of the judgment, without special authority so to do from his client or the owner of the judgment, and that what he did was an acceptance of the currency and check in satisfaction, still the court should have ordered the sheriff to bring the whole into court, for it was at the bank; under his control, and only through him could the judgment debtor touch it. This was so, as much in regard to the proceeds of the check as in regard to the currency, which the court did order him to bring in, so that the order should have covered the whole or nothing. But we do not think the attorney was authorized to receive the funds, sent by the sheriff, in satisfaction of the execution. The facts are these:

Zane, an attorney at law at the city of Springfield, obtained a judgment in the Sangamon Circuit Court, at the October term, 1860, for Benjamin M. Trumbull, against Thomas G. Taylor, upon which an execution issued, which was received by the sheriff by mail from Zane, in December of the same year. Zane states, in his affidavit, that about the first day of April, 1861, Benjamin M. Trumbull, the plaintiff in the judgment against

Taylor, informed him that he had sold the judgment to his brother, Lyman Trumbull, and that the same, with the execution, would from that time be subject to Lyman's control, and that Lyman would receive the money on the same. Lyman also informed him the judgment was his.

Zane also states, in his affidavit, that on the sixteenth day of May, 1861, about five months after the execution had been placed in the sheriff's hands, and about a month and a half after he was informed the plaintiff had sold the execution to his brother, a package was delivered to him, by the United States Express agent, at Springfield, Illinois, which he found to contain said execution, one hundred and twenty-five dollars, in bank notes, and two checks for current bank notes on the Springfield Marine and Fire Insurance Bank, amounting to $231, making in all the sum of $356, being the amount of the judgment and costs; and being unable to find Trumbull, he took the package to the bank, on which the checks were drawn, and the cashier counted out the bank notes on the checks. Upon further inquiry for Trumbull, he was informed that he was absent from the city, and would return on the night train, but that he deposited at Bunn's bank. Zane then went to the bank, and was there informed that he did not deposit there, and that bank notes would not be taken on general deposit, except from a regular depositor. Banking hours being about to close, he left the package containing the execution and bank notes, for safe keeping until morning, at the bank. Before banking hours, on the next morning, he saw Trumbull, who demanded the specie in satisfaction of the [*151] execution, and refused to receive bank notes. He then went to Bunn's bank, and as soon as it was open, got the package containing the execution and notes and took it to the Springfield Marine and Fire Insurance Bank, and proposed to return the currency he had received on the checks the preceding evening; which the cashier refused to do, and said it was the only currency the bank would pay out on them; and that the bills were current, and that he could not return the check.

Zane then put the execution and the bank notes in an envelope (both those he had received from the sheriff, as well as those paid on the checks) and sent the package to said sheriff by the first express returning to Logan county after he had received it, being on the first morning subsequent to the evening he had received it; and on the next returning express it was returned by the sheriff to him. He then took the package containing said execution and bank notes from the express agent, and deposited it in the Springfield Marine and Fire Insurance Bank, subject to the order of the sheriff of Logan county, and immediately wrote to the sheriff, informing him that he had deposited the package sent him by the sheriff in said bank, subject to his order, and that the said sheriff could get the same whenever he desired, and that he (Zane) would have nothing further to do with it. To which letter he received an answer from the sheriff, duly acknowledging the receipt of the letter; since which time he has seen nothing of the package.

The assignment of the judgment, notice of which was given to the attorney, was undoubtedly a revocation of his authority to receive the proceeds of the execution. If his principal had parted with the right to control the judgment, it can hardly be questioned that the power of the attorney closed with it. And he seems to have received no new power or employment from the assignee of the judgment. But admitting that he retained all his original powers, yet he was not authorized to receive anything but money, or at least that which was equivalent, and actually treated as coin, in satisfaction of the judgment. This principle has been recognized by this court, in the case of *Nolan* v. *Jackson*, 16 Ill. 272, and it is a principle indispensably necessary to the protection of parties against the imprudence or the misconduct of the attorney. The attorney might as well take cattle or corn, as anything but money, or he might take less than the amount of the judgment, in full satisfaction, as to take depreciated currency. If the sheriff had been injured by what the [*152] attorney did, he must look to the attorney for his indemnity. As in doing that act, if it could be construed into a receipt of the currency and check, in satisfaction of the judgment, he exceeded his authority, he must bear the responsibility of the act, instead of his client. The rule should have been made absolute, for the full amount of the judgment. The judgment is reversed, and the cause remanded.

Judgment reversed.

MANNING T. SMITH, Plaintiff in Error, *v.* HIRAM M. TRIMBLE, and ELISHA LINDER, Defendants in Error.

ERROR TO COLES.

If a non-resident is proceeded against by publication in a chancery cause, the court does not acquire jurisdiction over his person, unless a summons has been regularly issued, and returned by the sheriff.

The absence of a summons from the record, cannot be supplied by the return of a certificate of the clerk to a writ of *certiorari*, that there had been a summons which was lost, nor by the recital in the notice of publication, that it had been issued.

Upon a writ of error, this court looks only to the transcript of the record. If papers have been lost from the files or mutilated, they may be supplied in some cases by the Circuit Court upon satisfactory evidence, after a proper notice to the opposite party. This court has no authority to permit a party to supply, by proof, any part of the record.

When a bill is taken as confessed, the court may, in its discretion, require proof as to all or any portion of the allegations in the bill, and the evidence need not be preserved in the record, or it may render a decree on the *pro confesso* order without evidence.

A decree should ascertain the precise amount to be paid, and not leave it to computation.

IN July, 1859, a bill for injunction was filed by Trimble and Linder against Smith, charging that on the 1st day of January, 1857, they were indebted to Smith about two thousand dollars, being balance of purchase money for lands purchased by them of Smith, for which they gave their notes to Smith for about one thousand dollars each. That at that date, Trimble and Smith made a settlement of their individual indebtedness, and Smith was found indebted to Trimble in the sum of about $720, and Smith thereupon executed a written statement and delivered it to Trimble, showing the amount due, and containing mutual stipulations that said sum of $720 should be credited upon one of said joint notes.

The bill further charges, that Smith afterwards obtained a judgment upon the other note, for $792.52 costs, being the balance then due on said note; sued out execution and sold [*153] part of said land, and became the purchaser; and that the time of redemption would expire in October, 1859. That before the levy of said execution on said land, Trimble had sold his interest in the land to Linder, the other complainant, and Linder accounted to Trimble for said sum of $720, as so much money paid on joint account, supposing said sum of $720 had been credited on said note.

The bill further charges, that said Smith did not credit said sum of $720 on said note, but assigned it before it was due for a valuable consideration, and the assignees had brought suit on the note.

The bill prays that Smith may be made defendant, and enjoined from recovering on his judgment more than shall remain after deducting $720 and interest, and that complainant Linder may redeem said lands by paying said remainder, and that the sheriff may be enjoined from collecting any more, and from making a deed.

The injunction was granted by the master in chancery, and publication made as in case of non-residence. But no copy of affidavit of non-residence of Smith is on record, nor was any summons issued against him, nor any appearance made by him.

At some time, not specified in the record, a decree *pro confesso* was rendered, and cause submitted for final decree. Whereupon the court decreed a perpetual injunction for the sum of $525, part of said sum of $720, and that Linder pay the balance of said judgment and costs, being the sum of $ to said Smith, or the sheriff of Coles county, within twenty days from rendition of decree, and that all proceedings by Smith or said sheriff, under said execution, be enjoined.

M. C. McLAIN, and JAMES C. CONKLING, for Plaintiff in Error.

C. H. CONSTABLE, for Defendants in Error.

184

WALKER, J. It nowhere appears, in this record, that a summons was ever issued, in the case. A copy is not given in the transcript, nor does the *pro confesso* order or final decree find that one was ever issued. It has been repeatedly held by this court, and it must be regarded as the settled practice, that there must have been a summons issued, and it must be returned by the sheriff, or the defendant must have entered his appearance, to sustain a decree against a non-resident defendant. If a non-resident is proceeded against by publication, the court does not acquire jurisdiction, unless a summons has been regularly issued and returned by the sheriff. *Jacobs* v. *Smith*, 14 [*154] Ill. 359; *Randall* v. *Songer*, 16 Ill. 27; *McDaniel* v. *Correll*, 19 Ill. 226; *Chickering* v. *Failes*, 26 Ill. 507. The want of a summons in this case cannot be supplied by the return of a certificate of the clerk to a writ of *certiorari*, that there had been a summons, which was lost, nor by the recital in the notice of publication that it had been issued. We can look alone to the transcript of the record, nor have we any authority to permit the party to supply, by proof, any part of the record.

If any power exists to supply a portion of the record, it is in the Circuit Court, and not in this. We can only try the case on the record of that court. The Circuit Court has the power in some cases, and probably has in such a case as this, upon proper notice to the opposite party, and upon clear and satisfactory evidence, to supply any portion of the record which has been lost or mutilated.

It is insisted that the evidence upon which the court below acted, is not preserved in a bill of exceptions or by a certificate of the presiding judge. This bill was taken as confessed, and, consequently, the rule requiring the evidence to be preserved in the record, has no application in this case. When a bill is taken as confessed, the court trying the cause may, in its discretion, require proof as to all or to any portion of the allegations of the bill, or render a decree on the *pro confesso* order, without evidence.

The decree should have ascertained the precise amount that was required to be paid, and not left it to computation. Had this been the only error in this record, the decree might have been modified in this court, but owing to the want of jurisdiction of the court below, over the person of the defendant, either by actual or constructive service, the decree of that court is reversed, and the cause remanded.

Judgment reversed.

GERSHAM MONAHON, ISABELLA MONAHON, his Wife, and DEWITT C. ROBERTSON, Heirs at Law of Simon Robertson, deceased, Plaintiffs in Error, *v.* JOHN VANDYKE, Administrator of Simon Robertson, deceased, Defendant in Error.

ERROR TO COLES.

Proceedings for the sale of land by an administrator will be reversed, if the record does not show any petition by the administrator.

[*155] It is error for the Circuit Court to order a sale of land by an administrator, when the notice has been published but thirty days, while the statute requires a publication for six weeks, before the presentation of the petition.

THIS was an application by an administrator to sell real estate to pay debts. There does not appear, from the record, to have been any petition filed in the case. The first entry upon the record was made at the October term, A. D. 1843, of the Coles Circuit Court, on the 23rd day of October, and is as follows:

JOHN VANDYKE, Adm'r of Simon Robertson, dec'd. ⎱ In Chancery.
　　Petition to sell real estate. 　　　　　⎰

This day came the petitioner, by J. W. Ross, his solicitor, and on his motion, it is ordered that Albert Compton be appointed guardian *ad litem* for the infant heirs in said complainant's bill mentioned, who came into the court and waived the service of process and filed his answer herein, and it appearing to the satisfaction of the court that due notice of the pendency of this suit has been given by publication in the Charleston Courier; and it also appearing that the personal estate is insufficient to pay the debts of the decedent; it is therefore ordered, adjudged and decreed by the court here, that the administrator be authorized and required to sell (here follows a description of the property), or so much thereof as will be sufficient to pay the balance of the said claims against said estate, and that he make the report thereof to the next term of this said court, to which this cause is continued.

The following answer of the guardian *ad litem* appears upon file:

"Answer of George W. Robertson, DeWitt C. Robertson, Izabel H. Robertson, William Robertson and Abigail Robertson, by Albert Compton, the guardian *ad litem*.

"And the said infants, by their guardian *ad litem*, Albert Compton, came, and for answer in respect of a certain petition presented by John Vandyke, administrator of Simon Robertson, deceased, to the Coles Circuit Court, for the sale of the real estate of said intestate in Cumberland county and State of Illinois, say that they are ignorant of the premises in that behalf, and pray the court to protect their rights." (Signed by the infant heirs, by their guardian *ad litem*.)

The following notice appears on file:

"Notice is hereby given, that a petition will be presented to the Judge of the Coles Circuit, to be holden in the town of Charleston, Coles county, State of Illinois, on the 4th Monday in the month of October, A. D. 1843, for a decree to sell the following land belonging to the estate of Simon Robertson, deceased, lying in the county of Cumberland and State of Illinois, to wit: (here follows a description of the [*156] property), for the purpose of paying the debts of said estate, the personal estate being insufficient to pay the same; at which time and place, all persons feeling themselves interested are requested to attend and show cause, if any they have, why the prayer of said petition shall not be granted. September 23rd, 1843.

JOHN VANDYKE, Adm'r.

Certified to by W. W. Bishop, publisher.

The cause was continued from term to term, until the October term, A. D. 1844, when the following entry was made:

JOHN VANDYKE, Adm'r, etc.,
vs.   } Petition to sell land.
THE HEIRS OF SIMON ROBERTSON, deceased.

This day came the petitioner, by J. W. Ross, his solicitor, and filed his report herein, which is approved, ordered to be filed, and continued until the next term of this court for further report.

At the subsequent term of the said court the said cause was continued until the next term of the court, and thence from term to term, until the May term, A. D. 1847, when it was continued until the next term, but it does not appear since that time to have been upon the docket.

The following is the report of sale on file:

"To the Honorable Circuit Court, within and for the county of Coles and State of Illinois, in chancery sitting: The undersigned would report to this court, that in pursuance of, and in obedience to a decree entered at the October term, 1843, of this court, decreeing and ordering the undersigned, as administrator of the estate of Simon Robertson, deceased, to sell and convey at public sale, to the highest and best bidder, according to law, the real estate following, to wit: (here follows a description of the land sold), with other lands therein described, he did, under the authority of the aforesaid decree, on the 6th day of January, A. D. 1844, in the town of Greenup. having given previous lawful notice, between the hours of 10 o'clock a. m., and 5 o'clock p. m., sell at public vendue the west half of south-east quarter of Section 1, Town 9 north, Range 9 east, to Jeremiah Armstrong, who bid therefor the sum of one hundred dollars, he being the highest and best bidder; also the west half of north-east quarter of Section 1, Town 9 north, Range 9 east, to said Armstrong, who bid therefor one hundred and seventy-six dollars and seventy-five cents, he being the highest and best bidder for the same; also, the south-east of south-east quarter of Section 22, Town 9 north, Range 9 east, to William E. Smith, who bid for the same fifty dollars, [*157] he being the highest and best bidder. The undersigned would further report, that on the 18th day of May, 1844, having given previous lawful notice, authorized as aforesaid, he sold at public sale in the town of Greenup, the said lots Nos. 44 and 45, in the town of Greenup, to James Ewart, who bid for the same one hundred and twenty-six dollars, that being the highest and best bid; also, the said lot No. 46, for seventeen dollars and fifty cents, to J. H. Williams, he being the highest and best bidder for the same; also, the south-west quarter of the north-east quarter of Section 24, Town 9 north, Range 9 east, to William Wade, who bid for the same sixty dollars, that being the highest and best bid. That the above sales were made on a credit of nine months, and that deeds have been executed and delivered to each of the respective purchasers for the land by him purchased, pursuant to the authority of the aforesaid decree ordering the sale of the same.

JOHN VANDYKE, Adm'r of Simon Robertson.

The following are the errors assigned:

1. The court erred in rendering a decree ordering the sale of lands, in this: because there was no petition filed; because there was no proof showing an indebtedness, or the nature or the amount thereof; and because there was no sufficient notice to the parties interested, of the application for such decree.

2. The court erred in approving the sale of lands, in this: because the administrator did not give the notice required by law; because the administrator sold the land at a place not authorized by the decree, or the law of the land; because the administrator sold the land at a ruinous sacrifice; because the administrator sold more land than was necessary to supply the deficiency of the personal estate; and because the administrator sold the land upon a credit, not authorized by law, or the decree of the court.

3. The decree was not authorized by the pleadings and proofs in the case.

4. The decree of the court authorizing the sale of the land and approving the administrator's report of sale, was fraudulent, and contrary to law and equity.

5. The decree of the court is too vague, indefinite and uncertain, to authorize the proceedings thereon by the administrator.

C. H. CONSTABLE, and JOHN SCHOLFIELD, for Plaintiffs in Error.

O. B. FICKLIN, for Defendants in Error.

[*158] CATON, C. J.   There are several errors, for which this order must be reversed.   In the first place, we find no evidence in the record that any petition was ever filed.   This is made necessary by the statute, and without it the court could not legally make any order in such a case.

Also, the notice was insufficient.   The first insertion was but thirty days before the order was made, while the statute requires six weeks, before the presentation of the petition.

We might enumerate other irregularities, but it is quite unnecessary.

The order is reversed, and the cause remanded.

Judgment reversed.

CANFIELD S. HAMILTON, Plaintiff in Error, *v.* ARTOIS HAMILTON, Defendant in Error.

ERROR TO HANCOCK.

The statute requires that an instrument submitting a matter to arbitration, should be under seal.   The seal is an indispensable formality, and without it the court cannot enter judgment on the award.

Where an instrument submitting a matter to arbitration was recited in the record, as a bond, and the instrument and execution of it were fully set out, by which it appeared that there were no seals to the signatures, the Supreme Court could not intend that it was a sealed instrument.   If only the body of the bond had been set out in the record, the court might presume that it was properly executed.

THIS was a motion by the defendant in error to the Circuit Court of Hancock county, SIBLEY, Judge, presiding, for judgment upon an award of arbitrators.

The court allowed the motion, and entered judgment on the award against the plaintiff in error, who brings the cause to this court.

The opinion of the Court contains a full statement of the case.

WILLIAMS & GRIMSHAW, and GEORGE EDMUNDS, JR., for Plaintiff in Error.

WHEAT & GROVER, for Defendant in Error.

BREESE, J. This case originated in the Hancock Circuit Court, on a motion for judgment on a certain award.

The record recites as follows:

" And now this motion coming on for a hearing on the submission to arbitrators, the award of arbitrators, evidence, and arguments of counsel, and it appearing to the court that [*159] the said parties did, on the nineteenth day of September, one thousand eight hundred and fifty-four, enter into arbitration bonds, each to the other respectively; the bond of said Canfield S. Hamilton to said Artois Hamilton being in the words and figures following, to wit: Know all men by these presents, that I, Canfield S. Hamilton, am held and firmly bound unto Artois Hamilton, in the sum of three thousand dollars, to be paid to the said Artois Hamilton, his certain attorney, executors, administrators, or assigns, for which payment I bind myself, my heirs, etc., firmly by these presents. Sealed with my seal. Dated July 19, 1854.

" The condition of this obligation to such, that if the above bounden Canfield S. Hamilton, his heirs, etc., shall well and truly stand to, obey, abide, observe, perform, fulfill, and keep, the awards, orders, arbitrament final, and determination of Squire R. Davis, Richard Cannon, and Joab Green, or a majority of them, arbitrators, chosen by said parties to arbitrate, etc., to arbitrate and determine of and concerning certain matters of account between them, and also, all actions and causes of action, suits, bonds, specialties, judgments, executions, accounts, recoveries, quarrels, controversies, trespasses, damages and demands, whatsoever, both at law and in equity, at any time hereafter had, moved, brought, commenced, sued, prosecuted, done, suffered, committed, or depending, by and between said parties, so as the said award be made in writing, and so as said arbitrators commence said arbitration on Sept. 19, 1854, in the town of Carthage, then this obligation to be void, etc.

"And said Canfield S. Hamilton consents and agrees that said submission shall be made a rule of the Hancock Circuit Court.

CANFIELD S. HAMILTON."

" Signed, sealed, and delivered in presence of C. R. SCOFIELD.

A similar writing was executed by the other party, Artois Hamilton.

The statute regulating arbitrations and awards, provides for two descriptions of cases which parties may submit to arbitration. The one is, when persons, having the legal capacity, by an instrument in writing to be signed and sealed by them, and attested by at least one witness, submit to one or more arbitrators, any controversy existing between them, not in suit, and may agree in such submission, that a judgment of any court of record competent to have jurisdiction of the subject matter to be named in the instrument, shall be rendered upon the award [*160] made pursuant to the submission; and the other is, when a suit is pending in any court of record, the parties to it may submit the matters involved in the suit to the decision of arbitrators, whereupon an order of court is entered directing the submission to three impartial and competent persons, to be named in the order. Upon the award of the arbitrators, the court may enter up judgment as on the verdict of a jury. (Scates' Comp. 209.)

These are the only cases in which a court has jurisdiction to enter a final judgment upon an award of arbitrators. In all other cases of submission to arbitrators, the parties must be left to their common law remedies.

It is argued by the defendant's counsel, that this court must intend the instrument of submission was a sealed instrument, because, in the record it is recited as a bond, and that is well understood as being an instrument in writing under seal.

The record sets out, not only the body of the bond, but the manner of its execution also, and that shows there was no seal to it, but it is attested by one witness. If the body of the bond had alone been set out, as in *Cabell* v. *Vaughan*, 1 Saunders' R. 291, we might well say the Circuit Court found the instrument of submission to be a bond or writing under seal, and so properly executed, but the execution of it being also set out, and showing no seal, we must hold that it is defective for want of a seal, and not such an instrument as is provided for in the statute to which reference has been made. The seal is an indispensable formality, in order to give the court jurisdiction to enter a judgment on the award. This court has as much power to dispense with the requirement that the submission shall be in writing, as to dispense with the seal and subscribing witness. We can do neither—the statute must be obeyed.

The judgment is reversed, and the cause remanded.

Judgment reversed.

HENRY McHENRY, Plaintiff in Error, *v.* ELIZABETH YOKUM, and JESSE YOKUM, Administrators of Mathias Yokum, deceased, Defendants in Error.

ERROR TO MENARD.

A note was given for a piece of land which the payee conveyed by a warranty deed. Subsequently a right of dower was recovered against the land *Held*, that in an action upon the note, the value of this dower right could be set off as a partial failure of consideration.

The tables showing the probabilities of life, by which the value of dower [*161] rights can be computed, are recognized by the courts as the proper means of proving such value.

PLAINTIFF filed his note, payable to himself, signed by Mathias Yokum, for $1,485.40, with ten per cent. per annum from July 1st, 1854, in the court of probate in and for the county of Menard and State of Illinois, for adjustment, with a credit thereon, June 5, 1855, of $900. The defendants, as administrators, plead a set off in this: That said note was given for and in consideration for certain land deeded by plaintiff to Mathias Yokum, with full covenants; and that one Mrs. Penny had claimed and sustained her right of dower in and to the lands aforesaid, and her right of dower had, by order of the said court, been assigned, to the damage of said Mathias Yokum, in his lifetime, and to the administrators, etc., the full amount of said note. Thereupon the plaintiff demurred to said plea, and the probate court sustained the plaintiff's demurrer, and the defendants refusing to answer over, the court rendered judgment for plaintiff, for $1,053.20, from which judgment the defendants prayed an appeal to the Circuit Court.

A jury was waived, and trial by the court. Plaintiff introduced the note, and proved its execution. "One day after date, I promise to pay Henry McHenry or order, fourteen hundred and eighty-five dollars and forty cents, with ten per cent. interest from date until paid, this the first day of July, 1854. (Signed) Mathias Yokum." On the back of the note was the following indorsement: "June 5th, 1855, received $900 on the within note." And the plaintiff proved that the defendants were the administrators of Mathias Yokum, the maker of said note. As to the above facts there was no controversy or objection.

The defendants then proposed to introduce the said deed as evidence, to which the plaintiff objected. Objection overruled, and plaintiff excepted. The defendants then proved the note to have been given for the purchase money for the land mentioned in said deed; and that one Mrs. Penny, widow, seventy years old, had claimed, and by order of court, had dower assigned in the lands in said deed described, and that said dower was worth $350, and that the annual rent of said dower was worth $120. To all the evidence introduced by the defendants, the plaintiff objected; objection overruled, and plaintiff excepted. The court then computed the annual rent of dower from the assignment thereof up to the trial of this cause, at $120 per annum, and the value of said dower at $350, and allowed the same as an offset against said note. To which the [*162] plaintiff objected; objection overruled, and plaintiff excepted.

HERNDON & COWAN, for Plaintiff in Error.

LYMAN LACEY, for Defendants in Error.

CATON, C. J. This note was given for a piece of land which the plaintiff in error conveyed to the maker of the note by a full warranty deed, and it turns out that Mrs. Penny had a dower interest in the premises. Mrs. Penny was seventy years of age. The annual value of the dower was one hundred and twenty dollars, and the whole value of the dower was computed at three hundred and fifty dollars. And to this extent the defendant insisted the consideration of the note had failed; and we confess ourselves entirely unable to appreciate any reason why it is not so. He did not get all that he gave his note for, and to the value of that for which he gave the note and did not get, has the consideration failed. Had he got no title at all, then the whole consideration of the note had failed, and he was not bound to pay the notes and then rely upon his covenant of warranty to indemnify himself. This we have often decided, and the same principle has been applied where the consideration has partially failed.

But the plaintiff thinks it impossible to compute the exact value of this dower interest, so as to determine the extent to which the consideration has failed. The proof clearly shows what was the annual value of the dower and the age of the doweress. From this it is as easy to compute the cash value of the dower, as it is the interest on a note of hand, from tables which have been formed with great care, from well established facts, and these tables are recognized and acted upon by all courts, at least in this country and in England, whenever occasion requires.

We have no doubt the decision of the court was correct, and its judgment must be affirmed.

Judgment affirmed.

WILLIAM KERNEY, Appellant, *v.* CHARLES GARDNER, Appellee.

APPEAL FROM FULTON.

An agreement by a party to convey all his title, etc., to land, is a sufficient consideration for a note. If the party giving the note desires more than a quit claim deed, he should make his bargain accordingly.

Proof of a tender, though not of that clear and satisfactory character [*163] which convinces the mind beyond doubt, will be held sufficient.

THIS was an action of debt, commenced by Gardner and tried in his lifetime, against Kerney, for the September term, 1859, of the Fulton Circuit Court, on a promissory note. The declaration contains one special count and common counts for work and labor, for money paid, laid out, etc., and on account stated. The descriptive part of the special count is as follows:

"For that whereas the said defendant, heretofore, to wit, on the 8th day of August, A. D. 1851, at and within the county of Fulton and State of Illinois, made his certain promissory note in writing, bearing date a certain day and year therein mentioned, to wit, the day and year aforesaid, and then and there delivered the said note to the said plaintiff, by which said note the said defendant then and there promised to pay, one year after the date thereof, to the said plaintiff or order, the sum of two hundred and seventy-six dollars, with interest at ten per cent. per annum from date, for value received. By means whereof," etc. Here follows the breach.

At the September term, 1859, the defendant plead the general issue, and, at the September term, 1860, three special pleas, the first two of which are as follows, after the title of the cause, etc.:

"And the said defendant, for further plea to the plaintiff's declaration, says *actio non*, because he says, that the promissory note sued on, and in said declaration mentioned, was given for the balance of the purchase money of a certain tract of land described as the south-west quarter of section thirty-four, in township four north, of range three east of the fourth principal meridian, sold by Charles Gardner, the plaintiff herein, to the defendant, for the sum of three hundred and nine dollars; and at the same time of the execution of said note, and in consideration of the execution and delivery of said note, the said Charles Gardner, plaintiff herein, executed and delivered his agreement in writing, bearing date on the same day of said note, and thereby agreed to and with the said defendant to convey to him, the said defendant, all the right and title of him, the said Charles Gardner, to the tract of land aforesaid, upon the payment by the said defendant to the said plaintiff or order, the said sum of three hundred and nine dollars, in one year after the date thereof, and if such payment was not made, the said agreement was to be null and void. And the said defendant avers, that the said Charles Gardner has not conveyed his interest and title in said tract of land, or any part thereof, or offered to convey the same, to the defendant; but on the [*164] contrary, no deed or conveyance whatever has been made or offered to the defendant in performance of said contract. Wherefore the consideration of said note has failed; and this the said defendant is ready to verify. Wherefore he prays judgment," etc.

"And for further plea in this behalf to the plaintiff's declaration, the said defendant says *actio non,* because he says, that the consideration and the sole consideration of said note in the said declaration mentioned, was the purchase money agreed to be paid by the defendant to the plaintiff for a tract of land described as aforesaid in the foregoing plea; and the said sum mentioned in the promissory note aforesaid was the full sum to be paid by the defendant for said land. And the said Charles Gardner, plaintiff herein, at the same time of the execution of said note, executed and delivered an agreement in writing to the defendant, bearing even date with said note, and thereby agreed to deed all his (said Gardner's) right and title to the south-west quarter of section thirty-four, the tract aforesaid, to the said defendant, provided the said defendant paid to the said Charles Gardner, or order, the sum of three hundred and nine dollars (the said sum of three hundred and nine dollars being inserted in said agreement instead of the sum specified in said promissory note,) in one year from the date thereof, with the stipulation that if the said sum was not paid, the agreement was to be null and void. And the defendant avers, that the covenants to pay the amount of money in said promissory note, and to convey said land, were mutual and dependent, to be performed at the same time. And the defendant avers, that the said plaintiff has broken the agreement on his part to be performed, in this, that he never conveyed the said premises, or any part thereof, or offered to convey the same to the defendant. And the defendant further avers and says, that the consideration of said promissory note in the declaration mentioned has failed. And this he is ready to verify; wherefore he prays judgment," etc.

On the 26th of February, 1861, (at February term), the

plaintiff entered his stipulation in open court to offer in evidence on the trial only the note referred to in the declaration.

The fourth plea is as follows:

" And for further plea in this behalf, the defendant says *actio non,* because he says, that the said promissory note in the said declaration mentioned was given for the purchase money of a certain tract of land described as the south-west quarter of section thirty-four (34) in township four (4) north, of range [*165] three (3) east, sold by Charles Gardner, the plaintiff herein, to the defendant, William Kerney, by the style of William Kerney; and the said sum mentioned in the promissory note aforesaid was the full sum to be paid by said defendant for said land. And the said Gardner, plaintiff herein, at the same time of the execution of the said promissory note, executed and delivered to the said defendant an agreement in writing, bearing even date with the said note, and thereby agreed to deed all his right and title to the said south-west quarter of section thirty-four, in township four north, of range three east, to the said defendant (by the style of W. Karney) provided the said defendant [using the style of William Karney] should pay said plaintiff or order the sum of three hundred and nine dollars, [the said sum of three hundred and nine dollars being inserted in said agreement, instead of the sum specified in said promissory note,] in one year from the date of said agreement, with the stipulation that if the same should not be paid, the said agreement to be null and void, and which said agreement is in substance as follows:

" ' I, Charles Gardner, of the city of Springfield, Illinois, do hereby agree with William Karney, of Fulton county, Illinois, to deed all my right and title to south-west quarter of section 34, in township 4 north, of range 3 east, to said W. Karney, provided the said William Karney pays to me or order the sum of three hundred and nine dollars in one year from this date; if not paid, this agreement to be null and void, this 8th day of August, 1851.

CHARLES GARDNER.'

" And the said defendant says, that the aforesaid agreement in writing was and is the full and only consideration of and for the said promissory note in said declaration mentioned. And the said defendant further avers, that at the time of the execution and delivery of said promissory note, and of the said agreement in writing, the said real estate in said agreement described was vacant and unoccupied, and without any improvements whatsoever upon the same, and that at the said time the said plaintiff did not have the occupancy or possession of the said real estate, nor did he have any improvements thereon, nor has he ever had any such occupancy, possession or improvements, either before or since the entering into and delivery of the said agreement and promissory note. And the said defendant further avers, that at the time of the making and delivery by said plaintiff to said defendant of said agreement in writing, the said plaintiff did not have any right or title to said real estate in said agreement mentioned, [*166] nor has he had any right or title to such real estate at any time since the execution and delivery of said agreement in writing. And so the said defendant says, that the aforesaid promissory note was made and entered into without any good or valuable consideration. And this the said defendant is ready to verify; wherefore he prays judgment," etc.

To the second and third pleas the plaintiff filed the following replication:

"The said plaintiff, for replication to said defendant's pleas secondly and thirdly above pleaded by him, says *precludi non,* because he says, that the said note declared on in said plaintiff's declaration was given in pursuance of said agreement referred to in said pleas above pleaded, in consideration, as said defendant alleges, of such sale and transfer of the right, title and interest in and to said premises which he, the said plaintiff, had in and to said premises. And said plaintiff avers, that in pursuance of said agreement he caused to be made out a deed in and to said premises, to wit, the south-west quarter of section thirty-four, in township five north, range three east of the fourth principal meridian, on the thirty-first day of March, A. D. 1858, and on the sixteenth day of May, A. D. 1859, before the commencement of this cause, he caused said deed, so made as aforesaid, to be tendered to said defendant, to wit, on the day and year aforesaid. And of this the said plaintiff puts himself upon the country."

To the fourth plea the plaintiff filed a general demurrer, which was sustained by the court, and the defendant abided by the plea.

The issues, by consent of parties, were tried by the court, BAILEY, Judge, presiding, a jury having been waived.

On the trial, the plaintiff offered in evidence an instrument copied as follows:

"One year after date, I promise to pay Charles Gardner or order, two hundred and seventy-six dollars, with interest at ten per cent. per annum from date, for value received, this 8th day of August, 1851, as witness my hand and seal. This note is for money loaned. WILLIAM KERNEY." [SEAL.]

The court sustained the objection; whereupon the plaintiff called as a witness, J. Q. A. Jones, who testified, that some years ago he had possession, as a lawyer, of said note, and commenced suit on the same; that during the pendency of the suit, he met defendant in Lewistown several times and spoke to him about the note in witness' hand against defendant (not having the note present, however,) and in favor of Charles Gardner, and that defendant admitted to witness that [*167] he had given a note to said Gardner on a land trade, but stated at the same time that the same was without any consideration whatever, and that he (defendant) had never received any consideration for the note.

On cross-examination, the witness stated that he did not have the note present at any conversation spoken of; that he had never shown the note to defendant, nor had defendant ever seen the same while it was in his hands; that witness did not know but defendant had given several notes to plaintiff Gardner; and that he did not know, further than as stated, that defendant, in such conversation, referred to the note in controversy, but believed he did.

Plaintiff now again offered said note in evidence, to which defendant objected; but the court overruled the objection, and permitted the note to be read in evidence, and defendant excepted.

Plaintiff then called David S. Ray as a witness, who testi

fied, that on the 16th day of May, A. D. 1859, he tendered to the defendant a deed, the original deed introduced; that when he tendered such deed, the defendant refused to receive or accept the same.

On cross-examination, this witness testified that he received the said deed, before tendering the same, of one James Gardner, a brother of the plaintiff, Charles Gardner, and supposed him to be agent of the plaintiff. This supposition of the witness was objected to by defendant as evidence, but the court overruled the objection, and permitted the same to be received as evidence, and defendant excepted.

The witness, on further cross-examination, also stated, that after tendering said deed he returned the same to said James Gardner; that he (witness) never received any authority from the plaintiff to make the tender of said deed, and that he never had any conversation with the plaintiff in regard to said deed or tendering the same.

The plaintiff here offered said deed in evidence, to which defendant objected; but the court overruled the objection, and permitted the deed to be read in evidence, and the defendant excepted.

The plaintiff here rested; and this was all the evidence in the case.

The court thereupon found the issues for the plaintiff, and that he recover $276, debt, and $263.94, damages.

The defendant then moved for a new trial, which was denied.

The case comes to this court by appeal. Gardner's death since the judgment and appeal below, was suggested in this court, and his administrator made a party. The fol- [*168] lowing errors are assigned by Kerney:

1. The Circuit Court erred in sustaining the demurrer to the defendant's third special or fourth plea.

2. The court below on the trial, permitted improper evidence to be admitted and heard.

3. The Circuit Court erred in permitting the note to be read in evidence.

4. The court below erred in permitting the deed to be read in evidence.

5. The finding or verdict below was against the law and the evidence.

6. The Circuit Court erred in refusing to grant a new trial, and in rendering judgment.

7. The record and proceedings are otherwise informal, defective, erroneous and insufficient.

JUDD, BOYD & JAMES, for Appellant.

M. HAY, for Appellee.

WALKER, J. The first question which we propose to consider, is, whether the demurrer was properly sustained, to defendant's fourth plea. It averred, that the note sued upon, was given for the purchase money, on the sale of S. W. 34, T. 3 N., R. 3 E. of the fourth principal meridian, which was sold by appellee to appellant. That at the time the note was executed, appellee gave to appellant an agreement of that date, by which he obligated himself to convey all of his right and title in the land, to appellant, provided he should pay to him the sum of three hundred and nine dollars, which sum was inserted in the agreement instead of the amount specified in the note, within one year from that date. The plea further avers, that there was no other consideration for the execution of the note, and that when the note and agreement were executed, the land was vacant and unoccupied, and appellee did not have possession, or improvements thereon, nor has he ever had possession before or since making the agreement and note. And that appellee at the time had no right or title to the land, nor has he had since executing the agreement and note.

There is no covenant for title contained in the agreement described in the plea. Nor does it show any agreement to convey the land, but simply to convey all the right and title which he then had. If he had no title, there could be no failure of the consideration, as appellant by the agreement, [*169] assumed the risk of the want of title, in appellee. If he had been unwilling to risk such a title as appellee had, he should have refused to purchase, or he should have contracted for covenants of title, in the conveyance he was to receive.

But having contracted for such title only as appellee had, he has no right to insist upon anything more. That title, such as it was, constituted a sufficient consideration to support the note. A release or quit claim deed is all that is required by the contract. Such a deed fully answers its conditions.

It is again insisted, that as the note was rejected as evidence under the special count, because of variance, that it was improperly admitted under the common counts, its execution not having been sufficiently proved. Jones testified that some years previous to the trial, he had commenced suit on the note, and during its pendency, he spoke to appellant in reference to it, and that he admitted that he had given the note to appellee in a land trade, but stated that it was without consideration. That he, witness, had not shown the note to appellant. Does this evidence identify the note, and prove its execution? We think it does. The suit was pending, and a copy of the note was no doubt on file, or it was at least described in the declaration. It seems to be agreed by all parties, that this note was given for the purchase of this land, and no other appears to have been given to appellee. Appellant must have known that this was the note sued upon, as he said it was given in a land trade.

It is also urged, that the same evidence which proves the execution of the note, also proves that it was given without consideration. This evidence was heard on a preliminary question, and not upon the main issue in the case. That portion of the admission which related to the want of consideration, was not pertinent to the issue then being tried, and it was not introduced on the trial.

The next question is, whether the tender of the deed by Ray, was sufficient to authorize the maintenance of the suit. He testified that he received the deed from appellee's brother, and tendered it to appellant, who refused to receive it. He also says, that after tendering the deed, he returned it to James Gardner, of whom he had received it, but never had any conversation with appellee, in reference to the deed, nor did he receive authority from him to make the tender. The fact that the deed is found in the hands of appellee, after being in the hands of the others, and that they had previously had it, all

Kerney *v.* Gardner.

strongly tends to prove that appellee's brother had received the deed to be tendered to appellant. It can hardly be supposed that James Gardner would be in possession of this deed executed [*170] by his brother, and making a tender through Ray without authority. Appellant had the opportunity of receiving the deed, but rejected it, and although the evidence is not of that clear and satisfactory character which convinces the mind beyond doubt, yet we think it was sufficient, from which a tender might be inferred.

It is likewise objected, that the deed does not purport to convey the land.to appellant. After having carefully inspected the deed itself, we find that the name "Kerney" is not very legibly written, but seems to have been spelled with an "a," which is blotted. It however cannot well be made to spell any other than appellant's name. We are of the opinion that this objection is not well taken.

It is in the last place urged, that the deed should have contained covenants against the acts of appellee, after entering into the contract, and before the conveyance was made. The contract calls for no such covenant, and the court has no power to make agreements for the parties. If such acts had been done by appellee, as divested or incumbered his title, appellant should have shown it. The law will not presume that he has violated his agreement, but if he has, the other party must establish the fact. There was no proof that any change had occurred in the title after the sale was made, and when the complainant tendered the deed he fully complied with his agreement.

Upon this entire record, we perceive no error requiring the reversal of the judgment of the court below, and the same is affirmed.

Judgment affirmed.

JANUARY TERM, 1862. 170

Casselberry *v.* Forquer. Same *v.* Same. Same *v.* Same. Same *v.* Same.

CHARLES CASSELBERRY, Appellant, *v.* SUSANNAH FORQUER, Appellee.
THE SAME *v.* THE SAME.
THE SAME *v.* THE SAME.
THE SAME *v.* THE SAME.

APPEALS FROM ST. CLAIR.

A party cannot bring separate suits for several sums past due on a lease; if more than one payment is due, these payments should be consolidated into one suit.

A party cannot divide an entire demand, so as to maintain several actions for its recovery.

ON the 24th of May, 1854, Casselberry leased from [*171] William Forquer certain land in St. Clair county, for three years, for $150 a year, one-half payable semi-annually on the 25th of December and March ensuing. On the 3rd day of June, 1857, Susannah Forquer brought two suits on said lease, for $75 each, before the same justice of the peace, and filed her accounts, one for rent from 1st of March to 25th December, 1856, the other for rent from 25th December, 1856, to 1st March, 1857. On the 13th of June, 1857, judgments were rendered in each case for $75, and costs, against Casselberry, from which he appealed to the St. Clair Circuit Court. After two more installments were due, to wit, on the 4th of March, 1858, Mrs. Forquer brought a third suit on said lease, before a justice of the peace, and filed her account for rent from March 1st, 1857, to December 25th, 1857, and on the 12th of March, 1858, recovered another judgment for $75, and costs, which was also appealed to said Circuit Court. On the 28th of April, 1858, Mrs. Forquer brought a fourth suit on said lease, before a justice of the peace, and filed her account for rent from December 25th, 1857, to March 1st, 1858. She recovered another judgment for $75, and costs, which was also appealed to said Circuit Court. The cases were continued in said court till the September term, 1859, when they were submitted together to the court for trial.

205

Casselberry *v.* Forquer. Same *v.* Same. Same *v.* Same. Same *v.* Same.

On the trial, Mrs. Forquer introduced in evidence said lease, made by William Forquer to Casselberry. Also, the last will of William Forquer, duly proved and recorded in the County Court of said county, on the 7th of October, 1855, by which he devised to plaintiff said lease. The defendant then produced in evidence a decree in partition in the St. Clair Circuit Court, at its March term, 1856, wherein the parties to this suit, and the heirs and devisees of William Forquer, were complainants or defendants; ordering the sale of the leased premises, among other lands, and a deed made by the commissioners under said decree, of more than one-half of said leased premises to Joseph Vellinger, dated May 31st, 1856. It was admitted that, for a small advance on his purchase, Vellinger conveyed said land to Casselberry, by deed, dated April 27, 1857. Plaintiff below then proved that, after said decree and sales, said decree was reversed in the Supreme Court of this State, in January, 1859. Plaintiff then introduced in evidence the bill in chancery on which said decree was founded.

The court took the cases under advisement, and at the March term, 1860, rendered judgment for $75. and costs, in each case. Casselberry moved for a new trial in each case, because the sev-
[*172] eral findings were contrary to law and to evidence; which motions were severally overruled by the court, and excepted to, and the cases severally appealed to the Supreme Court, and by consent to be heard at Springfield.

All the cases are settled by the following opinion of the Court.

W. H. UNDERWOOD, for Appellant.

N. NILES, for Appellee.

BREESE, J. There is really but one question presented by this record, and that is, the right to sue separately for each of the claims after two of them had become due and payable. The question about the lease, and the rights of these parties under it, cannot be considered, for the court, in the partition case in chancery, the proceedings in which are made part of this case, never had any jurisdiction over the leasehold interest of Susannah Forquer to sell it, and the sale of it was therefore void.

When the several payments reserved by the lease were due, suit could be brought on each payment successively, as they fell due. But if more than one payment be due at the time of suit brought, they must be consolidated into one suit, otherwise a recovery in one could be pleaded in bar of recovery of the other. Here the facts show, that at the institution of each of these suits, two payments, of seventy-five dollars each, were due, and a separate recovery allowed. This cannot be done. In the case of *Camp* v. *Morgan*, 21 Ill. 258, this court said, the doctrine was well settled that a plaintiff cannot so divide an entire demand, or cause of action, as to maintain several actions for its recovery. When these suits were brought, there was an entire demand existing against the defendant in each case, of one hundred and fifty dollars, then due and payable. Suit should have been brought for the entire demand, all of them arising out of the same transaction.

The judgment is reversed, and the cause remanded, with direction to dismiss the several suits.

Judgment reversed

ANTHONY S. SEELY, Plaintiff in Error, *v.* THE [*173] PEOPLE, etc., who sue for the use of Alfred W. Neece, Guardian, etc., Defendants in Error.

AGREED CASE FROM GREENE.

Where a party executes a bond as surety with another, whose name appears to the bond, but which name has been forged, he will not be liable.

THIS was an agreed case, showing that suit was instituted upon the office bond of Lewis W. Leick, master in chancery of Greene county, against Anthony S. Seely, one of the securities thereon, in the name of the People, who sue for the use of Alfred W. Neece, guardian of Jesse H. Neece and Pemnah

Jane Neece. Said bond is payable to the People of the State of Illinois, and conditioned for the faithful discharge of the duties of the office of master in chancery.

The general issue was filed and stipulation thereon, authorizing all proper evidence to be offered thereunder, as though properly pleaded.

It appears, that Leick was nominated master in chancery, and filed the bond sued on, which is in evidence; that Leick collected money belonging to Jesse H. Neece and Pemnah Jane Neece, infants and wards as aforesaid of A. W. Neece; that A. W. Neece, as guardian for said wards, obtained judgment against said Leick, for $138.24; execution returned, no property found.

Samuel Heaton testified, that his name appeared as one of the securities on said bond, and that his name was a forgery thereto. Heaton's name was first in order, assigned and recited in bond. It is admitted that the last of said wards to come of age arrived at age, 25th January, 1860. This suit was instituted March 20th, 1861.

On this evidence, the court below found the issue for the People, for the use of Neece, the cause having been tried by the court without a jury. Defendant below excepted, and moved for a new trial, because said finding was contrary to law and evidence.

JAS. W. ENGLISH, for Plaintiff in Error.

STUART, EDWARDS & BROWN, for Defendants in Error.

CATON, C. J. This action was on the office bond of a master in chancery, against one of the sureties, whose name [*174] appears to the bond. The bond is joint and several. The facts relied upon in defense are these: In the body of the bond are three sureties named—first, Heaton; second, Seely, the defendant; and third, Morrow. When presented to the defendant for his signature, the name of Heaton appeared signed to the bond as a surety; and the defendant, supposing it to have been executed in fact by Heaton, signed his name to the bond as a co-surety with Heaton. It turns out that the name of

Heaton to the bond was a forgery. Although we have not been referred to, nor have we met with, a case precisely in point, yet we think upon principle, this should constitute a good defense to the action on the bond. By a fraud practiced upon the defendant, by means of the commission of a high crime, he was made to assume a different and greater liability than he intended, or supposed he was assuming, when he executed the bond. It is not like the case where the surety, when he signs the bond, is assured, and made to believe that others will afterwards sign it. In that case he acts upon the simple assurance that another will do an act which he knows may be defeated· or prevented by various accidents, and he must therefore take the risk of such assurance being fulfilled. But in this case he acted upon an apparent fact, which without the commission of a great crime by others, must have been true, and the commission of this crime the highest degree of caution might not suggest; and he cannot be charged with even slight neglect, in not having discovered the forgery. It cannot be said that his own credulity contributed in any degree to his being bound without Heaton. instead of with him. It is true that the obligee did not perpetrate, or in any way contribute to the fraud, so that one of two innocent parties must suffer, by reason of this forgery, but that reasonable degree of favor which the law extends to sureties, should exonerate the surety who has been fraudulently induced to execute the bond, not by a false promise, which a high or even a reasonable degree of prudence should have admonished him not to rely upon, but by a forgery, which would probably have deceived the most cautious person.

The judgment must be reversed, and the cause remanded.

Judgment reversed.

[*175] CHARLES SCHUCHMANN, Appellant, *v.* JACOB
KNOEBEL, Executor of William C. Kinney, deceased,
Appellee.

APPEAL FROM ST. CLAIR.

A partial failure of consideration may be pleaded to a promissory note given
for the purchase of land.

A party may also *recoup* in an action upon a note given for land, what he
has been compelled to pay in order to remove an incumbrance upon the
land.

THIS was action of debt, brought by Knoebel, executor,
etc., upon a promissory note under seal, made by Schuchmann,
dated February 24, 1858, for $2,200, payable to Wm. C.
Kinney two years after date, with interest, etc.

To this declaration Schuchmann pleaded, First, As to part
of the consideration of the writing obligatory sued on, that
before and at the time of making the same, Kinney sold and
conveyed to Schuchmann, by deed in fee simple, certain lands
in said county therein described, and in and by said deed covenanted, among other things, that said land was free from all
incumbrances. And defendant, in consideration of said conveyance and said covenant, then and there agreed to pay said
Kinney $9,000, a part of which was the sum mentioned in
the writing obligatory sued on, and the residue of said purchase money had been paid by Schuchmann. That at and
before said sale, the said lands were subject to the lien of a
judgment in said St. Clair Circuit Court, in favor of Ewald
Massow, and against the said Kinney and others, upon which
judgment an execution issued in due form of law, dated January 4th, 1858; and afterwards, to wit, on the 27th of March,
1858, after due notice the said first described tract was sold
by the sheriff of said county, in due form of law, to said
Massow, under said execution, for the sum of $1,093.99; and
afterwards, to wit, on the 26th of May, 1858, Schuchmann, as
subsequent purchaser from said Kinney, was obliged to pay

to the sheriff of said county, and did pay to him, $1,112.98, to redeem said land, from said sale. Defendant further averred, that at and before the execution of said writing obligatory sued on, and of said deed, the said lands were subject to an incumbrance of $30.61, for the state, county and special taxes, for the year 1857, and the said Schuchmann, after the date of said deed, was obliged to pay, and did pay, said taxes, to wit, on, etc., at, etc., aforesaid. Defendant further averred, that at the execution of the said writing obligatory and said deed, the said tracts of land were subject to a mortgage lien, dated August 23rd, 1851, and filed for [*176] record in the recorder's office in said county, on the 23rd of August, 1851, executed by the said Kinney and wife to the trustees of Shurtleff College, a corporation in said State, to secure the payment of a promissory note made by said Kinney to said trustees for the payment of $1,025, payable on or before the 1st of September, 1853, in the bonds or internal improvement script of the State of Illinois, the said bonds or script bearing interest on their face from the date prior to 1842, and engaging to pay to the order of said trustees, or their successors, the sum of fifty dollars cash annually by way of interest; and the said Schuchmann was necessarily obliged to pay, and did pay, to extinguish said mortgage, a large sum of money, to wit, $1,060, to wit, on the 24th day of February, 1859, at the county aforesaid, and before the commencement of this suit; wherefore defendant says that the consideration of the said writing obligatory has failed to the extent of the sums so paid by said defendant as aforesaid, etc.

Second plea. Set-off for $3,000, money paid by Schuchmann for Kinney in his lifetime at his request.

Third plea. That the writing obligatory sued on, was given to said Kinney in his lifetime, as part of the consideration for certain real estate mentioned in said first plea, which real estate was sold, etc., by said Kinney to said Schuchmann at the time, for the consideration and in the manner and form mentioned in said first plea; and by his deed therein mentioned, the said Kinney covenanted that said real estate was free from all incumbrances. Said plea avers that, at the time of making said deed, said real estate was not free from all incumbrances, but on the contrary, that said real estate was incumbered in manner and form as stated in said first plea; by reason whereof said defendant had been obliged to expend, and had expended the said sums of money mentioned in said first plea, in manner and form as therein stated, in extinguishing said incumbrances. And that neither said Kinney in his lifetime or said plaintiff, his executor, since his death, had kept said covenant, but they have broken the same, to the damage of said Schuchmann of $4,000, which the plea proposes to set off against the debt and damages sued for, etc.

Fourth plea. Payment in the usual form.

Plaintiff traversed second and fourth pleas, and demurred to first and third pleas, which demurrer was sustained by the court.

On the trial before the court, plaintiff below introduced the writing obligatory sued on, credited with $1,241, being the [*177] amount of the Massow judgment mentioned in first plea, paid by Schuchmann. Defendant introduced in evidence the deed, with covenant against incumbrances, made by Kinney to Schuchmann, as described in defendant's first plea, which deed it was admitted was given for the instrument sued on, and other notes. Defendant further introduced the mortgage, made by Kinney to the trustees of Shurtleff College, as stated in first plea, which was duly recorded in the recorder's office of said county, on the 23rd of August, 1351. Defendant also proved, that the balance due on said mortgage on the 24th of February, 1859, was one thousand and fifty dollars and forty-two cents, which defendant on the day last mentioned paid and satisfied, and extinguished said mortgage. This was all the evidence.

The court excluded the payment of said mortgage, and found for plaintiff the balance due on said writing obligatory, deducting only the credit for amount paid on the Massow judgment. Defendant moved for a new trial, because the finding was contrary to law and to evidence; which motion was overruled by the court, and to which decision of the court Schuchmann excepted. Final judgment was rendered and case appealed to Supreme Court, to be heard by consent at Springfield.

Appellant assigns for error:
That the court below erred in sustaining demurrer to his first and third pleas.

In the finding for plaintiff below, and in excluding the amount paid by appellant to extinguish the mortgage to the Shurtleff College.

In refusing to grant appellant a new trial.

WM. H. UNDERWOOD, for Appellant.

G. TRUMBULL, for Appellee.

BREESE, J. It is not, we conceive, a necessary subject of inquiry here, whether or not the defense set up by the first and third pleas, to which the demurrer was sustained, was permitted at common law. The decisions of the common law courts are not uniform on the point, and a resort to them seems to be unnecessary, inasmuch as our statute allows the defense. The tenth section is in these words: "In any action commenced, or which may hereafter be commenced in any court of law in this State, upon any note, bond, bill or other instrument in writing for the payment of money or property, or the performance of covenants or conditions by the obligee or payee thereof, [*178] if such note, bond, bill or instrument in writing was entered into without a good or valuable consideration; or if the consideration upon which such note, bond, bill or instrument in writing was made or entered into, has wholly or in part failed, it shall be lawful for the defendant or defendants, etc., to plead such want of consideration, or that the consideration has wholly or in part failed, etc., and if it shall appear that the consideration has failed in part, the plaintiff shall recover according to the equity of the case." (Scates' Comp., ch. 73, page 292.)

A part of the consideration for the note sued on, was, that the land sold was free from incumbrances. The pleas allege the fact of the existence of a certain incumbrance by mortgage, which the defendant had to pay and discharge, and thereby extinguish the incumbrance. To the extent then of this incumbrance there was a failure of consideration. *Morgan* v. *Smith*, 11 Ill. 199; *Whisler* v. *Hicks*, 5 Blackford, 100; *Smith et al.*

v. *Ackerman,* ih. 541; *Buell* v. *Tate,* 7 id. 54; *Pomeroy* v. *Burnet,* 8 id. 142.

We think too, the defendant, under the pleadings, might have *recouped* the amount thus paid. *Babcock* v. *Trice,* 18 Ill. 420. There is a natural equity as to claims arising out of the same transaction, that one claim should compensate the other, and that the balance only should be recovered. The damages claimed by the defendant, grow out of the contract for the sale of the land, and present a plain case for *recouping* damages. It is a salutary principle to permit parties to adjust the whole controversy in one action, out of which has grown the doctrine of *recoupment,* and at this day, almost universally applied. The defendant should have been allowed, either under his pleas of partial failure of consideration, or on the principle of *recoupment* under the other pleas, the amount he paid to extinguish the mortgage set out in his plea, and the plaintiff should have had a judgment for the balance only. To enable the defendant to get this allowance, this judgment must be reversed, and the cause remanded.

Judgment reversed.

The Ohio and Mississippi Railroad Company, Appellant, *v.* William Irvin, Appellee.

APPEAL FROM RICHLAND.

The law does not require any different words to be used in proving a case against a railroad company, from those used in ordinary cases; it is only requisite that the mind should be convinced of the existence of the necessary facts.

[*179] The presumption is, that the houses compose a village; if an animal is killed beyond the houses, the presumption is, that it is killed beyond the village; if the town extends beyond the houses, the defendant should show the fact.

Every one is supposed to have some idea of the value of such property as is in general use; and it is not necessary to have a drover or butcher to prove the value of a cow.

THE plaintiff below sued the defendant for the alleged killing of a cow by the trains of defendant. The cause came before the Circuit Court of Richland county, KITCHELL, Judge, presiding, by appeal from a judgment rendered by a justice of the peace. A verdict was recovered in the Circuit Court for the sum of $20. The plaintiff sought to sustain his action upon the statute requiring railroads to fence the lines of their roads. From the judgment of the Circuit Court the defendant below appeals to this court.

The plaintiff below introduced in proof the following testimony:

A. Philhour, being sworn, said: I stood on the platform at the depot; saw the train of the defendant coming in from the east; the cow was standing about one-fourth of a mile from me. I heard the locomotive whistle, and saw the cow knocked off. The road had been in operation six months. The cow was killed by defendant's train of cars at a place where the road should have been fenced. There was no fence there. It was within five miles of a settlement; it was not at a bridge or crossing; don't know whether it was within the limits of a town or not. It was outside of the houses of the town. I knew it was plaintiff's cow.

J. Stephens said: The cow belonged to plaintiff, and was worth twenty dollars.

Errors assigned:

1. There is no proof that the defendant was bound to fence the road, or liable for injuries in the event of not fencing.

2. There is no proof that it was not within the limits of a town, city, or village, that the alleged killing took place, and no proof that it was in any town or county in the State of Illinois.

3. There is no proof of the time when the alleged killing of the cow took place.

4. The proof of value is insufficient and illegal.

5. The court erred in refusing a new trial.

This cause was brought to the Second Grand Division by consent of parties.

215

WILLIAM HOMES, for Appellant.

A. KITCHELL, for Appellee.

[*180] CATON, C. J. This was an action against the railroad company, for killing the plaintiff's cow. The plaintiff relied not upon the negligence of the defendant in running its loco-motive, but upon its neglect to build and maintain a fence, as required by the statute, at the place where the cow was killed. The counsel for the appellant insists, that the proof does not show that at the point where the cow was killed, the company was required by law to keep up a fence. In this we think he is entirely mistaken. The law does not require a stereo-typed set of words to be used, in order to prove a case against a railroad, any more than in any other case. It is ·sufficient, if the testimony is such as reasonably to convince the mind of the existence of the necessary facts. It is said that the proof does not show that the cow was not killed in a town or village. The witness says, it was outside of the houses of the town. The presumption is, that the houses compose the vil-lage, and if the place where the cow was killed was beyond them, it was beyond the village. If the town extended beyond the houses, the defendant should have shown it. The witness did not say that the cow was not killed at a road-crossing, but he did state, that it was at a point where there should have been a fence, and as that could not have been true had there been a road-crossing there, it is sufficient to convince the judgment of a reasonable man, that there was no road-crossing there. But several witnesses swore to the value of the cow, without stating her color, size, age, breed, or other peculi-arities. This was quite consistent with the universal practice of courts, so far as our experience enables us to judge, and it was for the defendant, if it was deemed important, to have in-quired as to these particulars. Every one is presumed to have some idea of the value of property which is in almost universal use, and it is not necessary to show that a witness is a drover or a butcher, before he is allowed to give an opinion of the value of a cow. If it were a steam engine, or a diamond ring, it might be different.

We think the proof abundant to sustain the action, and the judgment must be affirmed.

Judgment affirmed.

JOHN M. ROBINSON, Appellant, *v.* ALVIN OL- [*181]
COTT, Appellee.

APPEAL FROM MACOUPIN.

If the indorsee of a note desires to hold t   indorser liable, he must proceed
to judgment against the maker. at the earliest opportunity. Any negligence or omission in that regard will release the indorser.

THIS was an action of assumpsit brought by the appellee against the appellant, to the September term of the Macoupin Circuit Court, for 1859, upon a promissory note made by one S. D. Martin to said Robinson, bearing date August 26. 1857, due three months after date, for one hundred and forty-two dollars and forty-four cents, and drawing ten per cent. interest per annum after maturity, and by said Robinson indorsed in blank.

The first and second counts in the declaration allege, that when the sum of money in said note specified became due and payable according to the tenor and effect thereof, the said Martin, the maker thereof, was so insolvent that a suit thereon for the collection of the said sum of money therein specified, would have been then and there wholly unavailing, nor has said Martin paid said money. The third count alleges, that the said Olcott, when the said sum of money specified became due and payable, according to the tenor and effect thereof, used due diligence to collect the said sum of money specified in the said note, by the institution and prosecution of a suit at law thereon, for the collection thereof in the Circuit Court of Macoupin county and State of Illinois, to the December term, A. D. 1857, of said court, against the said Martin, maker of said note, which said December term of said court was the first term of said court next after the maturity of said note; and on the 28th day of September, 1858, the said Olcott recovered a judgment on said note against said Martin, in said court, for the sum of one hundred and forty-four dollars and thirty-one cents damages. and also five dollars and seventy cents of costs, and that on the 18th day of October, 1858, then next ensuing, the said Olcott caused an execution to be issued on said judgment to the sheriff of Macoupin county, which said execution was returned by said sheriff, on the 3rd day of February, 1859, "unsatisfied, no property found in my county to levy this execution." To which are added counts for money lent and advanced, and had and received.

To which declaration the said Robinson filed a plea of the [*182] general issue. The cause was continued to the December term, 1860, when on the 28th day of said month, the cause was tried by the court by consent, without the intervention of a jury.

The plaintiff's evidence consists of—

First. The note mentioned in the declaration, and a blank indorsement thereon by the defendant.

Second. A summons issued by the clerk of the Macoupin Circuit Court, dated December 2, 1857, wherein Silas D. Martin is defendant, and Alvin Olcott is plaintiff, which was returned by the sheriff of said county, served December 1st, 1857. Said defendant was served to appear at said court on the second Monday of December, 1857.

Third. A declaration filed in said court, December 4th, 1857, wherein said Olcott is plaintiff, and said Martin is defendant, and in which the plaintiff declares upon the promissory note and indorsement above mentioned in one special count, to which are added the common money counts. On said declaration there is a copy of the note and indorsement sued on in this case.

Fourth. *A. McKim DuBois,* sworn as a witness for plaintiff, testified: That he was clerk of this court during the years 1857 and 1858, and that there is not on file, nor has there been at any time heretofore, any plea, demurrer or other paper filed by Silas D. Martin, nor was there any plea or demurrer or appearance by said Martin whatever, in the case of *Alvin Olcott* v. *S. D. Martin*, commenced at the December term of this court, A. D. 1857, in assumpsit, on note, and that all the papers in said cause have already been offered and read in evidence in this case. Here the plaintiff requested the witness to turn to the docket of the judge of this court for the December term, 1857, and read the entries in the case numbered 262 on said docket. The witness then read the following entries: "*John M. Robinson* v. *Silas D. Martin*, assumpsit." The witness further testified, that the only entry made by the judge of said court on said docket, was entered on the 28th day of December, A. D. 1857, in the words and figures following: "28 continued," and that there was no cause on said docket, of said term, of Alvin Olcott against Silas D. Martin. The witness then read the entries on the judge's docket for the March term, 1858, in said case, in the words and figures following: "No. 159, *Alvin Olcott* v. *Silas D. Martin*, assumpsit." Witness said that this was all the entry in said case at said term of said court, on the docket of the judge thereof, and that said cause was set for the 6th day of said term. The plaintiff then requested the witness to refer to the case numbered seventy-seven, entered on the docket of the judge [*183] of the Macoupin Circuit Court, at the September term, A. D. 1858. The witness then read the entries in the words and figures following: "No. 77, *Alvin Olcott* v. *Silas D. Martin*, assumpsit, judgment by default; clerk to assesses the damages." Witness then testified, that these entries were all that were made on the judge's docket in the case of Olcott against Martin. The plaintiff then read a judgment by default in the same case rendered at the September term, 1858. The witness then testified, that the December term of this court for the year 1857, commenced on the 14th day of December 1857, and ended on the 2nd day of January, 1858, and that the March term therof for the year 1858, commenced on the 22nd day of March A. D. 1858, and ended on the 3rd day of April, 1858.

Fifth. An execution, issued out of the Macoupin Circuit Court, and dated October 18th, 1858, and directed to the sheriff of said county, and commanding him to make of said Martin

$154.31, damages, for said Olcott, and also $5.70 costs. Said execution came to the hands of said sheriff, October 19th, 1858, which was returned by the sheriff on the 3rd day of February, 1860, no property found, and unsatisfied.

This was all the evidence offered by the plaintiff, and here he rested his case.

Jeremiah W. Owings was then called and sworn as a witness in the cause, on the part of the defendant, who testified, that he was acquainted with Silas D. Martin, the maker of the note offered in evidence by the plaintiff in this cause, during the years 1857 and 1858; that Silas D. Martin, during the year 1857, and until January or February, 1858, lived in Gillespie, Macoupin county, State of Illinois, and that said Martin was, during his residence at Gillespie, the owner of a buggy worth thirty dollars, and of about thirty hogs worth four dollars per head, and of two horses worth about one hundred dollars per head; that during that time said Martin was trading a good deal in horses, and sometimes had more than two, but never less than two horses; that all the time while at Gillespie, said Martin was in possession of two town lots in said town, on which he built a large house for a tavern stand, worth from four to five thousand dollars; that said Martin had household furniture during the year 1857, and until the month of January, 1858, at Gillespie aforesaid, to the value of four hundred dollars; that in the month of January or February, 1858, said Martin sold or exchanged said tavern stand and lots in Gillespie for a stock of dry goods in the town of Bunker Hill, in Macoupin county, worth about five thousand dollars; that witness [*184] saw Martin in possession of said goods during the summer of 1858, until the month of August, 1858, and that said Martin was in possession of the storehouse in Bunker Hill, and was doing business in it during that time, and that was the last time witness was at Bunker Hill while said Martin lived in said county; that said Martin left the State in the month of January or February, 1859.

Here the defendant rested his case; and this was all the evidence in the case. And thereupon the court found the issue for the plaintiff. The defendant then entered his motion for a new trial, which was overruled.

HORACE GWIN, JOHN I. RINIKER, and E. SOUTHWORTH, for Appellant.

PALMER & PITMAN, for Appellee.

WALKER, J. This was an action, by the assignee, against the assignor of a promissory note. It appears that suit was instituted against the maker, at the December term, 1857, of the Circuit Court. The summons was served in time for that term, no defense was interposed, or even an appearance entered by the maker of the note, yet the cause was continued, at that and the next succeeding term. Judgment by default was entered at the September term, 1858, and execution issued on the 18th day of October following, which was placed in the hands of the sheriff on the next day. It was returned on the 3rd of February, 1859, no property found, and unsatisfied.

According to the uniform and numerous decisions of this court, this cannot be held to constitute diligence, by the institution and prosecution of a suit. The assignee, to have recourse on the assignor, must, if he relies on diligence by suit, institute legal proceedings against the maker, at the first term after the maturity of the note, and must prosecute it to judgment at the earliest period within his power, and then issue execution without delay. If he, through negligence, permits a term to pass without obtaining judgment, he cannot have recourse on the assignor. If he resorts to legal proceedings, he must prosecute them with vigor, so long as such proceedings promise to be available. There is no averment, in the declaration or proof in the record, that the further prosecution of the suit against the maker at the first term would have been unavailing. On the contrary, the evidence shows that a judgment then recovered could have been collected. No excuse is given for failing to take judgment by default, and as no defense was made, we feel at a loss to see that any can [*185] exist. There is an entire want of diligence in this case, to fix the liability of the assignor.

Under the counts, containing an averment that a suit against the maker would have been unavailing, at the maturity of the note, owing to his insolvency, there appear to be no grounds for a recovery. The evidence, we think, is clear and abundantly satisfactory, that the maker then, and for a long period of time afterwards, was in possession of a large amount of property, liable to execution; much more than enough to have satisfied this judgment. He owned both real and personal property, either of which was amply sufficient to have paid the note, until as late as January, 1858, when he traded a tavern stand for a stock of goods which he held in the county until in August of that year. Had the judgment been obtained, as it might have been, at the term to which the suit was brought, this property could have been subjected to its payment. Then these counts are not sustained by the evidence, but the converse of the proposition is proved.

It would be manifestly unjust, to permit the assignee to hold the note, refuse to employ the requisite means for its collection until the maker, with ample means in his hands, becomes insolvent, and then hold the assignor liable. By the assignment the note becomes his, with the entire right to control its collection, and the assignor has no power to act, and unless the assignee is held to due diligence, he would be at the mercy of the assignor. This the law will not permit.

The judgment of the court below is reversed, and the cause remanded.

Judgment reversed.

The Illinois River Railroad Company, Plaintiff in Error, *v.* Beers & Sims, Defendants in Error.

ERROR TO CASS.

A subscriber to the capital stock of a railroad company, who agrees to be subject to the rules and regulations which may from time to time be adopted by the directors, cannot avoid payment, because the charter has been amended, reducing the number of days of notice to be given, if the amendment of the charter has been accepted.

Amendments to charters may be accepted in divers ways.

THIS was an action for subscription to the capital stock of plaintiff's corporation, on the part of the defendants, as partners.

The third count of the declaration was a general count [*186] upon the subscription, alleging that the defendants, on the first day of January, 1860, were indebted to the plaintiff in the sum of $500 for moneys due and owing on account of five shares of stock held by them in said corporation, and by virtue of divers calls made thereon before that time.

The general issue was pleaded, with leave to give in evidence special matter.

Upon the trial, the plaintiff gave in evidence, without objection, (trial being by the court), an act to construct a railroad from Jacksonville, in Morgan county, to LaSalle, in LaSalle county, Illinois; approved ———— 1st, 1854. (Acts of 1853, p. 53—Private Acts.)

Also, an act to amend the charter of the Illinois River Railroad Company, approved January 29th, 1857. (Acts of 1857, p. 105—Private Acts.)

Also, a further amendatory act, approved February 16, 1857. (Page 859—Private Acts.)

Also, a further amendatory act, approved February 14th, 1859. (Acts of 1859, p. 459—Private Acts.)

Plaintiff then called a witness who swore he was secretary of the company, and he produced the book of record of the company, containing its proceedings, showing the regular organization of the company by various entries therein.

Plaintiff next read in evidence the subscription of the defendants as follows:

" The undersigned, citizens of Cass county, Illinois, respectively subscribe to the capital stock of the Illinois River Railroad Company, to the amount of the number of shares opposite to our names, each share being one hundred dollars, our said subscriptions being subject to the rules and regulations which may from time to time be made by the corporation or directors of said company, but upon condition that each subscriber may, at his own option, be released herefrom, if Virginia should, by a change of the charter, cease to be a point on the road.

NAMES OF SUBSCRIBERS.	NO. SHARES.	AMOUNT $	PAID BY NOTE."
Beers & Sims.	5	500	$50

Plaintiff next read in evidence from the record book, an order adopted by the board of directors, 10th August, 1857.

Order recites that the board, having heretofore made calls upon the subscribers for the payment of a portion of their stock, according to which calls thirty per cent. of the amount subscribed by each subscriber is now due, including what has been paid; and whereas, part of said subscribers have not, as yet, paid the full amount thus due; and whereas, the work [*187] upon the road has been commenced, and the money is needed to pay for such work; and whereas, five per cent. more of said subscription has been called for by this board, which will become due on the first Monday of next September, and also five per cent. on each of the first Mondays of next October, November and December, it is therefore ordered, that each and all of the subscribers pay to the treasurer of said company, or to his agents, at such places as he may designate, on or before the first Monday of next September, thirty-five per cent., that is, the sum of thirty-five dollars, including what has been paid upon each share of one hundred dollars subscribed, and that they also pay to said treasurer, or his agents aforesaid, on each of the first Mondays of October, November and December, five dollars per share, and in default, etc., that the treasurer sue for the same; and it was further ordered, that notice of these calls be given by publication in the Cass County Times and Mason County Herald.

A further order of the board of directors, passed 10th day of November, 1857, was read in evidence, requiring the subscribers, (except those in Tazewell county), to pay on their subscriptions on the first Monday in January, 1858, five dollars per share; and also five dollars per share on the first Monday of each month thereafter, until the whole amount of stock subscribed should be paid in. The subscribers in Morgan and

Cass counties to pay their calls to Thomas Plartee, collector for said company, or his agents, at such places as he should fix upon, and that twenty days' notice should be given by the treasurer, by publication in some newspaper published in Cass and Morgan counties, of the time and place where such payments were to be made.

Also, a further order, passed on the 5th day of January, 1858, by said board of directors, reciting the failure of many of the subscribers to pay the calls that had been made upon their stock, and requiring that the subscribers, (except those in Tazewell county), should pay ten dollars per share on their subscriptions on the first Monday of February next, and ten dollars per share on the first Monday of every subsequent month, until the whole amount respectively subscribed shall be paid in, said payments to be made by the stockholders in Mason county to the treasurer of the company, or his agents, and by the stockholders residing in Morgan and Cass counties, to Thomas Plartee, collector for the company, or his agents, and that twenty days' notice of the time and place of making such payments should be given by personal notice upon the subscribers, or by publication in a newspaper published in the county where the stockholders should reside, and that in default of pay- [*188] ment, suit should be brought, etc. In this order it was further provided, that this call should not invalidate any former call, so as to prevent suit being prosecuted upon such previous calls, " it being the intention of this order to allow suit to be prosecuted either upon any previous call, or upon this call."

The plaintiff next gave in evidence publication of the notices required to be given under each of the foregoing orders for calls to the subscribers in Cass county. The notices set forth the orders respectively for such calls, and accompanying each is an additional notice from the collector designated, and fixing time and place for payment, in pursuance of the calls, and designating agents to whom calls might be paid.

The due publication of these notices in the " Cass County Times," a newspaper published in Cass county, Illinois, was proved. The residence of the defendants in Cass county, Illinois, was also proved. It was further proved, that said defendants voted as stockholders on the 5th of September, 1857, at an election for directors, representing five shares of the stock. The location of the road making Virginia a point, was also proved.

This was all the evidence; and the court upon the evidence rendered judgment for the defendants, on the ground, that there was no proof that ninety days notice of the calls had been given to the defendants, and that the amendatory act of 1857, changing notice of calls to subscribers to twenty days, was unconstitutional; to which plaintiff excepted, and moved for a new trial, which was overruled, and excepted to by plaintiff.

Plaintiff brings the case to this court, and assigns for error, that the court erred in not rendering judgment for plaintiff upon the evidence, and erred in rendering judgment for defendants, and in overruling motion for a new trial.

HAY & CULLOM, for Plaintiff in Error.

BREESE, J. The defendants, by their subscription to the capital stock of the Illinois River Railroad Company, expressly agreed " to be subject to the rules and regulations which might, from time to time, be made by the corporation or directors of the company. By the original charter of the company, granted Feb. 11, 1853—(Session Laws 1853, page 53)—ninety days' notice of calls on stock subscriptions was required. (Sec. 14.)

This charter was amended by the act of January 29, 1857 —(Session Laws, page 105)—the twelfth section of which [*189] provides that twenty days' notice shall be sufficient for such calls, instead of the time required in the original charter, (page 107.) It does not appear when the defendants became subscribers to the stock, nor is it material, the only question being as to the right of the legislature to pass the amendments of 1857, and whether these amendments were adopted by the company and so became a part of its charter. That the legislature can amend a charter, on the application of the company, there can be no doubt. That the amendments of 1857 were accepted by the company, is very clear. As was said in the case of the same plaintiffs against Zimmer, 20 Ill. 661, there are various modes by which amendments to charters may be accepted by corporations, or rather, by which such acceptance may be established, either for or against the corporation. The first, and perhaps the most satisfactory, is when an amendment is asked for in a general meeting of the shareholders, or when an amendment, after it is past, is accepted by a majority in interest at such a meeting. But this is not the only or the most usual mode in this country of accepting amendments to corporate charters. This is generally done by the board of directors, who are for the most part vested with all the corporate powers of the company.

The evidence in this case sufficiently shows, that the board of directors, in making these calls, was acting under this amended charter, and is evidence of acceptance. Being so, it was binding on the defendants, by the express terms of their subscription, they knowing that the company might obtain an amendment to their charter shortening the time.

We see no difference in principle, between this case and that of Zimmer above cited. The court should have found the issue for the plaintiff, for the amount of the calls as proved.

The judgment must be reversed, and the cause remanded for further proceedings not inconsistent with this opinion.

Judgment reversed.

JAMES PULLIAM, Plaintiff in Error, *v.* LUCY OGLE, Defendant in Error.

ERROR TO ST. CLAIR.

In disputed matters about the use of a farm, where the proof leaves the question of right uncertain, the verdict will not be disturbed.

THIS was an action of assumpsit, to recover for the use of a farm, in the St. Clair Circuit Court. There was a trial, [*190] and a judgment against Pulliam for twenty dollars. The plaintiff below, Ogle, was the aunt of defendant.

W. H. UNDERWOOD, for Plaintiff in Error.

G. TRUMBULL, for Defendant in Error.

CATON, C. J. This is a simple question of fact. Was the defendant indebted to the plaintiff for the use of her farm? The testimony shows that he was in possession of it, occupied it and used it for several years; but upon what terms, it does not very satisfactorily appear. He sometimes paid her money, and sometimes she had part of the crop. If she were to be credited with the full value of what the use of the farm is shown to have been worth, and only charged with what she is shown to have received, the balance in her favor would be vastly more than the jury have given her. Probably no accounts were ever kept between the parties, and no exact settlement was ever contemplated. It was a sort of family matter, which, so long as the parties continued on friendly terms, was all very well, but when they quarreled, and each came to look about to see which could rake up the most claims against the other, both found, as is very manifest, that their affairs had been conducted so much in confidence and so loosely, that they could not themselves tell, much less make others understand, how much one owed to or had a right to claim from the other. In such a case, whoever has to decide between the parties, can never be sure he is doing exact justice. It is at best but a guess, and probably the guess of a jury of their neighbors and countrymen, is quite as likely to be right as that of strangers. We cannot say the verdict was wrong, and shall affirm the judgment.

Judgment affirmed.

DANIEL RAYSOR, and MICHAEL Y. GIVLER, Plaintiffs in Error, *v.* THE PEOPLE, Defendants in Error.

ERROR TO MACON.

A recognizance taken out of court, or by a judge at chambers, does not become a record, upon which a *scire facias* can issue, until it is properly certified and filed.

228.

THIS is a proceeding by defendants in error, against [*191] the plaintiffs in error by *sci. fa.*, upon a forfeited recogniz- ance.

The *sci. fa.* alleges that the defendant, Raysor, was, on the 14th day of February, 1859, before Wm. L. Hammer, a justice of the peace, on a charge of perjury, and by said justice was held to bail in the sum of fifteen hundred dollars, and in default thereof was committed to jail.

That on the 23rd day of February, 1859, the said Raysor was before the Hon. Charles Emerson, then judge of the 17th Ju- dicial Circuit, State of Illinois, in pursuance of a writ of *habeas corpus*, for reduction of the amount of said bail, required by the said Wm. L. Hammer; and upon inquiry touching said matter of amount of bail, said judge did make a reduction there- in, and required and ordered bail in the sum of eight hun- dred dollars, in pursuance thereof; and afterwards, to wit, "on the 23rd day of February, 1859, at the county and State afore- said, the said Daniel Raysor, as principal, and Michael Y. Givler, as security, then and there entered into a recognizance jointly and severally binding themselves and their heirs, execu- tors and administrators, for the payment of the said sum of eight hundred dollars, to the People of the State of Illinois, condi- tioned for the appearance of the said Daniel Raysor, on the first day of the then next term of the Circuit Court, to be held in the said county of Macon and State aforesaid, and then and there answer and abide the order of the court touching the said charge of criminal offense for perjury, and thence not depart without lawful permission; which said recognizance was then and there signed by the said Daniel Raysor and Michael Y. Givler, the said judge having lawful authority to take the afore- said recognizance, and which said recognizance was then and there certified and approved by said judge, and by him, on the 23rd day of February, 1859, said recognizance was delivered to the clerk of the Circuit Court of said county, which was then filed and became a matter of record in said office of the Circuit Court of said county of Macon and State aforesaid. And after- wards, to wit, at March term, 1859, of the Circuit Court, began and held in the court-house, in said county of Macon,

State aforesaid, the said People being represented by the State's attorney, and the matter of the recognizance of the beforementioned Daniel Raysor and Michael Y. Givler, for the appearance, on the first day of the said March term of said court, of the said Daniel Raysor, to abide the proceedings and order of the court, as conditioned in the aforementioned recognizance, touching a charge of criminal offense, to wit, perjury, coming on to be heard; and the said Daniel Raysor, being three times [*192] solemnly called, came not, as by his said recognizance he was bound to do, but herein made default; and the said Michael Y. Givler, aforesaid security, being three times solemnly called to deliver the body of the said Daniel Raysor, failed therein, and made default. Wherefore, it was ordered by the said court, at the said March term thereof, that judgment of forfeiture be taken of their said recognizance, and that *scire facias* issue against the said Daniel Raysor and Michael Y. Givler, said recognizance being still in full force and unsatisfied. We therefore command you," etc.

To the said *scire facias* the plaintiffs pleaded *nul tiel* recognizance, and also *nul tiel record*.

Cause heard by the court.

The plaintiffs below introduced *Joseph Q. A. Oder*, who testified, that during the year 1859, he was clerk of the Circuit Court of Macon county, Illinois; that a recognizance, purporting to be signed by said defendants below, was filed in his office; that he had made a thorough examination and could not find the same; that the copy of recognizance set out in *hæc verba* in the *scire facias* herein, was a true copy thereof, according to his best recollection and belief, which said copy is in the words and figures following, viz.:

"Know all men by these presents, that we, Daniel Raysor, as principal, and Michael Y. Givler, as security, are held and firmly bound unto the People of the State of Illinois, in the sum of eight hundred dollars, for which payment, well and truly to be made, we bind ourselves, our heirs, executors and administrators, jointly and severally, firmly by these presents. Signed and sealed this 23rd day of February, 1859.

"The condition of the above obligation is such, that whereas the above bounden Daniel Raysor was, on the 14th day of February, 1859, committed to the common jail of Macon county and State of Illinois, upon a warrant of commitment, issued by Wm. L. Hamiuer, Esq., a justice of the peace in and for said county, upon a charge of perjury, in default of giving bail, by the said Raysor, in the sum of fifteen hundred dollars; and whereas, the said Raysor obtained a writ of *habeas corpus* from Charles Emerson, judge of the 17th Judicial Circuit, in the State of Illinois, for the purpose of reducing the amount of bail required as aforesaid, and to admit him to bail; and whereas, the said Charles Emerson, judge, as aforesaid, upon the hearing, upon the return of said writ of *habeas corpus*, did reduce the said bail to the sum of eight hundred dollars, and admit him to bail in the said amount. Now, if the said Daniel Raysor shall be and appear at the next term of the Circuit Court for the county of Macon and State of Illinois, upon the first day thereof, to answer [*193] whatever may be done in the premises, and abide the order of the court, and not depart without leave of the court, then this obligation to be void, otherwise of force.

(Signed)   DANIEL RAYSOR.   [SEAL.]
             MICHAEL Y. GIVLER.   [SEAL.] "

Said Oder, further testified, that said recognizance was not ' marked approved, nor certified so to be, by any person; that the same was left at his office by Wm. E. Nelson, Esq., on the day the same purported to be executed.

William E. Nelson, called, sworn and examined by the said People, testified that he was present on a certain occasion, when Daniel Raysor, one of the above defendants, was before the Hon. Charles Emerson, judge of the 17th Judicial Circuit, at chambers, upon writ of *habeas corpus ;* that said Raysor had been confined in the jail of said county, on a charge of perjury in default of bail; that said judge reduced the amount of bail which had been required, and fixed the amount to be given at $800. That a bond was then and there drawn up and signed by said defendants; that Judge Emerson expressed himself satisfied with the sufficiency of the security; that he did not know or recollect that said judge approved the bond in any other

manner. That said Raysor was discharged from custody upon
said bond or recognizance.

The plaintiff below then introduced the record of the proceedings of said court, had at the March term thereof, 1859,
showing judgment of forfeiture of a recognizance in the words
and figures following, to wit:

THE PEOPLE,
    vs.   } Perjury.
DANIEL RAYSOR.

And now come the people, by John R. Eden, their attorney,
and the defendant, Daniel Raysor, being three times solemnly
called, comes not, but makes default; and it appearing to the
satisfaction of the court that the said Daniel Raysor had heretofore entered into recognizance, together with Michael Y. Givler, his security, for his appearance at this term of this court,
in the sum of eight hundred dollars: it is therefore considered,
that said recognizance be forfeited, and that a writ of *scire facias*
issue against the said defendant and his security, returnable to
the next term of this court, commanding them personally to be
and appear at the said court, and show cause, if any they can,
why the People of the State of Illinois should not have execution against them for the amount of their said forfeited recognizance. All which evidence was heard by the court, subject to
[*194] the objections of the defendants below. Whereupon
the court rendered judgment against the defendants below, for
eight hundred dollars and costs, to which the said defendants
then and there excepted.

Error assigned: the court erred in rendering judgment
against the defendants below, upon the evidence in the cause.

N. W. TUPPER, and A. B. BUNN, for Plaintiffs in Error.

J. P. BOYD, for Defendants in Error.

BREESE, J. The criminal code of this State provides that
"all recognizances that have any relation to criminal matters,
shall be taken to the People of this State, shall be signed by
the person or persons entering into the same, be certified by the
judge, justice, of the peace, or other officer taking the same,

and delivered to the clerk of the Circuit Court on or before the day mentioned therein for the appearance of the witness or accused therein bound. Recognizances taken in courts of record need not be signed or certified as aforesaid." (Scates' Comp. 413, Sec. 205.)

A recognizance taken out of court, or by a judge at chambers, does not become a record until it is certified to that court by the judge. Not having been certified and filed in the mode prescribed, it did not become a record, and not being a record, no *scire facias* could be issued upon it, for it is only on records such a writ can issue. It is unnecessary to examine the other questions raised, as this objection goes to the substance of the proceeding. The judgment must be reversed.

Judgment reversed

Lewis Roach, and Leroy F. Staples, Plaintiffs in Error, *v.* Leonidas Chapin, Defendant in Error.

ERROR TO COLES.

A petition for a mechanics' lien is not obnoxious to a demurrer, because it avers that material was furnished to two persons, to erect a building on the land of one.

The rendition of a decree on the overruling of a demurrer to a bill, without first ruling the defendant to answer, is not error. The rendition of a decree upon a bill taken as confessed, is matter of discretion.

The act of February, 1861, provides that the former act in relation to mechanics' liens shall be held to include implied as well as express contracts, under which labor or material is furnished; provided they are done or furnished within one year from the commencement of the furnishing; and if these are done after the passage of the latter act, a petition need not aver that there was a time within which the materials were to be furnished.

Leonidas Chapin, complainant below, filed his bill [*195] to enforce a mechanics' lien against Lewis Roach and Leroy F. Staples, setting forth, that on the 20th day of March, A. D. 1861, and at sundry other times, as shown by a bill of particulars filed therewith as an exhibit, he furnished said

233

Roach and Staples, at their special instance and request, lumber for erecting a building on lots 10, 11 and 12, in block 76, in Noyes' Addition to the town of Mattoon, with an implied understanding between the parties that Chapin should have a lien on said premises for his payment for the materials furnished in such manner as the statute provides, in case Roach and Staples should otherwise fail to make payment for said materials upon the delivery thereof, and upon request made for the payment thereof; that the last of said materials were delivered on the 1st of May, 1861, and that payment for the whole of said materials thereupon became due, from the nature of the contract and understanding between the parties; that said Chapin had many times requested and demanded payment for said materials, and that said Roach and Staples had neglected and refused to pay, etc.; that complainant believes that the fee simple to said premises was vested in Roach, and that he had no certain security for the payment of the amount due him for said materials, $96.65, and interest thereon, since May 1st, 1861, except by the enforcement of a specific lien on said premises in such manner as the statute provides; concluding with a prayer that the court decree and order the enforcement of said Chapin's lien against said premises; and that said Roach and Staples be summoned to answer without oath, and that the court decree a peremptory sale without redemption of said premises at an early day, to satisfy the claim of Chapin for $96.65, and the interest thereon, together with costs, etc.

Then follows in the record the bill of particulars referred to as an exhibit in the bill of complaint, being an account of lumber delivered from March 20th to May 1st inclusive, and credits, and showing a balance due of $96.65.

At the October term, 1861, Roach filed his demurrer to complainant's bill.

At the same term, the court entered a decree overruling the demurrer of Roach, and reciting that Staples appeared and confessed the allegations of the bill to be true, etc.; that the said Roach appeared, but confessed nothing; and that on hearing the testimony of witnesses, it appeared to the satisfaction of the court that Chapin did furnish lumber and materials to said

Staples and Roach, for the purpose of erecting a house upon lots described in the bill, and that they were used for that pur- pose, and that there was a balance due on said lumber [*196] of $96.65, and that Roach was the owner in fee of said lots, whereon said building was erected, and it decreed that Roach and Staples should pay said sum, with interest and costs of suit, within ninety days from the rendition of the decree, in default of which, a special commission, appointed to execute said de- cree, should, after giving four weeks' notice of time and place, sell to the highest and best bidder the said lots, and execute a deed to the purchaser, etc.; that if the proceeds of the sale of said lots should not be sufficient to satisfy debt, interest and costs, complainant should have execution for the balance.

The following errors are assigned:

The overruling of the demurrer of Roach.

The rendering of a decree against plaintiffs in error.

The rendering of a decree without the answer of defendant, Staples, being filed.

The decree for a sale of all the premises set forth in the peti- tion without first finding that a part of the premises could be separated from the residue and sold without damage to the whole, and the value thereof was not sufficient to satisfy the amount due.

The rendering the decree upon the facts found to be true in said decree.

F. A. ALLISON, and SHERIDAN P. READ, for Plaintiffs in Error.

M. C. McLAIN, for Defendant in Error.

WALKER, J. This was a petition, filed to enforce a lien for materials furnished for the erection of a building. One of the defendants filed a demurrer, which was overruled and no answer filed. The other defendant came into court and confessed the truth of the bill. The court thereupon heard evidence, and rendered a decree, finding the existence of the lien as alleged, and that the sum due was $96.65, which was ordered to be paid in ninety days, and in case of default, the property described in the petition was ordered to be sold, after giving four weeks' notice of the time and place of sale.

It is insisted that the court erred in overruling the demurrer, because the petition alleges, that materials were furnished to two defendants, with which to errect a building on the land of one of them. In the case of *Van Court* v. *Bushnell*, 21 Ill. 624, this question was presented to, discussed and determined by this court. In that case it was held, that the fact that only [*197] one of the defendants owned the land, in no wise defeated the right to enforce the lien. That case is decisive of this question.

It is also urged, that the court erred in rendering a decree against Roach upon overruling his demurrer, without first ruling him to answer the petition. In the case of *Miller* v. *Davidson*, 3 Gilm. 518, it was said, that the correct practice in chancery causes, upon overruling a demurrer to the bill, is not to render a decree; but the order should be, that the defendant answer the bill, and if he neglect to do so, the bill may be taken as confessed. But the court, in that case, seems to have refrained from reversing upon that ground. It is further said in that case, that the chancellor may, in his discretion, render a decree at once upon a bill taken as confessed, on the overruling of the demurrer to the bill. The question whether the defendant in error should have been ruled to answer, being one of discretion, it will not be reviewed in this court.

We now come to the question mainly relied upon for a reversal. It is, that the petition contains no allegation, that there was any time specified, within which the materials were to be furnished. This, under the act of 1845, would have been a fatal objection on demurrer. But the General Assembly, by the act of the 18th of February, 1861, (Sess. Laws, 179,) provides that the former act shall be held to include implied as well as express contracts, under which labor is performed, or materials furnished, where no price is agreed upon, or no time is expressly fixed for payment, or for the furnishing of such labor or materials, provided the work is done or the materials furnished within one year from the commencement of the furnishing such materials. These materials are alleged to

.have been furnished after the passage of this act, and the case falls fully within its provisions. This, therefore, presented no ground for sustaining the demurrer.

We are also asked to reverse the decree, because it ordered that all three of the lots described in the petition should be sold, to produce the money. This objection is not well taken, as the decree does not make such an order. It orders, that all or "so much of the lots as may be necessary to satisfy said debt and costs" should be sold. Under this decree the master would have no power to sell any more, if it was susceptible of division, than would be sufficient to satisfy the decree.

The decree of the court below is affirmed.

Decree affirmed.

THE GREAT WESTERN RAILROAD COMPANY OF [*198] 1859, Plaintiff in Error, *v.* GUY HELM, Defendant in Error.

ERROR TO MACON.

A declaration against a railroad corporation for killing cattle need not negative the possibility that the animals may have been killed at a farm crossing. If the road is not properly fenced at such crossing, the company will be liable for injuries, and if it were properly fenced, that is matter of defense.

If a declaration avers a wrong with a *continuendo*, it may be obnoxious on demurrer; but the objection is too late if made after issue has been joined.

THIS is an action of trespass on the case brought by defendant in error, Helm, as plaintiff below, against the plaintiff in error, as defendant below, to the November term, 1861, of the Macon Circuit Court.

The declaration filed by defendant in error, contains but one count. It alleges, that on the 1st day of January, 1860, and from thenceforward to the commencement of the suit, the defendant was possessed, and had entire control of the Great Western Railroad of 1859, and had the right to run upon the same, locomotives and trains.

That during all that time it was the duty of defendant to erect and keep in repair fences sufficient to prevent cattle, horses, sheep and hogs, from getting on to said road, except at the crossings of public highways, within the limits of towns, cities and villages, and where the same run through unimproved land at a greater distance than five miles from any settlement, through land where proprietors had fenced, and except where proprietors had agreed to fence, and to construct suitable cattle guards, etc.

That nevertheless, defendant, more than six months after the road was in use, neglected to comply with these requirements; by reason whereof, four horses, four cows, four sheep, and four hogs, the property of plaintiff, of the value of $100, on, etc., and on divers other days and times, strayed and got on to the said road; but not at any of the various excepted places.

That the defendant, by its servants, on the day aforesaid, so carelessly, negligently and improperly run, conducted and directed the trains, etc., that the said locomotives and trains struck with great force and violence the four horses, etc., etc., by and through the neglect of the said defendant to erect and keep in good repair, etc., etc., and the same did then and there wound, injure, damage and kill.

The defendant pleaded not guilty.

[*199] The cause was tried by the court without a jury, and judgment was rendered for plaintiff for $81 and costs.

TUPPER & NELSON, for Plaintiff in Error.

J. S. POST, for Defendant in Error.

CATON, C. J. The principal objection to this declaration is, that it does not negative the possibility that the stock may have been killed at a farm crossing. The statute does not exempt the company from fencing their roads at farm crossings, nor does it exempt it from liability for killing stock at such crossings if the road is not there fenced; but it expressly provides that it shall fence at farm crossings, specifying the kind of fence which shall be made at such places; that is to say, bars or gates for the accommodation of the farmers. This specification of the kind of fence does not alter the case from what it would be if the law had prescribed live hedges or stone walls in certain localities. If the stock was killed at a farm crossing, where the company had made such a fence as the law required, which some one had left down or open without the fault of the company, whereby the stock got in and was killed, that was a matter of defense for the company, and need not be negatived.

It is hardly necessary to remark, that even if any objection could ever have been urged to the declaration because the wrong is laid with a *continuendo*, that should have been done by demurrer, and it is too late now, after issue was joined upon it, trial had and judgment rendered, to assign it for error here. The declaration is good, in substance at least, and is undoubtedly sufficient to sustain the judgment.

The judgment is affirmed.

Judgment affirmed.

LEVI WILSON, Plaintiff in Error, *v.* GEORGE WOOD, and HENRY A. HUNT, Defendants in Error.

ERROR TO RICHLAND.

A sold a stock of goods and a house and lot to B and C. The latter consented to relinquish the sale, and that A might find other purchasers, which he did, and sold to D and E, agreeing to give to D and E a title to the house and lot, which had been conveyed to B and C. These gave up the deed to themselves to D and E. On a suit by A, against D and E, on the notes given by them for the goods and the house and lot, they pleaded these facts, alleging failure of consideration, they not having received a conveyance of the house and lot. *Held*, that D and E were [*200] entitled to a conveyance to themselves, and if there was any special replication to the pleas, it should have been set out—that the handing over of the conveyance to themselves by A and B, was no conveyance, and that a finding sustaining the pleas should not be disturbed, but that A might resort in chancery to B and C, for a conveyance of the house and lot.

Wilson *v.* Wood *et al.*

THIS was an action of assumpsit. The declaration contains the common counts, and two special counts on the following notes; the first as follows:

" $500.   *August* 21, 1856.

   For value received, we jointly and severally promise to pay L. Wilson, or order, five hundred dollars, on or before the first day of June next.

HENRY A. HUNT,
GEORGE WOOD."

The other for $530, payable June 1st, 1858, and the same as the above in all other respects.

Also an account for goods sold, and the common money counts.

The defendants filed the general issue, and four special pleas, the third being for set-off, and the fifth the statute of limitations.

The first and second set up a failure of the consideration of the notes, the first a total failure and the second a partial failure, to the amount of $800; and with only this difference, both the first and second pleas are drawn alike. They set forth, that the notes were executed upon the express consideration that said plaintiff would make, execute and deliver to said defendants a general warranty deed "to a certain parcel of land," (describing the same,) "or cause the same to be done," and that "said deed of conveyance should be made before the said notes were to be paid, and on the express consideration that said deed" should be made before the payment of said notes. That said deed "has not been so executed," wherefore the consideration has failed, etc. Defendant also filed an account.

. The plaintiff joined in the general issue, and filed general replications to the other pleas, and defendants joined, etc.

 The cause was tried by a jury, and verdict rendered for defendants.

A motion was made by plaintiff for new trial and overruled, and plaintiff excepted.

The bill of exceptions sets forth the following evidence:

The notes sued on were admitted and read to the jury.

J. E. Martin testified, that he knew of the making of the

notes sued on; that one if not both were in his handwriting. That, at the time of making the notes, a sale of goods, and a house and parcel of ground, were sold to the defendant; [*201] that the plaintiff made the sale. The goods were a stock which witness and brother (Marshall Martin) had bought of the plaintiff about four months previously, and to which they had added by their own purchases, $400 or more of stock. The house and lot were the same bought by the witness and his brother (with the goods) from plaintiff, and which he procured to be conveyed to them by deed from John Parker, in whom the title had previously been vested. The sale to the defendants at the date of the notes, amounted to $910 for the goods, and $1,000 for the house and lot. Witness and his brother had not paid plaintiff for the house and lot, nor in full for the goods, when they were sold and turned over to the defendants, but by the contract and agreement of all parties, the defendants were to have the goods for $910, and the house and lot for $1,000, and the defendants were to pay witness and his brother $460, and the plaintiff $450, on account of the goods, and to give their notes to the plaintiff for $1,000, for the house and lot. That the reason why plaintiff made the sale was, that he did not seem satisfied with witness and his brother, and that they (witness and brother) themselves were not satisfied—they did not think they were selling goods fast enough, and the plaintiff was not getting his pay as fast as he thought he should, and the witness and his brother had agreed that if the plaintiff could find any other person to purchase the establishment, they would consent to sell, and the plaintiff, in pursuance of this agreement, made the contract of sale to the defendants. At the time of the sale, it was arranged and agreed with the defendants that the deed held by witness and his brothers should be given up, and another deed should be procured from Parker, and the witness' understanding was, that the way the deed was to be procured was through the instrumentality of the plaintiff, who was to get the title from Parker. Witness gave up the deed he had to the defendants, according to the agreement, and they have kept it ever since, so far as he knows, and the goods and house and lot were delivered to the defendants. He knows of their paying plaintiff $50 at one time, and $50 at another, on account of the $450 worth of goods. Witness says, the defendants never requested or called on him for any further deed or title, and he has never made any other. Whether Parker ever made them a deed or not, he does not know; he himself had never made a deed to anybody.

The defendants also filed an affidavit, setting up that they had paid or liquidated the sum of $600 to one Joel, on account of plaintiff, as part payment of the goods, etc., pur- [*202] chased of plaintiff, and as part payment on the first note, and also that they had paid at sundry times, to plaintiff, on account of the goods, etc., mentioned in declaration, divers sums, amounting to $200, which facts the plaintiff admitted without calling for witnesses, etc.

The defendants offered in evidence and read to the jury, two receipts given by the plaintiff to them, for money amounting to $350, and the plaintiff further admitted a credit to defendants of $52, for a mule.

The court gave instructions for plaintiff and for defendants, the latter of which are copied in the opinion.

A motion for a new trial was overruled.

The cause was tried in the Second Division by consent of parties.

A. KITCHELL, for Plaintiff in Error.

C. H. CONSTABLE, for Defendants in Error.

BREESE, J. This was an action of assumpsit in the Richland Circuit Court, on two promissory notes. Besides the general issue, the defendants put in two special pleas. The first set forth that the notes were executed upon the express consideration that the plaintiff would make, execute and deliver to the defendants, or cause the same to be done, a general warranty deed for a certain lot in the town of Olney, (describing it), and that said deed of conveyance should be made before the notes were to be paid, and on the express consideration that the deed should be made before the payment of the notes, averring that the deed has not been executed, and therefore the consideration has failed. The second plea is in all respects like the first, except that it alleges a partial failure of the consideration. General replications were filed to these pleas. The jury found for the defendants, and exceptions were taken to the refusal of the court to grant a new trial, and the suit is brought here by writ of error, the plaintiff assigning as error the instructions given by the court for the defendants, and overruling the motion for a new trial.

. From the bill of exceptions, it appears that at the time of making the notes, a sale of a stock of goods, and a house and lot in Olney, were made by the plaintiff to the defendants. The goods were a stock which the Martins, brothers, had purchased of the plaintiff about four months previously, and to which they had added, by their own purchases, four hundred dollars or more of stock. The house and lot were the same which the Martins bought of the plaintiff with the goods, and which the plaintiff procured to be [*203] conveyed to them by deed from one Parker, in whom the title was vested at the time of this sale and purchase. The notes were dated August 21st, 1856, and payable, one on the 1st of June, 1857, and the other on the 1st of June, 1858. At the date of the notes the sale to the defendants amounted to $910 for the goods, and $1,000 for the house and lot. The Martins had not paid the plaintiff for the house and lot, nor the full amount due for the goods when they were turned over to the defendants, but by the contract and agreement of all parties, plaintiffs, defendants and the Martins, the defendants were to have the goods for $910, and the house and lot for $1,000, and of this, the defendants were to pay to the Martins $460, and to the plaintiff $450, and this on account of the goods, and were to give their notes to the plaintiff for $1,000 for the house and lot, which are the notes in suit. It seems the reason why plaintiff made the sale was, that he was not satisfied with the Martins—and the Martins were not satisfied, they thinking they did not sell goods fast enough, and the plaintiff was not getting his pay as fast as he desired. The Martins then agreed with the plaintiff, if he would find some person to purchase the establishment, they would consent to sell, and accordingly, the plaintiff made the sale to the defendants. At the time of the sale to the defendants, it was arranged and agreed with them that the deed for the lot, which the Martins held, should be given up, and another deed should be procured from Parker through the instrumentality of the plaintiff, who was to get the title from Parker. The deed to the Martins was given up by them to the defendants, and it has been in their possession up to the time of the trial, so far as known, and the goods and house and lot were delivered up to the defendants. There was no proof that the defendants had ever requested or called on the Martins for any further deed or title, and they have never made any other. It was not shown whether Parker ever made the defendants a deed or not, or that plaintiff had ever procured from him a deed to the defendants. With the proof of some credits claimed by the defendants, the cause went to the jury on this evidence.

The court, on behalf of the defendants, instructed the jury as follows:

"1. If the jury believe from the evidence that the plaintiff was to make these defendants a title to the property (the lot of ground), and it appears from the evidence that a deed had been made to Martin for it, and Martin has never conveyed the same property to defendants, or to some one else who has since conveyed to the defendants, then the plaintiff cannot [*204] recover on the notes, if the jury believe the notes were given for a deed to said property.

"2. If the jury believe the notes were given in consideration that Wilson would make, or cause to be made, a deed for the house and lot, and that the said Wilson, or no one else for him, has ever made such deed, then the plaintiff cannot recover for the amount due on the notes sued on.

"3. If Parker conveyed the lot to Martin, the title conveyed to Martin thereby cannot be relinquished by a mere surrender of the deed; it can only be done by Martin making and delivering his deed; and if he has made no deed, whatever title he got from Parker, is still in Martin, and Parker or no one else could convey that title to defendants, except Martin."

These instructions, though not very carefully drawn, are appropriate to the issues and proofs in their support. If there was any answer to the defense set up in these pleas, it should have been replied specially. The pleas being good, and sustained by the proof, and the instructions conforming, there can be no ground for reversing the judgment. The defendants by this defense repudiate the contract, and consequently lose all right to the house and lot; and as the Martins, who hold the title, have been paid for it by the plaintiff in this arrangement with the defendants, the plaintiff must, on failing to recover these notes, be entitled to a conveyance of the lots on bill filed against the Martins, and probably, to the rents also, as against the defendants, in a suit brought for such purpose.

The judgment is affirmed.

Judgment affirmed.

LEVI FOULKE, Plaintiff in Error, *v.* WILLIAM C. WALKER, Defendant in Error.

ERROR TO EDGAR.

Where A and B convey a right of way to a mill to C, and B afterwards purchases one-half of the mill, B cannot become a witness for C, who has filed a bill to restrain A from obstructing the right of way; being an appurtenance to the mill, B was therefore interested, and was disqualified.

THIS was a bill in chancery, filed by the plaintiff in error in the Edgar Circuit Court, against the defendant, William C. Walker, to restrain and enjoin him from obstructing a certain passway leading to a grist mill of which the plaintiff was a part owner.

The bill sets out a deed from the defendant and wife, [*205] and one Dudley McClain and wife, to plaintiff, conveying to plaintiff a passway over their lands, as then located.

The bill alleges, that the defendant has placed obstructions in said passway, and is threatening to further obstruct it, unless restrained, and, as complainant believes, will so obstruct it, as to prevent his ingress and egress to his said mill, by which he will sustain great and irreparable damages, etc.

On the trial of the case, for the purpose of identifying where the passway was located at the time the conveyance was made, the plaintiff called as a witness *Dudley McClain*, one of the grantors in the deed, who being examined, testified on his *voir dire* that he was one of the grantors in the deed for the right of way to the plaintiff, which was shown him and identified.

" This indenture, made this 8th day of October, 1858, between William C. Walker, Rachel S. Walker, Dudley McClain and Rebecca McClain, of the first part, and Levi Foulke, of the second part, witnesseth, that the party of the first part, for and in consideration of one dollar to them paid, have granted, bargained and confirmed, and by these presents hereby grant, bargain and confirm unto the said party of the second part, and to his administrators and assigns, the right of way through the alley or passway, as now located on the lands of the parties of the first part, in the north-west quarter of section one, township thirteen north, range twelve west; which said alley or passway extends from the Chicago road to the mill lot, this day sold by the said parties of the first part to the said party of the second part. The said right of way hereby granted to the said party of the second part, to be and remain perpetual. In witness whereof, the said parties of the first part have hereunto set their hands and seals the day and year first above written."

It is signed by the parties, and properly acknowledged and recorded. The witness further testified, that the February preceding the commencement of the suit, he purchased of the plaintiff one undivided half of the grist mill, which had been sold by witness and defendant to the complainant, but did not purchase, or think he purchased, any interest in the right of way.

Whereupon the court refused to permit him to testify; to which ruling of the court the plaintiff at the time excepted.

A decree was rendered that the passway mentioned in the deed was only sixteen and one-half feet wide, eight and one-fourth feet on the land of Walker and the same on the land of McClain. That it had not been obstructed by the defendant, [*206] nor threatened to be obstructed; and dissolving the injunction, dismissing plaintiff's bill, and judgment for costs in favor of defendant.   To reverse which, the plaintiff brings the case to this court by writ of error.

The errors assigned are:

The refusal of the court to permit Dudley McClain to testify as a witness.

That the decree is contrary to the law and evidence of the case.

That questions are settled and adjudicated in the decree which were not raised by the pleadings in the case.

That there is no evidence incorporated in said decree to sustain it.

A. GREEN, for Plaintiff in Error.

JOHN SCHOLFIELD, for Plaintiff in Error.

WALKER, J.   This was a bill in chancery, filed for the purpose of restraining defendant in error from obstructing a passway, to and from a mill, owned by complainant and others. On the hearing, it appeared that the way had been conveyed to complainant, by defendant and McClain.   That afterwards, and before this suit was instituted, McClain purchased one-half of the mill.   On the hearing, plaintiff in error offered McClain as a witness, but he was excluded by the court, to which ruling of the court exceptions were taken, and this is now assigned for error.

The deed of conveyance, from defendant, to plaintiff in error, shows that the right of way became and was an appurtenance to the mill.   It could be used or appropriated to no other purpose.   It does not purport to convey a fee or any other estate in the soil, but a mere right of way in passing over it to and from the mill.   It being an appurtenance to the mill property, until it is severed by a conveyance of the way, it passed by the conveyance of half of the mill to McClain in the same proportion. He, by that purchase, became reinvested of an interest in the right of way, and having such an interest, he was disqualified to give evidence in the case.   The court below, therefore decided correctly, in rejecting him as a witness.   The decree of the court below is affirmed.

Judgment affirmed.   247

207 SPRINGFIELD,

Ohio and Mississippi. R. R. Co. v. Taylor.

[*207] The Ohio and Mississippi Railroad Company, Appellant, v. William H. Taylor, Appellee.

APPEAL FROM RICHLAND.

In an action commenced before a justice of the peace for killing cattle by a railroad company, the plaintiff should negative by proof that there was no public crossing where the killing occurred; and should show that the company was bound to fence at that point.

The proof should show that the injury was done by the road of the company sued.

Any person familiar with the kind of property injured, may prove its value; an expert is not an ind.spensable witness.

Proceedings were commenced before a justice of the peace, and taken by appeal to the Circuit Court.

Trial in Circuit Court, and verdict for $40. Motion for a new trial overruled.

The plaintiff below introduced the following testimony:

Jerry Taylor, being sworn, said: I sold the colt to plaintiff. It was wounded in August. It was near Pierce's farm—no town, city, or village there. I sold it for $25. I fix the value at $50. There was no fence there. One was necessary to keep off cattle. The road had been running for six months. It was a mile and a quarter to improved farms. I sold the colt for $25 because I needed the money.

Another witness said: I know of the killing of the colt spoken of here. It was in this county, on the 4th of August, on the railroad. It was at the place mentioned by Taylor. I don't know the value. I put it at $40. I have not bought, or sold, or seen any bought or sold of that age. I saw where it was killed.

This case was taken to the Second Grand Division by consent of parties.

Errors assigned:

There is no proof that the defendant was bound to fence, or liable for injuries in the event of not fencing the road.

There is no proof that plaintiff below was the owner or possessor of the colt when killed.

The defendant below is not, by the proof, in any way connected with the killing.

There is no proof that the killing was not at a public crossing.

There is no proof of the time when the colt was killed.

The proof of value of the colt is illegal.

The court erred in overruling the motion for a new trial.

WILLIAM HOMES, for Appellant.   [*208]

A. KITCHELL, for Appellee.

BREESE, J. The principal question in dispute before the Circuit Court, was, as appears by the testimony in the record, in regard to the value of the animal killed. It is however, alleged as error, that there was no evidence given by the plaintiff, and no proof in the cause, that the place where the injury occurred, was not at a public crossing.

Under the statute, railroads are not required to be fenced at such crossings; therefore, it was incumbent on the plaintiff to negative by proof, there being no pleadings in the case, that there was no public crossing where the injury occurred, but was at a point on the road, the company was required to fence, and this, in conformity to repeated rulings of this court. *O. & M. R. R. Co.* v. *Brown,* 23 Ill. 94; *Galena & Chicago U. R. R. Co.* v. *Sumner,* 24 ib. 631; *Ill. Cent. R. R. Co.* v. *Williams, ante,* 48.

There is also a defect in the proof to connect the defendants below, with the injury. The proof is, the animal was killed on the railroad. What railroad? There may be, for aught the court may know, more railroads in Richland county than the defendant's road. The jury could not know the fact that it was on the defendant's road without proof of it. They could take nothing of this kind for granted. It should have been proved. It is not one of the facts courts and juries are bound judicially to know, but must be proved. As to the proof of the value of the animal, we did not, in the case of the same plaintiff's against Irvin, (*ante,* 178,) consider it objectionable to give in evidence the opinions of persons presumed to be familiar with such kinds of property.

There being no proof in this cause, that the injury complained of, was done at a place where the road was required to be fenced, and no proof that it was on the defendant's road, the judgment must be reversed, and the cause remanded.

Judgment reversed.

[*209] Isaac A. Letcher, William Hadley, *et al.,* Plaintiffs in Error, *v.* James L. D. Morrison, Defendant in Error.

ERROR TO MADISON.

After a notice has been given to the administrator of a deceased debtor, of the existence of a judgment against the decedent, in accordance with Sec. 3, Chap. 47, Rev. Stat., the judgment creditor may issue an execution, and also an *alias* or *pluries,* without further notice.

Morrison purchased a piece of land under an execution against James Duncan, and filed his bill to set aside conveyances which vested the title to the land in John Duncan, alleging them to be fraudulent. Subsequently the land was sold by the administrator of John Duncan, under an order of court, as his property. Morrison received the proceeds of this sale for a claim which he held against the estate of John Duncan. *Held,* that this did not estop Morrison from asserting his title to the land.

This bill was filed by defendant in error, December 31, 1852, and sets forth that Edward Norton, on the 14th day of April, 1842, recovered a judgment in the St. Clair Circuit Court, against James Duncan, since deceased, and Rescarick Ayres, for $2,000. That just previous to the recovery of said judgment, and during the existence of the indebtedness, Duncan, with the intent to defraud said Norton, on the 22nd day of December, 1841, confederating with Isaac A. Letcher, conveyed to him the south-east quarter of section No. 20, except twenty-six acres out of the south-west corner of the said south-east quarter, containing 133 83-100 acres; also, the north-west quarter of Section 28, except five acres out of the south-east

250

corner, containing 155 acres—both in Township 3 north, Range 8 west, in Madison county, Illinois—upon the expressed consideration of three thousand two hundred and twenty-five dollars.

Bill charges, that in fact there was no consideration paid by Letcher to Duncan; that the conveyance was fraudulent; that Letcher did not take possession of said lands, and never exercised any acts of ownership over the same, except to place his deed on record; but that Duncan, the grantor, up to the time of his death, retained possession, and used the lands for his own benefit.

That on the 21st day of January, 1845, and while said judgment was in full force, etc., the said James Duncan and Isaac A. Letcher confederating with one John Duncan, (a brother of James, and who lived with, and who was wholly dependent upon the bounty of James, and who was destitute of any means), the said Letcher, at the solicitation of James and John, executed a deed to John for the said premises, upon an expressed consideration of twenty-five hundred [*210] dollars.

The bill charges, that no consideration was paid by John to Letcher; that the conveyance was made to defraud said Norton; that John never exercised any authority or control over said premises, until after the death of James, except that he resided thereon as a member of the family of said James Duncan.

That James Duncan departed this life, intestate, July 14th, 1846; that Charles Cook, public administrator of Madison county, administered upon the estate of James Duncan; that after the death of James, John occupied the premises to the time of his death, January 30, 1848; that letters of administration were duly granted to William Hadley on his estate.

The bill further charges, that various writs of *fi. fa.* were issued upon said judgment; and a sufficient sum of money made to reduce the amount upon the judgment to the sum of $737.-63, with costs; which amount was due September 23, 1850, the date of the sale hereafter mentioned; that there was no other property or estate out of which the amount due on said judgment could be made.

That at the time of issuing the *fi. fa.* of date June 17, 1850, more than one year had elapsed since the death of the said James; and that said Norton had given notice in writing to the said Cook, administrator, for more than three months, of his intention to sue out a *pluries.*

That on the 17th day of June, 1850, execution issued from the clerk's office of the Circuit Court of St. Clair county, directed to the sheriff of Madison county, and was by him levied on the lands which the said James Duncan had, as in bill stated, fraudulently conveyed to the said Letcher, as the property of the said James; that said lands were sold on the 23rd day of September, 1850, to the defendant in error,—the south-east quarter of Section 20, containing 133 83-100 acres, for the sum of five hundred dollars, and the north-west quarter of Section 28, for the sum of two hundred and thirty-seven dollars and thirty-seven cents, being the amount then due on said judgment; certificate executed; and the lands not having been redeemed, the sheriff of Madison county executed and delivered to him a deed therefor, May 11, 1852.

The bill further charges, that since the recovery of the said judgment, the said Rescarick Ayres has not had property or estate out of which the said judgment could have been made; and that he has refused to pay the amount due upon said judgment, or any part thereof.

[*211] The bill further charges, that Norton was unable to collect the whole amount of said judgment, except in the manner set forth in the bill; that personal estate of James Duncan was insufficient.

The bill prays, that the said deeds from James Duncan to Isaac A. Letcher, and from Isaac A. Letcher to John Duncan, may be set aside and esteemed for naught; and that the title be vested in defendant in error.

At the August term, 1853, defendants filed their demurrer to the bill, which was sustained, and leave given defendant to amend.

The answer of Mary Metcalf, disclaims all interest in the property mentioned in the bill; had sold all her interest in the

Letcher *et al. v.* Morrison.

estate of her brother, John Duncan, previous to the filing of the bill of complaint.

The answer of Isaac A. Letcher, believes it to be true that Norton obtained judgment as in the bill set forth; admits that James Duncan conveyed to him the tracts of land in the bill described, and at the time there stated. The conveyance was for a full and valuable consideration—the same as set forth in the deed; that at the time of the conveyance, he was a man of means, worth at least the sum of ten thousand dollars, and could on short notice have raised the sum of thirty-two hundred dollars. That the consideration of the deed from Duncan to himself ($3,225), was made up as follows: As early as the year 1828, he commenced advancing money to James Duncan, and from that time to 1841, he continued to make advances to him, and became liable for certain debts of Duncan to various persons—to Edward Chouteau, of St. Louis, since deceased, Joseph Sanbern, then of St. Louis, now of Quincy, Illinois, John O'Blennis, of St. Louis, John Darniel, of St. Louis, and William Atkins of Madison county—which he paid for said Duncan. That at the date of said deed, Duncan owed him about twenty-five hundred dollars, and he was liable, as indorser of notes of Duncan, to an amount of some eight hundred dollars more, which he afterwards paid. That the consideration of $3,225, expressed in the deed, was *bona fide*, and actually paid by him to the said Duncan, and to other persons for him. Denies that the conveyance was made to him by Duncan to defraud Norton, or any other person; but to secure to him a *bona fide* debt. He further states, that Duncan paid him rent while he owned the lands; paid in corn, pork, and other articles of personal property. That he made the conveyance to John Duncan for the true and full consideration of twenty-five hundred dollars, which said John Duncan paid to him. He denies all fraud or combination with James or John Duncan, to defraud said Norton; that on his part the [*212] transaction was *bona fide* and honest. That he was willing to sell said lands for $2,500, and did so, as it certainly was his right, and received the money, and personal property which was equivalent to money, from the said John Duncan. That he

did not know James Duncan in the transaction. Is ignorant
of proceedings under judgment; supposed judgment was long
ago satisfied. Knows nothing of the pecuniary ability of
Ayres.

The answer of William Hadley admits the recovery of
judgment by Norton against Duncan and Ayres. Admits conveyance by James Duncan to Letcher for $3,225; denies that
it was fraudulent. Admits that James Duncan resided on one
of the tracts of land after the conveyance; but whether as
tenant paying rent, or in what capacity, is ignorant. Admits
the conveyance from Letcher to John Duncan; denies that
the conveyance was made without consideration, or made to
defraud Norton. States that John Duncan after the conveyance to him, exercised acts of ownership over the lands; that
he cultivated some part of the land himself, and rented parts
to others. Denies that John was wholly dependent upon the
bounty of his brother James; and denies that he was destitute
of any means or pecuniary ability; believed that John
had money; denies all combination between Duncan and
Letcher to defraud Norton; admits that James Duncan departed this life at the time stated in the bill, and that Charles
Cook, as public administrator, took out letters upon his estate.
He admits that John Duncan occupied and enjoyed the
premises from the time of his purchase until he died, as his
own. He admits that letters of administration were granted
him on the estate of John Duncan; that, as such administrator, he obtained an order from the Circuit Court of Madison
county, at the ―― term, 1852, to sell the lands belonging to
John Duncan, deceased. That under said order, he sold the
south-east quarter of Section 20, Township 3 north, Range 8
west, at public auction, to Jonathan Duncan, for $800, and
has made him a deed therefor—fully believing, and now believing, that the fee simple title was in his intestate. He
further states, that he has been informed, and verily believes,
that the judgment recovered by said Norton, was fully paid
and satisfied long before the sale made by the sheriff of Madison county to the defendant in error, and that fact was known
to him before he made his purchase. He further states, that

on the 15th day of March, 1849, James Bishop, one of the heirs of John Duncan, became indebted to him in the sum of $85, and to secure the same, executed a mortgage on all his interest in said estate, recorded March 20, 1849; and [*213] Robert E. Duncan, another of the heirs, was indebted to him in the sum of $65, and executed to him a mortgage on all his interest in said estate, of the same date, recorded March 20, 1849. That said debts have not been paid, or any part thereof, and insists upon superior lien.

The answer of Charles Skinkle states, that he purchased from Jonathan Duncan all his interest and title in the lands described in the bill, for a valuable consideration without notice.

To which several answers replications were filed.

Decree *pro confesso*, as to the defendants failing to answer. The proof sustained the allegations of the bill.

The decree, after reciting the exceptions taken to various depositions, decreed that the exceptions taken by the complainant to the deposition of Isaac A. Letcher be sustained; that the exceptions of the defendants to the answer of John Keenan to the 26th direct interrogatory be sustained; and the remaining exceptions of said defendants are overruled. That the deeds from James Duncan to Isaac A. Letcher, and from said Letcher to John Duncan, as set forth in the bill, be taken and deemed as fraudulent and void, as against the said complainant, and those claiming title though or under him. That the title to the said property be vested in the complainant, and the defendants be forever barred, etc. Decree for costs against defendants. By agreement, cause to be heard at Springfield.

The receipt of Mr. Kœrner, referred to in the opinion, is as follows:

" Received, April 4, 1854, of William Hadley, administrator of the estate of John Duncan, deceased, the sum of two hundred and eighty-two dollars and fifty cents, being in full allowance of claim in the probate court of Madison county against said estate, with interest to date. The money being the proceeds arising from the sale of the following described tract of land: the south-east quarter of Section 20, Town 3 north,

Range 8 west. Sold under an order of the Circuit Court of
Madison county, as the land of said John Duncan, deceased.

GUSTAVUS KŒRNER,
Attorney for James L. D. Morrison."

H. W. BILLINGS, for Plaintiffs in Error.

J. AND D. GILLESPIE, for Defendant in Error.

[*214] CATON, C. J.* The transfer from James Duncan to
Letcher and from him to John Duncan, was so manifestly fraudulent, that we shall waste no time in discussing the evidence
on that subject.

Was it necessary that a new notice should be given to the administratrix whenever an alias or pluries or subsequent execution was taken out? Section three, of chapter forty-seven, Rev.
Stat., declares it shall be lawful to issue execution against estates of deceased persons; " *Provided, however,* the plaintiff
or plaintiffs in execution, or his or their attorney, shall give to
the executor or administrator, if there be any, of such deceased
person or persons, at least three months' notice in writing, of
the existence of such judgment, before the issuing of execution." We can find nothing in the language or the reason of
this statute requiring more than one notice, no matter how
many executions may be issued for the collection of the judgment. The statute does not even require the creditor to state
in his notice, that he intends to issue an execution upon the
judgment; much less to state the time when he will issue it;
but all that is required, is to notify the administrator of the
existence of the judgment. The object of the law evidently
was, to prevent the creditor from collecting his judgment by
execution, while the administrator was ignorant in fact of the
existence of the judgment. But after that fact was made known
to him, in the mode required by the law, the judgment creditor
has placed himself in the same position of right, as if the judgment debtor were still living, and the administrator is bound to

---

* Note.—Mr. Justice Breese did not sit at the hearing of this case, or take
any part in the decision of it.

Letcher *et al. v.* Morrison.

take notice of everything that is thereafter done, which the debtor himself would be required to notice if living.

The only remaining question is, whether the receipt given by Kœrner to the administrator, for the plaintiff, is an estoppel upon him. We do not think that even if this receipt had been given by Morrison himself, well knowing that the money had been raised by the administrator of John Duncan by the sale of this very land as the estate of John Duncan, that it would estop Morrison from setting up his claim to it. Had Morrison induced the administrator to sell it, and induced the purchaser to buy it, as the estate of John Duncan, then indeed would a court of chancery forever shut his mouth, so that he should never assert his claim to it, by reason of such a fraud practiced on the purchaser. But so far as this record shows, he knew nothing of this sale, [*215] at least till after it was completed, and the purchase money had passed into the hands of the administrator, as a part of the assets of the estate. It thus became a part of the general fund, and had to be distributed to the creditors of the estate generally. It does not appear even that it was sold specially to pay this debt, and if it did, the law says to the purchaser, *caveat emptor.*

But more than this, Kœrner was only authorized to receive this money generally for Morrison, and to give a general receipt therefor, and there is not a shadow of pretense for saying that he was authorized to sign any paper which should operate as a release of his interest in, or claim to this land, which, for aught that appears, was quite foreign to his mind when he requested Kœrner to collect this money for him.

The judgment must be affirmed.

Judgment affirmed.

THE PEOPLE, to the use of William P. Jarboe and others, distributees of the estate of P. Jarboe, deceased,
Plaintiffs in Error, *v.* ELIJAH LOTT *et al.*, Defendants
in Error.

ERROR TO GREENE.

The sureties upon an administrator's bond, applied to the probate court under the 79th and 80th sections of the statute of wills, to have the administrator give a new bond. The court took two new bonds from the administrator, the penalties of which being added together, equaled in amount the
penalty in the old bond. This was held to be a substantial compliance
with the statute, which requires that the new bond shall be in the like penalty as the first.

Where a new bond is given by an administrator or executor under the 79th
and 80th sections of the statute of wills, the sureties upon the first bond
are released from all liability for past as well as for subsequent acts.

If, instead of a new bond being given, the letters should be revoked, the
sureties would only be released from future liabilities.

Where administrators have given several bonds, and there is a complication
of interests, resulting from the death of one of the administrators
and of some of the sureties, whose legal representatives cannot be made
parties in a joint action at law upon the bonds, a court of equity will entertain jurisdiction.

The representatives of all of the deceased sureties should be made parties to
such a bill.   .

The 69th section of the statute of wills, in giving an action on an administrator's or executor's bond, against all or any portion of the obligors, has reference only to actions at law, and not to suits in chancery,

The last clause of that section, making certified copies of such bonds evidence, was only designed to change a rule of evidence, and not the practice
in courts of equity.

[*216] THE plaintiffs filed their bill on the 2nd July, 1858,
for settlement of the estate of the deceased, making E. Lott
surviving administrator of P. Jarboe, the administrator and
administratrix of H. M. Jarboe, deceased, who was the other
administrator of P. Jarboe, deceased—Job Collins, surety on
first administration bond, A. S. Seely, surety on second administration bond, and F. P. Vedder, surety on third administration bond, defendants, stating that P. Jarboe died intestate 8th

February, 1839, naming thirteen distributees of his estate; and
that at the time of his death he was in partnership with H. M.
Jarboe, as P. Jarboe & Son; that partnership effects survived
to him (H. M. J.) as surviving partner, to the amount of several thousand dollars, consisting of merchandise, notes, accounts,
and real estate, that the plaintiffs had no means of describing.
That H. M. Jarboe, as surviving partner, took possession of the
same, neglected the performance of his duty as surviving partner, had not applied the partnership effects to the partnership
debts, nor had his representatives after his death. That, on the
6th March, 1839, letters of administration were granted to H.
M. Jarboe and E. Lott, on their application; and charging
breach of the conditions of the administration bonds, in the following particulars:

1st. Had not complied with requirements of sections 95 and
123, statute of wills.

2nd. That they claimed and were allowed improper credits,
specifying them, in settlement of 7th August, 1840.

3rd. Also, 23rd August, 1841, in which mistake was made
against the estate, of $500, by erroneous subtraction and im-
proper credits allowed, (specifying them).

4th. In settlement, 12th February, 1842, some $6,000 of
demands against late partnership (specifying them) were improperly claimed as credits.

5th. That on 6th February, 1844, which was last appearance of the administrators in the County Court, they exhibited
their last account and vouchers; that the court suffered the account to be recorded, but wholly disapproved of the same, as
amounting to a fraudulent mismanagement and wasting of the
estate.

6th. Charging that administrators had not properly accounted.

7th. That administrators had sold real estate for $2,754.25,
and had rendered account for only $2,118.30.

8th. That on fair statement of account, there is a balance of
$3,000, principal, that ought to be accounted for, with com-
pound interest, because of mal-administration.

[*217] 9th. Claims allowed against the estate, the larger portion of which were on partnership account, which are disallowable on proper statement of account, many of which are not on file in the County Court; and amongst those not on file, one in favor of H. M. Jarboe, August 28th, 1840, for $3,703.51; and one in favor of E. Lott, allowed 25th October, 1839, for $134, charged to be groundless and unjust, no vestige of their having been proven or legally established in the court, and are charged to be disallowable, never having been proven according to law.

The first bond was executed by H. M. Jarboe and E. Lott, as administrators, one John Allen, deceased, and Job Collins, sureties on the same.

Third bond shows that the defendant, F. P. V., and one Henry Griswold, who has since departed this life, were co-sureties. Plaintiffs charge that they have rightfully, and according to the true intent and meaning of section 69, statute of wills, exhibited their bill in this case against defendants in this case, and have right to a decree against them, notwithstanding omissions of B. W. Holliday and representatives of estates of deceased sureties.

With full and specific reference to all and singular the claims referred to, plaintiffs charge that none of them are allowable, due from, or ever have been due from, or are chargeable, or provable or allowable, against the estate in due course of administration, expecting certain specified claims which amount to $2,422.20.

Inventory of effects is given at $5,630.32.

Answer on oath waived. Prayer for reference and statement of account on right principles, and for payment to the plaintiffs, use of, etc., or for such other and further relief as they may be entitled to.

The condition of the first bond is in full legal form; penalty, $5,000.

June 20th, 1842, Job Collins petitioned probate court that administrators be required to give counter security to bear him harmless. Citation issued, returnable 27th June, 1842, when administrators appeared and confessed themselves in fault, and the court adjudged that the security had sufficient cause for uneasiness, and that he was entitled to relief.

"Ordered, therefore, that the said administrators enter into bond in the penal sum of $3,000, with sufficient counter security to bear the said Job Collins harmless," and that bond be executed in ten days. Accordingly, referring to the premises, and with apt condition, the second bond was executed in penalty of $3,000, and filed as "counter security," and recorded; and it is expressly stated in the record, preliminary to [*218] the filing and recording of this bond, that it is "to bear Job Collins harmless, according to an order of the probate justice of the peace, made on the 27th day of June, 1842," and is so approved.

On July 18th, 1842, R. B. Allen, administrator of John Allen, suggested to the probate court that his intestate, in his lifetime, was security for administrators of P. Jarboe, deceased; that they were mismanaging the estate, and filed his petition for relief, praying that they should be required to give bond *de novo*. Citation issued, returnable 23rd July, 1842, when administrators appeared and agreed to give counter security by the 1st of August, 1842, and it was ordered that the penal sum in that bond be $2,000.

Probate office, July 23rd, 1842, widow of intestate filed her petition and complaint against the administrators, praying that their letters be revoked for mal-administration. Citation issued, returnable two days afterwards. Continued to 30th July, 1842, and then to August 15th, 1842.

July 30th, 1842, bond in penalty of $2,000, dated 23rd July, 1842, was executed, conditioned that the administrators had kept and would keep the condition of their first bond—signed by defendant and two securities. Philip Jarboe's counter bond, in case of R. B. Allen, was filed July 30, 1842.

February 6th, 1844, administrators tendered their account, which was utterly disapproved by the court, but was allowed to be recorded, and they were ordered to return into court certain papers that it was supposed they had abstracted, and to state an account as to the interest of intestate in the affairs of P. Jarboe & Son. This they never did.

Defendants in the case, excepting E. Lott, generally demurred
to bill, but bill was taken for confessed as to him.

The demurrers were severally overruled and withdrawn, and
the parties demurrant asked and were allowed time to answer.

June 2nd, 1860, administrator and administratrix of H. M.
Jarboe, deceased, answered, admitting deaths of P. Jarboe
and H. M. Jarboe, and administrations, as charged in bill.
Say they have no personal knowledge of facts alleged in the
bill as to settlement of estate of P. Jarboe, deceased, but
charge, on information and belief, that it is indebted to the
estate of H. M. Jarboe, deceased; admit partnership of P
Jarboe & Son; say it was hopelessly insolvent; owed
$14,000; its means, $2,157.59; that H. M. Jarboe paid, and
that there is due to his estate, from that of P. Jarboe, $5,000;
don't know whether the administrators gave notice of day for
[*219] adjustment of claims against estate, or made settlements
annually; insist that court can grant no relief in case for such
breaches of condition of bond; insist on validity of settlements
in August, 1840 and 1841, admitting error of $500 against the
estate.

As to settlement 12th February, 1842, they say
 that firm of P. Jarboe & Son, at death of P.
 Jarboe, owed $14,676.66
And means, of firm debts, goods and lands,
 amounted to only   5,305.34
             —————
Which left that concern insolvent $9,371.32
which was paid by H. M. Jarboe, and left a balance of
$4,687.66, to be charged to the separate estate of P. Jarboe, and
which was so properly charged in said settlement.

Insist that there is no balance due from the administrators to
the estate of P. Jarboe, deceased, and that the claims allowed
against it, in favor of H. M. Jarboe and E. Lott, were just and
legal.

Referring to an exhibit, say, that by that, Wm. P. Jarboe released to the administrators all his interest in the estate of P.
Jarboe, for good and sufficient consideration, and rely upon this
as a release and in lieu of his claim in this case. And that they

find, among papers of the estate of H. M. Jarboe, deceased, a promissory note, dated 29th July, 1835, made by E. Iott and P. Jarboe, for $5,000, at one day's date and twelve per cent. interest, and if unpaid, amounts to about $20,000, and ιeaves a larger balance against the estate. Respondents ask simple interest on the note, and refer to it as an exhibit.

Allege that a certain paper is a compromise of the administrators of P. Jarboe, deceased, with his widow and certain of his children, and Job Collins, as to a judgment that the administrators had against the widow and Wm. P. Jarboe, as to the dower interest of the widow in the lands of the decedent, and that she and Wm. and Alfred Jarboe and Job Collins, were to withdraw any interference with settlement of estate by administrators. And proceeding instituted against the administrators in probate court, and notice to set aside sale of partnership real estate of P. Jarboe & Son, to be withdrawn, and sale confirmed. And the administrators were to do certain other things. This agreement was dated 15th August, 1842, which was the last day to which Mrs. Jarboe's proceeding against the administrators, in the probate court, was continued. Nothing released in the paper by Wm. P. Jarboe.

The answer, plea and demurrer of F. P. Vedder ad-[*220] mits death and intestacy of P. Jarboe, and names of distributees of his estate and administration on estate, as charged in bill. Demurs to first breach of condition of bond alleged in bill; admits $500 error in second settlement, and pleads validity of the various settlements made by the probate court, as having jurisdiction; demurs to allegations of bill as to attempted settlement of February, 1844; denies allegations of bill as to amount of sales of real estate, and inadequacy of account; insists that accounts of Lott, $134, and H. M. Jarboe, $3,703.51, against the estate of P. Jarboe, were just, and properly allowed by the probate court; admits statements of the bill as to the first, second and third bonds, and insists that conditions of second and third bonds were for indemnity and protection of Job Collins and R. B. Allen, administrators of estate of John Allen, and not the persons to whose use this suit is brought; denies that he (respondent) is liable to complainants, use of, etc., on the conditions of his bond, and denies jurisdiction of the court in the premises; demurs to the allegations of the bill as to partnership relations of P. Jarboe & Son, and the liability of H. M. Jarboe, as surviving partner, to account, because these are not proper matters of adjudication in this suit.

The defendants, A. S. Seely and Job Collins, adopt the answers of their co-defendants, as their answer.

Replication to answer filed.

Cross-bill of Job Collins against his co-defendants, Seely and Vedder, filed April 23rd, 1861, says, that he and his said co-defendants are making common cause in the defense of this case, and that if they are entitled to any decree or relief in the case, that before he (Collins) can be rightfully subjected to pay anything by virtue of the condition of his bond, that the liabilities of the defendants, Seely and Vedder, should be severally and respectively exhausted to the amount of the several penalties of their bonds, and prays for such decree, and for rule to answer.

Demurrer to cross-bill filed.

L. E. Worcester testifies to the partnership of P. Jarboe & Son at the time of the death of P. Jarboe. Had done business on credit system to considerable amount, and the partnership effects survived to Harvey M. Jarboe and C. Swallow, in spring of 1840; sold lands to H. M. Jarboe, or E. Lott, for a stock of goods that had belonged to the partnership.

Master's report states that he has stated the account on most liberal terms for the defendants, and reports balance to [*221] 15th September, 1861, in favor of complainants, to the extent of $4,065.88.

The exceptions of complainants to master's report were taken because of the allowance of any other or further claim or claims, demand or demands, against the estate of intestate, than those admitted in the bill, and because the claims and demands thus allowed and excepted to severally and respectively, have been allowed without sufficient proof of the justice or payment of the same, and without the distributees of said estate ever having had any day in court to allow or contest the same.

Exceptions of Vedder and Seely to master's report show that the master erred in approving of the action of subsequent

264

courts, in disturbing the judgment of the County Court, allowing partnership claims against decedent.

Master erred in not regarding the release of William Jarboe and his mother, in stating said account.

Master erred in refusing to allow claims against the estate, which had been previously allowed by the probate court.

Decree without prejudice to the rights of the parties respectively:

1st. Overruling, severally, exceptions to the master's report.

2nd. That demurrer be sustained to the cross-bill, and that same be dismissed.

3rd. That bill of complainants be dismissed.

Plaintiffs assign for error the first and third provisions of said decree.

Job Collins assigns for error the second provision of said decree.

In the progress of the case in the court below, the defendants, excepting Lott, severally demurred to the bill, and on argument, as to jurisdiction of the court, parties, and equity of the bill, the court overruled the demurrer, which was withdrawn, and the demurrant parties obtained leave to answer. On the final hearing below, the court suggested lack of proper parties in the case, and dismissed the bill.

D. A. AND T. W. SMITH, for Plaintiffs in Error.

C. D. HODGES, and N. M. KNAPP, for Defendants in Error.

WALKER, J. The first question presented by this record is, what effect was produced upon the rights and liabilities of the parties, by the execution of their additional bonds, by the administrators? The seventy-ninth section, of the stat- [*222] ute of wills, authorizes the security on an administrator's or executor's bond, to file his petition in writing, in the probate court, when he shall believe he is in danger of loss, from the misapplication or waste of the assets of the estate, for a rule on the executor or administrator to give a new bond, or counter security to save him free and harmless, from loss. And the court is authorized on a hearing to dismiss the application, or direct the executor or administrator, in his discretion, either to give good counter security to save such petitioner harmless, or to give a new bond in the like penalty as the first; and that such new bond shall have relation back to the time of granting letters testamentary or of administration, and shall be as effectual in every respect, as if the same had been executed before the letters were granted. And upon refusal or neglect to give bond *de novo,* or counter security, the letters before granted may be revoked. The eightieth section prescribes the form of condition of such new bond.

In this case, the bonds of the fourth and thirtieth of July, 1842, given under the order of the probate court, on petitions filed for the purpose, conformed in every particular to the requirements of these sections, except that neither were in the same sum as the original. Then was this a fatal omission? It is apparent that the court approving them, must have designed the two new bonds when taken together, to form the amount of the original bond. The sums named in the two, when added together, make that sum. If the two were designed to operate as, and to supersede the former bond, we can see no reason why it should not be held to be a substantial compliance with the law. It can make no difference whether it is written on one or two pieces of paper. The condition of each is the same, and although the sureties became liable in different amounts, still the undertaking is the same. The law regards the substance and not the form of the agreement. If the fact that these bonds were in a less penalty than the one first given rendered them inoperative, they have never become binding, and are not capable of enforcement. But we are of the opinion that they were operative as statutory bonds.

The question then arises as to the effect produced upon the first bond given, by the execution of these. Was that bond abrogated, and the securities released, or did it remain in force? The design of the General Assembly in adopting these provisions, manifestly was to provide the means of enabling a security on such an obligation, when apprehensive of loss, to release himself from liability, or to obtain counter security for his indemnity   Had the probate court ruled the ad- [*223] ministrators to give counter security, and they had complied with the order, the obligations would have been executed to the securities, and not to the People.   They would have contained very different conditions, and upon a breach of the original bond, and damage resulting to the securities, they alone would have the right of recovery for their indemnity.   Or had the administrators failed to give the new bonds when thus required, their letters would have been revoked, and the securities would have been released from all future liability.   Then could it have been intended that the giving of such new bonds should have a less beneficial effect, by leaving them liable not only for the past but for the future acts of their principals?   We think not.

The statute, in terms, renders the sureties on the new bond liable for all of the acts of the administrators, from the date of the grant of their letters.   This seems to clearly manifest an intention to release the securities on the original bond, by the execution of the new one, not only from subsequent, but from all past acts of their principals.   And it was the evident design to render the first bond as inoperative as though it had never been given, and to transfer the liability to the new securities. The securities on the bond first given are not liable, and should not have been made parties to this suit.   ·

It is urged, that a bill in chancery will not lie in this case to declare and enforce the rights of the parties.   But that the remedy is by an action at law on the bond.   Whilst it may be true, that a settlement of the administrators' accounts might be as well adjusted by a jury as a master in chancery, yet there is such a complication of interests, resulting from the death of one of the administrators, and several of the securities, whose representatives cannot be made parties to a joint action on these bonds, that a court of equity may, we have no doubt, entertain jurisdiction of the cause and proceed to a final hearing and decree.   In fact, it is difficult to perceive how a court of law could do complete justice, between all of these parties, without great delay and vexatious litigation.

The next question presented is, whether the bill was defective

Watts *v.* Parker.

for the want of proper parties. We think it was. The representatives of the deceased securities have a direct interest in being heard in the adjustment of the administrators' accounts, as they would be liable to contribute in their representative character, for their proportion of any sum found remaining in the hands of the administrators, or misapplied or wasted by them. With only a portion of the parties to the bonds, or their representatives before the court, a decree doing full and [*224] complete justice to the several parties could not be rendered. The bill was defective in not making the representatives of Swallow, Seeley and Gregory, parties. Also, in omitting Holliday, a security to the second bond. For the want of these parties, the defendants' demurrer should have been sustained. The sixty-ninth section of the statute of wills, in giving an action on an administrator's or executor's bond, against all or any of the obligors, only has reference to actions at law. That section was not designed to change the practice in suits in equity. And the last clause of that section, making certified copies of such bonds evidence, was only designed to change a rule of evidence, and not the practice in courts of equity. The decree is therefore affirmed.

Decree affirmed.

SIMEON WATTS, Plaintiff in Error, *v.* SIDNEY PARKER, Defendant in Error.

ERROR TO BROWN.

The covenant that the grantor is seized of an estate in fee simple, is satisfied, if he has a seizin in fact, by having entered into possession, claiming a fee simple in the land. BREESE, J.

An entry into possession, under a paper title, claiming the fee, and the peaceable possession for more than twenty-six years, make a seizin in fee simple. BREESE, J.

Possession and payment of taxes for seven years under claim and color of title, will satisfy the covenant of seizin in fee simple. BREESE, J.

A deed purporting to claim land must be under seal. BREESE, J.

A party may show possession and payment of taxes under claim and color of title; although his chain of title may show a deed not under seal. BREESE, J.

Watts v. Parker.

On 17th October, 1861, Parker sued Watts in assumpsit, in the Brown Circuit Court. The declaration is upon a promissory note for $650, dated Mount Sterling, June 1st, 1860, due fifteen months after date, payable to Sidney Parker, with six per cent. interest from September 1, 1860, and ten per cent. after maturity if not paid when due. The declaration is in the usual form, with two special counts and the money counts.

Defendant below, Watts, filed the general issue, to which the similiter was added.

At same term, Watts also filed his other plea, which is set forth in the opinion of the Court, together with the issue formed upon it.

At November term, 1861, of said court, before HIGBEE, Judge, this cause came on for trial before said judge and a jury, who found for plaintiff Parker, and assessed his damages [*225] at $701.18, damages. Watts entered a motion for a new trial, which was overruled, and judgment rendered on the verdict, for said damages and costs of suit.

The bill of exceptions recites, that the plaintiff, on the trial, read said note in evidence, and rested his case.

That defendant then read, in evidence, a patent, in due form, conveying by the United States to Alexander Curry, lot 51, in old plat of Mt. Sterling, Brown county, Illinois, dated 10th of October, 1833. Also, a deed from Sydney Parker, plaintiff, and his wife, to Simeon Watts, defendant, conveying the part of lot 51, aforesaid, heretofore described, and also all that portion of the building known as the Parker House, which is comprised in the second and third stories of said brick building; containing a covenant that grantors were well seized of said premises as of a good, sure, perfect, absolute and indefeasible estate of inheritance in law in fee simple, and have lawful authority to grant, bargain, sell and convey the same in manner and form aforesaid, with other covenants. Which was read without objection; and defendant rested his case.

Plaintiff then read in evidence a deed for said lot 51, from Alexander Curry to Robert McCormick, dated 1st November, 1834; also, what purported to be a deed from Robert McCormick and wife to James Harper, dated 7th November, 1835, for said lot 51. Said paper was acknowledged as a deed, but had *no seals* affixed to signatures. Watts excepted at the time to the introduction of said paper, purporting to be a deed.

Plaintiff then read in evidence a deed for said lot from James Harper to George Harper, dated 22nd February, 1836; also, a deed for said lot from George Harper to William Reed, dated 17th February, 1840.

The plaintiff then introduced a record of the Brown Circuit Court, showing a sale and deed for said lot, by the administrator of William Reed, to George M. Pickett.

Plaintiff then read in evidence a deed for said lot 51, from said Moses and Hobbs, as administrators of William Reed, to George M. Pickett, dated 19th December, 1845.

Plaintiff then read a deed from George M. Pickett to Sidney Parker for said lot, dated 18th September, 1846.

Plaintiff then called *Robert N. Curry*, who testified, that about the year 1836 George Harper built a house on lot 51, and occupied it until about 1840, since which time the lot has been occupied nearly all the time and in possession by somebody; that after said Harper left said premises, William Reed occupied and held possession of the premises until his death, after which, [*226] Anthony L. Hobbs occupied and held possession for two or three years; after Hobbs left, George M. Pickett occupied and held possession of said premises until about 1849; that from and since 1849 Sidney Parker has had possession of said lot.

It was also proved by Robert N. Curry, that Robert McCormick died less than a year ago; that Curry was his administrator; that he never found any claim among McCormick's papers for said lot, nor heard of his claiming it after said deed.

It was proved that Watts took possession of said premises about the 1st September, 1860, and continued in possession up to time of bringing suit.

Plaintiff proved payment of taxes on said lot 51 from 1849 to 1859, both inclusive.

This was all the evidence in the case given on the trial by either party.

Defendant Watts asked the court to instruct the jury that a

seizin in fee simple is a seizin of a perfect paramount title, and unless plaintiff has proved such a title in himself on June 1st, 1860, they will find for defendant, and that twenty years' possession or seven years' payment of taxes does not create a seizin in fee. The court refused to give this instruction, to which Watts excepted.

The jury found the issues for plaintiff Parker, and assessed his damages at $701.18.

Errors assigned:

In admitting pretended deed from McCormick to Harpers, when said deed had no seal and was void.

In permitting to be read the record in the case of Hobbs against Reed and others.

In permitting to be read in evidence the deed from Hobbs and Moses to George M. Pickett.

In refusing to give the instructions asked.

In refusing to grant a new trial, and rendering judgment.

GRIMSHAW & WILLIAMS, and E. L. GROSS, for Plaintiff in Error.

J. S. IRWIN, for Defendant in Error.

BREESE, J. The question is not presented by this record, whether a maker of a note as part payment of the consideration money for land conveyed by deed to him, with covenant of warranty, and he put in possession, can plead, as a defense to the note, before an eviction, a failure of consideration, either total or partial, on the ground of want of title. [*227] The case assumes no such aspect. There was no demurrer to the pleas, but an issue in fact was made up on the plaintiff.'s first replication to the defendant's second plea, which is as follows:

"That the note in controversy was given as part of the consideration of part of lot 51, in the old plat of Mount Sterling, in Brown county, Illinois, described in the plea by metes and bounds; also all that portion of the building known as the Parker House, which is comprised in second and third stories of said brick building, and also the hotel furniture in said

Parker House, consisting of beds, bedding, etc., then owned by plaintiff and sold to defendant. That the sale of real and personal property was made at one time, as one sale, on 1st June, 1860. That the consideration for such sale was $4,500— $3,200 paid at time of sale; and for the remainder, defendant gave his two promissory notes, one of which is the note sued on; the other falls due first of September, 1862."

Plea further states, that at time of sale, on 1st June, 1860, plaintiff delivered to defendant his deed of conveyance, purporting to convey said real estate to defendant, with covenants in said deed that plaintiff was well seized as of a good, perfect, absolute and indefeasible estate of inheritance, in fee simple. Plea alleges that plaintiff was not, at time of execution and delivery of deed, or at any time since, well seized, etc., (negativing the language of the covenant,) but on the contrary, from the making of the deed and at all times, the title was in other and different persons. That of said sum of $4,500, the sum of $3,500 was agreed upon between said parties as the value of said real estate, and that consideration was expressed in said deed," and the consideration of said note has wholly failed.

To this plea the plaintiff replies: "that he was seized at the date of said conveyance of an estate of fee simple in and to said lands mentioned in said deed," with a conclusion to the country.

This replication admits that the note was executed for this lot, hotel and furniture, and narrows the issue down to the simple fact of seizin under a title in fee simple, an issue much more restricted than the one tendered by the plea. It was not urged that the issue thus restricted was an immaterial one, or any point of law raised upon it, but the issue to the country was accepted, and the parties went to trial.

The defendant asked the court to instruct the jury, and it was the only instruction asked, "that a seizin in fee simple is a seizin of a perfect paramount title, and unless plaintiff has proved such a title in himself on June 1st, 1860, they will [*228] find for defendant, and that twenty years' possession or seven years' payment of taxes does not create a seizin in fee." The propriety of this instruction is, really, the only question before this court.

272

Watts *v.* Parker.

The issue was not, as the defendant seems to suppose, on a title absolute and indefeasible, but whether the plaintiff had such a title as he had set out in his first replication, that is, that he was seized at the date of the conveyance of an estate in fee simple to the lot described in the plea. To constitute such a seizin, is it requisite it should be by a perfect paramount title, as the defendant desired the court to say to the jury?

We do not think so. The issue was not, that the plaintiff was seized of an absolute, indefeasible title to the lot, but that he was seized in fee simple only. To maintain this issue, we hold, it was only necessary for the plaintiff to show a seizin in fact by having entered into possession, claiming a fee simple in the lot. We have looked into the books on this question, and find some contrariety of opinion in the courts of the several States. We are inclined to think the doctrine held by the Supreme Court of Massachusetts to be quite as applicable to our condition, and to the exigencies of our State, as any other, and are inclined to adopt it as sound doctrine. That court held, in the case of *Marston* v. *Hobbs*, 2 Mass. 439, which was an action of covenant broken, brought on a deed containing this covenant, " that at the time of the execution of the deed the defendant was lawfully seized in fee of the premises," that it was not necessary to show a seizin under an indefeasible title. A seizin in fact was sufficient, whether he gained it by his own disseizin, or whether he was in under a disseizor. If, at the time he executed the deed, he had the exclusive possession of the premises, claiming them in fee simple by a title adverse to the owner, he was seized in fee and had a right to convey. The same doctrine is held by the Supreme Court of Ohio. It is there held, that a seizin in fact of the grantor, at the time the deed was executed, was a sufficient compliance with the covenant of seizin in the deed. If the grantor is in the exclusive pos-..ession of the land at the time of the conveyance, claiming a fee adverse to the owner, although he was in by his own disseizin, his covenant of seizin is not broken, until the purhaser, or those claiming under him, are evicted by title para-.ount. He has a seizin in deed, as contradistinguished from a seizin in law, sufficient to protect him from liability under his covenant, so long as those claiming under him continue so seized. *Adm'rs of Backus* v. *McCoy*, 3 Ohio, 220.

[*229] 'An actual, open and notorious adverse possession of land, in defiance of the whole world, may ripen into a perfect title in the disseizor, and when it has reached that state, it becomes an absolute and indefeasible title. Such was, in fact, the title exhibited by the plaintiff in this action. An entry into possession under a paper title—claiming the fee, and an undisturbed possession, by the several parties under whom the plaintiff claimed, for more than twenty-six years—the peaceable possession by the defendant, with no adverse claim asserted, make up, in our judgment, such a seizin in fee simple as maintains the issue, and warranted the court in refusing the instruction.

Something was said, about the ability to defeat the title shown by the plaintiff, by the fact that one of the heirs at law of Reed, through whom the title passed on its way to the plaintiff, and who is a married woman, can, when her disability is removed, or even now, recover the property. A perfect answer to this, is found in the fact, that she would have to make out her title through a paper void as a deed, it having no seal, and unable to give any proof of possession under claim of title.

As a part of this possession of more than a quarter of a century, the plaintiff showed abundant color of title, and payment of taxes under it, for more than seven successive years, and actual possession under it for that time, which, under the authority of the case of *Hinchman* v. *Whetstone*, 23 Ill. 185, is quite sufficient to satisfy the covenant of seizin in fee simple. This covenant is nothing more than an assurance to the purchaser that the grantor has the very estate in quantity and quality, which he purports to convey. A fee simple estate was conveyed by the deed to the defendant. He is in the peaceable possession, and no person claiming adversely to him. Justice requires that he should pay the purchase money. The judgment is affirmed.

Judgment affirmed.

CATON, C. J. I think the instruction was properly refused.

WALKER, J.   I concur in the conclusion in this case, but not
in all of the reasoning of the opinion.   I am not prepared to
hold, that a naked possession, although open, notorious and
against the whole world, claiming the fee, is in fact a seizin in
fee simple.

JAMES S. VERMILLION, Appellant, v. GARLAND [*230]
G. BAILEY, Appellee.

APPEAL FROM EDGAR.

On a bill filed for a settlement of partnership accounts, where the proofs and
statements leave everything in such doubt and uncertainty that it is impossible to do justice, the bill should be dismissed without costs.

ON the 17th of April, 1860, complainant filed his bill in
chancery in the clerk's office of the Edgar Circuit Court,
HARLAN, Judge, presiding, to settle a partnership in regard to
the construction and completion of two school-houses; alleging that complainant and defendant were equal partners in
the construction and completion of said houses, which were
completed in pursuance of the contract with the directors of
districts four and five, in townships thirteen and fourteen;
and that complainant put into said partnership, beside his
labor, for material, board, hauling, etc., $375.56, and received
pay for said labor, material, etc., only $356, and that defend-
ant, in materials, labor, board, etc., furnished only $142.75,
and received $348.05, and defendant received $135.79 more
than his share.   Complainant has shown defendant this error,
but he insists that he has not drawn over his due, but has
made a settlement of all their partnership transactions.

Common prayer for relief, asking that Garland G. Bailey be
made defendant to this bill, and that the People's writ issue,
which bill is sworn to.

Defendant in his answer alleges, he is wholly unable to
state the precise amounts furnished by himself or complainant
in material, labor, hauling, boards, etc., but thinks, from his

Vermillion *v.* Bailey.

best recollection, that complainant furnished, in all, not over $250. He cannot state the exact amount furnished by himself, only from his best knowledge and recollection; thinks from $250 to $275. Complainant received from said partnership, $565, from his best recollection, and from best recollection he worked one hundred and twenty-five days. Does not believe that complainant worked one-third as much as defendant. That both had hands sometimes, who were paid out of partnership funds and taken into the account in the settlement. That the books were kept by complainant, of their partnership transactions, and he cannot state, from memory, amounts, with precision, as he relied upon complainant to keep the accounts. Cannot say the books were correct or not correct, but the settlement was a final one.

[*231] Both their individual and partnership transactions, including a judgment due defendant from complainant, sworn to, May 18, 1860, were considered in settlement.

CONSTABLE & TROGDEN, for Appellant.

A. GREEN, for Appellee.

CATON, C. J. We have never met with a case, in which an attempt was made to prove the state of accounts between the parties, where the evidence was so unsatisfactory. After going carefully through with the testimony of each witness, and endeavoring to deduce something satisfactory from it, we feel utterly lost as to how the balance should be struck. What accounts the parties did keep are not presented, and probably if they were, they would be as uncertain as is the evidence. The defendant has only proved items of credit to the amount of three dollars and ten cents, and yet it was admitted at the settlement, that he had advanced over one hundred dollars. Probably no two accountants would go through with this testimony and strike the same balance. The more the testimony is studied, the more deeply are we impressed with its unsatisfactory character. We cannot resist the conclusion that neither has proved his case, as it really should appear. For instance, Wright swears, that he paid Vermillion & Co.'s order, two hundred and twenty dollars. Who got this money—who drew this order—to what was the money applied? No one can tell, nor is there the least attempt at an explanation. This is but one instance, among many, of the uncertainties arising from the testimony. Repeated attempts to strike a balance have been abandoned in despair.

In this state of evidence, we have no doubt the court below did the best thing that could be done, by abandoning all attempts to ascertain the rights of the parties from the proof of the accounts, and fell back upon the settlement made by the parties themselves, although with that, we are by no means satisfied. We *fear* there was some mistake in that settlement, and that by it the complainant may have been wronged. That settlement was not pleaded as an estoppel, nor was it designed to be conclusive between the parties, for the right to have any errors corrected, was expressly reserved when the settlement was made.

The settlement was proved by Horshborger, who testified: "I was present at the time referred to (the settlement). I was requested by Vermillion to make their calculations, which was mutually agreed to by both parties. There was about one hundred and twenty dollars yet due the firm, and accord- [*232] ing to the settlement, but seventy dollars of that was yet due Vermillion, and fifty dollars to Bailey. That is my best recollection. They both seemed to be satisfied, as far as I could see or know; Bailey seemed very easily satisfied." On cross-examination, he said, "there was some dispute about how the calculation ought to be made; Vermillion put in the largest amount of capital; do not recollect just how the calculation was made; Vermillion put in over three hundred dollars, and Bailey over one hundred dollars." "We charged Bailey individually, with half the amount Vermillion put in more than Bailey. The settlement was made on that basis, and the proceeds. I was not present when any note was given. I heard no note talked of." Other testimony tends very strongly to show, that a note for about thirty-five dollars, given by Vermillion to Bailey, was given on that settlement.

So far as disclosed by the witness, the principle on which the computation was made for this settlement, was correct, and yet many persons would be likely to fall into grave errors in carrying it out to a final conclusion. There is no class of accounts in which there is so great liability to fall into error, by those not familiar with keeping accounts, as those arising between partners; and we have serious apprehensions that errors may have been committed in the settlement. The truth is, the whole matter was so loosely presented to the court below, that it was impossible to know that by any decision, it was doing complete justice between the parties; and perhaps the safest course was to rely upon the settlement. But in view of the great uncertainty in relation to this whole matter, and the very unsatisfactory character of the determination finally forced upon the court, we think the bill should have been dismissed without costs. We shall therefore reverse so much of the decree as adjudges the complainant to pay costs to the defendant, and affirm the balance, and each party must pay one-half of the costs of this appeal.

Decree reversed.

Murray McConnel, *et al.*, Appellants, *v.* David A. Smith, Administrator of the Estate of Jerome McKee, Senior, deceased, *et al.*, Appellees.

APPEAL FROM SCOTT.

The ruling of this court in the case of *Wade* v. *King*, 19th Ill. 301, in relation to the admission of depositions taken in one suit, in another between the same parties, about the same controversy, examined and adhered to.

[*233] The opinion of the court in this cause as reported in the 23rd Ill., page 617, reconsidered, and the cause reversed, by reason of an inadvertence in examining the record.

This opinion is upon a petition for a rehearing. The former opinion will be found in the case as reported at page 111 of volume twenty-three of these Reports.

Breese, J. A rehearing having been granted in this cause, we have looked carefully into the points of objection to the several previous rulings of this court, and have come to these conclusions.

The objections raised heretofore to the decree, were, chiefly, the admitting as evidence in the cause, to prove the birth of a posthumous child of Jerome McKee, certain depositions, which, it is alleged, were not taken in the cause, and which were read without the consent of the complainants.

In looking into the record as to this point, we find that a motion was made by the solicitor of appellees on the hearing, that there be read as evidence in the cause, the depositions of W. H. Scoby and F. Vanderver, taken in Ohio, pursuant to a stipulation at the foot of the depositions. In the joinder in error, on this record as a reply to the appellants' assignment of error, the appellees say, that " the court below did not allow to be read on the hearing of the cause, the depositions of witnesses in Ohio, to prove the birth of Jerome McKee, Jr., posthumous child of Jerome McKee, Senior, deceased, notwithstanding which, appellees ask that the decree be affirmed." The record shows that these depositions were not allowed to be read, and of course formed no part of a basis for the decree.

These are the depositions, to which we referred, in the opinion delivered in this case as reported 23 Ill. 617, as the depositions of Scoby and Brown. They are really the depositions of Scoby and Vanderver, Brown being the commissioner before whom they were taken. In that opinion it is said, these depositions were taken, " to be read in evidence, in the ejectment suit, to enjoin which, this proceeding was instituted. They were taken in suits between the same parties, where the same property was involved, and this question was in dispute. These depositions were admissible as evidence under the rule laid down in the case of *Wade* v. *King*, 19 Ill. 301."

In this, the court erred, for it appears the depositions were not taken in the ejectment suits, the proceedings in which, these complainants enjoined by this bill, but in a suit brought some years previously, in chancery, in which some of these parties, but other and different parties and rights, were involved, and [*234] different questions. The principal question in that case, (*Smith et al.* v. *McConnell et al.*, 17 Ill. 135), was as to the right, of

McConnel *et al. v.* Smith, Adm'r, etc., *et al.*

the holder of a legal title, not being in actual possession, to maintain a bill to quiet his title, and compel a relinquishment of adverse claims; and that an administrator cannot in equity, obtain relief by the removal of adverse apparent titles to the lands of his intestate, or convert an equitable into a legal title. These were the two principal questions, and they were both decided against the appellants. The birth of this posthumous child, who was one of the complainants, being a question in the case, by consent, the depositions of Scoby and Vanderver on that point were read. In an ejectment case, subsequently brought' for a portion of the lands involved in this controversy, by *Detrick* v. *Migatt,* these depositions were read by consent. They never have been read in this case, as the record shows, and there is no proof that notice was ever given the complainants, that they would be taken. They seem to be *ex parte* altogether, and not within the rule in *Wade* v. *King.* There we say, and we adhere to the rule, that depositions in a former suit in chancery between the same parties involving the same questions, are admissible as evidence when the same questions are presented for judicial decision, if the parties interested had an opportunity of testing the truth of the testimony contained in them, in the various ways known to the law. This opportunity was not afforded the complainants if the depositions had been read. As they were not read on the hearing of this cause, we do not well see how the birth of this posthumous child was shown, and on that, hinged the decree. Certain testimony taken in one of the ejectment suits enjoined by these complainants, *Detrick* v. *Hatfield,* and preserved by the judge in his notes of that trial, was read in evidence, by agreement; that was the testimony of one John White, as to the possession of one of the tracts of land, and of H. W. Vansyckle, a part of which, is to this effect: "Jerome McKee died some years since in Ohio, leaving a wife, *as it is said, who had a child after his death,* neither of whom have ever been in Illinois."

This does not support the claim of the birth of a posthumous child, as it is hearsay, nor if one was born, that it was within such a period as to raise the presumption that it was the legitimate heir of Jerome McKee, deceased. There is no certainty about it.

Adhering to the views we have expressed, of the rights of the posthumous heir, if there be one, but believing that fact has not been legally established in this case, [*235] we reverse the decree on that point only, and remand the cause, with instructions to the Circuit Court, to direct an issue out of chancery, to try the fact of such birth, and to give parties leave to amend their several pleadings, and to defendants to make their answer a cross-bill, and to enable such posthumous - heir, if there be one, to make his cross-bill a bill to impeach the original decree in the case of McConnel and Vansyckle, against William McKee, Isabella McKee, and Samuel McKee.

Decree reversed and remanded.

CATON, C. J. I concur in this judgment, and all that is said in reference to the deposition. But under the record as it is now found in fact to exist, all that is said in this and the former opinion, as to the rights of the posthumous child, are but *obiter dicta*, as there is now no evidence that there is such a child. In this I do not concur.

Judgment reversed.

REUBEN COON *et al.*, Appellants, *v.* THOMAS L. NOCK Appellee.

APPEAL FROM SANGAMON.

The payee and indorser of a note, is not a competent witness to prove that an assignee had not paid any consideration for a note, or that it had not been delivered to the assignee.

THIS was an action of assumpsit, commenced in the Sangamon Circuit Court, RICE, Judge, presiding, at the June special term, by Thomas L. Nock, assignee of C. D. Loveland, the payee, on the following promissory note: " Six months after date, we promise to pay to the order of C. D. Loveland, one hundred and twenty-five dollars at Havana, Ill. Value received."

And on the back of which said note was the following indorsement: "For value received, I assign the within note to Thomas L. Nock, this January 17th, 1859."

The above note, together with others, were made and duly signed by Reuben Coon & Bro., and by Reuben Coon; said notes were made payable to C. D. Loveland, and by him duly indorsed to Thomas L. Nock, the appellant in this court.

The appellees, Reuben Coon & Bro., filed their plea of non-assumpsit, and filed a notice with said plea, by consent, noti-[*236] fying the appellant that they would undertake to prove there was usury, etc., in the original loan and contract in and concerning said notes. The plaintiff and defendant below formed their issues on said general issue, and said notice. They went to trial thereon, submitting said cause to the court without the intervention of a jury, by consent. The court heard the evidence and proofs on both sides, and gave judgment for said Thomas L. Nock for $1,381.68.

The defendants called as a witness, *C. D. Loveland*, the payee and assignor of said notes. The assignor swore that he indorsed said notes before they became due, and that the assignee had no notice of any defense. The said defendants then proposed to prove by said Loveland, the assignor and witness, that there was no consideration given for said indorsement, and that said notes so indorsed were never delivered to plaintiff below. The witness was asked said questions, which were objected to by the plaintiff, and the objections sustained by the court, and to which said rulings and decisions the said defendants excepted.

The defendants made a motion for a new trial, which was overruled by the court.

W. H. HERNDON, for Appellants.

STUART & EDWARDS, for Appellee.

WALKER, J. This was an action of assumpsit, on three several promissory notes, executed to Loveland, and indorsed by him to the plaintiff below. The indorsements bear date before the maturity of the notes. The defendants below interposed the general issue, and a notice that on the trial, they would insist upon the defense of usury, to defeat a recovery in part. On the trial, after the notes were read in evidence, and the plaintiff had rested his case, the defendants below called Loveland the payee, who testified that the notes where indorsed before their maturity, and without notice of any defense. Appellants then asked the question, "what did plaintiff give for said indorsement?" Also this question, "did you ever deliver said notes to plaintiff, after you indorsed the same?" Appellee objected to witness answering the questions, which objection was sustained by the court. This decision of the court below is assigned for error.

This record does not present the question whether the payee was a competent witness to prove the defense of usury against the assignee. Nor was it proposed to make any proof of usury. These questions were asked to establish a very different defense, and so far as we can see, entirely discon-[*237] nected from that of usury. It was an attempt to show that the assignee had not paid any consideration for the notes, and that they had not been delivered to him. The assignee was not competent to prove those facts, even if they constituted a defense. *Stacy* v. *Baker*, 1 Scam. 417. It was there held that the assignor was not competent to prove the fact of assignment, or any other fact, in a suit on the note against the maker. That case is decisive of this question.

No error is perceived in this record which requires a reversal of the judgment of the court below, and it is therefore affirmed.

Judgment affirmed.

JOHN VASCONCELLOS *et al.*, Plaintiffs in Error, *v.* MA-
THIAS FERRARIA *et al.*, Defendants in Error.

ERROR TO MORGAN.

The usages of a church, or the law of its organization as a religious society,
if they are to be considered in deciding legal controversies, should be proved as facts. In the absence of testimony, it will be presumed that religious
societies cannot dissolve their connection with the principal organization
without permission.

THE facts, as shown in this case, are similar to those reported
in volume twenty-three of these Reports, page 456, between the
same parties; except that in this case, the plaintiffs in error
offered, on the hearing, this additional proof, viz.:

Edward McMillan, Wm. D. Sanders, Wm. G. Gallaher,
and *George I. King,* testified, that they were acquainted with
the constitution, form of government, and usages of the Presbyterian Church in the United States of America, and that according to these, the members of a church not under censure,
may rightfully, by agreement, take a vote as to their adherence
or non-adherence to a particular presbytery; and that if the majority of the members of a church in such case vote not to adhere to a particular presbytery that they have been connected
with, after that fact is made known to the presbytery, the usage
is to strike the name of the church from the rolls of presbytery,
and the connection ceases.

These depositions were offered in evidence, and were excluded by the court, and the defendants excepted.

The court decreed in favor of the complainants as trustees,
and gave them possession of the property in controversy. The
[*238] defendants surrendered possession, and bring the case
up on stipulation to enter appearance.

Errors assigned:

That the court below erred in excluding the depositions of
McMillan, Sanders, Gallaher, and King.

The court below erred in decreeing in behalf of the defendants in error.

Vasconcellos *et al. v.* Ferraria *et al.*

The court below erred in not dismissing the bill of the said defendants.

D. A. AND T. W. SMITH, for Plaintiffs in Error.

M. McCONNEL, and I. J. KETCHUM, for Defendants in Error.

CATON, C. J. We are urged to review the decision made when this case was previously before the court. And inasmuch as the questions involved are of general interest to the churches in the State, we have deemed it our duty to carefully examine the facts, as well as the law arising upon the record, lest in the press of business under which that decision was made, we might have been mistaken in the conclusion then announced. In again examining the record, we find by mistaking a date, we supposed that the parties whom the plaintiffs in error represent, had, after the separation occurred, united themselves to a different body of Christians. The answer, however, discloses the fact, that the church had, previously to its connection with the Sangamon Presbytery, been united with the Illinois Presbytery, a different church organization, which we inadvertently supposed was their connection. The evidence shows that, by consent of the members of the church, a vote was taken, to determine whether the church would continue or withdraw its connection with the presbytery, which resulted in favor of withdrawal.

Since that time, the majority thus voting for withdrawal, insist that they are the church, and, as such, are entitled to the property. They deny the authority of the presbytery, and insist they are a complete independent organization. We, in the former opinion, held, that in the absence of proof to the contrary, a church must be presumed, after it has attached itself to the general organization, to have no right to sever the connection, unless by mutual consent, and that any portion of its members who continued to hold the tenets, and conform to the usages and authority of the general organization of the body, must be recognized as the church, and entitled to its property and effects. In the record as it was then presented to the court, there was no evidence of usage [*239] of the church, or the law of its organization, and such of course could not be considered in deciding the case. To entitle such law of the church to consideration, they must be proved as facts, whilst on the other hand, we know that one of the objects in the formation of all such bodies, is to render them permanent, and if there is an exception it must be shown. We may also notice the fact, that in their general organization, members, with officers, compose a church, and in this organization, a number of churches may compose a presbytery, and a number of presbyteries compose a synod, and all the synods compose the general assembly. And as none of these bodies can be formed except by agreement, the presumption would be, in the absence of evidence, that the connection could only be dissolved by consent.

After a careful review of all the adjudged cases, believed to throw any light on this question, and mature reflection to the extent of the time at our disposal, we are fully convinced that, unless the law of its organization, its government and usages, authorize a withdrawal from the general organization, its consent must be obtained, or those adhering to its tenets and submitting to its authority, in a divided church, will be regarded as composing the church, and entitled to all of its rights and privileges. We therefore see no reason to change or modify the rule there announced.

But this record presents evidence, on the question of a right of a church, under the constitution, government and usages of the Presbyterian Church of the United States of America, to withdraw from its presbytery without consent. This evidence was taken after the cause was remanded, but the court below, and the counsel of the defendants in error, seem to have understood our former opinion as holding the presumption conclusive, and the evidence was consequently rejected. The opinion is perhaps susceptible of such a construction, but it was not the design of the court to so announce the rule. The mode of argument on the trial in this court seems to indicate that the opinion was so understood. If the right to withdraw by a church at pleasure does exist, according to the constitution, government and usages of the general organization, it must be proved as a fact, and, like any other, must depend upon the evidence adduced on the trial.

This additional evidence, when considered in connection with the fact that the vote was had with the consent of the members of the church, and does not appear to have been protested against by any portion of the body, or appealed from, becomes material to the decision of the cause. It, therefore, should have been heard and considered by the [*240] court in forming the decree. If this evidence, as it purports to do, gives the constitution, government and usages of the church correctly, on this question, this church had the right, by general consent, to submit the question whether it would further adhere to its connection with the presbytery, or dissolve its relations with that body, and become an independent organization, taking with it all the rights of property it enjoyed at the time, if the decision should be in favor of separation. And so far as we can see, the mode adopted by the church was in accordance with the right, as shown by the evidence. And if so, the action of the church was regular, and the vote of the majority, unreserved by the action of the higher judicatories of the body, had the effect to render the church independent of that organization, and, by its withdrawal, they took all the rights and property of the church. The evidence in the record as it now appears, seems to establish this fact, and if so, the action of the minority was irregular and unwarranted, and by it they acquired no rights. But inasmuch as the counsel for the defendants in error seem to have acted under a misapprehension of what we designed to decide by the former opinion, and may have been prevented from taking further evidence, and from cross-examining the witnesses, instead of rendering a decree on the evidence, we shall reverse and remand the cause for further proceedings, that the parties may have the opportunity of being heard on all legitimate evidence they may see proper to adduce on another trial.

The decree is reversed, and the cause remanded.

Decree reversed.

Lucius Stebbins, and Luther L. Stebbins, Plaintiffs in Error, *v.* The People of the State of Illinois, Defendants in Error.

ERROR TO ADAMS.

Upon a change of venue in a criminal case, the court granting the order may take a recognizance from the defendant to appear in the court to which the venue has been changed.

A default and order of forfeiture was taken upon recognizance against the defendant and his surety, judgment was then taken upon the default against the defendant, and a *sci. fa.* issued against the surety alone. Upon the return of the *sci. fa.*, judgment was taken against both cognizors; and the judgment was reversed because the *sci. fa.* was issued against the wrong party.

Lucius Stebbins, one of the plaintiffs in error, was indicted [*241] in Pike county, and upon his petition the Circuit Court of Pike county granted a change of venue to Adams county, and took the recognizance of the plaintiffs in error for the prisoner's appearance in the Circuit Court of Adams county.

The Adams Circuit Court entered a default and order of forfeiture on the recognizance as to both, and a judgment was taken against Lucius Stebbins. Subsequently a *scire facias* was issued for and served upon Luther L. Stebbins, and at the March term of the Circuit Court of Adams county, Sibley, Judge, presiding, judgment was given upon the *scire facias* against both Lucius Stebbins and Luther L. Stebbins.

W. A. Grimshaw, and J. Grimshaw, for Plaintiffs in Error.

J. B. White, for Defendants in Error.

Breese, J. The principal question on the record is, as to the power of the Circuit Court of Pike county in a criminal case, to take a recognizance of the defendant, to appear in the Circuit Court of Adams county on a change of venue applied for by, and awarded to, the defendant.

It is admitted there is no such power expressly given by statute. We think the power exists independent of any statute, and is an inherent power in the Circuit Court, as in the Court of Queen's Bench, and has always been exercised by those. courts since the first organization of the State governments. There can be no doubt, the Circuit Court of Pike county, on a change of venue being awarded, could have committed the prisoner for safe 'keeping. Requiring him to enter into a recognizance is nothing more, and not so harsh a proceeding, and follows as a necessary consequence upon, or as an adjunct of, the power to commit.

The judgment, however, must be reversed, and the cause remanded, for the reason that the *scire facias* was awarded against the wrong party. The forfeiture was well taken, and will stand, but the *scire facias* and the proceedings under that, must be set aside for irregularity. Another *scire facias* can issue, directed to the proper parties.

Judgment reversed.

THE PEOPLE OF THE STATE OF ILLINOIS *ex rela-* [*242] *tione* GEORGE W. ROBERTS, Appellants, *v.* GEORGE W. RIVES, Appellee.

APPEAL FROM EDGAR.

Upon a petition for a mandamus, to compel a county clerk to issue a certificate of election to the relator, who was duly elected a justice of the peace, it is no defense that the clerk has already issued a certificate to the relator's competitor, and that he has been regularly commissioned by the Governor.

THIS was a petition for mandamus in the name of the People of the State of Illinois, on relation of George W. Roberts, against George W. Rives, clerk of the Edgar County Court, filed at the May term, 1861, of the Circuit Court of said county. The petition sets out, that at the regular township election for Paris township, in Edgar county, held at the court-house, in the town of Paris, pursuant to notice duly given, and in accordance with all the requirements of the statute in such cases provided, for the election of justices of the peace, and other township officers of said township of Paris, in said county of Edgar, that the said relator, George W. Roberts, was duly elected one of the justices of the peace for said township. That there was filed with the county clerk of said county, George W. Rives, a certificate of the election of said relator, and that he executed bond, with approved security, within the required time, and took the oath of office as required and prescribed by the statute, and requested said Rives, as county clerk, to certify to the Governor of the State of Illinois the election of said relator, as it was made the duty of said clerk to do by law; and that the said Rives, as county clerk, refused to make out and forward to the Governor of the State a certificate of the election of said relator to the said office of justice of the peace, as aforesaid, as it was his duty to do by virtue of the statute in such cases provided; and prays for an alternative writ of mandamus against said Rives, to compel him to certify to the Governor the election of the relator to said office, or show cause why he should not be required to do so. The petition was duly verified by the oath of the relator, and upon which petition an alternative writ of mandamus issued, and service was accepted by the defendant, Rives.

To which the defendant filed his answer, setting up, as a reason for refusal to certify to the Governor the election of said relator, that he had executed the necessary bond and taken the [*243] requisite oath of office (which is admitted by the defendant); that said relator was not duly and legally elected justice of the peace for said township of Paris, on the 2nd day of April, 1861, as alleged, or at any other time. And for another and further return to the writ, the defendant states, that at a town meeting, held at the county clerk's office, in the town of Paris, on the 2nd day of April, 1861, in pursuance of a notice given by the town clerk, to elect, among other officers, justices of the peace for said township of Paris, that one Newton Harlan, John II. Patton and John F. Anderson, were duly elected to fill the offices of justices of the peace for said township, and that their election was certified to him by the town clerk; that said Harlan, Patton and Anderson executed bond and took

People *ex rel.* Roberts *v.* Rives.

the requisite oath of office and oath against dueling, and that thereupon he had, as county clerk, certified their election to the Governor before he had any notice of the election of the relator, except by rumor, and that the Governor had severally issued commissions, as justices, to said Harlan, Patton and Anderson, as justices of the peace; and that afterwards, when the relator came to the office of the defendant and filed his bond, with security, and offered to take the oath of office of justice of the peace, he received his bond and administered to him the requisite oath, and filed said bond in his office, but refused to certify the same to the Governor, because said township was only entitled to three justices of the peace, and because said Harlan, Patton and Anderson had been legally elected and commissioned justices for said township, and that defendant would satisfy himself by complying with the request of the relator.   A further answer sets out the same as the last—the election of Harlan, Patton and Anderson—with an additional allegation, that the pretended election under which the relator claimed his election was illegal, unauthorized and void; that his election was not certified to defendant by any one having authority in that behalf, and because he had already certified to the election of Harlan, Patton and Anderson.

To these returns the relator filed replications, in which he reasserts that he was legally and duly elected, etc., as alleged in his petition, and traverses the statement in the return of the defendant. that he had no legal notice of the relator's election; also traversing the statements, in the return and answers of the defendant, that Harlan, Patton and Anderson were duly and legally elected, and denying that the pretended election held at the clerk's office, was legal, or held in conformity with the requirements of the statute.

On these issues a trial was had, in which the follow- [*244] ing evidence was introduced on the part of the People:

St. Clair Sutherland, being sworn as a witness, testified: that a notice shown him was one of the election notices posted up for the township election in the town of Paris; that he saw three of them, he thinks, at the most public places in the town of Paris; said that he was present on the second day of April, when the town meeting at the court-house was organized; that previous to the organization of the meeting, and between the hours of nine and ten o'clock A. M., he called upon A. J. Magner, township clerk, found him at the post office, and requested him to come and organize the town meeting; he said he was engaged and could not come. Witness returned to the court-house; thinks there were seventy-five or one hundred persons assembled there, most of them voters of the old township of Paris; but some were from what was formerly Sim's township, but then included in Paris township, as enlarged. It was between the hours of nine and ten o'clock A. M. that the meeting proceeded to organize by electing Milton M. Dill temporary chairman; and John Bovell was chosen moderator, and Theodore Read, clerk. All were allowed to vote, and they were unanimously elected; heard no opposing vote. The officers were all legal voters and residents of the township of Paris, within the old or former boundaries of the township. Proclamation was then made that the polls were opened, and that they were ready to receive votes. This all took place before any ·poll was opened or meeting organized at the county clerk's office. Some forty votes must have been cast before the meeting at the clerk's office was organized. Witness was a voter and resident of the township of Paris. Elections were sometimes held at the court-house and sometimes at the clerk's office. The buildings are detached, and about twenty feet apart. Tanner has his law office at the clerk's office.

Andrew J. Magner testified: that he was township clerk of the township of Paris. An election notice was shown him; said it was one of those which he had put up pursuant to the requirements of the law, giving notice of the time and place of holding the town meeting for the election of township officers for the town of Paris. Witness put them at the most public places. Sutherland called on him, on the morning of the second day of April, to go to the court-house and organize the town meeting. I am postmaster in the town of Paris, and was engaged in the post office, and could not go at that time, and told him so. Some time afterwards I went to the county clerk's office and organized a meeting. It was between nine

People *ex rel.* Roberts *v.* Rives.

and ten o'clock A. M.   Had no engagement with any one [*245] to organize a meeting there. It is a separate building, in the court-house yard, about twenty feet from the court-house. The county clerk and county judge occupy it for an office, and Mr. Tanner has his law office there. Elections are sometimes held at the court-house, and sometimes at the clerk's office. John J. Logan was chosen moderator, at the clerk's office, and A. Y. Trogdon, clerk. It was before ten o'clock the meeting was organized. Don't know whether any proclamation was made of the opening of the polls or not.

The notice identified was then read, as follows:

" ELECTION NOTICE.

" The citizens (legal voters) of Paris township, in the county of Edgar and State of Illinois, are hereby notified, that the annual town meeting of said township will be held at the court-house, on Tuesday, the second day of April next, being the first Tuesday in said month, for the purposes following: To elect one supervisor, one town clerk, one assessor, one collector, one overseer of the poor, three commissioners of highways, three justices of the peace, three constables, and to act upon any additional business which may in pursuance of law come before said meeting at the proper time when convened; which meeting will be called to order at eight o'clock in the forenoon, and be kept open until six o'clock P. M., unless sooner closed in pursuance of law. Given under my hand, at Paris, this 11th day of March, A. D. 1861.

A. J. MAGNER, *Town Clerk.*"

James A. Eads testified: was a voter of Paris township; was at the court-house about the time the town meeting was organized there. I voted at the court-house. Think my vote was numbered somewhere in forty. Went from court-house to clerk's office, and the meeting there was just being opened. Clerk's office is in a separate building, detached from the court-house. All were allowed to vote at the court-house. Persons voted there who lived in that part of Paris township which was formerly Sim's.

William F. Young testified: that he was township clerk of Paris township, or claimed to be under the election held on the second day of April, 1861. The minutes of said election were deposited with him. That the signatures to them were those of John Bovell and Theodore Read. The certificate was in the handwriting of Thomas Marks, an acting justice of the peace for Edgar county. Stated that he filed certificate of election for George W. Roberts and John J. Fouts with George W. Rives.

[*246] The minutes of the town meeting were then read in evidence. They show that the number of electors who voted were four hundred and five, and that for justices of the peace, George W. Roberts received 371 votes; John J. Fouts, 388 votes; Winston Griffin, 372 votes; Hardin Myers, 361 votes; Newton Harlan, 35 votes; John H. Patton, 17 votes; and John Anderson, 17 votes.

The bond was next read in evidence.

The written oath taken by the relator, George W. Roberts, was also read in evidence.

The defendant introduced and read the minutes of the town meeting at the county clerk's office on the second day of April, 1861. The minutes show one John J. Logan was chosen moderator, and A. Y. Trogdon, clerk. That the meeting was called to order by A. J. Magner, and that they proceeded to the election of township officers. That the polls were closed at forty minutes after four P. M., and that of the ballots cast for justices of the peace, at said meeting, John H. Patton received 277 votes; Newton Harlan, 280 votes; John H. Anderson, 218 votes.

To the minutes is attached the certificate of A. Y. Trogdon, clerk of the meeting.

The defendant also offered and read in evidence a record of the board of supervisors of Edgar county, so enlarging the boundaries of Paris township as to include all the territory formerly included in Sim's township.

Thomas C. W. Sale testified: that by his watch it was just half-past nine when the polls at the clerk's office were opened.

And upon the foregoing evidence the case was submitted to the court, who denied and refused to grant a peremptory mandamus, and rendered judgment against the relator for costs.

To which ruling and decision of the court the counsel for the People at the time excepted, and prayed an appeal, which was granted.

The errors assigned are: the court erred in refusing to grant a peremptory mandamus; and the judgment of the court was contrary to the law and evidence of the case.

A. GREEN, for Appellant.

E. S. TERRY, JAS. A. EADS, and THOMAS C. W. SALE, for Appellees.

CATON, C. J. The town meeting at the court-house was convened in pursuance of the notice, and in the place specified therein, and was organized strictly in pursuance of the provisions of the law, and beyond all doubt the business [*247] transacted at that meeting was legal and binding upon the town; and the election there held was valid. The meeting subsequently organized has not the least semblance of legality about it. It was at a place different from that mentioned in the notice, and after the regular meeting was organized, and more than forty votes cast. Indeed, it has the appearance of a secession from the regular town meeting, by a disappointed or discontented faction; and what took place there cannot deprive the relator of his right to a commission for the office to which he was elected, at a regular town meeting duly organized and held.

It is objected, that the defendant has already issued a certificate for another, to whom has been issued a commission for the same office. That cannot affect the rights of the relator. As well might it be contended that a certificate issued to one without color of an election, would prevent the clerk from issuing the certificate to the relator. We do not propose to turn the others out of office on an application for a mandamus. They are not parties to this record, and are not bound by this adjudication. All that the court can do, and all it is asked to do in this proceeding, is to compel the county clerk to issue to the relator a certificate of election, which the proof shows he was entitled to. Our right and our duty to do this was fully considered and

settled in *The People ex rel.* v. *Matteson,* 17 Ill. 167. A peremptory mandamus should have been issued.

The judgment of the Circuit Court is reversed and the cause
remanded, with directions to award the writ as prayed for.

Judgment reversed.

HANNAH ARNETT, and NANCY J. SANDERS, Plaintiffs in
Error, *v.* WILLIAM B. ARNETT, Defendant in Error.

ERROR TO CLINTON.

It is indispensable to the validity of a nuncupative will, that the testator
should request those present to bear witness that such was his last will.
Or that he should say or do something equivalent to such an expression.

THIS was a bill by William B. Arnett, to set aside an alleged
nuncupative will of Nathan Arnett, filed in the Circuit Court
of Clinton county.

[*248] Hannah Arnett and Nancy J. Sanders answered, alleging validity of will.

Trial by the court on feigned issue at law informally submitted.

The evidence consisted solely of two certified copies of the
record, and proof of said alleged will in the County Court of
Clinton county, which evidence is set out in the opinion of the
Court.

The court found for complainant, and overruled motion for
new trial, to which exception was taken at the time.

JOHN BAKER, for Plaintiffs in Error.

H. K. S. O'MELVENY, for Defendant in Error.

CATON, C. J. We are now called upon, for the first time,
to say how far the literal provisions of the statute must be complied with, in the attestation and proof of a nuncupative will.
And we appreciate it as a question of very considerable import-

ance, demanding our most cautious consideration. There is no dispute about the facts, for it is agreed by the parties that the record of the probate of the will, constitutes the entire proof in the case; and the only question is, whether the facts thus stated constitute a valid nuncupative will. This is the record and all the proof there is of the will, or its attestation; except that it was shown by legal testimony to have been reduced to writing within the time required by the statute:

"Be it known, that we, the undersigned, were present on the 22nd day of April, 1856, at the residence of Nathan Arnett, now deceased, in Clinton county, Illinois, then in his last sickness. The attending physician, Dr. A. R. Stickney, informed the said Arnett that if he had any disposition to make of his worldly affairs, it would be proper to do so.

"That the said Arnett said: 'I desire my personal property to be divided equally between my wife's sister, Aunt Hannah, and the two girls now living in my family. I desire my real estate to be left to Nancy Jane, a girl I have raised in my family, from the time she was two weeks old.'

"We declare that we were present and heard the above words spoken by the said Nathan Arnett during his last sickness, and that at the time of pronouncing the same, we believe him to be of sound mind and memory; and that the said Arnett departed this life on the 23rd day of April, A. D. 1856.

THOS. E. DAVIS,
SHERROD WILLIAMS."

The ninth section of our statute of wills provides: " a [*249] nuncupative will shall be good and available in law, for the conveyance of personal property thereby bequeathed, if committed to writing within twenty days and proven before the court of probate, by two or more credible, disinterested witnesses, who were present at the speaking and publishing thereof, who shall declare on oath or affirmation, that they were present and heard the testator pronounce the said words, and that they believed him to be of sound mind and memory; and that he or she did, at the same time, desire the persons present, or some of them, to bear witness that such was his or her will, or words to that effect."

While we should not be inclined to require an exact conformity to the literal requirement of this statute, in the publication of a nuncupative will, yet we are not authorized or inclined to dispense with a substantial compliance with all its provisions. It is not to be denied, that to allow oral testaments to be established in any case, is opening a door to frauds and impositions, which have sometimes, in spite of all legislative safeguards, been practiced. Yet, from the extreme necessity of the case, they have attained a firm foothold in our jurisprudence, and they must be treated by the courts with fairness and justice, with a view to give effect to the designs of the testator, when the will is pronounced and attested in conformity to the provisions of the law. But that law must be at least substantially complied with, or it is no will. In this case every requirement of the law was complied with, except the last member of the sentence quoted. That requires that the testator shall, at the time of pronouncing the words of the will, request some of the persons present to bear witness that such was his will, or words to that effect. It is not enough that the words of the will alone should be spoken in the presence of those who might bear witness to it, but the testator must also use some words indicating his desire or wish that those present, or some of them, should bear witness that such was his will. We will not now say that signs and gestures might not be so distinct and intelligible as to sufficiently indicate the desire of the testator, that he wished those present to bear witness to the will, as to amount, substantially, to words of that import, but it would have to be a very marked and unequivocal case to dispense with words actually pronounced, to the effect of those mentioned in the statute. But here we find nothing to satisfy this last clause quoted. No word was spoken, no sign made, no indication manifested, that the testator desired any one present to bear witness of his de-
[*250] clared wishes. There is nothing to show that he ever expected or wished that any one present should remember what he had said, or should ever repeat those declarations, or should ever go before any tribunal to prove that such was his will. If we say that such must have been his desire, from the nature of things, that is but conjecture at last, and the legislature has de-

clared that such conjecture shall not be sufficient. Understanding the operations of the human mind as well as any of us, the legislature knew that most probably any one who should, when *in extremis*, declare to those about him the disposition he wished made of his property, would also desire that those present would remember and bear witness to his wish, and to contribute what aid they might to carry out such wish. Such an inference must necessarily arise in almost every case where a will is declared by a dying man to those around him, but the law-makers thought it unsafe to rely upon such inference, however strong, and saw fit to require a direct expression of such wish by the testator at the time of pronouncing the words of the will. And yet, in the face of this express provision of the statute, we are asked to establish this will, upon mere inference, for there was not one word, sign or look, expressing the wish that those present should bear witness to the will. It may be and probably is true, that he did not know it was necessary to the validity of his will that he should call upon those present to witness it, but that cannot alter the law. The statute requires that a written will shall be attested by two witnesses, yet it would shock every lawyer to decide that one witness would do, because the testator supposed that was sufficient. In most cases, our convictions would be as strong that the will expresses the true wishes of the testator when witnessed and proved by one unimpeachable witness, as if witnessed by two, and yet it is not his will, because the law so declares. So here. The law required an additional formality to make this a nuncupative will, without which it should not have been admitted to probate, and for the want of which, it was the duty of the Circuit Court to set it aside and declare it void.

Judgment affirmed.

[*251] REUBEN M. WEIDER, and SUSAN WEIDER, Plaintiffs in Error, *v.* BENJ. CLARK, Defendant in Error.

ERROR TO McDONOUGH.

Where a fact is alleged in a bill and admitted by the answer, the admission is conclusive ; and evidence tending to dispute it, should not be considered.

Moore owned a tract of land which he had mortgaged to Clark for $1,400. Weider wished to buy this tract from Moore for $2,000, and another tract from Clark for $1,600. It was arranged that Moore should convey his tract to Clark for the $3,000, less the mortgage, and that Clark should then convey both tracts to Weider for $4,600 — Weider to pay $1,000 down, and give a mortgage for the balance. *Held,* that this was a sale of the whole premises from Clark to Weider, and that the mortgage being given for a part of the purchase money, Weider could not claim a homestead in the Moore tract to defeat a foreclosure.

THIS was a bill to foreclose a mortgage, filed in the Circuit Court of Hancock county, by Benjamin Clark against the plaintiffs in error. A change of venue was taken to McDonough county. The defendants filed a cross-bill setting up a homestead exemption.

The opinion of the Court gives a statement of all the points considered by the court.

GEO. EDMUNDS, and SCOFIELD, FERRIS & MANIER, for Plaintiffs in Error.

MACK & DRAPER, for Defendant in Error.

WALKER, J. The defendant, in his cross-bill, alleged that he was a householder, the head of a family, and resided on the premises in controversy, at the time when the notes and mortgage were executed. This was admitted by complainant's answer, and such portion of the evidence as shows, that he was not occupying the premises at that time cannot be considered, in opposition to that admission, so long as it remains. In determining the case, the admission must be regarded as true. But the question is, whether the notes and mortgage were given

for the purchase money of these premises, and if so, the provisions of the homestead exemption law cannot be invoked to
defeat the sale of the premises, for their satisfaction.

It appears from the record, that plaintiff in error had previously contracted with one Samuel Moore, for the tract in section seventeen, together with a small piece of timbered land, at
the price of three thousand dollars.   That defendant in error held
on it a mortgage to secure $1,400, which Moore owed [*252]
to him.   That plaintiff in error was unwilling to pay the money and receive a deed from Moore, until that mortgage was released.   And that defendant in error was unwilling to execute
a release, until the money should be paid.   It further appears
that plaintiff in error wished to purchase of defendant in error
the tract in section eighteen.   And to accommodate all parties,
it was agreed, that Moore should convey the quarter in section
seventeen and the timber tract, to defendant in error, who
should convey all three pieces to plaintiff in error for the sum
of forty-six hundred dollars, pay Moore for his land, and look
to plaintiff in error to have it refunded.   The conveyances were
thus made, defendant in error satisfied his mortgage against
Moore, paid him the balance, and received from plaintiffs in
error, one thousand dollars and his notes and mortgage to secure the balance of the forty-six hundred dollars.

That plaintiff in error agreed to pay defendant in error that
sum of money for these lands, there can be no question.   And
it is equally indisputable, that these notes and mortgage were
given to secure the balance.   Defendant in error paid Moore
for the land, and plaintiff in error does not pretend, that he
directly paid Moore anything on the land, but he insists, that
he paid Moore through defendant in error the purchase money
for that portion which he purchased of him; or that he borrowed the money of defendant in error to pay Moore for it.
We are unable to comprehend how that can be, when Moore
conveyed to defendant in error, who paid him, and when plaintiff in error received a deed from him and became liable to pay
him and not Moore.   Defendant in error paid Moore the purchase money, and there is no evidence in the record, that he
loaned plaintiff in error any portion of the amount paid to

Moore, or that it was called or treated as a loan except in the notes, to justify the reservation of eight per cent. interest.

The whole transaction, when stripped of mere forms, is clearly a sale of the land by defendant in error, and a purchase by plaintiff in error. The latter at the time paid the former one thousand dollars on the purchase. When Moore received his purchase money, it was paid to him by defendant in error. In no light in which the facts can be viewed, do we perceive that there is any evidence of a loan. We are therefore clearly of the opinion, that the notes and mortgage were executed to secure the purchase money of these several tracts of land, and that they are not subject to the defense of the statute exempting homesteads from sale.

[*253] It is, however, further urged, that the evidence shows that the decree is too large. It appears that plaintiff in error paid in a draft of $700 and through Sweeney about $300, on the fifteenth of April, 1855. This made the amount of the first note which fell due at or near that date, and this was no doubt designed to, and did satisfy and discharge that note. He again paid in December, 1858, the further sum of $321.22 through Foutch. This sum does not seem to have been paid on other indebtedness, and unexplained must be held to have been on the last note, to foreclose which this bill was exhibited. This last payment should therefore have been deducted. But the decree was rendered for the amount of the note with six per cent. interest, without that credit, which was error. The decree must therefore be reversed, and the cause remanded.

Decree reversed.

James A. Chadsey, Appellant, *v.* James G. McCreery, Appellee.

APPEAL FROM SCHUYLER.

A note payable to James G. McCreery, treasurer of the R. I. & A. R. R. Co., is not a note to the company, but to the individual named. The addition to his name is merely *descriptio personæ.*

Chadsey *v.* McCreery.

Where the name of a corporation consists of several words, the transposition, omission or alteration of some of them, may not be regarded as important, if it is evident what corporation is intended.

AT the October term of the Schuyler Circuit Court, appellant commenced an action of assumpsit against appellee, on a promissory note payable to James G. McCreery, treasurer of the Rock Island and Alton Railroad Company, the declaration containing special and common counts.

Defendant filed four pleas; the first as follows: "And the said defendant comes and defends the wrong, etc., and says, plaintiff *actio non*, because he says that the several causes of action in the said plaintiff's declaration contained, are one and the same cause of action, to wit, the cause of action specified in the said plaintiff's first count; and the said defendant avers, that at the time of signing the said note the said plaintiff falsely and fraudulently represented to the said defendant that he was treasurer of the Rock Island and Alton Railroad Company; that as such treasurer he was empowered to collect subscriptions to stock of said road; that the defendant was a subscriber for ten shares of stock of said road; that if this defendant [*254] would execute said note as a payment therefor, he (the said plaintiff) would cause certificates of said stock to be issued and given to this defendant. And the said defendant avers, that he had subscribed for ten shares of stock in the Alton and Rock Island Railroad Company, and believing the execution of said note to be a payment for said stock, and that he would be entitled to certificates for shares of said stock, executed and delivered said note to said plaintiff, which was the whole and only consideration for said note; whereas, in truth and in fact, there was and is no such company as the Rock Island and Alton Railroad Company, and the said plaintiff was not and never has been treasurer of such company, and the said plaintiff never was the owner or had the power to cause certificates of the stock of the Rock Island and Alton Railroad Company to be issued or given to this defendant—by means whereof, the consideration of said note has wholly failed. And this the defendant is ready to verify."

Second plea, "Failure of consideration."

Third plea, " Note executed without good consideration."

Fourth plea, " General issue."

The defendant filed his joint and several demurrer to the first, second and third pleas, which was overruled to the third and sustained to the first and second. Issues on third and fourth pleas. Trial, and verdict for plaintiff below for amount of note and interest. Motion for new trial overruled and judgment for plaintiff.

Errors assigned: the court erred in sustaining demurrer to first plea; in rendering judgment for plaintiff; and in overruling motion for new trial.

J. S. BAILEY, for Appellant.

M. HAY, for Appellee.

BREESE, J. This suit was not brought by a corporation, and consequently, no question of misnomer of a corporation can arise. The note is made payable to the appellee, who is described to be the treasurer of the Rock Island and Alton Railroad Company. It is mere description of the person, and if erroneous, cannot vitiate. The fact appears to be, that the true name of the railroad company is Alton and Rock Island. The transposition can be of no manner of consequence in this suit. There can be no doubt what road was meant of which the appellee was the treasurer. In 1 Kyd. 237, it is said, as the name of a corporation frequently consists of several words, the [*255] transposition, interpolation, omission or alteration of some of them may make no essential difference of their sense.

It is held, in a devise to a corporation, if the words, though the name be entirely mistaken, show that the testator could only mean a particular corporation, it is sufficient, as for instance, a devise to the inhabitants of the South Parish may be enjoyed by the inhabitants of the First Parish, "The First Parish" being the legal name. 3 Pickering, 237.

There is no evidence preserved in the record except the note, so we cannot know, but that it was abundantly proved what corporation was understood and meant, by the description in the note. That the Alton and Rock Island Railroad Company are liable to issue stock on the payment of this note, there can be no doubt. The judgment is affirmed.

Judgment affirmed.

P. B. PRICE, Appellant, *v.* M. McCONNELL, Appellee.

APPEAL FROM MORGAN.

A deed conveyed to M certain premises, extending to the west line of the west wall of a brick building upon the premises; so that it included the whole of the west wall; with the reservation that the owners of the ground on both sides should have the mutual use of the present partition wall. At that time there was a small one-story brick building on the lot adjoining on the west. Subsequently, M's grantors _conveyed this other lot to P, who tore down this small building, and erected one much higher, and extending further along on M's wall. *Held.* that the reservation in the deed to M, extended only to such portions of the west wall as were then used as a partition between the buildings, and that P had no right to the mutual use of any other, or greater part of this west wall.

THIS was an action on the case, brought by McConnell in the Circuit Court of Morgan county, based upon the following facts:

In 1850, the heirs of Gov. Duncan, deceased, were the owners of a lot in Jacksonville, upon part of which was built a large brick building, called the Morgan House, afterwards and now called the Mansion House, which building was and is three stories high, fronting south on the public square of said town, and running back north.

Adjoining this building on the west, also belonging to said heirs, was a small brick building, about one-third as high, and running about two-thirds of the depth of the same, built up against the west wall of said Mansion House, and occupying about one-third of said wall as a partition wall of said small house; but no joist of said building was inserted, or weight placed upon the wall of the Mansion House.

On the 1st of June, 1850, the heirs of Duncan, by the [*256] master in chancery of said county, sold the Mansion House and the land whereon it stood, to McConnell. The deed of the master in chancery to McConnell, which is set out in this record, shows that his purchase extended to the west line of the west wall of said house, including all the land and all the wall, and excluding this small house situated on the adjoining lands of said heirs. The deed is an absolute conveyance in fee, of all the premises and appurtenances, but contains the following reservation, while describing the west line of the property, to wit: the owner of ground on both sides to have mutual use of the present partition wall.

In 1851, McConnell leased this property to a tenant for ten years, who went into possession and occupied the same, until the committing of the grievances herein complained of, and until the commencement of this suit.

In 1858, the heirs of Duncan sold the adjoining land whereon the small house stood, to Price, the present party, and he went immediately into possession. In this deed was the following clause: " To have and to hold, etc., together with the use in common with the owners of the ground, occupied by the owners of the Mansion building, of the partition wall between the Mansion House and the premises hereby conveyed." Price then tore down this small house, and built upon the same ground a new house, higher and larger than the old house, which new house he extended above and further back than the Mansion House, and put three tiers of joist thereof in and through the wall of the Mansion House, and building but three walls to his house, and using the Mansion House wall as the fourth wall, and when he had built to the top of said wall, he built upon it, to make it higher to suit his house, and placed one-half of the weight of his house upon the wall of McConnell's house. North of the Mansion House, Price tore away a part of the side wall of a house McConnell had there on his own land, and extended his new house north, and on a line of the Mansion House, and upon McConnell's land.

This suit was brought by McConnell for the damage done by Price to the reversionary interest of said McConnell in this property, the same being in possession of his tenant. The case was tried before a jury, and a verdict and judgment rendered for five hundred dollars and costs, to reverse which, Price has brought the suit to this court by appeal.

D. A. SMITH, for Appellant.

M. McCONNELL, *pro se.*

WALKER, J. This was an action on the case instituted [*257] in the Morgan Circuit Court, for an alleged consequential injury to the building of defendant in error. It appears from the evidence in the record, that in June, 1850, he purchased the building in question, at a master's sale, of property belonging to the estate of the late Governor Duncan. The deed of conveyance contains this description and reservation: " Beginning at the south-east corner of lot number sixty-one, in the original plat of Jacksonville; thence running west forty-five feet three inches, more or less, measuring on the ground, to the west line of the main building of the " Morgan House," *the owners on both sides to have mutual use of the present partition wall;* from thence north one hundred feet; thence west sixteen feet nine inches; thence north eighty feet more or less to the alley; thence east seventy-two feet more or less to the north-east corner of said lot sixty-one; and thence south one hundred and eighty feet, more or less, to the place of beginning." The evidence also shows, that at the time this deed was executed, there was at the south end of the " Morgan House," and on the west side, a one-story brick building extending north, and adjoining to the " Morgan House" a portion of the distance of the length of that building. It also appears, that the joists of this one-story brick building were inserted into the west wall of the Morgan House at the time of the conveyance. Also, that the Morgan House was a three-story brick building, with a thirteen-inch wall, in the lower story, and a nine-inch wall in the two upper stories.

Plaintiff in error having, in 1858, purchased the adjoining ground, on the west of the Morgan, now the Mansion House, including the one-story building, "together with the use in common with the owners of the ground occupied by the owners of the Mansion House, formerly called the Morgan House building, of the partition wall between the Mansion House

and the premises hereby conveyed," proceeded to remove the
old building from his lot, and to erect a new three-story brick
building in its place. In doing so, he used the west wall of the
Mansion House, as the east wall of his. And to accommodate
his building, he pierced the west wall of the Mansion House
and inserted the ends of three tiers of joists, which defendant
in error claims, was without authority, and was injurious to
his property. That plaintiff in error also attached a shed
building, and in doing so, caused the earth to be removed
to the depth of the foundation of a shed building, annexed
to the Mansion House, and caused the foundation to be removed and replaced by another. He also removed the weather-
boarding from the west side of this shed building, and built
[*258] the space between the plaster and weather-boarding,
with brick as high as the eaves, which he sawed off and continued his own shed building above that of defendant in error.
In doing so, he constructed a valley or gutter where the eaves
had been removed, but it was insufficient to prevent leakage
and dampness, and caused a door in that building to sag. He
also placed some additional bricks on the parapet wall of the
Mansion House to increase its height.

Plaintiff in error, by his conveyance from Duncan's heirs, acquired all the right to use the west wall of the Mansion House
as a partition wall, which was reserved in the master's conveyance to defendant in error. Whether it extended to the whole,
as he contends, or it was limited alone to the wall separating the
Mansion House from the one-story brick building on the west,
as defendant in error insists, he succeeded to the right reserved
to Duncan's heirs. And he had the unquestioned right to use
whatever portion of the wall which was then reserved as a party
wall, for that purpose, so that he occasioned no damage to the
owner of the Mansion House. The use of such a wall is mutual,
but it must be reasonable, and such that neither of the parties
inflicts substantial injury upon the other. Nor has either the
right to remove or destroy the wall, nor to appropriate it exclusively to his own use.

But the main question in this controversy grows out of the
construction to be placed upon the reservation contained in

the deed from the master to defendant in error. If it can be ascertained, the intention of the parties to that deed must govern, in giving effect to the grant, as well as the reservation. It is also a rule of construction, that in cases of doubt, or when the language employed will reasonably bear either of two constructions, the instrument must be construed most strongly against the grantor. In this case the difficulty arises from the fact that, at the time the master made the conveyance, there was a portion only of the west wall of the Mansion House actually used as a party wall between the buildings, whilst the remainder only separated the estates. Had the lot west of the Mansion House been wholly vacant, then there could have been no doubt as to the intention of the parties. But as it was then situated, did the parties only intend to reserve the right to continue the use of that portion of the wall then enjoyed as a partition between the buildings, or the entire wall separating the estates, as the partition wall? The master's deed conveyed the entire west wall to defendant in error, but reserved this privilege out of the grant. The call of the deed is for the west line of the west wall of the building, and it will be observed that the reservation is [*259] not of that wall, or of the west wall of the building, but it is of "the present partition wall." This language seems to exclude the presumption that it was designed to reserve the whole of the west wall of the building as the partition wall.

If that had been the intention, it seems manifest that, as that wall had been already named as the boundary, some specific reference would have been made to it as the partition wall, but the language employed seems to refer to something different. If this was not the manifest intention of the parties, there is at least serious doubts as to what it really was. Here was a wall dividing the two estates, and a portion of that wall also formed and was then used as a partition wall of the two buildings situated on each side of the line. The reservation seems, from the language employed, more naturally to attach to the wall actually in use, than to the entire west wall of the building, but if it seemed to apply equally to one or the other, still if the deed must be construed most strongly against the grantor, the reservation must be limited to that portion of the wall separating the two buildings then in existence. The court, therefore, by the instructions given for defendant in error, in adopting this construction, committed no error.

The plaintiff in error, then, had no right to use any portion of the wall except that which was already appropriated to that purpose. He had no right to insert the ends of the joist of his building into any other portion of the wall of the Mansion House. He, by doing so, committed an injury to the reversionary interest of defendant in error, for which he had a right to recover damages. The evidence seems to establish the fact that he, in doing so, caused unnecessary injury to the wall. Whether the use of the entire wall as a partition was more convenient and less expensive to plaintiff in error, has nothing to do with the question. It is what were his legal rights—not what was convenient or profitable to him. The defendant in error had the undoubted right to use and enjoy his property in such a manner as he chose, independent of the opinion of others as to whether it is the most eligible that could be adopted, provided only that he inflicts no injury upon others.

In this case, no error is perceived in giving these instructions, and the evidence warrants the finding of the jury. The judgment of the court below is therefore affirmed.

Judgment affirmed.

[*260] Edward M. M. Clarke, Appellant, *v.* Julia Ann Quackenbos *et al.*, Appellees.

APPEAL FROM MORGAN.

Parties who claim that another is a trustee for their benefit, must clearly prove the fact. Especially so, if the trust is assumed to be in favor of those who have grossly ill-treated the person supposed to have created it.

This is a bill filed December 22, 1859, requiring defendant to account to complainants, as heirs of Eleanor Clarke, deceased, for moneys received from said Eleanor; and also to account to them as their agent, for moneys received from the sale of lands of William A. Clarke, deceased.

The bill alleges, that Mrs. Eleanor Clarke, widow of James B. Clarke, died intestate and unindebted, in December, 1856, at the residence of · E. M. M. Clarke, the defendant, in Jack⸺ sonville, Illinois, leaving the complainants and defendant, heirs and distributees of her estate. That many years since, as heir of an uncle, she became possessed of from $15,000 to $20,000, which was placed at interest for her by C. D. and G. A. Sackett, of New York, both of whom died in March, 1858. That she received the income thereof for her support, and boarded and stayed with her children from time to time as she was inclined. That the defendant induced her to reside with him at Jacksonville, under the pretext of obtaining ten or twelve per cent: interest on her money, and to withdraw all her moneys from New York, he pretending that he would thus invest them in Illinois, and also in the purchase of a residence for her. That she accordingly came to Jacksonville in the spring of 1856, and resided with him till her death in December, 1856, being then about eighty-five years old. That within about eight months after her removal, her funds were almost entirely withdrawn from the Messrs. Sackett in New York, and were placed in defendant's hands to and for her use, and to the aforesaid intent, uses and purposes. That upon her death, "defendant carried her body to the city of New York. Her funeral took place at once at Trinity Church, and after the funeral the said defendant promised to see such of the heirs as were in the city the next day, and give an account of the property and effects of his mother. He stated he was stopping at the Astor House, refused the hospitalities offered him by his several brothers and sisters who were in the city, and stated that he would meet them at the office of the Messrs. Sackett the next morning. He, failing to do so, some of the heirs called at his hotel, and lo! he had started that [*261] same morning at an early hour for Jacksonville, without leaving a message to or for the heirs, or any of them. Different ones of the heirs have written to him from time to time and frequently, inquiring as to his mother's estate, but he has not seen fit or found it convenient to answer any of their letters, and gives out and pretends at Jacksonville and elsewhere, that his mother left no property or estate of any kind or nature."

Bill charges, that defendant, about 19th of February, 1856, pur-- chased certain real estate in Jacksonville, described in the deed, of which a copy is filed. That the same was purchased and paid for with the funds of said Eleanor Clarke, and the deed "ought in good faith to have been made to her, but was fraudulently and at his instance made to him, and he in equity and good conscience is a trustee, holding the legal title to the same in trust and to the use of" her heirs at law.

Bill states, that to show the unprecedented frauds defendant is practicing upon complainants, they file a paper, giving a true statement of facts, and showing the relations of defendant to complainants, on the principles of trust and fair accounting, and call upon him to state on oath all that he knows of the allegations in their bill and the facts stated in said exhibit, beginning at date May 26, 1854; to state the amount of money he received from time to time of the Messrs. Sackett or of his mother, and whether the letters, papers, orders, etc., purporting to be signed by her are genuine, and the receipts, letters and vouchers purporting to be signed by him were so signed, and the letters purporting to be written to him were received, and the checks referred to, drawn and indorsed as stated, and whether a certificate of the Messrs. Sackett, copied in said exhibit, was in defendant's handwriting, and the papers, orders, letters, and accounts of the Messrs. Sackett are true and authentic, and the disposition he has made of the bonds and mortgages referred to, and what he received thereon, and when and from whom, and whether any of them are unpaid in whole or in part.

Bill charges, that defendant has received in cash, bonds and mortgages, more than $15,000, under the pretext of investing it for the use of his mother, and calls upon him to state what he has done with it, whether he now has it, or any part of it, and what loans or investments in property of any kind he has made of the same.

Bill charges, that there must have been a correspondence in writing touching the management and disposition of his mother's affairs, and that it came into his possession upon her death, and calls on him to produce the same, or disclose on oath [*262] what has become of it.

Bill charges, that defendant's mother " executed her last will and testament on the 30th of March, 1855, which seems not to have come to light, if in existence at the time of her death. Said defendant, at and immediately after the time of her death, came to the possession of her letters, papers and vouchers of every nature and kind, and he is called upon to disclose on oath everything he knows of said last will and testament, and to exhibit it as a part of his answer if in existence, and if not, to tell what has become of it.

Bill states, that defendant has been in the use of the real estate described since its conveyance to him, and that the rents have annually been worth $600—for which he is called upon to account.   And they file, as exhibit, a copy of a letter of defendant, dated July 29, 1860, as a part of this bill, and pray that he be held " to a full, just and true account of all and singular the matters and things referred to in said letter, with reference to the rights of complainants and defendants, as heirs and distributees of the items referred to in said letter." And that complainants regard it best to waive, and hereby expressly waive, the answer of defendant on oath.

Affidavit of defendant, at October term, 1860, that James P. F. Clarke desired his name as a complainant to be struck out from the suit.

Disclaimer of James P. F. Clarke states, that he was solicited and refused to unite in this suit, and his name was used without his knowledge, and the suit prosecuted without his sanction and in a manner involving great wrong to defendant, and desires that it be as to him dismissed. Filed October term, 1860.

Complainants' solicitors suggest the death of complainant Eleanor L. Smith, and file copy of her last will, and letters testamentary to John L. Jenks, sole executor thereof; and on their motion, court orders that this cause be revived in name of said executor as co-complainant.   And on motion of defendants' solicitors, court orders that the suit be, as to James P. F. Clarke, dismissed.

The answer admits, that defendant's mother died intestate at his residence in Jacksonville, in December, 1856, and that complainants and defendant, and James P. F. Clarke, are the heirs and distributees of whatever property she left.   That in the years 1850 and 1851, as an heir of an uncle, she received about $18,000 in cash and real estate, and placed her business with C. D. and G. A. Sackett of New York.   That she with-[*263] drew from them such moneys as she chose to do, but denies that such moneys were the income of her funds, or had any reference to it.   Denies, that she at any time boarded or stayed with, her children whenever inclined, but, on the contrary, asserts that although reared, educated and always occupying a position in society in New York and Brooklyn that secured for her, and her family while under her roof, the respect and esteem of a large circle of acquaintance; though uniformly kind, generous and indulgent to her children, and accustomed for far the greater portion of her life to all the comforts and luxuries enjoyed by the most affluent; and although to her latest days, a lady whose influence and example might well excite the envy of her sons and daughters; yet with all her children but defendant living in her immediate vicinity, and some of them and their husbands possessing great wealth, she was not privileged in her old age to board and stay with her children from time to time as she was inclined, but was compelled to forego the comforts and attentions demanded by both her habits in life and her advanced years, for such as she could procure from those who could be prevailed upon to receive their mother at board.

Answer denies, that defendant induced his mother to reside with him at Jacksonville.   Denies, that under the pretext of obtaining ten or twelve per cent. interest on her money, or under any pretext whatever, defendant induced her to withdraw her moneys, or any part thereof, from New York, pretending that he would invest them in Illinois at interest, and the purchase of a house or residence for her.

314

Answer admits, that she came, in the spring of 1856, to Jacksonville, and resided with defendant until her death, at which time she was in her eighty-third year. Admits, that previous to her death the principal portion of her funds, in the hands of the Messrs. Sackett in 1855, was received by defendant for the uses and purposes stated in the answer, but denies that it was so received for the intent, uses and purposes charged in the bill.

Answer admits the purchase by and conveyance to defendant, of the real estate described in complainants' bill, and that said purchase was made with the moneys so received by him in pursuance of the orders and instructions of his mother, but denies that said conveyance should for any reason have been made to her. Denies all fraud and fraudulent intent or purpose in procuring the conveyance to defendant, and denies that he is in law, equity or good conscience, a trustee holding the legal title thereof in trust and to the use of her heirs at law, and asserts and insists that defendant made said purchase and took said deed in his own name with the intent of vesting in him- [*264] self all legal and equitable right and title therein, and that such use of the moneys paid for said real estate was with the knowledge and in pursuance of the plans, purposes and designs of defendant's mother, as indicated in her agreement with defendant, all of which were well known to the adult complainants.

Answer admits, that defendant, since the death of his mother, has had the sole use of said real estate, but denies that the rents were anything like the value charged.

Answer alleges, that defendant's mother, from the death of her husband in 1842, reposed more confidence in and received more kindness and assistance from defendant, who resided in Illinois, than from her other children, and in almost every emergency has required his presence and assistance, which, without regard to his own affairs or expense, he has bestowed. That at her request he went to New York, in April, 1854, and remained till July, and while there, arranged with the complainants Hull for a permanent home for his mother with them. That she left her home at the said Hulls in October, 1855, having become greatly and justly dissatisfied with the treatment she there received, but before doing so, sought the aid of complainant, Henry L. Clarke, and wrote him a touching appeal, entreating him to come to her, yet that he never came nor even answered her, letter. That she also applied to complainants, Quackenbos and wife, to give her a home with them, and was informed that it would not be agreeable or convenient. That under these circumstances, pained, humiliated and distressed by the unkindness and ingratitude of those whom she had ever treated with the most affectionate indulgence, she left her home at the Hulls and obtained board in her extreme old age at a boarding-house in Brooklyn, having previously addressed defendant at Rushville, Illinois, to come to her assistance. That upon his arrival in New York, he found his mother, then eighty-one years old, living in a boarding-house in Brooklyn, ministered to entirely by strangers. Four of her children were then, as now, residing in New York. Their mother was unusually intelligent, and distinguished for her gentle manners and companionable qualities. She had cultivated tastes, and had always been accustomed, until the death of her husband, to live in a style adapted to the gratification of her tastes and in the enjoyment of all the comforts of life. Her distress from being forced to take refuge in a boarding-house, and her anxieties, were greatly increased by the apprehension which she had long entertained and frequently [*265] expressed, that her last years, like those of her mother and her uncle, would be years of physical suffering and mental imbecility, and from the dread of thus ending her days, she entertained a great repugnance to living among strangers. That in October, 1855, she was entirely neglected by her children and sons-in-law in and about New York, and was destitute of most of those comforts and all of those attentions indispensable to one of her very advanced age.

Answer alleges, in regard to that part of complainants' bill which insidiously and shamelessly suggests the destruction or the suppression by defendant of the last will of his mother, that she destroyed her said will in the summer of 1855, before she left her home at the complainants Hull. That defendant had no knowledge of said will until October thereafter, when he learned from his brother, James P. F. Clarke, that their mother had made and had destroyed her said will.

Answer states, that before the arrival of defendant, his mother had been living in a boarding-house three weeks or more, and within easy and ready access to her children and sons-in-law, yet not one of them, though well knowing where she was, had manifested the least regard for her feelings, or concern for her comfort and welfare. That defendant obtained board for himself and wife at the house where she was, and endeavored to allay the unnatural feelings of estrangement, and to bring about kindly relations between his kindred and mother. Her son James, upon being assured by defendant that their mother anxiously desired to see him, visited her. The said James was a widower and resided in the family of one of his own sons, and was not expected to offer his mother a home. Her other son, the complainant, Henry L. Clarke, was induced to visit his mother by the receipt of a note from her agents, the Messrs. Sackett. It being expected that the situation of his mother and her painful anxieties, when thus brought to his personal observation, would awaken a sense of duty, and cause him to offer his mother a home in his own comfortable mansion near the city, or would at least make him interest himself in her being properly cared for by others. But he was unmoved by the interview, and by it his mother was more deeply impressed with the conviction that in the midst of her children, and with abundant means for her support, she was disregarded, uncared for, and virtually repudiated by them.

Answer alleges, that said Henry did not again visit his mother, though she lived in boarding-houses in Brooklyn more than six months afterwards, nor did his wife or family. Nor did said Henry and wife, nor the said Quackenbos and wife, both of whom possessed great wealth and were surrounded [*266] with everything that could minister to their enjoyment, nor the said Hull and wife, during all that time, proffer any hospitalities whatever to their mother.

Answer alleges, that is was well known to all the relatives of defendant, that he was not at housekeeping, had no dwelling-house, no family but his wife, lived at board, and was in very

Clarke *v.* Quackenbos *et al.*

moderate circumstances; and states that defendant's mother, in view of her advanced age, the neglect of her children, and the presentiment that she would live, as her mother and her uncle had, until the decay of her physical and mental powers made life a wearisome burden to herself and others, applied to defendant and his wife to remove from Illinois to New York, and take care of her during the remainder of her days. And to this end proposed to purchase and furnish a residence there and make a gift of it to defendant, and also to give him to the extent all she possessed. But they could not return, for reasons assigned by them and which were satisfactory to her.

Answer alleges, that defendant's mother, in October, 1855, possessed about $12,500, in bank stock, bonds and mortgages, in the hands of the Messrs. Sackett, and also $2,400 due her from the complainants Hull, and secured by their bonds and mortgages. That she required defendant to secure for her a suitable home by returning to New York or in some other way. That he endeavored to procure for her a home with some one of her children there, but his efforts were unsuccessful, and he had either to leave his mother to the care of strangers, or provide a home for her in Illinois. The latter alternative required him to purchase a dwelling-house, enter upon a comparatively expensive style of living, devote his time to the care of his mother, and hazard the health of his wife, who had been for many years an invalid, by throwing upon her a great and unaccustomed burthen. It would also compel him to abandon the personal oversight and constant visiting of his lands, in which almost all he possessed was invested, and the value of which depended upon constant supervision.

Answer alleges, that it was finally agreed between defendant and his mother, on or about November 10, 1855, that she should give to him all of her means, excepting her bank stock and the Hull indebtedness, which together amounted to 3,000, and that he should purchase a dwelling-house in some large and pleasant town in Illinois, furnish it suitably, give her a residence with him, secure for her, while she lived, a comfortable and agreeable home by the personal attentions of [*267] himself and wife, and upon her decease deposit her remains by those of her deceased husband in her vault in Greenwood Cemetery.

Answer states, that defendant supposed that the home he was to provide would probably cost about $9,000; and it was his intention to invest whatever might remain after arranging his home, in such manner as to secure his ability to defray any reasonable expense that might afterwards be incurred in his fulfilling the said agreement, but alleges that no loan was or could be made, because all the money received by defendant was expended in carrying out the said agreement.

Answer alleges, that defendant's mother, in her fulfillment of said agreement, gave to the Messrs. Sackett the power of attorney and order or letter of instructions mentioned in complainants' exhibit B, and that it was in the execution thereof that defendant received the $1,671.20, on December 1, 1855, together with their certificate describing the bonds and mortgages, and showing the value thereof.

Answer states, that defendant has no means of knowing whether the copies of said power and of said letter of instructions are perfect or imperfect. Admits that a power and letter of similar import were drawn by the Messrs. Sackett, and executed by defendant's mother, in November, 1855, and states, that if said letter is in defendant's handwriting, he must have copied it. Admits defendant's receiving said $1,671.20, but states that he does not recollect the receipt therefor copied in said exhibit, and demands production of the original papers, and alleges that the bank check for that amount mentioned in said exhibit was for the same money and no other.

Answer admits the certificate of the Messrs. Sackett of November 30, 1855, describing the bonds and mortgages, and certifying their value and defendant's right to draw upon them for the proceeds of the sale thereof, but denies that the original certificate is in defendant's handwriting, and alleges that he still holds the original, and that if the paper copied in said exhibit is in his handwriting, he must have copied it.

Answer admits, that about February 16, 1856, defendant drew upon the Messrs. Sackett for $3,000, as is stated in alleged copy of his letter.

Answer states, that as to the orders of defendant's mother upon the Messrs. Sackett for $500 in gold, on May 4, 1856, and her receipt therefor, of May 5th and 6th, defendant has no knowledge, other than information from his mother, h e accounts of the Messrs. Sackett, and the fact that when he arrived in Brooklyn on May 17, 1856, to bring his mother to Jacksonville, [*268] she gave him that sum in gold, saying she had drawn it in anticipation of going, because she was informed that bank notes would not pass everywhere.

Answer admits the settlement of accounts with the Messrs. Sackett, on May 24, 1856, and defendant's receiving the cash, bonds and mortgages stated in the receipt in said account set forth, but denies that the check for $3,788.54 mentioned was for any other or different money than the cash mentioned in the said receipt.

Answer alleges, that the bonds and mortgages of complainants Hull, mentioned in said receipt, were delivered by defendant to his mother on said May 24, 1856, and were by her placed with the Messrs. Sackett, subject to her order, on May 30, 1856, and that the same are held by the executrix of one of the Messrs. Sackett. That on said May 30, 1856, defendant left with the Messrs. Sackett, for sale on his own account, the Haley bond and mortgage, and the Brown (Yellott) bond and mortgage, and afterwards assignments thereof to the persons who had agreed to take the said bonds and mortgages when in funds; the said Sacketts agreeing to hold said papers until they received the money for defendant.

Answer admits, that on June 2, 1856, defendant received from them, $1,089.02, and states that they received the same for defendant from the purchaser of said Haley bond and mortgage, for which he held their receipt of May 30, 1856, and that if defendant's receipt is signed as stated, it was so signed because they had for their own convenience entered in their books the money so received for him, in their account with his mother, instead of opening a separate account with defendant. And that the entry for that amount in check book of G. A. Sackett was for the same money received for defendant from the purchaser of said Haley mortgage.

Answer admits, that defendant received by the payment of his draft, $1,283.48 obtained from foreclosure of the Drake (Prosh) mortgage, and was paid to him pursuant to the aforesaid receipt of May 24, 1856, and that he also received by the payment of his draft $1,300, from the sale of the Brown (Yellott) mortgage, mentioned in the aforesaid receipt of May 30, 1856.

Answer denies, that defendant received any other or further moneys, choses in action, bonds or mortgages, than those admitted to have been received, and alleges that the moneys were received under and in pursuance of the aforesaid agreement, and are all the moneys that were received by defendant excepting the $625 on May 26, 1854, the $500 on October 30, 1855, and the $540 on November 30, 1855, the receipt [*269] of each of which sums are in the answer fully explained.

Answer states, that the object of procuring the certificate of the Messrs. Sackett, showing the value of the bonds and mortgages, and defendant's right to draw on them for the proceeds thereof, was to enable defendant to satisfy persons of whom he might purchase, that the requisite means would soon be at his command.

Answer alleges, that in the execution of the aforesaid agreement, defendant left Brooklyn, arrived at Rushville, visited Quincy, Peoria, and Jacksonville, examined and obtained the prices of such residences as would best promote the object in view, and on January 5, 1856, bargained for the property described in complainants' bill, for which he paid $1,000 on January 19, and $3,000 on February 19, and gave his note for $2,000, with interest at 10 per cent., which note he paid.

Answer alleges, that defendant wrote to Messrs. Sackett a letter on January 9, 1856, obtained possession of said property on February 19, 1856, expended thereon, in alterations and improvements, $1,211.15, for household furniture, $3,207.98, and subsequently expended on said property further moneys, amounting to $700.

Answer states, that when defendant went for his mother, in May, 1856, he found the relations between her and her children unchanged, not one of them, excepting the said James, having manifested the least interest or concern for her, nor did they, during the sixteen days defendant was then in Brooklyn, nor did any of them, excepting the said James, even come to bid their mother a parting farewell, at or before her departure for Illinois.

Answer alleges, that at the time defendant entered into the aforesaid agreement, he possessed about $2,000 of personal property, and a large amount of unimproved lands, in Brown and Schuyler counties, held chiefly by tax titles, in the vicinity of which at Rushville he resided, and by his personal attention to them and their sale, made a comfortable support, his annual expenses not exceeding $600, but that the change in his mode of living which said agreement required, more than doubled his expenses, as he felt obliged by it to provide for his mother a home suitable for her, such an one as would be in accordance with her tastes and wishes, and such as previous to her widowhood she had ever enjoyed. And that defendant did apply, invest, disburse, and use in his purchase of the property at Jacksonville and of the household furniture, in his expenditures in the improvements thereon, and in the [*270] different expenses he had to incur in his fulfillment of the said agreement, an amount of money exceeding that which he received.

Answer alleges, that the anticipations of defendant as to the disastrous effect of the said agreement upon his pecuniary interests, which, with the other reasons stated, made him reluctant to enter into it, have been more than realized, and that through the necessary neglect of his own affairs which it forced upon him, he has sustained great loss in his estate. That under the said agreement defendant received $12,632.24, of which sum he expended about $11,000 in the property at Jacksonville, the title to which was vested in him under the said agreement.

Answer states, that defendant, from motives of kindness and a sense of duty as well as to fulfill his obligations under the said agreement, left his home and business at Rushville and removed to Jacksonville, with the expectation and prospect that his wife and himself would have to devote a good share of their time in after years in smoothing his mother's pathway to the

Clarke *v.* Quackenbos *et al.*

grave.   And that had her life been protracted as was expected into that state of physical and mental imbecility so much dreaded by her, and had the necessary expenses oppressed him with debt beyond his power to discharge, not one of the complainants would have contributed to his relief.

Answer alleges, that when defendant accompanied the remains of his mother to New York, he found that the children who had disregarded and neglected their aged mother in life,. were unwilling to furnish at their residences a temporary shelter for her corpse.

Answer admits, that the funeral of defendant's mother took place at Trinity Church, New York, but not immediately as is charged, and alleges that it took place forty hours after defendant's arrival.

Answer alleges, that telegraphic notices were forwarded from Jacksonville to the relations on the day of the death of defendant's mother, and again two days afterward when defendant left there with her remains, and also during the journey to New York.   And that after he had arrived, notices of the time and place for the funeral were published in the newspapers.

Answer denies, that defendant promised to see the heirs in New York at any time and give an account of the property and effects of his mother.   Admits defendant stated that he was stopping at the Astor House.   Denies that he refused any hospitalities from any of the complainants.   Denies that any hospitalities whatever were offered to him by any of them. Denies he stated that he would meet them at the office of the Messrs. Sackett at any time.   Denies that he left New [*271] York on the morning after the funeral.   Denies that any of the heirs at any time called on him at his hotel.

Answer alleges, that defendant remained on that occasion in the city of New York six entire days, lodging and taking his meals at said hotel, and spending a portion of each day at the office of the Messrs. Sackett, which was his usual custom when in the city, as was well known to the complainants, not one of whom came to see him at said office.

Answer alleges, that notwithstanding the receipt by the complainants of the telegraphic notices, yet no provision whatever had been made by any of the complainants to relieve him of his charge, nor for the funeral ceremonies, nor did any of them appear before being summoned by one of the Messrs. Sackett, through life the attached friends of the deceased. And that when the said Sackett, from affectionate regard for the memory of the deceased, and his desire to relieve defendant, went in person to the complainants Quackenbos, whose capacious and elegant residence was nearest, and requested that the funeral of their mother might take place from their house, the request was declined, and the remains of the deceased were placed in Trinity Church until the funeral took place in the afternoon of the next day. Answer admits, that when defendant left New York four days after the funeral, he left no message for the complainants or any of them.

Answer alleges, with reference to the checks, orders, receipts, drafts, letters, and all other papers mentioned, that defendant has no means of knowing in many instances whether the said exhibit is correct, while in other instances it is incorrect and untrue, and he demands the production of all the original papers referred to therein.

Answer alleges, that in relation to letters, those of them by the Messrs. Sackett to defendant were received by him, and that he addressed letters to them upon the matters mentioned in the pretended copies of his letters, but insists and charges that the same are garbled and untrue copies.

Answer, in relation to the pretended copies of letters and parts of letters, denies that defendant's letter contains the passage, " I wrote to James a fortnight after mother's arrival in her new house," and alleges that if the last word in the sentence quoted is there in the original letter, it has been made to appear so by fraudulent alteration of the word " home" with the view of supporting the false statements and charges in complainants' bill.

Answer admits the passages quoted from the letters of the Messrs. Sackett, but alleges that those only that suited the pur- [*272] pose of complainants have been selected, and makes a correct copy thereof part of his answer.

Answer denies, that defendant's mother was induced by him

to come to Illinois upon any pretext whatever. Denies that there was any correspondence between defendant and his mother, touching the management and disposition of her affairs.

Answer admits and states, that during a visit of defendant to his mother in the spring of 1854, she drew from the Messrs. Sackett $625, for the purpose of lending it to the complainants Hull, for which and other moneys before loaned, they gave their bond and mortgage for $1,500. That the check mentioned in said exhibit, by Greenville A. Sackett, for $925, on May 26, 1854, was for the same money then loaned to the said Hulls, and was made payable to defendant because he was the bearer of his mother's order on the Messrs. Sackett, whose mode of meeting her orders was by bank checks payable to the person presenting her order, signed by said Greenville, who had the charge of their bank account. And that said bond and mortgage for $1,500 was drawn by defendant to save the Hulls the expense of the drawing thereof. Answer denies, that the said check, or the money on it, or any part thereof, went in any way to defendant's use.

Answer admits and states, that as to the check of $500, of August 15, 1854, defendant has no knowledge further than this, that it was agreed between the complainants Hull and their mother, shortly after the aforesaid loan of $1,500 was made by her, and at the time when she arranged for a permanent home with them, that she should lend to them $500 more, and they should erect a wing or addition to their house, so that she could have a room on the first or ground floor. And that in anticipation of such advance, defendant drew up for the Hulls, before his return to Illinois, a bond and mortgage for $500, and left it to be executed by them when they should require the money. That defendant afterwards learned that said $500 was advanced on said bond and mortgage.

Answer denies, that said check for $500, of August 15, 1854, or the money on it, or any part thereof, ever came in any way to defendant's hands or to his use, and alleges that defendant was not in New York when the said check and the order that produced it, were drawn.

Answer admits and states, as to the order of defendant's

mother on C. D. Sackett, of October 29, and the check of G. A. Sackett, of October 30, 1855, for $500, that they are one and the same transaction, the check being in payment of the order which was drawn on and paid out of her funds held by [*273] them jointly. That she never had an account with either of them individually. That defendant received and applied to his use the money on said check, and alleges that it was the same money which defendant's mother directed the Messrs. Sackett, by letter of July 21, 1855, to have in readiness for defendant when he should arrive in New York, and that said money was intended to reimburse defendant for the expenses of himself and wife in their visit at her request in the spring of 1854, or in the visit then required, or both.

Answer denies the allegation in complainants' bill, that defendant's mother paid over to defendant about $540, being the proceeds of sale of her five shares of bank stock, sold by her about November 30, 1855, to B. Treadwell, and alleges that defendant, at her request, carried the stock certificate, duly assigned, to said Treadwell, who gave his check therefor, on which defendant obtained the money and delivered it to his mother, who used and expended it in discharging her board bills and other expenses during the six months she remained after that time in boarding-houses in Brooklyn, and in advancing to her son James $100 of it, on May 22, 1856, previous to her removal to Illinois, and $50 in August following, after she had removed. Answer denies, that any part of said proceeds ever came to defendant's use.

Answer alleges, in illustration of the ingratitude of the complainants towards their mother, that all her children had enjoyed every advantage that wealth and kind parents could bestow. That each daughter had received her marriage portion of $2,000, and all were ever cordially welcomed to the paternal roof. That the complainant, William Hull, by borrowing the name and credit of her husband to upwards of $70,000, all of which her husband was compelled to pay, had reduced him to insolvency about two years before his death. That out of her own personal estate, acquired many years after her husband's death, she advanced the complainants Hull $2,800, part of which was made under her arrangement with them for a permanent home. That she also paid to the complainants, M. M. Quackenbos and Henry L. Clarke, $5,100, out of her said estate, to discharge claims set up by them against her deceased husband. That she also paid a debt of her husband to James P. F. Clarke, of $1,300, and also advanced $1,450 to the said James, towards his share of her estate, and also about $1,000 to the complainant, Mrs. E. L. Smith.

Answer states, that the ingratitude of complainants, and their disregard of their mother, was without the usual apology in cases of advanced age, as her temperament was uniformly cheerful and confiding, and her manners pleasant and [*274] agreeable. That her husband, before his death, had secured to her, from what remained of her property, about $4,000, and placed it in the hands of their sons, James and Henry, as trustees for her; and that after his death in 1842, the interest on that fund was her sole dependence for support until the year 1850, when she became possessed of the real estate hereinbefore mentioned, by the decision in her favor of a tedious litigation for more than twenty years in the court of chancery in which her rights as an heir of an uncle were involved. That defendant had from time to time rendered services therein for his mother, who, after the decision, sent for him to manage and dispose of the interest she had acquired. That he went to New York, and was engaged there upwards of a year in attending to her business, and effected sales of her interest in said real estate situated mostly in different counties in Western New York, from which sales his mother realized about $18,000, as hereinbefore stated. And that from the said fund and her aforesaid $4,000, she made the payments and advances hereinbefore mentioned, and paid, although under no legal or equitable obligation, the aforesaid claims of the complainants, Henry L. Clarke and M. M. Quackenbos.

Answer alleges, that defendant learned from his mother in 1845, that her only means of support was the interest on the aforesaid $4,000 in the hands of her trustee, Henry L. Clarke, and that it was not sufficient to supply her necessary wants. That he also learned from her that her children and sons-in-law

had devoted neither time, labor nor expense to ascertain anything about the estate of her deceased son, William A. Clarke,
of Arkansas, who had died in that State without issue and un-
married more than two years previously, and who had received
from his parents large advances in cash, and also a large amount
of wild lands in Kentucky. That defendant was unable to
learn whether her said son had or had not died intestate, nor
whether he had left any property, nor whether there had been
administration upon his estate. That all defendant could learn
was, that the said William had been greatly embarrassed and
was supposed to have been so at his death.

Answer alleges, that defendant, at his mother's request, undertook to visit the States of Arkansas and Kentucky, and
secure and protect her interests in the said estate.

Answer states, that defendant, before the commencement of
this suit, released to complainant, Charlotte Hull, at her request and for no consideration, all his interest in the bonds
[*275] and mortgages, etc., due from her and her husband to
the estate of defendant's mother.

Answer states and charges, that this suit is prosecuted in
pursuance of a dishonorable and corrupt agreement by which a
certain lawyer or lawyers in New York are to have the half or
quarter part of the avails thereof in case of success, and nothing in case of failure, and are to defray all costs and expenses of complainants therein; and that such agreement was
made in New York, and is in violation of the law of that State
as well as of good morals, the administration of justice, and
the law of the State of Illinois.

Answer further states, in order to show the tendency and
effect of said corrupt agreement to pervert the course of justice
and oppress the citizen, that although the heirs at law, before
this suit was brought, had released their interest in their
mother's estate in New York to the complainant, Charlotte
Hull, yet in furtherance of the schemes of said lawyer or
lawyers to worry and harrass defendant into an unjust compromise of this suit, letters of administration on her estate
were obtained in New York in April, 1860, and when defendant, in preparing for his defense in this suit, went to New

York, suit was brought against him in the Supreme Court of that State, in the name of such administrator, and he is thus compelled to defend two suits by the same parties in interest, for the same demands, at the same time, and depending on the same evidence, in tribunals of justice more than a thousand miles apart.

Answer denies all the allegations, statements, etc., in bill, that have not been admitted, denied, etc., and prays for dismissal of bill with costs, etc.

Deposition of Mrs. *Sophia E. Waite:*

That she is seventy-two years of age, and resides in Brooklyn, Kings county, New York, with her daughter, Mrs. Lyman, and so resided in 1855. That from October, 1855, to May, 1856, she conversed frequently with Mrs. Eleanor Clarke, who was then boarding with Mrs. Lyman. That Mrs. Clarke often spoke of going to Illinois to live with her son, and said " she had given her money to her son Edward to purchase a place in Jacksonville, and he had purchased it, and furnished a room expressly for her." That she said she was going there to spend the remainder of her days with her son, and he had promised that when she died he would bring her remains back and place them by her husband's in Greenwood Cemetery.

That she said "he was the only one of her children who had offered her a home, consequently she had given him all her property, and no other child should have any of it." [*276] She said " none of the other children had manifested any affection or interest in her welfare."

That Mrs. Clarke spoke of the manner the house was furnished, and particularly of her room in it, and always spoke of it as her son's.

That Mrs. Clarke boarded, in May, 1856, with Mrs. Woodruff, in Warren street, Brooklyn, and that she occasionally saw her there. That Mrs. C. expressed herself highly gratified with what her son had done, and expressed her anxiety for him to come and take her to his place in Illinois. That she spoke of this before her son came for her, in May, 1856, and said " she felt as if every tie was severed here."

That Mrs. Clarke felt very much depressed when speaking of

the conduct of her children, and expressed a great deal of feeling, having children nearer her who manifested no interest in her. That her feelings were not those of anger, but of grief, at their conduct.

To 10th interrogatory, as to the manners and qualities of mind and heart of Mrs. Eleanor Clarke, answers, "That she was a very pleasant, interesting and agreeable woman, and merited the respect of all her acquaintance. She was very intelligent and of strong mind, and uniformly pleasant and agreeable. That she saw her almost every day in her room while she was boarding with Mrs. Lyman. Mrs. Clarke was always perfectly lady-like in her manners, remarkably so. She was very fond of music, would come in the parlor often and play on the piano, and was of a very cheerful disposition."

To the cross-interrogatories, witness answers, I am not related to any of the parties. I never knew of any family quarrels between them. I only know what Mrs. Clarke said to me when she spoke of her children's conduct and their neglect of her. I do not know any of her children except her son, with whom she went to live at the West. I became acquainted with him while Mrs. Clarke was boarding with my daughter, in the latter part of 1855. The statements made by Mrs. Clarke were while she was boarding with my daughter, and with Mrs. Woodruff, between December, 1855, and June, 1856. I cannot state the particular time, but it was very frequently while I was in the room with her. She never mentioned or made any statements about her family matters to me in the presence of others. I know of no contract between her and her son, and I have never seen any correspondence between them.

Deposition of Mrs. *Elizabeth H. Woodruff:*

That her age is thirty-eight years, and she resides in New-[*277] ark, Essex county, New Jersey, but resided in Brooklyn, New York, in 1856. That she had conversations at different times with Mrs. Eleanor Clarke, who came to board at her house in Brooklyn, May 1, 1856, and remained till June following, having come to stay only till her son should come to take her to his home at the West. That she always talked with a great

Clarke *v.* Quackenbos *et al.*

deal of pleasure about her son Edward, and of his coming on to take her to his home in Illinois. That she wished to end her days with him, and then he should have all the property she left, as he was the only child that she had that showed any affection for her. She often spoke about his having a fine house handsomely furnished in Illinois, and spoke of his having one room furnished expressly for her, and told me how it was furnished. She told me that he wrote to her and mentioned in his letter about the room and furniture, and seemed perfectly delighted with it, and with the prospect of going to live with him. She always spoke of the property being his own. I don't think she ever said anything to me about her remains being brought back

To interrogatory 5th, " Did she in any of those conversations say anything about having given her money or means to her son Edward or to her son in Illinois, and about the rest of her children not getting any of it?" answers: " She did; she said she had given it to him; she wanted that he should have it all. She said she did not want the others to have one dollar, as they were not only not willing that she should live with them, but did not ask her to visit them. She always, when talking of this, shed tears." That she always spoke of her other children as not showing any feeling for her, and did not care for her, nor want her at their houses, and when they happened to meet her, did not treat her as a mother or friend.

To interrogatory 10th, as to the manners and qualities of Mrs. Clarke, answers: " Her society was very agreeable. She was very intelligent; the ladies in the house were very much pleased with her company, and I may say delighted with it. I could not see what fault any of her children could find with her, except that she could not conform to the late fashions in dress. She was certainly pleasant, not inclined to find fault nor make any trouble, very cheerful in her disposition, and very fond of music."

To the cross-interrogatories, witness answers, that she is not related to any of the parties, never heard of the family quarrels referred to, and knows nothing of any except what Mrs Clarke said to her while boarding with her, and does not remember whether any one was present. That the conversa-

tions occurred at any time through the day when she went in
[*278] to sit with Mrs. Clarke. That she was not present when
any contract was made, and has never seen any correspondence
between them to that effect, and knew nothing about Mrs.
Clarke's "disposition of her property, except what she told me,
that she had given it to her son Edward."

Deposition of *James P. F. Clarke:*

States that he is aged sixty-two years, resides in Brooklyn,
New York, and is a clergyman of the Protestant Episcopal
Church.

That the defendant is his brother, and has resided in Illinois
for the last twenty years, and they are children of James B. and
Eleanor Clarke. That his parents were wealthy, his mother
having inherited at least $40,000 from her father, and subse-
quently about $40,000 more from her uncle, John Fisher, a
portion of which last inheritance came into her possession after
the death of her husband, who, from the commercial crisis of
1837, and from large indorsements for his son-in-law, William
Hull, involving a loss of over $70,000, became completely im-
poverished. That previous to his father's misfortunes, his
children were all settled in life, the daughters having received
their marriage portions, and the sons having been pecuniarily
assisted by their parents, but that he is unable to specify the
amount in either case.

That his mother's sole dependence for support for some eight
years after his father's death, was a fund of from $3,000 to
$4,000, managed and controlled by Henry L. Clarke, until about
April, 1845, when, from her dissatisfaction with the manner and
with the amounts of the payments she received of him, she removed it from his control and placed it with her son-in-law, M.
M. Quackenbos, under the advisement of the defendant.

That his brother, William A. Clarke, died on his plantation
in Arkansas, in 1843, and that no exertions were made by any
one for about two years to ascertain anything respecting his
estate. That defendant, for the purpose of recovering it, subsequently visited Arkansas and Kentucky, but how often, or at
whose request, he is unable to state. That he heard of his do-

ing so from his mother, who showed him letters from defendant reporting his action there in regard to her business.

That he had no particular acquaintance with the business affairs of his mother until 1854, when he indorsed, filed and made for her a list of her papers. That he is not aware that any of the complainants in this suit devoted any time, service or money in the matter of the estate of the said William A. Clarke, deceased.

That the defendant " did account, to the entire satisfaction of my mother and of all the parties interested, for his [*279] whole agency in regard to his brother William's estate, and none of them, to his knowledge or belief, made any application to the defendant for information in regard to that matter prior to the commencement of this suit."

That his mother was involved for twenty years at least in a chancery suit relative to her rights in certain real estate, as an heir of John Fisher, and that at her request defendant, in 1848 and 1849, in order to expedite the same, informed himself of all the proceedings therein, and had much to do in advising and consulting with the counsel, but does not remember how long he was so engaged.

That after the decision in his mother's favor, she became involved in other suits respecting said property, and sent for the defendant, who came to New York and was engaged for a year in her business, and under a power of attorney disposed of her interests in said real estate, which was situated in Brooklyn and in different counties in the western part of New York. That the amount realized from the sales was about $18,000, and that her funds in the hands of the Messrs. Sackett, in 1855, consisted of what remained unexpended of that sum, and of the small amount she had previously possessed. That in the course of said business, defendant purchased some property in Brooklyn for his mother, from which she realized a profit of at least $1,000.

That his mother, from her own funds, paid a claim of M. M. Quackenbos and Henry L. Clarke, of about $5,000, on account of moneys they had paid as indorsers for her husband; she having with her husband signed an instrument to secure them, out of the property she expected by litigation to realize from her uncle's estate. And that she voluntarily and without solicitation paid him a debt due from his father, of $1,300.

That his mother boarded and made her home, from the spring of 1854 until October, 1855, with the complainants Hull near Sing Sing, about thirty miles from New York. That she advanced to the Hulls $1,000, and that defendant came there in the spring of 1854, and while there, an arrangement was made with the Hulls by which his mother was to have a home permanently (as witness understood) with them, and further moneys were advanced to them, and defendant drew the bond and mortgage for $1,500, executed by the Hulls, to secure the advances to that time. The money then advanced was drawn from the Messrs. Sackett, whose accounts show that on May 26, 1854, they paid $625 to defendant for his mother. That it was ar- [*280] ranged, during said visit of defendant, that his mother should advance $500 more to the Hulls, that they might erect a wing or addition to their house, so that she could have a room on the first or ground floor, and defendant drew the bond and mortgage to secure it when it should be made. That said addition was built, and the $500 was drawn from the Messrs. Sackett for that purpose by him, on August 15, 1854, as he believes. That if defendant had been at that time in New York he would doubtless have obtained it for his mother as witness did. That there was a further advance of $400. That the pecuniary circumstances of the Hulls were at that time moderate. That his mother paid $7 per week for her board, and was reasonably satisfied until the summer of 1855, when she became more and more dissatisfied until she determined upon a change of residence. That the causes were such as in the judgment of both the parties precluded the idea of her remaining with them.

That at his mother's request he wrote to defendant, informing him of his mother's unhappiness, and that she desired him to come to her, and that she had directed the Messrs. Sackett to have $500 in readiness to pay him on his arrival, but cannot recollect the precise time when he so wrote.

That he understood that his mother wrote to defendant in the summer of 1855, to come to her, and bring his wife with him. That he understood that Mrs. Hull wrote to defendant, informing him of the dissatisfaction and unhappiness of his mother, and that some arrangement must be made for another home for her. That he was informed by his mother that she had written to her son, Henry L. Clarke, expressing, in the strongest terms, the extremity of her distress, and evincing a desire to remove for a time at least to his house, and that her letter was answered by the wife of said Henry.

That his mother anxiously expected defendant at Sing Sing, and afterwards in Brooklyn, and that her anxiety was caused by her unhappy situation, and she did earnestly hope that defendant would remove from Illinois, and give her a permanent home in his family here. That she left the residence of the Hulls at Sing Sing in October, 1855, and came to Brooklyn, and procured board at a private boarding-house, and afterwards in another; the houses were kept by persons who were strangers to her. That he does not know that any direct appeal was made by her to the complainants, Quackenbos and Henry L. Clarke, for a home, but that she informed him that her wishes and feelings in regard to a change of residence were made known by her to them. That he does not know what was said by complainant Quackenbos when [*281] spoken to, but the alleged reason given for declining to receive her, was of such a nature as deeply to mortify and grieve her.

That he has been a widower for many years, and did not keep house in 1854, 1855 and 1856, nor for several years previously. That the complainants, Quackenbos and Henry L. Clarke, resided, and had for a long time before, in the city of New York and its vicinity, and both of them were then and had been for many years, reputed to be possessed of great wealth. Their dwellings were capacious, and their style of living such as is customary with gentlemen of wealth. That he does not recollect that the complainants, Hull, Quackenbos and Henry L. Clarke, visited their mother while she was at the boarding-houses in Brooklyn, except as to Henry L. Clarke, who did, at her special request, conveyed by the Messrs. Sackett, after the arrival of the defendant, visit her. That his mother was greatly

astonished and grieved by what she considered his unfilial coldness, and by his omission to make any offer of his aid in procuring her a home. That he does not know that his mother
was invited by the Hulls, or by Quackenbos and wife, or by
Henry L. Clarke and wife, to their houses while she was at the
boarding-houses in Brooklyn, or that she visited them. That
the alienation and estrangement, as he understood it, was on her
part as well as on theirs.

That his mother informed him, in the spring or summer of
1855, that she had destroyed her will, and he considered the
fact well known to all the family. That he mentioned it to
Mrs. Hull prior to his mother's removal from Sing Sing, and
also mentioned it to defendant on his arrival in Brooklyn in
in the fall of 1855.

That the defendant and his wife immediately procured
board where their mother was, and the subject of consideration
with defendant and his mother was the obtaining a suitable
home for her.

That his mother did frequently express a morbid dread and
horror of living with and spending her last days among strangers, and was at times needlessly distressed by such fears, and
frequently alluded to the case of her uncle.

That his mother's determination to make her future home
with defendant in Illinois, and that he was then and had been
for some time living at board, was known to all, witness believes, except possibly Mrs. E. L. Smith. That the agreement
that the defendant was to purchase and furnish a place or home
in Illinois, and return and take his mother there to live with
him, was well known in the winter of 1855 or soon after, to
[*282] the complainants or some of them. That he learned
from his mother that she was going there to spend the remainder of her days with defendant and his wife, and they were to
have the charge of her and take care of her so as long as she
lived, and he knows that she considered it her only resource if
she was to enjoy a home with any of her children.

That he understood from frequent conversations with his
mother, that the agreement was substantially this—all her
means were to be placed in defendant's charge, and to be ap-

plied by him to the purchase of such a residence in Jacksonville, without limitation as to the amount such purchase might require, and whatever remained of her means was to be invested by him at his discretion for her benefit. Said residence to be genteelly furnished, and to be her home during the remainder of her life, and her remains to be brought to New York for interment in her vault in Greenwood Cemetery.

That the defendant was fully authorized to furnish the residence spoken of out of her funds, and the title to it was to be and remain in him.

That his mother, in July, 1855, directed the Messrs. Sackett to have $500 in readiness as before stated, to meet the expenses of defendant and wife in the visit she desired from them, but he does not recollect that the money was to be obtained from the sale of some of her bank stock. That the defendant received the $500 soon after arriving, and probably on presenting the order of October 29, 1855, as the Messrs. Sackett never paid out her money without an order from her. That all his mother's available means were in their charge, and she drew from them from time to time whatever moneys she required. That she did advance to him, shortly before her removal to Illinois, $100 in bank bills, and transmitted to him $50 after her removal.

That defendant was a fortnight or more in Brooklyn, in May, 1856, and his mother accompanied him to Illinois. That he does not know and cannot recollect having heard that the complainants, Quackenbos and wife, Hull and wife, Henry L. Clarke and wife, or any of them, during that time, visited or tendered any hospitalities to their mother or to defendant, or came to bid them a parting farewell at or before their departure.

That he received a telegraphic dispatch communicating the death of his mother, from defendant, and his expected arrival with her remains, and endeavored to meet him, but failed in consequence of going to the Erie depot in Jersey City, instead of that in New York. That he was informed that dispatches were received by the Messrs. Sackett and immediately conveyed to the relatives. That no preparations were made [*283] for the funeral before defendant's arrival. That he was in-

Clarke *v.* Quackenbos *et al.*

formed that application was made by one of the Messrs. Sackett, after defendant had arrived, to the complainants Quackenbos, to have the funeral at their house. That the remains were placed in Trinity Church, and were there about two days to give time for the necessary preparations for the funeral.

That he was informed that defendant was detained in New York, on the occasion of the funeral, a week or more, and stopped at the Astor House. That the Messrs. Sackett were among the oldest and most intimate friends of his mother and of the defendant, who never failed to have frequent intercourse with them whenever he visited New York. That they died two or three years since, and always enjoyed the highest character for integrity and honor in their profession and otherwise.

That his name was used as a complainant in this suit without his knowledge and notwithstanding his refusal. That he was solicited, about the close of the year 1859, to unite in a suit about to be instituted against defendant, and to be conducted by lawyers whose only remuneration was to be the half or quarter part of what might be recovered, and that he positively refused to be made a party. That he was afterwards informed that the suit had been commenced, and that all the other heirs had united in such agreement respecting the suit, but does not know in what State the agreement was made, and does not remember the names of the lawyers, but thinks that the name of one of them was Silliman.

To cross-interrogatory 5th, "Have you and the defendant, in the family troubles referred to in this case, made common cause of hostility to the complainants or any of them?" answers, "He is not certain that he rightly understands the purport or object of the question. If it be meant to inquire whether he has so taken sides with any of the parties as to be induced to combine or collude with any of them, his answer, he thinks, need only be, that the defendant, as well as some of the complainants, have been alienated from him and more or less offended by the neutral position he has persisted in maintaining."

Deposition of *Robert S. Fleet,* complainants' witness:

That he is twenty-four years old, and resides in Brooklyn;

New York. That he was a clerk in the office of the Messrs. Sackett, and has possession or control of their books, papers, etc. That he acts as the agent of his sister, Mrs. Sackett, who is administratrix of C. D. Sackett.

That the Messrs. Sackett were the agents and attorneys of Mrs. Eleanor Clarke, up to November 30, 1855, when [*284] she directed them to pay over all her moneys to her son, the defendant. That her estate was valued at from $14,000 to $15,000, principally bonds and mortgages, and some bank stock. That he has no knowledge about any agency, admissions or inducements of defendant for such withdrawal or removal, and does not know at whose instance or request she moved to Jacksonville, Illinois.

That he understood from Mr. Sackett, after her removal to Jacksonville, that he paid over the entire estate of Mrs. Eleanor Clarke to defendant in money, the proceeds of collections and sales of her bonds and mortgages, bank stock and accounts.

That defendant was in New York some days on the occasion of his mother's funeral, but cannot state how many, and does not know of his promising any of those interested in her estate to adjust matters with them, and knows nothing of his leaving [New York] suddenly.

That he is acquainted with the handwriting of Mrs. Eleanor Clarke, and of the Messrs. Sackett, and of the defendant, and holds the papers referred to in the 8th interrogatory as agent for Mrs. Sackett, who would not like to part with them, and he therefore annexes copies.

That Mrs. Eleanor Clarke sold her five shares of bank stock, and he does not know to whom she paid the proceeds.

To cross-interrogatories 9, 10, 11, and 12, answers, that he thinks telegraphic despatches were sent to the Messrs. Sackett, of the death of Mrs. Eleanor Clarke, and of the time when defendant would leave [Jacksonville] with her remains, but there might have been none, and that the complainants, who were then in New York and Brooklyn, were notified by the Messrs. Sackett. That he has no personal knowledge of the matters referred to in 10th interrogatory, except that Henry L. Clarke and defendant met at Messrs. Sackett's office, that G. A. Sackett was sent up to the Quackenbos family to consult their views about the funeral, and that it was arranged [he thinks] at said office respecting the funeral. That he thinks he put a notice of the funeral in one of the Brooklyn papers, for the Messrs. Sackett, and the notice was published in the New York papers.

That the defendant was often in the office of the Messrs. Sackett, but cannot state how often, and does not know that any of the complainants called on him. That Henry L. Clarke was the only one whom he saw at the office at the same time defendant was.

Copies of letters of defendant to the Messrs. Sackett, referred to in the opinion:

[*285] RUSHVILLE, January 9, 1856.
C. D. & G. A. SACKETT, ESQRS.:

My Dear Friends:—From the time of my leaving New York I have indulged the confident expectation of hearing from you before the close of the first week in January. On every arrival of the mail since that period has elapsed, I have been greatly disappointed upon finding that you had not yet written. If there is anything you can do to facilitate the con· version of the mortgages into cash, I most earnestly beg you to do it. I have concluded a very advantageous bargain for a property at Jacksonville, and am under the necessity of paying $3,000 cash on or before the first of March next. As immediate possession will be given to me on the payment of that sum, I am exceedingly anxious to have it in my power to do so as soon as possible, that I may make the necessary arrangements in the house before going on for my mother, who I know is daily looking for me with much solicitude. If you entertain the slightest doubt of being able to get the mortgages cashed in due season, let me know it, that I may come on at once. That amount must be raised as soon as possible. If it cannot be done by an assignment of some of the mortgages, I must then go on to New York in the expectation of borrowing it by hypothecating them. Should I find myself unable to pay the money by the first of ᐟ March, I shall be in a most distressing embarrassment.

. Do write me on receipt of this.

Very truly yours,

EDWARD M. M. CLARKE.

RUSHVILLE, Ill., January 28, 1856.

C. D. & G. A. SACKETT, ESQRS.:

My Dear Sirs:—I telegraphed you at Jacksonville for the purpose of ascertaining whether any of the bonds were sold, because if I could at that time have drawn for the $3,000, I should have obtained possession of the property in a few days instead of waiting till the first of March next, and then it would have been in my power to have had the house in readiness for mother at least a month sooner. From your reply, I judge that it would be desirable to defer drawing upon you until about the 14th of February, so as to afford you ten days after the 20th of February to pay it, and yet I did not feel altogether certain that such was your desire. Your despatch was "draw on us at ten days after sight before 20th February." Had I drawn immediately upon receiving it, that would have been a literal compliance with its language, but I judge that you desired me to draw a few days before the 20th Feb., at ten days' sight. In this conclusion, however, I was not sustained by Mr. Ayres, the banker, [*286] at Jacksonville, to whom I showed the despatch, who said that its proper interpretation was, that I should draw so as that you would have, at the time of your acceptance of the draft, ten days before the 20th Feb'y to pay it, and that you wished me to draw about the 1st Feb. I now think that neither of us understood the despatch as you intended it. By our last mail (26th) I received your favor of 18th inst., in which, after saying that I will not be disappointed in the $3,000 I wanted by 1st March, you say, "In fact you may draw at any time before the 20th Feb'y next, at ten days after sight, advising us per letter for the amount. We mention the last day that we may not be obliged to hold the money, which is now ready, unemployed after the first week in March." I infer from this, that I may draw on any day that I may choose, and that you desire that I should not defer it longer than 20th Feb'y. I intend riding over to Jacksonville (38 miles distant) as soon after the 1st of Feb'y next as I conveniently can, and will draw upon you at that place, of which I will inform you at the time by letter. I have some reason to believe that I may obtain possession of the property on the 15th Feb'y, in which case we will be able to go on to New York for mother by the first of March next. I will write to her by the next mail. I trust that you will be able to dispose of some of the other mortgages before I reach New York. I particularly wish that you would give notice to all whose bonds are now due, that they must be discharged by 1st of March next. I can readily lend money here upon as good security as should be desired, at ten per cent.; and I have engaged for mother one loan of $2,000 before first of July next, and I could easily engage all that she has. Elizabeth sends love to Mrs. C. D. S., and desired to be had in kind remembrance by all.

Believe me to be very truly yours, etc.,

EDWARD M. M. CLARKE.
JACKSONVILLE, February 16, 1856.

C. D. & G. A. SACKETT, ESQRS.:

My Dear Friends:—I have just drawn upon you for $3,000, payable on the first of March next, but if convenient to you, it may as well be paid on presentation. I did not draw at ten days' sight, because I deemed it unimportant, as the draft will probably reach New York at the same time with this note (about 22nd inst.), and if you should desire it, will have about eight days before the first March. I shall leave here for New York as soon after possession is given me of the property as [*287] possible. I trust that mother is well—shall write to her in a day or two. Inform her that I have written to you, and say that we are well, and more anxious for, than she is to have, everything arranged as soon as can be, so that we may go on for her, etc., etc. I write in great haste, as the mail closes in a few minutes.

Address all future communications to me at this place. I am very anxious to know how mother is, and will be much obliged to you if you would inform me.

Very truly yours,

EDWARD M. M. CLARKE.

Decree: That the bill be dismissed so far as it charges fraud upon defendant, and dismissed so far as it relates to the estate of William A. Clarke, deceased. That the investments by defendant in the house, lot and furniture, belong to him under the agreement, and complainants have no right or claim therein, but that the proofs are not sufficient to show that defendant is entitled to the residue, and that defendant pay $1,580.80 to complainants within ninety days, etc., or, etc.

That the proofs show that defendant is entitled to the property at Jacksonville. That the balance must be distributed among the heirs at law. That so far as the bill charges fraud, it is dismissed, the charge not being sustained by the evidence. On the contrary, the facts show that defendant has, in the transactions out of which this suit originated, established a character for honesty and filial affection in pleasing contrast with that of others, who are alone entitled by the strict rules of law to a portion of the estate of Mrs. Clarke, deceased, which in good conscience they ought not to have.

The decree was pronounced by WOODSON, Judge.

The errors assigned are, that—

The court erred in rendering a decree in favor of the complainants in the suit.

The court erred in not rendering a decree in favor of the defendant in the suit, dismissing complainants' bill.

The evidence does not sustain the case presented by the complainants' bill.

The evidence does not authorize or warrant the decree, in so far as the court rendered a decree against the defendant in the suit.

The case presented by the complainants' bill does not authorize or warrant the decree.

The court ought to have allowed the defendant in the suit his cash expenses and reasonable remuneration for all services and losses incurred, rendered and suffered by him in [*288] carrying out the agreement set up in defendant's answer.

H. B. McCLURE, for Appellant.

D. A. SMITH, for Appellees.

Breese, J.   This case presents not a single feature to commend it to the favorable consideration of any court.

The answer of the appellant, sustained as it is by all the
proofs in the cause, shows a case of such heartlessness on the
part of the complainants—such want of filial regard—such absence of affection and reverence for an aged mother on·the very
brink of the grave, and who had been more than mother to all
of them—whose temper was of the kindest and most cheerful
nature—whose heart yearned for her children's love and sympathy—who had been accustomed to all the luxuries and attention which wealth cannot fail to command—within the circles
of whose gentleness and love, all ought to be happy—whose
gentle disposition created an atmosphere around her, which
should have warmed the coldest heart—who had, from the impulses of her generous nature, embarrassed herself to relieve
them—who was suffered, by them, surrounded, as they were, by
all the comforts of life, residing in luxurious mansions, with
rooms well furnished and to spare, to make her home with
strangers, at the advanced age of eighty-three, who denied to her
remains the shelter of their roofs,—presents such a picture of
cold and heartless nature, as to make humanity shudder!   We
cannot contemplate the painful picture with that coolness which
should characterize judicial conduct, and we shut it out from
our view with the remark, that their presumption, in claiming
the property of a mother thus abandoned, and neglected, is unparalleled.   The able counsel who argued the case on their part,
contented himself with contending, that although property and
means sufficient to procure and furnish a fit residence for this
aged mother, was undoubtedly, by her free gift, the property
of the appellant, yet as to the surplus remaining, he was but a
trustee for the complainants, her heirs at law.   This is the only
point we will notice.   This surplus it seems, amounted to
about fifteen hundred dollars, and for it, a decree has been passed to compel the appellant to account to complainants for it, all
pretense of fraud so freely charged in the bill against him, being
expressly ignored in the decree itself.

Under the circumstances of this case, there being such a full
[*289] denial of all the material statements of the bill, and the

proofs being so full and conclusive, in support of the position assumed by the appellant in his answer, that he was the donee of the entire fund, that we would require the strongest evidence to establish a trust in their favor—in favor of persons who had repudiated—disowned—contemned and spurned the donor. From the evidence, we think it is impossible to believe, that this venerable mother, feeling so sensitively as she appears to have done, the coldness and ingratitude of these her children, and protesting always, that they should enjoy none of the estate, should have so bestowed that estate as that any part of it should come to the complainants. There is no one fact in the cause to warrant this conclusion, and it should not exist in such a case as this, in mere inference from other facts, but should be positively established. The appellees attempt to make out this trust, by the testimony of James P. F. Clarke, who, to his credit be it said, refused, though a brother, and as well entitled to a share of this estate as the complainants, to become a party to the bill. This witness gives a full and apparently fair history, of the arrangements by which appellant came into the possession of their mother's whole estate. His testimony, in the most essential particulars, does not materially differ from the testimony of Mrs. Waite and Mrs. Woodruff, nor is it at variance with anything contained in the letters of appellant to the financial agent of his mother. From all these sources, keeping the circumstances surrounding the parties in view—the unnatural conduct of these complainants—the filial love and reverence of the appellant—the utter negation by the mother of any wish that these complainants should profit by her estate, we find in none of these, any satisfactory evidence of a trust in the surplus to be held for the appellees. We adopt the theory in relation to this surplus, presented by the appellant in his answer. That while for the maintenance of his aged and venerable mother, and for her reasonable enjoyment, growing out of the arrangement she had made with the appellant, she had the same kind of interest in the surplus, should there be any after purchasing and furnishing a residence, that she had in the establishment itself, yet such surplus, like the house and furniture, was the property of the appellant. It could not, in our judgment, go to these complainants, without doing violence to the arrangement, and to the manifest intention of the parties, the donor and donee of the fund.

Ingratitude is a most detestable vice, and most against justice, and sharper than a serpent's tooth, it wounds so deeply as to agonize by its sting. Does equity demand compensation shall be made to those who have so violated justice, and so stung [*290] to agony the bosom that nurtured them? We could not so hold without the strongest evidence. We would not infer it from circumstances, except of the most convincing nature, none of which do we find in this case. The evidence of Mrs. Waite, Mrs. Woodruff, James P. F. Clarke, and the letters of appellant to the financial agent, the Sacketts, fail to furnish, when looked at in the light of the circumstances in the case, any sufficient evidence of a trust in this property. The burden of proof was on the complainants to establish a trust, which they have failed to do. The decree is reversed, and the bill dismissed.

Decree reversed.

JULIA ANN QUACKENBOS *et al.*, Plaintiffs in Error, *v.* EDWARD M. M. CLARKE, Defendant in Error.

ERROR TO MORGAN.

SEE the preceding case for a statement of this. These cases are brought to this court upon the same decree pronounced in the Circuit Court, but by the different parties.

BREESE, J. This case is precisely similar in all respects to the case of *Clarke* v. *Quackenbos and others*, decided on appeal. The plaintiffs here, who were complainants below, not satisfied with the decree, bring the case here by writ of error, and assigned as the only error in the decree, that the court did not allow them interest on the amount decreed to be paid to them for a reasonable period, for the investment of, or accounting for the moneys, after they came to the hands of the defendant.

As we have found in the principal case that there was no trust of these moneys, the defendant could have abused none. As we could not conceive, from the evidence, that the mother of these plaintiffs ever intended or wished that they should enjoy any portion of her estate, but had bestowed the whole of it upon the defendant, endeared to her by the strongest ties of love and affection, and who had, on all occasions, exhibited to her the greatest filial regard, and had extended to her at all times the kindest offices, we have been disposed to give the most liberal interpretation to what the donor and donee have said and done, in order to effectuate the manifest intention of the donor. As we have said in that case, that whilst, for the maintenance and enjoyment of the mother, by virtue of the arrangement between her and the defendant, she had the same kind of interest in any surplus that [*291] might remain after purchasing and furnishing a house for her residence, that she had in such residence, still, such surplus, like the house and furniture, was the property of the appellant, and could, in no event, go to the plaintiffs without violating the arrangement and thwarting the manifest intention of the parties. Further reflection satisfies us that this view in no way conflicts with the testimony in the cause, but is in perfect harmony with it. That part of the decree on which the error has been assigned is, of course, affirmed, the decree itself being reversed, by the decision in the case of Clarke against these plaintiffs on the appeal brought by him.

Decree affirmed.

GEORGE W. RIVES, Appellant, *v.* ELIAS KUMLER, Appellee.

APPEAL FROM EDGAR.

It is not due diligence for the assignee of a note to delay issuing an execution against the maker of the note, for more than two months after obtaining his judgment—and without showing some excuse for such delay, he cannot hold the assignor.

An averment that a sheriff's return was signed, is unnecessary; this will be presumed.

In an action upon a promissory note, by the assignee against the assignor, the defendant filed a demurrer to the declaration, which was overruled, and he elected to stand by it. It was competent for the clerk to assess the damages.

It is error to award the plaintiff greater damages than he claims in his declaration.

THE opinion of the Court contains a full statement of the case.

JAMES A. EADS, for Appellant.

THOMAS C. W. SALE, for Appellee.

BREESE, J. This is an action of assumpsit, brought by the assignee against the assignor of a promissory note. The declaration averred the execution of a note by one Thornton to Rives, and by him assigned to the plaintiff below. That the note matured July 10, 1859, and judgment was obtained against the maker, for the amount of the note, at the October term, of that year, of the Circuit Court of Edgar county, where the maker resided, and that such term was the first [*292] term after the note became due. That he sued out an execution on the judgment and placed it in the hands of the sheriff of the county, on the 14th of January, 1860, which execution was returned by the sheriff, indorsed as follows: "Returned no property found, April 14, 1860;" that the debt remains unpaid; with the usual conclusion in assumpsit. Damages, fifteen hundred dollars.

The defendant demurred generally to this declaration, and there was judgment for the plaintiff on the demurrer, and a reference to the clerk to compute the damages. The defendant rested upon his demurrer. The clerk computed the damages, and reported them to the court, at fifteen hundred and thirteen and seventy-five one-hundredths dollars, for which, final judgment was entered, and costs and execution awarded. The defendant appeals to this court, and assigns his errors, overruling

Rives v. Kumler.

the demurrer to the declaration, and in directing the clerk to compute and report the damages, and also that the judgment is rendered for a greater amount of damages than is claimed in the declaration.

The demurrer brings up the question of due diligence. The suit was brought against the maker at the first term of the court next after the maturity of the note. This is one effort at due diligence. He is also required to use the means to enforce the judgment as soon as practicable by ordinary diligence. *Saunders* v. *O'Bryant*, 2 Scam. 370; *Bestor* v. *Walker*, 4 Gilm. 3; *Nixon* v. *Weyhrich*, 20 Ill. 600; *Chalmers* v. *Moore*, 22 ib. 359. The question arises, is it ordinary diligence, such diligence as a prudent man would exercise in a case where there was no recovery over, to delay the issuing of an execution sixty days after the rendition of the judgment? No excuse is shown for not issuing execution at an earlier day. In the case of *Bestor* v. *Walker*, above cited, the first and third counts in the declaration set out the recovery of a judgment against the maker of the note on the 7th of June, 1843, and the issuing of an execution thereon on the 30th of August thereafter. The court say, "there is some doubt whether this is not such a defect as might be fatal on error, were they the only counts in the declaration. In this respect, the court says, the allegations certainly do not show due diligence. For the purpose of reaching the indorser, the holder is required not only to institute and prosecute his suit to judgment at the earliest practicable time, but also to enforce that judgment by execution as soon as, by ordinary diligence, he can. If, in any such case, it appear, from the declaration, that the time intervening between the judgment and the execution be so great as to show clearly that the delay in the emanation of such process is the result of the plaintiff's [*293] negligence, and the declaration contains no matter of excuse for such neglect, the declaration must be held bad on demurrer."

We cannot think a delay of more than sixty days, in these times of great and rapid changes in the circumstances of the people of this State, engaged in active pursuits or otherwise, shows such diligence as a reasonably prudent man, watchful over his own interests, would exercise. Why was not an execution taken out at the end of the October term? Why, if the fact be so, was it not averred in the declaration, that such speedy action would not have availed, the maker not having then any property, or for some other sufficient reason? Sixty days, work wonderful changes in the business relations of our people, and in these stirring times, a delay of so many days, more than two months, cannot be considered due, or, what is the same thing, reasonable diligence.

We therefore think the demurrer should have been sustained.

As to the objection that it is not alleged the sheriff's return was signed, the presumption is that it was signed, and that is the effect of the averment.

The damages claimed were founded upon a promissory note for the direct payment of money, and it was competent, under our statute, for the clerk to compute them. We have repeatedly decided that a plaintiff in an original suit in the Circuit Court, cannot recover more damages than he has claimed in his declaration. *Brown et al.* v. *Smith,* 24 Ill. 197, and cases there cited. In suits originating before a justice of the peace and brought by appeal to the Circuit Court, we have held, that the Circuit Court may give a judgment in a sum beyond the jurisdiction of the justice of the peace, if it be increased by the accumulation of interest, as the interest is calculated on the note, and not on the justice's judgment, as for example, if suit is brought before a justice on a note for ninety dollars or a sum less than a hundred dollars, when it gets to the Circuit Court by appeal, if the interest upon it swells the amount due to more than one hundred dollars, the justice is not ousted of his jurisdiction. *Wilson* v. *Van Winkle,* 2 Gilm. 684. We know of no case originating in the Circuit Court where more damages can be recovered than are claimed in the declaration.

The judgment of the court below is reversed and the cause remanded, with leave to plaintiff to amend his declaration.

Judgment reversed.

DELAVAN MARTIN, Administrator of Albert Hous- [*294]
ton, deceased, Appellant, *v.* JAMES CHARTER, Administrator of Jonathan Charter, deceased, Appellee.

APPEAL FROM McDONOUGH.

It is a settled principle of law that the levy of an execution upon personal
property, sufficient to satisfy it, is of itself a satisfaction of the execution.
But this rule is changed by sec. 30, chap. 57, Rev. Stat. of 1845—which provides for the giving of a forthcoming bond. This statute is constitutional.

THIS was an action of trespass, brought to the October term of
the McDonough Circuit Court, 1856, for the taking of a horse,
the property of Albert Houston. Since the commencement of
the suit, both parties have departed this life.

The defendant pleaded the general issue, and a special plea,
that he was at the time of the supposed trespass, a constable of
said county, and had as such an execution in full force, etc., in
favor of one Hungate, and against Knowles and McGee, for
the sum of $65, and that at the time said execution came to
the hands of said constable, the horse mentioned in plaintiff's
declaration was the property of Knowles and liable to said
execution, and was by virtue of said execution, taken and sold,
etc.

The plaintiff added a similiter to the general issue, and to defendant's second plea, by leave, etc., replied, substantially, that
after said execution came to the hands of the constable, he
levied the same on two other horses and a threshing machine,
which were more than sufficient to satisfy said execution, and
that said constable took from Knowles, a delivery bond, with
good and sufficient security, for the delivery of the property so
levied upon, on a certain day therein mentioned to be sold to
satisfy said execution, and left said property in possession of
said Knowles, and that after the taking of said delivery bond,
and before the time for the delivery of the property therein
mentioned, the said Knowles sold and delivered the horse

mentioned in plaintiff's declaration to one Martin, who sold and delivered said horse to the plaintiff.

To which replication the defendant demurred. The demurrer was sustained, and the plaintiff abided by the same. Whereupon judgment was rendered for defendant.

The appellant assigns the following error: the court erred in sustaining defendant's demurrer to plaintiff's replication to defendant's second plea, and rendering judgment thereon.

BAILEY & VAN VLECK, for Appellant.

[*295] CATON, C. J. It is a well settled principle of law, no doubt, and often recognized by this court, that the levy of an execution upon personal property subject to execution, of value sufficient to satisfy it, is of itself a satisfaction of the execution. But we know of no constitutional provision depriving the legislature of the right to change this rule of law, in a given case or generally. And if there be no such prohibition, then has the legislature rightfully changed the law in this case? Section thirty of chapter fifty-seven, Rev. Stat. 1845, provides, that when the officer has levied an execution upon personal property, he may take a bond for the forthcoming of the property on the day fixed upon for sale, and then deliver it to the owner. And the next section provides, that if the property is not produced at the sale, in pursuance of the exigencies of the bond, the officer "may proceed to execute the same, in the same manner as if no levy had been made." That is precisely what was done in this case, and the judgment must be affirmed.

Judgment affirmed.

Justice WALKER took no part in the decision of this case.

EDWARD S. HINRICHSEN, Plaintiff in Error, v. LOUIS REINBACK, HARRY REINBACK, and CHARLES SAMPLE, Defendants in Error.

ERROR TO MORGAN.

A recovered a judgment against C, and was at the same time surety for B. upon an arbitration bond, for submitting differences between B and C to arbitration. C, obtained an award against B, and then filed a bill to have the amount of the judgment credited on the award. *Held*, that as A's liability to C was only contingent and might never arise, he should not be restrained from collecting his judgment, unless it was alleged that he was insolvent or about to leave the State.

JUNE 22, 1858, plaintiff in error filed his bill in chancery in the Morgan Circuit Court, alleging, that in August, 1840, Harry Reinback and Edward S. Hinrichsen, formed a partnership, under the style and firm of Hinrichsen & Reinback, and under said firm, did business at Franklin, in said county, till about the first day of January, 1851. That about the first of January, 1851, said firm was dissolved, and one Hiram Van Winkle came into said firm, with the said Edward S. Hinrichsen and Harry Reinback. Said last firm assumed the name of Reinback & Van Winkle, said Hinrichsen being a silent [*296] partner, and continued under said last named firm till March, 1853, when Hinrichsen & Reinback purchased the entire interest of Hiram Van Winkle in said firm. That in January, 1853, said Hinrichsen & Reinback, on account of said firm, executed a note to said Louis Reinback for the sum of $400; that said firm was indebted to the firm of Reinback & Hinrichsen, a firm composed of Louis Reinback and Michael Hinrichsen. Said last named firm having dissolved, Hinrichsen & Reinback, on the 15th day of February, 1853, in settlement of said debt, gave a note due one day after date, with ten per cent. interest, to Michael Hinrichsen, for $354.85, and a note for like amount of same date, payable to Louis Reinback. That in March, 1853, all the assets of the firm of Reinback & Van Winkle, and Hinrichsen & Reinback, were placed in the hands of Harry Reinback for collection and disbursement, amounting to $5,865; also the stock of goods on hand at that time, amounting to $1,610—the debts due from said firm being about $6,000, including the three notes above mentioned. That assets received by Harry Reinback were ample to pay all the debts against said firms.

That in the spring of 1855, Louis and Harry Reinback formed a partnership; and charges that said last named firm used the means of Reinback & Van Winkle in the business. That Louis Reinback, fraudulently intending to aid Harry Reinback to cheat complainant, commenced two suits at law against him and Harry Reinback; one on the two notes above mentioned, made payable to him, and the other in the name of Michael Hinrichsen, to his use, on the note dated February 16, 1853, for $354.85. Said causes were continued to the March term, 1857, of said court; at which term Hinrichsen filed his separate plea in said cases; said Harry Reinback made no defense,—and also filed his bill in chancery in said court, praying for an injunction, restraining said Louis Reinback from further prosecuting said suits; but by mistake it was made to apply only to the case of Louis Reinback; that judgment was therefore rendered against Hinrichsen in the case of Michael Hinrichsen, to the use of Louis Reinback; that therefore Hinrichsen presented his petition, praying an injunction to the last named case, which prayer was granted by the master in chancery. At the March term, 1857, defendants Louis and Harry Reinback filed their answer in said case, and moved the court to dissolve the injunctions, which motion was overruled. Said cause was referred to a special master, to state accounts, and cause continued; by stipulation [*297] of counsel, both cases were to be heard by the special master. Before said master had made up his statement of accounts, by agreement of parties, all matters in controversy between Harry Reinback and Edward S. Hinrichsen, were referred to arbitrators for final award. Accordingly, the parties entered into bond—penalty, $5,000—Louis Reinback being surety for Harry Reinback, and Michael Hinrichsen surety for Edward S. Hinrichsen, for the faithful performance of the award; by said agreement to arbitrate, the injunctions were to be dissolved. And at the October term, 1857, of said court, the same were dissolved. That said judgments, interest and costs amount, in the aggregate, to about $1,500; that execution, since issued on the same, has been levied on the property of Hinrichsen by Charles Sample, sheriff of said county. That said arbitrators to whom said matters were referred, having fully heard the evidence in the case, in March, 1858, made their award as follows:

EDWARD S. HINRICHSEN, ⎫
　　　　　　　　　　　　　⎬ On Arbitration.
H. REINBACK. ⎭

The undersigned arbitrators, after hearing the testimony and after due consideration thereof, do award that the said Harry Reinback account and pay to the firms of Hinrichsen & Reinback, and Reinback & Van Winkle, the sum of $1,296.90, that the parties be entitled to the proceeds of all unsettled and outstanding assets of said firms in equal amounts, and that the cost of this arbitration be divided between the parties, etc.

(Signed and sealed by arbitrators.)

That Reinback had due notice of the same; that Harry Reinback is still appropriating outstanding assets of said firms, and refuses to perform said award; and Louis Reinback is now endeavoring to collect the amount of said judgments off of Hinrichsen; that Hinrichsen is about to commence suit at law on said arbitration bond, and prays for an injunction, restraining Louis Reinback from further proceeding to collect his judgments until said case is heard; prays that the amount of judgment that may be recovered in said suit at law, be set off or credited on said judgments enjoined.

Master in chancery of said county granted said injunction, on complainant giving bond to defendants, in penalty of $3,000—with Michael Hinrichsen as surety.

Afterwards, on the 14th of March, 1860, said Edward S. Hinrichsen, by leave, filed his amended bill in this case, alleging, that Hinrichsen & Reinback purchased the interest of Van Winkle in the firm of Reinback & Van Winkle, and [*298] also agreed to pay all the indebtedness of said firm of Reinback

& Van Winkle; that as between themselves and the said Van Winkle, the said Edward and the said Harry were the only persons interested in the firm of Hinrichsen & Reinback, and Reinback & Van Winkle; that thereby said award is the same in legal effect as though it had directed Harry to pay $1,296.50 on the joint indebtedness of the said Edward's and the said Harry's indebtedness; that it was a matter of perfect indifference whether said sum should be paid on indebtedness of Hinrichsen & Reinback, or of the firm of Reinback & Van Winkle; that when the award was made, the only outstanding debts against the firms of Hinrichsen & Reinback and Reinback & Van Winkle, were the two payments already referred to, as now existing on the record of this court, and a debt of some $300 to John Spins, which last debt Hinrichsen paid before the filing of the bill in this case; that the only indebtedness now outstanding against either firm, are the two judgments offered, except a pretended claim, now in litigation, of some $257.

That the first injunction referred to in the original bill, was granted on condition that Hinrichsen and one Jacob Sample would execute injunction bond—penalty $2,000—conditioned for payment of any judgment the court might render. Said bond was duly given by Hinrichsen and the said Sample; that after the dissolution, on the —— day of ——, Louis and Harry Reinback brought suit on said bond on the common law side of this court. Suit still pending against Hinrichsen, impleaded with Jacob Sample, since deceased, seeking to obtain judgment against Hinrichsen, alleging, as a breach of the condition of said bond, the non-payment of said judgment. That in the second injunction suit in said original bill mentioned, said injunction was granted, on condition that said E. S. Hinrichsen and Thos. Spainhaver would execute a bond to defendants in the penal sum of $908.91, conditioned to pay any judgments that might be rendered; that said bond was duly filed; that after the dissolution of said last injunction, and after the commencement of this present suit, on the —— day of ——, 1859, L. and H. Reinback brought suit at law on the common law side of this court, on said bond, which is still pending against E. S. Hinrichsen and Thomas Spainhaver, alleging, as a breach of the condition of said bond, the non-payment of the judgment rendered in case of Michael Hinrichsen to the use of Louis Reinback. Judgment referred to in favor of Louis Reinback, was rendered by the Circuit Court of Morgan county, October, 1857, for $1,000.70 damages and costs of suit. The judgment in case of Michael [*299] Hinrichsen and Louis Reinback, referred to, was rendered March term, 1857, of said court, for $448.82, and costs of suit. That before the filing of amended bill, to wit, on the —— day of November, 1858, by interlocutory decree in this suit, the injunction granted was dissolved, and $75 damages was awarded for wrongful suing out injunction. Bond in this case was executed by E. S. Hinrichsen and Michael Hinrichsen. That on the —— day of ——, 185-, L. and H. Reinback brought suit in said court on said bond, to recover the $75—suit still pending.

Amended bill prays that L. and H. Reinback be enjoined from collecting said judgments against E. S. Hinrichsen and H. Reinback, out of property of E. S. Hinrichsen, except on condition of first crediting said judgments with aggregate sum of $1,448.25, being $1,296.90, with interest from date of award; that injunction be granted restraining Louis and Harry Reinback from attempting, in said first two suits now pending, to recover judgments against defendants therein, on account of non-payment of the common law judgments. Also, that the court will vacate said interlocutory order made in this case, and grant injunction restraining said Louis and Harry Reinback from prosecuting said suit. Amended bill sworn to.

May 22, 1860, defendants filed their joint and several answer in this case. That Sample is nominal party—not interested in suit. Louis and Harry Reinback admit recovery of judgment in favor of Michael Hinrichsen, to the use of Louis Reinback, March 17, 1857, for $448.80, and costs. Also judgment of Louis Reinback, against same defendants, Oct. 30, 1857, for $1,000.70, and costs of suit. Admit complainants enjoined the collection of said judgments as alleged in the bill. Admit cause was consolidated, and, August 13, 1857, referred to a special master. That after meeting before said master, by consent, said injunctions were dissolved, and at the same time

357

complainant, with Michael Hinrichsen as surety, and Harry Reinback, with Louis Reinback as his surety, entered into a bond, each to the other, in the penalty of $5,000, conditioned to abide the award of the arbitrators named in the bill, as to the matter of controversy between complainant and Harry Reinback in said suit; that said arbitrators made the award named in the bill.

Defendants, further answering, say, Louis Reinback is exclusively entitled to benefit of said judgments. That said Louis and Harry are abundantly solvent; that it is unjust to prohibit the said Louis from collecting his judgments, because of supposed insolvency of Harry, until complainant shall establish [*300] his demands against Harry. Louis denies that he has contemplated removal of his firm and effects from this State, to the prejudice of complainant, E. S. Hinrichsen; that the said award is void for uncertainty. That the averments made in the amended bill to aid said award, are untrue. Denies the right to aid said award by averment and proof. Admit all the allegations of original and amended bill as to proceedings had in this court, and deny all fraud. Defendants moved for a dissolution of said injunctions, and say the bill original and amended are multifarious, and therefore bad. Answer not sworn to.

Cause heard on original and amended bill, answer, replication of complainant thereto, and testimony referred to in decree.

It was admitted by defendants, on the hearing of this case, that Hiram Van Winkle, soon after the formation of the firm of Reinback & Van Winkle, went out of the firm and drew wages as a clerk from the time he first went there, and that he never had any interest in the said firm. Also, the debts due from said firms, or either of them, except the judgment of said Louis Reinback, mentioned, and a judgment of Ransen Van Winkle, now enjoined and in litigation in this court, had been fully paid.

The court entered a decree dissolving said injunctions, and dismissing complainant's bill.

Isaac L. Morrison, for Plaintiff in Error.

D. A. Smith, for Defendants in Error.

Breese, J. The scope of the bill filed by plaintiff in error, seems to be to compel Louis Reinback to appropriate the two judgments he obtained against the plaintiff in the Circuit Court in his actions at law, to the payment of the award in favor of the plaintiff against Harry Reinback, on the ground that Louis is the surety of Harry in the arbitration bond, and may, perhaps, be compelled to pay the amount. That to avoid circuity of action, it would be expedient, just and equitable that the one should be set off against the other *pro tanto.*

There is no proof of fraud, or of insolvency in either Harry or Louis—on the contrary, as it. regards Louis, he is admitted to be responsible. It is an unquestionable fact, that the plaintiff is the debtor of Louis Reinback, by judgment duly entered. That cannot be disputed. Without deciding whether the award is binding or not, the liability of Louis on the bond, is uncertain and contingent. He may never be required to pay a dollar on it. What equity [*301] then can there be in delaying Louis who is a judgment creditor, in the collection of his debt, on the bare probability, that at some future time, he may be called on to satisfy the penalty of his bond. Were he insolvent, or about to leave the State, there might be some pretense for the claim. Equity might, perhaps, take jurisdiction under such circumstances. *Buckmaster* v. *Grundy,* 3 Gilm. 626. The remedy, if the award be binding, is complete and adequate at law. There being no proof of insolvency or fraud, there is nothing appearing to justify the intervention of a court of equity, to restrain Louis from the collection of his judgments. The award stands against Harry Reinback to be enforced at law. The judgments are in favor of Louis, disconnected wholly from the award, and for which, the plaintiff is liable to Louis in his own right. We are at a loss to perceive any ground for the equitable interposition of the court.

The decree dismissing the bill, must be affirmed.

Decree affirmed.

THOMAS L. COOPER, and B. and J. M. BEESLY, Plaintiffs in Error, *v.* WILLIAM NOCK, Defendant in Error.

ERROR TO MASON.

In determining the question of usury, the intention of the parties should govern, without regard to the form of the contract.

An assignment of a note, in order to cut off a defense by the maker, must not only be before maturity. but must be *bona fide,* and if made for that express purpose, will be invalid.

The payee of a note, before its maturity put his name upon the back of it, but kept it in his possession until after it became due. He then delivered the note to the attorney of the plaintiff, who was a non-resident. This was not a *bona fide* assignment, and did not prevent the maker from setting up the defense of usury.

THIS was an action brought by the defendant in error, against the plaintiffs in error, in the Circuit Court of Mason county. Judgment was given for the plaintiff below for the whole amount claimed, the defense of usury having been specially pleaded. The defendant brings the case to this court, by writ of error. The opinion of this court states the case fully.

JAMES ROBERTS, for Plaintiffs in Error.

LYMAN LACEY, for Defendant in Error.

[*302] WALKER, J. This was an action of assumpsit, instituted on a promissory note. It was executed on the 3rd of February, 1859, for three hundred and thirty dollars, due in sixty days, with five per cent. interest per month after maturity, if not punctually paid, waiving all relief, valuation, stay, or exemption laws. The defense relied upon is usury. It appears from the evidence, that Loveland, the payee, loaned plaintiff in error, not exceeding three hundred dollars, and took the note for the sum therein named. That when the money was loaned, it was agreed, that the maker should pay five per cent. a month interest, and that thirty dollars by way of interest for the time the note was to run, was added in as principal.

Cooper *et al. v.* Nock.

It also appears from the evidence of the payee of the note, that he indorsed it in blank before it was due, but did not deliver it to any one, but retained it in his possession until after its maturity. He then placed it in the hands of the attorneys who brought the suit, with directions to fill up the assignment to defendant in error, who resided in the State of Mississippi. That the money which was loaned was Loveland's, and would be his when collected. He likewise testified that he always made it a practice to assign his notes to prevent the defense of usury or loss, but in this instance it was not done for that purpose, as he believed the makers would not interpose that defense.

In such transactions it is the intention of the parties, not the forms employed, which fixes its character. If it were otherwise, every species of fraud, oppression and wrong, might be perpetrated with perfect impunity. Hence in trials of questions of usury, it has ever been held that no device intended to cover up the real character of the transaction, can ever avail to defeat the statute. But in this case it stands confessed by the payee and beneficial plaintiff, that the transaction was usurious. And that the note hever left his possession until after its maturity. And that when the money is collected it will be his. As no transfer of the note took place, until after it fell due, any defense that existed against the note before the assignment was filled up, may be urged against it in the hands of the present holder.

The mere indorsement of the payee's name on the back of the note, with the intention of filling up the assignment at some future time, to the plaintiff below, without a delivery to him or to his agent, cannot be held to constitute such an assignment as will pass the title. Nor will it cut off this defense. The transfer of a note for such a purpose, will not prevent the maker, even when made before maturity, from relying upon his defense. It is, however, otherwise, when the assignment is made in good faith. The defendant [*303] in error, so far as we can see, at no time ever had any interest in the note. The assignment was, no doubt, intended to place it beyond the power of the payees to defeat the collection of the usury. To allow such shallow devices to defeat the statute and protect fraud upon its provisions, would amount to a denial of justice, and is too monstrous to meet the sanction of a court of justice. But the doctrine is well established and recognized, that upon an assignment, even before the note is due, if not *bona fide*, the same defense may be made in the hands of the holder as of the payee. 3 Kent, 91; 26 Ill. 494; 25 Ill. 218. In this case there can be no pretense that defendant in error is a *bona fide* holder, and the defense was proper and should have been allowed. The judgment of the court below is reversed, and the cause remanded.

Judgment reversed.

GEORGE FREELAND, and SAMUEL WHEELER, Appellants, *v.* THE BOARD OF SUPERVISORS OF JASPER COUNTY, Appellees.

APPEAL FROM CRAWFORD.

In an action upon a bond, judgment should be so entered, that the whole may be satisfied, upon the payment of the damages.

It is the duty of the clerk of the Circuit Court to make a full transcript of all of the record. This court is not permitted to act upon his statements, given in the transcript, that papers were filed or withdrawn.

If three defendants demur, and, after the demurrer is withdrawn, two of them plead, a judgment *nil dicit* should be entered against the party not pleading, and the jury should assess the damages against all. If but two plead, and the other abided by his demurrer, he could not be regarded as going to trial with the others.

THIS cause was submitted *ex parte.* The opinion of the Court states all the points arising in the case.

A. KITCHELL, for Appellants.

WALKER, J. This was an action on a bond, for the penal sum of six hundred dollars, conditioned for the payment of the amount of a debt and costs, due from one Burnett, to the county of Jasper. It was executed by appellants and Isaac

Clery. The obligors were all sued, but Wheeler was alone served with process. The sheriff also returned, that Freeland was not found, and makes no return as to Clery. A trial was had, resulting in a judgment, against Wheeler and Free- [*304] land, for $600 debt and $462.24 damages.

It is first insisted, that this judgment is erroneous in not providing that the whole judgment shall be satisfied, on the payment of the damages. This is manifestly wrong, as the payment of the damages assessed on such a bond, is a satisfaction. Otherwise the plaintiff could collect both sums, and receive the full amount of damages sustained by the breach, as well as the penalty. *McConnell* v. *Swails*, 2 Scam. 572. This point has been so frequently decided by this court, that it must be regarded as settled.

The clerk states, in the transcript, that the defendants filed, and afterwards withdrew, a demurrer. It is not set out, nor is the order permitting its withdrawal given in the transcript. Even if we were authorized to receive this mere statement of that fact, inasmuch as there were three defendants, and only one served, as is shown by the record, we could not determine whether two or three of the defendants had entered their appearance, by filing a demurrer. If only two, then which of the three. But even if we could ascertain, whether it was all or only two, we are not permitted to act upon the statement of the clerk. He can only make and certify a transcript of the record of the Circuit Court. When the demurrer was filed, it became a part of the record in this case, as well as the order permitting it to be withdrawn. They should have been copied into the transcript. He also states, that pleas of *non est factum* and payment, on behalf of Freeland and Wheeler, were ordered to be entered of record, and if ever entered, the clerk, in making the transcript, has failed to insert them. If all of the defendants filed their demurrer, and only two of them, after it was withdrawn, plead to the action, the regular practice would have been, to have entered judgment *nil dicit* against the party not pleading, and let the jury assess the damages against all of the defendants. If but two plead, and the other abided by his demurrer, he could not be regarded as going to trial with the others. If Clery never entered his appearance, and Freeland did, then the judgment was rendered against the proper defendants. As the cause will be remanded for a new trial, we deem it unnecessary to discuss the evidence in the case.

The judgment of the Circuit Court is reversed, and the cause remanded.

Judgment reversed.

[*305] WILLIAM B. CLARKE, Plaintiff in Error, *v.* THE BOARD OF SUPERVISORS OF HANCOCK COUNTY, Defendant in Error.

ERROR TO HANCOCK.

The board of supervisors alone, have the power to order an election to determine whether the county will subscribe to stock in a railroad company, and to issue the bonds therefor; and they cannot delegate their power. But this rule does not prevent the board of supervisors, after they have taken all necessary action in the matter, from directing that the bond shall be signed by the county judge. The county judge then becomes merely the instrument, by which the action of the board is manifested.

In ordering an election, to determine whether a county will subscribe for stock to aid in building a railroad, it is improper to submit the question, whether two different roads shall be so aided, by a single vote; so that the two propositions cannot be voted upon separately. The county may be restrained from issuing bonds in pursuance of such a vote: but when issued they are not necessarily void, in the hands of a *bona fide* holder.

Where county bonds, to aid the construction of a railroad, have been issued, in pursuance of an election held without warrant of law. as where it has been ordered by a person or tribunal having no such authority, they are absolutely void. But where the election has been properly authorized, and there has been informality in the manner of submitting the question to the people (such as submitting two propositions as to aiding two different roads, to a single vote), the bonds may be rendered valid, in the hands of an innocent holder, by the acquiescence of the people, and their subsequent ratification by the county, in levying a tax and paying interest upon them.

THIS was an action, commenced by the plaintiff in error against the defendant in error, in the Circuit Court of Hancock county

The declaration counts on divers interest coupons; plea, general issue. Trial by the court, SIBLEY, Judge, presiding, and judgment for defendant.

The bill of exceptions shows, that plaintiff read in evidence one coupon, as follows:

$80 $80
                          $80
CARTHAGE, Hancock Co., Ills., July 1st, A. D. 1856.

The Treasurer of Hancock county will pay the bearer, at the American Exchange Bank, in the city of New York, on the first day of July, A. D. 1857, eighty dollars, interest due on bond No. 1 to 100.

J. M. FERRIS, County Judge.

and three like coupons, Nos. two, three, and four, payable annually, after the day of payment of said coupon above set. forth; and plaintiff proved that the same were interest coupons of one bond of $1,000, dated July 1, 1856, payable in twenty years from July 1, 1856, purporting to have been issued by the county of Hancock, payable to the Mississippi [*306] and Wabash Railroad Company or bearer; and read in evidence a coupon, in the following form:

Eight per cent. stock.

Hancock County,   State of Illinois.
                    Rail Road Bond No. 35.

Pay to the bearer eighty dollars, on the first day of July, 1857, interest to that date.

JOHN M. FERRIS,
Judge of County Court of Hancock county.

and read four like coupons, payable annually, after the first day of July, 1857, and proved that said coupons were given for annual interest on a bond for $1,000, in all respects like the bond first above named, except that the same was payable to the Warsaw and Rockford Railroad Company or bearer; and proved that the signatures to the said coupons and bonds were in the handwriting of John M. Ferris, then county judge of said county; and proved that said coupons were, before the commencement of this suit, and after due, duly presented for payment, by plaintiff, at the treasurer's office of Hancock county, and that payment thereof was refused by said Hancock county.

Plaintiff also read from the records of the County Court of said county, of date August 21, 1855, an order which recites, that application had been made to the County Court for an election to be held in said county for the electors to vote for or against subscription, in the sum of two hundred thousand dollars, one hundred thousand dollars of which for the Mississippi and Wabash Railroad, and one hundred thousand dollars for the Warsaw and Rockford Railroad, and requesting said court to fix the time for which the bonds of said county, proposed to be issued therefor, should run, at twenty years, and to bear interest at eight per cent. per annum; whereupon it was ordered by said court, that an election be held in said county, at the various places of holding elections therein, on the 29th of September, 1855, by the electors of said county, for the purpose of deciding for or against said county taking stock in the sum of $200,000: $100,000 in capital stock of the Mississippi and Wabash Railroad Company, to be applied in construction of that part of said railroad lying between the cities of Warsaw and Macomb, by way of Carthage and Fountain Green; and $100,000 in the capital stock of the Warsaw and Rockford Railroad Company; the bonds of said county to be issued for stock to run for twenty years, and to draw interest at eight per cent.; and that the clerk of said court give notice of the holding of such election as notices are given for [*307] elections for state and county officers, and as required by the statute on said subject, approved November 6, 1849, and that the ballots at said election be "for subscription," or "against subscription;" and proved that the board of supervisors of said county, at a meeting thereof duly held on the 20th day of August, 1855, made and entered of record, an order of the same import, and to the same effect, as the said order of the County Court above set forth; and proved that notices were duly posted and given throughout said county, of an election to be held in pursuance of said orders of the County Court and board of supervisors, and submitting the question for and against subscription, as provided for by said orders.

Plaintiff also read in evidence, from the abstract election returns, from the office of the county clerk of said county, the following:

"Abstract of the vote of the election held on Saturday, the 29th day of September, 1855, on the proposition to subscribe, by the county of Hancock, the sum of two hundred thousand dollars, for stock in the Warsaw and Rockford Railroad, and the Mississippi and Wabash Railroad, one hundred thousand of which in each of said roads."

The total footings of said vote are as follows:

> For Subscription, 1975
> Against Subscription, 553

and proved that a majority of the legal voters of said county, as tested by their next preceding general election, voted in the affirmative of the question so submitted; that J. M. Ferris, as county judge of said county, acting under orders of the board of supervisors, hereafter mentioned, and not otherwise, subscribed to the capital stock of the Mississippi and Wabash Railroad Company, $100,000, payable in the bonds of said county, and to the capital stock of the Warsaw and Rockford Railroad Company the like sum, payable in like manner; that under orders of the board of supervisors hereafter mentioned, said Ferris, as county judge, executed one thousand dollar bonds, in pursuance of said orders, amounting to $200,000, and that half of them were payable to one road or bearer, and the other half to the other road or bearer; that to said bonds were attached coupons for the annual interest thereon for twenty years; that the county clerk of said county signed said bonds, and affixed the seal of the County Court thereto; that said Ferris, as county judge, under said orders signed the same, and alone signed, as county judge, the annual interest coupons for twenty years, at eight per cent. per annum; that said Ferris acted under said orders of the board of supervisors; that said bonds and coupons were, in fact, issued after the making of [*308.] said orders directing said subscriptions and the issuance of said bonds; that said county adopted, and was acting under township organization, prior to 1855, and prior to making the order submitting such propositions, and prior to making and issuing said bonds and coupons; that said bonds and coupons were issued to said railroad companies respectively, in payment of said subscriptions; that said county had paid some interest coupons, and had, on one or more occasions, voted for directors of said corporations.

Plaintiff also read from an act, entitled "An Act to amend an act, entitled 'An act to incorporate the Mississippi and Wabash Railroad Company,' approved February 10, 1853," approved February 24, 1859, the following:

"SECTION 11." "The votes taken in the county of Hancock, and in the city of Warsaw, for subscribing stock to said railroad company, are hereby declared to have been legally made, and the issuing of the bonds of said county and city, in the payment of said subscription, is hereby legalized."

And plaintiff read in evidence, from the records of the board of supervisors, the orders of said board, of date March 6, 1856, and November 18, 1856, directing the county judge of said county, to sign, execute and issue the bonds of said county, in sums of $1,000 each, to the amount $200,000; $100,000 thereof to the Warsaw and Rockford Railroad Company, and $100,000 thereof to the Mississippi and Wabash Railroad Company; said bonds to run twenty years, and to bear interest at eight per cent. per annum, payable annually, and to have coupons for the annual interest attached thereto; said bonds also to be signed by the county clerk, and to have the seal of the County Court affixed thereto.

This was all the evidence.

SKINNER, BENNESON & MARSH, for Plaintiff in Error.

J. GRIMSHAW, for Defendant in Error.

WALKER, J. The election, to determine whether the county would become a subscriber to the two roads, was ordered by both the board of supervisors and the County Court. These orders were made more than thirty days before the time fixed for the election, and under them, notice was given and the election held, resulting in a majority in favor of subscription. Afterwards the board of supervisors directed, by an order entered of record, that the bonds should issue, and that J. M.

Ferris should, as county judge, sign and execute the same. This he did, in pursuance to the order. It is now insisted, that inasmuch as the board of supervisors alone had the [*309] power to order the election, and to issue and deliver the bonds, that when issued by the County Court they were illegal and void. That as the board of supervisors were exercising a delegated authority, they were bound to pursue it strictly, and were powerless to appoint an agent to exercise that power. This is manifestly the rule, and if in this case it has been violated, the bonds are necessarily void.

All collective bodies, from the very nature of things, are to some extent compelled to employ agents, to record their resolutions, and to preserve the manifestations of their intentions. When they enter into contracts, or execute instruments of any description, where they are composed of large numbers, as a matter of convenience, if not from absolute necessity, they are compelled to designate a single individual to act on behalf of the body. The numerous signatures, if all were to sign an instrument, would occasion inconvenience and delay in executing an agreement. The body therefore must, generally by an order entered upon its records, designate some person to act on its behalf. He may be a member of their own body, or a person unconnected with the organization. This case illustrates the inconvenience of requiring each member of the board to sign the several bonds and coupons.

The board had ordered the election, canvassed the vote, decided that a majority had determined upon subscription, and had resolved, that the county would take the stock and issue the bonds. In all this they were exercising a power delegated by the General Assembly, and this power they could not have delegated to any other person or tribunal. Its exercise was confided to them alone, and they could only execute it legally. But after performing all these acts did they delegate any power, by their entering of record, that the bonds should issue to pay the county subscription, and requiring them to be signed by the county judge? This they might by resolution have required of their presiding officer, any member of the board, or of their clerk.

The law has failed to prescribe the mode of executing these bonds, or to designate any person who shall sign them. And in the absence of such a requirement, they, we think, had the unquestionable right, by order of the board duly passed, to authorize any person they might choose, to sign the instruments, to manifest their intention of completing the act. This was not properly an exercise of power, but was simply a mode of manifesting the fact that the power had been exercised by the board. We are, for these reasons, of the opinion that this objection is not well taken.

[*310] It is also insisted, that this question, whether the county would subscribe to these roads, was improperly submitted to a vote of the county. As submitted, the electors were required to vote for or against the subscription, or a gross sum, to be taken in equal parts in two different roads. We have held, on an application to restrain a county from issuing bonds, that it is illegal to submit two separate propositions in such a manner as that each may not be voted upon separately. *Fulton County* v. *Miss. & Wabash R. R.*, 21 Ill. 373. It was also held, on an application for a *mandamus*, to compel the issuing of bonds, to pay for a subscription thus voted, that the relief could not be granted. *The People ex rel.* v. *The County of Tazewell*, 22 Ill. 147. It is true, in this latter case, that was only one of several grounds, upon which the application was refused, but the doctrine announced was recognized.

The case under consideration presents the question, whether bonds issued under such a vote, and in the hands of innocent holders, are void, or are only voidable, and may be ratified by subsequent acts of the county, acting through its constituted authorities. And if capable of being ratified, whether any act has been done, having that effect. If an election were held without warrant of law, or if it were ordered by a person or tribunal having no authority, there could be no doubt that the whole proceeding would be absolutely void. Such an election, and every subsequent step, would be unauthorized and void, and therefore incapable of ratification by the county authorities. But an election held under the authority of an order by the proper authorities, and in the main conforming to the require-

Clarke *v.* Board of Supervisors of Hancock County.

ments of the statute, but wanting in some particular not essential to the power to hold an election, and acquiesced in by the people, and approved by their agents, the county authorities, would render bonds thus issued binding, when in the hands of innocent holders.

The objection to submitting two separate propositions, to subscribe for stock, in such a manner as the voter has no choice, but to vote for or against both propositions, may operate as a fraud upon the voters of the county. And when the issue of the bonds is resisted, they cannot be executed and delivered. In this case the election was ordered by the proper tribunal, it was held at the time and in the manner required by law, and for aught that appears, was in all things, except the submission of the proposition to take stock to the amount of the gross sum in the two roads, strictly legal. The people acquiesced in the election, the board of supervisors issued and delivered the bonds, and afterwards paid some installments of interest. Now in this case there was no want of authority to order the election, but simply an errone- [*311] ous mode of submitting the questions. And we have no hesitation in saying, that it was such a deviation from the correct mode as may be rendered valid by subsequent acts, so as to protect the rights of third parties, which may have been subsequently acquired. Had the proceedings been instituted by any citizen of the county, to restrain the issue of these bonds, the relief would have been granted. But when they have been issued, and purchased in market, and have passed into the hands of *bona fide* holders, good faith, justice, and every principle of fairness, require that these bonds should not be held invalid, for any but the most weighty reasons.

In the case of *Johnson* v. *Stark County*, 24 Ill. 75, this court held, that if the irregularity was only such as to avoid the liability, upon the grounds of a non-compliance with the law in holding the election, it must be insisted upon before the rights of third persons have intervened. That when such are the grounds of objection, the want of action by the tax-payer to restrain their being issued, and a ratification by the county authorities, either in express terms or by acts of recognition of

their validity, waives the right to object against the interests of
third persons.   In this case, the citizens of the county acquiesced in the issue and sale of the bonds, and the supervisors levied and collected taxes, with which several installments of interest were paid, before any resistance was made to the legality
of the bonds.   These acts clearly evince a recognition of their
validity on the part of the county.

This case does not, as it seemed to be supposed, fall within
the principle announced in the case of *Schuyler County* v. *The
People*, 25 Ill. 185, as in that case, there was no authority to
order the election by the body assuming the act.   But this irregularity only being such as would prevent the bonds from
being issued, and not sufficient to render them void, when
thrown into the market, we must hold that these bonds are valid,
and binding upon the county.   And that the court below erred
in rendering judgment in favor of the defendants, which is reversed, and the cause remanded.

Judgment reversed.

[*312] DAVID D. HULL, Appellant, *v.* JOHN PEER, *et al.*,
Appellees.

APPEAL FROM PIKE.

In a bill for the specific performance of a parol agreement for the sale of lands,
if the defendant denies the agreement, and does not set up the statute of
frauds as a defense, he cannot afterwards insist upon the statute in bar.

In a bill for a specific performance, the complainant need not, at his peril,
state the precise amount due.   He may state his case most favorably to himself, and if, upon the equities of the case, the court should decree a different
amount, he can then conform to its judgment.

A and B executed a note together, with the understanding that A should pay
it.   The payee insisted that B should appear upon the note as principal, and
A as surety.   It was held that nevertheless, as between themselves, A was
the principal and B the surety, in equity.

In decreeing a specific performance of a parol agreement for the sale of lands,
the court will require the complainant to do complete justice, upon the
broadest principles of equity, and will not be satisfied with a literal performance of the agreement by him.

On the 27th day of August, 1855, Billingsby Bowen filed his bill in chancery in the Circuit Court of Pike county, charging that about the year 1850, the complainant and David D. Hu· entered into a parol contract, whereby, for the consideration of one hundred and fifty dollars, the said Hull agreed to sell and convey to complainant the east half of the south-east quarter of section twenty-one, township four south, range seven west of the fourth principal meridian; that said Hull was at the time indebted to the school fund of said township in the sum of one hundred dollars, and it was agreed between complainant and said Hull that complainant should assume and pay the said sum of one hundred dollars for said Hull, in part payment of the consideration to be paid for said land; that afterwards, complainant and said Hull executed their note to said township for said sum of one hundred dollars, and being for the same sum of money agreed to be paid by complainant for said Hull to said township; that the agreement between Hull and complainant was, that complainant should pay this note, and that the amount thereof, when paid, should stand as a payment of one hundred dollars on said contract for the land; that no time was fixed by the contract for the land, for the payment of the balance of the consideration to be paid therefor, but that it was agreed between them, that complainant should pay said note to the township when called for, and pay the balance of said purchase money (fifty dollars) whenever thereafter it might suit the convenience of complainant to do so, and that upon payment of such balance [*313] and the said school note, said Hull was to execute a deed to him, conveying the title to said land.

Bill avers, that in pursuance of said contract, complainant paid said note to the township, in full, and took up the same; that said note was for the debt of said Hull to the township, and that complainant paid it in pursuance of his agreement to pay the same as part consideration for said land; that after he had paid said note, he notified said Hull thereof, and tendered to him the sum of fifty dollars, the balance of the consideration to be paid for said land, and requested said Hull to execute to him a deed for the land, but that said Hull refused and failed so to do. Complainant then offers to bring said sum of fifty dollars into court, and avers that the same is in court, ready to be delivered to said Hull, and subject to the order of the court.

Bill further charges, that said Hull, in part performance of the contract aforesaid, delivered the possession of said land to complainant, and that complainant has ever since had possession thereof under and in part performance of said contract, and that he is now residing upon said land with his family; that after he had so taken possession of said land, he removed thereon with his family, the land being vacant and unimproved when he so removed upon it; that complainant made valuable and lasting improvements thereon, consisting of a hewed log cabin as a dwelling-house for his family, which they now occupy as such, and by breaking and putting into cultivation forty acres of the land, fencing said forty acres, and digging a well thereon; that said Hull was cognizant of these improvements and made no objection thereto, but encouraged complainant to make the same, and stated to third persons that the land was complainant's; that complainant has been in the uninterrupted possession of said land since contract was made; that he, for a short interval, during a visit to Ohio, rented the same to a tenant, who held and occupied the same until his return, and who paid the rent to complainant without let or hindrance from said Hull; that complainant paid the taxes upon said land, and exercised all other acts of ownership thereon, during said period, without objection or warning from said Hull.

Bill makes Hull defendant thereto, and prays that he be required to answer the same; prays that he be compelled to convey the land to complainant, and for general relief.

The answer of the defendant to the charges in the bill, in respect to the alleged agreement to sell and convey to the complainant the land described, as said agreement is set forth [*314] in the bill, wholly denies the same; that respondent never agreed to sell or convey said land to complainant for the sum of one hundred and fifty dollars, or for any other sum as stated in said bill; that respondent never made any other or different agreement with complainant in regard to said land, or any land than as hereafter stated. Answer denies the allegations of the bill, respecting an agreement made between him and complainant, by which, as alleged, complainant was to assume the payment of a promissory note executed by respondent as principal to the school township, for the sum of one hundred dollars, and denies that respondent was to accept the same as part payment of the consideration of said land. Admits that he was indebted to said township in the sum of one hundred dollars, for which he executed his promissory note with security as stated in the bill. Admits that recently, and since a controversy has arisen between him and complainant respecting the land, complainant has, by some arrangement, taken up or paid said note, but that such payment was wholly unauthorized by respondent, and was done without any agreement or understanding with respondent; that respondent was at all times ready and willing to have paid the same whenever demanded of him, and that he had regularly, by himself or his agents, paid the interest thereon from year to year, as the same accrued and was demanded.

Admits tender of $50 to him, and demand of a deed by complainant for the land, and says complainant at the time spoke of a note he had taken up from the township. Admits he refused to make a deed, for the reason that there was no obligation upon him to do so. Admits that complainant went into the possession of a portion of the land described in the bill, about the year 1850, and that complainant at intervals has been in possession of portions thereof since that time, and that complainant has made some improvements upon said land, but not to the extent alleged in said bill; that the circumstances under which complainant went into the possession of said land and made said improvements will be more fully stated by respondent in subsequent portions of his answer. Denies that complainant went into possession of said land as owner, either equitably or legally, or that he made said improvements by virtue of any contract for the purchase of said land, but from other and different considerations from those stated in the bill. States that some of said improvements were made with the consent of respondent, but portions thereof were made without and against his consent, and after a controversy had arisen between him and complainant about the land.

[*315] Respondent states the facts to be as follows, in regard to what had occurred between him and complainant in regard to said land or any land: that complainant was a son-in-law of respondent (his wife having since died); that complainant was a poor man, of but little means or capital other than that with which, from time to time, he had been furnished by respondent; that respondent was desirous of assisting complainant as far as his duty to his own family and his other children would permit; that respondent had purchased the half section of land, of which the land described in the bill formed a part, and complainant was desirous of buying eighty acres of land from respondent, but no particular portion or eighty of said land was designated or agreed for between them; that respondent, in answer to the proposition of complainant, had informed him that if he (complainant) would give his note to the school treasurer of said township, instead of the note respondent had executed to said township (for one hundred dollars), and would jointly assist respondent in making a stock farm of said half section of land (for which purpose respondent had bought it), by building a house upon it, and residing there for the purpose of boarding respondent's hands whilst they were engaged in improving and taking care of stock, and would pay half the expenses of improving, that respondent would convey eighty acres of said land to complainant, but no particular part of said land was designated as the eighty to be conveyed to complainant; and respondent at the same time further proposed to complainant, that if he (complainant) would not buy the land upon these terms, that if he would help to improve it for the purposes of a stock farm, he should have the use of the land until he was fully paid for his labor and improvements; that these were the only propositions ever made by respondent to complainant in regard to said land; that complainant did not, at the time said proposals were made or afterwards, accept the same, nor did he in any manner comply with the terms of said proposals, but so far as said complainant afterwards acted under said propositions, by going into possession of a portion of said land and improving the same, it was under the alternative proposition to pay him for his labor and improvements, and not under the proposi-

Hull v. Peer et al.

tion to sell him said land. Respondent denies that complainant
ever complied· with any proposition ever made to him by respondent, for a sale of said land, or any part thereof, to him,
and affirms that both complainant and respondent understood
that no other contract whatever subsisted between them in regard to the land, than the understanding growing out of said
proposal by respondent to pay said complainant for the [*316]
improvements he might make upon said land in the manner
before stated, and that complainant, by his declarations and
conduct, has since so admitted; that after said proposals had
been made, complainant did go upon the land and make some
improvements, respondent's teams and hands assisting to a considerable extent. And that after complainant had been upon
the land for two or three years, he sold out his improvements to
respondent for about the sum of seventy dollars, and left for
the State of Ohio, where he remained some time, and then returned to this State; that in the sale of said improvements,
complainant had reserved the right of repurchasing them, and
of placing himself in his former position towards respondent
upon said land. Upon his return to this State, which was in
the fall of 1853, complainant manifested no disposition whatever to repurchase said improvements, but, on the contrary,
abandoned said land, and cultivated other land; that respondent, regarding the agreement between himself and complainant,
in regard to the improvement of said land, as abandoned by
complainant and at an end, made other and different arrangements for its improvement, and some time thereafter was surprised by an assertion to some claim, by said complainant, to
some part of the land in question; that after some negotiation
between respondent and complainant, said complainant then
agreed that he would pay back to respondent what respondent
had paid him for his improvements, and that then three disinterested persons should be chosen, who should say and determine
how long complainant should occupy said land in payment for
the improvements he had made upon it; that both parties assented to this proposition, and respondent has ever been ready
to comply with this agreement, but complainant, when they

met for the purpose of selecting persons to determine this matter, refused to comply with said agreement.

Answer alleges, that the use of the land has been sufficient compensation for all improvements made thereon by complainant.

Answer of respondent sworn to, and replication filed thereto.

Death of complainant suggested, and leave to revive in the name of the heirs.

Decree: That the complainants, within ten days, pay to defendant, or to master for him, the sum of ninety dollars; that upon such payment, defendant execute and deliver to complainants, and Isaac Bowen, and Martha Bowen, a deed [*317] for the land described in the bill, defining the interest to be conveyed to the respective parties, or in default, that the master convey, and decree for costs against defendant.

Defendant appealed and now assigns for error—

That the court erred in rendering its decree herein for appellees.

That the court erred in decreeing a specific performance of the alleged contract in the bill.

That the court erred in not dismissing the bill of complainants on the hearing, and in not decreeing costs against them.

C. L. Higbee, and M. Hay, for Appellant.

W. A. and J. Grimshaw, for Appellees.

Caton, C. J. The bill in this case, is for a specific performance of a parol agreement for the sale of land, for the consideration of one hundred and fifty dollars; and states the mode and terms of payment. It avers possession, improvements, part payment and tender of the balance. The answer, which is sworn to, the oath not having been waived, does not interpose the statute of frauds, but positively denies that any such contract, as is stated in the bill, or any other contract for the sale of the land, was ever made. Here is the great and leading issue, formed by the pleadings, and it requires evidence, equal to the testimony of two witnesses, to overcome this answer. This is upon the ground, that the complainant having required the defendant to answer an oath, has thereby made him a witness in the cause, and his testimony being against the allegations of the bill, it must be neutralized by evidence equivalent to it before he can commence establishing his case, by other and distinct proof.

In this case, it is proved by a cloud of witnesses, that the answer is false, when it denies the existence of any agreement for the sale of this land. There are at least five witnesses, who testify to statements made, repeatedly and at different times, by the defendant, that he had sold the land to complainant, though but two state the price and terms of the sale, as stated in the bill. These are Thomas Orr and Harvey Gallaher, though Fugate and Henry Johnson establish the mode and times of payment, as stated in the bill; but by them it does not appear that the defendant stated the price. Now here is the testimony of all these witnesses, going directly to impeach the truth of the defendant's testimony in his answer. The defendant must be a man, who habitually states the most reckless falsehoods, in his daily intercourse with his neighbors, or his answer is false, when he denies that an agreement for [*318] the sale of this land had been made between the parties. We are constrained to regard the answer as untrue, and unworthy of the least credit. It is true that one of the complainant's witnesses is very effectually impeached, in his general reputation, and were he unsupported by other witnesses, we should give little or no heed to his testimony; but the defendant's answer is shown by the other witnesses, and many of them, to be absolutely false, and is entitled to even less credence than the testimony of Gallaher.

The contract then was proved as averred, very clearly and satisfactorily, and so was the payment of the principal, and thirty dollars of the interest of the note; while the proof also shows, that the defendant paid twenty or twenty-five dollars of the interest on the note. There was proof of considerable other dealing between the parties, all having more or less connection with the land contract, and it is not entirely clear how the balance should be struck between them. The complainant averred the tender of fifty dollars to the defendant, before filing his bill, and he proves a tender by one witness of ninety dollars, and by another, he proves that the defendant had admitted a tender of one hundred and ninety dollars. The decree awards to the defendant the ninety dollars tendered, and requires him to convey. But it is objected that the allegations and proofs do not agree, and hence the proof of the tender of ninety dollars or more, is inadmissible, under an averment of a tender of only fifty dollars, stating, also, that that was the amount due the defendant on the purchase of the land. Now, strictly speaking, that was all that was due of the purchase money, under the literal terms of the contract, according to the testimony of Mr. Fugate. He says that Bowen was to substitute a new note, which the treasurer was to accept in place of the one hundred dollar note of Hull's, which he held, and this was to stand as a payment of one hundred dollars of the purchase money, and the proof abundantly shows, that after this, but fifty dollars was due. This was in fact done in a mode which met the concurrence and approbation of Hull. When they met at the treasurer's for the purpose of the substitution, the treasurer objected to taking a note in substitution, with Bowen as nominal principal, because Bowen was already owing the school fund seventy-five dollars, and hence it was necessary that some one else should, in appearance at least, be the principal of the new note; and he suggested that Hull should appear as principal in the new note and Bowen as surety, instead of making Bowen principal and Hull surety. This suggestion met the approbation of all par- [*319] ties, and it was so done, although this new note was always treated as Bowen's note by all parties, and in equity at least, if not at law, Bowen was in truth and fact the principal in that note, as much as if he had appeared so upon its face. Strictly and technically speaking this was a payment of the first hundred dollars, according to the literal terms of the agreement, and justified the averment that but fifty dollars remained due, and a tender of that amount. And yet it was no doubt the duty of a court of equity, to go behind this literal performance, in order to do complete justice upon the broadest principles of equity, and protect the defendant against loss upon that note, and compel the complainant to reimburse the defendant the interest he had paid on that note, before it would give him the benefit of his literal performance. So too, the court might, under some circumstances, and perhaps a close computation in this case would show, that it did require the defendant to pay interest on the remaining fifty dollars, at least for a part of the time, although not required to do so by the literal terms of the bargain as proved. Now the complainant was not bound to anticipate in his pleadings all the discretionary equities which the court might adjudge against him. To ascertain the amount of the balance which the complainant may have to pay, in order to obtain a specific performance, may be, and often is, in the nature of taking an account, and the complainant need not at his peril state the exact balance which may ultimately be found against him. In a case where the true balance is uncertain, and can only be ascertained by the adjudication of the court, upon testimony to be taken, the pleader may state the case most favorably to himself, and then comply with the decree, if it is less favorable than was his claim. So here, the complainant might reasonably say, that but fifty dollars of the purchase money was due, and so insist in his pleadings, submitting, however, to the determination of the court, which, upon the evidence, and considering all the equities of the case, adjudges that he shall pay more than that, in order to entitle him to a specific performance of the agreement.

Although in this case, there is probably enough shown of part performance, by possession, improvement and payment, to take this case out of the statute of frauds, had that been interposed, as that has not been done, it is unnecessary to discuss that question.

We are of opinion that the decree should be affirmed.

Decree affirmed.

[*320] NATHAN BEADLES, Plaintiff in Error, *v.* JOHN
BLESS, Defendant in Error.

ERROR TO FULTON.

A wager, that a railroad will be completed within a certain time, is not prohibited by the common law or by our statute; and a recovery can be had
upon it.

In an action to recover a wager, that a railroad would be built within a certain time, evidence, that the bet was talked of a good deal by the public,
to show that it may have influenced subscriptions to the stock, was properly excluded. The court cannot say that it was against public policy to
influence or discourage subscriptions to the road.

THIS was an action of assumpsit, commenced for the June
term, 1859, of the Fulton Circuit Court, on the following instrument, viz.:

"On the second day of June, A. D. 1856, I promise to pay to John Bless or
order, one hundred dollars, for value received, provided the Peoria and Hannibal Railroad shall not be completed between Farmington and Lewistown,
Fulton Co., Ill., by the 1st day of June, 1856, so far as the tieing and laying
of the rails of said road are concerned. Lewistown, July 13, 1855.

N. BEADLES."

The defendant below (Beadles) pleaded the general issue.

The trial was had at the February term, 1860, before BAILEY,
Judge, and a jury, when, in support of the issues on his part,
the plaintiff called as a witness, *H. B. Evans*, who testified,
that he knew defendant's handwriting, and that the signature
to the instrument was that of defendant. The plaintiff then
offered to read in evidence to the jury said instrument, (given
above), to the reading of which. the defendant objected, on the
ground that it was improper and irrelevant; but the court overruled the objection and admitted the note in evidence, and to
be read to the jury, which was done, and defendant excepted.

The witness Evans then continued his testimony as follows,
on behalf of plaintiff below: I have seen this contract or
instrument (the one copied above) before now. It was signed
by Beadles in my presence. Bless was present. Both re-

Beadles *v.* Bless.

quested me to take and put it away. I think there was a similar contract made by Bless to Beadles for the same amount, and payable provided the railroad should be completed, as recited in this contract, by the 1st of June, 1856. Don't recollect that the one to Beadles was left with me. These contracts were got up in my store in Lewistown, Fulton county, Ill. Bless and Beadles came into the store, talking about the completion of the Peoria and Hannibal Rail- [*321] road to Lewistown. Beadles offered to put up his watch against $100 in money, that the road would be completed to Lewistown by the 1st June, 1856. This was in 1855. I offered to hold the stakes. They finally agreed to put up their notes payable at the same time and on opposite contingencies—Beadles to Bless, if the railroad should not be completed by the 1st June, 1856, to Lewistown, and Bless to Beadles, if the road should be so completed by that time—and the contracts or notes were executed accordingly, and this one left with me to be delivered to Bless if the said road should not be completed according to its terms. The said railroad was not completed to Lewistown according to the terms of the contract, and has not been yet; and after 1st June, 1856, I delivered the contract present to plaintiff. I have been all along the track of said road, and the same is not yet completed to Lewistown by laying rails and tieing. Bless came to me and got the contract, after the time had expired when I was to give it up to him.

On being cross-examined, said witness testified as follows: Before these contracts were gotten up, the parties were talking about the early completion of the railroad. There seemed to be a difference of opinion. Beadles was then engaged in obtaining subscriptions to the stock of the road. Beadles was highly spoken of as a good manager to get subscriptions. Plaintiff was a stockholder. Think he was friendly to the road. Have heard him say he would be glad to have the road.

Defendant then offered to prove by this witness that this bet or transaction was talked of by the public about Lewistown a great deal when subscriptions were being obtained to the stock of said railroad. The plaintiff objected to this proof, and the

court sustained the objection, and refused to permit such evi.
dence to go to the jury, and the defendant excepted.

S. C. Judd was then called by the plaintiff, who testified,
that the body of the instrument above given was in his handwriting; that he drew this one and its counterpart, at the request
of the parties; that several persons were present at the time of
the transaction; that the other instrument (the one payable to
Beadles), according to his recollection, was payable in the event
the Peoria and Hannibal Railroad should be completed between
Farmington and Lewistown, Fulton county, Illinois, by the 1st
of June, 1856, so far as the tieing and laying of the rails were
concerned, and was for the like sum with the one payable to
Bless; that these instruments were drawn in Evans' store,
Lewistown.

[*322] This was all the evidence offered in the case by either
party.

The defendant then moved the court to exclude from the jury
all the evidence offered and admitted on the part of the plaintiff, on the grounds, that it showed no right of recovery whatever; that it showed the instrument offered was without consideration; and that it showed that the transaction, in consideration
of which and out of which the contract sprung and was created,
was a bet, and against public policy, and hence no recovery
should be allowed in the case. But the court overruled the
motion, and refused to exclude the said evidence; to which the
defendant excepted. The defendant brings the case to this court
by writ of error.

The jury rendered a verdict of $122, against the defendant.

JUDD, BOYD & JAMES, for Plaintiff in Error.

S. P. SHOPE, for Defendant in Error.

CATON, C. J. This action was on the following agreement:

"On the second day of June, A. D. 1856, I promise to pay to John Bless or
order, one hundred dollars, for value received, provided the Peoria and Hannibal Railroad shall not be completed between Farmington and Lewistown,

Fulton Co., Ill., by the 1st day of June, 1856, so far as the tieing and laying of the rails of said road are concerned. Lewistown, July 13, 1855.

N. BEADLES."

This, in form at least, is simply a contract for the payment of money, dependent on a future contingency. And in that aspect is quite unexceptionable. The testimony, however, gives the transaction something of the character of a wager, and shows that a similar agreement was given by the payee to the maker of this agreement, payable upon the opposite contingency. But if viewed in the light of a wager, as we understand the common law, the plaintiff has a right to recover upon it. It is not prohibited by our statute; it has no immoral, indecent, illegal or pernicious tendency. Such wagers are recoverable at the common law, although the parties have no interest in the event upon which the wager depends. No doubt many excellent jurists have regretted that such idle agreements should be recognized in, and enforced by the courts, yet such is the law, and it is not for us to reform it. But in this case, surely, we cannot safely affirm that these parties had no interest in the event, upon which the promise to pay depended. The plaintiff may have had a legitimate and proper interest in having the road completed, within the time specified in the agreement, and desired to stimulate the defendant to secure its completion, or failing in that, to indemnify [*323] himself to the extent of the one hundred dollars. Or the defendant might have had an equal interest in not having it completed in that time. The one may believe, that public policy and the public good required that the whole community should exert itself to complete the road; while the other might have entertained the opinion, that such a course would be detrimental to himself and the public. It is not for us to say which may have been right in their opinions. At all events, we cannot say that the wager, if it was one, was illegal or immoral; and as a simple question of law, we must hold it valid. Nor do we think the court erred in ruling out the evidence offered. What matter, if people did talk about the wager, or if it influenced some to subscribe to the railroad stock, and prevented others from subscribing. We cannot say that one or the other was the wisest course, or that there was anything immoral or illegal for either or both parties to exert their influence one way or the other on the subject.

The judgment must be affirmed.

Judgment affirmed.

Thomas H. Flynn, Executor, etc., of Thomas Morgan, Plaintiff in Error, *v.* Mudd & Hughes, and Francis Keys, Defendants in Error.

ERROR TO SCOTT.

An agreement, between the holder of a note and the principal, to extend the time of payment for a definite period which is founded upon a good consideration, will discharge the surety; unless the surety consents to the agreement at the time, or subsequently ratifies it.

To enable a surety to interpose the defense to a note that further time has been given to his principal, it is not necessary that his name should appear upon the note as surety; it will be sufficient if he was actually a surety, and this was known to the payee when the note was executed.

The payment of interest upon a note in advance, is a sufficient consideration to support an agreement for an extension of time to the principal, so as to discharge the surety.

Where the plaintiff introduces in evidence a note which has indorsed upon it, an agreement extending the time for payment, he will be bound by the agreement although it is not signed by him.

This was an action of assumpsit, brought by Thomas Morgan, plaintiff, in the Circuit Court of Scott county, at the December special term, 1858, on a promissory note, dated St. Louis, April 28, 1857, for $18,000—made by the defendants, [*324] payable to the order of one Wm. T. Hazzard, in four months after date, and by him assigned to said plaintiff. Process served on Francis Keys only, and by consent tried before Woodson, Judge, without a jury. Judgment rendered against said plaintiff in the court below for costs. A writ of error is now brought by Thomas H. Flynn, executor of the last will

Flynn, Ex'r, etc., *v.* Mudd & Hughes *et al.*

and testament of said Thomas Morgan, since deceased, to this court.

The declaration contains three special counts—for the note, interest and damages on protest, and the usual money counts.

The defendant Keys, besides the plea of non-assumpsit, filed two special pleas, in substance the same, in which he alleges, that he was simply security of Mudd & Hughes on said note, which the said plaintiff knew at the time he took the note; and that after plaintiff received said note, and before its maturity, to wit, on the 6th day of August, 1857, at St. Louis, Mo., said plaintiff agreed with said firm of Mudd & Hughes, that if they would pay him in advance the interest on said note up to the 28th day of March, 1858, he would extend the time for the payment of said note to said 28th March, 1858; and in pursuance of said agreement, the said firm of Mudd & Hughes did pay, on the 6th day of August, 1857, the plaintiff, in advance, the interest on the amount of said note up to the 28th March, 1858, to wit, the sum of $840; and in consideration thereof, the said plaintiff promised and agreed with the said firm to extend the time of payment of said note to the said 28th day of March, 1858. The said pleas then allege, that said Keys was in no way a party to said agreement, and it was made without his knowledge or consent.

To which special pleas the plaintiff filed a general demurrer, which the court overruled.

Whereupon the plaintiff, by leave of court, filed three replications, traversing the special pleas, and alleging that Keys was a principal on the note, and a joint payor of the same.

The following is the evidence adduced on the trial of said cause in the court below.

On behalf of the plaintiff, the note sued upon, to wit:

" $18,000.   St. Louis, April 27th, 1857.

" Four months after date, we promise to pay to the order of William T. Hazzard, eighteen thousand dollars, for value received, negotiable and payable without defalcation or discount, at the Bank of the State of Missouri, with six per cent. interest for forfeiture from date, if not paid at maturity.

MUDD & HUGHES.
FRANCIS· KEYS."

Flynn, Ex'r, etc., *v.* Mudd & Hughes *et al.*

[*325]　Assignment on said note:

"Pay Thomas Morgan, or order.　　　　　　　　WM. T. HAZZARD."

On behalf of the defendant, and excepted to by plaintiff in court below, *Adams*, witness, testified, that in the month of June, 1858, when and where the plaintiff, Francis Keys, and witness were present, in a conversation then and there between the plaintiff, Keys and witness, the said defendant stated that Francis Keys was security on the note sued upon in this case, and that plaintiff knew that fact at the time Keys signed it; that the said defendant, Keys, said that the note was signed by him after Mudd & Hughes had got the money for which the note was given, before he (Keys) signed the note, which plaintiff admitted; that the said Keys also stated, in the same conversation, in the presence of Morgan, that Mr. Grubb, one of the firm of Mudd & Hughes, requested him (Keys) to sign the note as security; and that at the same time Morgan had the note of Mudd & Hughes in his possession, and that afterwards, he (Keys) signed said note. That plaintiff, Morgan, stated in the same conversation, that he had extended the time of payment, and that Keys stated at the same time that he considered himself released from said note, because Morgan had extended the time of payment; and Morgan also stated, that he held Keys still bound to pay said note, and considered him as one of the principals on said note; and Morgan also further stated, that he would not have let Mudd & Hughes have the money for which the note was given without Keys signing said note. The witness also stated, that Morgan did not say that he received any consideration from Mudd & Hughes for extending the time of payment of said note.

Memorandum on the back of note sued upon, adduced in evidence by defendant, and excepted to by plaintiff in court below:

"Received of Mudd & Hughes payment in full for the interest on the within note to the 28th day of March next, at which time this note is to be due and payable; if not paid at that date, to draw interest according to the face and tenor of said note.

"St. Louis, August 6th, 1857."

Which was all the evidence in the case. Whereupon the court below rendered judgment against said plaintiff, and in favor of said Keys, for costs.

J. H. BERRY, and I. L. MORRISON, for Plaintiff in Error.

M. HAY, and N. M. KNAPP, for Defendants in Error.

WALKER, J. The doctrine, that giving further time [*326] to the principal debtor, by a valid agreement, without the assent of the surety, releases him from the contract, seems to be universally admitted and acted upon. Yet a diversity in the practice, as to the mode in which the surety may avail himself of the defense, exists in different courts. In some it is held, that the remedy is alone in chancery, unless it appears upon the face of the instrument, that he bears that relation to the contract, whilst in others it is held, that the fact that he is a surety may be averred and proved, although he appears as a principal.

In Great Britain the former rule appears to prevail, but on this side of the Atlantic, every defense which discharges the surety in equity, has generally been recognized as admissible in courts of law. There are, however, some of our courts that follow the English practice, although compared with the others, they are few in number. To render such a defense available, it is necessary that the contract extending the time for payment, should be such as would prevent the creditor from maintaining an action, on the original agreement, before the expiration of the extended time. To have that effect, it must be based upon a sufficient consideration, and must be for a definite period. *Gardner* v. *Watson*, 13 Ill. 347. But possessing these requisites, it must also have been entered into, between the principal debtor and the creditor, without the consent of the surety, or his subsequent ratification, to constitute a valid defense. And this defense is based on the principle, that the surety can only be held to perform the precise terms of his contract. He cannot be charged by the acts of others, beyond the terms of his agreement.

When he has agreed, that his principal shall pay money, or perform any other act, by a specified day, the change of time

389

Flynn, Ex'r, etc., *v.* Mudd & Hughes *et al.*

to a different day, is not the agreement into which he entered, and to enforce its performance, would be to permit other and unauthorized persons to make for him a contract. The principle is universally recognized, that any unauthorized alteration of an agreement, will release all parties, not assenting to or ratifying the change. And the surety must undeniably have the same right to interpose the same defense, when the terms of the agreement into which he has entered have been changed by other parties.

Again, any alteration, by which the rights of a surety are impaired, or the possibility of his resorting to them is delayed, places him in a different situation from that which he originally occupied. It might also impose upon him the whole burthen of the obligation, and deprive him of resorting to [*327] means of indemnity to which he looked, if the principal should in the meantime become insolvent. After the time for the performance has elapsed, the surety has the right to resort to equity, to compel the principal to proceed to the enforcement of the contract, or he may himself discharge it and look to his principal for indemnity. These are his legal rights, and to which he is supposed to look, when he assumes his liability, and to deprive him of them, might work great injustice and flagrant wrong. The necessary consequence of so extending the time, is the release of the surety, whatever the form of the contract, and whether the extension has been made before or after a breach. *Warner* v. *Campbell*, 26 Ill. 282. And we have seen that it is held by the greater number of the tribunals of this country, that such a defense may be made in a court of law.

This rule can work no injustice, as the creditor, if unwilling to release the surety, has only to refrain from entering into an agreement to give further time without the assent of the surety. The mere neglect to sue at the maturity of the contract, or even giving further time by an agreement not binding on the creditor, does not produce a release of the surety, as he may still compel the creditor to proceed to the enforcement of the agreement, or may discharge it, and resort to his remedy against his principal for his ultimate indemnity. By such an agreement he is deprived of none of his remedies, and is subjected to no new conditions, hazards or losses outside of his original undertaking.

Then was the agreement, to postpone the payment in this case, of such a character as released the defendant Keys? The evidence satisfactorily shows, that he was only a surety, and that the payee was aware of that fact at the time the instrument was executed. He admitted, that the money was loaned to defendants Mudd & Hughes, before Keys executed the note. He likewise admitted in the same conversation, that he had extended the time of payment. It also appears, that there was indorsed on the back of the note this memorandum: "Received of Mudd & Hughes, payment in full, for the interest on the within note, to the 28th day of March next, at which time this note is to be due and payable; if not paid at that date, to draw interest according to the force and tenor of said note. St. Louis, August 6th, 1857."

It is manifest from this evidence, that defendant Keys was only a security on the note. And we think it equally clear, that the advance interest was paid as the consideration, and to procure an extension of time, until the 28th of March, 1858. Morgan admitted an extension of time, and this memorandum found upon the back of the note, shows that such was [*328] the fact, as well as the period to which it was extended. It is, however said, that it was not signed by the payee, and is for that reason not binding. No one will for a moment doubt, that it is a sufficient receipt for the interest which accrued, prior to the 28th of March following. And why? Because it comes from the possession of the holder, and if it was untrue or improper, it would have been obliterated. It was in the possession and under the control of the person against whom it operated, and it must be supposed to be correct. And for the same reason the presumption must apply to every part of the indorsement unless rebutted, which has not been done.

At the time this interest was paid, the note had just matured, and it was not designed as a payment on the principal, because it was limited to the accruing interest. This excludes the inference that it was designed, or may be treated as a payment on the principal. This interest paid to the creditor in advance,

was a benefit to him, and was therefore a sufficient consideration, to support the agreement to extend the time of payment.
Had suit been instituted for the collection of the principal before the expiration of the time, this agreement would have defeated a recovery. And if so, Keys had no legal means of
compelling Morgan to proceed for its collection, or to have
himself paid the money, and proceeded against the principal
debtors for indemnity, before the time had elapsed. By this
agreement he was effectually prevented from resorting to those
remedies, which he doubtless had in contemplation when he
became a surety. Upon this entire record, after a careful examination, we are unable to perceive any error for which the
judgment should be reversed, and it is therefore affirmed.

Judgment affirmed.

GEORGE A. MONTAG, Plaintiff in Error, *v.* JAMES J.
LINN, Defendant in Error.

ERROR TO ADAMS.

The statute for the protection of occupying claimants is designed to protect
those who shall in good faith take peaceable possession of vacant land
under such a paper title as the records of the county show to be plain, clear
and connected, and without notice of any adverse title of record.

The protection of a party under this statute does not depend upon the original
deeds through which he deraigns his title being regular upon their face;
such deeds may contain material alterations, or be forgeries, and yet the
purchaser may be protected. where the records of the county show a clear
chain of title.

[*329] THIS was an application made to the Circuit Court of
Adams county, by the plaintiff in error, for the appointment of
commissioners to assess the value of lasting improvements made
by him upon land which the defendant in error had recovered
of him in ejectment. The court overruled the motion, to which
the plaintiff in error excepted, and has brought the case to this
court. The ejectment suit between these parties was tried at
the January term, 1860, of this court.

The opinion of the Court gives a full statement of the case.

GRIMSHAW & WILLIAMS, for Plaintiff in Error.

WHEAT & GROVER, for Defendant in Error.

BREESE, J. On a recovery in ejectment by the defendant here, against the plaintiff in error, of a tract of land in Adams county, the unsuccessful party entered his motion in the Circuit Court of that county, for the appointment of commissioners to value such lasting improvements as he had made upon the land, and, also, for an order to stay the issuing of a writ of possession until such valuation could be made and the amount thereof paid to him. The plaintiff in error relied on the provisions of that part of chapter 36, respecting "occupying claimants." (Scates' Comp. 220.) Due notice was given of the motion, and proof submitted that the plaintiff had made valuable and lasting improvements on the land, prior to the bringing the suit, by which he was ejected. The plaintiff showed as title to the land: First, A patent from the United States, dated Feb. 26, 1818, to one John Silver, a private in McIntosh's company of light artillery. Second, A deed from John Silver to John B. Cofield, dated in January, 1850, recorded in Adams county, Feb. 26, 1850. In this deed there was an alteration which this court held to be material, and rejected it, on a trial in this court. Third, The defendant read in evidence deed duly executed, purporting to convey the title from Cofield to the plaintiff, which was on record in the proper office in Adams county, without any notice to plaintiff of defendant's paramount title. He also proved that he had obtained peaceable possession of the land.

The defendant here, in opposition to the motion, proved paramount title to the land, by showing the original patent from the United States to John Silver; also, a deed from John Silver, dated Jan. 11, 1855, to Albert M. Noyes, recorded Jan. 24, 1856, in Adams county, and a deed from Albert M. Noyes to him, the defendant, dated Feb. 1, 1856, also recorded in Adams county. He also showed the [*330] deposition of John Silver, taken in the ejectment cause, who testified that he was the patentee, and that he never made any deed to Cofield, and if any such deed was in existence, it was a forgery.

The court, thereupon, overruled the motion, and refused to appoint commissioners or grant a restraining order, to all which the plaintiff here excepted, and brought the case here by writ of error, assigning for error, this refusal of the Circuit Court.

The material provisions of our "occupying claimant" law, bearing on this case, are the forty-seventh and forty-eighth sections (Scates' Comp. 220), the first of which provides "that every person who may be evicted from any land for which he can show a plain, clear and connected title in law or equity, deduced from the record of some public office, without actual notice of an adverse title, in like manner derived from record, shall be exempt and free from all and every species of action, suit or prosecution, for or on account of any rents, or profits, or damages, which shall have been done, accrued or incurred, at any time prior to receipt of actual notice of the adverse claim by which the eviction may be effected, provided such person obtained peaceable possession of the land." The forty-eighth section prescribes the manner of the appointment of the commissioners to assess the value of the improvements, and their whole duty in the premises, which it is not necessary to specify in detail. The question here is, did the plaintiff in error show a plain, clear and connected title in law or equity, deduced from the record of some public office, without actual notice of an adverse title in like manner derived from record?

The defendant in error, the successful party in the ejectment, contends that no such title was shown, and consequently the appointment of commissioners was properly refused—that the deed from the patentee to Cofield, through which he derived this title, and indispensable to its support, bore upon its face unmistakeable evidence of a material alteration, and so glaring as to excite the suspicion of any reasonably cautious man with regard to it. That taking possession of the land, under such a deed, was not in good faith, and did not make out a plain, clear and connected title. It is quite apparent, that it is not the design of the law to provide for cases in which an apparently good title may have been compelled to yield to a paramount title, and so the counsel for the defendant in error admitted on the argument. He admitted, that an ejected party is protected, who has a clear "set of title papers," not a good title, but who has "a *prima facie* [*331] apparent title," obtained in good faith, and who is a *bona fide* possessor under it.

We apprehend the statute designs to protect all persons, who, in good faith, shall take peaceable possession of vacant land under such a paper title as the records of the county show to be plain, clear and connected, and without notice of any adverse title of record.

It would not seem to be important that the original deeds through which the title is deraigned, should be clear on their face, but only that the records of the public office to which resort is had, should, upon their pages, show "a plain, clear and connected title." Lands are often bought and sold without reference to the original deeds, resort being had to the records of the county, and it is quite probable the plaintiff here, never saw the altered deed, but only the record of it, which would not show any alteration. His title, as deduced from the records of a public office, was plain, clear and connected, with no flaw in it, and it is only by inspection by the court of the original, that the alteration is manifested. The alteration itself was considered by counsel learned in the law to have been an unimportant one, as there were other words in the deed, which without the alteration, they supposed would have conveyed the land. If then, the original deed had been submitted to the plaintiff, who appears to be a person not acquainted with our language, or to counsel employed by him, it is quite probable he and they would have considered the deed unobjectionable by reason of the alteration. But the statute does not require that the title papers shall be perfect on their face, it only requires the records to show a plain, clear and connected title—so that; though a forged deed, placed on record, the party claiming under it, ignorant of the forgery, and having no notice of it, would be protected by this law, to the extent of the value of his lasting improvements. The records show a title *prima facie* good, and comes up to one of the admissions of the defendant's counsel. He may have no other set of title papers except such as the public records afford him.

The deposition of Silver was an after proceeding, of which the plaintiff had no knowledge until the trial of the ejectment suit. He could not know from the records, the fact, the deposition discloses, and is not chargeable with that knowledge. From the records, and by the records, the title was plain, clear and connected. His possession was taken peaceably under his title, with no notice of any adverse title, and he has, therefore, a right to have commissioners appointed to value his last-[*332] ing improvements made before notice of the paramount title, and to such other benefits as the statute confers.

The statute is of an equitable character, and seems designed to protect all persons, who shall be so unfortunate as to lose land, upon which they have entered in good faith, with no knowledge of any adverse or better title than they possessed, they themselves showing a plain, clear and connected title in law or equity, deduced from the record of some public office. There is so much justice and equity in such a statute, that assent is rendered to it instinctively. The judgment is reversed, and cause remanded, with directions to appoint commissioners, as moved, and also to enter an order staying the issuing of a writ of possession until such valuation shall be made, and the amount thereof paid to the plaintiff in error, should anything be due.

Judgment reversed.

GEORGE BALL, Plaintiff in Error, *v.* JAMES E. BRUCE, Defendant in Error.

ERROR TO EDGAR.

It is generally a matter of discretion whether the Circuit Court will rule a party to file security for costs; but if the affidavit upon which the motion is founded be insufficient, the Circuit Court has no power under the statute to make the rule, and its decision will be reviewed in this court.

Upon a motion for a rule upon the plaintiff to file additional security for costs, an affidavit is insufficient which only avers the insolvency of the plaintiff and his security; it should show, in addition, that the circumstances of the principal or security have changed since the approval of the former bond.

THIS is an action on the case, commenced at the April term, 1857, of the Circuit Court of Edgar county, by George Ball against James E. Bruce, for the seduction of one Eliza Alsup. At the September term following, there was a demurrer filed and sustained to the declaration. The case was brought to this court, and the decision of the court below reversed, and the case remanded; and at the October term, 1859, the defendant filed his pleas, and the issues were made up. A trial was had, and a verdict rendered in favor of the plaintiff. A motion for a new trial was made by the defendant's counsel and taken under advisement by the court, and at the next January term, 1860, the court set aside the verdict of the jury, and granted a new trial, and the case was then continued to the next April term, and on the eleventh day of that term the defendant, Bruce, filed the following affidavit:

"James Bruce *ads.* George Ball—Edgar county, ss. [*333]

"James E. Bruce being duly sworn, says that the plaintiff, Ball, and John F. Anderson (who was, as defendant believes, the security for costs of said Ball in this case,) are both insolvent, and not able to pay the costs in this cause, as this defendant verily believes.

JAMES E. BRUCE."

"Subscribed and sworn to, this 11th day of May, 1860.
W. J. GREGG, Clerk."

On motion of defendant's counsel on this affidavit, the court ruled the plaintiff to give additional security by the Monday following, which the plaintiff declined doing, and the court dismissed the case. The plaintiff at the time excepted, and brings the case to this court on writ of error, and assigns as errors:

That the court erred in ruling the plaintiff to give security for costs.

The court erred in dismissing said case because the plaintiff failed and declined to execute bond for costs.

The ruling and judgment of the court are contrary to law.

The court erred in maintaining said motion for security for costs, because it was not made at the first term at which it could have been made, and no reason shown in the affidavit for the delay.

A. GREEN, for Plaintiff in Error.

JAMES A. EADS, for Defendant in Error.

WALKER, J. This was a motion, in the court below, for a rule on plaintiff, for additional security for costs. It was based on this affidavit: "James E. Bruce being duly sworn, says that the plaintiff Ball, and John F. Anderson, who was, as affiant believes, the security for costs of the said Ball in this case, are both insolvent, and not able to pay the costs in this cause, as this affiant verily believes." The court below, upon this affidavit, ruled the plaintiff to give additional security by the following morning. He having failed to comply with this rule, the suit was dismissed and judgment rendered against him for the costs of suit, to reverse which, he prosecutes this writ of error.

It is insisted, that it is a matter of discretion, whether the court will rule a party to give security for costs. This may be true, as a general proposition, at the common law. And it was so held by this court, in the cases of *Gesford* v. *Critzer*, 2 [*334] Gilm. 698, and *Selby* v. *Hutchinson*, 4 Gilm. 319, on applications, in the first instance. This is, however, a second application, and for additional security, the plaintiff having given security, under a former rule of the court. When he complied with that rule, the sufficiency of the security must have been satisfactory to the court, or to the clerk approving it at the time, and for aught that appears the defendant may himself have been perfectly satisfied with its sufficiency at the time it was given.

This affidavit fails to disclose any fact, showing that the circumstances of the principal and security to the bond for costs had changed. after it was approved. There is nothing to show that they were not altogether as able to pay the costs as when the bond was first given. From anything appearing in the affidavit, it may have been filed to reinvestigate the question of the solvency of the surety, after the bond was filed, or it may have been an independent motion, upon the ground that the security had become insolvent after the execution of the bond. We think this affidavit was wholly insufficient, upon which to base a motion for additional security, although it may have been proper, on an application for security for costs in the first instance. Had the affidavit been sufficient for the purpose, and the court had ruled him to give security, either on the first or subsequent application, we should have regarded the case as falling within the rule announced in the cases referred to above. But until the court has before it a sufficient affidavit, he has no power to make the rule under the second section of the cost act, especially where its sufficiency is not admitted by justifying under it, or in some other mode.

The judgment of the court below is reversed, and the cause remanded.

Judgment reversed.

EDWARD L. HINRICHSEN, Plaintiff in Error, *v.* RANSOM VAN WINKLE *et al.*, Defendants in Error.

ERROR TO MORGAN.

A court of chancery will relieve against judgments obtained by fraud or by unavoidable accident; if there has been no fault or negligence on the part of the defendant in making his defense. But not if there has been such fault or negligence.

JULY 20, 1859, complainant filed his bill in the Morgan Circuit Court, alleging, that on March 24, 1862, com- [*335] plainant, Harry Reinback and Hiram Van Winkle were partners, as merchants, at Franklin, Illinois, under the name of Reinback & Van Winkle, complainant being only silent partner, and not taking active part in the business. In fall of 1852, the firm was dissolved, Van Winkle selling out his entire interest to other members, all the assets going into the hands of Reinback, with all papers, vouchers, etc., who was to collect in money due said firm, and pay the debts of said concern. That in schedule made out for use of complainant, at that time, no debt, such as is hereinafter mentioned, was included. One Ransom Van Winkle held a note against said firm, which was a part of said firm indebtedness; that Reinback managed the business loosely and negligently, and divers suits were brought against said firm; that in September, 1857, Ransom Van Winkle commenced his suit, in the Morgan Circuit Court, against said firm; that he filed his plea of the general issue, and then applied to Reinback for information as to said debt, who gave no satisfactory account of the same; that Hiram Van Winkle was then a resident of another county. Reinback failing to defend, judgment was rendered against defendants for $251.31; said suit based on a paper in handwriting of Hiram Van Winkle, as follows:

"FRANKLIN, March 24th, 1857.
"Rec'd of Rans. Van Winkle two hundred and forty-nine dollars and fifty cents, to be paid on demand.   REINBACK & VAN WINKLE."

No service on, or appearance in said suit by Hiram Van Winkle, but judgment was rendered against all the defendants. Complainant, after gaining all the information he could get in suit, sued out a writ of error from the Supreme Court, to reverse said judgment; but to prevent that, Reinback and Hiram Van Winkle, in fraud of the rights of complainant, released the error, and prevented the reversal. That Ransom Van Winkle is a careful business man, and would not have permitted said debt to remain without interest, if it was *bona fide* due.

Charges, that receipt was given for money left with firm temporarily; was not for their benefit, and was taken up by Ransom Van Winkle, and the receipt left outstanding, or if taken up, was again fraudulently given out to him to sue complainant.

Charges, that Van Winkle did not claim to hold complainant liable for said debt till suit was brought—that same was in fact controlled by Harry Reinback; believes if money is collected from complainant, that Reinback will be benefited by

the same; that said original judgment was recovered [*336]
by fraudulent combination of Ransom Van Winkle and Harry
Reinback; said firm does not owe said money in justice.   That
now Ransom Van Winkle insists on sheriff, I. S. Hicks, making the whole of said debt off of complainant; that the same
is, in fact, controlled by Harry Reinback; that said Hicks is
about to proceed to sell complainant's real estate; prays for injunction restraining sheriff from selling, and that the collection of said judgment be perpetually enjoined; bill waives oath
of Harry Reinback.

Master in chancery granted injunction December 28, 1859.
Ranson Van Winkle, Harry Reinback and Harry Van Winkle,
filed answers.

Harry Reinback's answer not sworn to.   Denies allegations
of fraud and negligence in managing partnership interest of
himself and complainant; adopts answer of other defendant as
his own.

Ransom and Hiram Van Winkle answer under oath.   Admit partnership, as alleged; say complainant had full access to
books, etc.; that if he was ignorant of anything, it was his own
fault.

Hiram does not remember that a list of liabilities was made
out at dissolution of firm; says he went to house of Ransom
and borrowed the money, and used it in said firm; gave the
paper set out in the bill; admits that he has resided in Macoupin county, Illinois, since July, 1857.

Admit rendition of judgment as alleged in the bill, on the
paper copied in the bill; admit release of errors as alleged;
deny fraudulent intent; say they have urged the collection of
judgment; note sued on was *bona fide* for money loaned, and
not a certificate of deposit; "that if it has been paid, respondents have no recollection of it;" that indulgence did not cancel obligation; had repeatedly demanded payment of said note
of Harry Reinback, before suit.   Reinback said he thought it
had been paid; could not show it had been paid; sued because
he thought debt due; denies that he sued it at instance of
Harry Reinback; says the money is for his benefit, and not for

the benefit of Harry Reinback; wants his money, and don't care who pays it; asks court to dissolve injunction.

On the hearing, the court entered a decree dismissing complainant's bill; and complainant appealed to this court.

Isaac L. Morrison, for Plaintiff in Error.

Breese, J. There is no question about the power of courts of chancery to grant relief against judgments obtained by [*337] fraud, or by the occurrence of such accidents as the party could not foresee and provide against. *Propst* v. *Meadows*, 13 Ill. 157; *Nelson* v. *Rockwell*, 14 id. 376. Proceedings to set such a judgment aside, being purely original, they may be instituted either at law or in equity, at the option of the injured party. 2 Leading Cases in Equity, Hare & Wallace, 97.

In the case of *The Marine Insurance Co. of Alexandria* v. *Hodgson*, 7 Cranch, 332, Chief Justice Marshall stated the rule which prevails in such cases in this language: "It may safely be said, that any fact which clearly proves it to be against conscience to execute a judgment, and of which the injured party could not have availed himself in a court of law; or of which he might have availed himself at law, but was prevented by fraud or accident, unmixed with any fault or negligence in himself or his agents, will justify an application to a court of chancery." But a party cannot ask for relief in equity on the ground that he has failed or omitted to make a legal defense at law. Ib. And this rule is absolutely inflexible, and cannot be violated even when the judgment in question is manifestly wrong in law and in fact, or when the effect of allowing it to stand, will be to compel the payment of a debt which the defendant does not owe, or which he owes to a third party, unless it shall appear it was obtained by fraud or was the result of accident or mistake. *Buckmaster* v. *Grundy*, 3 Gilm. 626; *State Bank* v. *Stanton*, 2 id. 332.

Testing this case by these principles, it is apparent no ground was shown for the interposition of a court of equity. No fraud is shown on the part of the plaintiff in the suit, or any of his agents—no unforeseen accident occurred, to deprive the complainant of the opportunity of making every possible defense to the suit—no deception was practiced by any one toward him, unless it was by his own partner and agent, H. Reinback, and which must be visited upon him. It was in the power of the complainant, in defending the suit at law, to plead payment of the note, and to call upon the plaintiff in the action to discover on oath the fact of payment. He did not do so—he did not avail himself of a defense which could have been made at law, if it existed.

The Van Winkles deny, on oath, all the matters charged in the bill, and there are no circumstances proved sufficient to discredit their answers. The presumption is very strong indeed, that the debt was unpaid, and that complainant was the responsible party.

Had it been shown, that the plaintiff in the judgment had colluded with Reinback, to throw complainant off his guard, by promising to retain counsel to defend the suit, then indeed, some semblance of fraud might be discoverable. But [*338.] there is nothing of the kind. Reinback, his partner, failing to employ counsel, he employed counsel himself, and went to trial on the general issue. Payment could have been shown under that plea, and a bill for discovery filed, to search the conscience of the plaintiff. He did not avail himself of it, and must bear the consequences of his own neglect. There is no ground for the interference of a court of equity. The decree must be affirmed.

Decree affirmed.

HARVEY BILDERBACK, Appellant, *v.* ALBERT H. BUR- LINGAME, Appellee.

APPEAL FROM RANDOLPH.

Held, that the following instrument was negotiable under the statute, and that in an action upon it, a consideration need not be averred or proved: "Due W. B. G. $450, to be paid in lumber when called for, in good lumber, at $1.25."

An instrument admitting a certain sum of money to be due, which may be
paid in merchandise, at a fixed price, becomes an absolute money demand,
if the payee fails to deliver the merchandise when it is called for. If there
were two payees, a refusal by one of them would be sufficient.

The cases of *Bradley* v. *Morris*, 3 Scam. 182, and *Lowe* v. *Bliss et al.*, 24 Ill.
R. 169, overruled.

THIS was an action of assumpsit, instituted in the Randolph
Circuit Court, against Henry Bilderback and Harvey Bilderback, by Albert H. Burlingame, the assignee of Wm. B. Goddard, returnable to the September term, 1860.

The return being "defendants not found," an alias writ was
issued to the same defendants, returnable to the April term,
1861. It was returned served "by reading to Harvey Bilderback."

The declaration was filed at the September term, 1860. It
contains but one special count, the substance of which is as
follows: That said defendants, (Henry Bilderback and Harvey
Bilderback,) on the 16th day of December, 1859 at, etc.,
"made their certain promissory note in writing," bearing date
etc, "and thereby then and there promised to pay to one Wm.
B. Goddard the sum of four hundred and fifty dollars, to be paid
in good lumber at one dollar and twenty-five cents, when called
for, and then and there delivered the said promissory note to
the said Wm. B. Goddard, and the said Wm. B. Goddard,
to whom the said payment of the said sum of money,
in good lumber, was to be made, as specified in said prom-
[*339] issory note, after the making and delivery of said
promissory note by the said defendants, and before the payment thereof, called for and demanded of the said defendants
the lumber as specified in said promissory note, but the said
defendants utterly refused to furnish or deliver said lumber as
required in said promissory note specified; and the said Wm.
B. Goddard, to whom the payment of said sum of money,
in lumber, in the said promissory note specified, was to be
made, after the making of said promissory note, and after the
demand of said lumber by the said Wm. B. Goddard, and the
refusal by the said defendants to deliver said lumber, and before the payment of the said sum of money therein specified,

to wit," etc., "on the 23rd day of May, 1860, at the county aforesaid, indorsed, by assignment, the said promissory note, by which said assignment, he, the said Wm. B. Goddard, then and there ordered and appointed the said sum of money in the said promissory note specified to be paid to the said plaintiff, and then and there delivered the said promissory note so assigned as aforesaid, to the said plaintiff, by means whereof," etc., "the said defendants became liable to pay to the said plaintiff the said sum of money in the said promissory note specified, according to the tenor and effect of said promissory note; and being so liable, they, the said defendants, in consideration thereof, afterwards, to wit, on the day and year aforesaid, at the county and State aforesaid, undertook, and then and there faithfully promised the said plaintiff to pay him the said sum of money in the said promissory note specified, according to the tenor and effect thereof."

The following is a copy of the plea in answer to the foregoing special count:

"Harvey Bilderback, one of the defendants in the foregoing case, by his attorney, comes and defends the wrong, etc., and says, for a plea to the first count of said plaintiff's declaration, that he did not make said promissory note, and undertake and promise, in manner and form as in said count is alleged, and of this he puts himself upon the country." Plaintiff joined issue.

The cause was submitted to the court, without a jury. The plaintiff offered the following written instrument in evidence under the first count of the declaration, to wit:

"$450.00.   December 16, 1859.
"Due Wm. B. Goddard four hundred and fifty dollars, to be paid in lumber when called for, in good lumber, at one dollar and twenty-five cents.
(Signed)   HENRY BILDERBACK.
                                         HARVEY BILDERBACK."

Defendant objected to the instrument, as being vari- [*340] ant from and inadmissible under said count. The objection was overruled, and the instrument admitted in evidence; to which the defendant expected. The assignment on the back of said instrument was written as follows:

"For value received, I assign the within note to Albert H. Burlingame.
  "*May* 23, 1860.   WM. B. GODDARD."

David McConechie was sworn, and examined by plaintiff,
and testifies that he carried the foregoing instrument down to
Mr. Bilderback, and that Bilderback refused to give lumber for
it; and that was about this time last year. Mr. Goddard gave
witness the note. Witness did not remember whether the assignment was then on it. Bilderback had lumber on hand; at
the time he sold witness lumber, on witness' own hook.

Reuben Goddard testified: He saw the note about this time
last year. Mr. Harvey Bilderback came up to Sparta, and
wished to make a settlement with Wm. B. Goddard, and Bilderback and Goddard made a settlement. A credit was indorsed on the note $56.65, dated May 18, 1860. Mr. Goddard
made a demand at that time for lumber on the note. Mr. Bilderback refused; and after subtracting the credit, Goddard and
Bilderback agreed on the amount that was coming. There
were then two other credits on the note, one for $81.25, and one
for $14.50, which were taken into account at the settlement, and
after subtracting those credits, Henry Bilderback admitted the
balance due Wm. B. Goddard, but would not pay it unless
Wm. B. Goddard would go security on a note of J. B. Parks
and Wm. M. Davids, which he (Henry Bilderback) held.

No other testimony was offered or admitted in the case.

The court found a verdict for plaintiff for $314.70. Defend-
ant moved for a new trial. Motion overruled, to which defendant excepted. Judgment was rendered for plaintiff for the
amount of the verdict.

Defendant, Harvey Bilderback, prayed this appeal and for a
bill of exceptions.

By consent of parties, the record is brought to the Second
Division.

The appellant assigns the following errors in the proceedings
of the Circuit Court:

Error in admitting the written instrument as evidence to
sustain the special count in plaintiff's declaration.

Error in the verdict.

And error in overruling the· motion for a new trial, and in rendering judgment for plaintiff.

THOMAS G. ALLEN, for Appellant. [*341]

J. B. UNDERWOOD, for Appellee.

BREESE, J. The points made on this record are to be determined by our statute, chap. 73, title, "Negotiable Instruments," (Scates' Comp. 291). The third section of that chapter provides, ·that all promissory notes, bonds, due-bills, and other instruments in writing, made or to be made by any person or persons, body politic or corporate, whereby such person or persons promise or agree to pay any sum of money or articles of personal property, or any sum of money in personal property, or acknowledged any sum of money or article of personal property to be due to any other person or persons, shall be taken to be due and payable; and the sum of money or article of personal property therein mentioned, shall, by virtue thereof, be due and payable to the person or persons to whom the said note, bond, bill or other instrument in writing is made.

The fourth section bestows upon such paper an assignable quality, and the fifth section authorizes the assignee to sue upon it, in his own name.

In the sense of the commercial law, the note, in the record, is not a promissory note, and a consideration, therefore, would have to be averred and proved, as it does not, on its face, import a consideration. The statute quoted has changed this law, and made such a writing negotiable. It has all the requisites of the statute. It is made by a person, who acknowledges a certain specific sum of money to be due to another person, which sum of money may· be discharged in certain property at a certain price. The case of *Bradley* v. *Morris*, 3 Scam. 182, cited by appellant's counsel, as governing this case, must be admitted to be, in most respects, precisely like this case. In that case, suit was brought on a note for $225, and an accepted order for $450, payable in lumber. The accepted order for $450, it was contended, was a bill of exchange, and ought to be governed by the rules applicable to such instruments. The court say, "It is true, it is in the form of a bill of exchange, and by statute is made transferable by indorsement or assignment; but here the analogy ends. The statute has not declared it to be a bill of exchange, and the law recognizes instruments of writing for the payment of money only as coming under this denomination. As this order, therefore, is not for the payment of money, but for the delivery of lumber to the value of a specified sum, it cannot be regarded as a bill of exchange; nor are the rules governing the rights and obligations of parties to [*342] such instruments applicable to it."

When this decision was pronounced, a statute, in all respects like the one we have cited, was in full force (R. L. 1833, page 482), and it seems strange such a decision should have been pronounced. The bill of exchange was for a specified sum of money, with the privilege to the exceptor to pay it in lumber. *Borah* v. *Curry*, 12 Ill. 66. It was a money demand, from which the exceptor could have discharged himself only by proving the delivery, or offer to deliver, the proper quantity of lumber, or by the payment of the money. It was not a bill for the delivery of lumber in any sense, nor like a covenant to deliver lumber, for a breach of which the party could recover damages. It was a privilege to the maker to discharge his exceptance in lumber, and on his failure so to do, the money could be demanded. The note in suit here, has a striking resemblance to this bill of exchange, it being a negotiable note, and indorsed by the payee. The indorser of the note stands in the same position as the drawer of the bill, and the maker of the note is under the same liabilities as the acceptor, and both are within the scope of the statute cited. The case of *Bradley* v. *Morris* cannot be the law, and cannot control this case.

The case of *Kelley* v. *Hemmingway*, 13 Ill. 604, is not, in any particular, such a case as this. In that case the note was decided not to be a promissory note and negotiable under the statute, for the reason that it was payable on a contingency which might never happen, and therefore the money was not certainly and at all events payable, a necessary ingredient of a promissory note, as well under our statute as by the commercial law.

We come now to the case of *Lowe* v. *Bliss et al.*, 24 Ill. 169, the latest case on the point raised here. That decision was by a majority of the court, there being one dissenting.

We are free to say, on more mature reflection, that so much of the opinion in that case, as decides that the instrument there presented was not admissible under the common counts without proving a consideration, is not in accordance with the statute quoted, because the note on its face was for value received, which imports *prima facie* a consideration. The majority of the court had more particularly in view the strict commercial law applicable to such cases. This instrument was evidence under the statute without proving a consideration. *Stacker* v. *Watson*, 1 Scam. 209. The payee of this note before it was indorsed, it is in proof, demanded the lumber of one of the makers of the note, which he refused to deliver, though he had lumber on hand at the time. On [*343] this refusal, the note became a money demand absolutely, and as such was assigned to the plaintiff. It is immaterial on whom the demand was made—it was on one of the makers of the note, and the refusal to pay the lumber, subjects either or both makers to its payment in money, and to the plaintiff in this suit, who is the undisputed assignee and owner of the note. The judgment is affirmed.

Judgment affirmed.

RICHARD WELLS *et al.*, Plaintiffs in Error, *v.* DANIEL D. HICKS, Defendant in Error.

ERROR TO PIKE.

Where the record of proceedings before the commissioners of highways, for the laying out of a road, shows that due notice has been given, by posting copies of the petition; upon an appeal regularly taken to the supervisors of the county, the supervisors acquire the jurisdiction necessary to determine the validity of the notices, and their decision upon that point cannot be collaterally attacked.

To prove that in proceedings for laying out a highway the copies of the petition were properly posted, it is not necessary to call as witnesses, the parties who posted them. Their *ex parte* affidavits attached to the petition are sufficient.

The statute, which requires the commissioners of highways to act within ten days after the expiration of the twenty days' notice, does not compel them to decide the matter within the thirty days; it is sufficient that they commence their work within that time. It would seem that this provision of the statute is directory and not mandatory.

That the statute regulating appeals, from the commissioners of highways to the supervisors, does not require notice to the party, whose land is affected by the location of the road, is an objection against which this court can afford no relief. It becomes the duty of the owner of the land, to take notice of, and follow up, the appeal.

THIS was an action of trespass, *quare clausum fregit*, brought by defendants in error against plaintiffs in error, in the Circuit Court of Pike county.

Defendants below filed several pleas justifying the alleged trespasses, upon the ground that the close in question was a public highway, and that the trespasses complained of consisted in the removal of a fence which was across, and obstructed the highway, doing no more damage than was necessary. Setting forth, in one of the pleas, that two of the defendants were commissioners of highways of the town in which the close was situated, and that they, with the other, as a servant, had moved the fence, as they lawfully might, for the reason aforesaid.

[*344] A general replication was filed to these pleas, and a trial had by jury. Verdict and judgment for the plaintiffs, for nominal damages and costs of suit. Motion for a new trial overruled, and judgment. Defendants bring the case to this court by appeal, and assign amongst other errors: that the court erred in excluding proper evidence from the jury; that the court erred in overruling the motion for a new trial, and in rendering judgment for plaintiff.

On the trial of the cause, the defendants, to sustain their pleas of justification, attempted to show the proceedings of the commissioners of highways, of the town of which the close in question was situated, and of three supervisors to whom an appeal had been taken from an order of the commissioners, establishing a road over the close in question, and for that purpose called the clerk of the town as a witness, who was asked to produce the papers on file in his office, pertaining to the laying out of the road in question. Said witness then produced from his files a petition for the road, in conformity with the law, praying the commissioners of highways to lay out the same. To this petition, three several affidavits were attached, one by James H. Crane, one by R. H. Clark, and one by Robert Davis, each swearing to the posting of a copy of the petition, and the place where and when it was posted.

On the back of said petition was an indorsement, as follows:

"PITTSFIELD, ILLINOIS, October 30th, 1856.

"The undersigned commissioners of highways for the township of Pittsfield, having had under consideration the within petition, have determined not to lay out the road, in said petition prayed for, in accordance with said petition.

JOHN L. CONNET, ⎫
SAMUEL BROWN, ⎬ Commissioners of Highways."
E. SANFORD, ⎭

The petition was indorsed by the town clerk, Nov. 15th, 1856.

Said witness further produced from his files an order for the laying out of the said road, prayed for in the petition; which purported to have been made by three supervisors of the county, on an appeal to them from the order of the commissioners of highways, refusing to lay out said road above referred to; which order of the supervisors recited, among other things, that it appeared "that proper petition has been made by the requisite number of legal voters, residing within three miles of said route, that copies of said petition have been duly posted as required by law, copies of said petition, affidavits of posting, &c., being hereto annexed, and that due notice of the appeal herein has been given by notice [*345] served upon said commissioners of highways of said town, and upon three of the petitioners herein, copies of said notices and affidavits of the service thereof being hereto annexed."

A plat and survey of the road was annexed, and copies of the petition for the appeal, copies of the notices thereof to the commissioners of highways, and to three petitioners, and affidavits of the service of these copies of the original petitions with the affidavits of the posting thereof in the manner required by law, also accompanied said order.

Defendants then offered to read said petition and the filing thereon to the jury; to which the plaintiff objected, because the posting of said petition had not been proved as required by law, and the objection was sustained by the court, and the court refused to permit said petition to be read to the jury, to which ruling of the court defendant excepted.

The jury found the issues for the plaintiff, and assessed his damages at ten cents. · The defendant moved the court for a new trial, because the court had refused to permit proper evidence to go to the jury, which motion was overruled, and the defendants excepted thereto, and judgment was thereupon rendered for the plaintiff for the amount of verdict and costs.

M. HAY, for Plaintiffs in Error.

W. A. GRIMSHAW, and J. GRIMSHAW, for Defendant in Error.

CATON, C. J. The first question is, does the record which was offered in evidence and ruled out by the court, show the posting of the notices, as required by the second section of the twenty-fourth article of the law? We think it does. In the first place, the record shows on its face that the requisite notice had been given. There is no question that the appeal was taken in strict conformity to the law, and hence the supervisors had jurisdiction to investigate that question of notice, as well as all other questions involved in the appeal, and they found and determined that due notice had been given, and according to the case of *Galena and Chicago Union R. R. Co.* v. *Pound,* 22 Ill. 399, that is conclusive in a collateral action, as this is. Besides that, there was proof of the notice by the affidavits of the parties who posted them. It was not necessary to bring the parties who posted the notices, before the court, to prove the fact of posting. That could be proved by an *ex parte* affidavit, the same as the service of a paper, which may become neces-
[*346] sary in the progress of a cause. Were the rule otherwise, the death or removal of the parties who have posted no-

tices, would endanger the location of all the roads in the country.

The next question which was argued is, whether the third section, which requires the commissioners to act within ten days after the expiration of the twenty days from the posting of the notices, is mandatory or directory. This question is not necessarily presented by the record. The notices were posted on the 20th and 22nd of September, and the final decision of the commissioners bears date on the 30th day of October, but it nowhere appears that they did not in fact examine the route, before the expiration of the thirty days from the posting of the notices, and that the examination was continued and the matter held under advisement, until it was finally decided, eight days thereafter. The statute does not say that they shall finally decide the matter, within the thirty days, but that they shall set to work within that time. If, however, the question were fully presented, we should be inclined to hold that the time specified in the statute is directory, and if they fail to examine the premises, as the law requires, they can be, compelled to do so. But it is unnecessary to decide that question directly now. While it is admitted that the appeal was taken strictly according to the provisions of the statute, it is complained that that does not provide for giving notice of the appeal, to the owner of the land. This is an objection against the statute, and unless we hold it is void for that reason, we can afford no relief for that cause. It was his duty to take notice of, and follow the appeal. *Johnson* v. *Joliet and Chicago R. R. Co.*, 23 Ill. 202.

The court erred in excluding the record. The judgment must be reversed, and the cause remanded.

Judgment reversed.

SANGER, CAMP *et al.*, Appellants, *v.* ISABELLA FINCHER, Administratrix of John Fincher, Appellee.

APPEAL FROM ST. CLAIR.

A contracted with B for a quantity of lumber and cross-ties. He then put B in possession of a saw-mill, and took a bond from B and C, conditioned for the return of the mill, upon the completion of the contract. A failed to pay for the cross-ties and lumber, and B failed to return the mill. *Held*, that in an action by B for the price of the lumber, A could recoup for the damages, arising from the breach of the condition of the bond.

[*347] Where the defendant attempts to recoup, for unliquidated damages, these damages must relate to the transaction, out of which the controversy has arisen.

B recovered a judgment against A, and subsequently died. A filed a bill against the administratrix, alleging that damages had accrued to him by reason of a breach of the condition of a bond executed by B and C, relating to the same matter for which the judgment had been obtained; but he failed to state whether the breach of the bond had occurred before or after the commencment of the action by B. *Held*, that the bill was demurrable, because it did not show but that the complainant had an ample remedy at law, by recouping his damages on the trial of B's action.

A party having an opportunity to interpose his defense at law, is estopped from seeking relief in equity, unless he can show that he was prevented by unavoidable accident, mistake or fraud.

APPELLANTS filed their bill against appellee, alleging, that on 1st September, 1853, they entered into a written agreement with John Fincher, by which he agreed to deliver and saw for complainants a large quantity of cross-ties and lumber, and was furnished by them and put in possession of a circular saw-mill of about the value of $2,000, to be surrendered by Fincher at the completion of said contract, in the same condition, to said complainants, for the surrender of which mill the said Fincher and one Wm. J. Scott, on the same day, entered into a bond with complainants, in the sum of $2,000. They allege that the mill was not surrendered, but clandestinely and fraudulently removed by said Fincher, and finally destroyed by explosion; that Fincher, when complainants were about to sue him for the recovery of said mill, died, wholly insolvent. Fincher, in his lifetime, had commenced a suit against complainants for a pretended balance for lumber delivered; on his death, Isabella Fincher, his administratrix, defendant to this bill, was substituted, and at the March term, 1860, of St. Clair Circuit Court, a judgment was obtained by said Isabella against complainants for five hundred and thirty-seven dollars and costs, which judgment was most unjust, but which they do not question now. But Fincher, in his lifetime, and his estate afterward, were all

the time largely indebted to complainants for the abstraction of
said mill, and said indebtedness is still unsatisfied, and much
exceeds the amount of the judgment recovered against the complainants. Nor is there any remedy on the security on the
bond, the said Scott being also insolvent.

Bill avers the issuing of an execution by said Isabella, to
sheriff of Cook county, against the property of two of the complainants, Henry A. Clark and Hart L. Stewart, prays for an
injunction, etc., etc.

To this bill the defendant filed a demurrer, which the court
sustained, dismissing the bill and dissolving injunction. Complainants appear from this decision, and assign as error, that
the court sustained the demurrer and dismiss the bill, [*348]
and dissolve injunction.

GUSTAVUS KŒRNER, for Appellants.

JEHU BAKER, for Appellee.

WALKER, J. The first question presented by this record, is,
whether the damages arising from a breach of this contract can
be recouped, in an action upon the agreement. It is urged, that
inasmuch as complainants held the obligation of intestate and
Scott, for the return of the mill in the same condition, that
damages resulting from a failure to return it, according to the
agreement, could not be set off against a recovery for the price
of the ties by Fincher. The answer to this position is manifest
when we consider, that by our statute all bonds executed by
several obligors are made joint and several. Upon the occurrence of a breach, the obligees might have maintained either a
joint or a several action upon it, at their option. It then follows, that if complainants might have recovered on this bond
against Fincher alone, for a breach, they had the undoubted
right to recoup such damages, in the suit at law by Fincher, for
a recovery of the price of the ties, if they were of such a character as is authorized in our statute.

But it is, however, urged that these damages were unliquidated. Our statute seems to make no distinction, as it allows
a set off of claims or demands. It has not limited the right to

liquidate claims or demands, and that damages for a breach of the condition of the bond, was a claim or demand, there can be no question. That the claim or demand should relate to the transaction out of which the controversy has grown, where the damages are unliquidated, seems to be the construction placed upon the act. It was held by this court, that unliquidated damages arising out of the same transaction, may be set off under the statute. *Edwards* v. *Todd,* 1 Scam. 462; *Nichols* v. *Ruckells,* 3 Scam. 300; *Kaskaskia Bridge Co.* v. *Shannon,* 1 Gilm. 15. The language of our statute is different from the British act, and the adjudications under their statute, are not authority under ours. We regard the cases referred to, as decisive of this question.

It was insisted upon the trial, that it fails to appear that the alleged breach of the condition of the bond occurred before the suit at law was instituted by Fincher. The complainants when they filed their bill, undertook to show such a case as entitled them to the relief sought. The bill alleges, that there [*349] had been a breach, but whether before or after the institution of the suit at law does not appear. For aught that appears in the bill, the damage had been sustained before the suit was instituted at law and if it was, then complainants had a complete remedy in that action by setting it off against that recovery. In the absence of an allegation to the contrary, it must be inferred, that the breach had occurred before that action was commenced, as the complainants have certainly presented all the facts which entitle them to relief. If the breach had been subsequent to bringing that suit, it would no doubt have been alleged. But even if that would have entitled them to the relief sought, which we by no means admit, in the absence of such an allegation, the complainants are not entitled to relief. Having failed to avail themselves of their defense at law, a court of equity will not interpose to afford such relief. A party having an opportunity to interpose his defense at law, is estopped from seeking relief in equity, unless he can show that he was prevented doing so by unavoidable accident, mistake or fraud. It is the policy of law to end strife, and when parties have had an opportunity in a court to fully and fairly present their claims, and fail to do so, they are barred from resorting to a different tribunal for relief.

For the want of equity on the face of this bill, the court below did right in sustaining the demurrer, and dismissing the bill, and the decree is affirmed.

Decree affirmed.

ALPHONZO WHITE, Appellant, *v.* J. M. HAFFAKER, Appellee.

APPEAL FROM MORGAN.

Although a note may bear ten per cent. interest, when a decree is entered upon it, the note is merged; and the decree can bear only six per cent interest. A solicitor in a case, cannot act as a special master to execute the decree.

COMPLAINANT filed his bill in the Circuit Court of Morgan county, stating that, 3rd June, 1854, he executed a deed to defendant, conveying certain lands, reserving vendor's lien to secure certain notes for purchase money, to bear ten per cent. interest, if not paid at maturity—one for $3,900, to mature 1st September, 1854, and the other for $3,900, to mature 1st January, 1856—specifying that his wife was lunatic, and not capable of releasing her dower, and that $2,600 of this last note was not to be paid, but was to be left outstanding, to secure [*350] the defendant against the dower right as long as the wife might live; and complainant offered in his bill to give such security and indemnity as the court might deem just and proper.

Defendant answered, admitting the foregoing allegations of the bill; says he is not liable, according to law, for interest at a greater rate than six per cent. per annum, because said notes were not given for money loaned, and says that Mrs. Huffaker is alive, within the jurisdiction of the court, and that she ought to be made party in the case before further or other proceedings are had.

The decree ascertains balance due, allowing interest at the rate of ten per cent. per annum, and also a like rate of interest on the decree to day of sale, to be appointed by special master. States that Mrs. Haffaker, wife of complainant, is insane, and a resident of Morgan county. Requires defendant to pay interest on the $2,600, at rate of ten per cent. per annum, to John Shuff, as agent for the complainant, or to the special master, annually. Appoints I. J. Ketcham, complainant's solicitor, special master and commissioner, to execute the decree.

From which decree the defendant appealed to this court.

D. A. AND T. W. SMITH, for Appellant.

I. J. KETCHAM, for Appellee.

WALKER, J. The record in this case presents the question, whether a decree may draw a greater rate than six per cent. interest. If it may, it is not by virtue of the statute, as it has made no such provision, nor may the court fix any greater rate of interest in its decree. Interest is the creature of either contract or positive legal enactment. It does not exist at the common law, and in the absence of contract or enactment it cannot be recovered. In this case the rate, by the contract of the parties, in accordance with the statute, drew ten per cent. interest. But had a higher rate not been expressed, then by the law it could only have drawn six per cent.

When a judgment or decree is rendered, the cause of action ceases to exist, as a vital binding right upon the parties. It becomes merged in the determination of the court, and to it alone can the parties look, to ascertain their rights and liabilities. Nor do the terms and conditions of the agreement enter into or form any part of the decree. It was the basis of, and upon which, the decree was rendered, and controlled the court [*351] in fixing the terms and conditions of the decree, but affords no means of interpreting it. Nor can the court make new contracts or impose conditions, for the parties. On the hearing it is proper that the court should ascertain the sum due upon the note, and decree its payment, leaving the law to regulate the interest, or at most decree no more than six per cent. Otherwise the court would have the right to deprive the complainant of all interest on the decree, which is given to him by the law. The statute only having allowed judgments and decrees to draw six per cent., it was error in the court below to decree, that the sum found should draw ten per cent.

It is likewise urged, that it was error to appoint complainant's solicitor a special master to execute the decree. In all legal proceedings, and at every stage of a cause, courts scrupulously guard against entrusting the execution of its mandates, to persons having any interest in the cause. The law, for wise purposes, acts alone through disinterested agents. It will not tempt those having an interest in any way to abuse its process, for the purpose of promoting selfish ends. The relation of attorney and client is so intimate, and the duty of attorney to protect the interest of the client is so rigid, that it can hardly be supposed that he would be willing, even if he were a disinterested person, to be entrusted with the enforcement of the legal rights of his client. His position would be embarrassing, and he would feel at every step that his preconceived notions of his client's rights, his anxiety to advance his interest, must, in case of dispute as to the mode of executing the decree, incline him to decide in his client's favor. Such a position, it seems to us, would never be sought, and it should not be imposed by the court.

Again, the 51st section of the chancery act authorized the court to appoint a special master, whenever it shall happen that there is no master in chancery, or when such master shall be of counsel, of kin to either party interested, or otherwise disqualified or unable to act. Thus it will be observed, that the master being of counsel, is declared by this enactment to be a disqualification to discharge the duties imposed upon the master. The master is the agent of the court, and must exercise his judgment in enforcing the decree, and as such must be left free from partiality or bias. This provision is wise, and well calculated to advance justice, and as the decree violates its provisions, it must be reversed. But a decree will be entered in this court, for the sum found to be due, to draw six per cent. interest, and with all of its other provisions, except that it shall be executed by the master in chancery of the court below, who

[*352] shall report his proceedings to that court for approval, for which purpose the cause is remanded.

Decree entered in this Court.

AMBERRY A. RANKIN, Appellant, *v.* G. B. SIMONDS, Appellee.

APPEAL FROM MENARD.

The interrogatories to and answers of a garnishee are a part of the record, and need not be preserved by a bill of exceptions.

Where no issue is raised upon the answers of a garnishee, they must be taken as true, and the rights of the parties must be determined by them.

The garnishee has a right to set up any claim he has against the defendant, to meet the fund in his hands, which he could set off or recoup in an action brought by the defendant to recover the fund.

Rankin, summoned as the garnishee of Elliott, answered, that he had funds of Elliott's, but that he had delivered to E. a note against the H. & S. R. R. Co. for collection; that E. owed the company an amount greater than the amount of the note and still retained the note, his account with the company being still unsettled. *Held*, that as the note had not been paid, Rankin might withdraw it at any time, and he could not be allowed to set it off against the fund in his hands.

Where garnishees are summoned in an attachment suit, the proper practice is to enter judgment against the garnishees and in favor of the defendant in the attachment suit, for the benefit of such attaching creditors as are entitled to the proceeds.

IN the Circuit Court of Menard county, Simonds sued out an attachment against Wm. H. Elliott, and took process of garnishment against A. A. Rankin and L. M. Green.

Judgment by default was rendered against Elliott for the sum of $1,121.13.

Interrogatories were then propounded to the garnishees, Rankin and Green, and answers given by Rankin, as follows:

Are you acquainted with the plaintiff and the defendant in the above suit? If so, when, where, and how long?

I have seen Mr. Simonds once; have known W. H. Elliott since 1856, in April of that year.

Are you acquainted with J. M. Green, Amberry A. Rankin and M. G. Moise, or any or either of them? If so, when, where, and how long?

I am acquainted with J. M. Green, and have been for many years; have seen Mr. Moise a few times, twice in St. Louis and about as often in this State. He was at my house once.

Did M. G. Moise place in your hands for collection an order, note of hand, draft or obligation, on W. H. Elliott, or W. H. Elliott place or put in your hands, for collection [*353] or otherwise, a note of hand on L. M. Green, or any other person? If so, when, where and for what amount was said note for, and on whom, and all about the facts connected with or bearing on the note, draft or writing?

Mr. Moise never put in my hands any note, draft or account on any man, nor Mr. Elliott either. But sometime in October, 1857, James Deskins came to my house and left a note on J. M. Green, for $1,665.27, the remainder of a two thousand dollar note to be collected for the use, as he said, of W. H. Elliott, of Linn county, Missouri, part payment to him for his farm that Deskins bought of him, and these are the facts in the case: Sometime in December, 1857, Mr. Elliott came to my house, and told me when I collected the money of Green, to send it to Messrs. Durkee & Bullock, of St. Louis, as a part of the money was going to Mr. Moise of St. Louis. And January first, or thereabout, I sent, by Jacob Bunn of Springfield, two hundred and twenty-five dollars to Durkee & Bullock.

Did you collect any money on said note, bill or writing? If so, in what, how much, and when, and of whom? Give the dates, facts and names particularly.

I stated above how much money I collected to this time, of J. M. Green.

Who placed J. M. Green's note in your hands, and what did he say it was for at that time? Did he state that the note left was to pay the $1,200 order now sued on in this suit, and did you not frequently write to M. G. Moise & Co., or one or both of them, acknowledging the trust?

Mr. James Deskins placed J. M. Green's note in my hands,

and he said at that time it was to pay W. H. Elliott $1,665.27, remainder, if called for; he did not say anything about the $1,200 in this suit. I did not know at that time of any twelve hundred dollars, or of Mr. Moise either, or of Mr. Moise & Co. I had not collected to this time only as stated above.

Were your collections on or under said note or writing after you thus wrote to M. G. Moise & Co., or one or both of them, or were they before? How much did you collect, of whom and when? State the dates exactly, and the facts.

My collections of Mr. Green have been $1,356.50, besides the $225 as above stated, and the most has been in certificates of purchase, which purchase was about the 12th of October, after the garnishee in Logan county, making $13 more than is coming to me, as will be seen by bill accompanying this.

Did you not, at one or more times, soon after the note had [*354] been placed in your hands, promise or say to M. G. Moise, that so soon as you collected the money you would hand it or pay it over to M. G. Moise & Co., or to Moise?

Some time in the latter part of 1858, Mr. Elliott wrote or told me when I collected the money of Green, to pay myself, which amounted to $690.47, and the Armstrong debt, which was $369.02; the remainder to go to Mr. Moise. Did not know me, and would not take me as security on a note of N. F. Stone for $125, or thereabout, and I had to come to Springfield and see Jacob Bunn to recommend me. So it was the middle or the last of the year 1858, that Elliott told me to pay to Moise, and I then wrote to Moise that Elliott had told me so to do, and I promised Mr. Moise, in the presence of Mr. Green and John Bennett, and the amount was then nearly agreed on; and the very next day, Mr. Elliott came to my house and forbid me paying Moise any money under any circumstances. The day of which I cannot tell, but think it in the fore part of July, 1859, but it was the next day after Mr. Moise left me in Petersburg.

Are there any credits on the said note, and who put them there? How much and at what time precisely were they put on? State fully the facts, the times, dates, etc.

The dates of the credits on the note can be seen on Mr. Green's report, as agreed to by both of us.

Did, or have you indorsed any credits or sums on said note, since you have been garnisheed? If so, in what were said indorsements or considerations made, had or paid? Did you make any arrangements with J. M. Green, by which he agreed to pay, etc.? What were they?

I, or Mr. Green, or H. B. Rankin, put all the credits on said note. The $1,231 was put on after the garnishee; and I made an agreement to take certificates as above stated, and the Green note for $74. And since all the transactions, garnishee, etc., W. H. Elliott has broken up, and I am compelled, in self-preservation, to put in all the claims I hold against Elliott; except my trouble and my expenses, I have as yet charged nothing.

A. A. Rankin, in addition to the statements hereinbefore made, states that all the effects he claims the right to deduct from the proceeds of the J. M. Green note, existed and had occurred before the service of the garnishee proven on him, said Rankin.

1. The cash item of $277.72 was allowed to Elliott the 1st April, 1857.

2. The claims for machinery originated the 1st April, 1853, in the purchase of certain carding machines, [*355] bought by me for Elliott, of Armstrong, of Springfield, Illinois, and sent to said Elliott in Missouri. The price of the machinery, and freight and expenses of a hand, which was paid by me to Armstrong, to the sum of $369.02.

3. The cash item of $269.54, originated on the 1st January, 1857, in the following manner: This affiant had sold land to the Hannibal and St. Joseph Railroad Company, and had the company's note for $269.54. A deed was to be executed by affiant and wife, to cover the real estate sold as above, and before the delivery of said deed, the $269.54 was to be paid. This deed was executed duly by said affiant and wife to said company, and the deed and note for $269.54 delivered to Elliott on or about the first January, 1859, who agreed to deliver the deed to the railroad company, and received the money. Neither the note nor the deed has been returned, or in any

manner accounted for to me. Elliott owed the company some
$600 or $800, and my understanding is, that he still retains the
note and deed; his account with the company is still unsettled.

4. This fourth item, being cash item of $412.75, originated
thus: Elliott was my agent, to sell my half interest in certain
town lots in the town of St. Catherine, Mo. We had a settlement on the first of April, 1857; after that date he continued to
sell until the 1st of July, 1859, when I revoked his authority
to sell, being advised at that time of Elliott's probable insolvency. By Elliott's admission to me, he sold property of mine,
being my half interest in the lots, amounting to $412.75, and
received the pay either in cash or labor, between the first of
April, 1857, and the 1st of July, 1859.

Of the above four items, the undersigned has never received
pay in whole or in part, nor has he any security for the same,
except as he may be allowed to retain the same from the J. M.
Green note. At about the 4th of July, 1859, Elliott was at my
house in Menard county, Illinois. He then expressly permitted and agreed with me, that for whatever claims I had
against him, I should retain any balance I had against him on
all accounts, without qualification, out of the proceeds of J. M.
Green note; at that date what was due me for the sale of my
interest in St. Catherine lots, was expressly mentioned, but the
amount was not ascertained until after Elliott's return from
Missouri. His account was forwarded to me, showing said balance of $412.75, all of which originated previous to 1st July,
1859.

The court upon these answers, (no issue being formed there-
[*356] on,) rendered judgment against the garnishee Rankin,
as follows:

> G. B. SIMONDS,
>   vs.   } Attachment.
> A. A. RANKIN, Garnishee of Wm. H. Elliott. }

And now at this day, this case, which was heretofore referred to the court for adjudication, coming on to be heard,
and the court having taken sufficient time to consider the argument of the counsel, doth find against the said A. A. Rankin, the sum of eight hundred and fifty-one dollars and thirteen

cents. It is therefore ordered by the court, that the said plaintiff recover of and from the said A. A. Rankin, the aforesaid sum assessed by the court, and also the costs herein expended, and that execution issue therefor.

Rankin appealed, and now assigns for error: That the court erred in not discharging said Rankin as garnishee upon his answer; that the court erred in its finding against the said garnishee, and in rendering judgment for costs against him.

HAY & CULLOM, for Plaintiff in Error.

W. H. HERNDON, for defendant in Error.

CATON, C. J. Although the question has never before been made, so as to call for a direct decision, it has always been the practice of our courts to treat the interrogatories to and answers of a garnishee as a part of the record without requiring them to be embodied in a bill of exceptions, and such we have no doubt is the correct practice. They constitute a part of the pleading in the cause, and as such are a part of the record as much as any other pleading. The statute expressly provides that an issue may be taken on the answer of the garnishee, and it follows that if the answer is not thus traversed by the formation of such issue, it must be taken as true, and by it must the rights of the parties be judged. This has been settled by repeated decisions of this court. The garnishee has a right to set up any claims which he has against the defendant, to meet the fund which he may have in his hands, which he could set off or *recoup* in an action brought by the defendant to recover such fund. By this rule we think the garnishee should have been allowed the several claims which he asserted in his answer, except the item for two hundred and sixty-nine dollars and fifty-four cents, which was for a note of that amount which he held against the Hannibal and St. Joseph Railroad Company, and which he had placed [*357] in the hands of the defendant for collection. This note, he admits, has not been collected, but he claims to be allowed for the amount, for the reason that the defendant owes that company more than the amount of the note. He still retains the note, and his account with the company is still unsettled. Now the title to this note is still in the garnishee, and he has a right to withdraw it at any time from the hands of the defendant who has not collected it and who is consequently not liable to the garnishee for its amount. Had the defendant settled with the railroad company, and delivered the note up as so much cash upon the amount which he owes to the company, then indeed the garnishee might well treat it as so much money in his hands. As it is, we think this claim should not be allowed.

We observe, too, that the judgment was not entered in proper form, and hence we will repeat what we said in *McLagan* v. *Brown*, 11 Ill. 519, as to the proper mode of entering a judgment against a garnishee. There the court said: "The proper practice would therefore seem to be, to enter the judgment against the garnishee in favor of the defendant in the attachment, for the benefit of such attaching creditors as are entitled to share in its proceeds." Here the judgment was entered against the garnishee, not in favor of Elliott the defendant in the attachment, to whom the fund in his hand belonged, but in favor of Simonds, the plaintiff in the attachment, and to whom the fund did not belong. In this case the fund in the garnishee's hand was greater than the amount of the judgment which Simonds recovered against Elliott, and his judgment against the garnishee would have been greater than the amount recovered against Elliott but for the deductions which the garnishee has a right to have allowed for claims against Elliott. And as it is, he has two judgments in part at least for the same demand against two individuals.

Whatever judgment is finally rendered against the garnishee, should be entered up in favor of Elliott to the use of Simonds, or so much of it as is sufficient to satisfy his judgment against Elliott, and the balance, if any, to the use of Elliott himself. The judgment must be reversed, and the cause remanded.

Judgment reversed.

AARON CARIKER, Plaintiff in Error, *v.* WILLIAM [*358]
L. ANDERSON, Defendant in Error.

ERROR TO MONTGOMERY.

A conditional judgment and a *scire facias* are requisite, as proper preliminaries to a judgment against a garnishee. The *scire facias* is to make known to the garnishee that a conditional judgment has been rendered against him, assuming him to be a debtor of the debtors in attachment, and that he must show cause why final judgment should not go against him.

A sufficient notice to a debtor under a foreign attachment should be shown of record.

It may not be error for a term of court to intervene between a default taken and a *scire facias* issued against a garnishee.

The date given in the indorsement of a service of process, should be taken as the time of service. A sheriff is not required to date his return. [Several decisions in reference to service of process, considered and examined.]

A garnishee is not properly a defendant in an attachment suit, to defend against the plaintiff's claim; the judgment should be entered against a
' garnishee in favor of the defendant in the attachment suit, for the benefit of the creditor or others in attachment, and if there is more due than will pay the attaching creditor, the creditor of the garnishee can control it.

THE action in this case was by attachment, in favor of Wm. L. Anderson against Robert J. Hayes. The original writ was served on Cariker as garnishee, and the following is a copy of the return by the sheriff: "Served on the within named Aaron Cariker, by reading the within, May 6, 1857." Signed by the sheriff.

Judgment by default was rendered against Hayes at March term, 1858, of the Circuit Court of Montgomery county; assessment by jury, and judgment for $265.25. At the same time, the default of Cariker was entered. On the 16th of December, 1858, what is called in the record a writ of " *scire facias* " was issued, and returned by the sheriff, served as follows: "I have executed the within writ by reading the same to the within named Aaron Cariker, Dec. 24, 1858."

At the March term, 1859, final judgment was rendered against Cariker for the amount of the original judgment, and also for costs.

Cariker *v.* Anderson.

The errors assigned are as follows:

There was no conditional judgment against the garnishee, as required by section 16 of the Attachment Act. Instead thereof, there was an order for a *scire facias.*

A term of the court intervened between the first default against the garnishee, and the issuing of the writ called in the record a "*scire facias.*" The default was entered and order for a *scire facias* was made at the March term, 1858; [*359] *scire facias* issued Dec. 16, 1858. The September term intervened.

There was no publication of notice as required by the 14th section of said act.

The officer does not show in his return of the writ of attachment that he was unable to find property of the defendant sufficient to satisfy the debt, which fact is required to exist before he is authorized to summon any one as garnishee.

No writ of *scire facias* was ever issued against the garnishee.

The returns of the sheriff on the original writ and, on the so-called "*scire facias,*" are wholly insufficient to justify the entry of the default against the garnishee. They do not show whether the dates refer to the times of service or the returns of the writs.

STUART, EDWARDS & BROWN, for Plaintiff in Error.

R. MCWILLIAMS, for Defendant in Error.

BREESE, J. Proceedings by attachment are in derogation of the common law, deriving all their validity from statutes, and must, in all essential particulars, conform to their requirements. It is objected here, that there was no conditional judgment against the garnishee—that a term of court intervened between the first default against the garnishee and issuing the writ of *scire facias*—that there was no sufficient publication of notice of the pendency of the suit—that the officer does not show, in his return of the writ of attachment, that he was unable to find property of the defendant sufficient to satisfy the debt—that no writ of *scire facias* was issued against the garnishee, and, last,

428

that the returns of the sheriff on the original writ, and on the so-called "*scire facias,*" are insufficient to justify the entry of the default against the garnishee.

Other points are made, arising out of the statute, which we will notice in the order presented by the assignment of errors. But this will be attended with some difficulty, on account of the great irregularity in the proceedings from the commencement until the final judgment.

It will be observed, this is a foreign attachment, and the writ which issued on filing the affidavit and bond, pursues the form prescribed in the second section of the statute, chapter 9, the mandatory part of which is in these words: "We therefore command you, that you attach so much of the estate, real or personal, of the said Robert J. Hayes, to be found in your county, as shall be of value sufficient to satisfy the said [*360] debt and costs according to the complaint; and such estate so attached, in your hands to secure, or so to provide that the same may be liable to further proceedings thereupon, according to law, at a court to be holden, etc., so as to compel the said Robert J. Hayes to appear and answer the complaint of the said William L. Anderson. And that you also summon Aaron Cariker as garnishee, to be and appear at the said court, etc., then and there to answer to what may be objected against him, when and where you shall make known to the said court how you have executed this writ," etc. The affidavit was filed on the 28th of April, 1857, and the writ issued on the same day, and on the 6th of May, 1857, it was returned as follows: "Served on the within named Aaron Cariker, by reading the within, May 6, 1857."

Now, by section thirteen of this chapter, it is provided, "when any attachment shall be issued out of the Circuit Court, and levied on served on a garnishee, and the sheriff returns the same, the clerk is required to give notice for four weeks successively in some newspaper published in this State, most convenient to the place where the court is held, of such attachment, and at whose suit, against whose estate, for what sum, and before what court it is pending, and that unless the defendant shall appear on the return day of the writ, judgment will be

---

---

entered and the estate attached will be sold. *Provided*, that in case of foreign attachment, if s'xty days shall not intervene between the first insertion of such notice and the first term of the court, then the cause shall be continued until the next term of the court. Any defendant in attachment may appear and plead, without giving bail or entering into bond." (Scates' Comp. 230.)

The twelfth section of this chapter makes it the duty of the sheriff, when he shall be unable to find property sufficient to satisfy any attachment issued, etc., to summon all persons within his county, whom the creditor shall designate, as having any property, effects or choses in action in their possession or power, belonging to the defendant, or who are indebted to the defendant, to appear before the court to which the writ is returnable, on the return day of the attachment, and there answer on oath, what amount they are indebted to the defendant in the attachment, or what property, effects or choses in action they had in their possession or power at the time of serving the attachment. The person or persons so summoned, shall be considered as garnishees, and the sheriff in his return shall state the names of all persons so summoned and the date of service on each.

[*361] The fourteenth section also provides for notice by publication by the clerk, differing but little from the provisions of the thirteenth section. Under that section, the clerk should have had a notice published immediately, and judgment could have been had at the following September term, as the plaintiff had filed his declaration at the May term. On motion of the plaintiff, the cause was continued to the next September term, at which term, on plaintiff's motion, the cause was continued for notice—an act wholly unnecessary, if the clerk had performed his duty. The next term, was the March term, 1858, at which term, the defendant Hayes was called and made default, and a jury of inquest called, who assessed the plaintiff's damages to two hundred and sixty-five and twenty-five one-hundredths dollars; and at the same term the garnishee, the plaintiff here, was called and made default, whereupon it was considered by the court, "that a *sci. fa.* issue against said de-

fendant, garnishee as aforesaid." At the next term, being the September term, 1858, this order appears in the record: "Now on this day comes the said plaintiff, etc., and the said garnishee being three times solemnly called, came not, and because said garnishee doth not appear, nor any one for him, it is considered by the court, that said plaintiff recover of the said garnishee, the sum of two hundred and sixty-five and twenty-five one-hundredths dollars, the amount of the original judgment against the defendant Hayes, together with his costs, etc., and may have execution hereof."

When default was taken against Hayes, the record does not show that he had been notified of the pendency of the suit. There is a notice pasted on the record, with the publisher's certificate, which the clerk certifies was filed in his office on the 15th March, 1858, but it does not seem ever to have been produced in court, or brought to the notice of the court. The entry of the judgment against Hayes was at the March term, 1858, but it nowhere recites, that proof of notice of the pendency of the suit was made. He was called, and made default, and the jury assessed the damages.

Section sixteen provides, where any garnishee shall be summoned by the sheriff or other officer in manner aforesaid, and shall fail to appear and discover on oath or affirmation as by this chapter is directed, it shall be lawful for the court, after solemnly calling the garnishee, and such court is authorized and required to enter a conditional judgment against such garnishee, and thereupon a *scire facias* shall issue against such garnishee, returnable to the next term of the court, "to show cause, if any he have, why final judgment should not be entered against him, upon such *scire facias* being duly [*362] executed and returned."

We look in vain to the record for this conditional judgment, and for the writ of *scire facias.* No such judgment was rendered, nor was any *scire facias* issued, the plaintiff contenting himself with an order for a *scire facias.* This error is well assigned.

As to the second error, it will be observed, that the interlocutory judgment was taken against the absent debtor, and the default entered against the garnishee, at the March term, 1858, and a *scire facias* ordered. At the September term following, the cause, on plaintiff's motion, was continued to the next March term. Intervening these terms, and on the 16th of December, 1858, a writ issued, which the clerk chooses to denominate a *scire facias*, which recites the recovery of the judgment against the absent debtor, and the amount, "and that Aaron Cariker having been duly served as garnishee, as appears to us of record; these are therefore to command you to summons the said Aaron Cariker, to be and appear before the Circuit Court, to answer to said garnishee, and not depart the court without leave," etc. Now, this is simply absurd. How could the person summoned as garnishee, answer the garnishee? The statute informed the clerk that the office of a *scire facias* is to make known to the garnishee that a conditional judgment had been rendered against him, assumed to be a debtor of the foreign debtor, and that he must appear and show cause why final judgment shall not be entered against him, for such an amount as might be shown he owed this absent debtor. Instead of this, the garnishee was required to appear and answer himself.

We are not prepared to say, that it was error to permit the September term to pass without having had a proper writ of *scire facias* issued, and made returnable to that term. A strict construction of the statute would perhaps require it, but it is sufficient now to say, there was no conditional judgment at any time against the garnishee, and no *scire facias* to show cause. Nor were any interrogatories filed. (Scates' Comp. 231, 232, Secs. 16, 18.)

The third error questions the sufficiency of the notice. We have already said, no notice was proved or exhibited on the default of the defendant being taken. The printed one pasted on the record, is not sufficient, for it appears on its face not to have been published four weeks successively, as the statute requires. The ·certificate of the printer states, that the first publication was on the 17th of October, 1857, and the last on [*363] the 4th of November following. Simple computation shows there was not a publication of four weeks.

We do not feel free to say that the fourth error is well assigned, looking to the proceedings in this case. The original writ of attachment issued under the second section, pursued the form there given, and the garnishee was made a party to the writ. This being so, it was unnecessary as to him, or for any purpose we can see, in which he may be interested, that the sheriff should have returned *nulla bona*, of the absent debtor. We do not now decide the point.

The remaining errors have already been considered and disposed of, and in concluding our view of the record as made up, we must say, that it is made up in a most unskillful manner— the plainest requirements of the statute disregarded, and for the whole proceeding from its inception, quite informal and incongruous.

As to the error last assigned, that the return of service by the sheriff was insufficient, we have to say, that we have taken occasion to review the various decisions made upon this point, and have come to the conclusion that the return in this case is in compliance with the statute, and in all respects sufficient. There is really no defect or uncertainty in it. By our practice act it is made the duty of the sheriff or coroner to serve all process of summons or capias, when it shall be practicable, ten days before the return day thereof, and to make return of such process to the clerk who issued the same, by, or on the return day, with an indorsement of his service, the time of serving it, and the amount of his fees. (Scates' Comp. 241, Chap. 83, Sec. 3.) The date in the indorsement of service, must be taken to be the time of the service, and nothing else. The sheriff is not required to date his return. The clerk makes that entry, or should do so.

The first case in which this question came up, was the case of *Simms* v. *Klein*, Breese, 371, new edition. The return was in this form: "J. R. Simms summoned by reading," signed by the sheriff, and dated, and was held sufficient. The next case was *Wilson* v. *Greathouse*, 1 Scam. 174, where this return, "Executed on the within defendant by reading the within," and signed by the constable, was held void, for the reason that the date of service, is not shown, and parol proof was not allowed to show the true time of service.

The next case was *Clemson and Hunter* v. *Hamm,* id. 176, where this return was adjudged void for the same reason: "Executed on Hunter—Clemson not found." N. Buckmaster, sheriff, M. C."

In the case of *Ogle* v. *Coffey,* id. 239, this return was ad-[*364] judged as coming within the rule in *Wilson* v. *Greathouse* and *Hunter* v. *Hamm,* and insufficient: "Executed Oct. 18, 1832, as commanded within." The court say, whether the date specified is intended for the date of the day of service, or is the day on which the summons is returned, is wholly uncertain. The court omitted a reference to the practice act, which we have quoted. The date should have been intended as of the day of service. But the manner of executing the writ was not stated, and therefore vitiated the return. It is not stated it was by reading.

In the case of *Belingall* v. *Gear,* 3 Scam. 575, this return was held insufficient: "Executed this 20th day of April, 1839, by reading. Moses Hallett, sheriff."

The court say the time and manner of service is shown, but omits to state on whom.

In conformity with the decision in *Ogle* v. *Coffey,* this court, in *Bancroft* v. *Speer,* 24 Ill. 227, held this return insufficient: "Served the within by reading the same to and in the hearing of S. B. Bancroft, June 21, 1858." The decision is placed principally on the ground that the date is indefinite—that it does not show whether the date refers to the time of the service or of the return. The practice act, section 3, makes all this clear. The date must be intended as the day of service, for that is all the date the officer is required to indorse upon the process. The service was not bad for this reason. In the case before us, the return on the original writ is in these words: "Served on the within named Aaron Cariker, by reading the within, May 6, 1857, and signed by the sheriff; and on the *scire facias* as follows: "I have executed the within writ by reading the same to the within named Aaron Cariker, Dec. 24, 1858," and signed by the sheriff. These returns are good in form and substance, and the date shall be intended as the day of service. This is according to the third section of the practice act. We must be permitted again to direct the manner in which proceedings should be carried on against a garnishee. A garnishee is in no proper sense, a defendant in the suit of the plaintiff, and cannot be called upon to defend against his claim. There is no privity between them. The object and design of the garnishee process is to subject the debt he may owe the absent or absconding debtor, or his property in the hands of the garnishee, to the payment of the plaintiff's debt. The garnishee, then, is the defendant to the suit, the law institutes in favor of his creditor, the absent debtor, and he is the plaintiff in that suit. In *Stahl et al.* v. *Webster et al.*, 11 Ill. 518, this court prescribed the mode of proceeding in such cases. We say, the practice has been to enter the judgment against [*365] the garnishee, in favor of the attaching creditor, and yet, there is a manifest impropriety in entering a judgment, as in this case, in favor of the attaching creditor, for a greater amount than he has recovered against the defendant in the attachment. How such a result is to be sometimes avoided, if the judgment against a garnishee is to be in favor of the creditor whose attachment has been served upon him, we do not well see. The proper practice would, therefore, seem to be, to enter the judgment against the garnishee in favor of the defendant in the attachment, for the benefit of such attaching and judgment creditors as are entitled to share in its proceeds. They would then have the right to control the judgment, and the money, when collected from the garnishee, would be liable to be distributed among the several creditors, according to the directions received from the clerk. There is a peculiar fitness in entering the judgment in favor of the party with whom the debt was contracted and to whom it is due; and if the judgment exceeds what is due the attaching and judgment creditors, the balance will be for his benefit. To the same effect is the case of *Gillilan* v. *Nixon et al.*, 26 Ill. 50; *Rankin* v. *Simonds, ante*, 352. This court hopes this mode will be strictly pursued by the Circuit Courts. For the reasons we have given, the judgment is reversed.

Judgment reversed.

SILAS W. ROBBINS, Plaintiff in Error, v. THOMAS LAS-
WELL, Defendant in Error.

ERROR TO SANGAMON.

When by agreement, persons have a joint interest of the same nature in a
particular adventure, they are, as between themselves, partners; although
some contribute money alone, and the others labor alone.

If parties agree to share profits, they are partners as to such profits; although
they do not agree to share in the losses.

A written agreement as to dividing profits may be extended tacitly by the
mutual understanding of the parties, or by their conduct in relation to it.

THIS was a suit in chancery, filed in the Sangamon Circuit
Court for the settlement of a partnership business founded upon the following agreement: .

" Memorandum of an agreement, made this 1st day of March,
1853, between Silas W. Robbins, of the first part, and Thomas
Laswell, of the second part: Witnesseth, that the said Robbins, party of the first part, has this day advanced to said Las-
[*366] well, party of the second part, two hundred and fifty-
four dollars, to buy young cattle, heifers, steers, yearlings, etc.,
with, and said Laswell is to feed, salt, handle and manage said
stock well in every respect, and to have proper oversight and
care in regard to said stock during the next grass season, and
if not sold in the fall for small beeves or otherwise, said Laswell is to winter well the next winter, and have them in good
order to go on the grass of the spring of 1854, and said Laswell is to sell them all in one year from this date, if deemed
practicable, and is to be at all expense and trouble in feeding
and salting said stock, supposed to be about forty head, and in
selling them, and the stock are to belong to said Robbins till
the sum of two hundred and fifty four dollars is returned, and
the profits to be equally divided between the parties, and said
Laswell guarantees that the portion of profits coming to said
Robbins shall not be less than twenty per cent. per annum on
the above sum.

" Witness our hands and seals, the day and date first above.

SILAS W. ROBBINS. [SEAL.]

THOMAS LASWELL. [SEAL.]"

On the back of said agreement was an indorsement as follows:

" The within agreement shall include the purchase of eleven head of yearlings, and five head of two year old bought at the sale of Ira C. Ash, made on the 29th day of April, 1853, and in payment the undersigned have executed their joint note to Antrim Campbell for $120.70, with six per cent. from date till paid, in twelve months from 29th April, 1853, being the date of sale, and as these cattle are bought on credit, the profits are to be equally divided.

" Witness our hands, this 30th day of April, 1853.

SILAS W. ROBBINS.
THOMAS LASWELL."

The bill was filed by said Robbins, setting forth said agreement and indorsement, and charges, that besides the sums specified therein, said Robbins advanced large sums of money upon the basis and terms specified in said agreement, between the date of said agreement and the last of February, 1856, amounting to upwards of five thousand dollars, including notes given; that said Laswell purchased cattle, hogs and horses, with the money so advanced, and made sales from time to time, but did not render full reports to said Robbins, and defrauded said Robbins by appropriating the money to his own use, and claiming the property as his own, and not taking good care of the cattle, etc.; that Robbins had endeavored to settle, but Laswell refused to do so, and declared his in- [*367] tention to keep money and property.

Interrogatories were propounded to said Laswell; an injunction and receiver, and a final settlement, were prayed for.

A receiver was appointed by the court, who reported that said Laswell refused to deliver the property to him.

The answer of Laswell admits the making of the agreement and indorsement thereon, but that they were intended to cover an usurious transaction, and denies that he is liable to account to said Robbins for money, cattle, hogs or horses in his possession, and refused to answer interrogatories.

Replication was filed, depositions taken, and at the Novem-

Robbins *v.* Laswell.

ber term, 1857, the cause was referred to the master in chancery to take testimony, state the accounts, and report.

The master afterwards filed his report to the court, and statement of accounts, by which it appeared that Laswell was indebted to Robbins in the sum of $1,902.41, not including a large number of cattle, hogs and horses which Laswell had in his possession when the suit was brought, he having excluded the horses from his account, and having reported that he had no means of ascertaining the value of the hogs and cattle in Laswell's possession. Said Robbins excepted to the report of master, which was overruled, and exceptions taken to decision; and afterwards, at the special February term, 1860, a final decree was rendered in favor of complainant for $411.83, to which complainant excepted, because the decree should have been for a larger sum, according to the evidence in the case.

J. C. Conklin, for Plaintiff in Error.

Stuart, Edwards & Brown, for defendant in Error.

Breese, J. The only or principal question of law presented by this record, arises out of the following agreement and indorsement thereon:

" Memorandum of an agreement, made this 1st day of March, 1853, between Silas W. Robbins, of the first part, and Thomas Laswell, of the second part: Witnesseth, that the said Robbins, party of the first part, has this day advanced to said Laswell, party of the second part, two hundred and fifty-four dollars, to buy young cattle, heifers, steers, yearlings, etc., with, and said Laswell is to feed, salt, handle and manage said stock well, in every respect, and to have proper oversight and care in regard to said stock during the next grass season, and if not sold in the fall for small beeves or otherwise, said Laswell is to winter well the next winter, and have them in good order to go [*368] on the grass of the spring of 1854, and said Laswell is to sell them all in one year from this date, if deemed practicable, and is to be at all expense and trouble in feeding and salting said stock, supposed to be about forty head, and in selling them, and the stock are to belong to said Robbins till the above sum of two hundred and fifty-four dollars is returned, and the profits to be equally divided between the parties, and said Laswell guarantees, that the portion of profits coming to said Robbins shall not be less than 20 per cent. per annum on the above sum.

"Witness our hands and seals, the day and date first above.

SILAS W. ROBBINS. [SEAL.]
THOMAS LASWELL. [SEAL.]"

On the back of said agreement was an indorsement ·as follows:

"The within agreement shall include the purchase of eleven head of yearlings, and five head of two year old bought at the sale of Ira C. Ash, made on the 29th day of April, 1853, and in payment, the undersigned have executed their joint note to Antrim Campbell for $120.70, with six per cent. from date till paid, in twelve months from 29th April, 1853, being the date of sale, and as these cattle are bought on credit, the profits are to be equally divided.

"Witness our hands, this 30th day of April, 1853.

SILAS W. ROBBINS.
THOMAS LASWELL."

Does this agreement constitute a partnership, and was it extended by the mutual understanding of the parties, and for what time? The theory. of the plaintiff in error is,' that this agreement, made the parties to it, partners not in the stock purchased, but in the profits arising from its sale, and that although limited by its terms to one year, and embracing only the stock to be bought with money therein specified, yet it was continued, by the mutual understanding and tacit agreement of the parties, to three years, and by the same understanding, was included all stock purchased within that time, and for which the defendant in error ought to account. It will be seen, by the indorsement on the agreement, the stock bought of Ash in April was, in express terms, made subject to this agreement, and it is to be determined, by the testimony in the cause, whether the stock subsequently purchased was to be embraced within it.

But first, as to the question of a partnership and its extension. The defendant in error contends, that such a relation has not been established by any certain proof—that the testimony to that point is too loose, uncertain and unsatisfactory [*369] to convince the mind of its existence, and that the plaintiff, holding the affirmative, should make it appear by clear and satisfactory evidence. He further urges, that if a partnership really existed, as to the stock purchased under the agreement of March, and which was made to include the stock subsequently purchased of Ash by a special indorsement thereon, that the conduct of the plaintiff in error, in his dealings with the defendant, is inconsistent with the theory that this contract was extended and enlarged by a parol understanding of the parties, so as to include all stock purchased during the three years, in which the parties transacted the business of buying and selling this kind of stock. He cites the fact, that the Ash cattle, by special indorsement on the agreement, were made to be included in it, and asks the question, how it was, that the greater interests which accrued subsequently, by large purchases of stock, were not manifested by some writing between the parties, and he concludes, from this fact, that there was no parol extension of the written contract of March.

We cannot say what may have influenced the parties, to have observed less caution as their business increased, but we do not suppose it was obligatory on them to put their mutual understanding in writing, if they deemed themselves able to show, by facts and circumstances, which speak louder than words, that their conduct could not be reasonably referred to anything else but the written contract. It may be, a mutual confidence had been inspired, and so strong as to render unnecessary the usual safeguards and strictness with which business of this nature is commonly surrounded. A fact is referred to by the defendant in error, as conclusive, in his judgment, that no partnership existed in the stock acquired after the date of the first contract, and that is, that at an arbitration in the spring of 1856, between these parties, the plaintiff in error was sworn as a witness, and then testified that he and the defendant were not, and had never been, in partnership " in a hoof of stock."

This does not, in our judgment, militate against the theory

of the bill. The plaintiff does not allege a partnership in the stock purchased. That he claims as his own, and for which he is to be reimbursed. He claims only, that the defendant was a partner with him in the profits to be realized from the sale of this stock, and which, by the agreement, could in no event be less to the plaintiff than twenty per cent. per annum on the money advanced by him.

Now, the question properly arises here, does this agreement make a partnership? As between themselves, we think there can be no doubt. It seems to be well settled, that when, by agreement, persons have a joint interest of the same [*370] nature in a particular adventure, they are partners *inter se,* although some may contribute money, and others labor. As in the case of *Reid* v. *Hollinshead,* 4 Barn. & Cress. 878, where Abbot, Ch. J., said "such a partnership may well exist, although the whole price is, in the first instance, advanced by one party, the other contributing his time and skill and security in the selection and purchase of the commodities." If, then, parties agree to share the profits, they are partners in the profits, although one contributes the capital or goods, and the other only trouble. Such is the case made by this record. The plaintiff in error furnished the stock by his capital employed in its purchase, and the defendant his time and trouble in preparing it for market, and making sales. It is not necessary that the parties should agree to share in the losses. Story on Part., Sec. 15; *Dob* v. *Halsey,* 16 Johns. 34; *Ferguson* v. *Alcorn,* 1 B. Monroe, 160.

These parties were partners in the profits of the first adventure, as specified in the written agreement. Was that agreement extended and enlarged, so as to embrace the stock purchased subsequently, and up to the fall of 1855?

We have examined all the testimony in the cause with great care, and it establishes, with sufficient clearness, that all the stock purchased, whether of cattle, hogs or horses, was to be controlled by the written agreement of March. This was the tacit understanding of the parties, since it is not shown by any act of theirs, or by any declaration of either party, that they had terminated, or desired to put an end to the written agreement of March, at the end of the year, the defendant admitting, on several occasions, that the plaintiff furnished the money, and when he was reimbursed his advances, the profits were to be equally divided between them. To what else, but to this written agreement, can the acts and conduct of these parties to be referred, no new or different agreement being set up or shown, and no extension in writing being necessary?

If a person leases a house for one year at a stipulated rent, and holds over another year, he will be adjudged to hold under the terms of the agreement for the first year, nothing to the contrary being shown. It is not at all probable, that the defendant would draw, and the plaintiff accept and pay orders for stock for three years, and to the amount of near four thousand dollars, unless it was the tacit understanding of these parties, that all these transactions were under the agreement of March, and to be controlled by it.

The defendant contends, however, even if the subsequent [*371] purchases of stock were included in this agreement, that they have been settled and adjusted, and an exhibit marked C is relied on to sustain this view.

This paper is proved to be in the handwriting of the plaintiff, and was produced by the defendant on the hearing, and is claimed by him, as the account rendered by the plaintiff against him, and as containing a full statement of their transactions growing out of their agreement. The paper bears no date, nor is it shown it was made out by the plaintiff for any purpose of a settlement, or delivered by him to the defendant. Being in the handwriting of the plaintiff, it is evidence against him, as a memorandum at least, but subject to explanations. We have examined this exhibit, and do not understand that it purports to be an account stated, or anything of the kind. It appears to be a rough memorandum made by the plaintiff, perhaps with a view to a future settlement, and was probably made in the spring of 1856, after their difficulties had arisen. It contains a statement to the effect that the defendant had received of the proceeds of the "California sale" the sum of fifteen hundred and four dollars and one cent, and the plaintiff had received, of the same proceeds, four thousand

and fourteen dollars. This certainly is not an account of their whole business, but of one sale only, and can charge the parties only so far as it goes. In it, a mistake against the plaintiff, of a large sum, is clearly shown by the testimony. In this memorandum, he is charged with having received, on the sale of cattle to one Huber, the sum of nineteen hundred and ninety dollars, whereas, he received but one thousand dollars of that sum, the remaining nine hundred and ninety dollars having been credited to the defendant and appropriated by him. The paper does not purport to be an accounting as to all the business of buying and selling stock, in which these parties were interested, nor does it afford any satisfactory evidence of the true state of the accounts. Taking it for what it proves, it would show, that out of the proceeds of a certain sale of stock, the plaintiff had received a certain sum of money, and the defendant a certain other sum. The stock remaining on hand, and the profits on the sales do not appear.

The evidence is quite convincing, that from the 1st of March, 1853, up to the spring of 1856, when the parties had a misunderstanding, the defendant was in the constant practice of purchasing cattle, hogs and horses, and drawing bills for their price on the plaintiff, or placing his name to notes executed for the price, all which were promptly paid by the plaintiff, and claiming that he was entitled to one-half the profits. The whole amount thus paid by him, including the first advance [*372] in March, 1853, reaches to about the sum of three thousand dollars, as appears from the testimony of the numerous witnesses whose depositions are in the record. But it is contended by the defendant, that no claim that hogs or horses purchased by the plaintiff, and received by the defendant, can be considered as within this written agreement, inasmuch as that specifies young cattle only.

The proof shows that the hogs and horses were paid for by Robbins, in the same mode that he paid for the cattle, and the defendant himself, in exhibit (C) which he introduced as evidence, has claimed for, and been allowed his share of the proceeds of the sale of hogs. No new contract having been set up, as to the hogs and horses purchased, and the defendant claiming and receiving credit for his share of the sale of hogs, and there being nothing shown but the written contract of March, 1853, to which to refer these transactions, we must, to effectuate justice, refer them all to this contract, as their real basis. The claim of the plaintiff to be reimbursed for them, and for his equal share of the profits arising out of their sale, if sold, would seem to be quite as meritorious and well grounded, as his claim to be reimbursed for the cattle, and to be paid his share of the profits on them. No other basis but that contract has been exhibited. The claim of the defendant, that all their dealings were adjusted and settled in exhibit (C), does not seem to be well sustained, as no full account of purchases or of sales is therein exhibited, and no accounting, as to the stock then on hand, or as to the horses.

The evidence shows a considerable amount of property belonging to the plaintiff, in the possession of the defendant, and which he refused to deliver up to the receiver appointed by the Circuit Court, on filing this bill of complaint. He now asks, on what principle is it that the court can decree that defendant should pay a specific sum to the plaintiff in money, if there be such property in his hands, and why not rather decree a division of the property, or pass an order for its sale and divide the proceeds? The answer to this, we think, is quite obvious. A division of the property, the whole of it being the property of the plaintiff, or of its proceeds on a sale, would not be just to the plaintiff. It would be giving the defendant that to which he is not entitled by the terms of the agreement. The stock undisposed of, is the property of the plaintiff, and if the defendant has neglected to sell it, so that profits might be had, to one equal half of which he would be entitled, and has refused to place it in the custody of the court, and has, as the proof shows, butchered and sold, and given [*373] away to his relations, a considerable portion, the strongest considerations of equity would prompt the court to decree against him, the value of such property as he has wrongfully endeavored to appropriate to his own use.

We think the theory of the plaintiff in his bill is sufficiently established by the evidence in the cause—that he bought the

Robbins *v.* Laswell.

stock of cattle, hogs and horses, which was his own property, and was to be reimbursed its value or cost, and such profits as might be made on the sale of it, were to be equally divided between the parties. This is established with reasonable certainty, and there is nothing, we can discover, in the conduct of the plaintiff, and in the dealings of the parties, inconsistent therewith. This court having jurisdiction, a partnership existing as to the profits, will hold the case and so adjudicate upòn it as to do complete justice between the parties. To that end, it is decreed that the plaintiff be reimbersed the full amount of his advances for cattle, hogs and horses, from March 1, 1853, to the end of February, 1856, and which came into the possession of the defendant by delivery or otherwise. That the plaintiff also have and receive of the defendant, one equal part of the profits, which may have been derived from the sale of all or any part of said property, and that the testimony taken in this cause be referred to the master in chancery of the Sangamon Circuit Court, who shall therefrom make up a report, showing, first, the whole cost of the cattle, hogs and horses purchased by the plaintiff, and which came to the possession of the defendant prior to March 1, 1856, under the agreement of March 1, 1853, and. extended and enlarged by the parol assent of the parties to the time first mentioned; showing, second, the amount of profits derived on the sale of any portion of said property, giving to the plaintiff one equal half part thereof, and to the defendant the other equal half part thereof; and third, to ascertain the value of the property so purchased by the plaintiff which was in the possession or control of the defendant, at the time of filing this bill, and which he refused to deliver up to the receiver appointed by the Circuit Court, and which inquiry will include the hogs, horses and other like property the said defendant may have disposed of to others without accounting for the same to the plaintiff; and for which sums, when ascertained, a decree shall pass in favor of the plaintiff, together with the costs of this suit.

We have not deemed it necessary to make any remarks upon the claims set up by the defendant, that a portion of this stock was purchased with a view to stocking the " Claywell farm," as it is called, inasmuch as all the testimony goes to [*374] show, that agreement was never consummated by the intended parties to it. That agreement having failed, the stock could not be retained by the defendant on that pretext, and he is bound to account to the plaintiff for them as his original property.

The decree of the Circuit Court is reversed, and the cause remanded, with instructions to the Circuit Court to proceed in the cause in conformity to this opinion.

Decree reversed.

Thomas J. Buntain, Appellee, *v.* David S. Curtis Appellant.

APPEAL FROM EDGAR.

A submission and award filed, that the award may be made a judgment, are a part of the record, and need not be preserved by a bill of exceptions.

An award should conform to the submission in order to make it obligatory. If it should not be as extensive as the submission it may be defective. If arbitrators should reject any matter comprised within the submission, it would be a ground of objection to the award.

Where a submission to arbitration requires an award by a certain day, if it appears that the time was extended by consent of both parties, an award after the day named will be sustained.

An award should be rendered upon all matters embraced in the submission, or it will be set aside.

This record is brought to this court on appeal from the Edgar Circuit Court, and presents the following facts:

On the 23rd day of March, 1858, Thomas J. Buntain and David S. Curtis, the parties to this proceeding, entered, under their hands and seals, into an agreement of submission to arbitration of certain unsettled accounts, and matters of trade between them, concerning the business transactions of the firm of Buntain & Curtis, and also of the firm of Curtis, Buntain & Co., to the decision and arbitration of certain persons therein

446

named, agreeing that each of them should be sworn and make his statement to the arbitrators in reference to all matters in controversy, to have privilege of introducing witnesses as each might desire, covenanting to keep the award that the majority of the arbitrators might make, in writing, under their hands, ready to be delivered by the 1st of May, 1858. It was further agreed, that the award of the said arbitrators should be made a judgment of the Edgar Circuit Court, and stipulating for the payment of two thousand dollars in damages by the one who should fail to keep and observe the award. At the September term, 1858, of the Edgar Circuit [*375] Court, the arbitrators filed their award in this cause.

The award of the arbitrators sets forth, that B. F. Lodge, Solomon Trogdon, Hiram Sandford, George E. Levings, and Samuel Connelly, arbitrators mutually selected by Thomas J. Buntain and David S. Curtis, to hear and settle the matters in dispute between them, growing out of their dealings or trading in cattle and hogs, on their joint account, under the style and firm of Buntain & Curtis, together with their dealings in such stock in partnership with H. D. Williams & Co., under the style and firm of Curtis, Buntain & Co., in the years 1855 and 1856, "being first duly sworn, did, on the 23rd March, 1858, proceed to the discharge of their duties, and continued in so doing from time to time, until the 1st of September, 1858; that they find that Thomas J. Buntain has received money and property amounting to the sum of $39,550.98, belonging to the said Buntain & Curtis, and Curtis, Buntain & Co., including interest thereon up to 1st September, 1858, as per schedule thereto annexed, marked A; that Buntain has paid out for the use of said firms, the sum of $44,042.63, including interest thereon to 1st September, 1858, as per schedule thereto annexed, marked B, showing $4,491.65 more paid out by him than received; that David S. Curtis has received money and property, $58,818.13, belonging to said firms, including interest as above, as per schedule C, and has paid out as per schedule D, the sum of $65,284.75, including interest as above, making $6,466.62 more paid out by him than received, and $1,974.97 more paid out by Curtis than Buntain. They award that Buntain shall pay Curtis $987.48, the one-half of the excess paid out by Curtis as above, and that each shall pay one-half the costs and charges of arbitration, and be jointly bound for any just demand against Buntain & Curtis."

The arbitrators then expressly except two items from said award, $640.44, with interest, that Curtis presented against Buntain, and $500 that Buntain presented against Curtis, declaring themselves unable to agree, but leaving them for further examination and settlement between the parties, together with their private dealings not included in the settlement and award.

At the special January term, 1860, Buntain moved the court to set aside the arbitrators' report, and files his reasons. After making several specific objections as to certain allowances of claims against him, states—

That the arbitrators have been guilty of divers other mistakes in stating the accounts between the parties.

[*376] That the award is broader than the submission.

That the award is not as comprehensive as the submission.

That the award is for the defendant to pay to Curtis $987.48, when a fair statement of the accounts, according to the showing of the parties, would show a large amount due from Curtis to Buntain.

Defendant (Buntain) asks that the award be rejected, and the rule making the same a judgment of the court be refused.

The court took the motion under advisement, and at the May term, 1861, of the Edgar Circuit Court, rendered a judgment on the award, that the plaintiff (Curtis) recover of the defendant (Buntain), overruling the motion and exceptions of defendant to the award, the sum of $987.48, and $121.72½, half of the costs of said arbitrators, and the costs of the court, and that said Curtis have execution therefor, etc.

Defendant prayed an appeal, which was allowed.

The errors assigned are—

That the court below erred in not rejecting the award of the arbitrators, and in overruling the motion of defendant to suppress the award, and in overruling defendant's exceptions to such award, and in rendering judgment on the award, as in said record set out.

And also that the court below erred in not setting aside the award, and either discharging the arbitrators and setting aside the submission as impossible, or recommitting the matters embraced in the submission to the arbitrators.

C. H. CONSTABLE, for Appellant.

S. P. READ, for Appellee.

WALKER, J. This was a judgment on an award, made by arbitrators selected by the parties, with an agreement in the submission, that their award should be made a rule of court. On filing the award, exceptions were taken as it is urged, but if so, they are not preserved in a bill of exceptions. It is first insisted, that the written submission, the award filed in the court below, or the exceptions thereto, are not a part of the record, unless made so by bill of exceptions. The statute having authorized parties by their submission, to have the award made a judgment of the court, it would seem to follow, that the submission and award, upon being filed for that purpose, and being the foundation of the judgment, became as much a matter of record, as the summons and declaration. The submission is as much the basis of the action as the declaration, and the award the foundation of the judgment as a verdict of a jury. By being filed with the clerk for the [*377] purpose of moving for a judgment, they clearly become a matter of record.

It is first urged, that the award does not conform to the submission. If this is true, and if it appears from inspecting those instruments, that the award in any essential matter departs from the submission, the exception is well taken. In support of the position, it is insisted that by the submission, the arbitrators were authorized to settle and determine certain "unsettled accounts and matters of trade existing between David S. Curtis of the first part, and Thomas J. Buntain of the other part, concerning the business transactions of the firm of Buntain & Curtis, and of the firm of Curtis, Buntain & Co." Whilst in the award the arbitrators say, they were selected and chosen, "to hear and settle the matters in dispute between them, growing out of their dealings in cattle and hogs, on their joint account, under the style and firm of Buntain & Curtis, together with their dealings in such stock in partnership, with D. H. Williams & Co., under the style of Curtis, Buntain & Co., in the years 1855 and 1856." Whilst this recital refers to the character of the business transactions of these firms, and its dates, we do not see that it follows, that they took into consideration either more or less than was submitted to them. There is no evidence in the record, and nothing appears in the award itself, to show that they took into consideration any matter not referred to their arbitrament.

Had they in the award said, that they had only considered the transactions of these firms relating to cattle, and it had appeared, that other firm transactions existed, then the award would not have been as extensive as the submission, and would have been essentially defective. Under the submission it was the duty of the parties to present to the arbitrators, all matters coming within the submission, and if rejected, it would have formed a ground of exception, upon proof of that fact in the Circuit Court. It does not, however, appear in this case, that such was the fact.

By the submission it was agreed by the parties, and the arbitrators were required to have the award ready for delivery in writing by the first day of May, 1858, but it was not ready until the first day of the following September. This is urged as a ground of reversal. It is undeniably true, that the arbitrators derive all of their power and authority from the submission. Without it, they would be unauthorized to act. And the parties may submit all or any portion of their matters in difference to such a tribunal, under such limitations and restrictions as they may choose to impose. And it is not for that tribunal [*378] or the courts to determine whether they are reasonable or not, if they contravene no legal prohibition or rule of sound policy. The submission is the agreement of the parties, and the arbitrators and courts can only carry it into effect, according to its terms and conditions. They can neither enlarge or restrict its terms. But the parties may undoubtedly waive or dispense with any of its terms, in precisely the same mode that they may those of any other contract, either by an express or implied agreement.

It is recited in the award, that the arbitrators met on the 23rd day of March, 1858, and proceeded to examine the accounts of the parties which were presented before them, together with the evidence of the parties themselves, with such other evidence as was presented before them. That they continued the examination and hearing of evidence from time to time until the first day of September, 1858.

Had it appeared, that both parties continued to attend the meetings of the arbitrators after the first of May, and had continued to introduce evidence without objection, it might have raised the inference, that the parties had enlarged the time for making and publishing the award. They had the undoubted right to waive that requirement of the submission by mutual consent. But this record fails to disclose such an agreement, either express or implied. The arbitrators only say, that they continued the examination and hearing of evidence from time to time, until the first of September. They do not state that it was evidence of both parties, and for aught that appears, it may have been that on the part of only one of them. If so it was wholly unwarranted by the submission, and would render the award void. They could only hear evidence after the first of May, by the consent of both parties, and it must affirmatively appear to have been given to sustain an award published, after the expiration of the time limited by the submission. No such evidence appears in this case, and the award therefore is not binding on the parties.

By the award itself it is stated, that two items of account, one in favor of each party, were not included in the award. The arbitrators say they were unable to agree upon them, and that they are left out of the award, and open to settlement between the parties, together with all their private dealings. This then presents the question, whether the award is defective, in not passing upon and determining all matters submitted to their award. Here are items which clearly fall within the matters submitted, and are of no small amount, claimed to be allowed by the party presenting them. The item claimed [*379] by appellant as a credit on his indebtedness to appellee, is $500, and that claimed by appellee, is $640.44. It was clearly the duty of the arbitrators, when these claims were presented, first to determine whether they were proper under the reference, to be investigated, and if they were, whether they were established by the evidence, and either allow or reject them. It may have been, that these very items were the moving cause of the submission to arbitration by the parties. It is not probable that a dispute existed as to all of the items of account between the parties, and the settlement of these may have been of grave importance to them.

If upon the final adjustment they had allowed appellant's and rejected appellee's claims, it must have reduced the sum found to be due from appellant, to $487.48. This would have been an important reduction to appellant.

If these items had been passed upon, this might not have taken place, yet we cannot say that such would not have been the result. But it is a general rule, that unless an arbitrator renders his award on all matters within the submission, and of which he had notice, the award is wholly void. Watson on Arbitration and Award, 121; *Whetstone* v. *Thomas*, 25 Ill. 361. The arbitrators in this case had notice of these items, and they refused to pass upon them. They were presented by the parties, and the arbitrators say that they are unable to agree, and leave them to be settled with the private dealings of the parties. This clearly implies that they were considered as partnership transactions and within the scope of the submission. Otherwise they would have rejected them as private accounts, not connected with the business of the firms. The award was then, not in accordance with the submission, and it should have been set aside. The court below erred in rendering judgment upon it, and the judgment is reversed, and the cause remanded.

Judgment reversed.

MORGAN GRIFFIN, Plaintiff in Error, v. LUCIEN EATON, Defendant in Error.

ERROR TO COLES.

Where it is manifest from an inspection of a record, that technicalities in the forms of actions have been abolished in the State where judgment was rendered, this court will treat the judgment as would the courts of the State where it was rendered, without regard to the rules of the common law by which different forms of action are designated.

THIS was an action of debt instituted in the Coles [*380] Circuit Court, HARLAN, Judge, presiding, on a record and proceedings and judgment had and rendered, in the Law Commissioner's Court of St. Louis county, State of Missouri.

A declaration was filed in debt.

Declaration recites proceedings had in the Law Commissioner's Court, and that " by the consideration and judgment of the said court, recovered against said defendant, the said sum of one hundred and sixty dollars, above demanded," which was then and there, to wit, on the 8th of June, A. D. 1859, " adjudged to the said plaintiff for his damages, which he had sustained," etc. Averment that judgment remains in full force, etc., with the *actio accrevit* to the extent of said sum of $160. Breach in the usual form. To plaintiff's damage, $50, etc.

Defendant filed his plea of " *nul tiel record*," to which plaintiff replied. Whereupon the cause was continued.

The cause was submitted to the court, which rendered a judgment in debt, in favor of plaintiff, against defendant, Griffin, for the sum of $160 debt, together with $18.80 damages, together with his costs, etc.

The following is a copy of the judgment in the Missouri Court:

" Now at this day comes the said plaintiff, and the defendant, although duly summoned and solemnly called, comes not, but makes default; wherefore it is considered by the court, that the petition of the plaintiff be taken as confessed, and it appearing to the court that this is an action founded upon a promissory note, the court doth find that the defendant is indebted to the plaintiff in the sum of one hundred and sixty dollars, the amount of said note and interest. It is therefore considered by the court, that the plaintiff recover of the defendant the sum aforesaid, in form aforesaid, by the court found, and his costs herein expended, and thereof have execution."

Appended to said record, is the following certificate:

" STATE OF MISSOURI, }
  COUNTY OF ST. LOUIS. } ss.

"I, John M. Fulton, clerk of the Law Commissioner's Court of St. Louis county, State aforesaid, do hereby certify that the foregoing transcript is a true and correct copy of the records, proceedings and pleadings in the case in which Lucien Eaton is plaintiff, and Morgan Griffin defendant, so full and entire as the same remain of record and on file in my office.

[*381] "And that said Henry Dusenbury is now, and has been for more than two years last past, the presiding judge of said Law Commissioner's Court.

     "In testimony whereof, I have hereunto set my hand
[L. S.] and affixed the seal of office in the city of St. Louis,
     this 18th day of February, 1860.

          JOHN M. FULTON, Clerk."

There is also subjoined the certificate of H. Dusenbury, law commissioner, that the foregoing certificate of John M. Fulton, clerk, is in due form.

The bill of exceptions shows that, to the introduction of said record in evidence, the defendant, by his counsel, objected, but the court overruled the objection and allowed the record to be used as evidence; whereupon the defendant excepted.

Plaintiff in error assigns the following specific errors as apparent in said record:

The court below erred in overruling the objection of defendant to the admission of the record of the Law Commissioner's Court, in evidence as aforesaid, and in receiving the same in evidence.

 The court below erred in rendering judgment against the

said Morgan Griffin for debt, damages and costs, as set forth in said record.

The court below erred in not rendering judgment in favor of said Morgan Griffin and against said Lucien Eaton, for costs of suit.

C. H. CONSTABLE, for Plaintiff in Error.

M. C. McLAIN, for Defendant in Error.

CATON, C. J. From an inspection of this record, it is manifest that in Missouri, where the judgment was rendered, distinctions in the forms of actions have been abolished, and that technically, the action was neither debt nor assumpsit, and in giving effect to judgments in that State, we should treat them precisely as their courts would treat them, and not apply the technical rules of the common law by which different forms of action are designated. The judgment on which this action was brought was not in fact or in form, either debt or assumpsit, but in substance the judgment was in assumpsit, according to our designation of actions. It was for the amount of the note and interest on which that action was brought, in a gross sum, which was the damages which the plaintiff had sustained, by reason of the default of the defendant to pay as he had agreed to. We are not to give [*382] to the words of the record, where the forms of actions have been abolished, the same strict and technical signification which we do here, where those forms are still retained, for the reason that they were not used in such technical sense.

We think the record was properly admitted, and the judgment must be affirmed.

Judgment affirmed.

DAVID MARCKLE, Plaintiff in Error, *v.* SAMUEL F. HAS-
KINS, Defendant in Error.

ERROR TO MORGAN.

If one bargains with an agent for a horse, knowing him to be such agent,
and that the principal had recognized the transaction, a warranty by the
agent is the warranty of the principal, who is the proper party to be sued
for a breach.

THIS is an action of assumpsit, first brought by Haskins
against Marckle, before a justice of the peace, who rendered a
judgment for the defendant, Marckle, the present plaintiff in
error.

From this judgment, Haskins, the plaintiff below, took an
appeal to the Circuit Court. In that court the case, by consent of the parties, was tried by the judge, without the intervention of a jury, who gave a judgment for the plaintiff in the
original action for seventy-five dollars. The defendant in the
Circuit Court brings the case here.

M. McCONNEL, for Plaintiff in Error.

I. L. MORRISON, for Defendant in Error.

CATON, C. J. The questions of law raised in this case admit of no dispute. If the plaintiff knew the defendant was
acting as the agent of his brother, at the time the bargain was
struck, and his brother had authorized him to sell the horse,
or subsequently ratified the bargain, then the warranty was
the warranty of the principal and not of the agent, and the
latter is not liable in this action. The only real controversy
is upon the facts. There are two principal questions of fact
in the case. First, was the plaintiff aware of the fact that the
defendant was selling the horse as the agent of his brother?
and, second, was the horse unsound at the time of the sale?
As is usually the case in trials upon horse trades, the testimony
[*383] is apparently conflicting and contradictory. On the
first question, the plaintiff's driver says, that he was present

Marckle *v.* Haskins.

during the whole time the parties were negotiating and till after the bargain was struck, and that the defendant claimed the horse as his own, and that nothing was said about his belonging to his brother. If what he says is true, that settles the first question.

Green says he was passing around among the parties on the morning of the trade, and heard them talking about price and pay, and that he heard the defendant say the horse belonged to his brother, but he heard nothing said about the soundness of the horse. It is very clear that this witness was not present when the trade was made, as testified to by the first witness.

Wiswell says that he told the plaintiff that. the horse belonged to the brother of the defendant, and from the character of the conversation between them, as stated by the witness, it raises a strong inference that it was before the bargain was closed, still it may have been afterwards, and there is no way of reconciling the apparently conflicting testimony consistently with the integrity of all the witnesses, except upon the conclusion that the conversations, as sworn to by these last two witnesses, took place after the bargain was struck, as testified by the first witness. Without this, some one has sworn to a falsehood, and the court will not arrive at this conclusion in regard to any unimpeached witness, where there is any reasonable hypothesis upon which the testimony of all the witnesses may be reconciled, consistently with the integrity of all. We know that witnesses are often mistaken, but courts reluctantly come to the conclusion that a witness against whose veracity nothing has ever been heard, has deliberately and knowingly sworn to a falsehood. This is evidently the view which the Citcuit Court took of this testimony, and we do not think it is so unreasonable as to require us to reverse the judgment for that cause.

There is no contradictory proof as to the warranty, and as to the unsoundness of the horse at the time of the sale, we think the proof decidedly preponderates in favor of the finding of the Circuit Court, so much so that we do not deem it necessary to review the evidence on that point.

The judgment of the Circuit Court is affirmed.

Judgment affirmed. 457

[*384] ANDREW LONG, and ALEXANDER BEALL, Appellants, v. THE COUNTY COURT OF SCOTT COUNTY, Appellee.

APPEAL FROM SCOTT.

The County Court succeeded to that of the county commissioner's, and a constable's bond is properly executed to the County Court; which court and its successors may maintain an action upon it.

ON the eighth of November, 1859, William Salisbury was elected constable of said county, and afterwards, as principal, with appellants as sureties, executed an official bond to the justices of said county, naming them and their successors in office, to the use of the People of the State of Illinois, for, etc., conditioned as the law requires. Suit was brought on this bond to the September term, 1861, of the Circuit Court of said county, in the name of "The County Court of Scott County," for use of, etc., there being four counts in the declaration, to each of which the appellants demur. Demurrer was overruled, and judgment against them.

The only error assigned, is the overruling of the demurrer.

D. A. AND T. W. SMITH, for Appellants.

KNAPP & BURR, for Appellee.

WALKER, J. This was an action of debt, instituted by the County Court, on a constable's bond, to recover for a breach in failing to pay an account for money collected by the constable, in his official capacity. The bond was executed by Salisbury the constable, and by Long and Beall as his securities, and was made payable to "William Leighton, Robert Husband, and Jesse Husted, county justices, together constituting the County Court of the county of Scott, and State of Illinois, and their successors in office, for the use of the People of the State of Illinois," etc., conditioned in the usual form for the faithful discharge of his duties as a constable. The declaration contained four counts, to which a demurrer was interposed, and overruled by the court, and the defendants refusing to answer further, judgment *nil dicit* was rendered, and the damages were assessed, from which this appeal is prosecuted.

The appellants raise the single question, whether the County Court of Scott county can maintain an action on this bond.

The law in force at the time of its execution, or at present, in counties not acting under township organization, [*385] does not in terms, prescribe the person to whom such a bond shall be executed. During the existence of the County Commissioners' Court, constables were required to make their official bonds payable to the county commissioners of their county, and to their successors in office, for the use of the People of the State of Illinois. The 15th section of the act of the 12th of February, 1849, (Scates' Comp. 309), provides, that the county judge, and two justices of the peace, designated and provided for by the act, as a County Court, shall "have, exercise and possess all the power, jurisdiction and authority heretofore conferred by law on the County Commissioners' Courts of this State."

It is, by this provision, manifest- that if the County Commissioners' Court had power or authority to take such a bond, the County Court may. They are invested by express language, with all the power and authority which was possessed by the Commissioners' Court. Constables were, as we have seen, required to make their bonds payable to the county commissioners and their successors, and when the law required that officer to execute his bond to them, it necessarily authorized and empowered them to receive it, and maintain an action upon it, for any breach which might occur. It then follows, that this bond was properly executed, as the County Court succeeded to all of the powers of the Commissioners' Court. *Shute* v. *Chicago and Milwaukee R. R. Co.*, 26 Ill. 436.

It also follows, as a consequence, that if the Commissioners' Court could have maintained an action upon a constable's bond payable to them, the County Court, as its successor, may do the same, upon such a bond payable to them. The power in the one case is as ample as in the other. Under the rules of the common law, the party holding the legal title or interest in the thing affected, must bring the suit. In this case the successors of the obligees have the legal title to this bond. It is by its terms payable to the persons named as the court, and to their successors, and by-law vested in them, and that of itself authorizes them to maintain the action.

This case is similar to that of *Fraizer* v. *Laughlin*, 1 Gilm. 347. It was there held, that the case was brought in the corporate capacity of the county commissioners, and the names of the individuals appearing as obligees in the bond, was entirely surplusage, and might be stricken out at any time. That was an action by that body, against a school commissioner and his securities. That case clearly determines the question, that the suit could be maintained in the corporate capacity of that body, and we have seen that the County Court has succeeded to all of their powers and authority. That case must be held de-
[*386] cisive of this. The judgment of the court below is affirmed.

Judgment affirmed.

Henry H. Hall *et al.*, Appellants, *v.* Henry Carpen, Appellee.

APPEAL FROM MORGAN.

A and B, each sent cattle to market, which were sold by the same broker, who, in accounting to the parties, paid A too much, and B, by precisely the same sum, too little; B sued A, to recover his deficit. *Held*, that there was no such privity between these parties, as would create a liability.

In June, 1860, appellee and appellants each shipped a lot of cattle to the city of New York for sale. On reaching the city, they separately employed to sell their respective lots of cattle, a cattle broker by the name of Wm. Florence. On the 25th and 26th of the same month, Florence sold by small lots, both lots of cattle, and in settling with the parties for the proceeds of their respective lots of cattle, Florence by mistake paid appellants $171 more than was due them on their cattle, and also paid appellee $171 less than was due him for his cattle.

Appellee sued appellants for the said sum of $171, in assumpsit, for so much money had and received for appellee's use. Appellants plead non-assumpsit, upon which issue was taken. By consent of the parties, the case was tried by the court without a jury, and the court gave judgment for the plaintiff below, $183.82 and costs; from which the appellants appealed, and the parties made this an agreed case, upon the clerk certifying the same, to be reviewed by the Supreme Court without any other or fuller record, and without exception to matters of form. The only question to be made is, whether such privity of contract exist between the parties as that the plaintiff below can rightfully recover anything in the case.

The error assigned in this case is, that the court erred in rendering a judgment for the plaintiff below, and in not rendering judgment for the defendants below.

MORRISON & EPLER, for Appellants.

D. A. SMITH, for Appellee.

CATON, C. J. The appellants consigned to a cattle broker in New York, a lot of cattle for sale, which were sold, [*387] and upon settlement, the broker by mistake paid them $171 too much; and about the same time, the appellee also placed in the hands of the same broker, a lot of cattle for sale, and upon settlement with him, the appellee was not paid enough by the sum of one hundred and seventy-one dollars, and Carpen sued the Halls for this amount, on the supposition that they had got his money. This is quite a mistake. The Halls have got the broker's money, and he has got Carpen's. There was no privity between these parties in any way, to connect the two transactions. They were as distinct and separate, as if they had been five years apart, and one mistake five times as large as the other; or as if one party had consigned hops, and the other corn, or even two separate brokers had been employed. But for the accidental circumstances that both parties consigned cattle to the same broker, about the same time, and that in their settlements, mistakes to the same amount were made, no one would have dreamed that the Halls had got Carpen's money. This money had no ear-marks to distinguish it. Who shall say that had no mistake been made, the same one hundred and seventy-one dollars which was paid to the Halls, would have been paid to Carpen? But even though this were capable of proof, and were actually proved, it would make no difference. There was no privity between these parties, which could make one liable to the other. *Trumbull* v. *Campbell*, 3 Gilm. 502. The judgment must be reversed, and the cause remanded.

Judgment reversed.

BENJAMIN F. SMITH, ALEXANDER THOMPSON, and WILLIAM H. COOPER, by their next friend, BENJAMIN F. SMITH, Plaintiffs in Error, *v.* JOB A. RACE, Defendant in Error.

ERROR TO MACON.

On an application by a guardian for license to sell the real estate of his wards, they need not be made parties to the proceedings, nor is the appointment of a guardian *ad litem* required.

The ruling in the case of *Mason* v. *Wait*, 4th Scammon, 127, adhered to.

The case *In re Sturms*, 25th Illinois, p. 390, examined and partially approved.

THIS was an action of ejectment by plaintiffs in error, against defendant in error; plaintiffs claiming the south-west quarter of the south-west quarter of Section 35, Town 17 north, Range [*388] 2 east of the third principal meridian, in Macon county, in fee simple.

Plea of general issue filed.

Trial by court, at July term, 1861, EMERSON, Judge, presiding. Judgment for defendant for costs on thirteenth day of said term.

Motion by plaintiffs to reinstate case upon docket, allowed by court upon payment of costs.

Cause reinstated, with leave to amend declaration.

Amended with ' additional count by Benjamin F. Smith and Alexander Thompson, claiming undivided three-fourths of land described in first count in fee simple.

Also, additional count by Alexander Thompson, claiming undivided one-fourth of land described in first count in fee simple.

Trial by the court, November term, 1861; issue found for defendant, on first and second counts, and for plaintiffs on third count.

Judgment for plaintiffs for one-sixth of premises described in declaration, and costs.

Motion by plaintiffs for new trial. Motion overruled.

It was admitted in evidence by the parties, that John E. French entered the land in controversy. That defendant Race was in possession of the same, as tenant of Alonzo Lapham's heirs. That the heirs of said French commenced an action of ejectment for the recovery of said land, in March, 1860, which suit was dismissed before the commencement of this suit.

Graham states, that John E. French died about the second of February, 1841; that the names of his children were Eliza Ann, Mary J., Marena Ellen, and Sarah M. French. That his wife was named Marena A. French. That she afterwards married Daniel Sturms, and died in 1850.

That Eliza A. French was born December 24, 1835; Mary J. was born February 14, 1837; Marena Ellen was born March 4, 1840; and Sarah M. was born July 23, 1841.

That Marena Ellen French died about June 4, 1854; Eliza A. Cooper, formerly Eliza A. French, died about June 9, 1857; and Sarah M. Thompson, formerly Sarah M. French, died July 6, 1860.

That Eliza A. married John Cooper, and died leaving only one child, William H. Cooper, who is now living. Mary J. French married Moses Reed, and is still living; and that Sarah M. French married Alexander Thompson, and died without issue; and that it was the best impression of witness that the heirs of John E. French resided in Indiana, in 1846 and 1847.

Plaintiffs introduced deed from Mary Jane and Moses [*389] Reed, to Benjamin F. Smith, for land in controversy.

Defendants introduced notice of intended application, by Daniel and Marena Sturms, to Macon Circuit Court, for power to sell and convey the lands of John E. French's heirs, including land in controversy.

Defendants introduced in evidence, a petition by Daniel and Marena Sturms, to Macon Circuit Court, October term, 1846, for power to sell and convey the lands of the heirs of John E. French, and invest the proceeds in other real estate.

Defendants introduced a decree of Macon Circuit Court, October term, 1846, in the matter of Daniel and Marena Sturms, guardians, etc., which recites, that notice of the intended application of petitioners had been regularly given, etc., in said county, and no person appearing to interpose any objections, it was ordered that petitioners sell the land in controversy among others, and invest proceeds in other real estate.

Defendants introduced an amended decree of said court in same case, made at June term, 1847, extending time of sale to September 13, 1847. Also, notice of the time, place and terms of sale of land by Daniel and Marena Sturms.

Defendants introduced a report of Daniel and Marena Sturms, to Macon County Court, October term, 1847, including sale of land in controversy to Alonzo Lapham. Report indorsed approved by the court.

Defendants introduced a deed from Daniel Sturms and Marena Sturms, guardians of Eliza Ann, Mary Jane, Marena Ellen, and Sarah M. French, of the county of Vermillion, Illinois, to Alonzo Lapham, of the county of Macon, Illinois, for the land in controversy.

Said deed recites the decree and amended decree of Macon Circuit Court, in the matter of the petition of Daniel and Marena Sturms, guardians of the minor heirs of John E. French, deceased, for an order to sell and convey lands.

Defendants offered tax receipt for the year 1853, to Margaret Lapham, for taxes on land in controversy. Also, tax receipts to William S. Crissey, guardian of A. Lapham's heirs, for 1854, 1855, 1856, 1857, 1858, and 1859. Also, certificate of redemption from sale for taxes of 1860.

Plaintiff objected to the introduction of all the foregoing evidence on part of defendants. Court overruled objection.

William S. Crissey, a witness for defendants, testified, that Alonzo Lapham was in actual possession of land in controversy, as early as 1848; that Lapham built a barn and fence on said land, and that he, his heirs and their tenants, had [*390] been in possession ever since.

Witness also stated, that he had paid taxes on said land for several years since 1848; that he was guardian for the heirs of Alonzo Lapham, and paid the taxes for said heirs. That Lapham died intestate, and that Margaret Lapham was his widow. Witness further stated, that he had paid the taxes on said land for four or five years since Lapham's death, and that Lapham died in 1851 or 1852.

Errors assigned:

The court erred in admitting in evidence the petition in the matter of Daniel and Marena Sturms, guardians, etc.

The court erred in admitting in evidence the decrees in the matter of Daniel and Marena Sturms, guardians, etc.

The court erred in admitting in evidence the report of Daniel and Marena Sturms.

The court erred in admitting in evidence the deed from Daniel and Marena Sturms to Alonzo Lapham.

- The court erred in rendering judgment for the defendant on the first and second counts in the declaration.

The court erred in admitting in evidence the tax receipts, and certificate of redemption from tax sale.

The court erred in rendering judgment against plaintiff, on the first and second counts in the declaration.

The court erred in overruling motion for a new trial.

A. B. BUNN, and B. F. SMITH, for Plaintiffs in Error.

J. S. POST, and TUPPER & NELSON, for Defendant in Error.

. WALKER, J.* Was the decree under which defendant derives his title void? If so, then his title must fail, as the

---

* NOTE.—See the case of *Gibson* v. *Roll,* in this volume.

guardian's deed to defendant's ancestor passed no title, to the premises in controversy. The only defect urged, as apparent on the face of that deed is, that the cause was not entitled as against the heirs of French, in their several names. In other words, the heirs were not made defendants to the petition of the guardian, for license to sell this real estate. It contains no prayer that they be made defendants, or that process may issue against them.

Our statute does not, in this proceeding, require the minor to be made a defendant, or the appointment of a guardian *ad litem.* The tenth section of the chapter entitled "Guardian [*391] and Ward," provides that "the Circuit Court may, for just and reasonable cause, being satisfied that the guardian has faithfully applied all the personal estate, order the sale of the real estate of the ward, on application of the guardian, by petition in writing, stating the facts, and having given notice to all persons concerned, of the intended application," etc. Another portion of the same section provides, that the order of the court may direct the sale for the support and education of the ward, or to invest the proceeds in other real estate. In this enactment there is no requirement, that the wards shall be made parties to the proceeding. But the sale is authorized on the application of the guardian, by petition, after having given the notice in the mode prescribed.

Then without making the wards, either petitioners or defendants, does the court acquire jurisdiction of the person? If so, the court may, after acquiring jurisdiction of the subject matter, determine whether the relief sought should be granted. Until jurisdiction of the proper parties, and of the subject matter is obtained, the court has no power to proceed in the cause, and an order so rendered would be inoperative and void. Whilst it is usual to make parties, whose interests are to be affected by the litigation, either plaintiffs or defendants on the record, yet no reason is perceived why the legislature may not have authority to enable parties laboring under legal disabilities, to act in their own name or in the name of others, entrusted by law with the managment and control of their property. In this class of cases, the guardian is authorized, in his own name, to institute and conduct this proceeding for the benefit of the minor.

In the case of *Mason* v. *Wait*, 4 Scam. 127, it is held, in a proceeding of this kind, that " it is not necessary, that the ward should have a day in court. The proceeding was not adverse to her interest, nor against her. It is her own application, by her legally constituted guardian. No summons to her was necessary; nor could she have any day, or guardian *ad litem* in court, unless upon suggestion, as *amicus curia*, it should appear, that the guardian was about to abuse the trust, or was seeking power to injure and misapply the estate. I think it altogether an erroneous view of such cases, to regard them as proceedings against the heir, to divest her of her interest or property. It is an application by her, or on her behalf, for power to do acts for her benefit and interest." This decision has doubtless been regarded and acted upon, by the courts and by the legal profession of the State, ever since its announcement, as the correct practice. And under that practice, large amounts of property have been purchased and sold, in [*392] perfect good faith, believing that this court had definitively determined such a practice to be legal and binding, upon the estate of the minor. On the faith of that opinion, covenants for title have no doubt been entered into, under the belief, by grantors, that they were acting with perfect safety.

The stability of titles, to real property, requires that judicial decisions affecting them should change as seldom as possible, and then only when a necessity almost imperative demands it. Whilst it may be true that cases of great injustice may have occurred under this practice, by unfaithful guardians, in procuring license to sell the real estate of their wards, still rather than endanger all the titles acquired since the decision of *Mason* v. *Wait* was announced, we regard it better to leave the practice as it now stands, trusting to the Circuit Courts and the friends of the minor to guard and protect his interest. We therefore feel disinclined to disturb that decision.

We are aware that the views here expressed are not in accordance with those announced in the case *In re Sturms*, 25 Ill. 390. In that case, it was improperly said, that the minors

were not parties to the original suit, and their interest could not
be affected by the sale of their land by the guardians. In that
we went too far, according to the case of *Mason* v. *Wait;*
but we still adhere to what was there said, when we held their
remedy was by original bill or by an action of ejectment. If
the decree was obtained by fraud, and the purchaser was a
party to it, or chargeable with notice, the heir may impeach
the decree by original bill, or if the adjudication was had without jurisdiction of the person or property, the remedy is by a
recovery in ejectment.

Then was the decree on the application of the guardian, regular and binding? It is insisted that it was not, because the
proceeding was had in the Macon Circuit Court, when the heirs
resided in Vermillion county. The tenth section of the act,
requires the application to be made in the county in which the
minors shall reside, unless the ward is not a resident of the
State, when such application shall be made to the Circuit
Court of the county in which the whole or a part of the estate
is situated. Graham testifies, that it is his "best impression
that the heirs of French resided in Indiana in the years 1846
and 1847." Although this evidence is not of the most positive character, yet in the absence of rebutting evidence, we
regard it as sufficient to establish the fact. It is in effect the
same as if he had said it was his best recollection, or memory
of the matter. We therefore conclude, that Indiana was the
[*393] place of the residence of the minors, when the application was made, and that Macon county was the proper county
to institute the proceeding.

The petition, upon which that application was based, seems
to have contained all the allegations necessary to give the court
jurisdiction. It was accompanied by a sufficient notice, which
was proved to have been given for the length of time, and in
the mode prescribed by the statute. The original, and further
decree, were regular on their face, and fixed the time, the place
and the terms of the sale. The guardian's report of the sale
was duly approved by the court, as required by the statute.
The guardian's deed is in proper form, and no want of jurisdiction or error appears on the face of that proceeding. It must,

therefore, be held that the title of the heirs to this real estate passed to the purchaser, at the guardian's sale. And the defendants in this suit, deriving and holding their title from the grantee of the guardian, were entitled to judgment in bar of the action. This view of the case renders it unnecessary to consider the question whether the action was barred, by the statute of limitations. The decree and sale under it divested the heirs of French of all title in the premises, and that is decisive of the case. The judgment of the court below is affirmed.

Judgment affirmed.

HENRY REINBACH, Appellant, *v.* WILLIAM and PHILIP WALTER, Appellees.

APPEAL FROM MORGAN.

A party who claims a homestead exemption as against a sheriff's sale, should show that the right existed when the lien attached; it is not enough for him to show that it was his homestead at the time of the sale.

It would appear that a stable, a horse lot, a smoke-house, and the grounds connected therewith, together with the dwelling-house, would constitute the homestead; but that a store, warehouse, and the grounds connected with these, would not.

APPELLEES declared in ejectment for two lots in Franklin, in the county of Morgan. Defendant pleaded not guilty. Trial by court by consent, and judgment for one lot and part of the other, in behalf of the appellees.

Bill of exceptions shows, that appellees, on trial below, produced and proved judgment of said court, *fieri facias* on same, sheriff's sale and deed for the premises sued for. [*394] Possession of premises admitted by appellant, and appellees rested:

Appellant produced and proved plat of his homestead. That the sheriff sold the lots in controversy by virtue of *fieri facias*. That the debt for which the appellees obtained judgment against him, was contracted after 4th July, 1851. That he was the owner of the premises indicated in the plat, at the time of the levy and sale, occupying the same as a residence with his wife and children, and that the entire premises, at that time, were not worth $1,000. That the storehouse was occupied and used by him as a merchant, sometimes individually, and sometimes by himself and partner, and that boarders in his family, who attended to business in the store, lodged therein. That there was a cellar under the "shed" referred to in the plat, where vegetables were sometimes kept for his family, and that they used the horse lot and stable.

It did not appear that the appellant was in possession of the premises at the time the judgment was rendered under which the execution was issued. The court rendered judgment as above, and the appellant excepted.

Errors assigned:

That the court below rendered any judgment against appellant.

That the court below rendered a judgment against him for a part of his horse lot, and the whole of his stable, which appertained to his homestead and exemption right.

D. A. AND T. W. SMITH, for Appellant.

MORRISON & EPLER, for Appellees.

CATON, C. J. As the defendant did not prove that any portion of the premises were his homestead at the time the judgment was rendered and when the lien attached, the homestead law has no application. The proof is, that it was his homestead at the time of the sheriff's sale. He may have moved upon the premises but the week before. Had he proved his possession at the time the lien attached, the same as it was at the time of the sale, we should be inclined to hold that the dwelling-house, the smoke-house, the stable, the horse lot, and the grounds connected therewith, for domestic and family purposes, constitute the homestead, and that the store and warehouse, and the grounds used for the business done in them, did not constitute a part of the homestead. It [*395] is impossible to say, from this bill of exceptions, how these grounds should be divided, as having been used for these several purposes. The judgment must be affirmed.

Judgment affirmed.

EUROPE A. LILLY, Appellant, *v.* GEORGE WAGGONER, Conservator of Elisha Waggoner, Appellee.

APPEAL FROM MOULTRIE.

A contract entered into during the lucid intervals of one who is a lunatic, is valid.

All persons of mature age are presumed to be sane, until after inquest found, when the presumption is changed, and proof is required to show sanity.

A deed executed several years before the maker was, by inquest, found insane, has the legal presumption of validity in its favor.

The evidence showing the insanity of a party at the time of the execution of a deed, must preponderate, or the legal presumption in favor of sanity, will sustain the act.

THIS suit was commenced by bill in chancery in the Circuit Court of Moultrie county, at the October term, 1858, by George Waggoner, as conservator of the estate of Elisha Waggoner, for the purpose of setting aside a conveyance of real estate made by said Elisha Waggoner to the appellant, Lilly, in the year 1851, upon the ground that said Elisha was insane at the time of selling and conveying the property.

The bill alleges, that, in 1858, an inquest was held upon said Elisha Waggoner, at the county of Moultrie, by order of the judge of the County Court, and a verdict of insanity rendered. That afterwards, on the 6th of September, 1858, George Waggoner was appointed by the County Court, conservator of the estate of Elisha Waggoner; that for a long period previous to the inquest, said Elisha was insane, and that during such insanity he conveyed the land described in the bill to the appellant, Lilly; that the said Lilly has not yet divested himself of the fee in said land; that Lilly knew of the insanity of said Elisha at the time of the conveyance; that said conservator

471

proposed, out of his own means, to give Lilly the amount to be paid for the land, if he, Lilly, would reconvey the land to Elisha, which Lilly has refused to do. Bill prays that the conveyance may be set aside, and an account of rents and profits be taken, etc.

The answer of Lilly admits the conveyance, and alleges that a full consideration was paid for the land; that he, Lilly, [*396] is in possession of the land, and has made valuable improvements on it; that the land has greatly increased in value since the conveyance to him by said Elisha, and that great injustice would be done to him by canceling the conveyance; that said Elisha was not insane at the time of making the conveyance, but legally competent to make it; denies that appellee offered to give him the amount he paid for the land; that appellee is the brother of said Elisha, and must have known of the conveyance; but no objection was made to it until several years after; that the purchase of said land was made by him in good faith.

To this answer there is a replication.

The case was, by consent, tried by the court upon the bill, answer, replication, exhibits, and oral proof. The testimony is summarily stated in the opinion of the court.

At the September term, 1859, of the Moultrie Circuit Court, the judge entered a decree declaring the deed from Waggoner to Lilly void, and ordering a reconveyance of the land to Waggoner; and that the purchase money be refunded to Lilly with interest. To which decree exceptions were taken. Motion for a new trial, and motion overruled. Exceptions taken, and appeal prayed.

The errors assigned are as follows: Court erred in rendering the decree in favor of the appellee; and in not rendering decree for appellant, and dismissing bill of complaint.

A. THORNTON, and STUART, EDWARDS & BROWN, for Appellant.

W. H. HERNDON, and H. P. H. BROMWELL, for Appellee.

WALKER, J. Does the evidence in this case establish the

fact, that Elisha Waggoner was of non-sane mind, so as to avoid his conveyance to appellant? It may be truly said, that there are few questions which present greater difficulties in their solution, than this of insanity. It assumes such a variety of forms, from that of the raving madman, to the monomaniac; from total dementia, to that of scarcely perceptible insanity, that it has almost been denied, that any person is perfectly sane, on every subject. But the law only regards it, when it renders the subject *non compos mentis*, or that condition of the mental faculties exists, which renders the subject incapable of acting rationally in the ordinary affairs of life. It is that degree of mental derangement which renders the person affected incapable of understanding the effect and consequences of his acts. It need not be of that total derangement, or rather obliteration of the faculties, which pre- [*397] vents the party from reasoning upon all subjects. Nor yet the want of power, at all times, upon correct premises, to arrive at accurate conclusions, but it is that want of power, which prevents a person from reasoning, or understanding the relation of cause and effect.

Persons of equal natural mental capacity, from difference in education, pursuits and opportunity, manifest different degrees of mental vigor. The law has never required the high order of reasoning powers that mark the gifted, or a large portion of the human family would be thus deprived of the legal capacity to transact their own business. But if the person manifest an ordinary degree of intelligence and judgment or even less, in reference to his business pursuits, and especially upon the subject in dispute, at the time of the transaction, it is all that is required.

A person may be a lunatic and yet have lucid intervals. And the law has at all times held, that a contract entered into, during a lucid period, is valid, whilst those made during a fit of insanity may be avoided. The reason is obvious, as a contract to be binding, must receive the assent of the parties. Not the mere formal assent, but the agreement of a mind capable of comprehending the nature of the transaction. Where one of the parties is *non compos mentis*, he has not entered into the agreement, because his mind has not comprehended the nature of the transaction, or the effect of his act. He lacks the mental capacity to understandingly give his assent to the transaction, whilst in the lucid interval, his mind acting with judgment, has understood the force and effect of his act.

Then does this evidence show, that this individual was insane, or if so, that the conveyance was made when he was laboring under its effects? The legal presumption is, that all persons of mature age are of sane memory. But after inquest found, the presumption is reversed, until it is rebutted, by evidence that he has become sane. When the transaction complained of occurred before the inquest is had, the proof of insanity devolves upon the party alleging it, but it is otherwise if it took place afterwards. In this case the conveyance was executed several years previous to the inquest, and the legal presumption is, that the deed is valid unless the proof establishes insanity at the time of its execution. Complainant's evidence is somewhat conflicting. But five or six of his witnesses speak of the grantor insisting that he was dead, was going to die, was dying, or that a change in his manner was perceptible after his sickness. Some of these witnesses, however, say, that he con- [*398] versed rationally on his business affairs, and none of them say that he did otherwise. One of these witnesses purchased of him a tract of land, and says that he fixed the prices of property at near its value. None of these witnesses say, that it was his habit of insisting upon the absurdities of which they testify, or whether it was only occasionally, or when they occurred. Whether it was during his sickness, or near the time of the sale, or some years later, is not disclosed by the evidence.

Again, one of the complainant's witnesses was present when the sale was made. He says, that appellant offered Waggoner four dollars per acre, which he agreed to take; that Waggoner's wife was present at the time, and made no objection; that witness had been acquainted with Waggoner several years; had conversed with him occasionally, but had never heard him speak of going to die. One of the physicians, who was examined, states that, from complainant's evidence, he thinks it difficult to tell whether Waggoner was sane or insane. That it discloses some marks of insanity, and if there was a cause for it, that there is some evidence showing simulated insanity, and that some of the tests of insanity are wanting. The other physician gives it, as his opinion, that he was insane, but that it was of the character, that in some cases the person affected would be capable, and in others incapable, of attending to his business.

Neither of these witnesses, however, give the opinion, that the grantor was so affected by insanity, as to be incapable of conducting his business. One of them speaks of some marks of insanity, whilst others are wanting, but thinks it difficult to determine the question. The other, whilst he thinks him insane, regards the insanity as of that character which in some cases renders a person incapable of transacting business, but abstains from giving an opinion as to the capacity of this person to transact business. Again, the justice of the peace who took the acknowledgment of this conveyance, says, he saw nothing to excite a belief that he was insane. He had taken other acknowledgments of deed from this grantor, and from his conversation and manner he supposed him to be sane.

It appears to us, that this evidence, on the part of complainant, fails to establish the fact that the grantor was insane when the deed was executed. It may create doubt, but that is insufficient to overcome the presumption of sanity. To have that effect, the evidence must preponderate. But if this were not so, appellant introduced eight witnesses, acquaintances of Waggoner, who saw and conversed with him, but at no time discovered any appearance of insanity, of which complainant's witnesses speak. Some of them purchased [*399] of him land or other property, but saw nothing to induce them to believe him insane. It appears, that immediately previous to the sale, Waggoner went, on two different occasions, to the house of one of the witnesses for the purpose of selling the land to appellant. That he then appeared to be rational. Noys testifies, that he purchased of him a piece of land, in April, 1851; had sold him goods and had seen nothing strange or unusual in his conduct, and believed him to be competent to trade and make contracts at the time. This witness says, he was about like the other Waggoners; was always somewhat singular from the time he first knew him.

When all the evidence in the case is considered, we can scarcely entertain a doubt of his sanity. And when we consider the evidence of one of his medical witnesses, who says, that if there was a reason for it, there would appear to be some marks of simulated insanity, we can readily perceive a motive in the rise of this land from four to twenty dollars per acre. And it, to say the least, seems singular, that none of the complainant's evidence was directed to his condition at the time the transaction occurred. And as the books lay down the rule, that a permanent injury received to the mind by sickness, usually produces *dementia,* or a total imbecility of mind, and not *monomania,* we cannot believe that he was insane from that cause, as such cases are believed to be of extremely rare occurrence.

But even if the evidence establishes the fact of his insanity, we think the evidence abundantly shows that he had lucid intervals. And from the testimony of the justice of the peace, who took the acknowledgment of the deed; of Philips, who was present when the contract was entered into; of Mrs. Lilly, who saw him immediately before; and of Samuel P. Lilly, who saw him immediately after the sale, we think it abundantly appears that he was then sane. And there is no evidence that opposes this conclusion. All of complainant's evidence is indefinite as to the time when the acts testified to occurred.

The decree of the court below is reversed, and the bill is dismissed.

Decree reversed, and bill dismissed.

BENJAMIN H. GATTON, Plaintiff in Error, v. [*400]
GEORGE B. DIMMITT, Defendant in Error.

ERROR TO MASON.

Oyer cannot be craved of an instrument not under seal, of which profert is not
made. If such an instrument is to be examined by this court, it should be
presented by bill of exceptions, demurrer to evidence, by an agreed case, or
by a special verdict.

A note given to a county, is properly assigned, by the clerk of the County
Court under its seal.

THE opinion of the court, by Mr. Justice BREESE, gives a
full statement of the case.

STUART, EDWARDS & BROWN, for Plaintiff in Error.

J. ROBERTS, for Defendant in Error.

BREESE, J. This was an action of assumpsit, brought in
the Circuit Court of Mason county, by Dimmitt, against
Gatton and J. M. Ruggles. Gatton alone was served with
process.

The declaration contains two special counts upon a promissory
note, and the common counts. The note declared on, was executed by Gatton and Ruggles, dated September 6, 1858, for the
sum of $733.86, payable to the *County of Mason*, three years
after date. This note was assigned by the clerk of the County
Court of Mason county, under seal of county, which assignment
purports on its face to have been made for the county, and in
pursuance of an order of the County Court.

To first and second counts, and each of them, the defendant Gatton filed a demurrer, craving oyer of the note and assignment, copies of which are set out in the demurrer, and assigning
as causes of demurrer to each of said counts—1st, That the
county had no power to transfer the note; and 2nd, that the
assignment indorsed on the note was not such as transferred the
interest of the county to plaintiff. To the other counts the de-

fendant Gratton pleaded the general issue. The demurrer to the first and second counts was overruled by the court.

The plaintiff dismissed the common counts, and the defendant Gatton saying nothing further as to the first and second counts, judgment on the demurrer was entered against him, and the damages assessed by the clerk, on which final judg-[*401] ment was entered. To reverse this judgment, he prosecutes a writ of error, and assigns for cause:

The Circuit Court erred in overruling the demurrer to the first and second counts of plaintiff's declaration.

The court erred in rendering judgment against plaintiff in error.

We have never understood, that oyer could be craved and had, of a promissory note, or of any writing not under seal, and of which profert is not made. 1 Ch. Pl. 431. In Kentucky, and in that State only, can oyer be craved of a writing not under seal. *Puggle* v. *Adams*, 3 A. K. Marshall, 429. If a party desires to bring the note or writing before the court, it is our practice to do so by bill of exceptions, demurrer to evidence, by an agreed case, or by a special verdict—never by oyer. This being so, neither the note or assignment is a part of the record, and we are only to consider the ruling of the court upon the demurrer to the first and second counts of the declaration, and the propriety of the final judgment as rendered. These make up the errors assigned.

The first count of the declaration is unobjectionable. It sets out in legal phrase the execution of the note by the defendants to the county of Mason, and the assignment by the county to the plaintiff in the suit. The count is perfect in all its parts.

The second count, after setting out the making of the note to the county, avers an assignment of the same to the plaintiff by the clerk of the County Court of Mason county, under the seal of the court, acting under a special order of the County Court, entered of record, authorizing him to assign the note.

The demurrer brings up the question of the power of the county to assign the note, and the legality of the manner of assignment. We have no doubt on either question. By section sixteen of chapter 27, Scates' Comp. 299, it is provided that all notes, bonds, bills, etc., whereby any person shall be bound to any county for the payment of money, or any debt or duty, etc., shall be as valid and effectual to all intents and purposes to vest in the county all the rights, interests and actions which would be vested in any individual, if any such contract had been made directly to him, etc.

An individual, to whom a promissory note is made, has an undoubted right to assign it; the same right by this statute is vested in the county.

As to the mode and manner of the assignment through the agency of the clerk, we can conceive no other mode by which it could be done. The county is a corporation incapable of acting except by its duly constituted agents, the most import- [*402] ant of which is, the court of the county. The court represents the county, for all purposes. Their acts are recorded by the clerk appointed for such purpose, and they are evidenced by the seal of the court, which is in his custody. The declaration avers, that the County Court made an order, entered of record at a regular term of the court, directing the clerk to assign the note, which he does under the seal of the court, and delivers the note to the plaintiff in the suit. This is the only mode by which the assignment could be made, and no objection can be taken to it.

The defendant resting on his demurrer, the court could do no less than enter an interlocutory judgment thereon, and direct the clerk to compute the damages. On his report coming in, final judgment was entered for the amount reported to be due, all which is in conformity with the practice in such cases, and with the statute.

The judgment is affirmed.

Judgment affirmed.

LOUISA MILLER *et al.*, Appellants, *v.* GABRIEL MARCKLE, Appellee.

APPEAL FROM MORGAN.

While a widow may release her interest in the homestead right, such a release will not affect the interest of the children.

IN September, 1858, appellee filed his bill in the Morgan Circuit Court, for the foreclosure of two mortgages on the west half of the north-east quarter of Section eighteen, in Township sixteen north, Range eleven west of the third principal meridian, situated in Morgan county, Illinois, executed by Wm. R. Miller to appellee; one was executed on the 17th day of January, 1857, to secure two notes executed by said Wm. R. Miller, the first in favor of E. F. Valentine, for the sum of $325, by him assigned to appellee, and dated Dec. 13, 1855, and the second was executed by said Miller to appellee, for $272.50, with indorsed payment of $220; and the other mortgage was executed on the 2nd day of October, 1857, to secure a note for $1,000, executed by said Miller to appellee on the same day.

At the October term of the court, said Miller filed his answer to the bill, admitting the execution of the said notes and mortgages, and that the first and second notes mentioned [*403] were made in good faith, but that the third note mentioned, and the mortgage to secure the same, were, by arrangement with appellee, made to delay his creditors; and he admitted nothing more in his answer.

At the March term, 1861, appellee filed his affidavit, showing that said Miller and his wife Louisa, at the time of filing his bill, were in possession of said premises as a homestead, and afterwards abandoned the same as such; that on the 26th of November, 1859, by virtue of a decree of said court, the same were sold by the master to affiant for $1,767.14; that on the 4th of March, 1861, said master conveyed the same to appellee; that the premises were worth at least that sum; that said Miller died in August, 1860, without asserting his homestead right to said premises; that on the 5th day of December, 1860, said Louisa, the widow of said Wm. R. Miller, executed to him a quit-claim deed of said premises, and that he had read to said Louisa the aforesaid master's deed, and demanded possession of the said premises. Also another affidavit, showing that he had served on said Louisa a notice, that he would, at the March term, 1861, make a motion for an order for a writ of execution and for possession of said premises.

On the 28th day of March, 1861, the appellants filed the affidavit of said Louisa, showing that the said Miller, at the time of the execution of the mortgages, was residing on the said premises as a homestead, as the head of his family, and residing with the same; that he had not released his right under the homestead exemption law to said premises; that the said Louisa was not a party to either of said mortgages; that she had not released her homestead exemption right to said premises; that the said Miller departed this life on the 26th of August, 1860, leaving, surviving him, his widow, said Louisa, and his children and minor heirs, Georgia Miller, David Miller, and John R. Miller; that she has been the head of her family, residing with the same, ever since the death of her said husband, and that said premises were then, and most of the time since the death of her said husband, occupied by her and her said infants as a homestead; that one or the other of her said infant children had resided on said premises ever since the death of said Miller; that all the time after the execution of said mortgages the premises were occupied by him as a homestead, either by himself or by his tenants paying him rent; that the said Miller moved from the premises on account of his apprehensions of violence against him by said appellee, who was repeatedly disturbing him in his possession.

And on the same date appellants filed the affidavit of James W. Miller, showing substantially the facts stated in the [*404] affidavit of said Louisa; that he, affiant, and one Isaac Barbor. occupied the premises as tenants of Wm. R. Miller, from the time Miller moved off of the same, which was in 1858, until the death of Miller; that he continued in the occupation of said premises as the tenant of Miller, under the contract of lease made with Miller, until Louisa, with her infant children, moved back on to said premises, and occupied the same as her homestead and homestead of the children.

At the September term, 1861, appellee filed his amended affidavit, showing that the decree of foreclosure in this cause was had to secure the payment of a part of the purchase money for the mortgaged premises; that Louisa, together with said infant children, were occupying and claiming said premises under the homestead exemption law, and that they were committing waste on the same, and prayed an injunction.

And at the same term, appellee filed his amended affidavit, showing that the decree of foreclosure and the master's deed of said premises had been served on the three minor children.

And he also then filed the affidavit of Z. Wells, showing that Miller had stated in his presence that he had made a note to E. F. Valentine for the premises in question, that Valentine had assigned it to the appellee, and that he (Miller) had mortgaged said premises to appellee to secure said note.

And at the same term, appellants filed the affidavit of David C. Miller, showing that the said Valentine note was executed by said Wm. R. Miller to Valentine in the year 1855, and that the mortgage securing the same was executed by said Wm. R. Miller to appellee in the year 1857, after the assignment of said note, and that he did not believe that the said note was given to Valentine for the purchase money of said premises; that the special master, who sold the premises under the decree, did not cause said premises to be appraised by a jury of the county, nor did the appellee set off to said Wm. R. Miller one thousand dollars worth of the said premises as his homestead, nor did the special master serve the said Miller with a copy of appraisal of said premises, as the statute provides in such cases; and that appellee became the purchaser of said premises for the sum of $1,767.14.

And at said term the court heard the motion of appellee for a writ of possession, and the cross-motion of appellants to vacate the decree of foreclosure and the sale of the premises under the same, upon the affidavits and exhibits aforesaid; and also the deed of Valentine to Miller conveying the said premises to said Miller, executed on the 12th day of January, 1857, acknowledging the receipt of $1,500, being the whole of the consideration for the same, (first having appointed [*405] C. Epler guardian *ad litem* of said infants), and decreed that the motion of appellee be allowed, and that appellants' cross-motion be disallowed and overruled, and that appellee have a writ of assistance to put him in possession of said premises. From which decree an appeal was taken by said Louisa, and the said infants by their guardian *ad litem.*

The errors assigned and relied on in this cause are:

The court erred in decreeing that the motion of appellee be allowed, and that he have a writ of possession.

The court erred in overruling the cross-motion of the appellants, and in not vacating the decree of foreclosure and the sale under the same.

MORRISON & EPLER, for Appellants.

D. A. SMITH, for Appellee.

BREESE, J. The appellants assign for error the allowance of the motion, founded on certain affidavits made by Marckle, for a writ of possession of the premises bought by him under the mortgage sale, and in not vacating the decree of foreclosure and sale on their motion and affidavits.

The wife, now widow of Miller, one of the appellants, was not a party to the bill to foreclose, nor has she, at any time, released her right of homestead exemption, in the mode prescribed by the statute, according to the construction put by this court on that statute. In *Kitchell* v. *Burgwin and Wife*, 21 Ill. 45, this court said, a formal release or waiver of the statute must be executed. It must appear that the privileges and advantages of the act were in the contemplation of the parties executing the deed, and that they were expressly released or waived in the mode pointed out in the statute. To the same effect is *Vansant* v. *Vansant*, 23 Ill. 541.

In the case of Vansant we said, when the householder dies, the exemption continues after his death for the benefit of the widow and family, some or one of them continuing to occupy such homestead until the youngest child shall become twenty-one years of age, and until the death of such widow. The appellee insists, that at the time of the decree, Miller did not insist upon his homestead right, and that since his death, his widow has released all her interest to the appellant. That release is a general one, and however it may effect her, cannot affect the interest of her children as secured by the Homestead Act.

[*406] But it is insisted, that one of the notes for which one of the mortgages was executed, was given to secure the purchase money of the land, and under the second section of the act the land cannot be exempt from sale.

This would appear so from the affidavit of Wells, and the circumstances of the case corroborate his statement, but it is *ex parte* altogether, and a vital question in this case. It is decisive of the claim set up by the widow and children. It is true the parties have not had a full opportunity of contesting that important fact, nor do they ask to do so, and we can, therefore, but find as the court below has found, that the first mortgage was given " for a debt or liability incurred for the purchase of the land mortgaged and sold under the decree," and that appellee must be allowed the benefit of his motion. The decree upon the mortgage given to secure the payment of one thousand dollars, and alleged to have been given to defraud creditors, was reversed by this court in the case of *Miller* v. *Marckle*, 21 Ill. 152, but that judgment is not insisted on here, nor is there any appeal from the original decree. The judgment of the Circuit Court on the motion is affirmed.

Judgment affirmed.

THOMAS J. BUNTAIN, Plaintiff in Error, *v.* JOHN W. BLACKBURN, Administrator of Paul N. Moyer, deceased, Defendant in Error.

ERROR TO EDGAR.

A bill to restrain the collection of a judgment, should not only show a good reason why the evidence was not saved by a bill of exceptions, but should also show what the evidence was which authorized the judgment complained of, and the grounds of his defense, the reason, if any, why it was not made, and such other facts as would make a case, or there will not be error in the dismissal of the bill.

THIS was a proceeding on the chancery side of the Edgar Circuit Court.

The record shows, that on the 7th day of December, 1857, Thomas J. Buntain, complainant, filed his bill in said court, praying injunction, etc. The bill represents that John W. Blackburn, as administrator of Paul N. Moyer, deceased, who was thereby made defendant to this bill, at the April term of the Edgar Circuit Court, 1857, obtained a judgment, as afterwards set forth, against complainant, for the sum of $89.04, and costs, on which execution had issued against [*407] the goods and chattels of complainant, which was in the hands of a deputy sheriff of Edgar county, who had levied the same on the lands of the complainant; that said sheriff would proceed to coerce the collection of said judgment, etc., unless restrained, etc. Bill shows how judgment was obtained; sets forth a contract for renting a mill; a breach of the contract, and a subsequent oral contract in lieu of the first. Shows occupancy of mill premises under said last contract, and repairs done to amount of $140; that repairs equaled rent, and that complainant overpaid the same, $40 in cash. That at a suit for rent, complainant set up said repairs and money paid as set-off, and asked judgment for surplus. That judgment was rendered against complainant for $79.21 and costs; that he appealed to Edgar Circuit Court; that at the May term, 1856, thereof, the case was tried, and judgment rendered against complainant.

Motion made for and new trial granted, and case tried at the October term, 1856, but no judgment then rendered. That no judgment was ever rendered in court while in session. That complainant is informed that on the last day of the April term, 1857, late in the evening, the judge being sick, and confined to his room, the papers in the case were delivered by the judge to an assistant clerk of the Edgar Circuit Court, with a memorandum in pencil on the back of papers, " Mot. overruled and judgment aff. $89.04;" that said papers were taken to the clerk's office, and judgment there entered as in open court, although the complainant is informed and charges, that the court had then adjourned, and that being unannounced, he knew nothing of said judgment until about the close of the September term, 1857. That, believing the case still under advisement, until the night on which the September term, 1857, closed, he inquired of the court as to the case, when he was informed of the judgment at the term previous; charges inability to apply for new trial, to appeal, or file bill of exceptions on which to base writ of error, the court having been adjourned; charges absence of remedy at law, issuance of execution, and collection of judgment unless restrained; prays redress, and for an injunction restraining deputy sheriff, and the defendant, John W. Blackburn, from all further proceedings under judgment, etc., until further order, etc.; waives answer under oath, and asks that injunction be made perpetual, etc., and for all other and proper relief, both special and general, etc.

At the special January term, 1860, of the Circuit Court, it appears, that the defendant demurred orally to complainant's bill, in which there was oral joinder, and that defendant then [*408] withdrew his demurrer and filed his answer to complainant's bill.

The answer of defendant is a formal general admission or denial of the allegations of bill—fixing the date of the judgment erroneously in 1858 instead of 1857.

The final order in the case is as follows:

" Now come the parties, and the court being advised in the premises, does now order and decree, that the injunction herein be dissolved, and cause is dismissed at the complainant's costs.

It is therefore ordered, adjudged, and decreed by the court, that the defendant recover of the plaintiff his cost and charges in this behalf expended, and hereof have execution," etc.

The errors assigned are six in number, as follows:

That the court below erred in entertaining the jurisdiction of the cause, when all the parties were not before it.

That it erred in dissolving the injunction and dismissing the cause, upon the coming in of the answer of one of the defendants, Blackburn, such answer being unsupported by the oath of defendant, or by *ex parte* affidavits, for that purpose.

That it erred in dissolving injunction and dismissing the cause, no motion to that end having been submitted, etc.

That it erred in dissolving the injunction and dismissing cause.

That court below erred in rendering decree against complainant for the payment of costs of defendant Blackburn.

And that the court below erred in. disposing of the case, until cause set down for hearing.

C. H CONSTABLE, for Plaintiff in Error.

S. P. READ, for Defendant in Error.

CATON, C. J This case depends entirely on the sufficiency of the bill. If that states such a case as should induce a court of equity to grant a new trial, then undoubtedly, the court erred in dissolving the injunction and dismissing the bill. The circumstances stated in the bill, we think, show a sufficient excuse for not having presented the evidence in a bill of exceptions, so that he could assign for error, the finding of the court upon the evidence. But the misfortune is, that he does not show what the evidence was before the court, on the trial at law. For aught that appears, the evidence was conclusive, showing the plaintiff's right to the judgment which he recovered, without the least shadow of a defense by the defendant. The complainant does not claim in his bill, that the court committed the least imaginable error upon that trial, [*409] or that the judgment of the court was wrong. But he does complain that he had a good defense to that action, which he

sets out in the bill, but he does not say that he presented that
defense on the trial at law, nor does he give the least excuse for
not having done so. The presumption is that he did not present his defense on that trial, through his own neglect. If this
was not so, he should have shown it in his bill. We cannot
presume it without averments. It makes no difference whether
the decree was made at the April or at the January term.

The decree was right, and must be affirmed.

Decree affirmed.

THOMAS J. BUNTAIN, Plaintiff in Error, *v.* COLLUM H.
BAILEY, Defendant in Error.

ERROR TO EDGAR.

A general objection to the introduction of an instrument as evidence, is not
sufficient; if it is obnoxious to a special objection, that objection must be
stated in the court below.

THIS case originated in a suit instituted before an acting justice of the peace in the county of Edgar, which resulted in a
judgment in favor of said Bailey, and against the defendant
Buntain, and was removed by Buntain into the Edgar Circuit
Court, by appeal.

At the October term, 1860, this cause was tried before HAR-
LAN, Judge, without the intervention of a jury. The record
shows, that on this trial, Buntain objected to the admission of
transcript and certificates thereon of the proceedings had before
Lambert Duy, Esq., claiming to act as a justice of the peace,
in and for Harrison township, Vigo County, Indiana, on which
suit was brought in evidence before the court, and the transcript
as certified admitted by the court.

The bill of exceptions shows that the cause was submitted to
the court for trial; that plaintiff offered in evidence a transcript of the proceedings had in Harrison township, county of
Vigo, and State of Indiana, before one Lambert Duy, claiming
to act as a justice of the peace in and for said township. The

transcript is set out at length, and purports to show judgment
in favor of plaintiff Bailey, against defendant Buntain.   The
first certificate appended to transcript is that of the said Lambert Duy, signing the same as justice of the peace, without
any seal, public or private, affixed.   Then follows what [*410]
purports to be a certificate of Andrew Wilkins, clerk of the
Circuit Court of Vigo county, as follows:

"STATE OF INDIANA, {
       VIGO COUNTY.   } ss.

" I, Andrew Wilkins, clerk of the Circuit Court in and for
the county and State aforesaid, do hereby certify, that Lambert Duy, Esq., before whom the annexed judgment appears to
have been rendered, was, at the time of rendering such judgment, an acting justice of the peace in and for said county, and
duly authorized by law to render the same, and am acquainted
with his signature, and believe the annexed signature, purporting to be his, to be genuine.   Witness my hand and the seal
of said court, this 17th day of May, A. D. 1860.

                                "ANDREW WILKINS, Clerk."

Then follows the certificate of Solomon Claypool, as sole
judge of the Vigo Circuit Court, as to the official character
and certificate of the clerk.   The oill of exceptions further
shows the defendant's objection to the introduction in evidence
of said pretended transcript, the overruling of the objection by
the court, and admission of transcript in evidence that such
transcript was all the evidence in the cause, and that the circuit judge rendered a judgment of affirmance of the judgment
of the justice of the peace of Edgar county, for $65.26, and
that the defendant, by his counsel, excepted, as well to the overruling of said objection, as to the admission of the transcript
in evidence, and to the rendition of the judgment by the court.

C. H. CONSTABLE, for Plaintiff in Error.

S. P. READ, for Defendant in Error.

BREESE, J.   This court has so frequently decided that
general objections to the instrument of evidence will not be
entertained, that it is unnecessary, in this case, to do more

than refer to the decisions. To go no further back, the case of *Sargeant* v. *Kellogg et al.*, 5 Gilm. 281, is understood to hold, that a general objection to the introduction of a certain instrument of evidence simply raises the question of its relevancy. But if it is obnoxious to a special objection, that objection must be stated. When various objections may be made to evidence, some of which may be removed by other proof, the party making the objection ought to point out specifically those he insists on, and thereby put the adverse party on his guard, [*411] and afford him an opportunity to obviate them. He ought not to be permitted, after interposing a general objection, to insist on particular objections in this court, which, if even suggested in the court below, might have been instantly removed.

The transcript when offered in evidence was objected to, without specifying any particular grounds. Under the authority of the case of *Frazer* v *McKee*, 1 Scam. 558, it would seem to be liable to but one objection, which, if pointed out on the trial, might have been removed, that is, the jurisdiction of the justice of the peace in the State of Indiana. Had that been the objection, it was quite easy to remove it, by producing the law of Indiana conferring the jurisdiction, and also, that the same law authorized the clerk to certify as to the official character.

To the same effect are the cases of *Peoria and Oquawka R. R. Co.* v. *Neill*, 16 Ill. 269; *Swift et al.* v. *Whitney*, 20 Ill. 144; *Conway* v. *Case*, 22 Ill. 127; *Funk* v. *Staats*, 24 Ill 633.

The judgment must be affirmed.

Judgment affirmed.

MICHAEL HALL, Plaintiff in Error, *v.* FRANK NEES, Defendant in Error.

ERROR TO COLES.

According to the strict rules of practice, a motion in arrest of judgment is a waiver of a motion for a new trial. A party who has filed both motions,

Hall *v.* Nees.

and calls up his motion in arrest and has it disposed of, and then allows judgment to be rendered, without directing the attention of the court to the other motion, will be held to have waived his motion for a new trial.

It is allowable to include in the same declaration, divers distinct words of slander, of different import.

This is an action on the case for words spoken.

The declaration alleges four several conversations between defendant and divers persons, in each of which defendant uttered several distinct "sets of words," charged as slanderous to plaintiff, as follows:

First conversation alleged:

"He (meaning plaintiff) stole my corn." "He (meaning plaintiff) and Smith Horton stole my corn." "He (meaning plaintiff) stole my hogs." "He (meaning plaintiff) stole my eggs and apples." "He (meaning plaintiff) keeps Smith Horton to steal my corn, and he (meaning plaintiff) [*412] conceals it." "He (meaning plaintiff) is a thief." "He (meaning plaintiff) keeps a whore house."

Second conversation alleged:

"Frank (meaning plaintiff) stole my corn." "Frank (meaning plaintiff) stole hogs from me." He (meaning plaintiff) stole hogs from me." "He (meaning plaintiff) and Smith Horton stole my corn." "Since he (meaning plaintiff) has come here (meaning the neighborhood of said defendant) my eggs and apples are all stolen," (meaning and intending thereby to charge that the said plaintiff stole the eggs and apples of said defendant.)

Third conversation alleged:

"He (meaning plaintiff) keeps Smith Horton to steal my corn, and he (meaning plaintiff) receives it and conceals it." "Smith Horton steals my corn, and he (meaning plaintiff) receives it." "Smith Horton stole my corn, and he (meaning plaintiff) conceals it." "Smith Horton steals my corn, and he (meaning plaintiff) conceals it and uses it," (meaning and intending thereby to charge said plaintiff with receiving for his own gain, and concealing stolen property, he, the said plaintiff, then and there knowing said property to have been so stolen.)

Fourth conversation alleged:

491

"He (meaning plaintiff) keeps a whore house." "His (meaning said plaintiff's) house is no better than a whore house." "He (meaning plaintiff) keeps a lot of whores," (meaning at the house of said plaintiff.) "He (meaning plaintiff) keeps his daughter and a hired girl there, (meaning at the house of said plaintiff) to keep a whore house.

There was a demurrer to the declaration and the several allegations thereof, which, after being filed, was withdrawn, without any judgment of the court thereupon, and defendant filed four pleas. General issue, and three pleas, justifying certain "sets of words" alleged in declaration.

Issue joined, (defendant withdrew his second plea), trial by a jury, and verdict as follows: "We the jury find the defendant guilty, and assess said plaintiff's damages at five hundred dollars."

Thereupon a motion for a new trial, and in arrest of judgment, was entered by defendant, which motions were taken under advisement by the court.

Thereupon the court rendered judgment for plaintiff, for five hundred dollars and costs of suit.

The motion in arrest, was put upon the ground that the declaration showed divers and distinct allegations of words [*413] spoken, divisible in their nature, some of which are not actionable.

H. P. W. Bromwell, for Plaintiff in Error.

John Scholfield, for Defendant in Error.

Caton, C. J. After the verdict in this cause was rendered, the defendant entered two distinct motions—one in arrest of judgment, and the other for a new trial; which were continued. At the next term, as the record states, the counsel for both parties called up the motion in arrest and argued it; upon which the court took time to consider until the next succeeding term, when the motion in arrest was overruled, and final judgment was rendered on the verdict. It is laid down as a general rule, in works on practice, that a motion in arrest of judgment is a waiver of a motion for a new trial. The motion for a new trial should be made and determined, where it is relied upon, before the motion in arrest is made. But if we were not disposed to adhere to this technical rule, and to allow both motions to be pending at the same time, there was clearly a waiver of the motion for a new trial in this case. After the defendant filed his motion for a new trial, he allowed it quietly to sleep among the files of the court, during several terms, without ever presenting it to the consideration of the court; while in the meantime, he called up and argued his motion in arrest, and pressed it to a decision, and allowed final judgment to be entered up. If he intended to rely upon his motion for a new trial, he should have called it up and asked a decision upon it, before the entry of final judgment at least. After the court had decided the motion which had been presented and argued, it was not its duty to hunt over the files in the cause to see if some other motion had not been slipped in, which should be decided before final judgment should be rendered. If the defendant really intended to rely upon the motion for a new trial, it has much the appearance of a trick, in allowing it to be passed over in silence, until final judgment was rendered, and now for the first time press it upon the attention of an appellate court, not upon its merits, but simply complaining that the Circuit Court did not decide it one way or the other. We do not feel inclined to encourage this kind of silent practice. The objections urged to the declaration, on the motion in arrest, would apply to all the most approved precedents to be found in works on pleadings.

That motion was properly overruled, and the judgment must be affirmed. *Judgment affirmed.*

THE TOWN OF LEWISTON, Plaintiff in Error, *v.* [*414] WILLIAM PROCTOR, Defendant in Error.

ERROR TO FULTON.

In an action to recover a penalty for obstructing a village street, after the ordinance establishing the offense and the penalty has been given in evidence without objection, evidence of a private act of the legislature legalizing the ordinances, was properly excluded from the jury. The statute might have been proper preliminary evidence, but after the introduction of the ordinances, it became irrelevant.

The plea of *nul tiel corporation*, is a plea in bar.

In actions before, and upon appeals from. justices of the peace, the defendant has a right to insist upon proof of every material fact necessary to a recovery, just as if all the requisite pleas had been filed. And the plaintiff, if a corporation, must prove its corporate existence.

A continuous and uninterrupted use of a highway by the public, for more than twenty years, creates a prescriptive right to the use of the road. And this right continues, until it is clearly and unmistakably abandoned.

A partial or transient non-user of a highway, by reason of the travel being diverted to other roads, is not sufficient to establish its abandonment.

The fact, that a village road has not been repaired by the corporate authorities, may be evidence tending to show that the corporation does not regard it as a highway. This will not be the case, however, if it appears, that, from the nature of the ground, the road has needed no repairs.

In an action, to recover a penalty, for obstructing a highway, if the complaint gives a local description, sufficient to fix the precise point obstructed, and also the *termini* of the road, the latter may be disregarded. But when the allegation is general, that a road leading from one point to another has been obstructed, the existence of the road, between the points named, must be proved, as a matter of essential description.

In prosecutions for obstructing highways, the rule is, that every averment must be established, by a clear preponderance of evidence. And it is error to instruct the jury that they must be satisfied of the defendant's guilt, beyond a reasonable doubt, before they could find against him. This latter rule obtains only in criminal prosecutions, affecting life or liberty.

THIS was an action commenced by complaint, before the police justice of the town of Lewiston, Fulton county, Illinois, for the violation of an ordinance, by placing and continuing obstructions, in one of the streets of said town.

The police justice rendered judgment against the defendant, Proctor, from which he appealed to the Circuit Court of Fulton county. From which court (the judge thereof having been of counsel in the cause), a change of venue was ordered, to Mason county.

At the October term, 1861, of the Mason Circuit Court, a trial was had before the court, HARRIOTT, Judge, and a jury. The defendant was found not guilty, and judgment was rendered against the plaintiff for costs.

On the trial, the plaintiff gave in evidence the charter of the town of Lewiston (Session Laws of 1857, p. 1038,) [*415] and proved the acceptance of and organization under the charter. The plaintiff then read, without objection, the ordinances of the town, defining the offense and fixing the penalty.

Plaintiff then offered in evidence an amendment to the charter (Session Laws of 1859, p. 635-6,) to which the defendant objected. The court sustained the objection as to section five, of the act, but permitted the remainder to be read.

Plaintiff then introduced a number of witnesses, who testified, as to the location of the road, and as to its being used as a public highway for many years.

The plaintiff then gave in evidence the record of the proceedings of the County Commissioners' Court of Fulton county, showing an order by the court, in pursuance of a petition duly presented to it, appointing commissioners to lay out a road, from Lewiston to the ford of Spoon river.

Also, a report of the commissioners that they had laid out the road.

Also, an order of the said County Commissioners' Court, that the said road be opened and declared a public highway.

Also, further, from the records of the County Commissioners' Court, showing an order of the said court, in pursuance of a petition duly presented, appointing commissioners to relocate the said road. And the report of the commissioners that they had reviewed and relocated the road. And an order of the court declaring the road as relocated, a public highway. The plaintiff then introduced a witness who testified that the said road, as relocated, passed over the point in controversy.

The defendant offered in evidence, the records of the County Commissioners' Court, showing the location of another road, which it was claimed had superseded the road alleged to have been obstructed. He then introduced a large number of witnesses, whose testimony tended to show that the travel on the old road had greatly diminished, and that it had been abandoned by the public, since the location of the new road. There were thirty-one instructions asked for by the plaintiff, and twenty-eight by the defendant, but the only questions arising upon them are stated in the opinion of the court.

See this case reported in 23 Ill. 533, and in 25 Ill. 153.

S. C. JUDD, for Plaintiff in Error.

N. BUSHNELL, for Defendant in Error.

WALKER, J. It is urged as grounds of reversal, that the [*416] court below rejected evidence, proper and pertinent to the issue. The plaintiff in error offered to read in evidence, the fifth section of the act of the 21st of February, 1859, which the court rejected, and exceptions were noted. To this decision we are unable to perceive any objection as its relevancy is not apparent. The ordinances creating the offense had been read to the jury without objection. Had an objection been interposed to the validity of these ordinances, then this section of the statute would have been proper preliminary evidence, to authorize their admission. But they having been admitted without objection, defendant could not afterwards question their validity. If the offense was committed after the adoption of this act, then this act established the validity of the ordinances which defined the offense, and imposed the penalty. But if it occurred before that time, then whether it was, when committed, innocent or penal, depended alone on the validity of the ordinances, independent of this enactment, as it could not have been the object, and no language is employed which indicates a design, to give this section a retrospective operation. It was only designed to cure any defects that might then exist, and to render them valid in the future.

It is again urged, that the court erred in admitting evidence, that the plaintiff had been acting as, and exercising the rights and privileges of a municipal corporation. This evidence was proper, if the plea of *nul tiel corporation* is in bar of the action, but it was not, if it is a plea in abatement. All matter of the latter character, must be interposed before a plea in bar, or it will be regarded as waived. It is said by Sergeant Williams in his notes to Saunders' Reports, (vol. 1, p. 340 *a*, n. 2), that "the defendant can only plead *nul tiel cor-*

poration in bar of the action, by a corporation." And it is believed that this rule has since been followed by the courts, both in Great Britian and in this country. When this plea is interposed, it operates as a special traverse of the averment, that the plaintiff is a corporation, and puts it upon proof of that fact. As in trials before justices of the peace, and in the Circuit Court, on appeals from their judgments, formal written pleadings are not required, and the defendant has a right to insist upon proof of all the material facts necessary to a recovery, precisely as if pleas were filed. It was necessary that the plaintiff should have proved its corporate existence. This evidence was therefore material, and should have been admitted.

It is also urged, that the court below erred in refusing to grant a new trial. First, because the jury found against the evidence; and secondly, because the court refused to give plaintiff's instructions as asked for, and in modifying [*417] them, and in giving improper instructions for the defendant. Other errors were assigned, but they are embraced in these, and will not, therefore, be separately discussed.

Is the finding of the jury in this case, manifestly against the weight of evidence? We think it is. Three witnesses on behalf of plaintiff, testified, that they had known the road in controversy, since 1837, and that it had during that time, been traveled as a public highway. Four others swear that they had known it to be thus used since 1838. Another since 1840, one since 1841, one since 1842, two since 1844, and one since 1857. Of the witnesses produced by defendant, one testified, that he had known the road since 1828, and that it had been used and traveled by the public since that time. Another had known it since 1831, to be thus used, and another after 1843. These witnesses all speak of what they know, were all citizens of the immediate vicinity, with every opportunity of being well informed, traveling it themselves, and seeing others do so, during the time of which they speak. Opposed to this affirmative evidence, a large number of witnesses state that the greater portion of the travel had abandoned this, and sought other routes; or say that they supposed the road had been abandoned as a public highway. We think the evidence most clearly rebuts all presumption, that the road had ever been abandoned as a public highway.

The question then arises, whether this road had a legal existence at the time it was obstructed by defendant. The evidence of user clearly shows that it had, by prescription. No less than nine witnesses testified to the use of the road by the public for a period of over twenty years. And from their evidence, it appears to have been continuous and uninterrupted during all that time. It is true that there was a great difference in the number who traveled it at different periods, still it was used and enjoyed by the public for the purpose of travel. This period, wherever the common law obtains, has always created a prescriptive right, as well in the public, as in private individuals. Such a right once obtained is valid, and may be enjoyed by the public to the same extent as if a grant existed, it being the legal intendment that its use was originally founded upon such a right. This right of user also continues until it is clearly and unmistakably abandoned. And in this case no such abandonment has been shown.

Again, the order of the Commissioners' Court of Fulton county, in December, 1830, by which commissioners to view and locate the road named in the order, were appointed, appears to be regular and valid. Nor is any objection perceived [*418] to their report, or the order confirming it, and establishing the road, and ordering it to be opened. The commissioners report, that they had made the location, "commencing at the south end of Main street, in Lewiston, thence a little south of west, to the first branch west of Lewiston," etc. The evidence shows that the road obstructed, commenced at the south end of Main street, and runs with the south line of the town, the direction of which is a little south of west. This would seem to identify this as the road which was obstructed.

The same court again, in 1845, appointed viewers to survey and relocate a road from Lewiston to Spoon river. The road was relocated, the report filed and approved, the road established and ordered to be opened forty feet in width. Stewart, who was one of the viewers, testified that they located the road from the mouth of Mechanic street, running west, or westerly, fifty-four rods, to the north-west corner of defendant's field, and over the exact point in controversy, and thence ran a south-westerly direction to the old Spoon river bridge. No objection is perceived to these orders locating these roads. The Commissioners' Court must be presumed to have had jurisdiction, until it is rebutted, and no such effort was made on the trial below.

It was attempted to be shown, that the public had acquired another and different road, which accommodated the same travel, and that this had been abandoned. In this, we think the defendant has entirely failed, as the evidence abundantly shows that this road was continuously used, up to the time of the obstruction. When an abandonment is relied upon, it must be clearly and satisfactorily proven, and that all use of it as a public road has ceased for a sufficient length of time clearly to indicate the intention. A transient or partial non-user will not suffice. In a town like this, the mere fact that there were some streets more used than others, is no evidence of abandonment. In all villages the streets are sufficiently numerous for the public to be accommodated in their travel by different routes, yet that cannot be regarded as an evidence that those but little used have ceased to exist.

It is insisted, that as this road, at the point of obstruction, had not been repaired by the corporate authorities, it was not regarded by them as a public highway. But all of the evi‧dence to that point, shows, that from the nature of the ground, it was never required. This being true, the law will not require a useless act. Had it been necessary, and it had never been repaired, that fact, with others, would have been proper for the consideration of the jury, in determining whether it was regarded, by those having charge of the highways, as a public road. Of itself, that fact is not sufficient to vacate [*419] a legally acquired public highway. On a question of dedication or prescription, it might be important, but not in a case of grant or condemnation under the statute.

It is again urged, that the proof fails to establish an obstruction of the road, described in the plaint. In the case of *Dimond*

v. *The People*, 17 Ill. 416, it was held, that the name of the
road was no essential part of the description, of either the road,
or the place of obstruction. And even if it was, proof that it
led from one of the points named to the other, would suffice.
When, however, a local description, sufficient to identify and fix
the precise point of obstruction, is given, as well as the *termini*,
the latter may be disregarded, and proof that a road existed at
the place of obstruction, is alone necessary. But when the allegation is general, that a road leading from one place to another
has been obstructed, its existence between the points named
must be proved, as a matter of essential description. In this
case the plaint does not fix the precise point of obstruction by
reference to lots or blocks, or by courses and distances from
other known objects. It only describes it, as a "certain street
of the town of Lewiston, county of Fulton and State of Illinois,
the said street being the road and street, sixth in number, south
from the court-house in said town, and running west from
Main street in said town." The second specification, in the
plaint, describes it, as being "known as the street running
west, or westerly from Main street, in said town, and sixth
in number south from the court-house in said town."

To maintain this action, it was necessary that the plaintiff
should have proved the existence of a road running west, or in
a westerly direction from Main street, or a street of the town as
described. That the road which was obstructed, was proved to
run from Main street nearly west, is without question. If it
ran a due west course, it fills the first description, or if it devi-
ates slightly from such a line, then it answers the second description in the plaint. We can perceive no material variance
between the plaint and the proof.

It is also insisted, that the court below erred, in modifying a
large number of the plaintiff's instructions, before they were
given to the jury. The modification complained of, was by informing the jury that they must be satisfied, that the defendant
was guilty, beyond a reasonable doubt, before they could find
for the plaintiff. This is undeniably true in all criminal prosecutions. And in the case of *Ferris* v. *Wood*, 4 Gilm. 499, it is
intimated, that the same rule obtains, in prosecutions for ob-

structing public highways. This rule can hardly be said to be sanctioned by the authorities. The rule announced by [*420] the ancient writers and decisions, is that there must be full proof, in all cases of prosecution to recover a penalty. In such cases the declaration must contain an averment of every fact, necessary to show the prosecutor entitled to recover, and every averment must be established by a clear preponderence of evidence. *Fairbanks* v. *The Town of Antim*, 2 N. H. 105 This seems to be the full scope of the rule, nor are we inclined to change it. When the judgment necessarily involves the life or liberty of the citizen, the benign rule, that the crime must be proved beyond a reasonable doubt, should prevail unimpaired, and the same doctrine is too firmly established to be shaken, by authority, if not on principle, in all proceedings by indictment. But when only a pecuniary forfeiture is involved, and the proceeding is on the civil side of the docket, the same reasons do not apply.

It is said, however, that the party may be imprisoned for such a forfeiture. So he may be taken in execution, on a judgment recovered in any form of action, in default of its payment. Imprisonment is no part of the judgment on such a forfeiture. Nor can a justice of the peace, under our constitution, imprison a defendant, as a part of his judgment in this proceeding. If the corporation has the power to take the body of a defendant, on a *ca. sa.*, it is no more than may be done in any other civil action. Again, it was held, when this case was previously before this court, (23 Ill. 433,) that town ordinances were not strictly penal statutes, within the meaning of the cost act.

It is likewise insisted, that the court below erred in giving the first and eighth of defendant's instructions. The first informs the jury, that unless the plaintiff has proved a legal highway the whole distance, from the south end of Main street to the north-west corner of defendant's field, that they should find for the defendant. The eighth is the same, except it fixes the western terminus at the western limit of the town, instead of at the corner of defendant's field. In describing the road, in the plaint, the corner of the field, or the western limit of the town, are not referred to as a part of the description. It is only described as running west, or westerly, from the starting point. Under the rules of evidence, the plaintiff was only required to prove a road as described in his plaint, and its obstruction as alleged. These instructions required more, and were, for that reason, erroneous, and should have been refused. Whilst the first of these instructions may not have been calculated to mislead the jury, the other evidently was, and if followed by them, accounts for this verdict. [*421] There was no proof, nor any effort to prove, that this street ran to the western limit of the town, and such proof was not required under the issue, yet the jury were told that, for want of such proof, they must find against the plaintiff.

For these various reasons, we are of the opinion, that the judgment of the court below is erroneous, and it is reversed, and the cause is remanded.

Judgment reversed.

WILLIAM E. D. MARSH, Plaintiff in Error, *v.* ASTORIA LODGE NO. 112, INDEPENDENT ORDER OF ODD FELLOWS, Defendant in Error.

ERROR TO FULTON.

Actions by the subordinate lodges of Odd Fellows should be brought in the name of the trustees of such lodges.

An organization in fact, and user under it, is sufficient in some actions to show a corporation in fact, although there may have been irregularities or omissions in the first instance.

If the right to sue is not expressly granted to a corporation, it may still exercise the faculty, if all the powers incident to corporations are conferred upon it.

The question in this case is presented by a plea which, in substance, avers that there is no such corporation, and not in abatement.

THIS was an action of assumpsit, commenced in the Circuit Court of Fulton county, at the June term, 1861, by Astoria

Lodge No. 112, Independent Order of Odd Fellows, against William E. D. Marsh, on an account.

The declaration contains the common counts for goods, wares and merchandise, sold and delivered to defendant at his request, also for money lent and advanced to, laid out and expended for defendant at his special instance and request, for money had and received by defendant for use of plaintiff, and for money found to be due on account stated.

At the September term, 1861, of said Circuit Court, the defendant filed his plea of the general issue to said declaration, and also the additional plea of "*nul tiel* corporation," upon which pleas the plaintiff took issue.

At the same term of said court, by consent of parties, a jury was waived, and a trial of the cause was had by HIGBEE, Judge of said court.

· The plaintiff, in support of the issues on his part, on the trial of the cause, called as a witness, *William T. Toler*, who, being sworn, testified, that he was present at a settlement, before the commencement of this suit, between a com- [*422] mittee appointed by the plaintiff for that purpose and the defendant, at which settlement defendant admitted that he, as treasurer of the lodge, had received dues from the members of the lodge to a considerable amount, and then had of such moneys and dues a balance of one hundred and forty-two dollars and fifty cents, and promised to pay the same. The plaintiff then offered to prove by witness, that said lodge was chartered under the Grand Lodge of the Independent Order of Odd Fellows of the State, and that the lodge had been, for some seven years or over, organized and acting as such lodge, and claimed to be acting under the Grand Lodge of such State; to all of which the defendant, by his counsel, objected, but the court overruled the objection, and permitted such evidence to be given, except as to the charter of the lodge, which testimony in reference to the charter was excluded, and the defendant excepted.

The witness then testified, on the part of plaintiff, that Astoria Lodge No. 112 was chartered by the Grand Lodge of the Independent Order of Odd Fellows, and had been for seven or more years acting and holding itself out as said subordinate lodge, by the name of Astoria Lodge No. 112, Independent Order of Odd Fellows, and that said lodge had regularly elected trustees; to all of which testimony defendant, by his counsel, objected, but the court overruled the objection, and permitted said testimony, (except as to the charter, which was excluded,) and defendant excepted.

The plaintiff then produced the records from the office of the recorder of Fulton .county, and offered to read in evidence therefrom, entries recorded therein as follows:

24204

"I hereby certify, that. at a regular meeting of Astoria Lodge No. 112, I. O. O. F., held at their Hall January 29th, 1855, the following named persons were elected Trustees for said Lodge for the term of one year, to wit: R. H. Bacon, Jacob Darling, Gilbert Rutledge, W. E. D. Marsh, W. T. Toler.

" Witness my hand and the seal of the lodge.

[L. S.]   JNO. N. STEELE, Sec'y."

" Recorded 20th February, 1855."

31657

"STATE OF ILLINOIS, }
   FULTON COUNTY, } ss.

" We, the undersigned, hereby certify that a corporate body by the name and style of ' Astoria Lodge No. 112, Independent [*423] Order of Odd Fellows,' is and has been since the 27th ' day of July, A. D. 1852, working and acting under a regular charter from the Grand Lodge of the State of Illinois, and that said Astoria Lodge holds their regular meetings on Monday evening of each week at their hall in the town of Astoria, county of Fulton, State of Illinois. ·We further certify, that at an election of trustees of said lodge, held at their hall, at a regular meeting, and in pursuance of the constitution and by-laws of said lodge, May 24th, 1858, the following named members of said lodge were elected trustees for the term of one year, to wit: Wm. E. D. Marsh, David Shrier, S. P. Cummings, Wm. Reeder, and Wm. T. Gallaher.

"In testimony whereof, we have hereunto set our [L. S.] hands and affixed the seal of said lodge this 21st day of July, A. D. 1858.

' Attest: WM. T. GALLAHER.   DAVID IVINS, Noble Grand."
    DAVID MARSH, *Treasurer.*

"Recorded July 23rd, 1858.

25440

"STATE OF ILLINOIS, }
  FULTON COUNTY.   }

"We do hereby certify, that on the 8th day of October, A. D. 1860, Henry Plank, W. T. Toler, W. E. D. Marsh, Geo. Thornburg and Samuel Hollingsworth, were duly elected trustees of Astoria Lodge No. 112, Independent Order of Odd Fellows, for the ensuing year. Given under my hand and seal, and the seal of our said lodge, at Astoria, this 8th day of October, A. D. 1860.

W. E. D. MARSH, N. G.
HENRY PLANK, Sec'y."

"Recorded November 21st, 1860."

. To which, and the receiving of which in evidence, the defendant objected, on the grounds that such entries were not the best evidence, that the certificates as recorded were not such as were required by law in the matter of incorporating lodges, that such entries were irrelevant and immaterial, that the original certificates had not been proven to have been executed, and that the record of the same had not been shown to have been made with the proper officer; but the court overruled such objection and permitted the entries or records and certificates to be read in evidence, and the defendant excepted.

The court thereupon found the issues for the plaintiff, and assessed the damages at the sum of $142.50.

The defendant then entered his motion for a new trial, and assigned in support of such motion the following reasons: the court erred in admitting improper evidence on the part of plaintiffs; the finding was against the law and the evidence. [*424] But the court overruled the motion for a new trial, and rendered judgment for the plaintiff for $142.50 and costs, to all of which defendant then and there excepted.

The defendant below, comes into this court by writ of error, assigning the following grounds of error:

The court below erred in admitting improper evidence on the part of the plaintiffs below.

The finding below was against the law and the evidence.

The Circuit Court erred in overruling the motion of the defendant below for a new trial.

The Circuit Court erred in finding for plaintiffs below on the issue of *nul tiel* corporation.

The court below erred in rendering judgment for the plaintiffs and against the defendant below.

The record and proceedings below are otherwise irregular, erroneous, informal and insufficient.

JUDD, BOYD & JAMES, for Plaintiff in Error.

S. P. SHOPE, for Defendant in Error.

BREESE, J. It is hardly necessary to examine in detail, the several errors assigned on this record. The conclusion we have arrived at, is, that under the statute of 1849, the suit is not properly brought. The act of February 8, 1849, entitled "An act for the incorporation of the Grand Lodge of the State of Illinois, of the Independent Order of Odd Fellows, and the subordinate lodges thereunto belonging," by the first section, declares the persons therein named and their successors to be a community, corporation and body politic by the name and style of "The Grand Lodge of the State of Illinois, of the Independent Order of Odd Fellows," and by that name to have perpetual succession. The second section provides that the said corporation and their successors, "by the name, style and title aforesaid," shall be capable to sue and be sued, etc. By the fourth section, the subordinate lodges instituted by this corporation, by the name and number of their respective lodges of the Independent Order of Odd Fellows in this State, are declared to be a community, corporation and body politic, capable for all time to take and hold property, real and personal, and of disposing of it in such manner as they think proper. The fifth section provides " that each of the subordinate lodges which now are or may be hereafter instituted, by the aforesaid corporation (the Grand Lodge), shall elect or appoint annually, five trustees, whose certificate of election shall be recorded in the office of the [*425] recorder in the county in which the subordinate lodges are situate," and " the said trustees and their successors shall be forever thereafter capable in law to sue and be sued, plead and be impleaded, answer and be answered unto, defend and be defended, in all or any courts of justice, and before all and every judge, officers or persons whatsoever, in all and singular actions, matters or demands whatsoever." The sixth section gives each of them a common seal, and in general to have and exercise " all such rights, privileges and immunities as by law are incident or necessary to corporations, and what may be necessary to the corporations herein constituted." (Session Laws, 1849, special acts, p. 46, 47.)

This act is the charter of all the subordinate lodges of this order, and the proof shows an organization in fact and user under it, and this is sufficient, in this collateral action, to show a corporation in fact, though there may have been irregularities or omissions in the organization.

The proof shows the election of the requisite number of trustees, and the record of the fact. This is evidence sufficient under the plea of *nul tiel corporation.* It establishes the fact of the existence of such a lodge, No. 112, but the plea goes further, and questions the right of the lodge to sue, in the name it has sued. It is in substance, that there is no such corporation as Astoria Lodge No. 112, capable of suing in this action. The Grand Lodge can sue by express grant, in their corporate name. The subordinate lodges cannot so sue. They must sue and be sued, in the name of the trustees, and in no other mode and by no other name. A corporation can have no faculty, not given by the act creating it. The faculty of suing is a most important one, and has not been specially conferred, and since it has been directly conferred on the trustees by special grant, it cannot be claimed as incident to the corporation under the general power conferred. Had not the faculty to sue, been conferred on the trustees, then indeed, would this corporation have had the right to sue under the grant, in the sixth section, of all the powers incident to corporations. *Metropolitan Bank* v. *Godfrey et al.*, and notes, 23 Ill. 609.

However just, and clearly established, is the defendant's liability in this case, yet, as the suit is not brought by the parties entitled to sue as plaintiffs, we are compelled to reverse the judgment. The suit should be brought in the name of "the trustees of Astoria Lodge No. 112, Independent Order of Odd Fellows."

Judgment reversed.

[*426] THE OHIO AND MISSISSIPPI RAILROAD COMPANY, Appellant, *v.* R. A. SAXTON, Appellee.

APPEAL FROM RICHLAND.

In an action for injuries to animals, it is necessary to show that the plaintiff in the action was the owner or had possession of the property injured.

THIS suit was commenced before a justice of the peace, to recover the value of a mule, which it was alleged had been killed by the appellant. The case was taken by appeal to the Circuit Court of Richland county, where there was a trial by jury, and a verdict and judgment for the appellee for eighty-one dollars, the value of a mule. The defendant below brings the case to the Supreme Court by appeal. By agreement of parties, the case was heard in the Second Grand Division.

W. HOMES, for Appellant.

A. KITCHELL, for Appellee.

WALKER, J. After a careful examination of the entire record in this case, we are unable to find any evidence which tends to prove, that appellee was the owner or had possession of the property for which suit was brought. If it was made, it was omitted in the bill of exceptions. In the absence of such proof, the verdict of the jury is manifestly against the evidence. The court below should, therefore, have granted a new trial, and for that error the judgment is reversed, and the cause remanded.

Judgment reversed.

EDWIN WRIGHT, Plaintiff in Error, *v.* JOSEPH GROVER
et al., Defendants in Error.

ERROR TO COLES.

Fraud must always be proved; the law never presumes it.

A complete transfer of personal property may be made, although the purchaser should not hold continuous possession. If the property is returned to the possession of the vendor, the fact may create suspicion, but is not conclusive of the fairness of the transaction.

THIS case originated in the trial of right of property, before Malden Jones, Esq., the acting sheriff of Coles county, in which Edwin Wright was claimant, and Joseph Grover, [*427] Lindle Madison, Benjamin C. Shaw and James H. Conner, were plaintiffs in execution; which resulted in a verdict against the claimant, who removed the case into the Coles Circuit Court, by appeal.

A trial of the cause was had by a jury, who returned a verdict against the claimant. Motion by claimant for new trial. Motion overruled; whereupon claimant excepted, and obtained leave to file his bill of exceptions, and judgment was rendered by the court upon the verdict.

The bill of exceptions shows, that on the trial of the cause before HARLAN, Judge, and a jury, the claimant offered in evidence a bill of sale, which is set out in *hæc verba* therein, executed by James M. Riddle, and witnessed by David H. McFadden, by which it is witnessed that Riddle, in consideration of the payment of $2,000, bargained, sold and delivered unto the claimant, Wright, various articles of personal property; that claimant then introduced the deposition of David H. McFadden, which proves that he (McFadden) was present when sale was made between Riddle and Wright; that after the sale, the property was brought back to Riddle's farm, and was there used as before, except that Wright claimed the property, and generally directed what should be done on the farm. Deponent identified the bill of sale signed by him as witness; that the property was taken from the farm to Mattoon before sale,

and afterwards returned, and remained on the farm while witness remained there—four or five months; that Riddle and
Wright both gave orders about the management of the property; that the property described in the sale bill was the same
taken to the farm and afterwards claimed by Wright; that
after the sale, witness considered the property as belonging to
Wright.

The defendant then called *James R. Cunningham*, who testified that he was attorney for defendants (the plaintiffs in execution); that he went with the officer to find property of Riddle and McFadden; found the property in controversy upon
the Wright farm; Riddle was using the same; Riddle lived on
Wright's farm; did not know whether a hired hand or not;
Riddle told witness' at time of levy that the property was
Wright's.

Harvey B. Worley testified, that he knew Riddle lived upon
Wright's farm, but did not know in what capacity; that
Wright lived sometimes on farm with Riddle and sometimes at
Mattoon, up to time of levy and since; used the horses frequently; had conversation with Wright before levy, in which
he said he had bought property from Riddle; that he had
[*428] leased the farm sometime before he bought the property;
that he took the property and applied the rent as part payment;
that Wright has no family, but lives with Riddle on farm;
some 300 acres in cultivation on the farm.

The claimant asked the following instructions from the
court:

1. That the law never presumes any transaction fraudulent.

2. That a party seeking to set aside a sale on account of
fraud, must allege and prove the same.

3. That any and all acts and declarations of the claimant
are to be considered by the jury in determining the possession
of the property after the date of the sale from Riddle to claimant; and if, from all the evidence, the jury believes that claimant was in possession of the property in controversy, or had
been in possession under a sale from Riddle to claimant, then
they should find for the claimant, unless the property had been
resold to Riddle.

4. That in defining what it takes to constitute a delivery, it is right and proper that the jury should take into consideration the situation of the parties at the time of the sale, and also take into consideration the situation of the article or articles sold.

5. That if they believe, from the evidence, that Riddle, the defendant in the execution, was *bona fide* indebted to Wright, the claimant of the property, that Riddle had the right to prefer creditors, and even exhaust all his effects in payment of said creditors' claim.

6. That although Riddle might have made the sale to Wright for the purpose of hindering or delaying creditors, yet if Wright, before or at the time of the purchase of the property from Riddle, had no knowledge of such facts, then the sale cannot be fraudulent as to creditors and purchasers, so far as the claimant's rights are concerned, and it devolves upon the defendants to show, by legal evidence, that Wright had such notice, either before or at the time of the purchase of said stock.

The court gave the third, fourth and fifth of said instructions, (refusing the third, however, as asked, but modifying it by inserting the words "and remained" after the words "or had been," in the fourth line from the bottom of instructions,) but refused to give the first, second and sixth. Whereupon claimant excepted to the modifying of the third instruction, and refusing to give the first, second and sixth.

The court gave the following instructions at the instance of defendants, to which claimant objected:

1. That actual possession must accompany and follow the sale of personal property, when the sale is practicable, [*429] to make the sale binding on judgment creditors and subsequent purchasers.

2. That sales of personal property, when the possession does not accompany the sale, but remains with the vendor or seller, are fraudulent and void as to creditors and subsequent purchasers; and the conditions of the parties at the time of the sale—the vendee residing with the vendor—does not take the sale out of this rule of law.

3. That the change of possession, to be effectual, must not be

merely nominal or momentary, but must be real, actual and open, and such as may be publicly known as a continual possession by the vendor, as ostensible owner after an absolute sale, though it be under articles of agreement with the vendee that the vendor shall be employed as his overseer, or under a contract of hire, is equally fraudulent and void.

4. A sale of personal property, to be binding upon creditors and subsequent purchasers, must be entered into *bona fide* and in good faith, and not with the intent of hindering or delaying creditors. Sales of personal property, to be effectual and valid against third parties, must be for a valuable consideration, moving from the vendee to the vendor.

5. That if there was not an open, positive change of the possession of the property, as evinced by the evidence, (if sold at all,) and that change of possession continued, so that creditors, or those who might have become purchasers, under ordinary circumstances, would have notice thereof, by virtue of such change and continued change of possession, that the law is against the claimant, Wright, and he cannot, under such purchase, hold the property against the execution of defendants.

6. That a bill of sale of personal property, where the possession remains with the vendor, is fraudulent and void in law, and is not good against creditors and purchasers without notice, unless acknowledged before a justice of the peace, in the precinct or township where the vendor resides, and recorded in the records of the county where executed.

7. That it is not necessary for a party to intend to commit fraud, in the sale of personal property, where there is no open, visible change of possession of such property into the hands of the purchaser, to constitute a fraud under the laws of Illinois; but if such possession does not accompany the sale, and continue openly with the vendee, it is a fraud against creditors and purchasers, and cannot be explained.

8. That in every sale of personal property there must be immediate, and actual, and continued change of possession, and [*430] unless this appear from the evidence, the sale shall be presumed to be fraudulent and void.

9. That it devolves upon the claimant to prove that the property is his, and that he must do so by affirmative testimony.

10. That the form of the verdict in such a case is this: " We, the jury, find the right of property *to be* (or *not* to be) in the claimant.

The grounds assigned for a new trial were as follows: the refusal to give claimant's instructions one, two and six; the refusal to give claimant's instruction number three, as asked, and the modifying the same; and the giving of defendants' instructions.

The claimant, who is plaintiff in error, assigns as specifications of error in the foregoing record, the following: the refusal of the court to give claimant's instructions Nos. 1, 2 and 6; the modifying of claimant's third instruction; the giving of defendants' instructions; and the refusal to grant a new trial.

CONSTABLE & ALLISON, for Plaintiff in Error.

O. B. FICKLIN, for Defendants in Error.

CATON, C. J. The court certainly erred in refusing to instruct the jury, that the law will not presume that a fraud had been committed. The law never does presume a fraud; that fact must always be proved, either by direct or circumstantial evidence. When there is no evidence of fraud, neither the court or jury have the right to infer or presume it.

Nor was it necessary to the validity of the complete transfer of the property, that the possession should be continued in the purchaser, as was held by the court, by the modification of the claimant's third and fifth instructions. *Brown* v. *Rielly*, 22 Ill. 45. If, after the delivery to the purchaser, he subsequently returned it to the vendor, it may be a circumstance tending to show only a colorable transaction, more or less cogent, according to the circumstances. But it certainly may be explained. The judgment is reversed, and the cause remanded.

Judgment reversed.

[*431] GEORGE M. RICHARDS, Plaintiff in Error, v. JANE
LEAMING et al., Defendants in Error.

ERROR TO SCOTT.

A note given for the purchase of land, if transferred, does not carry with it
to the assignee, the vendor's lien, so that the assignee can enforce it in his
own name.

THIS was a suit in chancery, brought in the Scott Circuit
Court, and based upon the following facts as set out in the bill:

Holloway W. Vansyckle sold to Peter Leaming two tracts
of land, and took from him, Leaming, several notes of hand
payable at a future day. The title to one of the tracts was in
Murray McConnel, and the title to the other was in said Mc-
Connel and David A. Smith, but all in trust for Vansyckle.
McConnel, at the request of Vansyckle, conveyed one of the
tracts to said Leaming, and McConnel and Smith joined in a
deed to Vansyckle for the other tract. While the title was in
this condition, Leaming died, leaving a widow and two children, the defendants in this case.

After the death of Leaming, in pursuance of his contract
and by arrangement with the family, Vansyckle conveyed all
this land (both tracts) by warranty deed, to the two last named
defendants, being the heirs at law of said Peter Leaming, deceased, the said widow and these children being in possession.
There is no controversy in this case about the title to the land,
or the mode or form of the conveyance; all but the last two
notes are paid, and three hundred dollars on one of them.

Holloway W. Vansyckle, before these notes became due, sold
and assigned them to complainant, and he filed this bill, setting
up a vendor's lien against the land for the payment of these two
notes, praying that a day be given to pay the same, and in default thereof, that said land be sold, or so much thereof as
might be necessary to pay the same. A demurrer to this bill
was filed, and overruled by the court.

The two last named defendants, being then minors, answered

by their guardian *ad litem;* their answer denying all the allegations of the bill, and putting the complainant on proof
· thereof. The defendant, Jane Leaming, who had filed the demurrer, then filed her answer, setting up some defense, charging that Vansyckle had not conveyed to the said heirs all the land, as, by his contract, he was bound to do, but charged that ·
he had conveyed but one of said tracts, and in this answer [*432]
she charged a new fact, not responsive to any charge in the
bill, to wit, that said Richards had agreed with her to wait for
the balance due on said notes until she could pay the same out
of the proceeds of said land.

To these several answers, replications were filed, and the
case was at issue.

Upon the trial, the complainant proved by a witness that the
land was sold as charged in the bill, and that the two notes
mentioned in the bill, were given by Leaming, deceased, in part
consideration for said land. The assignment of the notes to
Richards, the complainant, by said Vansyckle, was proven.
The notes and assignments were read in evidence. Three
deeds were read in evidence, clearly proving the conveyance of
all the land as stated in the bill.

There was proof of the allegations in the bill, and the defendants having failed to introduce any evidence whatever, the
court rendered a decree, that the bill be dismissed without prejudice.

To reverse this decree, and procure an order of this court remanding the cause, with instructions to the court below to
render decree in accordance with the prayer of the bill, the case
is brought to this court.

M. McConnel, for Plaintiff in Error.

A. G. Burr, for Defendants in Error.

Caton, C. J. The question in this case is, whether the vendor's lien for the purchase money of land, passes to the assignee
of the note given for the purchase money, by the simple assignment of the note, so that the assignee of the note can enforce
it in his own name and for his own benefit.

The vendor's lien arises from principles of equity alone, and finds no foundation or support in the principles of the common law, or our statute. Courts of equity have created this lien independent of any express contract, upon the mere supposition of the intention of the parties, and whenever from any circumstance, the court can infer that the vendor did not rely upon this lien, for his security, the courts have treated it as waived. Thus the taking of any security, either personal or material, or the neglect to enforce the lien for a considerable time, though short of the time prescribed by the statute of limitations, has been considered as a waiver of the lien. *Conover* v. *Warren*, 1 Gilm. 498; *Trustees* v. *Wright*, 11 Ill. 603. This species of incumbrance upon real estate has never been looked upon with favor in this [*433] State. It is a secret lien, not spread upon the records, which the policy of our law designs should exhibit the true condition of the title to all real estate; and not even resting in any contract or agreement, either in writing or parol. In the first case cited, this court said: "These equitable liens on real estate are generally unknown to the world, and frequently operate injuriously on the rights of creditors and purchasers, and ought not to be enforced, but in cases where the right is clearly and distinctly made out." And again, in the last case, it is said: "These secret liens on real estate, because generally in point of fact—however it may be in legal contemplation—unknown to the parties to be affected by them, are often productive of much injustice, and ought not to be encouraged." We ought not, therefore, to extend this lien beyond the requirements of the settled principles of equity law. In the common law, it has no existence. In England, where it was first created by the court of chancery, acting upon the conscience of the vendor, as it professed, the vendor's lien has never been held assignable in any way by the vendor, although it is held to pass by devise or descent. The right of this lien is confined to the person of the vendor alone, and the apparent exceptions above stated, are not in fact exceptions, for they are common attributes of nearly all personal rights, except those springing from torts. In Maryland, this question is discussed with much learning, by Chancellor Bland, in *Iglehart* v. *Armiger*, Bland. Ch. R. 519;

and the right is held not to pass to the assignee of the note given by the vendee, for the purchase money.   And in the same way was the question decided in *Briggs* v. *Hill*, 6 How. Miss. R. 362; and so by Chancellor Walworth, in *White* v. *Williams*, 1 Paige, 501.   And the Supreme Court of Ohio, in *Bush* v. *Kinsley*, 14 Ohio, 20, held the same rule, although they held that the lien was not absolutely extinguished by the assignment of the note, where the liability of the vendor continued upon the note, by reason of the indorsement, but was in a sort of abeyance and might be revived by the vendor, after he should have paid the note on his liability as indorser.   Kentucky alone has held a different rule, so far as our researches enable us to judge.   See *Thomas* v. *Wyatt*, 5 Monroe, 132.   The case of *Eskridge* v. *M'Clure*, 2 Yerger, 84, is not a case in point, for there the lien was created by a written memorandum at the bottom of the note, declaring that the land should be held as security, for the payment of the note.   This was in fact a written mortgage and was of course assignable, and was an incumbrance widely different from this secret, intangible, vendor's lien, which springs up without bargain and without promise, and very frequently, no doubt, without any intention or even suspicion of either party, at the time of the original [*434] transaction, but is the fruit of the will of the chancellor.   We are satisfied, that the law does not authorize the vendor to transfer this lien with the note, taken for the purchase money, even though he expressly professes to do so, and we are not inclined to make a law to enable him to do so.

The decree must be affirmed.

Decree affirmed.

JOHN H. Cox, Plaintiff in Error, *v.* WILLIAM H. REED *et al.*, Defendants in Error.

ERROR TO WABASH.

A party need not produce or prove a judgment that is not put in issue.

If heirs are brought into court by *scire facias* under the statute, to show cause why they should not be made parties to a judgment, it will be necessary to prove up the case *de novo* against them. Adults cannot demand that more shall be proved against them, when there are infant parties, than if all were adults.

The giving of a bond in satisfaction of a judgment, is in law a payment of it.

THIS case was heard in the Second Grand Division by agreement of parties.

This was an action (begun in Richland, and the venue changed to Wabash,) for breach of covenant of warranty in the deed of Joseph H. Reed, (the ancestors of defendants), dated September 1, 1838, to S. and J. Abernathy, for in lot No. 43, in Mansfield, Ohio.

The lot was afterwards sold and conveyed by F. Wharf, sheriff of Richland county, Ohio, in 1850, to James Weldon, under a judgment and execution of the Farmers' Bank of Mansfield, against S. and J. Abernathy and others, in the Court of Common Pleas of said county.

J. Weldon conveyed the same, December 17, 1850, to John H. Cox, the plaintiff; and Cox conveyed it, February, 11, 1851, to Harriet Pugh, with covenants of warranty.

The heirs of Samuel Lewis, by paramount title, older than the deed of Reed, recovered the same in the ejectment against Harriet Pugh, in September, 1855.

Cox, in 1857, being threatened with suit on his covenants to Harriet Pugh, settled and paid her over $1,100 damages, and the costs and damages recovered by the Lewis heirs, $160, and in 1858 brought this suit against the defendants, heirs of [*435] J. H. Reed, on the covenants in his deed, etc., to recover the damages plaintiff has suffered by the breach thereof.

The several counts in the declaration set forth, that J. H. Reed made a deed, with covenants of warranty, for lot 43, to Samuel and John W. Abernathy; that a judgment was recovered against them by the Farmers' Bank of Mansfield, and the lots sold or conveyed by Frederick Wharf, sheriff, to James Weldon; that Weldon conveyed to John H. Cox; that Cox conveyed, with covenants of warranty, to Harriet Pugh; that Harriet Pugh was by the paramount title of the heirs of Samuel

Lewis; that Cox paid her the damages incurred by breach of his covenants. The names of the heirs of said Reed, as also the heirs of said Lewis, are set forth, and Mary J. Musgrove, and Annette Musgrove, two of said defendants, were minors.

The defendant plead, 1st, *non est factum* to deed of J. H. Reed, and, 2nd, statute of limitations, (sixteen years.)

On these pleas issues were taken, and a trial had at the September term, 1859, before a jury, and a verdict for the plaintiff for $1,375.

The pleas were worded thus: "and the defendants, by their attorneys, came," etc., and signed by the counsel appearing for defendants; the issues were made upon the pleas in that form, and the verdict of the jury was, "we the jury find for the plaintiff;" without any designation by the counsel for the defendants as to who, if not all of the defendants, they did appear for, and without any notice being taken of the minority of Mary J. and Annette Musgrove.

After the return of the verdict and the discharge of the jury, and after the counsel for the plaintiff had left the court, and without any actual notice to them, the counsel for the defendants moved for a new trial, on the ground of the minority of the said Musgrove children, and the motion was allowed.

Afterwards, at the next term, being the first opportunity after the plaintiff had knowledge that the motion for a new trial had been made and granted, he moved to set aside the order for a new trial, and for leave to enter judgment against the other defendants who had appeared and plead, and showed for reason that there had never been any service on the said minors, that they were not in court, that no judgment had been asked or sought against them, and that judgment was only asked against the adult defendants, who by their counsel had appeared and defended; which motion being overruled, the plaintiff excepted.

And the plaintiff assigns for error, the refusal to allow him judgment on the verdict of the jury against the de- [*436] fendants, excepting said minors and *sci. fa.* for them.

On the last trial there were four issues, as follows: *non est factum* to the deed of J. H. Reed; statute of limitations;

non est factum to the deed of F. Wharf, sheriff, etc.; and *non est factum* to the deed of James Weldon. Issues tried by the court, by consent, without a jury.

To the introduction of the deeds and the depositions, there was a general objection made, but upon what grounds the bill of exceptions does not show. The statement in the bill is that "the plaintiff offered and introduced in evidence the following deeds, papers and depositions, to the introduction of which the defendants, by their counsel, at the time objected, and the evidence being heard and the cause finally submitted," etc.

The deed of J. H. Reed contains a covenant of warranty, binding his heirs.

The record of the judgment against S. and J. W. Abernathy and others, shows the judgment was confessed by an attorney in fact; that an execution was levied, and the lot sold by Wharf, as sheriff, to James Weldon; that a report of the sale was made and confirmed, and sheriff ordered to convey; that the proceedings were in the Court of Common Pleas, Richland county, Ohio, and certified by the clerk of the court, and the presiding judge.

The deed of Wharf refers to said judgment and sale, and conveys the lot to James Weldon. Deed was duly acknowledged and recorded.

The deed of James Weldon to John H. Cox, the plaintiff in error, conveys the same lot, and is duly acknowledged and recorded.

The deed of J. H. Cox (plaintiff), to Harriet Pugh, for said lot, is duly acknowledged and recorded, and contains covenants of title and warranty.

The record of the judgment of eviction by the heirs of Samuel Lewis against Harriet Pugh, shows that John F. Lewis and others (as named in plaintiff's declaration) recovered the possession by paramount title, as also judgment against Pugh and others, for $191.50 for rents, which record is duly certified by the clerk of the court and presiding judge, of the same Court of Common Pleas.

The deposition of G. F. Carpenter, proves the payment by

Cox of the damages to the amount of $1,100, and to Lewis' heirs, $160, which he was compelled to pay, to avoid suit by Pugh on the covenant, and which was less than the value of the property. Also proves the deeds to be genuine.

The deposition of J. F. Lewis proves that his father [*437] died seized of the lot, leaving the heirs named as plaintiffs in the suit against Pugh and others, and the same is also proved by Bartley.

The errors assigned are: that the court erred in granting a new trial to defendants, and in overruling the plaintiff's motion to set aside the order for a new trial; that the final judgment of the court was contrary to evidence; that the final judgment of the court was contrary to law; and that the judgment of the court should have been in favor of the plaintiff for his damages.

A. KITCHELL, for Plaintiff in Error.

C. H. CONSTABLE, for Defendants in Error.

CATON, C. J. We shall confine ourselves to the disposition of the points raised in the printed argument of the counsel for the defendants.

The first is, to the authentication of the judgment in Ohio, upon which the premises were sold and the sheriff's deed made. The answer made to this, we think, is conclusive. This is an action of covenant, in which, strictly, there is no general issue, putting the plaintiff upon proof of his whole case, but each fact, which of itself would defeat the plaintiff's action, must be specially pleaded. Here were three pleas of *non est factum,* putting in issue three of the deeds constituting the chain of title, and the statute of limitations. This is all of the declaration which was denied. There was no plea of *non infregit conventionem.* The existence of that judgment, as alleged in the declaration, was not put in issue, and consequently the plaintiff was not called upon to produce or prove it. All he was required to prove was. that which was denied by the defendants, and that was the execution of the deeds. When that was done, the breach of the covenants and the heirship of the defendants, were admitted, and the plaintiff only had to show how much he had been damnified by the breach of the covenant, so that the court might know for how much to render the judgment.

Another objection is made, that some of the defendants were infants. That appears from the declaration, but we do not quite understand the nature of the objection, on this account. They were not served with process, and are not parties to the judgment. When they are brought in by *sci. fa.* under our statute, to show cause why they shall not be made parties to the judgment, it will be necessary to prove up the [*438] case *de novo* against them. These adults, against whom the judgment was rendered, cannot claim that any more shall be proved under the issues which they have formed, when the defendants not served are infants, then would be required if they were adults. As to the defendants served, it was only necessary to prove up the case against all of the defendants, under the pleadings actually formed, and the court will not imagine that if the other defendants had been served, they would have put in other pleas or put the plaintiff to other proof, than is required by the pleas filed.

The giving the bond in satisfaction of the judgment against Cox, was in law a payment of it, as much for the purposes of this cause, as if he had paid it in coin. *Ralston* v. *Wood*, 15 Ill. 159.

The judgment is reversed, and the cause remanded.

Judgment reversed.

JOHN SIDWELL, Plaintiff in Error, *v.* ALFRED LOBLY, Defendant in Error.

ERROR TO CALHOUN.

Although the bill of exceptions does not purport to contain all the evidence, and therefore the refusal to grant a new trial on the weight of evidence, cannot be considered; yet as there was evidence, showing the refusal of an instruction erroneous, the judgment will be reversed.

If there is an actual delivery of property on the payment of money, with the design to make a sale of it, the title passes, except as to prior liens; as between the parties, the sale will be good, if a delivery of the property was all that remained to be done.

THIS was an action of replevin, brought by Lobly, who was plaintiff below, before a justice of the peace, and against Sidwell to recover possession of one cow and calf, one steer and one heifer. Trial and verdict for defendant; appeal to Circuit Court; trial and verdict for plaintiff; motion for new trial, overruled. Case agreed to be heard in Second Grand Division.

Wiley Miller testified, that he, as constable, held execution in favor of one Stebbins, against Lobly, for $21.96, and levied said execution on the property in controversy, and advertised the same for sale on 28th January. On day of sale, Sidwell and Lobly agreed as follows: the property in controversy was given up by Lobly to Sidwell, with an agreement that if he (Lobly) brought the money advanced by Sidwell to him in one month from then, the property should again be- [*439] come his by redemption.

John Sidwell, Jr., testified, that on 1st March following, Lobly begged for and obtained from Sidwell an extension of the time of payment for four weeks, and it was agreed, that the old contract should stand good for the extension.

Martin testified, he heard Sidwell, on 3rd April, 1860, tell Lobly he wanted his money or the cattle. Lobly said he should have them.

At request of plaintiff below, the court instructed the jury as follows:

"That if the jury believe, from the evidence, that Lobly agreed with Sidwell, either to pay him the amount due him by a certain time, or else deliver him the cattle in question as his property, while a failure to comply with said contract would subject Lobly to a suit for damages, it would not authorize Sidwell to take and retain possession of the cattle if the money was not duly paid."

And refused to give the following instruction for defendant below:

" That if they believe that plaintiff delivered up the property in controversy to defendant with his permission to pay the amount advanced and redeem the property in a given period, and said period elapsed without such payment, then defendant's right of possession and ownership was absolute on such failure.'

ALBERT G. BURR, for Plaintiff in Error.

N. M. KNAPP, for Defendant in Error.

WALKER, J. The refusal, of the court below, to give defendant's instruction, is, among other matters, assigned as error. It is this: "That if the jury believe that plaintiff delivered up the property in controversy to defendant, with his permission to pay the amount advanced, and redeem the property in a given period, and said period elapsed without such payment, then defendant's right of ownership was absolute on such failure." Whilst the bill of exceptions fails to state that all of the evidence in the case is embodied, and we are therefore precluded from examining the question, whether the court erred in overruling the motion for a new trial, because the verdict is alleged to be contrary to the weight of evidence, nevertheless we see that there was evidence in the case, upon which to base this instruction.

Miller testified, that the property was given up by defendant [*440] in error, to plaintiff in error, with the agreement, that if the former brought the money to the latter within a month, then the property was to be that of defendant in error.

If there was an actual delivery of the property, on the payment of the money, by plaintiff in error, in satisfaction of the execution, with the design that it should constitute a sale, then it was sufficient to pass the absolute title. This is true not only as between themselves, but as to all persons not having liens upon the property. Or if it was designed to be a complete sale and nothing more remained to be performed, but a delivery of the property, then as between the parties, the title passed, and vested in the purchaser. *Wade* v. *Moffitt*, 21 Ill. 110; *Howard* v. *Babcock*, ib. 295. Had the stock, under this arrangement, died before the time for payment, by defendant in error, had arrived, would any one doubt that plaintiff in error would have been compelled to sustain the loss? If the evidence of Miller is true, and it stands so far as we can see uncontradicted, the property was vested in plaintiff in error, conditionally, if it was redeemed, and absolutely if it was not, at the time specified. There was certainly evidence in the case tending to show that it was a sale, to become absolute upon a failure to pay the money, and there was evidence that it was not paid. This clearly required the giving of this instruction. The judgment of the court below is reversed, for this error, and the cause is remanded.

Judgment reversed.

THE COUNTY COURT OF CALHOUN COUNTY, for the use of Thomas Bradford, Plaintiff in Error, *v.* BALIS BUCK *et al.*, Defendants in Error.

ERROR TO CALHOUN.

There is no lawful mode of renewing an execution, except there has been a return to that already issued by the officer, of his doings thereon. A justice of the peace cannot renew an execution by any indorsement of his upon it.

A constable must, within the time appointed by law, return an execution with an indorsement of his doings thereon, for the truth of which he is responsible; but no particular form of indorsement is required.

All instructions must be based upon evidence.

One constable cannot hand over an execution to another, so as to relieve himself from the responsibility of its return according to the statute; if another constable returns the execution within the statutory time, it may save him from liability, to whom it was first delivered.

THIS cause was tried at the April term, A. D. 1860, [*441] of the Calhoun Circuit Court, before WOODSON, Judge, and a jury.

The opinion of the Court, by Mr. Justice BREESE, gives a full statement of the case.

W. A. GRIMSHAW, and E. L. GROSS, for Plaintiff in Error.

A. G. BURR, for Defendants in Error.

BREESE, J. As this case is somewhat novel in several of its aspects, we will make a full statement of it.

It appears by the record, that the defendant, Balis Buck, was constable of the county of Calhoun, in this State, and his co-defendants were his sureties on his official bond. The suit was originally brought before a justice of the peace on this bond, alleging a failure to return a certain execution within the time required by law. It seems that one Bradford, for whose use the suit was instituted by the county of Calhoun, had, on the 17th of April, 1858, before William B. Johnson, a justice of the peace, recovered a judgment against one McKinney and Gray, for thirty and fifty one-hundredths dollars and costs. Execution was issued and delivered to Buck, the constable, as Johnson testifies, on the 11th of May following, though the time was not indorsed on the execution. Johnson also testifies, that "towards the end of the life of the execution," Buck brought the execution to his office, and wished him to take it back, which he said he would do, if Buck would make a return of some kind on the back of the execution, and sign his name to it as constable, which Buck refused to do, and took the execution away with him.

On the 17th of July following, one M. H. Champlin, also a constable of Calhoun county, brought the same execution to the justice, Johnson, and requested him to "*alias it.*" To this, the justice replied, he would give him a new one if he would return the old one. Champlin replied, that he did not want that, but wanted the justice to write on the back of the old writ, "alias by order of the constable," and sign his name to it as justice of the peace. The justice remarked, if Champlin could make the money, he supposed it would be all right, but he did not think such a proceeding was law, but he did indorse on the execution the writing now on it: "Alias by order of the constable, July 17, 1858. Wm. B. Johnson, J. P." Champlin then took the execution away with him, and retained it until the 12th of October following, and then brought it to the justice, with these indorsements on it: "No property found to. M. Chap, constable. August 17th." Which is un- [*442] derstood to be an abbreviation of "M. H. Champlin," the constable's real name.

On this state of facts, the Circuit Court, to which the case had been brought by appeal, on motion of the defendant's attorney, instructed the jury, "That if they believe, from the evidence, that the justice of the peace received the execution in question from Buck, the constable, and before the expiration of return time, and gave it to another constable, that then neither Buck nor his sureties are answerable for any irregularities of either the justice of the peace or succeeding constable;" and "That there is no special form of indorsement necessary to constitute a return on an execution."

On behalf of the plaintiff, this instruction was asked: "The court instructs the jury that if they believe, from the evidence, that the execution was delivered to Buck, Buck had no right to transfer said execution to another constable, and could not thereby escape from the responsibility of returning said execution according to the statute." Which was given, with this modification: "But if he did transfer said execution to another constable, who, within the proper time, required by law, took it to the justice who issued it, who indorsed it as an *alias* execution, and gave it to the constable to whom it had been transferred, then the defendants are not liable."

The plaintiff, at the proper time, excepted to the instructions given for the defendant, and to the modification of the one asked by him.

The jury found for the defendants, whereupon the plaintiff moved for a new trial, assigning as reasons, these instructions of the court, and because the verdict was against the law and evidence. The motion being overruled, an exception was taken, and a bill of exceptions signed, and the case brought here by writ of error. The errors assigned question the correctness of these instructions.

It is the first case of which we have any knowledge, wherein a writ of execution has been attempted to be renewed, by such an indorsement of the justice of the peace who issued it, as is here shown. We can find no authority for it in the statute, and must regard it as of no effect whatever, however convenient the practice may be. It is insisted, by the defendants' counsel, that when the execution was indorsed, "alias by order of the constable," it was in fact returned by the constable, and within the statutory time. It was certainly within the seventy days when these acts were done, but they do not constitute a legal return of the writ. We know of no lawful [*443] mode by which an execution can be renewed, except by the actual return of the first or old execution with a proper indorsement of the officer thereon.

Our statute provides that all executions issued by a justice of the peace, shall be directed to any constable of the proper county, and made returnable to the justice who issues it within seventy days from the date; and that requirement is a part of the writ. (Scates' Comp. ch. 59, sec. 54, page 706.)

The constable must see to it that he makes his return within the time, and though it may be true, as stated by the court to the jury in the second instruction given for the defendants, that no special form of indorsement is necessary to constitute a return, still some indorsement is indispensable, and an execution cannot be said to be legally returned, without some sort of an indorsement upon it, for the truth of which the constable is responsible. The second instruction was calculated to mislead the jury; being told that no especial form was requisite, they may have inferred that no indorsement whatever of a return was necessary, and so they must have understood it.

As to the first instruction, we have often decided, that all instructions should be based on the evidence in the cause. This principle condemns the first instruction, for there is no evidence whatever that the justice, at any time, received the execution from constable Buck and gave it to another constable. The facts are, that Champlin obtained the execution from Buck himself, and not from the justice of the peace. This instruction, therefore, should not have been given, there being no evidence on which to base it.

As to the instruction asked by the defendants, we think it should have been given substantially as asked, certainly without the modification of the court. If we understand that instruction, it tends to say to the jury this, and nothing more, that Buck had no right so to transfer the execution to another constable, as to relieve him, to whom it was first delivered, from the responsibility of its return according to the statute. We do not deny the right of one constable, under certain circumstances, to hand over his writs to be executed by another constable, for the writs are all directed to any constable, and it cannot matter what constable executes them, so that they are executed and returned according to law. By so transferring his writs, the constable cannot relieve himself of responsibility, unless the writ be returned within the statutory time. Here there was no return until the lapse of more than ninety days.

By Sec. 118 of Chap. 59, it is provided, if any constable shall neglect, or fail to return an execution within ten [*444] days after its proper return day, etc., the party aggrieved may have his action, etc., against the constable and his sureties on the official bond of the constable, and shall recover thereon the amount of the execution, with interest, etc. (Scates' Comp. 713.)

The law makes it absolutely necessary that some return of an officer should be made to an execution, by which he may be charged, for until it is returned with a proper indorsement upon it, the plaintiff's hands are tied—he is incapable of any other action toward the collection of his debt which the law affords. He cannot, in default of personal property, to be manifested by the return, file a transcript in the clerk's office of the Circuit Court, so as bind the real estate of the defendant. He cannot issue an execution to another county—he cannot resort to garnishee process—he cannot issue a capias against the body of the debtor; of all these advantages and privileges is the plaintiff in execution deprived, by the neglect or refusal of the constable to return the writ, with a proper indorsement thereon.

These views dispose of the case, and must reverse the judgment. The cause will be remanded for further proceedings not inconsistent with this opinion.

Judgment reversed.

PERRY STEPHENS, Plaintiff in Error, *v.* PETER BICHNELL, Defendant in Error.

ERROR TO CLARK.

Upon the foreclosure of a mortgage given to secure the purchase money for premises, it is not necessary that the wife of the mortgagor should be made a party to the bill.

Where the mortgagor is insolvent, and the premises are not worth the amount due upon the mortgage, a strict foreclosure may be decreed.

Where a defendant to a suit in chancery has suffered a default, it is discretionary with the court to require evidence sustaining the allegations in the bill, and he cannot assign for error that the proof was insufficient.

Collins and Stephens purchased land jointly, giving their joint notes secured by a mortgage upon the same premises for the purchase money. They then partitioned the premises, each agreeing to provide for a specified proportion of the purchase money. Collins paid up his part and procured a release of the premises set off to him. *Held*, that it was proper for the mortgagee, in foreclosing, to take a decree against Stephens alone for the balance due.

THIS was a bill filed, in the Circuit Court of Clark county, [*445] by Peter Bichnell, the defendant in error, against the plaintiff in error, and Amos Collins and William Collins, to foreclose a mortgage. The bill states the sale of the premises by complainant to the defendants, Perry Stephens and Amos Collins, and the execution of notes and a mortgage upon the same premises to secure the purchase money. The mortgage was executed and acknowledged by Amos Collins and Stephens and his wife. That Collins and Stephens subsequently made a partition of the premises, and agreed that each should assume and pay off a certain proportion of the indebtedness secured by the mortgage. That Amos Collins had paid off his proportion of the payment, and that complainant had released to him the land allotted to him by the partition. That Stephens had failed to pay his part of the debt, that the land set off to him was not worth the amount due upon the mortgage, and that Stephens was insolvent. That Stephens had neglected to pay taxes, and thereby compelled complainant to pay them to protect himself, and that complainant had been compelled to pay the costs in a suit to enjoin Amos Collins and Stephens from committing waste on the premises, which costs were awarded against the defendant. That William Collins claimed some interest in premises, but that the nature and extent of it was unknown to complainant, but that such claim was fictitious and fraudulent. Prayed a strict foreclosure as to the portion of the mortgaged premises set off to Stephens by the partition.

Service was had on Stephens, and notice of publication as to Amos and William Collins. Default as to all the defendants, and a decree that Stephens pay the balance due upon the mortgage with interest, the amount paid by complainant for taxes and the costs in the injunction suit, within four months, or in default thereof, that he be forever barred and foreclosed of all equity of redemption in the premises.

Stephens brings the case to this court by writ of error.

C. H. CONSTABLE, for Plaintiff in Error.

JOHN SCHOLFIELD, for Defendant in Error.

BREESE, J. This case is submitted on the record and assignment of errors, and briefs and authorities. The principal errors are, the want of necessary parties to the bill, in decreeing a strict foreclosure, and insufficiency of the evidence. The case was, a bill filed by mortgagee against the mortgagors of certain lands for a strict foreclosure, and a decree *pro confesso* rendered. The mortgage was given to secure the payment of the purchase money of the lands, and was executed simultaneously with the [*446] deed, and the wife of one of the mortgagors was not made a party to the bill. Section four, of chapter 34, provides, where a husband shall purchase lands during coverture, and shall mortgage such lands to secure the payment of the purchase money thereof, his widow shall not be entitled to dower out of such lands, as against the mortgagee, or those claiming under him, although she shall not have united in such mortgage. (Scates' Comp. 152.) This was the rule at the common law. The seizin of the husband passing from him *eo instanti* that he acquired it, and being immediately revested in the grantor, the widow could not claim dower in the premises. *Stow* v. *Tift*, 15 Johns. R. 461; 14 Kent's Com. 38, 39, and cases cited in note (*a*). If then the widow would not be endowable, the wife, whilst the husband is living, can have no interest in the premises, and consequently she need not be a party to the bill.

The object in making the wife a party, is to bar her dower. *Gilbert* v. *Maggard*, 1 Scam. 471. So in the case of *Leonard* v. *Adm'r of Villars*, 23 Ill. 379, this court held, that the wife of a mortgagee was a necessary party to a bill to foreclose, but that was a case where the mortgage was not given to secure the purchase money, for the land mortgaged. In that case the wife had a dower interest, as against the mortgagee, and the equity of redemption of such dower interest remained in her, and she was, therefore, a necessary party to protect that interest.

As to decreeing a strict foreclosure, that was discretionary with the court, under the circumstances. It is alleged in the bill, and confessed, that the lands mortgaged are not equal in value to the purchase money due; it was then in the discretion of the court to decree a strict foreclosure, the effect of which is to vest the title absolutely in the mortgagee. The usual mode in this State, of foreclosing a mortgage, is by ordering the mortgaged premises to be sold, yet the power of strict foreclosure is frequently exercised, and probably, never refused when the interests of both parties manifestly require it, as when the mortgagor is insolvent, and the mortgaged premises are not of sufficient value to pay the debt and costs, as in this case, the bill averring both insolvency of the mortgagor and insufficiency of the mortgaged premises, and those allegations are confessed, and the bill prays a strict foreclosure. We have no statute prohibiting a strict foreclosure. *Johnson* v. *Donnel*, 15 Ill. 97; *Vansant* v. *Almon*, 23 id. 33.

It cannot now be urged here, that the evidence, on which

the decree passed, was insufficient, the rule being well settled, that when a bill is taken for confessed, the party [*447] against whom the decree is taken cannot complain and assign for error, the insufficiency of the evidence. , The nineteenth section of our chancery code provides that, " where a bill is taken for confessed, the court, before a final decree is made, if deemed requisite, may order the complainant to produce documents and witnesses to prove the allegations of his bill, or may examine the complainant on oath or affirmation, touching the facts therein alleged; such decree shall be made in either case, as the court shall consider equitable and proper."

With such a discretion vested in the court, it could not be urged, that the court acted upon insufficient proof, because, it would not be error to pass a decree without any proof. *Manchester et al.* v. *McKee, Ex'r,* 4 Gilm. 517.

As to the error assigned in not taking a decree against the two Collins, it is only necessary to say. there was no necessity for a decree against them, as they and Stephens had divided the land between them, and had paid complainant for their share, and the foreclosure was brought only against Stephens' interest. The defendants Collins, were so, nominally only, and they do not complain of want of notice or bring the case here. It was Stephens' interest in the land, that was affected. It was quite proper to decree that Stephens should pay the balance due on the mortgage, as the Collins had paid their proportion, and had been released. We see no error in the decree, and accordingly affirm the decree.

Judgment affirmed.

Hebert *et al. v.* Lavalle.

[*448] JOHN B. HEBERT, *et al.*, Appellants, *v.* FRANCIS
LAVALLE, Appellee.

APPEAL FROM ST. CLAIR.

The United States has, by grant, confirmed to the inhabitants of the village
of Cahokia the use of the "commons" adjacent to the village. The parishioners not living in the village, worshiping at the church in the village, do not, of right, participate in the use of those "commons."

Parties deriving title from original inhabitants of the village of Cahokia, do
not enjoy rights of common which might have pertained to their grantors,
if the grantees have abandoned the village. The "commons" were made
appurtenant to village lots, not to lands remote from the village.

Occupants of the common field lands, not inhabitants of the village of
Cahokia, cannot vote for the supervisor authorized to survey parts of the
"commons" into lots and lease the same, nor for the trustees of schools,
under authority of the act of 1841.

A stranger cannot question the acts of "commoners" amongst themselves,
even though they should enclose the "commons."

THE opinion of the Court, by Mr. Justice BREESE, gives a full
statement of the case. The cause was heard in the Second
Grand Division, by agreement of parties.

G. KŒRNER, for Appellants.

JEHU BAKER, and N. NILES, for Appellee.

BREESE, J. The complainants filed their bill in chancery for
an injunction, in the St. Clair Circuit Court, to the March term,
1860, (an injunction having been granted by the judge in
vacation,) alleging, that the complainants were all citizens of
St. Clair county, and residents of the Cahokia *common field;*
that by certain ancient grants under the French and English
Colonial Government, confirmed by acts of Congress under the
Confederation, and under the present Constitution, and by the
Constitution of the State of Illinois of 1818, and various Acts
of the General Assembly of Illinois, the inhabitants of the
village of Cahokia have enjoyed the right of pasturage, estovers,
etc., etc., in common, in a certain tract of land, known from

time immemorial as the *Cahokia Commons.* That by the same grants and confirmations, there was allotted to each head of family, of said village, a certain tract for cultivation, all of which tracts were enclosed under one common fence, and are known as the *Cahokia Common field.* That the grants were contemporaneous grants with the grant of lots to certain families then living in the settlement known as Cahokia, or Coes or Cahokia village, the village not being [*449] then laid out, surveyed and defined. That what is now known as Cahokia village, was surveyed and platted as late as 1808. That the village with attendant common field, which extended from Cahokia creek, to the Bluffs, east of the Mississippi river, was on the south, north and east surrounded by said commons, which commons were to support the cultivated fields of the inhabitants. That in the course of time, many of the inhabitants of the village of Cahokia, who had resided within the territory of what is now known as Cahokia village, and near there, removed into the common field, for the purpose of better cultivating their respective allotments, and that in the course of time, a majority of families who had resided in the village, and their successors, (the grants being to the inhabitants and their successors,) had removed on to the common fields. Complainants allege, that they hold their lands in the common field by titles of the original inhabitants, and that all *inhabitants of the common field are equally entitled to the enjoyment of the commons, in the use thereof,* and whatever proceeds may be derived therefrom, and that they have so claimed, from time immemorial.

That the General Assembly of Illinois, passed an act, 17th February, 1841, providing, that the commons, or any part thereof, might be surveyed in lots, and leased for any number of years not exceeding one hundred years; that the leases should be publicly sold after notice, and that the proceeds arising from the sales, should be appropriated to the education of the children of the inhabitants of the village of Cahokia; that by virtue of that act a portion of said commons was surveyed, platted and leased, the balance thereof, being about—— acres, remaining undisposed of; that by a subsequent act, 18th February, 1857, it was further provided, that the lots, laid out on the commons, might be leased at private sale, provided they should not be leased for a less price or sum per acre, than the average price at which the other parts of the commons were then leased.

Complainants, claiming as aforesaid, allege that they are informed and believe, that one Francis Lavalle, at present supervisor of the inhabitants of the village of Cahokia, has caused the balance, or part of the commons heretofore unsurveyed, to be surveyed, and at the instigation of, and by collusion with, certain inhabitants of the village, has already leased certain lots of said Cahokia commons at private sale, at mere nominal rates, and without reference to said average price, and is about to proceed to lease at private sale other of said lots collusively and fraudulently for a large number of years, usually ninety-[*450] nine years, to the very great detriment of all persons interested in the commons. That complainants are informed, that he has already made arrangements, with certain inhabitants of the village, who wrongfully claim the sole and entire use of the commons, and the proceeds thereof, to distribute the leases of the newly surveyed lots amongst them, at their choice, and at merely nominal rates, in a private manner, claiming, that under the last act of the legislature, no publicity whatever is necessary. Complainants allege, that by such a disposition of their valuable estate, their rights will irretrievably be prejudiced, as such leases may be assigned to innocent purchasers, and that the title of the lots may be clouded, by leases given, even to participants in the fraud. That Lavalle refuses to account to complainants for his actings and doings and to give an account of the proceeds of the leases made by his predecessors and himself, contending, that complainants have no part or interest in the commons—that the law contemplates public leases, and private leases only in case of forfeiture, etc., etc. That the supervisor is a trustee for all who are entitled to a share in the commons, and that he is abusing his trust.

Complainants prayed an injunction restraining supervisor to lease illegally, and from applying the proceeds to the exclusive use of the few persons residing in Cahokia, and that the defendant render an account, etc., etc.

The defendant filed a general demurrer. The court sustained the demurrer, dissolved the injunction, and dismissed the bill, and from this decision the complainants take this appeal.

The only error assigned, is the decision of the court below, in sustaining the demurrer, dissolving the injunction, and dismissing the bill.

A slight glance at the early history of this State, may throw some light upon the question presented by this record, one new to our courts, and with no aid to be derived from adjudicated cases.

Anterior to the voyage of the Jesuit Priest, Father James Marquette, with the Sieur Joliet, in the summer of 1673, prosecuted under the auspices of Mons. Talon, the Intendant of New France, as Canada was called, and then under the crown of France, but little, if any, authentic information existed, of the river Mississippi. The Jesuit Father, with his companions, proceeding from Canada, by way of Green Bay and the Wisconsin river, entered the Mississippi, on the tenth of June, 1673, and explored it to the mouth of the Arkansas, and returned, by way of the Illinois river, in September of that year. This was an exploration undertaken by the [*451] French Government, to be conducted on a larger scale subsequently, when, in 1678, Robert Cavalier De LaSalle obtained letters patent from Louis XIV, dated 12th of May of that year. By this patent, LaSalle was permitted " to endeavor to discover the western part of New France," the king having at heart this discovery, " through which, it was probable, a road might be found. to penetrate to Mexico." LaSalle was permitted to construct forts wherever necessary, and to hold them on the same terms as he held Fort Frontenac under his patent of March 13, 1675. Acting under this patent of 1678, LaSalle, with a small party, reached, by way of the Illinois river, on the ninth of April, 1682, the mouth of the Mississippi, and took formal possession of it, and of the country watered by the river, in the name of Louis XIV, and in his honor, called the country Louisiana.

In virtue of the authority, under his letters patent, LaSalle constructed Fort St. Louis, at the "Starved Rock," on the Illinois river, and other forts on the lakes, and Mississippi river. He seemed to have entire control of this portion of Louisiana, establishing his government at the Fort St. Louis, where it remained until sixteen hundred and ninety.

In the meantime, Jesuit missionaries advanced into the country, from the Seminary of Quebec, one of whom, James Gravier, as early as 1695, established the village of "our Lady of Kaskaskias," and there officiated at the altar, for several years, in the midst of populous tribes of Indians, laboring to convert them to christianity.

In the month of July, 1698, the Bishop of Quebec granted letters patent to the directors and superiors of the Seminary of Foreign Missions there, for the establishment of a mission for the Tamarois and Kahokias "living between the Illinois and Arancies," their country being considered as the key and passage to more distant tribes. They were empowered to send their missionaries there, and "to make such residences, and erect such missions as they might judge proper."

In pursuance of this authority, "the Mission of St. Sulpice" was established among the Tamarois and Kahokia Indians, and a village grew up, called "the village of the Holy Family of Caoquias," populated by Indians, fur traders, and tillers of the soil, all within the shadow of the Church of the Mission. This church was the nucleus of the village, the ground necessary for it, and land for the use of the villagers, being readily granted by the native owners.

From the time LaSalle took possession of the country in 1682, we discover no trace of a control by the crown of France, [*452] over it, until the grant to Anthony Crozat, by letters patent under date of September 14, 1712, of the whole commerce of the country, then for the first time, officially, called Louisiana. The Jesuit missionaries appear, up to this period, to have exercised all the control, necessary, over its people, subject to no power other than their superiors of the Seminary of Quebec.

Crozat made efforts to develop the lead mines of Missouri,

Hebert *et al. v.* Lavalle.

and imported many laborers and others, to the several missions on the Mississippi river, but failing to find the precious metals in which it was thought this country abounded, he, in 1717, surrendered his patent to the then occupant of the throne, the infant king, Louis XV, who ruled France, under the regency of the Duke of Orleans. He, in conjunction with the celebrated Law, established "the Company of the West," or "Company of the Indies," to whom was granted all Louisiana, with power, in conjunction with an officer of the crown, to grant away the royal domain. The early records of this State, preserved in the French language, are full of grants made by this company, up to 1732, when it was dissolved, and its powers and privileges reverted to the crown.

Among these records, is to be found a grant substantially as follows:

We, Pierre Duguet de Boisbriant, Knight of the Military Order of St. Louis, and First Lieutenant of the King in the Province of Louisiana, Commandant in the Illinois; and Marc Antonia de la Loire Des Ursins, Principal Commissary of the Royal Company of the Indies:

On the demand of the missionaries of the Caokias and Tamarois, to grant to them a tract of four leagues square in fee simple, with the neighboring island, to be taken a quarter of a league above the small river of Caokias, situated above the Indian village, and in going up following the course of the Mississippi, and in returning towards the Fort of Chartres, running in depth to the north, east and south for quantity. We in consequence of our powers have granted the said land to the Missionaries of Coakias and Tamarois, in fee simple, over which, they can, from the present, work, clear and plant the land, awaiting a formal concession which will be sent from France by the directors general of the Royal Company of the Indies. At the Fort of Chartres, this 22nd June, A. D. 1722. Signed Boisbriant—Des Ursins.

On this grant, documentary evidence presented by counsel in the argument of the case shows, that a village was established and village lots granted. On the explosion of "the Company of the West," on the 10th of April, 1732, their

[*453] powers and privileges reverted to the crown, from which emanated, thereafter, all grants of land.   In August, 1743, this grant made in 1722, was recognized by the French Government, acting through Mons. Vaudrieul, then Governor, and Salmon, Commissary, of the Province of Louisiana.

It will be perceived, there are no words in this grant, designating the land granted, or any portion of it, as commons—nor does it appear for what special use it was granted, but generally, for the use of the mission there established.   Upon it the missionaries established their church and village—granted portions of it for cultivation, whilst the largest portion was suffered to remain for the common use of the inhabitants, for pasturage, wood, and other purposes.   It is a peculiarity attending the early French settlements here, that the tillers of the soil did not reside upon their cultivated lands, but in the village. There were their barns and stables and out-lots for the protection of their cattle, and appurtenant to it was the common, on which their animals could range and feed.   The tillable land was granted in narrow strips, usually about one arpent in width, and in depth for quantity, some of which arpents were situate more than four miles from the village, going north.

After the conquest of the country by England, the result of the war commenced in 1756, and terminated by the treaty of Paris of 1763, no interference was attempted with any of the grants made by the India Company, or by the crown of France, in this part of Louisiana, nor by Virginia, after its conquest by her arms, in 1778.   Virginia ceded the country to the United States, by deed dated March 1, 1784, by authority of an act for that purpose, passed, October 20, 1783.   That act provides, " that the French and Canadian inhabitants, and other settlers of the Kaskaskias, Saint Vincents and the neighboring villages, who have professed themselves citizens of Virginia, shall have their possessions and titles confirmed to them, and be protected in the enjoyment of their rights and liberties." (Scates' Comp. 19.) On the 29th August, 1788, the Congress of the Confederation adopted a resolution, instructing the Governor of the Western Territory, to proceed without delay to the French settlements on the river Mississippi, and to examine the titles and possessions of those settlers, "in which they are to be confirmed." Hence originated a class of titles known in this State as "a Governor's confirmation," a specimen of which is found in the case of *Doe ex. dem., etc.,* v. *Hill,* Breese, 236, new edition, 304.

On the 3rd of March, 1791, the Congress of the United States passed an act for granting lands to the inhabitants and settlers at Vincennes and the Illinois country, in the territory [*454] north-west of the Ohio, and for confirming them in their possession, the fifth section of which provides, "that a tract of land containing about five thousand four hundred acres, which for many years has been fenced and used by the inhabitants of Vincennes as a common, also a tract of land including the villages of Cohos and Prairie du Pont, and heretofore used by the inhabitants of the said villages as a common, be, and the same are hereby appropriated to the use of the inhabitants of Vincennes, and of the said villages respectively, to be used by them as a common, until otherwise disposed of by law." Laws of U. S., vol. 1, page 221.

Here is the first recognition, by the act of any government, of a right of any of the inhabitants of the village of Cahokia, to land as common. Subsequently, commissioners were appointed by an act of Congress, to examine into this, among other claims to land in Illinois, and they examined, and confirmed this claim as a common to the inhabitants of Cahokia, on the 21st December, 1809, and so reported to the Congress, and Congress, on the 1st of May, 1810, passed an act, that all the decisions made by these commissioners entered in their transcript, bearing date December 31, 1809, and transmitted to the Secretary of the Treasury, be confirmed. 2nd vol. Laws of U. S., page 607.

This act is an operative grant of all the interest the United States may, at any time, have had in the land described in the transcript of the commissioners under that date, and confirms the land in terms, to the inhabitants of these "villages" respectively. Now it cannot be material to inquire, to what uses these lands were originally appropriated by the Priests of the Mission; the government, having power to confirm the title to them, or to grant them, having restricted the grant to the inhabitants of those villages as a common.

But it is argued, that the term village must not have the restricted signification which modern ideas of a village would place upon it, but that it may well be understood to mean "the settlement" or the parish, and in that sense it was understood by the missionaries themselves, as their letters on the subject referred to in the argument tend to show.

We do not understand, from anything in those letters, or from any facts in the case brought to our notice, that the parishioners — those who worshiped at the village church, and were under the spiritual control of its priest, and not living in the village, possessed any village rights belonging to the villagers. A parish is understood to be, the territorial jurisdiction of a secular priest, or a precinct, the inhabitants [*455] of which belong to the same church, or they may reside promiscuously, among people belonging to any church, and be resident in several villages. A village is any small assemblage of houses occupied by artisans, laboring people and farmers—in French villages, also by farmers. It is a defined locality with a name, and its inhabitants are called villagers. We have no right to suppose, that Congress, in making this grant to the inhabitants of the village of Cahokia, designed to include persons who resided on, and occupied lands, miles remote from the village, though the fact might be, that they worshiped at the parish church, and were under the spiritual teaching of the village priest. The term "inhabitants of the village," having a defined and well understood meaning, we do not see how it can be made, by any reasonable construction, to embrace other persons who are not, by their own showing, inhabitants of the village.

It is also argued by the complainants' counsel, that inasmuch as the complainants derive their titles to the lands in the common field, from original inhabitants of the village of Cahokia, they should have all the rights which, at any time, might have pertained to their grantors. This would be true undoubtedly, had they remained inhabitants of the village, and they would have been their "successors," in contemplation of the act of

1819. Laws of 1819, page 122. A removal from the village, by occupying their individual allotments in the common field remote from the village, was an abandonment of their village rights, for it is only to inhabitants of the village that a right of common has been granted. It was to them as inhabitants of the village, the right was granted, and we cannot see the justice of a claim which shall accord to those who have abandoned the village, rights equal to those who remain in it, as inhabitants of it. The act of Congress cited, appropriates this land as a common, to the inhabitants of the village—not to those who might own lands in the common field, and reside upon them. It was made appurtenant to the village lots, and not to arable lands remote from the village for which there were individual and exclusive grants.

It certainly could not have been in the contemplation of Congress, in conferring or granting these lands as a common, to the inhabitants of the village, that by any construction, a class of settlers living separate and apart as farmers on their own lands, should claim, or desire even the benefit of the commons. The object of the grant of commons to the inhabitants of the village, was, evidently to afford them such estovers, pasturage, etc., as they could not otherwise possess and enjoy, villagers being confined to small lots for dwellings, and the necessary outhouses. The domain of the proprietor of a farm is [*456] supposed to embrace within it, all these essentials to a comfortable subsistence, he being the exclusive owner of all he occupies. No necessity would seem to exist for such a convenience, and therefore is it, that the grant was made "to the inhabitants of the village" exclusively. In adverting to the legislation of our own State in reference to the commons, it will be found to be in harmony with the view we have taken of the question.

It is provided by section eight of article eight, of the constitution of 1818, that all lands which have been granted as a common, to the inhabitants of any town, hamlet, village, or corporation, shall forever remain common to the inhabitants of such town, hamlet, village or corporation. (Scates' Comp. 54.)

Substantially the same provision is found in the constitution of 1848, article eleven. (Ib. 72.)

A restriction to the inhabitants of the village, pervades all our legislation on the subject. Laws of 1819, page 122.

By the act of February 17, 1841, (Session Laws, pp. 65, 66,) it is provided that the supervisor elected by the inhabitants of the village of Cahokia, is authorized to cause to be surveyed in lots, etc., any part of the commons of Cahokia, and lease the same, etc. It is a pertinent inquiry here, can the occupiers of the common field lands, not being inhabitants of the village, but residing out of it on their individual lands, vote at the election of this officer, or vote for the trustees of schools as provided in the fourth section? Was such a claim ever advanced? We think this inquiry, answered, as it must be, in the negative, goes far to dispose of the case. They cannot vote for a supervisor of the commons, because they are not inhabitants of the village, nor, for the same reason, can they enjoy the benefit of the proceeds of the common to be derived from the leases; they are isolated from it by their residence.

The principle is well settled that a stranger cannot question the acts of commoners among themselves, no matter how subversive they may be of the objects of the grant, even if extending to an actual enclosing of the commons. And the complainants here being strangers, not inhabitants of the village, cannot be allowed to interfere with the acts of the commoners of which complaint is made. The demurrer goes to the very substance of the bill, and was properly sustained. The decree is affirmed.

Decree affirmed.

JONATHAN LEACH, Appellant, *v.* WILLIAM [*457]
THOMAS, Trustee, etc., Appellee.

APPEAL FROM LAWRENCE.

A judgment in favor of a corporation, if properly assigned, may be enforced
after the corporation has ceased.

A trustee appointed by a court, though not invested with legal title to property, has such equitable title as will enable him to proceed in his own name
in aid of the trust.

When a court of equity obtains jurisdiction, and gives to a party all that he
had asked by a motion in a proceeding at law, he cannot complain of a
proceeding that has not done him an injury.

ON the 25th of April, 1860, the appellee filed his bill of complaint against appellant, in the Lawrence Circuit Court alleging—

That at the May term, 1843, at the Circuit Court of Lawrence county, the president, directors and company of the Bank
of Illinois, recovered a judgment against appellant, for $223,
and costs of suit, upon which judgment execution was issued
to the sheriff of Lawrence county, and by him returned without any levy or other service indorsed thereon.

That on the 2nd of July, 1852, a second execution was issued,
and levied on the west part of the north-east quarter of Section 12, Town 3 north, Range 12 west, in said county, and returned indorsed "No sale for want of bidders."

That on the 10th of April, 1845, the president, directors and
company of the Bank of Illinois assigned, transferred and conveyed, by a written instrument, called an assignment, to A. G.
Caldwell and E. Z. Ryan, as assignees, all of the personal
estate, rights and credits, notes, bonds and payments of every
kind, due at the bank of Shawneetown and the branch at Lawrenceville; and filed a copy of assignment with his bill.

That the judgment aforesaid was for a debt due at Lawrenceville.

That at the December term, 1850, of the United States Circuit Court for the district of Illinois, in the case of the Bank

of Missouri against Ryan, Caldwell, Smith and Dunlap, as signees of the Bank of Illinois, the said court, by decree appointed said Caldwell, Joseph Gillespie and William Brown, trustees, to take charge of the effects of said Bank of Illinois.

That Caldwell alone had acted as trustee under said decree, and in July, 1851, departed this life.

[*458] That in July, 1851, said court appointed appellee, sole trustee, instead of said Caldwell.

That the assignees, in obedience to said decree, on the 29th of October, 1851, by their deed, assigned to appellee, as trustee, all the effects of said bank in their hands. Copy of the assignment filed.

That on the 22nd of April, 1859, appellee caused a *ven. expon.* to issue, and on the 21st of May, 1859, the sheriff sold said land to appellee, for $459.56, judgment and costs.

That appellant, at the September term, of Lawrence Circuit Court, 1859, served notice upon appellee, of his intention to move the court to quash the writ, upon which the sale was made, and set aside said sale—1st, Because said writ was issued contrary to law; 2nd, Because no judgment existed upon which said writ could legally issue; 3rd, Because no plaintiff was in existence at the time of issuing the same; and 4th, Because said land was not subject to execution, and was improperly sold.

That said motion is yet pending and undetermined.

The appellee shows that there is yet outstanding and unredeemed, of the Bank of Illinois, $30,000 in bills and certificates, and that there is due from said bank to the State of Illinois, $295,000.

That it is duty of appellee to collect and pay; that the land sold as aforesaid is part of the fund or means of redeeming the bills and paying amount due the State.

That Leach, the appellant, does not pretend that he does not owe the amount for which the land has sold.

That appellee is the trustee and representative of the creditors of the Bank of Illinois.

That appellant is justly indebted to trustee the amount the land sold for.

That by the act of the legislature, entitled "An act to reduce the public debt one million of dollars, and put the Bank of Illinois in liquidation," approved February 25th, 1843, the charter of said bank was continued four years from 4th of March, 1843.

That by an act of 25th of February, 1845, supplementary to the last recited act, the assignees were allowed four years to make final settlement, and by act of 10th of February, 1849, the time was extended to 1st of January, 1851.

That at the time of levy of the execution, and the sale of said land, appellant was in possession, claiming title to said land.

That since service of notice of motion, the appellee has examined records and made inquiry in regard to appellant's title to said land, but can find none; that he is informed [*459] that a son of appellant in his lifetime, now dead, claimed to be the owner.

Prays, that appellant be required to answer and say whether he has title to said land, or has had since the rendition of said judgment, and if he has parted with said title, to whom and when. That appellant be enjoined from further prosecuting his motion to set aside sale, and from selling the land, and if on hearing that he make his selection, if the court shall find appellant's title to be good, to pay the amount it sold for, or permit the sale to stand. Or if it should appear that the sale passed no title, that sale may be set aside, and a decree for the amount of the debt aforesaid be rendered against appellant in person, and execution be awarded; and, prayer for general relief.

Injunction granted, issued and served on the 31st of July, 1860.

The defendant below, and appellant in this court, filed a demurrer to bill of complainant and joinder. At September term, 1860, the demurrer was overruled, injunction made perpetual, and decree that the appellant pay to the appellee $437, amount of principal, and $59, costs of this suit, and on failure to pay, that the land be sold by the master, to wit: The west part of the north-east quarter of Section 15, Town 3 north, Range 12 west, or so much thereof as will pay the debt, to be

Leach *v.* Thomas.

taken off the north side, and that the defendant surrender the possession to the purchaser.

The errors assigned are, that—

The court erred in awarding an injunction to restrain appellant from prosecuting his motion to set aside sale of land under execution.

In overruling appellant's demurrer to the bill of complaint.

In making injunction perpetual.

In decreeing that there was to appellee as trustee, from appellant, principal and interest on judgments in appellee's bill mentioned.

In decreeing the land to be sold.

In ordering said land to be sold upon an insufficient, vague and uncertain description.

BOWMAN & HARROW, for Appellant.

W. THOMAS, for Appellee.

WALKER, J., delivered the opinion of the court. The fact [*460] that the charter of the bank may have expired before this judgment was paid, does not release the appellant from its payment, if there is any person who holds either the legal or equitable title. If the plaintiff had been a natural person, and he had assigned it, the assignee would have acquired an equitable title, and it could not be said that the death of the plaintiff would release or satisfy the judgment, and prevent the assignee from having satisfaction by an appropriate remedy. Corporations receive from the legislature an existence, endowed with many privileges and capacities of individuals, and of these usually the right to sue for and recover judgments for their debts. And having whilst their legal existence continues recovered a judgment, and assigned it by legal authority and afterwards ceasing to exist, cannot satisfy or discharge the debt.

The act of February 28, 1845, (Sec. 3, Sess. Laws, 246,) authorized and required the bank, if it should accept the terms and conditions of that law, within thirty days after such acceptance, to make an assignment of all their real and personal property to assignees named in the act; all of their personal estate, rights, credits and debts of every kind due them at Shawneetown, and the branch at Lawrenceville, to Albert G. Caldwell and E. Z. Ryan. The assignment was made on the 10th of April, 1845, by the bank to them, as required by the act. It required the assignees to collect the debts, and to make compromises as they might deem most advantageous. The act also gave the assignees four years from its passage to make a final settlement of its affairs. It also appears, that in a proceeding in the Circuit Court of the United States for the district of Illinois, against the assignees at the December term, 1850, William Brown, Joseph Gillespie and Albert G. Caldwell, were appointed trustees of the property of the bank. And the General Assembly, by an act approved February 15, 1851, (Sess. Laws, 120,) declared that they, or either one of them, who should give bond in pursuance to the decree, should be considered as legal successor or successors of the assignees of the bank.

The act also conferred upon such of them as should give bond, the right to sue and be sued, to prosecute and defend all suits already brought in the names of the assignees, to sue out an execution on all judgments rendered in favor of the bank or the assignees; which executions are required to issue in the names in which the judgments had been rendered, and be controlled and collected as they might have been by the bank or assignees. Caldwell only qualified, under the first decree, and in July, 1857, departed this life, when the [*461] court appointed appellee, sole trustee of this fund, who proceeded to, and has ever since acted in that capacity.

Whilst the assignment by the bank under the act of 1845, and the act of 1851, may have transferred, and no doubt did transfer the legal title in the property and debts of the bank, it does not follow that it vested in the appellee, under the decree of the court. It was obviously upon the supposition that such a decree did not, that induced the act of February, 1857, declaring the trustees to be successors of the assignees of the bank, and conferring that right.

But whilst the trustee appointed by a court, to take charge

of property, is not invested with the legal title to the property, he has by that means conferred upon him the equitable title with a power to execute the trust. And it is believed that the uniform practice of all courts of equity authorizes the trustee to proceed in his own name in all proceedings in equity. Hence it can matter but little whether he has the legal or equitable title. If it is the latter, he may enforce the claim by bill.

In this case, however, the appellee alleges that he is unable to find any title in appellant to the land of record. And alleges that he supposed that the appellee owned the land at the time of the levy, but is informed that a son of appellee, since deceased, had claimed to own the land, and prays a discovery of what title, if any, the appellee had to the premises. And as appellee showed himself the trustee of the fund, the court acquired jurisdiction to entertain the bill. And the court having acquired jurisdiction it was proper to proceed to complete justice, between all parties. By the decree the court in effect quashed the execution, the levy and sale, and thereby gave the appellee all that he could have obtained by his motion. When that was done, nothing more could have been attained by proceeding with the motion. And as it did appellee no injury, he cannot complain of the injunction.

Then as the court had acquired jurisdiction, and as the judgment was still unpaid, it was proper that the court should proceed to decree a sale of land for its satisfaction. There was no necessity of turning the appellee over to a court of law, to seek his remedy when all the parties were in court, complete justice could then be done. The decree of the court below is affirmed.

Decree affirmed.

GEORGE N. TITUS *et al.*, Plaintiffs in Error, *v.* [*462]
JOHN GINHEIMER *et al.*, Defendants in Error.

ERROR TO MADISON.

A railroad tank-house, locomotive and cars, are presumed to be annexed to
the realty, and in fact are a part of it, and are not liable to be sold by a
constable, on an execution from a justice of the peace.

THIS case was, by agreement, heard in the Second Grand
Division.

The appellants filed their bill in chancery in the Circuit
Court of Madison county, as mortgagees of the Chicago, Alton
and St. Louis Railroad, the rolling stock, etc., thereof.

The bill refers to the acts incorporating "The Alton and
Sangamon Raiload Company," and amendatory of that act, and
changing the name to "The Chicago and Mississippi Railroad
Company," the construction of the road from Alton to Joliet by
said company, and the operation thereof since about August,
1854.

The bill sets forth copies of the first mortgage bond and coupon; of second mortgage bond and coupon; refers to a further
amendatory act, alleges the issue of bonds thereunder, and sets
out copies of bond and coupon; refers to third mortgage to
secure these bonds; refers to another act, changing the name of
the company to the "Chicago, Alton and St. Louis Railroad
Company," and sets out the copy of deed of confirmation and
further assurance to secure the bonds secured by third mortgage;
the "deed of assignment by the Chicago, Alton and St. Louis
Railroad Company," to "William Fullerton, Henry J. Brown
and Edward Keating;" the copy of advertisement published by
said Fullerton, Brown and Keating, and alleges the purchase of
the road, etc., by Matteson and Litchfield; sets out the deed of
said Fullerton, Brown and Keating, to Matteson and Litchfield.

A copy of the charter of the St. Louis, Alton and Chicago
Railroad Company is set out.

The last clause of the fourth section of the charter is in these
words: "And all mortgages made or assumed by said company,

upon its rolling stock or personal property, shall be valid liens thereon, although not acknowledged as required by the statute touching the execution and recording of chattel mortgages." Bill also sets out the fourth section of said charter.

[*463] The bill next sets out the mortgage to the complainants, as trustees, a portion of the granting clause of which is as follows: "together with all its lands, tenements and hereditaments, acquired and appropriated for the purpose of a right of way, for a single or double track railroad, and the appurtenances thereof, and for depots, engine houses, car houses, station houses, warehouses, work-shops, superstructures, erections and fixtures, and also all and every the privileges, franchises and rights of said party of the first part, acquired at the date of said mortgage, or thereafter to be acquired by it; and also all the rails, bridges, ways, piers, depots, engine houses, car houses, station houses, warehouses, work-shops, erections, superstructures, fixtures, privileges, franchises and rights of said party of the first part, and all the lands, tenements and hereditaments and real estate acquired and appropriated, wheresoever and whatsoever, now owned by the said party of the first part, or hereafter to be owned by it; and also all the locomotives, tenders, baggage, freight and other cars, of or belonging to it, and all other cars, carriages, tools, machinery and equipments for the railroad of the said party of the first part; and also all goods and chattels employed in and about the operation of said road, now owned by the said party of the first part, or thereafter to be owned or acquired by it, in any way relating to or appertaining to said railroad, together with all the tolls, rents, issues, freight money, rights, benefits and advantages to be derived, received, or had therefrom by said party of the first part, in any way whatsoever."

By said mortgage, said trustees are authorized, in case of default, to sell " as well the said railroad and franchises as all other property and premises hereby granted and conveyed, or intended so to be, and all benefit and equity of redemption of the said corporation therein whatsoever, always with benefit of the franchise, and subject to the conditions thereof;" and also it is provided that they "shall have full power and authority to make and deliver to the purchaser or purchasers thereof, good and sufficient deed or deeds of conveyance, for the said lands, tenements and real estate, in fee simple or otherwise, according to the title and interest of said company therein, and good and proper conveyances and assignments of the other property hereby granted and assigned."

The bill next alleges the issuance of bonds secured by mortgage to complainants, to an amount exceeding three hundred thousand dollars; that the interest on these bonds has remained unpaid since July, 1858, and the interest on bonds secured by prior mortgages is and has been in arrear and unpaid since 1856; that many judgments have been obtained [*464] against the company, on which executions have been issued; that the company is largely indebted; that any sale of the property contained and embraced in the said mortgages, by the trustees therein, or to any of them mentioned, would, at the present time, be ruinous to the interest of all, or a large majority of the bondholders and creditors; that the preservation of all the property of the company, its line of road, and all the equipments thereof, and machinery, tools, etc., used in or necessary for the constant operation of the road, intact and undisturbed, by sale or otherwise, is essentially and absolutely necessary to the protection of the interests of the various bondholders, and other creditors of said company; that the company has no other means of paying any of its indebtedness than by the income derived from the constant operation of their said road, or by sale of the property embraced in said mortgages, and that by such a sale, now or within a short time made, not more than sufficient would be realized than would pay the first two mortgages, if so much as that; that all the rolling stock, engines, cars, tools, machinery, materials, wood, and other materials used in the operation, and now in the possession of the said company for such use, were either in their possession at the time of the execution and delivery of the last mortgage to the complainants, or have been purchased with the earnings of the road since that time, and substituted in lieu of those articles then actually in their possession and embraced in said mortgage.

The bill then shows the recovery of judgments by John

Ginheimer, before justices of the peace, the issuing of the executions to Missore, constable, and levy thereof upon tank-house erected by said company, and the advertisement thereof for sale on the 14th November, 1859; charges that the tank-house was erected by the company out of the earnings of the road, and is absolutely necessary to said company for the operation of its road, in order to get water from the Mississippi river for the supply of the locomotives running on the road; that George T. Brown recovered a judgment against said company, upon which execution had been issued and placed in the hands of William T. Brown, sheriff of Madison county, to execute, and that said plaintiff, and said sheriff by the direction of the plaintiff, threaten to levy and are about to levy said execution upon the cars, locomotives, and other property belonging to said railroad company.

Bill charges, that all the property belonging to said railroad company is embraced and protected by this aforesaid mort-
[*465] gage; that the same as in said bill before stated is necessary to be preserved and protected for the benefit of complainants and other mortgagees, and that said railroad company has no property in its possession which is not necessary and absolutely required for the successful use and occupation of its said railroad, and which, as complainants are advised and believe, is not embraced in their said mortgage.

Prayer for answer, process, injunction and general relief.

Injunction ordered by Rice, Judge, of the 18th Circuit.

Geo. T. Brown alone filed general demurrer to bill.

Demurrer sustained by the court, bill dismissed, and decree rendered in favor of defendants for costs.

Assignment of errors: the court erred in sustaining the demurrer to said bill; in dismissing said complainants' bill, and dissolving the injunction granted therein; in rendering decree against complainants; and in not making said injunction perpetual.

Stuart & Edwards, for Plaintiffs in Error.

G. Kœrner, for Defendants in Error.

WALKER, J. The various legal propositions involved in this record were discussed and determined in the case of *Titus* v. *Mabee*, 25 Ill. 257, at the present term, and it is therefore deemed unnecessary to again discuss them here. It was there held that railroad cars and locomotives were, when on the road for use, *prima facie* a part of the realty, and could not be severed and sold by the officer under an execution. This bill alleges, that the sheriff was threatening to seize and sell the cars, locomotives and other property of the road under an execution in his hands, and prays that he and the plaintiffs in execution may be restrained. Also that a constable, under an execution from a justice of the peace, had levied upon a tank-house belonging to the road, and was proceeding to sell it. All buildings and improvements of a permanent character placed upon or annexed to the freehold, usually become a part of it, and can only be separated from it by the owner.

That a railroad tank-house is of that character, is unquestionably true, and as such is not subject to levy and sale by a constable on an execution from a justice of the peace. His authority is only to seize and sell goods and chattels, and when he attempts to sell real estate or permanent fixtures, he acts in excess of his authority, and may be restrained by injunction. The court below erred in sustaining the demurrer and dismissing the bill. Until the evidence was heard, the pre- [*466] sumption is, that the tank-house, the cars and locomotives were annexed to, and formed a part of the real estate of the road. If after hearing the evidence it had appeared that they had been, and then were severed from the track and premises of the road, the bill should have been dismissed. The decree of the court below dismissing the bill, is reversed, and the injunction restraining the sale of the cars, locomotives and tank-houses, is continued until a hearing, and dissolved as to other property, and the cause is remanded.

Decree reversed.

DECISIONS

OF

THE SUPREME COURT

OF THE

STATE OF ILLINOIS,

OF CASES ARGUED AT

APRIL TERM, 1861, AT OTTAWA.

GEORGE W. OUTLAW, Plaintiff in Error, *v.* JOSEPH L. DAVIS, and JOEL KETCHUM, Defendants in Error.*

ERROR TO TAZEWELL.

A justice of the peace issues a capias upon an oath. an affidavit is not necessary, and the presumption is, that a justice requires all the necessary averments in the oath, such as are commanded by the constitution and laws.

The plaintiff in a suit where a capias has been issued by a justice of the peace, is not answerable with the justice in trespass *vi et armis*, even if the process has been issued without a sufficient oath; the magistrate is the proper person to pass upon its sufficiency. If a party acts maliciously, case is the proper remedy. Nor would a magistrate be liable in trespass, if he had jurisdiction to issue the process.

THE opinion of the Court by Mr. Justice BREESE, states the case fully.

ROBERTS & IRELAND, for Plaintiff in Error.

S. D. PUTERBAUGH, for Defendants in Error.

---

* This and the three following cases were heard at April term, 1861.

Breese, J. This was an action of trespass *vi et armis*, brought by Outlaw against Davis and Ketchum, and tried before Harriott, Judge, at the February term, 1860, of the Tazewell Circuit Court.

The declaration contained two counts.

[*468] The first count charged, that on the 23rd day of November, 1859, with force and arms, at Tazewell county, the said Joseph L. Davis being then and there a justice of the peace of said county, and the said Joel Ketchum procured the said Joseph L. Davis, as such justice of the peace of said Tazewell county, without having any jurisdiction thereof whatever, and without any affidavit being filed by the said Ketchum, or by any person or persons for him, that the said plaintiff was indebted to said Ketchum, and that the said plaintiff had refused to surrender his estate for the benefit of his creditors, or that the plaintiff had been guilty of fraud, issued a writ against the body of said plaintiff, called a *capias ad respondendum* in the name of the People of the State of Illinois, directed to any constable of Tazewell county, commanding him to take the body of the said plaintiff, and to bring him forthwith before the said Joseph L. Davis, unless special bail be entered; and if such bail should be entered, then to summon said plaintiff to appear before the said Joseph L. Davis, at Mackinaw, on the 7th of November, at two o'clock p. m., to answer the complaint of said Ketchum, for a failure to pay him a certain demand not exceeding one hundred dollars, and to make due return as the law directs, and then and there delivered the said capias into the hands of one E. B. Hibbard; the said Hibbard being then and there a constable of said Tazewell county, to execute, and the said Hibbard, in pursuance of, and in obedience to the commands of said writ as constable as aforesaid, then and there seized, and laid hold of the said plaintiff, with great force and violence, and then and there forced and compelled the said plaintiff to go from and out of his dwelling house in Tazewell county, to the office of said Davis in said county, and then and there imprisoned the said plaintiff, and kept and detained him in prison, for a long space of time, to wit, for the space of ten days, then next following, contrary

to the law of the State of Illinois, and against the will of the plaintiff. Whereby said plaintiff was greatly hurt and injured in his circumstances, and credit, to wit, at Tazewell county aforesaid.

The second count charged, that the said defendants, on the day and year aforesaid, at Tazewell county aforesaid, with force and arms, then and there again beat, bruised and ill-treated him the said plaintiff, and caused him to be arrested without any authority of law whatever, and then and there imprisoned him, and kept and detained him in prison, there, without any reasonable or probable cause whatever, for a long space of time, to wit, the space of ten hours, then next following, contrary to the laws of the State of Illinois, whereby the plaintiff was greatly injured and bruised, and was [*469] also greatly injured in his circumstances and credit, to wit, at Tazewell county aforesaid, to damage of plaintiff, of five hundred dollars.

To the first count of the declaration, defendants demurred, and judgment on the demurrer for the defendants.

To the second count of the declaration, the defendants pleaded separately, both pleas in substance as follows:

And the said defendant, Joseph L. Davis, by his attorney, Puterbaugh, comes and defends the force and injury, etc., when, etc., and says, *actio non*, because he says, that the said plaintiff ought not to have or maintain his aforesaid action thereof, in the second count of said declaration mentioned, because he says, that the said defendant was, and is now, an acting justice of the peace, in and for said county, and having jurisdiction of matters of such nature, the said defendant, Joel B. Ketchum, at the county and State aforesaid, on the 2nd day of November, A. D. 1859, made oath, that there was danger that the debt or claim of such Joel B. Ketchum against said George W. Outlaw, amounting to $94.69, will be lost unless the said George W. Outlaw be held to bail, and stated the cause of such danger, so as to satisfy the said Joseph L. Davis that there was reason to apprehend such loss. Thereupon Joseph L. Davis did issue a warrant commonly called a *capias ad respondendem*, in the name of the People of the State of Illinois, directed to any constable of said county, commanding him to take the body of the said plaintiff, and to bring him forthwith. before the said Joseph L. Davis, unless special bail be entered, and if such special bail be entered, then to command him to appear before the said Joseph L. Davis at Mackinaw, on the 7th day of November, at 2 o'clock P. M., to answer the complaint of said Ketchum, for a failure to pay him a certain demand not exceeding one hundred dollars, and to make due return, as the law directs; which said *capias ad respondendum*, the said Joseph L. Davis, as such justice of the peace, then and there delivered into the hands of E. B. Hibbard, the said Hibbard being then and there a constable of said Tazewell county, to execute, and the said Hibbard, in pursuance, and in obedience to the command of said writ, as constable as aforesaid, gently laid his hands upon said plaintiff and arrested him, using only necessary force, and brought said plaintiff before said Joseph L. Davis for trial, on the day and year last aforesaid, when the said George W. Outlaw confessed judgment for the amount of said claim, whereupon the said plaintiff was then and there released from such arrest, which is the same sup-[*470] posed trespass in the said second count in said declaration mentioned, whereof the said plaintiff hath complained of them, and this the said defendant is ready to verify. Wherefore he prays judgment, etc.

To these pleas the plaintiff demurred, and the demurrer was overruled by the court. The plaintiff abided by his demurrer; and thereupon the court gave judgment against the plaintiff for costs.

The errors assigned are, that the court erred in sustaining the defendants' demurrer to first count in declaration, and in overruling plaintiff's demurrer to defendants' pleas to second count of declaration.

The first question presented, is, was the first count good? It alleges that Ketchum procured, and Davis, as a justice of the peace, issued, the capias, without any affidavit being filed that the plaintiff was indebted to Ketchum, and that he had refused to surrender his estate for the benefit of his creditors, or that the plaintiff had been guilty of fraud.

Section 22 of Chap. 59, provides, that "if previous to the commencement of a suit, the plaintiff shall make oath that there is danger that the debt or claim of such plaintiff will be lost, unless the defendant be held to bail, and shall state, under oath, the cause of such danger, so as to satisfy the justice that there is reason to apprehend such loss, the justice shall issue a warrant, which shall be in the following form," etc. (Scates' Comp. 696.)

An affidavit in writing is not required, as in the Circuit Court, (sec. 2, ch. 14, Scates' Comp. 236,) but simply an oath which the justice is to administer, and the presumption must obtain, that he required all the necessary averments in the oath. As an affidavit was not required, the count averred too much, and was demurrable. It made a case not within the law, and the demurrer was to the merits and in bar. The point the plaintiff in error makes, is, that the declaration shows a case wherein the magistrate had not jurisdiction, consequently his acts are void, and he may be sued as a trespasser, and the constable also.

It has been decided by this court in the case of *Hull* v. *Blaisdell*, 1 Scam. 334, that an attachment issued by a justice of the peace for a sum beyond his jurisdiction, makes him and the officer executing it trespassers, and a similar principle was established in the case of *Tefft* v. *Ashbaugh*, 13 Ill. 603. This may be admitted to be the law, and yet they do not decide this case. How can it be known, from anything appearing in the declaration, that the necessary oath was not made? An affidavit in writing not being required, but a mere verbal oath, how can it be known, until the oath which the [*471] plaintiff made is shown, that the magistrate had not jurisdiction of the case? The oath may have come up to all the requirements of the law. The demurrer admits only that no affidavit was filed as charged in the declaration, but as that is not required, a want of jurisdiction is not thus shown.

We come now to consider the plea, and the matters arising on the demurrer to it.

The plea states, that Ketchum made oath before him, Davis, a justice of the peace, that there was danger that the debt or claim he had against the plaintiff here, amounting to $94.69, would be lost unless he was held to bail, stating the cause of such danger so as to satisfy the justice of the peace that there was reason to apprehend such loss.

The demurrer admits that an oath was made, and such cause of danger shown, sufficient to satisfy the justice of the peace that loss of the debt was apprehended. The statute in force at the date of these proceedings, chapter 59, section 22, has been quoted.

This statute, or one like it in all important particulars, has been in force from a period coeval almost with the existence of the State Government, and has never yet received a judicial exposition. The case *Ex parte Smith*, 16 Ill. 348, was not decided upon this statute. The capias, in that case, was issued by the clerk of the Circuit Court, on an affidavit which, though in conformity with the then existing statute, was held insufficient because it did not show the causes of the danger of loss of the debt, or any circumstances required by the constitution to subject the defendant to imprisonment for debt, such as that he had refused to deliver up his property on execution, or some fraudulent act or design. The case of *Gorton* v. *Frizzell*, 20 Ill. 291, was also decided upon a written affidavit appearing in the record. No facts appeared in it, showing any cause for the danger apprehended, as in *Ex parte Smith*.

This case is a different one—cause was shown sufficient to satisfy the justice that danger of loss of the debt was to be apprehended, and it may be, for aught this court can know, that the causes were, that he was fraudulently disposing of his property, or refused to surrender it for the benefit of his creditors. The circumstances detailed, which satisfied the justice of the peace, are not and cannot be known to us, and we have a right to presume, in favor of the justice, that inasmuch as they satisfied him, they must have been such as required by the constitution and law. *Ballance* v. *Underhill et al.*, 3 Scam. 457.

[*472] There is no want of jurisdiction then apparent in the plea, and as pleaded it presented a good defense.

It is urged by the plaintiff in error, that the oath required by the statute should be in writing, in order to detect perjury. If it was in writing, it would not then be what the statute requires; it would then be an affidavit, which is defined to be an oath or affirmation reduced to writing, sworn or affirmed to, before some officer having authority to administer it. As a precautionary measure, it might be well for the justice of the peace to reduce the oath to writing, but we cannot compel it.

But there is another aspect in which this case is to be viewed. The suit is brought against the magistrate, and the plaintiff who made the oath, jointly. On what principle is it that the complaining creditor can be made liable in an action of trespass *vi et armis?* Is he, ought he, to be held responsible for the act of the judicial tribunal to which he applies, in good faith and free from any malicious intention, for process to redress an injury, or for the recovery of a debt? He goes to a magistrate having jurisdiction of the subject matter of his complaint, and makes his statement on oath, which the magistrate adjudges to be sufficient to justify the issuing of the required process. The magistrate was honestly mistaken, from ignorance possibly, and the sworn statement is proved insufficient. To hold the complaining creditor liable in such a case, jointly with the magistrate committing the error, would be making him the judge of the sufficiency of his sworn statement, the province, exclusively, of the magistrate. The action of trespass, we do not think, was ever carried to this extent. If it is carried so far, it would make the suitor in court responsible for the correctness of the judgment of the court—a principle not to be tolerated. We have found no well adjudged case that holds the suitor liable in trespass, jointly with the magistrate.

In the case of *West* v. *Smallwood*, 3 Meeson & Welsby, 417, which was an action of the same description as this— trespass and false imprisonment—it appeared that the plaintiff was a builder, and had been employed by the defendant to build some houses for him, under a special contract. A dispute arose, and the plaintiff discontinued the work, whereupon the defendant went before a magistrate and laid an information against him under the Master and Servant's Act, 4 Geo. IV. The magistrate granted the warrant, and when brought up on it, he was discharged, and brought his action. Lord Abinger, who tried the cause on the circuit, was of opinion [*473] that the action was misconceived, and non-suited the plaintiff, and now in the Exchequer, a motion was made to set aside the non-suit and for a new trial, and it was argued in support of the motion, that if a complaint be made, and the magistrate be put in motion by the party complaining, in a matter over which he has no jurisdiction, he is a trespasser, and all who act with or under him are trespassers also. That the act of 4 Geo. IV, gave the magistrate authority only in cases where the relation of master and servant existed, and, therefore, the magistrate had no right to grant a warrant unless he was clearly satisfied that relation did exist.

Lord Abinger said, he retained the opinion he had at the circuit. Where a magistrate has a general jurisdiction over the subject matter, and a party comes before him and prefers a complaint, upon which the magistrate makes a mistake in thinking it a case within his authority, and grants a warrant which is not justifiable in point of law, the party complaining is not liable as a trespasser, the only remedy against him being by an action on the case, if he has acted maliciously.

Baron Bolland was of the same opinion, for the same reasons, and says, in the case of an act done by a magistrate, the complainant does no more than lay before a court of competent jurisdiction, the grounds on which he seeks redress, and the magistrate, erroneously thinking that he has authority, grants the warrant. Baron Alderson said, the party must be taken to have fairly laid his case before the magistrate, who thereupon granted a warrant adapted to the complaint. Then what has been done by the defendant to make him a trespasser? He would be liable only in case, if he was actuated in what he did by malice.

We think, then, if the magistrate, having jurisdiction of the general subject, did not require a sufficient statement, on oath, of the party complaining, such party could not possibly be guilty of a trespass with force and arms. If he had acted maliciously, case would lie against him.

As to the liability of the magistrate, we cannot pronounce

his capias void, because we do not know, under-the pleadings as they stand, what was contained in the oath made by the suitor. We have presumed the statements in it were such as the constitution required, and he had jurisdiction to issue the capias. If his action was irregular and erroneous, yet, having jurisdiction, he cannot be liable civilly in this form of action. *Flack et al.* v. *Ankeny*, Breese, 145, (old ed.); *Lancaster* v. *Lane*, 19 Ill. 242; *Booth et al.* v. *Rees*, 26 Ill. 45.

We think the demurrer was properly sustained to the first count of the declaration, and properly overruled as to [*474] the defendant's separate plea, and therefore affirm the judgment.

Judgment affirmed.

OLIVER M. BUTLER *et al.*, Plaintiffs in Error, *v.* SOLOMON DUNHAM *et al.*, Defendants in Error.

ERROR TO KANE.

The legislature has the constitutional right to authorize counties, towns and cities to aid in the construction of railroads. by lending credit, issuing bonds or taking stock. Fraud in the election authorizing such action must be set up in apt time, and before rights have accrued.

THIS bill alleges, that each of the complainants are owners of real estate and tax-payers in the limits of the town of St. Charles, and that the total amount of property assessed to them is $100,000, and is about one-fourth the taxable property of said township. That the joint property of complainants in said township, will be liable to an assessment for taxes for the year 1859, for about the said sum of $100,000, for state, county, and township taxes.

That the village of St. Charles contains between 2,000 and 3,000 inhabitants. That the voters in said village are the majority of voters of said township of St. Charles. That the inhabitants of said village, against the wishes of complainants, procured at the last session of the legislature, the passage of an act entitléd "An act to incorporate the St. Charles Railroad Company," which was approved February 18, 1859.

That O. M. Butler is now acting supervisor of the town of St. Charles, duly elected. That R. N. Botsford is the acting town clerk for said town, duly elected, etc., and both said But-ler and Botsford are made defendants.

That in pursuance of authority to be obtained in pursuance of an election to be held at a time and place, in said notice mentioned, said defendants are about to issue bonds to a large amount, of the said township, making the same a charge on said township, and on the property of its inhabitants, the prin-cipal and interest to be paid by tax on all the real and personal property in said township.

That on information and belief it is not designed to have any stock taken in said railroad company, except such part as shall be taken by the said township; but it is designed to [*475] make the said township a railroad corporation, for the purpose mentioned in said act.

That as they are advised, the complainants charge that said township is a municipal corporation for the government of its people; not a private corporation for pecuniary purposes; and that it is contrary to the constitution of this State to make such a private corporation for the purposes of speculation; compel-ling the inhabitants and property owners of said town to invest their property without their consent, and against their wishes, etc., which municipal corporation is changed from the legiti-mate constitutional and legal objects thereof.

That the farming community of said town, and especially complainants, have ample railroad facilities. That no benefit would accrue to complainants by building said branch railroad, but the same would be an injury.

That said defendants, and those acting with them, declare it is the intention to issue said bonds by authority of said act, ac-cording to the determination of said election, to be held in pur-suance of said notice, and to use and apply the proceeds, when issued, in repairing an old railroad belonging to the Galena Railroad Company, connecting said village with the said Galena road, with the pretense that that would be using said bonds in accordance with said act.

That the track last mentioned is not used by said Galena Company, and has not been for a long time, for the reason that it would not pay running expenses and repairs. They have freely given the use of the said old track to the citizens of St. Charles, also running equipage, conditional that they would run the same and keep it in repair.

That nineteen of complainants have lands in said township, of about the assessed value of $15,000; all of which lands lie nearer some one of said depots, than to the depot at St. Charles, so that said railroad will be of no advantage to said property of said nineteen complainants, and that each and all of said nineteen complainants live without the town of St. Charles, have no vote at elections mentioned in said act, and if said bonds are issued, they will be injured and have no voice in the matter. That should said contemplated road be built, it can never pay running expenses; that all moneys invested in said road will be lost.

That said village has for many years been provided with a railroad, and all equipments necessary for running it, free of expense; that the same has been abandoned, as it would not pay running expenses and repairs, and was worthless as a moneyed investment. That complainants have all the railroad facilities to carry their produce to market and to travel upon. That they are not obligated by the constitution or law to provide [*476] ways of travel, etc., to the people of St. Charles, etc. That no benefit of any kind can accrue to complainants or their property, private, public, legal, commercial, moral or religious, by the building of said railroad. It is in no sense a railroad. It cannot be called a public road, but a matter of accommodation, local in its character, to the village of St. Charles; said road will not increase the value of the property of complainants, but will decrease its value, by taxes, etc. That money invested in said road will be sunk and lost, and it will be a continual tax upon the property owners of said town to keep it in repair.

The complainants became property owners in said town under the pledge of the law of the constitution of this State, that their property should be burdened only with taxes legitimate and necessary for the support of the government, and that it should not be taken for private use against their will, and not for public use without just compensation. That the using said bonds and encumbering complainants' property by taxes hereafter to be raised, to pay principal and interest of the same, is a direct violation of the constitution, etc. Complainants show, on information and belief, that O. M. Butler, acting supervisor of said town, and R. N. Botsford, acting clerk, are about to issue the bonds of said town to the amount of several thousand dollars under said law mentioned, bearing a high rate of interest, pledging all the property in said township for the payment thereof. Complainants had well hoped that said defendants would have regarded their duty, etc., but they not regarding their duty, etc., but combining and confederating, etc., whose names, etc., have called an election at the village of St. Charles, on the 20th day of May, 1859, to get an excuse for issuing said bonds, and intend to issue the same; sometimes pretending that the proceeds shall be applied to building a plug railroad, to connect with the Air Line Railroad at Geneva, sometimes pretending the same to be applied to building a plug railroad, to connect with the Galena and Chicago Union Railroad, near Clintonville, and sometimes they are to be applied to repairing the plug branch railroad, running from St. Charles to the Junction, all of which acting and doings are contrary to equity, etc.

Here follows usual prayer for summons, etc., that defendants answer without oath. And also that a writ of injunction may issue, restraining defendants' agents, attorneys, and successors, from issuing, signing, selling or disposing of any bonds, pledging the township of St. Charles for their redemption, in pursuance of the act of the legislature mentioned, or [*477] from doing any other act or thing by which the township of St. Charles may be made liable for any railroad, and that the injunction be made perpetual.

The complainants, by their solicitor, moved the court for an injunction, which motion was sustained by the court.

By a supplemental bill the complainants allege, that since

filing the original bill, to wit, May 20, 1859, a town meeting of the inhabitants of said township was held under and pursuant to the notice, and that a vote was then and there taken by such of the inhabitants of said township as attended said meeting for the purpose, as alleged in said notice, of ascertaining whether the citizens, etc., were desirous that said township should subscribe for, or cause to be subscribed for, any, and if any, how much of the capital stock of said railroad company. That at such meeting one hundred and nineteen votes were cast against a railroad, and that two hundred and fifty-eight votes were cast for a railroad, two hundred and fifty of said votes being for $6,000 capital stock, and a few of said votes being for $15,000 capital stock. ' That nearly or quite all of said one hundred and nineteen votes were composed of complainants and of the remaining farmers of said township. That nearly or quite all of said two hundred and fifty-eight votes for a railroad were given by persons residing in said village. Complainants don't know of a single farmer who voted in favor of a railroad.

That defendants aforesaid now propose and threaten to issue bonds of said township, in all the sum of $6,000, as soon as the injunction in this case shall be dissolved.

At the May term, 1859, of said court, the following proceedings were had in said cause:

The respective parties come by their solicitors. etc., the court being fully advised of the defendants' motion to dissolve the injunction herein heretofore entered in this cause, overrules said motion, to which ruling of the court the defendants, by their counsel, except.

A demurrer was filed by the defendants in the usual form, to said original and supplemental bills. The court overruled said demurrer.

It is ordered that the default of defendants be taken for want of answer, and that complainants' bill be taken as confessed against defendants, and that the injunction heretofore ordered be made perpetual, etc.

C. B. WELLES, R. N. BOTSFORD, and J. L. BEVERIDGE, for Plaintiffs in Error.

A. M. HERRINGTON, and M. FLETCHER, for Defendants in Error.

[*478] BREESE, J. All the questions presented by this record have been decided by this court.

In the case of *Prettyman* v. *The Supervisors of Tazewell County*, 19 Ill. 406, which was an application similar to this, for the exercise of the restraining power of the court, we held that the legislature had the constitutional right to authorize counties, towns and cities to aid in the construction of railroads, by lending their credit, in the form of bonds, or by taking stock in the roads. That a complaint of fraud in the election, or the question of taking stock or issuing bonds, must be made in apt time, and before any rights have accrued under the election. To the same effect, is the case of *Robertson* v. *The City of Rockford et al.*, 21 Ill. 451; *Johnson* v. *The County of Stark*, 24 id. 75, and *Perkins* v. *Lewis et al.*, id. 208.

We see nothing in this case to take it out of the ruling in these cases. The court should have sustained the demurrer and dismissed the bill, as it is without merits. The decree of the court below is reversed, and the bill dismissed.

Decree reversed, and bill dismissed.

WILLIAM BRADY, Plaintiff in Error, *v.* GEORGE SPURCK, Defendant in Error.

ERROR TO PEORIA COUNTY COURT.

In an action upon covenants contained in a deed, brought by the last grantee of the land, he need not allege or prove that the intermediate assignees have kept their covenants.

A judgment in favor of the last grantee of land, against the original covenantor, upon the covenants contained in his deed, can be pleaded in bar to any action brought by an intermediate grantee.

The covenants of seizin and of power to sell are covenants *in presenti*, and if the grantor has no title when he enters into them, they are broken at once. They then become mere choses in action, and are not assignable at law.

The covenant of warranty is prospective, and runs with the land into the hands of all those to whom it may come by purchase or descent; and is broken only by an eviction, or something equivalent thereto.

A declaration upon the covenants in a deed averred the making of covenants of seizin, of power to sell, and of warranty, only; the breach included not only these, but also covenants against incumbrances and for quiet enjoyment. The defendant assigned as a ground for demurrer, that this one count set forth more than one cause of action. *Held*, that as all these causes of action were of the same nature and could be answered by one plea, they might be joined in one count. That these separate breaches were to be regarded as so many distinct counts. That the demurrer being to the [*479] whole count, and one of the breaches being properly assigned, the demurrer should be overruled.

Several causes of action of the same nature may be joined in one count. The defendant can plead specially to each cause of action.

The rule as to joining causes of action is, that when the same plea may be pleaded, and the same judgment rendered on all the counts, they may be joined.

A quit-claim, or any other deed which is effectual to convey land, passes to the grantee the covenants running with the land, unless there be words in the deed limiting the conveyance.

In an action of covenant upon the covenant against eviction in a deed, the plaintiff alleged particularly the manner of his eviction, by showing the foreclosure of a mortgage given by the covenantor, and a sale under the decree. *Held*, that as it was not averred that a deed had been given under the decree, or that the time for redemption had expired, or that any actual eviction had occurred, a demurrer to the declaration should have been sustained.

The declaration in an action upon covenants in a deed of conveyance, claimed an eviction by showing the foreclosure of a mortgage given by the covenantor, and a sale under the decree, but did not show that any deed had been given under the sale, or that the time of redemption had expired, or that an actual eviction had occurred. *Held*, that if the plaintiff had removed the mortgage, the measure of damages would have been the amount so paid, provided it did not exceed the purchase money and interest—but as it did not appear that the plaintiff had paid off the incumbrance or had suffered any eviction, nominal damages only should be awarded.

THE declaration alleges, that Brady conveyed and warranted to Haskell, for consideration of $550, Lots 8, 9, and 10, in Block 3, Eastman's Addition to Peoria. Haskell, for $300, conveyed Lot 8 to Spurck; and for $500, Lots 9 and 10 to Grow; and Grow, for $25, same to Spurck.

Averments of breach of covenant, and eviction by paramount title. Further averments of mortgage from Brady to East-

man on said premises, and foreclosure for $287.42. Sale by
master, and purchase by Eastman for $91.91½ for each lot.

A general and special demurrer to declaration was filed by
defendant.

Special causes of demurrer are, that the declaration is double,
and that declaration does not show that grantors of plaintiff
warranted said premises, nor whether the said grantors have
kept the covenants of the defendant.

Demurrer overruled; jury waived; assessment of $540 dam-
ages by the court.

Motion to set aside assessment—overruled, and final judgment.

The plaintiff below offered in evidence, the deed from Brady
and wife to Haskell, warranty; deed from Haskell and wife to
one George Spurcks, warranty; deed from Haskell and wife to
Grow, warranty; deed from Grow to Spurck, warranty, not
[*480] sealed; and proceedings in case of *Eastman v. Brady,*
in Peoria Circuit Court, to foreclose mortgage.

There was a motion by defendant below to set aside assessment, etc., for following reasons:

Evidence insufficient.

Finding not supported by evidence, and should have been for
nominal damages only, and not for amount so found, etc.

Admission of deed from Brady to Haskell, to prove amount
of damages.

No evidence of any actual eviction.

Motion overruled.

Assignment of errors is as follows:

The court below erred in overruling the demurrer of the said
William Brady, to the declaration, and giving judgment for said
George Spurck thereon.

In admitting improper evidence upon the assessment of
damages.

In assessing the damages of the said George Spurck at $550,
and afterwards refusing the motion of the said William Brady
to set aside such assessment, etc.

And in giving judgment for the said George Spurck, and
against the said William Brady.

BONNEY & ROUSE, for Plaintiff in Error.

M. WILLIAMSON, for Defendant in Error.

BREESE, J. This was an action of covenant. The declaration contains one count only, and upon the following covenants, contained in a deed from the defendant to William H. Haskell, the plaintiff claiming as the last covenantor through deeds of conveyance of the premises, from Haskell: "And the said William Brady covenants to and with the said William H. Haskell, his heirs and assigns, that he, the said William Brady, was then the true and lawful owner of the premises hereby granted, and had good right, full power and lawful authority to sell and convey the same in fee simple, and that he, the said William Brady, will covenant and forever defend the aforesaid premises, etc., to the said William H. Haskell, his heirs and assigns, against all lawful claims."

The breach is as follows: "And the plaintiff avers, that at the time of the execution of the deed to Haskell, said Brady was not lawfully seized in fee simple of the premises, nor had he then and there good right and lawful authority to sell and convey the same in manner aforesaid, nor could the said Haskell or the plaintiff, by force of said deed, lawfully [*481] possess or quietly enjoy the same free from all incumbrances, nor has he, the said Brady, warranted and defended the same premises to them, against all lawful claims whatsoever, but on the contrary thereof, the plaintiff says that at the time of the sealing and delivery of the deed, the paramount title and freehold in the premises was in other persons than the said Brady, by virtue of which paramount title, the said plaintiff was evicted out of, and kept out of the premises, and afterwards, to wit, on the fifth day of July, 1860, was evicted out of, and kept out of and from the said premises, and so the said Brady has not kept his said covenants, but has broken the same." The declaration then avers the existence of a mortgage on the property, executed by Brady before the execution of the deed to Haskell, proceedings in court to foreclose and sell, decree of foreclosure and sale, and a sale under the decree, and the purchase by one Eastman, of the premises, on the 7th July, 1860.

The defendant demurred generally to the declaration, and assigned special causes: first, that the declaration is double, containing two causes of action in one count; second, that the declaration does not show that the grantor of the plaintiff warranted the premises to him, "nor whether the said grantors have kept the covenants of the defendant."

Disposing of the last cause first, it will be observed that the suit is brought, not by an intermediate covenantee, but by the last assignee, and a judgment and recovery in his favor, could be pleaded in bar to any action any intermediate covenantee might bring against the first grantor or covenantor. So that it is not necessary that it should be alleged and shown, that they have kept their covenants with the defendant. They are not in the case. The plaintiff being the last assignee is the only person injured.

Upon the question of duplicity. The declaration sets out the defendant's covenants with Haskell, which were, that he was then the lawful owner of the premises, and had power to sell and convey in fee simple, and a general warranty. The breach is, that he was not lawfully seized in fee simple, nor had he good right and lawful authority to sell and convey the same, nor could said Haskell or the plaintiff lawfully possess or quietly enjoy the same free from all incumbrances, nor has the defendant warranted and defended the premises to them, against all lawful claims, but on the contrary he has been evicted by a paramount title.

The deed containing the covenants, is not before us, it not having been made a part of the record by oyer. The declaration before us avers the making a covenant of seizin, of power [*482] to sell and of warranty only. The breach, includes not only these, but two others, on which the plaintiff has not counted, namely: a covenant against incumbrances and for quiet enjoyment. So far as the covenants of seizin and power to sell are concerned, they are covenants *in presenti*, and if the grantor had no title at the time he entered into them, they were broken as soon as made. They then became a mere chose in action, not assignable so as to enable the assignee to sue, at law, in his own name. *Furniss* v. *Williams*, 11 Ill. 229;

Rawle on Covenants for Title, 285. But the covenant of warranty is prospective, and is understood to be broken only upon an eviction or by something equivalent thereto, and runs forever, with the land, into the hands of all those to whom it may subsequently come, by descent or purchase. The plaintiff could sue upon this, and the breach assigned upon it is well assigned. But could he join a breach of other covenants not in the deed, and which did not pass to him, with this covenant, as he has done?

The rules of correct pleading allow several causes of action of the same nature to be joined in one count, and a recovery had *pro tanto*. The defendant can plead specially to each cause of action. *Godfrey et al.* v. *Buckmaster*, 1 Scam. 456. Different causes of actions cannot be joined in the same declaration. The rule is, that when the same plea may be pleaded and the same judgment rendered on all the counts, they may be joined. These distinct breaches are to be regarded as so many distinct counts, to which the defendant could plead specially, or they might be met by a general plea of covenants performed. The demurrer is general to all the breaches, and one of them being good—that on the covenant of warranty—the plaintiff must have judgment. This rule is so well settled as not to require a reference to authorities.

Upon the other point, that the declaration does not show that the conveyance of the lots to the plaintiff was by deed of warranty, we hold, that it matters not by what kind of deed the premises were conveyed. Any deed which would convey the land, would convey the covenants running with the land. A quit-claim deed is as effectual to convey land, as a deed with full covenants. *McConnel* v. *Reed*, 4 Scam. 121. Unless there be words in the deed limiting the conveyance. *Butterfield* v. *Smith*, 11 Ill. 486.

The other question made, is as to the assessment of damages. The defendant abided by his demurrer, asking no leave to plead over, and we must take the facts to be true as alleged, that the plaintiff was evicted by a paramount title. But the manner and quality of that eviction is alleged, and the demurrer reaches that also. It is a substantial part of the [*483] declaration, from which it appears, there has been no actual eviction, or attornment to the purchaser under the decree, or that the plaintiff has been turned out of possession, or even threatened to be turned out, or that there is an adverse title. Nor is there any averment that a deed has been made to such purchaser, or that he has any muniment of title by which he could oust the plaintiff. Nor is there any averment that the time of redemption had expired. Had the mortgage not been foreclosed, on the principle that the mortgagee is the owner of the fee, he could have maintained ejectment and recovered the premises, but having resorted to a court of equity to foreclose and sell, can the purchaser under the decree without a deed, and before the time of redemption has expired, assert or set up a hostile title, to which the plaintiff could, rightfully, and without suit, succumb? The covenant is not against incumbrances, but on an eviction, and from the plaintiff's own showing, we do not think there was an eviction, or anything equivalent to it. We cannot say, under the plaintiff's showing, that his title has been defeated, by a paramount legal right, and must hold, that the mortgage and proceedings under it was a mere incumbrance which the plaintiff might have removed, and then looked to the defendant for indemnity. If he had removed it, then the measure of damages would have been, not the purchase money and interest, which the court allowed, but the amount necessarily paid to remove the incumbrance, not, however, to exceed in any event, the purchase money and interest. The question then is, was not the court wrong, in measuring the damages? Clearly it was wrong. The facts do not make a case in which anything more than nominal damages should have been awarded, as there is an absence of proof that the plaintiff had paid off the incumbrance.

The judgment is reversed, and the cause remanded.

Judgment reversed.

ROBERT HOLLOWAY *et al.,* Plaintiffs in Error, *v.* JOHN CLARK, Defendant in Error.

ERROR TO WARREN.

A clerk's or sheriff's deed on a tax sale is sufficient to show claim and color of title, if it appear on its face to be regular. The person relying upon it, is not bound to show that the pre-requisites of the statute have been complied with.

A quit-claim deed is sufficient to show claim and color of title under [*484] the limitation act of 1839.

H. obtained claim and color of title in 1842, and conveyed to B. in 1845, B. allowed the land to be sold for the taxes for 1847, and bought it himself; he then paid the taxes from 1849 to 1856 inclusive. P., the minor heir of a person who had died seized of the patent title, in 1853 redeemed from the sale of 1847, by paying to the clerk double the amount of the purchase money and all the taxes, with interest, for five years, being up to the time of the redemption. *Held,* that this redemption by P. entirely obliterated the tax sale of 1847, and the payment of taxes by B. for the five years, and that the grantees of B. could not defend under the limitation act of 1839, without showing payment of taxes for seven years, exclusive of the five years from 1848 to 1853.

The provisions of the limitation act of 1839, empowering minors to redeem land sold for taxes, within three years after attaining their majority, by paying to the person who has paid the tax, the amount with interest, do not take from the minor the right to redeem within one year after his majority, by paying double the amount, etc., to the collector, according to Sec. 69, Chap. LXXXIX, Rev. Stat. 1845.

A person whose lands had been sold for taxes during his infancy, for the purpose of redeeming them, after he attained his majority, paid the necessary amount to the clerk. The purchaser accepted this money from the clerk. *Held,* that by that act, he admitted the right of the infant to redeem under the statute.

THIS was an action of ejectment, commenced by the plaintiffs in error, against the defendant in error, in the Warren Circuit Court, to recover possession of S. W. 17, 8 N., 3 W., on the 28th day of May, 1857.

The cause was tried by TYLER, Judge, and the issue found for defendant, and judgment rendered against the plaintiffs for costs.

On the trial, the plaintiffs proved a regular title in fee ·from the Government, commencing by patent, dated October 6, 1847, to the plaintiffs, ending with a deed from James W. Perkins to plaintiffs, dated 24th April, 1857.

It appears by the evidence that the plaintiff's title was vested in James W. Perkins, heir of James Perkins, from 13th July, 1844, to the 10th March, 1852; that he then conveyed to Peter S. Hoes, who held the title till 23rd November, 1852, when he conveyed to Clarissa Perkins, the mother of James W. Perkins; that Clarissa Perkins died seized of the land, 10th August, 1854, whereby the land passed by inheritance again to James W. Perkins, who subsequently conveyed to plaintiffs. Possession was admitted.

The defendant then offered to read, as claim and color of title, a deed from the county commissioners' clerk, to A. C. Harding, dated 22nd March, 1841, reciting a sale for taxes of 1838, the sale made by the clerk on the 9th March, 1839; and also another deed as claim and color of title from the sheriff to A. C. Harding, dated 30th December, 1842, reciting a sale for taxes of 1839, made 18th May, 1840, by the sheriff.

[*485] The plaintiffs objected to each of these deeds, but the court overruled the objection, and allowed them both to be read, to which the plaintiffs excepted.

The defendant then read a quit-claim deed from A. C. Harding and wife to Nathan Brainard, dated 26th August, 1845.

The defendant then proved the payment of the taxes of 1848, on the 28th May, 1849; taxes and costs, $6.04; also the taxes and costs of 1849, $2.16; also the taxes and costs of 1850, $2.84; also the taxes and costs of 1851, $2.41; also the taxes and costs of 1852, $2.65; also the taxes and costs of 1853, $4.80; also the taxes and costs of 1854, $3.54, made January 29th, 1855.

The defendant then read in evidence a contract, dated 10th April, 1856, between Nathan Brainard and Joseph Godfrey, showing a sale of the premises by Brainard to Godfrey, for the sum of $500, in annual payments, the first due 1st January, 1857, and that upon the payment, a deed was to be made, with covenants against his own acts.

The defendant then proved an assignment of contract by Godfrey to defendant before the suit was commenced, and for a good consideration.

It was admitted that the land was vacant and unoccupied before July, 1856, when the defendant took possession under the assignment of the contract, and has been in possession ever since.

The plaintiffs then proved that the land was sold on the 30th May, 1848, for the taxes of 1847, to Nathan Brainard, for the sum of $3.77.

They further proved a deposit with the county clerk, as redemption money, by James W. Perkins, as a minor heir of James Perkins, on the 19th February, 1853, the sum of $7.54, as double the amount of the purchase money, and the sum of $19.15 for the taxes of 1848, 1849, 1850, 1851, and 1852, with the interest thereon.

The plaintiffs then proved, that no payment was made by Godfrey or other persons, upon the contract with Brainard, at the time it was made, and that the first payment was made January 1st, 1857.

They further proved, that after the contract was made with Godfrey, and before the first payment thereon, Brainard received and accepted the redemption money from the county clerk, and receipted therefor on the books of the office.

The court found the issue for the defendant. The plaintiffs moved for a new trial, which was overruled, and the plaintiffs excepted.

Judgment was rendered for the defendant, to which [*486] plaintiffs excepted.

The plaintiffs in error now bring the case to this court by writ of error, and assign as errors the following, to wit: The Circuit Court erred in finding the issue for the defendant; in overruling the motion for a new trial; and in rendering judgment for the defendant and against the plaintiffs in error.

W. C. GOUDY, for Plaintiffs in Error.

GEORGE F. HARDING, for Defendant in Error.

WALKER, J. The tax deed, as well as the quit-claim deed, relied upon in this case, were color of title. They, on their face, purport to convey and transfer the title to the land. Nor is a person relying upon a clerk's or sheriff's deed, on a tax sale, as has been repeatedly held by this court, bound to see that all the pre-requisites of the law have been answered, before he can rely upon it as claim and color of title. If it appears on its face to be regular, that will suffice. When it so appears, the party is not required to go beyond the deed to see whether it actually passes title or is void. If it was otherwise, this statute would be useless, and would fail to afford the protection designed to be extended by the General Assembly in its adoption.

So of a quit-claim deed, if the grantee were required to see that it passed paramount title, before he could rely upon it as color, he would not need the protection of the statute. All know, that a quit-claim deed is as effectual to pass title, as a deed containing full covenants. A deed of release passes all of the grantor's title, and a deed of bargain and sale, with full covenants for title, conveys no more, or greater estate. The covenants form no part of the operative part of the deed, to pass title, but obliges the grantor, on the failure of the title, or breach of any covenant, to make it good, by compensation in damages. All persons in the community know that a quit-claim deed conveys the grantor's title, and it purports to have, and has, that effect. We all know that the language used in a deed of bargain and sale cannot enlarge the estate granted, but only purports to convey the grantor's title. This the quit-claim deed does, by another mode of expression. In law, they both purport to accomplish the same thing, independent of the effect of the covenants. We have, therefore, no hesitation in saying that a deed of release is claim and color of title, within the limitation law of 1839.

It appears from this record, that Brainard, under whom de-[*487] fendant below claims title, paid all taxes legally assessed upon the land in controversy, from the year 1849 to 1856, inclusive, a period of full seven years. That he, during that time, held a quit-claim deed from Harding. It also appears that

James W. Perkins, a minor heir of James Perkins, deceased, who died seized of the patent title to this land, on the 19th day of February, 1853, redeemed this land, from the sale for taxes in 1847, by paying to the clerk double the amount of the purchase money, together with all of the taxes which had accrued, after the sale and up to the date of the redemption. His father had died in 1844, and the patent title thereby vested in his son, who, being a minor, had, under the statute, the right, within one year after arriving of age, to redeem from any tax sale which occurred after his father's death. Brainard recognized this right by receiving the redemption money, after the expiration of seven years from his first payment of taxes, and after he had contracted to sell the land to defendant below. Perkins, unquestionably, whilst a minor, or within one year after attaining his majority, had the right to redeem from the tax sale of 1847, upon the terms and in the mode prescribed by the statute. By such a redemption, the law has provided that the sale shall be canceled. And it, by the same means, obliterates the payment of the taxes precisely as it does the sale. The person redeeming, pays the taxes to the clerk, to whom he is required to make the payment by the statute, on a redemption. The statute calls it a payment of taxes, and we are not authorized to call it anything else. When this redemption was made, and the sale and Brainard's payment of taxes was canceled, the relation of the parties became precisely the same as if the sale, or payment of taxes by Brainard, had never occurred. By that redemption, all of his rights, whether under the tax sale or his payment of the taxes, were entirely obliterated and ceased to exist. And this too, whether he received the money or not, as it is the redemption in pursuance to law, and not his acceptance of the money, which produces that effect.

To render his color of title available, therefore, it was necessary that he should have paid all taxes legally assessed for seven successive years after the redemption was made. The previous payments having been canceled by the redemption, they cannot be counted as a part of the payment for seven years. Such a payment of taxes, thus canceled, could not have been contemplated by the General Assembly as forming a portion of those required to be computed. Those payments had been rendered null for every purpose. On the redemption having been made, the money paid for that purpose became that of [*488] Brainard, absolutely and unconditionally. Perkins could not at any time have resumed it, or in any manner have controlled it. The clerk, under the law, was Brainard's agent to receive the money, and when legally paid, he is as much bound as if the clerk had been expressly appointed by him for that purpose. And this was as effectual to obviate the effect of the payment of taxes as if the minor had paid it directly to Brainard, under the provisions of the limitation act of 1839. The provisions of this act were not designed to, nor do they, take from the minor the right to redeem from a tax sale, in the ordinary mode, but it was designed to afford the means of destroying the bar, of the statute, to the same extent as if he had made an entry before the bar became complete.

It was also the design of the statute to give the minor three years after arriving at age within which he might exercise this right, whether there had been a sale or not, whilst under the general law he was compelled to redeem within one year after his majority. This provision does not conflict with, but it enlarges the rights which the minor previously had under the law authorizing a redemption, as he may resort to either mode in case of a previous tax sale. This redemption was, we have no doubt, as effectual as if the payment had been made under the provisions of this limitation law. Then, excluding the payments included in the redemption, there is not a payment of all taxes legally assessed for a period of seven successive years, but three only, concurring with the color of title, under the statute. There not being a payment of taxes for seven successive years, under color of title, the bar of the statute has not been created, and the court below erred in rendering judgment for the plaintiffs. That judgment is therefore reversed, and the cause is remanded.

Judgment reversed.

DECISIONS

OF

THE SUPREME COURT

OF THE

STATE OF ILLINOIS,

OF CASES ARGUED AT

APRIL TERM, 1862, AT OTTAWA.

JAMES B. GORTON, Appellant, *v.* JOHN M. BROWN, Appellee.

APPEAL FROM COOK.

An action on the case will not lie for improperly causing a writ of injunction to be issued. The remedy is on the injunction bond.

The case of *Cox* v. *Taylor's Administrators*, 10 B. Monroe, 17, not recognized as authority.

THIS was an action of trespass on the case, commenced by the appellee, Brown, against the appellant, Gorton, in the Circuit Court of Lake county, from which the venue was changed to Cook.

The declaration charges, that the appellant, on the 30th day of October, 1854, falsely, maliciously, and without any reasonable or probable cause whatsoever, filed his bill of complaint on the chancery side of the Lake Circuit Court, and at the same time falsely, maliciously, and without any reasonable or probable cause whatever, caused to be issued out of, and under the seal of said court upon said bill, and the indorsement of the master in chancery of said county thereon, a writ of injunction against and to the said appellee, Brown, whereby he, the said Brown, was restrained and enjoined from selling, or in any way or manner disposing of, or interfering with a certain lot of lumber purchased of Smith & Murphy, of Manitowoc, Wisconsin, and which was in said injunction alleged to be owned [*490] by said Brown and Gorton as partners. Also enjoining said Brown from collecting any debts due on account of any of said Smith & Murphy lumber which had been sold on credit; which said injunction was, on or about the day of the issue thereof, served on said Brown.

Declaration also charged, that at and before time of filing said bill, said Brown was engaged in the lumber trade at Waukegan, in said county of Lake. That he had a cash capital of $2,000, in his said business, and a good credit. That the quantity of lumber which he was so enjoined from selling or interfering with, amounted to 100,000 feet of best quality of pine lumber, worth then in the market, $35 per thousand.

· That after the issuing and service of said injunction, such proceedings were had in said chancery suit, in said court, as that said injunction was, on the 7th day of August, 1856, unconditionally dissolved by said court; and that at the September term of said court, 1857, said bill was, by said Gorton, dismissed at his own costs.

That said Gorton, at the time of filing said bill and obtaining said injunction, knew that he was not a copartner or joint owner with said Brown in said lumber. That by reason of the commencement of said suit, and procuring and service of said injunction, and the retaining of said injunction from the time of the service up to the time of the dissolution thereof, said Brown was greatly injured, and wholly ruined, in his credit and reputation, and lost the benefit of the sale of his said lumber during the time the said injunction was in force; and said lumber, while the sale thereof was so enjoined, became greatly damaged, rotted, and spoiled, so that at the time of the dissolution of said writ, the same could not be sold in the market for so much per thousand feet into $10 or $15. And that he, said Brown, was also compelled to expend large sums, to wit, $500, in employing counsel to defend said chancery suit, and obtain the dissolution of said writ.

' To this declaration Gorton plead—

1st. The general issue.

2nd. That said cause of action did not accrue within two years preceding the commencement of said suit.

Issue was joined on both of these pleas. And the cause was tried at the October term, 1860, of the Circuit Court of Cook county, before MANIERRE, Judge, and a jury. There was a verdict and judgment for the plaintiff below for two thousand dollars.

On the part of Brown, the plaintiff below, the court gave the jury, among others, the following instructions:

3. If the jury believe, from the evidence, that the defendant willfully and maliciously commenced said chancery [*491] suit, and caused said writ of injunction to be issued and served, he not being at the time the copartner of the plaintiff, nor having reasonable or probable grounds for believing that he was jointly interested with him in the lumber, then the law is for the plaintiff; and in estimating the plaintiff's damages, the jury are not confined to the exact amount in dollars and cents proven by the plaintiff, but may give such damages as they believe, from the evidence, in view of all the facts and circumstances of the case, the plaintiff has sustained, by reason of the commencement of said suit, and the issuing and service of said writ of injunction.

4. If the jury believe, from the evidence, that the defendant was not, at the time that he commenced said chancery suit, and the issuing and service of said writ of injunction, the copartner of said plaintiff, or jointly interested with him as alleged in his bill, and had no reason or probable ground for believing that he was, and commenced said cause maliciously, then the plaintiff is entitled to recover such damages as the jury believe from the evidence he has sustained, by reason of the issuing of said writ, and the service thereof, and commencement of said chancery suit; and in estimating such damages the jury will consider the condition, as shown by the evidence, of the lumber at the time of the service of said writ,

as well as its condition at the time of dissolution of said injunction, and allow such damages, by reason of the injury thereto, as they believe, from the evidence, was sustained by the plaintiff by reason thereof.

5. If the jury believe, from the evidence, that the plaintiff was engaged in the lumber business in Waukegan, prior to and after the time of the commencement of said chancery suit, and issuing and service of said writ of injunction, and had prior thereto established a business and business credit in said lumber trade, and that the defendant, knowing that fact, for the purpose of destroying said business and business credit, commenced a chancery suit against said plaintiff, charging a copartnership to exist between them, or a joint interest in said property, and caused a writ of injunction to be issued and served on said plaintiff and his property, without probable cause for believing that a partnership existed, for the purpose aforesaid, and that by means thereof said business and credit were injured, then the law is for the plaintiff; and the jury, estimating the plaintiff's damages, are not confined to the exact amount in dollars and cents as shown by the evidence, but may give such damages in addition [*492] thereto as they believe, from a just view of the whole case as detailed in evidence, the plaintiff has sustained.

The defendant thereupon requested the court to instruct the jury, among other things, as follows:

6. If the jury believe, from the evidence, that Gorton in good faith supposed himself to be a part owner of the lumber and shingle bolts mentioned in the injunction described in plaintiff's declaration in this case, and obtained said writ of injunction for the purpose of protecting what he believed to be his equitable rights, then he had probable cause for commencing said suit and obtaining said writ of injunction, and this action cannot be maintained.

8. If the jury believe, from the evidence, that at the time of filing the bill and suing out the writ of injunction mentioned in the plaintiff's declaration, the defendant Gorton believed in good faith that the allegations in said bill were true, and that he was entitled to the relief therein sought, then he had

probable cause for his said action, and this suit cannot be maintained.

Which said instructions the court refused to give as asked, but modified the sixth instruction, by inserting, after the word "faith" in second line, the words "and without willful ignorance," and by striking out the words "he had probable cause," and inserting in their place the words "this action," in the place of the words so stricken out, and also by striking out the words "and this action," after the word injunction.

And modified said eighth instruction, by inserting after the words "good faith," the words "and without willful ignorance," and also by striking out the words "he had probable cause for his said action," after the word "then," in the last clause of said instruction.

11. If the jury believe, from the evidence in this case, that the bill was filed and injunction obtained and served in said plaintiff's declaration mentioned, more than two years before the commencement of this suit, then this suit is barred by the statute of limitations, and the law is for the defendant.

12. If the jury believe, from the evidence, that the writ of injunction in the plaintiff's declaration mentioned, was dissolved by the court more than two years before the commencement of this suit, then this suit is barred by the statute of limitations, and the plaintiff cannot recover.

Which said last two instructions the court refused to give.

Motions for new trial and in arrest, were overruled, on condition that Brown remit five hundred dollars, from verdict, which having been done, judgment was rendered on the verdict.

Gorton appeals to this court, and assigns the follow- [*493] ing errors upon the record:

1. The court erred in refusing to instruct the jury as a matter of law, what was probable cause, as asked in 6th and 8th instructions by the defendant.

2. The court erred in instructing the jury that they might give exemplary damages. See 1st, 2nd, 3rd, and 5th instructions asked by the plaintiff and given by the court.

3. The court erred in giving the instructions asked for by the plaintiff.

4.   The court erred in modifying the 6th and 8th instructions asked for by the defendant.

5.   The court erred in refusing to give the instructions numbered eleven and twelve, in regard to the statute of limitations, asked for by the defendant.

6.   The jury disregarded the law of the case as expressed in the instructions of the court.

7.   The court erred in admitting improper evidence on the part of the plaintiff.

8.   The court erred in excluding proper evidence offered by the defendant.

9.   The court erred in refusing a new trial in said cause, there being no evidence of malice on the part of the defendant.

10.   The verdict of the jury and the judgment rendered in said cause, are contrary to the law of the case, and the evidence given on the trial thereof.

11.   The court erred in not sustaining defendant's motion in arrest of judgment, and in rendering judgment on the verdict.

BLODGETT & UPTON, for Appellant.

W. S. SEARLES, for Appellee.

BREESE, J.   Preliminary to all other questions presented by this record, is the question, can this action be maintained? We have searched the precedents and books of pleadings from the earliest times to the present, and find but one case where it has been held, that an action can be maintained for maliciously suing out a writ of injunction. We are well aware that elementary writers and respectable courts have held that an action on the case will lie for an abuse of the process of the courts, where special damages are alleged, and against a party for prosecuting a causeless action prompted by malice, by which the defendant has sustained some injury, for which he has no other recourse or remedy. Such actions, however, for the most [*494] part, are actions wherein arrests have been made and bail demanded, or the party put to some other expense and inconvenience, which cannot be compensated in any other mode than by an action. Such actions, except where a malicious arrest is charged, are not favored by the courts, and ought not to be, for in a litigious community, every successful defendant would bring his action for a malicious prosecution, and the dockets of the courts would be crowded with such suits. Even for instituting a criminal prosecution, and failing in it, courts regard a subsequent action for malicious prosecution with disfavor, for the reason that they have a tendency to discourage just prosecutions for crime. There is little doubt that very many aggravated cases of crime have not been prosecuted, from the dread, in the event of an acquittal, of this action to follow, and damages recovered, ruinous to the prosecutor. But the action will lie, for it is reasonable, that when an injury is done to a person, either in reputation, property, credit, or in his profession or trade, he ought to have an action of some kind to repair himself. Most of the cases we have examined are cases for falsely, maliciously, and without probable cause, suing out process, regular and legal in form, to arrest and imprison another. Such arrest is tortious and unlawful, and the party causing it ought to be answerable in damages for the wrong done, but even in such case, some damage must be alleged and proved.

As we have said, we have found but one case where the action was held to be maintainable for suing out an injunction in chancery, and that was a case decided by the Supreme Court of Kentucky. It is the case of *Cox* v. *Taylor's Administrators*, and reported in 10 B. Monroe, 17.

The declaration in that case was adjudged insufficient, because it did not allege that the injunction or restraining order, whereby the plaintiff was prevented from the proper use and enjoyment of his land, was obtained or caused to be issued or continued without any probable cause therefor. Had this allegation been in the declaration, as it is in the one before us, it would have been sufficient. It was argued by the defendant, that the remedy, by an action on the case, was merged in that on the bond which is given on obtaining an injunction. In reply to this, the court said, that although a bond was given, on obtaining the injunction, that an action upon it, and on the case, are not coextensive or commensurate, either as to the nature of the wrong, or as to the extent or criterion of damages recoverable, and therefore there was no ground for this argument, and the court likened it to a case of official bonds by sheriffs or others, both remedies would [*495] exist, and thought the same should be the case with regard to injuries occasioned by injunctions for which the party might have an action on the case, if no bond were required.

This is the only case we have been able to find going near to sustaining this action. It is a solitary case — it stands alone; and that fact is some evidence that it is out of the track of well received judicial decisions. On the principle that this action is not to be encouraged, it seems surprising such a decision should have been made, especially where the injured party had a more efficient remedy, and in pursuing which, he would not be required to show a want of probable cause.

We hold the remedy on the bond given on obtaining the injunction, is all the remedy to which the injured party can resort. It is designed by the statute, to cover all damages the party enjoined can possibly sustain, and it is in the power of the judge or officer granting the writ to require a bond in a penalty sufficient to cover all conceivable damages. This bond is a high security which the law requires the complainant in a bill ·for an injunction to execute, to indemnify the defendant, in case the injunction shall be dissolved. It is a familiar principle, when a party has taken a higher security, his suit must be brought on that security. *Touissant* v. *Martinnant*, 2 T. R. 104; *Cutler* v. *Powell*, 6 ih. 324. The bond becomes, when forfeited, the cause of action, and is intended by the law, to measure the damages of every kind which the party may sustain by wrongfully suing out the injunction in case it is dissolved. It is not at all like the official bonds of sheriffs. They are made payable to the People of the State, not to any particular person, and consequently, do not merge a remedy one may have outside of the bond, and besides, it is the policy of the law to multiply the remedies against public officers. Not so with the injunction bond, that is made payable to the defendant. He is the only person interested in it. It is his security. It is all the law gives him as his security, and he is bound to sue on the bond. Were no bond given or required, then the action might lie. · This action on the case, under the circumstances shown, cannot and ought not to be maintained. It is against public policy. For these reasons, the judgment is reversed.

Judgment reversed.

JOHN TIMMERMAN, *et al.*, Plaintiffs in Error, *v.* [*496] GEORGE W. PHELPS, Defendant in Error.

ERROR TO McHENRY.

On the death of the sheriff his deputy continues to act until a successor to his principal is qualified. The return to process signed by a deputy, without reference to the sheriff, where the court below found that it was "duly served," will be sufficient to uphold a default. If the sheriff was not dead, the defendant below should have taken steps to show that fact.

The case of *Ditch* v. *Edwards*, 1 Scam. 127, commented upon and explained.

THIS was a suit in chancery to foreclose a mortgage. Bill filed December 12th, 1857, by George W. Phelps against John Timmerman, David C. Wagner, and Elizabeth Timmerman, in the McHenry Circuit Court.

The only service of process upon the defendants to the bill was as follows:

" I have duly served the within on the within named John Timmerman, David C. Wagner, and Elizabeth Timmerman. by reading the same to them in their presence and hearing, and by delivering to each of them a true copy of the same, this 24th day of May, 1858.

W. C. STODDARD, *Deputy Sheriff*.".

There was no appearance by defendants.

The decree was rendered by default, ordering a sale of the mortgaged premises. The defendants below bring the case to this court and ask a reversal, upon the following errors as-

The court erred in rendering the decree without proper service of process upon defendants.

There was no proper service of process.

GLOVER, COOK & CAMPBELL, for Plaintiffs in Error.

LELAND & BLANCHARD, for Defendant in Error.

CATON, C. J. The process in this case was served by a deputy sheriff, and the return signed by him as such, without using the name of the sheriff. Upon this return a default was entered, and the bill taken as confessed, and a final decree rendered, in which it is stated, that it appeared to the court that process had been duly served on the defendant. By our law, upon the death of a sheriff, the authority of the deputy does not cease, but continues till a successor is qualified. If the sheriff was dead, then the deputy had direct [*497] authority to serve the summons from the statute, and not a derivative authority from the sheriff, and having no principal in whose name he could return the process, necessarily he must sign the return in his own name, and in the character which the statute has given him, which is that of deputy sheriff. Even if the court was not bound to take notice of the death of its chief executive officer, it was competent to receive proof of that fact, and to decide upon such proof. Here the court has substantially found that the sheriff was dead at the time this summons was served, for it found that the summons was duly served, and that could only be so when it was made to appear to the court that the sheriff was dead. This finding is conclusive, unless the defendant, on a motion to set aside that default, would show that the court unadvisedly found that fact, and then that question could be brought before this court. In the case of *Ditch* v. *Edwards*, 1 Scam. 126, it does not appear that there was anything in the record from which this court could conclude that the Circuit Court had found that the sheriff was dead. Upon no other conclusion can that decision be sustained. We cannot presume that the court intended to say that in no case could a deputy sheriff sign a return except in the name of his principal, for that would be to presume the court ignorant of the statute. The decree is affirmed.

Decree affirmed.

SAMUEL CLAYCOMB, Appellant, *v.* WILLIAM V. CECIL, Appellee.

APPEAL FROM PEORIA.

In a proceeding for a mechanics' lien the law implies a contract to pay for the work when it shall be done, if other terms are not specified.

A sale under a mechanics' lien, as there is no redemption from it, should not be authorized within a less period than the lifetime of an execution; and if the amount of the judgment is large, a longer time should be given.

THIS was a petition to enforce a mechanics' lien against a building situated on a lot in Monmouth, Illinois, and filed in the Warren Circuit Court.

The original petition sets forth, that the petitioner was employed by the defendant to burn a kiln of brick, to be used in erecting a building on lot No. 1, in block No. 10, in Monmouth, in said county, and also to lay up a large quantity of brick and stone in a building on said lot, and specifies the nature of the contract, etc.

By leave of court, the petitioner filed an amended [*498] petition, in which he sets forth, in several distinct paragraphs, the several contracts made by him with Claycomb for burning brick, for laying up brick or putting them in the wall, for laying stone caps and sills in the wall, and for furnishing lime and sand, etc., for a wall.

The petition alleges, that on or about the 1st day of May, 1857, Claycomb, who was the owner of lot one, in block ten, in Monmouth, engaged the petitioner to make and burn 84,000 brick, for the purpose of building and erecting, in part, a building on said lot, and that Claycomb agreed to pay him what the making and burning of the brick was reasonably worth, within a reasonable time thereafter, to wit, on or before the 10th day of July, 1857; that he did make and burn the brick before that time; that the brick were put into and used for the erection of a building on said lot, and which "is now on the lot," and said brick forms a part of the material of said building.

The petition further alleges, that the making and burning of said brick was worth $1.50 per thousand; that the whole amount is $126, which Claycomb refuses to pay, and which is now justly due to petitioner.

Also that on or about 1st July, 1857, defendant employed petitioner to build, lay, and put 357,996 brick into a wall, for the purpose of erecting said building on said lot, and agreed to pay therefor, when the work was completed, what it was reasonably worth, and the wall was to be built during the summer and fall of the year 1857; that he did build, lay and put said brick into a wall on said lot, within the time specified; that it was worth $4 per thousand, and amounted to $1,431.98, which defendant refuses to pay.

That on the 1st June, 1857, defendant purchased of petitioner 700 bushels of sand, and agreed to pay what it was reasonably worth; that the sand was bought for and used in the erection of said building on said lot, and was worth twelve cents per bushel, amounting to $84, which defendant refuses to pay.

That on or about the 1st day of July, 1857, defendant employed petitioner to raise, set, and put in forty-nine pair of cut-stone window and door caps, and door-sills in said building, which was erected on said lot, and promised to pay therefor what it was reasonably worth; that they were to be set in said building, as the erection of the same progressed, and, when finished, petitioner was to be paid; that the building was put up by petitioner, and the caps and sills were put in and finished during the fall of 1857, and were reasonably [*499] worth seventy-five cents per pair, amounting to $36.75, which defendant refuses to pay.

The petition then alleges, that all of said contracts were parol contracts, and not in writing, and that the whole amount due petitioner is $1,702.73.

The cause was removed to Peoria county.

The answer denies that defendant employed the petitioner to make and burn 84,000 brick, or that he employed him to burn any brick whatever, or that he ever did make or burn any brick on any contract with him.

Denies that he did employ petitioner to build, lay, and put 357,996 brick into a wall, for the purpose of any building whatever.

Admits that he was the owner of lot 1, in block 10, in the city of Monmouth, and expressly denies that he ever employed petitioner to raise, set, and put in forty-nine pair of cut-stone window and door caps and sills in the building described in the petition, and denies any agreement to pay for the same.

The answer then alleges, that on the 12th day of April, 1856, defendant made a written agreement with Alexander M. Warwick, and Cecil, the petitioner, (who were then in partnership,) to make and burn 250,600 brick, during the year 1856, and lay them up; that under this agreement, Warwick & Cecil burned about 150,000 brick, which they afterwards used in building a school-house; that defendant paid Warwick & Cecil for burning those brick. " That Warwick & Cecil were to lay all of the brick that would be necessary to build a large hotel, several stories high, and were to lay said brick at $2.50 per thousand, as set out in said agreement."

He admits that he was to pay petitioner $1.25 per thousand for burning about 84,000 brick, which brick were put in said building, and said Cecil " began, continued, and completed said building, under the agreement made with Warwick & Cecil, and under no other agreement whatever."

That Cecil & Warwick afterwards pretended to dissolve partnership, but as defendant had paid them a large amount, they did not pretend that they were working under any other contract.

That he made out an account against Warwick & Cecil, and presented it to Cecil before the building was completed, and Cecil acknowledged it to be correct.

A replication was filed, denying all the matters set forth in the answer.

The case was tried at the November term, by the Peoria
Circuit Court, and a verdict rendered for the plaintiff for
[*500] $1,156.60, and a decree entered that the same be a lien
on said lot, and the lot sold to satisfy the same, etc.

McCoy & Harding, for Appellant.

H. M. Wead, and A. G. Kirkpatrick, for Appellee.

Walker, J. No defect is perceived in the petition. It alleges, a contract was entered into for the materials and labor to
be employed in the construction of this building and upon the
particular lot. That they were to be furnished and employed
in this building, which was to be completed, within the period
allowed by the statute, to create such a lien; that it was completed within the time specified; that appellee was to be paid
what the labor and materials were worth, and at its completion. This fills the requirements of the statute, and if they
were proved as alleged, a mechanics' lien was created upon the
premises.

It is, however, insisted, that the proof fails to sustain the
petition, and that the sworn answer of appellant is not overcome by sufficient weight of evidence. The proof all concurs,
that the building was completed, as far as appellee's contract
extended, either in November or December, 1857, and that
he furnished the labor and a portion of the materials, and their
value is established by several witnesses. It also appears, that
appellee and Warwick had been partners, but the latter testified, that the partnership terminated in January, 1857; this
labor and materials had not been furnished by the firm, and
that he had no interest in the contract. McMahon testified,
that appellant stated to him, that he had employed appellee to
perform the labor, and had agreed to pay him. Foot testified,
that appellant also informed him, that he had employed appellee to erect the building. Claycomb, appellant's witness, testified, that appellee said to him, whilst the work was progressing,
that Warwick was not in partnership with him. Squire testified,
that appellant informed him, in January, 1857, that appellee
and Warwick were not in partnership, and that he had settled

with them. This evidence abundantly establishes the fact, that the work was not performed by the firm, nor under the contract with them, of April, 1856, but under a contract with appellee.

The evidence also shows, that appellant admitted, that by the contract, the work was to be completed before cold weather, in the fall of that year. That the building was erected on the lot described in the petition. And notwithstanding there is no evidence that appellant, in terms, agreed to pay appellee upon the completion of the work, the law implies such [*501] a contract, if no other terms were specified, and it is sufficient to support the allegation, that the labor and materials were to be paid for at that time. *Brady* v. *Anderson*, 24 Ill. 110.

But this decree provides, that the property shall be sold within ninety days after the sheriff shall have received a copy of the decree, in the same manner as sales are made on executions at law. In the case of *Link* v. *Architectural Iron Works*, 24 Ill. 551, it was held, that as this sale is made without redemption, the court should, in the decree, fix a reasonable time within which the money shall be paid, and in default of payment within that time, decree the sale of all or so much of the premises as would be necessary to produce the money. It was also said, that it was no more than equitable, that the defendant should have at least the lifetime of an execution within which to pay the money, to prevent an irredeemable sale of his land. (See also *Strawn* v. *Cogswell*, decided at the present term.) By the terms of this decree, the sheriff might have advertised and sold the premises, at the expiration of twenty days after the adjournment of the court, upon being furnished with a copy of the decree at the time when the court adjourned. Whilst every case must, to some extent, depend upon circumstances, and the right to fix the time for the payment of the money is discretionary with the chancellor, yet, in equity, the exercise of all equitable discretion by him is subject to be reviewed by the appellate court. In this case, the time was too short. Owing to the amount involved, it would not have been unreasonable to have given six months. For this error, the decree of the court below must be reversed, and the cause remanded, with instructions to the court below to enter a decree in conformity with this opinion.

Decree reversed.

THE CHICAGO FIRE AND MARINE INSURANCE COMPANY, Appellant, *v.* MARGARET M. KEIRON, Appellee.

APPEAL FROM THE SUPERIOR COURT OF CHICAGO.

A certificate of deposit payable in "Illinois currency," cannot be satisfied by depreciated paper; it must be met by bills passing in the locality in the place of coin. It might be otherwise if the certificate had been made payable in Illinois bank paper.

The words "Illinois currency" mean something different from gold or silver, or their equivalents, and may be used in reference to things of different values, when applied to the uses of traffic; and on enforcing a contract [502] using these words, it is proper to show what meaning the parties intended to give them in their use of them. CATON, C. J.

THIS was an action of assumpsit upon an instrument commonly called a certificate of deposit, which is set out in the record, as follows:

"No. 10,773. STATE of ILLINOIS,
" *Chicago Marine and Fire Insurance Company,*
Chicago, April 23, 1861.
" John Woollacott, Esq., has deposited in this office three hundred dollars, Illinois currency, payable in like funds to his order, on return of this certificate.

" $300. HAMILTON B. DOX, *Secretary.*
" *Registered.* SAMUEL S. ROGERS, *Assistant Secretary.*"
" EUGENE C. LONG."

On said certificate were the following indorsements: " Pay Margaret M. Keiron, or order. John Woollacott."

The declaration contained six special counts upon this certificate of deposit, and the common money counts.

Plea, the general issue.

Trial by jury, and verdict for plaintiff for $298.10. Judgment on the verdict.

Motion for new trial by defendant overruled, and exception.

The bill of exceptions shows, that on the trial plaintiff offered in evidence the certificate of deposit described in her declaration, with the indorsements thereon.

The plaintiff then called a witness, who testified as follows: I called on defendant at its banking house in Chicago, June 13th, 1861, the day before this suit was begun, with the certificate of deposit, or instrument sued on, and offering it to H. B. Dox, the cashier of defendant, demanded payment of it. He said they would pay it in Illinois currency. I asked him what kind of Illinois currency, and he said, such as they had on hand. I asked what it was worth. He said, fifty or sixty cents on the dollar.

I then spoke to Mr. Scammon, the president of defendant. I asked him if he could not pay this certificate, remarking, at the same time, that it was a small amount, or something to that effect, and he said they could do no better with it than with any others, although it was a small one, and that he could make me no better offer than Mr. Dox had done. I refused these offers. I did not see the bills. No specific bills were offered.

I asked for current funds. I don't think I designated any particular funds, but only what would pass current. May have demanded gold, but think current funds. I know [*503] Dox familiarly and well, and showed him the certificate.

I made no compromise. `I would have taken anything that would pass current, but when they offered me what would only pass at fifty or sixty cents, that ended it.

The testimony on the part of the defense, in reference to the value and condition of Illinois currency in this case, was much the same as that reported in this volume, in the case of the *Marine Bank* v. *Chandler et al., post.*

The plaintiff then asked for, and the court gave to the jury, the following instructions:

1. A deposit commonly signifies a bailment of property for custody, without compensation, the title remaining with the depositor, and the depositary acquiring no title in the thing deposited, but only a right to its mere possession and custody. Hence the depositor is entitled to a return of the specific chat-

tel on demand, and to an action to recover its possession when wrongfully withheld. As a consequence of this principle, if the property is lost, stolen or destroyed, while in the custody of the depositary, and without gross and willful negligence on his part, the loss falls on the depositor.

2. But when the subject matter of the deposit or loan is money, wheat or other property, and it is delivered to the depositary for use or consumption, the law implies a contract to return not the identical thing deposited or lent, but the equivalent of the same kind, nature or quality. In such cases, the title to the thing deposited rests in the depositary *ipso facto*, and is at his risk. The only right of the depositor is to a return in kind or value, and this right is not impaired by reason of the subsequent loss or destruction of the property in the hands of the depositary.

3. Such is ordinarily the relation implied by law from the dealings between a banker and his customer, where no special agreement is made by them varying their rights. The money, checks or bills which may be the subject of the deposit, become the property of the bank, and the depositor becomes a creditor. If stolen, lost or destroyed, or if they become of no value by reason of subsequent depreciation, the bank must sustain the loss. The depositor's legal title in the deposit having passed by operation of law, his right is resolved into a mere *chose in action* or claim against the bank for the value of the deposit, usually fixed by the credit given, as in the case of an ordinary loan of money. Indeed, a general deposit with a bank is denominated a gratuitous loan, payable to the depositor on demand.

4. In this case, therefore, the first question for the jury to [*504] consider, is, what was the nature of the relation arising out of the dealings between these parties, as disclosed by the evidence? Was it the ordinary relation of a customer with his banker? If so, then what was the subject matter of the deposit? Was it money, or currency, or something else? And first, as to the relation of banker and customer?

6. If this relation is found to have existed, the jury should next inquire into the nature and subject of the deposit. Was it money, or current bank bills, or depreciated bills of Illinois

banks circulating at the time as money? If the latter, then were these bills received on deposit as money or currency, to be accounted for on demand in like current funds or money? Or were they received as depreciated bills *eo nomine,* upon an agreement, expressed or implied, that they should be accounted for in identically like bills of the Illinois banks, whether current or uncurrent at the time of demand? In determining this question, the jury should inquire into the course of dealing between the parties, the state and condition of the currency at the time the deposits were made, the nature and value of the deposits, and whether or not any express arrangement existed, regulating and fixing the basis of their mutual dealings with each other.

7. On this point, the court instructs the jury, that if they find, from the evidence, that the deposits were made in Illinois bank bills, passing current at the time, in all business transactions, as money, and as such, though known to be depreciated, were accepted and credited by defendant, without any agreement or understanding that the deposit or collection should be paid in like funds as those in which the deposit or collection was made, then the law implies a promise to pay in Illinois or other bank bills, current at the time of the demand, though the bills deposited were subject to a discount for specie when deposited, and subsequently became entirely discredited and greatly depreciated. Such a contract can only be discharged by the payment or tender of bank notes current at the time of demand, or their equivalent in money, and the measure of the plaintiff's damages in this case would be such value on the 13th of June, the time of demand, with interest thereon at date. And if no bank notes were then in circulation as money, the engagement became absolute for the payment of money. For where an amount of money is made payable in a particular thing, the contract can only be discharged in the identical description of property called for, or in money. Nothing else can be substituted.

To the giving of which instructions the defendant ex- [*505] cepted.

Chicago Fire and Marine Insurance Co. *v.* Keiron.

The defendant then asked the court to give the following instructions:

1. If the jury believe, from the evidence, that the words "Illinois currency," in the certificate of deposit offered in evidence by the plaintiff, referred to and meant the bills issued by the banks created under the banking laws of Illinois, and that such bills were, at the time of the deposits, of a fluctuating and depreciated value as compared with coin, then the plaintiff is only entitled to recover the average value of such issues of Illinois banks, as were used as currency after the first day of April, 1861; the average value of such issues to be de-determined at the time of the demand made for the payment of the certificate, on or about the 20th day of June, 1861, and interest from that date to this time.

2. If the jury believe, from the evidence, that the parties to the certificate made a special agreement in regard to the Illinois currency, and knew it was depreciated at the time of deposit, and that the depositor assumed the risk of the further depreciation by leaving his funds on deposit with the defendant, after a further depreciation, then plaintiff can only recover the value of the funds deposited at the time of the demand.

3. If the jury believe, from the evidence, that the deposit was made in Illinois bank notes, and that it was to be paid back in like funds, and that the notes deposited were depreciated below their par value, or worth below their face in specie, then the plaintiff can only recover the real value of such funds as were deposited at the time of a demand made upon the certificate.

Which the court refused to give; to which refusal of the court the defendant excepted.

Errors assigned:

1. In admitting the certificate of deposit, offered by plaintiff below, in evidence under the money counts.

2. In giving improper instructions to the jury for the plaintiff.

3. In refusing to give proper instructions to the jury, asked by the defendant.

4. In refusing to grant defendant's motion for a new trial.

5. In rendering judgment on the verdict for the plaintiff, when, by the law, it should have been for the defendant.

Hoyne, McGagg & Fuller, for Appellant.

M. W. Fuller, for Appellee.

Walker, J. The certificate of deposit, upon which [*506] this suit was instituted, was for Illinois currency, and payable in like funds. This presents the question, as to the meaning of the term " Illinois currency." Is it the paper of the free banks of Illinois, or any bank paper used for, and answering all the purposes of the constitutional coin of the country? Is it that bank paper used in buying and selling the various commodities of trade, and in the payment of debts by the business community specified? The legal definition is, " bank notes, or other paper money, issued by authority, and which are continually passing, as and for coin." Wharton's Law Lex. 236. This is also the commercial as well as the popular meaning of the term. Then, what is " Illinois currency "? Does it designate the paper money, without reference to the banks by which it is issued, and which passes in this State in lieu of coin, or the paper of the banks chartered in this State?

When it is remembered, that the currency or circulating medium of the country is not of uniform value, and that bank paper at par with coin, in one locality, has a depreciated value at a different point, it would seem that the term was designed not to specify the paper of a particular class of banks, but rather a particular description of bank paper. A character of paper which was current, and not a denomination of bills without reference to their currency. If this was not the sense in which the term was used by the parties, it seems to us they would have employed altogether different language. It would have been Illinois bank paper. The term currency, however, must control, and whether it be paper of Illinois, or other banks, it must be current, such as passes in the locality in the place of coin.

It was held, that a bill, payable in New York currency, was met with any funds current in the city, whether on New York,

New England, or other banks. *Judah* v. *Hains,* 19 J. R. 144. This seems to be commercial usage, the general understanding of community, and the legal effect of such a contract. If depreciated bank bills were offered in payment, whether issued by Illinois banks or not, the tender could not be said to have been in currency, and yet the certificate calls for currency. It calls for and must be discharged in currency, or in current coin. It cannot be paid in broken bank paper, no difference what it is called. The certificate says that currency was received, and the same was to be paid, and nothing else will discharge the certificate.

The judgment of the court below is affirmed.

Separate Opinion by CATON, C. J. There is one question [*507] arising in all these bank cases, in the determination of which I cannot agree with the majority of the court, and I shall content myself by a statement of my views in this case alone, without encumbering the record with them in each case. I think that it was competent to show by parol proof on the trial, that the terms " currency," or " Illinois currency," to pay which, in terms, the promises were made, had a local signification well understood by all parties, and that they did not mean gold or silver, or their equivalent. The broad and comprehensive meaning of the word currency, is such as to show, that it may with propriety be used in reference to things of different values, when applied to a medium of exchange of property. Its primary signification is a passing or flowing—something which flows along or passes from hand to hand. When used in reference to a circulating medium, or a representative of values in trade or commerce, it does not necessarily mean cash, but is equally applicable to anything which is used as a circulating medium, and is generally accepted in trade as a representative of values of property. Among many of the native tribes on the head waters of the Niger, a certain kind of shells, called *kurdi,* is used as such currency or circulating medium ordinarily, about 2500 of which represent the value of a dollar; among others, strips of cotton cloth are used as currency, and among many, both are in use, as well as money. 3 Barth. 128. Now a promise made there, to pay so many dollars in currency, would mean so many dollars in shells or cloth, the actual value of which, as compared with specie, it would be competent to show, if we would enforce the contract as the parties understood it. So long as it is possible that the parties to the contract meant that something of less or even more value than money, should be paid, simple justice between man and man requires that they should be permitted to show that fact. They. made an agreement which both parties understood. And shall the court make another agreement for them, different from their own, and enforce that agreement, in violation of what both parties intended? By doing this, we wrest the meaning of the parties from the contract, and enforce an obligation which they never contemplated. The very fact that the promise was made to pay "Illinois currency" shows that something else was intended than cash, else the promise would have been simply for so many dollars. This qualifying expression was put in for a purpose—to carry out some definite understanding which the parties had. It means some particular kind of circulating medium or funds, which the proof shows was well understood in the community, in view of which understanding the parties made their agreement. It is the duty of the courts, [*508] and such is the dictate of common justice, to carry out the intention of parties and to enforce contracts as they are actually made. If "Illinois currency" could have but one meaning, if it could only mean so many dollars in gold or silver, as would be the expression of so many dollars in the current coin of the United States, the case would be different, but here is an expression used, which might have a local signification, the very form and use of which shows that they did mean by its use something different from cash, and I think that sheer justice, as well as the well-settled rules of law, require that the parties should be allowed to show, what was universally understood in the community by the use of such term, as the sense in which it was used in this promise. The necessity of this rule of law is most forcibly illustrated by these very cases, and the history of the times in which these contracts were made, of which no man who lived in Illinois can affect to be ignorant. We all know that at the time our only circulating medium was bank bills

issued upon the security of government bonds, which, in consequence of the rebellion in the South, had depreciated in value,
and that these bank notes had correspondingly depreciated in
value, to the extent of ten, twenty and thirty per cent. below a
specie standard. This "Illinois currency" constituting, as it
did, the currency of the country, everything was bought and
sold in reference to this depreciated value of this currency, and
promises were made to pay in this currency; no one intending
or expecting that they would be paid in specie. We all know
that this term was not understood by any one to mean cash, but
a circulating medium which was in everybody's hands, of a less
value than cash. The witnesses who testify on this subject,
state only what is in the distinct remembrance of all. And
now shall we shut our eyes against this light and knowledge,
and insist, against the facts as we know them to exist, not only from the legal testimony, but from our own knowledge, and
say that the parties intended this promise should be performed
by the payment of cash instead of Illinois currency, which was
of less value than cash? Is that the perfection of reason which
is the boast of the law? I cannot so appreciate it. The value
of the thing which the party promised to pay at the time the
promise should have been performed, was the true measure of
damages. This was the ruling of the court below, and this was
the extent of the plaintiff's recovery. I concur in the affirmance of the judgment, but cannot approve of the principles
laid down in the principal opinion.

Judgment affirmed.

[*509] SMITH D. HINMAN, Plaintiff in Error, *v.* THOMAS
L. RUSHMORE *et al.*, Defendants in Error.

ERROR TO SUPERIOR COURT OF CHICAGO.

Actions in attachment must be commenced where the defendant has property,
or where he can be found, and service must be upon him or his property.
The court does not acquire jurisdiction by issuing two writs, one of which
is to another county than that where the process is returnable, although
there may be property to attach in such other county.

.THIS suit was brought by the defendants in error against the plaintiff in error, under the attachment act of Illinois, the plaintiff in error being a non-resident.

On filing the affidavit and bond required by the statute, in the clerk's office of the Superior Court of Chicago, a writ of attachment was issued to the sheriff of Cook county; and on the same day, on the application of the plaintiffs below, another writ of attachment was issued to the sheriff of Livingston county. The former writ was returned without being executed; the other was returned levied on real estate of plaintiff in error.

After proof of publication of the notice required by the statute, default was entered for want of appearance and plea, and judgment rendered for the amount proven to be due. Afterwards, on the suggestion of counsel for the defendant, that the court had no jurisdiction in the case, by reason of the failure to execute the writ issued to the sheriff of Cook county, the judgment was set aside, with leave to the plaintiffs to file special motion to vacate such order and reinstate the judgment.

Such special motion was filed; and on the hearing thereof by the court in banc, the order setting aside the judgment was vacated, and the judgment restored.

The plaintiff in error thereupon removed the cause to the Supreme Court, alleging for sole cause of error, that the court below had not acquired jurisdiction in the case. It is understood that this is the only question arising in the cause; it being expressly stipulated that the proof was sufficient to authorize the judgment, provided the court had jurisdiction to render the same.

HURD, BOOTH & POTTER, for Plaintiff in Error.

H. T. STEELE, for Defendants in Error.

CATON, C. J. This is a manifest attempt to pervert [*510] what is supposed to be a literal expression of the statute, to purposes never designed by the legislature. For the purpose of giving jurisdiction to the court in Cook county, where the defendant had no property, the party issues a writ of attachment to that county, and also to another county at the same time, where the defendant had property. The first, of course, is returned not served; the last is returned served by the attachment of property of the defendant. It is a rule of law, in order to give the court jurisdiction in an attachment case, there must be service on the defendant or his property, and the action must be commenced where the defendant has property, or where he can be found. The thirty-first section of the act was never designed to enable the court to acquire jurisdiction, but it was designed in aid of another writ where the court has jurisdiction by virtue of the service of the other writ. This is a palpable perversion of the statute and of the writ.

The judgment is reversed.

Judgment reversed.

JOHN O'DONNELL, Plaintiff in Error, *v.* PHINEAS HOWES, Defendant in Error.

ERROR TO WINNEBAGO.

In ejectment, before the court can take jurisdiction, it should appear, by affidavit, that the declaration and notice to appear and plead, have been served. A sheriff's return will not give jurisdiction.

THE record from the court below, sets forth a declaration in ejectment by Howes against O'Donnell, in the usual form, filed 12th March, 1861, in March term, with the usual notice to plead appended.

There is also appended to the declaration and notice, the following sheriff's return:

STATE OF ILLINOIS, }
WINNEBAGO COUNTY. }

I have this day served this writ of ejectment, by delivering a copy of the same to the within named John O'Donnell, this 12th day of March, 1861.

M. J. UPRIGHT, *Sheriff.*
By J. E. DENNIS, Deputy.

The following was also appended: [*511]

STATE OF ILLINOIS, }
WINNEBAGO COUNTY. }

James E. Dennis, being first duly sworn, deposes and says that he has this day, to wit, the 12th day of March, A. D. 1861, delivered to the within named John O'Donnell, a true copy of the within declaration and notice, and that said defendant is in possession of the within described lands.

M. J. UPRIGHT, Sheriff.
By J. E. DENNIS, Deputy.

No jurat appearing.

Upon these papers a rule to plead was entered at March term, 1861, and a judgment by default was entered at the ensuing June term, 1861.

The errors assigned, are:

It does not appear that a copy of the declaration or any notice to appear and plead, was served.

An affidavit of service was not filed.

It does not appear that the court acquired jurisdiction of the cause, or of the person of defendant below.

BURNAP & HARVEY, for Plaintiff in Error.

J. MARSH, for Defendant in Error.

WALKER, J. This was an action of ejectment, with the declaration and notice in the usual form. The only evidence of service, is the sheriff's return, which was indorsed on the declaration, and is this: " I have this day served this writ of ejectment, by delivering a copy of the same to the within named John O'Donnell, this 12th day of March, 1861." The thirteenth section of the ejectment act provides, " that the plaintiff, on the day specified in the notice, or on some day thereafter, upon filing the declaration, with an affidavit of the service of a copy thereof, and of the notice required by the statute, shall be entitled to enter a rule, requiring the defendant to appear and plead within twenty days after entering such rule, etc. This section only authorizes the plaintiff to enter the rule, and a default, to be taken upon filing an affidavit of service. The whole proceeding is statutory, and essentially changes the action as it existed at the common law, and having, amongst other changes, described the mode of making service and return, it must be regarded. No authority is given to issue a summons, or to make service in the manner required in ordinary causes. In this proceeding, the statute has prescribed the practice, and the parties or the [*512] courts have no right to say whether it is the best, but must comply with its requirements. This service fails to do so, and is insufficient.

The judgment of the court below must be reversed.

Judgment reversed.

GEORGE C. BARNES, Appellant, *v.* GEORGE SIMMONS, Appellee.

APPEAL FROM MARSHALL.

In an action upon a note, the books of a banker, showing entries made by third parties without the knowledge of the litigants, are not proper evidence. Such books are not public records, nor do they fall within any recognized class of written or documentary evidence.

THIS was a suit on a note. Declaration in the usual form, against Barnes.

Parties went to trial upon declaration, general issue, and notice of set-off.

Trial by jury; verdict for Simmons for $429.66.

On the trial, Simmons offered copy of note in evidence to maintain the issues on his part, and rested.

The defendant then called *Richard H. Maxwell*, who testified, that about a year ago he heard a conversation between the parties. Barnes said he had borrowed $400 of Simmons, and had given his note for it, but had not got the money; That Simmons' money was in the bank of Wm. L. Crane & Co., and Barnes feared it would be impossible to get the money out of the bank, as he believed it was insolvent; that

Barnes had been unable to get it out; that Barnes had so told Simmons before that time, and Barnes wanted Simmons to give up the note; that Simmons said nothing denying what Barnes said, but refused to give up the note, but told Barnes to get all the money or effects he could, do the best he could to get the money out of the bank, and Simmons would do what was right about it.

Simmons, then called one *Henry Crane*, who testified, that he was clerk in the bank of Crane & Co., in winter of 1857-8; that the books of the bank show that Simmons gave up his certificates of deposit, and that on same day Barnes is credited the amount of them; that the books of the bank show that Barnes has drawn out all the money from the bank. States that he has no knowledge of his own that Barnes ever received any of the money on the checks; that he sup- [*513] poses so from the books and the possession of the checks by the bank, and from these only; that the books of the bank show that Barnes has drawn out all the money from the bank; that the checks appeared to have been drawn by Barnes and paid by the bank in the course of regular business

Simmons here offered in evidence that part of the books of the bank of Crane & Co., containing the account of Barnes; also, the certificates in favor of George Simmons; and also, the checks drawn upon the bank by Barnes—to all of which, Barnes objected and excepted.

Barnes moved to set aside verdict, and for new trial; motion overruled; judgment for plaintiff for $419 and costs; where-upon Barnes prayed an appeal.

Leland & Blanchard, for Appellant.

Richmond & Burns, for Appellee.

Walker, J. This record fails to disclose any evidence, necessary to authorize the admission of the books of the bank. They were not those of either party, and no necessity is perceived for their being admitted. The banker, or his clerk, who transacted the business, were doubtless competent witnesses, and must be relied upon, to prove the facts contained in the books. The entries were there made without their agency, consent, or, for aught that appears, without knowledge of the parties, and consequently were not binding upon them. They were not public records, nor do they fall within any class of written or documentary evidence. They are the entries of other persons not connected with the parties, and who had no right to bind them by what they did. The entries in these books are precisely like the declarations of those making them, and are hearsay evidence, and inadmissible. They are not made under the sanction of an oath, and not subject to cross-examination. In no point of view, and for no purpose, are they admissible in this case. The judgment of the court below is reversed, and the cause remanded.

Judgment reversed.

[*514] JOHN F. WRIGHT, Appellant, *v.* EDWIN CURTIS, and JOSEPH BAKER, Appellees.

APPEAL FROM IROQUOIS.

If a declaration avers that a note is made payable to the plaintiffs by the name and style of Curtis and Baker, such a note may be read in evidence, although they declared in the names of Edwin Curtis and Joseph Baker, without alleging that they were partners, or that the note was made payable in any joint character.

THIS was an action of assumpsit, brought to the Iroquois Circuit Court, where a judgment was rendered, in favor of the plaintiffs, below, the appellees, on this note:

"$155.00.　　　　　　　　NEW YORK, October 17, 1860.

"Six months after date, I, the subscriber, of Middleport, County of Iroquois, State of Illinois, promise to pay to the order of Curtis & Baker, one hundred fifty-five dollars, at their office in New York, value received.

"JOHN F. WRIGHT."

The defendant below appealed.

The note was payable to "Curtis & Baker." The suit is in the names of "Edwin Curtis" and "Joseph Baker" as individuals. There is nothing showing that the individuals Edwin Curtis and Joseph Baker are the same persons to whom the note was made payable. There is nothing showing that the plaintiffs were partners, or in what manner they were jointly interested in the note sued upon.

C. KINNEY and S. G. BOVIE, for Appellant.

F. BLADES, and G. B. JOINER, for Appellees.

WALKER, J. Appellees declared in the names of Edwin Curtis and Joseph Baker. The note produced and read in evidence, was payable to "Curtis & Baker." The declaration contained no averment, that plaintiffs were partners, and the note was payable to them as such, nor that it was made to them in any other joint character. When the note was produced, it did not purport to be payable to Edwin Curtis and Joseph Baker. There was, however, an averment that the note was made payable to plaintiffs by the name and style of "Curtis & Baker," and when it was produced, it fully sustained the averment. There was no variance, and the judgment of the court below is affirmed.

Judgment affirmed.

JOHN F. WRIGHT, Appellant, *v.* JAMES M. [*515] MEADE, SAMUEL A. STOWELL, and LEVERETT C. STOWELL, Appellees.

APPEAL FROM IROQUOIS.

THIS case is similar in all respects, save in the names of appellees, to the preceding one.

WALKER, J. This record presents the same question as that of *Wright* v. *Curtis and Baker,* and is, therefore, governed by the same rules. The judgment of the court below is affirmed.

Judgment affirmed.

ANNIE BOWEN, Appellant, *v.* WILLIAM P. DUTTON, Appellee.

APPEAL FROM COOK.

This court will not reverse a judgment, merely because another might be more acceptable.

THIS suit was originally tried before a justice of the peace, and judgment was rendered by the justice for the appellee, and an appeal taken to the Circuit Court, where the suit was submitted to the court for trial by the consent of parties, and judgment was rendered for the appellee for the sum of fifty dollars, and an appeal was prayed and allowed.

This cause was tried before MANNIERE, Judge.

T. SHIRLEY, for Appellant.

D. C. AND I. J. NICHOLS, for Appellee.

CATON, C. J. This is strictly a question upon the evidence, and we do not feel inclined to disturb the finding of the court, even though there may be some doubt as to which way the judgment should have been. There was certainly evidence to sustain the finding. Taking the testimony of Little and Madge, and the plaintiff's case was sustained. Their testimony shows a personal understanding by the defendant to deliver her the goods on being paid twenty-five dollars which he had advanced for her. This agreement he refused to fulfill when she offered to pay him that amount. And this breach [*516] of that agreement afforded a cause of action. That promise was made for a consideration to himself, which made the promise a personal one, no matter to whom the goods, in fact, belonged. Mrs. Allen contradicts these witnesses, but we will not reverse the judgment because the court still believed them. The judgment must be affirmed.

Judgment affirmed.

JAMES J. MILLAY *et al.*, Plaintiffs in Error, *v.* MARVIN DUNN, Defendant in Error.

ERROR TO LA SALLE.

Where it appears that a party is to deliver grain and have the price of it at a certain place indorsed on a contract, the party to whom it is to be delivered, has not, prior to delivery, any authority to take possession of the grain.

THIS was an action of replevin in the LaSalle Circuit Court, commenced by Dunn against Millay and Pierce.

The declaration alleges, that on September 25, 1861, defendants wrongfully took about five hundred bushels of ear corn, and two hogs, and unlawfully detained same until, etc.

Defendants filed four pleas.

The court sustained plaintiff's demurrer to fourth plea, and rendered judgment thereon.

Defendants withdrew first, second and third pleas.

The error assigned is, that the court erred in sustaining demurrer to the fourth plea, and rendering judgment thereon.

The fourth plea is substantially as follows:

And for another and further plea in this behalf, by leave of court, etc., said defendants say, as to so much of said declaration as charges the taking and detaining the corn therein mentioned, *actio non*, etc., because they say, that on the nineteenth day of October, A. D. 1859, the plaintiff, and said Nathaniel S. Pierce, made and entered into an agreement in writing, in the words and figures following:

"Article of agreement, made the nineteenth day of October, one thousand eight hundred and fifty-nine, between Nathaniel S. Pierce of the town of Adams, county of LaSalle, and State of Illinois, of the first part, and Marvin Dunn of said town, of the second part, witnesseth, that said party of the first part has contracted and agreed to sell to said party of the second part, all that certain piece or parcel of land, situated in said town, and which is bounded or described as follows, to wit, etc; and the party of the first part agrees to ex- [*517] ecute and deliver to said party of the second part a warrantee

deed for the said land, provided and upon condition that said
party of the second part, his heirs or assigns, pay to party of
the first part, his heirs or assigns, for the same land, the sum
of eight hundred dollars, at ten per cent. interest, as follows,
etc., (description of land, and terms of payment, are omitted in
this statement); and the party of the second part further
agrees with the party of the first part, for the better security
of the payments, that the growing crops shall be and remain
the property of the party of the first part, until the said payment or payments are made and canceled by the party of the
second part; and the party of the first part agrees with the
party of the second part, that the grain, or so much thereof as
to satisfy the said payment or payments, as they may become
due, shall be delivered at Somonauk Station, and the party of
the second part shall have the current price of that place indorsed on the within contract, on delivery of the grain."

"Signed and sealed," etc.

And defendants aver, that said sum of seventy-five dollars
and the interest on said whole sum in said agreement mentioned,
were, at the said time, when, etc., due and unpaid — that said
corn in said declaration mentioned was raised and grown upon
said tract of land in said agreement mentioned, and that said
Nathaniel S. Pierce in his own right, and the said Millay, as
the servant and agent of said Pierce, took said corn by virtue
of said agreement, for the purpose of delivering the same at
Somonauk Station, in accordance with said agreement, as they
lawfully might, and defendants allege that said hogs have not
been replevied; and this the said defendants are ready to verify, wherefore they pray judgment, etc.

LELAND & LELAND, for Plaintiffs in Error.

GRAY, AVERY & BUSHNELL, for Defendant in Error.

BREESE, J. The only question presented by this record is, as
to the decision of the court in sustaining the plaintiff's demurrer to the defendant's fourth plea. And that depends upon
the construction to be placed on the agreement set out in
that plea. It is contended by the plaintiff in error, that by

the terms of the agreement, the grain raised upon the land was to be his not absolutely, but as security for the purchase money of the land, and that he was the party to deliver it at Somonauk Station. We do not so understand the contract. This portion of it is as follows: "And the party of [*518] the first part (who is the plaintiff in error) agrees with the party of the second part (the defendant in error) that the grain, or so much thereof as to satisfy the said payment or payments as they may become due, shall be delivered at Somonauk Station, and the party of the second part (the defendant in error) shall have the current price of that place indorsed on the within contract on delivery of the grain."

Language could not be plainer to indicate the party who was to deliver the grain. That party was to have the current price of that place indorsed on the contract on delivery of the grain, and he is described as the party of the second part, the defendant in error. It is too plain for disputation.

The interference of the plaintiff with the grain, by taking it into his possession, was unauthorized. The defendant was the party to deliver the grain and to procure the indorsement of the price, at that station, to be placed on the contract, by which the payments were to be adjusted.

The demurrer to the plea was properly sustained, and the judgment must be affirmed.

Judgment affirmed.

Lovina Jennings, Appellant, v. Elizabeth Jennings *et al.*, Appellees.

APPEAL FROM ROCK ISLAND.

A testator gave to his wife all his estate, to be disposed of in any way that would best support her for life, but if his sons, John and Thomas, should take care of their mother, they were to have certain lands, but if they failed to support their mother, then she could sell the land, or any part of it to support herself; but if the sons complied with these conditions they were to take immediate possession of the land; there were bequests to other children : *Held*, that the testator intended to charge his entire estate with the support of his widow ; that the question of support was a condition subsequent, the word " comply ". being used in the sense of "assent," and when John and Thomas assented, the estate passed to them, burthened with the condition of support of the mother ; and that the widow of John being his heir. and proffering to support the widow, had a right to inherit and possess the estate, and could compel the grantee of the widow to reconvey to her.

THE complainant filed her bill of complaint in the Circuit Court of Rock Island county, in August, 1860, HOWE, Judge, presiding. Defendants appeared and filed a demurrer to the bill, which was sustained, and the bill dismissed at January term, 1861. Complainant excepted to the ruling of the court [*519] in sustaining the demurrer and dismissing the bill, and prayed an appeal to this court.

Complainant's bill sets forth, that she is the widow of John Jennings, who died May 3, 1857, in said Rock Island county; that said John Jennings was a son and heir-at-law of David Jennings, who died January 29, 1856, in said county; that said David Jennings, at the time of his death, was owner in fee simple, of real estate in said county, to wit: One hundred acres on the east end of the south-west quarter of Section 31, Town 18 north, Range 2 east of the 4th principal meridian, in said county; and of other property both real and personal; that Elizabeth Jennings is the widow of said David Jennings; that said David Jennings died testate, leaving a will, made part of the bill of complainant; that said will was filed, proved and recorded in the probate court of said county, February 7, 1856; that by said will the said David Jennings devised unto the said John Jennings the above described real estate, upon the condition that the said John Jennings—together with one Thomas Jennings, who is also a son and heir-at-law of the said David Jennings, and to whom was devised other real estate in said will mentioned—should support and take good care of their mother, the said Elizabeth Jennings, during her lifetime; that upon the death of the said David Jennings, the said John Jennings, by virtue of the said will, entered upon and took possession of the above described real estate, and continued in the peaceable possession thereof till his death aforesaid, and made permanent and valuable improvements thereon by and with the consent of the said Elizabeth Jennings, and from the time of the death of the said David Jennings took good care of the said Elizabeth Jennings, and treated her with great kindness and affection, and furnished her with all the food and raiment that she desired until the time of his death; that there was no issue of the marriage of complainant with the said John Jennings; that by the laws of the State of Illinois, upon the death of the said John Jennings, at least an undivided one-half descended to complainant; that at the time of the death of the said John Jennings, complainant was on a visit to her relatives and friends in the State of Pennsylvania, but upon hearing of the death of her said husband, immediately returned to said Rock Island county and arrived at her home, the residence of the said John Jennings, within about two weeks after his death; that complainant, immediately upon her return home, in a kind and respectful manner, offered to take good care of the said Elizabeth Jennings during her lifetime, in the same manner and style that her husband had previously done, and that she was ready, able and willing so to do.

That said John Jennings died intestate, and that E. [*520] H. Johnson was duly appointed administrator of his estate, June 10, 1857; that said E. H. Johnson, as administrator aforesaid, and for and on behalf of complainant, immediately upon his appointment aforesaid, offered, in a respectful manner, to take good care of the said Elizabeth Jennings during her lifetime, in the manner required by the will; that always since the death of her husband, complainant has been ready, able and willing to take care of the said Elizabeth Jennings, and offered to take care of her in the manner required by the will.

That the said David Jennings, by his will, gave the said Elizabeth Jennings power to sell the said real estate only upon the express condition that " the said John Jennings and Thomas Jennings should fail to give her a good support." That the said Elizabeth Jennings, well knowing that said John Jennings did, after the death of the said David Jennings, and until the death of the said John Jennings, support and take good

care of her, and well knowing that after the death of said John
Jennings, complainant, as the widow of the said John Jennings,
was able and desired and offered to continue to support her, did,
soon after the death of said John Jennings, unlawfully and
forcibly expel complainant from the said premises and every
part thereof and ever since has kept complainant out of the
possession of said premises and every part thereof. And that
upon the 31st day of August, 1857, by warrantee deeds, did
unlawfully and fraudulently convey the said one hundred acres
to David B. Jennings, Thomas Jennings and Andrew Jennings
—to one of them forty acres, to the others thirty acres each.
That said David Jennings, Thomas Jennings and Andrew Jennings did then, each and all of them, well and fully know that
said conveyances were wrongful, unlawful and fraudulent.

The bill prays that all the above parties be summoned as defendants, and required to answer the bill, and that upon a final
hearing thereof, the court would order, adjudge and decree the
above mentioned conveyances to be canceled and held for
naught; that complainant, by proper decree, may be placed in
possession of said premises, upon the same terms that her husband possessed them, and that complainant may be allowed to
take care of and support the said Elizabeth Jennings, and that
she may be allowed all the rights and privileges enjoyed by her
husband in his lifetime under said will; and for general relief.

A copy of the will is set out in the opinion of the court.

Appellant, who was complainant below, assigns for error the
[*521] order of the court below in sustaining the demurrer
and dismissing the bill.

A. WEBSTER, for Appellant.

WILKINSON & PLEASANTS, for Appellees.

WALKER, J. The controversy in this case arises on the construction of the will of David Jennings. It is this:

" Know all men, that I, David Jennings, being old and in-
firm, knowing that my time in this state of things is short, I
hereby make my last will and testament.

" *First:*—I will to my wife all my real estate and personal
620

property, in a word, all that belongs to me, to have the disposing of in any way that will best support her while she lives; but if my sons, John and Thomas, take good care of their mother during her lifetime, they shall have the farm on which we live, between them, but if they should fail to give her a good support, she can sell the land or any part of it to support herself. But if John and Thomas comply with these conditions they can take possession of the land immediately after my death. It is my will that John should have one hundred acres on the east end of the south-west quarter of section thirty-one, township nineteen, two east, and Thomas to have sixty acres on the west end of the same quarter; also forty acres of the south-east quarter of same section, which will make one hundred acres to each one; and further, what money or property may be left at my wife's death, besides the above described land and John's horses and wagon, I wish to be divided among my other children, namely: Rachel, Andrew, David, Elizabeth and Sarah. It is also my will, that John and David B. Jennings shall be executors of the estate, to do the necessary business thereof. Given under my hand and seal, this eighteenth day of February, one thousand eight hundred and fifty-two."

The bill avers, and the demurrer admits, that after his death, and the probate of the will, Elizabeth Jennings, resided with John Jennings, in pursuance of the provisions of the will, until the time of his death. That complainant, the widow of John, then offered to keep and support Elizabeth, in the same manner she had been, by John, and as required by the will, but that she refused to receive such support. That John Jennings had no children at the time of his death, but left complainant his widow, who, as his heir, under the statute, was entitled to one-half of his real estate. That Elizabeth, after the death of John, sold and conveyed the premises in controversy, to David, Thomas and Andrew Jennings, sons of the testator, [*522] and that they had full notice of all the facts. The bill prays, that this deed be vacated, and that by decree, the complainant might be put into possession of the premises, upon the same condition, in which they were held by her deceased husband,

and that she be permitted to·support Elizabeth Jennings, in the mode provided by the will.

The facts being admitted by the demurrer to the bill, the question is presented, whether by the provisions of this will, John Jennings took such a vested interest in the premises, as descended to his heirs at his death. This depends upon whether the condition is precedent or subsequent. If the former, then the condition must be fully. performed in all of its parts before such an estate can become vested, and a want of a performance of the condition, from any cause whatever, cannot be relieved against, either at law, or in equity. See 4 Kent, 125, and the authorities cited. If the condition, however, is subsequent, and the estate vested upon the death of the testator, he leaving the condition to be subsequently performed, it is otherwise. This question can only be determined, by ascertaining the intention of the devisor, as manifested in the will. And in cases of doubt, the rules of construction require, that the entire instrument, and all of its provisions, shall be considered, to ascertain its meaning.

It is apparent from this will, that the controlling motive, in making this provision, was to secure to his wife a support during her life. This devise was evidently made to secure this object. By it he devises all of his property, real and personal, to his wife, to be at her disposal, in any mode that would best support her during her life. Had the devise stopped at this point, it would not seem that the design was to pass a fee simple estate in her, but only to create a power of sale, coupled with an interest. It would have been a power to sell all or so much as might become necessary for her support. But if any doubt existed as to the meaning of this clause, it is made clear by the last clause in the sentence, which declares, that if John and Thomas shall fail to give her a good support, " she can sell the land, or any part of it, to support herself." It then seems to have been the purpose of the testator to charge all of his estate with the support of his widow.

If John and Thomas assented to the terms of the will, which provided, that if they should support their mother during her life, then this property should become theirs.

When the testator provides, that if John and Thomas comply with these conditions, they could take possession of the land immediately after his death, he cannot mean, that they [*523] should first furnish her a support during her life, as such a condition would prevent their entering into possession until a full performance of the conditions. The word "comply" could only have been used in the sense or stead of "assent," as no other interpretation can be given to the language employed, and give this clause of the will any effect.

The intention then being to charge these premises with the support of the wife, it must remain as the primary fund, out of which, when the other means provided in the will should fail, to be subjected to sale, to effectuate the testator's intention. The provision, that if the two sons named should afford the support, that they should have the property, was only a means by which the property might be relieved from the burthen. And their assent to the terms of the will, and their entering upon the execution of the condition, vested the property in them, subject, however, to the charge imposed, from which it could only be relieved by a performance of the condition. If, after assenting to the condition in the will, John and Thomas had sold the premises thus devised to them, it would have passed subject to this charge; so, upon their death, it would have descended to their heirs or devisees, under the same burthen.

If, after their assent, and after entering upon the performance of the condition, they had at any time failed to afford to their mother the support required by the will, she would, under the power conferred by the will, have the right to sell all or any portion of the premises, for the specified purpose. Or if they had sold it, or it had descended to their heirs or devisees upon their death, she would have had the same right to sell it, if the support had been refused. By assenting to the terms of the will, and entering into the possession, and by continuing to perform the conditions of the will, and thus becoming vested with the title, liable, it is true, to be defeated, they no doubt become personally liable for the support of their mother, a refusal to afford which, would have rendered them liable to a recovery by suit. The will does not require the widow to reside with these devisees. She had the option to live with whom she pleased, and they would be liable to defray the expense. This was her right, and that was their liability. Then the persons holding the property, by purchase or by descent, would, to prevent its sale to afford the support, have to see that the support was afforded by the devisees, or pay it themselves, to prevent the widow of the testator from exercising her power of sale. But before they could be put in default, they should have a fair and reasonable opportunity, on demand properly made, to dis- [*524] charge the liability.

It would seem, from the terms of this will, that it was the design of the testator, to impose an equal share of the burthen on John and Thomas, and their several shares of the real estate. And in the event of the failure of either to perform his portion of the duty, his portion of the property should be liable to sale, according to the provisions of the will. This is the only just and equitable construction that can be given to this provision of the instrument. If it were held, that a failure of one of them to comply, should defeat the devise to both, great and manifest injustice might result, such as never could have been designed by the testator. It then follows, that the portion of land devised, by this will, to John, upon his death, descended to his heirs at law, subject to a moiety of appellee's support, required by the will.

The bill alleges, that all of the purchasers had notice of, and fully knew, that the conveyance was wrongful, unlawful and fraudulent. The purchasers, to derive title, were compelled to trace it through the will, and must, therefore, have been fully apprised of complainant's rights. It is also alleged, that they had purchased fraudulently. Although this allegation is not very specific as to notice, it is believed to be sufficient to authorize the introduction of evidence, for the purpose of showing that they were chargeable with either actual or constructive notice of complainant's rights, and of the circumstances upon which her claim is founded.

The bill also alleges, that complainant had offered to support appellee according to the terms imposed by the will, and that the administrator of John Jennings had made the same offer. That both of these offers were declined. This places her in no default, and the allegations of the bill show complainant to be entitled to her share of the premises, as an heir of her husband, which is liable to be defeated by a failure to perform the conditions imposed by the will. As an heir of her husband, she would be entitled to one-half of the premises devised to her husband, after the payment of his debts. This then would render her liable to one-fourth of the expense of the support of appellee.

The decree of the court below is reversed, and the cause is remanded, with leave to defendants to file answers, and the cause to proceed to a hearing, if they shall desire to take such steps.

Decree reversed.

THE MARINE BANK OF CHICAGO, Appellant, *v.* [*525] CHAS. CHANDLER, Appellee.

APPEAL FROM THE SUPERIOR COURT OF CHICAGO.

Where it appears that a bank received for a customer by collecting or by receipt of deposits, funds, which were current, and passed as money in general business transactions, without directions to hold the identical funds, it will have to account to the owner for the sums so received, without diminution or discount, notwithstanding the bills received by the bank were at the time or have since depreciated in value.

The special custom of bankers in a particular locality, cannot change values as fixed by law; and if some persons have been in the habit of receiving depreciated paper in payment of dues, the right to enforce payments in such paper does not exist. Such a right can only arise by contract.

A general agreement to receive depreciated paper in business transactions, may be abandoned by common consent, and when this appears, a party who disregards such agreement cannot hold another to it.

THIS was an action of assumpsit for money had and received, money lent, money due upon account stated, and money paid, etc., commenced in the Superior Court of Chicago, to the July term thereof, 1861, by defendant in error, against the appellants, for damages laid at $20,000.

The declaration is in the usual form, containing only the money counts, attached to which is a copy of the account upon which the suit is brought, and is for an alleged deposit of $20,000—by the defendant in appeal, with the plaintiffs as bankers.

Defendants below filed the plea of the general issue, and the trial took place before the court and a jury.

The trial took place at the November term of said court, A. D. 1861, when the jury rendered a verdict for the plaintiff below, and assessed the damages at the sum of $16,375.83.

Whereupon, defendants moved for a new trial, which was overruled by the court.

The court entered a judgment upon the verdict.

Thereupon, defendants prayed the appeal herein taken, to the Supreme Court, which was allowed.

The substance of the testimony of Lewis C. Ellsworth, and that of Mr. Dox, the cashier of the Marine Bank, is given.

Mr. Ellsworth says: " I am a banker of the firm of H. A. Tucker & Co., and one of the partners of said firm. I have been engaged in the business of banking in Chicago for several years past."

Plaintiff's counsel here showed the witness a draft, of which the following is a copy:

[*526] WISCONSIN FIRE AND MARINE INSURANCE COMPANY'S BANK,
$957.   *Milwaukee, April 11th,* 1861.

At sight of this first of exchange, (second unpaid,) pay to the order of Jacob L. Platner, nine hundred and fifty-seven dollars, in current Bk. notes, on account of this Bank.   (Signed)
To MESSRS. H. A. TUCKER & Co., }   D. FERGUSON,
      Chicago, Ill. }   Cashier.

On the back of which draft are the following indorsements: " Jacob J. Platner," " Jacob Strader," " Pay to Marine Bank, Chicago. Charles Chandler & Co., per J. B. Pearson."

" This draft was paid by H. A. Tucker &. Co., to defendant. on the 19th of April last.

" I have personal knowledge of the payment of the draft on 19th of April. The draft was paid in the daily exchange between the two banks. It was paid in Illinois currency, which at that time was current bank notes of Illinois banks, organized under the laws of the State. The exchanges at that time, of the banks with each other, were made in bills of the Illinois banks. The exchanges were made every day, by defendant sending in all checks and drafts against H. A. Tucker & Co., and H. A. Tucker & Co. would make up their account of all checks and drafts against defendant, and the difference, if any existed in favor of either, was paid in Illinois bank notes. The bills of all the banks in the State were then current, except nine banks discredited or thrown out in November previously (1860), and thirty banks thrown out and discredited on the 30th of March, 1861, and these notes had ceased to pass current. After these banks had ceased to be current, the bills of all the other banks were the currency in circulation in April, 1861. These bills or notes were used at this time in all the transactions of business, and were such as paid debts to H. A. Tucker & Co., and were received by others in payment of debts. In April and May the entire circulation was made up of Illinois banks. On the 19th of April, 1861, there was a difference between the value in market of these bills and coin. It is my impression that coin was worth ten or fifteen per cent. in these bills. Nominally it was ten, but really it was fifteen per cent. I think it cost that to convert the bills into coin. The bills of these banks continued to circulate as money until the 18th of May, 1861, and down to that day almost the entire circulation was made up of these notes. These notes or bills continued to decrease in value from the 19th of April to the 18th of May, 1861.

" I have been about ten years engaged in the banking business in Chicago, as paying and receiving teller most of the time. It is the general usage and custom of banks, to keep their customers' money or funds in one common, not [*527] separate, fund. This is the custom of all banks here, and has been. Everything received in the ordinary course of business is put into one common fund.

" I have been in the State since the free banking has been in force, and been engaged as a banker during the last ten years.

The bills of these banks have made up the principal part of the circulation here. There were some Wisconsin bills circulated here. The bills of Eastern banks and coin have always been treated by bankers as worth more than our bills, the difference being from one to forty and fifty per cent., down to the 18th of May last. The bills which have been in common use here, buying goods and paying debts, have been bills of Illinois banks.

"If a deposit was made in Eastern bills or bank funds of Eastern banks, or in gold, and no premium was paid to the depositor, it was the custom of the bankers to credit coin or Eastern funds as such, and if the party wished to draw for coin or Eastern funds, it was specially called for in the checks. He drew out like funds to those deposited, if he was paid no premium to reduce the deposit to currency, the same as other funds in general circulation.

"I resided here in June last, and was engaged in the banking business; had means of knowing the value of Illinois bank notes at that time. The average value of all the bills of all the banks which were in circulation after the 1st of April, 1861, was, on 21st of June, 55 to 60 cents on a dollar. On the 18th of May, the Illinois banks ceased to circulate as money, and became the subject of barter as a commodity, and so continued to the present time. I include, in making this average, the entire body of bills, good, bad and indifferent, which were in circulation. In the spring of 1861, the currency was composed of the poorer class of the banks. The bills of the same banks which were in circulation in April and May, 1861, were in circulation in 1860, except those rejected in November and March previously.

"Currency depreciated from the 20th of April till the time it went out of circulation, and till the 1st of June. In April and May the depreciation was from ten to twenty per cent., compared with coin, and in June the depreciation was from ten to sixty per cent. The bills of no bank, except the Marine Bank, were in circulation at par in June. The bills which were in circulation in the winter of 1860, and spring of 1861, were the same that were in circulation in April and May, and they were used previous to the 18th of May in the payment of debts and in business as money. They composed the currency almost exclusively at that time; they were received on deposit. [*528]

"Where a deposit was made, generally, it was credited as currency; if in coin or Eastern currency, it was so noted. Where a check was drawn, payable generally, it was paid in Illinois bank bills. Up to the time when bills were thrown out in November and April, the bills of those banks had circulated as money after the rejected bills had ceased to circulate as money. Illinois bank bills have constituted the principal part of the currency for some nine or ten years. I think those bills have been as near par, from time to time, as one-half per cent. since the passage of the law. In November, the banks here had on deposit and in their vaults, the bills of the banks which were then rejected.

"When the thirty banks were thrown out in March, the banks here had the bills of those banks on deposit right with the common fund of their depositors, but they did not undertake to pay them out on the checks of their depositors. The banks entered into an agreement not to pay out the bills of those banks on account of their depreciation. They ceased to be current after the banks here rejected them, but they were current to the time of rejection.

"For one or two years there was a large amount of Georgia bank bills in circulation. The issues of the Wisconsin banks have constituted a part of the circulation during the last ten years, sometimes for some months quite a large amount of them. The bank notes of the Bank of Iowa constituted a very small portion of the circulation previous to the 19th of April. Some of those notes, and also of banks of Kentucky, Ohio and Indiana, also constituted a part of the circulation in April last and previously. When I speak of Eastern currency, I mean New York and the New England States. There were also some bills of Michigan and Pennsylvania in circulation. The notes of Indiana, Pennsylvania, Ohio, Michigan and Kentucky have always been considered as worth more than our circulation. When those notes were intermixed with their deposit, it was customary to credit a premium. Georgia bank notes passed as currency never at a premium, although the most of it was readily convertible.

During April and May last, there was $30,000 or $40,000 of Georgia currency in circulation.

"It is the custom of country bankers to keep accounts with bankers here. The course of business between them consists in the country bankers sending checks and drafts on other banks and business houses, together with currency at times, which are placed to their credit, and drawn against by them [*529] as they might need, and it has been customary for merchants and produce men generally to place money to the credit of country banks with whom they were dealing at the time. No charge is made either way by the bankers here or there for the receiving or having the money thus deposited. The arrangement is an accommodation for the country banker in having his money here so that he can draw drafts to parties with whom he deals, so as to avoid the risk of sending money here. The city banker has usually a balance to the credit of the country bankers, which may be an advantage. Whatever is thus placed to the credit of the country banker, he can draw against it. The banker here uses the money thus placed to his credit in the same way as money deposited with it by its other customers. As a general thing, a deposit account is desirable to the banks. Banks make money out of the buying and selling of exchange, and discounting business paper for business men here; the larger the amount of the deposit the more it can do. The larger the general balance on hand is, gives the bank so much more that they can use in discounts and exchanges. From the month of November to the 18th of May, the fluctuation in the discount on circulation for gold was from two to twenty per cent., varying from time to time between these extremes.

"After the bills were rejected in November and April, the bills in the hands of the banks here were sorted out by them and laid away. They were not attempted to be paid out by the banks. The bills, after rejection, were put away as so much dead money. In 1853 and 1854, and perhaps 1855, the bills of the Georgia banks disappeared from circulation, mostly. In the spring of 1861, the bills of Iowa constituted no perceptible part of the circulation. The bills of free banks were more in circulation at that time than the bills of State banks. Our banks were receiving and paying out $75,000 to $100,000 per day. It was very rarely that we saw anything else in circulation than Illinois and Wisconsin bank notes. There was not much difference in the value of the two. Sometime in April, Wisconsin bills ceased to circulate here. After April 1st, the circulation was almost entirely Illinois bills.

" The bank notes thrown out in November and March were assorted by the banks from among their deposits and laid away as dead. And the same was the case with the bills of the residue of the Illinois banks after the 18th of May. They likewise then became dead, and were thereafter bought and sold as a commodity by brokers."

The defense, by agreement with plaintiff, stated that the balance due upon the accounts between the parties, was the sum of $15,971.23, as appeared from the book of defendant, [*530] some payments having been made since the presentation of the plaintiff's check on the 21st of June, on checks which he had before drawn, but which had not then been presented.

The defendant then offered in evidence an agreement signed by the plaintiff, of which the following is a copy:

No. 1.

CHICAGO MARINE AND FIRE INSURANCE COMPANY.

The undersigned agree to receive and pay out as currency, in payment of debts, and general transactions of business, during the present war, the notes of all the banks of this State at present taken by the following named banks and bankers of Chicago, provided the bankers named below agree to do the same.

> CHICAGO MARINE AND FIRE INSURANCE COMPANY.
> B. F. CARVER & CO.
> F. GRANGER ADAMS.
> HOFFMAN & GELPCKE.
> H. A. TUCKER & CO.
> WESTERN MARINE AND FIRE INSURANCE COMPANY.
> EDWARD I. TINKHAM & CO.

This agreement to be terminated upon the transfer of our account with the Chicago Marine and Fire Insurance Company.

> CHARLES CHANDLER & CO.

HAM. B. DOX.

The defendant also offered in evidence an agreement, of which the following is a copy:

No. 2.

Chicago, April 26th, 1861.

We, the undersigned citizens and business men of Chicago, agree to receive and pay out as currency, in payment of debts, and general transactions of business, during the present war. the notes of all banks of this State at present taken by the following named banks and bankers of this city, provided the bankers named below agree to do the same:

Chicago Marine and Fire Insurance Company.
B. F. Carver & Co.
F. Granger Adams.
H. A. Tucker & Co.
Western Marine and Fire Insurance Company.
Hoffman & Gelpcke.
Edward I. Tinkham & Co.

In accordance with the above, we the undersigned bankers do hereby ratify and confirm the agreement therein expressed.

J. YOUNG SCAMMON,
President of Chicago Marine and Fire Insurance Company.
H. A. TUCKER & Co.
F. G. ADAMS.
B. F. CARVER & Co.
HOFFMAN & GELPCKE.
EDWARD I. TINKHAM & Co.
J. H. WOODWORTH, *Pres't.*

[*531] *H. B. Dox* testified as follows: " I am cashier of the Marine Bank."

Witness is told to look at agreement numbered " 2," a copy of which is given above, and states: " The first signature to the said agreement is that of J. Y. Scammon. He was president of the Chicago Marine and Fire Insurance Company. This is his signature attached to the agreement." Witness proves the signatures of all the parties.

" My name is signed to the paper No. 1 as secretary. This paper was signed about the 27th of April. The agreement was sent to plaintiff about the 29th of April, to be signed by him. We sent with it a circular that we would not receive this kind of currency on deposit unless he signed the agreement. The circular was attached on the other half of the same sheet upon which the agreement was printed, so that he could separate the circular from the agreement and enclose us the agreement signed by him. The circular also notified him that the business would not be continued unless he signed it. This is a copy of the circular enclosed with the agreement.

· No. 3.

CHICAGO MARINE AND FIRE INSURANCE COMPANY.

CHICAGO, April 27th, 1861.

Dear Sir:—I enclose a copy of an agreement entered into by the bankers and business men of Chicago, for your signature, should you be disposed to co-operate with us. Our board of directors have ordered that no deposits of money be received, or open accounts kept, with parties who do not assent to this agreement. Should it be declined, please direct a transfer of your account, collections, etc. I also enclose a list of the names of parties who have to-day deposited under this agreement.

Yours respectfully,   HAMILTON B. DOX, *Sec'y.*

" I can't say when I first saw the agreement signed by plaintiff, after it was returned, or after he had signed it."

(Defendant read in evidence the two papers above, numbered one and two.)

Witness adds: " The circular sent to plaintiff was on the other half of the sheet on which an agreement to be signed by plaintiff was contained. This is the circular (looking at the paper numbered 3, already referred to above,) which was sent to the plaintiff. Our correspondents to whom the circulars were sent, tore off the part to be signed by them, and returned only that part with their signature thereon, keeping the other part. [Defendant then read the circular, in evidence.] Chandler & Co. never had any business with defendants before the month of April last. The account was opened on the 18th of April, 1861. At that time the currency was in a disturbed and unsettled state here. I don't think it ceased before the [*532] 18th of May last, at which time the whole currency broke down and ceased to circulate as money.

" I have seen the evidence of debt introduced. The defendant received for plaintiff the same kind of currency it received on its own claims. We received Illinois currency in payment of debts due the bank during the same time plaintiff's account continued, and the same kind of currency that we received was that which was, in general, in use among banks and business men, and by the great bulk of business community. The currency was then composed of Illinois bank bills.

"After the thirty banks were thrown out, the nominal amount of Illinois banks in circulation, was $6,500,000. I arrive at this from the State Auditor's reports. I speak from public rumor. The bills of the thirty banks which were discredited in March, and which defendant had on hand, were not mixed with its other funds, but were separated therefrom, and kept separately. They were not, after thrown out, paid or offered to depositors on their checks. . I have been engaged as a banker seven years. The usage and custom of bankers is to intermix all the moneys collected for its customers as well as those kept on deposit. They were not kept separately. The funds which were received on collections made for plaintiff, went into the common funds of the bank. The funds with which plaintiff's funds were intermixed, were composed of Illinois bank notes. They were made up of such bank notes as had been in general circulation in the spring of 1861, except discredited notes. They were the same kind that we received for our debts, and paid debts with, and were received by others for the same purpose.

"The rate of discount for specie on the currency received from plaintiff was as follows, at the rates specified: "April 16th, rate of discount 8 per cent.; 17th, rate of discount 10 per cent.; 20th, rate of discount 10 per cent.; 22nd, sold very sparingly at 12 per cent. discount; 24th, not freely at 15 per cent. discount; 29th, sold sparingly at 10 per cent. discount; May 1st, 10 per cent. discount; 4th, 10 per cent. discount; 6th, 10 per cent. discount; 8th, 10 per cent. discount; 9th, 10 per cent. discount; 10th, no sales, 10 per cent. discount; 13th, but little sold, 10 per cent. discount; 15th, $1,500 sold at 10 per cent. discount; 17th, for what was sold, 25 per cent. discount; 18th, 25 per cent. discount. After that, no rate; the currency ceased to circulate as money, and was no longer used as such. Exchange was readily sold, on 16th April, at the rate named; after the 20th April, it was sold sparingly; after the 18th of May, and down to the 21st of June, it had no value except for sale to brokers, who bought it up for the pur- [*533] pose of converting the same and obtaining the bonds of the banks from the State Auditor. The average price for purposes of sale, from the 18th of May to time of demand in this case, (21st June,) I should say, was between fifty and sixty cents. During that time, and since then, there was no such thing in circulation, as currency, as the bills of Illinois banks. The great body of it has risen in value since that date. The rise in Southern stocks has caused this. Since the 18th of May, the bills fluctuated in value as the stocks on which they were based fluctuated. After the 18th of May, there was nothing in use which had been used as currency before. These drafts have been paid by the defendant. [It was here admitted that all the plaintiff's drafts have been paid.] They were all paid out of the common fund of the bank, which consisted of like funds with those which have been described. No objection was ever made to such payment by plaintiff. There would be no profit from an account with an interior bank unless the balance is large. It would be no advantage to a bank unless, they helped to create that balance.

" In April and May last, the bankers were averse to taking a new account, on account of the state of the currency exposing the bank to additional risk, and the feeling in the business community was such at that time that these funds could not be employed in the transaction of business. The course of these funds was into the banks. The funds could not, at that time, have been employed in the business of the bank to only a limited extent. They could not be employed in the purchase of exchange, and in loaning on securities to a limited extent. Two of the banks thrown out in April were restored to circulation, and were treated as currency. My estimate of the average value of Illinois bills, in June, does not include the bills of the banks which had been discredited before the first of April. Our charge for sterling bills was $5 per pound, and the fifteen cents was the difference in bank bills and specie; but I will not speak positively on this point. The defendant, at the time of plaintiff's demand in June, offered to pay its debts in the bills which were current in April and May. The bills of the discredited banks were kept in a separate place, and not mixed up with the funds of the bank.

" I have no knowledge, except from bank books, that plaintiff was not a customer till April last. I have not seen his name on the books. There is no profit from collections unless there is a reliable average balance all the time with the bank. It is customary for the banks to use a certain part of the average surplus of deposits in its general business in buying exchange [*534] and in loaning money, and advancing to its customers on securities.

" After this agreement was signed, the bankers signing it received and paid out the money described in it in payment of debts, and in the general transaction of business, till the circulation broke down after May 18th. After that time I don't recollect an instance in which Marine and Fire Insurance Company or defendant received those bills in the payment of debts or in the general transaction of business. If deposited, they were only taken by them as special deposits. At that time both institutions had a large amount of bills receivable ($800,-000 or $900,000), which had mostly matured before. A small part matured after the 18th of May, perhaps from one-eighth to one-fourth of the whole amount after the 18th of May. I think none of the bankers named in the list continued to take any of these bills. They were alike refused by all as currency. I was cashier of the Marine Bank of Chicago, and secretary of the Marine and Fire Insurance Company. Scammon was president of both. The same officer was paying teller and receiving teller, and assistant cashier of both; the paying teller and receiving teller acted for both; both had same persons as directors, and stockholders had same interest in both. They held equal shares in both; no one could have stock in one and not in the other. The certificate of stock is a joint certificate in both. There were no separate shares in either. The stock shows on its face that the share is in both, and that a transfer of it transferred a share in each. Everything that was done was known to the officers of both institutions.

" There was a meeting of the bankers at the defendant's

office, preliminary to the making of the agreement signed by them. This meeting was held on the 26th of April. Three officers of defendant were present thereat, the vice-president and myself. Scammon at that time was in Springfield. At the time this circular was inclosed to the plaintiff, Scammon was not here. We had such a large amount of Illinois bills we had to keep a police officer. The risk was also on account of the depreciation, and thereby raising a question with depositors as to the extent of the liability of the bank. Plaintiff's deposits went into the common deposits of the bank. No attempt to keep them separate was made, or ever is made, in such cases. I think plaintiff was there seeking a settlement of his account. Before the demand was made by him, he was trying to effect a settlement of his account. The paying teller, at the time of demand, had an assortment of the different grades of bills with which to pay depositors. The better grades in April and May were assorted and held by the cashier to keep. That which was paid out was, during those [*535] months, the worst. This assorting took place every day, and the best separated and put away. The better grades were thus reserved; the worst grades were put into paying teller's hands to pay out. After the 18th of May, we would take out of that fund to put with and pay out to depositors. The checks on defendant and Marine and Fire Insurance Company were paid out of the same fund. Checks on the defendant were always paid by the Insurance Company. The funds in the hands of the teller, on the 21st of June, to pay checks with, were not so good as those in the hands of the cashier. The reserved fund was the best.

"The cashier had all kinds to pay with, while the reserved was the best. The teller had in his hands on that day between $100,000 and $200,000. The assorting teller had $600,000 to $800,000, and the reserved fund contained $300,000 to $400,000. The assorting was made immediately after the 18th of May, and was completed about that time. The reserved fund was the best, but as the assorting teller had some of the higher grades, the paying teller would go to the assorting teller. On the 21st of June, the paying teller had in his hands more than an average

in value of all the bills of what were actively in circulation in April and May. On the 21st of June the paying teller had not in his hands of an average of all the bills then on deposit in the bank; his assortment was much below the average. The instructions to the teller were made to pay plaintiff's checks in the lower grades of currency, because his deposits were made when we were receiving only the lower grades. During the seven years last past, the word *currency* meant, among bankers, such bank notes as passed current among bankers and business men. Currency, bankable funds, and current bank notes, have meant, and mean, the same thing among them. Since 1856, the currency has been composed almost exclusively of Illinois bank notes, with some Wisconsin. There were some Iowa in circulation, passing in small lots. There was also some of Kentucky, passing in same way. Currency, bankable funds, and current bank notes, mean the same thing; that is to say, the bank notes which pass current as money. The word has always been used in the same sense through all varying circumstances, and means the paper circulation passing as money. It has always been at a discount for coin, and is still. Par currency here means just the same as currency. Par funds means the same thing as currency. If demand is made in currency worth one hundred cents on the dollar, I should think it would be payable in cur-
[*536] rency. The currency passes at one hundred cents on the dollar, and ordinarily means a dollar. The teller was not authorized to pay the plaintiff in anything but an average of the lower grades then in the bank. The state of mind referred to by me in the business community, was in reference to the circulation of these bills, which prevented bankers from issuing these deposits in their business to anything like the usual extent. There had been an uneasy feeling in regard to it all the previous winter, but it became still more marked and apparent after the 10th of April.

" The first disturbance in the currency began in November last, from the 16th to the 20th. Nine banks were thrown out after the 16th of November. Those were almost exclusively based upon the stocks of the Southern States; no material amount of Northern stocks. After that there continued to be an uneasy feeling in reference to those which were based on same stocks. The confidence, or want of confidence, in the bills, was governed by the price of stocks in New York, and also by the appearance of the political horizon.

"The first assorting by us was in November, after the nine banks were thrown out. At that time the defendant and Marine and Fire Insurance Company held from $60,000 to $90,000 of the bills of rejected banks. The bankers could not, during the winter, tell which would depreciate, and which would not, until we had the State Auditor's Report in January last, which showed the securities for each bank, and the circulation. During the Winter and early months of Spring the stocks of all the banks were varying and fluctuating. Previous to the meeting of the bankers, at which the thirty banks were thrown out, we could not tell with any certainty what banks would be thrown out by the bankers. Of those thirty, we had $170,000. I have no means of telling how much of the issues of the same banks was held by the other city bankers. After that meeting, the currency was very unsettled, and the feeling in consequence was very unsettled and anxious in regard to it; and that anxiety was largely increased after the 19th and 20th of April. When hostilities had begun, this feeling continued likewise to grow worse till the 18th of May, when the whole circulation depreciated, and was thrown out, and ceased to circulate. At that time the defendants, or Marine and Fire Insurance Company, had on hand between $1,200,000 and $1,300,000. That amount included all the funds of all kinds in the bank, reserved fund and all.

"After the 18th, I don't recollect that any money of this kind was offered on deposit. The defendants received and continued to receive checks on themselves in payment of [*537] debts due the bank, and they have received them ever since in payment.

"Prior to the 18th, this currency had flowed into the city from the country in an unusual degree, so that both defendants and the Marine and Fire Insurance Company had to increase their clerical force. I know that a great many of the country bankers would not receive bills of the banks which we

were receiving here, though they were received by others. The
draft and current of the circulation was into the city at that
time. Before we gave instructions to the paying teller, we
looked at the account, and judged as near as we could when the
money was deposited by each depositor, and we went on the
basis that those who had deposited in April and May were only
entitled to the lower grades of the currency, for the reason that
was all we did get in those months; and the instructions to the
teller were given accordingly. . Those whose deposits had come
in before April, were entitled to a better class of currency. No
special instructions were given to teller in plaintiff's case. The
average value of what was actually in circulation in April and
May, was from fifty to sixty cents on the dollar; but that estimate does not include the bills which had been rejected; but
taking the whole body of the bills together, it was from sixty
to seventy cents on the dollar. This estimate includes good,
bad and indifferent, whether in actual circulation, or assorted
and withheld from circulation.

"I can't say that I have any personal knowledge of what was
deposited by plaintiff. I could not say when the deposits were
made by the person whose checks the plaintiff deposited, whether
in April or May, or previously;.have no knowledge on the subject. All the drafts deposited by plaintiff, drawn on other
banks, were paid by those banks in the course of our daily exchanges. The defendant was ordinarily the creditor in all those
settlements. The defendant had more customers who gave
checks and drafts on other banks, and deposited with others,
than the others had on us. If we had done less with other
banks, plaintiff would have been better off. None of the November discredited, belonged to the Marine Bank. This all
belonged to the Marine and Fire Insurance Company. None
of the $170,000 belonged to defendant. All of it belonged to
the Marine and Fire Insurance Company. I don't recollect
how much of the currency we had on hand, on May 18th, belonged to defendant. I don't know that any of it did. After
the 18th; neither the Marine and Fire Insurance Company, nor
the defendant, received checks on other banks, or Illinois bank
[*538] notes, in payment of debts due them, nor would the

other banks. I don't know of a single instance in which those bills were used as currency or money after the 18th. Defendant was organized under the general banking law, some time after that law went into force."

Defendant below here offered the following in evidence, which were read as such, viz.:

Letter from plaintiff to defendant, April 29th, 1861:

Macomb, Ill., April 29.

H. B. Dox, Esq., *Cashier Marine Bank, Chicago:*

Dear Sir:—We notice in the Reports a list of current money, in the *Tribune* of this morning, that they report the three following banks as good: Grayville Bank, Shawanese Bank, Southern Bank of Ill. Do you take these? Please inform us, and oblige

Yours truly,   CHAS. CHANDLER & CO.
Per H. C. TRUMAN.

Letter from plaintiff to defendant, May 10th:

Macomb, Ill., May 10, 1861.

H. B. Dox, *Cashier Marine Bank:*

Enclosed find for Col. and our credit:

O. S. Camp,......................$1,600.00.

Yours truly,   CHAS. CHANDLER & CO.
Per J. H. CUMMINGS.

Letter from plaintiff to defendant, May 14th:

Macomb, Ills., May 14th, 1861.

H. B. Dox, *Cash. Marine Bank:*

Dear Sir:—Please *send us, per express, currency,* $2,000.

Yours truly,   CHAS. CHANDLER & CO.
Per J. H. CUMMINGS.

Letter from plaintiff to defendant, June 10th:

Macomb, Ill., June 10th, 1861.

H. B. Dox, *Cashr., Chicago, Ill.:*

Please render our account current, as we wish to compare with our books.

Yours truly,   CHARLES CHANDLER & CO.
Pr. J. H. CUMMINGS.

The court gave the following instructions, which were read to the jury; to the giving of which instructions the defendants excepted:

1. A deposit commonly signifies a bailment of property for custody without compensation, the title remaining with

the depositor, and the depositary acquiring no right in the thing deposited, but to its mere possession and custody. Hence the depositor is entitled to a return of this specie chattel on demand, and to an action to recover its possession when wrongfully withheld. As a consequence of this princi-[*539] ple, if the property is lost, stolen or destroyed, while in the possession of the depositary, and without gross or willful negligence on his part, the loss falls on the depositor.

2. But where the subject matter of the deposit or loan is money, wheat or other property, and it is delivered to the depositary for use or consumption, the law implies a contract to return, not the thing deposited or lent, but an equivalent of the same kind, nature or quality. In such cases the title to the thing deposited rests in the depositary *ipso facto*, and it remains at his risk. The only right of the depositor is to a return of an equivalent in kind or value, and his right is not impaired by reason of the subsequent loss or destruction of the property in the hands of the depositary.

3. Such is ordinarily the relation implied by law, from the dealings between a banker and his customer, where no special agreement exists varying their rights. The money, checks or bills which are the subject of the deposit, become the property of the bank, and the depositor becomes a creditor. If stolen, lost or destroyed, or if they become of no value by reason of depreciation, the bank must sustain the loss. His legal title having passed by operation of law, his right is resolved into a mere *chose in action*, or claim against the bank for the value of the deposit, usually fixed by the credit given, as in the case of an ordinary loan of money. Indeed, a general deposit with a bank is termed a gratuitous loan, payable to the depositor on demand.

4. In this case, therefore, the first question for the jury to consider, is, what is the nature and character of the relation arising out of the dealings between these parties as disclosed by the evidence? Is it the ordinary relation of a customer with his banker? If so, then what was the subject matter of the deposit? Was it money, or currency, or something else? And,

first, as to the relation of banker and customer; on this point the court instructs the jury:

5. That if the defendant was engaged in banking, and in receiving general deposits from its customers; if the plaintiff, as an interior banker, kept a deposit account with the defendant, and deposited drafts, checks and currency to his own credit, to be drawn against from time to time, in accordance with the usage of banks; that if the moneys thus deposited were, according to like usage, mingled and intermixed with the moneys of other depositors, and used by the defendant in the course of its business, then and in that case the relation implied by law is that of banker and customer, or debtor and creditor, and the title to the currency or money deposited vested in the defendant, and in the absence of any special arrangement or understanding varying or modifying [*540] the rights of the parties, the subject of the deposit remained at the risk of the defendant.

6. If this relation is found to have existed, the jury should next inquire into the nature and subject of the deposit. Was it money, current bank bills, or depreciated bills of Illinois banks, circulating at the time as money? If the latter, then were these bills received on deposit as money or currency, to be accounted for on demand, in like current funds or money? Or were they received as depreciated bills *eo nomine* upon an agreement, expressed or implied, that they should be accounted for in identically like bills of the Illinois banks, whether current or uncurrent at the time of demand? In determining this question, the jury should inquire into the course of dealing between the parties, the state and condition of the currency, the nature and value of the deposits, and whether or not any express arrangement existed regulating and fixing the basis of their dealings with each other.

7. On this point the court instructs the jury, that if they find, from the evidence, that the deposits were made in Illinois bank bills, passing current at the time in all business transactions as money, and as such were accepted and credited by the defendant, then the law implies a promise to pay in Illinois or other bank bills current at the time of demand, though

the bills deposited were subject to a discount for specie when deposited, and subsequently became entirely discredited and greatly depreciated. Such a contract can only be discharged by the payment or tender of bank notes current at the time of demand, or their equivalent in money; and the measure of the plaintiff's damages, in this case, would be such value on the 21st of June, the time of the demand, with interest thereon to date. And if no bank notes were then in circulation as money, the engagement became absolute for the payment of money. For when an amount of money is made payable in a particular thing, the contract can only be discharged in the identical description of property called for in money. Nothing else can be substituted.

8. It must, therefore, be manifest to the jury, that the rights of the parties here strictly depend upon the nature of the deposit, and their intentions concerning it. Whether the deposit of bills was made and accepted as currency on the basis of money, and credited as such, or as a commodity or species of property, to be accounted for in the like kind and quality, rather than in money. The law will allow parties to deal with each other on any basis which is legal, and their intentions will govern in the determination of their respective [*541] rights. No principle prevented these parties from dealing with each other in Illinois bank bills as a specific commodity or as currency. If the deposits were intended to be received as currency, and were credited at their nominal value as such, then the law will enforce the payment in currency, though the bills were depreciated below their nominal value, and have since gone out of circulation altogether. Parties make their own contracts, and mere inadequacy of consideration is never a defense to them, unless so gross as to be evidence of fraud. If, on the other hand, the parties were dealing in these bills as a species of merchandise, to be repaid in kind or value, then the law will enforce the agreement, and not impose a different one upon them. When the subject of deposit is ascertained, then the law will imply a promise to pay in kind, or an equivalent in value. If money, then in money; if currency, then in currency; if in stock or depreciated bank notes as a species of

property, then in each case the like, and not in something else of a different nature or value. Where the deposit is property, then a merchantable article of average value of the kind deposited must be delivered under the contract, and less than that will not be a legal tender.

9. Therefore, if the jury find, from the evidence, that by the course of dealing between the parties, or by their express agreement, the deposits were made in depreciated bank bills, and as such accepted, to be repaid by the defendant in the same kind of bills, without regard to their value as currency, or in money at the time of the demand, then the measure of plaintiff's damages is the value in money of an average lot of such Illinois bank bills as were in circulation after the first of April, of the nominal amount due the plaintiff, with interest at 6 per cent. to this date.

10. As a part of the evidence tending to establish the character of the arrangements and relations between the parties, a paper, signed by the plaintiff, and in the following words, has been given in evidence, viz.:

CHICAGO, April 26th, 1861.

"We, the undersigned, citizens and business men of Chicago, agree to receive and pay out as currency, in payment of debts, and in the general transactions of business, during the present war, the notes of all the banks of this State at present taken by the following named banks and bankers of this city, provided the bankers named below agree to do the same."

To this is attached the following instrument, purporting to be signed by all the banks and bankers therein named:

"In accordance with the above, we, the undersigned, bankers, do hereby ratify and confirm the agreement there- [*542] in expressed."

11. Among the bankers referred to, are two incorporated companies, and their assent is expressed by the signatures of their respective presidents. It is claimed by the plaintiff that if those officers had no authority, express or implied, to execute the agreement, the plaintiff is not bound by the promise alleged, as his promise is conditional. This is the law, and before any weight as evidence shall be given to this agreement,

in determining the basis of the dealings between the parties, the jury must be satisfied, from the evidence, that it was signed by authority of said companies, and is binding upon them; unless signed by all the parties named, it is not in force as against the plaintiff, and the defendant can derive no benefit under it. Therefore,

12. If the jury find that no express authority existed, and that the only evidence from which an authority could be implied is the fact that those institutions continued to do business with such bank notes as are described in the said agreement, in the same manner as they had done before, then such fact is not in itself sufficient for that purpose. And unless the jury should further find that the making of such an agreement was within the scope of the duties of the officers signing it, they will reject it altogether from their consideration.

13. If the jury find that the instrument was duly executed by the parties, then its operation is by way of *estoppel*, so far as third persons were induced to act upon the faith of it. In this view it is not material whether it was actually signed by the defendant as well as by the plaintiff, in order to give the defendant a right to claim under it. But to entitle the defendant to make that claim, it must be proved that the defendant dealt with the plaintiff solely with reference to and on faith of it. But if the defendant did not rely upon it, and its dealings with the plaintiff had no reference to it, then the plaintiff is not estopped from alleging the want of mutuality or binding obligation of the same, and the jury should disregard it.

14. But the evidence in this case may show that the business relations between the parties were of a two-fold character, viz., that of principal and agent, with respect to the checks and drafts sent by the plaintiff for collection, and of depositary of the moneys after they were collected by the defendant. If the defendant was thus employed, and as agent received bills and drafts for collection, then the law imposed upon the defendant the duty of making such collections in money, unless authorized to collect the same in the depreciated currency then in circulation as money. Such authority may be implied from [*543] the course of dealing between the parties. If the jury

find that such authority was given, and that the defendant was instructed to collect in such bills and put the same to the plaintiff's credit as a depositor, and did so, then the liability of the defendant is that of a depositary of the plaintiff's funds, and is to be ascertained and settled by an application of the principles already stated. In other words, the case is left before the jury precisely as if the defendant had received no paper for collection, and as if the several deposits had been made in Illinois currency by the plaintiff, and not through the medium of collections. That is to say, were the deposits made as currency treated as money in the dealings of the parties, or in depreciated bills as such, as already more clearly defined in these instructions?

Defendant asked the court to give the following instructions to the jury, which the court refused to do; to which decision in refusing to give such instructions, defendant then and there excepted:

1. If the jury believe, from the evidence, that the funds received by defendant were received in payment of notes, drafts or bills sent to defendant for collection, and that the said notes, drafts or bills were collected for plaintiff at his instance or request, either express or implied, in depreciated Illinois bank notes or currency, and not specie, then the law is for defendant in this action, the declaration being only for money, and not depreciated currency or other specie commodity or property.

2. If the jury believe, from the evidence, that defendant, acting at the instance and request of plaintiff, received by way of collection for him the funds sued for in this action, and such funds were depreciated bank notes or currency at the time they were collected, then the plaintiff could only recover, in any event, the value of the funds collected, or the balance on hand at the time of demand made on the 21st of June, 1861, with interest.

3. If the jury believe, from the evidence, that at any time during the continuance of the business transacted between the plaintiff and defendant, that the plaintiff stipulated or agreed that during the war they would receive and pay out Illinois bank notes in payment of debts, and ordinary transactions of

business, and the defendant, relying upon such agreement, accumulated a balance of collections, made upon account of plaintiff, in such Illinois bank notes, and that the funds sued for
were received in Illinois bank notes, upon plaintiff's collections
and account, then the plaintiff can only be entitled to receive
such notes, or in case of refusal of defendant to pay him such
[*544] notes, then their value in money or coin at the time of
demand made on the 21st of June, 1861.

But if, upon demand made, the plaintiff was offered Illinois
bank notes in payment of his balance, then the plaintiff cannot
recover in this action, the tender having discharged the defendant of any default, or failure to perform his contract.

4. If the jury believe, from the evidence, that the defendant collected, at the request of plaintiff, or by his assent, large
amounts of Illinois bank notes or currency, depreciated in
value at the time below that of specie, in payment of bills,
drafts, or notes, sent to defendant by plaintiff for collection, and
held the proceeds subject to his demand, according to his request, or instructions, and according to the ordinary usage of
bankers in such cases, then and in that case there was existing
the relation of agent on the part of defendant to the plaintiff
as their principal; and if defendant exercised the ordinary diligence of other bankers in like cases, then and in such case the
law does not cast the risk of further depreciation or loss on the
funds received, upon defendant; and the plaintiff can only recover the actual or average value of the depreciated medium
at the time of the demand made by the plaintiff.

5. If the jury believe, from the evidence, that the defendant
acted in pursuance of the request, or by direction or assent of
plaintiff, in making collections of checks, notes or bills in Illinois bank notes or currency, when they were depreciated at a
value below that of specie, and the defendant acted with ordinary diligence, according to the usage and custom existing
among bankers in Chicago—this constituted the relation of
principal and agent, and defendant was not liable to plaintiff
except for the same or like funds to those received; and if such
funds were tendered to plaintiff on demand made, it was a suf-

ficient discharge of the liability arising out of the contract between them.

6. If the jury believe, from the evidence, that plaintiff sent to defendant for collection, notes, bills and drafts, with the knowledge that the financial business of this place was done with a depreciated currency, fluctuating in value from causes out of the control of the defendant, and expressly or impliedly authorized the defendant to receive payment of such collections in such currency, and that defendant did so receive payment of them in such depreciated currency, and, by direction of plaintiff, placed such funds so received to his credit; and if the jury further believe, from the evidence, that defendant mingled the funds so received with its own funds of a similar character, according to the usage and custom of bankers in like cases, and that all defendant's like funds, in- [*545] cluding those collected for the plaintiff, depreciated in value after such collection, from causes not within the control of defendant, then the loss of such depreciation of the funds collected by defendant for plaintiff, must be borne by the plaintiff; and he is only entitled to recover of the defendant such sum of money as the jury shall believe, from the evidence, was the average value in coin, on the 21st day of June, 1861, of the notes of all the banks of Illinois that were used as currency after the first day of April, 1861, with interest from that date for the balance due from defendant to plaintiff for such collections.

7. If the jury believe, from the evidence, that it is the usage and custom of banks and bankers to mingle all the funds received by them in a common mass, and that according to such usage the defendant mixed the funds received on account of plaintiff with its own, and that its own funds with which plaintiff's were mingled were composed of the notes of the banks of Illinois, received by it in its ordinary course of business for itself and its customers, which were afterwards depreciated in value from causes not within defendant's control, then the loss by such depreciation on plaintiff's funds must fall on him.

Therefore, if the jury believe, from the evidence, that at the time defendant made the collections for plaintiff, and the several other deposits were made by him, the circulating medium of this vicinity and city was the depreciated notes of the banks of this State and Wisconsin, and that plaintiff knew it, and expressly or impliedly authorized defendant to collect his notes, drafts and checks in those bills, place them to his credit, and mix them with the like bills belonging to defendant, and that the parties dealt with each other with the understanding that defendant should collect such currency or depreciated paper money, and that plaintiff should only demand like funds of defendant in payment of such collections, whether of current value at the time of demand or not, then the loss by the depreciation of such funds after they were received by defendant must fall on the plaintiff, for the balance due from defendant to the plaintiff for collections made for him, which nominal balance is agreed to be the sum of

The jury found plaintiff's damages at $16,375.83—a new trial was denied, and a judgment was rendered on the verdict.

The following are the errors assigned:

1. The court erred in permitting the evidence offered to go in, under the money counts of the declaration, against the objections of defendant.

2. The court erred in giving his instructions to the jury.

[*546] 3. The court excluded and refused to give the instructions asked for by defendant.

4. A new trial should have been awarded to defendant, the verdict in the case being against the law and the evidence.

5. A new trial should have been awarded, upon the ground that the whole record and evidence shows that the plaintiff recovered as for "money had and received," the same as if money, and not bank notes, or indebtedness, had been the real and only foundation and cause of action.

6. The court, in all its ruling, treated depreciated -bank notes or currency, the same as money, and allowed the jury to assess damages as upon a cause of action founded upon money, instead of a contract, or cause of action, payable in other commodities only.

7. The court refused to instruct that money only could be

the subject of the recovery in action, and that if bank notes were non-specie paying, or depreciated, they could not be regarded as money by the court or jury, in any case whatever.

8. The court refused to instruct that, in cases of agency, the plaintiff, or principal, took all the risk of loss or depreciation on currency, where the agent followed his directions in receiving and holding it; and that in this case, such was the relation legally existing between the parties.

9. The court gave no instructions as asked, but delivered a general essay, or principle, which had no application to the facts in the case.

10. The whole recovery is a subversion of the clearest and most fundamental principles of law. 1st. In setting up false standards of value in actions for money. 2nd. In establishing a false measure of damages. 3rd. In charging an agent in respect to losses of his principal. 4th. Putting bank notes, not equivalent to coin, or specie, in the place of money.

C. BECKWITH, FULLER & McCAGG, and THOMAS HOYNE, for Appellant.

J. GARY, for Appellee.

WALKER, J. In determining this case, it will be proper, first to determine, whether the deposits made by appellee were a bailment only, for safe keeping by the bank, or were made to be passed to appellee's credit, in the usual course of banking business. If for the former purpose, then the appellee must be responsible for any depreciation in the value of the funds which occurred, before a demand was made, if appellant in good faith preserved the identical funds placed in the hands of the bank. If the relation of the bank to [*547] appellee, was simply that of a bailee for safe keeping, and the identical funds were preserved, and a loss ensued by depreciation, no rule of law, principle of reason or justice, can hold the bank liable for such a loss. Such a liability would be inconsistent with the undertaking, which would only require a return of the thing deposited, uninjured by the acts or neglect of the bailee. The fact that the deposit consisted of bank bills, would not distinguish it from a deposit for safe custody, of articles of property, in the rights, duties and liabilities incurred by the parties.

If, on the contrary, the deposits were designed by the parties to have become a loan to, or indebtedness by the bank, the relation of the parties would have been that of any other debtor and creditor. Banks, in the transaction of their business, may occupy either of these relations. But, when the funds are deposited to be held and returned in the same bills or coin, the deposit becomes a special one, entirely different from a general one, which authorizes the bank to use the funds in the course of their business. In this case, the evidence shows, that the deposits arose from collections, made by the bank, for the appellee. The latter, at various times, forwarded to the former, perhaps without an exception, bills, notes and checks, which, when collected, were placed to appellee's credit.

The funds thus received were placed in the general fund of the bank, and paid out indiscriminately in the course of the business of the bank. The evidence likewise shows, that these funds when collected were current, and passed as money in the payment of debts, and the various other business transactions. They at that time answered all the purposes of money, and appellee was credited by them as money. From all of the evidence in the case, it appears, that the parties considered and treated it as money, until the 18th of May, when it became so much depreciated that it ceased to circulate as such, and was thenceforth considered and treated as a commodity, bought and sold by the banks and brokers at a heavy discount. Nor was there any evidence tending to show, that the bank had any directions to hold the identical funds received at the risk of appellee. Nor is there any pretense that the bank has lost a farthing, on the money collected. It went into the common fund of the bank, and for aught that appears, every dollar may have been paid out at par, before it ceased to circulate as money.

But as the relation, of the parties to each other, was that of debtor and creditor, even if no portion of the funds had been [*548] disposed of by the bank, the liability would have been the same. As well might the purchaser of a horse, of grain or other commodity, when called on to pay, insist that the artic'e had depreciated in value, since the purchase, and that he should be relieved from paying the amount of the depreciation. No one would ever suppose, that if a merchant were to purchase a quantity of grain or other produce, and give the seller a credit at the market price, and it afterwards declined in the market, that the loss would fall upon the seller, or that he should re- ceive the same quantity and quality of grain. The same is true of almost every character of business transactions involving a sale. To establish as a rule, that in cases of that character, the loss by depreciation in price, or otherwise, should fall upon the seller and not the buyer, and give it a practical operation, would well nigh revolutionize every description of business, and would produce incalculable injustice and wrong.

The proof of the depreciated value of the paper when re- ceived, cannot change the liability of the debtor for bank bills, any more than if it had been for produce, at a higher rate than its market value. Nor can the special custom of banks in particular locality, change the laws of the land, regulating the value of the currency and fixing the standard value of the cur- rent coins. That parties may contract to receive any commo- dity, in lieu of money, in payment of indebtedness, is undenia- bly true. This can only be done by special agreement and not by usage. No custom can compel a creditor, in the absence of a special agreement, to receive anything but the constitutional currency of the country. The fact that the business men of the particular place, have been in the habit of receiving depre- ciated paper money in payment of their demands, by no means proves that all creditors in that locality have agreed to receive the same, much less a person residing hundreds of miles dis- tant. To have such an effect, a special agreement must be proved.

The doctrine of agency has no application to a case of this character. There is nothing to show, that the bank was the agent of appellee, beyond the fact that it collected the money. But even if it did appear that the bank acted as the agent of appellee, it also appears that the former appropriated the funds when collected, to its own use, and made itself debtor for the amount, by passing it to the credit of appellee, and by mingling the funds thus collected with those of the bank, and using them as its own. The proof shows, that it was the custom of the bank to so appropriate such funds, and to pay when called for by the creditor. It would hardly be contended, [*549] if an attorney were to collect a debt for a client, in bank bills, and appropriate them to his own use, that if the bank afterwards failed, that he would be exonerated from payment. No difference is perceived in the two cases.

It is further insisted, as appellee signed the agreement to receive and pay out the bills of Illinois banks, during the continuance of the present war, that he was bound to receive such paper in discharge of this debt in June, when he made the demand of payment. The testimony shows, that after the 18th of May, 1861, appellant and all the other parties to that agreement, refused to receive such funds. From this fact it may be reasonably inferred, that by mutual consent this agreement was ended, and all parties released from its further observance. When appellant and all of the parties to this agreement disregarded its stipulations, no reason is perceived why appellee should be bound by its provisions. Appellant has no right to enforce an observance of the agreement against appellee, when all other parties to it are released.

No error is perceived in giving appellee's instructions, or in refusing those asked by appellant. The verdict is warranted by the evidence, and the judgment is affirmed.

Judgment affirmed.

INDEX.

ACTION.

1. The statute has not made it the duty of a constable to collect money except by virtue of process; and an action will not lie upon his bond for money collected by him without process for that purpose. *Henckler* v. *County Court,* 39.

2. Before a party can recover for injury to property, he must show that he is either the absolute or qualified owner of it. *Ohio and Mississippi R. R. Co.* v. *Jones,* 41.

3. In an action against a railroad corporation resulting from injuries to property because of an omission to fence its road, it should appear that the road has been open for use for six months prior to the injury. Ibid. 41.

4. If an action is brought against a railroad company under the statute, and the negligence charged results from an omission to erect a fence, the declaration should show that the accident did not happen at a place where the company is not bound to maintain a fence. *Illinois Central R. R. Co.* v. *Williams,* 48.

5. In an action upon an insurance policy; which contains a condition that in the event of a loss, the company may at its option restore the building: it is unnecessary to negative the performance of this condition, in the declaration. It is a condition subsequent, and if performed, the company should allege it in defense of the action. *Ætna Insurance Co.* v. *Phelps,* 71.

6. A party may maintain trespass, if he has, at the time of the act, such a title as draws after it a constructive possession. *Gauche* v. *Mayer,* 134.

7. A had placed goods with an auctioneer for sale, reserving to himself the right to resume possession at his pleasure, the auctioneer not having any claim to or charge upon such goods: *Held,* that A had a right of action in trespass against a sheriff for making a levy upon those goods as the property of another, the sheriff having been notified of the facts before the levy. Ibid. 134.

8. A party cannot bring separate suits for several sums past due on a lease; if more than one payment is due, these payments should be consolidated into one suit. *Casselberry* v. *Forquer,* 170.

655

9. A party cannot divide an entire demand, so as to maintain several actions for its recovery. Ibid. 170.

10. A wager, that a railroad will be completed within a certain time, is not prohibited by the common law or by our statute; and a recovery can be had upon it. *Beadles* v. *Bless*, 320.

11. In an action to recover a wager, that a railroad would be built within a certain time, evidence, that the bet was talked of a good deal by the public, to show that it may have influenced subscriptions to the stock, was properly excluded. The court cannot say that it was against public policy to influence or discourage subscriptions to the road. Ibid. 320.

12. Actions by the subordinate lodges of Odd Fellows should be brought in the name of the trustees of such lodges. *Marsh* v. *Astoria Lodge*, 421.

13. An organization in fact, and user under it, is sufficient in some actions to show a corporation in fact, although there may have been irregularities or omissions in the first instance. *Marsh* v. *Astoria Lodge*, 421.

14. If the right to sue is not expressly granted to a corporation, it may still exercise the faculty, if all the powers incident to corporations are conferred upon it. Ibid. 421.

15. The question in this case is presented by a plea which, in substance, avers that there is no such corporation, and not in abatement. Ibid. 421.

16. A declaration upon the covenants in a deed averred the making of covenants of seizin, of power to sell, and of warranty, only; the breach included not only these, but also covenants against incumbrances and for quiet enjoyment. The defendant assigned as a ground for demurrer, that this one count set forth more than one cause of action. *Held*, that as all these causes of action were of the same nature and could be answered by one plea, they might be joined in one count. That these separate breaches were to be regarded as so many distinct counts. That the demurrer being to the whole count, and one of the breaches being properly assigned, the demurrer should be overruled. *Brady* v. *Spurck*, 478.

17. Several causes of action of the same nature may be joined in one count. The defendant can plead specially to each cause of action. Ibid. 478.

18. The rule as to joining causes of action is, that when the same plea may be pleaded, and the same judgment rendered on all counts, they may be joined. Ibid. 478.

19. An action on the case will not lie for improperly causing a writ of injunction to be issued. The remedy is on the injunction bond.
The case of *Cox* v. *Taylor's Administrators*, 10 B. Monroe, 17, not recognized as authority. *Gorton* v. *Brown*, 489.

ADMINISTRATOR.

1. An attorney, who is an administrator, is not entitled to an allowance against the estate for professional services he may have rendered it. If

he perform such services, they will be regarded as a gratuity. *Willard* v. *Bassett*, 37.

2. Infants are bound by proceedings by an administrator to sell real estate, although they are not nominally made parties to the proceeding. The case *Ex parte Sturms*, 25th Illinois R. 390, overruled in part. *Gibson* v. *Roll*, 88.

3. If the proceedings of a guardian to sell the estates of infants have not been regular and in conformity to law, they must have an opportunity to correct the errors. But such proceedings are not adverse to the interests of the infant, and if they have been regular, the infant will be bound by them. The case of *Mason* v. *Wait*, 4 Scam. 127, examined. Ibid. 88.

4. A proceeding by an administrator to sell the real estate of his decedent, is adverse to the infants, and he must follow the statute in his petition, and give proper notice; if he does this, the sale will be good. The court is to pass upon the sufficiency of the statements in the notice, which calls upon parties to object to the proceedings. Ibid. 88.

5. Proceedings for the sale of land by an administrator will be reversed, if the record does not show any petition by the administrator. *Monahon* v. *Vandyke*, 154.

6. It is error for the Circuit Court to order a sale of land by an administrator, when the notice has been published but thirty days, while the statute requires a publication for six weeks, before the presentation of the petition. Ibid. 154.

7. The sureties upon an administrator's bond, applied to the probate court under the 79th and 80th sections of the statute of wills, to have the administrator give a new bond. The court took two new bonds from the administrator, the penalties of which being added together, equaled in amount the penalty in the old bond. This was held to be a substantial compliance with the statute, which requires that the new bond shall be in the like penalty as the first. *People, etc.*, v. *Lott*, 215.

8. Where a new bond is given by an administrator or executor under the 79th and 80th sections of the statute of wills, the sureties upon the first bond are released from all liability for past as well as for subsequent acts. Ibid. 215.

9. If, instead of a new bond being given, the letters should be revoked, the sureties would only be released from future liabilities. Ibid. 215.

10. Where administrators have given several bonds, and there is a complication of interests, resulting from the death of one of the administrators and of some of the sureties, whose legal representatives cannot be made parties in a joint action at law upon the bonds, a court of equity will entertain jurisdiction. Ibid. 215.

11. The representatives of all of the deceased sureties should be made parties to such a bill. Ibid. 215.

12. The 69th section of the statute of wills, in giving an action on an administrator's or executor's bond, against all or any portion of the obligors, has reference only to actions at law, and not to suits in chancery. Ibid. 215.

13. The last clause of that section, making certified copies of such bonds evidence, was only designed to change a rule of evidence, and not the practice in courts of equity. Ibid. 215.

See ATTORNEY AND CLIENT. EXECUTION. PRACTICE, 22.

AGENT—AGENCY.

1. When the attorney of a party becomes the purchaser at a forced sale, he stands in the shoes of his client; and though the attorney designed to purchase for his own benefit, the client may claim the purchase for himself. *Moore* v. *Bracken*, 23.

2. It is error to instruct the jury, that if, the defendant purchased lumber from the plaintiffs without disclosing the fact that he was purchasing as the agent of another, he became personally liable for the price of the lumber—because the plaintiffs may have known all the time that the defendant was merely an agent; in which event he would not be personally liable. *Warren* v. *Dickson*, 115.

3. If one bargains with an agent for a horse, knowing him to be such agent, and that the principal had recognized the transaction, a warranty by the agent is the warranty of the principal, who is the proper party to be sued for a breach. *Marckle* v. *Haskins*, 382.

See ATTORNEY AND CLIENT, 1.

AGREEMENT.

1. An agreement to submit a case upon briefs, to be decided in vacation, order and decree to be entered as of that or the next term, will be construed as a submission of the whole controversy, and not of the submission of a motion to dissolve an injunction. *Anderson* v. *White*, 57.

2. When parties make a new agreement, revoking an old one, and a horse is paid as a part of the consideration on the new agreement, one of the parties cannot refuse to execute it because the other has not executed a reconveyance of land, no time being fixed for that purpose. A reasonable time will be allowed for performance, and a tender of the reconveyance was not an indispensable preliminary to the enforcement of the new agreement. The parties must be restored to their original rights before either can insist upon a rescinding of the new contract. Ibid. 57.

3. A sold a stock of goods and a house and lot to B and C. The latter consented to relinquish the sale, and that A might find other purchasers, which he did, and sold to D and E, agreeing to give to D and E a title to the house and lot, which had been conveyed to B and C. These gave up the deed to themselves to D and E. On a suit by A, against D and E, on the notes given by them for the goods and the house and lot, they pleaded these facts, alleging failure of consideration, they not having received a conveyance of the house and lot. *Held*, that D and E were entitled to a conveyance to themselves, and if there was any special replication to the pleas, it should have been set out—that the handing over

of the conveyance to themselves by A and B, was no conveyance, and that a finding sustaining the pleas should not be disturbed, but that A might resort in chancery to B and C, for a conveyance of, the house and lot. *Wilson* v. *Wood*, 199.

4. When by agreement, persons have a joint interest of the same nature in a particular adventure, they are, as between themselves, partners; although some contribute money alone, and others labor alone. *Robbins* v. *Laswell*, 365.

5. If parties agree to share profits, they are partners as to such profits; although they do not agree to share in the losses. Ibid. 365.

6. A written agreement as to dividing profits may be extended tacitly by the mutual understanding of the parties, or by their conduct in relation to it. Ibid. 365.

See CONTRACT.

AMENDMENTS.

1. A person who holds, the beneficial interest in a mortgage should be, made the complainant, yet when the use is declared, the suit need not be dismissed if the bill should be amended by, striking out the name of the nominal complainant; and such an amendment would not produce injury. *Winkelman* v. *Kiser*, 21.

2. In appeals from justices, the Circuit Court cannot amend summons by changing the names of parties. *Henckler* v. *County Court* 39.

APPEALS.

1. An appeal from the decision of a justice of the peace, gives the appellate court jurisdiction of the party, although he was not served with process in the case appealed from; and the appellate court can proceed to a trial on the merits. *Ohio and Mississippi R. R. Co.* v. *McCutchin*, 9.

2. A railroad company cannot appeal to the Circuit Court from an assessment of its property for taxation by a board of supervisors. If any remedy exists, it may be by *certiorari*. *Same* v. *Lawrence County*, 50.

3. The provision of the constitution granting the right of appeal, needs legislative action to make it available. Ibid. 50.

4. Where, the record of proceedings before the commissioners of highways, for the laying out of a road, shows that due notice has been given, by posting copies of the petition; upon an appeal regularly taken to the supervisors of the county, the supervisors acquire the jurisdiction necessary to determine the validity of the notices, and their decision upon that point cannot be collaterally attacked. *Wells* v. *Hicks*, 343.

5. To prove that in proceedings for laying out a highway the copies of the petition were properly posted, it is not necessary to call as witnesses, the parties who posted them. Their *ex parte* affidavits attached to the petition are sufficient. Ibid. 343.

6. The statute, which requires the commissioners of highways to act within

ARBITRATION AND AWARD.

ASSESSMENT.

2. The provision of the constitution granting the right of appeal, needs legislative action to make it available. Ibid. 50.

3. For purposes of taxation property should be assessed at its present value, and not at its prospective value. *The State* v. *Illinois Central R. R. Co.* 64.

4. In assessing the value of a railroad, for purposes of taxation, the inquiry should be, what is the property worth, to be used for the purposes for which it was designed, and not for any other purposes to which it might be applied? Ibid. 64.

5. In such a case, if the property is devoted to the use for which it was designed, and is in a condition to produce its maximum income, one very important element for ascertaining its present value, is the amount of its net profits. Ibid. 64.

6. This, however, should not be the absolute standard of value. There should be taken in connection with it, the inquiry, what would a prudent man give for the property as a permanent investment, with a view to present and future income? Ibid. 64.

See TAXES.

ASSIGNMENT—ASSIGNEE.

1. An assignment of a judgment is a revocation of the authority of plaintiff's attorney to collect or control it. *Trumbull* v. *Nicholson*, 149.

2. An assignment of a note, in order to cut off a defense by the maker, must not only be before maturity, but must be *bona fide*, and if made for that express purpose, will be invalid. *Cooper* v. *Nock*, 301.

3. A note given to a county, is properly assigned by the clerk of the County Court under its seal. *Gatton* v. *Dimmitt*, 400.

ASSUMPSIT.

A and B, each sent cattle to market, which were sold by the same broker, who, in accounting to the parties, paid A too much, and B, by precisely the same sum, too little; B sued A to recover his deficit. *Held*, that there was no such privity between these parties, as would create a liability. *Hall* v. *Carpen*, 386.

ATTACHMENT.

1. A sufficient notice to a debtor under a foreign attachment should be shown of record. *Anderson* v. *Cariker*, 358.

2. Actions in attachment must be commenced where the defendant has property, or where he can be found, and service must be upon him or his property. The court does not acquire jurisdiction by issuing two writs, one of which is to another county than that where the process is returnable, although there may be property to attach in such other county. *Hinman* v. *Rushmore et al.* 509.

ATTORNEY AND CLIENT.

1. Where the attorney of a party becomes the purchaser at a forced sale, he stands in the shoes of his client; and though the attorney designed to purchase for his own benefit, the client may claim the purchase for himself. *Moore* v. *Bracken*, 23.

2. An attorney, who is an administrator, is not entitled to an allowance against the estate for professional services he may have rendered it. If he perform such services, they will be regarded as a gratuity. *Willard* v. *Bassett*, 37.

3. An attorney has no power to receive depreciated money, in satisfaction of a judgment. *Trumbull* v. *Nicholson*, 149.

4. If an attorney should accept from the sheriff depreciated money, in satisfaction of an execution, the owner of the judgment is not bound by such acceptance; and may compel the sheriff to return the amount in legal currency. If the sheriff has been injured by the conduct of the attorney, he must look to him for redress. Ibid. 149.

5. An assignment of a judgment, is a revocation of the authority of the plaintiff's attorney to receive the money on the execution, or to control the judgment. Ibid. 149.

6. A solicitor in a case, cannot act as a special master to execute the decree. *White* v. *Haffaker*, 349.

BANKS AND BANK BILLS.

1. A certificate of deposit payable in "Illinois currency," cannot be satisfied by depreciated paper; it must be met by bills passing in the locality in the place of coin. It might be otherwise if the certificate had been made payable in Illinois bank paper. *Chicago M. & F. Ins. Co.* v. *Keiron*, 501.

2. The words "Illinois currency" mean something different from gold or silver, or their equivalents, and may be used in reference to things of different values, when applied to the uses of traffic; and on enforcing a contract using these words, it is proper to show what meaning the parties intended to give them in their use of them. CATON, C. J. *Chicago M. & F. Ins. Co.* v. *Keiron*, 501.

3. Where it appears that a bank received for a customer by collecting or by receipt of deposits, funds, which were current, and passed as money in general business transactions, without directions to hold the identical funds, it will have to account to the owner for the sums so received, without diminution or discount, notwithstanding the bills received by the bank were at the time or have since depreciated in value. *Marine Bank* v. *Chandler*, 525.

4. The special custom of bankers in a particular locality, cannot change values as fixed by law; and if some persons have been in the habit of receiving depreciated paper in payment of dues, the right to enforce payments in such paper does not exist. Such a right can only arise by contract. Ibid. 525.

becomes merely the instrument, by which the action of the board is manifest. *Clarke* v. *Board of Supervisors*, 303.

14. In ordering an election, to determine whether a county will subscribe for stock to aid in building a railroad, it is improper to submit the question, whether two different roads shall be so aided, by a single vote; so that the two propositions cannot be voted upon separately. The county may be restrained from issuing bonds in pursuance of such a vote; but when issued they are not necessarily void, in the hands of a *bona fide* holder. Ibid. 303.

15. Where county bonds, to aid the construction of a railroad, have been issued, in pursuance of an election held without warrant of law, as where it has been ordered by a person or tribunal having no such authority, they are absolutely void. But where the election has been properly authorized, and there has been informality in the manner of submitting the question to the people (such as submitting two propositions as to aiding two different roads to a single vote), the bonds may be rendered valid, in the hands of an innocent holder, by the acquiescence of the people, and their subsequent ratification by the county, in levying a tax and paying interest upon them. *Clarke* v. *Board of Supervisors*, 303.

16. The giving of a bond in satisfaction of a judgment, is in law a payment of it. *Cook* v. *Reed et al.* 434.

17. An action on the case will not lie for improperly causing a writ of injunction to be issued. The remedy is on the injunction bond.
The case of *Cox* v. *Taylor's Administrators*, 10 B. Monroe, 17, not recognized as authority. *Gorton* v. *Brown*, 489.

See ARBITRATION.

BOOKS OF ACCOUNT.

In an action upon a note, the books of a banker, showing entries made by third parties without the knowledge of the litigants, are n ot proper evidence. Such books are not public records, nor do they fall within any recognized class of written or documentary evidence. *Barnes* v. *Simmons*, 512.

CAPIAS.

1. A justice of the peace issues a capias upon an oath, an affidavit is not necessary, and the presumption is, that a justice requires all the necessary averments in the oath, such as are commanded by the constitution and laws. *Outlaw* v. *Davis et al.* 467.

2. The plaintiff in a suit where a capias has been issued by a justice of the peace, is not answerable with the justice in trespass *vi et armis*, even if the process has been issued without a sufficient oath; the magistrate is the proper person to pass upon its sufficiency. If a party acts maliciously, case is the proper remedy. Nor would a magistrate be liable in trespass, if he had jurisdiction to issue the process. Ibid. 467.

CERTIFICATE.

The certificate of a county clerk, showing that A. B. was not a justice of the peace, at the date of an acknowledgment, purporting to have been taken by him, is some though not conclusive evidence of such fact. *Ross* v. *Hole,*104.

CERTIORARI.

1. The only office which the common law writ of certiorari performs, is to certify the record of a proceeding from an inferior to a superior tribunal· It is the duty of the inferior body to whom it is directed, to transmit a complete transcript of the record, properly certified, to the court awarding the writ; without any statement of facts *dehors* the record. *Commissioners of Highways* v. *Supervisors, etc.* 140. .

2. The superior tribunal, upon an inspection of the record alone, determines whether the inferior tribunal had jurisdiction of the parties and of the subject matter, and whether it has exceeded its jurisdiction, or has otherwise proceeded in violation of law. Ibid. 140.

3. This proceeding is wholly different from a trial under our statutory writ of *certiorari*, inasmuch as that is a trial *de novo*. Ibid. 140.

4. Upon an appeal to the board of supervisors from the decision of the commissioners of highways, as to the laying out of a road, it is not necessary that the supervisors should examine the entire road. It will be sufficient if they examine that portion of the road against which the objections are urged. Ibid. 140.

5. Where the commissioners of highways make themselves parties to a proceeding to reverse a decision of the supervisors, by a writ of certiorari, and are unsuccessful, a judgment against them for costs is proper. *Commissioners of Highways* v. *Board of Supervisors*, 140.

6. If they were acting in behalf of the town, they should have appeared in its name and not in their own. Ibid. 140.

CHANCERY.

1. A person who holds a beneficial interest in a mortgage should be made the complainant, yet when the use is declared, the suit need not be dismissed if the bill should be amended by striking out the name of the nominal complainant; and such an amendment would not produce injury. *Winkelman* v. *Kiser*, 21.

2. A decree should not be pronounced against a party not before the court· Ibid. 21.

3. A decree should not be entered against the purchaser of mortgaged premises, whether he be or not a purchaser with notice; the decree should direct a sale of the premises and a distribution of the proceeds. If he held the equity of redemption, the sale might bar it, if he failed to redeem. Ibid. 21.

4. It is erroneous to decree a sale of premises in thirty days, where there is not any redemption from the sale. *Moore* v. *Bracken*, 23.

5. In chancery all matters, whether of discretion or of positive law, are subject to review in a superior court. A bill of review may also be filed in the same court to correct an error in the original decree. Ibid. 23.

6. Where the attorney of a party becomes the purchaser at a forced sale, he stands in the shoes of his client, and though the attorney designed to purchase for his own benefit, the client may claim the purchase for himself. Ibid. 23.

7. An agreement to submit a cause upon briefs, to be decided in vacation, order and decree to be entered as of that or the next term, will be construed as a submission of the whole controversy, and not of the submission of a motion to dissolve an injunction. *Anderson* v. *White*, 57.

8. When parties make a new agreement, revoking an old one, and a horse is paid as a part of the consideration on the new agreement, one of the parties cannot refuse to execute it because the other has not executed a reconveyance of land, no time being fixed for that purpose. A reasonable time will be allowed for performance, and a tender of the reconveyance was not an indispensable preliminary to the enforcement of the new agreement. The parties must be restored to their original rights before either can insist upon a rescinding of the new contract. Ibid. 57.

9. Where a purchaser, under a verbal contract for the sale of land, takes possession by consent of the vendor, and makes valuable improvements, and within the time agreed upon for payment, tenders the purchase money, the case is taken out of the statute of frauds, and the purchaser is entitled to a specific performance of the oral agreement. *Blunt* v. *Tomlin*, 93.

10. It is no defense for third parties who subsequently purchased of the vendor with full notice, and before the time for payment expired, that the vendor had disaffirmed the verbal contract, and sold to them before the purchase money was actually paid or tendered. The purchaser is entitled to protection, if he paid or tendered the money within the time agreed upon. Ibid. 93.

11. Where a purchaser of land under an oral agreement, has five years in which to make his payments, so that the contract conflicts with two sections of the statute of frauds, he may nevertheless be entitled to a specific performance. The same facts which would take the case out of one section of the statute, will take it out of the other. In such a case, the court should be more cautious in examining the evidence of the oral contract. Ibid. 93.

12. A party who makes a tender for a deed under a contract, need not part with the money, until he receives his deed. If the vendor offers to take the money but refuses to make the deed, this is a refusal of the tender, and it is a useless ceremony to count out the money after that. *Blunt* v. *Tomlin*, 93.

13. A tender made in pursuance of a contract for a deed, fixes the rights of the parties, as conclusively as if the money had been actually paid. Ibid. 93.

14. Where an answer is filed for infant defendants, by one purporting to

be their guardian *ad litem,* and the decree recites that he was so appointed, but the record shows no separate order of appointment, it will be presumed that the appointment was regularly made. *Tibbs* v. *Allen,* 119.

15. Where the record shows a notice by publication in a chancery cause, which recites the fact that an affidavit of the non-residence of the defendants was duly filed, but the affidavit does not appear in the record, this court will regard that recital as an official declaration by the clerk, and will presume that the affidavit was duly filed. Ibid. 119.

16. Where there are infant and adult defendants, and the adults alone prosecute a writ of error, they cannot assign for error those proceedings which only affect the interests of the infants. Ibid. 119.

17. Upon a bill for a partition brought by one of the heirs at law, in which it is suggested that the widow is entitled to dower in the lands sought to be divided, but the prayer does not ask that her dower be assigned, the court cannot decree an assignment of dower and appoint commissioners to set it off. Nor can the court give the widow an estate in fee in one-third of the land, in lieu of her life estate, for dower. Ibid. 119.

18. Where the affidavit and report of commissioners appointed to make partition bear date one day prior to the order of their appointment, and no specific objection is raised to this, it will be regarded as a mistake of the clerk in making up the record. Ibid. 119.

19. Commissioners appointed to make partition, should take the·oath as provided by the statute, "to make partition in accordance with the judgment of the court as to the rights and interests of the parties." It is irregular for them to be sworn, merely to divide the land impartially. Ibid. 119.

20. Commissioners appointed to make partition, reported, "that from all the circumstances surrounding the pecuniary condition of the family, and the locality of the lands, they cannot be divided without prejudice to the owners." *Held,* that this report was not in conformity with the statute, and did not justify the court in ordering a sale of the lands. Ibid. 119.

21. A bill in chancery for a partition should set out the title of the petitioner, or show the interest he claims in the premises sought to be divided. Ibid. 119.

22. The decree in a chancery proceeding for partition, should set out the respective interests and titles of the parties, and it is error for the decree to provide for an equal division among the defendants without finding that they have equal interests in the land. Ibid. 119.

23. Infants are not bound by a decree unless all of the evidence necessary to establish it, is preserved in the record. Ibid. 119.

24. Where a default has been taken and a decree entered *pro confesso,* which recites that the defendants have been regularly notified of the pendency of the suit, by summons or advertisement, a *bona fide* purchaser under the decree will be protected, although the record may not furnish

any evidence of a summons or advertisement. *Reddick* v. *State Bank*, 145.

25. Upon a writ of error in a chancery cause, the Supreme Court will not presume that any evidence was given in the court below, except what appears in the record. Ibid. 145.

26. Strict proof is required against infant defendants, and the record must furnish the evidence to sustain a decree against them, whether their guardian answers or not. No confession by their guardian can bind them. Ibid. 145.

27. If a non-resident is proceeded against by publication in a chancery cause, the court does not acquire jurisdiction over his person, unless a summons has been regularly issued, and returned by the sheriff. *Smith* v. *Trimble*, 152.

28. The absence of a summons from the record, cannot be supplied by the return of a certificate of the clerk to a writ of *certiorari*, that there had been a summons which was lost, nor by the recital in the notice of publication, that it had been issued. Ibid. 152.

29. Upon a writ of error, this court only looks to the transcript of the record. If papers have been lost from the files or mutilated, they may be supplied in some cases by the Circuit Court upon satisfactory evidence, after a proper notice to the opposite party. This court has no authority to permit a party to supply, by proof, any part of the record. Ibid. 152.

30. When a bill is taken as confessed, the court may, in its discretion, require proof as to all or any portion of the allegations in the bill, and the evidence need not be preserved in the record, or it may render a decree on the *pro confesso* order without evidence. Ibid. 152.

31. A decree should ascertain the precise amount to be paid, and not leave it to computation. Ibid. 152.

32. A petition for a mechanics' lien is not obnoxious to a demurrer, because it avers that material was furnished to two persons, to erect a building on the land of one. *Roach* v. *Chapin*, 194.

33. The rendition of a decree on the overruling of a demurrer to a bill, without first ruling the defendant to answer, is not error. The rendition of a decree upon a bill taken as confessed, is matter of discretion. Ibid. 194.

34. The act of February, 1861, provides that the former act in relation to mechanics' liens shall be held to include implied as well as express contracts, under which labor or material is furnished; provided they are done or furnished within one year from the commencement of the furnishing; and if these are done after the passage of the latter act, a petition need not aver that there was a time within which the materials were to be furnished. Ibid. 194.

35. After a notice has been given to the administrator of a deceased debtor, of the existence of a judgment against the decedent, in accordance with Sec. 3, Chap. 47, Rev. Stat., the judgment creditor may issue an execu-

tion, and also an *alias* or *pluries*, without further notice. *Letcher* v. *Morrison*, 209.

36. Morrison purchased a piece of land under an execution against James Duncan, and filed his bill to set aside conveyances which vested the title to the land in John Duncan, alleging them to be fraudulent. Subsequently the land was sold by the administrator of John Duncan, under an order of court, as his property. Morrison received the proceeds of this sale for a claim which he held against the estate of John Duncan. *Held*, that this did not estop Morrison from asserting his title to the land. Ibid. 209.

37. On a bill filed for a settlement of partnership accounts, where the proofs and statements leave everything in such doubt and uncertainty that it is impossible to do justice, the bill should be dismissed without costs. *Vermillion* v. *Bailey*, 230.

38. Where a fact is alleged in a bill and admitted by the answer, the admission is conclusive; and evidence tending to dispute it, should not be considered. *Weider* v. *Clark*, 251.

39. Moore owned a tract of land which he had mortgaged to Clark for $1,400. Weider wished to buy this tract from Moore for $2,000, and another tract from Clark for $1,600. It was arranged that Moore should convey his tract to Clark for the $3,000, less the mortgage, and that Clark should then convey both tracts to Weider for $4,600—Weider to pay $1,000 down, and give a mortgage for the balance. *Held*, that this was a sale of the whole premises from Clark to Weider, and that the mortgage being given for a part of the purchase money, Weider could not claim a homestead in the Moore tract to defeat a foreclosure. Ibid. 251.

40. Parties who claim that another is a trustee for their benefit, must clearly prove the fact. Especially so, if the trust is assumed to be in favor of those who have grossly ill-treated the person supposed to have created it. *Clarke* v. *Quackenbos*, 260.

41. A recovered a judgment against C, and was at the same time surety for B, upon an arbitration bond, for submitting differences between B and C to arbitration. C obtained an award against B, and then filed a bill to have the amount of the judgment credited on the award. *Held*, that as A's liability to C was only contingent and might never arise, he should not be restrained from collecting the judgment unless it was alleged that he was insolvent or about to leave the State. *Hinrichsen* v. *Reinback*, 295.

42. In a bill for the specific performance of a parol agreement for the sale of lands, if the defendant denies the agreement, and does not set up the statute of frauds as a defense, he cannot afterwards insist upon the statute in bar. *Hull* v. *Peer*, 312.

43. In a bill for a specific performance, the complainant need not, at his peril, state the precise amount due. He may state his case most favorably to himself, and if, upon the equities of the case, the court should

55. Collins and Stephens purchased land jointly, giving their joint notes secured by a mortgage upon the same premises for the purchase money. They then partitioned the premises, each agreeing to provide for a specified proportion of the purchase money. Collins paid up his part and procured a release of the premises set off to him. *Held*, that it was proper for the mortgagee, in foreclosing, to take a decree against Stephens alone for the balance due. Ibid. 444.

56. A trustee appointed by a court, though not invested with legal title to property, has such equitable title as will enable him to proceed in his own name in aid of the trust. *Leach v. Thomas*, 457.

57. When a court of equity obtains jurisdiction, and gives to a party all that he had asked by a motion in a proceeding at law, he cannot complain of a proceeding that has not done him an injury. Ibid. 457.

58. An action on the case will not lie for improperly causing a writ of injunction to be issued. The remedy is on the injunction bond. The case of *Cox v. Taylor's Administrators*, 10 B. Monroe, 17, not recognized as authority. *Gorton v. Brown*, 489.

CHURCHES.

The usages of a church, or the law of its organization as a religious society, if they are to be considered in deciding legal controversies, should be proved as facts. In the absence of testimony, it will be presumed that religious societies cannot dissolve their connection with the principal organization without permission. *Vasconcellos v. Ferraria*, 237.

CIRCUIT COURTS AND CLERKS.

1. The Circuit Court should not, in cases of appeal from a justice of the peace, authorize an amendment of the summons, by changing the names of parties. *Henckler v. County Court*, 39.

2. It is the duty of the clerk of the Circuit Court to make a full transcript of all of the record. This court is not permitted to act upon his statements, given in the transcript, that papers were filed or withdrawn. *Freeland v. Board of Supervisors*, 303.

3. It is generally a matter of discretion whether the Circuit Court will rule a party to file security for costs; but if the affidavit upon which the motion is founded be insufficient, the Circuit Court has no power under the statute to make the rule, and its decision will be reviewed in the Supreme Court. *Ball v. Bruce*, 332.

4. Upon a motion for a rule upon the plaintiff to file additional security for costs, an affidavit is insufficient which only avers the insolvency of the plaintiff and his security; it should show, in addition, that the circumstances of the principal or security have changed since the approval of the former bond. Ibid. 332.

See APPEALS. JURISDICTION. JUSTICES OF THE PEACE. PRACTICE.

CITIES.

See Towns and Cities.

CLAIM AND COLOR OF TITLE.

1. The covenant that the grantor is seized of an estate in fee simple, is satisfied if he has a seizin in fact, by having entered into possession, claiming a fee simple in the land. *Watts* v. *Parker*, 224.

2. An entry into possession, under a paper title, claiming the fee, and the peaceable possession for more than twenty-six years, make a seizin in fee simple. *Watts* v. *Parker*, 224.

3. Possession and payment of taxes for seven years under claim and color of title, will satisfy the covenant of seizin in fee simple. Ibid. 224.

4. A deed purporting to claim land must be under seal. Ibid. 224.

5. A party may show possession and payment of taxes under claim and color of title; although his chain of title may show a deed not under seal. Ibid. 224.

6. A clerk's or sheriff's deed on a tax sale is sufficient to show claim and color of title, if it appear on its face to be regular. The person relying upon it is not bound to show that the prerequisites of the statute have been complied with. *Holloway et al.* v. *Clark*, 483.

7. A quit-claim deed is sufficient to show claim and color of title under the limitation act of 1839. Ibid. 483.

8. H. obtained claim and color of title in 1842, and conveyed to B. in 1845. B. allowed the land to be sold for the taxes for 1847, and bought it himself; he then paid the taxes from 1849 to 1856, inclusive. P., the minor heir of a person who had died seized of the patent title, in 1853 redeemed from the sale of 1847, by paying to the clerk double the amount of the purchase money and all the taxes, with interest, for five years, being up to the time of the redemption. *Held*, that this redemption by P. entirely obliterated the tax sale of 1847, and the payment of taxes by B. for the five years, and that the grantees of B. could not defend under the limitation act of 1839, without showing payment of taxes for seven years, exclusive of the five years from 1849 to 1853. Ibid. 483.

9. The provisions of the limitation act of 1839, empowering minors to redeem land sold for taxes, within three years after attaining their majority, by paying to the person who has paid the tax, the amount with interest, do not take from the minor the right to redeem within one year after his majority, by paying double the amount, etc., to the collector, according to Sec. 69, Chap. LXXXIX, Rev. Stat. 1848. Ibid. 483.

10. A person whose lands had been sold for taxes during his infancy, for the purpose of redeeming them, after he attained his majority, paid the necessary amount to the clerk. The purchaser accepted this money from the clerk. *Held*, that by that act, he admitted the right of the infant to redeem under the statute. Ibid. 483.

COMMONS.

1. The United States has, by grant, confirmed to the inhabitants of the village of Cahokia, the use of the "commons" adjacent to the village. The parishioners not living in the village, worshiping at the church in the village, do not, of right, participate in the use of those "commons." *Hebert* v. *Lavalle*, 448.

2. Parties deriving title from original inhabitants of the village of Cahokia, do not enjoy rights of common which might have pertained to their grantors, if the grantees have abandoned the village. The "commons" were made appurtenant to village lots, not to lands remote from the village. Ibid. 448.

3. Occupants of the common field lands, not inhabitants of the village of Cahokia, cannot vote for the supervisor authorized to survey parts of the "commons" into lots, and lease the same, nor for the trustees of schools, under authority of the act of 1841. Ibid. 448.

4. A stranger cannot question the acts of "commoners" amongst themselves, even though they should enclose the "commons." Ibid. 448.

CONDITIONS.

A testator gave to his wife all his estate, to be disposed of in any way that would best support her for life, but if his sons, John and Thomas, should take care of their mother, they were to have certain lands, but if they failed to support their mother, then she could sell the land, or any part of it, to support herself; but if the sons complied with these conditions, they were to take immediate possession of the land; there were bequests to other children: *Held*, that the testator intended to charge his entire estate with the support of his widow; that the question of support was a condition subsequent, the word "comply" being used in the sense of "assent," and when John and Thomas assented, the estate passed to them, burthened with the condition of support of the mother; and that the widow of John being his heir, and proffering to support the widow, had a right to inherit and possess the estate, and could compel the grantee of the widow to reconvey to her. *Jennings* v. *Jennings*, 518.

CONFESSION.

When a bill is taken as confessed, the court may, in its discretion, require proof as to all or any portion of the allegations in the bill, and the evidence need not be preserved in the record, or it may render a decree on the *pro confesso* order without evidence. *Smith* v. *Trimble*, 152.

CONSIDERATION.

See NEGLIGENCE. PROMISSORY NOTE. RAILROADS.

CONSTABLE.

1. The statute has not made it the duty of a constable to collect money ex-

cept by virtue of process; and an action will not lie upon his bond for money collected by him without process for that purpose. *Henckler* v. *County Court,* 39.

2. There is no lawful mode of renewing an execution, except there has been a return to that already issued by the officer, of his doings thereon. A justice of the peace cannot renew an execution by any indorsement of his upon it. *Calhoun County* v. *Buck et al.* 440.

3. A constable must, within the time appointed by law, return an execution with an indorsement of his doings thereon, for the truth of which he is responsible; but no particular form of indorsement is required. Ibid. 440.

4. One constable cannot hand over an execution to another, so as to relieve himself from the responsibility of its return according to the statute; if another constable returns the execution, within the statutory time, it may save him from liability to whom it was first delivered. Ibid. 440.

CONSTRUCTION OF STATUTES.

1. A town or village, within the meaning of the statute requiring railroad corporations to construct fences, may exist, although there is no plat of the same, dedicating streets, etc., in the manner pointed out by the statute in that regard. *Illinois Central R. R. Co.* v. *Williams,* 48.

2. In construing an amendatory statute, it is a fixed rule that the old law must be considered, the mischief arising under that law, and the remedy for it, which the new law may be supposed to provide. *Maus* v. *Logansport, Peoria and Burlington R.R. Co.* 77.

3. The act of February 14th, 1855, amendatory of the revenue law, which directs that the track or superstructure of a railroad shall be denominated "fixed and stationary personal property," was intended to create a species of personal property not before known to the law. For non-payment of taxes upon this property, the collector may levy upon the rails and remove them from the track, for the purpose of selling them. Ibid. 77.

4. This act has reference only to the collection of the revenue, and does not change the character of such property for other purposes. Ibid. 77.

5. Section 14, of the amendatory act of 1853, which provides that real property shall be liable for taxes on personal property, and *vice versa*, has no application to this "fixed and stationary personal property;" such property must bear its own burden of taxation. *Maus* v. *Logansport, P. & B. R. R. Co.* 77.

6. It is within the province of the legislature to provide that property, which is attached to the freehold, so as to become a part of it by the common law, may be regarded as personal property, for all purposes, or for any special purpose. Of this character is the act of Feb. 14th, 1855, which directs that the tract and superstructure of a railroad, together with the improvements at stations, shall be denominated personal property, for the purposes of collecting the revenue. Ibid. 77.

7. The sureties upon an administrator's bond, applied to the probate court under the 79th and 80th sections of the statute of wills, to have the administrator give a new bond. The court took two new bonds from the administrator, the penalties of which being added together, equaled in amount the penalty in the old bond. This was held to be a substantial compliance with the statute, which requires that the new bond shall be in the like penalty as the first. *People* v. *Lott*, 215.

8. Where a new bond is given by an administrator or executor under the 79th and 80th sections of the statute of wills, the sureties upon the first bond are released from all liability for past as well as for subsequent acts. Ibid. 215.

9. If, instead of a new bond being given, the letters should be revoked, the sureties would only be released from future liabilities. Ibid. 215.

10. Where administrators have given several bonds, and there is a complication of interests, resulting from the death of one of the administrators and of some of the sureties, whose legal representatives cannot be made parties in a joint action at law upon the bonds, a court of equity will entertain jurisdiction. Ibid. 215.

11. The representatives of all of the deceased sureties should be made parties to such a bill. Ibid. 215.

12. The 69th section of the statute of wills, in giving an action on an administrator's or executor's bond, against all or any portion of the obligors, has reference only to actions at law, and not to suits in chancery. Ibid. 215.

13. The last clause of that section, making certified copies of such bonds evidence, was only designed to change a rule of evidence, and not the practice in courts of equity. Ibid. 215.

14. The statute for the protection of occupying claimants is designed to protect those who shall in good faith take peaceable possession of vacant land under such a paper title as the records of the county show to be plain, clear and connected, and without notice of any adverse title of record. *Montag* v. *Linn*, 328.

15. The protection of a party under this statute does not depend upon the original deeds through which he deraigns his title being regular upon their face; such deeds may contain material alterations, or be forgeries, and yet the purchaser may be protected, where the records of the county show a clear chain of title. Ibid. 328.

16. Where the record of proceedings before the commissioners of highways, for the laying out of a road, shows that due notice has been given, by posting copies of the petition; upon an appeal regularly taken to the supervisors of the county, the supervisors acquire the jurisdiction necessary to determine the validity of the notices, and their decision upon that point cannot be collaterally attacked. *Wells* v. *Hicks*, 343.

17. To prove that in proceedings for laying out a highway the copies of the petition were properly posted, it is not necessary to call as witnesses, the parties who posted them. Their *ex parte* affidavits attached to the petition are sufficient. Ibid. 343.

18. The statute, which requires the commissioners of highways to act within ten days after the expiration of the twenty days' notice, does not compel them to decide the matter within the thirty days; it is sufficient that they commence their work within that time. It would seem that this provision of the statute is directory and not mandatory. *Wells* v. *Hicks*, 343.

19. That the statute regulating appeals, from the commissioners of highways to the supervisors, does not require notice to the party, whose land is affected by the location of the road, is an objection against which this court can afford no relief. It becomes the duty of the owner of the land, to take notice of, and follow up, the appeal. Ibid. 343.

20. The County Court succeeded to that of the county commissioners', and a constable's bond is properly executed to the County Court; which court and its successors may maintain an action upon it. *Long* v. *County Court*, 384.

See EJECTMENT. MECHANICS' LIEN. SECURITY FOR COSTS.

CONTESTED ELECTION.

See MANDAMUS.

CONTINUANCE.

A continuance will not be granted because a witness has said that h would be present at the trial and had been subpœnaed by the opposite party. The party desiring the testimony of the witness, should secure his presence at the trial. *Moore* v. *Goelitz*, 18.

CONTRACT.

1. When parties make a new agreement, revoking an old one, and a horse is paid as a part of the consideration on the new agreement, one of the parties cannot refuse to execute it because the other has not executed a reconveyance of land, no time being fixed for that purpose. A reasonable time will be allowed for performance, and a tender of the reconveyance was not an indispensable preliminary to the enforcement of the new agreement. The parties must be restored to their original rights before either can insist upon a rescinding of the new contract. *Anderson* v. *White*, 57.

2. A promise by the defendant that he will settle with the plaintiff as soon as he receives his pay for certain work, is a conditional promise; and does not waive the statute of limitations, unless it is proved that he has received his pay. *Mullett* v. *Shrumph*, 107.

3. A subscriber to the capital stock of a railroad company, who agrees to be subject to the rules and regulations which may from time to time be adopted by the directors, cannot avoid payment, because the charter has been amended, reducing the number of days of notice to be given, if the amendment of the charter has been accepted. *Illinois River R. R. Co.* v. *Beers*, 185.

4. Amendments to charters may be accepted in divers ways. Ibid. 185.

5. *Held*, that the following instrument was negotiable under the statute, and that in an action upon it, a consideration need not be averred or proved: "Due W. B. G. $450, to be paid in lumber when called for, in good lumber, at $1.25." *Bilderback* v. *Burlingame*, 338.

6. An instrument admitting a certain sum of money to be due, which may be paid in merchandise, at a fixed price, becomes an absolute money demand, if the payee fails to deliver the merchandise when it is called for. If there were two payees, a refusal by one of them would be sufficient. Ibid. 338.

7. A contracted with B for a quantity of lumber and cross-ties. He then put B in possession of a saw-mill, and took a bond from B and C, conditioned for the return of the mill, upon the completion of the contract. A failed to pay for the cross-ties and lumber, and B failed to return the mill. *Held*, that in an action by B for the price of the lumber, A could recoup for the damages, arising from the breach of the condition of the bond. *Sanger* v. *Fincher*, 346.

8. A contract entered into during the lucid intervals of one who is a lunatic, is valid. *Lilly* v. *Waggoner*, 395.

9. All persons of mature age are presumed to be sane, until after inquest found, when the presumption is changed, and proof is required to show sanity. Ibid. 395.

10. A deed executed several years before the maker was, by inquest, found insane, has the legal presumption of validity in its favor. Ibid. 395.

11. The evidence showing the insanity of a party at the time of the execution of a deed, must preponderate, or the legal presumption in favor of sanity will sustain the act. Ibid. 395.

12. In a proceeding for a mechanics' lien the law implies a contract to pay for the work when it shall be done, if other terms are not specified. *Claycomb* v. *Cecil*, 496.

13. Where it appears that a party is to deliver grain and have the price of it at a certain place indorsed on a contract, the party to whom it is to be delivered, has not, prior to delivery, any authority to take possession of the grain. *Millay et al.* v. *Dunn*, 516.

14. A general agreement to receive depreciated paper in business transactions, may be abandoned by common consent, and when this appears, a party who disregards such agreement cannot hold another to it. *Marine Bank of Chicago* v. *Chandler*, 525.

See CHANCERY. SALE OF LAND.

CONVEYANCE.

See CLAIM AND COLOR OF TITLE. DEED.

COPARTNERS.

See PARTNERS.

CORPORATIONS.

1. Where the name of a corporation consists of several words, the transposition, omission or alteration of some of them, may not be regarded as important, if it is evident what corporation is intended. *Chadsey* v. *McCreery*, 253.

2. Actions by the subordinate lodges of Odd Fellows should be brought in the name of the trustees of such lodges. *Marsh* v. *Astoria Lodge*, 421.

3. An organization in fact, and user under it, is sufficient in some actions to show a corporation in fact, although there may have been irregularities or omissions in the first instance. Ibid. 421.

4. If the right to sue is not expressly granted to a corporation, it may still exercise the faculty, if all the powers incident to corporations are conferred upon it. Ibid. 421.

5. The question in this case is presented by a plea which, in substance, avers that there is no such corporation, and not in abatement. Ibid. 421.

6. A judgment in favor of a corporation, if properly assigned, may be enforced after the corporation has ceased. *Leach* v. *Thomas*, 457.

COUNTIES, COUNTY COURTS AND CLERKS.

1. Upon a petition for a mandamus, to compel a county clerk to issue a certificate of election to the relator, who was duly elected a justice of the peace, it is no defense that the clerk has already issued a certificate to the relator's competitor, and that he has been regularly commissioned by the Governor. *People* v. *Rives*, 242.

2. The board of supervisors alone, have the power to order an election to determine whether the county will subscribe to stock in a railroad company, and to issue the bonds therefor; and they cannot delegate their power. But this rule does not prevent the board of supervisors, after they have taken all necessary action in the matter, from directing that the bonds shall be signed by the county judge. The county judge then becomes merely the instrument, by which the action of the board is manifested. *Clarke* v. *Board of Supervisors*, 305.

3. In ordering an election, to determine whether a county will subscribe for stock to aid in building a railroad, it is improper to submit the question, whether two different roads shall be so aided, by a single vote; so that the two propositions cannot be voted upon separately. The county may be restrained from issuing bonds in pursuance of such a vote; but when issued they are not necessarily void, in the hands of a *bona fide* holder. Ibid. 305.

4. Where county bonds, to aid the construction of a railroad, have been issued, in pursuance of an election held without warrant of law, as where it has been ordered by a person or tribunal having no such authority, they are absolutely void. But where the election has been properly authorized, and there has been informality in the manner of submitting the question to the people (such as submitting two propositions as to aiding two different roads, to a single vote,) the bonds may

broken at once. They then become mere choses in action, and are not assignable at law. Ibid. 478.

9. The covenant of warranty is prospective, and runs with the land into the hands of all those to whom it may come by purchase or descent; and is broken only by an eviction, or something equivalent thereto. Ibid. 478.

10. A declaration upon covenants in a deed averred the making of covenants of seizin, of power to sell, and of warranty, only; the breach included not only these, but also covenants against incumbrances and for quiet enjoyment. The defendant assigned as a ground for demurrer, that this one count set forth more than one cause of action. *Held*, that as all these causes of action were of the same nature and could be answered by one plea, they might be joined in one count. That these separate breaches were to be regarded as so many distinct counts. That the demurrer being to the whole count, and one of the breaches being properly assigned, the demurrer should be overruled. Ibid. 478.

11. Several causes of action of the same nature may be joined in one count. The defendant can plead specially to each cause of action. Ibid. 478.

12. The rule as to joining causes of action is, that when the same plea may be pleaded, and the same judgment rendered on all the counts, they may be joined. Ibid. 478.

13. A quit-claim, or any other deed which is effectual to convey land, passes to the grantee the covenants running with the land, unless there be words in the deed limiting the conveyance. Ibid. 478.

14. In an action of covenant upon the covenant against eviction in a deed, the plaintiff alleged particularly the manner of his eviction, by showing the foreclosure of a mortgage given by the covenantor, and a sale under the decree. *Held*, that as it was not averred that a deed had been given under the decree, or that the time for redemption had expired, or that any actual eviction had occurred, a demurrer to the declaration should have been sustained. Ibid. 478.

15. The declaration in an action upon covenants in a deed of conveyance, claimed an eviction by showing the foreclosure of a mortgage given by the covenantor, and a sale under the decree, but did not show that any deed had been given under the sale, or that the time of redemption had expired, or that an actual eviction had occurred. *Held*, that if the plaintiff had removed the mortgage, the measure of damages would have been the amount so paid, provided it did not exceed the purchase money and interest—but as it did not appear that the plaintiff had paid off the incumbrance or had suffered any eviction, nominal damages only should be awarded. Ibid. 478.

See APPEAL. JURISDICTION. JUSTICES OF THE PEACE.

CRIMINAL LAW.

1. An indictment upon a lost paper, which it is averred was a forgery, should set out the substance and effect of the instrument; that the

court may see that it was such an instrument, that the forgery of it would constitute a crime. *Wallace* v. *People*, 45.

2. Where an indictment concludes against the form of the statute, etc., it clearly indicates a prosecution under a statute, and not at common law. *Town of Paris* v. *People*, 74.

3. The offense of keeping and maintaining a "*calaboose,*" by an incorporated town, is not an offense against the statute, for which an indictment will lie. *Town of Paris* v. *People*, 74.

4. Upon a change of venue in a criminal case, the court granting the order may take a recognizance from the defendant to appear in the court to which the venue has been changed. *Stebbins* v. *People*, 240.

5. A default and order of forfeiture was taken upon recognizance against the defendant and his surety, judgment was then taken upon the default against the defendant, and a *sci. fa.* issued against the surety alone. Upon the return of the *sci. fa.*, judgment was taken against both cognizers; and the judgment was reversed because the *sci. fa.* was issued against the wrong party. Ibid. 240.

6. In prosecutions for obstructing highways, the rule is, that every averment must be established, by a clear preponderance of evidence. And it is error to instruct the jury that they must be satisfied of the defendant's guilt, beyond a reasonable doubt, before they could find against him. This latter rule obtains only in criminal prosecutions, affecting life or liberty. *Town of Lewiston* v. *Proctor*, 414.

CURRENCY,

1. A certificate of deposit payable in "Illinois currency," cannot be satisfied by depreciated paper; it must be met by bills passing in the locality in the place of coin. It might be otherwise if the certificate had been made payable in Illinois bank paper. *Chicago Marine and Fire 'Ins. Co.* v. *Keiron*, 501.

2. The words "Illinois currency" mean something different from gold or silver, or their equivalents, and may be used in reference to things of different values, when applied to the uses of traffic; and on enforcing a contract using these words, it is proper to show what meaning the parties intended to give them in their use of them. CATON, C. J. Ibid. 501.

3. When it appears that a bank received for a customer, by collecting or by receipt of deposits, funds, which were current, and passed as money in general business transactions, without directions to hold the identical funds, it will have to account to the owner for the sums so received, without diminution or discount, notwithstanding the bills received by the bank were at the time or have since depreciated in value. *Marine Bank of Chicago* v. *Chandler*, 525.

4. The special custom of bankers in a particular locality, cannot change values as fixed by law; and if some persons have been in the habit of receiving depreciated paper in payment of dues, the right to enforce

5. Where a default has been taken and a decree entered, *pro confesso,* which recites that the defendants have been regularly notified of the pendency of the suit, by summons or advertisement, a *bona fide* purchaser under the decree will be protected, although the record may not furnish any evidence of a summons or advertisement. *Reddick* v. *State Bank*, 145.

6. A decree should ascertain the precise amount to be paid, and not leave it to computation. *Smith* v. *Trimble*, 152.

See CHANCERY. MORTGAGE.

DEEDS.

1. Where it appears that the treasurer of schools, the obligor of a bond, presented it signed and sealed in blank for approval, the penalty not being expressed, but was afterwards inserted in his presence and with his approval, but in the absence of his sureties: *Held*, that while he was estopped by his consent, his sureties were not holden. *People* v. *Organ*, 27.

2. An executed deed may be avoided by erasure, interlineation or other material alteration; or by an intentional destruction of the seal. Ibid. 27.

3. A deed signed and sealed in blank, with verbal authority to fill the blank, will be void, unless it has been subsequently acknowledged or adopted by the party executing it. Ibid. 27.

4. A deed may be valid though not recorded; and may be offered as proof in ejectment; and then the fact of knowledge of its existence may be brought home to subsequent purchasers, as touching their good faith, and the duty of making inquiries as connected with them. *Ross* v. *Hole*, 104.

5. A deed executed several years before the maker was, by inquest, found insane, has the legal presumption of validity in its favor. *Lilly* v. *Waggoner*, 395.

6. The evidence showing the insanity of a party at the time of the execution of a deed, must preponderate, or the legal presumption in favor of sanity will sustain the act. Ibid. 395.

7. A quit-claim, or any other deed which is effectual to convey land, passes to the grantee the covenants running with the land, unless there be words in the deed limiting the conveyance. *Brady* v. *Spurck*, 478.

See COVENANTS.

DEFAULT.

1. A party who voluntarily submits to a default, impliedly admits that the demand against him is just. *Lucas* v. *Spencer*, 15.

2. Upon a default, a writ of inquiry issues to have the damages assessed, which may be executed in court or be directed to the sheriff to execute

in vacation. It would be regular for the sheriff to summon a jury from the bys·anders, and have the damages assessed in the presence of the court. *Ætna Ins. Co.* v. *Phelps*, 71.

3. On the death of the sheriff his deputy continues to act until a successor to his principal is qualified. The return to process signed by a deputy, without reference to the sheriff, where the court below found that it was "duly served," will be sufficient to uphold a default. If the sheriff was not dead, the defendant below should have taken steps to show that fact. *Timmerman et al.* v. *Phelps*, 496. The case of *Ditch* v. *Edwards*, 1 Scam. 127, commented upon and explained.

DEMURRER.

See CHANCERY. PLEADING.

DEPOSITIONS.

Depositions taken in one suit, may be used in another between the same parties, about the same controversy. *McConnel* v. *Smith*, 232.

DILIGENCE.

1. If the indorsee of a note desires to hold the indorser liable, he must proceed to judgment against the maker, at the earliest opportunity. Any negligence or omission in that regard will release the indorser. *Robinson* v. *Olcott*, 181.

2. It is not due diligence for the assignee of a note to delay issuing an execution against the maker of the note, for more than two months after obtaining his judgment—and without showing some excuse for such delay, he cannot hold the assignor. *Rives* v. *Kumler*, 291.

DIVISION WALLS.

A deed conveyed to M. certain premises, extending to the west line of the west wall of a brick building upon the premises; so that it included the whole of the west wall; with the reservation that the owners of the ground on both sides should have the mutual use of the present partition wall. At that time there was a small one-story brick building on the lot adjoining on the west. Subsequently, M.'s grantors conveyed this other lot to P., who tore down this small building, and erected one much higher, and extending further along on M.'s wall. Held, that the reservation in the deed to M. extended only to such portions of the west wall as were then used as a partition between the buildings, and that P. had no right to the mutual use of any other or greater part of this west wall. *Price* v. *McConnell*, 255.

DOWER.

1. Upon a bill for a partition brought by one of the heirs at law, in which it is suggested that the widow is entitled to dower in the lands sought

to be divided, but the prayer does not ask that her dower be assign°d, the court cannot decree an assignment of dower and appoint commissioners to set it off. Nor can the court give the widow an estate in fee in one-third of the land, in lieu of her life estate, for dower. *Tibbs* v. *Allen*, 119.

2. A note was given for a piece of land which the payee conveyed by a warranty deed. Subsequently a right of dower was recovered against the land. *Held*, that in an action upon the note, the value of this dower right could be set off as a partial failure of consideration. *McHenry* v. *Yokum*, 160.

3. The tables showing the probabilities of life, by which the value of dower rights can be computed, are recognized by the courts as the proper means of proving such value. Ibid. 160.

See CHANCERY, 17.

EJECTMENT.

1. An action of ejectment is within the purview of the statute requiring security for costs; and if the plaintiff is a non-resident he must give security for costs before instituting suit; which is commenced by serving the declaration and notice. *Farnsworth* v. *Agnew*, 42.

2. If it appears from the bill of exceptions, that a plaintiff in ejectment was a non-resident at the time of the service of the declaration and notice, although the affidavit of the defendant to that fact is not saved in the bill of exceptions, the judgment dismissing the action for want of security will be upheld. Ibid. 42.

3. A deed may be valid though not recorded; and may be offered as proof in ejectment; and then the fact of knowledge of its existence, may be brought home to subsequent purchasers, as touching their good faith, and the duty of making inquiries as connected with them. *Ross* v. *Hole*, 104.

4. In ejectment, before the court can take jurisdiction, it should appear, by affidavit, that the declaration and notice to appear and plead, have been served. A sheriff's return will not give jurisdiction. *O'Donnell* v. *Howes*, 510.

ELECTIONS.

See COUNTY CLERK. MANDAMUS.

ERASURES.

See BOND. DEED.

ERROR.

1. It is erroneous to decree a sale of premises in thirty days, where there is not any redemption from the sale. *Moore* v. *Bracken*, 23.

686

2. In cases tried by the court, errors may be assigned as to the law and fact upon the judgment. *Metcalf* v. *Fouts*, 110.

3. Upon a writ of error in a chancery cause, the Supreme Court will not presume that any evidence was given in the court below, except what appears in the record. *Reddick* v. *State Bank*, 145.

4. The absence of a summons from the record, cannot be supplied by the return of a certificate of the clerk to a writ of *certiorari*, that there had been a summons which was lost, nor by the recital in the notice of publication, that it had been issued. *Smith* v. *Trimble*, 152.

5. Upon a writ of error, this court looks only to the transcript of the record. If papers have been lost from the files, or mutilated, they may be supplied in some cases by the Circuit Court upon satisfactory evidence, after a proper notice to the opposite party. This court has no authority to permit a party to supply, by proof, any part of the record. *Smith* v. *Trimble*, 152.

6. Proceedings for the sale of land by an administrator will be reversed, if the record does not show any petition by the administrator. *Monahon* v. *Vandyke*, 154.

7. It is error for the Circuit Court to order a sale of land by an administrator, when the notice has been published but thirty days, while the statute requires a publication for six weeks, before the presentation of the petition. Ibid. 154.

8. It is error to award the plaintiff greater damages than he claims in his declaration. *Rives* v. *Kumler*, 291.

9. Although the bill of exceptions does not purport to contain all the evidence, and therefore the refusal to grant a new trial on the weight of evidence, cannot be considered; yet as there was evidence, showing the refusal of an instruction erroneous, the judgment will be reversed. *Sidwell* v. *Lobly*, 438.

10. This court will not reverse a judgment, merely because another might be more acceptable. *Bowen* v. *Dutton*, 515.

ESTATES.

1. The covenant that the grantor is seized of an estate in fee simple, is satisfied, if he has a seizin in fact, by having entered into possession, claiming a fee simple in the land. *Watts* v. *Parker*, 224.

2. An entry into possession, under a paper title, claiming the fee, and the peaceable possession for more than twenty-six years, make a seizin in fee simple. Ibid. 224.

3. Possession and payment of taxes for seven years, under claim and color of title, will satisfy the covenant of seizin in fee simple. Ibid. 224.

4. A deed purporting to claim land must be under seal. Ibid. 224.

5. A party may show possession and payment of taxes under claim and color of title; although his chain of title may show a deed not under seal. Ibid. 224.

6. On an application by a guardian for license to sell the real estate of his wards, they need not be made parties to the proceedings, nor is the appointment of a guardian *ad litem* required. *Smith* v. *Race*, 387.

See ADMINISTRATOR. ATTORNEY. PROBATE COURT.

ESTOPPEL.

1. Where it appears that the treasurer of schools, the obligor of a bond, presented it signed and sealed in blank for approval, the penalty not being expressed, but was afterwards inserted in his presence and with his approval, but in the absence of his sureties: *Held*, that while he was estopped by his consent, his sureties were not holden. *People* v. *Organ*, 27.

2. Morrison purchased a piece of land under an execution against James Duncan, and filed his bill to set aside conveyances which vested the title to the land in John Duncan, alleging them to be fraudulent. Subsequently the land was sold by the administrator of John Duncan, under an order of court, as his property. Morrison received the proceeds of this sale for a claim which he held against the estate of John Duncan. *Held*, that this did not estop Morrison from asserting his title to the land. *Letcher* v. *Morrison*, 209.

EVIDENCE.

1. After usurious money has been paid, the parties are not competent witnesses in a suit to recover it back. *Lucas* v. *Spencer*, 15.

2. A party who voluntarily submits to a default, impliedly admits that the demand against him is just. Ibid. 15.

3. A party who sues a railroad company, under the statute, for injuries to cattle, resulting from omission to fence a road, should show that the road had been opened more than six months prior to the injury complained of. *Ohio and Mississippi R. R. Co.* v. *Meisenheimer*, 30.

4. Parol evidence is admissible, to show that the consideration of a note has wholly or partially failed. *Morgan* v. *Fallenstein*, 31.

5. The certificate of a county clerk, showing that A. B. was not a justice of the peace, at the date of an acknowledgment, purporting to have been taken by him, is some though not conclusive evidence of such fact. *Ross* v. *Hole*, 104.

6. A deed may be offered in evidence in ejectment, though not recorded. Ibid. 104.

7. Proof of a tender, though not of that clear and satisfactory character which convinces the mind beyond doubt, will be held sufficient. *Kerney* v. *Gardner*, 162.

8. Where A and B convey a right of way to a mill to C, and B afterwards purchases one-half of the mill, B cannot become a witness for C, who has filed a bill to restrain A from obstructing the right of way; being an appurtenance to the mill, B was therefore interested, and was disqualified. *Foulke* v. *Walker*, 204.

.9. The payee and indorser of a note, is not a competent witness to prove that an assignee had not paid any consideration for a note, or that it had not been delivered to the assignee. *Coon* v. *Nock*, 235.

10. Where a fact is alleged in a bill and admitted by the answer, the admission is conclusive; and evidence tending to dispute it, should not be considered. *Chadsey* v. *McCreery*, 253.

11. A general objection to the introduction of an instrument as evidence, is not sufficient; if it is obnoxious to a special objection, that objection must be stated in the court below. *Buntain* v. *Bailey*, 409.

12. In an action to recover a penalty for obstructing a village street, after the ordinance establishing the offense and the penalty has been given in evidence without objection, evidence of a private act of the legislature legalizing the ordinances, was properly excluded from the jury. The statute might have been proper preliminary evidence, but after the introduction of the ordinances, it became irrelevant. *Town of Lewiston* v. *Proctor*, 414.

13. In an action upon a note, the books of a banker, showing entries made by third parties without the knowledge of the litigants, are not proper evidence. Such books are not public records, nor do they fall within any recognized class of written or documentary evidence. *Barnes* v. *Simmons*, 512.

EXCHANGE.

See INTEREST.

EXECUTION.

1. After a notice has been given to the administrator of a deceased debtor, of the existence of a judgment against the deceased, in accordance with Sec. 3, Chap. 47, Rev. Stat., the judgment creditor may issue an execution, and also an *alias* or *pluries*, without further notice. *Letcher* v. *Morrison*, 209.

2. It is a settled principle of law that the levy of an execution upon personal property, sufficient to satisfy it, is of itself a satisfaction of the execution. But this rule is changed by Sec. 30, Chap. 57, Rev. Stat. of 1845—which provides for the giving of a forthcoming bond. This statute is constitutional. *Martin* v. *Carter*, 294.

3. There is no lawful mode of renewing an execution, except there has been a return to that already issued by the officer, of his doings thereon. A justice of the peace cannot renew an execution by any indorsement of his upon it. *Calhoun County* v. *Buck et al.* 441.

4. A constable must, within the time appointed by law, return an execution with an indorsement of his doings thereon, for the truth of which he is responsible; but no particular form of indorsement is required. *Ibid.* 441.

5. One constable cannot hand over an execution to another, so as to relieve himself from the responsibility of its return according to the statute; if another constable returns the execution within the statutory time,

it may save him from liability, to whom it was first delivered. Ibid.
441.

6. A railroad tank-house, locomotive and cars, are presumed to be annexed
to the realty, and in fact are a part of it, and are not liable to be sold by
a constable, on an execution from a justice of the peace. *Titus et al.* v.
Ginheimer et al. 462.

EXECUTORS.

See ADMINISTRATORS. ESTATES.

FAILURE OF CONSIDERATION.

See PROMISSORY NOTE.

FORECLOSURE OF MORTGAGE.

See MORTGAGE. SCIRE FACIAS.

FOREIGN JUDGMENT.

Where it is manifest from an inspection of a record, that technicalities
in the forms of actions have been abolished in the State where judgment
was rendered, this court will treat the judgment as would the court of
the State where it was rendered, without regard to the rules of the
common law by which different forms of action are designated. *Griffin*
v. *Eaton*, 379.

FORGERY.

See BOND, 5.

FRAUD—STATUTE OF FRAUDS.

1. Where a purchaser, under a verbal contract for the sale of land, takes
possession by consent of the vendor, and makes valuable improvements,
and within the time agreed upon for payment, tenders the purchase
money, the case is taken out of the statute of frauds, and the purchaser
is entitled to a specific performance of the oral agreement. *Blunt* v.
Tomlin, 93.

2. It is no defense for third parties who subsequently purchased of the vendor with full notice, and before the time for payment had expired, that
the vendor had disaffirmed the verbal contract, and sold to them before
the purchase money was actually paid or tendered. The purchaser is
entitled to protection, if he paid or tendered the money within the time
agreed upon. Ibid. 93.

3. Where a purchaser of land under an oral agreement, has five years in
which to make his payments, so that the contract conflicts with two
sections of the statute of frauds, he may nevertheless be entitled to a
specific performance. The same facts which would take the case out of

one section of the statute, will take it out of the other. In such a case, the court should be more cautious in examining the evidence of the oral contract. *Blunt* v. *Tomlin*, 93.

4. A party who makes a tender for a deed under a contract, need not part with the money, until he receives his deed. If the vendor offers to take the money but refuses to make the deed, this is a refusal of the tender, and it is a useless ceremony to count out the money after that. Ibid. 93.

5. A tender made in pursuance of a contract for a deed, fixes the rights of the parties, as conclusively as if the money had been actually paid. Ibid. 93.

6. The statute of frauds must be pleaded, if it is to be relied upon by the defendant. He cannot set it up, for the first time, in an instruction. *Warren* v. *Dickson*, 115.

7. In a bill for specific performance of a parol agreement for the sale of lands, if the agreement is denied, without setting up the statute of frauds as a defense, that statute cannot afterwards be insisted upon to bar the suit. *Hull* v. *Peer*, 312.

8. A court of chancery will relieve against judgments obtained by fraud or by unavoidable accident, if there has been no fault or negligence on the part of the defendant in making his defense. But not if there has been such fault or negligence. *Hinrichsen* v. *Van Winkle*, 334.

9. Fraud must always be proved; the law never presumes it. *Wright* v. *Grover*, 426.

10. A complete transfer of personal property may be made, although the purchaser should not hold continuous possession. If the property is returned to the possession of the vendor, the fact may create suspicion, but is not conclusive of the fairness of the transaction. Ibid. 426.

See CHANCERY.

GARNISHEE.

1. The interrogatories to and answers of a garnishee are a part of the record, and need not be preserved by a bill of exceptions. *Rankin* v. *Simonds*, 352.

2. Where no issue is raised upon the answers of a garnishee, they must be taken as true, and the rights of the parties must be determined by them. Ibid. 352.

3. The garnishee has a right to set up any claim he has against the defendant, to meet the fund in his hands, which he could set off or recoup in an action brought by the defendant to recover the fund. Ibid. 352.

4. Rankin, summoned as the garnishee of Elliott, answered, that he had funds of Elliott's, but that he had delivered to E. a note against the H. & S. R. R. Co. for collection; that E. owed the company an amount greater than the amount of the note and still retained the note, his account with the company being still unsettled. *Held*, that as the note

had not been paid, Rankin might withdraw it at any time, and he could not be allowed to set it off against the fund in his hands. Ibid. 352.

5. Where garnishees are summoned in an attachment suit, the proper practice is to enter judgment against the garnishees and in favor of the defendant in the attachment suit, for the benefit of such attaching creditors as are entitled to the proceeds. Ibid. 352.

6. A conditional judgment and a *scire facias* are requisite, as proper preliminaries to a judgment against a garnishee. The *scire facias* is to make known to the garnishee that a conditional judgment has been rendered against him, assuming him to be a debtor of the debtors in attachment, and that he must show cause why final judgment should not go against him. *Cariker* v. *Anderson*, 358.

7. A sufficient notice to a debtor under a foreign attachment should be shown of record. Ibid. 358.

8. It may not be error for a term of court to intervene between a default taken and a *scire facias* issued against a garnishee. *Cariker* v. *Anderson*, 358.

9. The date given in the indorsement of a service of process, should be taken as the time of service. A sheriff is not required to date his return. Ibid. 358.

10. A garnishee is not properly a defendant in an attachment suit, to defend against the plaintiff's claim; the judgment should be entered against a garnishee in favor of the defendant in the attachment suit, for the benefit of the creditor or others in attachment, and if there is more due than will pay the attaching creditor, the creditor of the garnishee can control it. Ibid. 358.

GUARANTOR AND GUARANTEE.

1. If the indorsee of a note desires to hold the indorser liable, he must proceed to judgment against the maker, at the earliest opportunity. Any negligence or omission in that regard will release the indorser. *Robinson* v. *Olcott*, 181.

2. Where a party appears to have executed a bond with another as surety, but whose name has been forged, he will not be liable. *Seely* v. *People*, 173.

3. An agreement, between the holder of a note and the principal, to extend the time of payment for a definite period, which is founded upon a good consideration, will discharge the surety; unless the surety consents to the agreement at the time, or subsequently ratifies it. *Flynn* v. *Mudd*, 323.

4. To enable a surety to interpose the defense to a note that further time has been given to his principal, it is not necessary that his name should appear upon the note as surety; it will be sufficient if he was actually a surety, and this was known to the payee when the note was executed. Ibid. 323.

5. The payment of interest upon a note in advance, is a sufficient consideration to support an agreement for an extension of time to the principal, so as to discharge the surety. Ibid. 323.

6. Where the plaintiff introduces in evidence a note which has indorsed upon it, an agreement extending the time for payment, he will be bound by the agreement although it is not signed by him. Ibid. 323.

GUARDIAN AND WARD.

1. Infants are bound by proceedings by an administrator to sell real estate, although they are not nominally made parties to the proceeding. The case *Ex parte Sturms*, 25th Illinois R. 390, overruled in part. *Gibson* v. *Roll*, 88.

2. If the proceedings of a guardian to sell the estates of infants have not been regular and in conformity to law, they must have an opportunity to correct the errors. But such proceedings are not adverse to the interests of the infant, and if they have been regular, the infant will be bound by them. The case of *Mason* v. *Wait*, 4 Scam. 127, examined. Ibid. 88.

3. A proceeding by an administrator to sell the real estate of his decedent, is adverse to the infants, and he must follow the statute in his petition, and give proper notice; if he does this, the sale will be good. The court is to pass upon the sufficiency of the statements in the notice, which calls upon parties to object to the proceedings. Ibid. 88.

4. Strict proof is required against infant defendants, and the record must furnish the evidence to sustain a decree against them, whether their guardian answers or not. No confession by their guardian can bind them. *Reddick* v. *State Bank*, 145.

5. On an application by a guardian for license to sell the real estate of his wards, they need not be made parties to the proceedings, nor is the appointment of a guardian *ad litem* required. *Smith* v. *Race*, 387.

HIGHWAYS AND STREETS.

1. The only office which the common law writ of certiorari performs, is to certify the record of a proceeding from an inferior to a superior tribunal. It is the duty of the inferior body to whom it is directed, to transmit a complete transcript of the record properly certified, to the court awarding the writ; without any statement of facts *dehors* the record. *Commissioners of Highways* v. *Supervisors, etc.* 140.

2. The superior tribunal, upon an inspection of the record alone, determines whether the inferior tribunal had jurisdiction of the parties and of the subject matter, and whether it has exceeded its jurisdiction, or has otherwise proceeded in violation of law. Ibid. 140.

3. This proceeding is wholly different from a trial under our statutory writ of *certiorari*, inasmuch as that is a trial *de novo*. Ibid. 140.

4. Upon an appeal to the board of supervisors from the decision of the commissioners of highways, as to the laying out of a road, it is not

necessary that the supervisors should examine the entire road. It will be sufficient if they examine that portion of the road against which the objections are urged. Ibid. 140.

5. Where the commissioners of highways make themselves parties to a proceeding to reverse a decision of the supervisors, by a writ of certiorari, and are unsuccessful, a judgment against them for costs is proper. Ibid. 140.

6. If they were acting in behalf of the town, they should have appeared in its name and not in their own. Ibid. 140.

7. Where the record of proceedings before the commissioners of highways, for laying out of a road, shows that due notice has been given, by posting copies of the petition ; upon an appeal regularly taken to the supervisors of the county, the supervisors acquire the jurisdiction necessary to determine the validity of the notices, and their decision upon that point cannot be collaterally attacked. *Wells v. Hicks,* 343.

8. To prove that in proceedings for laying out a highway the copies of the petition were properly posted, it is not necessary to call as witnesses, the parties who posted them. Their *ex parte* affidavits attached to the petition are sufficient. Ibid. 343.

9. The statute which requires the commissioners of highways to act within ten days after the expiration of the twenty days' notice, does not compel them to decide the matter within the thirty days ; it is sufficient that they commence their work within that time. It would seem that this provision of the statute is directory and not mandatory. Ibid. 343.

10. That the statute regulating appeals, from the commissioners of highways to the supervisors, does not require notice to the party, whose land is affected by the location of the road, is an objection against which this court can afford no relief. It becomes the duty of the owner of the land, to take notice of, and follow up, the appeal. Ibid. 343.

11. In an action to recover a penalty for obstructing a village street, after the ordinance establishing the offense and the penalty has been given in evidence without objection, evidence of a private act of the legislature legalizing the ordinances, was properly excluded from the jury. The statute might have been proper preliminary evidence, but after the introduction of the ordinances, it becomes irrelevant. *Town of Lewiston v. Proctor,* 414.

12. In actions before, and upon appeals from, justices of the peace, the defendant has a right to insist upon proof of every material fact necessary to a recovery, just as if all the requisite pleas had been filed. And the plaintiff, if a corporation, must prove its corporate existence. Ibid. 414.

13. A continuous and uninterrupted use of a highway by the public, for more than twenty years, creates a prescriptive right to the use of the road. And this right continues, until it is clearly and unmistakably abandoned. Ibid. 414.

14. A partial or transient non-user of a highway, by reason of the travel being diverted to other roads, is not sufficient to establish its abandonment. Ibid. 414.

15. The fact, that a village road has not been repaired by the corporate authorities, may be evidence tending to show that the corporation does not regard it as a highway. This will not be the case, however, if it appears, that, from the nature of the ground, the road has needed no repairs. Ibid. 414.

16. In an action, to recover a penalty, for obstructing a highway, if the complaint gives a local description, sufficient to fix the precise point obstructed, and also the *termini* of the road, the latter may be disregarded. But when the allegation is general, that a road leading from one point to another has been obstructed, the existence of the road, between the points named, must be proved, as a matter of essential description. Ibid. 414.

17. In prosecutions for obstructing highways, the rule is, that every averment must be established, by a clear preponderance of evidence. And it is error to instruct the jury that they must be satisfied of the defendant's guilt, beyond a reasonable doubt, before they could find against him. This latter rule obtains only in criminal prosecutions, affecting life or liberty. Ibid. 414.

See Towns and Cities.

HOMESTEAD EXEMPTION.

1. Moore owned a tract of land which he had mortgaged to Clark for $1,400. Weider wished to buy this tract from Moore for $2,000, and another tract from Clark for $1,600. It was arranged that Moore should convey his tract to Clark for the $3,000, less the mortgage, and that Clark should then convey both tracts to Weider for $4,600—Weider to pay $1,000 down, and give a mortgage for the balance. *Held*, that this was a sale of the whole premises from Clark to Weider, and that the mortgage being given for a part of the purchase money, Weider could not claim a homestead in the Moore tract 'to defeat a foreclosure. *Weider* v. *Clark*, 251.

2. A party who claims a homestead exemption as against a sheriff's sale, should show that the right existed when the lien attached; it is not enough for him to show that it was his homestead at the time of the sale. *Reinback* v. *Walter*, 393.

3. It would appear that a stable, a horse lot, a smoke-house and the grounds connected therewith, together with the dwelling-house, would constitute the homestead; but that a store, warehouse, and the grounds connected with these, would not. Ibid. 393.

4. While a widow may release her interest in the homestead right, such a release will not affect the interest of the children. *Miller* v. *Marckle*, 402.

HOUSEKEEPER.

A, being in feeble health and a resident of Missouri, was brought by B to Illinois, and lived in the house of B, as a guest, furnishing his own room and a part of his food, but occupying the room at the sufferance

of B. A had two daughters, within the age prescribed by the fourth
section of the act, entitled " An Act to amend an act relative to wills
and testaments, executors and administrators, and the settlement of
estates," page 597, Revised Statutes of 1845, one of whom remained
with him, the other living apart from him with a relative—A, during
his lifetime, declaring his intention to return to Missouri, to pursue his
former occupation: *Held*, that A was not a housekeeper within the
meaning of the said fourth section, and that his children could not receive the same amount of property that would have been by law allowed to the widow of A. *Veile* v. *Koch*, 129.

HUSBAND AND WIFE.

Upon the foreclosure of a mortgage given to secure the purchase money
for premises, it is not necessary that the wife of the mortgagor should
be made a party to the bill. *Stephens* v. *Bichnell*, 444.

INDICTMENT.

1. An indictment upon a lost paper, which it is averred was a forgery,
should set out the substance and effect of the instrument; that the court
may see that it was such an instrument, that the forgery of it would
constitute a crime. *Wallace* v. *People*, 45.

2. Where an indictment concludes against the form of the statute, etc., it
clearly indicates a prosecution under a statute, and not at common
law. *Town of Paris* v. *People*, 74.

INDORSEMENT—INDORSER—INDORSEE.

See GUARANTOR. PROMISSORY NOTE.

INFANTS.

1. Infants are bound by proceedings by an administrator to sell real estate,
although they are not nominally made parties to the proceeding. The
case *Ex parte Sturms*, 25th Illinois R. 390, overruled in part. *Gibson*
v. *Roll*, 88.

2. If the proceedings of a guardian to sell the estates of infants have not
been regular and in conformity to law, they must have an opportunity
to correct the errors. But such proceedings are not adverse to the interests of the infant, and if they have been regular, the infant will be
bound by them. The case of *Mason* v. *Wait*. 4 Scam. 127, examined.
Ibid. 88.

3. A proceeding by an administrator to sell the real estate of his decedent
is adverse to the infants, and he must follow the statute in his petition,
and give proper notice; if he does this, the sale will be good. The
court is to pass upon the sufficiency of the statements in the notice,
which calls upon parties to object to the proceedings. Ibid. 88.

4. Where an answer is filed for infant defendants, by one purporting to be

their guardian *ad litem*, and the decree recites that he was so appointed, but the record shows no separate order of appointment, it will be presumed that the appointment was regularly made. *Tibbs* v. *Allen*, 119.

5. Where the record shows a notice by publication in a chancery cause, which recites the fact that an affidavit of the non-residence of the defendants was duly filed, but the affidavit does not appear in the record, this court will regard that recital as an official declaration by the clerk, and will presume that the affidavit was duly filed. Ibid. 119.

6. Where there are infant and adult defendants, and the adults alone prosecute a writ of error, they cannot assign for error those proceedings which only affect the interests of the infants. Ibid. 119.

7. Infants are not bound by a decree unless all of the evidence necessary to establish it, is preserved in the record. Ibid. 119.

8. Strict proof is required against infant defendants, and the record must furnish the, evidence to sustain a decree against them, whether their guardian answers or not. No confession by their guardian can bind them. *Reddick* v. *State Bank,* 145'

9. On an application by a guardian for license to sell the real estate of his wards, they need not be made parties to the proceedings, nor is the appointment of a guardian *ad litem* required. *Smith* v. *Race*, 387.

10. If heirs are brought into court by *scire facias* under the statute, to show cause why they should not be made parties to a judgment, it will be necessary to prove up the case *de novo* against them. Adults cannot demand that more shall be proved against them, when there are infant parties, than if all were adults. *Cox* v. *Reed et al.* 434.

INJUNCTION.

See CHANCERY.

INSANITY.

See CONTRACT, 8, 9, 10, 11. DEEDS, 5, 6.

INSTRUCTIONS.

1. It does not follow that a judgment will be reversed, because an improper instruction has been given for the plaintiff and appellee, if the other instructions on his behalf, put the whole case fairly before the jury. *Warren* v. *Dickson*, 115.

2. Although the bill of exceptions does not purport to contain all the evidence, and therefore the refusal to grant a new trial on the weight of evidence cannot be considered; yet as there was evidence, showing the refusal of an instruction erroneous, the judgment will be reversed. *Sidwell* v. *Lobly*, 438.

3. All instructions must be based upon evidence. *Calhoun County* v. *Buck et al.* 440.

INSURANCE.

In an action upon an insurance policy, which contains a condition that in the event of a loss, the company may at its option restore the building, it is unnecessary to negative the performance of this condition in the declaration. It is a condition subsequent, and if performed, the company should allege it in defense of the action. *Ætna Ins. Co.* v· *Phelps*, 71.

INTEREST.

1. By the act of 31st January, 1857, relating to interest, a forfeiture of all interest, legal or illegal, is incurred for usury; no other penalty can be recovered for a breach of the law. *Lucas* v. *Spencer*, 15.
2. If a party has had an opportunity, which he has neglected, to prevent the recovery of a judgment, which includes usurious interest, he cannot relieve himself by a resort to chancery. Ibid. 15.
3. The sixth section of the interest law of 1845, only applies to cases where the money has been paid; and not as a defense to usury due and unpaid. Ibid. 15.
4. After usurious money has been paid, the parties are not competent witnesses in a suit to recover it back. Ibid. 15.
5. A custom on the part of a creditor to charge interest on an account past due, will not authorize its recovery, unless the debtor was informed of the custom. *Rayburn* v. *Day*, 46.
6. In determining the question of usury, the intention of the parties should govern, without regard to the form of the contract. *Cooper* v. *Nock*, 301.
7. Although a note may bear ten per cent. interest, when a decree is entered upon it, the note is merged; and the decree can bear only six per cent. interest. *White* v. *Haffaker*, 349.

INTERLINEATIONS.

See Bonds, 2, 3. Deeds, 1, 2.

JUDGMENT.

1. It is erroneous to decree a sale of premises in thirty days, where there is not any redemption from the sale. *Moore* v. *Bracken*, 23.
2. In debt, recovery must be had against all or none of the defendants. *People* v. *Organ*, 27.
3. An attorney has no power to receive depreciated money, in satisfaction of a judgment. *Trumbull* v. *Nicholson*, 149.
4. If an attorney should accept from the sheriff depreciated money, in satisfaction of an execution, the owner of the judgment is not bound by such acceptance; and may compel the sheriff to return the amount in legal currency. If the sheriff has been injured by the conduct of the attorney, he must look to him for redress. Ibid. 149.

14. A party need not produce or prove a judgment that is not put in issue. *Cox* v. *Reed et al.* 434.

15. If heirs are brought into court by *scire facias* under the statute, to show cause why they should not be made parties to a judgment, it will be necessary to prove up the case *de novo* against them. Adults cannot demand that more shall be proved against them, when there are infant parties, than if all were adults. Ibid. 434.

16. The giving of a bond in satisfaction of a judgment, is in law a payment of it. Ibid. 434.

17. A judgment in favor of a corporation, if properly assigned, may be enforced after the corporation has ceased. *Leach* v. *Thomas*, 457.

18. A judgment in favor of the last grantee of land, against the original covenantor, upon the covenants contained in his deed, can be pleaded in bar to any action brought by an intermediate grantee. *Brady* v. *Spurck*, 478.

See EXECUTION. GARNISHEE. LEVY—SALE.

JURISDICTION.

An appeal from the decision of a justice of the peace, gives the appellate court jurisdiction of the party, although he was not served with process in the case appealed from ; and the appellate court can proceed to a trial on the merits. *Ohio and Mississippi R. R. Co.* v. *McCutchin*, 9.

JUSTICES OF THE PEACE AND CONSTABLES.

1. An appeal from the decision of a justice of the peace, gives the appellate court jurisdiction of the party, although he was not served with process in the case appealed from ; and the appellate court can proceed to a trial on the merits. *Ohio and Mississippi R. R. Co.* v. *McCutchin*, 9.

2. Upon an appeal from a justice of the peace, the Circuit Court should try the cause *de novo*, and it is error to dismiss the suit because the justice rendered judgment against two defendants when he had only obtained jurisdiction over the person of one of them. *Stephens* v. *Cross*, 35.

3. If a justice of the peace renders judgment against two defendants when only one has been brought into court, and the defendant who was served appeals the case and fails to prosecute his appeal, the Circuit Court may affirm the judgment as to him, and reverse it as to the other who has not been served. Ibid. 35.

4. The Circuit Court should not, in cases of appeal from a justice of the peace, authorize an amendment of the summons, by changing the names of parties. *Henckler* v. *County Court*, 39.

5. The certificate of a county clerk, showing that A. B. was not a justice of the peace, at the date of an acknowledgment, purporting to have been taken by him, is some, though not conclusive evidence of such fact. *Ross* v. *Hole*, 104.

6. In actions before, and upon appeals from, justices of the peace, the de-

fendant has a right to insist upon proof of every material fact necessary to a recovery, just as if all the requisite pleas had been filed. And the plaintiff, if a corporation, must prove its corporate existence. *Town of Lewiston* v. *Proctor*, 414.

7. There is no lawful mode of renewing an execution, except there has been a return to that already issued by the officer, of his doings thereon. A justice of the peace cannot renew an execution by any indorsement of his upon it. *Calhoun County* v. *Buck et al.* 440.

8. A constable must, within the time appointed by law, return an execution with an indorsement of his doings thereon, for the truth of which he is responsible; but no particular form of indorsement is required. Ibid. 440.

9. One constable cannot hand over an execution to another, so as to relieve himself from the responsibility of its return according to the statute; if another constable returns the execution within the statutory time, it may save him from liability, to whom it was first delivered. *Calhoun County* v. *Buck et al.* 440.

10. A justice of the peace issues a capias upon an oath, an affidavit is not necessary, and the presumption is, that a justice requires all the necessary averments in the oath, such as are commanded by the constitution and laws. *Outlaw* v. *Davis et al.* 467.

11. The plaintiff in a suit where a capias has been issued by a justice of the peace, is not answerable with the justice in trespass *vi et armis*, even if the process has been issued without a sufficient oath; the magistrate is the proper person to pass upon its sufficiency. If a party acts maliciously, case is the proper remedy. Nor would a magistrate be liable in trespass, if he had jurisdiction to issue the process. Ibid. 467.

See County Clerk. Mandamus.

LANDLORD AND TENANT.

1. A party cannot bring separate suits for several sums past due on a lease; if more than one payment is due, these payments should be consolidated into one suit. *Casselberry* v. *Forquer*, 170.

2. A party cannot divide an entire demand, so as to maintain several actions for its recovery. Ibid. 170.

LEASE.

See Landlord and Tenant.

LEVY—SALE.

It is a settled principle of law that the levy of an execution upon personal property, sufficient to satisfy it, is of itself a satisfaction of the execution. But this rule is changed by sec. 30, chap. 57, Rev. Stat. of 1845—which provides for the giving of a forthcoming bond. This statute is constitutional. *Martin* v. *Charter*, 294.

LIEN.

A note given for the purchase of land. if transferred, does not carry with it to the assignee, the vendor's lien, so that the assignee can enforce it in his own name. *Richards* v. *Leaming et al.* 431.

LIMITATION.

1. If the maker of a note says to the payee, that if he will wait awhile he will pay the note; and that he will pay when he "makes a raise," not being at the time in a condition to pay; the note will be taken out of the statute of limitations. *Horner* v. *Starkey*, 13.

2. A promise by the defendant that he will settle with the plaintiff as soon as he receives his pay for certain work, is a conditional promise; and does not waive the statute of limitations, unless it is proved that he has received his pay. *Mullett* v. *Shrumph*, 107.

3. A clerk's or sheriff's deed on a tax sale is sufficient to show claim and color of title, if it appear on its face to be regular. The person relying upon it is not bound to show that the prerequisites of the statute have been complied with. *Holloway et al.* v. *Clark*, 483.

4. A quit-claim deed is sufficient to show claim and color of title under the limitation act of 1839. Ibid. 483.

5. H. obtained claim and color of title in 1842, and conveyed to B. in 1845. B. allowed the land to be sold for the taxes for 1847, and bought it himself; he then paid the taxes from 1849 to 1856, inclusive. P., the minor heir of a person who had died seized of the patent title, in 1853 redeemed from the sale of 1847, by paying to the clerk double the amount of the purchase money and all the taxes, with interest, for five years, being up to the time of the redemption. *Held*, that this redemption by P. entirely obliterated the tax sale of 1847, and the payment of taxes by B. for the five years, and that the grantees of B. could not defend under the limitation act of 1839, without showing payment of taxes for seven years, exclusive of the five years from 1848 to 1853. *Holloway et al.* v *Clark*, 483.

6. The provisions of the limitation act of 1839, empowering minors to redeem land sold for taxes, within three years after attaining their majority, by paying to the person who has paid the tax, the amount with interest, do not take from the minor the right to redeem within one year after his majority, by paying double the amount, etc., to the collector, according to Sec. 69, Chap. LXXXIX, Rev. Stat. 1845. Ibid. 483.

7. A person whose lands had been sold for taxes during his infancy, for the purpose of redeeming them, after he attained his majority, paid the necessary amount to the clerk. The purchaser accepted this money from the clerk. *Held*, that by that act, he admitted the right of the infant to redeem under the statute. Ibid. 483.

702

LODGES.

See ACTION. CORPORATION.

MANDAMUS.

Upon a petition for a mandamus, to compel a county clerk to issue a certificate of election to the relator, who was duly elected a justice of the peace, it is no defense that the clerk issued a certificate to the relator's competitor, and that he .has been .regularly commissioned by the Governor. *People* v. *Rives*, 243.

MARRIED WOMAN.

See HUSBAND AND WIFE.

MECHANICS' LIEN.

1. A petition for a mechanics' lien is not obnoxious to a demurrer, because it avers that material was furnished to two persons, to erect a building on the land of one. *Roach* v. *Chapin*, 194.
2. The rendition of a decree on the overruling of a demurrer to a bill, without first ruling the defendant to answer, is not error. The rendition of a decree upon a bill taken as confessed, is matter of discretion. Ibid. 194.
3. The act of February, 1861, provides that the former act in relation to mechanics'. liens shall be held to include implied as well as,express contracts, under which labor or material is furnished; provided they are done or furnished within one year from the commencement of the furnishing; and if these are done after the passage of the latter act, a petition need not aver that there was a time within which the materials were to be furnished. Ibid. 194.
4. In a proceeding for a mechanics' lien the law implies a contract to pay for the work when it shall be done, if other terms are not specified. *Claycomb* v. *Cecil*, 497.
5. A sale under a mechanics' lien, as there is no redemption from it, should not be authorized within a less period than the lifetime of an execution; and if the amount of the judgment is large, a longer time should be given. Ibid. 497.

MONEY.

1. A certificate of deposit payable in "Illinois currency," cannot be satisfied by depreciated paper; it must be met by bills passing in the locality in the place of coin. It might be otherwise if the certificate had been made payable in Illinois bank paper. *Chicago M. & F. Ins. Co.* v. *Keiron*, 501.
2. The words "Illinois currency" mean something different from gold or

silver, or their equivalents, and may be used in reference to things of different values, when applied to the uses of traffic; and on enforcing a contract using these words, it is proper to show what meaning the parties intended to give them in their use of them. CATON, C. J. Ibid. 501.

3. Where it appears that a bank received for a customer by collecting or by receipt of deposits, funds, which were current, and passed as money in general business transactions, without directions to hold the identical funds, it will have to account to the owner for the sums so received, without diminution or discount, notwithstanding the bills received by the bank were at the time or have since depreciated in value. *Marine Bank of Chicago* v. *Chandler*, 525.

See JUDGMENT, 3, 4.

MORTGAGE—MORTGAGOR—MORTGAGEE.

1. A person who holds the beneficial interest in a mortgage should be made the complainant, yet when the use is declared, the suit need not be dismissed if the bill should be amended by striking out the name of the nominal complainant; and such an amendment would not produce injury. *Winkelman* v. *Kiser*, 21.

2. A decree should not be pronounced against a party not before the court Ibid. 21.

3. A decree should not be entered against the purchaser of mortgaged premises, whether he be or not a purchaser with notice; the decree should direct a sale of the premises and a distribution of the proceeds. If he held the equity of redemption, the sale might bar it, if he failed to redeem. Ibid. 21.

4. Moore owned a tract of land which he had mortgaged to Clark for $1,400. Weider wished to buy this tract from Moore for $2,000, and another tract from Clark for $1,600. It was arranged that Moore should convey his tract to Clark for the $3,000, less the mortgage, and that Clark should then convey both tracts to Weider for $4,600—Weider to pay $1,000 down, and give a mortgage for the balance. *Held*, that this was a sale of the whole premises from Clark to Weider, and that the mortgage being given for a part of the purchase money, Weider could not claim a homestead in the Moore tract to defeat a foreclosure. *Weider* v. *Clark*, 251.

5. Upon the foreclosure of a mortgage given to secure the purchase money for premises, it is not necessary that the wife of the mortgagor should be made a party to the bill. *Stephens* v. *Bichnell*, 445.

6. Where the mortgagor is insolvent, and the premises are not worth the amount due upon the mortgage, a strict foreclosure may be decreed. Ibid. 445.

7. Where a defendant to a suit in chancery has suffered a default, it is discretionary with the court to require evidence sustaining the allegations in the bill, and he cannot assign for error that the proof was insufficient. Ibid. 445.

704

MOTIONS.

MUNICIPAL CORPORATIONS.

NEGLIGENCE.

NEGOTIABLE INSTRUMENTS.

1. *Held*, that the following instrument was negotiable under the statute, and that in an action upon it, a consideration need not be averred or proved: " Due W. B. G. $450, to be paid in lumber, at $1.25." *Bilderback* v. *Burlingame*, 338.

2. An instrument admitting a certain sum of money to be due, which may be paid in merchandise, at a fixed price, becomes an absolute money demand, if the payee fails to deliver the merchandise when it is called for. If there were two payees, a refusal by one of them would be sufficient. Ibid. 338.

See PROMISSORY NOTE.

NOTICE.

A sufficient notice to a debtor under a foreign attachment should be shown of record. *Cariker* v. *Anderson*, 358.

See PRACTICE.

NUNCUPATIVE WILL.

It is indispensable to the validity of a nuncupative will, that the testator should request those present to bear witness that such was his last will. Or that he should say or do something equivalent to such an expression. *Arnett* v. *Arnett*, 247.

OCCUPYING CLAIMANTS.

1. The statute for the protection of occupying claimants is designed to protect those who shall in good faith take peaceable possession of vacant land under such a paper title as the records of the county show to be plain, clear and connected, and without notice of any adverse title of record. *Montag* v. *Linn*, 328.

2. The protection of a party under this statute does not depend upon the original deeds through which he deraigns his title being regular upon their face; such deeds may contain material alterations, or be forgeries, and yet the purchaser may be protected, where the records of the county show a clear chain of title. Ibid. 328.

ODD FELLOWS.

See ACTION, 12. CORPORATION.

OYER.

Oyer cannot be craved of an instrument not under seal, of which profert is not made. If such an instrument is to be examined by this court, it should be presented by bill of exceptions, demurrer to evidence, by an agreed case, or by a special verdict. *Gatton* v. *Dimmitt*, 400.

PAROL AGREEMENT.

See CHANCERY.

PARTITION—PARTITION WALLS.

1. Where the affidavit and report of commissioners appointed to make partition bear date one day prior to the order of their appointment, and no specific objection is raised to this, it will be regarded as a mistake of the clerk in making up the record. *Tibbs* v. *Allen*, 119.

2. Commissioners appointed to make partition, should take the oath as provided by the statute, "to make partition in accordance with the judgment of the court as to the rights and interests of the parties." It is irregular for them to be sworn, merely to divide the land impartially. Ibid. 119.

3. Commissioners appointed to make partition, reported, "that from all the circumstances surrounding the pecuniary condition of the family, and the locality of the lands, they cannot be divided without prejudice to the owners." *Held*, that this report was not in conformity with the statute, and did not justify the court in ordering a sale of the lands. Ibid. 119.

4. A bill in chancery for a partition should set out the title of the petitioner, or show the interest he claims in the premises sought to be divided. Ibid. 119.

5. The decree in a chancery proceeding for partition, should set out the respective interests and titles of the parties, and it is error for the decree to provide for an equal division among the defendants without finding that they have equal interests in the land. Ibid. 119.

6. A deed conveyed to M. certain premises, extending to the west line of the west wall of a brick building upon the premises; so that it included the whole of the west wall; with the reservation that the owners of the ground on both sides should have the mutual use of the present partition wall. At that time there was a small one-story brick building on the lot adjoining on the west. Subsequently M.'s grantors conveyed this other lot to P., who tore down this small building, and erected one much higher, and extending further along on M.'s wall. *Held*, that the reservation in the deed to M. extended only to such portions of the west wall as were then used as a partition between the buildings, and that P. has no right to the mutual use of any other, or greater part of this west wall. *Price* v. *McConnell*, 255.

See CHANCERY. INFANTS. PRACTICE.

PARTNERS—PARTNERSHIP.

1. The giving of a note and mortgage by one of two copartners in settlement of a joint debt, does not discharge an account against the firm, unless they were received in satisfaction of it. *Rayburn* v. *Day*, 46.

2. If a note is given not under seal, by one of several parties, it will not satisfy the account, unless the parties so intended; and a recovery may be had upon the account, if the note is surrendered. A recovery cannot be had on the account if the note is still held by the creditor. Ibid. 46.

3. On a settlement of partnership affairs, if it is agreed that one of the partners shall collect a note and accounts, for the benefit of both, it will be presumed, that the money, as fast as received, should be divided between the parties. *Metcalf* v. *Fouts*, 110.

4. On a bill filed for a settlement of partnership accounts, where the proofs and statements leave everything in such doubt and uncertainty that it is impossible to do justice, the bill should be dismissed without costs. *Vermillion* v. *Bailey*, 230.

5. When by agreement, persons have a joint interest of the same nature in a particular adventure, they are, as between themselves, partners; although some contribute money alone, and the others labor alone. *Robbins* v. *Laswell*, 365.

6. If parties agree to share profits, they are partners as to such profits; although they do not agree to share in the losses. Ibid. 365.

7. A written agreement as to dividing profits may be extended tacitly by the mutual understanding of the parties, or by their conduct in relation to it. Ibid. 365.

1. If a declaration avers that a note is made payable to the plaintiffs by the name and style of Curtis and Baker, such a note may be read in evidence, although they declared in the names of Edwin Curtis and Joseph Baker, without alleging that they were partners, or that the note was made payable in any joint character. *Wright* v. *Curtis*, 514.

PAYMENT.

1. The giving of a note and mortgage by one of two copartners in settlement of a joint debt, does not discharge an account against the firm, unless they were received in satisfaction of it. *Rayburn* v. *Day*, 46.

2. If a note is given not under seal, by one of several parties, it will not satisfy the account, unless the parties so intended; and a recovery may be had upon the account, if the note is surrendered. A recovery cannot be had on the account, if the note is still held by the creditor. Ibid. 46.

3. The giving of a bond in satisfaction of a judgment, is in law a payment of it. *Cox* v. *Reed et al.* 434.

See ATTORNEY AND CLIENT. JUDGMENT.

PERSONAL PROPERTY.

1. The purchaser of personal property is not to presume, by a vague statement made, that the vendor is a trifling fellow, and had not money, in the opinion of the person making the remark, to buy the property; that the title of the vendor is defective. A purchaser is not bound to take mere suspicions unsupported by facts, in his business affairs, as a

warning ; though the statement of facts touching the manner of the acquisition of property by his vendor, might be sufficient to put him on his guard. *Gosney* v. *Frost*, 53.

2. A party may maintain trespass, if he has at the time of the act, such a title as draws after it a constructive possession. *Gauche* v. *Mayer*, 134.

3. A had placed goods with an auctioneer for sale, reserving to himself the right to resume possession at his pleasure, the auctioneer not having any claim to or charge upon such goods: *Held*, that A had a right of action in trespass against a sheriff for making a levy upon those goods as the property of another, the sheriff having been notified of the facts before the levy. Ibid. 134.

4. A complete transfer of personal property may be made, although the purchaser should not hold continuous possession. If the property is returned to the possession of the vendor, the fact may create suspicion, but is not conclusive of the fairness of the transaction. *Wright* v. *Grover et al.* 426.

5. If there is an actual delivery of property on the payment of money, with the design to make a sale of it, the title passes, except as to prior liens; as between the parties, the sale will be good, if a delivery of the property was all that remained to be done. *Sidwell* v. *Lobly*, 438.

6. A railroad tank-house, locomotive and cars, are presumed to be annexed to the realty, and in fact are a part of it. and are not liable to be sold by a constable, on an execution from a justice of the peace. *Titus et al.* v. *Ginheimer et al.* 462.

7. Where it appears that a party is to deliver grain and have the price of it at a certain place indorsed on a contract, the party to whom it is to be delivered, has not, prior to delivery, any authority to take possession of the grain. *Millay* v. *Dunn*, 516.

PLEADING.

1. If an action is brought against a railroad company under the statute, and the negligence charged results from an omission to erect a fence, the declaration should show that the accident did not happen at a place where the company is not bound to maintain a fence. *Ill. Cent. R. R. Co.* v. *Williams*, 48.

2. In an action upon an insurance policy, which contains a condition that in the event of a loss, the company may at its option restore the building, it is unnecessary to negative the performance of the condition, in the declaration. It is a condition subsequent, and if performed, the company should allege it in defense of the action. *Ætna Ins. Co.* v. *Phelps*, 71.

3. The statute of frauds must be pleaded, if it is to be relied upon by the defendant. He cannot set it up, for the first time, in an instruction. *Warren* v. *Dickson*, 115.

4. A partial failure of consideration may be pleaded to a promissory note given for the purchase of land. *Schuchmann* v. *Knoebel*, 175.

5. A declaration against a railroad corporation for killing cattle, need not

negative the possibility that the animals may have been killed at a farm crossing. If the road is not properly fenced at such crossing, the company will be liable for injuries, and if it were properly fenced, that is matter of defense. *Great Western R. R. Co.* v. *Helm,* 198.

6. If a declaration avers a wrong with a *continuendo,* it may be obnoxious on demurrer; but the objection is too late if made after issue has been joined. Ibid. 198.

7. An averment that a sheriff's return was signed, is unnecessary; this will be presumed. *Rives* v. *Kumler,* 291.

8. Oyer cannot be craved of an instrument not under seal, of which profert is not made. If such an instrument is to be examined by this court, it should be presented by bill of exceptions, demurrer to evidence, by an agreed case, or by a special verdict. *Gatton* v. *Dimmitt,* 400.

9. It is allowable to include in the same declaration, divers distinct words of slander, of different import. *Hall* v. *Nees,* 411.

10. The plea of *nul tiel corporation,* is a plea in bar. *Town of Lewiston* v. *Proctor,* 414.

11. In an action to recover a penalty, for obstructing a highway, if the complaint gives a local description, sufficient to fix the precise point obstructed, and also the *termini* of the road, the latter may be disregarded. But when the allegation is general, that a road leading from one point to another has been obstructed, the existence of the road between the points named, must be proved as a matter of essential description. Ibid. 414.

12. A declaration upon the covenants in a deed averred the making of covenants of seizin, of power to sell, and of warranty, only; the breach included not only these, but also covenants against incumbrances and for quiet enjoyment. The defendant assigned as a ground for demurrer, that this one count set forth more than one cause of action. *Held,* that as all these causes of action were of the same nature and could be answered by one plea, they might be joined in one count. That these separate breaches were to be regarded as so many distinct counts. That the demurrer being to the whole count, and one of the breaches being properly assigned, the demurrer should be overruled. *Brady* v. *Spurck,* 478.

13. Several causes of action of the same nature may be joined in one count. The defendant can plead specially to each cause of action. Ibid. 478.

14. The rule as to joining causes of action is, that when the same plea may be pleaded, and the same judgment rendered on all the counts, they may be joined. Ibid. 478.

15. In an action of covenant upon the covenant against eviction in a deed, the plaintiff alleged particularly the manner of his eviction, by showing the foreclosure of a mortgage given by the covenantor, and a sale under the decree. *Held,* that as it was not averred that a deed had been given under the decree, or that the time for redemption had expired, or that any actual eviction had occurred, a demurrer to the declaration should have been sustained. Ibid. 478.

16. The declaration in an action upon covenants in a deed of conveyance,

710

claimed an eviction by showing the foreclosure of a mortgage given by the covenantor, and a sale under the decree, but did not show that any deed had been given under the sale, or that the time of redemption had expired, or that an actual eviction had occurred. *Held*, that if the plaintiff had removed the mortgage, the measure of damages would have been the amount so paid, provided it did not exceed the purchase money and interest—but as it did not appear that the plaintiff had paid off the incumbrance or had suffered any eviction, nominal damages only should be awarded. Ibid. 478.

17. In an action upon covenants contained in a deed, brought by the last grantee of the land, he need not allege or prove that the intermediate assignees have kept their covenants. Ibid. 478.

18. If a declaration avers that a note is made payable to the plaintiffs by the name and style of Curtis and Baker, such a note may be read in evidence, although they declared in the names of Edwin Curtis and Joseph Baker, without alleging that they were partners, or that the note was made payable in any joint character. *Wright* v. *Curtis*, 514.

See RAILROADS.

PRACTICE.

1. A continuance will not be granted because a witness has said that he would be present at the trial and had been subpœnaed by the opposite party. The party desiring the testimony of the witness, should secure his presence at the trial. *Moore* v. *Goelitz*, 18. .

2. In debt, recovery must be had against all or none of the defendants. *People* v. *Organ*, 27.

3. Upon an appeal from a justice of the peace, the Circuit Court should try the cause *de novo*, and it is error to dismiss the suit because the justice rendered judgment against two defendants when he had only obtained jurisdiction over the person of one of them. *Stephens* v. *Cross*, 35.

4. If a justice of the peace renders judgment against two defendants when only one has been brought into court, and the defendant who was served appeals the case and fails to prosecute his appeal, the Circuit Court may affirm the judgment as to him, and reverse it as to the other who has not been served. Ibid. 35.

5. The Circuit Court should not, in cases of appeal from a justice of the peace, authorize an amendment of the summons, by changing the names of parties. *Henckler* v. *County Court*, 39.

6. An action of ejectment is within the purview of the statute requiring security for costs; and if the plaintiff is a non-resident he must give security for costs before instituting suit; which is commenced by serving the declaration and notice. *Farnsworth* v. *Agnew*, 42.

7. If it appears from the bill of exceptions, that a plaintiff in ejectment was a non-resident at the time of the service of the declaration and notice, although the affidavit of the defendant to that fact is not saved in the

bill of exceptions, the judgment dismissing the action for want of security will be upheld. Ibid. 42.

8. Upon a default, a writ of inquiry issues to have the damages assessed, which may be executed in court or be directed to the sheriff to execute in vacation. It would be regular for the sheriff to summon a jury from the bystanders, and have the damages assessed in the presence of the court. *Ætna Ins. Co.* v. *Phelps*, 71.

9. Where an answer is filed for infant defendants, by one purporting to be their guardian *ad litem*, and the decree recites that he was so appointed, but the record shows no separate order of appointment, it will be presumed that the appointment was regularly made. *Tibbs* v. *Allen*, 119.

10. Where the record shows a notice by publication in a chancery cause, which recites the fact.that an affidavit of the non-residence of the defendants' was duly filed, but the affidavit does not appear in the record, this court will regard that recital as an official declaration by the clerk, and will presume that the affidavit was duly filed. Ibid. 119.

11. Where there are infant and adult defendants, and the adults alone. prosecute a writ of error, they cannot assign for error those proceedings which only affect the interests of the infants. Ibid. 119.

12. Upon a bill for a partition brought by one of the heirs at law, in which it is suggested that the widow is entitled to dower in the lands sought to be divided, but the prayer does not ask that her dower be assigned, the court cannot decree an assignment of dower and appoint commissioners to set it off. Nor can the court give the widow an estate in fee in one-third of the land, in lieu of her life estate, for dower. Ibid. 119.

13. Where the affidavit and report of commissioners appointed to make partition bear date one day prior to the order of their appointment, and no specific objection is raised to this, it will be regarded as a mistake of the clerk in making up the record. Ibid. 119.

14. Commissioners appointed to make partition, should take the oath as provided by the statute, "to make partition in accordance with the judgment of the court as to the rights and interests of the parties." It is irregular for them to be sworn, merely to divide the land impartially. *Tibbs* v. *Allen*, 119.

15. Commissioners appointed to make partition, reported, "that from all the circumstances surrounding the pecuniary condition of the family, and the locality of the lands, they cannot be divided without prejudice to the owners." *Held*, that this report was not in conformity with the statute, and did not justify the court in ordering a sale of the lands. Ibid. 119.

16. A bill in chancery for a partition should set out the title of the petitioner, or show the interest he claims in the premises sought to be divided. Ibid. 119.

17. The decree in a chancery proceeding for partition, should set out the respective interests and titles of the parties, and it is error for the decree to provide for an equal division among the defendants without finding that they have equal interests in the land. Ibid. 119.

18. Infants are not bound by a decree unless all of the evidence necessary to establish it, is preserved in the record. Ibid. 119.

19. When a bill is taken as confessed, the court may, in its discretion, require proof as to all or any portion of the allegations in the bill, and the evidence need not be preserved in the record, or it may render a decree on the *pro confesso* order without evidence. *Smith* v. *Trimble*, 152.

20. A decree should ascertain the precise amount to be paid, and not leave it to computation. Ibid. 152.

21. If a non-resident is proceeded against by publication in a chancery cause, the court does not acquire jurisdiction over his person, unless a summons has been regularly issued, and returned by the sheriff. Ibid. 152.

22. After a notice has been given to the administrator of a deceased debtor, of the existence of a judgment against the decedent, in accordance with Sec. 3, Chap. 47, Rev. Stat., the judgment creditor may issue an execution, and also an *alias* or *pluries*, without further notice. *Letcher* v *Morrison*, 209.

23. Depositions taken in one suit may be used in another between the same parties, about the same controversy. *McConnel* v. *Smith*, 232.

24. In an action upon a promissory note, by the assignee against the assignor, the defendant filed a demurrer to the declaration, which was overruled, and he elected to stand by it. It was competent for the clerk to assess the damages. *Rives* v. *Kumler*, 291.

25. In an action upon a bond, judgment should be so entered, that the whole may be satisfied, upon the payment of the damages. *Freeland* v. *Board of Supervisors*, 303.

26. If three defendants demur, and, after the demurrer is withdrawn, two of them plead, a judgment *nil dicit* should be entered against the party not pleading, and the jury should assess the damages against all. If but two plead, and the other abided by his demurrer, he could not be regarded as going to trial with the others. Ibid. 303.

27. It is generally a matter of discretion whether the Circuit Court will rule a party to file security for costs; but if the affidavit upon which the motion is founded be insufficient, the Circuit Court has no power under the statute to make the rule, and its decision will be reviewed in the Supreme Court. *Ball* v. *Bruce*, 332.

28. Upon a motion for a rule upon the plaintiff to file additional security for costs, an affidavit is insufficient which only avers the insolvency of the plaintiff and his security; it should show, in addition, that the circumstances of the principal or security have changed since the approval of the former bond. Ibid. 332.

29. The interrogatories to and answers of a garnishee are a part of the record, and need not be preserved by a bill of exceptions. *Rankin* v. *Simonds*, 352.

30. Where no issue is raised upon the answers of a garnishee, they must be taken as true, and the rights of the parties must be determined by them. Ibid. 352.

31. The garnishee has a right to set up any claim he has against the defendant, to meet the fund in his hands, which he could set off or recoup in an action brought by the defendant to recover the fund. *Rankin* v. *Simonds*, 352.

32. Rankin, summoned as the garnishee of Elliott, answered, that he had funds of Elliott's, but that he had delivered to E. a note against the H. & S. R. R. Co. for collection; that E. owed the company an amount greater than the amount of the note and still retained the note, his account with the company being still unsettled. *Held*, that as the note had not been paid, Rankin might withdraw it at any time, and he could not be allowed to set it off against the fund in his hands. Ibid. 352.

33. Where garnishees are summoned in an attachment suit, the proper practice is to enter judgment against the garnishees and in favor of the defendant in the attachment suit, for the benefit of such attaching creditors as are entitled to the proceeds. Ibid. 352.

34. A conditional judgment and a *scire facias* are requisite, as proper preliminaries to a judgment against a garnishee. The *scire facias* is to make known to the garnishee that a conditional judgment has been rendered against him, assuming him to be a debtor of the debtors in attachment, and that he must show cause why final judgment should not go against him. *Cariker* v. *Anderson*, 358.

35. A sufficient notice to a debtor under a foreign attachment should be shown of record. Ibid. 358.

36. It may not be error for a term of court to intervene between a default taken and a *scire facias* issued against a garnishee. Ibid. 358.

37. The date given in the indorsement of a service of process, should be taken at the time of service. A sheriff is not required to date his return Ibid. 358.

38. A garnishee is not properly a defendant in an attachment suit, to defend against the plaintiff's claim; the judgment should be entered against a garnishee in favor of the defendant in the attachment suit, for the benefit of the creditor or others in attachment, and if there is more due than will pay the attaching creditor, the creditor of the garnishee can control it. Ibid. 358.

39. Oyer cannot be craved of an instrument not under seal, of which profert is not made. If such an instrument is to be examined by this court, it should be presented by bill of exceptions, demurrer to evidence, by an agreed case, or by a special verdict. *Gatton* v. *Dimmitt*, 400.

40. A general objection to the introduction of an instrument as evidence, is not sufficient; if it is obnoxious to a special objection, that objection must be stated in the court below. *Buntain* v. *Bailey*, 409.

41. According to the strict rules of practice, a motion in arrest of judgment is a waiver of a motion for a new trial. A party who has filed both motions, and calls up his motion in arrest and has it disposed of, and then allows judgment to be rendered, without directing the attention of the court to the other motion, will be held to have waived his motion for a new trial. *Hall* v. *Nees*, 411.

42. A party need not produce or prove a judgment that is not put in issue. *Cox* v. *Reed et al.* 434.

43. If heirs are brought into court by *scire facias* under the statute, to show cause why they should not be made parties to a judgment, it will be necessary to prove up the case *de novo* against them. Adults cannot demand that more shall be proved against them, when there are infant parties, than if all were adults. Ibid. 434.

44. Actions in attachment must be commenced where the defendant has property, or where he can be found, and service must be upon him or his property. The court does not acquire jurisdiction by issuing two writs, one of which is to another county than that where the process is returnable, although there may be property to attach in such other county. *Hinman* v. *Rushmore et al.* 509.

45. In ejectment, before the court can take jurisdiction, it should appear, by affidavit, that the declaration and notice to appear and plead, have been served. A sheriff's return will not give jurisdiction. *O'Donnell* v. *Howes*, 510.

See AMENDMENT, 1.

PRESUMPTIONS.

1. Fraud must always be proved; the law never presumes it. *Wright* v. *Grover et al.* 426.

2. A justice of the peace issues a capias upon an oath, an affidavit is, not necessary, and the presumption is, that a justice requires all the necessary averments in the oath, such as are commanded by the constitution and laws. *Outlaw* v. *Davis et al.* 467.

PRINCIPAL AND AGENT.

See AGENT. AGENCY.

PRIVITY

A and B, each sent cattle to market, which were sold by the same broker, who, in accounting to the parties, paid A too much, and B, by precisely the same sum, too little; B sued A to recover his deficit. *Held*, that there was no such privity between these parties, as would create a liability. *Hall* v. *Carpen*, 386.

PROBATE COURT.

See ADMINISTRATOR. COURTS. ESTATES.

PROMISSORY NOTE.

1. If the maker of a note says to the payee, that if he will wait awhile he will pay the note; and that he will pay when he "makes a raise," not

15. The payee of a note, before its maturity, put his name upon the back of it, but kept it in his possession until after it became due. He then delivered the note to the attorney of the plaintiff, who was a non-resident This was not a *bona fide* assignment, and did not prevent the maker from setting up the defense of usury. Ibid. 301.

16. An agreement, between the holder of a note and the principal, to extend the time of payment for a definite period, which is founded upon a good consideration, will discharge the surety; unless the surety consents to the agreement at the time, or subsequently ratifies it. *Flynn* v. *Mudd*, 323.

17. To enable a surety to interpose the defense to a note that further time has been given to his principal, it is not necessary that his name should appear upon the note as surety; it will be sufficient if he was actually a surety, and this was known to the payee when the note was executed. Ibid. 323.

18. The payment of interest upon a note in advance, is a sufficient consideration to support an agreement for an extension of time to the principal, so as to discharge the surety. Ibid. 323.

19. Where the plaintiff introduces in evidence a note which has indorsed upon it, an agreement extending the time for payment, he will be bound by the agreement although it is not signed by him. Ibid. 323.

20. *Held*, that the following instrument was negotiable under the statute, and that in an action upon it, a consideration need not be averred or proved : " Due W. B. G. $450, to be paid in lumber when called for, in good lumber, at $1.25." *Bilderback* v. *Burlingame*, 338.

21. An instrument admitting a certain sum of money to be due, which may be paid in merchandise, at a fixed price, becomes an absolute money demand, if the payee fails to deliver the merchandise when it is called for. If there were two payees, a refusal by one of them would be sufficient. Ibid. 338.

22. Although a note may bear ten per cent. interest, when a decree is entered upon it, the note is merged ; and the decree can bear only six per cent. interest. *White* v. *Haffaker*, 349.

23. A note given to a county, is properly assigned, by the clerk of the County Court under its seal. *Gatton* v. *Dimmitt*, 400.

24. A note given for the purchase of land, if transferred, does not carry with it to the assignee, the vendor's lien, so that the assignee can enforce it in his own name. *Richards* v. *Leaming et al.* 431.

25. If a declaration avers that a note is made payable to the plaintiffs by the name and style of Curtis and Baker, such a note may be read in evidence, although they declared in the names of Edwin Curtis and Joseph Baker, without alleging that they were partners, or that the note was made payable in any joint character. *Wright* v. *Curtis*, 514.

RAILROADS.

1. A party who sues a railroad company, under the statute, for injuries to

cies of personal property not before known to the law. For non-payment of taxes upon this property the collector may levy upon the rails and remove them from the track, for the purpose of selling them. *Maus* v. *Logansport, Peoria and Burlington R. R. Co.* 77.

14. This act has reference only to the collection of the revenue, and does not change the character of such property for other purposes. Ibid. 77.

15. Section 14, of the amendatory act of 1853, which provides that real property shall be liable for taxes on personal property, and *vice versa*, has no application to this "fixed and stationary personal property;" such property must bear its own burden of taxation. *Maus* v. *Logansport, Peoria and Burlington R. R. Co.* 77.

16. It is within the province of the legislature to provide that property, which is attached to the freehold, so as to become a part of it by the common law, may be regarded as personal property, for all purposes, or for any special purpose. Of this character is the act of Feb. 14th, 1855, which directs that the track and superstructure of a railroad, together with the improvements at stations, shall be denominated personal property, for the purposes of collecting the revenue. Ibid. 77.

17. The law does not require any different words to be used in proving a case against a railroad company, from those used in ordinary cases; it is only requisite that the mind should be convinced of the existence of the necessary facts. *Ohio and Mississippi R. R. Co.* v. *Irvin*, 178.

18. The presumption is, that the houses compose a village; if an animal is killed beyond the houses, the presumption is, that it is killed beyond the village; if the town extends beyond the houses, the defendant should show the fact. Ibid. 178.

19. Every one is supposed to have some idea of the value of such property as is in general use; and it is not necessary to have a drover or butcher to prove the value of a cow. Ibid. 178.

20. A subscriber to the capital stock of a railroad company, who agrees to be subject to the rules and regulations which may from time to time be adopted by the directors, cannot avoid payment, because the charter has been amended, reducing the number of days of notice to be given, if the amendment of the charter has been accepted. *Illinois River R. R. Co.* v. *Beers*, 185.

21. Amendments to charters may be accepted in divers ways. Ibid. 185.

22. A declaration against a railroad corporation for killing cattle need not negative the possibility that the animals may have been killed at a farm crossing. If the road is not properly fenced at such crossing, the company will be liable for injuries, and if it were properly fenced, that is matter of defense. *Great Western R. R. Co.* v. *Helm*, 198.

23. In an action for killing cattle by a railroad company, the plaintiff should negative by proof that there was no public crossing where the killing occurred; and should show that the company was bound to fence at that point. *Ohio and Mississippi R. R. Co.* v. *Taylor*, 207.

24. The proof should show that the injury was done upon the road of the company sued. Ibid. 207.

25. Any person familiar with the kind of property injured, may prove its value; an expert is not an indispensable witness. Ibid. 207.

26. Where the name of a corporation consists of several words, the transposition, omission or alteration of some of them, may not be regarded as important, if it is evident what corporation is intended. *Chadsey* v. *Mc-Creery*, 253.

27. A note payable to James G. McCreery, treasurer of the R. I. & A. R. R. Co., is not a note to the company, but to the individual named. The addition to his name is merely *descriptio personæ*. Ibid. 253.

28. The board of supervisors alone, have the power to order an election to determine whether the county will subscribe to stock in a railroad company, and to issue the bonds therefor; and they cannot delegate their power. But this rule does not prevent the board of supervisors, after they have taken all necessary action in the matter, from directing that the bonds shall be signed by the county judge. The county judge then becomes merely the instrument, by which the action of the board is manifested. *Clarke* v. *Board of Supervisors*, 305.

29. In ordering an election, to determine whether a county will subscribe for stock to aid in building a railroad, it is improper to submit the question, whether two different roads shall be so aided, by a single vote; so that the two propositions cannot be voted upon separately. The county may be restrained from issuing bonds in pursuance of such a vote; but when issued they are not necessarily void, in the hands of a *bona fide* holder. *Clarke* v. *Board of Supervisors*, 305.

30. Where county bonds, to aid the construction of a railroad, have been issued, in pursuance of an election held without warrant of law, as where it has been ordered by a person or tribunal having no such authority, they are absolutely void. But where the election has been properly authorized, and there has been informality in the manner of submitting the question to the people (such as submitting two propositions as to aiding two different roads, to a single vote), the bonds may be rendered valid, in the hands of an innocent holder, by the acquiescence of the people, and their subsequent ratification by the county, in levying a tax and paying interest upon them. Ibid. 305.

31. A railroad tank-house, locomotive and cars, are presumed to be annexed to the realty, and in fact are a part of it, and are not liable to be sold by a constable, on an execution from a justice of the peace. *Titus et al.* v. *Ginheimer et al.* 462.

32. The legislature has the constitutional right to authorize counties, towns and cities to aid in the construction of railroads, by lending credit, issuing bonds or taking stock. Fraud in the election authorizing such action must be set up in apt time, and before rights have accrued. *Butler et al.* v. *Dunham et al.* 474.

REAL ESTATE.

A testator gave to his wife all his estate, to be disposed of in any way that would best support her for life, but if his sons, John and Thomas, should take care of their mother, they were to have certain lands, but if they failed to support their mother, then she could sell the land, or any part of it, to support herself; but if the sons complied with these conditions, they were to take immediate possession of the land; there were bequests to other children: *Held*, that the testator intended to charge his entire estate with the support of his widow; that the question of support was a condition subsequent, the word "comply" being used in the sense of "assent," and when John and Thomas assented, the estate passed to them, burthened with the condition of support of the mother; and that the widow of John being his heir, and proffering to support the widow, had a right to inherit and possess the estate, and could compel the grantee of the widow to reconvey to her. *Jennings* v. *Jennings*, 518.

See ADMINISTRATORS. GUARDIANS. INFANTS.

RECOGNIZANCE.

1. A recognizance taken out of court, or by a judge at chambers, does not become a record, upon which a *scire facias* can issue, until it is properly certified and filed. *Raysor* v. *People*, 190.

2. Upon a change of venue in a criminal case, the court granting the order may take a recognizance from the defendant to appear in the court to which the venue has been changed. *Stebbins* v. *People*, 240.

3. A default and order of forfeiture was taken upon recognizance against the defendant and his surety, judgment was then taken upon the default against the defendant, and a *sci. fa.* issued against the surety alone. Upon the return of the *sci. fa.*, judgment was taken against both cognizors; and the judgment was reversed because the *sci. fa.* was issued against the wrong party. Ibid. 240.

RECORDING ACT.

See DEED. EJECTMENT.

RECOUPMENT.

1. A party may *recoup* in an action upon a note given for land, what he has been compelled to pay in order to remove an incumbrance upon the land. *Schuchmann* v. *Knoebel*, 175.

2. A contracted with B for a quantity of lumber and cross-ties. He then put B in possession of a saw-mill, and took a bond from B and C, conditioned for the return of the mill, upon the completion of the contract. A failed to pay for the cross-ties and lumber, and B failed to return the mill. *Held*, that in an action by B for the price of the lumber, A could recoup for the damages, arising from the breach of the condition of the bond. *Sanger* v. *Fincher*, 346.

3. Where the defendant attempts to recoup, for unliquidated damages, these damages must relate to the transaction, out of which the controversy has arisen. Ibid. 346.

4. B recovered a judgment against A, and subsequently died. A filed a bill. against the administratrix, alleging that damages had accrued to him by reason of a breach of the condition of a bond executed by B and C, relating to the same matter for which the judgment had been obtained; but he failed to state whether the breach of the bond had occurred before or after the commencement of the action by B. *Held*, that the bill was demurrable, because it did not show but that the complainant had an ample remedy at law, by recouping his damages on the trial of B's action. Ibid. 346.

5. The garnishee has a right to set up any claim he has against the defendant, to meet the fund in his hands, which he could set off or recoup in an action brought by the defendant to recover the fund. *Rankin* v. *Simonds*, 352.

RELIGIOUS SOCIETIES.

The usages of a church, or the law of its organization as a religious society, if they are to be considered in deciding legal controversies, should be proved as facts. In the absence of testimony, it will be presumed that religious societies cannot dissolve their connection with the principal organization without permission. *Vasconcellos* v. *Ferraria*, 237.

ROADS.

See HIGHWAYS AND STREETS.

SALE.

If there is an actual delivery of property on the payment of money, with the design to make a sale of it, the title passes, except as to prior liens; as between the parties the sale will be good, if a delivery of the property was all that remained to be done. *Sidwell* v. *Lobly*, 438.

See LEVY. PERSONAL PROPERTY.

SALE OF LAND

1. Where a purchaser, under a verbal contract for the sale of land, takes possession by consent of the vendor, and makes valuable improvements, and within the time agreed upon for payment, tenders the purchase money, the case is taken out of the statute of frauds, and the purchaser is entitled to a specific performance of the oral agreement. *Blunt* v. *Tomlin*, 93.

2. It is no defense for third parties who subsequently purchased of the vendor with full notice, and before the time for payment had expired, that the vendor had disaffirmed the verbal contract, and sold to them before the purchase money was actually paid or tendered. The purchaser is entitled to protection, if he paid or tendered the money within the time agreed upon. *Blunt* v. *Tomlin*, 93.

722

3. Where a purchaser of land under an oral agreement, has five years in which to make his payments, so that the contract conflicts with two sections of the statute of frauds, he may nevertheless be entitled to a specific performance. The same facts which would take the case out of one section of the statute, will take it out of the other. In such a case, the court should be more cautious in examining the evidence of the oral contract. Ibid. 93.

4. A party who makes a tender for a deed under a contract, need not part with the money, until he receives his deed. If the vendor offers to take the money but refuses to make the deed, this is a refusal of the tender, and it is a useless ceremony to count out the money after that. Ibid. 93.

5. A tender made in pursuance of a contract for a deed, fixes the rights of the parties, as conclusively as if the money had been actually paid. Ibid. 93.

6. Where a default has been taken and a decree entered, *pro confesso*, which recites that the defendants have been regularly notified of the pendency of the suit, by summons or advertisement, a *bona fide* purchaser under the decree will be protected, although the record may not furnish any evidence of a summons or advertisement. *Reddick* v. *State Bank*, 145.

7. Proceedings for the sale of land by an administrator will be reversed, if the record does not show any petition by the administrator. *Monahon* v. *Vandyke*, 154.

8. It is error for the Circuit Court to order a sale of land by an administrator, when the notice has been published but thirty days, while the statute requires a publication for six weeks, before the presentation of the petition. Ibid. 154.

9. An agreement by a party to convey all his title, etc., to land, is a sufficient consideration for a note. If the party giving the note desires more than a quit-claim deed, he should make his bargain accordingly. *Kerney* v. *Gardner*, 162.

10. A partial failure of consideration may be pleaded to a promissory note given for the purchase of land. *Schuchmann* v. *Knoebel*, 175.

11. A party may also *recoup* in an action upon a note given for land, what he has been compelled to pay in order to remove an incumbrance upon the land. Ibid. 175.

12. In a bill for the specific performance of a parol agreement for the sale of lands, if the defendant denies the agreement, and does not set up the statute of frauds as a defense, he cannot afterwards insist upon the statute in bar. *Hull* v. *Peer*, 312.

13. In a bill for a specific performance, the complainant need not, at his peril, state the precise amount due. He may state his case most favorably to himself, and if, upon the equities of the case, the court should decree a different amount, he can then conform to its judgment. Ibid. 312.

14. A. and B. executed a note together, with the understanding that A. should pay it. The payee insisted that B. should appear upon the note
723

as principal, and A. as surety. It was held that nevertheless, as between themselves, A. was the principal and B. the surety, in equity. Ibid. 312.

15. In decreeing a specific performance of a parol agreement for the sale of lands, the court will require the complainant to do complete justice, upon the broadest principles of equity, and will not be satisfied with a literal performance of the agreement by him. Ibid. 312.

16. A sale under a mechanics' lien, as there is no redemption from it, should not be authorized within a less period than the lifetime of an execution; and if the amount of the judgment is large, a longer time should be given. *Claycomb* v. *Cecil*, 497.

SANITY.

1. A contract entered into during the lucid intervals of one who is a lunatic, is valid. *Lilly* v. *Waggoner*, 395.

2. All persons of mature age are presumed to be sane, until after inquest found, when the presumption is changed, and proof is required to show sanity. Ibid. 395.

SATISFACTION OF JUDGMENT.

1. It is a settled principle of law that the levy of an execution upon personal property, sufficient to satisfy it, is of itself a satisfaction of the execution. But this rule is changed by Sec. 30, Chap. 57, Rev. Stat. of 1845 —which provides for the giving of a forthcoming bond. This statute is constitutional. *Martin* v. *Charter*, 294.

2. A. recovered a judgment against C., and was at the same time surety for B., upon an arbitration bond, for submitting differences between B. and C. to arbitration. C. obtained an award against B., and then filed a bill to have the amount of the judgment credited on the award. *Held*, that as A.'s liability to C. was only contingent and might never arise, he should not be restrained from collecting his judgment, unless it was alleged that he was insolvent or about to leave the State. *Hinrichsen* v. *Reinback*, 295.

3. The giving of a bond in satisfaction of a judgment, is in law the payment of it. *Cox* v. *Reed et al.* 434.

SCIRE FACIAS.

1. A recognizance taken out of court, or by a judge at chambers, does not become a record, upon which a *scire facias* can issue, until it is properly certified and filed. *Raysor* v. *People*, 190.

2. Upon a change of venue in a criminal case, the court granting the order may take a recognizance from the defendant to appear in the court to which the venue has been changed. *Stebbins* v. *People*, 240.

3. A default and order of forfeiture was taken upon recognizance against the defendant and his surety, judgment was then taken upon the default against the defendant, and a *sci. fa.* issued against the surety alone.

724

Upon the return of the *sci. fa.*, judgment was taken against both cognizors; and the judgment was reversed because the *sci. fa.* was issued against the wrong party. Ibid. 240.

4. A conditional judgment and a *scire facias* are requisite, as proper preliminaries to a judgment against a garnishee. The *scire facias* is to make known to the garnishee that a conditional judgment has been rendered against him, assuming him to be a debtor of the debtors in attachment, and that he must show cause why final judgment should not go against him. *Cariker* v. *Anderson*, 358.

5. It may not be error for a term of court to intervene between a default taken and a *scire facias* issued against a garnishee. Ibid. 358.

SEAL.

1. The statute requires that an instrument submitting a matter to arbitration, should be under seal. The seal is an indispensable formality, and without it the court cannot enter judgment on the award. *Hamilton* v. *Hamilton*, 158.

2. Where an instrument submitting a matter to arbitration was recited in the record, as a bond, and the instrument and execution of it were fully set out, by which it appeared that there were no seals to the signatures, the Supreme Court could not intend that it was a sealed instrument. If only the body of the bond had been set out in the record, the court might presume that it was properly executed. Ibid. 158.

SECURITY FOR COSTS.

1. An action of ejectment is within the purview of the statute requiring security for costs; and if the plaintiff is a non-resident he must give security for costs before instituting suit; which is commenced by serving the declaration and notice. *Farnsworth* v. *Agnew*, 42.

2. If it appears from the bill of exceptions, that a plaintiff in ejectment was a non-resident at the time of the service of the declaration and notice, although the affidavit of the defendant to that fact is not saved in the bill of exceptions, the judgment dismissing the action for want of security will be upheld. Ibid. 42.

3. It is generally a matter of discretion whether the Circuit Court will rule a party to file security for costs; but if the affidavit upon which the motion is founded be insufficient, the Circuit Court has no power under the statute to make the rule, and its decision will be reviewed in this court. *Ball* v. *Bruce*, 332.

4. Upon a motion for a rule upon the plaintiff to file additional security for costs, an affidavit is insufficient which only avers the insolvency of the plaintiff and his security; it should show, in addition, that the circumstances of the principal or security have changed since the approval of the former bond. Ibid. 332.

SERVICE OF PROCESS.

1. An averment that a sheriff's return was signed, is unnecessary; this will be presumed. *Rives* v. *Kumler*, 291.

2. The date given in the indorsement of a service of process, should be taken as the time of service. A sheriff is not required to date his return. [Several decisions in reference to service of process, considered and examined.] *Cariker* v. *Anderson*, 358.

3. On the death of the sheriff his deputy continues to act until a successor to his principal is qualified. The return to process signed by a deputy, without reference to the sheriff, where the court below found that it was "duly served," will be sufficient to uphold a default. If the sheriff was not dead, the defendant below should have taken steps to show that fact. *Timmerman* v. *Phelps*. 496.

The case of *Ditch* v. *Edwards*, 1 Scam. 127, commented upon and explained.

4. Actions in attachment must be commenced where the defendant has property, or where he can be found, and service must be upon him or his property. The court does not acquire jurisdiction by issuing two writs, one of which is to another county than that where the process is returnable, although there may be property to attach in such other county. *Hinman* v. *Rushmore et al.* 509.

5. In ejectment, before the court can take jurisdiction, it should appear by affidavit, that the declaration and notice to appear and plead, have been served. A sheriff's return will not give jurisdiction. *O'Donnell* v. *Howes*, 510.

SHERIFF — SHERIFF'S SALE.

1. A party who claims a homestead exemption as against a sheriff's sale, should show that the right existed when the lien attached; it is not enough for him to show that it was his homestead at the time of the sale. *Reinback* v. *Walter*, 393.

2. It would appear that a stable, a horse lot, a smoke-house and the grounds connected therewith, together with the dwelling-house, would constitute the homestead; but that a store, warehouse, and the grounds connected with these, would not. Ibid. 393.

3. On the death of the sheriff his deputy continues to act until a successor to his principal is qualified. The return to process signed by a deputy. without reference to the sheriff, where the court below found that it was "duly served," will be sufficient to uphold a default. If the sheriff was not dead, the defendant below should have taken steps to show that fact. *Timmerman et al.* v. *Phelps*, 496.

The case of *Ditch* v. *Edwards*, 1 Scam. 127, commented upon and explained.

See OFFICER. SERVICE OF PROCESS.

SLANDER.

It is allowable to include in the same declaration, divers distinct words of slander, of different import. *Hall* v. *Nees*, 411.

SPECIFIC PERFORMANCE.

1. In a bill for the specific performance of a parol agreement for the sale of lands, if the defendant denies the agreement, and does not set up the statute of frauds as a defense, he cannot afterwards insist upon the statute in bar. *Hull* v. *Peer*, 312.

2. In a bill for a specific performance, the complainant need not, at his peril, state the precise amount due. He may state his case most favorably to himself, and if upon the equities of the case, the court should decree a different amount, he can then conform to its judgment. Ibid. 312.

3. A and B executed a note together, with the understanding that A should pay it. The payee insisted that B should appear upon the note as principal, and A as surety. It was held that nevertheless, as between themselves, A was the principal and B the surety, in equity. Ibid. 312.

4. In decreeing a specific performance of a parol agreement for the sale of lands, the court will require the complainant to do complete justice, upon the broadest principles of equity, and will not be satisfied with a literal performance of the agreement by him. Ibid. 312.

STATUTES CONSTRUED.

See CONSTRUCTION OF STATUTES.

STATUTE OF FRAUDS

See CHANCERY. FRAUDS.

SUMMONS.

If a non-resident is proceeded against by publication in a chancery cause, the court does not acquire jurisdiction over his person, unless a summons has been regularly issued, and returned by the sheriff. *Smith* v. *Trimble*, 152.

SUPREME COURT.

1. This court will not disturb a verdict, which the evidence justifies. *Bromley* v. *People*, 20.

2. In cases tried by the court, errors may be assigned as to the law and fact upon the judgment. *Metcalf* v. *Fouts*, 110.

3. It does not follow that a judgment will be reversed, because an improper instruction has been given for the plaintiff and appellee, if the other instructions on his behalf, put the whole case fairly before the jury. *Warren* v. *Dickson*, 115.

4. It is error to instruct the jury, that if the defendant purchased lumber from the plaintiffs without disclosing the fact that he was purchasing as the agent of another, he became personally liable for the price of the lumber—because the plaintiffs may have known all the time that the defendant was merely an agent; in which event, he would not be personally liable. *Warren* v. *Dickson*, 115.

5. Upon a writ of error in a chancery cause, the Supreme Court will not presume that any evidence was given in the court below, except what appears in the record. *Reddick* v. *State Bank*, 145.

6. The absence of a summons from the record, cannot be supplied by the return of a certificate of the clerk to a writ of *certiorari*, that there had been a summons which was lost, nor by the recital in the notice of publication, that it had been issued. *Smith* v. *Trimble*, 152.

7. Upon a writ of error, this court looks only to the transcript of the record. If papers have been lost from the files, or mutilated, they may be supplied in some cases by the Circuit Court upon satisfactory evidence, after a proper notice to the opposite party. This court has no authority to permit a party to supply. by proof, any part of the record. Ibid. 152.

8. In disputed matters about the use of a farm, where the proof leaves the question of right uncertain, the verdict will not be disturbed. *Pulliam* v. *Ogle*, 189.

9. It is error to award the plaintiff greater damages than he claims in his declaration. *Rives* v. *Kumler*, 291.

10. It is the duty of the clerk of the Circuit Court to make a full transcript of all of the record. This court is not premitted to act upon his statements, given in the transcript, that papers were filed or withdrawn. *Freeland* v. *Board of Supervisors*, 303.

11. Although the bill of exceptions does not purport to contain all the evidence, and therefore the refusal to grant a new trial on the weight of evidence cannot be considered; yet as there was evidence, showing the refusal of an instruction erroneous, the judgment will be reversed. *Sidwell* v. *Lobly*, 438.

See EVIDENCE. PRACTICE.

SURETIES.

See BONDS, 1. GUARANTOR. PROMISSORY NOTE. SALE OF LAND, 14.

TAXES—TAXATION—TAX TITLE.

1. For purposes of taxation property should be assessed at its present value, and not at its prospective value. *The State* v. *Illinois Cetrnal R. R. Co.* 64.

2. In assessing the value of a railroad, for purposes of taxation, the inquiry should be, what is the property worth, to be used for the purposes for which it was designed, and not for any other purposes to which it might be applied? Ibid. 64.

3. In such a case, if the property is devoted to the use for which it was designed, and is in a condition to produce its maximum income, one very important element for ascertaining its present value, is the amount of its net profits. Ibid. 64.

4. This, however, should not be the absolute standard of value. There should be taken in connection with it, the inquiry, what would a pru-

dent man give for the property as a permanent investment, with a view to present and future income? Ibid. 64.

5. In construing an amendatory statute, it is a fixed rule that the old law must be considered, the mischief arising under that law, and the remedy for it, which the new law may be supposed to provide. *Maus v. Logansport, Peoria and Burlington R. R. Co.* 77.

6. The act of February 14th, 1855, amendatory of the revenue law, which directs that the track or superstructure of a railroad shall be denominated " fixed and stationary personal property," was intended to create a species of personal property not before known to the law. For non-payment of taxes upon this property, the collector may levy upon the rails and remove them from the track, for the purpose of selling them. Ibid. 77.

7. This act has reference only to the collection of the revenue, and does not change the character of such property for other purposes. *Maus v. Logansport, Peoria and Burlington R. R. Co.* 77.

8. Section 14, of the amendatory act of 1853, which provides that real property shall be liable for taxes on personal property, and *vice versa*, has no application to this "fixed and stationary personal property;" such property must bear its own burden of taxation. Ibid. 77.

9. It is within the province of the legislature to provide that property, which is attached to the freehold, so as to become a part of it by the common law, may be regarded as personal property, for all purposes, or for any special purpose. Of this character is the act of February 14th, 1855, which directs that the track and superstructure of a railroad, together with the improvements at stations, shall be denominated personal property, for the purpose of collecting the revenue. Ibid. 77.

10. A clerk's or sheriff's deed on a tax sale is sufficient to show claim and color of title, if it appear on its face to be regular. The person relying upon it, is not bound to show that the prerequisites of the statute have been complied with. *Holloway et al. v. Clark*, 483.

11. A quit-claim deed is sufficient to show claim and color of title under the limitation act of 1839. Ibid. 483.

12. H. obtained claim and color of title in 1842, and conveyed to B. in 1845. B. allowed the land to be sold for the taxes for 1847, and bought it himself; he then paid the taxes from 1849 to 1856, inclusive. P., the minor heir of a person who had died seized of the patent title, in 1853 redeemed from the sale of 1847, by paying to the clerk double the amount of the purchase money and all the taxes, with interest, for five years, being up to the time of the redemption. *Held*, that this redemption by P. entirely obliterated the tax sale of 1847, and the payment of taxes by B. for the five years, and that the grantees of B. could not defend under the limitation act of 1839, without showing payment of taxes for seven years, exclusive of the five years from 1848 to 1853. Ibid. 483.

13. The provisions of the limitation act of 1839, empowering minors to redeem land sold for taxes, within three years after attaining their majority, by paying to the person who has paid the tax, the amount with

interest, do not take from the minor the right to redeem within one year after his majority, by paying double the amount, etc., to the collector, according to Sec. 69, Chap. LXXXIX, Rev. Stat. 1845. Ibid. 483.

14. A person whose lands had been sold for taxes during his infancy, for the purpose of redeeming them, after he attained his majority, paid the necessary amount to the clerk. The purchaser accepted this money from the clerk. *Held*, that by that act, he admitted the right of the infant to redeem under the statute. Ibid. 483.

TENDER—TENDER OF MONEY.

Proof of a tender, though not of that clear and satisfactory character which convinces the mind beyond doubt, will be held sufficient. *Kerney* v. *Gardner*, 162.

See Chancery. Sale of Land.

TESTAMENTS AND WILLS.

See Wills and Testaments.

TITLE TO LAND.

Morrison purchased a piece of land under an execution against James Duncan, and filed his bill to set aside conveyances which vested the title to the land in John Duncan, alleging them to be fraudulent. Subsequently the land was sold by the administrator of John Duncan, under an order of court, as his property. Morrison received the proceeds of this sale for a claim which he held against the estate of John Duncan. *Held*, that this did not estop Morrison from asserting his title to the land. *Letcher* v. *Morrison*, 209.

TOWNS AND CITIES.

1. A town or village, within the meaning of the statute requiring railroad corporations to construct fences, may exist, although there is no plat of the same, dedicating streets, etc., in the manner pointed out by the statute in that regard. *Illinois Central R. R. Co.* v. *Williams*, 48.

2. The offense of keeping and maintaining a "*calaboose*," by an incorporated town, is not an offense against the statute, for which an indictment will lie. *Town of Paris* v. *People*, 74.

3. The legislature has the constitutional right to authorize counties, towns and cities to aid in the construction of railroads, by lending credit, issuing bonds or taking stock. Fraud in the election authorizing such action must be set up in apt time, and before rights have accrued. *Butler et al.* v. *Dunham et al.* 474.

· TRESPASS.

1 A party may maintain trespass, if he has at the time of the act, such a title as draws after it a constructive possession. *Gauche* v. *Mayer*, 134.

2. A had placed goods with an auctioneer for sale, reserving for himself the right to resume possession at his pleasure, the auctioneer not having any claim to or charge upon such goods: *Held*, that A had a right of action in trespass against a sheriff for making a levy upon those goods as the property of another, the sheriff having been notified of the facts before the levy. Ibid. 134.

3. The plaintiff in a suit where a capias has been issued by a justice of the peace, is not answerable with the justice in trespass *vi et armis*, even if the process has been issued without a sufficient oath; the magistrate is the proper person to pass upon its sufficiency. If a party acts maliciously, case is the proper remedy. Nor would a magistrate be liable in trespass, if he had jurisdiction to issue the process. *Outlaw* v. *Davis et al.* 467.

TRUSTS—TRUSTEES—TRUST DEEDS.

1. Parties who claim that another is a trustee for their benefit, must clearly prove the fact. Especially so, if the trust is assumed to be in favor of those who have grossly ill-treated the person supposed to have created it. *Clarke* v. *Quackenbos*, 260.

2. A trustee appointed by a court, though not invested with legal title to property, has such equitable title as will enable him to proceed in his own name in aid of the trust. *Leach* v. *Thomas*, 457.

3. When a court of equity obtains jurisdiction, and gives to a party all that he had asked by a motion in a proceeding at law, he cannot complain of a proceeding that has not done him an injury. Ibid. 457.

USURY.

1. By the act of 31st January, 1857, relating to interest, a forfeiture of all interest, legal or illegal, is incurred for usury; no other penalty can be recovered for a breach of the law. *Lucas* v. *Spencer*, 15.

2. If a party has had an opportunity, which he has neglected, to prevent the recovery of a judgment, which includes usurious interest, he cannot relieve himself by a resort to chancery. Ibid. 15.

3. The sixth section of the interest law of 1845, only applies to cases where the money has been paid; and not as a defense to usury due and unpaid. Ibid. 15.

4. After usurious money has been paid, the parties are not competent witnesses in a suit to recover it back. Ibid. 15.

5. In determining the question of usury, the intention of the parties should govern, without regard to the form of the contract. *Cooper* v. *Nock*, 301.

6. The payee of a note, before its maturity put his name upon the back of it, but kept it in his possession until after it became due. He then delivered the note to the attorney of the plaintiff, who was a non-resident. This was not a *bona fide* assignment, and did not prevent the maker from setting up the defense of usury. Ibid. 301.

VENDOR AND VENDEE.

1. The purchaser of personal property is not to presume, by a vague statement made, that the vendor is a trifling fellow, and had not money, in the opinion of the person making the remark, to buy the property; that the title of the vendor is defective. A purchaser is not bound to take mere suspicions unsupported by facts, in his business affairs, as a warning; though the statement of facts touching the manner of the acquisition of property by his vendor, might be sufficient to put him on his guard. *Gosney* v. *Frost*, 53.

2. A note given for the purchase of land, if transferred, does not carry with it to the assignee, the vendor's lien, so that the assignee can enforce it in his own name. *Richards* v. *Leaming et al.* 431.

VERDICT.

1. The Supreme Court will not disturb a verdict, which the evidence justifies. *Bromley* v. *People*, 20.

2. In disputed matters about the use of a farm, where the proof leaves the question of right uncertain, the verdict will not be disturbed. *Pulliam* v. *Ogle*, 189.

WAGER.

1. A wager that a railroad will be completed within a certain time is not prohibited by the common law or by our statute; and a recovery can be had upon it. *Beadles* v. *Bless*, 320.

2. In an action to recover a wager, that a railroad would be built within a certain time, evidence, that the bet was talked of a good deal by the public, to show that it may have influenced subscription to the stock, was properly excluded. The court cannot say that it was against public policy to influence or discourage subscriptions to the road. Ibid 320.

WALLS.

See DIVISION WALLS. PARTITION WALLS.

WARRANTY.

If one bargains with an agent for a horse, knowing him to be such agent, and that the principal had recognized the transaction, a warranty by the agent is the warranty of the principal, who is the proper party to be sued for a breach. *Marckle* v. *Haskins*, 382.

WIDOW.

While a widow may release her interest in the homestead right, such a release will not affect the interest of the children. *Miller* v. *Marckle*, 402.

WILLS AND TESTAMENTS.

1. *Held*, that the following words of devise in a will gave the devisee an estate of inheritance: " I will and bequeath to my oldest daughter, Margaret Jane Elizabeth Holliday, eighty acres of land where my house and well stands, never to to her and and heirs forever, never to be mortgaged nor sold forever." *Holliday* v. *Dixon*, 33.

2. In construing wills, the court will gather the meaning of the testator from the language used, if it be possible to do so. Ibid. 33.

3. A, being in feeble health and a resident of Missouri, was brought by B to Illinois, and lived in the house of B, as a guest, furnishing his own room and a part of his food, but occupying the room at the sufferance of B. A had two daughters, within the age prescribed by the fourth section of the act, entitled " An Act to amend an act relative to wills and testaments, executors and administrators, and the settlement of estates," page 597, Revised Statutes of 1845, one of whom remained with him, the other living apart from him with a relative—A, during his lifetime, declaring his intention to return to Missouri, to pursue his former occupation: *Held*, that A was not a housekeeper within the meaning of the said fourth section, and that his children could not receive the same amount of property that would have been by law allowed to the widow of A. *Veile* v. *Koch*, 129.

4. It is indispensable to the validity of a nuncupative will, that the testator should request those present to bear witness that such was his last will. Or that he should say or do something equivalent to such an expression. *Arnett* v. *Arnett*, 247.

5. A testator gave to his wife all his estate, to be disposed of in any way that would best support her for life, but if his sons, John and Thomas, should take care of their mother, they were to have certain lands, but if they failed to support their mother, then she could sell the land, or any part of it to support herself; but if the sons complied with these conditions, they were to take immediate possession of the land; there were bequests to other children: *Held*, that the testator intended to charge his entire estate with the support of his widow; that the question of support was a condition subsequent, the word "comply" being used in the sense of "assent," and when John and Thomas assented, the estate passed to them, burthened with the condition of support of the mother; and that the widow of John being his heir, and proffering to support the widow, had a right to inherit and possess the estate, and could compel the grantee of the widow to reconvey to her. *Jennings* v. *Jennings*, 518.

WITNESS.

1. After usurious money has been paid, the parties are not competent witnesses in a suit to recover it back. *Lucas* v. *Spencer*, 15.

2. Where A and B convey a right of way to a mill to C, and B afterwards purchases one-half of the mill, B cannot become a witness for C, who has filed a bill to restrain A from obstructing the right of way; being an appurtenance to the mill, B was therefore interested, and was disqualified. *Foulke* v. *Walker*, 204.

WRIT OF INQUIRY.

Upon a default, a writ of inquiry issues to have the damages assessed, which may be executed in court or be directed to the sheriff to execute in vacation. It would be regular for the sheriff to summon a jury from the bystanders, and have the damages assessed in the presence of the court. *Ætna Ins. Co.* v. *Phelps*, 71.

THIS TIME
it's love

Love Stories from the Unmasked Podcast

TACCARA MARTIN

Author's Note

I am so excited to introduce you to, "This Time It's Love," the second love story to come out of the fiction podcast, **Unmasked**. Unmasked follows the incredible journey of a woman named Kenya as she courageously, and messily, navigates the world of healing after finding herself in a series of toxic relationships. In season one, you'll encounter Jaxon Hart, Kenya's ex-husband, whose presence in her life was undeniably toxic.

As a domestic abuse survivor and relationship coach, I've encountered numerous women who, like myself, found themselves entangled with their own versions of "Jaxon." We've all attempted to shape ourselves into what we believed these men needed to love us better, to love us more. We've all stayed in relationships a little too long, clinging to the hope that our love alone could inspire a man to change. But that change never came. Still, we stayed, searching for answers to questions like, "How did he get this way?" or "Can a man like him truly change?"

"This Time It's Love" answers both questions in a unique yet relatable way.

Please note, this book delves into themes of toxic relationships, difficult childhoods, religious abuse, and matters involving questions of faith. It also touches on grief and loss, although death is not explicitly part of the story nor depicted on the page. And since I make my characters' journeys all encompassing, there will be sex. A good amount of it. I encourage you to use caution if any of these topics trigger anything for you.

While listening to the Unmasked Podcast isn't required to enjoy this book, diving into the podcast episodes might provide a deeper connection to the characters and a sense of empathy for their journeys.

If you're interested in immersing yourself in the intriguing world of Unmasked, perhaps even guessing who could be the subject of the next love story, do yourself a favor and head on over to **https://midcenturymodern.media** to learn more and begin listening.

Get ready to embark on a captivating journey with Jax and Dash as they uncover the redemptive and healing power of love and family.

Table of Contents

Prologue

Jaxon

10 Years Old

Bad day number 983. Today was supposed to be my first day back to school after the winter break, but since we got home so late from Daddy's preaching engagement last night, Momma said I'd just start back school on Tuesday. I wish I had gone to school, though. Whenever Momma and Daddy had long road trips, they ended up fighting. It's like they couldn't be in the same space for longer than a few hours before one or both of them said something to make the other mad. Today seemed different, though.

I could hear Momma crying and screaming in the living room, "She's dead! That poor girl is dead because of you!"

Who was she talking about? Who was dead? I'm sure she would have come and told me if it was someone from our family. Then again, when it came to things happening with my dad, you never really knew what to expect. A few minutes later, I'd get my answer.

"You'd better watch your mouth, woman!" my dad shouted back. "You don't know what God was

7

protecting that woman from by calling her home early!"

"*God* didn't call her home! You having sex with that child and getting her pregnant is what did it! Don't you *dare* blame that on God!" My mom shot back. It was the first time I'd heard her talk back to my dad like that and my dad didn't have a comeback for her. Probably because it was true. But whenever he couldn't think of an intelligent explanation for his behavior, he resorted to using scriptures to quiet anyone who challenged him.

"Now listen here, that's the last time! I won't have you disrespecting me in my own house! The Bible says..."

I always tuned my dad out whenever he started quoting scriptures. Not because I didn't believe in the Bible or God. I just wasn't sure my dad believed. He used scriptures and God as a tool for manipulation, not a guide for loving people. Ever since I turned eight years old, I began to question if my dad really loved God. If he really loved *us*. All the wonderful things that he preached about God; all the things he said a man of God should be, none of that existed in our home. It didn't feel like I had a comforter... or a present help.

Before we all went our separate ways for winter break at school, my best friend Torian let me

8

borrow his Boys II Men CD. I'd been keeping it on repeat in my CD player ever since. With the constant arguments between Momma and Daddy showing no signs of slowing down, I found myself reaching for the play button more often than not.

We grew up in a pretty peaceful neighborhood. We weren't a middle-class family, but we always had what we needed. My mom worked tirelessly as a physical therapist's aide, played the piano for funerals and weddings for extra money, and around Christmas time, she even cleaned houses. Even though Momma didn't make the type of money that the doctors she worked with did, her paychecks and the extra money she made, were the only constants in our household.

Daddy's contributions were less predictable. The only time he brought home money was when he had a preaching engagement lined up. But those opportunities were becoming scarce, so it fell onto Momma's shoulders to keep the ship afloat, and she did it with a sense of grace and strength that I admired. For the life of me, I couldn't understand why she continued to put up with my dad's mess. She was so strong and capable of so much more. She didn't need him. *We* didn't need him.

In the blink of an eye, the upbeat tempo of 'Motown Philly' filled my ears, transporting me far away from the chaos in the next room. The shouting echoing from my dad and the soft cries of my momma, each retelling the latest episode of my father's transgressions, were drowned out by the music. It was like the melodies created a bubble around me, shielding me from the harsh realities of my home life, and giving me a brief respite from the storm.

Even with the music blasting in my ears, I couldn't shake the eerie feeling behind someone being dead. I couldn't stop wondering who it was or how my momma was doing, since my dad didn't seem too shaken up about it. Just as the song came to an end, I heard the front door slam. I threw my headphones on the floor and jumped up to look out my bedroom window. My dad was leaving. I saw him throw his brown suit coat over the passenger's seat of our truck and jump in the car like he was running away from something. Maybe away from us. Finally.

I walked out of my room and just stood in the hallway for a few moments, waiting to hear if it was safe to approach Momma. Normally when she was upset, she wanted privacy until she could gather herself. I'd have to wait until I heard her say, "It's OK, baby. You can come out," before I entered the living room. But that night, she never said anything. I just heard sobs coming from the kitchen area.

Suddenly, the hallway to our modest, two-bedroom home with wall-to-wall wood paneling, seemed to stretch a mile long. I was afraid to walk any further; scared of the condition I'd find my mother in. My daddy never hit my mom. His words were always heavy-handed enough to leave a lifetime of scarring. I slowly began taking steps towards the living room and kitchen area, and I heard Momma's sobs get quieter. She heard me coming.

"Momma?" I called out. "Can I play you a song?"

We had a keyboard in our living room that Momma would play whenever Dad hosted Bible studies at our house. She had such an incredible talent for the piano. She didn't grow up playing Motown or even in the church. She was classically trained, playing pieces from Beethoven, Bach, and Tchaikovsky. She could have easily been performing at grand concert halls. In fact, she always wanted to, but Daddy insisted that her gift was meant for the church, for supporting his ministry and nothing else.

So when she wasn't accompanying my dad's sermons with her music, she'd pass on her skills to me. She had this dream that someday I'd be the one playing the music while Daddy preached. Maybe there was a time when that idea seemed appealing. But now, I just loved making Momma smile.

"Sure, baby," she sniffled. "What you gon' play for me today?"

"You… You got any requests, madam?" I asked while bowing to greet her as if I were an orchestra conductor. And even though I was wearing my yellow and brown striped shirt with an uncombed nappy head, she lowered her head as if to bow back.

"Whatever the Lord lays on your heart, son. Play whatever he puts on your heart," she said through tears.

I yanked off the black vinyl cover that shrouded the keyboard, my mind racing to find the perfect tune that would lift her spirits. As I eased onto the round stool and positioned my feet on the pedals, a spark of inspiration struck me. And no, it wasn't going to be "Precious Lord Take My Hand." This time, I was going to play something purposeful, a song with an intention.

Momma had never allowed me to see her cry. Even if I heard her cry, she'd always have a fresh face and a bright smile before I actually saw her face. No matter how much she cried, she never let herself be seen as anything but strong. And *this* was the moment. The moment that I'd decided to never end up like my dad. Never treat women the way he did my mom.

I had no desire to fall in love. I didn't want to be responsible for anyone's emotions and I didn't want to give anyone control over mine. My father was a man who would take and take until there was no more, with no regard for anyone other than himself. I know Momma wasn't perfect, but growing up and seeing their marriage up close made me feel like marriage was nothing but constant disappointments. So, the night that I saw my momma crying at that table, too broken to hide her tears from me, was the night that I decided love was too much of a burden to carry.

It took me all summer this past year to nail the intro. The original track featured a beautiful orchestra, mostly strings, so I had to painstakingly program the synthesized strings into our keyboard. But I was determined to master it, no matter how long it took, because it was my granddaddy's favorite song, and Momma loved to play it on Sunday afternoons. And as if on cue, we belted out the words in unison to the song, "A Change Is Gonna Come," By Sam Cooke.

Chapter One

Jaxon

Sometimes I felt like I was living a dream. I remember being a young kid watching Boomerang and seeing Eddie Murphy's character in this lavish house with a different woman every night. I wanted to grow up and be just like that. Including having Halle Berry lying next to me in the bed. But how things ended up wasn't so bad either. I got to wake up every morning next to a beautiful woman, in a beautiful home, in a town right outside of Atlanta, Georgia. She even had pretty feet.

Anyone who knew me from back in the day would never believe that I, Jaxon Hart, was a domesticated man living with a woman. I've always been allergic to monogamy. Relationships always seemed to get in the way of... well ... *everything*. Whenever a woman got too close to me or too clingy after we'd been seeing each other for a little while, it wasn't the monogamy or commitment itself that made me keep my distance. It was the emotional responsibility of someone's heart and the baggage that followed when I inevitably broke it. Even as a musician, that was a song and dance that I didn't particularly enjoy.

Remy Fontaine was different. I met her when my band was playing at Sanctuary, an upscale restaurant and wine bar that I frequented. She was wearing a knee-length, red dress that clung to her curves like a second skin and commanded attention. Every pair of eyes were magnetized by her presence. It was like the scene out of "Mo Betta Blues" when Clarke walked into the club and no one could keep their eyes off of her.

As she floated past me while I was sitting at the bar, a glint of gold caught my eye. There was a gold zipper in the back of her dress that traced her spine and stopped just short of *hallelujah*. Simply by observing her walk and her essence, I could tell she wasn't the type of woman that was simply looking for a good time. She carried herself with class and a level of professionalism that let me know she wasn't to be played with or played. So, I just watched her as she sat down in the front row where she'd get the best view of that night's set. She folded her arms across her chest as if to say, 'Impress me.' It was all the motivation I needed to ensure that she not only got a great show that night—she'd get the *best*.

My band was known around town for covering some of the most melodious and energizing songs of the 70's, 80's, and 90's. We took requests from the audience, but we intuitively played everything they wanted to hear. With a gorgeous woman in the front row, I wanted to do things a little different.

Impress her even. So, instead of opening the set with the usual rendition of Franky Beverly and Maze's "Before I Let Go," I started off a little slower. Once the announcer called my name and introduced the band, the crowd went wild as Tevin Campbell's "Can We Talk" began to play over the speakers. The recent social media challenge that had various R&B singers covering the popular 90's ballad, had reinvigorated the song's popularity.

I always enjoyed playing for predominantly black crowds. It wasn't that I didn't relish playing for all audiences—quite the contrary. But there was an inexplicable spark, a certain vivacity that permeated the room when black audiences congregated in the name of R&B. And Sunday nights at Sanctuary were a religious experience.

For nearly two hours, our band played hit after hit as the audience danced and sang along in unison. Remy remained seated and just took in the atmosphere from her front row seat, nursing a glass of red wine. She blushed as I seductively serenaded a seventy-year-old Ms. Mattie Stevenson for her birthday. When I asked her what song she wanted me to sing for her, Mattie shocked the crowd by yelling, "Cause I Love You," by Lenny Williams. I obliged, but made it extra special by having Ms.

Mattie sit on my lap for the duration of the song. When the song was over, I kissed Ms. Mattie on the cheek and threw a wink at Remy.

I hadn't had the nerve to introduce myself. You had to step to a woman of her caliber correctly, and I didn't have *half* of what I felt I needed to do that. So instead, I just kept making her blush from the stage, making sure she felt like a VIP the entire night.

"Don't think I didn't see you flirting with a certain lady executive Sunday night either, Jaxon!"

It was the Tuesday following the night Remy was at Sanctuary. I was there preparing to hold auditions for a new drummer when Lucy came in teasing me about my obvious infatuation with the lovely lady in the VIP section. Lucy, or Lu as I liked to call her, was the owner of Sanctuary, but she was also my best friend. I know many would argue that men and women couldn't be friends without sex getting in the way, and I wouldn't dare disagree. But Lu and I had already been there and done that. We dated momentarily, if that's what you'd call it, but we quickly realized that we loved our friendship more than our situationship. And when I fell on hard times and needed to rebuild my life, professionally and financially, Lu opened a residency for me at Sanctuary. The wine bar was doing *OK,* but Lu let me know that business hadn't quite recovered from the pandemic. So, her idea to add musical experiences to the venue actually saved us both.

"What are you talking about?" I asked, pretending to be clueless.

"Negro! Don't play dumb! I saw you putting on the performance of your life for Ms. Remy Fontaine, and the chemistry was electric! Did you get her number?"

"Wait…" I paused. Because I had no clue that *she* was who I was flirting with that night. "Remy Fontaine. Remy Fontaine of Nova Records?! *That* Remy Fontaine?"

"The one and only! I thought that's why you were being so extra!"

"Nah. I just wanted to make sure the lovely lady had a memorable experience. Nothing more," I lied. I wouldn't dare say that Remy intimidated the shit out of me, and I knew for a *fact* that she was out of my league. Controlled confidence was the only expression she'd get out of me.

"Well, whatever it was, it worked because this came for you yesterday." Lu handed me a white, legal-sized envelope that was addressed to Mr. Jaxon Hart, with nothing in the return address area.

I opened the envelope to find a letter on Nova Records' letterhead, inviting me to a discovery meeting. And it was signed by Remy Fontaine herself. I couldn't figure out what a discovery meeting was, let alone what we'd be discussing or discovering. After doing a quick search on my phone, I discovered that Remy Fontaine was an even bigger deal than I realized. An executive at Nova Records, a black-owned imprint of the more famous record label, Dream Records, Remy was responsible for making sure certain artists' songs ended up on TV and movie soundtracks. I had no idea what she could possibly want with me, but it was clear that, while I was fixated on her physical appearance, she was sizing me up for something entirely different. Something more professional. So I had to make sure to take advantage of this opportunity by *not* taking advantage of her.

If you'd met the younger me, Remy wouldn't have stood a chance. The moment I set my eyes on her, I would've been sweet-talking her and not giving it a second thought before diving headfirst into...well, *her*. When I began playing in bands and touring, I made it a point to live my life in a way that didn't require much commitment from me. Constantly hopping from one place to another, chasing after big dreams, and always having a string of gorgeous women at my fingertips. As I aged, the drama that was associated with that lifestyle became harder to explain or rationalize. Lack of self-control and constantly looking over my shoulder due to jealous women had become my norm, and it just wasn't worth it anymore. I decided to take control over every aspect of my life.

I became more thoughtful about my choices, preferring to keep a leash on my desires rather than letting them run free. I made a promise to myself that I would no longer let women, or any other distractions for that matter, influence me to make decisions that could jeopardize my future. This is why I tried to avoid anything other than a professional relationship with Remy. Her position and her influence made her someone who could do a lot for my career. Sex and intimacy would only mess that up. So while I was sure that any amount of time spent with Remy would be rewarding, the long term benefits of a professional relationship far outweighed those of an intimate one.

A week later, I found myself in her impressive corner office on the 10th floor, surrounded by stunning views of the Ferris wheel in midtown Atlanta. While waiting for her to arrive, her assistant, Tony, went to get me a Pelligrino, and I took in the sleek surroundings of her office—the glass desk adorned with two computer monitors and the cozy living room area on the other side of the office, complete with a fireplace. It was truly a luxurious space to be in. A few minutes later, she sauntered in wearing a chic, black dress accented by another gold zipper that traced her spine. This must be a signature look of hers. One that she spent fortunes to maintain. It was worth it.

She knew she intimidated me. Something I felt like she actually enjoyed. But she was also giving off flirty vibes. Despite this, I knew better than to let things get inappropriate since she had introduced herself in such a professional manner. Nova Records was a big deal, signing some of today's most prolific artists. So if she wanted me to play on someone's track or compose a song for someone, I wasn't going to let my usual antics of, "love 'em and leave 'em" mess that up for me. She was impossible, though. And I had no idea what I was in for, dealing with her.

After pleasantries and her professionally sizing me up to her satisfaction, she asked me if I had ever considered scoring music for TV or movies. I must have confused her because I laughed. Loudly. Her facial expression didn't change, though. I saw a slight twitch in her mouth, resembling a smile, but she never broke eye contact. She actually peered into my eyes more intensely like she was reading me.

"Scoring music? You mean you don't simply go to royalty-free music sites and add music to the productions?" I asked, attempting to recover my size thirteen foot from my mouth.

"For smaller budget productions, sure," she answered in a measured, elegant tone. Her coral-colored lipstick accentuated her thick lips. "But for larger productions, we work with professional musicians to create the mood of the scene. I've seen otherwise boring productions be elevated beyond imagination by simply adding music scoring. It's a magical experience. And I believe you have what it takes to make…"

She paused and smiled at me, noticing my infatuation with her...mouth. "Magic?" I offered, completing the sentence I distracted her from.

"Yes! Magic," she repeated.

"What's the catch? What would I have to do to put myself up for projects like that?"

I couldn't shake the feeling that there had to be a catch. Something about this, her in general, seemed too good to be true. I'd flirted with countless women, probably thousands, and it'd led to some incredible nights. But never had I flirted with a woman who, in turn, dangled a life-changing opportunity in front of me. It was almost too much to handle.

"No strings attached," she assured me. Her voice trailed off, and I watched as her gaze gradually descended from my face, lingering at my midsection, before finally settling on my feet. It was as if she were slowly cataloging images of me, savoring each one to etch them into her memory. A wave of unease washed over me, the feeling of being objectified making me shift restlessly in my seat. "You simply have to do as I say."

I leaned forward, placing my elbows on my knees and clasping my hands, "Do as you say?"

"Take the meetings I tell you to take; dress how I recommend you dress; charge what I tell you to charge when it comes to your fee for engagements. This is a tricky world, Mr. Hart, and I believe you have what it takes to make it. But *I* have what it takes to usher you into it."

"And what's in this for you?" I inquired. "I find it odd that you've summoned me here out of the goodness of your heart. I don't mean to be cynical, Ms. Fontaine, but I'd like to understand everything that will be required of me before committing to following your every command. Respectfully," I grinned.

Sidestepping my barrage of questions, she extended an invitation to dinner instead. Apparently, there was a mixer happening to celebrate the opening of a new movie studio and, instead of answering a bunch of questions, she wanted to show me the world I could have instead of telling me. I was skeptical at first, assuming she was playing games and had some sinister ulterior motives, but I walked away from the evening feeling pleasantly surprised.

By the end of the mixer, Remy had introduced me to some movie and TV executives that were decision-makers for some of the largest budgets in entertainment. She even set me up with her favorite producers to help me create a demo that would, according to her, have executives eating out of my hands. I didn't know what to say other than thank you because I was literally stunned. I'd never had anyone invest in me to that degree without wanting *something* in return. But no matter how grateful I was, or how shamelessly she flirted with me, I never crossed any lines with her. I never wanted to make things inappropriate or awkward between us. She saw something in me and, for the first time, I had met a woman I didn't want to disrespect or disappoint.

My "good guy" impression lasted all of two months before Remy showed up at my house, furious.

It was 3 a.m. on a Sunday morning, and I was finally home after a long night performing at Sanctuary. I had just stepped out of the shower and had thrown on a pair of gray sweatpants to go to the kitchen when my doorbell rang. I looked at the time on my stove, making a mental note that whoever was on the other side of that door was either the police or someone had the wrong address. I almost didn't answer when the knocks turned into banging.

Not wanting to startle my neighbors, I yelled, "Hold on! It's three o'clock in the morning so somebody better be bleeding or dead!" One glance through the peephole had me eating my words.

It was Remy. I didn't see her at the club, so she couldn't have followed me home. But how did she get my address? Of all the questions swirling around in my head, the most important one was, what the hell was Remy Fontaine doing *here*?

Neglecting to put on a shirt, I unlocked the door and opened it for her. "Remy? What are you..."

Cutting me off, she lunged straight into a fiery diatribe that was both sexy and entertaining to watch. "So, is this what you do?"

Blinking, I said, "I'm sorry?" Because I was genuinely clueless as to what she was talking about.

"I am a rich, powerful, *beautiful* woman!" she exclaimed.

"Agreed," I confirmed, grinning in her direction.

"And never in my life has a man *not* tried to sleep with me with the level of strength and control you have! What the entire *fuck, Jaxon!?*"

She went on like this for what seemed like five minutes before she stopped to catch her breath. "Are you done?" I asked. She hadn't realized that, while she was yelling and flailing her hands all over the place, her coat had inched open, exposing what appeared to be a nipple. She was naked.

"Well…yes! What do you have to say for yourself?" she demanded. And I had nothing. At least nothing honest that I wanted to share.

Struggling to find the right words, I slowly stepped towards her and gently buttoned the top button of her beige tweed coat. She was beautiful and incredibly hard to resist. But I'd been in these types of situations before. There was always a woman who'd tried to mold me into a version that fit their world better. But invariably, I fell short. I'd been a player all my life and I was wary of getting entangled with her, knowing she held the power to either elevate or obliterate the opportunities presenting themselves to me.

I respected her. I was grateful for her. And it was crucial for her to understand that I had no intention of risking our relationship, or the mutual respect we shared, for a fleeting moment of physical gratification. No matter how beautiful…and naked she was.

She was noticeably flustered and one hundred percent drunk, so I didn't want to push her any further over the edge. "What do you want from me, Remy? What do you want me to say to…*this*?"

"I want you to *want* me!"

"Remy, I think we have an amazing *working* relationship, but I'm not the man you want."

"Why not?!" she pouted.

"Because I'm no good for you. I'd take these opportunities that you've handed me. I'd perform great for you and your executives, having them all pining for me. I'd even make love to you as if you were the only woman I would ever need…"

"I'm not seeing the problem here," she countered.

"Then I would inevitably destroy you. I've got a lifetime of broken women in my past to prove it, and I respect you too much to subject you to that."

"And what if I destroyed you *first*?"

I let out a sardonic breath. "I would *never* let that happen. I'm not the kind of man who lets himself get close enough to anyone to allow that to happen."

"Somebody's got some brokenness of their own in the past, I see," she diagnosed. "But I'm not here to fix you or mold you, Jaxon. I'm not even here to love you or make you love me. Do I see potential in you? Yes. Do I have what it takes to elevate your profile? Absolutely. But don't get it twisted. I didn't get to where I am today by being some lovesick little girl who falls for every sexy musician who crosses her path. I like you. I enjoy spending time with you. And I don't want anything from you that you don't *want* to give me."

"And what if I said I've already given you everything I wanted to give you?"

She laughed wryly, "Then I'd say you were a better keyboard player than you are a liar. You're wearing gray sweatpants, Jaxon."

I had run out of excuses and I couldn't think of anything else that would convince her that this was a terrible idea. I wasn't a new and improved man that could simply stop being who I'd always been, just because a beautiful woman propositioned me. I was well aware of who I was. And when faced with the choice between a once-in-a-lifetime opportunity or a passionate night with Remy Fontaine, she wouldn't be my choice.

"Remy. You're sensational. My body won't let me deny that, as you so eloquently pointed out. But I *will* hurt you. It's inevitable. And I value the work we've been doing together too much to let this…my body, your beauty…get in the way."

"By the looks of it, *hurt* would be guaranteed," she suggestively pointed out. She stepped farther into the apartment, setting her purse at her feet. "Let's make a deal. Whatever happens behind closed doors between us, is for that night or that day or that moment only. Whenever either of us begins to feel differently about this arrangement, we get out. No hard feelings. No questions asked."

"Remy," I cautioned her, "women have tried and failed when attempting to settle into arrangements like this with me. Not to be cocky, but it always ends badly...*for them.*"

"What about no hard feelings and no questions asked, do you *not* understand, Jaxon?"

"What part about, I will hurt you, don't *you* understand?"

She rolled her eyes and, at that moment, I could tell she was done talking. I saw fire in her eyes as her breathing intensified. She bit her bottom lip, hypnotizing me by the lip gloss that emphasized her plump lips. Everything about her gaze said that she wasn't taking "no" for an answer. While I was stuck in a mesmerizing stare down, I stood motionless as Remy unbuttoned her coat. I didn't react, but I took a deep breath in, and my chest rose as I anticipated what would be revealed when she got to the last button.

She let her coat fall to the floor and I took two steps back, leaning against the wall opposite my front door. I wanted to take all of her in with my eyes. She was stunning. Breathtaking, really. As a young man, I had idolized Robin Givens and Remy even had *her* beat. She was fiercely confident and knew what she wanted. Her body was a masterpiece, a testament to the majestic works of God's hands. Every curve, every line seemed to have been crafted with meticulous precision, resulting in a silhouette that was both powerful and delicate at the same time.

Even if I wanted to continue to deny her, the throbbing hardness in my pants made it clear that I wasn't going to. Before she could change her mind or become embarrassed about completely offering herself up to me like this, I dropped to my knees and helped her out of her black leather stilettos with red bottoms. She never broke eye contact with me as she placed her hands on my shoulders to steady herself to step out of each shoe. First the left heel, then the right, bringing her glistening clit four inches closer to me and only one inch away from my mouth.

After helping her out of her shoes, the temptation to immediately dive into her was driving me insane. But like I said before, her body was an exquisite masterpiece that demanded my appreciation and admiration. So I savored the moment, leisurely admiring every curve and contour of her figure. Kneeling at her feet, my fingertips, then my lips, then tongue, delicately traced an invisible map along her legs. Our intense gaze was abruptly broken as she threw her head back, releasing a guttural moan that echoed raw, unadulterated need. Overwhelmed, she thrust her arms forward, seeking support from the wall behind me.

There I remained on my knees, dwarfed by Remy who towered above me. Her breasts swayed above my head, creating a magnetic pull as my hands wavered, torn between the multitude of enticing options that lay before them. Yearning to explore the entirety of her body, I didn't know where to start. The look in her eyes wasn't that of someone who was desperate for attention but there was a hint of vulnerability there. She wanted me. She wanted me to want her. But she wasn't begging me. She was summoning me.

Remy carried herself with a regal allure, and she was commanding me to fulfill her every desire. There was no pretending with her. No expectations of a happily ever after. Here, standing before me, was a beautiful goddess with a beautiful, practical invitation to be whatever she needed, with no strings attached. No questions asked.

And that's how Remy Fontaine won over this player's heart.

Chapter Two

Jaxon

One Year Later

"You want anything from Black Coffee?" Remy asked, snatching me out of my morning musings. Black Coffee was a local, black-owned coffee shop here in Atlanta that had become one of our favorite spots to get coffee.

"Nah. I'm trying to cut back on caffeine, remember?"

"Oh yeah, I forgot," she yawned as she walked into the bathroom to get ready for her day.

I had never expected things to move so quickly with her. What started out as a casual friendship soon turned into something more — something that neither of us were quite ready for. But we settled into a rhythm quite effortlessly.

Within months of us partnering professionally, I was given the opportunity to score music for two different television pilots. Six months into our personal relationship, Remy and I had been spending a lot of time together when my landlord let me know that he was putting the loft that I was renting on the market, giving me the first right of refusal to purchase. I had some money saved, and a brother's credit wasn't too shabby. But a $500K mortgage wasn't something I was ready to take on. Remy suggested that I move in with her instead of me worrying about finding another spot right away, but the idea of living with another woman scared me.

Living with my ex-wife was even an accident. Hell, marrying her was an accident as well. I met Kenya when I was playing at a church years ago, and she was one of the singers and worship leaders there. She was always helpful and always willing to pitch in to help when needed, but she had absolutely zero interest in me or my games. Nothing I did worked on her, and the fact that she resisted me when the other ladies at the church were practically proposing every week made me pursue her harder.

In 2014, Atlanta had a deadly snow storm that brought the city to its knees. Buses full of children and cars were stranded along highways overnight, some people didn't make it through the night. Kenya and I were downtown with some of our church leaders at a meeting when we were advised that snow was beginning to come down pretty heavily. By the time we'd made it out of the conference center, the streets were packed with people and cars trying to make it home. And with many people opting to simply wait it out in the hotel, Kenya and I were left with the last king suite available. Straight out of a Lifetime movie, I know.

She was still guarded and refused to go to the room with me until she knew she would be falling asleep. But throughout the remainder of the evening, we started talking and getting to know each other. She was fun and cool and sexy; one of those women that could easily hang with the guys because she wasn't trying hard to get attention. We had the same sense of humor, same love for music and movies, and there was an ease to how we vibed. I spent one carefree night laughing and having a good time with her, and after that one night, I actually believed I could love her.

The day after the storm passed, and the roads were finally clear of cars, I offered to drive her home. She had taken a car service there originally, but there was no telling when they'd be able to come back to get her. We fought over what songs to play on the radio but ultimately settled on some old school Will Downing. That might have been when I started to make my move. You couldn't go wrong with Will. Anytime I wanted to impress a woman or get her to let her guard down, a candlelit dinner with the smooth and sultry sounds of his voice did it every time.

We were going back and forth about which female singer had the best duet with Will Downing, but as we pulled into her building, the conversation came to a halt. There were crowds of people walking around the parking lot with plastic trash bags, furniture, and discarded belongings sprawled out everywhere. When we stopped to ask someone what was going on, we were told that the entire building was flooded. The icy conditions had led to the pipes in her building bursting, causing widespread destruction. In a moment, Kenya found herself homeless with all her possessions ruined. Her family was in California at the time, leaving her without an immediate place to go. So, I invited her to stay at my place until she could get back on her feet.

What was supposed to be a single night morphed into a week. Then two weeks turned into several months as her apartment underwent renovations. Along the way, we fell into a routine, a semblance of a shared life. However, once our relationship became intimate, she started pressing me about marriage. What ensued—the arguments, the betrayals, her emotional devastation—could have all been avoided if I hadn't brought her home with me that fateful day. It's a decision that continues to haunt me.

I hadn't lived with a woman since then and, after my divorce, I vowed to never do it again. The expectations, the lack of privacy and solace after a long day, those things were non-negotiable to me, and women never took too kindly to that. But the only woman who could have changed my mind would've been Remy. She wasn't like other women in that she begged for my attention as soon as I walked through the door. Sure, she greeted me. But after that, she left me alone to decompress. She had her own decompressing to do.

She didn't ask me to do "couple-type" things with her, because she enjoyed the persona of being her own woman. And when neither of us felt like engaging at all, the woman had a basement complete with a kitchen and spare bedroom. It was the easiest decision I ever made.

Twenty-year-old me would have fully taken advantage of Remy and this entire situation. But forty-year-old me understood how these situations created certain types of power dynamics between men and women. So, I treated this like another one of our business arrangements. I asked her to write me a lease in my name and told her to include a reasonable amount for monthly rent. She thought I was being ridiculous, but I didn't care how much money she had. I didn't care that she *could* take care of things on her own. I simply wanted to contribute to keep the scales between us balanced.

I was making myself a cup of ginger tea when Remy yelled from the bedroom, "Will you be home for dinner tonight?"

She casually strutted into the kitchen, rocking a sleek, black leather pencil skirt with a slit that stopped just shy of her thigh. Her ensemble was complete with a vibrant Paco Rabanne t-shirt, featuring a playful mix of black, blue, and pink. And those black buckle-up gladiator heels added an extra touch of flair. A mischievous chuckle escaped me as she playfully spun in a circle, as if she was asking, "Well, how do I look?"

"You look stunning. Digging the edgy vibe. But I'll be home late tonight. I've got a set at Sanctuary."

I loved the comfortable way we were able to exist with one another. We never fought. We had an open and honest friendship that enhanced our relationship. And even though there was no label on anything, I hadn't made any attempts to sleep with another woman. Even if Remy and I *hadn't* had sex in more than a month.

"Ugh! Really!?" she yelled as she ran around the house packing her laptops and grabbing snacks for her day. "I thought we agreed that you would cut back at Sanctuary! Especially with the kind of money you're making now!"

Okay, if we argued about anything, it was about the amount of time that I spent at Sanctuary. Remy understood that Lu helped me by creating that residency for me at the wine bar. But she seemed to gloss over the fact that my residency saved Lu, too. It wasn't about the money for me anymore. It was about making sure that Lu and her staff would be OK. And right now, I didn't see how that could happen without my help. At least until I found a reasonable replacement.

"I *have* cut back, Rem. I only do shows twice a week now. Besides, this is a slow night, so the music keeps patrons around and buying drinks longer."

I stopped her in the midst of her frantically running around the house and steadied her for a beat. "Jaxon, I've got to go, or I'm gonna be late for my meeting!" she hissed.

"You know," I whispered in her ear while brushing her neatly-trimmed bob away from her shoulders, "you *could* come see me play like you used to."

She softened into me, tilting her neck to the left and inviting me in for the kiss I was angling for. "You know I don't like the attention I get when people recognize me there," she whined.

"Okay then," I said as I softly kissed her neck once more. "Wait up for me."

"Okaaay," she giggled.

"What?" I teased, this time using my teeth when I kissed her neck. "I didn't hear you."

"Okay! Jaxon." She squirmed and wiggled out of my grip. "I will wait up for you. Now move out of my way so I can go!" Then she grabbed her coat and her laptop bag and rushed out of the door.

This role reversal situation was quite a novelty for me. Usually when I was dating someone, I tended to be guarded and occasionally indulged in a bit of deception. But, for once, there was no need for me to hide anything or put on a facade. Surprisingly enough, being completely open with Remy from the start actually made her embrace me even more. Even still, I wouldn't call what Remy and I had between us romantic. Convenient, maybe. Comfortable, even. But not romantic.

I was grabbing my clothes for the day, getting ready to take a shower, when I heard my phone vibrating. It was eight o'clock in the morning, and I usually didn't get calls this early. I stepped out of the walk-in closet and grabbed my phone on the nightstand and saw that the number was blocked. It was the third call I'd received like this in three days, but everybody knows black people don't answer unlisted or blocked numbers, so I sent it to voicemail and figured that the person would leave a message if it was important.

The last time I got calls like this, it was a woman trying to convince me that she was pregnant with my baby after I wouldn't return her calls. Since I had a vasectomy in my 30's, I knew the call was only meant to get a reaction out of me. But now that I'd been consistently seeing Rem for the past year, there would be no reason for calls like that. So sorry to whoever that might be. I'm a one-woman man...At least I am *now*.

Chapter Three

Jaxon

At least once a month, Remy and I got dressed up to attend the listening parties of up and coming artists. Whenever an artist released a new album or single, record labels would host listening parties for industry executives, press, and fans that also happened to be social media influencers. It was an expense that many labels had cut back on, but Nova Records believed that some things in the music industry should never change. Listening parties were a staple and could make or break a new artist, so they invested heavily in the outcome of them. If I wanted to remain top of mind for the industry executives that decided my fate, I had to get dressed up to do the song and dance.

For Remy, it was a chance for her to make sure she kept her finger on the pulse of all the music that would be hitting the radio air waves and music streaming services. It didn't matter what was going on or what we had planned, with Remy, business was always at the forefront. Everything had a business component, or it wasn't of value to her.

We cleaned up well, if I said so myself. When we stepped out together, people thought we were the embodiment of a power couple. I wore a navy-blue suit with a blush top underneath. She wore a mauve-colored, sequined dress that left nothing to the imagination. Remembering that we hadn't had sex in a month, Remy should know that if she wanted me to be on my best behavior tonight, she owed me some assurances for when we got home.

She was a beast. When she was engrossed in her work or juggling multiple projects, everything else seemed to fade into the background. I admired her intensity, so I never voiced any complaints. However, if this arrangement that we had was going to continue, my needs had to be considered as well. Going without sex for a month wasn't something I'd done since high school, especially when I was used to having several women vying for my attention at Sanctuary. This was becoming unbearable, and that dress she was wearing was making me dizzy.

"So, that's what you chose to wear tonight?" I said, walking behind her as we made it down the stairs of the house.

When we landed in the foyer, she stopped in the mirror by the door to check her lipstick one more time. "I'm sorry?" she replied, puckering her lips to ensure maximum coverage.

With a deliberate, prowling grace, I moved to stand behind her in the mirror's reflection. I wanted her to feel my presence, my need, and the unspoken question that hung heavily in the air between us. My left arm found its way around her waist, pulling her closer, while my thumb traced a tantalizing path to her lips, parting them gently.

"So," I murmured, my voice a low, husky whisper, "this is the dress you chose for tonight?" My words were laced with desire, each syllable dripping with the effect she had on me. "Did you know what this would do to me, Rem?" There was a hint of playful accusation in my tone.

"I knew *exactly* what this dress would do to you," she admitted, her voice a seductive whisper that wrapped around my senses like a smoky caress. A sly grin spread across her face as she bent over, feigning the need to adjust her shoe buckle. Unwilling to let her tease me any longer, I grabbed her waist, my desire for her intensifying. She caught my gaze in the mirror, offering a view that was both exquisite and agonizing.

"And if you're a good boy tonight," she continued, turning to adjust my collar. "I'll let you do whatever you want to me afterwards." The air between us sizzled with anticipation when she turned to straighten her dress, walk out of the door, and down the steps to meet our driver that was waiting. I, on the other hand, needed to stand there and settle my nerves…in my pants.

This was a game we played well. The mesmerizing game of passion and power. I would do something meant to unsettle her or knock her off her game, and she'd know just how to bounce back and reclaim control of the situation. She was constantly testing me and challenging me, and I was always checking to make sure I still had an effect on her. It was a game that neither of us ever truly mastered, ensuring the scales of power perpetually teetered. Neither of us ever getting bored, or the upper hand for long.

The party was set to take place at Symmetry, a high-end event venue that Remy had a vested stake in. She held a firm belief that lounges and clubs were the lifeblood of music, the pulsating heart that kept it thriving. She wanted a say in which artists' music would define the space. Symmetry, on the other hand, was more than just a venue; it was a luxurious haven perched high above the city's chaos. Every corner was steeped in luxury, from the low, sultry lighting that draped the room in a soft, golden hue, to the plush velvet sofas that seemed to beckon for hushed conversations and shared confidences.

The air was heavy with expectancy for Petah Pan, the rapping, R&B singing artist of the hour. The atmosphere was electric, charged with the energy of the city's elite who called this place their playground. A heady mix of high-end perfume, the rich scent of single malt, and the intoxicating promise of power and exclusivity. It was a space where music, power, and passion converged, creating a vibe that was uniquely...Remy.

I was taking in the atmosphere when I heard Remy's unmistakable voice approaching, "Jax! There you are! I wanted to introduce you to Lela Glover. She's the showrunner for a confidential TV show set to premier next year! I was just telling her how gifted your hands were...on the piano, *of course*." Everyone laughed at her obvious innuendo.

I took Lela's left hand and politely kissed it. "Pleasure to meet you, Ms. Glover."

"Ohhh! The pleasure is all mine, sir!" Lela giggled. "Tell me, Remy, is this one yours?"

"Jaxon belongs to no one but himself, Lela. He chooses where he wants to be, and he *always* chooses wisely." Remy shot me a knowing look before continuing, "I'll leave you two to get acquainted." Then she confidently sauntered off, fully expecting me to *choose* wisely.

Remy was challenging me. She relished in reminding me that I had the freedom to choose where I wanted to end my nights. But she was confident that, when it came down to it, I would always come home to her. So, when she casually tossed out that comment to Lela and then walked away, it wasn't just a parting shot. It was most-certainly a challenge. A dare, even. She introduced me to a beautiful woman, confidently asserted that I could have any woman I desired, and then dared me to make a different choice than she assumed I would.

This wasn't the first time Remy had suggested I do as I pleased in a situation like this. A couple of months ago, we were at an awards ceremony. Remy had received the Atlanta Women in Business Achievement Award and the after party was just getting started. As usual, I was off in the corner and enjoying the vibe when Renea Burkhalter approached me. Her and her husband owned a premier winery and B&B in North Georgia and Remy was heavily courting her to be a sponsor for Symmetry.

Renea didn't hesitate in revealing that she and her husband were in an open marriage. This amused Remy, who even playfully suggested I take up a stay at the Burkhalter B&B. At first, I was livid, feeling as if she was trying to pimp me out or something. But when I pulled her aside and demanded to know what the hell she was doing, she simply replied with utmost confidence, *"Jaxon, how many times do I have to remind you? With me, you aren't a caged animal. And neither am I with you. If Mrs. Burkhalter offers something you're interested in, I won't stand in your way. Or hers."*

It was Remy's outlook on our arrangement that made *her* all the more enticing, not Renea Burkhalter. Never in my life had I been with a woman who so freely allowed me to be...*me*. To be free without any restrictions or restraint. But before I could dive head first into flagrant philandering and debauchery, Remy leaned in and whispered provocatively in my ear, *"But remember this. Just because you're not in a cage, doesn't mean you're not on a leash."* That was the point where our game of passion and power intensified. Sure, I could do whatever or whoever I wanted. But Remy's statement, no, warning, let me know that there would be consequences and rewards assigned to the choices I made. I hadn't been on the wrong side of the consequences just yet.

"So...Jaxon," Lela purred. "Have I seen or heard your work anywhere recently?"

"Not too many places. Most of the things I'm currently working on are in development, so I can't speak about them."

"Pity. I was really hoping to get introduced to the *marvelous* works of your hands."

I don't know what had gotten into me, but I suddenly felt like playing along with Remy tonight. "You know," I offered, "there's a piano in the back VIP area. I'd be happy to play something for you."

Lela audibly swooned, "Wow! Really? That would be epic."

In true gentleman style, I extended my left arm for her to loop hers through. Swiftly, I snagged two champagne flutes from a passing waiter and guided Lela towards the rear where the grand piano was. As we walked away, I glanced back over my shoulder to see if Remy was watching. She was. I shot her a sly, flirtatious grin and a wink, and I saw her mouth slightly curl up in a smirk. She raised her glass in my direction, in what appeared to be a toast and her silently gesturing, "game on" as Lela and I disappeared into the back.

It was a quiet and dimly lit room, just off the side of the main lounge area and bar. Even though there was no door to close this space off from the main area, the noise seemed to disappear into the background. I gently placed my glass on the glossy surface of the piano and took a seat. There had always been something enchanting about the scent that wafted up when you lifted the lid of a piano, the mingling of polished wood and well-worn ivory keys. I paused for a moment, letting the unique aroma fill my senses.

Just as I was losing myself in the nostalgia, Lela's soft footsteps pulled me back to reality. She came up behind me, her hands gently kneading my shoulders, her touch both comforting and electrifying. "Do you know 'If This World Were Mine' by Luther Vandross?" she asked.

Another glass of champagne wasn't the best idea. It was obvious that she'd already had enough to drink. "It's actually by Marvin Gaye and Tammi Terrell, but yes. I know that one well." I began the low rumblings of the notes that introduced the first few lyrics.

"I *love* this song," Lela murmured. With a graceful movement, she moved from behind me and made herself comfortable next to me on the piano bench.

"Me too, it's right up there with my all-time favorites," I agreed.

She shot me a teasing look. "And just what would you know about this song? Isn't it a bit before your time?"

"No more than it is for you," I retorted playfully, lifting my champagne glass for another sip. "Actually, my mom is a big fan of this song. I used to play it for her when I was a kid. It never failed to bring a smile to her face."

Lela turned to me, her gaze intense. "So, you can sing, compose music, plus you're fine as hell. Why on *earth* are you still single?"

At that, I couldn't help but chuckle, "I'm just not the settling down type, I guess."

Her curiosity piqued, she probed further. "Okay then, so what's your deal with Remy?"

"My deal?"

"Yes, your deal! I see you two together all the time, but you never seem to officially label yourselves as more than friends."

"Alright…what's your question exactly? You seem to have already drawn your conclusions," I said, my eyebrow arched in amusement.

Lela huffed, clearly annoyed that I wasn't giving her the straightforward answers she was probing for.

"What is it you want to know, Lela?"

Suddenly, I felt her tense beside me. Her breathing became noticeably faster, as if her heart was pounding in her chest. Then, out of nowhere, I felt her right hand grip my thigh, attempting to inch its way higher. But before she could reach any further, I stood up abruptly.

"Lela, Maybe we should go back out…"

Before I could even complete my sentence, Lela sprang up from the piano bench and launched herself at me. The move was so sudden and swift that I barely had time to register what was happening. Her body pressed firmly against mine, effectively pinning me to the wall behind us. This time, she didn't hesitate or seek consent, her hand boldly exploring the contours of my manhood through the fabric of my pants.

"Lela," I whispered. "You, my dear, have been drinking."

"Yep! And it makes for a *great* lubricant, don't you think?" she replied, her words punctuated by a mix of hiccups and giggles.

"It does," I confirmed. "But I'm afraid you've *lubricated* yourself for nothing, love. I don't *do* public spaces," I lied. I just couldn't do that *there,* in Remy's lounge… with *her.*

This was why it was so hard to remain faithful when I was married. My ex-wife didn't believe that things like this happened to me all the time. I would be at a show or a gig, minding my own business, when some beautiful woman would come up out of nowhere and grab my junk like it was a joystick! It didn't matter how often I resisted or how many times I said, "no," these women rarely took no for an answer. And since I didn't like turning down a gift when offered, I usually gave in to their advances in the end.

"You're no fun," she pouted.

"I assure you, I'm every bit of the fun you've probably imagined. This just isn't the time nor the place. I hope you can understand," I explained, hoping she was at least sober enough to listen to reason.

As we were exiting the back where the piano was, I saw Remy attentively watching the door from the other side of the room. Admittedly, our rather disheveled appearance made it seem as if Lela and I were doing something unseemly back there. Before Lela was out of reach, I grabbed her by the left arm and pulled her back to me in a spin, kissing her on the cheek and thanking her for allowing me to serenade her. Then she handed me her business card and walked away smiling. Remy was already on her way over to me.

"That was fast. What happened? It's been too long, and little Jax couldn't control himself?" Remy teased.

"You think I had sex with her?"

"I don't know, did you?"

"Why, Remy? Why do you want to know?"

Remy peered into my eyes, tilting her head as if she was trying to read me. Then she reached up, pulling my neck down to her mouth before she sank her teeth into my neck, drawing out an instinctive groan from deep within me. Music was playing loudly so people weren't paying any attention to us. I'm sure many assumed we were simply dancing when her hand dipped to my groin as she subtly massaged the firm bulge in my pants that threatened to burst a hole through the fabric.

I took both hands and wrapped them around her neck, pulling her bottom lip into my mouth as I sucked and teased. Her strokes became more intense when I broke our connection. "Rem," I said breathily, "What are you doing?"

"Oh. So you *didn't* fuck her."

Unsure of how she arrived at that revelation, I asked, "How can you tell?"

She let out a soft laugh, then leaned in to gently press her lips against mine, ensuring she gave my lower lip a lingering bite as she pulled back — a move she knew always got my pulse racing. I was acutely aware that she was teasing me, while also reprimanding me, but this was quickly escalating into a form of torment.

"Can we go home...*now*?" I asked through gritted teeth. I wanted her, and I wasn't even above begging at this point.

She smiled at me before saying, "Not yet, baby. I've still got some mingling to do." Then she walked away, leaving me there standing...hard. She had won this round, but I had something for her later.

Chapter Four

Jaxon

I still couldn't believe that this was my life. I was sitting across from Bruno Estrella, Emmy award-winning director and producer of some of my favorite films and TV shows, and he was asking *me* for my opinion on the musical direction of his next project. When I was a little boy, all my father wanted was for me to end up with my name in lights. But instead of my name appearing on a Hollywood marquee, he would have preferred a television credit from me preaching on a Christian television network or something.

Since my father was a Pentecostal preacher, my mom and I would travel with him from city to city as he preached fire down from heaven in various churches. Sometimes he preached for money, sometimes for a warm meal and a place to stay. Other times, over-zealous pastors' wives would offer up honorariums of a sensual nature for my dad's troubles. When I got old enough to realize what he was doing, he told me that it was impolite to reject someone's expression of gratitude to us. *"Even if it seems wrong,"* he'd say. *"That's all they know to do. People will honor and bless you because they are seeking the favor and a blessing from God. So it's on us to receive their gift in whatever form and not block their blessing."* It didn't seem right or fair to my mom. But I figured my father knew God and the Bible better than me, so I didn't question it.

When things were good between my dad and my mom, it was amazing. But when things were bad, I had to create ways to escape so I didn't hear the violence and turmoil that would happen outside my bedroom door. Music became my own personal haven. From Franky Beverly and Maze to Earth Wind and Fire; to New Edition and Jodeci. Music gave me the ability to see beyond my circumstances. It transported me to a place that allowed me to be free and creative and safe.

I was explaining to Bruno how certain sounds would ignite specific feelings for a scene he was describing, when my phone rang. "I'm so sorry," I said, rushing to silence my phone out of embarrassment.

"It's fine. In this business, we are slaves to our phones. Do you need to get it?"

"No, sir. Just a blocked number that keeps calling but doesn't leave a message."

"They must not know that black people don't answer calls from blocked numbers!" he joked. And we both laughed at the unspoken but shared truths of the black community.

We wrapped the meeting with the promise of his people calling my people. But overall, I felt very good about what would come next. Once a film executive liked you, they pretty much brought you along for other projects they were working on. Things moved fast, and changing your team members could be a costly endeavor if you had to train someone and wait until they were up to speed or familiar with your working style. Bruno liked how easily I picked up and flowed with his energy, something you learned working in the church.

As an organist or a keyboard player in church, it was expected of me to know every popular song on the radio, and even those that hadn't been played in decades. If someone got on the mic to sing a solo, and they didn't bother to learn what key they were singing in, I had to pick at the notes to find the key, *quickly*. If they skipped a part of the song, I had to know the songs well enough to be able to quickly jump to wherever they were, and bring the other musicians along with me. If they changed keys in the middle of the song, something reserved for the worst singers, I had to learn to adjust to that, too. As much as I had grown to despise my church upbringing, it definitely helped me in ways I didn't realize it could.

I was headed out of the building when my phone rang again from another blocked number. At this point, the person was calling back-to-back, so I assumed they weren't going to stop. I was holding the door for a woman that was walking up behind me when I answered the call with verifiable annoyance in my tone.

"What!" I demanded, willing the person on the other end of the phone to quickly spit out what they were calling me for. But it was silent. I heard someone breathing, but no one spoke. "Hello!" I yelled. "Who is this calling and playing games on my phone?!"

"Jaxon?" a timid voice called out. She sounded young. Too young to have any history with me.

"Who's asking?"

"It's me...Mila?"

"Look, little girl. I don't know what kind of games your mommy has you playing, but I'm not your daddy, OK?"

I heard sniffles come from the other end, and I was kicking myself for making a little girl cry when she said, "My name is Mila Hart, and my mommy and daddy are both dead."

My mouth hung open, and the line went silent again. Mostly because she had stopped talking, and I didn't know how to respond to what she had just said. I didn't know anyone named Mila Hart, and she said her mommy and daddy were *both* dead, so she couldn't think I was her father.

I softened the tone of my voice now that I realized what she must have already been going through. "I...I'm sorry. Mila? How did you get this number? I don't think you're calling the right number, sweetheart."

I heard shuffling in the background when a different voice sounded over the line. "Hello, Mr. Hart?" the voice called out, this woman sounding more mature. "This is Danica Taylor from Child Protective Services. We've been trying to reach you because..." her voice trailed off as if she was bracing for impact. "Sir, your mother and father have been killed in a car accident, and Mila...we have Mila here. She was the only survivor, and she's been in the hospital for more than a week, and we haven't been able to reach any next of kin for her. She's about to be released from the hospital and...well, sir, if you don't take her, we will be forced to place her into foster care."

"Perhaps there's been a mistake, Ms. Taylor. My mother has been gone for quite some time, and my father," I paused because I didn't know any other way to say he could rot in hell. "I haven't spoken to my father in a few years. Still, he definitely didn't have a daughter the last time I spoke to him. Especially one as old as she sounds. She has to be at least, what, ten years old?"

Danica let out an exasperated sigh, "Sir. Is your father Jaxon Hart, III?"

"Yes, but…"

"Then sir, I'm afraid to tell you that your father and his wife have been killed in a car accident and your baby sister is all alone, with you as her only next of kin. She's twelve, by the way."

I was speechless. I didn't know how to process everything that had just been dropped in my lap. I hadn't spoken to my father in over seven years, and when I did, he never once mentioned a wife or a daughter. We talked about music, sports, and his plans to retire from his ministry and move to Mexico. But we never once talked about a wife or a daughter!

"Mr. Hart?" the social worker called out. "Are you still there?"

I snapped out of my spiraling thoughts, "Ye… yes. I'm here. I just…Danica, is it? Can you give me your phone number? I'm going to need to call you back." Danica gave me the numbers to her office and her cell, and made sure that I knew that Mila had forty-eight hours to be claimed before she was placed into the system. She needed to be *claimed.* Like she was misplaced luggage waiting for someone to walk by that would recognize her.

Everything was spinning. I was still standing motionless outside of Bruno's offices, but I couldn't move my feet. My father's old ass found a woman dumb enough to fall in love with him and got remarried, had a daughter named Mila, and then died in a car accident. Leaving Mila with me. I didn't know if I should laugh, cry, or grieve first. With everything that I had going on in my life, and the way my schedule was set up, this was the worst possible time for any surprises of this magnitude.

Then, as if a breeze of *holy shit* washed over me, I thought about the other factor that would make this the biggest inconvenience of the century. "Fuck," I muttered to myself, "I gotta talk to Remy."

Chapter Five

Jaxon

I walked into our home to find Remy in the kitchen, engrossed in scanning takeout menus. Cooking was something she rarely did, declaring it to be a gesture she reserved for her man or husband, and I had never pushed the subject. It was just another aspect that kept our arrangement uncomplicated. But at this moment, her culinary preferences were the least of my concerns.

The shock of my father's passing was still a whirlwind in my mind, a storm I couldn't quite navigate. On top of the confusion and the unfamiliar emotions it stirred, there was the immediate issue of Mila, my little sister. When I was about eleven, my dad used to tell me that having kids should be reserved for later in life. He believed that a man's younger years should be dedicated to serving God and helping others. It was only once a man was older and settled, he'd say, that he should consider starting a family. *"Having kids young ruins things. Gets in the way,"* he'd often repeat, and it always left me wondering about his true sentiments towards me. Given that he was a mere twenty-year-old when he and my mom brought me into the world.

As insensitive as it might've sounded, dealing with my father's affairs and trying to piece together the man he was had to be put on hold for now. The immediate concern was Mila. She was the urgent situation that needed addressing, and honestly, I was completely stumped on how to even broach this topic with Remy. Here I was, suddenly thrown into the deep end with a sister I'd never met and a responsibility I'd never asked for. And Remy, well, the thought of even starting this conversation with her was daunting, to say the least.

How do you tell someone that their carefree life was about to take a 180-degree turn? How do you explain that the weekend getaways and weekday party life we relished might soon be replaced with homework and PTA meetings? I couldn't even guess what she would do or say. Remy didn't even allow me to get in the way of her free time and self-care indulgences, so she was going to lose her shit when I told her this. But no matter how much I dreaded it, this was a conversation that needed to happen. For Mila, for me, and for whatever future Remy and I might still have together.

"Jaxon, what is it? You're scaring me!" Remy exclaimed. My obvious distress with red eyes and tear-stained cheeks was a side of me she had never seen before.

I guided her to sit at the kitchen island with me, and with a heavy heart, I broke the news — my father and his wife had died in a car crash. We spent a good half an hour digesting that piece of information, primarily because until then, I had never spoken about my father. She had assumed he was already dead. She was curious about who he was to me, where he had been living, when we last exchanged words, and why I never brought him up. I answered her as honestly as I could, but her rapid-fire questions added another layer of complexity to the situation. There was still more I needed to share, and I wasn't certain that it would be met with the same level of grace and empathy.

"There's more, Rem," I confessed, struggling to hold back tears that were *definitely* not invited to this conversation. "He had a daughter."

"You mean you have a sister? Aww! That's kinda sweet! How old is she?"

Alright, her reaction was more positive than I'd anticipated. "She's about eleven or twelve, I think?" I knew the social worker had told me her age, but there was honestly so much going on in that moment that everything was still sort of a blur. " Anyway, she reached out to me today, and I felt awful because I'd never even heard of her, but she knew me. She even had my phone number."

"Oh, the poor thing. So, she wants to get to know you now that her dad's gone?"

I dropped my head, resting my elbows on my knees as I found the strength to continue. "She's an orphan now, Rem. She's all by herself, and the people at social services are giving me a two-day window to claim her, or they'll have to put her into foster care."

Remy backed away from me, removing her hand from mine. "Claim her? Like she's just some piece of property?!" she exploded. This was the reaction I had been bracing myself for.

"I know, Remy. It's just as much of a shock to me as it is to you, but…"

"But what, Jaxon?" she interrupted. "I *know* you're not asking me if she can come *here!*" She paused, and I took a moment to take in the environment of Remy's home. The plush white carpet, barely touched furniture, and priceless art screamed decadence. Clearly no place for a child.

"That is a child, Jaxon," Remy continued. "A little girl. What are you…*we*…going to do with a little girl?!"

I jumped up and began pacing the floor, not able to sit and deal with Remy's yelling like *I* was the child in this scenario. I didn't always have the nicest words to say when I felt like I was being backed into a corner, so I tried to remove myself from situations that would drive me to that place. "I don't know, Rem. I was hoping for ideas or support or something? I don't *know*! I'm a bit out of my element here!"

Within seconds, Remy had gotten up from her seat and was standing next to me, glaring up as if she was challenging me. "Sup...support? Jaxon, support wasn't part of our deal. We have a good thing going on here, and introducing a kid into the mix wouldn't just complicate matters. It would completely ruin them!" She folded her arms across her chest and leaned back against the kitchen island. "Well, a kid would at least ruin things for me," she said, her words sucking the air completely out of the room.

"Wow, so you're saying that if I want to take her, *we're* done?"

"I'm *saying* that kids were never part of the arrangement, Jaxon."

She had a point. Children were never part of our arrangement. Hell, I'd never even considered having kids in the first place. But I also never expected to be thrown into a predicament where I'd have to choose between the life and luxuries I was used to, or a child. My little sister, a girl I'd never even met, was suddenly all alone in the world. And as expected, Remy was livid. I could see it in her eyes; this just might be the thing that made us walk away now that so much had changed in a literal instant. No hard feelings. No questions asked.

"Let's not make any decisions just yet, OK?" I proposed. Let me go meet her and then we can talk more."

"Go meet your sister, Jax. Go meet your sister and bury your father. But I've made my decision. There isn't anything else for you and I to discuss."

Chapter Six

Hadassah

"Mrs. St. James, I love your hair!"

"Thank you, Solange! Now let go of Marcus' hand before you end up pregnant!"

Fridays at school were always chaotic. The Fridays before a holiday break were a special kind of torture. It was the Friday before Thanksgiving break, and the kids were excited about the weekend and all of their teenage plans. The teachers were too tired from the week of tests and parties to enforce many of the rules. But our kids weren't bad, so there was rarely anything to enforce.

The Bridget "Biddy" Mason STEM charter school, named after the formerly enslaved turned prominent business woman and philanthropist, sat in a small suburb of Atlanta called Cinnamon Grove. The city of Atlanta had become synonymous with prominence and luxury with high-rise buildings, outdoor shopping centers, and vegan eateries. However, the cities that remained stagnant, because developers didn't see any value in their gentrification, still served as home to thousands of children who didn't see any way out of their conditions. As one of the founders of this school, we built it with a vision to give those students the opportunities they needed to thrive, regardless of their surroundings. The goal was to have a network of charter schools like this, but that dream died a little over five years ago. And with so much political opposition to charter schools these days, I didn't have the time nor the energy to fight the government alone.

The school was thoughtfully designed, keeping in mind those bright students who perhaps hadn't yet discovered how to unlock their intellectual potential. Built on land that used to be forbidden to black people, the first thing that struck you was the vibrant blend of colors adorning the walls. Shades of royal blue, deep purple, and rich gold were carefully chosen to stimulate creativity and curiosity, as well as to enhance concentration and foster a sense of calmness, crucial for a learning environment.

My husband, Dr. Lamar St. James was one of the other founders of Biddy Mason. He was passionate about exposing our kids to black inventors and innovators that weren't talked about in traditional, western learning environments. So when the school was being designed, he had the developers create what we now called 'Innovation Alley,' our innovation lab that featured a timeline of tributes to black inventors from Lewis Latimer to Mae Jemison, their inventions etched alongside their portraits. I, on the other hand, had a passion for charity work and good causes, so 'Philanthropy Lane' highlighted black philanthropists who had generously contributed to education and scientific research, inspiring students with stories of kindness and giving back.

This place was everything we ever dreamed of twelve years ago. Back during a time where life was simple, and the future was hopeful. Lamar and I met at a teachers' conference just after he had successfully defended his dissertation. He was going to be receiving his PhD and couldn't stop grinning at his accomplishment. At the conference, he had electrified the crowd with a talk that he gave on the hidden effects of gentrification. Highlighting the neighborhoods that were deemed hopeless and worthless, and the children that remained in them. He had a passion and a dream to prepare young boys and girls for the inevitable future that was not preparing a place for them in it, and his passion was contagious. *He* was contagious.

As with most professional conferences, there was no shortage of parties with men and women alike on the prowl. Not me, though. I enjoyed watching people and, when the opportunity presented itself, I actually engaged in stimulating conversations.

71

I was sitting at the hotel bar when I felt a breeze of air as if someone had just come up next to me. *"Not into the party scene tonight, huh?"*

I had looked up to find Lamar St. James staring down at me, looking like a scoop of *Jesus be a chastity belt*. He was fine. About six feet with smokey gray eyes, and long dreadlocks that reached the center of his back. He was wearing a brown suit with a beige turtleneck that showed just enough of his chest muscles to confirm that his body was indeed a temple. One that I'd love to worship at.

"I...I'm sorry?" I'd stuttered. I couldn't tear my eyes away from his chest quickly enough to find my words.

He'd flashed me a devilish grin. *"I saw you earlier after my talk. By the way you were mingling and talking to different people, I assumed you'd be joining them at the after parties."* He'd leaned in and whispered as if he was sharing a forbidden secret, *"I hear the one on the tenth floor has Hennessy."*

I'd grinned, *"I'm not big on large gatherings. At least pointless ones. I'm much more inclined to enjoy an engaging conversation or an intimate debate. I only tend to engage when I'm genuinely interested."*

"Well, can I genuinely interest you in some engaging banter with me?" he'd asked, not waiting for my answer before presumptuously pulling out the seat next to me and sitting down.

"Since you're already taking a seat, sure. Why not?"

We must have talked for hours that night. Sharing stories of our past and vulnerably casting visions for our future.

Lamar had used the back of his right hand to caress my cheek. *"You're magnetic."*

"I was going to say the same about you."

"Where do you live?"

And without hesitation or even wondering why he wanted to know, I'd answered, *"Atlanta. You?"*

He'd grinned, *"Tennessee, but I'm moving next month."*

"Oh, yeah? Where to? Not too far away, I hope."

He'd moved in closer and whispered, *"Atlanta. Not far at all."*

I'd laughed heartily. *"Oh, really now! And what brings you to Atlanta?"*

"This magnetic woman named Hadassah. Her friends call her Dash, though."

I'd laughed it off, assuming he was joking. We'd spent the rest of the night talking and enjoying each other's company. Three weeks later, I'd gotten a call from him asking to take me out that weekend. He had uprooted his entire life after one night spent talking to me. We didn't even kiss. He never made any inappropriate advances or asked me up to his room, unfortunately. We spent an entire night dreaming and enjoying each other's company, and that made him want to keep doing the same for the rest of his life.

But now, even though the hallways of our school were filled with the laughter and chatter of countless kids, the spaces he once occupied seem a bit hollower. Despite the vibrant world we'd crafted within these walls, his absence was felt, leaving a void that was hard to ignore.

"Hey, Mrs. St. James! I wanted you to be the first to know," Jamison said, pausing for effect, *"that I got accepted into Morehouse!"*

"Jamison! That is amazing! When did you find out?!" I yelled while simultaneously embracing him in a hug.

"I just got the email. Isn't that crazy?!"

74

"Crazy in the best way, boy! I'm so proud of you. I knew you could do it," I said, hugging him one more time so I could quickly wipe away a tear that had escaped from my eye.

Jamison Davis was one of our star students. When he first came to us in the fifth grade, he was rebellious and full of anger. His mom had just gone to prison for killing his father, her abuser, and Jamison and his older brother, Julian, were left all alone. Since Julian was nineteen, he was able to keep Jamison with him. But with the path Julian was on, it would only be a matter of time before Jamison ended up just like him. I wanted to kick Jamison out of school. He was fighting every day, and the teachers were out of ideas on what to do with him. But Lamar wouldn't give up. He didn't believe we had tried everything. I can still remember how it all began.

One morning, I walked into the administration office to find Julian Davis in the office with Lamar. I was confused, but I didn't want to interrupt, assuming Jamison had just gotten into another fight. I was grabbing a cup of coffee when I heard the door to Lamar's office open and their conversation spilling out into the hallway. *"All I'm asking for, Julez, is your cooperation. If you can meet me halfway, I'll make sure your baby brother stays off the streets."*

"*Aight, man,*" Julian agreed. "*I'll work on him at home. Make sure he does what he's supposed to do and shit.*"

Once Julian was out of earshot, I ran into Lamar's office and shut the door. "What was that about? You finally threatening to kick Jamison out of school?"

Lamar just smiled at me. "*No, woman. I asked Julez for his help and support. Just like we would any parent or guardian of a student we were having problems with. Julian never got involved because we never invited him to get involved. Now, he's acting like a man with responsibilities, and I treated him as such.*"

"*OK? So, what does this mean? What's the plan?*"

His glare turned serious, "*Take another sip of coffee.*"

"*Oh Lord,*" I said, knowing this only meant it was something I wasn't gonna like.

"*One more sip.*"

"*Lamar!*" I laughed. "*Boy, if you don't quit playin' with me!*"

"OK. OK! I just made Julian a deal. He works odd hours."

"By work, do you mean sellin' drugs into the wee hours of the night?"

"Baby," he said as if he was issuing a warning. *"We don't judge. We love, remember?"*

"Ugh. Fine," I pouted. *"Continue."*

"Since he works late hours, he said that he can't be home to always help him with homework so he could use some help with that."

"Oh! The after-school program! Easy."

"And dinner," he threw in shyly.

"I'm sorry, what?"

"He could use help making sure he has dinner, too. So, I was wondering if... maybe..." Lamar sang.

"You know what, Lamar? I know you did not volunteer me!"

"Twice a week, baby. Twice a week, would you mind making pasta or spaghetti or something that can last a few days for the boy? Something that he can heat up without his brother being there? If we can do that, Julez said he'd get up every morning

77

and check on Jamison to ensure he has everything he needs for the day. Including lunch money."

"Lamar."

"Hadassah Jenai St. James," he added my middle name for emphasis. *"Give me thirty days. And if at the end of thirty days my plans for Jamison don't work, we will move to expel him from the school. No questions asked."*

"Fine, Lamar," I said defiantly. *"You have thirty days."*

It'd been close to seven years, and Jamison was still here. Lamar became a surrogate father to Jamison and so many of the kids around here. Now, passing his office, sitting exactly as he left it five years ago, I was reminded of the lives he loved, touched, and then left.

As I strolled into the breakroom, intending to snag a bottled water from the fridge, I was met with a sea of flowers and colorful balloons. It was our administrator, Genevieve's birthday today, a fact made pretty evident by the words 'Happy Birthday Gen' scrawled across the remnants of a white cake, its raspberry filling peeking out from the sides. The cake looked delicious, so I swiped a finger full of the raspberry filling and licked it. "Mmm," I moaned. Satisfied, I turned around, ready to retreat to the sanctuary of my office.

"I saw that!" Corinne said, startling me so much that I spilled water from my bottle.

Corine was my best friend and my indispensable assistant principal. She embodied a new generation of educators, the type that our students playfully labeled as "baddies" due to her striking figure that might cause some parents to hesitate about their sons being in her class. However, without her, our school wouldn't be where it was today.

With an MBA in International Business and a PhD in Education, her mind was as sharp as her fashion sense. Her passion for guiding young minds towards excellence was nothing short of inspiring. Of course, when we first brought her on board, a number of mothers voiced their concerns, hiding behind thinly veiled doubts about her qualifications for the role. But after her stellar performance in her first year, marked by the remarkable strides she took in raising the school's standing within the community, they had no choice but to respect her. I just hated how society had decided that beautiful women who valued their appearance couldn't also be educated and brilliant.

"So what!" I said while licking the remaining evidence of the cake off my finger. "If I buy it, I can lick it."

"That's what *he* said," Corinne retorted, making us both instantly burst out with laughter.

The night of my husband's funeral, no one could get me to talk, eat, much less laugh. I avoided everyone, hoping they would leave me alone and just disappear. Corinne wasn't having it. She got me to eat *and* laugh by making me smoke weed and watch hours of the show, "The Office." When I asked Corine where she got weed from, she shamelessly admitted that she kept it whenever she confiscated it from the kids at school. It was now our main source of inappropriate innuendos and inside jokes.

"And girl, you are rockin' those braids! You should take them out for a spin next week for Genevieve's birthday party! We're all going to Sanctuary for a live music night."

"I don't know," I said hesitantly. "I'm not really in the celebratory mood."

"I know! *Duh!*" Corinne teased. "That's why you go to parties...to *get* in the mood!"

Corinne was unique among my friends. She never attempted to push me to "move on" or "get past" the grief. However, she didn't allow me to wallow in my sorrow alone either. Instead, she simply stayed by my side, her presence a comforting constant. She observed me with gentle care, always ready to provide whatever I needed; be it silence, conversation, or simply companionship. Her ability to hold space for my emotions, no matter when or what they were, made her more than a friend. She was my sister. It'd been five years since my world changed forever, and I wouldn't have been able to make it this far without my students, this school, or the solace I found in Corinne.

"Just make me a promise?" she continued.

"What?" I said, rolling my eyes with fake annoyance.

"Promise me you'll at *least* think about it? I know you ain't doin' nothin' else for the break anyway!"

She was right. I had no plans for anything except catching up on HGTV and Million Dollar Listings. That reminded me. I needed to schedule an in-home massage, too. My time away from the school was sacred. I loved my students. I loved walking into this building and being greeted with energy and enthusiasm for knowledge. But I was also exhausted. We hosted fundraisers and galas to keep tuition free or low cost, but I'd be the first to admit that it had gotten harder post-pandemic. People either had smaller budgets for donations, were on a different side of the political charter school debate, or simply didn't see the value in the work we were doing. And after this past semester and fundraising season, I wanted to do nothing but lay around my house in yoga pants and speak to no one for seven glorious days. But if Corinne had it her way, I'd at least have one day out of the house to be with grownups.

"Fine," I relented. "I'll think about it."

Chapter Seven

Jaxon

In the span of two days and after what seemed like an endless back-and-forth of phone calls and text messages with Danica Taylor from Social Services, I was finally on my way to meet Mila. I learned that her full name was Milagros, a beautiful Spanish name meaning 'miracles,' but she went by Mila.

I left the house around 5 a.m., headed towards Savannah, Georgia. It would take four hours to get there, and I had several new albums and podcasts to keep me occupied on the drive. But an hour into the journey, I hadn't played a thing. I just drove in silence, trying to sort through all of my feelings and emotions that I was, or wasn't, dealing with. I didn't even know my dad was living back in Georgia. The last time we spoke, about seven years ago, he lived in Tennessee. Obviously, that wasn't the only thing he'd neglected to mention. Mila, who must have been around five years old at that time, was never once mentioned in our conversation.

Even though my father and I weren't close, there was something about his untimely death that suddenly made me want to know him more. Understand him, even. I wanted to know why he kept Mila a secret from me. I wondered why kindness never found its way into his words when he spoke to me and Momma. I questioned how he could just pack up and leave us when I was merely a boy, without ever extending a helping hand or looking back. I found myself pondering over what stories he might have told Mila and her mom about me. Did he paint a picture of a son he was proud of? Or did he simply gloss over my existence? And the question that echoed the loudest in my mind — why did he never entertain the idea of being a family with *me*?

All these questions, like puzzle pieces, seemed to be crucial in forming a complete picture of who my father really was. And now, more than ever, I wanted to fit those pieces together. But all I had left to provide me with anything resembling answers was Mila. All that I had left of my father was being carefully stored and incubated in a twelve-year-old little girl. I wasn't sure how that would work, though. I had only spoken to Danica. Mila was too shy to speak, especially seeing as how I nearly bit her head off the first time she heard my voice. She was probably shaken up and traumatized, so I didn't want to add any additional pressure on her to help me resolve *my* daddy issues.

This morning, Danica sent me some pictures of Mila. She was still pretty bruised up from the accident, and she wanted me to be prepared for what I saw. If I was going to have any negative reactions to the bandages and bruising, she wanted me to get them out of the way before coming face-to-face with Mila. I could understand that. And I thanked Danica for being considerate of Mila's feelings.

Despite the bandages on her face and the cast that cradled her arm, my little sister was beautiful. Her hair was a riot of curly ringlets, framing a face that bore hazel brown eyes and an innocent smile that could melt hearts. Looking at her, I couldn't help but see the resemblance she bore to my dad, and in turn, to me. It was uncanny, and yet, somehow comforting. Even through the photographs, I could sense a strong connection to this little girl. I hadn't even met her, and she'd already managed to wrap me around her finger.

Erykah Badu's "Love of My Life" was playing in the car when I pulled up to the Warm Springs Family Farm, a group home and farm that fostered children who were also trauma survivors. Since I wasn't exactly in the position to take Mila in right now, I asked Danica to do whatever she could to place Mila in an environment that fostered learning and creativity. If she was anything like me, creativity would offer a lifeline where people failed. With the constant arguments I was having with Remy about the situation, I knew it would be crazy to think I could take Mila in right now. After all, she and I were practically strangers — she didn't really know me, and I had only just learned about her. How could I assume she'd even want to come live with me?

As much as I wanted to ensure Mila's stability and safety, I knew rushing to get her would be a recipe for disaster, if not done properly. We needed to establish a connection first, lay down the groundwork for a relationship. I was ready to do whatever it took to ensure her safety and give her some sense of stability, but it was crucial that we got acquainted before making any more drastic changes to her life. I wanted to meet her, know her, and let her know me, too.

I got to the door and rang the doorbell, daisies in my hand like a nervous kid, and an older woman with stringy, silver hair opened the door to greet me. "You must be Mr. Hart."

"Yes, ma'am," I confirmed.

"My name is Gladys Singletary, and I'm one of the owners of this home. My husband Bo is out back doing a science lesson. Danica from Social Services is waiting for you in our classroom. If you'll follow me, I'll take you to her."

We ambled towards the rear of the house, navigating through a living room that was buzzing with the unmistakable evidence that children lived there. Scattered around were stuffed animals and toys, looking as though they'd been tossed aside just moments ago. But what truly caught my attention were the framed pictures hanging proudly on the walls. The hand-drawn images, filled with bold colors and abstract shapes, were clearly the works of children hung like masterpieces in a gallery. It made me smile that Mila was in a creative space.

When we got to the group home's classroom, Danica from Social Services was there waiting. She was younger, probably in her early thirties, and she had black hair with blue streaks and matching blue glasses. In an attempt to break the ice, I asked Danica if she was a fan of the hit 80's sitcom, Punky Brewster, but she just stared at me with confusion. This was how it began. The road to minivans and dad jokes.

"How are you, Mr. Hart?" Danica asked, sounding as if she knew I was nervous.

"I'm...I'm fine, I guess. As well as can be expected." I took a look around the room to make sure I didn't miss another person when I walked in, but it was just us. "Is Mila here?"

"She's outside playing. I wanted us to have a discussion before I asked Ms. Gladys to bring her back."

"How is she? Is she eating? Adjusting okay?"

I was preparing to launch into a full inquisition when Danica reached across the table and gently placed her hand on mine. "She's fine, I promise. She's a little shy, a lot shaken up, but extremely smart and funny once she opens up to you."

She had been through this before. It was clear that Danica had spent countless hours comforting both children and adults in the aftermath of tragedy or trauma. Her approach was gentle, her demeanor soothing. I didn't care about the blue streaks in her hair; I was instantly grateful for her presence and glad my sister had someone like her around.

"She talks about you quite a bit," Danica went on.

"Really?" I responded, taken aback. "I need you to understand, I wasn't aware she..." I hesitated, not wanting to steer the conversation towards the communication breakdown between my dad and me. "I hope he told her good things about me."

"It sure sounds like he did!" Danica chimed in cheerfully. "She never stops raving about your impressive music career and how you've toured with all sorts of famous artists and bands! She seems quite proud of her big brother."

A smile spread across my face, but it was fleeting. My mind was immediately racing with questions. *How does he know? Has he been keeping tabs on my career all this time? Who was feeding him information about me?* My mother had passed away from cancer a few years ago, and she hadn't spoken to him in over two decades. After all the years he'd been absent, without so much as checking in on us or offering support, she wouldn't have dared to divulge any details about my life to him. And Danica's comment about Mila being proud of me — did that mean my dad was proud of me, too? These thoughts added to the mountain of questions that had been piling up ever since I found out about his passing.

"Sir, I hate to be forward, but…"

"It's okay," I whispered, suddenly overcome with emotion. "You can be straight with me, Ms. Taylor."

"What will you do? What are your plans for her?"

"I don't know. I honestly don't know. My first priority is just to meet her and let her know that she has me."

"Yes, but," Danica cautiously interjected. "After that, what will you *do*? She needs stability, and while Warm Springs is an excellent facility, it's not a permanent solution, Mr. Hart."

"Look, Ms. Taylor, I appreciate the severity of the situation, but my life is not set up to welcome a child into it. I work late hours, I travel on school nights, I live with a woman who, under no uncertain terms, has blatantly stated I can't bring a child there! I'm not in between a rock and a hard place. I'm in between a boulder and a mountain, neither of which are able to be moved simply by snapping my fingers."

Danica just looked at me with her warm, gentle smile and said, *"Because you have so little faith. If you have faith as small as a mustard seed, you can say to this mountain, 'Move from here to there,' and it will move."*

I jumped up from the table, instantly anxious by her recital of the popular Bible verse. "Matthew 17:20. I know the verse well," I said, pacing around the classroom.

"Sir, are you OK? Did I say something to offend —"

"Can we talk about plans later? I'd just like to meet Mila, if that's OK with you."

"Sure," Danica said, sounding confused. "I'll go and get her from outside."

I stood nervously in the corner as the classroom door inched open. I could see timid footsteps slowly making their way inside the door. "It's okay," I heard Danica saying to assure Mila. "He's really nice, and he didn't even bite me!" I heard Mila's laugh from outside the door.

Finally, the door came all the way open, and I was face-to-face with this petite person. We both hesitated, each waiting for the other to take the first step or say the first word. She was so still and appeared to be so frail, that I couldn't quite gauge her emotions; was she simply nervous, or was she still reeling from some sort of shock?

Her hair was neatly parted to one side, and a cascade of curly ringlets artfully concealed the bandage on her cheek. She was dressed in a charming little dress and matching shoes, an outfit that seemed carefully chosen for our introduction today. I took two steps forward as a show of willingness to know her, but not wanting to be too presumptuous to where I made her uncomfortable.

"Hi, Mila. You look very pretty today."

Her big, brown eyes darted up towards me, as if to say 'thank you for noticing.' Tears began to pool in her eyes, but she managed a soft whisper, "You look just like Daddy. You dress like him, too."

My heart shattered instantly for her. I had been standing face-to-face with this little girl for barely two minutes and already, I wanted to erase all the pain from her life. Just two brief minutes with me, and all she thought about was her daddy and his dressy suits that he wouldn't be caught dead without. I might not talk much about him, but you'd never hear me say my daddy didn't stay fly in his suits. He believed that how we presented ourselves to people, was how we presented God to them. So it was imperative that we always looked our best. I might not have inherited his hypocritical connection to God, but I stayed fresh and fly in my suits.

Once the initial awkwardness of our meeting had passed, I found myself sitting with Mila in the classroom for another hour. I ordered a pizza, but made sure to order enough for all the kids in the group home, creating a casual atmosphere for us to chat. After I shared some fun facts about myself, I invited Mila to open up, to share any details about herself that she wanted me to know.

Mila was twelve years old. Her parents were named Jaxon and Aurelia Hart. She believed Chloe and Halle Bailey were magical. Last year, her mom took her to a BTS concert, and she even got to go backstage. And the final fact she shared, with the most adorable grimace I had ever seen — she absolutely, unequivocally *hated* math. She told me she faked fainting spells on multiple occasions to get out of tests. Danica was right; Mila was funny. And I studied her, trying to find a connection or pieces of me in her.

We were laughing about her super powers of persuasion when Mila's face turned serious. "Jaxon? Can I ask you a question?"

I took a sip of my soda as I braced myself for what I assumed would be a question about her coming to live with me. "Sure, Mila. You can ask me anything."

"Do you still have a mommy?"

"I do still have a mommy, Mila. And so do you, too. It's just that, our mommies don't live with us anymore on earth. They live in our hearts."

"Do you think our mommies are in heaven?" she innocently asked.

It wasn't lost on me that she had questioned me about our mothers, but not our father. She seemed to be searching for a common bond between us as well, and I couldn't help but wonder if she felt the same detachment from our dad as I did. Had she also learned to find solace in her mom's arms or immerse herself in music when Dad was off on one of his rants? Perhaps we shared more similarities than I initially thought.

Chapter Eight

Jaxon

"Black can't be your favorite color!" Mila exclaimed. "It's technically not even a real color, so you're going to have to pick something different."

"Well, if this crayon box right here has a black crayon that I can color with, then I reject your rejection of my favorite color, little girl."

Mila shook her head as if she was giving up on me. "Men are hopeless.," she murmured.

This was my third time driving out to see Mila, and today we were out having lunch, just the two of us. After our first visit, I'd returned home, attempting to convince Remy once more about having Mila stay with us, even if just for a short while. But Remy was adamantly against the idea. I didn't pressure her, nor did I attempt to guilt-trip her into making a decision she was uncomfortable with. Remy, if nothing else, was a woman of her word and a woman who meant business. From the beginning, she made it clear to me what she was willing to do and what she wasn't, and I had to respect that.

I don't think I'd ever encountered anything like this before. For the first time, my usual charm and persuasive tactics had hit a wall. I'd always had a knack for swaying women, using just the right words at the perfect moment to get them to cater to me and do whatever I wanted. It had become something of a hobby for me, a game I enjoyed playing. However, it seemed I was now out of my depth.

Growing up, I observed how a well-timed phrase, spoken in the right tone, could have women bending over backward to fulfill any request. My father was a master at this, expertly using faith and scripture as tools to manipulate unsuspecting women into paying his bills or even sharing his bed. He was a true master of deception, and I was his protégé. Even if I hadn't realized it. Yet, here I was, all those tricks and strategies doing nothing to serve me when it came to my situation with Remy. I found myself at a loss, unable to sway her decision. This was definitely a new, humbling experience for me.

After finishing our meal and coloring pages that the restaurant had given us, we jumped back into my truck to head back to the Warm Springs group home. "What's your favorite song, little girl?" I asked, hoping to find a shared love for music. But it was silent, and she didn't answer. I glanced over to make sure she was OK or check if she had fallen asleep as soon as we got into the car, but she was just looking straight ahead with a tiny smirk on her face. "Oh, so you ignoring me?"

"I didn't know you were *talking* to me," she shot back in a sassy tone, her arms folded across her chest.

I pretended to roll my neck with a fake attitude like the girls used to in school. "Well, you're the only person in the car, so who else would I be talking to, *little* girl?"

"You'd be talking to whoever's name is little girl because *my name* is Milagros Hart. Miss Mila if ya nasty."

We both laughed hysterically at the Janet Jackson reference. "Oh, so you know a little somethin' about Janet Jackson, huh?"

"OMG yes! Janet Jackson is my mom's favorite! Every Saturday morning, she would wake me up to clean the house with Janet Jackson's music," she said with excitement. But moments later, I noticed a subtle change in her expression. Her excitement faded, replaced by a touch of sadness as she corrected herself, "Well...she *was* my mom's favorite."

Even after several visits, she didn't mention her mom or Dad much. Something I assumed she did to keep from getting sad, and I didn't want to pry. But God I hope she wasn't about to start crying. I didn't know how to deal with women's tears. I never knew whether to say something kind or pat them on the shoulder until they stopped. So instead of waiting for the water works to commence, I searched my phone for a familiar tune, connected my Bluetooth to Apple CarPlay, and let the sounds of Janet Jackson's "Rhythm Nation" fill the space. When I turned to see if the song was cheering her up, she looked up and gave me the biggest smile, a silent, 'Thank you' I imagined.

The group home was about fifteen minutes away, but the last few minutes driving in silence felt like an eternity. I wanted to say something. Let her know that it was OK to cry or feel sad. But I didn't want to slip and say the wrong thing and make the situation worse. Trying to keep my focus on the road, I glanced at her and noticed her knuckles had turned a ghostly white, her arms rigidly placed on either side of her on the seat. It looked as though she was bracing herself for a crash. Her body was trembling, and tears were carving paths down her face. What had just happened? She was fine a few minutes ago.

"Mila? Mila, are you okay?" I asked, my voice filled with concern. But she remained silent, her breathing becoming increasingly labored as her quiet sobs grew louder with each passing moment. "Mila, sweetheart, you need to tell me what's wrong," I pleaded, feeling helpless as she seemed lost in a world of her own, unreachable. I couldn't focus on her and focus on the road at the same time, so I pulled into the parking lot of a diner that we were approaching in the distance. It was one of those older spots without a name. Just a big, red sign that said, "Diner" on the building.

The thought of dialing 9-1-1 crossed my mind, but I hesitated, not wanting to escalate the situation and potentially traumatize her further. My heart pounded against my chest like a drum. I wasn't equipped to handle this. I felt lost, unsure of how to help her. And then, as if guided by a faint whisper, a name came to me: "Danica."

As Janet Jackson's "Love Will Never Do (Without You)" played through the car speakers, I scrambled to grab my phone. I hastily paused the music to make a call. Within seconds, the ringing tone echoed through the speakers — I hadn't even thought to disconnect the Bluetooth from my phone.

"Mr. Hart! Funny hearing from you!"

"Danica! Something's wrong with Mila!" I interrupted, making a mental note to address the flirty sound of her voice later.

"Oh my God! What's wrong?" she yelled, her voice rising to the level of urgency to match the moment.

"I don't know! She mentioned her mom and then she started crying and hyperventilating! What should I do?" I yelled, panic permeating my every nerve. "Danica, if anything happens to her…"

"It's OK, Mr. Hart. She's having a panic attack. We'll get through this together," Danica calmly said, instantly bringing a sense of calm to me.

Danica advised that we'd be in a better position to work through the necessary exercises if we were standing, so I unbuckled my seatbelt, jumped out of the car, and bolted to the passenger's side of the truck.

"Mila, sweetheart, could you do a favor for Ms. Danni? I want you to take a deep breath in, as if you're trying to breathe in all the air in the world, okay?" I began following Danica's breathing prompts as a show of support, silently urging Mila to breathe with me.

"Jaxon, is she breathing?"

"Yes, she's breathing," I confirmed, relief washing over me.

"That's my brave girl, Mila! Now, I want you to let that breath out slowly while counting to ten. Make sure you don't run out of air until you reach ten, alright?" Although Mila didn't vocalize her response, her nod was enough confirmation.

"Danica, she's nodding yes," I relayed.

"Good, Mila! Breathe in again just like you did before, honey! You're so brave and so strong. You are safe and you are loved, right Jaxon?" I was so focused on making sure Mila was breathing that I missed my cue. "*Right, Jaxon?*" Danica repeated.

"Oh! Uh. Yes," I clumsily recovered. "Mila, sweetheart. You are safe. And you are...loved, OK?"

Ten minutes passed, and by then, Mila's breathing had steadied. I had gotten her out of the car just so she could stretch and breathe, but she just stood there, hugging herself as tears continued to flow down her cheeks. Something stirred inside me, a feeling of protectiveness that I hadn't experienced before. Not sure what had come over me, but I wrapped my arms around Mila, joining her in that self-embrace.

For the first time, I felt an unfamiliar sensation — a sense of powerlessness to the unfolding situation. But unlike before, I didn't want to escape or shirk the responsibility. Instead, I found myself wanting to do whatever was necessary to ensure her safety. She didn't deserve any of this turmoil; her innocence was actively being drained out of he,r and I wanted to shield her from any future pain, panic, or tears. Not because I couldn't handle her hurt, but because I didn't want *her* to have to.

As I held Mila, I realized how different this situation was from my past experiences. In an effort to try to understand Mila or relate to her, I kept trying to compare her emotions or mannerisms to all the women I knew. But Mila wasn't a woman that I was trying to win over, and there was nothing I wanted from her other than her trust. It was a humbling experience, one that made me question the deceptive strategies I'd learned from my father. For the first time, I wanted to use my words and actions for comfort and reassurance, not manipulation.

As soon as Danica was reassured that we were alright, she ended the call. She promised to inform Gladys at the group home about the incident and guide her on the necessary care steps for such scenarios.

I was about to help Mila back into the car when I felt a small hand slip into mine. I paused, looking down at our intertwined hands and then up at her. I was touched by the sight of her tiny hand enclosed within mine. "Can we walk the rest of the way?" she asked, her voice barely above a whisper.

She was scared, and I hadn't realized it until now. My mind had been so consumed with my own issues with Remy and driving to visit Mila as often as possible, that I had overlooked her unique needs. She had been in a car accident where she lost both her parents, so the fact that car rides might be triggering should have been obvious. But clearly I had so much more to learn.

"Sure, sweetheart," I responded, my voice softer than usual. Then, I secured my truck, ensuring it was locked and safe, and then notified the manager of the diner where we were parked that I would return for my vehicle. With Mila's small hand gently nestled in mine, we began our journey. The road back to the group home wasn't particularly scenic or extraordinary, but the moment felt significant. Together, we navigated the path ahead, our shared silence speaking volumes about the bond that was slowly but surely forming between us.

Mila was a little girl, weighed down by grief and trauma, and it felt like her emotional needs were being overlooked. Suddenly I knew what I had to do, what my responsibility was to her. No matter the hurdles, no matter the challenges, I was determined to bring my little sister home with me.

She deserved more than the cold confines of the group home. She deserved warmth, love, and a place where she could heal. And I wanted to give that to her. Mila would come to live with me, and it wasn't going to be easy, but I was ready. For her, I would move mountains if I had to.

Chapter Nine

Hadassah

I hated the notion of grief. I hated that something that seemed so innocuous could breeze in and out of your life, completely knocking the wind out of you without a moment's notice. Like an uninvited guest, slipping in and out of your life with no warning, leaving you breathless and disoriented. Grief had a way of dredging up emotions you'd tried so hard to hide or forget, spoiling your day or even an entire season of your life. So, I made a choice: I chose not to feel. I actively steered clear of situations and people that threatened to stir any emotions within me.

Some might find this impossible, especially since my job involved being around hundreds of lively, beaming kids. But I prided myself on my stubborn streak and resilience. And since no one really wanted to hear about the constant pain I dealt with every day, often prodding me about what I was doing to "move on," I'd become quite the expert at putting on a facade. Pretending to be okay. Pretending to be someone I wasn't.

This was something I never had to do with Lamar. He understood every inch of me better than anyone else ever could. I couldn't have a bad day without him noticing and knowing exactly how to cheer me up. If I needed time alone to decompress or center myself, he could always sense that, too. It wasn't every day that you found someone who loved you enough to study you the way he did. And if I couldn't have *him* here to share my feelings with him, if I couldn't have him as my sounding board, then I didn't want to *feel* anything at all.

"What are you planning to do over your Thanksgiving break?" Dr. Johana inquired. She was the trauma therapist who had been assigned to help students navigate their emotions following Lamar's tragic passing, but we eventually hired her as one of our school counselors. I had decided I didn't need therapy or to talk to anyone. I just wanted to bury myself in the work that Lamar and I had started together. If I could finish what we'd started, I'd be fine. But Dr. Johana wasn't having it. Despite my initial reluctance, even outright avoidance of her well-intentioned assistance, she voluntarily paid a weekly visit to my office just to check on me.

Over time, our relationship evolved. What started as a purely professional interaction morphed into something akin to friendship. After that first year, we began meeting outside of school, opting for more casual settings. Our favorite spot? A local black-owned coffee shop in the city called Black Coffee. It was a comforting place, a safe haven where we could talk openly, away from the prying eyes of the faculty at school.

"Oh, I'm planning to do absolutely nothing!" I cackled, pausing to take a sip of my toffee latte. Johana wasn't buying it. Her eyes peered into mine as if she was waiting for me to crack. "What!" I shrieked, waiting for her to tell me what she was angling at.

"You know *what*, Dash. We talked about this! You're supposed to be finding more opportunities to get out of the house and be around people!"

"But I *am* around people! All day! *Every* day!"

"I'm talking about *outside* of school. Don't play dumb with me."

I smacked my lips out of fake frustration. "I know what you mean but, as an introvert, I feel like you are unfairly prescribing me activities that are destined to drain me and pull me into an even deeper depression!"

"So, you've been feeling depressed lately? Tell me about that," Johana pounced.

"No! No!" I protested. "That is *not* what I said! I just meant that being around people unnecessarily exhausts me, and I don't want to spend my time of rest *intentionally* seeking to be worn out!"

"I understand that, Dash. But going out with friends, surrounding yourself with people who love you and care about you, that isn't unnecessary. That's *essential.*"

The bell above the door of the coffee shop chimed, signaling the arrival of four women who were wrapped up in their own world of laughter and conversation. "I get it, Jojo," I conceded, releasing a deep sigh as I allowed the sight of the lively group to transport me back to a time when I was the life of the party. A time when I'd host glamorous sleepovers at luxury hotels or eagerly volunteer to plan weddings or baby showers. I had to admit, that vibrant woman seemed like she died in that crash, too.

"Corinne *did* invite me to a birthday party at Sanctuary this week," I added, trying to offer Johana a semblance of victory for the day. "Maybe I *could* go, let my hair down a bit, I guess."

"Yes! That's what I'm talking about. We *all* just want you to be okay, to enjoy life a little, you know?"

I huffed wearily. "I know, Jojo. Geez. Guess I'm going to Sanctuary this week."

And that's how the game is played. By agreeing to her suggestion, I managed to make Johana feel like she'd made some progress. The truth? I'd attend the party, sure. I needed some new material for our next chat, after all. But truly 'letting my hair down?'That wasn't really on the agenda. I was open to a drink and a few laughs, but not much more.

As an introvert, social interactions felt like an elaborate game of role-play to me. To survive these encounters, I'd create an alter ego—a confident, self-assured temptress who commanded the room's attention but only spoke when absolutely necessary. This persona was mysterious, alluring, and unapproachable—a winning combination. I'd mingle with friends, maintaining the facade of being engaged and having a great time. And as long as there was liquor flowing and someone else stealing the spotlight, people didn't pay much attention to me. Most of the time, they were just glad I actually showed up. I might or might not have flaked on them a few times in the past. So, that was the plan. I'd attend Genevieve's birthday party and navigate the night through the lens of my alter ego.

After wrapping up our coffee date and paying the bill, I pulled out my phone while walking to my car.

With a hint of resignation, I texted: *Fine, bitch. I'll see you at Sanctuary.*

Her response was almost instantaneous, bubbling with excitement.

(Corinne) *OMG, yay! I can't wait to see you! It's gonna be so much fun!*

(Me) ***Party hat emoji*.**

Chapter Ten

Jaxon

Tonight marked my first live performance in over a month and I had just finished the first set of the evening. Juggling the complexities of Mila's situation had demanded my full attention. Fortunately, Lu had graciously given me some time off from the wine bar, assuring me she wouldn't fill my spot. But to keep the vibe alive and ensure the wine bar never missed a beat, my boy Spiro stepped up to cover for me whenever I was away. He'd toured with big names like Adele and sung background for artists like Eric Benet, so Spiro wasn't just a fill-in; he was a powerhouse performer. I knew without a doubt that Lu's spot was in excellent hands.

Remy had become impossible in the midst of all this. She went from being this sexy, cool woman that I could see as a partner, to this cold, shell of a woman that seemed to want nothing to do with me so long as I was choosing someone else before her. I always imagined that things would end up like this between us, distant and cold. But I thought it would be because I messed around with another woman or got bored with this arrangement, *not* because I was trying to help my only living relative on the planet.

She stopped sleeping with me and she'd even begun staying out all night, coming home at two and three in the morning, and then sleeping in the guest apartment in the basement. I tried everything to get through to her, but she was effectively done with me. I hated what that did to me. I wasn't hurt or heartbroken, just stunned that *this* was what it came down to. After the last year of us hanging out, making appearances together in a very power-couple like fashion, I didn't even recognize the woman that Remy had morphed into. Her behavior made the decision easier. It was time to look for a place of my own for me and Mila.

I had to snap myself out of the shock I was experiencing. Hart men didn't chase after women, nor did we beg them for anything. Besides, it was all about Mila now. All of my time, attention, and energy would be focused on her for the foreseeable future. So I didn't have time to waste thinking about what the hell had happened with Remy. I needed to reconnect with that part of me that was nonchalant and didn't give a damn. The part of me that could make a woman yield to my every desire without breaking a sweat. I missed what that kind of power, focus, and control did for my ability to turn off distractions, and I needed to channel that energy. Tonight was my last night of unrestrained freedom, and I was ready to bring that side out...*to play.*

"You look nice," Lu noticed. "But then again you always do in your fly suits."

I smirked at the compliment, knowing that Lu had a thing for a brother who knew how to wear a suit. "Thank you, love. You know I can't show up to your fine establishment just looking any old kinda way," I said, popping my collar for emphasis.

While Lu and I would never cross into romantic territory again, we didn't hold back on light-hearted flirting. Even though I couldn't find it in myself to love Lu in the way she deserved, my respect for her was unparalleled. After losing her home and restaurant to Hurricane Katrina, she had relocated to Atlanta and rebuilt her life from scratch for her and her twin boys. Today, she owned one of the most vibrant wine bars in the city that served classic New Orleans style cuisine.

Whenever I wrapped up a set at Sanctuary, my usual routine was to dart off to the back room. It wasn't that I didn't appreciate the adulation from groupies; I simply preferred to avoid the repetitive, mundane questions like, "Oh my God, where did you learn to play and sing like that?!" The admiration was flattering, sure, but the conversation? Not so much.

Tonight, though, things were going to be slightly different. Lu owned a cozy two-bedroom townhouse just a block away from Sanctuary. She typically rented it out on Airbnb, but she'd agreed to let me lease it so I could have a home for Mila. Tomorrow, I'd bring Mila home, unpack her stuff, and this place would transform into our private retreat. But tonight, that same townhouse was going to serve a different purpose. Tonight, it would be my lair. I had a plan up my sleeve. All that remained was to scout a worthy contender.

"Good evening, Jax," Melissa purred. "Great set tonight!"

Not her. Melissa could *not* be the woman I played with tonight. She was a regular here, and I could tell she was the type who, given just a *taste* of what I had to offer, would cling to me relentlessly. If I satisfied her even once, she'd want it forever.

"Thanks, Liss. Always a pleasure to see you, gorgeous." That didn't stop me from flirting with her shamelessly, though. After all, she kept bringing her friends to see me perform. Who was I to deny her the thrill of feeling like she might have a chance?

Suddenly, Lu came barreling around the corner from the back office. "Jax, I need you guys to get back on stage five minutes early tonight, okay? The crowd's more lively and antsy than usual, and only *you* have the magic touch to soothe them, darling," Lu flirted.

"Oh, you *know* I've got it," I shot back, both of us bursting into laughter at the blatant innuendo.

I resumed my quiet observation of the crowd, gauging the room's energy when the most captivating woman made her entrance. She had a natural beauty to her vibe that reminded me of Sza, before she had all of the work done. Her hair tumbled over her shoulders in thick waves, framing a pair of voluptuous lips painted with nothing more than a nude gloss.

She claimed a seat at the bar, her presence commanding attention. Men were drawn to her, and I watched as they flocked, one by one, offering drinks and inviting her to join their tables. Yet, she only responded with a gracious smile, her lips mouthing a polite "no thank you, I'm fine."

Mesmerized by her mouth, I decided that she needed a nickname. Something that suited her essence, and I arrived at 'Shiloh.' A beautiful Hebrew name that translated to 'tranquil,' 'abundance,' or 'his gift.' It was perfect—a subtle nod to the gift that she was the world, and the gift she would be to me tonight. I'd call her Shy for short.

My gaze traced her from a distance, drinking in the sight of her silver satin dress. It hung loosely where it should, draping off her body, yet clung to her enticingly where it mattered most. As she sat, her back elegantly arched while leaned forward, elbows planted on the bartop, engrossed in her phone, I caught a tantalizing glimpse of her right thigh. The slit in her dress was like an open secret, guiding my eyes along a path that promised miracles, signs and wonders of pure, unadulterated pleasure.

After about fifteen minutes or so, she was joined by a group of friends and she seemed to be in her element. She wasn't overly boisterous or drawing attention to herself. Rather, she had a certain aura that drew people in, a magnetic pull that was hard to resist. She carried herself with an air of discernment, as if she were selectively sifting through the evening's events, deciding what deserved her time and attention. The way she absorbed the energy around her, processed it, and chose what to engage with was fascinating. It was like she was curating her own personal entertainment for the night, and it was intriguing to watch. A challenge I eagerly accepted.

I turned in my seat and got up so I could make my way back to the stage. I wasn't going to approach her, yet. But I wasn't above walking by and making my presence and interest known, either. I dropped a hundred dollar bill on the bar top and grabbed a chilled bottle of Prosecco from the back, placing the bottle into a silver bucket of ice. Holding 4 champagne glasses, I casually strolled to the table where they were seated and said, "You lovely ladies look like you're celebrating something tonight. This one is on the house," but I only looked at her. My Shiloh. And I held her gaze to make sure sure she knew that I didn't give a fuck about anybody else at that table. I was there for *her*.

"Oh, Lord!" I heard Lu yell from behind the bar. "He's baaaack!"

Hadassah

My alter ego strikes again! It never failed. Whenever I channeled my inner vixen, who I liked to refer to as 'Sza the Stallion,' doors seemed to open, and opportunities just fell into my lap. From complimentary drinks to spontaneous marriage proposals, all it took was for *her* to confidently walk into a room and allow her essence to do the rest. So when a tall, fine brother wearing a tan suit with a carefully unbuttoned white shirt approached our table, I wasn't taken aback. His presence was as welcome as it was expected. But have *mercy*, I was so very grateful. Thanks Sza, girl.

There was something interesting about this man. Of course he was fine and he had a look that reminded me of the sexy black model and actor Chris Flanagan. But this man's appeal wasn't what you'd expect. He didn't carry himself with an air of expectation or entitlement, like most men that night seemed to. He didn't make the rookie mistake of assuming I was single, or even alone. Instead, he confidently presented us with the champagne and then retreated, leaving a trail of intrigue behind him. His gaze, however, had been fixed on me—intentional, yet not overly forward. It was a refreshing change, and I found myself drawn to it.

My curiosity piqued when I saw this very same man take center stage, introducing himself as Jaxon Hart—our entertainment for the evening. Given the smoldering way he had looked at me earlier, he had already claimed the role of my *personal* entertainer for the night. And as he began playing "In a Sentimental Mood," the version by Duke Ellington and John Coltrane, I surrendered myself to the melody. Closing my eyes, I let the music whisk me away to a different era, a different place.

The year after Lamar and I got married, I had the crazy idea to go to Mardi Gras. Knowing I was introverted and detested the idea of large crowds, Lamar thought I had to have been insane to suggest this. But it was a bucket list item, and dammit I wanted my beads! Lamar hated telling me no, so we packed up the car and drove to New Orleans for Fat Tuesday. I was so excited, I made him watch the movie "Girls Trip" twice on the way there.

"You do know this movie is set during Essence Fest, not Mardi Gras, right?" Lamar had teased. "And just to be clear, I'm your husband, not one of your girlfriends while you got me out here agreeing for you to bare boobs for beads!"

"That's not the point! Well, not the boobies part. The movie! I just want to soak up the vibe before we get there! It's like hype music, but in movie form."

Lamar had chuckled, shaking his head at my quirky logic, "Alright, fine. Get your hype on, then."

"And my boobies?" I asked, knowing good and well I was joking…probably.

Lamar let out a sigh and then shook his head laughing, "Permission granted."

"Yay!!"

As expected, within our first two hours in New Orleans, I was done. But not just done, I was having a full on panic attack from so many people. Where did they come from and why were so many of them naked?!

Back in the comfort of our hotel suite, I had laid on the bed with a warm towel over my eyes. Lamar emerged from the bathroom to find me clad in nothing but a white tank top, blue boy shorts, and my camel-colored Ugg boots.

"Do you want me to say it?" he'd asked.

"If you dare say 'I told you so,' Lamar, I swear..."

"I wouldn't dream of saying that! I would, however, point out that you are an exquisite treasure. Treasures like you aren't meant to be lost in the masses. You talk a big game and act all fearless, but deep down, you cherish solitude and anonymity."

"You think you know me so well," I'd retorted.

"I don't *think*. I *know*."

"But I didn't get to flash my boobies for beads!" I'd whined.

"Why, Mrs. Hadassah St. James," he'd said, holding up a handful of colorful beaded necklaces. "I've got beads right here!" He bent down to nibble on my neck and ear while tickling me. Then he dropped his tone to a low rumble, "Now, how about that show?"

For the next three days, we stayed in our hotel room, only venturing out to eat or see sites in less populated areas. And one night, while walking down a relatively empty street, a trumpet player sat on the corner and played, "In a Sentimental Mood." For five, exquisite minutes, New Orleans was ours as we danced in the middle of the street. That was the night we claimed "In a Sentimental Mood" as *our song.*

Chapter Eleven

Hadassah

Realizing what that song would probably do to my mood, Corinne ordered shots. Lamar's mother played *our song* at the burial interment after his funeral and I didn't stop crying for two hours. But tonight I was fine. Between Me, Sza and a little confidence brought to you by a lot of THC, it was going to take more than a song to knock me off my game tonight. I still took that shot of tequila, though.

A gentle smile spread across my mouth as a familiar tune began to play. It was "The Way You Make Me Feel" by Michael Jackson, but it wasn't the normal rhythm. It was slower. Sensual. And the lead singer was singing the words in an octave lower than the original rendition. Noticeably feeling this version of the song, grooving in my seat and rocking back and forth, I caught a glimpse of Jaxon smiling right at me as he sang.

Laughing off his transparent flirtation, I rolled my eyes and deliberately turned my gaze elsewhere. I didn't want to give him the satisfaction of knowing he had caught my attention. But he was good; and I'm not just talking about his musical genius. His thick, black lips, perfectly framed by a meticulously groomed goatee, hinted at an array of other talents he likely possessed. And as much as I tried to ignore it, there was an undeniable magnetism about him that was hard to escape.

As the band began playing the opening chords of "Whip Appeal" by Babyface, I watched as couples and groups of single ladies gravitated towards the dance floor. I *loved* that song. When I was thirteen, you couldn't tell me that me and Babyface weren't going to end up married. His lyrics had this ability to make you feel like he was singing just for you everytime he opened his mouth.

I'd always admired artists who could communicate so eloquently through their craft. Jaxon, it seemed, was no different. Every note he sang that night felt like it carried a secret message meant just for me. And each time he delivered a suggestive lyric, his eyes would find mine, checking to see if I was still watching him. I was.

The night's final song took me back to my teenage days when we'd stay up late just to catch our favorite song on the radio. When we'd hurriedly hit the play and record button simultaneously, desperate to capture the song on the B-side of our homemade mixtape. It was Shai's "If I Ever Fall In Love." The song wasn't as sensual as the others, but it still hinted at something more, something I couldn't quite put my finger on.

"Dash, we're so happy you made it out tonight!" Corinne's voice rang out. "And look at you! The perfect wing woman, turning down all these guys, leaving them no choice but to flock to *me*!" she said, her words punctuated with a playful shriek.

"Well, we all have to play our part, right?"

"We're headed over to Drew's house for the after party, you wanna come?" she asked. Andrew Sanders, the former NFL Linebacker and unbelievably beautiful Gym teacher at Biddy Mason, was known to have people over for night caps and board games where they'd change all the rules to make it a drinking game. Corinne was batting her eyelashes as if she was really begging me to come, but she knew I'd probably be calling it a night.

As predicted, my friends seemed perfectly content all evening, never once questioning my silent demeanor. As long as I flashed a smile and laughed along with their nasty jokes, they were easily convinced that I was having as much fun as they were. Not even Genevieve noticed. She was in her fifties, about ten years older than most of us in the group, but she *stayed fly.* She was a slender woman with golden skin, green eyes, and a body that let you know she'd been fly all her life. By now, she would have cozied up beside me and made sure I was okay while no one was looking. But tonight, she was in her element, and I loved that for her. I loved that she was enjoying herself and not worried about me.

I almost didn't come tonight. I almost let my aversion to *living* keep me from enjoying a few simple pleasures. I thought I would be inundated by old men with missing teeth and too much cologne. However, contrary to my initial expectations, tonight turned out to be a pleasant surprise. I genuinely enjoyed myself. And the reason behind this unexpected delight? It had everything to do with my private performance. *He* was the reason for my memorable evening.

I found myself wanting to thank him, maybe even offer to buy him a drink while my courage was still intact. But I knew that would open a door I wasn't ready to walk through. He'd expect more — my phone number, a date, daily good morning texts designed to make me smile. And that was something I wasn't prepared for. I wasn't ready for the burden of emotions or the expectations that came with them. At least...That's not what I'd want after just *one* encounter. One spontaneous night.

"Alright, well, we're about to head out. Our Uber's nearly here. You sure you'll be okay?"

Corinne asked, concern lining her voice as she searched my eyes for assurance that I was indeed OK.

"Yes, I'll be fine, I promise. My driver will be here shortly. I'm just going to make a quick stop in the ladies' room before I leave. You girls go ahead, have fun at Andrew's, and tell him I said hello," I assured her.

"Okay, bye!" They all chorused, as they hurried out the door to catch their Uber.

I found myself frozen in front of the ladies' room mirror, locked in a silent stare-down with my own reflection. What was I thinking? Was I genuinely toying with the idea of surrendering myself to this man for the night? My alter ego had never ventured this far before. She was merely a coping mechanism, a persona I slipped into when I had to navigate through uncomfortable events or situations that triggered my anxiety. But this... this was straying into unfamiliar territory.

Still, a part of me was craving this, yearning for a taste of the unknown. I wanted to let loose, to experience a spark of joy, even if it was fleeting. I was under no illusion that this would be a remedy for my pain. It wouldn't heal the deep-seated trauma caused by the sudden collapse of my family, the abrupt disintegration of my world as I knew it. But it *could* offer a brief respite, a momentary sense of completeness...even if it was just for one night. I just wanted to feel... *something.*

I quickly grabbed my phone to text my driver, letting him know I wouldn't need him after all. Then I reapplied my nude gloss, smoothed out my dress, and prepared to leave the ladies' room. However, as soon as I stepped out, I walked straight into... *him.*

"My apologies," he murmured, his voice a low, seductive rumble. "I didn't intend to bump into you like this."

"But you *did* intend to bump into me?" I countered, tilting my head up to look at him. Even in heels I only reached his chest, so he had to be much taller than six feet. Maybe six-foot-two?

"Well, I certainly hoped to. Couldn't you tell by..." He trailed off, smoothly sidestepping to let a group of ladies pass by. He positioned himself casually against the wall, one hand tucked into his pocket while the other rested above me, looking every bit like a Morris Chestnut-Elba. Leaning in closer, he brushed my hair off my shoulder, his lips grazing my ear as he continued, "my performance? Didn't it clue you in on just how much I wanted to *bump into you?*"

My breath hitched as his voice vibrated through me, his warm whisper sending shivers down my spine. But I needed to stay in character. I was the confident, enigmatic temptress who wasn't easily won over. "Your performance was exactly that," I retorted, refusing to reveal that whatever he was doing was having an effect on me. "It was a performance. And the one thing I've learned about performers is that they can turn it on or off at will. So, while your act might have *seemed* tailored for me, I'm only moved when I know I'm receiving something that no one else can have."

With that, I sauntered off, leaving him leaning against the wall, a picture of surprise and intrigue. But with a challenge, nonetheless.

Jaxon

I followed behind her, watching her hips sway back and forth as the satin clung to the coke bottle that was her temple. I wasn't done with her. I wanted her, and the fact that everyone else in the building wanted her too made my hunger for her even more intense. She took the same seat at the bar that she'd sat in earlier and waited for the bartender to greet her. I stood off to the side and observed as she ordered two fingers of Remy Martin cognac, something I hadn't heard anyone order in quite a long time. *So, she's a vintage kind of lady. I can work with that.* Even though she did happen to channel coincidental thoughts of Remy, I brushed it off.

As soon as the bartender slid her drink across the counter, I smoothly settled into the seat beside her. I caught the eye of a younger man who had been eyeing the same spot, and I held up my hand and gave him a knowing look; a silent 'I've got this.'

She was a secret that drew me in, willing me to uncover it. Her smile was friendly but never too inviting, maintaining an air of mystery. Her fingers absent-mindedly traced her bare ring finger—a hint of a marriage or divorce, perhaps? The way she moistened her lips before savoring her first sip was intoxicating. I bet she tasted like a blend of sweet honey and cinnamon.

Leaning closer, enough to where my breath on her neck would meet her before my words did, I whispered softly in her ear, "Speaking of turning you on..."

A soft giggle escaped her, and she seemed taken aback by my bold statement. She didn't look at me or turn in my direction, but simply responded with a playful, "Yes? You were saying?" before taking another sip of her drink.

"Well, you wanted something unique, something no one else has," I reminded her.

"I believe you're mistaken. I didn't *ask* you for that. I merely implied that I'm not easily impressed or moved by one-size-fits-all gestures. If you want me, you're going to have to give me something no one else has."

"Ah yes, I remember now." I paused, absorbing her presence—her breaths, her smiles, her hidden pain. Despite her cool and composed demeanor, something in her eyes hinted at a vulnerability beneath the surface. I watched her subtly avoid the gaze of other men passing by. She seemed lost in thought, and I found myself willing to spend every penny just to know what was on her mind. "What's your name?" I asked, hoping to peel back another layer of her mystery.

She took a deep breath, "Does it matter?"

I smirked, "It does to me. But if you prefer not to tell me, that's fine. I already gave you a nickname anyway."

"Oh! We're already at the nickname phase of our relationship, huh?" She took another sip of her drink before continuing. "Well, aren't you gonna tell me what it is?"

"If I reveal it, what's in it for me?"

"You get to continue talking to me. How's that?"

"I can dig that. I enjoy talking to you, even if you're not saying much."

"You noticed that, huh?"

"When it comes to you, there's nothing I'd miss. You are worth not just remembering, but studying."

"You sure do know how to make a girl blush. More of your performance, I presume?"

"Shiloh," I interrupted.

"I'm sorry?"

"Your nickname. It's Shiloh, or Shy for short."

She smiled. "Shiloh. I like that. What does it mean?"

"It's Hebrew. It means tranquil, abundance, or his gift. From the moment I saw you, I thought of you as my gift."

She threw her head back and laughed heartily at that, clearly thinking I was doing too much. I couldn't help but follow the curve of her neck as it disappeared into the neckline of her dress, offering just a hint of her cleavage.

"OK, Mr. Jaxon Hart. I know this suave act probably gets you plenty of ladies whenever and wherever you please, but that's not what I'm looking for. You don't have to wine and dine me or whisper sweet nothings to get me ready for what happens next. We clear?"

I studied her expression to see if I could decipher exactly what she was saying. Was she saying what I thought she was saying? Was she offering me an evening with her without my having to pull out all of my usual stops?

"What are you saying, Shy?"

She looked around the bar and observed the various people around. The couples grabbing their coats and heading out of the door. Then she turned her gaze back to me. "I'm saying… yes."

That was all I needed to hear. Consent. I peered into her eyes and with a voice that was almost a growl, I said, "Wait here." I left to pack up my equipment and pay my band, eager to take this goddess back to *my* sanctuary, my playground for the night.

Chapter Twelve

Hadassah

Since Jaxon's house was just a block away from Sanctuary, we agreed to walk.

"You mind if I smoke?" I asked, completely taking him off guard.

His eyebrows raised at the question. "A cigarette?"

"No! A pre-roll!"

"Weed. That's surprising," he said, gently guiding me to the inside of the sidewalk as we strolled. He was a gentleman. Interesting.

"Yeah. Something I picked up after...well, after a lot hit my life at once. But I don't care how stressful my life gets, if you ever catch me smoking a Newport, shoot me in the head!"

He watched me. Not staring in a creepy way, he studied me. I kept stealing glimpses of him watching my moves and mannerisms as if I was an equation and he was trying to solve me for X.

Not wanting to be too emotionally vulnerable with him, I redirected his focus by surprising him with a tease. Purposefully wetting the tip of the joint with my tongue as my lips curled around it sent a surge of desire through him.

"Not judging, but what happened that drove you to smoking weed?"

"No," I retorted quietly.

I looked up at him just in time to see the confused look on his face, accentuated by his furrowed eyebrows. "Huh?"

"Nothing personal, OK?"

"Okay…?"

A car blasting a Drake song sped past us when I asked, "You do this often?"

"Do what often?" It was clear he wanted me to spell it out, to acknowledge the palpable tension between us and what would inevitably come next.

"*You know* what I'm asking you. I mean, you're a musician, so I assume the answer is yes, but…I don't know. I…I guess I'm just making conversation."

Nervousness was creeping in, and my words were becoming jumbled and flustered. My thoughts began to spiral, and I was beating myself up for even attempting this when I felt him reach for my hand. I jumped slightly at his touch.

Stopping us in our tracks, he turned my body to face him. "Full disclosure, I've taken *many* women home in the past. But it's been more than a year since I have done anything like this, and no one has ever set foot in the place I'm taking you tonight. This is my last night of freedom, and I'm choosing to spend it with you. This entire experience will be unique to *you*." Then he leaned into my petite frame, planting a sweet kiss on my cheek, before continuing our walk, my hand still clasped in his.

"So, this is a new place for you? The house, I mean?"

"Something like that."

He was much too confident. Much too good at putting a woman's nervous system at ease. And so, I decided that he was one of those players who had perfected the game of seduction. The ones that never had less than a few women in rotation.

"Do you have a—"

"For someone who doesn't want to get personal tonight," he interrupted, "you sure do ask a lot of questions, Shy."

"I'm sorry," I said nervously. "I guess I-"

"You can relax, baby. You don't have to pretend anymore," he assured me. "Tonight, you want something that's different from your norm. Perhaps you want to feel something that you haven't felt in a while, and you required two shots of cognac and some THC to be brave enough to go after it."

"You got all that from a few spoken words, huh?" I quipped.

"Like I said, I've been studying you all night."

"Interesting. I sat for hours with my friends and they didn't pick up anything close to what you just did."

"Familiarity. People tend to stop paying attention to what they think they already have figured out. They stop studying you, and then, before you know it, they're taking you for granted."

"He's insightful, too," I murmured and he squeezed my hand at that.

We finally reached the front of Jaxon's townhouse—and he turned to me. "This is me," he said, gesturing towards the building. "We can either go in, or we can stand here while I call you a rideshare. But if you choose to stay, once we cross that threshold, Shy, you're *mine*."

Reaching out, he gently took my right hand, bringing the delicate inner wrist to his mouth. He planted a soft kiss there, and my pulse quickened beneath his lips. Then, with the same arm, he guided it around his neck as he dipped his head to capture my lips in a tender kiss. He tugged lightly on my bottom lip with his teeth while simultaneously pulling me closer into his embrace. I was tentative, my movements clumsy and slow, but I didn't resist.

Our breaths became labored and I pulled away. My mouth was no longer touching his lips, but my forehead was still pressed against his. "First," I panted, my chest rising and falling rapidly, "I have rules."

"Okay," he smiled, taking a step back to give us some breathing room. "Let's hear your rules."

"First, you will *never* know my name. What happens tonight is only for tonight, no matter how good you are in bed or how many times you make me come. Second, no oral. It's too intimate and..."

"That's not what you're here for?" he offered, completing my sentence.

"Right. And thirdly," I continued, my voice barely above a whisper as it threatened to crack with emotion, "don't kiss me like that again."

"Like how?"

A single tear escaped down my right cheek. "Like you love me... Like you're about to *make love* to me. It's..." My voice trailed off as another tear threatened to escape my eye before I blinked it away. "Just not like that, okay?"

I saw a pang of something akin to pity eclipse his face, but he quickly brushed it aside.. "I think there was some confusion when I said 'once we go in, you're mine,' because that's precisely what I meant. Now, I won't pry into why you're seeking a manufactured experience tonight, but I won't pretend not to *see* you either."

"*See* me?" I questioned, my voice laced with timid uncertainty. "What do you mean?"

He chuckled dryly, "You haven't been listening to me, have you? I've been studying you. Even up until right now, observing your mood and mannerisms. You're a force to be reckoned with, no doubt about it. But you're not the heartless enchantress that you're pretending to be, either. You may have convinced *yourself* that you don't want intimacy, but one taste of your lips, and I know you long for it. Long for *me*.

"So, here's how tonight will go down. If you choose to walk through those doors with me, I won't just fuck you like a disposable plaything. I will savor every moment *with* you while pleasing you with every inch of me. Baby, I promise you *all* of the intimacy as I please you in ways you can't even imagine. And that nonsense about no oral? Sweetheart, I intend to use my tongue in ways you didn't even know were possible."

I stood there, dumbfounded, as he shredded my ground rules and placed them at my feet. "My house, *my* rules," he added.

He closed the gap between us, glancing around to ensure we were alone. His gaze barreled into me as his right hand raised my skirt and gently traced my inner thigh, seeking my core. Once he reached the gates of my entrance, he used his pinky and ring fingers to slide my lace thong to the side, and he moaned at first touch.

"Mmmm. There it is. Warm, inviting, and wet with anticipation for me," he purred.

Holding my gaze, he asked in a low, smoky tone, "Mine. Am I clear?" Not waiting for my response, he used two fingers to venture into the depths of me, exploring every inch.

My breath struggled to escape my lungs as a symphony of shock, pleasure, or perhaps delight raged through me. I let out a soft whimper as my fingers found his shoulders, gripping them for support and my head fell into my chest.

"Jaxon, what are you doing to me?" I panted as his fingers moved rhythmically inside me, each thrust sending waves of pleasure coursing through my body. His eyes never left me, and he tensed as my nails dug into his neck. He stalked my pleasure, the look in his eyes telling me he was going to enjoy drawing this out all night long.

My insides pulsated as I rocked into his hand, the wetness that was escaping down my legs signaled I was about to unravel. Then, he swiftly withdrew his fingers. "You can't come yet," he teased, letting my dress slip back into place. I bit my bottom lip as he brought his finger to his lips and licked the remnants of my essence.

Guiding me up the steps, he fished around his pocket for the key card while I stood in front of him, my gaze fixed straight ahead. His erection dangerously close to the edge of my back. Opening the door, he leaned in, pressing a soft kiss against my cheek from behind.

"Now," he instructed in a husky whisper, "go inside, go up the stairs, and head straight into the master bedroom at the end of the hall. You can't miss it. Then, I want you to take off all your clothes, take a shower or bath, whichever you'd like. Then slip into the bed and wait there for me."

This man was going to ruin me. And not in the romanticized sense of being 'ruined for all other men.' No, this was different. One fleeting glimpse at the sheer length and girth of his erection, and I found myself questioning the resilience of my gag reflexes. I had no idea what I'd signed up for, or how far I was willing to push my boundaries with this unexpected surge of confidence and boldness. But I was inside his house now—I was *his* for the night, and there was no turning back.

Obediently, I ventured into the master bedroom, a space so lavishly decorated that it was hard to believe a man had any hand in its design. Regardless of how sexy he was or how effortlessly he wore a suit, this room screamed of a woman's touch. Maybe he was getting married or settling down soon. The thought brought me back to his words when we were outside, *"This is my last night of freedom, and I want to spend it with you."* It seemed we were both seeking some form of an escape tonight—a shared desire to momentarily forget our realities and lose ourselves in each other.

The bathroom was an extension of the bedroom's opulence. The shower had dual shower heads on either side, and a bench for sitting, shaving, or...other things. And, further confirming the presence of a woman *somewhere,* I discovered unopened travel-sized bottles of women's body wash, untouched loofah sponges, and pristine shower caps tucked away under the bathroom sink. This *house* might have been new to him, but the art of seduction—the act of making a woman feel pampered, cared for—was evidently not new territory for Jaxon Hart.

When I stepped out of the shower, I noticed that there were no towels around. Panic surged through me as I frantically hunted for something—anything—to dry and drape myself in. Nothing. Swinging the bathroom door open, a billowing cloud of steam rushed out like it was desperate to escape. I called out, "Hello... Hey, Jaxon? I need a towel!"

Moments later, he walked into the room, cradling a tray with an assortment of oil-filled bottles. "You don't need a towel," he declared, his voice a commanding whisper. "Now lay down on the bed, like I asked."

I just stood there frozen, not out of some feigned defiance, but from sheer speechlessness. A potent wave of arousal washed over me, leaving me breathless. These little girls on the internet might be complaining about mens' dominance and forcefulness, but I found an undeniable attractiveness in it. The way this man asserted his authority, confidently issuing directives, was intoxicating. His commands weren't abrasive demands, but an enticing call to surrender, stirring a yearning within me that I hadn't known before. The raw, unapologetic power he exuded, and the promise of being desired with such intensity, left me weak at the knees.

And so, I stood there, caught in the throes of a desire so potent it left me speechless. His dominance wasn't about control; it was about passion. A passion that could consume you, and I reveled in it. It was provocative, it was exciting, and above all, it was sexy as hell.

He sat the tray on the edge of the bed, then closed the distance between us. He pulled me into a sensual kiss, his tongue teasing mine in a tantalizing dance that nearly unraveled me. Then, just as abruptly as before, he pulled away, jolting me from my momentary bliss. "Now, will you lay down, please?"

I obeyed, reaching to pull back the covers when his growl stopped me. "Don't you dare cover that beautiful body up."

I bit my lip as a whirlwind of emotions swept over me. He crawled on top of the bed and bent over me, and I thought he was going to kiss me again, when instead, he began softly blowing his warm breath all over my body. Beginning at my neck, down to my breasts, then my stomach and torso area, my...nether regions. My body rose and fell with heavy breaths, chills covered my body, and I ached for him like I couldn't believe.

I wasn't sure what I had been expecting, but this...this was beyond anything I could have imagined. If he was going to lead me on a journey of fantasy and foreplay, I was gonna need more weed!

"Open your legs for me."

"I...I'm sorry?" I stammered, my mind racing to catch up with my mouth.

"Spread your legs, Shy," he commanded, paying no attention to my confusion.

So, I did as I was told. I laid on the bed and spread my legs for him. "Good girl," he praised, his gaze appreciative as it roamed over me. "You're breathtaking, do you know that?"

"I do, but tell me again?" I teased, as my middle finger traced slow, wet circles around my pulsating center. I wanted to drive him crazy and, if he was the kind of animal I thought he was, this would push him over the edge.

He stood silently for a few minutes, a captive audience. Realizing I had his full attention, I bit my lip, intensifying my movements with eyes closed, ignoring his presence. It worked - opening my eyes revealed passion ignited in his gaze as he marveled at my intimate act.

Then came the growl again, I was beginning to like the sound of that. "Move your hand," he ordered. And with one swift motion, his mouth replaced my fingers and his tongue lavished my clit as if it held the elixir of life. My arms flung out across the bed and my back arching in ecstasy as he licked, sucked, and teased me to the brink of climax. And then, just as he had before, he pulled away, leaving me bereft of his touch.

"OK, you have *got* to stop doing that!" I protested, my body humming and shaking with unfulfilled desire.

His response was silence. He quietly removed himself from between my legs, a mute promise of return in his smoldering eyes. I watched as he moved towards the tray, retrieving the oil-filled bottles he had brought in. He picked up one that had clear liquid cradling an assortment of flowers and rose petals, then poured a few drops into his hands.

I smiled seeing that his mustache still bore the evidence of my pleasure, soaked with my essence.

With my right leg perched on his shoulder, he began his sensual exploration. His hands, warm and sure, massaged and traced a path up my body, starting from my ankles and working their way up to my calves. Each stroke was deliberate, unhurried, sending shivers of anticipation all over my body. Every so often, he would pause, pressing soft kisses to my skin where his hands had just been, each touch leaving a trail of goosebumps in their wake. I found myself captivated by the sight of him—the tension in his muscles, the focus in his eyes, the raw desire radiating from him. But what held my gaze captive was the bulge in his pants, a threatening promise of what was to come.

As he moved to lavish the same attention on my other leg, I couldn't help but let out a sigh of anticipation. The night was young and there was still so much left to explore.

"Your body is a work of art," he whispered as he poured more oil into his hands and then gently bent over to massage it into my stomach and then my breasts. His thumb traced sensual circles around my nipples, pinching and squeezing them until they were so hard, they pointed to the heavens. This man had transformed my body into his temple, and he was there to worship.

Words eluded me. Every command he issued, I followed. Every way he moved my body, I yielded. I was mute, lost in the whirlwind of passion and pleasure that had swept over me. It had been so long since a man had desired me and had me in such a vulnerable state, that I found myself paralyzed by the intensity of it all. And yes, beneath the waves of pleasure, there was a hint of guilt. A twinge of guilt that I quickly pushed aside.

As if sensing my internal struggle, Jaxon's voice cut through my thoughts. "Where are you going, Shy?"

His question startled me. "What? Huh?"

"Your eyes," he said, his gaze intense. "They're telling me you're drifting away. You're not here with me, and I need your undivided attention, baby. Focus on me."

His words hung in the air for a moment before Alexa chimed in, "Now playing 'Focus' by H.E.R." The timing was so perfect we both burst into laughter.

But when the laughter subsided, the atmosphere shifted. The music seemed to ignite something within him, unleashing an animalistic fervor. He set about ravishing me, his mouth descending onto my nipples, sucking and biting while his tongue teased. His hands roamed my body, exploring every inch of me, before finally stopping at my core. I gasped as he entered me with one finger, then two, issuing waves of pleasure.

"Shit!" I yelled, as he dropped to cover me again with his mouth, his fingers never leaving their place inside me.

"My first scream of the night. I was beginning to worry I wasn't doing my job," he smirked.

"You gotta work for it," I panted, barely able to string two words together.

"I'm not above putting in work, baby. Trust me, there are more screams where that came from," he said, flashing me a devilish grin. Then he knelt down to reclaim my clit.

His tongue was long and thick as it licked me from end-to-end and his fingers rhythmically went in and out, circling my core. I panted, "You better not stop this time!" I was there. Close. So close to my release I was shaking. My leg wrapped around his back, and my foot glided up and down his spine as I arched in preparation for my orgasm. "Oh my God. Oh my…"

"That's it," he praised. "Come for me, baby."

"Yes! Yes! Shit! Yes!" I screamed, convulsing and panting. I grabbed a pillow and pulled it over my head out of embarrassment. I didn't want him to see me that...*open.*

He yanked the pillow from my head and licked me from my belly button all the way up through the center of my breasts, stopping to nibble on my right ear before whispering, "And I'm just getting started. Now roll over."

I rolled over onto my stomach, folding my arms under my head as I turned my gaze to him. He reached into the side drawer, pulling out a condom and placing it on the bed next to him. He paused, his eyes locking onto mine with a hunger that was palpable. But there was something else lurking in his gaze, an emotion or feeling I couldn't quite place.

As if reading my thoughts, his voice broke the silence. "I wish I knew you, Shy. I wish we'd been friends turned lovers who had loved each other for years before this moment."

His words caught me off guard, and I searched his eyes for meaning. "Why do you say that?"

"Because," he said, his voice soft but firm. "I had plans for you. Plans to play with you tonight. But you're not the kind of woman who can handle that kind of *play* without love. And I don't want to rob you of that tonight. No matter what you *think* you're looking for."

I don't know what he had in mind, but his sentiment was sweet. He was a beast inside, but he was subduing his beast on the account of me. What he saw *in* me. "Don't tell me you're regretting this."

His response was immediate. "Quite the contrary. I'm savoring this." As he spoke, his hands began to roam my body, massaging my back with slow, deliberate movements that sent shivers down my spine.

He had a level of control that I couldn't believe. His dick *had* to be throbbing. He had to be torturing himself by the constant start and stop of this because I was certainly being tortured by the anticipation. Finally, I saw him reach for the condom to unwrap it and then cover himself with it. This was it. This was how the ending and the undoing of me began.

He slowly crawled on top of me, using his arms to steady himself as he hung over me. "Roll over, baby, I wanna watch your face while you take me in."

"No," I whispered. "You can't look at me, OK?" I was feeling all sorts of emotions, and I couldn't be sure I wouldn't cry the first time a man entered me since Lamar.

He kissed the nape of my neck, tracing a path down my spine with his tongue, and I felt him at my entrance. His presence was demanding, yet gentle. His hands coaxed my legs apart before he reached around my waist, lifting me to meet him. Our breaths hitched simultaneously as the first wave of pleasure crashed over us when he breached the opening of my slick folds. My head fell onto the pillow, my fingers digging into the sheets as sounds I'd forgotten I could make escaped my lips.

"Stay with me, baby," he pleaded, his voice strained with desire. "I'm not all the way in yet."

"You won't break me, Jaxon. Don't hesitate. Don't question. Just... please me. Now!" I demanded. Before I could finish my sentence, he had thrusted his way fully inside, and I cried out from the concoction of pleasure mixed with pain. His thrusts were long, measured, and deep, and all I could offer were incoherent moans as he owned me with each stroke.

"So good," he murmured possessively, lost in our shared pleasure. A low curse slipped from his lips as he dropped his head to my back. "Fuck!" he murmured, his teeth grazing my skin as he bit into my back.

I attempted to inch towards the top of the bed, discreetly trying to find relief from the literal hole this man was tearing through my walls when he grabbed a handful of my hair, pulling my head back to bring my mouth to his. "Don't think I don't feel you tryna run from me," he teased. "Get back here." Then he returned to my neck, biting and marking me as if this was his last night on Earth, and I was his final meal.

My back arched while I moved in rhythm with his thrusts, each one crashing us together in a symphony of pleasure. "I'm going to come again, Jaxon," I warned.

"Not yet," he commanded, pausing his movements but staying inside me. "Take what you want tonight... Take whatever you need, okay?" His words reverberated through me. With a shake of my head, I silently agreed to his unspoken proposition. He rolled onto his back, carefully maintaining our connection, and guided me to straddle him.

Being on top usually left me feeling awkward, uncertain of whether or not I was doing it right. But with Jaxon, it was different. His hands steadied me, guiding me along the length of him. He held back, but there was undeniable tension building inside him. Gradually, I found my rhythm, my body moving in sync with his, and I heard Van Hunt's "Seconds of Pleasure" come over the house speakers.

His hands traveled from my hips to my waist, finally coming to rest on my breasts. He rose up to take each one in his mouth, his tongue and lips working their magic while I surrendered to the ecstasy of his warmth.

He laid back, reclaiming my hips and my ass with his hands. "You're going to undo me," he growled. "I can't hold back any longer, baby. Promise me you'll tell me if I hurt you, okay?"

I met his gaze, my eyes flashing with determination. I panted, "Hurt me!"

Without warning or reply, his right hand moved to my neck, holding me in place as he thrusted into me, hard and fast. His movements reached the very core of me, eliciting a sharp gasp, but I could barely breathe. His grip around my neck grew tighter, and I had never experienced such a mixture of pleasure and pain and ecstasy! My nails dug into his chest as I did what he'd demanded—I took what I needed. Each thrust unearthed emotions I'd buried for the past six years. Every suppressed tear, every hidden scream, I reclaimed them all with every crash into him. As heat rose inside me, signaling my impending release, I looked down to find Jaxon watching me, his eyes filled with a mixture of desire and admiration.

He moved his hand from gripping my neck and placed his thumb in my mouth, and I sucked and bit it. "Yes, that's it, Shy. Take it all," he urged.

Tears streamed down my cheeks as I whispered, "I love you. I love you so much. Tell me you miss me. That you love me. Please?" The plea slipped out before I could stop it.

A veil of confusion passed over his face, quickly replaced by an understanding that ran deeper than words. "I love you, baby. I miss you so much," he murmured. Then, he reached up, pulling my mouth to his, his tongue seeking mine in a dance as old as time.

His arms wrapped around me, drawing me into a bear hug as he maintained his rhythm. I felt him swell inside me, teetering on the edge of release. Harder. Faster. Hotter. The sweat from our bodies mingled as it dripped from my breast onto his skin.

"One more time, baby. Come with me, baby."

We both cried out as warmth began to radiate from us. He held me so tightly against him that I was immobilized, ruined by him with each thrust.

"Mine," he cried out, the word a primal declaration. "Come for me like you're mine." His erection twitched and swelled as I tightened around him, his final thrust echoed by a moan of satisfaction. "Fuck! Yes!" His head buried in my neck, lost in the waves of pleasure as he found his release.

"Fuck! Shit! Yes!" I screamed, my own climax washing over me. " Lamar! Baby!" I screamed.

And then, everything stilled. The realization of what I'd just said hit me like a punch to the gut. Panic seized me, and I scrambled to climb off of him, my mind a whirl of confusion. I had to get away. I started searching the room for my clothes so that I could quickly get dressed and get the hell out of there! What the hell was I thinking doing this? I was so silly for thinking I could pretend that everything...this...would be OK. That *I* would be OK after this!

"I'm sorry," I cried. "I'm so sorry for this. I'll just get my things and go, and you'll never hear from me again, OK?"

He didn't respond. But before I could completely exit the bed, Jaxon grabbed me and pulled me back to him, enveloping me in his chest. That's when I fell apart. Relinquishing every piece of my resolve, I curled up like a baby, sank into his chest, and sobbed. It was four in the morning, but he held me there for the rest of the night until the tears stopped, and we both drifted off to sleep.

Chapter Thirteen

Hadassah

I had woken up with swollen eyes from all the crying I was doing, and a sore throat from all the screaming I had been doing just moments before that. On my first day of middle school, I had gotten my hair pressed and wore white jeans with a matching white jean top, all to debut my new sophisticated look for the seventh grade. There was a big set of stairs that went from the sidewalk down to the school entrance and, when I stepped off of the bus and started to walk down the steps, I fell. All the way down. In front of the *entire* school. Everyone laughed while I ran into the building and hid in the cafeteria my entire first day. This—breaking down and crying like an idiot in this man's arms—was arguably more embarrassing than that.

When I woke up, he was nowhere to be found, and I was actually a bit relieved. It gave me the perfect opportunity to get up, put on my clothes, and run out. If I was never going to see him again, it was the perfect way to end things—saying nothing at all. The alarm clock on his nightstand said that it was nine in the morning, and I was shocked that I had actually managed to sleep past 3 a.m. It was the longest I had slept in years, and I couldn't remember the last time I actually slept in like a normal person. There was a large chaise lounge in the corner of his bedroom, and I noticed that my dress from the night before had been neatly laid out with my shoes on the floor beneath it. *That was sweet of him,* I thought.

I sat up and turned to get out of the bed, bringing the furry throw blanket at the end with me to cover myself with, when the bedroom door opened. Jaxon had come in with two cups of coffee and a bag that looked like it had pastries inside. "Look...this is...*was* nice," I stammered, "but I really need to get going."

"Who said I was done with you?" he grinned.

"And who said I was open to extending things beyond last night?" I argued. I actually liked to verbally spar with him.

He kept coming closer to me, and the smile slowly disappeared from my face. Once he got too close, I fell back onto the bed. He was wearing a navy-blue jogging suit with a matching blue Atlanta Braves hat, and I was feeling the dressed down look on him *just* as much as the suave one. "One-night stands are typically supposed to end once the night is over, aren't they?"

Jaxon smirked, handing me one of the cups of coffee, then took the seat next to me on the bed. "I know we said last night was a one night only thing, and I respect that, but you are no 'one-night-stand' kind of woman. *You,* Shy, are a one night of 'I may never get an opportunity to see this person again, so I will cherish and treasure every moment I have with her' kind of woman." He leaned over to kiss me on the cheek before finishing with, "And don't you ever forget that."

I blushed at his words, "You're good at that."

"Good at what, kissing you?" he joked, and I lowered my head and chuckled. "You don't laugh often enough."

"See! *That* is what I'm talking about!"

"What?" he laughed. "I'm just sitting here talking to you."

"You're sitting here *reading* me. Seeing into me. It unnerves me."

"I like that you're honest about it."

"I don't know how else to be." I shrugged before taking a sip of the hot, warm, life-saving elixir that is coffee. "Mmmm," I moaned. "This is exactly what I needed."

"But that's not *all* you need, is it?" he probed.

I knew what he was doing. He was gearing me up to ask about last night, and I couldn't even begin to go into it. I lowered my head and closed my eyes. "Please don't," I begged quietly.

"I don't mean to pry," he said softly, taking my hand and putting in his, "but you told me you loved me last night. Asked me to tell you I loved you. Then you…"

I snapped, cutting him off, "You don't have to say it! You don't have to finish. I know what happened, and I'm sorry."

"Don't misunderstand me, Shy. I'm not asking for an apology. Maybe just an explanation, if you can?"

I tilted my head back, looking up at the ceiling, and let out a sigh. Tears burned in my eyes, and one escaped before I could catch it. That's when I felt him lean in. I wanted to get up and leave, but before I could follow through with that thought, he kissed my tears away. I closed my eyes and leaned into him, giving him access to the tears as they fell. It felt so good to be seen and cared for that way.

"He was my husband, OK?" I whispered, my eyes still closed, unable to open them or look at him. I felt him squeeze my hand a little tighter. "It's been six years. Six years today, to be exact."

He let out a sympathetic sigh and whispered, "Baby. I'm so sorry."

"I'm fine. It's fine. I just got caught up in the memory of the day, and it got the best of me. But I'm fine now."

"You're sitting in my bed shaking, trying to fight back tears, for whatever reason I can't be sure. But, one thing is for certain; you're *not* fine."

"I wanted to forget," I continued. "Last night? I wanted to forget everything and just *feel* something other than grief for once, but I wasn't expecting *you*. What I'd feel with you. It was a little too much, and I'm sorry."

"Stop apologizing," he bit back, seemingly offended by my incessant need to apologize. "Grief isn't something you ever need to apologize for."

I appreciated the fact that he wasn't attempting to gloss over my grief or speed past it. When most people learned of my widowhood, they usually stumbled over their words, their discomfort palpable. They'd steamroll past the topic with a well-meaning yet hollow "I'm sorry." But he was different. He acknowledged my grief and my pain, and that meant more than any empty condolences.

He removed my coffee cup from my hand and placed both his and mine on the nightstand next to me. Then he got up and knelt in front of me, "I tell you what," he propositioned, "I don't have anything to do until this evening after 4 p.m. If I promised to abide by *most* of your rules from last night, will you stay a little longer? I'll draw you a bath, make you a better breakfast than pastries, and let you tell me all about Lamar. Would that be OK?"

This was a different side of him than I'd seen last night. Last night he was a very confident player on the prowl. Today he seemed like he genuinely cared about me and wanted to spend time with me. It all could have been a performance, but I honestly didn't care. All of this, how he was taking care of me, was something I hadn't experienced in a long time, and I wasn't ready for it to end either. "Okay then," I said smiling.

I decided that this would be a do-over for last night, sans tears. Besides, I didn't have any other plans for my birthday anyway.

Jaxon

I had to admit it, I wasn't ready to let her go. Without knowing her name or barely anything about her at all, she had captivated me. I went into last night fully intending on making her my plaything for the evening, capturing her senses and leaving her soul craving me for days, even months, to come. But there was something in her eyes and her demeanor that wouldn't let me. I saw her, and I knew there was more to her than what she was letting on. I just didn't realize it would be something as deep, as tragic, as losing her husband.

He sounded like such a great man. The way her face lit up when she talked about him was admirable. It was easy to see that they had a great love, and her heartache wasn't just from losing him, but from the possibility that she would likely never find a love like that again. She didn't cry when speaking about him, though. It was interesting that, as long as she was talking about him, she smiled and would light up the room. But I noticed that when she would try to suppress thoughts of him or keep memories to herself, that's when the tears came.

I sat at the edge of the bathtub and rubbed her feet as she told me countless stories about their early years and how they met. She was transported to another place as she shared things she probably had hidden away for safekeeping. Her eyes were closed, so I was able to unashamedly roam my eyes up and down her body and marvel at her imperfect perfection. She tried to use soap bubbles to cover them, but I saw glimpses of what appeared to be stretch marks, and I silently wondered where those were from. Did she have a child waiting for her just as I had one waiting for me later?

"You know," I said, taking her left foot in my hand after I finished massaging her right, "you shouldn't ever stop talking about him."

She looked up at me confused, "Why do you say that?"

"Because. I've only known you for less than twenty-four hours, but this is the most I've seen you smile this bright. I mean, you're beaming, Shy. Do you ever talk to anyone about him?"

She took a long moment to consider what I asked. "I have a therapist friend that I talk to *sometimes,* but it's different. Everyone wants to know how I'm doing, but as soon as I begin to talk about Lamar, *their* face gets sad as if they're the ones who lost him. And then that in turn makes me sad, so I resolved to stop talking about him. It's just easier than finding myself comforting someone else during what's supposed to be my time of grief."

"Well, forget those people." I really wanted to say fuck those people, but I didn't want to be crass. "You loved him for more than ten years. Nobody gets to tell you to get over it or stop talking about him. That's how you keep your heart light and his memory alive."

She was shocked at my insight, assuming that just because I was attractive that I couldn't be insightful too. Little did she know that most of the insightful wisdom I carried with me was from my mom. She was the most caring and wise woman I knew, and I saw a spark of joy on Shy's face as I talked about my mom, sharing a little bit about me and my background with her as well. I shared how I was married once and that I'd never forgive myself for how I hurt my ex-wife. I even told her how I'd never been the "settling down" type, so I was determined to remain single for the rest of my life. I didn't know what I was expecting but, after sharing that honesty about me and women, she didn't even flinch. She just listened as I opened myself up to her.

I left her in the bathtub and, while she was relaxing, I made her breakfast. While plating the food as if I was a gourmet chef, I grinned to myself at her observation of my ability to read her or discern what she was feeling. It wasn't some party trick I'd picked up on the road. It was a trauma response to growing up in a house with an abusive father and a mother who suffered from chronic depression as a result. We lived on a knife-edge, always bracing for dad's unpredictable mood swings. On days when he woke up with that dark cloud hanging over him, when he stomped around the house, silent but seething, we knew trouble was brewing. And Momma, bless her heart, would find ways to whisk us away from the house, keeping us out all day until the storm had passed.

When it was just me and Momma at home alone, I would watch *her*, making sure *she* was OK. I'd take care of her when she was sad, make her food when she couldn't get out of bed, or play her a song when she needed her spirits lifted. I had learned to decipher her moods just as well as I had my dad's and, even though I was just a little boy, I think a part of me always feared that she would harm herself as a result of my father's abuse. One day she even tried, leaving me with him while her sister checked her into a hospital for, what they told me was, stress and being overwhelmed. But even then my father didn't let her rest, threatening to do irreparable harm if she didn't come home immediately. I'm certain that her love for me was the only reason she came back. When she walked through the door, she vowed to never leave me alone with him again, and I honestly believe that I was the only reason she chose life every day.

I was done plating the eggs and chicken sausage that I made, adding a side of fruit for color, when Shy walked into the kitchen wearing one of my t-shirts. The sight instantly excited me, sending fire to my groin. "That looks *good*," she smiled, gesturing at the plates in my hand.

"You look better," I responded, already mentally undressing her with my eyes.

Her eyes roamed my body, and they got wider when she saw my erection staring back at her through my sweatpants. "You always cook with your shirt off?" she teased.

I grinned back, setting the plates on the counter behind me. "Only when it gets too hot in the kitchen."

"Oh, and it's definitely, *really* hot in here," she said, closing the distance between us. She used her hand to trace the ridges of my six pack, then she leaned in to kiss, then lick, then bite my chest. I wasn't planning to sleep with her again. I had every intention of talking and getting to know her better, as much as she'd allow. But her mouth all over me was literally driving me insane. Maybe we'd talk more later.

My hands instinctively found their way to her hips, pulling her against me, the evidence of my desire pressing unmistakably into her belly. A thrill shot through me as I realized she wasn't wearing any panties. With a swift motion, I hoisted her onto the empty counter in front of me. The new position granted me an unobstructed access to her petite yet seductive frame. Bending down, I caught the hem of her t-shirt between my teeth, teasingly raising it while my thumbs began an intimate exploration of her body.

They danced over her nipples, gently rubbing and caressing, transforming them into hardened peaks under my touch. The sensation of her arousal beneath my fingertips was turning me into a mad man. She was dripping wet, and I saw the evidence begin to pool onto my kitchen counter.

Taking her left breast into my mouth, my tongue tracing circles around her pointed peaks, I slid my right hand between her legs. I bit her nipple, hard, while sinking two, then three fingers into her, and her head shot back as she screamed out for me.

"Tell me your name," I demanded, my thumb tracing delicate circles over her sensitive pearl. "Tell me, or I'll stop."

"Don't stop," her response was a plea wrapped in a command. "Don't you dare fucking stop!"

She unabashedly rocked into me while I licked, bit, and sucked anywhere... everywhere...all at once. "Tell me," I growled, getting more violent with the strokes of my hand.

"Dash!" she screamed. "Call me Dash!"

I slowed the rhythm of my hand between her legs and smiled with satisfaction. "OK, then, Dash. Come here," I demanded, before picking her up and removing her from the counter. She bit her bottom lip as she watched me licking the evidence of her pleasure off of my hands.

I turned her around to face the counter, bending her over. "I'm going to fuck you now. It won't be soft, and I won't be gentle. Is that OK?"

"Yes," she whispered, her body vibrating with anticipation of me entering her.

I removed a condom from my wallet and quickly opened it when Dash turned around, "Wait, let me put it on," she asked, and my eyes went dark with desire.

I watched as she sensually untied the drawstring to my joggers and pulled them down to unveil my rigid arousal. Her eyes never left mine while her delicate fingers hooked around the waistband of my briefs, pulling them down to reveal

169

me in all my hardened glory. As she knelt in front of me, a mischievous smile played on her lips before she leaned in, her tongue gently lapping at the pearl of moisture that had gathered at the tip. A surge of pleasure shot through me as I threaded my fingers through her hair, tilting my head back and surrendering to the wave of ecstasy that was building inside me.

Her hands began their intimate dance, stroking my length while her mouth continued to explore, sending sparks of pleasure coursing through me with every lick. A brother could get used to this, watching her lavish me with such attention. She was truly remarkable, and I knew I didn't deserve her. Even if just for today. And yet, there was no denying the sweet torment she was inflicting upon me, pushing me closer to the precipice of pleasure with each passing second.

Her head moved in a rhythmic dance as she traced circles around my tip with her tongue. I could feel the control slipping from my grasp, "Baby..." I warned, my voice a strained whisper, "You're about to make me..." The sentence hung unfinished in the air, swallowed by a gasp that escaped my lips as I staggered slightly. In one audacious move, she took me entirely, so deep that I could swear I brushed against her tonsils. Over and over again, she rocked

170

back and forth, each motion sending waves of pleasure through me.

"Dash!" I grunted, the urgency in my voice palpable. "You have *got* to stop."

"No," she shot back, her tone equally determined and defiant. Stopping only to peer deep into my eyes. Hell…my soul. "You're not the only one who likes control. And if this is the last day I get with you, then I'm leaving *you* something to remember *me* by, too." Then her face disappeared again as she resumed her sweet torment.

She was driving me to the brink of release, and I damn near asked her to marry me. She removed me from her mouth with a grin, then licked her lips. And…oh my goodness. She spit on it. I lost it after that, becoming an animal under her spell.

I grabbed a fistful of her hair, winding it around my hand, before guiding myself back into her mouth. The guttural sounds of her gagging were music to my ears, and I reveled in it. "Is this what you wanted, Dash? Is this how you wanted me to relinquish control to you?" I said, my voice shaking from the blood that was rushing from everywhere to my core.

"Tell me where you want this. Tell me where you want me to come, Dash." I didn't want to say it, but I refused to violate her mouth like that. I meant what I said; she was a once in a lifetime kind of woman, and even in the midst of this intense, power play, I still wanted her to feel cherished.

She paused momentarily to remove my shirt that she was wearing, revealing her beautiful, swollen breasts to me, and my eyes lit up with passion. "Bad girl," I grinned. Without missing a beat, she drew me back into the warm haven of her mouth. With skilled finesse, she coaxed every hidden desire, every pent-up yearning, right from the depths of my being to the brink...to the edge of a seismic release.

I stepped back and emptied myself where she asked me to, then pulled her up to bring her mouth to mine. I kissed her passionately, even with *everything* between us. Then, with a gentle pull, I led her to the shower. I didn't just clean her off, I worshiped her body with every drop of water. Bathing her as if I was her humble servant. Then, when I was finished, I bent her over the seat in my shower, took her from behind, and did as I promised. I fucked her. *Hard.*

Her screaming echoed all through the house, and it suddenly hit me that I hadn't even met my new neighbors yet.

Chapter Fourteen

Jaxon

Dash stayed over until I had to officially take custody of Mila and bring her home with me. In between the countless times we found ourselves back in bed, we talked. We kept most of the personal information at bay, the things that could be used to identify us, but we still shared so much in those hours that I felt like I knew her. From favorite colors to favorite childhood cartoons, we talked about the things that made us who we are today, without actually sharing the intimate details of who we are today. It was nice and something I'll hold close to me, but it was time to transform into the responsible man with a child to take care of. No more games. No more distractions.

When it was time to get Mila, we had arranged to meet at a local restaurant where we could all share a meal together. Danica had become such an important part of Mila's life, and I wanted to give Mila the opportunity to say a proper goodbye, while not making Danica feel like she was just a transactional part of our lives.

"So, what's the game plan after this?" Danica asked with a lively pep in her voice.

"Shopping!" Mila declared at the top of her lungs.

"Exactly," I chimed in, "we need to grab some school essentials for her until I can sit down with an estate lawyer to square away things at my dad's place and get the rest of her belongings."

"Oh, how exciting!" Danica exclaimed. "I bet you're going to be the prettiest little girl at your new school!"

Instantly, Mila's spirit seemed to deflate, her excitement evaporating. "I don't want to go to a new school," she confessed in a barely audible whisper.

"I understand, sweetie," Danica comforted. "You've been through so much change, and it's completely natural to feel scared about yet *another* change. But how about we make a deal? For every week that you put in a good effort at school, and at least try to make the best of it, I will treat you to ice cream. Deal?"

Mila's head bobbed with enthusiasm, "Deal!"

Watching Danica effortlessly connect with Mila was a real eye-opener for me. It hit me like a ton of bricks that I had so much to learn about making a little girl feel safe and secure. Sure, playing the cool older brother was a piece of cake—cracking jokes, playing games, and generally being the fun guy. But when it came to creating a warm, nurturing space where a little girl could blossom and grow—well, that was a different game altogether. And I was most certainly out of my depths.

Our trip to the mall was a whirlwind of activity. Mila's face lit up like a Christmas tree when I told her she could pick out her own clothes and even some fashion jewelry. To her, it was like being set loose in a candy store because her mom had never let her make her own fashion choices. As we strolled through the aisles, I felt like I was on track for the 'Best Big Brother' award. But truth be told, I was flying by the seat of my pants. I didn't have the foggiest idea about girls' fashion. So, I figured Mila would be the best judge of what she wanted and needed.

I was feeling very confident on my first day as legal guardian and big brother extraordinaire when Mila announced that she needed new bras. The group home had given her two, but only one fit properly. "Girls need more than one bra, Jax!" she informed me, and I grinned at her ease in giving me a nickname. It was a subtle sign that she was starting to trust me, starting to feel comfortable around me. And that meant the world to me.

Even still, if I never heard the word bra come out of my little sister's mouth again, it would be too soon. "O…OK, but," I stammered nervously, "I don't have to like, see you try it on or anything, right? Like you can just pick some and we can buy them and go, right?"

She seemed to find that funny. "No, silly!" she said, giggling. "You wait outside while I try them on. Then I'll tell you which ones I like. Deal?"

"Deal," I said, smiling down at her.

Seeing that I might have been a bit out of my depth, the store's shopping attendant walked over. "Can I help you find anything specific?" she asked.

The reality of our shopping trip didn't hit me until I took a moment to look around. Suddenly, I realized that Mila had led me straight into a full-fledged adult lingerie store. The place was teeming with sultry bras, lace panties, and all sorts of risqué lingerie. Now, I was no expert when it came to little girl's fashion, but I'd seen my fair share of Target commercials to know that we could have easily picked up a suitable bra for a girl her age there.

"Uh…Umm…" I couldn't find my words.

"We would like three bras, please! Lace ones!" Mila chimed in confidently.

"Uhh, well, hold on," I said. "Forgive me, ma'am, but I believe what my precocious little sister means to say is, we need three *age-appropriate* bras for a twelve-year-old young lady that's starting a new school tomorrow. *No lace.*"

"Aww! You're no fun!" Mila pouted.

"Sure! We can help you with that! Do you know your size, sweetie?"

"No, my mommy just said I needed something to cover my mosquito bites."

We all laughed at Mila's mom's characterization of her budding womanhood. Then I wasn't able to unsee it.

"Well, it just so happens that we have a special mosquito-bite-friendly section for young ladies just like you! We even have some with a little bit of lace that I think your big brother would approve of."

Mila vibrated with excitement. "Yes! Let's see whatcha got!"

I watched as they disappeared into the mosquito-bite-friendly zone of the lingerie store and yelled, "I don't need to see them. Just make sure they're age-appropriate, please!" The attendant turned to flash me a grin and gave me a thumbs up. Mila just waved.

I found myself seated in what seemed to be the designated 'men's corner' of the store. It looked like a spot where husbands and boyfriends would hang out, twiddling their thumbs while their significant others shopped. As I idly scrolled through my phone, my mind wandered back to the woman I'd just spent an unforgettable night with.

Dash—it was such a distinctive name that I couldn't help but wonder if it was a nickname or something she'd made up at the spur of the moment. Curiosity piqued, I decided to do a little snooping around on social media. I opened up Facebook, keyed in 'Dash' into the search bar, and hit enter. Nothing. A similar search on Instagram and TikTok also drew a blank.

I wasn't quite sure what I would have done if I had stumbled upon her profile. We had been pretty clear about our intentions—or lack thereof—to see each other again. But if there had been a chance to sneakily grab a screenshot of a picture or two, well, that would have been a small token to remember her by.

My head shot up as I saw Mila and an attendant making their way towards the front of the store, arms laden with five bras instead of the agreed-upon three. "Okay, hear me out!" Mila started, laying the groundwork for her persuasive argument. "I know you said only three, but they have this special deal where you buy four bras and get the fifth one free! You seem like the kind of guy who knows the value of a good bargain, so I went ahead and got the five."

I couldn't help but chuckle at her smooth negotiating skills. They were actually working! Was I seeing the early signs of a future litigator in my baby sister? "You've read me like an open book, Ms. Hart," I replied, playing along with her game. "You're absolutely right. I'm a sucker for a good deal. So, accepting your proposal is a no-brainer."

Mila's response was an ear-piercing squeal of delight. She grabbed my hand and started pulling me towards the cash register. "Quick! Before you change your mind!" she cried out, her excitement infectious.

Watching her face light up like that was truly a sight. Given all the pain and hardship she'd had to endure in such a short span of time, bringing a little joy into her life felt like the least I could do. Throughout our entire drive home, she was all chatter and giggles, going on and on about how she planned to match her new bras with her outfits. Her non-stop chatter was almost enough to make me wish for a pair of earplugs.

She spoke at a breakneck speed, her words tumbling out in a rush of excitement. It was hard to keep up with her, but the best part was, she didn't really expect me to. She was perfectly content to hold the conversation all by herself, talking and squealing and talking some more. As we pulled into my driveway, I took a deep, steadying breath, bracing myself for another round of her enthusiastic chatter.

Earlier that day, I had cleaned the house and made sure that any and all evidence of Dash had been picked up or removed. Under my bathroom sink, I discovered her lace thong, and I tucked it away for safekeeping. A small, intimate reminder of our time together. She had left several memories behind that day, but this little piece of fabric was perhaps the most treasured. It was a tangible token of an unforgettable encounter.

We opened the door to the townhome, and I saw a big smile wash over her face. "Is this ours?"

"It is," I smiled. "Do you like it?"

"It's really pretty! Did you decorate all by yourself?"

I laughed at her obvious assumption that I likely didn't. "What, you don't think I have the skills to decorate like this?"

"Nope!" she quipped, then she ran past the stairs and straight ahead into the kitchen area, which opened to the living room. "Wow! How big is this TV!" she yelled.

I walked over to the kitchen and set all of the shopping bags onto the counter, "It's seventy-five inches, I think."

"Woooow!" she shouted, stretching her arms the length of the TV to see how far her tiny hands could reach. "We get to live here *every day!?*"

"Every day," I confirmed. "Do you want to see your room?"

"Yes, please!"

As I guided her around the house, I introduced her to the various spaces where she could play and relax. One of these was a multi-purpose room that functioned as my office and studio but also housed theater seats and a popcorn machine for an authentic cinema experience. She extracted a promise from me to host movie nights there every Friday, a pact sealed with a solemn pinky promise.

After our tour, she took a bath and emerged in a pink satin pajama set, her feet in matching fluffy slippers. She attempted to teach me how to wrap her hair, but I failed miserably. I made a mental note to ask Lu for a hair stylist recommendation this week.

In anticipation of Mila's arrival, I had read several books on adoption, hoping they would provide some insight into establishing a connection and bond with her. While she wasn't technically an adopted child, our situation echoed many elements of the adoption process. One book suggested that a good starting point was simply getting to know Mila without any preconceived notions about her or children in general. So, I asked Mila to tell me the essentials—what she liked for breakfast, the school subjects she found challenging, whether she liked hugs or preferred other expressions of affection. My hope was that these questions would convey my genuine desire to understand her better

Yet, as much as I hoped, I also feared—feared that she would reject my attempts and see through the facade to the performer that I really was. The fraud her father felt too ashamed to acknowledge.

It was getting close to ten at night, and I asked her the question I probably should have led with, "What time do you normally go to bed?"

She grinned, and it sort of looked like mine when I was plotting something. "Eleven?" she *proposed.*

"Try again," I said, laughing at her attempt to get over on me. "Let me ask you this way, what time did your mommy and daddy make you go to bed?"

"Eight o'clock usually," she said in quiet defeat.

"OK then. After tonight, that's your bedtime, OK?"

"Can we do 8:30 instead?" she begged, and I was unable to resist the way her big brown eyes looked up at me.

"Fine. 8:30 and not a minute later." I was already starting to sound like a parent.

I took a shower and crawled into bed, checking my email once more for all the details of Mila's new school, when I heard a faint knock on the door. "Yes?" I called out and the door slowly inched open.

"I...Jaxon? I'm scared. Can I sleep with you?"

My heart melted. I thought Dash would be the undoing of me if I spent more time with her, but

Mila was easily winning that race. Thankfully I had changed all of the linens and pillows on the bed today because without giving it a second thought, I peeled back the covers, and Mila scampered over to leap onto the opposite side of the bed. She nestled her head into the pillows, blissfully unaware they'd cradled Dash's head merely twelve hours ago.

Chapter Fifteen

Hadassah

Six Years Ago

"Mommy! Mommy! We made you bwekfis!" Ty screamed, running to bring me my annual birthday breakfast in bed that Lamar started doing after our first year together. Now, Ty raced his daddy for the honor of being the first person to wish me a happy birthday.

At five years old, Ty was the spitting image of his daddy with his smokey gray eyes and sandy blonde hair. Lamar and I often argued over whether or not we would loc Ty's hair like his. I wasn't against little boys with dreads, I just wanted him to be able to choose the loc journey for himself. Lamar wanted a carbon copy of himself.

"You made me bwekfis! I'm so proud of you! And it looks amazing! Tell Mommy what you made, baby?"

"OK! We made you peanut butter toast with bananas and coffee!"

"My favorite!" I beamed. It wasn't my favorite. It was Ty's favorite. But since he had unilaterally decided that peanut butter and banana toast was

everybody's favorite in our family, we just all went along with it.

I looked up to find Lamar smiling at Ty bouncing all over me on the bed. He knelt to give me a sweet kiss, *"Happy birthday, baby."*

"Thank you, my love," I grinned.

"So," he said while continuing to kiss me on my cheek, then my ear. *"What's on your agenda for today?"*

"Absolutely nothing!" I shot back. *"I plan to lay in this bed and watch HGTV and eat ice cream until I fall asleep. Then wake up and do it all over again until nightfall."*

"But you're not gonna eat ice cream before your bwekfis, right Mommy?!" Ty interjected.

"Not before my breakfast, baby. Mommy promises."

"OK!" he screamed and then jumped off the bed to go put on his clothes, and we both just shook our heads and smiled.

"What do my two favorite boys have planned today?" I asked, pulling Lamar into another passionate kiss, one that didn't require censorship since the baby had run off.

"Mmmm... You keep kissing me like that, and the only thing I'll be doing is you," he joked, kissing me once more. *"First, I'm gonna take little man shopping for a birthday present for you. Then I promised him we could see a movie."*

"Let me guess, Miles Morales Spiderman?"

"You already know!"

Ty was obsessed with Spiderman already but, as soon as he found out there was a black Spiderman character, he hadn't been able to stop talking about it or watching the movie. There was a cinema in our town that only played positive black movies and inspiring cartoons for kids, so we took our students there, and now Ty, any chance we'd get.

My husband was a giver. A pleaser in every way. So when we were sure that Ty was busy watching cartoons for a little while, Lamar gave me my other birthday present that was part of our annual tradition—orgasms. Setting my coffee mug on the nightstand, he gently kissed me. He kissed me like it was the first time he had ever touched me, taking my face into both hands and letting out an audible moan when his tongue touched mine. His fingers traced the contours of my cheeks, holding my face as if it were a delicate piece of art.

"You are so beautiful," he said, with love and admiration in his eyes. *"It may be your birthday, but you give me the gift of you every day. I'm so lucky to be with you,"* he said, as he took his time to unbutton his shirt that I had worn to bed the night before.

When the shirt was fully unbuttoned, he didn't immediately gawk at my breasts, nor did he rush to devour them. Instead, he bent down to press his lips against the stretch marks adorning my stomach, whispering a silent "thank you" for allowing my body to go through hell to bless him with a son. After he had succeeded in sexing me silly and putting me back to sleep, he and Ty left me alone for the day.

With the boys off on their own adventure, the house was finally left to me, in a peaceful and quiet tranquility. The journey to motherhood hadn't been an easy one for us. We had tried to get pregnant right after we got married, but I suffered two miscarriages. At first, I figured I wouldn't have kids, treating my students at Biddy Mason as my surrogate kids. But two years of unsuccessful attempts later, that infamous little stick surprised me with a positive result when I least expected it.

Our family was complete. From Friday night game and movie nights to Sunday night book club where we read whatever book Ty picked out and discussed it over dinner on Sundays. Things weren't perfect, but we had our own little slice of heaven, and I felt incredibly blessed.

Corinne wanted to come over and hang out with me, but thankfully I was able to get her to understand my need for quiet and solitude today. Turning thirty-five wasn't exactly a milestone year, but I had been through and overcome a lot over the years, and I was feeling incredibly blessed to be alive. I just wanted to sit with that for today in solitude.

My morning with Lamar had done more for me than I had realized, lulling me into a deep, restful sleep that lasted an uninterrupted, blissful four hours. Blinking away the remnants of sleep, I glanced at my phone and saw that it was 3 p.m., and I had eight missed calls. Hopefully, my friends and family would understand my need for solitude today. I didn't feel up to repeating my plans - or lack thereof - to everyone. Today, I simply wanted to bask in the peace of doing absolutely nothing. So, I decided to follow the unwritten post-birthday protocol that everyone seemed to adhere to. I would craft a heartfelt thank you message on Facebook, acknowledging all the birthday calls and text messages. Alleviating guilt for not responding to EVERY call and text message I received today.

I saw a voicemail message from Lamar, and that was the only one I was interested in hearing. *"Hey, babe. We just got done buying you the perfect birthday gift and..."*

"You're gonna love it, Mommy!" I heard Ty chime in from the back seat.

"Yes, you are gonna love it. Since it took a little longer than expected, we're going to catch a later showing of Miles Morales, so we won't be home until around 7 p.m.. I ordered you dinner from your favorite Mediterranean restaurant, and that should be there by 4 p.m. I hope you're resting and taking a nice, long nap, baby. I love you."

"Love you, Mommy!" Then the message ended.

Since my dinner would be here in a little while, I went and took a nice, long shower, and it was ecstasy. I could have stayed in there all day, but the doorbell broke the spell of serenity as the person annoyingly rang it over and over again.

"Just leave the food by the door!" I yelled, draping myself with a robe so I could run down the stairs to grab what I assumed was my food order being delivered early. *"Ringing my doorbell like the damn police!"* I added, sounding *just* like my mother

I swung the door open with noticeable frustration when I realized it wasn't my food delivery. It actually *was* the police. Only…I knew these officers. They were often on duty near the school and helped out during fundraisers. Only today, the look on their faces told me that this was the last house call they ever wanted to make.

"Mrs. St. James," one of the officers said. *"Do you mind if we come in? It's about your husband and your son."*

Chapter Sixteen

Jaxon

As we stepped through the welcoming doors of Biddy Mason Charter School, we were immediately immersed in a vibrant display of black excellence. The students, teachers, and even the images adorning the walls echoed an inspiring narrative—one that celebrated black accomplishments beyond the realms of hip hop and sports. It was something I'd never seen before.

On our drive to the school, I had turned to Mila and asked her what she wanted the school's staff to know about her. I felt it was crucial to let her establish her own boundaries. As a young boy, I *hated it* when my mom would tell her friends and sometimes the entire church our business, and somehow she always ended up talking about me. So I'm glad I gave Mila a voice in this. She confided that she wasn't ready for anyone to know about her parents' passing just yet. The idea of people pitying her made her uncomfortable, and I could understand and respect that.

So, we crafted a story about her life that she felt comfortable sharing. The rest of her story would remain hers to tell if and when she decided to share more. This way, Mila retained control over her own narrative.

As we settled into the school administrator's office, Mila confidently launched into her rehearsed introduction. "My name is Milagros Hart, but I prefer to be called Mila. And this is Jaxon Hart, or Jax, as I like to call him. I'm twelve years old, and I love the color pink, but sometimes purple is my favorite, too. I'm obsessed with BTS, and since Jax is a musician, I'm starting to like that. My favorite subject is science—unless it involves math. What's your name?"

"Well! Delighted to meet you, Mila. And you too, Jax," the administrator replied with a warm smile. "I'm Ms. Genevieve, the school administrator. And guess what? I like the color purple, too! We've been eagerly awaiting your arrival all week, and I have some special surprises *just* for you!"

I watched as Ms. Genevieve presented Mila with a personalized backpack on wheels. This school was truly first-class, and it amazed me that there was no tuition fee. "This is your Biddy Mason backpack, packed with everything you need to succeed here. Every student receives a laptop, generously donated by the staff at Cola World; an iPad, courtesy of a local mega-church that sponsors our school; and all your books, covered by registration fees. We've gone digital with our books, and they're all loaded onto your iPad for easy access."

"Wow!" Mila's eyes sparkled.

"Do you have any other questions, Mila?" Genevieve asked.

Mila hesitated, her head bowed as if embarrassed by her next question. I gently squeezed her hand in silent support. "How will I make friends? I've never started a new school without my friends before." My heart ached at her vulnerable admission.

"Well, your first friend will be your buddy, Arrin. She's in the same grade as you, and she even likes science! In fact, she won the Percy Julian Inventor Award this year for her science project!

"Wow!" Mila exclaimed.

"Here she is now," Ms. Genevieve said as Arrin came bursting into the office. "Arrin will give you the grand tour of our school, show you where everything is, and answer any other questions you may have, OK?"

With a wave of their hands, the girls vanished into the bustling school corridor. Mila, with her shiny new rolling backpack, blended into the crowd. I lingered in Ms. Genevieve's office for a bit longer, honoring my pact with Mila to reveal only what she was comfortable sharing.

Mila had also expressed her wish for her panic attacks to remain private. So, without going into specifics, I requested that the school staff keep a watchful eye on her, especially during times when she seemed overwhelmed or unusually quiet. After wrapping up the paperwork and tying up all the loose ends, I left, promising to be back at 4:30 p.m. sharp to pick up Mila.

Hadassah

For the first time in five years, I was late to school. After the sting of death took everything from me, I didn't get out of bed for three months. Then, when I finally did return to school, I only came into the building once the kids and teachers had already gone to their classrooms. I didn't want to risk running into anyone and seeing their pitying faces while they all asked, "how are you holding up, dear?" But since that first year of playing hide and seek from my students, I hadn't been late. That said, I hadn't been *fucked* properly in a few years either.

Jackson had folded, twisted, and bent me in ways that I had forgotten my body knew. So when it was time to get up this morning for work, I felt like I had been hit by a truck! As soon as I walked—no—hobbled, through the doors, Corinne rushed me with a series of questions that sounded a lot like an incoherent stream of consciousness, "Oh my goodness, are you ok? When we didn't hear from you this morning we thought something was wrong, then you called and said you were gonna be late..." Corinne lowered her voice and leaned in closer to me as if she was sharing a forbidden secret, "Were you depressed about... *you know*...the anniversary and your birthday?"

I shook my head, pushing the doors open to my office and setting my stuff down. "*No,* I wasn't sad or depressed about my birthday or the anniversary, Corinne."

I stopped to pick up a picture of me, Lamar, and Ty that sat on my desk and smiled, tracing the shapes of both my boys' faces. "I think you'll be *very* pleased to know that I actually did something adventurous for my birthday!"

Corinne gasped, "Bitch, and I'm *just* now hearing about it? Tell me everything. What did you do, go to a spa? Get a massage? Treat yourself to a nice dinner?"

"I treated myself to a nice *dick!*" I teased.

We both screamed like little highschool girls. "I *know* you are lying to me! You gave up your widowgenity? To who?!"

"I'm sorry, my what?"

"Your widowgenity! Aww! Let's call in Genevieve, our girl is growing up!"

I cackled while Corinne ran out to go grab Genevieve but she came back empty handed.

Corinne, our resident hopeless romantic, was firmly of the belief that life could never be complete without a man...or at least a *piece* of one, as she often seemed to attract. For the past two years, she'd been on a mission to convince me it was time to "get back out there," but it never seemed right to me. I could never grasp why women like Coretta King or Betty Shabazz chose not to remarry. But after losing Lamar, it all clicked into place. I felt no urgency to find a new man or a new love. I had experienced an extraordinary love, the best there ever was. So, the frantic pursuit of finding something else, only to be disappointed by the cesspool of the dating world, was of no interest to me.

"OK, well never mind!" Corinne said, storming back into my office. "Genevieve is with a new student and her dad, who looks cute from the back, by the way! But we'll have to fill her in later. So...*bish whet?!*"

I gestured towards my desk, suggesting that she and I sit. "OK, so…remember when you guys left Sanctuary Saturday night and I said my driver was a few minutes away? Well, I canceled the driver."

Genevieve gasped, "You what? Why? What did you do?"

"I may or may not have propositioned the leader of the band after you left. I didn't want to spend another birthday alone or feeling sad that my family was gone. I wanted to feel something different, and Jaxon facilitated that for me."

"Aww! So that fine man who was flirting with you and practically serenading you from the stage…*him?* "

"Yes, *him,*" I confirmed.

Corinne's voice got a bit somber and softer, retreating from the school girl excitement she once had. "And…how was it?" she asked carefully. "Not necessarily how was the sex, but how were you *after* the sex?"

With a playful smirk on my face, I sat there, debating if I should tell her *everything* but, what the hell. "At first, I attempted to act tough and nonchalant, as if this was an everyday occurrence for me. But he saw right through my act. Our time together turned into an intriguing game of power, vulnerability, and surrender. And truth be told, he won. He coaxed me into opening up about Lamar, about myself. He even let down his guard and shared a bit about his own life.

"The experience was sweet, yet intense, tender yet passionate, a mix of raw emotions and primal attraction. It was everything I needed at that particular moment."

"Wow," Corinne said, her mouth hanging onto every word. "And...what about...did you feel any guilt about it? With this being your first time and all?"

She knew me so well. "It came in waves. But I got the most emotional when I immaturely considered the fact that Lamar was watching me, somehow. Watching this man, who wasn't him, do all those things to me."

Corinne noted my tardiness with a smirk, "Well, you're late this morning, so there must have been quite a few...*things*."

I couldn't help but chuckle. "Many, many things indeed," I confirmed.

"Aww, your widowgenity!" Corinne whined again.

"OK Ok, for the love of God what is a widowgenie?"

"Widowgeninity, and it's the first time you have sex after being made a widow!"

"That's not a thing, is it?"

"It absolutely is a thing! Even *if* I made up the word to express such a thing. Actually, Genevieve and I both made it up the first year after Lamar died. We sort of took bets on when you'd lose it. She won."

We both erupted in laughter, and I just shook my head, amused. These ladies were a handful, but I adored them to bits. They had morphed into the family I never knew I was missing. That's just the way things were at Biddy Mason—we were undeniably a tight-knit group, a family. Even if they did take bets on when I'd get laid.

I got up to go grab an entire pot of coffee from the breakroom when I saw a man who eerily looked like Jaxon from behind. His gait, his stance, everything about him echoed Jaxon. But seeing as how I was likely still under a dickmatic spell, I shrugged it off and carefully made my way to the breakroom.

My legs were killing me.

Chapter Seventeen

Jaxon

"Level with me, B. Is Remy responsible for me suddenly getting passed over for so many projects?"

I went to sit down with Bruno Estrella because I needed him to be candid with me about what was going on with my work lately. I hadn't worked in the film and television industry long, but Bruno was one of the only people who took me under their wing, other than Remy. So when people seemed to go cold on me for no reason other than projects being put on hold, I knew Bruno would be straight with me. At least, I thought he would.

I had cut back hours at Sanctuary so I could take care of Mila, but the money from my other projects were supposed to be carrying me. With them suddenly drying up, I couldn't help but feel like Remy's hands were all over this.

"You know how this business works, Jaxon," Bruno sighed. I could tell he was choosing his words wisely, "One minute, the people love you. The next minute, they're on to the next hot thing."

"Yeah but, I went from having several meetings a day, to things mysteriously being put on hold and meetings being canceled within a span of a week!

You can't tell me this isn't a coincidence, Bruno. I mean, I know we haven't known each other long but, come on, man. Just tell me if I need to have a conversation with Remy?"

Bruno sat back in his chair, folded his arms over his growing beer belly, and said, "You should talk to Remy."

That was all the confirmation I needed. I was well aware of Remy's influential status, but I never took her as malicious or vindictive. Her blatant indifference made it even harder for me to believe that she could be actively sabotaging my progress. This is why I had developed an aversion towards letting a woman do anything for me. The moment our relationship hit a rough patch, their once "loving" and freely given gestures transformed into manipulative tools used as leverage over me.

I was getting ready to go to Bruno with more questions when my phone rang. It was the school, and it hit me that I was late picking up Mila...*again.*

Hadassah

Just over a week had passed since we returned from our Thanksgiving Break, and both the students and teachers were comfortably easing into what we fondly referred to as the "coasting" season. This was a period where our primary focus shifted to wrapping up the semester and providing students with a much-needed mental break after months of diligent work.

While many schools traditionally conducted midterm finals around this time, Biddy Mason adopted a different approach. We believed in giving our students a chance to demonstrate their knowledge and understanding through practical application. So, during midterms, students were encouraged to create projects that showcased what they'd learned throughout the semester. We reserved the traditional final exams strictly for the end of the academic year. Something that the students actually loved about the school.

"Have you seen the news yet?" Corinne asked while coming into my office to shut the door.

"No. What news?" I cautiously questioned.

Corinne pulled her phone out of her hot pink blazer pocket and began typing furiously. Then, she held the phone to my face showing me a headline that read, 'Congresswoman Dede Atkins is One Step Closer to Making Charter Schools Unlawful in the State of Georgia.'

Dede Atkins, our district's congresswoman, staunchly believed that charter schools were the downfall of our education system. She vehemently opposed the opening of Biddy Mason, but her efforts were overruled due to the pressing issue of overcrowding in existing schools. However, with the current political climate becoming more polarized and giving rise to contentious voices, she might be able to rally support for her cause.

People who lacked an in-depth understanding of the education system often pointed fingers at Charter Schools, accusing them of siphoning off resources from schools in underprivileged communities, exacerbating the education divide. However, Biddy Mason was intentionally not government-funded to avoid contributing to this very issue. Lamar understood that resources were particularly scarce in the communities most in need. Therefore, he and Corinne devised a business and operating model that relied heavily on external fundraising, making it the lifeblood of our school's survival. We even shared resources with neighboring schools when possible.

"Wait a minute. What?" I gasped. "What does this mean?"

Corinne sighed, "It means that if this measure passes, regardless of how we are funded, Biddy Mason would lose its accreditation."

"I don't understand what this woman's issue is with us! She has been intentionally gunning for us since we launched!"

"She's bitter! Remember, she ran for the board of education and lost, largely because she had no formal education experience. Then, she ran for mayor of Atlanta and lost that, too! The only thing she could get elected for is congresswoman in a district with the smallest population! And all she's been able to accomplish is fighting people who make *her* look bad on issues that actually help the community! *You*, on the other hand, came in with your beautiful black family and made actual change for these people. Because of the partnerships I've made with large organizations, and the success you've had with the students, companies are bringing jobs here so they can employ parents and allow them to work close to their kids' schools! You are the lifeblood of this community, Dash. And Dede Atkins knows it!"

I appreciated what Corinne was saying, but it was still scary, to say the least. Suddenly, everything Lamar and I had worked so hard to build was in jeopardy. I wouldn't even know what to do...what I'd do...if this all went away. The vision of Biddy Mason was all I had left of Lamar, and this school had come to fill a void left by Ty. If this all went away, it would be like I was losing my family all over again, and I wasn't sure I would recover from that.

A knock sounded at the door before opening, "Mrs. St. James? The little girl we told you about, Mila, her dad is late getting her…"

"Again?" I exclaimed, cutting off Erikah Lucas, our after-school counselor. I hadn't met this little girl, yet. Usually, we'd have a welcome party for all the new students and parents but, since she joined later in the year, we hadn't had one yet. But I guess it was time I met her and her parents because we had a very strict policy about tardiness.

"Yeah. Would you mind having a conversation with Dad? I hate to be a tattle-tale, but I think it's time."

"I understand, Erikah. Bring her into my office, and we'll wait for him together."

"I guess I'll leave you to it, then? We will get together this weekend to discuss a plan of attack for that raggedy heffa, Dede Atkins!" Corinne said as she left my office.

I looked up to find Ms. Lucas bringing the prettiest little girl my way. She had thick, curly ringlets with big brown eyes. I imagined Zoe Saldana looking like her as a little girl.

"Principal St. James, this is Mila Hart," Ms. Lucas said introducing us, "And Mila, this is Mrs. St. James, our amazing principal."

"It's a pleasure to meet you, Mila," I said, extending my hand to her for her to shake it. She did. "Come on in and have a seat!" I pointed to the sofa that sat in the corner of my office and invited Mila to sit down next to me, but she just stood there. "Mila? Is everything OK?"

"Am I in trouble?" she asked, her voice quiet and shaky.

I smiled gently. "No, sweet heart. You're not in any kind of trouble. I promise. I just want you to be comfortable until your ride gets here. Does that sound good?"

I watched her shy, apprehensive look turn into a big smile as she plopped down on the sofa in my office. She was a sweet little thing. I just smiled at her while I observed her cross her legs and fold her hands in her lap like she had been through some sort of etiquette class.

"Is that your family?" she asked, pointing to the picture of me, Lamar, and Ty on my desk.

I smiled, getting up to get the picture off my desk to show her. Sitting beside her, holding the picture and pointing to my boys' faces, I said, "Yes. That's Mr. St. James. He actually opened this school. And this is Ty, our son." I had to clear my throat after that admission. My voice was strangely cracking in a way it hadn't done in a long time.

Had this been four or five years earlier, I wouldn't have been able to endure this conversation without breaking down in tears. Most people learned not to probe, especially when it came to Ty. Discussing Lamar was always somewhat easier than speaking about Ty. Some might argue that talking about him should ease the pain, but those were often the same people who had never experienced the gut-wrenching loss of a child. It felt like reliving the agonizing intensity of labor and childbirth repeatedly, only to be cruelly awakened with the news that your baby was gone. And I didn't know how to keep communicating that to people. So, I opted to keep certain memories of my baby boy to myself, for safekeeping. However, children, being naturally curious, seldom refrained from asking questions, and Mila was no exception.

"How old is he?" Mila continued.

As I simply gazed at her and let a smile creep onto my face, a tear was on the brink of escaping in response to her question. A wave of emotions unexpectedly washed over me from out of the blue!

I cherished my students and relished witnessing their intellectual growth. However, I maintained a safe emotional distance, never allowing another child to touch my heart as deeply as my own son did. I didn't want to love another child, only to have them leave at the end of a school year or graduation or...something else.

Mila, with her infectious spirit, seemed like the kind of kid who would capture your heart and hold it hostage forever. Perhaps that was the effect she was having on me in that moment.

The door flung open before I could answer Mila's question, saving me from a sudden outburst of tears. "Mrs. St. James, her ride is here now."

"Thank you, Ms. Lucas!" I said, standing up. I reached for Mila's hand so we could walk outside together.

Once we reached the parking lot designated for parents to collect their children, I came to a startling halt at the sight that greeted me. There he was—Jaxon. "J...Jaxon?" I stuttered.

"You know my Jax?" Mila excitedly shrieked.

Jaxon remained silent but flashed a knowing smile as he sauntered towards me. What on Earth was he doing here? Suddenly, Mila's words struck me like a lightning bolt, 'My Jax.'

"Quite the coincidence bumping into you here," Jaxon smirked. "So, you're a teacher here or something?" He motioned towards the car, signaling for Mila to get in.

Once Mila was safely inside the car and out of earshot, I turned to Jaxon, fury simmering beneath my feigned smile. I had insisted on not sharing personal information about us, but his omission about having a child *screamed* 'fuck boy!'

"Actually," I countered, my eyes narrowing, "I am the principal and co-founder of this school, Hadassah St. James. I'm only here because you're consistently late picking up your daughter, which is draining our resources and time! Our teachers are underpaid as it is, and our policy explicitly states that parents must respect our teachers' time and efforts by adhering to pickup times! I should have known *this* is the guy you'd be! How do you lie or forget about a whole child?"

Jaxon closed the gap between us, almost charging at me. "Firstly," he began, his voice calm yet strained as he spoke through his teeth, "lower your fuckin' voice. She doesn't need to get any ideas about the shit between us. Secondly, she's my little sister, *not* my daughter. She was orphaned, and

I am her sole relative. I didn't lie about her. The night we met was my last night of freedom before taking on my guardianship responsibilities. So, yes, I'm still adjusting to the sudden responsibility of raising a child alone and, damn it, I'm doing my best." He leaned in closer than I thought was possible and whispered, "Lastly, just because I fucked you, doesn't mean you know anything about me. So before you come for me again with your preconceived notions and accusations, make sure they're not being filtered through the lens of me fucking you senseless, OK?"

With that, he turned on his heel, returned to his car, and drove off.

Chapter Eighteen

Jaxon

As soon as those words left my mouth, I felt terrible. I don't like when I'm *that* guy. The guy who belittles women with cutting remarks, using words as a weapon to carve deep wounds into their self-esteem. No matter the indiscretions in the past when it came to women, talking to them like they weren't valued was probably the worst because of my words. Words have a nasty habit of lingering, their echoes reverberating long after they're spoken. And when those words were steeped in disrespect, their impact could be more damaging than anything physical.

I knew first-hand because it was what I remembered most about my father. A man whose words were as rare as they were harsh, rarely had a kind word for me. His compliments, if you could call them that, were always laced with ulterior motives. Since it was seldom that I was useful to him, words of affirmation were never spoken to me. At least not from him.

"Jax, how do you know Mrs. St. James?" Mila asked, breaking through the silence in the car, but I was so deep in thought that I neglected to respond.

I still couldn't believe that was her, though.
Dash. My Shilo. I had looked into this school before
we moved here, but since the school's leaders were
a husband and wife duo, and I didn't know her real
name, it didn't register that she was the same
person. *Still, she was just as stunning as I
remembered and, my God.* Pencil skirts did her
body good. I'd be lying if I said that seeing the
school that she and her late husband built didn't
make me feel inadequate as hell. She had built a life
and a legacy with this man that would stand the test
of time. No wonder she only wanted one night with
me. How could I compare to...*him?*

"Jaaax!" Mila whined, "Are you listening to
me? Why were you late again, and how do you
know Mrs. St. James!?"

"Mila! Wait! Can't you see that I'm thinking?!"
I snapped, and I saw her reflection in the rearview
mirror as she jumped at the sound of my voice. Her
head went down, and I knew I had hurt her feelings.
Fuck, I was 0-0 today. First Dash, and now her.

"Mila, sweetheart. I'm sorry. I didn't mean to
raise my voice at you. Will you forgive me?"

She didn't answer me. In fact she was quiet the
entire drive home. I played BTS through my
Bluetooth in the car, hoping it would cheer her up.
But she just sat and stared out the window as we

drove. I was constantly late picking her up, the hairstylist I'd found only showed me how to do one hairstyle for her hair every morning, and she warned me that she was getting sick of the same ponytail, and now I had resorted to raising my voice out of frustration. I was failing at parenting, and I didn't know what to do or how to make things right with her.

When we got home, I grabbed Mila's rolling backpack, and she ran into the house, up the stairs, and slammed the door. I was getting ready to close the door behind me when I saw an older woman carrying groceries. She moved slowly, but it looked like she was going to the townhouse right next to mine. It was confirmed when I saw her carefully walking up the stairs next door.

"Can I help you with that, ma'am?" I asked, keeping a distance until she could discern whether or not I was safe for her.

"Oh, would you mind?" she exclaimed with a bright smile on her face. She had to be in her sixties, judging by the limited range of motion and her yellowish, gray hair. You could tell she used to wear jerry curls back in the day because of the way her hair was permanently tinted with a yellow hue. "I always have trouble with this darn key card! I swear you young folks just can't keep things simple with all this new technology," she mused while I held her bags for her.

"Well, on behalf of my entire generation, I'm sorry to inconvenience you with all this technology, Miss…" I paused, hoping she'd fill in the blank with her name.

"You can just call me Nana Shirley. That's what everyone else around here calls me."

"You mean like Nana Shirley's Small Cakes?"

"Exactly like it," she confirmed with a smile.

"OK, so…wait…You are *thee* Nana Shirley?"

"The one and only! At least the one who owns the Small Cakes franchise."

I couldn't believe it. Nana Shirley's "Small Cakes" was a local treasure. Whether it was a wedding or a birthday party, her cakes always played a part. I didn't have many celebratory memories that didn't include her. Or her cakes, at least.

"My ex-wife was obsessed with your German chocolate cakes," I said, still a bit starstruck at the person I was standing in front of. I had played with and met some of today's most impactful artists, but I never let their celebrity make me geek out over them. But Nana Shirley had me grinning like a schoolboy.

"Ex-wife, huh?" She asked inquisitively, "I bet there's a story there."

"A long one. Too long for today, I'm afraid Ms...I mean, Nana," I sighed. "I've got to get back next door and figure out how to make a twelve-year-old be my friend again."

Nana laughed dryly, "Good luck with that! Most twelve year olds I raised seemed to take a vow of silence until they turned twenty-five! And I should know 'cause I've raised seven of them."

"So, I've read in all these parenting books I bought."

"Oh, now don't go letting all them books raise your child for you. Just talk to her. Be straight with her. And don't try to bullshit her. One thing little girls hate is when you try to bullshit them," Nana quipped, laughing to herself.

I smiled at Nana's advice because she made it seem like it was just that simple. Talk to her. Don't bullshit her. I could do that just fine. Maybe I was approaching this parenting thing all wrong. Perhaps I wasn't supposed to be trying to parent her at all. There had to be a way to find balance between being a guardian and simply being her big brother, and if all I needed to do was treat her like a regular person instead of a fragile little girl, then that's what I'd do.

I thanked Nana Shirley for her advice, and she told me I could come to her anytime. She even offered to babysit when I needed it since most of her restaurant duties had been handed over to a very capable management team. I told her that I hoped I wouldn't need that but, when I told her that Mila was my sister and not my daughter, she just laughed and said, "Oh, trust me. You'll need it!"

When I got back to my house, it was eerily quiet. Normally, Mila would come home and blast music while she did her homework, but it was just quiet. I walked upstairs to her bedroom and, even though the door was closed, I heard sniffles. She was crying.

Knocking softly I called out, "Mila? Can I come in?"

"It's your house! Do whatever you want!"

She was mad at me. And the fact that her silence had transitioned into a full blown pre-teen attitude, made me realize how unprepared I was for this. The crying, the yelling, and the emotions were all things that I avoided when it came to women.

217

I inched the door open and found her on the floor, her knees bent to her chin, sobbing, and my heart ripped in two. "Mila, honey. I'm sorry. I'm so sorry."

"I…" she stuttered through sniffs, "I miss my mom!" and the sobs continued.

I rushed to the floor to sit next to her, not making any sudden moves in case she wasn't comfortable with me getting too close or hugging her. "I know. I miss my mom, too."

She looked up at me, her eyes big and red from tears. "Did your mommy make you feel better when your daddy yelled at you?"

"Fuck," I murmured, not even realizing it slipped out. My dad yelled at her, too. He had used harsh words and made her feel worthless, too. "Yes. My mommy made me feel better when…" I trailed off for a second. "When *our* daddy yelled."

There's a moment in life when you catch a glimpse of yourself in the mirror, and what stares back at you isn't quite what you expected. That moment hit me like a freight train today. I realized, with a gut-wrenching clarity, that I was morphing into the one person I swore I'd never become—my dad. And I hated myself for it.

I had become a mirror image of him—the same flaws, the same mistakes. I was walking down the very path I had promised myself I never would, and this small, seemingly insignificant exchange was a magnifying glass to my own shortcomings. It was as if someone had turned up the spotlight on my worst fears, illuminating the harsh reality I was too afraid to face. I was messed up, just like him. And the thought filled me with a dread that was impossible to shake off.

Mila deserved so much better than a rerun of my father's mistakes, and I was given the opportunity to course correct for her. To give her a male figure that didn't resemble our dad. I owed it to her to be a better version of myself, to break free from this vicious cycle.

So, there I stood at the crossroads, finally awakened to the harsh reality. It was time for a change, time to rewrite the narrative. For Mila, for myself, for the promise of a future where the apple fell extremely far from *that* tree.

"I'll tell you what," I said, using my hand to lift her little chin up so she could look at me. "I will do my very best to not make you feel like Daddy did, OK?"

I saw what looked like a smile forming in her cheeks, and then she brought her pinky up to my face, her brows furrowed and eyes narrowed. "Pinky promise?"

I smiled, interlocking my pinky with hers. "Pinky promise," I smiled. I got nervous and shifty at what I was about to ask her next, "Mila, would it be weird if I gave you a hug?"

She shrugged her shoulders as if it didn't matter, but I saw the smile on her face get bigger at the question. Then she lunged at me without notice and wrapped her tiny arms around my stomach, giving me the warmest, tightest hug.

"Thank you," I said. "I needed that hug."

She gave me an encouraging pat on the back and said, "Well, if you need another one, you know where to find me!" And we both fell out laughing.

"How about you do your homework, and I'll order something for us to eat for dinner since I was so late picking you up?"

"Pizza?"

Social services would probably come take her away if they knew how much pizza I gave this child, but it was the only thing she would eat! "Sure. Pizza it is."

I stood up to get off the floor, hoping she didn't hear my knees cracking, when she yelled, "Not so fast, mister!"

"What?!" I laughed.

"How do you know Mrs. St. James!? She looked like she knew you, but she also looked like she was mad at you, and normally when women are mad at you, it's because you did something to hurt their feelings, and that's *just* how Mrs. St. James looked at you!" She was smart *and* discerning, and I wondered what she had been through that made her have to become this way.

I hung my head, let out a sigh, and proceeded to give my baby sister the no bullshit but cliff notes version of how me and her principal met. "I actually met her the day before you came to live with me. She was at the club that night and heard me perform."

When it seemed she was satisfied with my answer, I wiped the sweat from my brow and went to go order this girl a pizza before she asked me how babies were made.

Chapter Nineteen

Hadassah

Coach Sanders, we need you on volunteer duty to make sure all the volunteers get to the right place, and Mrs. St. James will need to have a person with her for protection at all times. Since you're the biggest guy on staff, as well as the most affordable, Coach, I'm afraid you're pulling double duty once the volunteers are situated." Our Holiday Bazaar was in a week and Genevieve was running down everyone's assignments and responsibilities.

The Holiday Bazaar was something that we came up with to engage local businesses in the community. We had festive games, prizes, and entertainment for the families, while they also got to patronize and support local businesses. Initially, we were only able to convince two businesses to sign up. But now, especially since we'd seen more businesses come to the area, we maxed out our vendors this year with more than eighty. The funds raised from the Bazaar was how we were able to provide so many free resources to our students and their families.

"I have no problem protecting our fearless leader," Coach Sanders gushed. "You don't have a problem with that, do you?" he asked. But I was mentally somewhere else. "Dash?"

"I'm sorry. What?" I jumped, obviously not paying attention.

"I said, do you mind me being your protection during the Holiday Bazaar?" Coach repeated.

"Oh! No, Coach! Me and you always end up acting a fool together anyway!" I laughed, hoping my candor covered up the fact that I'd spaced out.

Throughout the day, I found myself constantly distracted. The interaction with Jaxon from our last encounter lingered in my thoughts, and I couldn't shake it off. I was puzzled as to why it bothered me so much. After all, he was just a one-night stand I didn't expect to cross paths with again. Yet, the fact that he was Mila's father...brother didn't mean I couldn't maintain professionalism, right? With that realization, I made a firm decision to do just that.

Whenever I had to see Jaxon or engage with him, I would be my best, professional self. I'd act like we had nothing between us except Mila's education and well-being. I wouldn't pay attention to his thick lips or his muscles that were bursting out of his gray suit or the fact that he was starting to let his hair grow, and he looked a little bit like Luke James. No, I would be professional and ignore all of that. Especially with the way he spoke to me. Verbally accosted me.

An unsettling feeling tugged at me as I recalled Jaxon's sudden transformation. I found it difficult to reconcile the stark difference between the man standing before me that day and the one who had tenderly held me during our night together. That night was a precious memory etched into my mind—Jaxon was gentle, caring, and compassionate. He treated me with a kindness that was rare, a softness that hinted at a depth of feeling I hadn't expected. But now, his demeanor had shifted so dramatically it was as if that man had been an illusion.

Grief, my unwelcome companion, had taught me to numb my feelings, to avoid the raw pain it brought with it. That's why I had chosen to close myself off from emotions, to distance myself from situations and people who threatened to disrupt the intentional vacancy in my heart. Yet, here I was, *feeling* things I didn't want to feel. Thinking about someone I didn't want to want.

I was fine until I saw him again. I was able to suppress him along with everything and everyone else. But as soon as he was in front of me, it was as if my vault of emotions was ripped open, my deepest secrets and longings exposed.

"In other news," Corinne announced, "Mr. Douglas was caught vaping in the theater again, and this time students caught him on video, so we've had to place him on administrative leave. But...I think it's safe to say he *won't* be returning."

I snapped out of my Jaxon-induced stupor, "Oh, no! What about the spring musical?" I gasped, "Nobody is equipped to finish what he started, so does this mean we'll have to cancel?"

Corinne placed her hand on my shoulder. "Let's take this offline and see what we can come up with. Mr. Douglas usually designates a student director, so the kids may just need an advisor to oversee rehearsals."

A wave of relief washed over me, causing my tense shoulders to relax, *slightly*. This school was a constant whirlwind of challenges. From disgruntled parents questioning the curriculum to politicians taking issue with me personally, it was a wonder I didn't have a drinking problem. But this was the work of someone who put the needs of their entire community before their own. This chaotic reality was what Lamar and I had willingly chosen. Absorbing the pressures and criticisms that came with the territory, and still striving to make a difference every single day.

Trying to find a music teacher mid-year was going to be another challenge that I would have to take on. With only a few months left in the school year and even less time until the spring musical, anyone would be crazy to accept a job under these conditions. *Hmmm...If only there was a musical genius that could potentially step in to help temporarily. One whose little sister had just joined the school?* It would be nearly impossible to be in such close proximity to him. But then again, I was desperate.

Jaxon

To make ends meet, I started putting in more hours at Sanctuary. From Monday to Wednesday, during the lunch peak, I was serving food and helping out behind the bar, since Mila was at school. Then, from Thursday to Sunday nights, Nana would watch Mila so my band could play for the crowds. As long as the drinks were being ordered and flowing, Lu gave me a percentage of the bar sales. Splitting the bar revenue was her idea, saying it would keep us both honest about my impact on the restaurant. And it proved to be effective. If the band wasn't playing, the people didn't flock to the restaurant.

Lu didn't have to do this for me. She didn't owe me any favors. But she knew firsthand the struggles of raising kids on your own, so she was willing to help out however she could.

"Incoming!" Lu shouted from the back.

It took me a minute to register what she was saying when it dawned on me that the bell to the front door had rang, signaling someone entering the building. "Remy," I said in a less than pleasant tone. I was standing behind the bar, but I could see her as clear as day.

"So, he *does* still remember me. Hello, Jaxon," Remy said as she walked towards me wearing a black dress, black heels, and shades that hid her eyes.

Nothing had changed about her. She was still fine with a gorgeous body and a walk that rivaled Jessica Rabbit but, *I* had changed. Since I'd taken in Mila...since I had met Dash...Remy didn't move me the way she used to. "What are you doing here, Rem?" I asked through gritted teeth, trying to keep my tone even.

"I need a reason to visit you, now?"

"When you've been playing games and pulling the shit you've been pulling the past couple of weeks? Yes, Remy. You absolutely need a reason to visit me. Now, what do you want?"

Remy stood behind one of the barstools with her gaze fixated on me. She removed her glasses as if she needed a better view. Like she was attempting to search my eyes for something. "Jaxon, can I sit?"

I pointed to all the seats at the bar and gestured for her to be my guest. "Can I get you anything to drink?"

"Pelligrino, please?"

I went into the fridge behind me at the bar and grabbed the overpriced water for her, placing it on the bar with a glass and a napkin. "Now," I said, remembering my goal to try to be softer when speaking to women. "What can I do for you, Remy?"

I watched her take a sip of water and square her shoulders as if she was giving herself an internal pep talk. "I need a favor. A new director needs music scoring for a project, and he specifically requested you. Apparently your name is floating around several venues these days."

I let out a dry laugh, "Hell, I wouldn't know it, the way these projects have suddenly dried up and nobody will take my calls."

She held her head down, and I thought it was because she felt bad about what she had been doing, but she looked back up at me and her expression went cold. "See what happens when I'm not the first choice? I told you there would be consequences for not choosing me…"

"Remy, don't do that!" I cut in, "That was specifically dealing with other women...grown ass women, and you *know* it. Mila is a child. My sister! And you acted like I told you I was leaving you for another chick. You *acted* like you didn't care since we weren't *really* a couple anyway!"

Remy just continued speaking as if I didn't say anything about Mila, "And I told you that I would likely be the one to destroy you *first,* remember?"

"And what? You think you can stop me by ripping away all the opportunities you introduced me to? Sweetheart, I was making a way for myself before you, and I'll have no problem doing it without you."

I turned to take the empty bottle of water to the trash when Remy grabbed my arm. "What about this," she said in a low, seductive voice. "Give me two weekends a month with you and that magnificent dick, and we'll call it even. All the opportunities you had filling your calendar a month ago will magically reappear!"

I looked at her hand on my arm and then back up to her face with an intentional glare and whispered, "Let me say this one time, and I want you to listen *very* carefully. You will never get another opportunity to hold anything you have over my head again. You play too many games, and

229

while I willingly played with you before, I'm done. Now, grow up, and get out of this bar. Anyone who wants to work with me can speak to my management from here on out."

She cleared her throat, "And who is your manager?"

Before I could make up the name of this new fictitious manager, Lu came from the back in the kitchen and busted the door open yelling, "I am!" Her little four-foot-eleven self was scary, and not even Remy would step to her.

Remy collected her things and nearly ran out the door when Lu promptly turned to me and said, "I want ten percent of everything, but I'll negotiate the best deals for you."

I just shrugged my shoulders laughing, "Aye, do your thing. I trust you."

It was the truth. I'd trust Lucy before I would trust anyone else to handle my business and have my best interests at the forefront of everything. "Good," Lu continued. "Send me all of the Hollywood contacts you've accumulated, and I'll resubmit your demo work under an alias. Once we get some bites, I'll secure all of the contracts, and no one will be the wiser. And even when they do find out it's you, no one will be able to say they knowingly crossed Remy Fontaine."

Sitting there and watching Lu morph into a beast of a businesswoman made me question why I never went to her before. But man was I grateful to have her in my corner now.

Chapter Twenty

Jaxon

Checking in on Nana Shirley and helping her get deliveries or groceries off of her doorstep became a regular part of my routine. I'd like to believe my mom would have been proud seeing me look in on Nana this way. After all, it was the easiest way to get free samples of her cakes. Everytime I would bring something in for her, she would send me home with a cake for Mila.

"So, how's she adjusting to school?" Nana asked, handing me a German chocolate cake for the road.

"She's getting there, I think. She is still pretty quiet about everything, and I don't want to push her."

"That's probably for the best," Nana confirmed. "She'll come around in her own time."

Apart from Lu, Nana was the only one who knew about the circumstances surrounding me and Mila. I needed advice and insight, and who better to ask than Nana? She had raised seven girls and practically fed all of Georgia. I told her, "I'm hoping that once Mila starts therapy, she'll start opening up to me more."

"She will. Just gotta be patient with her," she said, snuggling up to my side and squeezing me into a side hug. "Just like I'm sure your parents had to be patient with you!"

I chuckled, "My father wasn't a very patient man, so I was just whatever he told me to be."

"Oh?" Nana's facial expression shifted from jolly to pity or concern. Tilting her head she asked, "He was mean to you?"

"You could say that. I could handle it though. It was my mom that I always worried about." I wasn't sure why I was sharing all of that information. Something about Nana made me feel comfortable and safe.

"Men in those days were so backwards. They wanted a woman to dote on them and nurture a loving home, never realizing that everything they wanted for themselves needed to be demonstrated by them, *first.*" I watched as her gaze drifted off into the distance, and she laughed to herself, "My husband tried to rule my house with an iron fist *one time,* and it was the last time he did!"

"Oh, wow," I laughed. "What did you do, Nana?"

"Honey! I put castor oil in everything I cooked for him. The man didn't leave the toilet closet for a week! And when he finally had the nerve to ask me if I was putting something in his food, I just looked at him and asked, *'Now what was this you were saying about a husband ain't supposed to submit to a wife?'"* We both fell out laughing. "Then I smiled and handed him another roll of toilet paper and went on my way, honey!"

"And that worked?"

"He couldn't cook, so I'd say so! Milton learned to treat me with respect and honor. Until the day he died he would say, *'Your wife is your partner. And if you don't wanna partner with your lady, then you ain't got no business asking her to marry you. 'Cause if she can't partner with you, she can't trust you."*

I allowed Nana's words to linger in the air, soaking them in as I watched the affection dance across her face while she spoke of her husband. "If she can't partner with you, she can't trust you." Her words were laced with wisdom and experience. The idea that a woman felt more secure when she was included in plans and processes touched a nerve.

It made me think about how Dash often spoke of her and Lamar's partnership, their shared decisions in every aspect of life. The idea of being *that* connected to someone is foreign to me. I'd never experienced a love like that before. My ex-wife, Kenya, had tried, but I was too insecure then. I would never admit this out loud but, standing next to Kenya often made me feel like I was less. She was educated, a powerhouse at work, and on her way to partner at a prestigious marketing firm. She was beautiful, could sing, and everyone loved her. But because I didn't know myself back then, I ended up undermining and sabotaging our relationship every chance I got. Even today, I struggled to comprehend why I caused her so much hurt.

After sitting with Nana Shirley for much longer than I intended to, I gave her a soft kiss on the cheek and headed for the door. I was headed to my house when my phone rang. It was Mila's school.

"This is Jaxon?" I answered, looking at my watch to make sure I wasn't late again. I wasn't.

"Hello, Mr. Hart? This is the school nurse at Biddy Mason. I think…we need you to come down to the school!"

I heard frantic breathing and crying in the background, and my heart plummeted to my feet, "What happened?" I barked.

"She's…We think she's having a panic attack! Does she have panic attacks because nothing was on fi…" I hung up the phone while the lady was still talking. I didn't care what else she had to say. I just needed to get to Mila.

The school was only ten minutes away, but each turn, each traffic light seemed to stretch time, turning seconds into minutes, minutes into an eternity. Mila was in distress, and I found myself mentally rehearsing apologies to the school for not informing them about her condition. Looking back, it seemed ridiculous that we'd let Mila decide to keep her panic attacks a secret. The school should have been prepared to handle situations like this.

I was beating myself up over it, feeling like I had failed her once again. But I quickly realized this wasn't about me or my guilt. This was about Mila. She needed me to be present and focused on helping her through her panic attack, not wallowing in my own feelings of inadequacy. So, I took a deep breath, pushed my guilt aside, and focused on what mattered most—getting to Mila safely.

I pulled into the school parking lot, barely stopping to park before I jumped out and ran into the double doors in front of the building. Panting, I grabbed the first person I saw and asked, "Where is she?" The woman looked startled, and it hit me how crazy I must have sounded…on a school campus. I took a deep breath and tried again, "I'm sorry. The nurse's office, where can I find it?"

The woman eased her shoulders and flashed a comforting smile, then gestured to the door behind her, indicating that Mila was inside. I darted into the nurse's office, which in hindsight, was quite easy to spot if I had only taken a moment to look. There, I found Mila, huddled on the floor, tears streaming down her face. My heart clenched at the sight of her, rocking back and forth, consumed by her distress.

"Mila? Honey? It's me, Jax," I said gently, as I got down on the floor and settled behind her, inching closer with each soothing word. "I'm going to pick you up, and we're going to do the bear hug exercise we practiced with Danica, alright?" I paused, waiting for her nod of approval. It was crucial she felt in control, a point Danica had always stressed.

Once Mila nodded, granting me permission to proceed with the breathing exercise, I rose and bent over to slide my arms under hers, preparing to lift her off the cold floor. "We're going to stand up now, okay sweetheart? On the count of 3...1, 2, 3." As Mila stood, her frantic breathing began to slow. "Good job, sweetheart. You're doing great."

Once she was upright, I enveloped her in the warmest, most reassuring bear hug I could muster, whispering into her ear, "You are safe. You are incredible. And you are loved. Mila, you are safe. You are loved." I wasn't certain if I was even saying the right words or phrases, but they seemed to be working. Her hyperventilating had stopped, and according to the nurse, her heart rhythm was returning to normal.

This was the most terrifying situation I'd faced in a long while and, surprisingly, I felt a sense of pride. I had confronted it head-on, refusing to let fear dictate my actions.

Hadassah

I wasn't entirely sure if Jaxon even noticed me when he rushed into the nurse's office. I just stood quietly in the corner, observing him as he tenderly comforted Mila. His gentle touch, his soothing words, they took me back to the night we had spent together. The way he cared for me that night, it was the same man comforting Mila now. He was back, and I was relieved to see that side of him again.

As if he was reading my thoughts, Jaxon turned around to find myself, Corinne, and Genevieve in the corner. Partly concerned, partly turned on, maybe?

"Wow," Genevieve swooned. "I...I mean...Let me show you to the meditation room where Mila can rest for a moment."

"Meditation room?" Jaxon asked, seeming perplexed that we would have such a thing.

"Yes," I interjected. "Children have just as much of a need for meditation as adults. Even more so if you ask me."

Jaxon picked Mila up, and we all melted as this fragile little girl seemed to bury herself into his neck. He didn't say much in response to me chiming in. He simply replied, "I see. Would you mind showing me the way?" He asked, looking at me, but Genevieve jumped to volunteer.

"I...I'll show you, sir. Right this way." I watched as Jaxon secured Mila's legs around his waist and then followed Genevieve out the door.

"Biiiitch!" Corinne whispered. "The man who took your widowgenity was just right here! Looking dead at you like a whole ass meal!"

I smacked my lips and proceeded to walk out of the door towards my office. "Girl! Can we please find a different way to refer to Jaxon? Preferably anything that doesn't have the word widow in it?" I whisper-yelled while closing my office door.

Although, one could get away with calling him the *widow-maker* because of his monstrosity of a penis.

"I guess you're right," Corinne continued. "We could also call him…"

"How about by his name?! It's what everyone else around here calls him, and I don't want to tip anyone else off to our *history.*" Before she could say anything else, there was a knock on the glass of my office door. It was Jaxon, and I gestured for him to open it.

"Pardon my interruption, Dash…I mean…Mrs. St. James but, could I have a brief word with you while Mila is resting?"

I was instantly flustered, and I was barely able to hide it. "Uh… yeah! Sure. Come on in. Can I get you anything to drink or a seat? Have a seat here on my sofa! Unless you prefer a chair, then we could sit over…"

He held up his right hand as if he was signaling for me to take a breath. "I'm fine, thank you," he said softly.

"Well!" Corinne piped, "I will go ahead and leave you two to chat, and I'll see you later, Da…I mean, Mrs. St. James!" I rolled my eyes as I watched her shut the door behind her.

Suddenly, it was just the two of us. Alone together for the first time since that unforgettable night. His gaze seemed to pierce right through me, and I could feel a warmth spreading across my face. Was I blushing? Damn, he looked so good.

"I'm sorry, Dash," he said out of the blue.

"Sorry? For what?" I stammered, taken aback not only by his apology but also because I'd been caught off guard while daydreaming about his touch.

"The way I spoke to you the other day," he continued. "You didn't deserve that and..." he trailed off before regaining his train of thought, "I'll be honest, I can be a bit of an asshole when I feel threatened or challenged or..."

"Insecure?" I chimed in, finishing his sentence.

He chuckled, "Well, yes, if I'm being truthful."

"And, are you?"

His eyebrows knit together in confusion. "Am I..."

"Honest! Are you being honest with me right now?"

"I'm being more honest with you now than I've ever been with anyone in my life. Do you know how hard it is for a guy to admit he felt insecure?"

"Yeah," I murmured softly. "I can understand that. And I appreciate your honesty."

With two steps, he moved closer to me. "Look, I know we never planned to see each other again, and the fact that you're Mila's principal complicates things even more. But I want you to know that I'm sorry, and I promise not to let my temper get the best of me again. Mila deserves a better man than that in her life."

"She does," I agreed. Then I let out a heavy sigh, "Look, I don't know your situation, but we're in a bit of a bind and could use your help."

"For you? Anything."

I blushed, "Before you agree to *anything*, let me explain what it entails. Our music teacher is on leave and he was in charge of our spring musical. Now we need a musical director to help finalize the program and guide the students in their song choices."

"You want me to be a teacher? Dash, I don't have any teaching credentials."

"You wouldn't be a traditional teacher, so it's okay. The pay is $60,000 a year, but we can't guarantee that this will extend beyond the current school year. Still, if you want to be more present in Mila's life, this could be a solution." I held my breath, waiting for his response.

"Do you think I could do it?" he asked, clearly nervous.

"Absolutely! It's no different than directing the band at Sanctuary. It just involves a lot more sugar than you're probably used to, judging by those abs." *Did I just say that out loud?* "I...I'm so sorry. I didn't mean..."

He moved even closer, his lips just inches from mine, "You what? You didn't mean it, Shy?"

Lowering my voice I retorted, "Don't call me that, please. This is my job. *My* sanctuary. If this is going to work, us working together, you will have to remain professional."

"Hey! I'm not the one making lewd comments, risking a sexual harassment complaint!"

I couldn't help but laugh, "I did *not* make any lewd comments, fool!"

"Don't worry," he said softly, "I won't tell."

He knew exactly what he was doing, invading my personal space and stirring up feelings I'd been trying to suppress. I closed my eyes for a moment, taking him in, and I could feel him getting even closer. "I don't know if I can work anywhere near you every day and not want...every day with you."

"Jaxon," I breathed. But before I could continue, my office door swung open, and Coach came bustling in.

"Mrs. Saint James, they told me to come and get you so you could sign off on the Santa's Workshop display?"

"Sure, Coach," I said, barely able to break eye contact with Jaxon. "I…I'll be right there."

"Ooo…Kay," he said, finally letting it register that he might have been interrupting something. Then he shut the door and walked out of my office.

"I'd better get going," Jaxon said, backing away slowly from me. I missed him already.

"Will I…we see you at the Holiday Bazaar?" I muttered, attempting to make it seem like I wasn't looking *forward* to seeing him.

"Are you kidding me?" he grinned, "Mila won't stop talking about it. Her attitude has been on ten lately, but all I have to do is mention this holiday thing, and she brightens right up. So, yes. We'll be there."

"Good! Then we'll see you there."

"See you then," he said, sneaking in one more playful nickname mention as he flashed me a sexy grin. "And I'll think about the job, OK, Shy?"

With a grin, I shook my head and walked him to the door, "Goodbye, Mr. Hart."

Chapter Twenty-One

Hadassah

Holidays typically brought me down a notch, but this year was different. The Holiday Bazaar had somehow managed to keep my spirits soaring. I decided to make a statement with my outfit, opting for a bold, monochromatic look. I dressed in a chic red turtleneck, paired with matching high-waisted slacks. To tie it all together, I draped a stylish, red wool coat over my shoulders.

Usually, I'd go for a more casual attire for the bazaar, but this time around, we had invited the press, and I had a hunch some critics might pop in as well. I wanted to ensure that I left an impression, a good one at that. And if I do say so myself, I was looking pretty damn good. Before I left the house, I said a silent prayer for protection—protection over Biddy Mason and protection over my heart.

When I arrived at the school, the parking lot had been transformed into a winter wonderland with carnival games, photobooths, and food. Lots of food. Cars lined the street and families walked all along the sidewalk, rushing to get to the Bazaar, and the holiday spirit was infectious.

A group of eighth grade girls came rushing towards me. "Mrs. St. James! You look so pretty!"

"Thanks, Tasha! You girls look like you're having fun with your faces painted!"

"Yes!!" they all dragged out in unison.

I reached into my coat pocket and pulled out four candy canes. "Here you go, ladies. Have an amazing evening, OK?"

"Thank you, Mrs. St. James!!" they all yelled as they ran off.

It was incredible to see our dreams come to life. I cherished the memory of how this all started—just a simple idea scribbled on a yellow legal pad. And now, we'd created something that's actively shaping the future. Before the rush began, before the onslaught of cameras and questions, I stole a quiet moment to soak it all in. I closed my eyes, immersing myself in the sounds of joyous laughter, chattering families, and the festive hum of holiday music. Then, in a soft whisper audible only to me, I said, "Thank you."

"It's a beautiful sight, isn't it?"

The deep, familiar voice that came from behind me made me jump.

I'd recognize Jaxon's voice, his presence anywhere. "It is," I replied, managing a smile. I chose not to turn towards him, so I remained facing the crowd with him standing behind me. His warm breath tickled my neck, sending a cool shiver down my spine. But I fought the urge to react. I didn't want him to know he affected me. And after the way I'd awkwardly rambled during our previous office encounter, I had to regain my confidence. Or at least pretend to appear like I had everything under control.

"You look beautiful tonight, Dash."

"Thank you," I said, a grin spreading across my face.

Then, without thinking, I blurted out, "And you smell like sin." Why did I keep doing that?! Why did I keep letting my inner thoughts slip out like I had no control over them? Mortified, I dropped my head, my hand instinctively shooting up to my forehead.

"What's wrong, Shy? You say the quiet part out loud again?"

Taking a deep breath, I began, "Jaxon, it was really nice to see you..."

Suddenly, a voice broke in, "Mrs. St. James!" I turned around to see Mila running up to us, her face beaming. "Look, I got my face painted!"

"Did you now? It looks beautiful, Mila! You're the most adorable little Rudolf that I ever did see." I couldn't help but admire the intricate detailing of the reindeer ears and tiny antlers that formed a cute mistletoe between her eyes. "You two enjoy yourselves tonight, okay?" Without waiting for a response, I quickly walked away, eager to escape the magnetic pull of Jaxon's presence and Mila's smile.

It frustrated me how I seemed to lose myself whenever he was around. It bothered me that I couldn't keep my composure when he was near. And as if that wasn't enough, Mila made it terribly hard not to fall for her. If anything could keep my emotions for Jaxon in check, it would be my reluctance to get close to Mila. I didn't want to love another child. It would feel like I was betraying Ty's memory.

But Jaxon did look irresistible tonight. He was wearing a black turtleneck that accentuated his muscular build, paired with a cream-colored jogger suit that left little to the imagination. A well-dressed man with a captivating scent was my weakness, so I knew I had to keep my distance. Especially if we were going to be colleagues.

"Great turnout, Hadassah. Too bad this will all be for nothing!" The winter chill of Atlanta seemed to intensify with the arrival of Congresswoman Dede Atkins' voice, the official who was fighting to ban charter schools in Georgia.

I turned to face her, forcing a sarcastic smile onto my face. "Congresswoman Atkins, I know you find joy in spoiling Christmas for children, but take a night off of the broomstick and have some hot cocoa. You never know, it just might brighten your dark soul!" I closed the gap between us and added, "And it's Mrs. St. James to you. If you can't respect that on my property, then you're free to leave."

She put her hands on her hips, indignation rising up in her. "You seem to think that hosting a few community events will keep your little charter school safe, but it won't! You people suck resources from public schools and create educational disparities among communities! Plus, with no teacher unions and no government oversight of your curriculum, who knows what you're teaching these impressionable young minds! You could be raising a generation of extremists, for all we know!"

"You people?" I struggled to not curse this woman out. Her words left me stunned. Here was a black woman who had the potential to do so much good for people of all backgrounds, yet she chose to attack an institution committed to doing more than she'd ever achieved. It was infuriating, and I was tempted to ask where she was on January 6th!

Keeping a smile on my face, I replied, "Congresswoman Atkins, I'm not sure why you're so strongly against me and the work my husband began, but I assure you, your motives are misplaced. And *trust* that the voters will make their feelings clear about us, our curriculum, *and* our love for our teachers." Pausing for effect, I looked at her with something close to pity. "We could be allies, but you choose to undermine us. Once the community sees your true intentions, not only will we defeat your ridiculous measure at the polls, but you'll be lucky to secure a spot on the PTA, let alone be re-elected to Congress."

I walked away, leaving her standing there with a gaping mouth, and it felt invigorating. I suppose I should have tapped into my inner 'Sza the Stallion' before leaving home, but that fiery spirit was definitely ignited after that encounter! As someone who leaned more towards introversion, confrontation wasn't really my thing. But it irked me when people mistook my non-confrontational demeanor for fragility or fear of expressing myself. After losing Lamar, I realized I had to get better at asserting my boundaries. That meant letting go of the fear that voicing my desires or thoughts would inevitably lead to conflict. And guess what? It had made me a stronger, better version of myself. *So, take that, Dede Atkins. Old wench.*

"There you are!" Coach Sanders announced walking towards me. "How am I supposed to protect you if you don't show up to our designated meeting spot? You know Genevieve will have my neck if I let anything happen to you!"

I laughed, "And I could have used you a few minutes ago!"

His expression turned serious. "Why? Did something happen?"

"Nothing like that, Drew," I assured him, placing my arm in his as we walked through the crowd. "Congresswoman Atkins made her appearance, and it would have been nice to have you block her and cuss her out like the security guard Otis from the show "Martin"!" We both burst into laughter.

Drew Sanders was so easy to talk to and be around. Despite being a celebrity, he never let it get to his head. He had two Super Bowl rings and was once a top contender for the Heisman Trophy, but you'd never guess it from his demeanor. A true gentle giant, brilliant with kids, and always the life of any party. He'd tried to step up and be the surrogate for the students that Lamar was, but he said all the time that his were impossible shoes to fill. Still, we were fortunate to have him at Biddy Mason.

The line for Santa photos was so long, it wrapped around the entire school parking lot. But as soon as the "Cupid Shuffle" started blasting from the speakers, the line broke up and a wave of excited screams filled the air. Parents, kids, and teachers all rushed to the makeshift dance floor in the heart of all the action. I found myself laughing as everyone moved in sync to the rhythm... right, then left, now kick. The atmosphere was buzzing with energy, and in that moment, I was overwhelmed with emotion, my eyes filling with tears. "Look at what we've accomplished," I whispered to myself. "Just look at what we've done."

Suddenly, out of nowhere, Genevieve and Corinne appeared, each grabbing an arm and dragging me onto the dance floor. And I danced.

Jaxon

Dash was simply captivating. I hadn't planned on spending the night watching her, but somehow, my senses kept gravitating towards her. It felt like an invisible force pulling me in. I watched her dance, her friends encircling her, egging her on and cheering her every move. I don't think I'd ever seen her so joyous, so carefree. My gaze followed her movements, in sync with the beat. The way her hips swayed to the rhythm, her laughter echoing around, it felt as though everyone else vanished, leaving only her, shining brightly in the distance. I could have been imagining things, but I could have sworn I saw her watching me, too.

I longed for a moment alone with her, a chance to whisk her away to some secluded corner like sneaky teenagers stealing kisses when no one's looking. But she wasn't alone. She had a man shadowing her the entire time. I knew she was influential, but private security? She was consistently impressing me.

I found myself drawn to her, experiencing feelings I'd never known before. Every instinct told me to resist the urge to get closer, to distract myself with other women. But after spending a year with Remy, being practically faithful, and then meeting Dash, someone I could envision myself being genuinely loyal to... Well, who was I kidding? To win her over, I'd have to live up to the ghost of a legend that was Lamar St. James, and the only legacy I had was one of pain and regret.

As the song shifted to the classic "Jump On It" by the Sugarhill Gang, her bodyguard couldn't resist joining the crowd in the dance. Dash, visibly exhausted, made her way towards the drink area near the teachers' refreshment table. An opportunity presented itself—a chance to approach her, talk, or maybe even tell her how amazing it was to see her letting loose. I didn't have a script; all I knew was I was dying to be close to her.

The teachers' refreshments were located in the quad near the cafeteria, and I recalled a dimly lit walkway leading from there back into the building. After ensuring Mila was safe in line for a carnival game with her friend Arrin and Arrin's mom, I informed them I'd be right back. Then, without a second thought and before I lost my nerve, I practically ran over to Dash. Quietly yet swiftly, I grabbed her by her hand and guided her behind the refreshment table and along the remembered walkway.

Every planned word had fled my mind, so I did what my body screamed out for—I kissed her. Gently at first, allowing our minds and pulses time to adjust to this sudden intimacy. A soft moan slipped from her lips as she leaned into me, her nails lightly tracing up my back before digging in.

Suddenly, she pulled away, panting, "Jaxon, what are you—" I didn't let her finish. I wasn't about to let overthinking spoil our moment, so I drew her back into another kiss, deeper, fiercer, my tongue parting her lips to explore her mouth.

"I missed you," I whispered into her ear, my tongue tracing a path down her neck. "I missed this," I murmured, pulling down her turtleneck to dig my teeth into her skin.

"Fuck! Jaxon," she whimpered, igniting a torturous twitch in my pants. Sweats for that matter. "This is not a good idea!" Despite her words, her hands roamed all over me, confirming her desire matched my own and was turning me into an animal.

Lifting her up, she instinctively wrapped her legs around my waist, and I pressed her against the brick wall lining the walkway. "Fucking people. Fucking clothes," I gasped. "Everything is in the way of me doing what I crave to you right now," I growled as she slowly grinded against me, her legs providing leverage for her pleasure.

She was petite, so I was able to hold her against the wall with one hand while using the other to untuck her top from her pants, exposing her plump breasts covered only by the red lace of her bra. Freeing her left breast, I drew her hard nipple into my mouth and feasted. Licking and sucking and biting, she was unraveling, and I marveled at the sight of her throwing her head back and sliding up and down the length of my shaft while she chased her release.

"Jaxon," she moaned, her teeth grazing my ear while her arms clung to my neck in a sex-starved death grip. The distant glow from the school's football stadium draped us in an intimate darkness, the muted light adding a thrilling edge to our sexy rendezvous.

If I hadn't perfected the art of self-restraint, of keeping my own climax in check so that a woman could reach hers first, I would have come undone right there and then. In my pants. She was the epitome of seduction, an irresistible mix of touch and taste that I craved with an addict's desperation.

"There you go, baby," I encouraged, feeling her breathing hitch as she neared her climax. "If I had more time, one more night, this would only be round one. Come for me, baby." With that, she let go.

"Damn it! Fuck! Shit!" She breathed out in a husky whisper, her body trembling from the waves of pleasure coursing through her. "I hate you so fucking much right now!"

"Lies," I countered with a devilish grin, loosening my hold on her but keeping her close enough for a few more tantalizing seconds, my throbbing arousal teasing her sensitive center.

"Where is Principal St. James?" We heard Ms. Genevieve's voice echoing from afar. "She's up next for her speech!" The sound jolted us back to reality, reminding us that our stolen moment was over.

"I...I should get back," she mumbled, a bashful smile playing on her lips.

Gently, I helped her rearrange her disheveled clothes, her top neatly tucked in and her turtleneck and coat smoothed back into place. As she turned to leave, I couldn't help myself—I grasped her left arm, pulling her back into my arms for one last heated kiss. My hands cradled her face, drawing her closer, tasting her, savoring her. This desire was becoming too much, too reckless.

"Jaxon, I really need to go," she murmured softly, gently pulling away from me.

"I know. Go give 'em hell, alright?" I held onto her hand a few seconds longer before adding, "And my answer is yes, I'll take the job."

Smiling, she walked away, leaving me alone in the dimly lit walkway. I lingered there, allowing my body to gradually adjust to the biting cold and the void left by her absence.

Chapter Twenty-Two

Hadassah

The Holiday Bazaar was a resounding success. When I woke up on Saturday morning, my phone was flooded with notifications—text messages containing links to social media posts and news articles, all praising our contributions to the local community. Thanks to our efforts, the event had injected over two million dollars into local businesses. Although Congresswoman Atkins attempted to cast a shadow over our triumph through some obscure news outlet, her negativity was drowned out by the positive buzz we'd created. We had shown our town the destructive agenda she was pushing, and people were beginning to rally behind us.

It was a rainy Saturday morning, but I decided to sit in our screened in patio area and have my morning coffee, allowing the sounds of wind and rain to soothe me while I wrote in my journal. I'd gathered quite a collection of journals over time, each one playing a different role in my life. One served as an outlet for my day-to-day emotions, a place to express my thoughts freely. Then, I had individual journals for Ty and Lamar, where I wrote heartfelt letters to them whenever I found myself missing them. Journaling had always been my personal compass, helping me stay balanced and grounded amidst the chaos of life.

Today, though, my thoughts were all over the place, a jumbled mess that I couldn't seem to piece together enough to pen down anything that was coherent or made sense. In fact, my emotions were in a similar state of disarray, making sense of them felt like trying to catch smoke with bare hands. I couldn't stop thinking about Jaxon and everything that transpired the night before. He had invaded every area of my senses, and I needed an exorcism to get him out of my system. I still smelled him, tasted him, and if I closed my eyes, I could feel his hands all over me.

What was he doing to me? How could this man, who was everything I absolutely did not need, come in and disrupt the years of work I had been doing to keep myself closed off to feelings and emotions? I was losing my mind, spiraling at the thoughts that were assaulting me. This called for an emergency intervention, and I knew exactly who I'd assign the task. I grabbed my cell from the pocket of my yoga pants to call in the calvary.

(Me) *You busy? I need you.*

(Corinne) *Mimosa emergency or carb crash emergency?*

(Me) *Both.*

(Corinne) *Shocked face emoji* Say less. I'll bring a bottle of my Black Girl Magic Prosecco for Mimosas and pancakes from Main Street Cafe. See you in an hour.*

And just like that, the calvary was on the way. We had our own unique system for rating the level of our emergencies—we used comfort food as the gauge. If all we needed was a drink, then it was just a minor inconvenience that required a pep talk. But if we were calling for both carbs and alcohol, you could bet someone was on the brink of a full-blown meltdown.

I was a private person. I wasn't like some women who couldn't wait to share their every thought or every intimate detail of their lives to social media. I enjoyed stolen moments and secret kisses. I loved sharing something special with someone, and no one else knew it but us two. I loved having a part of me and my life that no one else had access to. But that was before. Before when everything made sense. Now, I really could use help processing these feelings and emotions.

Less than an hour later, Corinne was on my doorstep with breakfast, pastries, and Prosecco. I had never been more relieved to see her at my front door. "OK, bitch," she belted out, "tell momma what's going on. Who did it, and who do I need to fight?!" We laughed and I closed the door behind her and followed her into the kitchen.

Lamar and I purchased a house near the school because we wanted to be a part of the community we were serving. Since the school was in a less-developed area, we were able to get a good deal on a fixer upper home that, during the Summer breaks, Lamar would work tirelessly upgrading. We eventually had to hire a contractor because the repairs were taking too long, and I had found out we were expecting Ty. We didn't want to have a baby living through a construction zone, so we bit the bullet and hired help.

Over the course of four years, our fixer upper house was transformed into our dream house. Complete with a playground and zipline out back for the boys. The only area where I wanted complete control of the design was the kitchen, and Lamar didn't argue with any of my choices. No matter how expensive the designs or finishes, Lamar would say, *"Whatever my lady wants, my lady gets."* And every time I walked into this kitchen, with its matte black cabinetry and rustic gold finishes, I was reminded of those words.

"So? The suspense is killing me!" Corinne whined.

I let out a sigh, took a big gulp of my mimosa, and dove right in. "I can't stop thinking about him," I said in a pouty voice.

"Aww, sweetie! That's normal! He was your husband! Anyone would be going through what you're going through right…"

"No," I cut her off, "Not Lamar. Jaxon." I watched Corinne's face closely for a reaction. But she just stood there, her face expressionless.

"You mean the one-night-stand turned forbidden fruit because he's one of your students' parents, Jaxon?"

"He's not her father. He's her brother," I defended.

"Same difference! He's her guardian and…Dash, that could get messy!"

"I know! That's why *you're here!* Can you not judge right now and just be here for me?!" I yelled.

She quickly fixed her face and gave me a brief hug. "You're right. I'm sorry. Let's start over." Taking a sip of her drink, she turned back to me. "Why can't you get Jaxon out of your mind? What's changed all of a sudden?"

"That's the thing," I countered, "I don't think it's sudden. It's been a slow burn."

"Ooh!

I finally filled Corinne in on all the juicy details surrounding my encounter...encounters... with Jaxon. I started with every sexy, filthy detail of the first night we shared. Then, I moved onto the events of the previous night at the Holiday Bazaar. How he whisked me away from the crowd and led me to a dark corner. How he allowed me to unabashedly get mine without requiring anything in return.

"Daaaaaaang!" she swooned, sounding like Josie from Love Jones after Nina and Darius' first hookup.

"I knoooow!!" I groaned.

"So, what does this mean? What's next?"

"Honestly, I have no idea! I didn't want this. I didn't *need* this! I had a plan. I was going to concentrate on the work Lamar and I began. The kids at Biddy would become my surrogate family, and the work would be my life partner, ruling out the chance of loving another man ever again!"

"Dash, even for a workaholic like me, that sounds unrealistic! And down right dumb! Lamar would not have wanted that for you. I spent so much time with you two over the years, and one thing was crystal clear—Lamar would have done *anything* to see you happy. Hell, Dash. He passed away while executing the perfect birthday for you. How can you believe that a man like him would want you to shut yourself off from the possibility of finding love again?"

"Because *he* never said it. He never told *me* that!" I yelled, a sob looming at the back of my throat. "You're talking about a man with whom I shared every decision and every plan, after our marriage! We discussed everything, but this... this was the one topic we never touched!"

Corinne just sat there with me at the kitchen island, gently taking my hand in hers. "I know," she replied softly. "And I bet you feel like falling for another man would be a betrayal to Lamar because you still feel his presence."

"Exactly!" I cut in. "Lamar's spirit permeates not just the halls of Biddy Mason, but the streets of this entire community! What man could handle such... I don't know... pressure? Who could love me, knowing that I'm still deeply in love with my late husband?"

"Honey, your husband is an integral part of your life's narrative. Everything about him, even his passing, has shaped who you are. Anyone fortunate enough to fall in love with you, will understand that there wouldn't be a 'you' without the chapters that helped shape your story. Even the painful ones."

I adored her. I loved how she understood me, how she didn't judge me for still holding on to him after all these years. Wiping away tears from my face, I continued, "But Jaxon isn't *that* guy, Rinne."

Her eyebrows furrowed. "What do you mean, '*not that guy?*'"

"He's told me as much! Multiple times. The first night we met he told me he wasn't the 'settling down' type. Then, I caught a glimpse of his meanstreak the first day I found out he was Mila's brother. Two very obvious red flags that are telling me to run as far and as fast away from him as possible."

"But that dick keep snatchin' you and yankin' yo' ass back, huh?"

"Corinne!" I gasped, playfully slapping her wrist before doubling over with laughter.

Everything about Jaxon was a red flag. His looks, his voice, and he was a damn musician. He was the kind of guy the "After School Specials" and moms warned girls about. *"Steer clear of that man! He may look charming, but he gon' waste your time, girl."* Yet, I couldn't shake off the magnetic pull I felt towards him. I couldn't make sense of how he could be so tender, loving, and caring one moment, and then turn into the guy who spoke to me with such harshness the other day. Yes, he had apologized, but I knew plenty of women who wished they could rewind time and pay attention to those initial warning signs before falling for someone harmful. They all regretted brushing those first glimpses of a darker side under the carpet.

"So, even if he's not *that guy,"* Corinne continued, "is it so bad to just have a good time with him for a while? You've certainly earned it!"

"Having fun in my condition is a recipe for disaster." I grabbed both of her hands and dramatically looked her in the eyes and whispered, "Corinne! I'm *feeling* things!"

Corinne dropped her chin and narrowed her gaze. "Feeling things like what? 'Cause from the sound of it, all you're feeling is *horny*! Why not get the sexin' out of your system and see if that alleviates these mysterious *feelings*?" she suggested, waving her hands around to signify a mystical energy.

Maybe she had a point. Perhaps I was getting all worked up for nothing, and I was simply experiencing hormones! That had to be the obvious explanation, come to think of it. Before that night with Jaxon, I hadn't been touched in almost six years! That's why he was able to have me wide open over him! So, if I could adjust my thinking concerning him, then I could engage in *whatever* activities with him and just enjoy it for what it was. We wouldn't have to worry about feelings or emotions because we would set boundaries and ground rules. Yeah! I could handle this!

We sauntered into the family room at the back of the house. Our initial plan was to binge-watch our guilty-pleasure reality shows, but truth be told, I just relished the simple joy of chatting and reconnecting with my friend. Corinne was the epitome of a "ride or die." She'd whip up a meal for you when you were under the weather, would be the first one knocking on your door if she hadn't heard from you in a while, and possessed a combination of beauty and brains that made her irresistible to most. It often baffled me why she was still single, because my friend was genuinely a catch. But one thing was for certain, she wouldn't settle for just *any* man and that's what kept a lot of men at bay.

Sitting on the couch, Corinne turned to me and held up her right pinky. "Let's make a pact: There will be no falling in love with Jaxon Hart. You can spend time with him. Let him sex you up and dick you down. But he's not the forever guy. He's the guy that reintroduces you to the possibility of joy and pleasure again. He's the guy that you can call for judgment-free fellatio but…"

I wrapped my pinky finger around hers and completed her sentence, "but he's not the forever guy."

"Good girl. And why is that?" she asked, sounding like a teacher quizzing the class.

"Because he told me so."

"Very good! Gold star for you, Dash!"

We both laughed, but I took her words to heart. There would be no falling in love with Jaxon Hart.

Jaxon

"No fair! You cheated!" Mila shouted. She was pouting because we were playing a game of Twister, and I kicked her leg from under her, causing her to fall.

When I settled into this house, I gave Lu a little extra money to leave behind all the family-friendly games she'd bought for her short-term renters, since this was previously used as an AirBnB. The media room was filled with oversized versions of Twister, Connect Four, and Jenga. It was a great temporary solution until we could retrieve Mila's belongings.

Today, I had appointments with my father's probate attorney, so I promised Mila that we could have a game morning until it was time for my calls.

I would be lying if I said that Dash wasn't consuming my every thought since she walked away from me last night. I'd liked women before. I'd even been low-key infatuated with them. But never had I encountered a woman who managed to take such a firm hold on my thoughts. There was a brewing conflict going on inside me. On one hand, Dash was a respected woman in the community, and the town would have my head if I hurt her, so it was best for me to leave her alone. On the other hand, I wanted to do everything in my power to captivate her, impress her, and work to be the man she needed. Even though I'd never been *that man* for anyone else.

It wasn't that I had never tried to be faithful and committed to a woman before. When I married Kenya, there was a brief period of time where I had tried to be the man she needed me to be. But I was a man at war with myself back then, and Kenya suffered as a result. Whenever I felt like I couldn't measure up to the other men in her life, I'd find comfort elsewhere. I leaned on other women to bolster my self-esteem and cover up my insecurities. I'm fully aware that I wasn't fair to her, and the guilt of it was so overwhelming it made me want to escape my own reflection. Shame was a feeling I was very uncomfortable with but, so was integrity at one point. If I was going to choose one over the other, I was really trying to work on choosing integrity more.

While I was tied up with the lawyers, Lu kindly took Mila and her boys out for a pizza hangout. I was touched by how my close friends rallied around me, reminding me of the crucial role that these non-romantic relationships played—they had essentially become my family. I was well aware that Mila and I were all we had, both of us being orphans. So, it was vital for me to create a stable circle of friends for her, making sure she never felt the void of not having a family.

While on a call with the lawyer, I quickly realized I was way out of my depth. They bombarded me with questions about my dad's will, death certificate, tax returns, list of debts, and all sorts of stuff I had no idea about. When she and my dad were married, my mom was the one who handled all the legal documents and kept things organized. So, being asked about my dad's business, since everything was in his name, had me utterly clueless. Things were easier with my mom. She had neatly packed everything into a Trust for me to handle once she passed. But given that I barely knew my dad, and hadn't spoken to him in almost ten years, I had no idea where to start.

We wrapped up the call with me assuring the lawyers that I would drive down to my dad and his wife's house in Savannah to find all the needed documents. From what they said, he hadn't left much behind, but whatever was there would be set aside for Mila's future.

All of this was a first for me. I was still adjusting to the fact that I was now basically a parent to a twelve-year-old, a stark contrast to my partying days and being knee-deep in a different woman every weekend. This little girl had burst into my life and turned everything on its head, and surprisingly, I didn't mind it. I wasn't annoyed by the early morning wake-ups with her joyfully jumping on the bed. I didn't mind when she acted sassy about her breakfast or my lackluster ponytail skills. I even grew accustomed to her non-stop chatter and endless questions. In just a short time, this little girl had become more than just a responsibility—she had become my friend, my family.

When Dash offered me a job at Biddy Mason, it was a no-brainer to say yes. Spending every day with Mila had shown me that I could handle kids pretty well, and since music was my thing, this job seemed like it would be a walk in the park. The only reason I asked Dash for some time to mull it over was because I wasn't sure how she felt about seeing me on a daily basis. Being in close proximity to me. But judging by her reaction last night, maybe she wouldn't have a problem with it after all.

The doorbell rang, and I picked up my phone to see who was at the door on the security camera. It was Lu and Mila, and I had to check the time because they were actually back early.

Upon opening the door, Mila darted past me without a word and ran up the stairs to her room. "What happened? Is everything alright?" I asked Lu.

"I think she's fine. She was complaining of a tummy ache after pizza, so I brought her back."

"Got you," I said, relieved. I almost thought she'd had another panic attack. "Well, I appreciate you looking out for her. She loves hanging with you and the boys."

"Anytime!" Lu said smiling. "You know we love us some Lala!"

Laughing, I asked, "Lala, that her nickname or something?"

"It is when she's with me!" Lu replied. Then she turned around and headed back to her car. I watched her get in and waved at the boys before she drove off.

Feeling a bit worried, I headed upstairs to check on Mila. "Mila, sweetheart, can I come in?" I asked, waiting by the door. But she didn't respond. "Mila? I'm coming in, okay?"

Before I could turn the knob, she opened the door from the inside. I stepped back to let her out, but she just stood there. Tears were streaming down her face as she blurted out, "I think I'm dying!" and then started sobbing uncontrollably before lunging into me in a hug.

I gave her a gentle squeeze and crouched down to look her in the eye. "Honey, I promise you, tummy aches don't kill people, okay? You might've just had a bad reaction to the cheese on the pizza. How about I make you some tea or something?"

"You don't understand!" she yelled back, making me second guess all the sentimental things I'd said earlier about not minding her sass.

"What am I not getting, sweetheart?" I asked.

"In the bathroom," was all she managed to say.

With a sigh, I went towards her bathroom, a sense of dread building up as I wondered what I would find there.

At first glance, everything seemed normal. The bathroom was spotless, just as she'd left it before she'd gone out for pizza. All the towels were neatly arranged. Just as I was about to turn back to ask her what she was referring to, something in the trash can caught my eye. I didn't need to pick it up to know what it was. I recognized it immediately.

And I was losing my shit.

Chapter Twenty-Three

Jaxon

I tried to get ahold of Lu, but her phone was going straight to voicemail, so I sent her a text.

(Me) *Lucy, I need you. Please call me ASAP. It wasn't just a tummy ache!*

Five minutes passed, and I'd heard nothing from Lu. Of all things on all days, Mila had experienced her first... well, step into womanhood, and I was unprepared. I was at a loss for what to do or say. Had her mom discussed 'the birds and the bees' with her? Obviously not since she didn't even understand what a period was. The poor baby assumed it meant a death sentence. Something many women I know wouldn't necessarily disagree with.

I even tried texting Dash, but got no reply. Chances were she didn't recognize the number since we'd never swapped contacts before. I had to dig through the school's internal directory to find her details. It was unusual for principals to list their cell numbers on the school's website, but Dash's profile mentioned that she wanted parents to feel involved in their kids' education, starting with direct access to her. Given the number was still up there, I guessed not many parents had made use of it. Regardless, she didn't get back to me, and I was running out of options to help Mila. Remembering that there was a CVS a block over, I decided to run there to get whatever supplies she might need.

Sweating like a pig and gasping for air, I barreled into CVS. Everyone at the checkout counter stopped and stared. I probably looked like a crazed lunatic chasing after his next victim, but I didn't care. Mila needed me, and this was my chance to step up in a dad-like way. In hindsight, I probably should have driven there, but I'm not above admitting that I was delirious and not anything close to my right mind.

"Can... Can I help you... sir?" the confused store attendant asked.

I was still standing in the entrance, trying to catch my breath. "Girl stuff," I barely managed to croak out. I'd never spoken the words tampons or maxi pads in public before.

The man's eyes lit up as if he'd just solved a complex math problem. "Ah, yes. Aisle Five."

"Thanks, bro," I replied, relief washing over me. Then I darted past him towards aisle five. My confidence dwindled when I was met with an ocean of products all labeled "feminine hygiene."

I'd always heard people talk about being frozen by too many choices, but I never thought I'd be stuck in a drugstore aisle, haunted by the decision of which feminine product to buy. I cast a desperate look around, hoping some kind-hearted woman would swoop in and guide me through this maze of pads and tampons. But no one came—probably because I was panting like a dog, dripping with sweat and looked like I'd seen a ghost.

"I can't do this," I muttered to myself, finally admitting defeat. Then, I turned on my heels and sprinted out of the store, heading straight for home. I was sure someone was already dialing 9-1-1, convinced a madman was on the loose.

Once I got back home, I ordered every type of feminine hygiene product available, along with a few other goodies, on the DoorDash app. I just couldn't wander through the feminine care aisle any longer. Mila must have thought I was losing it, because ever since I spotted her pink, wadded-up underwear in the trash, all I managed to say was, "This is completely normal. Don't freak out, okay?"

"I'm not freaking out, *you are!*" she yelled.

I was absolutely freaking out. It had been an hour, and I hadn't gone back up to check on her since then. I simply kept yelling up the stairs, "Mila? I'm gonna find someone to help us, OK!?"

"Stop yelling at me!" she shot back.

I was pacing the floor, wracking my brain on what to do and who to call for help to explain this new chapter of her life when it suddenly clicked. Just five minutes later, Nana Shirley was bustling into the house, tote bag in hand, and heading straight upstairs to check on Mila.

"I appreciate this so much, Nana," I said.

She just waved me off with one hand as she climbed the stairs, saying, "Don't even mention it. Seven daughters, remember?" She laughed before I heard her knocking on Mila's door.

The doorbell rang, and I checked the security camera feed on my phone to find that my delivery was on my doorstep. After placing the bags of feminine products and goodies for Mila on the table, I hunted for a gift box that I could use. I had seen something on social media that had gone viral, and I wanted to try to recreate it for her.

Unable to find a gift box or bag around the house, I improvised by taking a basket used for linens and dumped them all out. Then, I lined the basket with all four brands of maxi pads. Then I created another layer with an assortment of candy, all of Mila's favorites. The next layer was an assortment of teas, hot cocoa and marshmallows.

Finally, I placed a card on top of the basket. It read: "With Love, the Period Fairy." Then I placed the basket by Mila's door for her to find later.

More than an hour had passed, and they were still up there. Only now, I heard Nana running a bath. I don't know what kind of sorcery this woman knew, but Mila had been laughing the entire time. I was flipping through channels on the television when I got a text message.

(Shy) *Jaxon?*

(Me) *Yes?*

(Shy) *How did you get this number?*

(Me) *School directory.*

(Shy) *Everything OK?*

(Me) *It is now.*

(Shy) *So, you don't need me anymore?*

(Me) *Are you really asking me that?*

(Shy) *Why? What would be your answer?*

(Me) *Always. Every day.*

(Shy) **Crying laughing emoji* Boy, please! Stop tryna spit game and open your front door.*

I switched to the security camera app on my phone and spotted Dash outside, dressed in white leggings, a royal blue Nike hoodie, and a matching blue cap. I was digging her hip-hop B-Girl vibe. With a sudden burst of energy, I sprang up and bolted for the door.

"What are you doing here?" I whispered, stepping outside and closing the door behind me so Nana or Mila wouldn't hear me.

"You texted that you needed me. I didn't see it immediately because I was passed out, taking a nap. But once I woke up and saw your message, I rushed over. Is that okay?"

"*More* than okay... but... you know you could've just texted back, right? You didn't have to come all the way over here," I said, grinning. "But don't get me wrong, I'm *so* happy to see you. Just didn't want you to be disappointed when I told you Nana Shirley already came to the rescue."

"You call your grandma Nana? That's cute," she teased.

"Stop it. She's my neighbor, and she's become like a second mother and grandmother to us." I moved closer and whispered, "She's *the* Nana Shirley, from Nana Shirley's Small Cakes?"

"No way!" she gasped.

"Yep! And she's upstairs right now, helping Mila take a bath."

"Mila... is she okay?"

I smiled, "Yes. Our little girl became a woman today."

"Oh, bless your heart! You must've been freaking out!" She was trying her best not to laugh.

"You saw that frantic text I sent, right? I was completely buggin'."

"I can only imagine!" Dash paused, her eyes flickering uneasily. "But... she's okay now, right?"

"Yeah, she's fine. Would you like to come in to say hi and meet Nana..."

Before I could finish, she cut me off, "No! I'm good. As long as she's okay, I don't need to see her." She took a deep breath, "Besides, explaining why her principal is here would be tricky, don't you think?"

I grinned. "Guess you have a point. But I feel like you're holding something back. Are you okay?" I asked, closing the gap between us. I gently tilted her chin up to meet my gaze, "Everything okay, Shy?"

"I'm fine, Jaxon. I'm..." she sighed, "I'm just relieved everyone's okay, that's all."

"I'm not entirely convinced, but... okay," I said, holding her gaze a bit longer than necessary to search her eyes for answers.

"Maybe if you'd give me some space, I could think and speak clearly!"

I leaned in closer. "So, you're saying you lose control around me? Can't find your words?"

She looked up at me, her eyes smoky and inviting. "What if I do? Lose control around you, I mean."

Without a second thought, I drew her into a kiss, my tongue tracing the edge of her lush pink lips. I tugged her bottom lip gently into my mouth, savoring the taste of her. When I abruptly broke our connection, her eyes stayed closed, as if she was reluctantly emerging from a sweet dream.

"Mmm...There you go teasing me again," she gasped, her breath coming out in ragged pants. Scizing the moment, I leaned in to claim her neck with another heated kiss.

"Trust me, baby," I groaned into her skin. "What feels like teasing to you, is pure torment for me." I pulled her even tighter against me, trying to dissolve the boundaries of clothing and skin between us. My hands roamed freely over the curve of her backside, appreciating its firm, voluptuous shape—just as I remembered. Pulling away, I asked, "Tomorrow. What are you doing tomorrow?" Then I let her go, stepping back as if to resist the gravitational pull between us.

"I'm free. You?"

"Mila's going to be with Nana all day. And since there's no school on Monday, I could ask if she can stay over. Can I see you tomorrow, Shy?" Before she could respond, I reeled her back into my arms, stealing another electrifying kiss.

"If you don't let me go now, I might not make it home!" she warned, her words carrying the undertone of a dare.

"Don't tempt me."

"I'm not," she laughed, stepping back and smoothing out her hoodie before heading towards her truck. "Tomorrow, then."

Chapter Twenty-Four

Hadassah

"Were you a Black Planet or a Myspace girl back in the day?"

"What?!" I said, feigning shock. "I was Myspace all day, honey! You couldn't tell me nothin' about my bootleg web development skills! What about you?"

"I'm black so…Black Planet for me."

"And what does that make me?!"

"It makes you who you are. We aren't playing this little game you made up to psychoanalyze each other," Jaxon said in a calm but matter of fact way.

His communication style was always clear-cut. He spoke with a steady, measured tone and didn't beat around the bush. He'd tell you exactly what he was thinking, even if it wasn't what you wanted to hear.

Our day had been filled with lounging in bed, chatting, giggling, and…*other things*. Mila went off to visit Nana Shirley at noon, and five minutes later, I was knocking on Jaxon's door! Ever since my heart-to-heart with Corinne, I'd started to feel more at ease about whatever was going on between Jaxon and me. As long as I didn't overthink or over analyze it, I could just relax and enjoy it for what it was. Jaxon wasn't *that* guy. But even though I had this new found awareness of what the situation with him was, today still felt different.

When we weren't wrapped up in each other, we were getting to know one another through light-hearted questions. We hadn't really delved into serious topics much, but it was enough to reveal a different side of Jaxon. Normally, he was more guarded, always trying to maintain control of the situation, and himself. But during our time together this time, he was genuinely opening up to me, which was a pleasant shift in his demeanor. I just hoped this didn't mean he was attempting to give me something I wasn't ready for. Something like an actual relationship.

"Love Jones or Brown Sugar?" I asked, with my answer already locked and loaded.

"Oh, come on, man! I'm a musician…It's definitely gonna be Brown Sugar."

"Really?! I actually just lost respect for you a little bit."

"You can't be serious. The nostalgia factor of Brown Sugar alone would make anyone fall in love with that movie."

"You have lost your *black* mind because the way Mr. Darius Lovehall spits that poetry and chases Nina down to fight for her love…Honey Darius, Larenz, whoever…can *get it*, you hear me?!"

"Wooww," he whined, acting like he was offended. "Good to know who my competition is."

The moment those words left his lips, silence engulfed us. It was like we both instantly understood the implication behind his remark, and it was evident that Jaxon had gotten swept up in the moment when he said it.

"I'm…I didn't mean that…"

"It's fine, Jaxon," I said, cutting him off. "Can I tell you something?"

"Of course," he replied.

"I know you're not the settling down type or the relationship guy, and that's why I'm here. I don't want anything serious right now, and that makes you safe for me. That's why I don't flinch at your stories about groupies or the women who constantly throw themselves at you. When I'm with you, I like to pretend you're my man, and we're just doing what we normally do when we're together. So statements like that won't scare me or push me away, as long as it only happens during times like this."

I wasn't entirely sure why I found myself opening up to him so much, but he had a way of making conversation feel easy. Just like I never passed judgment on him for who he was or what he'd been through, he extended me the same courtesy. He didn't look at me differently because of my quirks or the unconventional ways I dealt with my grief. That was something I truly valued.

"You mean like role play?" he snickered.

"Actually? Yeah! Exactly like role play," I replied.

Then, he surprised me by bringing up our last encounter, "Is that why you asked me to tell you I loved you and missed you last time?"

"Damn!" I shot back. "Way to dive right into the deep end!"

He insisted it was a fair question, but I pointed out he'd jumped from role play to me sobbing during sex! We were laying in the bed, him on his back and me on his chest, and he squeezed me tight and kissed my forehead before saying, "Don't be mad, Shy. I didn't mean for it to come off like that.

You don't have to answer if you don't want to. But I'll still tell you I love you while you're with me."

I climbed on top of him, my legs throbbing from everything we'd been doing the past four hours, then gave him a quick kiss. "Only if I ask you to. Anything else would just be weird."

Grabbing two handfuls of my cheeks he said, "But you *asking* me to do it isn't weird at all," and we both fell out laughing.

I crossed my arms on his chest, made myself comfortable on them, and gazed into his eyes, "I have another question, but it's a bit serious."

"OK..." he said, bracing for what I was about to say.

"That day at the school when you first found out I was the principal at Mila's school, you scared me. How you talked to me. I didn't like that. And I know I wasn't exactly pleasant, so I do apologize for how I even came at you. But, even if we are just...*whatever this is*...That can't happen again OK?"

"OK. That wasn't really a question, though."

"You're right. How often do you talk to women like that?"

I wasn't sure what prompted me to be so assertive with Jaxon, but there was something about not being overly attached to someone that gave you the courage to stand your ground and honor your own boundaries.

"It hasn't happened in a while. But before I continue," he said, raising himself up onto his elbows to achieve better eye contact, "I'm sorry, Hadassah. You didn't deserve that at all, and it will not happen again."

"I don't know why, but I trust you. Maybe it's because of Mila."

"You think so?"

"Yeah! Seeing you with her, you're...different. I didn't know you before, but there's just something about your bond. It's like you really care about her, love her even."

Jaxon chuckled, "Love, huh?"

"Are you saying you've never loved anyone other than yourself?" I asked, surprised at my own boldness.

He paused, mulling over my question. I laid my head back on his chest, giving him space to think without my gaze pressing into him.

"I guess...I've loved people before. My mother. I had deep feelings for my ex-wife, but I didn't love her the way she deserved. And...I suppose I do love my little sister. I can't quite explain it. When I first saw her big brown eyes and curly hair, I just melted."

"That's parenthood for you," I agreed. "The love is immediate and overwhelming," I murmured, mostly to myself.

"Why don't you ever talk about him, Shy?"

I knew what he was getting at. My last comment had steered the conversation towards Ty, but I wasn't ready to open up about him yet. "Because he's mine. That part of my story is mine to keep."

Jaxon fell silent, perhaps taken aback by my firm boundary. I heard him take a deep breath. "I understand. I was just curious...wanted to know if..." He stumbled over his words, struggling to find the right ones. "Is he with his dad?"

A sob threatened to break free, but I held it back and whispered, "Yes. He's...Yes," that's all I could muster.

I felt Jaxon's arms tighten around me in a comforting squeeze. "I'm sorry. I didn't mean to upset you."

"I'm not upset, just... It's hard. I'm not the type who needs to talk things out constantly. I write in my journal, and when things get really tough, I pretend or...role play."

His fingers gently traced the bare skin of my back as he listened. "Role play? Like we're doing now—playing house?"

"Yes," I chuckled softly. "But more like, when I'm home alone, I imagine that the boys are just out grabbing food or hanging out and I'm waiting for them to come home."

"And then? When they don't...you know..." His voice was gentle.

"By then, I've cried, written in my journal, and screamed enough to tire me out. Then I fall asleep, only to wake up to my reality."

"Does that help you cope?"

"It has so far," I answered. "At least it *was.*"

I had to change the subject. I wasn't prepared to revisit my grief or talk about how I cope with the loss of my family. What I needed was an escape, a way out of the heaviness I had carried with me for so long, and this was my day. My opportunity to hide from it all. So, before our conversation took a deeper turn into more serious territory, and I found myself tearing up in his arms again, I decided to make a playful move. With a mischievous twinkle in my eye, I lightly bit at his nipple, deftly changing the trajectory of our chat.

"Ouch!" he giggled. "What changed? Why isn't your coping tool working as well now?"

"You," I said, kissing his chest while my left arm stroked his hardening shaft. "I mean, my usual coping mechanisms still work. But since meeting you, things feel a little different."

His touch intensified as his hands explored my body, pausing at my thighs to give them a firm squeeze. "Different how?" he probed, desire evident in his tone... and in my hand.

Suddenly, he rolled me over, shifting me from his chest and onto my back. A wave of longing swept over me, leaving me gasping for air. My legs started to twitch, my knees rocking involuntarily as my back arched with anticipation and yearning. "Umm... Just different. Like, you've ignited something in me and umm...ahhh!" My sentence was cut short by a sharp intake of breath as he pinned my wrists to the mattress and bit into my neck.

"I'm sorry, could you repeat that?" he teased, his eyes sparkling with playful mischief.

I squirmed under his grip, playfully trying to escape. But instead, he pinned my legs down by straddling me. He held both my hands above my head with one of his, and then reached behind the bed to retrieve what looked like handcuffs that were attached to the bed somehow. Warmth rippled down my spine and spread to my core as I watched him secure my wrists into the leather straps. "What... what are you doing?" I managed to ask, but he remained silent, a mischievous smile playing on his lips.

Silent but determined, he climbed off the bed, his erection not shy about the thrill he was experiencing. I watched him walk to the edge of the bed and kneel down, pulling two additional straps from underneath the bed. He was restraining my legs as well, and I gasped from the anticipation of it all.

"OK, are you gonna give me a safe word or..."

He peered up from the edge of the bed where he was strapping my legs in. "Shhhhh..." he said, silencing my inquisition. "If you need me to stop or if you want more of something, simply ask me. But you must begin each request with, 'Shiloh Says.'"

A grin spread across my face. "Like Simon says?"

"Exactly," he said smiling. Then he rejoined me on the bed.

I hadn't realized it until now, but I rather enjoyed being dominated. I liked being given commands and being praised for my obedience. I even loved the consequences when I didn't comply. The spankings, the biting, the teasing. He had mentioned before that he liked to...*play*...but I didn't know what type of play he enjoyed, and I certainly didn't realize how prepared he was today. How serious he was. But there I lay, my heart racing with fire and my mouth wet anticipation.

I had never been in this position before—literally or figuratively. I tried to keep my thoughts from spiraling as I felt his fingers begin to trace the inner contours of my legs, starting from the delicate skin around my ankles. His touch was slow, gentle yet purposeful. A deep yearning for him stirred within me as his hands playfully skimmed my skin. My pulse quickened as his hands journeyed past my thighs and ventured towards my intimate center. As he reached the peak of my desire, I silently pleaded for him to end my torment by lingering there. But he didn't. Just like our previous encounters, he suddenly withdrew his hands, leaving my core pulsating and craving relief.

He started again at my ankles, but this time, he blazed a new trail up my body with his lips, alternating between using his tongue and teeth as he peppered my body with kisses. His calculated and bold advances were driving me to the brink of insanity. Initially, I was apprehensive about his intentions and what this would lead to. Now, I was burning with longing. The need radiated from my skin as he licked and kissed his way up my body, and I felt myself unraveling as I noticed his hand stroking his hardened arousal in the dim light. This was pure torture in the best possible way.

"Jaxon," I whimpered, as he teased my intimate folds with his lips, then his tongue. But when his tongue grazed my sensitive bud, he pulled away yet again, gently blowing circles around my clit as if trying to douse my desire.

"Jaxon!" I cried out, my soft pleas morphing into desperate demands. "Why do you insist on torturing me like this?" That's when he covered my mouth with his before abruptly pulling away.

"You mean like that?" he teased. Then he went back down to my ankles and re-started his trail up my legs again. This time, he only used teeth and instead of stopping at my center, he bit his way up to my stomach, then my breasts, pausing to bite my nipples. Hard.

"Fuck!" I gasped, instinctively trying to move and reach for his head, only to be reminded of my current predicament—my limbs were bound and useless for now.

He resumed his attention to my thigh area, teasing, nipping, and lavishing my inner thighs that were glistening with the moisture from my arousal. I found myself admiring his dark, smooth skin, his muscular build, the sharp contour of his jawline. An overwhelming desire to run my fingers through his soft curls came over me. I craved him. My body, my very core, was yearning for him, and in that moment, I remembered what little power I did still have.

"Hey, Jaxon?" he paused, looking up from his exploration of my thighs, anticipating my command. "Shiloh says... *feast.*" His expression transformed, and his eyes darkened with hunger as he shifted his focus to the epicenter of my desire, teetering on the edge of release. I felt every sensation and every tingle coursing through my body with each touch. And I knew that as soon as he touched me, as soon as his tongue touched my pulsating clit, I would be finished.

And then, without any hesitation or protest, he obeyed my order. He feasted, indulging himself fully, leaving no trace of my arousal untouched.

Chapter Twenty-Five

Jaxon

This woman was going to be my undoing, and even as I felt it, I couldn't pull myself away. Each time we were together, she revealed a little more of herself that made me feel protective over her. I found myself thinking that maybe, just maybe, I *could* love someone other than myself... *her*.

What was intriguing was she seemed oblivious to the impact she was having on me. It made me compare my attraction to her with my feelings for Remy. Remy was a mystery, a puzzle I pursued in an attempt to unravel. Ours was a relationship of constant power struggles, and she was the first woman who had managed to one-up me. But with Dash, there were no mind games, no hidden agendas. I found myself being surprisingly candid with her. I wasn't scared to let her see my flaws, trusting her to accept me as I am. And when she opened up to me, she trusted that I wouldn't frown at her wounds. For once, I was with a woman I didn't feel the need to charm with my usual playboy tactics. I could just be myself with her. And her with me.

From the moment Dash arrived, we were all over each other. We barely had time to say hello before our clothes were discarded and scattered on the floor. Within seconds, I was carrying her into the living room of my townhouse to take her right there on the floor. We had made love three more times since then, but now that we were upstairs in my bed, I wanted to take my time with her. It was time to play.

I was introduced to playful dominance by a previous lover who was quite into S&M. Her preference leaned towards the more intense, impact play. She reveled in the flogging and whipping, and I was more than willing to indulge her. However, when it came to incorporating these techniques on my own terms, I tweaked them slightly to better fit mine and my partner's temperament. Blame it on slavery, but whips and chains aren't my thing. I don't take pleasure in causing physical pain to a woman under the guise of pleasure. Don't get me wrong, I'm not against a bit of spanking, but I believe there's an appropriate time and place for it. What I did take pleasure in, though, was the power. The thrill of having someone completely at my mercy, responding to my every command. Dominance and submission.

My game plan with Dash was to gently guide her into this realm of passion and control, letting her set the pace based on her comfort level. She had been through so much that left her powerless, I wanted to introduce her to her own inner power and control, using this game I created for us. At first, she was a bit shy, uncertain about what to request or even what she truly craved. But the moment I handed over the power, allowing her to use her voice to steer me, she became a force to be reckoned with. She was chomping at the bit for me to satisfy her deepest desires. Once she witnessed how enthusiastically I responded to her every command, she reveled in the control, and watching her embrace it had me coming undone.

Dash and I spent an entire day and well into the early hours of Sunday morning holed up in my bed. We ordered takeout and ate it right there, too. By the end of it all, I was thoroughly spent, not a drop of energy or fluid left in me. But I wouldn't have traded that day for anything else. I felt as though we'd grown closer, understanding each other a little more. Even though we weren't aiming for anything serious, I found myself delighting in our pretend game...the imaginary scenario where Dash was mine, and I was hers.

With school on winter break, Mila was spending time at Nana Shirley's house, where she was learning how to bake cookies. Meanwhile, I took advantage of the empty house to prepare a special Christmas surprise for her. With Christmas just around the corner, my friend Lu gave me the go-ahead to use the BnB's guest Christmas tree. I pulled it out from the attic and set it up, leaving the decorations for Mila and me to hang together. I planned to do some gift shopping before picking her up from Nana's.

During English class, Mila and her classmates were tasked with writing letters to Santa, outlining their Christmas wishes. I was touched by how humble Mila's wishlist was. Unlike most kids her age, she didn't ask for dolls or fancy gaming consoles. Instead, she wished for a laptop, a small keyboard to learn piano, and a Christmas tree with beautifully wrapped presents underneath. She didn't even mind if they were used, according to her letter. My father, as I remember, never made much of Christmas or any holiday, really. He used to say holidays were too commercial, and Christmas had especially lost its true meaning. So, we rarely celebrated beyond attending church.

Even after all these years, it seemed my father never changed. Mila was such a good kid who asked for so little, and it irked me that my father remained the same, even after having another child. I often found myself wondering if he ever regretted his past actions or felt remorse for not building a relationship with me. But judging by Mila's silence about him and her reactions mirroring my own childhood responses to my dad, it was clear he hadn't changed one bit. Mila deserved holiday memories filled with sugar cookies and excited late-nights spent waiting for Santa, and I was determined to give her that. Especially this year since, the day after Christmas, we were set to start clearing out my father's house.

When Mila first saw the tree, she let loose a shriek that wasn't just a subdued 'yay,' but an ear-splitting scream that sounded more like Santa was murdered, not coming to town. Nana Shirley and I burst into laughter as she ran around excitedly shouting, "Thank you! Thank you! Thank you!" Nana brought us steaming mugs of hot chocolate and then left us to our tree decorating, creating a cozy bonding moment just for us.

"Ever decorated a Christmas tree before?" I asked Mila, hoping to gently coax more about her past life from her.

"Just once. Daddy was away preaching on the road, and Mommy said it wouldn't hurt to have a small tree since he wasn't around," she shared.

I was all too familiar with my dad's lengthy 'road trips,' and I knew they usually meant something other than preaching. But I didn't want to cast a shadow over our festive moment, so I steered the conversation back to happier memories. "Really? What colors did you deck the tree out in?" I inquired, my tone brimming with interest.

"Red and gold! They were Mommy's favorite colors. She said they reminded her of her home in Spain," Mila paused in her decorating, seemingly lost in a memory. "She promised to take me there one day."

I hadn't known her mom hailed from Spain. Suddenly, the name Milagros clicked into place. Her mom had gifted her a name deeply rooted in her own heritage. It struck me then that this was the most she'd ever spoken about her parents or her life before moving in with me.

TLC's Christmas song, "Sleigh Ride" began playing over the Bluetooth speakers, providing the perfect chance to lift Mila's spirits. I playfully initiated a dance-off, where I'd bust out old-school moves and challenge her to copy them. I was surprised by her rhythm and grace. She nailed every dance move, even outshining me a few times with her natural flair.

Finally, after adorning the tree with ornaments, lights, and candy canes, our decorating mission was complete. We switched off the lights in the house, sitting back to admire the festive twinkling lights as they cast a magical glow from the tree to the ceiling. Lying on the living room floor, where just hours before Dash and I had been entwined, Mila and I gazed upwards, as though stargazing indoors.

"It's perfect," Mila whispered, snuggling closer to rest her head on my shoulder. We ended up dozing off right there, and I woke to the sound of her soft snores as she nestled under my left arm.

Chapter Twenty-Six

Jaxon

"It's too loose!" Mila yelled while I wrestled with her hair and she watched me in the bathroom mirror. It was Christmas Day, and we were hustling to get ready for a brunch date with Lu and some of our Sanctuary colleagues who didn't have family around.

"Fine then, Mila, how do you want me to style it? I'm really sorry I'm not an expert at this," I said, trying to keep my tone light.

"But, my mom usually lets me wear it down on special days!" she retorted, her voice louder than necessary.

In that moment, it dawned on me that I hadn't considered asking her about any traditions or preferences she might have had for the day. We'd spent Christmas Eve staying up late, engrossed in our favorite holiday movies, and roasting marshmallows with Nana. When the clock struck midnight, we'd excitedly torn into our presents. Mila had even thoughtfully selected a gift for Nana.

Her delight at seeing all her presents neatly wrapped under the tree was heartwarming, something I had to thank Lu for. But when she unwrapped the keyboard and looked up at me, asking me to teach her to play, my heart was assaulted with something resembling affection. I had just assumed she already knew how to play. When I asked her what sparked her interest in the instrument, she gave me a look that said 'isn't it obvious?' and replied, "You, duh!" before moving on to her remaining gifts. Her gratitude was palpable, and it stung a bit each time I realized that she was already twelve and had never truly experienced a full-blown Christmas like other kids her age.

"OK! What does *down* mean or look like, Lala?" I said, attempting to change her attitude by calling her the nickname Lu gave her.

"Hey! Auntie Lucy calls me that!"

"I know! I think it's cute. Can I call you that, too?"

"I guess!" she said with a smile spreading across her face. Then that smile quickly turned mischievous. "You can call me that, but *only* if you let me wear my hair down today!"

I was already attempting to let her wear her hair "down" but I let her think she was winning this little game. "OK, fine. One beautiful little girl coming right up."

"Yaay!" Mila cheered.

I had no idea how to do any hairstyles that didn't involve a simple ponytail. With no time to fall down a YouTube tutorial rabbit hole, I asked Mila for her help. She began by dividing her hair into four sections, securing each one with a spare rubber band and leaving one section loose to start. She then filled the sink with warm water, dipped her hair brush in it, and handed it to me, dripping wet. "You need to make sure my hair is really wet. It hydrates it and makes it easier to comb," she advised.

"Got it, boss," I responded, shaking out the brush to get rid of some of the excess water. Mila's hair was a mix of textures, and her curls sprang to life as soon as they came into contact with water.

I started brushing her hair with the wet brush, dipping it back into the water between strokes, only to be chastised for doing something wrong. "Start at the ends and work your way up to the roots! You'll cause breakage, and then boys won't like my hair!"

"Hold on, what's this about boys liking you? You should style your hair in whatever way makes *you* happy, not for anyone else."

"But my best friend Arrin says that it's very important for me to become popular now, before high school, or I'll be invisible forever!"

I shook my head, trying not to dismiss her very real concerns. Kids could be harsh, and social hierarchy was a reality, but twelve seemed too young to worry about this stuff.

"Mila," I sighed, moving onto the next section of her hair. "I get that being liked feels important, and being popular can make you feel powerful. But do you know what's even more important?"

"What?"

"Being liked for who you are. When people appreciate you without expecting you to change or do things you're not comfortable with, you feel better about yourself. If you let people control you for popularity's sake, you risk losing sight of what makes you unique or special."

She sat silently, absorbing my words. For a moment, I felt like some kind of teen whisperer. I wasn't sure where this sudden wisdom was coming from, but I was speaking her language in a way that made her listen. I knew I hadn't suddenly been gifted with a parenting gene that equipped me with the perfect advice. I think part of me was telling Mila things I wished someone had told me when I was her age.

During my school days and a large part of my life, I was always striving to be adored and accepted. I couldn't figure out the secret to getting my dad's approval. I learned how to play all sorts of instruments, always made sure I was the best-dressed in the room, and worked tirelessly to hone my singing voice. All of this was done with the hope that one day my dad would say he was proud of me or that he loved me. Now, even as an adult, I still struggled with the fear of being rejected. I found myself doing everything possible to control how people perceived me. It was something I didn't want Mila to experience, especially not at her age.

I wasn't half bad at this. I had finished all four sections of Mila's hair, and we were both standing there smiling. She was obviously happy with her look, I was in large part surprised that I was able to pull it off. She barely even winced which meant I was getting better at not being so rough when brushing her hair. I finished off her style with hair mousse and watched her shake her curls all around her head.

"You look beautiful, you know that?"

"Of course I do!" she said as she sashayed out of the bathroom, swinging her shoulder-length curls back and forth. At least I didn't have to worry about her confidence.

Nothing could make you begin to examine yourself as a man quite like the presence of a little girl that looked up to you. Especially a little girl that was starting to wonder about boys. I'm self aware enough to realize that any advice that I'd give to Mila about boys, would essentially be warning her about men who thought like me, and I was beginning to not like myself. My hypocrisy. I wanted to be a man that was worthy of Mila. Worthy of being the kind of man that she would look at and say, 'I want a man that treats me like my big brother.' And a man like that, is a man worthy of Dash, too.

Hadassah

After Lamar died, the staff at Biddy Mason started a tradition where we would host holidays together, as long as we didn't have commitments with extended family. Nobody wanted me to be alone, and I appreciated the noise during these times. The noise of love and laughter helped me to block out the grief that tended to consume you during these times. Christmas will be hosted at my house this year. And after years of allowing darkness to cloud my holidays, I actually managed to put up a tree.

"Silent Night" by the Temptations played in the background as I sat in the corner and smiled, enjoying the sounds of Coach Sanders, Corinne, and a few other teachers from the athletic department trash-talk each other during a game of Spades. I'm pretty sure Corinne lied about knowing how to play because Coach Sanders was *big* mad after her last renege. Genevieve and her husband were on the screened-in porch enjoying a glass of wine by the outdoor fireplace, and I smiled everytime I caught them cuddling. They'd been married for more than twenty years, and he still found opportunities to grab his wife's booty.

A few of the other staff's children played on the playground outside while the dads shamelessly enjoyed the zipline. Today was turning out to be a pretty perfect day, and for the first holiday in a long time, I didn't wake up with overwhelming sadness in my heart. I felt different, and I didn't dwell on it too long because I didn't want to ruin the feeling or scare it away.

I went into the kitchen to clear some of the dishes when I heard heavy footsteps walking up behind me. Feeling the obvious presence of a man, getting a little too close for comfort, I turned around quickly to see who it was. "Coach Sanders! You startled me," I said, grabbing a dish towel to dry my hands. "Can I get you anything?"

"Nah, I'm good," he said smiling. "I just had to get up from that card table before I flipped it over. Corinne needs to stop acting like she knows how to play. Knowing good and well she should be playing Go Fish with the kids!" He was obviously upset, but I couldn't help laughing in his face.

Spades wasn't just a card game. Spades was a black cultural tradition in most households, and many would swear you weren't "really black" if you didn't know how to play. I learned how to play when I was ten years old at a family reunion. At first, my daddy would sit me on his lap and show me the difference between a good book and a bad one. Then, he'd let me pick out the 'books' I thought were good on my own. Once he saw I had the hang of it, we became the reigning Spades champions, making me the only partner my daddy ever wanted to play with. *"Who needs enemies, when you have a spoiled daddy's girl?"* My mommy would tease, and Daddy and I would eat it up. I spent Christmas Eve with them, but they had always been supportive of me spending time with my Biddy Mason family as well.

"You know Corinne is not gonna admit that she doesn't know what she's doin'!"

"Exactly," Coach confirmed. "That's why I had to leave before you ended up having to report me to HR on Monday!"

Still laughing and talking, I watched as Coach began bringing dishes to the counter next to the sink to help me load one of the dishwashers. When I designed this kitchen, one of my requirements was to install two dishwashers for when we had large gatherings. I was more than grateful for it today because there were dishes everywhere. No matter how many paper plates we had, more dishes kept getting dirty. But doing dishes wasn't simply a chore for me. As an introvert, I needed small things like this to take my mind away from crowds and chaos for a little while to give me time to recharge.

"You don't have to help me, Coach! I've got this."

"Oh, I *know* you've got it," he said grinning. And I could swear it sounded like he was flirting. "I just wanted to do my part to help the pretty lady."

He was definitely flirting, and I wasn't sure how to feel about it. Other than weird. "Oh I appreciate it, but…"

"Nonsense," he cut in. "Everyone sees how hard you always work, even on your days off. Let us take care of you for a change," he said '*us,*' but the spark in his eyes said he was only speaking about himself.

Had I been missing clues that Coach Sanders liked me? Had he flirted with me before and I just never noticed? Before I could examine my thoughts or Coach's feelings any further, there was a big commotion in the living room that sent us both running to see what was going on. Mr. Darby from the math department and our guidance counselor, Ms. Sneed, were both in Corinne's face yelling at her over this last round of Spades. Apparently, Mr. Darby actually had flipped the table due to Corinne's shenanigans, and we were all dying laughing.

Everyone was laughing and yelling amongst themselves, making this the perfect opportunity to steal away. I ducked onto the porch since Genevieve and her husband had gone back into the house. There was something peaceful about hearing the crackling fire from the fireplace against the crisp air. It had the ability to instantly quiet my senses and let me just be. But since I had a house full of people, I was never alone for long. I heard the door from inside open and turned to see Corinne tiptoeing out to join me.

"You OK out here?" she asked, taking off her shoes and cozying up to me on the outdoor sofa.

"I'm fine. Just taking a few moments to myself. Processing the fact that your Coach seemed like he was flirting with me," I said nonchalantly.

Corinne turned to me, and I just looked straight ahead. "Wait, what? He *finally* said something?"

I snapped my head to look at her. "What do you mean *finally?* You know something I don't?"

"Well, he may have asked if I thought it was a good idea to try to ask you out."

"What?" I gasped. "And what did you say? Did you tell him about Jaxon?"

"I told him no, and hell no! I just said that on top of it being just plain weird, it's also your place of business. Your one escape from everything you've been through. He shouldn't want to disrupt that."

I was grateful for Corinne's wisdom because I wouldn't know how to let him down easily. Coach was a beautiful specimen of a man, and any woman would be crazy to not see him and want to jump on that immediately. But he was friends with Lamar and someone that I looked at like a brother. Anything romantic between us was not even in the realm of possibility from my perspective. Nothing would make me feel like I was cheating on Lamar more.

Corinne leaned over and playfully slapped me on the leg. "You look good, Dash. Happy."

Taking her arm and wrapping it in mine, I rested my head on hers."Thanks, girl. I guess I do feel...*happy?* Or something? I haven't felt anything but...*whatever* I've been feeling for the past few years that I barely recognize the feeling of anything different."

We sat there quietly for a moment, and I thought about Corinne's words. I actually was happier. I felt like I was finally on the other side of things. Nothing had magically changed, and I still felt sadness from time to time, but it no longer consumed me or lingered like it used to. And I couldn't explain it, but an immediate twinge of guilt surged through me as well. It was like I felt guilty for moving forward, and I didn't want my boys to feel like I was leaving them behind. Especially in this house. I shared with Corinne that I always felt like their spirits were here watching over me, and sometimes I felt like it would hurt their feelings to hear about me moving on.

"I can understand how you would feel like that," Corinne said empathetically. "But I also feel like your boys would..." her sentence was cut off by the sound of the doorbell.

"Hmm," I said inquisitively. "I wasn't expecting anyone else."

Corinne jumped up and blocked me from going into the house. "OK, so about that. I may have gotten Jaxon's information off of his new hire profile and invited him over, telling him it was a way for him to get to know the staff before he joins officially?"

"Corinne!" I whisper-yelled. "What in the entire *hell* were you thinking?! This was our home! My home with Lamar!"

318

"I just thought that maybe you could use some more…you know…*happy* for Christmas!"

"I appreciate the sentiment, but *not* while my staff is in my house!"

The doorbell rang again, and I pushed her out of the way to go open the front door. On the way to the front of the house, I couldn't tell if I was excited, mad, frustrated, or all of the above. I knew nothing would happen tonight, but having Jaxon in my house instantly made me tense up. Especially since I had just told Corinne about the very real guilt I was feeling simply from experiencing happiness. Asking Jaxon to come work at the school was already too close for comfort. Having him in my home was simply madness! I was never supposed to see him again, and now he was being invited into several areas of my private life. I tripped over someone's boot in the walkway and decided then and there that I was definitely excited, mad, *and* frustrated at the same time.

Before opening the door, I stopped and looked in the mirror that hung in the foyer and fixed my hair, then made sure my frustration wasn't noticeable on my face. Taking a deep cleansing breath, I opened the door to greet my uninvited guest.

"Mr. Jaxon Hart," I said, and my heart immediately began racing.

"Mrs. St. James. I hope you don't mind me crashing your Christmas," he said, handing me a gift box that was normally used to wrap bottles of wine in. "I brought a little something as a thank you." I grabbed the box and opened the door a little wider, gesturing for them to come in.

"Hi, Principal St. James!" Mila said excitedly. "Your house is really pretty! You are such a boss!"

"Well thank you for noticing, Mila! And Merry Christmas. The kids are upstairs playing video games if you want to go play with them. Follow the noise up there, and you can't miss them."

"OK! Jax, will you hold my coat?"

I watched Jaxon's face turn into a smile as he playfully sighed, "OK." Then she darted up the stairs, disappearing into what was still considered Ty's playroom.

I stood at the front of the house for what seemed like hours, staring into his eyes. Unable to process that he was standing here in my house. "Wha...What made you come? This must be...strange or weird or..." I was rambling.

"Corinne was kind enough to invite me, and it wasn't the worst idea to meet the people I'd be working with." He peered behind me, observing the room to see if anyone was coming our way before taking a step closer and whispering, "And I wanted to see you, Shy," squeezing my hand for emphasis.

Heat instantly rose to my cheeks, and I heard Coach Sanders' loud voice walking up behind me again. "Well, Dash! Who do we have here!?"

Taking a step back, attempting to break the fiery connection between me and Jaxon, I cleared my throat before saying, "Coach Sanders, this is Jaxon Hart! He's going to be helping us with the Spring Musical since we have that vacancy."

"Oh, yes! Mila's father, right?"

"Brother, but…yes. I'm her guardian," Jaxon replied, offering his hand for a handshake to Coach Sanders.

Coach took his hand. "Well. Welcome to the Biddy Bunch. Let me take you in to introduce you to the rest of the crew, since you obviously know our fearless leader. You know how to play Spades?" I shook my head at the implication and sensed a slight nod of jealousy permeating from Coach as they walked off into the living room. I was gonna murder Corinne.

Kids were running and jumping around upstairs while the adults watched football, played games, and trash-talked downstairs. I was enjoying the love and laughter filling the air, but I was also getting tired. As an introvert, there was usually a stopwatch attached to my energy levels, and after spending two days cooking and preparing, and now all day today surrounded by people, I was ready for some peace and quiet.

I was in the kitchen cleaning up while everyone else was watching "Best Man Holiday" in the livingroom, and I laughed to myself at the fact that it seemed like Coach Sanders had taken Jaxon under his wing in an attempt to cock block. Everytime Jaxon looked in my direction, Coach Sanders was redirecting him by asking him questions about himself or his sports preferences. Coach also didn't like the fact that Jaxon didn't know who he was in the NFL, adding more fuel to his competitive streak he had brewing. With a smile still eclipsing my face, I turned from the sink and was startled to find Jaxon there smiling from the kitchen doorway.

"How long have you been standing there?" I asked.

"Long enough. You look beautiful today," he said softly, making a point to not let anyone outside of the kitchen hear him.

"Thank you," I said blushing. "You enjoying meeting everyone?"

"I am. Everyone seems nice, and they all think the world of you."

"I pay them all very well to say nice things about me," I joked.

"Stop deflecting," he said sharply. Then he stepped further into the kitchen to get closer to me. "You're amazing, and there isn't a person who knows you that doesn't believe that. Present company included."

I don't know which was burning hotter, my cheeks or my core, but heat was all around me and I struggled to breathe. I saw Corinne step into the kitchen, but she quickly turned around and headed back out into the living room.

"Jaxon," I whispered. "These people are my family and my employees. I can't risk a scandal."

"I know. I'm going to go now because I can't be near you without wanting to touch you."

As soon as he said he was leaving, I missed him. "Oh. OK. Yeah. I get that," I muttered as he used the back of his right hand to stroke my cheek.

"You busy tomorrow?" he asked.

I looked up at him to meet his gaze. "Mila goin' to Nana's again?" Assuming he wanted to carve out some more time to *play.*

"No," he chuckled. "I am driving down to Savannah to take care of some business for my father and…I don't know…you wanna maybe take a road trip with us?"

The thought of being in a car with Jaxon and Mila for more than a few hours scared the hell out of me. Sweat began to bead at the top of my lip, and my heart began racing as I considered the idea that I would be in a car with a child that wasn't my own for the first time since Ty was alive. I didn't sign up for that. I don't know why he was doing this, but I wasn't trying to take family outings with him and Mila. This was not a relationship, and I was almost upset at him for even asking.

"Look," he spoke up, noticing the distress on my face. "I…I didn't mean to make you uncomfortable. Forget I even asked. Don't even know what I was thinking. I…I'm gonna go, and I'll see you on the first day of school after winter break." He was nervously rambling, and I could tell that I had made him feel some type of way.

Grabbing his hand I said, "Jaxon, stop. It's not that I don't *want to* take a road trip with you. I

324

just…You just have to understand that I haven't been in the car with a man and a child since…"

"Dash," he sighed with pain in his voice. "I'm sorry. I…"

"It's not your fault. You didn't know. But Jaxon, you must know that inviting me to something like that breaks the rules. Once you involve Mila, it's no longer role play. It's real. And I don't know if I can handle '*real*' *right* now." Especially not with him. Not when I was desperately avoiding falling in love with him. Or that little girl.

There was something in his eyes. Pain, maybe fear. And it made me want to use everything in my power to make it go away. I let out a sigh, closing my eyes, knowing that what I said next was going against everything I knew to be right. "I'll think about it, OK?"

Then, he took my hand and kissed it, went to grab Mila and their coats, and headed home.

Chapter Twenty-Seven

Jaxon

It was early in the morning, around 7 a.m., and we were on the road headed to Savannah. In the backseat, Mila was belting out Shanice's "I Love Your Smile" with surprising accuracy, and I made a mental note to encourage her singing once we got back home. In the front passenger seat, Dash was sitting to my right, seeming a bit uneasy as she looked out the window with a faint smile. Her hands were folded neatly in her lap.

Certain her mind was going a million miles a minute, I had the urge to reach over and take her hand, to reassure her. But with Mila already curious about Dash's presence, I didn't want to stir up more questions. So, I decided to give Dash space and ask her where her head was when the time was right.

Mila suddenly chirped, "I need to pee!" And I figured that this was a good time to stop for food and gas.

As Mila and I hopped out of the car, Dash stayed put, and it was frustrating me that I couldn't quite read her expression. "Mrs. St. James, will you come to the bathroom with me? There will be strangers inside, and my mommy always says it's not safe to go alone," Mila enthusiastically asked.

I quickly tried to squash that idea, letting Mila know that I would go with her to the restroom when Dash interrupted, "No, it's okay. I can go with her." And I searched her face, trying to gauge if she was *really* okay with this.

"Dash, are you sure?"

"When Mila's around, it's Hadassah. And yes, I'm sure. Be right back." With that, Dash got out of the car, and they both disappeared into the gas station.

She was acting distant, and it made me question my decision to invite her on the trip. Was I fooling myself? Probably. I was so wrapped up in the holiday spirit when I was at her house, that I overlooked the glaring issues with having her join us. Her admission of not being in a car with a child since her son should have been the biggest red flag. But after our last encounter, where we opened up to each other more, I found myself wanting to be near her any chance I could get. I couldn't stop wanting to talk to her or touch her, and that desire was leading me to make impulsive, even selfish decisions.

When the ladies emerged from the convenience store, they had handfuls of candy, chips, and drinks, and I just shook my head laughing. "So, *that's* what took you two so long!"

"Yep!" Mila giggled. "I hope you don't mind, but we used *your* card."

I looked between Mila and Dash, trying to figure out which one of them stole my debit card. It wouldn't have been hard to do since I usually kept my card in the center console of my truck. But still, the fact that they both wore a devious grin as I tried to get the truth out of them made it impossible to figure out. It also made it impossible to stay mad since they were both undeniably adorable.

"I see how it is. I'm on a road trip with a couple of common criminals," I joked. And they both just continued to giggle while they climbed back into the truck.

Mila was ecstatic about the candy Dash let her get. But when I told her she had to wait a couple of hours before she could eat more than the two pieces of candy she'd already devoured, she laid down and went to sleep.

Even though light jazz played in the background, the car was quiet, and the tension was palpable. I looked over to Dash and grabbed her left hand, stroking it a bit to get her attention. "How are you?"

She peered up at me, knowing I wasn't asking in the polite sense. I was asking how she was handling all of this. "I…I think I'm OK. Why do you ask?" She averted her gaze when she asked that question. She knew why I was asking.

"Just talk to me, Shy. I can tell you're agitated and distant, and your mind is barely here."

"I'm sorry. I don't…I don't talk about him. I don't *want* to talk about him. But…" she let out a sigh before continuing. "Jaxon I don't know how to say this without sounding like the worst possible human being in the world."

"Just say it. No judgment between us, right?"

"Yeah, but we also said nothing *real* between us either, and now look at us on a damn family road trip!" she snapped, and I caught a glimpse of an icier side of Hadassah St. James. "I'm sorry," she said after a few moments. "I didn't mean to come off like that. This is just hard for me." As if on cue, Mila snored from the backseat, and we both smiled.

"No, *I'm* sorry," I said, removing my hand from hers and placing it back on the steering wheel. "I shouldn't have insisted you come with us. I was being selfish, and I see that now. If you want me to turn around and take you home, just say the word and…"

She reached over and placed her hand on my knee. "It's fine. I'll be OK. This is just one of those things I need to work through."

I gently placed my hand over hers in my lap, then I began speaking to her in a tone that was soft and reassuring. "OK then, Dash. Role play with me. I'm your man. We do this all the time." I straightened in my seat and shifted a bit as if I was preparing myself to put on a different persona. "I'll go first," I said, clearing my throat. "Full disclosure, I'm not good with feelings, and this is something that *I* need to work through. So if you tell me how you're feeling, it would actually be helping me learn how to navigate you and your feelings in moments like this. That, and I can't read minds, so the things that I'm *assuming* you're thinking are actually driving me crazy."

Dash snickered with a faint smile, but it didn't last long. She put her head down and whispered, "Guilt. Whenever I find myself enjoying the company of another child, I feel guilty. Like my son is watching me, and I don't want him to feel like I could love another child the way I love him."

That truth hit me like a bus. I had just assumed that Dash was struggling with the loss of her son in general, not wrestling with tortuous thoughts of her son watching her and not feeling loved. Even in his absence. I wanted to hold her, love the grief and hurt away. But that's not what this was. It wasn't who *we* were. And since I didn't know what to say or how to respond, I just drove quietly as we both took in the sights of charming, small towns and picturesque, countryside views.

I never enjoyed living in the country or smaller towns. I didn't like feeling disconnected from the rest of the world. However, whenever I had the opportunity to visit or even drive through a small town, I was able to appreciate what it represented. I still found a sense of peace in landscapes that were dotted with traditional Southern architecture, historic sites, and quaint shops. It was a reminder of how comfort could be found in simplicity. Especially when there was nothing simple about this moment between Dash and I right now.

Hadassah

I knew this was a bad Idea. I was painfully aware of what something like this would do to my senses after all the work I'd done over the years. But something about the look in Jaxon's eyes the night before made me feel like he didn't just want me to go with him today, but he needed me. He also looked annoyingly sexy in an all-white jogging suit that was the perfect contrast against his chocolate skin and perfectly shaved beard and goatee.

331

Back when I was married to Lamar, I rarely took the wheel whenever we drove anywhere together. There was something comforting about sitting in the passenger seat, letting my mind wander while my man took control of the road. Lamar was always a careful and thoughtful driver, which made me feel secure. We made sure Ty had the best car seat, and Lamar would always ease off the accelerator whenever our little one was with us in the car. But after a devastating car crash stole my boys from me, it became difficult to trust anyone but myself to hold the reins of my life.

Jaxon was still a mystery to me. I knew only what a background check could reveal about him, which we conducted when we hired him at the school. Given our complicated relationship, it was probably for the best that I didn't know anything else about him. Yet, every time I was near him, I found myself torn between wanting to understand him better and desperately avoiding anything that might make me fall for him.

I knew very little about Jaxon's relationship with his father. I never wanted to probe beyond what he willingly shared with me. But I'd be lying if I said I didn't have questions surrounding how he came to be the guardian of a sister he knew nothing about, after losing a father whose death was also news to him. Students at Biddy Mason came from all sorts of backgrounds, but this was a first.

"She's really special, you know that?" I asked, attempting to break the awkward silence that filled the tiny space between us.

"She is. Makes me a little sad that I didn't get to know her before now," he admitted.

"Do you mind if I ask why you're just now learning about her? I mean...I know I have my secrets, too, so if you don't want to share, it's..."

"It's fine, Shy," he interrupted, squeezing my hand and giving it a gentle rub with his thumb. He'd gotten used to my nervous rambling and had already learned the perfect way to still me in those moments.

I listened as he told me about his childhood and how he grew up. How his father was a preacher that knew every scripture in the Bible but struggled to follow its teachings. How his mother was a strong woman that was beaten down by his father's emotional cruelty. And how when she'd finally gotten the nerve to leave him, she was diagnosed with cancer.

"I've always blamed my father for the cancer," he confessed, looking in his rearview mirror before signaling a lane change. "My mother was the sweetest and most gentle soul you would ever meet. She never drank, and she never let smoke touch her lips. But what she did do was take on all of my father's abuse and toxicity…and it killed her."

"Jaxon, I'm…"

"I didn't ask for sympathy, Shy. You asked what happened, and there it is!" he snapped, and it was easy to see that this was a sore subject for him.

Jaxon was a resilient man, not just because life had toughened him up. His strength was born from a childhood that prioritized toughness over tenderness, thanks to a demanding father. It was hard to ignore this fact about him, but I knew I couldn't let his past make me more vulnerable to him than I already was. Men like Jaxon had a kind of magnetic appeal to women, as though their emotional scars were a silent call to our nurturing instincts. Once a woman caught a glimpse of a man's wounded spirit, she was drawn in, like a moth to a flame, eager and indiscriminate.

There was something incredibly alluring and dangerously enticing about a man marked by a difficult past. And there was nothing more intoxicating, yet risky, than a woman who firmly believed she could heal a broken man.

Don't get me wrong, I'm not naive or easily swayed by sob stories. I was well aware that there were lousy men out there who, for whatever reason, had chosen to be emotional menaces and downright harmful to our culture. However, I'd always found it intriguing how we, as women, didn't hesitate to criticize black men who turned out to be no good—and rightly so. But at the same time, no one was asking why they turned out that way. This was a topic that I was so passionate about, I convinced Lamar to introduce empathy training for our students and parenting classes for those raising young boys.

Every Friday morning at Biddy Mason, instead of homeroom, we divided classes by gender and asked teachers to give lessons that were usually reserved for the opposite sex. Young girls learned things like how to change a tire or carpentry skills. Boys were taught how to cook and things that men were notoriously oblivious to, like how to be considerate or how to be empathetic. Of course, we gave the students options so they didn't feel like they were forced to learn skills they didn't want to. But most appreciated that we didn't assume that they wanted to learn certain types of skills over others. I couldn't help but wonder who the little boy in Jaxon might have become if he'd had the chance to grow up in an environment like that.

I knew it was hypocritical, but I wasn't ready to let this go. "Are we still 'role playing' right now?"

He let out a huff, and a sly grin eclipsed his face. "Yes, Hadassah."

"Then talk to me like I'm your girl. Like you trust me and we do this all the time."

I watched him as he bit his bottom lip, appearing to contemplate what I was asking. This line of questioning was making him nervous, and it was obvious by the way he was gripping the steering wheel. "I just find it interesting that you have refused to talk about anything that makes you squirm but, when it comes to me, you dig like a dog after a bone."

"I know," I agreed. "You just don't talk about anything, other than music or the nostalgia you get from old movies and stuff. And…And I guess I was trying to get to know you more. While also giving you an outlet 'cause I know your black ass doesn't talk to anybody."

"Anybody like a therapist, you mean?"

"Anybody at *all*. But especially a therapist."

That part was obvious. While I knew that therapy was becoming less of a taboo topic in our community, it was easy to identify those that hadn't embraced the idea. If you weren't paying attention, you could be easily fooled by Jaxon's demeanor. Since Jaxon was a great listener and occasionally offered sound advice, one could assume that he was a well-adjusted individual who didn't have a problem with talking about feelings. However, when someone was doing all the listening, it meant they weren't required to talk. If he was asking all the questions, no one got the opportunity to ask any of him. And that's how he interacted with me. That's how he always appeared to be so caring and understanding. Not that it wasn't genuine, but it was definitely a tactic all the same.

"Fine," he relented. "But you go first."

"I…I'm sorry?"

"I didn't stutter. If you want me to share something meaningful with you, then you go first."

My heart started racing because I wasn't expecting him to turn the tables on me. Talking to this man was like playing a game of chess, and he constantly had the advantage.

"What do you want to know?" I asked, my voice trembling with anxiety and a real fear that he was going to ask me about Ty.

I never understood why people made such a big deal about talking about the loved ones we lost. I got how it could be cathartic or therapeutic for some. But for me, it just made the loss feel heavier. Especially when it came to Ty. When I described his caramel skin and his kinky, sandy blonde hair that matched his daddy's; or his raspy voice that sounded like he had been yelling all day, all it made me want to do was scream and curse the world for taking my little boy too soon. Talking about Ty and his favorite Miles Morales movie that he would never get to watch again was torture to me.

Jaxon gently took my left hand in his, bringing it to his lips for a light kiss. Then he flipped my hand over, peppering more soft kisses on the inside of my wrist. As a tear slipped down my cheek, he squeezed my hand and held it close to his chest. "Tell me about your happiest day with your family?" he asked.

I felt a wave of relief wash over me. He didn't ask me to describe Ty or what he was like, like the people at the grief groups my friends insisted I attend. Instead, he prompted me to share something that was much easier for me to talk about... joy. So, for the next hour as we drove, I reminisced about the memorable road trips Lamar, Ty, and I had taken together.

Our goal was to visit every state in the US before Ty turned twenty-one, but we only made it to ten of them. Growing up, I always wanted to rush to our destination, not caring much for the journey. I was the little girl that would annoyingly hound my parents about whether or not we had made it yet. But as an adult, especially with my boys no longer with me, I realized that the road trip itself was the best part of the whole experience.

Tears of joy streamed down my face as I recounted several of my favorite memories with my boys. And I realized that, for the first time since Ty's death, I actually talked about him in a way that didn't make me sad. All I felt was happiness, and I was deeply touched by Jaxon's thoughtful approach in asking that question the way he did. Then, I was reminded of Corinne's words to me the day we sat in my kitchen, *"Anyone fortunate enough to fall in love with you will understand that there wouldn't be a 'you' without the chapters that helped shape your story. Even the painful ones."*

Chapter Twenty-Eight

Jaxon

When we got to my dad's house, I felt strange as I stepped out of the truck and into the driveway. The house was a modest brick home with bay windows and a wrap around porch, complete with a porch swing. This house was much nicer than the one that I lived in with my father and mother, and a shard of jealousy pricked my heart for the life that this home and my father appeared to give Mila.

The attorneys mailed me the keys to the house, so as soon as I unlocked the doors, Mila darted past me and ran straight to her room upstairs. I, on the other hand, took a moment to take the place in. The house looked like it was suspended in time like a ghost town. When I was a little boy, my father used to preach sermons about the great rapture and how those who were saved would be swept away to be with God in Heaven, while the sinners would remain left on earth.

"Two people will be working in the field, and one person will be caught up, while the other will be left standing there, wondering what just happened!" He had preached. That sermon would be used every time he wanted to get a rise out of the congregation and make people give their lives to Christ. I just grew up with an existential fear that

one day, I would come home from school and my mom would be gone.

One day, I had come home from school an hour late because I was hiding my report card from my mom. Avoiding the inevitable whooping I had coming, I stayed out at the playground with my friends and played a little while longer. When I had finally gotten home, my mother was nowhere to be found. Dinner was cooling on the kitchen counter and music was playing from the living room, but I couldn't find my mom.

Panic began to overtake me as I frantically searched all over the house for her. And since it wasn't a big house, I was going crazy trying to figure out what had happened. When my search came up empty, I stood in the middle of the kitchen crying out to God to take me, too. I assumed that my mom was taken in the rapture and, while I didn't believe my dad was going to Heaven, I knew that if what my dad preached was real, my mom would surely make it in.

I was so busy crying and pleading to God on the ground, that I missed the sound of the screen door opening and closing as my mother walked back into the house. *"Baby? What's wrong?"* I had heard my mother say. And I jumped up and ran into her arms, vowing to never be bad again.

When I explained to her what made me think she was gone forever, pointing to the food left on the counter and the radio playing in our empty house, she understood why I would feel that way. And then explained that she had just gone next door to borrow some sugar and got stuck talking to the neighbor. But looking around my dad's house, food and dishes left as if waiting for someone to return, I got the same eerie feeling that I did when I was a little boy. The feeling that someone had been removed before their time. Before they had expected to be gone.

"Are you OK?" Dash asked, startling me as she placed her hand on my shoulder and pulled me from my trance.

"I'm fine. Just taking everything in. Trying to decide where the best place is to start."

I knew I had to gather important documentation for my father's attorneys, but I promised Mila that we could take anything she felt was valuable, too. So I carried in an assortment of boxes and envelopes to hold anything we'd take with us, leaving them at the front door so everyone could grab a box when needed.

The house was dusty, but not unclean. Still standing near the front door, my eyes trailed the layout of the home. To my right, there was a dining room with a China cabinet and a table that looked to be set for special occasions. To my left, there was a den that looked like it was a mixed use space with a sofa, an old desk, and religious books all over the hardwood floors. Slowly, I began walking towards the back of the house where it opened up to an open floorplan with a living room that led straight back into the kitchen.

As I walked down the hallway, pictures with wooden frames lined the wall. I smiled as I saw Mila's baby pictures. In one of them, she wore a pink lace dress with tulle along the bottom. Her cheeks were chubby, and drool was running down her little face. She seemed happy and well cared for. In another photo, I noticed a picture of my father and his wife that appeared to be their wedding day. Mila's mother, Naomi, was a beautiful Spanish woman with long, black hair, green eyes and thick, curly eyelashes. So much about her reminded me of Mila, and it was nice to see what or who had made up the other parts of her. Naomi looked like she could have been a model or an actress that rivaled the likes of Ana De Armas or Salma Hayek. It was easy to see why my father had been taken with her. Judging by her looks, at least.

I was wandering around the living room, observing the family photos, and Mila's awards that hung on the walls when Dash suggested, "Why don't you ask Mila where your dad's office is or where they might have kept important information?"

My heart twinged with pain because I didn't want to *have to* ask Mila anything. I hadn't heard from her since we'd gotten here, but I knew this was going to be hard enough. We were going to be packing up the only life she'd ever known and saying goodbye to her home. There was no funeral. No one to comfort her and help her understand what was happening when all this began. She was alone. And now we were going to be packing pieces of her parents away and closing this very stressful chapter of their lives. Asking a child to be responsible for *any* of this seemed cruel.

"I'll ask her if I absolutely need to. But I don't want her to have to worry about any of this. She's living with enough, and she's still not talking about it so, I'd like to spare her this," I said, and Dash nodded with understanding.

I could tell that Dash was tiptoeing around me. I was noticeably shaken, and I was trying to hold it all together, but this was new territory for me. I was assaulted by the plethora of emotions that were running through me—grief, sadness, anger, regret. I felt it all, and I didn't know what to do with any of it. And since Dash didn't want to do or say the wrong thing, she just watched me and took her cues from my demeanor.

Hours passed, and I managed to find much of the information that my father's attorney's needed in their den area while packing it up. Dash was upstairs with Mila packing up her room, and I was grateful that Mila had a distraction. The laughter and running around let me know that, while this was probably a really sad day for her, she was being reminded of the joy from the memories of her parents that she could carry with her. The kind of joy that Dash knew about all too well.

I was finishing packing up things in the kitchen when I decided to go upstairs to see what the girls were doing. When I got up there, I stood in the doorway and watched as Mila held up various dresses and asked Dash if she should keep them or donate them. I had arranged for a charity to come and take everything that we'd left behind and instructed Mila to donate anything that she didn't want but was in good condition.

"Looks like you ladies haven't gotten much done," I said jokingly.

"Yes, huh!" Mila chirped back. "I packed two whole boxes of clothes and three boxes of toys!" Of course she had packed more toys than clothes.

"She's a tough negotiator," Dash laughed. "She had legitimate reasons for wanting to hold on to these clothes and I honestly didn't have an argument for her!"

Seeing that there were still tons of clothes and various items to either pack away or donate, I sent Mila downstairs to get more boxes. Turning to Dash, I said, "You look like you're having fun," and I didn't wait for her to respond because I knew what that meant for her. What *fun* meant for Ty and her. I just took her hand and gave it a little squeeze.

We were both in this awkward space where we were dealing with emotions that we had no idea how to handle. Me wondering which version of my father I hated more—the one that I had or the father that Mila grew up with? And Dash, trying to decide if letting Mila 'in' was worth the betrayal she felt her son might proverbially experience from her moving on.

Hadassah

Witnessing Jaxon taking in his father's home for the first time was interesting to watch. He wandered around like a little boy in search of something. Perhaps his father. Maybe himself. And suddenly, the man who was full of wisdom and comforting words a few hours ago was now speechless. Yet, he still managed to find words to ask me questions to keep my mind at ease. Questions that kept me from spiraling about the joy I was experiencing hanging out with Mila.

She was impossible to *not* love. Her infectious laugh, her vibrant personality, her admiration for her big brother, she was perfect. Tears stung my eyes as I tried to make sense of everything I was feeling. I wanted to shut my heart off from the world in memory of Ty. But seeing this little girl with virtually no one, playfully carry on in a house that held the remnants of her shattered life, I couldn't help but wonder if my vow to never love another child again was a disservice or an injustice to my baby boy instead. Mila was joy personified, and her vibrance made me not want to withhold anything from her. Not even my heart.

"It's hard not to have fun with her. She's a riot," I said, finally responding to Jaxon's observation of how much fun I was having with Mila.

"Well, she definitely likes you."

"I'm her principal," I quipped. "She *has* to like me a little bit. Besides, she's probably just enamored with the idea that I'm here."

"I'm sure that's true, too. But I think she's grateful to have you here as well," he said.

He was grateful to have me here, too. He didn't say it. He didn't have to. It was in the way his eyes softened when they met mine, in how he kept himself busy with random boxes or clothes whenever our gazes locked and his eyes threatened to reveal his secret. The secret that this was hurting him more than he let on.

As we went through the items, I noticed something odd. There were loads of photos of Jaxon's dad with his new family, but none that included Jaxon. This seemed strange to me because anyone who looked at Jaxon could see his dad in him.

"He was always impeccably dressed," I said, trying to avoid the glaring fact that Jaxon was conspicuously missing from the photos.

Jaxon snickered, but a smile never formed on his face. " 'Dressed to the nines,' as my mom would say. He was big on presentation. Looking the part, even if you weren't shit." He sat a photo back down on the built-in bookshelf and laughed to himself. "I guess that's where I get it from, why I always try to dress so well."

Hearing him express such self-deprecation shattered a piece of my heart. I wasn't sure if he was referring to his father or himself, but the ambiguity made it all the more painful. I wondered if he saw himself as worthless, using his impeccable sense of style as a shield to hide his perceived inadequacies. If he was indeed talking about himself, this would be the second time I'd seen cracks in his usually impervious armor, signs of his hidden vulnerability.

The first time was back at school when we reconnected. I could see how the reality of my professional status and the revelation of who Lamar really was had bruised his ego. His insecurities were laid bare. Today, his pain surrounding his father was palpable, raw, and unfiltered. It wasn't like Jaxon to reveal such deep emotions to anyone, let alone me. He was always careful, always calculating, always in control. He never allowed himself to be seen as vulnerable or without the upperhand. Yet here he was, stripped of his usual bravado, his emotions swirling around him like a tumultuous storm.

It was clear that something within him was fracturing. But amidst the chaos, I felt us growing closer. This shared moment of vulnerability was drawing us together in a way nothing else could, no matter how hard we fought it.

"You're the spitting image of him," I pointed out, noticing a hint of a smile trying to break through his stoic expression.

His gaze was fixed on a photo of his father, dressed in a sharp brown suit and a matching hat.

He ran his fingers over the picture, tracing the contours of his father's face. "Guess he got that part right," he said, his words holding a bittersweet undertone.

They shared the same deep, warm skin tone, the same expressive eyes, even their lips were shaped similarly. And if you were lucky enough to catch Jaxon in a smiling mood, you'd see his dad's smile reflected on his face. Their smiles were like carbon copies—charismatic, warm, and capable of melting the coldest of hearts. But despite all these similarities, Jaxon was conspicuously missing from his dad's collection of family photos. Seemingly from his life altogether. It was as if he'd been deliberately left out, which only added another layer of hurt to an already painful situation, and he was refusing to open up to me.

I had shared a bit of my story with him on the way here, but he still managed to sidestep his part of the deal where he promised to share a bit of his truth with me. As much as I wanted to avoid knowing him, wanting him, I couldn't deny what being here with the two of them meant to me. What it must have meant to him.

"Is it weird being here?" I was trying to get him to express some sort of emotion because right now he was this brooding mess that I couldn't seem to get through to.

This was how it began. This was how unsuspecting women around the world ended up trying to love a broken man whole. She would encounter him in an emotionally intense moment that would send a rush of oxytocin through her system, nudging her nurturing instincts into overdrive. And because oxytocin had a way of traveling from your nipples and into your panties, the nurturing urge usually confused the surge of desire and passion with empathy, making us women believe that we'd found our soulmate. If only we could get him to an emotionally safe and healthy place in time for the wedding!

Before Jaxon could respond to me, there was a knock on the door followed by the ringing of the doorbell. "Anybody home?" a man's voice called out.

"Mr. Shoe!" we heard Mila yell out as we rushed down the stairs to see what the commotion was.

"Mila," Jaxon called out. "We seriously need to talk about you waiting to answer doors until an adult is present."

"But you *are* present!" Mila sang, gesturing towards us as we landed at the bottom of the stairs.

The man at the door looked to be in his sixties at least, and it was obvious that he was a family friend by the way Mila clung to his waist. The gentleman had kinky, white hair that was the perfect contrast against his dark, milk chocolate skin. His eyes looked like they held secrets and stories of a much different time.

"Mr. Shoe, is it?" Jaxon asked, interrupting the catch up session that was happening between Mila and the older gentleman.

"Yes," he said, holding out his hand to greet him. He had a slow, southern drawl that made everything he said sound like home. "I'm Marvin Shoe, but you can just call me Shoe. I live two houses down. Mila plays chess with me from time to time, and I looked in on her and Naomi whenever Senior was traveling."

Jaxon's eyebrows raised inquisitively. "Senior?"

Chuckling, Mr. Shoe responded, "Yes. That's what we called Mr. Hart. He would always say the name Jaxon was reserved for two people, his father and his son."

Jaxon let out a huff before introducing himself, "Jaxon Hart, Mr. Shoe. I imagine I'm the son he was referring to."

The man stopped and covered his mouth with his hand as if he had just seen a ghost. "You're Jaxon Hart? Senior's boy? I was so sorry to hear about their passing! Him and Naomi were dear friends to me."

"I appreciate that," Jaxon cordially replied.

I watched Jaxon's face, a complex mix of emotions, as he ushered the elderly man into the living room and offered him a seat. This man was a walking memory, having known Jaxon's father over the years. He had even met Jaxon as a young boy. Though Jaxon didn't recall those times, his mood became noticeably brighter as he absorbed the man's stories about his father and reminisced about his own childhood.

I decided to take Mila upstairs to continue packing, but also to give Jaxon some privacy. As we ascended the stairs, I heard Jaxon's voice, tinged with a hint of vulnerability, "What did my father tell you about me?" And in that moment, he was that little boy again, yearning for his father's approval, desperate to know that he had made his daddy proud.

353

Chapter Twenty-Nine

Jaxon

I felt a sense of relief when Dash took Mila upstairs, but I was still a bit on edge as I sat down to talk with a man who seemed to know my father far better than I did. Mr. Shoe was originally from Alabama, but his family had moved to Georgia after the Vietnam War. He and my father used to work together in a factory and, according to Mr. Shoe, my dad would often share the "Good News" with and preach to their coworkers while they were busy on the assembly line.

"I always knew there was something different about your father," Shoe said, walking around the living room and picking up pictures of him that sat on the mantle. "But I could never put my finger on it. He was a complicated man. Guarded most of the time, and he never let anyone get too close. But when he talked about his kids, he would open up like a book."

Shock spread across my face, but it quickly turned into a puzzled expression. I couldn't help but ask, with a hint of disbelief in my voice, "He talked about his kids? Even about me?" The idea that my father would have anything nice to say about me was hard for me to imagine.

"Shoot, yeah! He *especially* talked about you. Senior always said you were a great musician that could follow anyone on them keys. Said you had a special calling. A gift that could read people, connect to whatever they were thinkin' or feelin'. And with music, that helped you to follow them when they sang. Didn't matter if they started off key or sang the wrong words, Senior said you could always *feel* where they were goin'. Yes, sir! That's what your daddy used to always say about you."

I took a moment to process what Shoe had just said. It was astonishing on so many levels and for various reasons. First of all, I never knew my father to have close friends. And second, I'd never heard him speak kindly of anyone unless he had something to gain from them. That included me. So, hearing from Mr. Shoe that my father practically bragged about me to him left me pretty stunned.

Whenever I accompanied him to his preaching gigs and played music while he spoke, he always had some criticism or suggestions on how I could do better. I never felt like I was good enough or like I had mastered anything because he never acknowledged when I did well. And yet, here he was, all this time, praising me to people I didn't even know. This was hard to process, and I wasn't exactly sure what to do with this information.

Dash had ordered pizza for everyone, and I spent another hour chatting with Shoe about his friendship with my dad. In that brief time, I learned so much about the man who had always been a mystery to me. I couldn't help but feel sympathy for my dad—the son of a cotton farmer, whose mother passed away giving birth to him, and whose father blamed him for it and punished him all his life.

"Your daddy would get drunk and share things with me, and I just listened. I think it tortured him somehow. Something in him broke a long time ago, and I don't think he knew how to fix it, son. Though I reckon he tried. Naomi was good for him. She knew how to settle him when he would have his episodes, and he'd always say she saved his life."

My dad's 'episodes' became as regular as clockwork, especially when he had been drinking. He was never officially diagnosed, but Mom and I always thought he might be grappling with something like manic depression or bipolar disorder. His moods swung wildly between two extremes. He was never the life-of-the-party kind of guy, but he had his moments of light-heartedness where he'd crack jokes and play around. But just as quickly, a random word or sound could set him off, turning him into a completely different person in a heartbeat.

If there was anything that honed my ability to sense people's feelings and anticipate their needs, it was growing up under the constant watch of my father's shifting moods. I learned to read his emotional state like a weather vane, adjusting my own actions and reactions to help ensure his day went smoothly. There's no one more attuned to the emotional climate than someone who's survived abuse or lived with someone whose moods were a ticking time bomb. But apparently, Naomi had learned to diffuse the bomb.

The story of how my dad met Naomi was actually pretty sweet. They were both on a mission trip in Ecuador, building homes for the less fortunate. Naomi, who had been there a few times already, was the team leader and knew the local language and customs like the back of her hand.

One night, my dad ended up at a bar, and after a few drinks, he managed to offend a group of locals with his broken dialect. He was convinced they were going to hurt him, if not worse. That's when Naomi stepped in. She calmed the men down and made my dad buy them a round of drinks. After that incident, she made sure my dad took Spanish lessons from the locals so he wouldn't mix up the dialects again.

"Naomi grew up with brothers, so tough men didn't scare her," Shoe reminisced. "I think that's what attracted Senior to her. She didn't back down from him easily. And when she began to see how his moods affected him, and the people around him, she was the only one brave enough to sit with him in it. Show him how to manage it instead of using alcohol to hide from it."

It was a charming story of a beautiful woman rescuing my dad, likely adding years to his life. Meanwhile, he had taken away the best years from my mother's life. My emotions were a tangled mess. I was bitter about the life my father got to live after leaving us, but also felt a pang of sadness that he was no longer here for me to confront him about some of the things he did.

"You look like him, you know?" Shoe said, and I instinctively pulled at the turtleneck that felt like it was beginning to tighten and suffocate me.

"Not sure if that's a blessing or a curse," I said dryly.

"Judging by the looks of that beautiful woman you got wandering 'round here, I'd say a blessing indeed, son!" He laughed.

"Oh, Dash? She's not...She and I aren't like..." I stuttered unconvincingly.

Shoe just laughed at my mutterings. "I don't know when you kids are gonna learn. All that datin' around and kickin' it stuff only leads to misery. When you've got a woman like that in your grips, you hold on to that, son. Don't borrow from another man's future if you don't intend on making her part of yours." And with that, Mr. Shoe's bones creaked and cracked as he lifted himself up off the sofa and began to head home.

We stood at the door and talked for a few more minutes before I offered to walk him to his door. Mr. Shoe lived alone, his children living far away in the city of Atlanta, and I couldn't help but feel like he was losing a bit of family with my father and Naomi being gone, too. We exchanged phone numbers and he offered to be there anytime I needed to talk. Something I'd planned to take him up on.

When I got back to my dad's house, Dash stood at the door, searching my face for what I assumed was emotion. On the drive down, she had worn a black, Nike jogging suit with a hoodie. But in the midst of all the excitement, I missed that she had removed her hoodie and was only wearing a white tank top, the black lace of her bra peeking from the top.

"Is everything OK?" I asked, because she was standing awkwardly with her hands behind her back as if she was hiding something.

"Everything's fine," she whispered, her tone measured and even as if she was trying to remain calm, while ensuring I remained calm. "Mila's sleeping, and I wanted to wait until you were alone to show you something we found while packing up your parents'...your dad's bedroom."

Confused, I tilted my head and furrowed my brow, "Okaaaay. You're sort of scaring me, Dash. What did you find?"

Without uttering a single word, she strolled into the living room and took a seat on the couch, motioning for me to join her. As I sat down, she handed over an old wooden cigar box labeled 'P. Witlock's Old Virginia Cheroots.' But what caught my eye was the name 'Jaxon' scribbled across the top lid in black marker, with the box sealed shut by black electrical tape. I couldn't help but wonder, what could be so important inside that it needed to be sealed off like this?

But curiosity often walked hand-in-hand with apprehension. Typically, boxes like these were used to hold cherished memories, keepsakes of moments or people we wanted to remember. But given the complicated relationship I had with my dad, and the sea of unspoken words between us, there was a real chance that the box held nothing pleasant. I wasn't sure I was ready to face whatever was in it. So, I turned to Dash, expressed my gratitude for the box, and suggested that we call it a night.

Hadassah

We had initially planned on getting a hotel for the night, but when Mila dozed off in her own bed, we couldn't bear to disturb her. Giving her one last night in the familiarity of her room seemed the least we could do. On the surface, Mila appeared to be coping admirably, but after spending this time with her, Jaxon's worries about her reluctance to discuss anything meaningful were justified. In the same vein, I was worried about his own avoidance of deeper, more serious conversations.

With sofas in both the den and the living room, Jaxon chose the den—the closest spot to the front door, while I claimed the living room couch. We were exhausted and had managed to pack up a great deal of the house today, leaving his dad and wife's room and the kitchen for the next day. If I hadn't been here, Jaxon probably would have still been packing up Mila's room, since Mr. Shoe had showed up unexpectedly. But by the number of times Jaxon thanked me for my help today, he knew he couldn't have gotten all this packing done without me either. Something that I could easily do for him, but hadn't gotten around to doing for Lamar and Ty.

Lamar's office at Biddy Mason was a sacred space, untouched since the day he took his last breath. At home, his clothes still hung on his side of the closet, his razor and toothbrush forever waiting for him on the bathroom counter. I seldom stepped into Ty's room, but I left it as it was—bed unmade, toys scattered on the floor, as if any moment he would come back from school and I could gently chide him about neglecting his chores. That part of my life stood still, suspended in time. But I had no problem helping Jaxon and Mila turn the pages of these chapters.

I was deep in sleep when the rustling of paper roused me. Realizing the noise was coming from the den where Jaxon was, I decided to investigate. What I found was a heart-wrenching scene. Jaxon was hunched over the old cigar box. His hand repeatedly traced over his name that had been etched onto it, and if I hadn't been paying close attention, I might have missed the tear stains marring the letters, fresh tears still silently making their way down his face.

He was aware of my presence, yet he didn't meet my gaze, nor did he try to hide his tears from me. This beautiful man. His wide shoulders, usually held high, now sagged with an unseen weight. His captivating brown eyes were shut tight, the creases in his thick, furrowed brows hinting at the torture within. His lower lip was caught between his teeth, seemingly the only barrier holding back the flood of his sobs dangerously close to flooding over. He was in agony, wrestling with a pain I couldn't fathom, and I stood helpless, unable to do anything for him.

"I can open it," I offered gently, hoping to shoulder some of his burden. "Let me carry this weight for you, Jaxon. If there's something inside the box that you'd rather not see, I'll take it on and carry it so you don't have to."

I was acutely aware of what my words were implying. It wasn't just an offer of comfort, I was offering myself to him, to be a balm for his raw and ragged pain. This blurred the lines between friendship and something more profound, something that 'friends with benefits' rarely ventured into, I would assume. But in that moment, all personal agendas, all self-imposed rules were put aside. I wasn't preoccupied with the potential implications of my actions or what they could mean for our future. All I felt was an overpowering need to soothe his hurt, to be the anchor in his storm. If I was the only solace he had today, then so be it. I would willingly become his place of peace. His refuge.

He still didn't look up at me. Instead, I saw his hands clench around the box before he rose and handed it over to me. "If it's anything bad, don't show me," he begged, his voice barely more than a whisper. I nodded in understanding and accepted the box from him.

I placed the box on the worn desk in the den and began to tear away the black tape sealing it shut, my nails digging into each side. Each tear brought me closer to a truth that I felt privileged he trusted me with. My heart pounded and palms sweated, as though the box held my secrets rather than his. As I finally lifted the lid, I glanced over at Jaxon. He was sitting behind me on the sofa, legs spread wide, hands clasped between them, head bowed. He was avoiding this like a child that didn't want to watch a band-aid being ripped off.

Tears began to stream down my face as I held up each piece of paper one by one. Programs of Senior's preaching engagements where he had circled his and his son's name as the guest speaker and musician. Newspaper clippings where Jaxon was on stage playing behind famous artists. He had even printed images off of the computer. Images that looked like they were taken from Jaxon's

365

Instagram and Facebook pages when he was years younger.

I glanced at Jaxon, finding him watching me with a look that was equal parts anticipation, hope, and a dash of fear. "Jaxon," I managed to choke out.

"What? What is it?"

All I could do was hand him the box, encouraging him to discover its contents for himself. As he sifted through the papers, each one a testament to his father's hidden admiration, I watched with a mix of wonder and affection.

"I didn't even know he kept this," Jaxon murmured, holding up a medal from an eighth-grade talent show. "He always said singing worldly music would send me straight to hell...he never supported it. When I told him that me and my friends were singing Boys II Men for the talent show, instead of a gospel song he recommended, he cursed and said God wouldn't be pleased. But when we won, and he didn't say anything at all, I just thought that meant he was angry or disappointed."

"He could have been disappointed that you didn't choose the path he wanted for you. But he also could've been proud of your tenacity and your talent at the same time," I offered gently, hoping to provide some solace amidst his swirling emotions and unanswered questions.

Suddenly, Jaxon sprang up, retreating to the kitchen. I quietly followed, finding him clutching the cigar box. His back was turned to me, and I just...watched him, the rise and fall of his broad shoulders, each breath he took heavy with emotion. A sound, primal and raw, rumbled from his throat, a growl that sent shivers down my spine. Then, in a sudden burst of energy, he flung the box onto the floor. The loud thud made me jump, my heart pounding in my chest as I braced for what might come next. I didn't know what to do, so I knelt down to pick up the papers, placing them back into the box and setting it on the counter.

"It feels like lies," he muttered bitterly. "I know what this should mean. I know it should make me *feel* good. But it all feels like lies because he never had the guts to tell me himself! To apologize? He never said a damn thing! He died letting me believe he never liked me, let alone loved me!" Overwhelmed by his raw pain, I rushed over to him, wrapping my arms around his waist.

The scent of him, a mix of musk and sadness, filled my senses, stoking a flame that danced on the edge of friendship and desire. His pain was palpable, a tangible entity that gnawed at my heart, compelling me to draw him closer, to wrap him in a cocoon of warmth and understanding.

His breath hitched as I held him tighter, my fingers tracing soothing circles on his back as his heartbeat thrummed against my own. He resisted my grip initially, standing upright and choosing not to participate in the embrace. He was clearly battling a tumultuous storm of emotions, but I stood my ground, pressing my cheek against his chest, offering him silent comfort. After what felt like an eternity, he finally yielded. Fiercely, he pulled me into an embrace, his head buried in the crook of my neck. I guided us to lean against the counter, using it to steady myself under his weight. He was inches taller than me and pounds heavier, but in that moment I carried him and took on the weight of his pain.

I could feel hot tears soaking my shirt, streaming down my collarbone as Jaxon wept silently. The taste of his tears on my lips was a bitter reminder of his torment, yet the strength of his grip around me echoed a silent plea for relief. And I answered that plea without hesitation, without reservation. In the face of his anguish, I found myself surrendering to an undeniable pull, a magnetic force that was drawing us closer than ever before. This was the moment—the moment I found myself falling for this man. It felt like a betrayal, a treachery that I couldn't resist, even if I wanted to. And I didn't.

Our journey began as a quest for pleasure. I wanted to experience the intoxicating rush of physical connection, and he was my chosen tool, my conduit to feel again. I *chose* him to awaken my senses that had long been dormant. And once we began, I was convinced that I could control this dance, that I could retreat and sever these ties once I had taken what I craved from him. But now, our hearts were headed straight for a dangerous collision, and I found myself unable to look away, unable to resist the seductive pull of him. Of...us.

In the blink of an eye, Jaxon's mood morphed, transforming what was once a manifestation of pain into a pulse of pleasure. His grip on me tightened, his lips tracing a path down my neck, his teeth grazing my skin in a tantalizing tease. This was hardly the moment for such a charged reaction. We needed to pause, to discuss, to untangle the web of emotions that he was grappling with. That was the logical voice in my head, but as his hands roamed my body, that voice was being told to shut the hell up!

Without breaking our connection, Jaxon pressed his growing arousal against my stomach, scattering kisses across my face, using his tongue to trace a wet path from my earlobes down to the swell of my cleavage. I felt his arms shift behind me, heard the shuffling of boxes being pushed aside from the counter. Then, interrupting our kiss, he dropped to his knees, hooked his arms under my thighs, and hoisted me onto the cool kitchen countertop.

"Jaxon, this isn't…we should stop. Talk. How are you feeling?" I panted as he used both of his hands to rip my tank top down the front, exposing my black lace bra.

"How am I feeling?" he growled. "I'm feeling like you should shut up and left me fuck you now, Shy." Effortlessly, he unclasped the front-facing hook of my bra, then he used his teeth to tease my left nipple before he ravished it, making sure to not leave the other out of the fun.

His hand had slipped into my pants, two fingers diving beneath the lace of my panties, and I rocked to a rhythm that was uniquely ours. My eyes fluttered open to find Jaxon's gaze fixed on me, unblinking as he stoked the fires of my pleasure. His determination to regain some semblance of control was written all over his face, in the clench of his jaw and the bite of his lip. He was using my impending climax as a lever, a means to shift the balance of power away from his own emotional chaos. But I wasn't about to let him hide behind this facade.

Ignoring the screaming protest of my body, I seized Jaxon's hand, abruptly halting his pleasurable assault. His expression flickered with confusion, and I could see a sting of rejection in his eyes until I spoke up, "No more role playing. Don't play games with me tonight, Jaxon. Don't hide behind the mask of the alpha male, chasing dominance and control. Be present with me tonight. Whatever that means, just be here, okay?"

As he considered my words, I watched as his eyes softened, his hardened exterior melting away in an instant. He didn't speak, and I couldn't decipher his thoughts or anticipate his next move until he leaned in, pressing a gentle kiss on my lips. First, a feather-light touch, then he deepened the kiss, his tongue exploring my mouth in slow, deliberate strokes.

"Fine," he conceded, using the one word to express his agreement to stop all the games. He scooped me up, my legs instinctively wrapping around his waist as he carried me out of the kitchen and back into the living room. This man was massive, using one arm to lay a blanket on the floor while still holding me and kissing me with his right arm. Once he had the blanket and a pillow where he wanted, he gently laid me down and promised, through actions rather than words, to be real with me.

There was no show of force or dominance. There was no aggressive play. I lay there as Jaxon slowly undressed me, peeling off my pants and panties with a gentle touch, his eyes drinking me in as though seeing me for the first time. "You're breathtaking," he whispered, aligning his body with mine, his arousal teasing the sensitive juncture between my thighs.

The room was cloaked in darkness, illuminated only by the glow of moonlight seeping through the large picture window. Yet, even in the muted light, I could make out the defined silhouette of him. His physique was sculpted to perfection, like an African god—powerful, majestic. And I felt a primal urge to surrender myself to him, to be his willing offering.

His gaze swept over me, intense and predatory. It was as if his eyes had the power to peel away my layers, to delve beneath my skin and touch the raw essence of my being. His look wasn't just seeing; it was probing, exploring, claiming—a silent demand that left me breathless with anticipation.

"If you don't want me to pretend, then you can't pretend either, Shy." Unsure of what he meant,

I shook my head in the affirmative, willing to do just about anything this beautiful man asked me.

His left hand traced the length of my inner thigh before reaching my core. "Open for me, baby," he coaxed, using his hand to guide my legs apart while his lips claimed mine. His gaze was intense, challenging me to look away. He kissed me again, biting my lower lip gently before asking, "Will you keep your eyes open for me this time?"

"Wha...Huh?" I stuttered, my thoughts a jumbled mess.

"If I can't pretend to not..." He stopped as if he was about to reveal a secret but caught himself before it slipped out. "If I can't pretend to be in control tonight, then neither can you. When I'm inside you, with each stroke, promise me you won't look away." My breath hitched as I grasped the depth of his request. He wasn't just about to penetrate me; he was about to possess me.

He held my gaze as he freed himself, skillfully rolling a condom down his impressive length with one hand. As I felt him inch closer, a wave of nervous anticipation washed over me."Shit!" I gasped as I felt him eclipse my walls. He entered me slowly, bit by bit.

The weighty feel of him never failed to catch me off guard. The building pressure, each time he delved deeper inside me, was an indescribable sensation that left me gasping for breath. I frantically searched for something—anything—to muffle my moans, terrified that we'd wake Mila. Usually, I was a silent lover, but this man, Jaxon, stirred something within me that had me making sounds from the very core of my being.

His touch ignited a wildfire, a raw and untamed passion that resonated in every moan that escaped my lips. Each thrust, each rhythmic grind against my body, drove me further into a state of unadulterated ecstasy. His name was a chant on my lips, a sweet surrender to the paralytic pleasure he was providing.

Tonight, Jaxon didn't hold back. He was unselfish, pouring himself into me without any restraint. And in turn, I opened myself to him, taking in everything he had to offer. His pain, his anguish, his pleasure, his love—I welcomed it all, opening myself wide to receive every fragment of his being. I wrapped my legs around his waist to draw him closer, offering him the depths of me. And with every stroke, he shed a piece of himself, revealing layers of his soul I'd never seen before. The intimacy of the moment was overwhelming, and as I accepted everything he gave me, I realized that this was more than just a physical connection. It was raw, it was real, it was us—and, it was perfect.

I threw my head back and my body arched from the blend of pleasure and pain he was giving. I grabbed the pillow from behind my head and placed it over my face to muffle the screams that were only getting louder. "Baby! Fuck! Shit! Ahhh!"

"Don't you dare fucking cover your face, Shy. I need to see your eyes. I need...you," he whimpered, snatching the pillow from my face diving into me deeper as he chased that need.

"I'm here," I murmured, and he plunged even deeper, filling me completely. "Jaxon!" I cried, biting into his neck to stifle a scream. In response, he thrusted harder.

His movements became more forceful, yet he maintained a steady rhythm. His eyes never left mine, and I saw tears well up. Real tears eclipsed his eyes as he grunted, "Fuck! Baby! You feel so good."

Caught up in an orgasmic-induced trance, I said, "It's yours, baby." And I felt his dick jump at the sound of those words.

He bent down to kiss me fiercely and his eyes held an ancient sorrow as he drove into me, deeper.

Harder. Unrelenting. "Tell me..." he murmured, his voice strained.

"Tell you what, baby?" I gasped, breathless. He was so deep inside me, his girth so filling, that forming complete or coherent sentences felt nearly impossible.

Desperately, I found the leg of the sofa, attempting to inch away from him, but Jaxon was relentless. He snaked both his arms under mine, his grip firm on my shoulders, anchoring me in place. There was no escape from his hold as he sought both satisfaction and solace within our shared passion. His pursuit was fervent, a mix of desire and need that left us both breathless. Each thrust was a plea, a silent confession of his craving for both physical release and emotional tranquility.

Our bodies moved in sync, creating a rhythm that was as sexy as it was captivating. Like the scenes from a movie where the love interests make love for the first time. Every gasp, every moan was a testament to the depth of our connection. The room was filled with our shared breaths and the aromas of our shared euphoria, the sound of skin against skin, and the unspoken words of love that hung heavily in the air.

His eyes darkened, his thrusts slowing before he kissed me again, this time with a passion that was tender. "Tell me you love me," he managed to say, and I realized it was his turn.

His eyes, usually so full of confidence and bravado, were now vulnerable and pleading. He craved love. Despite the day's shocking revelations about his father, he craved a love untainted by past wounds and unsaid truths. Tonight, he sought something genuine, something unconditional—I was determined to give him just that. To be his haven, just as he had been mine on our very first night together.

And so, I vowed to drown him in love, to wash away the pain of the day with the warmth of my affection. I'd match his vulnerability with my own, bare my soul to him. In the heat of our passion, amidst the tangled blankets and hushed moans, I'd show him a love that was pure, unadulterated, and above all, real.

I cupped his face, searching his eyes for any sign of confusion, but found none. Instead, he thrust into me harder, and repeated his demand, "Tell me, Dash. Tell me you love me."

The air was charged with tension as I felt his body responding to me, struggling to hold on to his inevitable climax. Hold on to this moment. He delved deeper into me, and I pleaded for him to stay there forever. As his body started to shudder, I felt him harden even more. Our fingers entwined in a silent promise. His lips found mine in a fervent kiss, and with a final surge, I felt him unravel.

"Fuck! Dash!" he cursed, panting and barely able to catch his breath. "I need you. I need you so much right now," he whimpered, releasing my hands, he enveloped us in the blankets strewn on the floor, gently rolling over so I was perched atop him, our connection unbroken.

I looked into his eyes and wiped a tear from his face, kissing away the ones on his other cheek before whispering, "I love you, Jaxon Hart. And I'm so proud of the man you've become."

And I meant it.

Chapter Thirty

Jaxon

We pulled out of Savannah on a Monday afternoon and it was evident that what had transpired there had changed us, leaving an indelible mark on our hearts. We entrusted Mr. Shoe with our instructions for the realtor and details of our intended charity donations before loading Mila's belongings into the truck. A sense of melancholy washed over me as I looked at Mila's life, now condensed into five boxes and six large trash bags. It was a sobering reminder of how quickly life could change, and I felt a pang of sadness for the little girl whose world had been so drastically reduced.

As Dash and I rode in the front of the truck, Mila listening to music on her phone in the back, we were in an undeniable state of bliss. There was a sense of calm serenity, a shared understanding that passed between us as we drove. We were careful not to be overly affectionate in front of Mila, but we didn't hide the fact that something was brewing between us. A rhythm was forming, a comfortable dance of shared looks, stolen touches, and soft smiles. Dash even seemed at peace with this new dynamic.

I noticed a change in Dash since we'd gotten on the road this time. The shadow of guilt and sadness that seemed to always hang over her had disappeared. In its place was a lightness, a certain ease that I hadn't seen in her before. The shift actually gave me hope. Hope that maybe this was the start of something more, something deeper. However, no matter how much I found myself yearning for this 'something more,' the thought of it scared me because it was unfamiliar. Yet, for some reason, it was a journey I was willing to take…with *her*. And for the first time in my life, I felt like I could love someone wholly.

I couldn't help but wonder what things would be like once we started working together. The school was still on holiday break for Christmas and New Year's, but next week would bring another change. Dash would essentially become my boss, and I didn't think about the implications of that dynamic until now. Until I was starting to catch real feelings for her and didn't want to spend a moment without her.

"So," I said, breaking the silence between us as light jazz played in the background. "How is *this* going to work once we start working together?"

Dash looked at me as if to say she hadn't thought about it before now either. "You know what? That's a great question. I guess we should set some ground rules, huh?"

We both laughed as she pulled out her phone and began to type out everything we were listing as part of our ground rules. "And absolutely no sex of any kind while at school," she offered, writing it down without consulting me, and I definitely wanted to protest that.

Looking back to make sure Mila couldn't hear anything above her noise-canceling headphones I said, "At *all*? Come on now! You know that's every man's fantasy, right?"

"Welp! You'll just have to fulfill that fantasy elsewhere," she laughed.

It was her place of business, and she had an entire community that respected and championed her. I could never jeopardize that, no matter how intimidating it was. So whatever rules and stipulations she hit me with, I had no problem agreeing to.

"And what if I wanted to steal a kiss?" I negotiated.

"Kisses can be stolen between the hours of 6 a.m. and 7:30 a.m., and after 4:30 p.m. All times where kids are not likely to be there and most of the staff aren't around my side of the building," she bargained. We pinky promised each other, sealing this new agreement.

This was all new territory for me. Not only was I admitting to myself that I had genuine feelings for Hadassah St. James, but I was also learning to compromise in a way I'd never done before. Typically, if I wasn't in control, I wanted no part of it. But once I saw how a woman could bloom, becoming more flexible and giving when she felt heard, I started to see the value in compromise. It's something I'd mastered with Remy but wanted to give an honest try with Dash.

I had never let my guard down with a woman the way I had with her. Aside from my mom, no woman had ever seen me shed tears. And even my mom hadn't witnessed that since I became an adult. At seventeen, I vowed never to let love make me soft. To me, love—whether it was between men or women, fiction or not—just didn't seem to work. Especially not black love. Seeing how love reduced my mother to her most vulnerable state, I swore I'd never let myself fall into that trap.

But recently, I'd realized that in my attempt to dodge the inevitable impacts of love, I'd ended up doing the very thing I was trying to avoid. I'd used the women who fell for me...reduced them for my gain. Broke them for my benefit. And since Mila entered my life, I'd had to reconcile with the fact that everything I taught her would be aimed at giving her a strong sense of self so she didn't fall for the traps that I'd led women into. That stung. Teaching her one thing while doing the exact opposite was the type of hypocrisy I despised most about my dad. I didn't want to be that man to her. I didn't want her growing up with a skewed perception of men because of what she saw in me. I had to be better.

Sitting here with Dash, knowing she was loved by and married to a veritable community icon, both intimidated and energized me. She was the kind of woman who inspired men to be better. I'd watched many great men in my life, and one thing was clear: they didn't just choose a beautiful woman to adorn their arm. The truly great ones picked women who could partner with them and help them build. A woman like Hadassah was destined to stand alongside great men. I knew if I wanted her, I'd have to become the kind of man worthy of her. Great enough to deserve her.

The music changed in the background and Israel Houghton's song, "You Are Alpha and Omega," began playing, and you could feel the tension rise in the car. Dash and I had never talked about religion before, and I wasn't sure what her views were.

"I've always loved this song," I shared. "My mom taught me how to play this when I was seven years old."

Dash didn't immediately respond, and I couldn't pin down what had changed her mood. "It's pretty," she said. But she didn't look at me or turn my way to indicate she wanted to talk about it. Instead, she just stared out the window, her expression unreadable as she nervously toyed with her hands.

"I know we never really talk about it but, you ever go to church?"

"I used to go, but I couldn't find anything to be grateful for after the loss of my family." She huffed sarcastically. "How could I sing praises to a God that would steal, kill, and destroy the best parts of me?"

I gripped the steering wheel a little tighter at that statement. I'm no theologian, and I am the last person to be offering religious counsel. I wasn't even sure *if or what* I believed anymore. Still, I always felt a bit uneasy when someone made statements about God that seemed disrespectful or irreverent. However, I still tried to be empathetic and understanding in this moment because I knew Dash was speaking from a place of grief.

"Well, it's the enemy that comes to steal, kill, and destroy, if we're being technical. But perhaps the blessing in all of this is that *you're* still here. *You* still have a purpose, Hadassah," I said, reaching over to caress her cheek with the back of my hand. She was still stoic, until her eyebrows furrowed as if she'd had a delayed reaction to what I had just said. Then, she turned to look at me as if I had just cursed her entire bloodline.

I knew how contradictory it sounded, me of all people, promoting anything that even hinted at religion. But it really got under my skin to hear her talking about herself as if her life was over just because Ty's and Lamar's were. It was as if she didn't believe she deserved to live or be happy anymore. Her disappointment with God was understandable. Her grief was warranted. But her anger was being misplaced, and it was causing her to make decisions that were robbing her of a future.

She didn't say anything, but her murderous gaze was burning a hole into the side of my head. It was the kind of gaze women gave just before they were about to key your car or slash your tires. Unfortunately, I'd seen this look far too many times, and I would do anything to remove it from her face in an instant.

"Look Dash," I said, attempting to deescalate the situation, "I am no expert in grief, and I won't ever pretend to know what you're going through, but..."

"That's right!" She bit back. "You can't pretend to know anything about me, my loss, or my grief...so don't even try!"

I'd never seen her act like this before. Sure, she had her moments of being upset, and there were times when she could be particularly frosty when she was making a point or activating 'boss mode.' But right now, she was coming off as downright aggressive. I knew I had offended her somehow, but I was at a loss as to how exactly I had managed to do so. I couldn't figure out why bringing up God or church had upset her so much that her words and tone had taken such a sharp turn. How in an instant, it felt like last night never happened.

Hadassah

He had no right. The nerve of him to question me this way and suggest that how I was grieving was inadequate. Or that my being *here* instead of my boys was a *blessing?!* I was self aware enough to know that I was responding to something he had triggered within me. But I also took offense to the way he seemed to 'offer Christ to me' with an err of self righteousness. Especially since he was a man who admittedly ran through countless women, and not more than twenty-four-hours ago was he sexing me crazy! The audacity.

I was no stranger to God. We shared a deep connection, a strong bond... that is, until the day my family was taken from me. People often suggested turning to God as a cure for my grief, as if I wasn't already pleading with Him every single day. Begging Him to ease the unbearable pain of loss, or if He couldn't bring them back, at least reveal to me the greater purpose behind taking my boys.

"How is it that you can even fix your mouth to suggest something like that to me after you just sat in the home of your father? A man who, according to you, used the Bible as a tool to take advantage of people?"

He took a few minutes to respond. I'm sure he was trying not to say the wrong thing. "One person's actions, or how they choose to use the Bible, doesn't deny its purpose, power, or intent, Hadassah."

He wasn't yelling or trying to match my energy, but it was clear he was getting annoyed. The fact that he used my full name, Hadassah, instead of my nickname, was a dead giveaway. His chest heaved with each deep breath, and the way his jaw clenched so tightly, it looked like he might just shatter his teeth.

"Listen, whatever *your* twisted relationship is with religion, you can keep to yourself. But I don't need you trying to save me or fix me, Jaxon. Between the two of us, I'm not the one who's broken!"

As soon as those words slipped from my mouth, I regretted them. It was like watching myself from the outside, spewing hurtful things and daring myself to twist the knife just a bit more. And so, I did.

"Actually, I think it's best if we take a step back for now. We're going to be working together, and it's not a good idea for us to be... *this* close."

He turned to me, his gaze locked onto mine in disbelief. His truck slowed on the freeway, causing other drivers to honk and swerve around us. "Dash, what are you saying?" His face crumpled with hurt.

"I'm saying that this was a mistake. We need to just... be co-workers. Nothing more."

The rest of the drive was spent in heavy silence. And just like that, I had succeeded in pushing him away, just as I'd planned from the very start of all this.

Chapter Thirty-One

Jaxon

This was probably my shortest relationship to date. Not that Dash and I were ever in an actual relationship. But the night we spent together in Savannah actually had me believing that we were on a path towards something more significant. Something real. I was even planning to discuss it with her on the road. As scary and potentially humiliating as it seemed, especially for me, I was going to ask Hadassah St. James to be my girlfriend. But the idea to do so left as abruptly as it came. She had said, in no uncertain terms, that she wanted us to simply be friends. And I'd never had a woman say that to me before.

Typically, I was the one who ended things in relationships. Sure, there had been times when women called it quits once they figured out that my 'casual only' rule wasn't just talk. But most of the time, if I felt a woman was getting too clingy or trying to control things, I'd start to back off. My usual escape routes were saying I had a band tour coming up or that I needed some 'me time' to deal with personal stuff. However, I stopped ghosting women a few years ago. I realized that even the most sophisticated and composed women could spiral into worst-case scenarios and create unnecessary drama when kept in the dark or when things didn't go the way they intended. I didn't sense any of those red flags when it came to Dash. She didn't display any behavior that would hint at a sudden change of heart or a dramatic twist the way she had done and I was more than a little fucked up about it.

It was New Year's Eve, and it had been nearly a week since we'd gotten back from the road trip to Savannah. After an especially quiet drive home and two uncomfortable bathroom stops, she got out of the car and didn't even turn to look at me. She just said, 'goodnight' and walked to her door. I'd tried calling and texting for the last three days, but she hadn't bothered to answer. Now I think she'd even blocked me.

Mila said she had never stayed up past midnight, so I promised her that I would watch all of the "High School Musical" movies with her and then we'd watch Ryan Seacrest on the 'New Year's Rocking Eve' special. I loaded us up on Twizzlers, Starburst, Snickers and Reese's Cups, and Nana hooked us up with cupcakes on her way to her church's annual New Year's Eve Shut-In Service. She asked if we wanted to attend, but once I told her about my experiences with God and my love/hate relationship with the church, she backed off. She said she understood that some things were between a man and his God to work through.

Growing up, church lock-ins were a big deal, even though they only happened once or twice a year. These events were often used as an opportunity for the congregation to come together and pray for miracles or for something we were collectively hoping for. While the kids got to watch movies and popcorn and candy all night, as the church musician, I rarely got to join them. I was expected to stay up all night, playing the same old songs over and over while the adults prayed and spoke in tongues. If I dared to complain, my dad would threaten to punish me.

As a kid, I often resented my musical talent because it felt like my father used it both as a tool and a weapon. All I wanted was to hang out with my friends and I promised myself that once I was grown, I'd never play for another church lock-in, or even a church again. So, I guess this all-night New Year's celebration was just as much a novelty for me as it was a treat for Mila. We were both getting to do something we'd never done before. It was also a distraction from the amazing night I had with Dash, and the way she dropped me the next day.

Since we'd be going back to school in a few days, I resolved to stop calling her, giving us both the space needed to regroup and get ready for the start of the semester. I had no clue what I was doing, and while I had been reading a bunch of material to get me ready to deal with multiple children at one time, I didn't know what to expect. The movie "High School Musical" was as much research for me as it was a treat for Mila.

This situation with Dash was new territory for me, so I was trying to figure out how I was going to respond to her at this point. Normally, I would go out and simply find another woman to occupy my time with. It usually worked to stop me from tripping off someone. But since I had Mila, that wasn't exactly possible. And since I cared for Dash, and we'd soon be working together, I honestly had no desire to be with anyone else. New territory for me, indeed.

"Jax! You said we'd start the movies at 6 p.m. to give us time to watch High School Musical 1 and 2 before Ryan Seacrest!" Mila yelled from the top of the stairs.

I was running three minutes late for our movie night, and she was already giving me grief. "Just chill, little momma! I'm coming."

I was grabbing bowls from the kitchen when I literally had to stop myself and give myself a pep talk. "Dawg...She hurt you. She used words and your flaws against you. Which proved she couldn't be trusted to keep your vulnerabilities safe. Especially during times where they were most sensitive!"

That right there, those words from myself, was all I needed to hear to jolt me back into reality. To bring me back to who the fuck I was. I'm Jaxon Hart, and nobody gets to use my vulnerability against me. Not even her.

Hadassah

New Year's Eve used to be the night where me, Lamar, and Ty would all climb in our bed and watch scary movies until we fell asleep. Now, Genevieve, Corinne, and I got together and hosted an annual girls' sleepover, usually themed by the movies we watched. Tonight's theme was "Sex and the City." As the glamourous one of the group, Genevieve claimed the spot of Carrie, wearing a pink headband with pink tulle that looked like a wedding veil. Corinne jumped at the chance to be Samantha, and I was dubbed Miranda. We all agreed that Charlotte was too prudish to be part of our friend group.

I hadn't spoken to Jaxon since the trip, and I was honestly avoiding him like the plague. He was nothing but kind to me the night I needed him, and I was the complete opposite for him. The next day, at least. I don't know why I said those things, and my

394

therapist was out of town for the holiday so I couldn't unpack it with her, either. Deep down, though, I knew what the issue was. I'd broken my rule, and despite telling myself that I wouldn't be bothered by the consequences, they hit me harder than I expected.

Admitting to myself that I was falling for this man, felt like I was telling my boys that I was making room for someone else and pushing them aside. Surprisingly, it felt good, even comfortable. But I didn't know how to handle these feelings, especially alongside the guilt weighing me down. Jaxon and I had fallen into a rhythm almost naturally, but suddenly, I found myself worrying that things were moving too quickly. Thoughts of his past and the women he'd taken to bed then left broken in his wake began to taunt me. Who was I to think I'd be any different than those women when all was said and done?

That one question was what kept me from answering his phone calls and text messages. I could not think so highly of myself that I would believe I could change a man who was an admitted womanizer. Instead, I decided to focus on what I promised myself I would—the school and the kids. After tonight, that is. After the girls night that promised to leave me with such a hangover from

Cosmos that Jaxon Hart wouldn't even be an afterthought.

"So, are we just gonna sit here acting like this woman didn't just get back from a sexy getaway with Daddy Yum-Yum?" Genevieve asked. We were all watching the first "Sex and the City" movie at Genevieve's house, but everyone was acting strangely weird and quiet.

"I was wondering the same thing, but y'all know I don't like to start no mess," Corinne chimed in.

"Now Corinne, you know that's a lie and both of you get on my nerves!" We all laughed, and the tension finally started to feel broken. "And it wasn't a sexy getaway! It was a sad road trip to help him settle his dead father's affairs."

"Not sexy at all," Corinne said.

"No, but seriously," Genevieve commented with a concerned tone. "We know it's none of our business, but we are worried about you. This being your first *anything* since Lamar and all. How are you doing?"

"And how was the sex?" Corinne added.

I stared back at the TV, Carrie and her girls were in Mexico after Big had stood her up at the altar, and I was trying to figure out the best words to describe everything that had happened in the recent days. How it all crumbled before it had the chance to begin. "I told him I loved him."

Corinne squealed with excitement, "Awww!"

But then, I continued, " I hurled the most insulting things at him less than twenty-four-hours later."

"Hold on...what? Can you back up a bit?" Genevieve interjected, clearly confused. "How did you end up saying such hurtful things to him?"

Corinne, though, seemed more focused on my confession of love. She grabbed my shoulders, turned me to face her, and asked dramatically, "Wait, you love him?"

I knew Corinne would be surprised. After all, she was the one who had warned me against falling for him. But honestly, I wasn't sure if I was in love. "We shared something intense and passionate. It felt like love, but it also felt like lust. There's something different about him that scares me," I admitted.

I didn't delve into the details about Jaxon's past or his relationship with his father. Those weren't my stories to tell. But I did share the powerful moments we'd shared, how easily I could fall for that little girl, and how I'd confessed my love after a night of what felt like making love.

Genevieve chimed in, "Sounds like bereavement sex, also known as sympathy sex."

I hadn't heard of that before, but it seemed to fit our situation perfectly. One moment Jaxon was crying on my shoulder, the next he was making love to me. It was all so sudden and confusing. I asked Genevieve, still looking puzzled, "Is bereavement sex really a thing?"

"It is absolutely a thing! When you're grieving, your body craves something to alleviate the pain, and sex is a great way to do that. It releases chemicals in your brain that can help numb the senses that feel the hurt the most," she explained. "Could it be that what you felt was shared grief, not love?"

It was a possibility. I'd suppressed my need for intimacy for so long that when it was finally awakened, I might have mistaken the passion and pleasure for love. "You could be right," I admitted.

But Corinne wasn't convinced. She furrowed her brows and said, "Nah. I don't think so. I'm not buying it. I know you're trying to stay level-headed about this, but there's been a change in you, and we shouldn't dismiss it that easily."

"What exactly do you think has changed about me?" I asked, eager to understand what they were seeing. I'd sensed a shift in myself, too, but couldn't put my finger on it.

"Well, it's hard to pinpoint, but you just seem lighter. Not as burdened with trying to be the...and I mean this affectionately...the perfect widow," Corinne whispered the word widow as if the softer she said it, the less it would offend me.

"The perfect widow? What on Earth does that mean, Rinne?" I retorted, taken aback by her words.

Corinne raised her hands defensively. "Now Dash, I'm saying this out of love. But sometimes, it feels like you're wearing the label of 'widow' as if you're following a 'how to be a widow' handbook!" I stared at her, my heart pounding, fighting the urge to throw my Cosmopolitan cocktail at her. "Dash," she continued, "for the first time since Lamar passed away, you seem unburdened and free, not weighed down by grief and suffering."

"Yeah, Dash, sometimes it feels like you want to wallow in sadness. And as painful as it is to see, we let you because we understand that asking you to move on might push you away."

Her words hit me hard, forcing me to reflect. Had I been intentionally prolonging my pain, exacerbating my grief, all to feel closer to my lost family? The thought was sobering. Nobody wanted to be sad. Nobody woke up every morning and chose sadness over joy, like they were picking an outfit for the day. I woke up every day and chose memories, and it manifested as sadness. I was starting to see that now.

"So, what did he say that made you lash out at him? And what triggered it?" Genevieve questioned, bringing me back from my introspection. Embarrassed, I recounted the conversation that led to my outburst.

"Wait, so it was a mention of church and Fred Hammond that made you go off on that fine ass man?" Genevieve exclaimed in disbelief, and I couldn't give her a sensible explanation.

"It was Israel Houghton, and I know how ridiculous it sounds. The only explanation I can think of is that I was coming to terms with enjoying his company. But I was also worried about them being disappointed in me. Even if I wasn't scared to let another man love me, even if I believed Lamar wouldn't mind me moving on, would Jaxon be someone Lamar would approve of? And considering all the women Jaxon has been through, what made me think he wouldn't do the same to me? One night of passionate lovemaking can't change a man's nature!"

"Whew! Preach!" Corinne rejoiced. "I've done the legwork, honey, and I'm here to tell you; outlook not good. Do not recommend. Very ghetto." And we all laughed as Corinne got up to go refill our Cosmos. "And another thing," she continued, this time coming back with the entire carafe of the Cosmo mix. "Maybe you do need to talk to Jesus! You've been so busy writing your own rules to grief and doing things your way, maybe there are different answers and a different purpose that you're not seeing in any of this. All because you're walking around pouting with God like you're punishing *Him*."

She had been drinking, and her words were starting to mush together, but she was onto something. Something I wasn't quite ready to face just yet. I'd deal with my faith and all the questions that came with it when I felt ready, not a second before. I didn't want to be someone who turned to religion just because they felt lost or desperate. Choosing to believe in God, going to church, embracing religion—these were conscious decisions. And I wasn't ready to confront those choices while I was still nursing so much pain and anger towards God.

We finished watching the first Sex and the City movie, but I couldn't really focus on it the way I wanted to. I knew I owed Jaxon an apology, but I was trying to decide if I wanted to simply apologize and leave things platonic and as drama-free as possible, or try to give *something* with him a chance? At this point, who's to say he even wanted to give anything a chance with me after the things I said?

We started the second movie where Carrie, Samantha, and the girls go to the UAE, but Corinne fell asleep no more than fifteen minutes in, leaving me and Genevieve to talk. Genevieve wasn't the kind to dish out advice left and right. She had a way with her expressions that made people feel comfortable opening up to her. So when she started giving advice without anyone asking, you knew it was time to sit up and listen—she was about to share something really insightful.

"So... you like him, huh?" she asked. But I could tell her question was packed with more meaning than the words let on.

"I do like spending time with him. But it's confusing. Part of me thinks it's just lust, you know? He's the first guy in a long time that's got me all excited like this. But then, there's this other part of me that wonders if it could be something real? Something more serious?"

"And what makes you so sure it's *not*...something real?

"Gen, I'm not the kind of woman who believes she has some magical power that can change a man. I'm pragmatic. I don't dabble in uncertainties, and when a man tells me he's only interested in something casual, I believe him. That's because I'm someone who doesn't just throw words around—if I say something, I mean it."

Genevieve sat her cup of tea down on the coffee table and placed her hands over mine and said, "You're also someone who's never been a widow before." The air between us seemed to stop flowing. "And maybe, just maybe, you don't know who you are anymore on the other side of that trauma. Hadassa B.T. (Before Trauma), was all the things you're trying to remember and hold on to about you. When Hadassah A.T. (After Trauma) is someone completely different altogether. You don't go through and survive the things you have and stay the same. I'm not saying Jaxon is 'the one' or 'the forever guy.' But I am saying get to know who Dash is, A.T., before you rule him out completely."

Chapter Thirty-Two

Jaxon

It was my first day at Biddy Mason Charter School, and to say I was nervous would be an understatement. Despite the multiple guide books and lesson plans provided by the school administrator, nothing could have prepared me for this. It was, without a doubt, the most outrageous thing I'd ever agreed to—all in an attempt to impress a woman. Sure, the extra money was appealing and the chance to be more involved in Mila's life was enticing, but I must have been under the potent enchantment of Dash's thighs to have agreed to this.

On regular school days, I wouldn't be expected to be at school until 2 p.m. to prepare for the after-school rehearsals, but since it was my first day of school, I took Mila to her homeroom and then reported to Ms. Geneveieve's office. Ms. Genevieve was a *bad* woman…in the best of ways. Every time I saw her, she was dressed in a different variation of beige or white—it seemed to be her signature style. Her voice was low and melodic, reminiscent of the soothing tones of Phylicia Rashad. And when she moved, her curves swayed rhythmically with each step she took, making it clear that she worked out, stayed hydrated, and prayed up. Ms. Genevieve was not one to be played with.

"Here is all the sheet music that Mr. Douglas left, and he even left detailed notes about what parts the students were struggling with," Genevieve said, handing me various stacks of envelopes and forms that I needed to fill out. "I know you don't technically have to report back until 2 p.m., so when you do come back, have your emergency information and your I-9 completed," she instructed. Something told me she wasn't one to ask many questions. She made demands.

I was pleasantly surprised that she understood how nerve wracking this might be for me, so she gave me several words of advice and offered her support whenever I needed. "We're a family here at Biddy Mason, and we never want you to feel like you're struggling," she assured me. Which was something completely different from the music industry. Grown ass men would fight for positions and scheme to sabotage competition. But Genevieve painted a picture of this environment that really did make it seem like family.

"The Spring Musical is a big deal around here," she continued. "So there will be a lot of eyes on you to make this a success. So, whatever you need, just let me know, and I'll try to make it happen for you.

Mrs. St. James is a big supporter of the arts, and she is determined to make it a key part of the school's future."

I heard what she was saying, but I sort of tuned her out at the mention of Hadassah St. James. I wondered if she knew about me and Dash and she was just really good at playing it off, or had Dash kept me and us all to herself? I came to learn that if a woman didn't talk to any of her friends about you, she didn't take you seriously, and I, for a brief moment, desperately wanted to be taken seriously by her. But now that she had shown her teeth, I was doing my best to push those thoughts away.

As Ms. Genevieve was walking me through my schedule, I couldn't help but get distracted by all the people, especially the women, pacing up and down outside her office. With most of the offices having glass windows, it gave off a friendly and open vibe. But it also made it pretty hard to focus when there was constant movement in your line of sight.

"Don't mind them. You're just the first piece of new meat that's come around in a while," Genevieve said jokingly. Then her face turned a bit serious. "So, you're *him,* huh?" she asked, but it didn't sound much like a question. She definitely knew about me and Dash.

"Him, who?" I replied, feigning ignorance.

She shifted uncomfortably in her seat, fixing me with a look that was far from welcoming and seemed to say, 'don't mess with me.' "The man who has our girl," she hesitated, searching for the right word, "open?"

"I'm not sure what you've heard but, I don't have *anything* when it comes to Mrs. St. James," I said truthfully. After that incident in my truck, I had to take a hard look at who Hadassah was to me, and who she could possibly be in my life. I didn't like the feelings that she stirred up, and she was incredibly lucky that I wasn't the old me that would have matched her energy with my words...in a very savage way. But Mila was present, and I had been determined to be a better man for her, so it was best that I just washed my hands of her and that entire situationship before I reverted back to a different version of myself. So whatever emotions Dash might be dealing with now, they had nothing to do with me.

People only got one chance to show me their true colors, and if I hadn't already accepted this job at the school, I would've made sure our paths never crossed again. My plan was simple: go in every day, do my work, and keep things strictly professional with Hadassah St. James, just as she'd asked. Once I made it clear to Genevieve that anything involving Hadassah should stay strictly within professional

407

boundaries, I left to take care of some errands before my 2 p.m. return time.

I hadn't seen Lu since before the holidays, and she had actually been making some big strides with my career as my new manager. She admittedly had no experience working in the film and TV industry, but she had a sharp business mind and a fearlessness that I trusted about her. After I gave her all of my Hollywood contacts, she made me create a new scoring demo with entirely new sounds so people wouldn't associate it with Jaxon Hart. Simultaneously, Lu had me create an LLC for me that would be used to float my abilities for music scoring, making us seem more like an agency than a one-man show. Once she started reaching out to people, it was only a matter of time before the inquiries started coming back in.

"Sooo," Lu sang. "How was your first day of school?"

"I haven't technically done anything but paperwork, but so far, so good."

"Have you figured out a dynamic with *her,* yet?" she inquired, and I was already annoyed with the direction this conversation was headed.

"Our dynamic is professional from here on out. That's it."

Lu was removing the barstools from the bar top but she stopped to peer at me. "That was fast, even for you! What happened?"

I let out a sigh and helped her remove the remaining stools from the bar. "Can we just not and say we did? I really don't want to get into it."

The reality was, I couldn't escape from it. Thoughts of Dash and our last chat kept playing on repeat in my mind as I tried to make sense of what went wrong. What I had done to provoke such a strong response from her. But I wasn't about to be the guy moping around over a woman who clearly wanted nothing to do with me. I needed to shift my focus back to what mattered: Mila, and landing these film and TV contracts so that I wouldn't need the school paycheck after the spring musical.

"OK! Fine by me!" Lu said, before sitting down at the bar and inviting me to sit with her.

Since the bar didn't open until dinner time, we had the place to ourselves to go over new opportunities that were being introduced. I wasn't picky about the projects that I took on, but I did draw the line at things I couldn't relate to like horror and sci-fi. Since I didn't consume that kind of entertainment, it was hard for me to identify the feelings that the scenes were supposed to convey, and I didn't want to waste my time attempting to take on projects that I knew I couldn't do justice.

Today, however, Lu presented me with a new film from a director that I admired named Pete Chatmon. He had a different take on films and was passionate about telling stories that depicted specific types of journeys, and I dug that about him. He had a series of indie films, two shorts and two features, that he needed scored, and even though the budget was lower than I'd like, I wanted to do it. Pete was the kind of director that took his people with him if he liked you, and I would do anything to work with him.

My entire face lit up with excitement. "Lu, you have *got* to get me this gig. Tell me what I have to do?!"

She was amused by my child-like enthusiasm and had no problem rubbing this in. "So who's the best bootleg manager you never knew you needed?" she teased.

I rolled my eyes, pretending to be irritated, and whined, "You are, Lu."

She baited me a little bit longer, threatening to raise her percentage, before she told me that I was the frontrunner for the project. "He is sending over an emotionally charged scene and he wants to see what you can do with it. You nail it, this gig is as good as yours."

I wasn't sure what to expect when I gave Lu control of my career, but this wasn't it. She stepped in and took absolute command, leaving a trail of success in her wake. When she first hired me for Sanctuary, we both had our doubts about how things would pan out. She didn't want my romantic entanglements causing drama at work, a concern I started taking more seriously when I realized it could jeopardize her business. And I didn't want her to think that just because I was her employee, she could use it as leverage over me. But as we'd worked together, we'd formed a bond that went beyond any issues from our pasts, developing a relationship that felt like family.

I wrapped up my meeting with Lu at 1 p.m., giving me plenty of time to take the fifteen-minute drive to the school. I planned to get there in enough time to walk the theater, review all of the props and instruments we were working with, and acclimate myself to the campus as a whole. Since this was the first day, I was going to use today's rehearsal to get to know everyone and find out how we could best work together.

I've experienced situations on tours or in bands where there was a change in section heads mid-tour or during an important project, which easily disrupted the team dynamic. Oftentimes, it happened because someone came in with a chip on their shoulder or something to prove, asserting themselves without trying to understand the existing team dynamic. This had the potential to disrupt chemistry and negatively impact performances. So, I approached this new venture as if I were a new musical director joining an established band, recognizing the importance of earning my place by getting to know the students and understanding what it takes to bring out their best performances.

When the kids came into the classroom, they were all surprised to see me standing there, even though they were prepared for a new musical director. The only student who was excited to see me was Mila. She ran in and gave me a hug before taking her seat, and I was surprised that she wasn't ashamed to show me affection in front of her friends. Instead of standing quietly as they all waked in, I played the song, "Get Ya Head in the Game," made popular by the High School Musical movie and, one-by-one, kids began to mimic the dance moves. One student even grabbed a basketball to try to emulate Corbin Bleu.

Once the theater was pretty full, I turned the music down to introduce myself. "Hello, everyone. My name is Mr. Hart. Whenever we're in this room, everyone can call me Jax. When we are around other teachers or," I lowered my voice like I was telling them a secret, "if Mrs. St. James comes around, you have to call me Mr. Hart, OK? It will be our little secret." All the kids looked around at each other as if they were blown away by this, and I think I heard a few kids say I was cool. And for the next two hours, I got to know them, and they got to know me. This might turn out to be a cool gig after all.

Chapter Thirty-Three

Hadassah

Jaxon's first day turned out to be quite the eventful day since all the women, and some men too, were buzzing about the new Music Director, Mr. Hart. Since his hiring was somewhat last-minute and unconventional, many of the staff had done their homework to find out more about him. Some of the women were even planning to visit Sanctuary next time he was set to perform. Despite my best efforts to avoid crossing paths with Jaxon, I couldn't escape the whispers and chatter about him in the hallways and breakroom.

"I bet he's married!"one teacher speculated.

"I heard he's a widower or something? That new girl, Milagros, is his daughter, right?" another added.

"Nooo! Mila's his little sister and, from what I know, he's a single guy raising her all on his own," the after-school teacher corrected. "He seemed sort of unreliable as a parent at first, which makes me wonder how he persuaded Mrs. St. James to give him this job?"

At that, I quickly retreated to my office. I didn't want anyone reading any hidden meanings on my face, unsure if my reasons for hiring him would be evident. It wasn't *just* because we'd been intimate that I considered him. I'd seen him create some amazing musical arrangements and knew he had real talent. But if anyone asked if that was my *only* reason, particularly given his initial reputation as a "difficult parent" when Mila joined the school, I'd have to plead the fifth.

"Well, well, well! Who are *you* hiding from?" Corinne teased, startling me as I tried to sneak into my office without being noticed.

"Wouldn't be a certain tall, dark, handsome musical director down the hall, would it?" Genevieve joined in.

Corinne plopped on the couch like a big kid, "Oh! You mean, Daddy Yum-Yum, Genevieve?"

Shaking my head and making sure the coast was clear, I whisper-yelled, "You know what? I can't stand either of you! And I'm not hiding. I'm...simply trying to get ready for our staff meeting this afternoon!" I tried to play it cool, but there was no fooling them.

Corinne, the hopeless romantic between the three of us and who also rooted heavily for everybody black and in love, prodded further. "Wellll?" she sang like a schoolgirl with a crush.

"Have you spoken to him or seen him yet? Did you lock eyes and realize just how much you…"

"Stop, Corinne," I cut her off. "No, I haven't seen him. No, we still haven't talked. I wanted to give him space and time to get acclimated before I hit him with anything else. Besides, we have our first one-on-one check-in this Friday, and I don't want to muddy those waters with anything unprofessional. Maybe after his first week I'll try to connect with him outside of work."

"Good luck with *that*," Genevieve muttered, disguising her words as a cough.

Corinne and I both looked at her and said in unison, "What's that supposed to mean?"

Genevieve walked to my office door, glancing out the window to ensure no one was nearby. "Based on my conversation with him this morning, when I gave him his paperwork and keys, he made it clear he doesn't want anything to do with you outside of work. And he seemed pretty serious."

"Daaaaamn!" Corinne sang.

OK. So, he was still upset. I had said some terrible things about his past, and he was clearly still reeling from it. Probably playing my words on repeat in his mind, each replay making him resent me a little more. I'd never been in an abusive or toxic relationship, but I'd attended numerous trainings about the struggles women faced in these situations, why it was so difficult for them to break free, and how to identify signs of abuse in children. The most damaging impacts of abuse weren't necessarily the bruises that appeared after a beating. It was the lingering words, the harmful messages that stayed with victims for days, even years later. Those words were often lies used by abusers to convince their victims that they were worthless. Once these lies took root in their minds, it was incredibly difficult to unlearn them. Because eventually, victims started believing those lies, regardless of how far removed they were from the truth. I got the feeling that I stirred up some of the lies Jaxon wanted me to help him forget.

When I thought about what he endured with his father and the hurtful things he likely had to hear and deal with throughout his life, it made sense that he'd decided to never let anyone get close enough to cause him that kind of pain again. Then along comes me, breaking down his barriers, then beating him over the head with the remnants of his past. I wasn't one of those women who thought it was my job to heal or manage my man's emotional triggers tied to his personal traumas. But I do believe that when I can, I should do my best to protect him from those painful memories. And I failed him miserably.

"Well, then," I continued. "That's that! We'll be co-workers and nothing more. Actually makes things much easier for me." Corinne and Genevieve looked at each other as if they could sense I was lying…to myself.

"So, you're completely fine. No issues. And there will be no drama, right?" Genevieve said with a concerned tone.

"I'm fine, ladies. No issues. Absolutely no drama. My name is Hadassah St. James, and I am a goddamn professional!" I exclaimed unconvincingly.

Every Monday at 4:30 p.m., after all the children had been picked up from after school activities, we had our weekly staff meetings. With it being Jaxon's first, I had a feeling that today's meeting would have 100 percent attendance. We normally used these meetings to go over our calendar of events, semester initiatives, and any feedback from the community. Still abuzz with everyone these days, was the initiative that Congresswoman Dede Atkins was pushing to get rid of all charter schools by stripping us of our accreditation. This could be detrimental to our entire community, and I'd been so preoccupied with my Jaxon drama that I let my priorities slip.

Clearing my throat, I brought everyone's attention to me at the front of the room so we could get started. "Good afternoon, everyone, and welcome back! Hope you all had a restful holiday, but now, we get back to Biddy business!" I tried my best to sound upbeat and unaffected, even though Jaxon was sitting just three seats away, looking at me with an expression that was completely unreadable. And my goodness did he look good.

I fought hard to keep my body from responding to the sight of him. The way his broad shoulders and muscular arms filled out the blazer, casually paired with a hoodie, was positively enticing. He'd freshened up his fade, leaving a small fro on top, adorned with soft, twisted coils. His beard was meticulously groomed, and his mustache perfectly framed those irresistible lips.

The appeal of this man... It was nothing short of sinful. His presence stirred within me a whirlwind of thoughts and desires that required absolution. Each glance at him was like a dance with temptation, each thought of him a sweet surrender to the forbidden. My heart pounded in my chest, my breath hitched, and I found myself both shaken and stirred by the pull of his charm.

I cleared my throat to continue, and my voice sounded like I hadn't had water in days. "As I'm sure you've all heard, we hired a new music director to help with the spring musical, Mr. Jaxon Hart." I offered a warm smile to Jaxon and prayed he wasn't about to make this awkward. "Mr. Hart, would you like to introduce yourself to the rest of the staff?"

Jaxon narrowed his eyes towards me, and I noticed a flicker of nervousness wash over his face before he cleared his throat and stood from his seat. "Hello, everyone. As Mrs. St. James said, my name is Jaxon Hart, and I'm happy to be here with such an esteemed group of educators. I'm sure it's no secret that I have no clue what I'm doing when it comes to being a teacher, so I hope you all are OK if I reach out for advice from time-to-time."

"We don't mind at *all!*" Ms. Brooks, our science teacher, suggestively swooned. She was the type that had a five-year plan to be married, and she would do whatever it took to make that dream a reality, even unabashedly throwing herself at unsuspecting men. *Heffa.*

Redirecting the attention from this thirsty thot of a science teacher, "We are *all* available to support you, Mr. Hart. Biddy Mason is a family, and helping each other succeed is how we help our community succeed." He returned to his seat and nodded his head at me but stopped short of saying thank you or anything that would be meant specifically for me.

As the meeting progressed, I painstakingly moved through the remaining items on our agenda. Yet, my focus was relentlessly drawn towards him. Each time I stole a glance, an acute sting of heartbreak would clutch at me as I grappled with the bitter reality—this man was not checking for me! At best, I pissed him off, and he was simply taking some time to cool off, punish me even. At worst, I hurt his feelings. And one thing I knew about hurting a man's feelings, you only got once. I couldn't tell which was the case for him.

I caught him a few times, scrolling on his phone while I was speaking and, sure, other teachers were doing the same, their attention divided between the meeting and their devices. But it stung a bit deeper when it came from him. It felt personal, targeted—as if he was making a conscious effort to shut me out. Each indifferent gaze he cast my way was a dagger to my heart, each nonchalant scroll on his phone a cruel reminder of my unrequited feelings. The room filled with chatter and occasional laughter, but all I could hear was the deafening silence of his indifference. He was oceans away from me, and it was like that night in Savannah never happened.

"And finally, we need to figure out what we are going to do to fight this initiative being brought by Congresswoman Atkins. Did anyone come up with any solutions or ideas to help us raise more awareness and get people to vote?" I looked around, and no one had any ideas to offer.

Most people often felt lost when it came to initiatives like these, especially when they were introduced by politicians trying to win over their supporters. These politicians usually targeted marginalized communities, seeking to disenfranchise them. A lot of folks we worked with didn't understand that their vote had the power to stop these proposals in their tracks. The media tended to keep people's attention focused on who was going to be the next president, and our communities didn't realize that the everyday things that affected them weren't decided by the president alone. These decisions were actually made by local officials, like Congresswoman Atkins. And without the awareness of our community, and their votes to stop Congresswoman Atkins, Biddy Mason would cease to exist.

"You mean besides quite literally fighting her? 'Cause I will ring that lady's bell from sea to shining sea, honey!" Corinne yelled, and the entire room went up in laughter.

"Let me rephrase," I said, trying to hold back a laugh and remain professional. "Does anyone have any *non-violent* ideas to help raise awareness?" The room was back to being silent. No one had any ideas on how to help us boost awareness, and I was starting to feel defeated.

Normally, Lamar and I would sit up all night and strategize, and by the end of it all, he'd have a plan in place with a project schedule and marching orders. I hated the pressure that came with feeling like I had to solve all these problems on my own.

"You guys," I pleaded with the teachers in the room. "This is important. We could all be out of jobs, and children could get left behind in a system that wasn't designed for them to thrive if we don't do something about..."

I was in the middle of my impassioned speech when I was interrupted. "Uh, excuse me, Mrs. St. James. Have you thought about a fundraiser event that gets the community involved?" Everyone went silent as the newest member of our staff dared to speak up.

"Well, Mr. Hart, we have done similar things in the past, but...what did you have in mind, exactly?"

Jaxon sat up straight in his seat and began speaking to the room, not necessarily me directly.

"Well, I've seen where politicians hold outdoor fundraising events and bring popular artists to rally the community for a specific cause or initiative."

Corinne's eyes lit up as Jaxon's idea sparked an idea of her own. "Yeah! And since all of this is politically motivated, perhaps we find a PACT to support us and use the funds from the fundraiser to get the PACT to work *for us*!"

"We can call it 'Bucks for Biddy Mason,'" Jaxon suggested, and everyone in the room exploded with excitement. It *was* a great idea.

"I really appreciate that input, Mr. Hart. Let's explore your ideas around that. I'd love to hear your thoughts, especially surrounding artists. Do you have a moment after the meeting today for a quick chat?"

I saw a condescending smirk appear on his face as he said, "I actually have to pick up Mila from her friend's house right after this, so perhaps we can later this week. Thursday, maybe?" He was keeping his distance, but the look on his face made it seem like it was amusing to him. So, this was his game. He didn't just know I wanted him; he reveled in it.

Jaxon had returned to being the same arrogant jerk that I first crossed paths with at the club that night. His warmth had vanished, replaced by a chilling indifference. There was a dark satisfaction in his eyes, a predatory gleam that spoke volumes, and still, I couldn't read him anymore. His every move was calculated, each gesture designed to tantalize and torment. The look in his eye said he was committed to stringing me along, playing me like a fiddle while he sat back and enjoyed the show.

Fine, Mr. Hart. Game on.

Chapter Thirty-Four

Jaxon

I wasn't the kind of man that thought he had everything figured out or had it all together. I was just well-versed in all things related to me. So the idea of talking to someone about my problems, someone who *wasn't me,* always struck me as odd. If I was at the center of everything, then I should be able to solve the problems that had to do with me. That philosophy had always worked... until now. Until Mila. I didn't know how to give her the internal tools to access what she needed to help herself, and I could tell she needed help.

She and I were growing closer as siblings and as a family, but she still refused to talk about her mom or her relationship with our dad. Though, something told me they weren't that close. Whenever I tried to broach the subject with her, she would shut down or had figured out how to change the subject like an avoidant pro. But she was hiding so much behind those big brown eyes and curly eyelashes, and I was honestly afraid the secrets would destroy her. The way secrets destroyed a little piece of me. So, even though I didn't feel the need to discuss *my* problems with a professional, I didn't want Mila to go through life holding on to things that a therapist could help her process and release.

I had received a few therapist recommendations from Danica, Mila's social worker. However, while in Savannah, Dash suggested that Mila might feel comfortable talking to the school counselor since the two had already begun building a rapport. I actually agreed. And since Dash had more experience with children and their needs than I did, I didn't see a reason to doubt her or the school's counselor. Today was Mila's first appointment, and we were both nervous about what to expect.

Biddy Mason had an entire mental health wing, complete with a meditation room, which Mila had already begun visiting since her panic attacks. The wing also had various activities designed to help students find what worked for them to create a sense of peace and calm. I had never seen anything like it, and it made me wonder what all went into inspiring something like this. To have a vision this big, then to see it come to fruition, it was nothing short of amazing, and I had to shake off the jealousy that was rising up for Lamar. The perfect man that Dash, and everyone else, had immortalized.

The waiting room to Dr. Johana's office, the school counselor, was vibrant and colorful with various pictures and toys that lined the wall on the floor. Paintings of motivational quotes with phrases like 'You're Amazing Just the Way You Are,' or 'If You See Someone Without a Smile, Give them One of Yours," accented the walls and I was grateful that Mila was surrounded by staff and faculty that legitimately wanted to see her thrive.

I watched Mila as she flipped through the pages of a magazine designed by the school's newspaper club, or the 'Pub Club.' While going through the mountain of paperwork and information to work here, I read that the student-led group published a monthly magazine that highlighted inspiring students and their accomplishments. The issue Mila was holding had a special needs child on the cover.

"Are you OK?" I asked. Because while she appeared to be reading the publication, she was actually just staring at pages, appearing to be somewhere else entirely. She just shrugged her shoulders in response which told me she was *very* nervous.

I got on one knee so I could meet her at her level, and raised her chin so her eyes could meet mine. "You don't have to be scared, OK? I know this is weird, and it feels funny, but we all just want to make sure you're OK. Do you understand?"

She looked back down at the magazine, flipping through the pages as if she was really engrossed in what was there. I didn't want to cause an incident before her first therapy appointment, but I also didn't want her to go into this session mad at me. I didn't want her to feel like anything was wrong with her because I was making her talk to a therapist. "Mila, sweetheart. Can you talk to me? Say something."

She looked at me, and I could tell tears were starting to form in her eyes. "Are you mad at me?" she asked innocently.

My face initially looked rigid as I furrowed my eyebrows, but I quickly softened my expression so she could sense empathy instead. "No! Of course not! Why would you think I was mad at you?"

She was scared at first, but I gave her hand a little squeeze, rubbing it for a little extra comfort, and she opened right up. A trick that often worked for Dash whenever she was spiraling, too.

"Whenever Mommy used to get mad at Daddy, she would tell him that he needed counseling, and he would yell at her. He used to say if he couldn't fix his own problems then what was somebody else gonna tell him about how to do it?"

I hated that man. Everytime I felt like I was distancing myself from him and his image, someone or something always managed to remind me, yet again, that this apple didn't fall far from his rotted tree.

Before I could respond to what she'd said about my dad, the door opened to Dr. Johana's office. "Mila? You ready to come talk to me?"

Mila retreated into me and squeezed my hand tightly, signaling that she wasn't quite ready. I turned her face to me and lifted her little chin, "I'm not mad at you. I'm incredibly proud of you, and you should be proud of yourself. You are not talking to Dr. Johana because you are broken or because anyone is mad at you. You are talking to her because we love you and we want you to know that it's OK to be sad or feel happy or even hurt sometimes. Does that make sense?"

She shook her head yes, and I was grateful because I couldn't think of a better way to explain why she was there. I watched her take Dr. Johana's hand, and I couldn't believe the strength of the connection I felt to her. We were connected by the silence and secrets that accompanied a chaotic home. We didn't have to speak our truth to know we shared a bond only familiar to those who had learned to tiptoe through life without making waves for others.

"I'll be here when you get done, OK?" I said, before Dr. Johana waved and shut the door behind them.

I had fifty minutes to kill until Mila's session was over, so I headed to the auditorium to review plans for the next rehearsal. Mr. Douglas had arranged a musical in the spirit of the movie "Wakanda Forever," and some of the song numbers were overly ambitious for the amount of time we had left. Since this wasn't my original vision, I was updating some of the music so it was simpler for the kids to learn, but would translate well to an adult audience.

It was my third day at work, and so far, I'd done a good job of avoiding Mrs. St. James. I managed this by showing up just before my after-school class started, minimizing any free time in which I might bump into her or she could "run into" me. I steered clear of the break room, which was just a few steps from her office door. And when my class ended, I made sure to exit through the front door, away from where the staff and faculty parked their cars. But since the Meditation Wing was on the route past her office, today marked the first time I'd seen her twice in the same day.

As I walked past her office, headed to the theater, I noticed her in there talking to Coach Drew

Sanders. She was wearing a black sweater dress with black thigh high boots, and I was envious that Coach got to be that close to those curves and her scent that always smelled like an escape. I hadn't realized it, but my steps slowed dramatically as I observed the ease of connection that seemed to flow between them. They were naturally comfortable with each other, and I suddenly wanted to know if they were sleeping together. If he'd had the chance to touch and taste her the way I did.

I must've lost track of where I was going, because next thing I knew, there was a loud crash, and I was sprawled on the floor. Trying to stealthily watch Hadassah and Coach Sanders, I'd collided with the big metal trash can outside the admin offices. So much for staying under the radar. Now everyone was rushing out of their offices to see what the fuss was about. And there I was, lying on the floor with today's lunch special smeared all over my gray pants.

Stunned and trying to stifle a laugh, Genevieve asked, "Are...Are you OK, Mr. Hart?"

I wanted to lay there like the men who got tackled on the football field and wait for the pain to subside, but the humiliation was hurting me more than my pain was. "I'm fine. Just missed a step while I was headed to the theater," I lied and I wanted to punch Coach Drew in the nuts for bending down to offer me a hand to help me up.

"Thanks, man," I said, but the look in my eye said, 'fuck away from me and my girl, bro!'

"Everything is fine. Nothing to see, everyone," Hadassah said, as I bent down to pick up the large metal trash can and placed it up right. From the corner of my eye, I caught a glimpse of her bending to help pick up some of the trash that was sprawled across the floor. Great. More torture as I avoided staring at the way her dress dipped perfectly at the sway of her back, accentuating her ass.

The spectators scattered, leaving Hadassah and me standing alone. Coach Drew said he'd chat with her later and went off to find the janitor. I gritted my teeth, watching him give her arm a friendly squeeze before he left.

She fidgeted with her fingers, her gaze darting around as if searching for the right words. "Are you sure you're alright?" is what she finally settled on.

"I'm fine. I guess I just got distracted, and...well..." I chuckled, spreading my arms and gesturing to the ground where my *distraction* had caused a big mess.

She was stunning, absolutely irresistible. It took all my willpower not to pull her close and confess how much I missed her. But she'd hurt me in a way I never saw coming. I hadn't even thought she could be so cruel. Now that I knew what she had the capability to do with her words, how could I ever trust her again? How could I trust her to not hurt me that way again? The answer was simple...I couldn't.

I noticed the janitor and Coach Drew walking towards us, their laughter echoing down the hallway. I chose to ignore their amusement as Coach recounted the embarrassing story of my fall. "Well, I need to get some sheet music from the theater. Have a good afternoon, Mrs. St. James," I said, keeping my voice flat and emotionless.

I was walking away when I heard her call out, her footsteps trailing behind me. "Jaxon, wait."

I stopped in my tracks but didn't immediately turn to face her. I needed a moment to mask the hope in my eyes with the lingering pain she had caused. That was the only way I could keep my guard up around her. Finally, I turned and said, "Yes? Mrs. St. James?"

Her face was a picture of confusion. "You...you're being so formal. Is that how it is between us now? After...*everything*?"

"Isn't that what you wanted?" I retorted with a grin. I could see her trying to decipher or read my expression, but she'd lost that privilege. I was no longer an open book for her to read.

"Look, I know I said some unfortunate things, Jaxon. I was caught off guard and hurting, and you..."

Cutting her off, I said, "I appreciate your apology, if that's what this is supposed to be. But it's all good. *We're* good. And I am grateful for this amazing opportunity to work here. I'll see you on Friday at my first official meeting with the boss, right?" I saw pain eclipse her face, but it washed away quickly.

"Yeah! Of...of course. Friday at 4 p.m.?" she stammered, before quickly walking away and back into her office. And that mutherfucker Coach Sanders followed.

After taking care of a few things in the theater, and hiding out from Hadassah and whatever was going on between her and Drew, I headed back to Dr. Johana's office to pick up Mila. The hallways were mostly empty and dark, the motion detectors activated to conserve energy. Hadassah's office was now empty, and I was torturing myself with the idea that she had left with Drew.

I arrived just in time to see Dr. Johana open her office door and Mila to come running out.

"Hey, Jax!" she exclaimed, a stark contrast between the Mila I dropped off and the Mila I was looking at less than an hour later.

Smiling at Dr. Johana I said, "Looks like things went well?"

"I don't like to measure things by good or bad," she replied softly, "but all things considered, I believe she and I will work well together."

Mila asked to run to the restroom before we left and, after I excused her, Dr. Johana took it upon herself to inquire more about me. "So, how has all this been for *you?*" she asked pointedly.

I wasn't sure where her question was coming from, but I answered her in the most guarded way possible, without coming off combative. "As well as could be expected. Going from being a bachelor to practically a single dad is quite the adjustment."

Not responding immediately, she smiled like she was mentally downloading all of my secrets and was preparing to read me my mail. "I can imagine it would be. But I was more so talking about your dad." She stepped closer to make sure that what she was about to say was just between us. "You know,

Mila isn't the only one who lost a parent recently. And since I imagine your sudden life change hasn't left you much space for grief, I want you to know that I'm here for you, too."

I took a step back because I didn't like her being this close or this comfortable with making deliberate eye contact with me. "Look, Dr. Johana, I appreciate what you're trying to do here, but I'm not your focus. Do you have any tips on how I can do a better job relating to Mila and getting her to open up more?"

"*You* can open up more," she said pointedly. "Children can sense when you are guarded, making them guarded, too. When you share a bit of your truth, your fears, and even your hurts, it makes them comfortable doing the same. Have you tried being open and honest with her in the way you wish for her to be with you?"

I let her know that I was an open book with Mila. Wherever she asked questions, I gave her honest answers because I would have appreciated the same when I was her age. But I never shared anything that felt too grown up for her to handle. It wasn't fair for her to shoulder the burdens of adults while she was still figuring out how to be a child.

"Sure, there are things that kids shouldn't know about," Dr. Johana counseled. "But I'm not talking about those kinds of things. When you feel down or find yourself relying on unhealthy ways to cope, or when you're just puzzled by your own feelings, it's a good idea to share these experiences with Mila. There's a good chance she's going through similar things and isn't sure if she can trust you with her feelings."

I understood what she was saying. It felt a bit like sorcery, how she could identify the things I was dealing with even though I hadn't really shared them with anyone, not even Hadassah. So, I took her words to heart and assured her that I'd do my utmost to make our home a safe haven for Mila to express her feelings. Considering all the years I'd spent studying women, this shouldn't be too hard, right?

Chapter Thirty-Five

Hadassah

The first week back at school had been such a whirlwind of activity that it was all a bit of a blur. Jaxon's idea for a fundraising event to draw more attention to our campaign to save charter schools was brilliant. Corinne sprang into action immediately, planning and making calls. She even set up some interviews with local news stations for me. That's Corinne for you—once she set her sights on a goal, she was unstoppable. Before you could blink twice, she'd have a full plan, marketing strategy, and funding for whatever project she was tackling. Without her, Biddy Mason would have crumbled in the months after Lamar's passing. I was so grateful to have her as my right hand.

It was Thursday after school, and I couldn't stop thinking about Jaxon's smug reply during our staff meeting on Monday when I asked him about discussing the fundraiser. "How about Thursday," he said, and I wanted to strangle his muscular neck right then and there. I felt like a teenager with a crush, wandering the school halls, hoping to bump into him or catch sight of him.

The whole thing was absurd. I was his boss. I could easily walk over to the theater where he held rehearsals and simply order him to meet me in my office after his practice. Sure, it sounded like the start of a very cliché porn scene, but it was the only idea I could come up with to get him to talk to me. Even if nothing were to happen between us again, we were now co-workers, and it was ridiculous that we were avoiding each other. Well, that *he* was avoiding me. It had been over a week since our trip from Savannah, and he had stopped answering my calls or texts. I think he even blocked my cell number because the only way we could get ahold of him now was through the school's phone.

Indignation in my steps, I stomped over to the "Off Broadway" wing where the theater was, to tell Jaxon to come to my office once he was finished. That part of the building was designed to give students interested in entertainment the resources they needed to consider careers in the field. We had a recording studio that we used for our after-school radio station and morning announcements and a 3D and graphic design studio for kids interested in design. There was also a newsroom set up for students who wanted to learn the ropes of reporting and writing for the news. Once a quarter, we got local celebrities to come in and give workshops to students. When the areas weren't in use, we were able to rent them out to raise money for the school.

As I neared the theater, the sound of a gorgeous singing voice filled the hallways. The voice was raw and unpolished, but stunning as she belted out the chorus to Whitney Houston's "The Greatest Love of All." Trying to stay unnoticed, I stood at the side, peeking through the open theater door when the music abruptly stopped. I craned my neck a little further around the door to see what was happening.

The main group of kids sat in the theater seats, waiting for their turn to sing, while the soloist stood on stage, singing her heart out to the crowd. I saw Jaxon rise from the piano to talk to the little girl face-to-face. It was Mila.

"Why'd you stop singing?" I heard Jaxon ask her gently.

"I messed up!" she responded, hiding her face from her classmates.

"It's okay to mess up sometimes. Everyone messes up!"

She looked at Jaxon with raised eyebrows. "Even you?"

"*Especially* me," he replied with a smile, and my heart did a flip. Why was he so good with kids?

Then, turning to the other kids in the audience, he asked, "Who else messes up sometimes? Raise your hand!" All the kids raised their hands, and I watched as Mila's eyes lit up, realizing she wasn't alone. I was gonna need new panties.

Suddenly feeling embarrassed about my plan to summon him, I turned to head back to my office. I'd just talk to him tomorrow at our scheduled meeting, keeping things professional as he'd asked. I was checking a text message on my phone when I bumped into Dr. Johana, the school counselor.

"I'm so sorry, Jo! I was distracted and didn't see you there," I apologized, catching my breath.

Johana smiled and nodded towards the theater area. "Distracted, huh? I bet," she said with a knowing smile.

I rolled my eyes. "Now don't you start anything. I was just doing my rounds and checking on our new music director's... *progress*."

"Oh honey," she laughed, "We *all* enjoy observing that man," and we both broke into a fit of laughter.

Linking arms with her and heading away from where Jaxon was rehearsing, I asked, "So, what's your take on him and Mila? Do you think you can help them?"

Johana gave me a serious look, "Now, Dash. You know I can't discuss anything about Mila's session with you that isn't directly related to her education."

I quickly waved off her assumption, "Oh! No. I didn't mean for you to share any private information," well, at least I didn't think I did. "I was just wondering if there were any concerns?" I hoped that would clarify any confusion about why I was asking about him.

"Oh! No. He's cautious and very guarded, sure. But he seems genuinely committed to providing a healthy environment for Mila. I was pleasantly surprised." Dr. Johana smiled.

I was glad to see Jaxon was invested in Mila and her success. After seeing him with her and the other students today, it seemed like I was getting a glimpse into another side of Jaxon, even if he wasn't necessarily intending to reveal it.

Dr. Johana looked at me and gave my hand a little squeeze. "You seem good. You *look* good! Anything new going on that's responsible for the change?"

I could never really tell where Johana's line of questioning was headed, so I kept my answer as brief and unrevealing as possible. At least until I was ready to share. If things were going to remain like this with Jaxon, perhaps there wouldn't be anything to share at all. "Oh! I guess I just got some rest during the holiday! I've been good, though," I assured her. Then I quickly said my goodbyes before she probed any further. Sharing my escapades with Corinne and Genevieve was one thing, but Dr. Johana would have more questions than I was prepared to answer.

When I returned to my office, Drew was there waiting for me. Ever since Corinne had told me about him having a bit of a crush on me, I couldn't help but notice his increased presence. He seemed to be finding more reasons to swing by my office and even call me after work hours. Sure, Drew was a good looking guy, but I had never thought of him in that way. As a former linebacker, he still had his footballer's build. His towering six-foot-four frame, muscular physique, and long dreadlocks reminded me of Demario Davis, the linebacker for the New Orleans Saints, but Drew was undeniably more attractive. Even so, I couldn't shake off the fact that he and Lamar were once as close as brothers, and it puzzled me that this didn't seem to bother him.

"Hey, you!" I greeted him as I walked into my office.

"Hey yourself," he replied with a smile that suggested he was genuinely pleased to see me.

I wanted to keep things casual since I wasn't sure if he knew that Corinne had let me in on his little secret. So, I played it cool. "Did I forget about a meeting we had or something?"

Drew seemed a bit uneasy, "Uh…No. Nothing like that. I was just checking in to see how you're doing."

I gave him a friendly smile, though slightly puzzled. "I'm fine. Thanks for checking in."

"It's no problem. I like knowing you're okay." As I was tidying up some files and packing my laptop to head home, I felt Drew inching closer behind me. I turned around, surprised by his proximity.

"Drew, is everything alright?" I asked, my eyebrows furrowed.

"I'm sorry, Dash. I'm messing this up, aren't I?"

"Messing up what, *exactly*?" I asked, even though I had an idea about what he was trying to say.

"Look," he began, avoiding eye contact. "I know we've been friends for a while, and I would never want to disrespect you or Lamar's memory. But I can't ignore the fact that you're the most beautiful and captivating woman I've ever met and..." Drew took a step closer, which made me back up a bit. I think he noticed my discomfort because his eyes softened, and he backed off.

"I'm sorry, Dash. I didn't mean to...I'm sorry. I think you're amazing, and I was wondering if it would be weird if I asked you out on a date. And now, I guess I've made it weird, huh?"

It was weird. But not just for the reasons that many would assume. Drew had been in my home and helped Lamar hang doors during summer breaks. He'd been one of the first people to hold Ty when he was born. He was the man I called to fix things around the house when I was afraid to call a stranger in to help. And he came to me with all of his dating woes. Women flocked to him like bees to honey, but he had been part of my life in this platonic capacity for so long that it did seem weird to even attempt to envision him differently.

I chuckled and reached out to hold his hand. "Drew, you're one of my closest friends, and I really appreciate how you've always been there for me, and for this whole school, actually." I glanced at the floor before meeting his gaze again. "I wouldn't be able to forgive myself if our friendship got ruined by us trying something that we both already know isn't a good idea."

He pulled me into a hug before stepping back and gently touching my cheek with the back of his hand. "You're right. You are absolutely right," he said smiling, heading towards the door of my office. Just as he was about to leave, he turned around and said, "You're still fine though, Hadassah. And if you ever reconsider, don't hesitate. Just let me know, okay?"

I laughed and waved him goodbye as he walked out of the office door.

Chapter Thirty-Six

Jaxon

I had just survived my first week as a music director, wrangling over forty energetic kids. I was exhausted, but there was a satisfying feeling about it all. It felt worthwhile. The music world I'd grown accustomed to was all about glitz and glam, flashy cars, and the constant stream of gorgeous women. But working with these kids? It gave me a sense of purpose that I hadn't expected. I didn't leave them feeling spent or like I needed to wash off the remnants of the day. I was their teacher, sure, but they were also teaching me a few things about myself.

I'd always assumed I'd be a lifelong bachelor because it *seemed* simpler. But in reality, there was nothing simple about that lifestyle. It's why so many musicians wound up six feet under, nursing a bottle of alcohol, or hooked on drugs. You always needed a little 'something extra' to get by. But with these kids, I found myself leaving each day feeling invigorated, which was largely unexpected.

I'd just finished up rehearsal for the day and I was headed over to Hadassah's office for our first one-on-one meeting. Since the majority of my employment had been informal, these types of meetings were also new to me. Sitting down with your boss every week and discussing 'how things were going,' seemed like a waste of time. If things were going bad, I'd let her know. If things were great, I'd send it in an email. No meeting required.

I was a touch nervous heading into this meeting since she and I were barely on speaking terms, and to be frank, I was avoiding her like my life depended on it. But after some thought, I realized it was pretty childish for me to dodge her like I had been. We were both grown-ups and knew what we were signing up for when we started our little fling with no guarantees for anything more. So it made no sense for things to be this way. At the end of yesterday's practice, I decided to pop by her office to offer an olive branch. But when I got there, she was already busy...with Drew, and I was beginning to think of ways to plot this man's death and hide his body so no one would find him.

I hung back outside her office, watching as she clasped his hand. My blood went from simmer to boil when I saw him draw her into a hug. I wanted to launch a boulder through the glass of her door when I caught sight of his hand stroking her cheek. She had moved on. Not that it was any of my business or that I had any claim over her, but I couldn't help wondering if I'd happened to stumble into something that had already been brewing before she and I met. Had her and Drew been inevitable? Either way, it didn't matter. It just further solidified my resolve to keep things strictly professional with her.

When I arrived at her office today, her door was shut, but the glass window gave me a clear view of her. She always seemed so laser-focused and determined, like she could tackle anything she put her mind to. She was a whirlwind of activity in this place, always needed for *something*. Trying to keep up with all her commitments was impossible, but she still found time to rap lyrics to Kendrick Lamar with students in the hallway. There seemed to be nothing she wasn't good at or couldn't handle, but I caught sight of her rubbing her temples. This was a sure sign she was burning the candle at both ends, and I wished I could just sit with her on her couch, lift her feet onto my lap, and massage away her stress. But I had to push those thoughts away.

I straightened up, put on my best poker face, and knocked on the door twice before stepping in. "Good afternoon, Mrs. St. James," I greeted, flashing a smile, hoping to seem nonchalant despite how her glossy lips drew my attention.

"Mr. Hart," she replied, her tone cordial. "Close the door and take a seat." It was clear she'd also put up walls, keeping our interactions sterile. Her expression was similar to the one she wore the night we first met. Poised, resolute, and bold.

"So, how was your first week at Biddy Mason? I trust the staff and faculty have been welcoming?" she asked.

Aside from that nigga Drew? I thought. "Everyone's been fantastic. Super friendly. They haven't even brought up my clumsy fall the other day." She tried to hold back a laugh, but the memory was too amusing, and we both ended up chuckling.

That small moment of humor helped break the ice, and I saw her demeanor relax a bit. "Well, that's good to hear," she said, releasing a sigh. "The parents have been given great feedback from the students as well. You should be proud!"

Her words were registering, but my eyes kept drifting towards her lips, and I feared my resolve would disintegrate. But I'd resisted plenty of women before. She shouldn't be any different. She shouldn't have such an effect on me. But who was I kidding? She was having *every* effect on me.

I cleared my throat and forced myself to look into her eyes instead of her enticing lips. "I am proud. I'm actually enjoying this more than I thought I would," I admitted. As I glanced around her office, a picture on a bookshelf in the corner caught my eye. It was a family photo with her, Lamar, and Ty. I quickly composed myself, hoping she hadn't noticed my wandering gaze or the expression on my face from the sting that pricked my heart at seeing their family portrait.

After just a week on the job at Biddy Mason, it was clear that Lamar St. James' legacy still lingered. From the grand portrait that greeted you at the entrance, to the various rooms and structures named after him and their son, Ty, it seemed like Hadassah didn't really need to move forward. She had everything around her to keep their memories alive and keep anyone else at arm's length. I might have been the broken one between us, but she carried the most baggage.

"So, how do these one-on-one meetings work? Do I have a scorecard or something that you read from?" I asked, trying to get rid of the awkward silence between us.

"Nothing like that, Mr. Hart. This is just an informal time for us to go over any concerns or action items that we have. Since this is our first meeting, and there isn't much for us to go over, I was hoping I could ask you for a favor."

I sat up straight, my curiosity piqued, and I tried to mask the excitement building within me. "A favor? What are we talking about?"

"Well," she started, her voice shaking slightly. "Thank you again for your brilliant idea for the fundraiser. Corinne has already hit the ground running with the planning and she's making good progress." Her eyes fell to her desk and she began fiddling with a pen, a clear sign that she was nervous.

"Just say what's on your mind, Shy," I said assuredly, not realizing that I had reached across her desk and grabbed her hand.

She quickly withdrew it, placing both hands in her lap. "We're looking for a musical act, and we were hoping you might be able to pull some strings with your contacts in the industry?"

"I'm sorry, Mrs. St. James. For…your hand. Reflex, I guess," I said in a disjointed sentence.

Touching her came as natural to me as breathing, and anytime there was even the slightest opportunity to be near her, my body reacted. Usually, I could keep my impulses in check, but there was something about the way she looked at me when she needed me that always seemed to dissolve my self-control.

"It's fine, Jaxon. So, do you?"

I realized I had drifted off again, my gaze returning to her lips. "I'm sorry, can I...what?" She chuckled, and I found myself taking a sharp intake of breath, rubbing my face to hide my reaction as she moistened her lips. Was she doing this deliberately?

"I was asking if you knew any musicians who might be willing to perform for free at the fundraiser? You know, 'Bucks for Biddy Mason,' as you've named it?"

"Oh, right!" I regained my composure. "I think I can hit up a few decent artists for you. They might not be A-listers, but I've got a couple of folks in mind. Let me make some calls and I'll update you next week?"

As easy as that sounded, convincing artists to play for charity was a heavy lift if it wasn't for a big named cause. No matter how well you knew someone, many people still needed to know what was in it for them before they agreed to helping you out. And since Biddy Mason wasn't exactly a big named cause, it would take a mountain of favors to pull it off. But I still carried a weakness for Shy, no matter how it appeared on the outside, and I wanted to come through for her. Be the hero in someone's story for once.

"That sounds perfect. Thank you, Jaxon. I really appreciate it," she said, flashing me a grateful smile. My heart clenched at the sight.

There was so much I wanted to say, so much I wanted to do. But all I could do was nod and mumble a quick, "You're welcome."

A quiet moment stretched between us, each of us seemingly content to simply exist in the other's company. Her breathing quickened, her nerves visibly heightening, but I kept watching her. She had gone light on makeup today, allowing me a clear view of the freckles scattered like tiny chocolate drops across her cheeks. I caught her gaze and held it, an exchange of emotions—hurt, hope, and desire—passing between us.

"Jaxon," she murmured, her voice breaking the silence. "I just wanted to..."

I stood abruptly, cutting her off before she could finish. "I should probably get going. Thanks again, Mrs. St. James, for this incredible opportunity. I have my night gig later, so I'll catch you on Monday?"

Her presence was intoxicating, and I wasn't sure how much more I could take without reaching out to touch her again. I didn't want to be drawn to her. I didn't want to find her irresistible. But just because I didn't want a relationship with her didn't mean I could suppress the raw, primal response she ignited in me every time we were near each other. She was about to apologize, try to return things to how they were before, but I couldn't trust her. And I certainly couldn't trust myself around her. So, I decided to leave before I could make a fool of myself by falling for a woman who had the potential to shatter me.

As I stood up to leave, my eyes caught sight of the family picture on her bookshelf again. It was a stark reminder of the line that we couldn't cross, of the reality that existed outside the confines of this office. With a final nod, I turned and left her office, mentally preparing myself for the task ahead. Not only did I have to arrange a musical guest for the fundraiser, but I also had to figure out how to keep my feelings for Hadassah in check.

I pulled my phone from my pocket and took a deep breath as the ring tone echoed in my ear. I was dreading this call, and if there was any other way to secure a notable artist for the school on such short notice, I would have pursued it. But time was against me. As soon as I heard the voice on the other end of the line, I had the urge to hang up immediately. However, I had given Dash my word, and regardless of where we stood, I wanted her to at

least be able to rely on that. So, with a heavy heart,
I spoke up, "Hey, Remy. I need a favor."

Chapter Thirty-Seven

Jaxon

On rare occasions, Lu got a break from Sanctuary and was able to enjoy a weekend without having to deal with the stress that came with running one of the hottest restaurants and lounges in Atlanta. Tonight, we were out to dinner celebrating her success in closing some major deals for me that I would be starting in the fall. It wasn't money that I'd be getting right away, but it did mean that I would have guaranteed income after I wrapped up my contract with the school.

After the most recent contract came through, Lu called me and told me to meet her on Sunday at Tré Steakhouse, one of the most exclusive restaurants in the city. It was normally impossible to get a reservation there, but since we were both cool with the head chef, we were always able to get in on short notice. We even found a sitter that could watch all three of our kids, so we were most-certainly not letting a night of freedom go to waste.

"I can't believe you came through, Lu," I said, raising my glass to toast her success. "Here's to you and your bad ass negotiation skills."

She smiled and raised her glass back to me. "Here's to *us* and your bomb ass musical abilities that will keep me rich!" She took a sip of her wine, and after swallowing she added a caveat, "As long as you keep your dick in your pants!"

I chuckled, but I could sense the serious undertone in her voice. Lucy had been a witness to several of my relationships that had ended poorly, and we were both acutely aware of how my typical behavior could harm my future. Now that she was acting as my manager, her future was tied to mine. She couldn't risk tarnishing her reputation because of me, and I had too much respect for her to let that happen.

"I'm a single parent now, remember? I can't carry on the way I used to, especially now that I'm responsible for Mila. I won't risk her well-being." I took Lu's hand and looked at her earnestly. "Aye, you have my word, Lu. I'm done letting meaningless situations bring me mountains of grief. All of this—you, Mila... it's just too important for me to mess up."

"So you're a changed man, huh? This wouldn't have something to do with a certain school principal, would it?"

I let out a dry laugh, "For one, I never said I was a changed man. I just said I was done letting my old ways get in the way. And second, I already told you I'm not messing with her anymore. The only women in my life are you and Mila."

Lu chuckled at my declaration but, as our food arrived, I leaned back, mulling over her comment about me being a different person, a changed man. I never really thought about it that way because, growing up with a dad like mine, you'd understand that men like that don't really change, they simply adjust to new circumstances. I figured that was precisely what I was doing since Mila came into my life. However, if I *could* change, it wouldn't be such a bad thing. Especially if it meant I could be good for Hadassah.

We had been sitting and enjoying our meal, me a steak, Lu seafood pasta, when I heard a familiar voice coming from behind me. "Funny seeing you here!" she said, a glaring stare on her face that she tried to disguise as a smile, but it was *not* working. Lu and I looked rather cozy, so I could only imagine what she assumed was going on here.

"Hadassah, hi!" I said, my voice a few octaves higher than necessary. "What...what are you doing here?"

She smiled but she was still showing signs of emotions that I wasn't quite familiar with. Jealousy, maybe? "I am meeting a friend out for dinner. It's their birthday," she replied.

I wanted to know what friend she was talking about because, let me find out it was that mother fucker, Drew. "Oh, really? You must have had reservations for a while," I said nosily, hoping she'd share more about who she was with.

"Oh! Not really. Drew Sanders, you know, from school? He knows a guy, so we never have to wait when we want to dine here," she said, and I felt like she threw that in to get under my skin. He wasn't the only man who *knew* a guy. And it had better not be the same guy I knew.

The audacity of her to show up here looking like that. She was wearing a cream bodysuit that accentuated every curve, and I could feel my heart hammering and pulse quickening as I looked at her, her eyes meeting mine. She had on a coat that paired perfectly with her bodysuit, but it did nothing to hide her body's shape. Don't misunderstand me. Hadassah St. James was more than just a beautiful face and amazing body. There was so much more to her than the alluring goddess standing before me, and I'd never get tired of studying all the ways to make her smile. I loved... adored... everything about her. She was perfectly delightful in every way.

Hadassah and I were stuck in a wordless battle of stares when Lu thought to remind me that she was sitting there as well. "Hi! I'm Lucy. I've heard a lot about you. You know, since you're Jaxon's new boss and all."

My hand washed over my face, and my heart began to race. Why did she have to say that? We were already in a dimly lit booth, sharing what looked like an intimate meal with wine glasses on the table. Lu sharing that as if I only talked about Dash in a work capacity made it seem like Lu and I were something...*else*. Not that it mattered, since Dash and I were nothing to each other but co-workers anyway. Still, I didn't like the look on Dash's face as she observed the remnants of what appeared to be a romantic evening on the table.

Dash shifted in her stance a bit, seeming like Lu's introduction made her uncomfortable. But she was still putting on a confident performance for us. "Lucy. Can't say I've heard much about you. But it's a pleasure to meet you all the same," she lied, and for the first time in a while, I was afraid that I was sitting between two women who were going to say something that would start a fight.

Instead, Hadassah straightened her shoulders, said goodnight, and proceeded to walk towards her table, where a group of ladies sat waiting. A few I recognized from the school. I was just glad that Drew wasn't sitting over there.

I turned around to find Lu glaring at me, her left eyebrow suspiciously raised. "Yeah. Y'all don't mess with each other at all, huh?"

I waved her off, took a sip of my wine, and sulked in my seat for the remainder of the evening, stealing glances of Hadassah every chance I got.

Hadassah

So she was the infamous Lucy. While inadvertently poking around Jaxon's townhouse, I stumbled upon a few letters addressed to a 'Lucy.' I'd initially brushed it off, assuming she was an ex, especially since traces of a woman's presence were noticeable when we first met. But seeing them together, in public, I won't deny, it made me feel some type of way. Especially since I always assumed Lu was a man, not short for a woman named Lucy.

It was Johana's birthday, and she said she wanted to be treated on a fancy date. Since this restaurant usually cost more than most of our paychecks combined, Corinne and I decided to take her out on a throuple date. Genevieve was home celebrating her wedding anniversary with her fine ass husband.

I had stepped out of the house confidently, sure that I was going to have a good time with my girls, and I even enjoyed the looks of the men as I walked past them. And then, there I was, heart pounding in my chest as my eyes landed on Jaxon, tucked away in a dimly lit booth with a woman. They were laughing, their joy echoing in the hushed atmosphere, and it was a harsh reminder of what I couldn't have. Lu was breathtaking, her skin a rich shade of ebony that glowed under the soft lighting. Her eyes were alive with laughter, her lips, painted a daring red, curled into a captivating smile, enhancing her allure.

A surge of jealousy washed over me, its sharp edge cutting deep. But more than that, an ache of sadness tugged at my heartstrings. I wanted Jaxon, craved his presence with an intensity that left me breathless. Yet, as I watched him with this beautiful woman, a sinking feeling settled within me, the realization that he was slipping further out of reach. I couldn't understand what I'd done that had caused him to ice me out to this degree, and I wondered if he would ever let me in again.

"Was that who I think it was?" Corinne leaned in to whisper once I sat down.

I let out an exasperated sigh, "Yes. Yep! That was him. Could I get a drink menu, please?" I yelled, nearly hyperventilating after the sight of Jaxon.

Johana looked confusedly between me and Corinne. "Umm, does anyone want to tell me what's going on?"

In the midst of all the commotion, I had forgotten that Johana didn't know about anything that had transpired between me and Jaxon and, well, now was as good a time as any to spill the tea. I grabbed Corinne's drink, finishing it before waving over a waiter that was walking by. "Two more of these please," I said to the young man, pointing to Corinne's empty glass on the table.

"That bad, huh?" Johana said under her breath.

Corinne snorted in amusement, *"Or...that good*...depending on who you're asking."

I didn't know where to start, so I just word-vomited everything out in a random stream of consciousness, "OK so, on my birthday we all went to Sanctuary to listen to some live music. I had a good time, and since I hadn't *felt* anything in so long, I decided to let myself feel," I paused, using my head to nod in the direction of Jaxon and Lucy, "him!"

Johana raised her eyebrows in even more confusion. "I'm sorry, you decided to feel *him*? Him, who?"

I leaned in and lowered my voice, "Jaxon! The new music director! And I know you're gonna say it's a bad idea and that now I have to do some deep inner work or whatever, but that's why I didn't tell you! I don't want to do deep inner work unless it involves Jaxon Hart doing *deep inner work* on me!" I covered my face with both of my hands, feigning shame and embarrassment.

Corinne busted out laughing while Johana just blinked from what I could only imagine was pure shock.

"So, you've slept with our new music director. That's what I'm hearing right now?"

Corinne took it upon herself to chime in to defend me. "In her defense, he wasn't our music director when it first happened."

"And," I jumped in to continue, "*nothing* has happened since he's started working with us."

Johana looked at me, searching. "But judging by how you're looking and reacting right now, that's not exactly what you want, is it?"

I paused, letting her question hang in the air as I grappled with my swirling emotions. Honestly, I wasn't certain of what I wanted. All I knew was the pang I felt inside at the sight of him sitting across from someone else, sharing a moment that wasn't with me. The sight gnawed at me, stirring a whirlpool of emotions I struggled to identify. Was it jealousy? Longing? Or perhaps a strange mix of both?

And what stung more was his apparent happiness. He looked content, his laughter resonating in the dimly lit room, his eyes crinkling at the corners as he shared a joke with her. His ease was unsettling, almost as if my presence didn't ruffle him in the slightest. It felt like a punch to the gut.

For a moment, I was transported back to the ladies' room mirror when he and I first met. I was locked in a battle with my own reflection, and I remembered the craving for the unknown, the yearning for a taste of joy, however fleeting. That night, I had been considering breaking my own rules, all for the chance to feel...whole. And seeing him tonight made me want to break those rules again. The rules to throw caution to the wind and do something that I normally wouldn't ever do—run to him and tell him how much I'd missed him. Because this... this was a different kind of longing, and it was killing me. It was a longing for something I couldn't have—Jaxon.

As I sat there, lost in my thoughts, Johana extended her hand across the table, her fingers gently coaxing me out of my reverie. "Listen," she said, her voice sincere and reassuring, "I really couldn't care less about you sleeping with that man. Ethically speaking, it's a good thing you haven't, considering he's now working for you. But here's the thing—what truly matters is that you've made an attempt to feel again! Do you realize how monumental that is?"

Her words hung in the air, prompting me to think. I guess she was right. It was indeed a huge step. Until now, I hadn't connected this development to our prior conversations, but Johana had always maintained that my body would signal when I was ready to re-engage with life, to experience emotions again. And it seemed like that moment had finally arrived. I had spent so much time cocooned in my own world, avoiding feelings, choosing numbness over emotions. Now, however, I was contemplating a change, a deviation from my self-imposed norms.

But Johana had a point. This wasn't just about a fleeting moment of intimacy or breaking a rule. It was about allowing myself to feel again, to experience life in all its messy glory. It was about taking that first tentative step towards healing, towards finding a semblance of completeness, even if it was just for a night. And in that moment, I realized just how significant that was. Even if my mother would call me a common hussy for it.

Noticing that minutes had passed and we still hadn't gotten our drinks, Corinne yelled, "Where is our waiter with those drinks? Since Dash the Dalmation came over here and gulped down mine!" We all laughed.

"Since I guzzled your drink down, let me go to the bar and just order you a new one," I said. I needed to walk off my nerves anyway so I could rejoin the ladies and we could celebrate Johana in style.

The restaurant's ambiance was striking a balance between upscale sophistication and an industrial chic vibe. The walls were adorned with exposed brick, offset by the warm hues of oak woods and sleek black metal fixtures dotting the space. The bartop was a unique piece, a butcher block encased in glass that gleamed under the subtle lighting. As I leaned over to catch the bartender's attention, I reveled in the cool sensation of the glass against my arms—a welcome distraction.

I didn't even notice the gentleman who had taken a seat next to me at the bar. It wasn't until his confident, deep voice filled the air that I was jolted back to reality. "Bartender," he called out, his voice booming, resonating through the room. Startled, I jumped slightly, the suddenness of his voice catching me off guard.

Rather than turning to face him, I chose to stare straight ahead, my gaze fixated on the flatscreen above the bar where some game was playing. I offered a light laugh, doing my best to play off my surprise. "You startled me," I admitted, trying to keep the conversation light and casual.

I had no intentions of picking up a man tonight, but as the stranger next to me leaned in closer, his words laced with a flirtatious undertone, I couldn't deny that the attention felt good. It was a brief respite from the storm of emotions threatening to consume me. I found myself wondering if Jaxon had noticed. Was he watching as this man attempted to charm me? Did he feel a surge of jealousy? I wasn't sure why I cared. I wasn't one to play such games, to use someone else's interest as a tool to incite jealousy. But there was something about Jaxon, something that stirred up feelings within me that I couldn't comprehend. He was like a puzzle that was as intriguing as it was infuriating. And as much as I tried to resist, I couldn't help but be drawn to him.

Just then, I noticed the bartender making his way towards us, drawn by the man's commanding call. I turned towards the stranger, a playful smirk pulling at my lips. "Guess you really know how to get someone's attention, huh?" I quipped, appreciating his assertiveness.

"Sometimes you just have to be a bit more vocal about what you need. Or *want*."

That made my head snap and look at him. "If I didn't know any better, I'd say you were flirting, young man."

"Damn! Young man? So I look like a child to you?" he said, flashing a sinful grin.

He was undeniably good-looking, but still so young. Towering at six feet, with a bald head and a baby face complete with dimples. He couldn't have been older than thirty-five. Yet, his demeanor had an air of maturity that could give a run to most men in their forties. He even footed the bill for the drinks Corinne and I ordered. When I almost tripped while leaving the bar, he gallantly offered to carry our drinks to the table for me.

While walking, I spotted Jaxon preparing to leave, chivalrously helping Lucy into her coat. As I braced myself to look away, my eyes met his.

Responding to his gaze, I flashed a gentle smile, and waved goodbye.

I stood there and watched them disappear into the valét area before taking my seat, when I saw a hand in my peripheral view as if it was beckoning for mine. "My name is Matthew, by the way," the young man said, bringing my attention back to him and my friends.

I recollected my thoughts and held my hand out to him, and he brought it to his lips to kiss. "I'm Dash," I blushed.

"And yes, she's single!" Corinne piped, and I closed my eyes, letting out a sigh and shook my head in embarrassment.

Matthew grinned. "Well, that answers my next question." He looked around the table to my friends and asked, "Would you ladies be at all offended if I asked Dash to join me at the bar?"

"Not at all!" Johana and Corinne said in unison, shamelessly flirting with him while kicking me under the table.

Holding my hand up in protest, I flashed him the most sincere but stern smile. "Uh, I am flattered, Matthew, but I'm out with my girls, celebrating my friend's birthday. And I'm also starving. So, why don't we do this," I stood back up from my seat to look him in the eyes. "How about you go hang over there where I found you and wait for me. Feel free to even buy some ladies a drink while you wait. I'll hang with my girls and, once we're done, I'll come join you. That is, if you don't meet someone else who catches your eye in the meantime."

Matthew grinned, but I could tell that he was the kind of man that women didn't ordinarily turn down or make wait. "So, it's like that, huh?" he asked, bringing my hand to his lips to kiss again.

"I'm afraid so!" I shrugged, then took my seat and waited for him to walk away.

Corinne leaned in and whispered, "Daaaaaamn, Dash! When did you become a pimp like that? Just sending brothas to the corner and telling them to wait for you there?!"

Johana just laughed, shaking her head before saying, "Ladies and gentlemen, I believe we've just witnessed a legend at work. A Masterclass, indeed!" she cheered, clapping her hands and mimicking a crowd applause.

"This recent display of dominance has been brought to you by S&M play with Jaxon Hart!" I said to myself, grinning at the pure shock on

Johana's and Corinne's faces. But it was true. That night that Jaxon let me take control had awakened something in me that didn't even require me to channel Sza the Stallion! I actually enjoyed the thrill of control, the way the dominance caught some off guard. It was something I could get used to.

I finished my meal with my girls, even sitting through the obnoxious restaurant staff singing the birthday song as they brought out a big piece of chocolate cake. When the evening was dying down, I looked across the restaurant to find Matthew still seated at the bar, scrolling something on his phone. After I walked the ladies to the door and we said our goodbyes, I went to join Matthew at the bar.

Chapter Thirty-Eight

Jaxon

"I am not a creep. I am not a stalker. This is perfectly normal," I said to myself as I watched Dash flirt with a man at the bar from outside the restaurant window.

When I put Lu in her car to send her home, I asked if Mila could stay the night so I could take care of some business. But one look in my eyes and Lu already knew what was going on. She'd seen me watching Dash and had no problem calling me whipped after my mood instantly changed as soon as she left our table. And now, here I was, standing outside of a restaurant looking like Joe from the Netflix show, *You*.

Usually, I was the one that women stalked and tried to figure out what or *who* I was doing. I'd even had women pop up on dates to *surprise me* while I was out with another woman. It wasn't until right now that I could imagine what they were experiencing. How they could possibly be feeling to make them believe that this type of behavior was reasonable or rational. Of course it wasn't rational, but when you felt this way about someone, rationality went out the window. Because now, I was the crazy, irrational person who was pining for a woman outside of a restaurant after I couldn't get over my hurt feelings, unable to get over myself and tell her how I felt.

I didn't know how to process hurt feelings with the feelings that plagued me when it came to Dash. She quickly and quite easily became like a close friend to me and I was able to share almost anything with her. I had never had that before. I mean, with Lu, it was different. We became like family, and now, the thought of loving her outside of a familial capacity seemed weird. But Dash, I didn't just want to be her best friend or even her boyfriend. I wanted to be her everything. And the fear that she would ultimately do to me what I'd done to countless women in my past had me confused. Scared even. All I knew was that I didn't want Hadassah to go on believing that I didn't like her or didn't want her.

She seemed to be having a good time, laughing and enjoying a glass of wine with this man. He seemed like a gentleman, nice-looking enough. But the fact that she was smiling and sharing her joy with someone who wasn't me had me ready to throw a car through the window. I saw her get up and go to the restroom and I grinned at the opportunity to make my move. I walked back into the restaurant and grabbed a seat at the bar before she could return. Nodding at the man who was occupying her time.

When Dash rounded the corner, returning from the restroom, she found me sitting on the other side of the seat she'd just vacated, right between me and whoever this dude was she was hanging with. I was done giving her the opportunity to forget about me. She was mine. I wanted her. And unfortunately, this man was about to be a casualty of my hunger.

"Jaxon, wha...what do you think you're doing?" she asked and I still hadn't turned around to meet her gaze.

"Just enjoying a drink, Shy."

"You don't *have* a drink," she said through gritted teeth.

The man in the other seat chimed in, his eyebrows almost unified, "Umm, I take it you two know each other."

I turned to the man and a wicked, knowing grin spread across my face. "Biblically," I said, before turning back to face the TV screen.

"Jaxon!" Dash gasped, turning to the man to flash him an apologetic look. " Matthew, I'm sorry. This is a man who thinks that, since we've had sex, he has some sort of claim over me. But he's sorely mistaken."

Dash turned back towards me, nothing close to a smile on her face. "Jaxon? Point taken. Cute little game you've played here tonight, but you made it perfectly clear what you do and *don't* want. So you're gonna have to eat that. I think you should leave."

Finally, I turned in my seat to look at her. "Yeah, about that. I've given it some thought, and... *no.*"

There was rage in her eyes, but there was a fire, too. I could tell that she was getting excited by this exchange just from the way her chest was rising and falling with her heavy breaths. We were locked in a stare and I licked my lips to torture her a bit.

"No? What do you mean, no?"

"Look, I don't know what is going on between you two but, Jaxon, is it? The lady asked you to leave her alone and…"

I fixed him with a stare, giving him a scowl from the depths of my soul as I gave him a stern body check from his feet to his head. "Matthew, is it? I'm sure she's told you her name is Dash and that she's single. She's even beautiful and charming enough to have you believing that she might give you some play."

Dash's eyes got wider in disbelief. "Jaxon, you have got *some* nerve, you know that?" She shifted on one leg and crossed her arms to display her annoyance.

I ignored her, leaning in to finish what I was saying to Matthew, this time in a whisper laced with my signature growl that I *knew* Dash loved. "But she won't be sleeping with you. Not tonight. Not ever. In fact, after you both say your goodbyes tonight, I'm going to show up at her house, and you know what?"

Matthew let out a sardonic breath. "What's that?"

I smiled at his apparent interest in what I was saying. "She's gonna let me in. Then, I'm gonna do very dirty, unspeakable things to her...And she's gonna let me. So, if I were you, I wouldn't waste my time on this fruitless endeavor. She may be single, but she's definitely not on the market." Without saying another word, Matthew got up from the bar and walked away.

Dash was still staring at me, blinking and not saying anything at all. The look in her eyes said plenty.

I pulled out the seat next to me and held my hand out, gesturing for her to sit. "Have a seat, Shy. I wanna tell you something."

She sat her purse on the bar next to me and took the seat, barely able to look in my direction. "I can't believe you just did that. Don't tell me you're the kind of man who lets a woman know you don't want her, but won't let any other man get close either?"

She was angry. Fuming. And I knew I had to figure out how to de-escalate the situation before she walked away for good. "I'm sorry," I said, uttering two words that I usually only said with an agenda. But this time, I meant it. "I didn't mean to turn this into a game or make you feel like I didn't want you. Because that couldn't be further from the truth."

I spun around in my seat, turning to face her and my legs brushed against hers. She remained straight forward, but I had to open my legs to make it easier to look directly at her. "Hadassah, I don't just want you. I crave you. I think of you all the time. I hate having you mere yards away at school without being able to see you."

She looked at me and tilted her head as if she was seeking understanding. "But you *could* see me. You could have seen me every day. You simply chose not to."

"Shy, I couldn't risk seeing you because if I did, I would have grabbed you and devoured you on sight. You consume me and there is nothing I hate more."

Raising her eyebrow, she said, "Nothing you hate more?"

I let out a dry chuckle. "Yeah. I don't like *not* being in control. And everytime I'm around you, it chips away a little more at my resolve."

Something that appeared to resemble a blush attempted to curve the edges of her mouth up. "Then why? Why the cold shoulder and shutting me out?"

I let out a sigh. "At the risk of sounding like Mila right now, you hurt my feelings, Dash. I'm not a perfect man. Hell, I am broken. But I trusted you with my brokenness and you tossed it back in my face like I was nothing. Like I was *less*."

She turned away from me, and I noticed her demeanor soften at that revelation. I had never told a woman that she'd hurt my feelings before. I couldn't even recall ever allowing a woman close enough *to* hurt my feelings. Yet, I was taking another chance at being vulnerable with her, hoping that maybe hearing how her actions affected me, would help it to not happen again.

It was a crazy thing to admit, but I actually learned this idea from Mila. She was having what I could only guess was a hormonally bad day, and she had dropped a plate of spaghetti on the kitchen floor one night while we were sitting down to dinner. I snapped, yelling for her to be more careful, and she just stood in the middle of the kitchen and yelled, *"If I'm already anxious and upset at myself for making a mess, do you think yelling at me is making me feel better or worse?!"* Then, she stomped upstairs, slamming the door to her room.

After cleaning up the mess, I took her a warm plate of spaghetti and apologized. It dawned on me that Mila's presence in my life had me apologizing way more than I ever had in the past. *"I'm sorry that I yelled at you and made you feel worse. I guess I didn't think about how I could be making you feel."*

She'd taken the spaghetti with garlic bread on the side and set it on the computer desk in her room, before turning to me. *"I accept your apology. But only if you try harder to use more empathy."*

Her word choice made me chuckle. It was a big word for a twelve-year-old. *"Empathy, huh?"*

"Yes! Dr. Johana says that empathy is trying really hard to imagine how someone else is feeling outside of yourself, so you learn how to make room in your heart for other people." And that's the story of how a pre-teen schooled me on empathy.

I turned back around to face the TV screen above the bar, and Dash and I both just stared straight ahead for a few moments. "I've never said that to a woman before," I said, my voice low and strained.

She looked at me with a confused stare, "Said what?"

"That something hurt my feelings. I'm sharing that with you because I need you to know what this…what you mean to me."

"Then you shouldn't play games with me like you did. I'm…*We* are too old for that. Grow the fuck up and tell me how you feel!"

"I just did! What else do you want me to say?"

Dash grinned and I could see the wheels turning in her head. She removed her left arm from the bar top and placed it in my lap, angling for my groin. I stiffened, turning to her to flash her a, 'you can't be serious' glance, but she just looked straight ahead, stroking me from the outside of my pants. And my goodness was she good at this!

Looking straight ahead at the TV, she said, "Tell me *everything.*"

I put my elbows on the bartop and dropped my head into my hands, and my breathing became labored. "Dash...Hadassah..." I panted, my heart rate speeding up in tandem with her strokes.

"You know you wrong for this, right?" It was her turn to play games and the daring glare in her eyes had me feeling like I was locked in one of Remy's games.

People were walking by, music was playing, plates clinked in the background and she could care less as she mercilessly stroked my hardness underneath the bar. I pleaded with her to stop, but she kept going, chasing what was inevitably about to be one of the most embarrassing days of my life.

I'd had enough. I jumped up abruptly, breaking away from her grip and bent down, grabbing the back of her neck to pull her lips to mine. I kissed her deeply, hungrily. Then I pulled away quickly. I adjusted myself in my pants before whispering, "I'm going to the restroom. Join me or be gone when I get back." Then I walked away from the bar and headed to the restroom.

Hadassah

I left the restaurant. Sure, he apologized, but that was no excuse for not handling things like a grown up. If someone said something that offended you, you went to them and talked about it so it didn't fester. You didn't passive-aggressively shut them out and make them believe they meant nothing to you. I wasn't sure if I was ready to accept his apology, but I wasn't above making him suffer for the way he handled that. How he handled me.

I was the type of person who, as soon as I walked through the door, everything came off. Clothes, jewelry, hair, all of it. Tonight was no different. As soon as I walked into the door, a satisfied grin on my face, I went straight to my room, shed everything, and hopped in the shower. Since I was still rocking braids, my hair stayed in tact. As I washed the remnants of the day away, Jaxon's words began to echo in my mind. *"I'm not a perfect man. Hell, I am broken. But I trusted you with my brokenness, and you tossed it back in my face like I was nothing. Like I was less."*

I couldn't dispute his feelings or opinions. I had, in a way, broken a trust with my words, and I was fully aware of it. In fact, I had meant to.

Whenever someone dared to question how I was dealing with my grief, or challenged me over anything really, I was known to respond sharply. Sharp was putting it mildly. I didn't like having to justify myself, so I would hurl the harshest comment that would effectively silence them and make them think twice before bringing up the subject again. I understood it was wrong. I knew it was a brutal way to avoid discussions about my feelings, but perhaps I was a bit broken and damaged, too. Maybe it was time for me to confront that.

When I'd gotten out of the shower, my doorbell rang and I actually anticipated this moment. I went into my walk-in closet and grabbed my robe, securing the belt tightly around my waist. I briefly toyed around with the idea of not answering, but I figured I'd had my fun for the night.

When I finally made it downstairs to open the door, he was standing there fuming, and I could have sworn I saw steam coming out of his head.

"So, you talk about me playin' games, and this is what you do? You just leave and can't even answer your phone, Dash?"

At least he was calling me Dash instead of Hadassah. He couldn't have been *that mad.* "What's the matter, Jax? Not in the mood for a little taste of your own medicine?" I teased.

"That wasn't a taste of anything but some bullshit, Dash. I was trying to be real with you and—"

"Oh, so you were being real with me by gloating about our intimate moments to a complete stranger before running him off?"

"Don't do that. Don't act like we're not in this place right now because—" He couldn't finish whatever he was saying because his mouth quite literally hung open.

I had unfastened the belt of my robe to reveal my damp nakedness beneath it. "I'm sorry, too, Jaxon."

It was a cheap move and I didn't care. I knew we had things to discuss, and I owed him more than my body in this moment. However, nothing would be resolved if we stood in the door shouting. My simply nakedness added a bit of color to the ordeal.

Jaxon didn't seem moved at the sight of me. He didn't even...*look* at me. He maintained eye contact as if he was in the middle of an interrogation. "Sorry, for what, Hadassah?"

487

"I'm sorry for mishandling your heart and your trust. I am not proud of the way I spoke to you, and I promise I will work on making sure that doesn't happen again." He smirked at that admission, and his eyes finally began to take in the sight that stood before him. "Now, would you please get into this house before all my neighbors see me naked?"

He stepped just inside the threshold, closing the door behind him. But he didn't come much farther. "I guess I'm sorry for tonight, too. Homie didn't deserve the way I crushed his hopes and dreams of being with you." We both laughed.

"I'm sure he'll be *just* fine. Besides, I'm certain it wasn't going anywhere."

Jaxon closed the distance between us and pulled me closer to him. "And this? Where is *this* going?"

I looked up at him, not sure if he was really asking *that* question or if he was simply trying to decipher where the remainder of the night was headed. I chose to simply accept the latter. "Well, right now we're going up stairs." I took his hand and began to lead him to the stairs. "I've been a bad girl tonight, Jax. And I promise to hold still while you punish me."

Chapter Thirty-Nine

Hadassah

I woke up the next morning as if the night before was a dream. I had not experienced several rounds of pleasure like that in a long time. Ever, really. Every time Jaxon and I were together it was like things between us got deeper and more complex. What began as one night of unadulterated fun and pleasure, evolved into supposed meaningless sex. And after that, sex evolved into what seemed like, felt like...love.

I'm not a silly woman. My mother had had all the talks with me. *"Sex always feels like love. Especially when it's good,"* she'd say. My mother never gave the usual, 'boys are only after one thing' talk as much as other girls' moms when I was younger. She would always paint broad pictures of the types of relationships people had and tell me that every relationship had a purpose. And every person had a different idea about what that purpose was for them. It was my job to figure out what someone's purpose was in my life, and it was best to do it *before* sex got involved. Sex had the tendency to ruin things, especially women. For this reason, I didn't allow sex to drive me or influence how I handled myself in relationships. I used it for what it was intended...pleasure.

Whatever this was with Jaxon, was no longer just about sex. At least, not anymore. Over the past few months, as our relationship evolved, I'd noticed changes in him, too. I'm not so vain as to think that I was the cause of his transformation. It was just clear to me that something was shifting within him and I could sense it during our intimate moments. I could see it in his eyes and in the way he looked at me. Even in the way he spoke to me. He was gradually shedding his guarded, macho persona that kept me at arm's length, never allowing a glimpse into his thoughts. He was beginning to let me in.

Just as I began to allow myself to get lost in the girly musings of happily ever after, Corinne's words came back to smack me upside the head, *"There will be no falling in love with Jaxon Hart."* It was the mantra I repeated every time I felt myself longing for him when I knew he was nearby. But there was a growing conflict inside me between the love and loyalty I held for Lamar, and the developing feelings I was experiencing when it came to Jaxon. I had already pledged my heart to someone, and I never *once* considered that my vow wouldn't last until death. My death, not his.

"So, is this where you sleep every night?" Jaxon asked, pulling me from my silent reverie.

I was laying on his bare chest and traced circles near his rib bones. "Sometimes. This is the guest bedroom."

Jaxon snickered softly. "I figured as much. It feels welcoming but in a *stay for a while but not too long,* kind of way."

Jaxon had a way of making statements that revealed the questions lingering in his mind but didn't say. It was obvious that he didn't want to pry beyond what I was comfortable with and I appreciated that. But I had been more guarded than him regarding my life and my pain, so I guess I owed him some answers.

"Sometimes I sleep in here when I don't want to be reminded. When I want to feel like I'm not expecting them to come through the doors at any moment." I stared at the ceiling and willed the tears not to flow. "And if I'm honest, I don't think I...I couldn't..."

He squeezed me tightly and then peppered light kisses on my forehead. "I understand, Shy. That's *his* bed. Your shared bed with your husband. I understand how that might feel like a betrayal.

He was doing it again, reading me like an open book. I felt translucent with him, like there was nothing I could possibly hide or keep to myself. He saw everything and made no secret about his discoveries. When he rolled on top of me, trapping me beneath his muscular frame, my nether regions cried out in exhaustion, but I was relieved to maybe be changing the subject.

My eyes opened wide at the hunger that seemed to eclipse his face. "*Again?!*" I whined. "I don't think I can—"

Jaxon covered my mouth with his thick lips, and I moaned into him. "Relax, baby. I'll let you rest a little while longer. I just wanted to look at you for a bit. Do you mind?"

I likely had crust in my eyes and my breath smelled like a baby's dirty diaper, but he wanted to just *look* at me? I began to shift uncomfortably at the sudden intrusion. "This is weird."

"You're beautiful."

"I know, but that doesn't make this any less weird," I said wryly.

He looked like he was studying me. Trying to unearth more of the secrets behind my eyes that I tried to keep hidden. "What would you say if…" He looked away as if he suddenly changed his mind. "Never mind."

I took his face between my palms and turned his head towards me. "You can tell me. You can trust me with...whatever it is."

He didn't say a word. He kissed me fervently, searching for strength between our bodies and our breaths. "I've never done this before," he whispered.

I searched his eyes for an explanation. "Done what?"

He dipped his head to kiss me one more time. "I think I'm falling in love with you, Hadassah. And I don't want this, us, to be a secret situationship anymore."

I blinked hysterically at what he was saying because he was quite literally taking me off guard and off balance. "Jaxon, what are you saying to me right now?"

"I thought it was obvious. I want you to be my girlfriend. I want to try something different. With you, Shy."

I sat up in the bed looking over at him, bringing the sheet to my neck as if it were a shield. I tried to say something, but words wouldn't form. Couldn't form. Was he seriously asking me to be his girlfriend? To say I wasn't expecting this would be the understatement of the decade, but it actually felt impossible to conceive. He was a playboy and had, on numerous occasions, told me as much. The fact that Jaxon now wanted to be *the guy* that got to fill a position that was left vacant after Lamar died had me spinning.

"Look," Jaxon continued, "I know I haven't been the best man in the past. I mean…I've downright been a shitty man for most of my life when it comes to women. But…when I'm with you, since I've been with you, I feel different. Like I could *be* different."

I let out a dry laugh because there was no way that I was hearing this correctly. But he just watched me expectantly.

"What, Shy? Say something."

I looked over at him, and I could tell that my reaction wasn't what he was expecting. He was trying to figure out where my head was, but I could see that my response was shattering him and we were about to have a repeat of Savannah all over again.

Straightening my face, I looked him in his eyes and asked a simple question. "How do you know, Jaxon? How do you know you can *be different* with me than you have with any other woman?"

He let out a sigh and drug his hand down his face. "I just know, OK? I know me!"

"Do you?" I shot back. "Because not too long ago you were warning me of the perils of falling in love with the great Jaxon Hart and his addictive magic stick!"

"I know! And at the time, I believed that. That had always been my truth at that time. But now, with you? I've never felt like this before, Dash. And I really be—"

"Exactly," I said, cutting him off. "You've never felt like this before. Met a woman like me before. So, all we really know, Jaxon, is that you've never *ruined* a woman like me before!"

He jumped up, pulling on his pants that had been discarded on the floor, and began pacing the floor of the guest bedroom. "Fuck, Dash! I'm sayin'. Why are you acting like you're too good or better than me? Or..." He paused and sat down on the edge of the bed like he was bracing for what he'd say next. "Like *he* was better than me."

And there it was. Jaxon had always exuded such confidence that I hadn't realized until now. How long had he been comparing himself to Lamar's ghost? Draped in the sheet that was my only cover, I left the bed and moved to his side, kneeling on the floor in front of him.

"Jaxon, I need you to hear my heart when I say this to you. I've developed genuine feelings for you, too. And it's terrifying because I never planned on loving anyone after Lamar, even after his death. But *this* can't be the next move for us."

He looked at me with an almost child-like innocence. "Why not?"

"Because, Jaxon. You didn't offer me anything different than you've offered any other woman. You don't know if you've changed, you know how you *feel.* And feelings are fickle. You can't offer someone a broken version of yourself and expect them to jump up and down for joy. Whatever it was that had you disregarding and discarding women left and right? Go fix that shit first and *then* come and offer me something real and meaningful."

I moved between his legs and wrapped my arms around his waist. "I'm not claiming to be better than you, Jaxon. I'm not even saying Lamar was better. What I am saying is that I've experienced better than what you're offering me right now, and I won't let you experiment with my heart just because you feel good in this moment. I'm going to need more assurances than that."

He kissed the top of my head before gently moving me aside so he could collect the rest of his things. He quietly put on his clothes and his shoes before heading out the door without even saying goodbye.

I had managed to break this man's heart once again.

Chapter Forty

Jaxon

"OK, everyone! Big smiles for the big finale!"

It was the Monday following the weekend that Hadassah told me she wouldn't be my girlfriend, and I was trying my best to hold it together with these kids. The Bucks for Biddy Mason fundraiser, and subsequent vote that would decide the school's fate, was two weeks away and the children were scheduled to perform the song, "We Are the World," which was also from the spring musical. Corinne hoped the performance would boost ticket sales to the musical. I just needed this all to be done so I could fulfill my contract with the school and leave all of this behind me.

The bell rang, which meant the after school session was over, and all the kids bolted out of the auditorium. "Walk, you guys. There's a game on ESPN tonight and I'm not taking anyone to the hospital!"

Mila lingered around my piano, waiting for me to finish packing my things. "Jax? Why doesn't Mrs. Dash come over anymore?"

I snapped my head up and quickly looked around the room to see if anyone else was within earshot. "What did I tell you about talking about that stuff at school? Or calling her Dash for that matter?"

"Sooorry," she whined.

"It's OK. We just need to be more careful about that sort of thing, OK? What goes on in the house—"

"Stays in the house!" she yelled, completing the sentence of our number one family rule. Our only family rule, but it was important nonetheless.

"I just kinda miss her coming around and she's nicer when we're not at school!"

I turned to look at Mila, noticing her big, brown eyes staring at me expectantly. "I didn't realize you noticed since she didn't come around that much anymore."

Mila put her head down and started aimlessly swinging her leg back and forth. "I noticed. It's nice not being the only girl around."

Mila had been seeing Dr. Johana pretty consistently, but she still hadn't come around to sharing her feelings about losing her parents with me. However, this seemed like an opening, like she was open to sharing her thoughts with me.

"Does having Dash around make you think about your mommy?"

Mila's face lit up with the biggest smile. "She reminds me of Mommy! I like that she talks to me like I'm a mature lady."

I chuckled at her enthusiasm to be regarded as an adult. Since she'd endured more than many grown-ups at her age, it was refreshing to see her genuinely acting like a child. Still, I hadn't realized how attached she had become to Dash and instantly, I understood why women often held off on introducing their children to the men they were dating. If the kids grew attached to them and the relationship fell apart, then they experienced the heartbreak just as intensely as their parents. The pressure of having a child's future being impacted by my every decision was damn-near debilitating.

I had spent the last twenty-four hours processing what Dash had said and, while she didn't exactly say anything wrong or unkind, I still instinctively avoided her. I couldn't face her. Never had a woman so matter-of-factly reject me, and I was having a hard time wrapping my mind around it. While I maintained that my playboy persona was something I chose, part of me still avoided serious connection out of fear of rejection. More men did this than they cared to admit, but since meeting

Dash, I hadn't been able to keep my feelings and emotions under control.

Since I had *just* recently apologized for shutting Dash out and making her feel unwanted, I felt the need to make sure she knew that my current silence had everything to do with me and not her. So, I pulled out my phone and sent her a text message.

(Me) *Hey...I know this seems like last time, when I shut down and shut you out, but I promise you it's not. You said some heavy stuff and I need time to process it all. I just didn't want you to think that my silence meant I didn't want you or don't care about you anymore. Because I do. I want you so bad it hurts.*

Almost immediately, I saw the bubbles appear like she was about to respond, but a call rang through before I could read the response.

"Hey, Lu. What's up?"

"Okay, are you sitting down?"

"No, but what is it?"

Lu smacked her lips, frustrated that I wouldn't play along. "How do you feel about California?"

"Expensive as hell. Why do you ask?"

"What if it wasn't so expensive because you had a fat ass paycheck?"

I laughed at the excitement that was practically oozing through the phone. "A fat paycheck might soften the blow a bit. What's this about, Lu?"

"Well, I was able to get you on a dream project. Big budget, big production, and you get to work with a live orchestra! The only caveat is, you will need to move to California for nine months."

"Nine mo…Lu, what about Mila? She just got acclimated to a new school and making friends."

"You would be there during the school year, and you'd be in an area with great schools! It might be hard for her at first, but what little girl wouldn't want to live near Hollywood?"

This was a lot. I wiped my hand down the back of my neck and tried to breathe through everything Lu was saying, but the room felt like it was spinning. This was definitely the opportunity of a lifetime, but I wasn't solely responsible for myself anymore. I didn't have the freedom to just pick up and move 3,000 miles away for nine months. Mila had her school, her friends, her therapist, and a ton of baggage to unpack. Uprooting her again could make things worse for her and I cared about her too much to let that happen.

"I don't know, Lu," I said, as she waited for my excitement to match hers. "I just need to think more about this and how it could impact Mila. When do we have to give them an answer?"

"They didn't say. I just assumed it would be a no-brainer. You think a week is long enough for you to decide?"

"I think so. Let me have some conversations with Mila's therapist and get her perspective. I just wanna do right by her, Lu."

"I understand. And I'm proud of you for putting her needs before yours. Maybe you *are* changing!" At that, I laughed and then hung up the phone.

I could sense the changes in myself. The effortless way I prioritized Mila over my own needs; how I opened up to Dash and allowed myself to experience intimacy with her that I'd never experienced, even though she did push me away; even the immense joy I got from working with these kids every day—all these were clear signs of my growth over the past months. Looking back, I could see that even my time with Remy shaped me, although I hadn't realized it until now.

My experiences with Remy tempered me. The shift in power dynamics, the instinctive awareness of her moods and feelings, the natural rhythm we found together—all created a sense of stillness and calm with a woman that I normally would have ran away from. Maybe that's why I didn't feel the need to cheat or seek other women when we were together. Even if the relationship was one of convenience, fueled by games of power and play, it was still unique to us.

As I grappled with this idea of moving across the country, I inevitably arrived back at my feelings for Dash. For the first time, I was faced with a decision where I considered the feelings of a woman, and I had to ask myself if I would really allow my feelings for her to influence my decision to stay or go? And if I were to stay, would that mean that I would do whatever it took to prove my ability to love her the way she deserved? I was gaining a clearer understanding of the man I'd become, and perhaps my struggle to articulate the certainty of my inner changes was what made Dash wary of entrusting her heart to me. I couldn't blame her for that. I just wished that I could request some assurances from her as well. Something that made me feel safe with the idea of staying for her.

I looked back at my phone to find Dash's response to the text message I sent her before Lu's call distracted me.

(Shy) *Prove it.*

Chapter Forty-One

Hadassah

"And that's why our charter school, and everything we stand for, will stand the test of time!" The faculty behind me exploded with cheer as I gave a rousing speech at a press conference meant to boost awareness of the fundraiser we were hosting to save Biddy Mason.

Corinne had managed to garner attention from news crews across the country, after it became known that more conservative groups were rallying to support the school's closure. The moment certain individuals got wind how much money we independently raised to uplift black and brown students, who would otherwise be overlooked, their fury seemed to intensify. Their anger was directed at our success. Our students' success. The mere thought of providing opportunities for brown kids to escape poverty was enough to infuriate some people, and witnessing this reaction was disheartening, to say the least.

As the news crews gathered in the auditorium, all of the teachers and administrators stood behind me as a show of force and support. Even local police officers and firefighters showed up in uniform as a show of solidarity. We had an entire community rallying for us to win and it meant the world to me. One person missing from the crowd behind me though, was Jaxon. He stood off to the side and watched as I answered question after question with poise and confidence. I was proud that I didn't flinch or waiver in my resolve. By the look in his eyes, he was proud, too and it dawned on me that I missed having my man cheering for me on the sidelines. Something that Lamar and I did for each other interchangeably.

When the press conference was over, we all headed to the teacher's lounge and popped bottles of champagne. The fundraiser was just a few days away, and the staff wanted to celebrate a great turnout from the media. With that much attention, the energy was electrifying. Everyone was hopeful that good press coverage would automatically equal strong voter turnout in support for us. But anyone who studied politics and exit polls could tell you that people were extremely fickle and unpredictable.

"Did you see all those people? There is *no way* they will be able to ignore us!" Corinne exclaimed.

"Please. This is America. They make money off of ignoring us," Coach Drew countered.

"How about we just take this time to celebrate the day? Our fearless leader stared down the mouth of the lion today and didn't flinch!" Genevieve shouted, and the entire crowd erupted in cheers again.

My nerves were all over the place so, when no one was looking, I retreated into my office to steal a few quiet moments alone. Even more than I hated crowds, I hated public speaking. It wasn't just the speaking in front of a room full of people that got to me. It was the energy it took to speak to a room full of people. Each of them with their own questions and agendas, all looking to pull something out of me. It was exhausting and Lamar was so much better at it than me.

Not more than five minutes after I'd been sitting in my office alone, I heard a knock on the door. I was laying on my couch with my eyes closed when I looked up to see Drew standing there.

"Dear, Lord. Give me strength," I murmured to myself, adjusting my clothes as I raised up from the couch.

I painted on a smile and invited him to come in. "Drew! Hey, come in!"

"I won't hold you. I saw you slip away from the celebrations and just wanted to check on you to make sure you were OK."

Drew really was a catch, something I began to notice more after he made his feelings for me known. Even after I gently let him down, he didn't change up the way he interacted with me or cared for me. He didn't try to avoid me, he simply carried on like nothing happened. Like an adult.

"Oh, I'm fine, Drew. Just needed a few moments of quiet, ya know?" I hinted.

"Yeah," he chuckled. "You never were one for crowds, huh?"

I tilted my head to the side and smiled that he actually knew that. "I didn't realize you knew that about me."

"I notice a *lot* about you, Dash. Casualty of unrequited affections, I guess," he mused.

"Drew, I—"

He raised his hand to cut me off before I went into a diatribe. "I didn't mean anything by that, Dash. I was just making a statement. You don't owe me anything. I'm just happy to be your friend."

"Even still, Drew, I appreciate it all the same. You're a good friend to me, and I admire the fact that you didn't change the dynamic of our relationship simply because we couldn't be more than friends."

Drew leaned against the wall that was next to my office door. "Oh nah. I'm too grown for that. No disrespect but, I do *OK* in the ladies' department. I will be just fine, sweetheart."

I laughed, but hearing him call me sweetheart sent a shiver down my spine. Jaxon was the only one who had called me that in recent days, and my body made it known that it only wanted him to do that for the foreseeable future.

"I'm sure you'll be just fine," I joked, then I politely excused Drew so I could get back to resting my eyes for a few moments.

Jaxon

Strip clubs were great and all, but seeing Hadassah St. James take on the media the way she did was some of the sexiest shit I had ever seen. I knew that my position at the school wasn't guaranteed long term, so I opted to not join the faculty onstage during the press conference. But being able to observe her do her thing from the wings was a sight to behold. She was a *bad girl,* and she was taking no prisoners.

I was drinking a bottle of water when I saw her slip away from the crowd and into her office. Not long after, I saw Drew sneak behind to join her. I was going to fight this man one day, I was certain of it. I stalked around outside of Dash's office, waiting to see if Drew would make any moves, but she kept her distance and he kept his hands to himself. There was nothing suggestive. Nothing that would make it seem like there was something romantic between them. But I still felt my blood pressure rising the longer they were in there alone together.

"Yes, he likes her. No, she doesn't like him back," a whisper from behind me, and I jumped at the sound. Partly because I wasn't expecting someone to be there, but also because it seemed that I was caught. I made a mental note about the comment about Drew liking Dash, though.

Clearing my throat, I said, "Oh! Genevieve. Hey, how are you? I didn't see you standing there," I said, my voice jumping between octaves on the pentatonic scale.

"Mmm-hmmm," she sounded as if she knew a secret that I didn't know.

I narrowed my eyes at her, "Something you'd like to say, Ms. Genevieve?"

"No, Mr. Hart. Something *you'd* like to say?" she shot back. And while it sounded like a question, it came across more like an order.

You could tell that Genevieve was the matriarch around here. She reminded me of Gammy, Jada Pinkett's mom, with her blueish-gray eyes and the way she rocked her pixie cut. And just like Gammy, she was nobody to mess with.

"I was just stopping by to see about Dash...Mrs. St. James. But it seems like she's busy, so I'll catch her another time," I said, opting to head for my car instead of back into the teacher's lounge but Genevieve kept walking behind me.

"Mr. Hart," she called out. "Do you have a second?"

I dropped my head and let out a huff. "Sure, Ms. Genevieve. What can I do for you?"

She raised her left eyebrow, drew her neck back, and looked me up and down as if to say, 'who do you think you're talking to, young man?'

"I'm sorry for the attitude," I said smiling.

"That's more like it," she said while nodding with a satisfied smile. "Now, back to you and our fearless leader."

"Back? I didn't realize we were there to begin with." Genevieve didn't take kindly to my playing dumb, so I cleared my throat and straightened up.

"She likes you, Jaxon. I'd even venture to say she's falling for you. And she's scared."

I ignored the fact that Genevieve knew anything about me and Dash. "And I'm not supposed to be scared, too?"

"You're not *acting* scared. You're acting indifferent. Yet you lurk around in dark corners, hoping for a glimpse of her any chance you get!"

"That obvious, huh?"

"*Beyond* obvious," she quipped. "Look, Jaxon. You told her you were a player. You made her believe that the only thing she could trust about you was the certainty that you would break her heart. Now, you want her to believe something different, and that doesn't happen overnight. But one thing is for sure, Dash is used to men *fighting* for her affection. *You* are used to women falling all over you for yours. What I do know is that Hadassah St. James will never fall for a man who she can't trust to catch her. She would rather stand flat footed and alone than fall flat on her face, hoping a man will be there to shield her from the impact."

It was beginning to unnerve me that so many people had this level of insight into me and my pseudo-relationship with Dash. I had never been the guy that kept a community of people around, never wanting to let them in or be fully "seen." However, I had to admit that it did feel nice to have a village like this. People who chased you down just to make sure you knew they cared. I could understand why Dash felt so tied to this place and these people; she was safe there.

I took Ms. Genevieve's hand and kissed it lightly. "I appreciate that bit of wisdom, Ms. Genevieve. And I promise I won't let it go to waste. But this is between me and Mrs. St. James, and I'll speak to her about it when the time is right."

Then, I walked out of the building to head home. Then I walked back into the building to the after-school area to get Mila. So much for dramatic exits.

Chapter Forty-Two

Hadassah

The day before any fundraising event was known to be pure chaos and today was no different. Volunteers needed instructions, vendors needed directions, and I couldn't shake the feeling that *something* was going to go terribly wrong. Most people wouldn't know it, but I had a terrible fear of public speaking. Up until ten years ago, I avoided crowds altogether. But as the needs of the school grew, and the demands for more vocal leadership in the community got louder, I stepped up and did what I had to do for our students. I still hated it, but I considered it a privilege to stand up for those who had no one else fighting for them. Even if it did trigger my debilitating anxiety.

I saw Genevieve storming towards me, and I could tell she had just about had enough. "Girl, where did you find these volunteers? If I have to repeat myself *one* more time, I'm sending everybody home, and I'll just get this thing together *myself*!"

Genevieve may or may not identify as a control freak. Whenever there was an event or a fundraiser, her low patience and zero tolerance for incompetence was beyond obvious. She was organized, meticulous, and ferocious when it came to order and excellence, and if anyone got in her way, there would be hell to pay.

I grabbed Genevieve by the arm and walked her out of earshot of the volunteers. "Now Genevieve, need I remind you that these are highschool students? They don't know any better, but they are offering us *free* help, and I think we need to give them a little more grace, OK?"

Genevieve looked at me like she hated me with a hate that not even grace could cover. "Like I said, *one more time*, and I'm sending them all home." She rolled her eyes and then stormed off into the teacher's lounge. Probably to sneak a shot of tequila that we kept hidden for stressful days like this.

"Mrs. St. James! Is Petah Pan *really* comin' tomorrow?" Jamison asked. He was still reeling from his acceptance to Morehouse and Corinne even got Morehouse to sponsor Petah Pan's appearance.

"He is! And did you know that Petah Pan also went to Morehouse?"

Jamison's eyes spread as big as golf balls. "No way!"

"Yes, way!"

Rap artists weren't exactly known for their book smarts, but Petah Pan was different in that he grew up in the suburbs and embraced the 'cool nerd' vibe. He reminded me of Kanye before he went *Kanye* on us. Petah Pan rapped about going to college, college parties, and cramming for exams like it was a cool underground culture. As young people began to catch on to his lyrics, minority applications for colleges went up, and non-black applications to HBCU's went up as well. For once, we had a hip-hop artist that politicians didn't wage war against, and we were thrilled he was showing up for our students.

Corinne was in the cafeteria blowing up balloons, and I promised to help her, so I went over there to fulfill my duties. "Oh, girl! Just in the nick of time!" she yelled, immediately shoving a handful of balloons into my hands. "You can use the green helium tank, and I'll use this red one here. Don't blow them up too full or they'll pop."

"Yes, ma'am!" I joked, giving her a solute like she was a drill sergeant giving orders.

"Don't start with me. You know how I get during these things!"

I laughed at her because how Corinne got during these things was downright neurotic. I don't know what the school administrator equivalent to a Bridezilla was, but Corinne was definitely it.

"I know *exactly* how you get! And while it can be nerve wracking for the rest of us, it's also a relief for me to know that you care as much, if not more, than I do."

Corinne stopped blowing up balloons and smiled affectionately. "I really do. This school, the kids, the community, it's everything I ever dreamed of being part of. I feel like this place is my calling—my purpose, and I'd be devastated if it went away."

Corinne was beaming. I hadn't noticed it before, but she lit up with such passion when she spoke about Biddy Mason. She loved this place like it was her own. I was ashamed to admit it, but I honestly couldn't remember the last time I felt the same way about the school.

Corinne gently placed a hand on my shoulder. "Where'd you just go, Dash?"

"What do you mean?"

"I mean, one second we were talking about how this place was a safe haven for so many, including me, and then you just…checked out!"

I shook my head and smiled. "I'm sorry, girl. I guess my mind drifted back to a time where this school meant as much to me as it seems to mean to you," I admitted.

Corinne's eyes widened at that admission. "What are you saying? I don't understand."

I sat down on one of the cafeteria tables and let out a deep sigh. "I don't know. I guess I've just been on autopilot for so long that I misplaced my passion for what we do here, and I'm afraid that I'm losing my edge."

She studied my face to see if she could decipher where I was going. "Are you saying that you don't care what happens to the school anymore?"

"No! God, no!" I snapped back quickly. "All I'm saying is that I've just recently noticed that my passion for what Lamar and I once built has been dormant, and I can't say for how long. But don't confuse that with my love for these kids and this community. The impact that our closure would have would be devastating!"

Corinne let out a sigh of relief. "Oh! Girl, I thought you were about to start talking crazy like giving up the fight and letting this place go, or something like that!"

I could never let this place go. Giving up on what we'd built would feel like a betrayal of the ultimate kind to Lamar. Losing this place would feel like losing him and Ty all over again. I just wish there was a way to separate my feelings for the school from my feelings for my boys. Wandering these halls lately, it began to feel like a shrine to their memories and not the honorarium it was designed to be. And for the first time in the years since Lamar's passing, I thought about clearing out his office, making room for something...someone new.

Chapter Forty-Three

Hadassah

It was the day of the fundraiser, and it took five pep talks and three puffs of a pre-roll to get me ready for the day. Corinne offered me a Xanax, but I detest prescription drugs. While I didn't want to be overly anxious about today, I still wanted a clear head. Xanax had some crazy side effects, and I wasn't trying to make a fool of myself on national television. This moment was too big for me to mess it up with an accidental slip of the tongue due to heavy medications.

Corinne had done a great job organizing this. Kids were running around with their faces painted, bouncy houses kept the younger ones entertained, and Jaxon even played music with his band from the stage while we waited for the main act, Petah Pan, to show up. I'm still not sure how Jaxon pulled off his appearance. He was probably the reason half these people even bothered to show up, but either way, I was grateful.

I watched as Corinne effortlessly worked the crowds and made sure everything was in order. I barely had to lift a finger, and I was actually able to just enjoy the day and take it all in, while getting ready to give my big speech. Petah Pan's tour bus arrived, and Corinne even made sure she personally escorted him to the makeshift VIP area we'd set up for him. I saw the way he watched her walk and I just shook my head and laughed. She wasn't slick.

"Hi, Mrs. St. James!!" Mila ran over to me and gave me the biggest hug, and it hit me just then how much I'd missed her.

"Mila! You look so pretty!"

"Thank you! Jax got me braids just like you!"

Emotion washed over me as I soaked up Mila's excitement and I was transported to a time when I wanted a little girl to dress up like me and wear matching hairstyles. I used to say that Ty would be the best big brother to a little girl. He would go crazy everytime we mentioned the idea of a little brother or sister, begging us to hurry up and 'make one.' Before everything happened, Lamar and I even talked about trying for another baby. My hand instinctively reached for my belly as I remembered how much I enjoyed being pregnant. How much I enjoyed the game of hope and possibility as a human life miraculously grew inside me. Mila's infectious smile and her precocious personality was the exact reason why I tried to resist her from the very beginning. She made me feel things. Want things that I'd long given up on.

I placed my hand on Mila's head and admired the neatly platted braids that she got like mine, hers accented by colorful beads. "Your hair looks way better than mine, though! I wish I could wear pretty beads like you!"

She giggled and gave me one more big hug. When I looked up, I noticed a sweet young woman standing off to the side watching us.

"Mila, is this your...Jax's friend?"

She looked over her shoulder at the dark-haired woman with hot pink streaks and matching pink glasses. "Oh! This is Danica, or Dani. She's my social butterfly!"

"Social butterfly?" I laughed.

The young woman stepped towards me, offering her hand to shake. "Social worker. Mila just likes to joke and call me the social butterfly because my hair and glasses always make random strangers come up to me and socialize."

"It is quite the conversation starter! Well, it's a pleasure to meet you as both Mila's social worker *and* her social butterfly," I said jokingly.

"Mila talks about her super pretty and super fashionable principal all the time, so I feel like I know you already!"

I looked back and forth between Mila and Danica. "Oh, really, now? I hope all good things!"

"The best of things." Danica moved in closer, and I nearly stepped back at the intrusion into my personal space. "Also, I really appreciate how you helped them pack up their father's house. Having you there meant a lot to Mila. I'm sure Jaxon, too, but he's a tough nut to crack, so I couldn't say for sure. But your presence was needed *and* appreciated. From what I'm told."

I smiled as Danica, the social butterfly, talked, but my mind drifted off to what she had just said about Mila mentioning my going to Savannah with them. Part of me was flattered to be spoken of fondly. The other part of me worried about who else Mila might have shared this information with.

While Biddy Mason wasn't known for its gossip mill, I still had a reputation to uphold as their principal. Anything like that getting out could stir up unnecessary drama. I had to calm my spiraling thoughts because this was not the time to be freaking out. I'd just have to remind myself to ask Jaxon if he'd had "the talk" with Mila yet. Not "*the* talk" as in birds and the bees. But the one where you talked about what sorts of things you shouldn't share with people you didn't explicitly give permission.

Once I wrapped up my conversation with Mila and Danica, I went by the face painting booth where art students from Biddy Mason painted children's faces. No matter what the event, face painting was always the biggest hit because of the skills of the artists. Children were asking for elaborate designs, but our talented students delivered every single time! Our art program was state of the art in that we had a true painter and sculptor that created a rewarding program for our students. Children who once believed that art was a dead end or that it didn't pay, were able to see a different side of art that had nothing to do with music or dance. They were introduced to rich history and culture as they were reminded that they shaped the culture of tomorrow. We even hosted art exhibits where students got to sell their pieces, showing them that art could be rewarding in more ways than one. News crews were all around and one publication even asked if they could do a feature on the art program we had.

I was taking in the view of at least a thousand people as families played and children danced to the music, when I heard a thunderous voice coming up from behind me. "You look stunning, Haddassah." I'd recognize that voice anywhere.

Blushing, I turned to face him. "You don't look too bad yourself, Jax." Which was the understatement of the century. Because this man looked exceptionally, magically delicious.

As the principal, I was expected to show up looking fly. So I rocked a monochromatic look with an emerald green turtleneck and matching satin slacks. But Jaxon? He looked like he'd stepped out of a magazine in his navy blue suit with a matching tie, his jacket did nothing to cover his muscles. That suit fit this man so well, so beautifully, that his arms threatened to bust out of the coat if he turned the wrong way. Alas, this was just the meticulously tailored Jaxon I'd come to know and...*like? A lot.*

I turned back to admire the sea of people that filled the school parking lot and grounds while Jaxon closed the distance between us, stepping in closer behind me. I could feel his breath on the back of my neck, and I closed my eyes momentarily to inhale, breathe him in. "I miss you," he said, making my eyes snap open.

"I...I miss you, too. I guess," I stuttered.

"You guess?" he questioned, stepping even closer so there was no space left between us.

"I mean...I do. I just, I guess I haven't *missed* anyone in a long time. I genuinely had to evaluate feelings in the moment."

He was still and motionless, but heat and tension reverberated through us. "I see. So, I wanted to ask you something."

I felt him shift behind me as if what he was about to ask was really important. "OK...fire away," I said, smiling and waving at students and parents that walked by.

"I'd like to...go out with...take you out. I guess. I mean...would you like to go on a date with me?" he stammered nervously.

My face lit up with excitement and the giddiness of a teenage girl being asked out on her first date. Trying to temper my reaction, I simply asked, "A real date, huh? I thought the infamous heartbreaker didn't *do* dates. Too confusing, right?"

He chuckled lightly with a low rumble, and my nether parts gyrated. "Well, maybe I'm at a place in my life where I'd like to mix things up a bit. Do things differently, you know?"

I was getting ready to match his flirty energy when a loud, high-pitched voice came up from behind us. Jaxon and I simultaneously turned towards the commotion, and I clenched my fists and grinded my teeth at the sight of Congresswoman Atkins with a rather striking, well-dressed woman walking beside her.

"Congresswoman Atkins. How nice of you to show up today," I lied through gritted teeth and a smile faker than her weave. After a few times meeting Dede Atkins, I had decided that she looked like one of those church women who never wore make up that was the right shade or found clothes that were fit for her body type, but had the audacity to always talk about other womens' skirts being too tight on their behind.

"Well, I couldn't help myself. Besides, I wanted to accompany my good friend since she had business here today." Congresswoman Atkins looked over at the woman standing next to her.

"Have you met Remy Fontaine from Nova Records? She supplied the talent tonight!"

I looked at Jaxon and then back at the woman Dede Atkins was introducing me to, offering my hand. "I...I don't believe I've had the pleasure. Pleased to meet you, Ms. Fontaine."

Remy Fontaine extended her hand to me. "The pleasure is all mine. So, Jax! This is where you landed, I see." Remy looked around before turning back to look me up and down with a petty body check, adding, "Cute."

"Anyway," Congresswoman Atkins continued, "Remy and Nova Records have been a Godsend to my campaign and my initiatives, donating $150,000 towards defeating my adversaries in the polls!"

I kept a straight face and offered a painted smile. "Well, if money could buy everything, you'd have class. And—"

Not sure what had come over me, but I had lost all composure, and I was getting ready to verbally tear into that woman until Jaxon interrupted before I could continue. "Remy, why are you doing this?"

Confused, I stepped away from the three of them, Jaxon, Remy, and Dede, and looked between them to see if I could read on their faces what the hell was going on. "Can somebody fill me in here? Jaxon?"

Remy Fontaine wore a pleased smile on her face like she and Jaxon had a secret between the two of them. "So, Jaxon didn't tell you?" she asked, which came off like an assumption more than a question. "I see he's still up to his same games."

"Remy?" Jaxon warned. "Stop this. Mrs. St. James has nothing to do with what is going on between us."

I clenched my fists and bit my bottom lip to stop me from going the fuck off. "Between who? What, now?"

We all stood there silent for a moment, and I wanted to smack the spit out of Congresswoman Atkins for bringing this woman to my event. But even moreso, I wanted to understand what the hell Jaxon was talking about when he'd said "between us." The way he'd been pining after me, I thought *I* was the other party that made up an "*us*" with him. I was the one whose affections he was supposed to be fighting for. Who was this woman, and what claim did she have on my man? On Jaxon?

Jaxon took my hand, and I instinctively recoiled. "Don't touch me. Don't you dare touch me!" And with that, I walked away.

Chapter Forty-Four

Jaxon

Calling Remy and asking her for the favor of getting Petah Pan to show up for the fundraiser did not come without strings. The only way I could get her to agree to help me was if I went to dinner with her. At her penthouse in the city. Yes, she had her house in the suburbs, but Dream Records had corporate housing for all their executives as well. It was in one of those high rise buildings that came with all sorts of amenities like valet service, exquisite dining options, a gym, and a full service laundry department. I agreed to the dinner as long as we ate in one of the public dining areas, and not her penthouse specifically.

While at dinner, Remy flirted with me shamelessly, but her attempts were futile. The allure she once had was gone once I saw what she was capable of. She had ruined nearly every opportunity I was working towards and expected me to be grateful to be in her presence. Instead, I was pissed, and I'd lost respect for her. Remy didn't owe me anything nor did she have to do any of the things that she'd done for my career. But to childishly rip opportunities away was a side of her that I never thought I'd see. Especially since she was so respected in the industry for her professionalism.

People didn't know that behind closed doors, this woman was basically Diddy in Dior.

When the final course was complete and I was preparing to take care of the check, 'cause I definitely wasn't giving her another thing to hold over my head, Remy asked, *"Who is she?"*

Blinking with a straight face, I simply said, *"My refusal to sleep with you or let you back into my life has nothing to do with another woman, Remy. You closed that door all by yourself."*

"I did no such thing. All I wanted was to be first and—"

"I'm not about to get into this with you again, Rem. It's pointless." Draining what was left of my drink and getting up from the table, I left her with, *"Now I've kept up my end of the bargain. You do yours,"* and then walked away.

Perhaps she didn't take too kindly to being left sitting alone in the restaurant that was connected to her penthouse building, because she had turned her viciousness up all the way. The way she taunted and stared down Dash and made it seem like that dinner was more than what it was, made me want to revert back to old Jaxon. The old me that would have found creative ways to ruin her entire world. Lucky for Remy, I was trying to be on this evolved man path; otherwise, I would have accepted her challenge and made her pay. Instead, I rushed off to go find Dash and explain what Remy was referring to. I couldn't bear to have her thinking that what I felt for her wasn't real or that I had feelings for someone else.

I saw her walk towards the main school building, and I chased behind her. "Dash! Mrs. St. James...Hadassah! Would you just stop?"

"I have nothing to say to you! Leave me alone!"

I finally caught up to her as she was searching her purse for her keys to the building. "Dash, please listen to me. It's not what it looks like. What Remy said, it's not what you think."

Dash finally turned around, tears streaming down her beautiful face. "Then what is it, Jaxon? You have two minutes to tell me so that I can go in and fix my face and put on a smile for these people!" The tears continued to flow, and my heart ached for her.

"Baby. Remy and I used to date. We lived together. It's a really long story but, when I had to take custody of Mila, she wanted nothing to do with me...or my baby sister. She thought that by forcing me to choose between her and a child I'd never met,

I'd automatically choose her. When I chose Mila, she set out on a mission to destroy me."

Dash and I had never really discussed Remy. I didn't have a reason, nor was I intentionally trying to hide it from her. But once I had decided that I was going to take Mila, I honestly had a sore spot when it came to Remy. Especially with how she tried to ruin my career after I didn't choose to be with her. Now, I wish I would have talked about her more so that Dash wouldn't have been blindsided by what Remy was doing. Perhaps if I'd taken Remy's threats more seriously, I would have been prepared for her attempt to ruin Dash, too.

Dash wiped the tears from her face. "But that's the thing, Jaxon. She's not just trying to destroy you, is she? She's trying to destroy me *because* of you! My family! The only home I've known for all these years. *You* did that. *Your* dirt brought this to my doorstep, and so help me God. If she wins, I will *never* forgive you." Dash turned on her heels, proceeded to unlock the door to the building, and went in, leaving me standing outside.

Her words pierced my heart in a way I didn't even want to admit to myself. My dirt did bring this to her doorstep, and now the fate of the school hung in the balance because, once again, I'd let my decision to get involved with the wrong type of woman impact my future. A future I was hoping for with Dash. At every turn, every time I got close to getting her to see me differently from who I used to be, something came up to push Dash away, getting in the way of our chance at happiness. I was beginning to wonder if it was a sign. Maybe who I am was inevitable, and I needed to stop trying to convince myself that I could be someone different. Maybe I needed to make a clean break and start over in California with Mila.

When I turned to walk back towards the actual fundraiser, Coach Drew was standing behind me.

"Is there a problem I need to be concerned about?"

I snickered, but there wasn't an ounce of humor on my face. "Nah, man. Nothing concerning you going on at all."

Drew stepped a little closer, and my fist curled at the implication. I hope this man wasn't about to try to fight me over a babe. "Let me rephrase. Dash does concern me. Her husband's legacy concerns all of us. And if you think you're gonna come in here and disrupt what we have because you can't keep it in your pants, I'm here to let you know you're mistaken."

I looked Drew up and down, this time grinning wickedly in his direction. I lowered my voice and checked him through gritted teeth. "Listen here, playa. I know I threaten you, making you panic because you think you might have missed your chance to shoot your shot. I've seen you sniffin' around Dash's office, trying to get in wherever you think you can fit in. I hate to break it to you, but you're too late. I appreciate your care and concern, though. I recognize that Biddy Mason is a tight-knit family. But let's just say, I'm in the family now. Mmm k, homie?"

Drew was noticeably pissed, but I had him stuck looking for a witty comeback. I was getting ready to walk off and leave him standing there speechless when he retorted, "Interesting imagination you have there. Especially since she just told you to leave her alone and left you standing out here." Then Drew turned around and walked off, leaving *me* speechless.

Despite the drama, the concert with Petah Pan was a hit. He did a thirty-minute set, and the entire neighborhood came out to see his performance. Towards the end of his performance, he brought Corinne out on stage to perform his hit song, "Tinker Ya Bell," and I could be wrong, but it seemed like there was some chemistry between the two of them. As he spat lyrics and the crowd joined in, Corinne tastefully danced around the stage, and Petah stumbled over his words from watching her body move. He had to pretend like he was letting the crowd help him with the lyrics to cover up his fumble. I laughed at the obvious mistake, and my eyes instinctively looked over to Dash, hoping to meet her gaze, but she was avoiding me. She continued to do so the rest of the evening.

While Mila and her friend Arrin danced to the music, my mind went back to one of my first conversations with Remy, before we took our relationship out of the professional and into the personal realm, and I told her that I would inevitably destroy her. She had responded with, *"Not if I destroy you first."* And I never once imagined that she could. Especially not like this. I had my health. Mila was the happiest I'd seen her since I first met her. But I still felt destroyed. Like I had lost something that I couldn't get back. And my heart ached like I was already grieving.

"One day, love is gon' bite you so good and so fast, you ain't gon' know what hit you," my momma used to say to me. She never agreed with my player ways and prayed for the day that I fell in love. I couldn't be sure, but since I'd never felt this way about anyone before, I was tempted to admit that her prayers had finally been answered. *I think it finally happened, Momma. This time, it's love.*

Chapter Forty-Five

Jaxon

"Is it far?" Mila asked, inquiring about the distance between Georgia and California.

"It *is* far. We couldn't walk or drive there. We'd have to take an airplane."

Mila's eyes lit up with excitement. "Really? I've never been on a plane before, so it will be like an adventure!"

"So, as long as we can take a plane, you're OK moving to California?"

She took a few seconds to think about what I'd asked before replying, "As long as we can ride a plane *and* as long as I can wear a skirt to the airport!" my little litigator negotiated.

"We'll see about the skirt but, depending on the weather, I don't see a problem."

I wasn't sure if she really understood what was happening. She'd never been anywhere beyond Tennessee, and even then it was only by car. So her idea of what "far" meant was kind of subjective. But I still didn't want to make things harder for her than they already were. I decided to hold off on any more talks until we saw Dr. Johana again. I wanted an expert's opinion on how this could affect her. I kept telling myself I'd ask her at school, but with all the hustle and bustle of getting ready for the spring musical, it kept slipping my mind.

Dr. Johana had been a true blessing to us, becoming an essential part of our support system. She'd done such a great job helping Mila work through her emotions, that she'd started opening up about her life before we came into it. With her next therapy session being her eighth, I was expected to join in. Apparently, it was a regular part of the process for parents or guardians to participate and discuss progress and any important matters. I made a promise to myself to be receptive to the therapy process as well, for Mila's sake. I wasn't quite sure what to expect, but I felt proud to take on new challenges that would ultimately benefit me in the long run.

Tonight, we were having dinner with Nana Shirley. She was making gumbo, and since Mila said she'd never had it before, Nana demanded we come over. Not wanting to arrive empty handed, I brought a bottle of Black Girl Magic Merlot for me and Nana and sparkling cider for Mila. Nana even let Mila drink hers out of a wine glass so she could feel like a grown up.

Nana Shirley made the kind of gumbo that had *everything* in it, even crab legs, so Mila was initially freaked out by her bowl that seemed to contain everything but the kitchen sink. I watched as she negotiated what she was going to eat first and how. She went straight for the crab legs, savagely breaking the legs open and cleaning the shell dry. We laughed at the mess she was happily making all over her bib.

"Impressive!" Nana cheered. "It took me a week to figure out what to do with them crab legs!"

Mila just smiled and kept on devouring the assortment of flavorful foods that had become a black delicacy. We both watched Mila with smiles on our faces as she slurped and moaned through that entire bowl like a pro. The spice didn't even seem to bother her.

"She's growing up right before your eyes," Nana leaned in to whisper. "I know you just met her, and life is coming at you real fast as you try to build a life and a future for her, but don't forget to look up and see what you got in front of you in the moment. It all goes by so fast," she drawled in her country accent.

"Who are you tellin'? Before coming here tonight, I noticed that her sneakers were too tight on her feet! I *just* bought those shoes for Christmas!"

"I see nobody told you the trick about buying shoes a half size too big so they have a chance to grow in them?"

"No ma'am," I said, lowering my head in mock shame.

"Well, now you know! Kids grow like weeds, so you gotta stay a few steps ahead in everything, all the time."

That statement was true in more ways than one. As much as I felt like I knew as a forty-year-old man, nothing made me feel dumber than meeting and raising a twelve-year-old girl. To make matters more complicated, I had to balance my ignorance with not wanting to make Mila responsible for educating me in this area. I'd always heard men say how they didn't learn how to treat women until they had a daughter, and so many people, myself included, celebrated that sentiment. The idea that men didn't truly develop empathy and concern for women until they had a little girl that could be subject to falling for the same type of man he was. Sitting here and watching Mila grow up before my eyes actually made me sick to my stomach to think that my eyes weren't opened to the fragility of a woman until I met her.

The lessons I was getting a crash course in as a result of having Mila were making me judge myself pretty harshly. Growing up with a healthy respect for women would have ensured I wasn't using a pre-teen as a surrogate for my education in women. I likely would have made healthier relationship choices through the years. Hell, who knows? Maybe I would have even been married with kids right now if my life had started out differently. If I'd had better role models as a young man, perhaps I would have paid a little more attention to the love songs I sang and played. Because none of them ever glorified men like me. The kind of man I had been.

When R&B was at its peak, men would have used those songs to captivate women like Dash. She was the kind of woman you called and told her to put on her red dress, high heels, and spray on that sweet perfume for a surprise night out. She was the type of woman that I would make a fool of myself for. A woman I'd love to fight for, make love to and serve breakfast in bed…for as long as we both shall live.

Snapping me out of my pointless musings, Nana asked, "Mila told me about her big solo for the musical you got comin' up. You all ready for the big night?"

"Just about. I've been meaning to tell you, after the musical, we may be heading to California. I got a pretty big job opportunity, and I'm thinking I might take it. If Mila's therapist thinks it would be OK for her, that is."

Nana stared at me for a moment, and I think I saw a bit of sadness eclipse her face. "Are you runnin' to somethin', or from somethin'?" she asked, and the question took me completely by surprise.

"Ma'am? What do you mean?"

She let out a dry chuckle before she got up to clear the dishes from the table. I helped, following her into the kitchen. "You just got the girl settled. She's makin' friends. And I know you've had a young woman sniffin' around here, too. Seems to me that the only way a man would abruptly give that up, is if he's runnin' from somethin' or to somethin'."

I considered what she said as I loaded the dishes into the dishwasher for her. I wasn't running. I was given an opportunity and, at my age, opportunities like that didn't come often. Sure, things going sour with Dash hurt my feelings a little bit. But I wasn't running *from* her or the situation. It was just clear that our time together had run its course, and I needed to move out of the way to give her space.

"Are you rationalizing your decisions or contemplating them?" Nana asked, reading my mind like only a mother could.

I laughed at her observation. "I'm not...I guess I don't know what I'm doing. I'm thinking?"

I dove head first into the situation with Dash. My lifestyle and my schedule made it so I didn't build friendships with many people longterm. I had acquaintances that I could call in the industry, but few solid people that I could unburden myself to when I needed to talk through things. Lu had been that person for a while, but having Nana's wisdom was like having the words of a mother to give perspective on things. And just like a mother, she never pulled any punches or beat around any bushes. She was real and gave it to me straight every time.

As I wrapped up my long story of all the twists and turns that made up the story of me and Hadassah St. James, Nana simply said, "You are some kinda stupid, huh?" A statement more than it was a question.

I threw my head back in laughter. "Damn, Nana! Why I gotta be stupid?"

She smiled back, but there wasn't a hint of playfulness in her demeanor. "First of all, as soon as you heard that woman was a widow, you should have left her alone. When you found out she lost a son, you should have just offered to be a friend. You are too old to not know that anyone who has been hurt that way is too vulnerable to get involved in something that could overtake their emotions. Especially if you were the first man she's been with! You fumbled a big opportunity to prove that you could have been more for her, and I have to say, I'm a little disappointed in you."

Damn. I never thought I'd see the day when a woman, other than my mother, was telling me she was disappointed in me, and it actually stung. "So, you don't think I have another chance with her?"

"Now, I'm no psychic, so I can't say for certain what she's feelin' or what she'd be open to. What I will say is she's probably having a hard time receiving a different side of you because you never showed her anything other than the side of you that thought and made decisions with your penis. You men are so competitive about getting a woman strung out on your sex that you never care to understand what that exchange does for her. You knowingly stirred up something in her that you have no clue how to manage. And that's because a man's aim isn't usually to control his sexual prowess, but to use it to conquer women.

"But now you've fallen in love, and you're at a loss because you started off on the wrong foot. You didn't try to nurture or build anything with her. Instead, you both opted to spend time together avoiding the real emotions and longing that was simmering between you... Avoiding Love."

I felt like I was sitting at the feet of my mother and all her wisdom. Like God somehow knew that my mother wasn't done with me, and so he transplanted a piece of her into Nana Shirley. My mother would have been disappointed in me as well. Out of everything she ever taught me, she never raised me to be even a little bit like my father. I wasn't supposed to grow up to avoid love or deny my mother the right to grandchildren by having a vasectomy. I was supposed to break the generational curses and choose love in a way that my father never did. Going an entire lifetime not knowing how to cultivate relationships in a healthy way was shameful, but I wanted to change that. I wanted to choose differently. Even if Dash didn't receive me after this, if we never met again, I owed her my gratitude for at least opening me up to the possibility of love. Real love.

I finished cleaning up Nana's kitchen for her while Mila watched TV. Nana sat and watched me, but we were both pretty silent for the next twenty minutes or so. Placing the damp towel over a cleaned sink, signifying the kitchen was closed in a black household, I looked over to Nana and saw her watching me with an intense gaze. "What, Nana?" I asked, smiling at the way her belly rose and fell with her chuckles.

"So, are you runnin' from somethin', or towards it?"

I walked over to her, bending down to kiss her on the cheek. "I'm running towards it, Nana…I'm running towards *her*."

Chapter Forty-Six

Jaxon

Waiting for Dr. Johana to finish up with a patient, I sat with Mila in the waiting room as she put together a puzzle that sat on the children's table. Since Mila's come to live with me, I've been discovering so many of her talents. It was becoming very clear that we might have a genius on our hands. Of course, I was biased. However, seeing how effortlessly Mila picked up notes in songs, and how she just sat here and put together a 100-piece puzzle in less than fifteen minutes, it was evident that she had a mind that was extremely rare. She had even been spending time with me, learning to play the keyboard in her spare time. So, yes, I was incredibly biased about Mila's smarts, but Mila was also a very impressive young lady.

Mila had just completed the puzzle when Dr. Johana's door opened and a little boy with curly red hair came running out with excitement.

"Hey, Mila!" He waved.

"Hey, Markie!" she replied, then pointed to the door, letting him know that his mom was waiting outside in the hall. Markie proceeded to skip out of the waiting room and into the hallway.

"Mila? Jaxon? Are you two ready for your session?"

"Yep!" Mila yelled, jumping up from the table. I, on the other hand, was only ready to run in the other direction and out the door.

Dr. Johana smiled as Mila ran to give her a hug and she extended her hand to me to shake.

Once the doors were closed, it felt like the entire room was closing in on me. I appreciated the cool shades of blues and grays on her wall, accented by leather camel-colored sofas and chairs. It made me feel a bit calmer about what was coming. I guess that's what the space was designed for.

"Have a seat wherever you'd like, Jaxon," Dr. Johana offered, pointing to the various seating options in the room. "You can choose between the sofa or any of the chairs."

"Sit next to me, Jax! Please?" Mila begged, and suddenly, choosing a chair seemed like a life altering decision.

I wanted to feel at ease, but at the same time, I didn't want to feel trapped or suffocated. I had never been in a situation where I sat in someone's office just to talk about my emotions, so I was trying to figure out how to make this whole experience as stress-free as I could. In the end, I decided to go for the sofa and casually extended my arm, inviting Mila to join me. Without hesitation, she dashed over and plopped down right beside me. Having a little person cling to me like a shadow was definitely a new and interesting experience for me, too.

We started off the session with Mila pouring out everything she had learned from Dr. Johana. She talked about how it didn't have to be scary to share your feelings, stressing the importance of feeling safe and comfortable with whoever you choose to confide in. But the most crucial lesson was to always stay true to your emotions and give them the respect they deserved, no matter where they come from or where they might take you. It almost felt like Dr. Johana was using Mila's wisdom as a tactic to make me feel at ease about opening up, too. Well, let me tell you, I wasn't about to let a twelve-year-old show me up. Challenge accepted.

Dr. Johana turned to me, offering a gentle smile. "Jaxon, before we continue, Mila worked on a letter that she wants to read to you."

I drew in a deep breath, leaning back to prepare myself for whatever Mila was about to say. As a kid, I remember crafting heartfelt letters to my mom, trying to lift her spirits after a tough week. Mom was my safe space, the only person I could trust with my raw, unfiltered emotions. When writing these letters, I would honestly express how much I despised the way my father treated her. Yet, she never scolded me for speaking my truth. Instead, she gently reminded me that disrespecting my father was like disrespecting God himself. *"You don't have to like him,"* she'd say, *"but don't go blocking your blessings by showing him disrespect."* So, whenever my father was around, I gave him the one thing, even if he never deserved it...respect.

Dr. Johana handed Mila an envelope that was sitting in a manila folder, and Mila unfolded it before standing in front of me.

"Dear Jax,

Thank you for taking care of me. I am so happy that you're my big brother. You're also my best friend. I really appreciate how you are patient with me, most of the time, and how you work really hard to make me feel safe.

I want you to know that I am here for you, too. You are safe with me, too. If you ever want to talk about Daddy or your mommy, I am happy to be your best friend like you are to me.

I can't wait to live in Hollywood with you. It will be scary, but I know that I will be safe as long as I am with you.

Please don't ever leave me because you are my only family and I would miss you very much.

Love Always,

Milagros Hart. Miss Mila, if ya nasty."

I didn't know what to say. And even if I did, I don't think I could physically say anything from the raw emotion that was trapped in the back of my throat. Before I could react, Mila ran and jumped into my arms, offering a big hug. That's when the dam broke and the tears began to fall uncontrollably. How could someone so tiny render me speechless like this?

My arms wrapped around her tiny frame, and I'd swear they could fit around her twice. I loved her, and it was the purest form of love I'd ever held for anyone. She was my blood and, despite the thirty plus year age difference, she was my friend, too. Over the past few months we had formed a bond that I would literally kill someone over if they tried to take her from me. So no, I wouldn't dare leave her. And as I squeezed her tightly in my arms, I vowed to myself that I would never let her feel anything remotely close to what I felt as a child. From me, she would only ever feel loved and cherished.

Dr. Johana's question rescued me from a complete meltdown. "How did Mila's words make you feel, Jaxon?"

I cleared my throat, and as I looked up, Dr. Johana was standing in front of me with a box of tissues. Mila stepped to the side and sat back down next to me on the sofa. "I...guess I am at a loss for words right now." I turned to Mila as I wiped the condensation from my eyes. "Thank you, Mila. I couldn't ask for a better little sister, and I promise that I will always be there for you, too."

I turned back to Dr. Johana, hoping this would mark the ending of the little episode I'd just had. "But," she continued "How do you *feel*, Jaxon?" Guess she wasn't done.

I wiped my hand down the back of my neck, and Dr. Johana handed me a colorful piece of cardboard shaped like a circle with the words 'Feeling Wheel' written in the center. "I feel a lot of things, man. Proud, happy, angry, sad, jealous, and curious with so many questions. So many damn questions," I said, feeling wetness touch my cheek again.

"I get that," Johana offered softly. "Let's take them one at a time. Why curious? What kind of questions do you have?"

I mulled over my own curiosity, all the burning questions that had been simmering inside me. Not just since Mila moved in with me, but also from the moment my father walked out of my life. My mind was a whirlwind of queries, but I'd kept them bottled up, not wanting to burden Mila with my personal perplexities. But sitting here now with both of them, my pride seeping into the tissues clenched in my hand, it seemed as good a time as any to lay my emotions and questions out on the table.

I turned to Mila to take her little hand in mine, and I saw tears eclipse her eyes as well. "Mila, can I ask you something?" She nodded her head in the affirmative while she chewed on her bottom lip. "Did Daddy...was Daddy nice to you?"

She nervously looked down and started playing with her hands, then at Dr. Johana for permission to share. "It's OK, Mila. Remember? Jaxon is on our safe list." Mila's expression relaxed at her assurance.

Looking back at me, Mila responded, "He was nice most of the time. Sometimes, when he got mad, I would hide and listen to BTS really loud." I dropped my head, and more tears fell as I grappled with the revelation that she had the same responses and coping mechanisms to my father as I did.

"Mommy always knew how to make him feel better," Mila continued. "She would pray, and then sing to him in Spanish. She was the only one that could make him smile."

I let out a dry chuckle, making Mila and Dr. Johana both look up at me in surprise. "What's funny, Jaxon?"

"Nothing. I mean, it's not funny. I'm sorry. My reaction came from a sarcastic place."

Dr. Johana studied my expression. "Is sarcasm how you normally cope with things?"

I looked up at her, and fire overtook my expression. "No. But I'm afraid if I don't use sarcasm in this moment, I may hurt Mila's feelings and upset this entire process."

I didn't know where the sudden burst of anger came from, but suddenly I couldn't control my emotions. Abruptly, I jumped up from my chair and began pacing the floor back and forth while Mila and Johana watched me intently.

"Help us understand what's going on with you right now, Jaxon," Dr. Johana requested softly.

I ended my restless pacing and plunked down on a chair across the room, a safe distance from them both. I didn't want my unexpected surge of emotions to make them think that I was directing it at them. There was something suddenly boiling beneath the surface of my hardened exterior, and I had no point of reference for what it was, but it was begging to be set free.

"She got a life that I never got. A father that was able to be soothed and calmed before his wrath caused her irreparable damage. She got the mother who was strong enough to fight his demons with him. And I know it's the worst thing I could possibly say or feel right now, but I'm jealous and angry at..." I paused, not sure if the words that were about to come out were my real feelings or simply a manifestation of this moment.

Dr. Johana probed further. "Angry at who or...what?"

"Her. My mother. Angry that she never left. If she wasn't going to stand up to him, why couldn't she stand up *for me*?"

It was the first time I'd ever said that to anyone. I don't even think I'd ever thought about this idea to myself. My mother had always been revered as a practical saint in my eyes, and I could never blame her for choosing love. I guess I just wish it didn't feel like she was choosing him over me. She had everything she needed to fight. I didn't And I didn't understand how her prayers for protection never resulted in God telling her that she needed to participate in that protection by leaving. Leaving and protecting me.

Mila walked across the room, and emotionally, I wanted to recoil. I didn't want her to see me or experience me in this vulnerable state. But I remembered her words from her sweet letter, *"I'm here for you, too."* So as she walked towards me, her big brown eyes accented by big curly ringlets all over her head, I opened my arms wide to welcome her into an embrace. She ran to me.

"I'm sorry your mommy didn't sing to your daddy for you," she whispered, and it dawned on me that she said *your* daddy instead of just 'Daddy.'

I don't think she meant it intentionally, but the sentiment was true all the same. We did have different daddies. At least different versions of the same man. And if these last few months told me anything about being different versions of myself, it was that nothing *had* to stay the same. Everything and everyone was faced with situations and seasons that either challenged them to change, or gave them permission to stay exactly the same. I guess if my recent experiences with Mila and Dash could challenge me to change, perhaps Mila's mom did that for my dad.

I pulled back from our embrace and looked Mila in the eyes. "Don't you ever apologize for that, okay? I know I said a lot today, but it's not on you to fix or make up for. Jax just has some work I need to do so I can be better for you, okay?"

She shook her head in the affirmative. "But don't do it for me, Jax! Be better for you, OK?"

I smiled at her correction, but she was right. If I was going to continue this quest of becoming a better version of myself, then I couldn't let my motivation come from outside of me. It had to start within, and anyone outside of me only got the extension of the work I was doing for me.

We wrapped up our session with Dr. Johana, who shared some insightful tips with Mila on discerning safe people in her life and embracing her true self. She also guided me on how to untangle the complex web of emotions I held regarding my parents. Initially, I felt a pang of guilt about the sentiments I'd revealed about my mom, but Dr. Johana reassured me that my feelings weren't just normal, but also healthy. She even suggested that my relationship struggles and issues with women might be rooted in my failure to fully confront my feelings towards my mom. When she advised me to consider seeing a therapist of my own, I initially hesitated. But ultimately, I decided to follow through on it, and she gave me some referrals for black male therapists in the area. She wanted me to see someone who could at least begin this work with me. Today was cathartic, and I was grateful for the chance to learn more about myself and my new best friend, Mila.

Chapter Forty-Seven

Hadassah

Today was the day. The Tuesday in March that the fate of our beloved Biddy Mason was on the line. The community was casting their votes to decide whether our school would keep its doors open or be forced to close down. Our students had a day off, given that the school was doubling as a polling location. But for our staff, it was all hands on deck. We were there, offering help and guidance to voters as they streamed in one after another. Each person who walked through our doors felt like a ticking time bomb, their decision holding the power to change our lives forever.

As I stood there, watching the steady flow of people, my heart pounded away in my chest like a drum. It was a strange mix of fear and anticipation, every beat echoing the question, 'Are they voting to save us or shut us down?' Each ballot cast felt personal, as if they weren't just deciding on the fate of a building, but on the future of a family. Because that's what we were at Biddy Mason—a family. And the thought of losing our home was devastating, leaving me feeling sick to my stomach.

When no one was paying attention, Genevieve and Corinne managed to swipe a bottle of tequila from the break room and sneak it into my office. We took shots over our lunch, a desperate, half-hearted attempt to drown out the worries that were gnawing at us. While the girls were plotting day drinking, I had ordered sushi for us while the rest of the staff had pizza.

Genevieve pointed her chopsticks at me in the form of a stern warning. "Now, you know if Coach Drew finds out you ordered sushi and didn't tell him, he's gonna throw a fit!"

I smacked my lips at the assertion. "Please! That's why I ordered Papa Gino's! The only thing Drew likes more than sushi, is Papa Gino's pizza! That man would marry Gino's daughter just to get free access to the pizza whenever he wanted!" We all laughed.

"Speaking of hot and ready," Genevieve interrupted. "What's the deal with you and a certain Disney-themed rapper, Corinne?"

Corinne choked on her food, taking a gulp of water to wash it down. "Ex...Excuse me? What are you talking about?"

"Ahhh, yeah! Don't play dumb now, Rinne! What *is* the deal with you and Petah Pan, huh?" I teased.

Corinne cleared her throat and took another sip of water. "There is nothing going on between me and said rapper. Xavier and I are just friends."

Genevieve and I looked at each other as if to say, 'Who's Xavier?!'

"So, we're on a first, slash, government name basis with him now?" I asked.

"We are on a friendship basis where we are getting to know each other and, yes, that usually involves sharing names with each other."

"Awww!" Me and Genvieve chorused in unison.

Geneive grabbed Corinne's hand and studied her face, "So, you like him, honey?"

Corinne jumped up from her place on the sofa and began jumping up and down like a giddy girl. "You guys, I *really* like him! Like, we haven't even kissed yet because I don't want to mess anything up! He's kind, and intelligent, and thoughtful, and considerate. Nothing like these other rappers out here!"

"Girl! I knew that as soon as I heard his lyrics. He's got an old soul to him in the way he respects women and actually wants to inspire kids to do better," I said.

Corinne wasn't the type to be easily swept off her feet, so the fact that Petah, or Xavier, had her open like this was a welcomed change to her usual 'hard-to-get' demeanor. I'd seen men propose to her after ninety days, and Corinne still turned them down. She rarely trusted mens' motives because they always had an unhealthy obsession with her body. She always said that she'd know a guy was right for her when he tried as hard to make love to her mind as he did her body. I guess Xavier was doing something right.

As I sat there, the sharp taste of alcohol on my tongue, my mind drifted back to the journey that had led me here—a rollercoaster ride of ups and downs, of love and loss. It started with Lamar, the man who had known me better than anyone else, who had loved me for who I was, with all my flaws and imperfections. Then came the birth of Biddy Mason, our brainchild, our shared dream. A place where kids could learn and grow, a haven for the community. Shortly after, we welcomed our blood child, Ty. He was the most beautiful little blessing that we didn't deserve but were grateful for...every single day. But just as we were basking in the success of our venture, planning to do so much more for our family and community, tragedy struck.

However, amidst the darkness, a glimmer of hope emerged in the form of Jaxon. He came into my life when I least expected it, offering solace, a shoulder to lean on. As the memories washed over me, I was grateful for him coming into my life when he did. The way he did. No matter what the future held for us, he had played an important role in helping me move forward and turn the page on my grief.

"I can't believe that we might not be here this time next year," Genevieve offered in a somber tone. She was a very well-kept woman, so she didn't *need* this job. But she still found a purpose here, so that's why she showed up every day. I was more concerned about what would happen to the other staff members if the measure to close us down won in the polls.

Corinne piped up, indignation in her voice. "I'm not gonna buy into that lie. Congresswoman Atkins wants us to give up and throw in the towel, but we have an amazing school here! Do you see all the smiling faces filing in and out of these hallways today, marveling at how beautiful the school is?"

I let out a dry chuckle. "Yeah! Most of them admittedly had never been inside the building before!"

I wasn't naive. Cattiness and two-faced smiles was the language of politics. Just because people smiled and said nice things did not mean they had good intentions. So I wasn't going to trick myself into believing that the people smiling through these halls wanted us to have the good that we provided for these kids every day.

"Dash, you seem so indifferent about all this these days," Corinne said.

"I'm not indifferent. Maybe I'm just tired. The last few months, hell the last few years, have been exhausting! I think the exhaustion is just making me come across jaded."

Corinne looked me in the eyes and said, "If Lamar and Ty's memory wasn't holding you here, would you want to be here anymore?"

I froze, and my office suddenly got so quiet that you could hear my heart thumping through my blouse. I didn't immediately say no. I didn't even get angry at the question. I legitimately thought about it because it was a question that I didn't know how to answer. It suggested that I wouldn't be here if the memory of Lamar and Ty weren't connected to it and...*was that the only thing keeping me here?*

Genevieve cleared her throat. "Maybe let's change the subject, yeah? How do you feel about Jaxon moving to California, Dash?"

This time I was the one to choke on my food. Gulping down a sip of water I said, "I don't know what I feel since this is the first time I'm hearing about it."

It had been well over two weeks since Jaxon and I had a real, meaningful conversation. Yet, something as big as relocating across the country wasn't just small talk you forgot to mention. My mind kept looping back to that night of the fundraiser. The tension from that evening was still fresh as if it had just happened. I told Jaxon that he'd brought his dirt to my doorstep. I didn't mince my words. Even now, I didn't regret saying it. But I never thought my words would sting him so much that he'd consider something as drastic as packing up his entire life and moving thousands of miles away. Then again, this was someone who shut me out after I had hurt his feelings. *Could something I said really have pushed him to make such a radical decision?* The thought left a bitter aftertaste, a mix of regret and worry.

"Wait...Jaxon is leaving? Genevieve, how did you find out?" Corinne said in shock, her voice elevated from the tequila that was now coursing through her bloodstream.

"Jaxon told me! He said it so matter of factly that I assumed everyone knew!"

I took another sip of my water, chasing it with a shot of tequila. "Nope! Everyone definitely did *not* know," I said quietly.

Apparently, Jaxon was getting copies of Mila's school records for her new school when he let the news slip to Genevieve. Mila had come so far in the past few months that moving seemed like it could upend her entire world all over again. If he was doing that to her, because he needed to get away from me, I would never forgive myself.

Once the polls closed, I headed home to prepare myself for what was to come. I took a shower, washed my hair, and chilled a bottle of wine in the fridge for later. Whatever the news would be, I didn't want to be sober when it hit. Earlier in the day, the polls were reporting the measure being defeated. But as the day went on, and more votes were tallied, it became harder to predict a clear winner. Of course, there were other elections being decided today, but the only thing keeping my heart and stomach in knots was this one particular measure.

I found myself glued to my phone, fighting the urge to send Jaxon a text to ask him what he was doing or why the hell he was making such a drastic move to California?! But every time I was about to dial his number or type out a message, I stopped myself. I needed to figure out why I felt this irresistible pull to reach out to him. I liked Jaxon, but it was clear that it was best I stayed away from him. That night at the fundraiser was a real eye-opener for me. It forced me to acknowledge some uncomfortable truths about him that I had been conveniently ignoring.

Jaxon had a ton of baggage, and it wasn't just metaphorical anymore—it had literally landed right at my front door. As much as I cared for him, as much as I wanted to be there for him, I knew deep down that I had no business getting involved with someone who wasn't actively working through their issues. No matter how much my heart ached for him, I couldn't magically make him whole again. He needed to want that for himself—to recognize his own need for healing and actually put in the work to get there.

This realization was a bitter pill to swallow, but it was a necessary one. I had spent too long avoiding feelings, steering clear of situations and people that threatened to stir up emotions within me. But this... this wasn't something I could ignore or brush under the carpet. This was about Jaxon, about us, and about the harsh reality that sometimes, no matter how much you cared about someone, you couldn't fix them. They had to want to fix themselves.

Just as I was settling down in front of the TV for the special news report, my doorbell chimed. The results we'd all been biting our nails over were finally in. Within moments, the news flashed across the screen—the motion to outlaw charter schools in Georgia had passed by a landslide. My heart sank to the floor—our school was going to be closing its doors forever. The reality hit me as if Lamar and Ty had been ripped away from me all over again.

The persistent ring of the doorbell jerked me out of the paralyzing shock that had held me captive. On opening the door, I found Corinne standing there, arms brimming with pastries and a bottle of Prosecco. This was indeed a 'Carb Crash Emergency.' But even her well-meaning gesture couldn't quite dispel the heaviness that the crushing news had planted in my heart. I let her in, shut the door, and sunk to the floor and sobbed.

Chapter Forty-Eight

Hadassah

The days and weeks that trailed the election seemed to blur into one another. I found myself moving through them like a zombie, working alongside staff and administrators to pinpoint the schools our students would be dispersed to next year. Our teachers were caught in a mad scramble, hunting for new jobs they could switch over to as well. People kept checking in with me, peppering me with questions about how I was holding up. But truth be told, I felt nothing. I was numb.

Grief, loss, and hopelessness were emotions I was all too familiar with. They weren't strangers; they had been constant companions, often casting a dark shadow over phases of my life. So, in a twisted way, I was better equipped to shoulder everyone else's pain rather than having them try to bear mine. I was strong when everyone else felt the need to fall apart. As parents and students from previous graduating classes came in to pay their respects and reminisce about how much Lamar meant to them, I was their source of comfort. For the community that had held me up all these years, I was more than willing to be that source of strength for them.

The auditorium buzzed with chatter and commotion as everyone gathered for the beloved spring musical. The spring musical had become a tradition after the third year that Biddy Mason was founded, and each year the town looked forward to the creative ways the theater and musical staff would transform popular music into a production fit for kids. Normally, the musical served as a showcase for donors and philanthropists to see what we were doing with the funds they donated. Tonight, however, the musical would serve as a farewell celebration.

Tears ran down my face as I saw the stage be transformed into a scaled down version of Wakanda. The colorful costumes, made from authentic Ankara that were adorned with African beads, brought the production to life in a unique and dramatic way. Jaxon had arranged a subdued version of the popular Beyonce song, "King Already" for the musical's opening, and the crowd went wild as the dancers and singers stormed the stage with uniformed precision.

Halfway through the performance, the lights dimmed, the music slowed, and Mila Hart graced the stage. She wore a beautiful white dress with lace, and her curly hair was down and accented by a lace headband that matched her dress. Jaxon played a beautiful opening to the song, and just as it died down, the spotlight shined brightly on Mila, and she opened her mouth to sing her solo. As she began to sing the opening lyrics to Whitney Houston's, "The Greatest Love of All," I felt a pang of something akin to jealousy as she sang about children being the future. Which children? Whose future?

As Mila's solo drew to a close, the crowd burst into applause. Her voice, as sweet as an angel's, hung in the air, leaving everyone spellbound. Nana, Danica and I all rushed onto the stage, arms filled with bouquets of flowers for our little star. I watched as Jaxon beamed with pride from his keyboard, and I think I even saw a hint of a tear in his eye.

We hadn't seen each other much outside of school. Our conversations were usually brief, filled with awkward silences. I was at a loss for words around him, and all he ever seemed to manage to say was that he was sorry, feeling like the school's closing was partly his fault after what had happened with Remy. His apologies felt sincere, and I did believe he meant them. But I just didn't know what to do with them, how to process them. Watching him shower Mila with praise after her mesmerizing performance, it was pretty evident—she was the only woman who truly needed him in her life at the moment. He was her rock, her support system, and right then, that was all that mattered.

The show was a resounding success. I was standing at the door of the auditorium, greeting parents, students, and community members as they left, when Mila came running up to me.

"Mrs. Dash! I Mean! Mrs. St. James!!" She looked around to see if Jaxon was within earshot, afraid she'd get in trouble for calling me Dash in public.

"Hey, sweet girl! You did an amazing job tonight! We are all so proud of you!"

"Thank you! Jax said I sounded just like Janet Jackson!"

I leaned down to pull her little ear close to me to whisper a secret. *"You sounded better!"* And she beamed with pride.

"Really?" she said, her eyes big and bright.

I shook my head and grinned, "Really!"

My back was toward the crowd filing out of the auditorium when I saw Mila's face freeze as if she'd seen a ghost. I thought she was getting ready to have another panic attack until her little voice whisper-yelled, "Woooow! Petah Pan!?! You heard me sing?!"

I turned on my heels to find Corinne and Petah Pan, or Xavier, hand-in-hand as they left the auditorium.

"I sure did, lil' momma. You did your thing up there. Don't stop singing, OK? Who knows, maybe you'll end up on tour with me one day!"

Mila returned back to her speechless state except to say, "Wooow!" again.

As they continued to walk by, I pinched Corinne in her side and mouthed 'call me!' as she grabbed Xavier's hand tighter and proceeded to walk out of the door. Clearly, I had missed a few things these past few weeks.

I walked back to my office to grab my things but, on the way, I stopped at a door that I had closed six years ago and hadn't opened since. Lamar's office. Pulling out my keys, I looked around to see if anyone was coming. Once I saw that the coast was clear of anyone who would question what I was doing, I unlocked the door and walked in. The janitorial staff still came in and dusted, but I asked them to leave everything else where it was. Just as Lamar left it.

I sat in his chair and looked around at the various trophies that adorned the shelves. The last bit of notes that sat scribbled on his desk. His coffee mug that still had the last drop of dried coffee at the bottom and read, 'Knuck If You Buck.' I laughed and cried at the sight of it because Lamar couldn't dance one bit, but let that song come on and he lost all sight of couth and decorum. He was a man of many contradictions, and I loved that about him.

As I sat there, soaking in my surroundings, it hit me—there wasn't a single thing in this room that I hadn't already etched into my heart and mind. I had created a shrine to Lamar and inadvertently turned my grief for him into something I worshiped. My sorrow for Ty had morphed into a security blanket of sorts, one that I clung to fiercely, hoarding it as if it were the last lifeline to my sanity. If I was going to be turning the page and closing the chapter on Biddy Mason, then it was time I released the physical items that were tricking me into believing that they were the source of my connection to my boys.

I got up from Lamar's desk and said one final goodbye to the space, making a mental note to have Genevieve box up all his things. Then I walked out and shut the door before heading back to my office. When I got there, Jaxon was waiting for me.

"Hi," he said. His face somber and void of emotion.

"Hi," I whispered back.

"Danica took Mila and Arrin out for ice cream and—"

"You did a great job tonight. She did amazing as well. You should be really proud."

"I am." Cautiously, Jaxon took a few steps and closed the distance between us.

I wasn't completely numb, so being this close to him still had an effect on me. I had just come to the conclusion that I couldn't allow myself to give in to the effects he had on me. No matter how impossible he made it.

He grabbed my hand and brought the inside of my wrist to his mouth to plant a soft kiss there. It reminded me of our first night together. "Look, Shy. I am about to tell you something that will go against anything I've ever said about myself. It may shock you, and you may not even believe me, but I feel the need to share my truth with you."

I took a step back and let out a nervous laugh. "O...OK?"

"I love you."

I took another step back, and I saw his feet trail mine as he took two more steps towards me. *He said that, right? He loved me?* I kept moving back until my feet hit my office door behind me.

Trapping me between the glass wall and Jaxon's large frame.

He bent down, planting kisses all over my face, each one echoing the words he kept repeating. "I..." His lips brushed against my cheek softly. "Love..." He moved to my nose, his kiss as tender as a whisper. "You..." And then he drew me into him, pressing a desperate, heart-wrenching kiss onto my lips, his tongue gently parting them. A warmth spread through me, making me feel like I was melting right into him. He felt familiar, comforting—like home.

As he withdrew his mouth from mine, my eyes lazily parted, begging to not be ripped away from this moment. I craned my neck to look up at him as I whispered, "I love you too. So much. But—"

He placed his hand softly on my lips, silencing the rebuttal that was inevitably coming next. "I know. You told me. You would never forgive me if...I get it. And I am so sorry. I just wanted you to know that I'm not giving up on you. On us. While you're here, plotting your next big move," he stopped to grin as if he had an inside joke all to himself. "Because I know whatever you do next will be big. I will be in California going to therapy, attending church, and becoming the best male role model that I can be for Mila...and the best man I can be for you. I recognize that my leaving could leave the door open for you to fall in love with someone who you feel deserves you. But I'm going to prove that I can love you the way that…In a way that would make Lamar and Ty rest a little easier in peace."

A sob got caught in my throat at those words. I closed my eyes and threw myself into his chest and simply said, "OK."

He backed away slightly, taking my chin to tilt my head up to meet his gaze. "But, Shy. I'm not the only one that has work to do. I own my shit. I'm working on being a better me because I know I have been a trash human being in some instances. But you have some healing to do, too. And I'll be damned if I bring myself back to you, all healed and fine, for you to cut me with your unhealed wounds."

I didn't have a rebuttal to the carefully crafted speech he'd just laid out. Mostly because he wasn't wrong. It was mighty self-righteous of me to carry on as if Jaxon was the only one who had issues and healing to take accountability for. If I wanted to be a healthier me, I had to stop using my grief as a crutch and excuse to not face my own truths.

Chapter Forty-Nine

Hadassah

We coasted through the final weeks of school. Teachers opted to take it easy on students for finals and testing, allowing them to process their grief for the closing of the school. I, on the other hand, was exhausted from the meetings and crying and paper shuffling that needed to be done in the final weeks. Everyone expected me to appeal or seek a special waiver for the school to remain open. However, it was clear that the city had no interest in keeping our doors open with government funding. I had to keep retelling my rehearsed message of timing and seasons. Biddy Mason had served a purpose for a season in this community, but our season had ended.

It was a Saturday morning, and Corinne and Genevieve woke me up, demanding I meet them at Black Coffee for an early morning surprise. Reluctantly, I agreed. But only because Black Coffee had the best sticky buns in the state of Georgia, and I was in need of a carb crash, fast. I arrived to find Genevieve and Corinne beaming at a table near the store's fireplace.

"Alright, bitches," I said, walking towards their table. "I put on a bra and lip gloss for y'all. This had better be good!"

"Yeah! Yeah!" Corinne said, waving me off while handing me a hot cup. "Here's your chai latte. Now sit down so we can get right to it."

I looked between her and Genevieve and their excitement was palpable. "OK? I'm here. Tell me what this is all about?"

Corinne grabbed mine and Genevieve's hand like we were about to enter into a prayer circle. "We found a way to save the school!" she exclaimed, and my eyes got enormously big at the news.

Confusedly, I yelled, "What?!? How?!" I almost knocked over the latte that they had ordered for me.

"Well?" Corinne sang. "Petah Pan's mom is the former school superintendent of schools for the county that Biddy Mason resides. While we were at dinner with her last week, she made a comment about not understanding why Biddy Mason couldn't be reclassified as a private school instead of a charter school. When I explained to her that most of our students wouldn't be able to afford a tuition that a school like Biddy Mason would require, she basically dismissed the notion, stating that grants and donations could still serve as the core source of funding."

The shock on my face must have been disturbing because Genevieve shook my arm as if she was trying to wake me from a dream. "Dash? Are you alright? Didn't you hear what Corinne just said?"

"I...yeah! Of course! That's amazing news!" I said, trying to recover my obvious fumble.

This was good news. The *best* news that I could have hoped for. But why wasn't I happy? Why wasn't I excited about it? Corinne had single-handedly found a way to save our school, and Petah Pan had offered to generously donate the funds needed for all of our returning students for the next school year. I should be jumping up and down and screaming cheers of joy. Perhaps it was due to the whirlwind of emotions that I had been going through since the election—my mind didn't know how to react to yet another piece of news. Or...maybe I wasn't excited because deep down I knew that Biddy Mason wasn't my home anymore.

The ladies looked at each other as if they could sense something bubbling beneath the surface. Our hands remained locked around the table as my silence choked the excitement out the air.

"But that isn't what you want anymore, is it, Dash?" Genevieve asked, searching my eyes for confirmation.

A tear fell into my latte as I silently shook my head no.

Corinne gasped. "What? Are you serious? Why?"

"I guess I had gotten so used to the idea of closing this chapter, that I actually did it. I already closed it. And I don't think I want to reopen it again, ladies. The school or the grief that I was held prisoner to while I was there. I would never admit this publicly, but Congresswoman Atkins did me a favor. This *needed* to be done for me if I was ever going to move on."

The ladies were completely taken aback by my revelation, but I had never been more sure. More confident in a decision.

"So, what are you saying? What does this mean for Biddy Mason?" Corinne anxiously asked, a tinge of fear and panic in her voice.

I smiled at her, caressing her hand the way Jaxon used to do me to calm my nerves. "*You* are going to open the school as one of the founding members…and as their principal, Corinne."

"Me?! What? Dash, I can't. You and Lamar bled for Biddy—"

"And so do you," I interrupted. "No one loves that school and those kids more than me...*except you*, Corinne. Your passion and energy is exactly what that school and this community needs. I'm just tired, sweetie. It's time for a new chapter. A new adventure, ya know?"

Genevieve and Corinne nodded, their expressions a mix of agreement and understanding. Once the initial shock faded, they got where I was coming from and realized it was the right path for me. Lamar and Ty had left behind life insurance policies I hadn't even touched. The money was just sitting there in savings, slowly accumulating interest, waiting for me to decide what to do next.

But I needed to figure things out at my own pace, in my own style. No pressure of preserving someone's legacy or memory as my only reason for being. I wasn't just a memory keeper, I was a person with my own life to live. And that's exactly what I intended to do, on my own terms and in my own way. We sat there for another two hours, mapping out press releases and transition plans for the school. And with each minute that passed, a weight was being lifted off my shoulders. I was moving on, but the legacy of me, Lamar, and our school's namesake, Biddy Mason, would live on. And Corinne was the perfect person to carry that mantle.

Chapter Fifty

Jaxon

"It's too tight!" Mila yelled. We were getting ready for church, and I was attempting a half up, half down hairstyle, but apparently my ponytail skills had gotten too good because I was now being yelled at for them being too tight on a regular basis.

"I'm sorry! Hold still so I can fix it."

"We're gonna be late, and you know I won't be able to go to children's church if we're too late!"

We had been going to church with Nana the past few months now, my attempt at reintroducing myself to God from a different perspective, and Mila loved children's church. If we were late, and she had to sit next to me in the adult service, she didn't speak to me for days. And boy could this girl hold a grudge.

Even though we were scheduled to move in two weeks, I had started seeing one of the therapists that Dr. Johana had recommended. When I asked why I couldn't simply continue to see her? She told me that, due to my relationship with my father, I hadn't developed the skills to build healthy relationships with men. The right male therapist could help me begin to learn those skills. It took a few tries to find someone I was comfortable with, but I found a black man that understood the intricacies of my past because he had dealt with similar issues. I understood that therapists were supposed to have it all together for their patients. But there was something about our shared experiences that made me more comfortable with him.

The therapist was also why I had begun taking Mila to church more. Initially, she would go with Nana, and I would use Sunday mornings to sleep in or catch up on work. However, my therapist recommended that I try taking Mila myself, realizing that all of the negative feelings I had toward God and church came from an unreliable source—my father. So I began to get up on Sunday mornings to take Mila to church, and the routine had actually brought us closer together.

I had gone to California a few times in the past weeks to sign contracts and get a place ready for Mila, but I had kept my intentions that I shared with Dash on track. I was working to become a man that would be worthy of her. I didn't call her or text her anymore after the spring musical. I withdrew my presence with a promise to return when I felt that I was ready. When I knew that I could trust myself to keep every promise I would ever make to her, beginning with this one. The one to earn her.

That didn't mean I didn't miss her terribly. The kids today would call me a simp because I was turning away gorgeous women left and right at Sanctuary and keeping my head down while I was in California. For the first time in my life, I was determined and focused with one goal in mind, and I wouldn't let myself get distracted by meaningless encounters the way I used to. Suddenly, the risk wasn't worth it.

We were both dressed and heading out the door when I heard Mila yell, "Dash!" And I looked up to see Dash standing there.

"What...Hadassah, what are you doing here?"

After my brain fully recovered from the shock of seeing her standing there, and registered the condition she was in as she stood before me, I turned to Mila and told her to go next door to ride to church with Nana, before opening the door and inviting Dash in. She was crying and appeared disheveled, and I couldn't begin to know what was going on. I removed my suit coat and pulled her into a hug, not caring that she was likely ruining the sky blue shirt and tie that I had on.

"Shy, baby. What's wrong?" And she abruptly broke our embrace to look me in the eye.

"Let me just say this, and I'll go. OK?"

Hadassah

I was sitting with Johana at my house this morning, reeling from all of the sudden life-altering changes that I was facing. She asked me one question, and that one question was all it took for the dam inside me to irreparably burst open.

"If Ty could dream the perfect life for his mommy, a life that he would be overjoyed to share with you, what would that life look like?"

For what seemed like an eternity, I proverbially released all the dreams and hopes I'd ever had for my life. And in that soul-baring moment, I realized that my life, though punctuated with grief, had been truly beautiful. How many people could say they'd lived multiple lives in one lifespan? With Lamar, we had crafted a family and built our dream life from scratch. Even though our shared journey was cut short, it was uniquely ours, and we savored every precious moment of it. But here's the thing—I was still breathing, still standing, which meant there was more life waiting to be lived.

I had the ability to choose to live this next chapter differently from what I'd always imagined, because it was an entirely new adventure. And new adventures, they had a right to be different, to break the mold. In that moment, I made the decision to no longer let grief dictate how I lived the rest of my life. That choice was mine. And I chose to embrace the new, the unexpected, the different. Because life was about the stories we weaved, and I had plenty more chapters left in me.

Through teary eyes, I smiled at Jaxon saying, "His name was Ty. Tyshawn Duke Ellington St. James." Jaxon reached his hand out for me but I stifled my sobs while jerking my hand back.

"Just...let me get through this," I said. If I was going to hold it together, he couldn't comfort me. Not yet.

"When he was born, his daddy cheered because his caramel skin and his kinky, sandy blonde hair matched his own. He didn't just have an heir. He had a twin, and he was through the moon over it. Tyshawn was obsessed with Spiderman and, when they released the first Miles Morales movies, he made us watch it every day. He was convinced that since this Spiderman was black, all he had to do was watch Miles Morales in order to develop super powers just like him. We stopped short of allowing him to get intentionally bitten by a spider, though he tried." We both laughed as Jaxon handed me a paper towel to dry my tears.

"Why are you telling me this, Shy?" Jaxon asked, leading me to the sofa to have a seat.

"Because. You were right. I do have some healing to do. And it was unfair of me to put all of the problems in our relationship on you. I'm broken. I'm the one who needs mending. And I'm here sharing this with you because I haven't had the desire to talk to anyone about Ty. I didn't trust that anyone would be safe enough for me to fall apart with and say things like 'I don't know if I could ever love another baby because of what losing Ty did to me,' until you. You made me feel safe and allowed me to say things without judgment. Even when it hurt you as a result."

Jaxon gently, cautiously placed his hand on mine and squeezed it. "Thank you for trusting me. I promise I won't betray it."

"I know you won't. That's why I'm here. I wanted to say thank you for giving me space and time to process everything. But also thank you for keeping your word and showing me that you were being intentional about working on yourself. You taught me what that looked like, so I'll be following your lead."

We sat and talked for another twenty minutes before it dawned on me that I had interrupted him and Mila as they were leaving to go to church. But Jaxon had abruptly jumped up to run upstairs, leaving me to sit in the living room. I glanced down at my left hand and noticed that the tan line from my wedding band was gone. The once prominent line, a symbol of my love for someone else, had faded away. It felt like a poignant symbol, a physical representation of my choice to turn the page on my past with Biddy Mason.

I looked up to find Jaxon coming back down the stairs in a black sweatsuit, matching the one that I'd worn over to his house. "What are you doing? I'll leave so you can go to church. I'm sorry for interrupting you."

Jaxon didn't respond to the apology. He simply extended his hand and helped me up from the couch. He took my arm and looped it through his and led me to the door. "I changed because I didn't want you to feel silly for how you were dressed. So I opted to match your style today."

"OK...but where are we going?"

He smiled and kissed me on the cheek and said, "Come on, Shy. Today you're going to be my guest at church."

Epilogue

Jaxon

One Year Later

The doorbell rang, and I opened it to find Drew with a care basket filled with ice packs, my favorite candy, and bourbon. "You ready? Today's the day that our little boy becomes a man!"

"Forget you, dick. I'm not getting circumcised, and I told you I don't need you here."

Drew walked past me and laughed. "And miss out on this joyous occasion? Seeing you walk like a wounded duck after making the biggest mistake of your life?! Oh nah, playa. You couldn't have paid me to stay away."

After spending a year in California, Dash and I came back to Atlanta to finalize the sale of her home. Initially, we agreed to keep our distance as we worked through our respective healing processes. I kept my word, working on being a better version of myself every day. And Dash, she kept her promise, too, focusing on her own healing journey. We even set aside time each week to talk about what we were learning about ourselves and how we hoped it would help inform our behavior in future relationships. If two years ago someone would have told me that I would be in a committed relationship, proudly going to therapy, all while raising my teenage little sister, I would have laughed them out the door. Today, it's my life's greatest joy.

A long-distance relationship was something I said I'd never be able to do. And after finding something so special with Dash, I knew the distance wouldn't be sustainable. I loved her. I wanted every moment possible with her. So, we both opted to travel back and forth when the distance became too much for us to bear. After a month away from Mila and I, Dash missed us too much and came for an extended stay. I could count on one hand how many times she left us.

Together, we had built something pretty amazing—a love and a relationship that was real and raw. It was the kind of connection I hoped everyone got to experience at least once in their lifetime. Our love was about growth, respect, and mutual support—a far cry from the manipulative games I learned growing up. And honestly, it was a journey I wouldn't trade for anything.

Last month, I asked Dash to marry me. We were laying out at Laguna Beach, watching Mila play in the sand. There was nothing particularly romantic about it. It was just a moment where I was happy and filled with an overwhelming sense of joy, and I wanted to savor it. So I looked down at her and said, "Marry me," before turning my eyes back to Mila.

Dash looked at me with a sweet smile. "Get a vasectomy reversal, and I'll think about it."

I laughed. "First of all, I thought you didn't want any more kids. Second of all, don't play with me. If you're serious, I'll look into it."

"First of all, I changed my mind. You and Mila did that. Second of all, make it happen and we will see. And next time, I'm gonna need a little more effort put into a proposal." I kissed her softly on her forehead and made myself a promise: That I'd do everything in my power to make that happen for her. To give her a baby.

Initially, I wasn't even sure if getting the reversal was worth it, not optimistic about her being able to get pregnant after a procedure like that. But the doctor showed me several case studies of women getting pregnant after vasectomy reversals, so I caved. And today, Drew and Dash were responsible for getting me to and from the clinic for this glorious occasion. To be sure we had all of our bases covered, Dash had also begun fertility treatments to harvest her eggs.

After the reopening of Biddy Mason, most of the staff chose to stay. However, Coach Drew landed a job as a sports commentator on ESPN, which took him to Los Angeles as well. Since he didn't know many people in the city, he started hanging out with me and Dash, and somehow, we all became friends. There was an awkward phase at first, mainly due to his misplaced crush on Dash, but we eventually moved past that. As time went by, I found myself respecting Drew more and more. I hadn't invested in male friendships when I was younger, so Drew turned out to be the male friend I didn't even know I was missing.

Drew also played a crucial role in bringing Dash and me closer together, serving as a bridge between Dash and Lamar, and then between Dash and me. I believe Drew's presence in our lives and his ability to make peace with the relationship that Dash and I had built, ultimately made Dash feel more secure about being with me. And hopefully, marrying me. It was as if Drew's blessing served as a surrogate for Lamar's, making everything fall into place for us.

When Dash, Drew, and I returned from the clinic, heavy drugs still coursing through my veins, I was greeted with our group of friends that had become my family since moving to Atlanta and working at Biddy Mason. Large, obnoxious signs that read "Congratulations" and "Happy Bar Mitzvah," courtesy of Drew, hung all over the house with balloons everywhere. The decorations were covering up the real reason everyone was here.

Drew slapped me on the back and handed me a pillow. I walked, limping, over to the couch with Dash and gestured for her to have a seat. Then, I placed the pillow on the ground so that I could kneel in front of her, trying to make myself as comfortable as possible.

She looked down at me with a confused expression on her face. "Jaxon, what are you doing?"

"Shhhh!" Drew interrupted, "Let the man speak, Dash! He only has so much time that he can be on that knee before it gives out!" Causing the crowd to erupt with laughter.

"Hadassah," I said, taking her left hand in mine. "From the day that I met you, I have regretted not having known you and loving you sooner. The day that I thought I could lose you, and the way it ripped my heart in two, was the day that I knew I couldn't bear to live without you. I went away to become a better man for me, and by extension, you. But I'm letting you know that if you marry me and agree to be my wife, I will never stop working to earn your love and respect. I will never stop working to make you happy and your boys proud."

Barely able to hold myself in place from the pain that was radiating from my groin, I reached for Drew to hand me the Tiffany's blue box that he was holding for me. I opened it to reveal a two carat, platinum soleste emerald cut halo engagement ring, accented by a one carat diamond band. It was a ring that she'd been eyeing for months and she didn't know I'd seen it.

From behind me, I heard Corinne swoon, "Oh my goodness!"

"You just couldn't wait to do this, could you?" Dash asked, grinning.

"No, I couldn't. I want you part of my life, for the rest of my life…and that's urgent than a muthafuka," I said, taking a line from her favorite movie, "Love Jones."

I shifted to my other knee, the discomfort getting to me. "Now, Shy. You've reached me in places I didn't know were possible, and I want you there forever. Will you marry me?"

Mila jumped onto the sofa where Dash sat, wrapped her arms around her neck and screamed,

"PLEAAAAASE?!" Making everyone else swoon and smile.

But as the room fell silent, we all turned our attention back to Dash. She hadn't given an answer. With tears in her eyes, and her bottom lip in her mouth, she shook her head, yes.

She *said* yes.

The End

About the Author

Taccara Martin is a contemporary romance writer and an award-winning fiction podcast producer who has, alongside her husband, Kenyon, gained over 100,000 social media followers using the timeless magic of words.

A survivor of domestic and narcissistic abuse, Taccara infuses her narratives with a deep passion for healthy love, weaving stories that mirror the intricate realities of relationships, even when they aren't perfect.

She's married to her "forever book boyfriend," Kenyon, and openly shares how he fuels her endless romance inspiration. Together, they live just outside Atlanta, Georgia and share a blended family of six amazingly creative kids.

Learn more by visiting https://taccaramartin.com

Printed in Great Britain
by Amazon

43639129R00334